IF FOUND, please notify and arrange return to owner. This text is an in[...]
for the owner's career and/or exam preparation.

Name: ____________________

Address: ____________________

City, State, ZIP: ____________________

Telephone: ____________________ E-mail: ____________________

Gleim Publications, Inc., offers six university-level study manuals:

Auditing & Systems Exam Questions and Explanations, 8th ed.	$19.95
Business Law/Legal Studies Exam Questions and Explanations, 4th ed.	16.95
Business Law/Legal Studies Outlines and Illustrations, 1st ed.	16.95
Federal Tax Exam Questions and Explanations, 7th ed.	19.95
Financial Accounting Exam Questions and Explanations, 8th ed.	19.95
Managerial Accounting Exam Questions and Explanations, 5th ed.	16.95

The following is a list of Gleim examination review books:

CIA Review: Part I, Internal Audit Process	$22.95
CIA Review: Part II, Internal Audit Skills	22.95
CIA Review: Part III, Management Control and Information Technology	22.95
CIA Review: Part IV, The Audit Environment	22.95

CIA Test Prep software ($35 per section) is also available to complement your study.

CMA/CFM Review: Part 1, Economics, Finance, and Management, 8th ed.	$22.95
CFM Review: Part 2CFM, Corporate Financial Management, 8th ed.	22.95
CMA Review: Part 2CMA, Financial Accounting and Reporting, 8th ed.	22.95
CMA/CFM Review: Part 3, Mgmt. Reporting, Analysis, and Behavioral Issues, 8th ed.	22.95
CMA/CFM Review: Part 4, Decision Analysis and Information Systems, 8th ed.	22.95

CMA/CFM Test Prep software ($35 per section) is also available to complement your study.

CPA Review: Financial	$24.50
CPA Review: Auditing	24.50
CPA Review: Business Law	24.50
CPA Review: TAX-MAN-GOV	24.50

CPA Test Prep software ($35 per section) and *CPA Review* audiotapes ($75 per section) are also available to complement your study.

Order forms for these and all of our other publications are provided at the back of this book.

All orders must be prepaid. Shipping and handling charges will be added to all orders. Library and company orders may be purchased on account. Add applicable sales tax to shipments within Florida. All payments must be in U.S. funds and payable on a U.S. bank. Please write or call for prices and availability of all foreign country shipments. Orders will usually be shipped the day after your request is received. Allow 10 days for delivery in the United States. Please contact us if you do not receive your shipment within 2 weeks.

Gleim Publications, Inc. guarantees the immediate refund of all resalable texts and unopened software and audiotapes purchased directly from Gleim Publications, Inc. if they are returned within 30 days. Shipping and handling charges are nonrefundable. Returns of books purchased from bookstores and other resellers should be made to the respective bookstore or reseller.

Groundwood Paper and Highlighters -- This book is printed on high quality groundwood paper. It is lightweight and easy-to-recycle. We recommend that you purchase a highlighter specifically designed to be non-bleed-through (e.g., Avery *Glidestick*™) at your local office supply store.

REVIEWERS AND CONTRIBUTORS

Karen Hom, B.A., University of Florida, is our book production coordinator. Ms. Hom coordinated the production staff and provided production assistance throughout the project.

Grady M. Irwin, J.D., University of Florida Holland Law Center, has taught in the University of Florida College of Business. Mr. Irwin wrote some Publisher questions and provided many answer explanations and extensive editorial assistance throughout.

Travis Moore, M.B.A., University of Florida, provided technical and editorial assistance, reviewed the final manuscript, and prepared the page layout.

Nancy Raughley, B.A., Tift College, is our editor. Ms. Raughley reviewed the entire manuscript and assisted in all phases of production.

John F. Rebstock, B.S.A., is a graduate of the Fisher School of Accounting at the University of Florida. He has passed the CIA and CPA exams, and is a CMA candidate. Mr. Rebstock reviewed the entire edition.

A PERSONAL THANKS

This manual would not have been possible without the extraordinary effort and dedication of Jim Collis and Terry Hall, who typed the entire manuscript and all revisions as well as prepared the camera-ready pages.

We appreciate the production and editorial assistance of Shannon Bunker, Jerry Coutant, Lana Cox, Jennifer Cutting, Tiffany Dunbar, Brian Fitzgerald, Eric Hall, Rusty Helton, James McGinn, Jan Morris, Brenda Rowland, and Tricia Slaton.

We appreciate the assistance of Marcia Bremer, a graduate of Florida State University, and employee of the Florida Auditor General. Ms. Bremer conducted research and wrote questions concerning assurance services.

Finally, we appreciate the encouragement and tolerance of our families throughout the project.

Send e-mail to update@gleim.com or visit our Internet site (www.gleim.com) for the latest updates and information on all of our products.

Eighth Edition

AUDITING & SYSTEMS

Exam Questions and Explanations

by

Irvin N. Gleim, Ph.D., CPA, CIA, CMA, CFM

and

William A. Hillison, Ph.D., CPA, CMA

with the assistance of
Grady M. Irwin, J.D.

ABOUT THE AUTHORS

Irvin N. Gleim is Professor Emeritus in the Fisher School of Accounting at the University of Florida and is a member of the American Accounting Association, Academy of Legal Studies in Business, American Institute of Certified Public Accountants, Association of Government Accountants, Florida Institute of Certified Public Accountants, The Institute of Internal Auditors, and the Institute of Management Accountants. He has had articles published in the *Journal of Accountancy, The Accounting Review,* and *The American Business Law Journal* and is author/coauthor of numerous accounting and aviation books and CPE courses.

William A. Hillison is Professor of Accounting at Florida State University, where he holds the Arthur Andersen Chair. His primary teaching duties include graduate and undergraduate auditing and systems courses. He is a member of the Florida Institute of Certified Public Accountants, American Accounting Association, and Institute of Management Accountants. He has had articles published in many journals including the *Journal of Accounting Research*, the *Journal of Accounting Literature*, the *Journal of Accounting Education, Cost and Management, The Internal Auditor, The American Journal of Small Business,* and *The Journal of Forecasting*.

Gleim Publications, Inc.
P.O. Box 12848
University Station
Gainesville, Florida 32604
(352) 375-0772
(800) 87-GLEIM
FAX: (352) 375-6940
E-mail: sales@gleim.com
Internet: www.gleim.com

This is the first printing of the eighth edition of ***Auditing & Systems Exam Questions and Explanations***. Please e-mail update@gleim.com with AUD EQE 8-1 as the subject or text. You will receive our current update as a reply.

EXAMPLE:

To: update@gleim.com
From: your e-mail address
Subject: AUD EQE 8-1

ISSN 1092-4159
ISBN 1-58194-010-6

First Printing: August 1998

ACKNOWLEDGMENTS

Material from Uniform Certified Public Accountant Examination questions and unofficial answers, Copyright © 1972 - 1997 by the American Institute of Certified Public Accountants, Inc., is reprinted and/or adapted with permission.

The authors also appreciate and thank the Information Systems Audit and Control Association for permission to use sample CISA questions from *Study Guide - Certified Information Systems Auditor*.

The authors also appreciate and thank the Institute for Certification of Computing Professionals for permission to use sample CDP questions from the *CDP Instruction Manual*.

The authors also appreciate and thank The Institute of Internal Auditors, Inc. for permission to use The Institute's Certified Internal Auditor Examination questions, Copyright © 1977-1997 by The Institute of Internal Auditors, Inc.

The authors also appreciate and thank the Institute of Certified Management Accountants for permission to use problem materials from past CMA examinations, Copyright © 1977-1997 by the Institute of Management Accountants.

The authors appreciate questions contributed by the following individuals: Lynn Bailey, David Bradley, John Brooks, George Fiebelkorn, D. Finkbiner, Jim Heian, Kenneth Macur, Deborah Pavelka, Ken Plucinski, Nathan Schmukler, C.J. Skender, James Swearingen, and Don Wells.

PREFACE FOR ACCOUNTING STUDENTS

The purpose of this study manual is to help you learn and understand auditing and systems concepts and their application. In turn, these skills will enable you to perform better on your undergraduate examinations, as well as look ahead to the CDP, CIA, CISA, CMA, CFM, and CPA examinations.

One of the major benefits of this study manual is comprehensive coverage of auditing and systems topics. Accordingly, when you use this study manual to help prepare for auditing courses and examinations, you are assured of covering virtually all topics that could reasonably be expected to be studied in typical college or university auditing courses.

The question-and-answer format is designed and presented to facilitate effective study. Students should be careful not to misuse this text by referring to the answers before independently answering each question. Accordingly, we have provided two removable bookmarks at the back of this book to use to cover the answers while considering the questions.

The majority of the questions in this book are from past CDP, CIA, CISA, CMA, and CPA examinations. In addition, hundreds of publisher-written questions test areas covered in current textbooks but not directly tested on accounting certification examinations.

All of the questions in *Auditing & Systems Exam Questions and Explanations* have been modified, if necessary, to accommodate changes in professional pronouncements, to clarify questions, and/or to emphasize an auditing or systems concept or its application.

Note that this study manual should not be relied upon exclusively to prepare for the professional examinations. You should primarily use review manuals specifically developed for each examination. The Gleim *CIA Review, CMA Review, CFM Review,* and *CPA Review* are up-to-date and comprehensively cover all material necessary for successful completion of these examinations.

Thank you for your interest in this study manual. We deeply appreciate the many letters and suggestions received from accounting and auditing students and educators during the past years, as well as from CDP, CIA, CISA, CMA, and CPA candidates. Please send us your suggestions, comments, and corrections concerning this manual. The last two pages of this book have been designed to help you note corrections and suggestions throughout your study process.

To continue providing our customers with first-rate service, we request that questions about our books and software be sent to us via mail, e-mail, or fax. The appropriate staff member will give each question thorough consideration and a prompt response. Questions concerning orders, prices, shipments, or payments will be handled via telephone by our competent and courteous customer service staff.

Please read the introduction carefully. It is short but nonetheless very important.

Good Luck on Your Exams,

Irvin N. Gleim
William A. Hillison

August 1998

PREFACE FOR ACCOUNTING PRACTITIONERS

The first purpose of this study manual is to permit you to assess your technical proficiency concerning auditing standards, ethics, and special skills such as systems and statistical sampling. The second purpose is to facilitate your review and update of auditing standards and techniques with our compendium of nearly 1,800 objective questions. The third purpose is to provide CPE credit for your self-assessment and review/update study effort.

This approach to CPE is both interactive and intense. You should be continually challenged to answer each question correctly. When you answer a question incorrectly or have difficulty, you should pursue a complete understanding by reading the answer explanation and consulting reference sources as necessary.

In this Eighth Edition, we have included the CPE questions at the back of the book as Appendix B: Auditing & Systems CPE. Please read the instructions carefully before you begin.

Most of the questions were taken from various professional examinations, but many have been revised, adapted, etc., to provide broader, up-to-date coverage of the auditing and systems body of technical knowledge. While some are from the CPA exam, many are from other exams, such as CISA, CDP, CMA, and CIA. Thus, you have an opportunity to consider the appropriateness of pursuing these other accounting certifications. In addition, hundreds of publisher questions cover material not directly tested on the accounting certification examinations.

Finally, we ask for any supplemental comments, reactions, suggestions, etc., that you may have as you complete our CPE program. Please attach them to the Course Evaluation (handwritten notes are fine).

CPE candidates should read carefully the "Introduction: How to Use This CPE Program" in Appendix B: Auditing & Systems CPE.

To continue providing our customers with first-rate service, we request that questions about our books and software be sent to us via mail, e-mail, or fax. The appropriate staff member will give each question thorough consideration and a prompt response. Questions concerning orders, prices, shipments, or payments will be handled via telephone by our competent and courteous customer service staff.

Thank you for your interest, and we look forward to hearing from you. If you would like information on other CPE programs available from Gleim, please call us for a free brochure.

Best Wishes in Your CPE Endeavors,

Irvin N. Gleim
William A. Hillison

August 1998

TABLE OF CONTENTS

ACRONYMS: All acronyms used in this book are listed in the index. See pages 18 - 23 for definitions of and cross-references to APB, AR, AT, AU, BL, CS, FASB, QC, PR, SAS, SFAS, SSAE, SSARS, and TX pronouncements.

Visit the Gleim Home Page

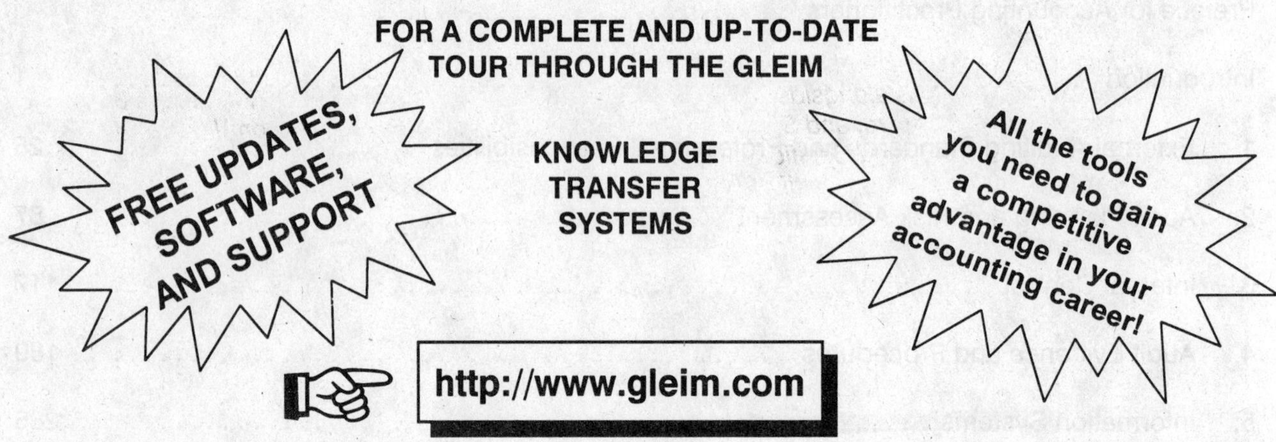

Visit the **GLEIM HOME PAGE** at http://www.gleim.com. Our extensive web page is updated regularly to provide convenient and current information. Useful features include

- The latest information on the CPA, CMA, and CIA exams
- Free demonstration versions of our software
- Listings of bookstores that carry Gleim's ***CPA Review***
- Continuing Professional Education self-study course catalog
- Technical support request form
- Information about other Gleim products
- Order forms
- Gleim's ***CPA Review: A System for Success*** booklet
- Direct connection to the Gleim e-mail update service (update@gleim.com)

Visit Gleim on the Internet today, and learn how you can study for success!

INTRODUCTION

The format and content of this study manual are innovative in the accounting text market. The first purpose is to provide auditing students with a well-organized, comprehensive compendium of objective questions covering the topics taught in typical auditing and information systems undergraduate courses. The second purpose is to provide accounting professionals with a comprehensive presentation of objective questions for self-diagnostic use and/or review of auditing standards and procedures.

The Gleim exam question and explanation books really work! You can pretest yourself before class to see if you are strong or weak in the assigned area. You can retest after class to see if you really understand the material. The questions in these books cover **all** topics in your related courses, so you will encounter few questions on your exams for which you will not be well prepared.

The titles and organization of Chapters 1 through 9 are based on the current auditing and information systems textbooks listed in Appendix A. Appendix A contains the table of contents of each of the listed books with cross-references to chapters and modules in this book. Some textbooks may have been inadvertently omitted. If you are using a textbook that is not included in our list, please fax, mail, or e-mail us the table of contents so that we may provide you with a cross-reference. In your correspondence to us, please include your name, address, school, professor, and course name.

OUR USE OF MODULES

Each chapter of this book is divided into subtopics to assist your study program. We call these subtopics "modules." Modules permit broad and perhaps overwhelming topics to be divided into more manageable study components.

Choosing modules and arranging questions within these subtopics was difficult. As a result, topics and questions may overlap somewhat. The number of questions is large enough for comprehensive coverage but does not present an insurmountable task. We have defined each module narrowly enough to cover a single topic but broadly enough to prevent questions from being repetitious.

Within each module, the multiple-choice questions are presented in a sequence moving from the general to the specific, elementary to advanced, etc., to provide an effective learning sequence. Duplicate questions and redundant explanations have been kept to a minimum.

SOURCES OF OBJECTIVE QUESTIONS

Past CIA, CISA, CMA, CIA, and CPA examinations and sample questions are the primary sources of questions included in this study manual.

Gleim Publications will continue to prepare questions (coded in this text as *Publisher*) based upon the content of auditing and information systems textbooks, SASs, SSARSs, etc. These *Publisher* questions were developed to review topics not adequately covered by questions from the other sources. We will continue to develop challenging, current questions to provide you with complete review materials. Also, professionals and professors from schools around the country have contributed questions. See page iv for a list of their names. We invite professors and students to submit questions for future editions.

IDENTIFICATION OF THE SOURCE OF EACH QUESTION

The source of each question appears in the first line of its answer explanation, in the column to the right of the question. Summary of source codes:

CDP	*CDP* Instruction Manual
CIA	Certified Internal Auditor Examination
CISA	Study Guide -- CISA
CMA	Certified Management Accountant Examination
CPA	Uniform Certified Public Accountant Examination
Publisher	Your authors
Individual name	Name of professional or professor who contributed the question

If you, your professor, or your classmates wish to submit questions, we will consider using them in future editions. Please send questions you develop, complete with answers and explanations, to the following address:

Gleim Publications, Inc.
EQE Question Bank
P.O. Box 12848, University Station
Gainesville, FL 32604

Writing and analyzing multiple-choice questions is an excellent way to prepare yourself for your exams. We will make every effort to consider, edit, and use questions you submit. However, we ask that you send us only serious, complete, carefully considered efforts.

UNIQUENESS OF OBJECTIVE QUESTIONS

The major advantage of objective questions is their ability to cover a large number of topics with little time and effort when compared to essay questions and/or computational problems.

A multiple-choice question is actually a series of statements of which all but one are incorrect given the facts of the question. The advantage of multiple-choice questions over true-false questions is that they require more analysis and result in a lower score for those with little or no knowledge. Random guessing on questions with four answer choices results in an expected grade of 25%. Random guessing on a true-false test results in an expected grade of 50%.

Students and practitioners both like multiple-choice questions. Because they present alternative answers from which only one needs to be selected, students find them relatively easy to answer. Professors also like objective questions because they are easy to grade and because much more material can be tested in the same period of time. Most professors will also ask students to complete essay or computational questins.

ANSWER EXPLANATIONS ALONGSIDE THE QUESTIONS

Our format presents objective questions and their answer explanations side by side. The answer explanations are to the right of each question. The example below is from the CPA exam.

Proper segregation of duties reduces the opportunities for persons to be in positions to both

A. Journalize entries and prepare financial statements.

B. Record cash receipts and cash disbursements.

C. Establish internal controls and authorize transactions.

D. Perpetrate and conceal errors and fraud.

The correct answer is (D). *(CPA, adapted)*

REQUIRED: The effects of the segregation of duties and responsibilities.

DISCUSSION: Proper segregation of duties and responsibilities reduces the opportunity for an individual to both perpetrate and conceal an error or fraud in the normal course of his/her duties. Hence, different people should be assigned the responsibilities for authorizing transactions, recordkeeping, and asset custody.

Answer (A) is incorrect because accountants typically journalize entries and prepare financial statements. Answer (B) is incorrect because accountants may record both cash receipts and cash disbursements as long as they do not have custody of the cash. Answer (C) is incorrect because management establishes internal controls and ultimately has the responsibility to authorize transactions.

The format in this study manual is designed to facilitate your study of objective questions, their answers, and the answer explanations. The intent is to save you time and effort by eliminating the need to turn pages back and forth from questions to answers.

Be careful, however. Do not misuse this format by consulting the answers before you have answered the questions. Misuse of the readily available answers will give you a false sense of security and result in poor performance on examinations and decreased benefit from your studies. The best way to use this study manual is to cover the answer explanations with the bookmark provided for this purpose in the back of the book (or a sheet of paper) as you read and answer each question. As a crucial part of the learning process, you must honestly commit yourself to an answer before looking at the answer explanation. Whether you are right or wrong, your memory of the correct answer will be reinforced by this process.

FREE UPDATES, SOFTWARE, AND SUPPORT: THE GLEIM HOME PAGE (www.gleim.com)!

Our extensive web page is updated regularly to provide convenient, up-to-date information. Some of the features include

- Free Demonstration Versions of Our Software
- Updates and Corrections for Gleim Books and Software
- Listings of Bookstores that Carry Gleim's ***CPA Review***
- Technical Support Request Form
- Links to Other Helpful Sites
- Information about Other Gleim Products
- Order Forms

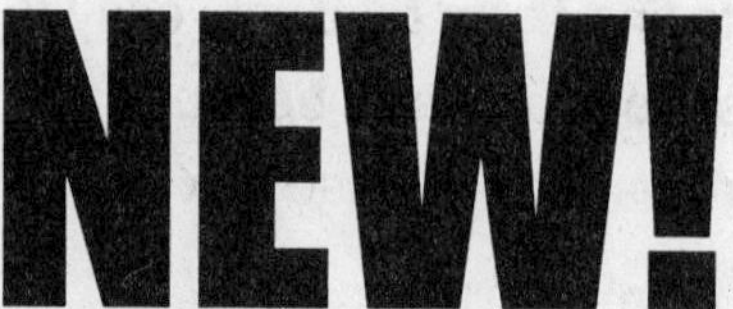

update@gleim.com

GLEIM
E-MAIL
UPDATE
SERVICE

Your message (in the subject or body of your e-mail) to Gleim must include the acronym of your book or software (see below), followed by the edition-printing for books, or version for software. The edition-printing is indicated on the book's spine. The software version is indicated on the diskette label.

	Book*	Software*
Exam Questions and Explanations		
Auditing & Systems	AUDEQE	
Business Law/Legal Studies	LAWEQE	
Federal Tax	TAXEQE	
Financial Accounting	FINEQE	
Managerial Accounting	MANEQE	
CIA Review:		
Part I, Internal Audit Process	CIA I	CIATP I
Part II, Internal Audit Skills	CIA II	CIATP II
Part III, Management Control and Information Technology	CIA III	CIATP III
Part IV, The Audit Environment	CIA IV	CIATP IV
CMA/CFM Review:		
Part 1, Economics, Finance, and Management	CMA/CFM Part 1	CMA/CFMTP 1
Part 2CFM, Corporate Financial Management	CMA/CFM Part 2CFM	CMA/CFMTP 2 CFM
Part 2CMA, Financial Accounting and Reporting	CMA/CFM Part 2CMA	CMA/CFMTP 2CMA
Part 3, Management Reporting, Analysis, and Behavioral Issues	CMA/CFM Part 3	CMA/CFMTP 3
Part 4, Decision Analysis and Information Systems	CMA/CFM Part 4	CMA/CFMTP 4
CPA Review:		
Auditing	CPA AUD	CPATP AUD
Business Law	CPA LAW	CPATP LAW
TAX-MAN-GOV	CPA TAX	CPATP TAX
Financial	CPA FIN	CPATP FIN
A System for Success	CPA SFS	

*Add the printing-edition of your book or version of your software to this acronym to get your update.

OVERVIEW OF ACCOUNTING CERTIFICATION PROGRAMS

The CPA (Certified Public Accountant) exam is the grandparent of all the professional accounting examinations. Its origin was in the 1896 public accounting legislation of New York. In 1917 the American Institute of CPAs (AICPA) began to prepare and grade a uniform CPA exam. It is currently used to measure the technical competence of those applying to be licensed as CPAs in all 50 states, Guam, Puerto Rico, the Virgin Islands, and the District of Columbia. More than 60,000 candidates sit for each CPA exam which is given twice a year in May and November.

The CIA (Certified Internal Auditor), CMA (Certified Management Accountant), and CFM (Corporate Financial Management) examinations are relatively new certification programs compared to the CPA. The CMA exam was first administered in 1972, and the first CIA exam in 1974. The CFM was first administered in December 1996. Why were these certification programs begun? Generally, the requirements of the CPA designation instituted by the boards of accountancy, especially the necessity for public accounting experience, led to the development of the CIA, CMA, and CFM programs.

Certification is important to professional accountants because it provides

1. Participation in a recognized professional group
2. An improved professional training program arising out of the certification program
3. Recognition among peers for attaining the professional designation
4. An extra credential for the employment market/career ladder
5. The personal satisfaction of attaining a recognized degree of competency

These reasons hold particularly true in the accounting field due to wide recognition of the CPA designation. Accountants and accounting students are often asked if they are CPAs when people learn they are accountants. Thus, there is considerable pressure for accountants to become *certified*.

A new development is multiple certifications, which is important for the same reasons as initial certification. Accounting students and recent graduates should look ahead and obtain multiple certifications. Obtaining multiple certifications will help to broaden your career opportunities. The table of selected CIA, CMA, CFM, and CPA examination data on page 12 provides an overview of these accounting examinations.

RATIONALE FOR ACCOUNTING CERTIFICATION PROGRAMS

The primary purpose of the CIA, CMA, CFM, and CPA examinations is to measure the technical competence of candidates. Competence includes technical knowledge, ability to apply such knowledge with good judgment, and comprehension of professional responsibility. Additionally, the nature of these examinations (low pass rate, broad and rigorous coverage, etc.) has several very important effects.

1. Candidates are forced to learn all of the material that should have been presented and learned in a good accounting educational program.
2. Relatedly, candidates must integrate the topics and concepts that are presented in individual courses in accounting education programs.
3. The content of each examination provides direction to accounting education programs; i.e., what is tested on the examinations will be taught to accounting students.

EXAMINATION CONTENT

The content of these examinations is specified by their governing boards with lists of topics to be tested. In the Gleim review manuals -- *CIA Review, CMA/CFM Review,* and *CPA Review* -- the material tested is divided into subtopics called study units. A study unit is a more manageable undertaking than an overall part of each exam. The listings of topics on pages 13 through 15 provide an overview of the content of these exams.

CIA, CMA/CFM, CPA EXAMINATION SUMMARY

	CIA	CMA/CFM	CPA
Sponsoring Organization	Institute of Internal Auditors 249 Maitland Avenue Altamonte Springs, FL 32701 (407) 830-7600 www.theiia.org	Institute of Certified Management Accountants 10 Paragon Drive Montvale, NJ 07645-1759 (201) 573-9000 (800) 638-4427 www.ima.org	American Institute of Certified Public Accountants Harborside Financial Center 201 Plaza III Jersey City, NJ 07311-3881 (201) 938-3419 www.aicpa.org
Passing Score	75%	70%	75%
Average Pass Rate by Exam Part	45%	40%	33%
Cost	$300 (50% student discount)	$240 (50% student discount; requires IMA membership)	$35-315 (Varies by state)
Year Examination Was First Administered	1974	1972	1916
Major Exam Sections and Length	I. Internal Audit Process (3½ hours)	1. Economics, Finance, and Management (3 hours)	1. Business Law & Professional Responsibilities (3 hours)
	II. Internal Audit Skills (3½ hours)	2. Financial Accounting and Reporting (3 hours) 2CFM. Corporate Financial Management (3 hours)	2. Auditing (4½ hours)
	III. Management Control and Information Tech. (3½ hours)	3. Management Reporting, Analysis, and Behavioral Issues (3 hours)	3. Accounting & Reporting -- Taxation, Managerial, & Governmental and Not-for-Profit Organizations (3½ hours)
	IV. The Audit Environment (3½ hours)	4. Decision Analysis and Information Systems (3 hours)	4. Financial Accounting & Reporting -- Business Enterprises (4½ hours)
Length of Exam	14 hours	12 hours (CMA or CFM) 15 hours (CMA and CFM)	15½ hours
When Administered	2 weeks after CPA Wed, Thur	On Demand	1st week of May, Nov Wed, Thur
Candidates Sitting for Exam:	Total number of candidates sitting for two examinations; many are repeaters.		
1990	4,363	4,839	143,572
1991	4,597	6,404	140,042
1992	4,961	7,464	136,541
1993	5,103	7,879	140,100
1994	4,557	8,259	131,000
1995	4,649	8,675	126,000
1996	4,646	8,679	122,232
1997	5,169	7,481	121,437

Other professional accounting-related designations include: CBA (Certified Bank Auditor), CDP (Certificate in Data Processing), CFA (Chartered Financial Analyst), CFE (Certified Fraud Examiner), CISA (Certified Information Systems Auditor), Enrolled Agent (one enrolled to practice before the IRS).

CIA REVIEW

Gleim makes your study process straightforward with 10 study units per exam part. Pass the first time with Gleim.

Part I: Internal Audit Process
- Introduction to Internal Auditing
- Independence, Status, and Objectivity
- Standards and Proficiency
- Internal Control
- Planning and Administering the Audit Assignment
- Audit Evidence and Procedures
- Managing the Internal Auditing Department
- Information Technology Auditing
- Ethics
- Fraud

Part II: Internal Audit Skills
- Problem Solving
- Decision Making
- Pronouncements on Audit Evidence
- Types of Audit Evidence
- Flowcharting and Data Gathering
- Using Electronic Media
- Working Papers
- Communicating Results
- Mathematics
- Statistics and Sampling

Part III: Management Control and Information Technology
- Internal Control Concepts
- The Controlling Process
- Budgeting
- Responsibility Accounting
- Product Cost Control Systems
- Decision Analysis I
- Decision Analysis II
- Information Technology I
- Information Technology II
- Information Technology - Control

Part IV: The Audit Environment*
- Standards and Statements
- Assets
- Liabilities and Shareholders' Equity
- Financial Accounting - Special Topics
- Finance I
- Finance II
- Managerial Accounting - Cost Behavior and Allocation
- Managerial Accounting - Additional Topics
- Regulatory Environment I
- Regulatory Environment I

*Persons who have passed the CPA or CMA exams (and many other professional exams) are not required to take Part IV of the CIA exam.

Each of the four parts consists of 80 multiple-choice questions and is 3½ hours in length (8:30 - 12:00 and 1:30 - 5:00).

The first two parts of the CIA exam focus on the theory and practice of internal auditing. The body of knowledge of internal auditing and the auditing skills to be tested consist of

1. The typical undergraduate auditing class (as represented by auditing texts, e.g., Arens and Loebbecke, Taylor and Glezen, etc.)
2. Internal auditing textbooks (e.g., Sawyer and Sumners, *The Practice of Modern Internal Auditing,* and Atkisson, Brink, and Witt, *Modern Internal Auditing*)
3. Various IIA (Institute of Internal Auditors) pronouncements (e.g., The IIA *Code of Ethics*, Standards for the Professional Practice of Internal Auditing, and Statement of Responsibilities of Internal Auditing)
4. Reasoning ability, communications, and problem-solving skills, and dealing with auditees within an audit context (i.e., the questions will cover audit topics, but test audit skills)

The remaining 50% of the exam, parts III and IV, assures that internal auditors are conversant with topics, methodologies, and techniques ranging from individual and organizational behavior to economics.

Management cannot personally observe the functioning of all officers, employees, and specialized functions (finance, marketing, operations, etc.). Each has a unique perspective. Only internal auditing is in a position to take a total company point of view.

CMA and CFM REVIEW

Gleim makes your study process straightforward with 10 study units per exam part. Pass the first time with Gleim.

Part 1: Economics, Finance, and Management
- Microeconomics
- Macroeconomics
- International Business Environment
- Domestic Institutional Environment of Business
- Working Capital Finance
- Capital Structure Finance
- Risk
- Organizational Theory
- Motivation and the Directing Process
- Communication

Part 2CMA: Financial Accounting and Reporting*
- Accounting Standards
- Financial Statements
- Conceptual Framework
- Assets
- Liabilities
- Shareholders' Equity
- Other Income Items
- Other Reporting Issues
- Financial Statement Analysis
- External Auditing

*Persons who have passed the CPA exam are not required to take Part 2 of the CMA exam.

**CMAs in good standing need only pass this part to earn the CFM designation.

Part 2CFM: Corporate Financial Management**
- Financial Statements and Annual Reports
- Financial Statements: Special Topics
- Long-Term Capital Financing
- Financial Markets and Interest Rates
- Investment Banking and Commercial Banking
- Financial Statement Analysis
- Business Combinations and Restructurings
- Risk Management
- External Financial Environment
- Accounting Standard Setting

Part 3: Management Reporting, Analysis, and Behavioral Issues
- Cost and Managerial Accounting Definitions
- Product Costing and Related Topics
- Cost Behavior
- Statements on Management Accounting
- Planning
- Budgeting
- The Controlling Process
- Standard Costs and Variance Analysis
- Responsibility Accounting
- Behavioral Issues

Part 4: Decision Analysis and Information Systems
- Decision Analysis
- Cost-Volume-Profit Analysis
- Capital Budgeting
- Decision Making Under Uncertainty
- Quantitative Methods I
- Quantitative Methods II
- Information Systems I
- Information Systems II
- Internal Control
- Internal Auditing

The CMA and CFM exams have broader coverage than the CPA exam in several areas. For example,

1. Management information systems is tested more extensively on the CMA exam.
2. SEC Financial Reporting Releases and Cost Accounting Standards Board pronouncements are covered on the CMA exam but not on the CPA exam.
3. Topics like economics, finance, and management on Part 1 and Part 2CFM are covered lightly, if at all, on the CPA exam.
4. The CMA exam tests internal auditing to a far greater degree than does the CPA exam.
5. The CMA exam tests business ethics, but not business law.

CMA questions are generally more analysis oriented than CPA questions. On the CPA exam, the typical requirement is the solution of an accounting problem, e.g., consolidated worksheet, funds statement, etc.

Each part of the CMA/CFM consists of 110 multiple-choice, computer-administered questions, of which five will be unscored for pretesting.

CPA REVIEW

Gleim makes your study process straightforward with 19 to 21 study units per exam part. Pass the first time with Gleim.

Business Law
AICPA Ethics
CPAs and the Law
Agency
Partnerships
Corporations
Estates and Trusts
Contract Formation
Contract Performance
Rights and Duties
Guarantors
Bankruptcy
Securities
Employment
Environmental Regulation
Commercial Paper
Sales
Secured Transactions
Documents of Title
Real Property and Insurance
Personal Property, Bailments, and Computers

Auditing
Engagement Responsibilities
Risk Assessment
Strategic Planning Issues
Internal Control Concepts
Internal Control -- Sales-Receivables-Cash Receipts Cycle
Internal Control -- Purchases-Payables-Cash Disbursements Cycle
Internal Control -- Payroll and Other Cycles
Tests of Controls
Internal Control Communications
Evidence -- Objectives and Nature
Evidence -- The Sales-Receivables-Cash Cycle
Evidence -- The Purchases-Payables-Inventory Cycle
Evidence -- Other Assets, Liabilities, and Equities
Evidence -- Key Considerations
Evidence -- Sampling
Reports -- Standard, Qualified, Adverse, and Disclaimer
Reports -- Other Modifications
Special Reports
Related Reporting Topics
Review and Compilation
Governmental Audits

TAX-MAN-GOV
Gross Income
Deductions
Tax Computations
Tax Procedures
Property Transactions
Corporate Taxable Income
Corporate Tax Computations
Corporate Tax Special Topics
S Corporations
Partnerships
Estates and Trusts
Exempt Organizations/Preparer's Responsibilities
Governmental Concepts
Governmental Accounting and Reporting
Not-for-Profit Concepts
Not-for-Profit Accounting and Reporting
Cost Accounting
Budgeting
Analytical Methods

Financial
Concepts and Standards
Revenue Recognition
Financial Statements
Other Income Statement Items
Financial Statement Disclosure
Statement of Cash Flows
Cash and Investments
Receivables and Accruals
Inventories
Property, Plant, and Equipment
Intangibles and Other Assets
Payables and Accruals
Accounting for Income Taxes
Employee Benefits
Bonds and Notes Payable
Leases and Contingencies
Equity Accounts -- Corporations
Equity Accounts -- Other
Business Combinations
Foreign Currency Issues and Other Topics

1. The table below presents the CPA exam schedule and exam composition by question type.

Section	Day	Time	Objective		Essay/Problem
			MC	Other	
Business Law	Wednesday	9:00-12:00	50-60%	20-30%	20-30%
Auditing	Wednesday	1:30-6:00	50-60%	20-30%	20-30%
TAX-MAN-GOV	Thursday	8:30-12:00	50-60%	40-50%	0
Financial	Thursday	1:30-6:00	50-60%	20-30%	20-30%

2. The "other objective question format" (OOF) is any question that can be answered on an answer sheet that can be optically scanned, except four-answer multiple-choice.
3. Essay questions will be graded for writing skills.
4. Calculators will be provided for both Thursday sessions (Sharp Model EL-231L).
5. Every aspect of the exam is explained and analyzed in *CPA Review: A System for Success*. Faculty and student organizations should order this free booklet in bulk for distribution.

EXAMINATION SCHEDULES AND FUTURE DATES

The CPA exam is given during the first week of May and November on Wednesday and Thursday. The CIA exam is given on a Wednesday and Thursday 1 or 2 weeks after the CPA examination. The CMA and CFM exams are offered in a computer-based, on-demand format.

Note that all four examinations can be taken within a 3-week period, which is ideal owing to the great amount of overlap of the material tested.

	1998	1999		2000	
CPA EXAM	Nov. 4, 5	May 5, 6	Nov. 3, 4	May 3, 4*	Nov. 1, 2*
CIA EXAM	Nov. 18, 19*	May 19, 20*	Nov. 17, 18*	May 17, 18*	Nov. 15, 16*
CMA EXAM	Computer-Based/On-Demand	Computer-Based/On-Demand		Computer-Based/On-Demand	
CFM EXAM	Computer-Based/On-Demand	Computer-Based/On-Demand		Computer-Based/On-Demand	

*Predicted dates. Check your registration card for actual dates.

When to Sit for the Exams

Sit for all four examinations as soon as you can. The CIA, CMA, and CFM exams can be taken in your last undergraduate quarter or semester, and both offer a 50% reduction in fees to full-time students. In many states you may also take the CPA exam in your last quarter or semester. If you are graduating in May, consider taking the CPA exam the first week of May, the CIA exam 1 or 2 weeks thereafter, and the CMA or CFM exam in early June. Your preparation program for all of these exams is very synergistic and not appreciably more work than preparing for just the CPA exam.

EXAMINATION PASS RATES

The pass rates on the CIA and CMA exams are about the same and are somewhat higher than the pass rate on the CPA exam. Nationally, the pass rate on the CPA exam is about 33% on each of the four parts. The pass rates on the CIA and CMA exams average 40%-45% per part (see the tables on page 11).

Unfortunately, a great deal of confusion surrounds CPA exam pass rates. There is considerable variation in the pass rate from state to state, even though the national rate is fairly constant. Nationally, about 20% pass all four parts on the first sitting, even though the pass rate on each part is about 33%. Approximately 20% of all candidates sitting for each CPA exam successfully complete the exam (this includes those passing the entire exam on one sitting and those passing their final parts for successful completion). Over 80% of *serious* CPA candidates eventually complete the CPA exam.

There is confusion between CPA pass rates and condition rates. While 75% is the passing grade for each part, *conditional* status is assigned to candidates who pass some, but not all, parts. The combined pass and condition rate is therefore higher than the pass rate. Relatedly, the qualifications and the requirements of conditional status vary from state to state.

Many schools and CPA review courses advertise the quality of their programs by reporting pass rates. Obviously, the best rates are emphasized. Thus, the reported percentage may be that for first-time candidates, all candidates, candidates passing a specific section of the examination, candidates completing the examination, or even candidates successfully completing the exam after a specified number of sittings.

CPA Exam	Pass Rates -- First-Time Candidates						Pass Rates -- Repeat Candidates					
	5/95	11/95	5/96	11/96	5/97	11/97	5/95	11/95	5/96	11/96	5/97	11/97
Auditing	29.5	32.9	29.5	31.0	27.2	26.5	32.8	35.7	30.7	33.4	33.8	35.8
Business Law	33.6	31.8	31.1	31.9	30.6	28.4	35.7	31.5	31.2	37.8	34.9	35.1
TAX-MAN-GOV	31.3	30.0	29.8	29.5	27.7	22.8	31.2	30.2	30.1	33.5	30.5	29.3
Financial	32.4	33.5	30.8	32.3	28.4	24.1	30.1	32.0	29.9	34.3	26.7	26.2
*All**	17.0	17.0	15.5	16.3	15.1	12.5	29.4	28.3	28.1	30.6	28.8	26.5

*Percentage of first-time and repeat candidates who pass all remaining parts on a particular exam.

Reasons for the Low Pass Rates

Although a very high percentage of serious candidates successfully complete each of the examinations, the 33% CPA pass rate and the 40% - 45% CIA and CMA pass rates warrant an explanation. First, the pass rates are low (relative to bar and medical exams) because these examinations reflect the high standards of the accounting profession, which contribute greatly to the profession's reputation and also attract persons with both competence and aspiration.

Second, the pass rates are low because most accounting educational programs are at the undergraduate rather than graduate level. (See the table on page 14 and look under the 150-Hr. Requirement column.) Undergraduate students are generally less career-oriented than graduate students. Undergraduates may look on their program as a number of individual courses required for graduation rather than as an integrated program to prepare them for professional practice. We encourage accounting undergraduates to take accounting seriously by helping them look ahead to professional practice and the CIA, CMA, CFM, and CPA exams.

Third, the pass rates are low because accounting programs and curricula at most colleges and universities are not given the budgetary priority they deserve. Accounting faculties are often understaffed for the number of accounting majors, the number and nature of accounting courses (problem-oriented vs. descriptive), etc., relative to other faculties. However, you cannot use this as an excuse or reason for not achieving your personal goals. You must do your best to improve your control systems and study resources.

CIA Exam Pass Rates						
	5/95	11/95	5/96	11/96	5/97	11/97
Part I	44.9	44.4	45.0	50.3	58.2	47.7
Part II	44.7	44.1	41.9	43.2	45.1	49.7
Part III	49.9	43.7	45.1	43.9	43.3	46.9
Part IV	45.1	43.9	44.4	42.5	44.3	44.1

CMA/CFM Exams The CMA/CFM exams are administered on-demand at Sylvan Testing Centers.	
Part 1	45%
Part 2CMA	37%
Part 2CFM	41%
Part 3	49%
Part 4	40%

COST TO OBTAIN AND MAINTAIN PROFESSIONAL CERTIFICATION

The cost to take the CIA exam is a $60 registration fee plus $70-per-part examination fee, which totals $340 (assuming you pass all parts the first time you take them). Full-time students save 50%. A $20-per-year record-keeping fee is charged to maintain CPE records for nonmembers of The Institute of Internal Auditors (The IIA). Membership in The IIA is not required.

The cost to take the CMA/CFM exam is $80 for each of the parts and a $50 application fee plus Institute of Management Accountants (IMA) membership dues, which varies from $27 for students to $135 for regular members. Membership in the IMA is required. Students may take the examination once at a reduced fee of $40 per part and do NOT pay an application fee.

The cost of the CPA exam varies by state. The table on page 21 lists the examination fee in each state. Additionally, most states require an annual fee to maintain the CPA certificate and/or license.

WHERE TO TAKE THE CPA EXAM

If you are not going to practice public accounting, you may wish to become certified in a state that

1. Issues a CPA certificate separate from a license to practice
2. Does **not** require experience to receive a CPA certificate
3. Does **not** require continuing professional education of CPA certificate holders
4. Does **not** require residency to sit for the CPA exam

You may also be concerned with the 150-hour requirement to sit for the CPA exam. Consult the table on page 14. This topic and more specific recommendations are presented in Chapter 1 of the free 112-page Gleim booklet, *CPA Review: A System for Success*.

STEPS TO BECOME A CPA

1. Decide when you are going to take the CPA exam (the sooner, the better!).
2. Determine the state board to which you will apply to sit for the CPA exam. Read "Where to Take the CPA Exam" above.
3. Obtain, complete, and submit your application form, including transcripts, etc.
4. Commit to thorough, systematic preparation for the exam as described in our free booklet, *CPA Review: A System for Success*.
5. Work systematically through each study unit in the four Gleim *CPA Review* books (*Business Law*, *Auditing*, *TAX-MAN-GOV*, and *Financial*).
6. Use Gleim's ***CPA Test Prep*** software: over 5,000 CPA questions, all updated to current tax law, FASB Statements, etc.
7. Sit for and PASS the CPA exam while you are in control, as described in Chapter 8 of *CPA Review: A System for Success*. Gleim will make it easy. Call (800) 87-GLEIM for more information.

STATE BOARDS OF ACCOUNTANCY

All 50 states (and the District of Columbia, Guam, Puerto Rico, and the Virgin Islands) have an administrative agency that administers the laws and rules which regulate the practice of public accounting in each state. Each of these 54 jurisdictions contracts with the AICPA to use the AICPA's Uniform CPA Examination.

While the 54 jurisdictions agree on using the same examination, the rules and procedures for applying to take the exam and becoming licensed to practice public accounting vary considerably. Accordingly, you should call or write to your state board for a CPA exam application form. With the form you will receive that board's rules, regulations, and directions to you as a CPA candidate.

The next page contains a list of the state boards, their addresses, phone numbers, and the following information relevant to most CPA candidates.

CPA REQUIREMENTS BY STATE (next page)

Residency: Some states have in-state guidelines to meet in order to sit for the CPA exam: R = residency, E = employment, O = office (business), C = U.S. citizenship requirement.

150-hour requirement: As of August 1998, 44 states have legislated the requirement for 150 semester hours to take the CPA exam, which is generally a baccalaureate plus 30 hours. The effective dates of this requirement are listed on the table on the next page. Contact individual boards for exact information.

Education beyond high school (in years) required to take exam/apply for certificate: A number = years of education beyond high school; B = bachelor's; A = emphasis in accounting; + = hours in excess of bachelor's. The slashes are used to separate various levels of education, which affect the amount of experience required to practice (see Experience, below).

Experience (in public accounting) required to practice: Years of experience correspond to education which is listed in the column just to the left. Varying education requirements and varying experience requirements are separated by slashes. For example, Alaska permits persons to take the CPA exam if one of the following requirements is met:

1. A bachelor's degree not in accounting
2. A bachelor's degree with an accounting major

After passing the CPA exam, either 3 or 2 years' experience is required before a CPA certificate is issued.

1. Three years if the exam was taken with a bachelor's degree not in accounting
2. Two years if the exam was taken with a bachelor's degree in accounting

Exam application deadline -- first time: New candidates

Exam application deadline -- re-exam: For candidates with conditional status (see below)

Exam conditioning requirements: Number of parts to pass, followed by minimum grade on other parts, if any

Exam fee: For all four parts, usually less if conditioned

Ethics test: An E indicates a separate ethics test is given (not during the CPA exam). A dash indicates no ethics test. A pound sign (#) means the ethics test is required at the time of certification.

CPA certificate issued separately from a license to practice: Indicated by a "Y"

CPA REQUIREMENTS BY STATE
as of August 1998

NOTE: Each State Board is currently updating requirements to accommodate the 1997 changes in the CPA exam. Contact your State Board for complete up-to-date information.

	STATE BOARD	ADDRESS	Telephone #	Residency	150-Hr. Requirement	Education	Experience	Application Deadline First Time	Application Deadline Re-Exam	Condition Requirements	Exam Fee	Ethics	Separate Certificate
	AK	P.O. Box 110806 • Juneau, AK 99811	(907) 465-2580	--	2001	B/BA	3/2	60 days	60 days	2, 50	$100	E	Y
	AL	770 Washington Ave., Ste. 236 • Montgomery, AL 36130	(334) 242-5700	C	1995	B+	2/5	2/28; 8/31	3/31; 9/30	2, 50	$190	--	Y
	AR	101 East Capitol, Ste. 430 • Little Rock, AR 72201	(501) 682-1520	R/E	1998	BA/+	2/1	60 days	30 days	2, 50	$160	--	Y
	AZ	3877 N. 7th St., Ste. 106 • Phoenix, AZ 85014	(602) 255-3648	--		BA/+	2/1	2/28; 8/31	2/28; 8/31	2, 50	$175	#	--
	CA	2000 Evergreen St., Ste. 250 • Sacramento, CA 95815	(916) 263-3680	--		B/BA	3/2	3/1; 9/1	3/1; 9/1	2	$160	E	--
*	CO	1560 Broadway, Ste. 1370 • Denver, CO 80202	(303) 894-7800	--	2002	BA	1	3/1; 9/1	3/1; 9/1	2, 50	$200	#	--
*	CT	30 Trinity Street • Hartford, CT 06106	(860) 509-6179	--	2000	BA	3	60 days	60 days	2, 50	$220	#	--
	DC	P.O. Box 37200 • Washington, DC 20013-7200	(202) 727-7468	--	2000	BA	2	90 days	60 days	2, 50	$120	--	Y
*	DE	Cannon Bldg., Ste. 203, P.O. Box 1401 • Dover, DE 19903	(302) 739-4522	--		2/BA/+	4/2/1	3/1; 9/1	3/1; 9/1	2, 50	$195	#	Y
	FL	2610 NW 43rd St., Ste. 1-A • Gainesville, FL 32606	(352) 955-2165	--	1983	BA+	0	2/1; 8/1	3/1; 9/1	2, 50	$235	#	--
*	GA	166 Pryor Street, S.W. • Atlanta, GA 30303	(404) 656-2281	--	1998	BA	2	2/1; 8/1	3/1; 9/1	2, 50	$200	--	--
	GU	P.O. Box P • Agana, GU 96910	(671) 475-2672	C/R/E/O	2000	BA/+	2/1	60 days	60 days	2, 50	$35	--	--
*	HI	P.O. Box 3469 • Honolulu, HI 96801	(808) 586-2694	--	1978	BA+	2	3/1; 9/1	3/1; 9/1	2, 50	$270	--	Y
*	IA	1918 SE Hulsizer Avenue • Ankeny, IA 50021	(515) 281-4126	R/E/O	2001	0/BA/+	3/2/0	2/28; 8/31	2/28; 8/31	2, 50	$210	E	Y
	ID	1109 Main St., Ste. 470 • Boise, ID 83720-0002	(208) 334-2490	R	2000	BA/+	2/2	3/1; 9/1	3/1; 9/1	2, 50	$175	E	--
	IL	320 W. Washington St., 3rd Fl. • Springfield, IL 62786	(217) 785-0800	--	2001	BA	1	3/1; 8/1	3/1; 9/1	2, 50	$180	E	Y
*	IN	302 West Washington St, E034 • Indianapolis, IN 46204	(317) 232-3935	R	2000	BA/+	3/2	3/1; 9/1	3/1; 9/1	2, 50	$220	--	--
*	KS	900 SW Jackson St., Ste. 556 • Topeka, KS 66612	(913) 296-2162	R/E/O	1997	BA/+	1-2	3/1; 9/1	3/1; 9/1	2, 50	$200	E	Y
	KY	332 W. Broadway, Ste. 310 • Louisville, KY 40202	(502) 595-3037	R	2000	BA	1-2	3/1; 9/1	3/1; 9/1	2, 50	$140	#	--
*	LA	601 Poydras St., Ste. 1770 • New Orleans, LA 70130	(504) 566-1244	R	1996	BA/+	2/1	3/1; 9/1	3/1; 9/1	2, 50	$200	--	Y
*	MA	100 Cambridge St, Rm. 1315 • Boston, MA 02202	(617) 727-1806	--	2002	BA/+	3/2	3/15; 9/15	3/15; 9/15	2, 50	$220	--	--
**	MD	500 N. Calvert Street, Room 308 • Baltimore, MD 21202-3651	(410) 333-6322	--	1999	BA	0	60 days	60 days	2, 50	$98	E	--
*	ME	35 State House Station • Augusta, ME 04333	(207) 624-8603	R	2002	B/+	2/1	3/1; 9/1	3/1; 9/1	2	$225	--	Y
**	MI	P.O. Box 30018 • Lansing, MI 48909-7518	(517) 241-9249	R/E/O		BA/+	2/1	3/1; 9/1	3/1; 9/1	2, 50	$145	--	Y
	MN	85 East 7th Place • St Paul, MN 55101	(612) 296-7937	R/E/O		0/2/B/BA/+	6/5/3/2/1	3/1; 9/1	3/1; 9/1	2, 50	$150	E	Y
*	MO	P.O. Box 613 • Jefferson City, MO 65102	(573) 751-0012	R/E/O	1999	BA	2	3/1; 9/1	3/1; 9/1	2, 50	$200	#	Y
	MS	653 North State Street • Jackson, MS 39202-3304	(601) 354-7320	R/O	1995	BA+	1	3/1; 9/1	3/1; 9/1	2, 50	$200	--	Y
	MT	111 N. Jackson, P.O. Box 200513 • Helena, MT 59620	(406) 444-3739	--	1997	B/BA+	2/1	3/15; 9/15	3/15; 9/15	2, 50	$225	#	Y
	NC	P.O. Box 12827 • Raleigh, NC 27605	(919) 733-4222	C	2001	B	2	1/31; 7/31	2/28; 8/31	2, 50	$175	E	--
	ND	2701 S. Columbia Rd • Grand Forks, ND 58201	(800) 532-5904	R	2000	0/BA	4/0	3/15; 9/15	3/15; 9/15	2, 40	$140	E	Y
	NE	P.O. Box 94725 • Lincoln, NE 68509	(402) 471-3595	R/E/C	1998	B+	2	3/31; 9/30	3/31; 9/30	2, 50	$200	E	Y
	NH	57 Regional Drive • Concord, NH 03301	(603) 271-3286	--		B/B+	2/1	3/15; 9/15	3/15; 9/15	2, 50	$225	--	--
*	NJ	P.O. Box 45000 • Newark, NJ 07101	(973) 504-6380	--	2000	BA	2	3/1; 9/1	2/1; 8/1	2, 50	$290	--	--
	NM	1650 University NE, Ste. 400A • Albuquerque, NM 87102	(505) 841-9108	--		B/BA	3/1	3/1: 9/1	3/1: 9/1	2	$125	E	Y
	NV	200 South Virginia St., #670 • Reno, NV 89501	(702) 786-0231	--	2001	B	2	3/1; 11/1	3/1; 11/1	2, 50	$150	#	--
*	NY	Cultural Ed Center, Rm. 3013 • Albany, NY 12230	(518) 474-3836	--	2009	BA/+	2/1	2/1; 8/1	3/1; 9/1	2	$345	--	--
*	OH	77 S. High St., 18th FL., Ste. 222 • Columbus, OH 43266	(614) 466-4135	R/E/O	2000	BA/+	2/1	3/2; 9/1	3/2; 9/1	2, 50	$245	E	--
	OK	4545 Lincoln Blvd., Ste. 165 • Ok. City, OK 73105	(405) 521-2397	R	2003	BA	0	60 days	60 days	2, 50	$120	--	--
	OR	3218 Pringle Road SE, Ste. 110 • Salem, OR 97302-6307	(503) 378-4181	--	2000	0/BA/+	4/2/1	3/1; 9/1	3/1; 9/1	2, 50	$150	E	--
**	PA	P.O. Box 2649 • Harrisburg, PA 17105	(717) 783-1404	R/E/O	2000	BA/+	2/2	2/15; 8/15	3/1; 9/1	2	$103.75	--	Y
*	PR	P.O. Box 3271 • San Juan, PR 00902-3271	(787) 722-2122	C/R/E/O	2000	0/B/BA	6/4/0	3/1; 9/1	60 days	2	$275	--	--
*	RI	233 Richmond St., Ste. 236 • Providence, RI 02903	(401) 277-3185	R/E	1999	BA/+	2/1	3/15; 9/15	3/15; 9/15	2	$260	#	--
*	SC	P.O. Box 11329 • Columbia, SC 29211-1329	(800) 272-3926	--	1997	BA+	2	3/15; 9/15	3/15; 9/15	2, 40	$200	--	--
	SD	301 E. 14th St., Ste. 200 • Sioux Falls, SD 57104	(605) 367-5770	--	1998	BA/+	2/1	3/1; 9/1	3/1; 9/1	2, 50	$200	#	Y
*	TN	500 J. Robertson Pkwy., 2nd FL. • Nashville, TN 37243-1141	(615) 741-2550	R	1993	B/BA+	1	3/1; 9/1	3/1; 9/1	2, 50	$200	E	--
	TX	333 Guadalupe Tower III, Ste. 900 • Austin, TX 78701	(512) 305-7800	--	1997	BA/+	2/1	2/28; 8/31	2/28; 8/31	2, 50	$170	#	--
	UT	160 E 300 S., Box 45805 • Salt Lake City, UT 84145	(801) 530-6628	--	1994	BA+	1	2/1; 8/1	3/1; 9/1	2, 50	$251	E	Y
*	VA	3600 West Broad Street • Richmond, VA 23230	(804) 367-8505	--		BA/+	2/1	3/1; 9/1	60 days	2, 50	$162	E	Y
	VI	1-B King Street • Christiansted, St. Croix, VI 00820	(809) 773-0096	R/E/O		0/B/BA	6/3/2	3/15; 9/15	3/15; 9/15	2	$150	--	--
*	VT	109 State Street • Montpelier, VT 05609-1106	(800) 272-3926	--		0/2A	2/2	3/15; 9/15	3/15; 9/15	2, 50	$315	#	--
*	WA	P.O. Box 9131 • Olympia, WA 98507-9131	(360) 664-9191	--	2000	BA	1	3/1; 9/1	3/1; 9/1	2, 50	$200	E	Y
	WI	P.O. Box 8935 • Madison, WI 53708	(608) 266-5511	--	2001	BA	3	3/1; 9/1	3/1; 9/1	2, 50	$132	E	--
	WV	201 L&S Bldg., 812 Quarrier St. • Charleston, WV 25301	(304) 558-3557	R/E/O	2000	BA	2	2/15; 8/15	2/15; 8/15	2, 50	$170	E	Y
	WY	First Bank Bldg., 2020 Carey Ave. • Cheyenne, WY 82002	(307) 777-7551	R/E/O	2000	BA	2	3/1; 9/1	3/1; 9/1	2, 50	$200	E	Y

*CPA Examination Services, a division of the National Association of State Boards of Accountancy, administers the CPA exam including exam application in these 22 states. Call (800) CPA-EXAM

**LGR Examinations administers the CPA exam including exam application in these 3 states. Call (800) 877-EXAM

CERTIFIED INFORMATION SYSTEMS AUDITOR PROGRAM

The Certified Information Systems Auditor (CISA) program, sponsored by the Information Systems Audit and Control Association (ISACA), is available for IS audit, control, and security professionals.

To earn the CISA designation, candidates are required to

- Successfully complete the CISA Examination;
- Adhere to the Information Systems Audit and Control Association's *Code of Professional Ethics*; and
- Submit evidence of a minimum of five (5) years of professional information systems (IS) auditing, control, or security work experience. Substitution and waivers:
  - A maximum of one year of IS audit, control, or security experience may be waived for candidates with
    - one full year of audit experience, or
    - one full year of information systems experience, and/or
    - an Associate's degree (60 semester college credits or its equivalent).
  - Two years IS audit, control, or security experience may be waived for candidates with a Bachelor's degree (120 semester college credits or its equivalent).
  - One year of IS audit, control, or security experience may be waived for each two years experience a candidate has as a full-time university instructor in a related field (i.e., computer science, accounting, IS auditing). Experience must have been gained within the 10-year period preceding the application for certification or within five (5) years from the date of initially passing the examination. Application for certification must be submitted within five (5) years from the passing date of the CISA Exam. All experience will be verified independently with employers.

The CISA examination is offered each year in June and consists of 200 multiple-choice questions, administered during a four-hour session. The purpose of the examination is to test a candidate's understanding, evaluation, and application of

- Generally accepted IS audit standards, statements, and practices and IS security and control practices
- IS strategies, policies, and procedures, management practices and organizational structures
- IS processes, including hardware and software platforms, network and telecommunication infrastructure operational practices, utilization of IS resources and business processes
- Logical, physical, environmental, data validation, processing and balancing controls and the business continuity planning and testing process
- IS development, acquisition, and maintenance

A scaled correct score of 75 is required to pass the examination. The exam is offered in the following languages: Dutch, English, French, German, Hebrew, Italian, Japanese, Korean, and Spanish.

Passing the CISA Exam can be achieved through an organized plan of study. To assist individuals with the development of a successful study plan, ISACA provides several study aids and review courses to exam candidates. The practice of taking the CISA Exam prior to meeting the experience requirements is acceptable and encouraged. The CISA designation will not be awarded until all requirements are met.

If you have any questions, please contact the CISA Examination Registrar by telephone +1.847.253.1545; fax +1.847.253.1443, or e-mail <certification@isaca.org>.

USING EXAM QUESTION AND EXPLANATION BOOKS TO IMPROVE GRADES

Use the other Gleim exam question books to ensure your understanding of each topic you study in your accounting and business law courses. Access the largest bank of exam questions (including thousands from past certification exams) that is widely used by professors. Get immediate feedback on your study effort, while you take your "practice" tests.

AUDITING & SYSTEMS EXAM QUESTIONS AND EXPLANATIONS (Eighth Edition)

FINANCIAL ACCOUNTING EXAM QUESTIONS AND EXPLANATIONS (Eighth Edition)

MANAGERIAL ACCOUNTING EXAM QUESTIONS AND EXPLANATIONS (Fifth Edition)

FEDERAL TAX EXAM QUESTIONS AND EXPLANATIONS (Eighth Edition)

BUSINESS LAW/LEGAL STUDIES EXAM QUESTIONS AND EXPLANATIONS (Fourth Edition)

CITATION OF AUTHORITATIVE PRONOUNCEMENTS

This book cites authoritative pronouncements using the abbreviations in the following list. The internal auditing abbreviations and acronyms are listed in Chapter 13, Internal Auditing.

APB — APB Opinions were issued by the AICPA Accounting Principles Board from 1959 to 1973. A total of 31 opinions were issued.

AR — SSARSs are codified using the AR prefix.

ARB — Accounting Research Bulletins were issued by the Committee on Accounting Procedure until 1959. A total of 51 ARBs were issued.

AT — SSAEs are codified using the AT prefix.

AU — SASs are codified in the professional standards volumes using the AU prefix.

BL — Bylaws of the AICPA are abbreviated as BL.

CS — Statements on Standards for Consulting Services are codified using the CS prefix.

FASB — The Financial Accounting Standards Board issues Statements of Financial Accounting Standards and Interpretations. The latter interpret existing pronouncements rather than establish new, superseding, or amending positions.

QC — Statements on Quality Control Standards are codified using the QC prefix. These AICPA pronouncements set standards for quality control by CPA firms.

PR — Standards for Performing and Reporting on Peer Reviews are codified under the PR prefix. They apply to the parties involved in practice-monitoring programs.

SAS — Statements on Auditing Standards issued by the AICPA Auditing Standards Board are codified using the SAS prefix. These interpretations of generally accepted auditing standards have the status of GAAS.

SFAS — Statements of Financial Accounting Standards are issued by the Financial Accounting Standards Board (FASB), which was established in 1973. Many SFASs supersede prior SFASs, APB Opinions, and Accounting Research Bulletins.

SSAE — Statements on Standards for Attestation Engagements pertain to attestation standards (AT 100), financial forecasts and projections (AT 200), reporting on pro forma financial information (AT 300), reporting on internal control (AT 400), compliance attestation (AT 500), agreed-upon procedures engagements (AT 600), and management's discussion and analysis (AT 700).

SSARS — Statements on Standards for Accounting and Review Services are a series of AICPA pronouncements setting standards for engagements in connection with unaudited financial statements or other unaudited financial information of nonpublic entities.

TX — Statements on Responsibilities in Tax Practice are codified using the TX prefix. They are AICPA pronouncements recommending nonenforceable standards for tax practice and the CPA's responsibilities to the client, the public, and government.

When a pronouncement is cited in the text, the pronouncement number follows the abbreviations. For example, AU 110 refers to Auditing Standards Section 110.

The first time an authoritative pronouncement is cited, the abbreviation and number are followed by the pronouncement title, e.g., AU 339, *Working Papers*. In subsequent citations within a related series of questions, the title is usually omitted.

The next two sideheadings give two-way cross-references:

- Chapters in this book referenced to authoritative pronouncements
- Authoritative pronouncements referenced to chapters in this book

COVERAGE OF AUTHORITATIVE PRONOUNCEMENTS

The listing below and on the next page indicates coverage by chapter in this book.

Chapter 1 External Auditing Standards and Professional Responsibilities
- 110 Responsibilities and Functions of the Independent Auditor
- 150 Generally Accepted Auditing Standards
- 161 The Relationship of Generally Accepted Auditing Standards to Quality Control Standards
- 201 Nature of the General Standards
- 210 Training and Proficiency of the Independent Auditor
- 220 Independence
- 230 Due Professional Care in the Performance of Work
- 310 Appointment of the Independent Auditor
- 311 Planning and Supervision
- 312 Audit Risk and Materiality in Conducting an Audit
- 313 Substantive Tests Prior to the Balance Sheet Date
- 315 Communications between Predecessor and Successor Auditors
- 316 Consideration of Fraud in a Financial Statement Audit
- 317 Illegal Acts by Clients
- 319 Consideration of Internal Control in a Financial Statement Audit
- 380 Communication with Audit Committees
- 410 Adherence to Generally Accepted Accounting Principles
- 411 The Meaning of *Present Fairly in Conformity with Generally Accepted Accounting Principles* in the Independent Auditor's Report
- 431 Adequacy of Disclosure in Financial Statements
- 504 Association with Financial Statements
- AT 100 Attestation Standards
- AT 500 Compliance Attestation
- AR 100 Compilation and Review of Financial Statements
- PR 100 Standards for Performing and Reporting on Peer Reviews
- Statements on Standards for Consulting Services
- Statements on Quality Control Standards
- Statements on Responsibilities in Tax Practice
- AICPA Code of Professional Conduct
- Assurance Services

Chapter 2 Audit Planning and Risk Assessment
- 310 Appointment of the Independent Auditor
- 311 Planning and Supervision
- 312 Audit Risk and Materiality in Conducting an Audit
- 315 Communications between Predecessor and Successor Auditors
- 316 Consideration of Fraud in a Financial Statement Audit
- 317 Illegal Acts by Clients
- 319 Consideration of Internal Control in a Financial Statement Audit
- 326 Evidential Matter
- 329 Analytical Procedures
- 331 Inventories
- 333 Management Representations
- 339 Working Papers
- 350 Audit Sampling
- 508 Reports on Audited Financial Statements
- Conduct Rule 201

Chapter 3 Internal Control
- 313 Substantive Tests Prior to the Balance Sheet Date
- 316 Consideration of Fraud in a Financial Statement Audit
- 317 Illegal Acts by Clients
- 319 Consideration of Internal Control in a Financial Statement Audit
- 322 The Auditor's Consideration of the Internal Audit Function in an Audit of Financial Statements
- 325 The Communication of Internal Control Related Matters Noted in an Audit
- 326 Evidential Matter
- 331 Inventories
- 350 Audit Sampling
- 380 Communication with Audit Committees

Chapter 4 Audit Evidence and Procedures
- 311 Planning and Supervision
- 312 Audit Risk and Materiality in Conducting an Audit
- 313 Substantive Tests Prior to the Balance Sheet Date
- 316 Consideration of Fraud in a Financial Statement Audit
- 317 Illegal Acts by Clients
- 319 Consideration of Internal Control in a Financial Statement Audit
- 326 Evidential Matter
- 329 Analytical Procedures
- 330 The Confirmation Process
- 331 Inventories
- 332 Auditing Investments
- 333 Management Representations
- 334 Related Parties
- 336 Using the Work of a Specialist
- 337 Inquiry of a Client's Lawyer Concerning Litigation, Claims, and Assessments
- 339 Working Papers
- 341 The Auditor's Consideration of an Entity's Ability to Continue as a Going Concern
- 342 Auditing Accounting Estimates
- 390 Consideration of Omitted Procedures after the Report Date
- 508 Reports on Audited Financial Statements

530 Dating of the Independent Auditor's Report
560 Subsequent Events
561 Subsequent Discovery of Facts Existing at the Date of the Auditor's Report
901 Public Warehouses -- Internal Controls and Auditing Procedures for Goods Held
AR 100 Compilation and Review of Financial Statements

Chapter 5 Information Systems
319 Consideration of Internal Control in a Financial Statement Audit

Chapter 6 Statistical Sampling
350 Audit Sampling

Chapter 7 Audit Reports
110 Responsibilities and Functions of the Independent Auditor
150 Generally Accepted Auditing Standards
310 Appointment of the Independent Auditor
316 Consideration of Fraud in a Financial Statement Audit
317 Illegal Acts by Clients
331 Inventories
333 Management Representations
334 Related Parties
336 Using the Work of a Specialist
337 Inquiry of a Client's Lawyer Concerning Litigation, Claims, and Assessments
341 The Auditor's Consideration of an Entity's Ability to Continue as a Going Concern
342 Auditing Accounting Estimates
380 Communication with Audit Committees
410 Adherence to Generally Accepted Accounting Principles
411 The Meaning of *Present Fairly in Conformity with Generally Accepted Accounting Principles* in the Independent Auditor's Report
420 Consistency of Application of Generally Accepted Accounting Principles
431 Adequacy of Disclosure in Financial Statements
504 Association with Financial Statements
508 Reports on Audited Financial Statements
530 Dating of the Independent Auditor's Report
534 Reporting on Financial Statements Prepared for Use in Other Countries
543 Part of Audit Made by Other Independent Auditors
544 Lack of Conformity with Generally Accepted Accounting Principles
551 Reporting on Information Accompanying the Basic Financial Statements in Auditor-Submitted Documents
552 Reporting on Condensed Financial Statements and Selected Financial Data
558 Required Supplementary Information
560 Subsequent Events
561 Subsequent Discovery of Facts Existing at the Date of the Auditor's Report
623 Special Reports
625 Reports on the Application of Accounting Principles
634 Letters for Underwriters and Certain Other Requesting Parties
711 Filings under Federal Securities Statutes
AT 100 Attestation Standards
AT 200 Financial Forecasts and Projections
AT 700 Management's Discussion and Analysis
AR 100 Compilation and Review of Financial Statements
Conduct Rule 203
Conduct Rule 301

Chapter 8 Special Reports and Other Reporting Issues
150 Generally Accepted Auditing Standards
324 Reports on the Processing of Transactions by Service Organizations
504 Association with Financial Statements
543 Part of Audit Made by Other Independent Auditors
550 Other Information in Documents Containing Audited Financial Statements
551 Reporting on Information Accompanying the Basic Financial Statements in Auditor-Submitted Documents
552 Reporting on Condensed Financial Statements and Selected Financial Data
558 Required Supplementary Information
622 Engagements to Apply Agreed-upon Procedures to Specified Elements, Accounts, or Items of a Financial Statement
623 Special Reports
625 Reports on the Application of Accounting Principles
634 Letters for Underwriters and Certain Other Requesting Parties
711 Filings under Federal Securities Statutes
722 Interim Financial Information
801 Compliance Auditing Considerations in Audits of Governmental Entities and Recipients of Governmental Financial Assistance
AT 100 Attestation Standards
AT 200 Financial Forecasts and Projections
AT 300 Reporting on Pro Forma Financial Information
AT 400 Reporting on an Entity's Internal Control over Financial Reporting
AT 500 Compliance Attestation
AT 600 Agreed-Upon Procedures Engagements
AT 700 Management's Discussion and Analysis
AR 100 Compilation and Review of Financial Statements
AR 200 Reporting on Comparative Financial Statements
AR 300 Compilation Reports on Financial Statements Included in Certain Prescribed Forms
AR 400 Communications between Predecessor and Successor Accountants
AR 600 Reporting on Personal Financial Statements Included in Written Personal Financial Plans

Chapter 9 Internal Auditing
The IIA Code of Ethics
Statement of Responsibilities of Internal Auditors (SRIA)
Standards for the Professional Practice of Internal Auditing (SPPIA)
Statements on Internal Auditing Standards (SIASs)

PRONOUNCEMENT CROSS-REFERENCE

The following is a directory listing the modules in this study manual that cover the professional standards. The module number(s) follow(s) the pronouncement title. Most pronouncements are covered by at least two multiple-choice questions.

Sec. No. Statements on Auditing Standards

110 Responsibilities and Functions of the Independent Auditor - 1.1, 1.2, 1.7, Chap. 7
150 Generally Accepted Auditing Standards - 1.2, 7.1, 7.2, 7.5, 8.1
161 The Relationship of Generally Accepted Auditing Standards to Quality Control Standards - 1.10

201 Nature of the General Standards - 1.2, 1.3
210 Training and Proficiency of the Independent Auditor - 1.3
220 Independence - 1.3
230 Due Professional Care in the Performance of Work - 1.3

310 Appointment of the Independent Auditor- 1.4, 2.1, 7.7
311 Planning and Supervision - 1.10, 2.1, 2.2, 2.5, Chap. 4
312 Audit Risk and Materiality in Conducting an Audit - 1.4, 2.3, Chap. 4
313 Substantive Tests Prior to the Balance Sheet Date - 1.4, 3.4, Chap. 4
315 Communications between Predecessor and Successor Auditors - 1.3, 2.1, 2.2, 2.4, 2.5
316 Consideration of Fraud in a Financial Statement Audit - 1.7, 1.9, 2.4, Chap. 4, 7.6
317 Illegal Acts by Clients - 1.5, 2.4, 3.2, 4.12, 7.5, 7.7
319 Consideration of Internal Control in a Financial Statement Audit - 1.1, 1.4, 1.6, 2.2, 2.3, 2.5, 3.1 - 3.5, 3.7, 3.11, 3.13, 3.14, 4.1, 4.12, 5.13
322 The Auditor's Consideration of the Internal Audit Function in an Audit of Financial Statements - 3.4, 3.13
324 Reports on the Processing of Transactions by Service Organizations - 8.5
325 The Communication of Internal Control Related Matters Noted in an Audit - 3.2, 3.7, 3.12
326 Evidential Matter - 2.2, 3.9, Chap. 4
329 Analytical Procedures - 2.5, 4.2, 4.11
330 The Confirmation Process - 4.1, 4.3
331 Inventories - 2.2, 3.10, 4.1, 4.4, 4.6, 4.14, 6.2, 7.5
332 Auditing Investments - 4.8, 4.9
333 Management Representations - 2.4, 4.1, 4.12, 7.7
334 Related Parties - 4.16, 7.4, 7.5, 7.10
336 Using the Work of a Specialist - 4.14, 7.5, 7.12
337 Inquiry of a Client's Lawyer Concerning Litigation, Claims, and Assessments - 4.13, 7.5, 7.7
339 Working Papers - 2.5
341 The Auditor's Consideration of an Entity's Ability to Continue as a Going Concern - 4.2, 7.4, 7.5, 7.11
342 Auditing Accounting Estimates - 4.1
350 Audit Sampling - 2.3, 3.5, Chap. 6
380 Communication with Audit Committees - 1.3, 3.12
390 Consideration of Omitted Procedures after the Report Date - 4.15

410 Adherence to Generally Accepted Accounting Principles - 1.4, 7.2
411 The Meaning of *Present Fairly in Conformity with Generally Accepted Accounting Principles* in the Independent Auditor's Report - 1.4, 7.1, 7.2, 7.4, 7.5
420 Consistency of Application of Generally Accepted Accounting Principles - 7.3 , 7.4, 7.11
431 Adequacy of Disclosure in Financial Statements - 1.7, 7.4, 7.6

504 Association with Financial Statements - 1.3, 1.8, 7.1, 7.5, 7.6, 7.9, 8.3, 8.4
508 Reports on Audited Financial Statements - 2.4, 4.16, Chap. 7
530 Dating of the Independent Auditor's Report - 4.15, 7.8, 7.9, 7.11
534 Reporting on Financial Statements Prepared for Use in Other Countries - 7.2
543 Part of Audit Made by Other Independent Auditors - 7.5, 7.9, 7.12, 8.3, 8.5
544 Lack of Conformity with Generally Accepted Accounting Principles - 7.2, 7.5
550 Other Information in Documents Containing Audited Financial Statements - 8.2
551 Reporting on Information Accompanying the Basic Financial Statements in Auditor-Submitted Documents - 7.4, 8.2
552 Reporting on Condensed Financial Statements and Selected Financial Data - 7.12, 8.2
558 Required Supplementary Information - 7.7, 8.2
560 Subsequent Events - 4.9, 4.15, 7.4, 7.5, 7.8, 7.11
561 Subsequent Discovery of Facts Existing at the Date of the Auditor's Report - 4.15, 7.11

622 Engagements to Apply Agreed-upon Procedures to Specified Elements, Accounts, or Items of a Financial Statement - 8.1
623 Special Reports - 7.2, 7.7, 8.1, 8.4

Sec. No.

Statements on Auditing Standards

625 Reports on the Application of Accounting Principles - 7.2, 8.1
634 Letters for Underwriters and Certain Other Requesting Parties - 7.5, 7.9, 8.4, 8.7
711 Filings under Federal Securities Statutes - 7.11, 8.2, 8.7
722 Interim Financial Information - 4.2, 8.1, 8.3, 8.4, 8.7
801 Compliance Auditing Considerations in Audits of Governmental Entities and Recipients of Governmental Financial Assistance - 8.8
901 Public Warehouses -- Internal Controls and Auditing Procedures for Goods Held - 4.6

Statements on Standards for Attestation Engagements

AT 100 Attestation Standards - 1.13, 7.9, 8.1, 8.9
AT 200 Financial Forecasts and Projections - 1.5, 7.5, 8.1, 8.6
AT 300 Reporting on Pro Forma Financial Information - 8.6
AT 400 Reporting on an Entity's Internal Control over Financial Reporting - 8.1, 8.5
AT 500 Compliance Attestation - 1.13, 8.9
AT 600 Agreed-Upon Procedures Engagements - 8.1
AT 700 Management's Discussion and Analysis - 8.10

Statements on Standards for Accounting and Review Services

AR 100 Compilation and Review of Financial Statements - 1.8, 1.9, 4.2, 7.6, 8.4, 8.5, 8.7
AR 200 Reporting on Comparative Financial Statements - 8.4
AR 300 Compilation Reports on Financial Statements Included in Certain Prescribed Forms - 8.4
AR 400 Communications between Predecessor and Successor Accountants - 8.4
AR 600 Reporting on Personal Financial Statements Included in Written Personal Financial Plans - 8.4

Statements on Standards for Consulting Services

CS 100 Consulting Services: Definitions and Standards - 1.12

Statements on Responsibilities in Tax Practice

TX 102 Introduction - 1.11
TX 112 Tax Return Positions - 1.6, 1.11
TX 122 Answers to Questions on Returns - 1.11
TX 132 Certain Procedural Aspects of Preparing Returns - 1.11
TX 142 Use of Estimates - 1.11
TX 152 Departure from a Position Previously Concluded in an Administrative Proceeding or Court Decision - 1.11
TX 162 Knowledge of Error: Return Preparation - 1.11
TX 172 Knowledge of Error: Administrative Proceedings - 1.11
TX 182 Form and Content of Advice to Clients - 1.11

Statements on Quality Control Standards

QC 20 System of Quality Control for a CPA Firm's Accounting and Auditing Practice - 1.3, 1.10
QC 30 Monitoring a CPA Firm's Accounting and Auditing Practice - 1.10

Standards for Performing and Reporting on Peer Reviews

PR 100 Standards for Performing and Reporting on Peer Reviews - 1.10

Code of Professional Conduct

Conduct Rule 101 - 1.3, 1.5, 1.6
Conduct Rule 102 - 1.5, 1.6, 1.8
Conduct Rule 201 - 1.2, 1.5, 2.1
Conduct Rule 202 - 1.2, 1.5
Conduct Rule 203 - 1.4, 1.5, 1.8, 7.2
Conduct Rule 301 - 1.7, 7.4
Conduct Rule 302 - 1.6, 1.8
Conduct Rule 501 - 1.5, 1.8
Conduct Rule 502 - 1.5, 1.8
Conduct Rule 503 - 1.5, 1.8
Conduct Rule 505 - 1.5

RECENT SASs AND THEIR AU NUMBERS

		AU Numbers
SAS 62	Special Reports	623
SAS 63	(Superseded by SAS 68)	
SAS 64	Omnibus Statement -- 1990*	
SAS 65	The Auditor's Consideration of the Internal Audit Function in an Audit of Financial Statements	322
SAS 66	(Superseded by SAS 71)	
SAS 67	The Confirmation Process	330
SAS 68	(Superseded by SAS 74)	
SAS 69	The Meaning of "Present Fairly in Conformity with Generally Accepted Accounting Principles" in the Independent Auditor's Report	411
SAS 70	Reports on the Processing of Transactions by Service Organizations	324
SAS 71	Interim Financial Information	722
SAS 72	Letters for Underwriters and Certain Other Requesting Parties	634
SAS 73	Using the Work of a Specialist	336
SAS 74	Compliance Auditing Considerations in Audits of Governmental Entities and Recipients of Governmental Financial Assistance	801
SAS 75	Engagements to Apply Agreed-Upon Procedures to Specified Elements, Accounts, or Items of a Financial Statement	622
SAS 76	Amendments to SAS 72, Letters for Underwriters and Certain Other Requesting Parties	634
SAS 77	Amendments to SASs 22, Planning and Supervision, 59, The Auditor's Consideration of an Entity's Ability to Continue as a Going Concern, and 62, Special Reports**	
SAS 78	Consideration of Internal Control in a Financial Statement Audit: An Amendment to SAS 55	319
SAS 79	Consideration of Internal Control in a Financial Statement Audit: An Amendment to SAS 58	508
SAS 80	Consideration of Internal Control in a Financial Statement Audit: An Amendment to SAS 31, Evidential Matter	326
SAS 81	Auditing Investments	332
SAS 82	Consideration of Fraud in a Financial Statement Audit	316
SAS 83	Establishing an Understanding With the Client (amends AU 310)	310
SAS 84	Communication Between Predecessor and Successor Auditors (supersedes old AU 315)	315
SAS 85	Management Representations***	333
SAS 86	Amendment to SAS No. 72	634

*Integrated with AU 341, 508, and 543.
**Integrated with AU 311, 341, 544, 623.
***Supersedes old AU 333 and also slightly amends AU 508.

CHAPTER ONE
EXTERNAL AUDITING STANDARDS AND PROFESSIONAL RESPONSIBILITIES

The first module in this chapter provides an overview of the nature of independent, external auditing. The next three modules concern the 10 generally accepted auditing standards. Module 1.3 covers the three general standards, which are not addressed elsewhere in the book. The three standards of field work and the four standards of reporting are dealt with in a single module (1.4) because these standards and their applications are covered further in

Chapter 2 -- Audit Planning and Risk Assessment
Chapter 3 -- Internal Control
Chapter 4 -- Audit Evidence and Procedures
Chapter 7 -- Audit Reports

Modules 1.5 through 1.8 concern the AICPA *Code of Professional Conduct*, and Module 1.9 covers the legal liability of CPAs. Module 1.10 addresses the quality control and peer review standards applicable to CPA firms (GAAS apply to individuals) that help them to comply with GAAS. Module 1.11 contains questions on the AICPA Statements on Responsibilities in Tax Practice. Module 1.12 covers the AICPA Statement on Standards for Consulting Services. Module 1.13 deals with AT 100, *Attestation Standards*, which established the 11 attestation standards. These standards are an extension of the 10 GAAS. They apply to attest services rendered by a CPA in the practice of public accounting. These services also include compliance attestation (AT 500). A new category of services, assurance services, is the subject of Module 1.14.

1.1 Introduction to Auditing

1. The primary reason for an audit by an independent, external audit firm is to

A. Satisfy governmental regulatory requirements.

B. Guarantee that there are no misstatements in the financial statements and ensure that any fraud will be discovered.

C. Relieve management of responsibility for the financial statements.

D. Provide increased assurance to users as to the fairness of the financial statements.

The correct answer is (D). *(CMA, adapted)*

REQUIRED: The primary reason for an independent, external audit.

DISCUSSION: The objective of an audit is to express an opinion as to whether an entity's financial statements present fairly, in all material respects, its financial position, results of operations, and cash flows in conformity with generally accepted accounting principles (GAAP). An audit performed by an independent, external audit firm provides assurance of the objectivity of the auditor's opinion.

Answer (A) is incorrect because governmental regulation has increased [e.g., the requirement of the Foreign Corrupt Practices Act (FCPA) that certain companies maintain adequate internal control], but the primary objective of the audit continues to be an opinion on the fairness of the financial statements. Answer (B) is incorrect because the auditor is neither a guarantor nor an insurer. Answer (C) is incorrect because, according to both AU 110, *Responsibilities and Functions of the Independent Auditor*, and the FCPA, management is responsible for the financial statements.

2. Independent CPAs perform audits on the financial statements of public companies. This type of auditing can best be described as

A. An activity whose purpose is to search for fraud.

B. A discipline that attests to financial information presented by management.

C. A professional activity that measures and communicates financial and business data.

D. A regulatory function that prevents the issuance of improper financial information.

The correct answer is (B). *(Publisher)*

REQUIRED: The statement that best describes independent auditing.

DISCUSSION: The objective of the audit is to express an opinion on (attest to) the fairness of presentation and conformity with GAAP of management's financial statements.

Answer (A) is incorrect because the auditor plans and performs the audit to provide reasonable assurance of detecting material misstatements, whether caused by error or fraud. However, (s)he need not search for all instances of fraud, and the ultimate objective is to determine whether the statements are fairly presented. Answer (C) is incorrect because the accounting, not auditing, process is a professional activity that measures and communicates financial and business data. Answer (D) is incorrect because an auditor lacks regulatory authority.

3. Users of a public company's financial statements demand independent audits because

A. Users demand assurance that fraud does not exist.

B. Management may not be objective in reporting.

C. Users expect auditors to correct management errors.

D. Management relies on the auditor to improve internal control.

The correct answer is (B). *(Publisher)*

REQUIRED: The reason for an independent audit.

DISCUSSION: Management and financial statement users may have an adversary relationship because their interests in the firm are different. The independent auditor provides assurance that the financial statements are not biased for or against any interest.

Answer (A) is incorrect because the independent auditor is ultimately concerned with the fair presentation of the financial statements in conformity with GAAP, not just with the detection of fraud. However, the audit should be planned and performed to provide reasonable assurance that material misstatements are detected. Answer (C) is incorrect because management is responsible for error correction. Answer (D) is incorrect because poorly designed internal control is not necessarily inconsistent with a fair presentation of the financial statements.

4. An audit of the financial statements of Camden Corporation is being conducted by an external auditor. The external auditor is expected to

A. Express an opinion as to the fairness of Camden's financial statements.

B. Express an opinion as to the attractiveness of Camden for investment purposes and critique the wisdom and legality of its business decisions.

C. Certify the correctness of Camden's financial statements.

D. Make a 100% examination of Camden's records.

The correct answer is (A). *(CMA, adapted)*

REQUIRED: The responsibility of an external auditor for an audit of financial statements.

DISCUSSION: The fourth standard of reporting requires the auditor to express an opinion regarding the financial statements taken as a whole or to make an assertion to the effect that an opinion cannot be expressed. The opinion concerns the fairness with which the statements have been presented in conformity with GAAP.

Answer (B) is incorrect because the external auditor does not interpret the financial statement data for investment purposes or evaluate management decisions. Answer (C) is incorrect because the external audit normally cannot be so thorough as to permit a guarantee of correctness. Answer (D) is incorrect because a 100% examination is seldom, if ever, feasible.

5. Brandnew Company is going public, and its stock will be listed on a stock exchange. Audited financial statements are required to be filed with the Securities and Exchange Commission (SEC). Who is expected to be the primary user of the audited financial statements?

A. The stock exchange.

B. Brandnew Company's investors.

C. The SEC.

D. Brandnew Company's board of directors.

The correct answer is (B). *(Publisher)*

REQUIRED: The primary user of audited financial statements of a publicly held corporation.

DISCUSSION: An audit's primary objective is to provide assurance to current and potential creditors and investors and other users of financial statements that the financial statements present fairly, in all material respects, the financial position, results of operations, and cash flows of the company.

Answer (A) is incorrect because a stock exchange can require disclosures suitable for its purposes. Investors may not have this power. Answer (C) is incorrect because the SEC can require whatever disclosures are desired. Answer (D) is incorrect because the board of directors can require whatever disclosures are desired.

6. The National Commission on Fraudulent Financial Reporting (the Treadway Commission) made a number of recommendations to overcome fraudulent financial reporting. Which of the following was not one of the commission's recommendations?

A. A stronger internal auditing function.

B. More emphasis on fraud detection by independent public accountants.

C. Better training by colleges and universities about the symptoms of fraud and fraudulent reporting.

D. More stringent regulation by the FASB.

The correct answer is (D). *(D. Bradley)*

REQUIRED: The item that was not a recommendation made by the Treadway Commission.

DISCUSSION: The commission called for more regulation, but it did so with the SEC and other regulatory bodies in mind. The FASB establishes accounting principles but has little influence on prevention of fraudulent reporting.

Answer (A) is incorrect because the commission recommended a stronger internal auditing function. The tone at the top of organizations is an important factor in evaluating the possibility of fraudulent reporting. More effective control by both management and auditors helps to prevent and detect fraud. SASs 53 through 61 were issued in part because of the recommendations of the commission. Answer (B) is incorrect because more emphasis on fraud detection by independent public accountants was a recommendation of the commission. Answer (C) is incorrect because better training by colleges and universities about the symptoms of fraud and fraudulent reporting was a recommendation of the commission.

7. The Committee of Sponsoring Organizations (COSO) of the Treadway Commission issued a document in 1992 that has been embraced by numerous organizations, including the AICPA and the GAO. That document is titled

A. The Yellow Book.

B. Internal Control--Integrated Framework.

C. Statements on Auditing Standards.

D. *Code of Professional Conduct*.

The correct answer is (B). *(Publisher)*

REQUIRED: The document issued by the COSO.

DISCUSSION: Many professional and regulatory bodies have recognized the COSO's internal control framework by incorporating its terms, definitions, and concepts into their policies, procedures, pronouncements, and literature.

Answer (A) is incorrect because the Yellow Book, or *Government Auditing Standards*, is issued by the GAO. Answer (C) is incorrect because Statements on Auditing Standards are issued by the Auditing Standards Board of the AICPA. Answer (D) is incorrect because the *Code of Professional Conduct* has been adopted by the members of the AICPA.

8. Who establishes generally accepted auditing standards?

A. American Institute of Certified Public Accountants.

B. Financial Accounting Standards Board.

C. The Institute of Internal Auditors and the Institute of Management Accountants.

D. Securities and Exchange Commission.

The correct answer is (A). *(Publisher)*

REQUIRED: The organization that promulgates generally accepted auditing standards (GAAS).

DISCUSSION: AICPA Conduct Rule 202, *Compliance with Standards*, requires adherence to standards promulgated by bodies designated by the AICPA Council. Thus, the Auditing Standards Board (ASB) is the body designated to issue auditing pronouncements. The ASB issues Statements on Auditing Standards (SASs), which are deemed to be GAAS.

Answer (B) is incorrect because the FASB issues Statements on Financial Accounting Standards, etc. Answer (C) is incorrect because The IIA has promulgated Standards for the Professional Practice of Internal Auditing (SPPIA), a Statement of Responsibilities of Internal Auditing (SRIA), The IIA *Code of Ethics*, and Statements on Internal Auditing Standards (SIASs). The IMA's Management Accounting Practices Committee issues Statements on Management Accounting (SMAs). Answer (D) is incorrect because the SEC issues Financial Reporting Releases and Accounting and Auditing Enforcement Releases.

9. The authoritative body designated to promulgate standards concerning an accountant's association with unaudited financial statements of an entity that is not required to file financial statements with an agency regulating the issuance of the entity's securities is the

A. Financial Accounting Standards Board.

B. General Accounting Office.

C. Accounting and Review Services Committee.

D. Auditing Standards Board.

The correct answer is (C). *(CPA, adapted)*

REQUIRED: The body that promulgates standards for an accountant's association with unaudited statements.

DISCUSSION: The Accounting and Review Services Committee is the senior technical committee authorized to issue pronouncements in connection with the unaudited financial statements or other unaudited financial information of a nonpublic entity.

Answer (A) is incorrect because the FASB is charged with establishing GAAP. Answer (B) is incorrect because the GAO is the federal agency that issues *Government Auditing Standards* (the Yellow Book). Answer (D) is incorrect because the ASB is the AICPA senior technical committee responsible for issuing auditing and attest standards and procedures.

10. CPAs within each state have formed state societies or associations of CPAs. Which of the following statements about these associations is false?

A. Most associations have their own codes of professional ethics that closely parallel the AICPA *Code of Professional Conduct*.

B. The state societies are independent of the AICPA.

C. All CPAs in the state must be members of the state association or society.

D. Members of state associations may also be members of the AICPA.

The correct answer is (C). *(Publisher)*

REQUIRED: The false statement concerning state associations or societies of CPAs.

DISCUSSION: Membership in state societies as well as the AICPA is voluntary. State societies typically function through small, full-time staffs or committees composed of their members. They promote the interests of the membership through communication and continuing education programs.

Answer (A) is incorrect because many state societies have adopted codes of ethics that are similar to the AICPA *Code of Professional Conduct*. Answer (B) is incorrect because the state societies are independent of the AICPA, although they cooperate in promoting the mutual interests of CPAs. Answer (D) is incorrect because members of state societies may also belong to the AICPA.

1.2 Nature of Generally Accepted Auditing Standards

11. Which of the following best describes what is meant by generally accepted auditing standards (GAAS)?

A. Pronouncements issued by the Auditing Standards Board (ASB).

B. Rules acknowledged by the accounting profession because of their universal application.

C. Procedures to be used to gather evidence to support financial statements.

D. Measures of the quality of the auditor's performance.

The correct answer is (D). *(CPA, adapted)*

REQUIRED: The best description of GAAS.

DISCUSSION: According to AU 150, *Generally Accepted Auditing Standards*, GAAS are concerned with the quality of the auditor's performance, including his/her professional qualities and exercise of judgment in connection with audit engagements. The 10 standards include three general standards, three standards of field work, and four standards of reporting.

Answer (A) is incorrect because the ASB issues pronouncements that are not included in GAAS. Answer (B) is incorrect because adherence to good practice is not universal. Answer (C) is incorrect because "procedures relate to acts to be performed, whereas standards deal with measures of the quality of performance of those acts and the objectives to be attained by the use of the procedures" (AU 150).

12. Generally accepted auditing standards (GAAS) are

A. Sufficiently established so that independent auditors generally agree on their interpretation.

B. Generally accepted based upon a pronouncement of the Financial Accounting Standards Board.

C. Generally accepted by the business community.

D. Generally accepted as a consequence of approval by the AICPA membership.

The correct answer is (D). *(CPA, adapted)*

REQUIRED: The correct statement about GAAS.

DISCUSSION: The 10 GAAS are binding on AICPA members as a result of adoption by the AICPA membership (AU 150). They are also considered standards of the profession by state boards of accountancy and the courts, so they are also binding on non-AICPA members. The AICPA has also adopted rules providing for enforcement of GAAS as part of the *Code of Professional Conduct*.

Answer (A) is incorrect because, although the 10 GAAS were adopted by the membership, the SASs, which are now issued by the ASB and are deemed to have the status of GAAS, are often controversial. Answer (B) is incorrect because auditing standards are issued by the AICPA, not the FASB. Answer (C) is incorrect because adoption by the accounting profession, not acceptance by the business community, determines whether an auditing standard is binding.

13. Which of the following statements best describes the primary purpose of Statements on Auditing Standards (SASs)?

A. They are guides intended to set forth auditing procedures applicable to a variety of situations.

B. They are procedural outlines intended to narrow the areas of inconsistency and divergence of auditor opinion.

C. They are authoritative statements, enforced through the *Code of Professional Conduct*, and are intended to limit the degree of auditor judgment.

D. They are generally accepted auditing standards.

The correct answer is (D). *(CPA, adapted)*

REQUIRED: The primary purpose of SASs.

DISCUSSION: SASs are interpretations or clarifications of the 10 GAAS, but they are also deemed to have the status of GAAS. Conduct Rule 202, *Compliance with Standards*, requires members who perform professional services to "comply with standards promulgated by bodies designated by Council." This rule therefore does not distinguish between the 10 GAAS and the SASs.

Answer (A) is incorrect because SASs are intended to establish auditing standards rather than auditing procedures. Answer (B) is incorrect because SASs narrow areas of inconsistency in auditing, but they are standards and are therefore broader than procedural outlines. Answer (C) is incorrect because compliance with SASs is enforced by the AICPA through the *Code of Professional Conduct*. However, the intention is not to limit the auditor's judgment but to provide guidelines for its exercise.

14. Through legal precedent, the generally accepted auditing standards established by the AICPA apply

A. Only to CPAs who belong to local CPA societies.

B. To all CPAs.

C. Only to those CPAs who choose to have quality reviews.

D. Only to CPAs conducting audits subject to AICPA jurisdiction.

The correct answer is (B). *(Publisher)*

REQUIRED: The legally determined applicability of GAAS.

DISCUSSION: GAAS apply to all CPAs, whether or not they are members of the AICPA. GAAS are deemed to be standards of the profession (explicitly or implicitly) by state boards of accountancy, which issue, renew, suspend, or revoke licenses and otherwise regulate CPAs in all states. Furthermore, the courts in both civil and criminal cases involving independent accountants also treat GAAS as standards of the profession.

Answers (A) and (C) are incorrect because GAAS are binding on all CPAs who perform independent, external audits. Answer (D) is incorrect because AICPA jurisdiction concerns only membership in the AICPA. The right to perform the attest function is controlled by state boards of accountancy, all of which require compliance with GAAS.

15. In deciding to undertake an audit engagement, the CPA would most likely consider which generally accepted auditing standard(s)?

A. The four reporting standards.

B. The three field work standards.

C. The second field work standard requiring consideration of internal control.

D. The three general standards.

The correct answer is (D). *(Publisher)*

REQUIRED: The GAAS most likely to be considered in choosing to accept an audit engagement.

DISCUSSION: The three general standards require the auditor to (1) have adequate technical training and proficiency as an auditor, (2) have an independent mental attitude, and (3) use due professional care in planning and performing the audit and preparing the report. An auditor who cannot meet any one of these requirements should not accept the audit engagement. Conduct Rule 201, *General Standards*, requires an AICPA member to "undertake only those professional services that the member or the member's firm can reasonably expect to be completed with professional competence."

Answer (A) is incorrect because the standards of reporting apply to communicating the results of an engagement. Answer (B) is incorrect because the standards of field work apply to the conduct of the engagement. Answer (C) is incorrect because the second standard of field work requires understanding of internal control.

16. What is the nature of the generally accepted auditing standards classified as standards of field work?

A. They require persons performing the audit to be competent.

B. They identify the criteria for the content of the auditor's report on financial statements.

C. They identify the criteria for audit planning and evidence gathering.

D. They state the need to maintain an independence in mental attitude in all matters relating to the audit.

The correct answer is (C). *(Publisher)*

REQUIRED: The nature of the standards of field work.

DISCUSSION: The three standards classified as standards of field work relate to (1) planning the audit and supervising assistants, (2) obtaining a sufficient understanding of internal control, and (3) gathering sufficient competent evidence.

Answer (A) is incorrect because the competence of persons performing the audit relate to the general standards. Answer (B) is incorrect because criteria for the content of the auditor's report concern the standards of reporting. Answer (D) is incorrect because independence relates to the second general standard.

17. Which statement is not one of the generally accepted auditing standards of reporting?

A. The report shall state whether the financial statements are presented in accordance with GAAP.

B. The report shall state whether the audit was conducted in accordance with GAAS.

C. Informative disclosures in the financial statements are to be regarded as reasonably adequate unless otherwise stated in the report.

D. The report shall contain either an expression of opinion regarding the financial statements taken as a whole or an assertion to the effect that an opinion cannot be expressed.

The correct answer is (B). *(Publisher)*

REQUIRED: The statement that is not one of the generally accepted auditing standards of reporting.

DISCUSSION: The scope paragraph of the auditor's standard report states that the audit has been conducted in accordance with GAAS, but that statement is not specifically required by a standard of reporting. The fourth reporting standard does state that, when an auditor's name is associated with financial statements, the report should contain a clear-cut indication of the character of the auditor's work, if any (AU 150).

Answer (A) is incorrect because the first standard of reporting requires that the report state whether the financial statements are presented in accordance with GAAP. Answer (C) is incorrect because the third standard of reporting concerns informative disclosures. Answer (D) is incorrect because the fourth standard of reporting concerns the expression of an opinion.

18. Auditing Interpretations are issued by the Audit Issues Task Force of the Auditing Standards Board (ASB) to provide timely guidance on the application of pronouncements of the ASB. They are

A. Less authoritative than pronouncements of the ASB.

B. Equally as authoritative as pronouncements of the ASB.

C. More authoritative than pronouncements of the ASB.

D. Nonauthoritative opinions that are expressed without consulting the ASB.

The correct answer is (A). *(CPA, adapted)*

REQUIRED: The authoritative weight of Auditing Interpretations.

DISCUSSION: The Auditing Interpretations are numbered in the AU 9000 series and immediately follow the related sections in the codification of professional standards. They are not as authoritative as ASB pronouncements, but members should be aware that they may have to justify departures from interpretations.

Answers (B) and (C) are incorrect because interpretations are less authoritative than pronouncements of the ASB. Answer (D) is incorrect because Interpretations provide timely guidance on the application of pronouncements, are considered authoritative, and are reviewed by the ASB.

1.3 GAAS -- General Standards

19. An individual just beginning an auditing career must obtain professional experience primarily to achieve

A. A positive employment evaluation.

B. Seasoned judgment.

C. A favorable peer review.

D. A specialty designation by the AICPA.

The correct answer is (B). *(CPA, adapted)*

REQUIRED: The purpose of requiring professional experience in the auditing profession.

DISCUSSION: AU 210, *Training and Proficiency of the Independent Auditor*, states that a junior assistant just beginning an auditing career must obtain professional experience with proper supervision and review by a more experienced supervisor. An auditor charged with the final responsibility for an engagement must be capable of exercising the seasoned judgment developed through professional experience.

Answer (A) is incorrect because a positive employment evaluation is possible before significant professional experience has been obtained. Answer (C) is incorrect because a peer review is an external evaluation of a public accounting firm's practice. Answer (D) is incorrect because, although the AICPA may provide for specialty designations, professional experience will continue to be necessary for the development of the professional proficiency of all independent auditors.

20. Within the context of quality control, the primary purpose of continuing professional education (CPE) and training activities is to provide a CPA firm with reasonable assurance that personnel within the firm have

A. Technical training that assures proficiency as an auditor.

B. Professional education that is required to perform with due professional care.

C. The ability to fulfill assigned responsibilities and the qualifications for advancement.

D. Knowledge required to perform a peer review.

The correct answer is (C). *(CPA, adapted)*

REQUIRED: The primary purpose of CPE and training activities relative to a CPA firm's quality control.

DISCUSSION: According to QC 20, the firm should adopt policies and procedures to obtain reasonable assurance that "personnel participate in general and industry-specific CPE and other professional development activities that enable them to fulfill responsibilities assigned, and satisfy applicable CPE requirements of the AICPA and regulatory agencies." Furthermore, personnel chosen for advancement should "have the qualifications necessary for fulfillment of the responsibilities they will be called on to assume."

Answer (A) is incorrect because technical training does not assure proficiency as an auditor. Professional experience complements formal education to develop seasoned judgment. Answer (B) is incorrect because professional education alone does not assure performance with due professional care. Answer (D) is incorrect because CPE is important to all personnel, not just to peer reviewers.

21. The first general standard requires that an audit of financial statements be performed by a person or persons having

A. Seasoned judgment in varying degrees of supervision and review.

B. Adequate technical training and proficiency.

C. Knowledge of the standards of field work and reporting.

D. Independence with respect to the financial statements and supplementary disclosures.

The correct answer is (B). *(CPA, adapted)*

REQUIRED: The subject of the first general standard.

DISCUSSION: The first general standard requires adequate technical training and proficiency as an auditor. AU 210 states that this requirement can be met through education and experience.

Answer (A) is incorrect because the first standard of field work requires that the audit to be planned and that assistants be properly supervised. Answer (C) is incorrect because, although the auditor should have knowledge of the field work and reporting standards, the first general standard does not state this requirement. Answer (D) is incorrect because the second general standard requires the auditor to be independent.

22. Competence as an independent auditor includes all of the following except

A. Having the technical qualifications to perform an engagement.

B. Possessing the ability to supervise and evaluate the quality of staff work.

C. Warranting the infallibility of the work performed.

D. Doing additional research or consulting others.

The correct answer is (C). *(CPA, adapted)*

REQUIRED: The statement not consistent with professional standards of competency.

DISCUSSION: The auditor is not a guarantor. The auditor's responsibility is to express (or disclaim) an opinion on whether the financial statements, taken as a whole, are presented fairly. The audit is planned and performed to provide reasonable, but not absolute, assurance that the financial statements are not materially misstated.

Answer (A) is incorrect because adequate technical training and proficiency as an auditor are required by the first general standard. Answer (B) is incorrect because due professional care requires that the auditor with final responsibility for the engagement be "responsible for the assignment of tasks to, and the supervision of, assistants" (AU 230). Answer (D) is incorrect because, according to an Interpretation of Conduct Rule 201, the need for additional research or consultation with others is a normal part of the performance of professional service.

23. According to the standards of the profession, which of the following activities may be required in exercising due professional care?

	Consulting with Experts	Obtaining Specialty Accreditation
A.	Yes	Yes
B.	Yes	No
C.	No	Yes
D.	No	No

The correct answer is (B). *(CPA, adapted)*

REQUIRED: The activity(ies) that may be required in exercising due professional care.

DISCUSSION: A CPA should undertake only those services that (s)he reasonably expects to complete with professional competence and should exercise due professional care in performing those services. According to an Interpretation of Rule 201, additional research or consultation with others may be necessary to gain sufficient competence to complete a service in accordance with professional standards. However, professional standards do not require specialty accreditation, although many CPAs choose to specialize in specific services.

Answers (A), (C), and (D) are incorrect because due professional care may require additional research or consultation with others but not specialty accreditation.

24. The second general standard of GAAS requires the auditor to be independent. Independence implies that the auditor

A. Must be impartial with respect to the client.

B. Must adopt the attitude of a prosecutor during the audit.

C. Has an obligation solely to third parties.

D. May have a direct ownership interest in the client's business if it is not material.

The correct answer is (A). *(Publisher)*

REQUIRED: The meaning of the second general standard.

DISCUSSION: AU 220, *Independence*, states that an auditor must be independent. Aside from being in public practice, (s)he must be "without bias with respect to the client under audit." The findings of an auditor who is not impartial will lack the credibility that makes them valuable to financial statement users.

Answer (B) is incorrect because, under AU 220, "Independence does not imply the attitude of a prosecutor." Instead, it implies a "judicial impartiality" to achieve fairness. Answer (C) is incorrect because the auditor's obligation is to the entity being audited as well as to third parties. Answer (D) is incorrect because an Interpretation of Conduct Rule 101, *Independence*, prohibits a member from having any direct or material indirect financial interest in an enterprise for which attestation services are rendered.

25. GAAS require the auditor to be independent in mental attitude. An auditor is independent if (s)he is

A. Intelligent.

B. Independent in fact and in appearance.

C. Independent in fact and consistent.

D. Logical and intellectually honest.

The correct answer is (B). *(Publisher)*

REQUIRED: The true statement about auditor independence.

DISCUSSION: Auditors must be independent in both fact and appearance. This crucially important quality gives credibility to the auditor's opinion. If an auditor does not maintain the appearance of independence, however unbiased (s)he may be in fact, the public will be reluctant to believe that (s)he is unbiased (AU 220).

Answers (A), (C), and (D) are incorrect because intelligence, consistency, and logic are not dimensions of auditor independence.

26. Beth Babett, CPA, is associated with a client's financial statements but is not independent with respect to that client. If she is requested to perform an audit on the financial statements, she should

A. Recommend that the engagement be downgraded to a review.

B. Disclaim an opinion.

C. List the procedures performed in the audit report.

D. Express a piecemeal opinion.

The correct answer is (B). *(Publisher)*

REQUIRED: The action taken by a CPA who lacks independence in connection with an audit.

DISCUSSION: The CPA may perform audit procedures according to an agreement with the client. However, a CPA who lacks independence is precluded from expressing an opinion on financial statements because any procedures (s)he performs are not in accordance with GAAS. Hence, the CPA should disclaim an opinion on the financial statements and state specifically that (s)he is not independent (AU 504).

Answer (A) is incorrect because a review engagement is an attest service that requires the CPA to be independent. Answer (C) is incorrect because the public might be misled into believing that the CPA has performed an audit and is expressing an opinion on the statements if audit procedures are listed. Answer (D) is incorrect because a piecemeal opinion (expressing an opinion on only part of the financial statements) is not acceptable if the CPA has disclaimed an opinion or expressed an adverse opinion on the statements taken as a whole.

27. Audit committees have been identified as a major factor in promoting both the internal and external auditor's independence. Which of the following is the most important limitation on the effectiveness of audit committees?

A. Audit committees may be composed of independent directors. However, those directors may have close personal and professional friendships with management.

B. Audit committee members are compensated by the organization and thus favor a shareholder's view.

C. Audit committees devote most of their efforts to external audit concerns and do not pay much attention to internal auditing and the overall control environment.

D. Audit committee members do not normally have degrees in the accounting or auditing fields.

The correct answer is (A). *(CIA, adapted)*

REQUIRED: The most important limitation on the effectiveness of audit committees.

DISCUSSION: The audit committee is a subcommittee made up of outside directors who are independent of corporate management. Its purpose is to help keep external and internal auditors independent of management and to assure that the directors are exercising due care. However, if independence is impaired by personal and professional friendships, the effectiveness of the audit committee may be limited.

Answer (B) is incorrect because the compensation audit committee members receive is usually minimal. They should be independent and therefore not limited to a shareholder's perspective. Answer (C) is incorrect because, although audit committees are concerned with external audits, they also devote attention to the internal auditing function. Answer (D) is incorrect because audit committee members do not need degrees in accounting or auditing to understand audit reports.

28. The SEC has strengthened auditor independence by requiring that management

A. Engage auditors to report in accordance with the Foreign Corrupt Practices Act.

B. Report the nature of disagreements with former auditors.

C. Select auditors through audit committees.

D. Acknowledge its responsibility for the fairness of the financial statements.

The correct answer is (B). *(CPA, adapted)*

REQUIRED: The SEC requirement.

DISCUSSION: The SEC requires that the management of a public company report the nature of disagreements with former auditors by filing Form 8-K. Such disclosure inhibits management from changing auditors to gain acceptance of a questionable accounting method. Also, a potential successor auditor must inquire of the predecessor auditor before accepting an engagement (AU 315). Thus, the inquiry provides an opportunity to confirm the information given in the 8-K report. However, confidential client information may be communicated only with the client's consent.

Answer (A) is incorrect because the SEC does not require an audit report in accordance with the FCPA. Answer (C) is incorrect because the SEC does not require selection of auditors through audit committees. Answer (D) is incorrect because the SEC does not require management to acknowledge its responsibility for the fairness of the financial statements. However, management's representations include this acknowledgment.

29. The auditor should not initiate discussion with the audit committee concerning

A. The extent to which the work of internal auditors will influence the scope of the audit.

B. Details of the procedures that the auditor intends to apply.

C. The extent to which change in the company's organization will influence the scope of the audit.

D. Details of potential problems that the auditor believes might cause a qualified opinion.

The correct answer is (B). *(CPA, adapted)*

REQUIRED: The subject not appropriate for discussion.

DISCUSSION: The auditor should not discuss with the audit committee the specific procedures to be applied during the audit. The auditor exercises professional judgment in determining appropriate procedures. To remain independent (s)he must not subordinate this judgment to others. Also, audit testing is done on a sample basis, and the client should not have knowledge of how samples are selected.

Answer (A) is incorrect because, according to AU 380, *Communication with Audit Committees*, certain communications with those responsible for oversight of the financial reporting process are required. For example, the auditor should communicate the responsibility assumed under GAAS, including the extent to which the work of internal auditors will influence the scope of the audit. Answer (C) is incorrect because the audit scope is a legitimate subject for discussion with the audit committee. Answer (D) is incorrect because potential problems should be discussed with the audit committee.

30. The exercise of due professional care requires that an auditor with final responsibility for an engagement

A. Examine all available corroborating evidence.

B. Be responsible for the assignment of tasks to, and supervision of, assistants.

C. Attain the proper balance of professional experience and formal education.

D. Design the audit to detect all instances of illegal acts having direct and material effects on financial statement amounts.

The correct answer is (B). *(CPA, adapted)*

REQUIRED: The meaning of due professional care.

DISCUSSION: According to AU 230, *Due Professional Care in the Performance of Work*, "Due professional care imposes a responsibility upon each professional within an independent auditor's organization to observe the standards of field work and reporting." The first standard of field work requires proper supervision of assistants (AU 150). Thus, AU 230 states, "The auditor with final responsibility is responsible for the assignment of tasks to, and the supervision of, assistants."

Answer (A) is incorrect because cost-benefit considerations ordinarily require the auditor to examine evidence on a test basis. Answer (C) is incorrect because the first general standard requires the audit to be performed by persons having adequate technical training and proficiency as auditors. The attainment of proficiency begins with formal education and extends into the auditor's subsequent experience (AU 210). Answer (D) is incorrect because the auditor is required to plan and perform the audit to obtain reasonable, not absolute, assurance of detecting illegal acts having direct and material effects.

1.4 GAAS -- Field Work and Reporting Standards (See also Chapters 2, 3, 4, and 7.)

31. GAAS consist of general standards, standards of field work, and standards of reporting. The standards of field work include which one of the following?

A. The audit is to be performed by a person or persons having adequate technical training and proficiency.

B. In all matters relating to the assignment, an independence in mental attitude is essential.

C. The work is to be adequately planned, and assistants, if any, are to be properly supervised.

D. Due professional care is to be exercised in the planning and performance of the audit and preparation of the audit report.

The correct answer is (C). *(CMA, adapted)*

REQUIRED: The standard of field work.

DISCUSSION: The first standard of field work states that the work is to be adequately planned and that assistants, if any, are to be properly supervised. The second and third standards of field work require obtaining a sufficient understanding of internal control and sufficient competent evidential matter, respectively.

Answer (A) is incorrect because the first general standard provides that the audit is to be performed by a person or persons having adequate technical training and proficiency. Answer (B) is incorrect because the second general standard states that, in all matters relating to the assignment, an independence in mental attitude is essential. Answer (D) is incorrect because the third general standard provides that due professional care is to be exercised in the planning and performance of the audit and preparation of the audit report.

32. Early appointment of the auditor enables preliminary work to be performed by the auditor that benefits the client because it permits the audit to be performed in

A. A more efficient manner.

B. A more thorough manner.

C. Accordance with quality control standards.

D. Accordance with generally accepted auditing standards.

The correct answer is (A). *(CPA, adapted)*

REQUIRED: The benefit to the client from early appointment of the auditor.

DISCUSSION: AU 310, *Appointment of the Independent Auditor*, indicates that an early appointment of the auditor is advantageous to both the auditor and the client. Early appointment aids the auditor in planning the work, especially that to be done before the end of the year. The client benefits from more efficient scheduling of the audit and an early completion of the work after the end of the fiscal year.

Answer (B) is incorrect because thoroughness is directly related to the requirement to collect sufficient competent evidential matter, not to the date of appointment. Answer (C) is incorrect because adherence to quality control standards is necessary regardless of the date of appointment. Answer (D) is incorrect because adherence to GAAS is necessary regardless of the date of appointment.

33. With respect to the auditor's planning of a year-end audit, which of the following statements is always true?

A. An engagement should not be accepted after the fiscal year-end.

B. An inventory count must be observed at the balance sheet date.

C. The client's audit committee should not be told of the specific audit procedures that were performed.

D. It is an acceptable practice to carry out part of the audit at interim dates.

The correct answer is (D). *(CPA, adapted)*

REQUIRED: The statement about the year-end audit that is always true.

DISCUSSION: Much of the audit work, including obtaining a sufficient understanding of internal control, assessing control risk, and the application of substantive tests to transactions, can be conducted prior to the balance sheet date (AU 313).

Answer (A) is incorrect because an engagement may be accepted after year-end. Answer (B) is incorrect because, if observation at year-end is not feasible, the auditor may observe inventory at another date. Answer (C) is incorrect because the audit committee (usually consisting of outside directors) may sometimes be told of specific audit procedures already performed, e.g., how a major defalcation was discovered. However, specific procedures should not be discussed with the client prior to the audit.

34. Which of the following elements underlies the application of generally accepted auditing standards, particularly the standards of field work and reporting?

A. Relevant internal controls.

B. Corroborating evidence.

C. Quality control.

D. Materiality and audit risk.

The correct answer is (D). *(CPA, adapted)*

REQUIRED: The element(s) affecting the application of GAAS.

DISCUSSION: Materiality and audit risk affect the application of GAAS, especially the field work and reporting standards, and as a result are reflected in the auditor's standard report. The auditor must make judgments about materiality and audit risk in determining the nature, timing, and extent of procedures to apply and in evaluating the results (AU 312).

Answer (A) is incorrect because the second standard of field work concerns internal control. Answer (B) is incorrect because the third standard of field work concerns evidence. Answer (C) is incorrect because quality control is covered by a separate series of pronouncements, Statements on Quality Control Standards.

35. GAAS for reporting do not include which of the following standards?

A. The report shall identify those circumstances in which GAAP have not been consistently observed in the current period in relation to the preceding period.

B. Informative disclosures in the financial statements are to be regarded as reasonably adequate unless otherwise stated in the report.

C. Sufficient competent evidential matter is to be obtained through inspection, observation, inquiries, and confirmations to afford a reasonable basis for an opinion regarding the financial statements under audit.

D. The report shall state whether the financial statements are presented in accordance with GAAP.

The correct answer is (C). *(Publisher)*

REQUIRED: The standard that is not a reporting standard.

DISCUSSION: The standard requiring the auditor to collect sufficient competent evidential matter is the third standard of field work, not a standard of reporting.

Answer (A) is incorrect because the second standard of reporting states that the report shall identify those circumstances in which GAAP have not been consistently observed in the current period in relation to the preceding period. Answer (B) is incorrect because the third standard of reporting states that informative disclosures in the financial statements are to be regarded as reasonably adequate unless otherwise stated in the report. Answer (D) is incorrect because the first standard of reporting states that the report shall state whether the financial statements are presented in accordance with GAAP.

36. The first standard of reporting requires that "the report shall state whether the financial statements are presented in accordance with generally accepted accounting principles." This standard should be construed to require

A. A statement of fact by the auditor.

B. An opinion by the auditor.

C. An implied measure of fairness.

D. An objective measure of compliance.

The correct answer is (B). *(CPA, adapted)*

REQUIRED: The interpretation of the first reporting standard.

DISCUSSION: AU 410, *Adherence to GAAP*, states, "The first reporting standard is construed not to require a statement of fact by the auditor but an opinion as to whether the financial statements are presented in conformity with such principles." The opinion is based on the auditor's judgment as to whether the principles selected and applied have general acceptance and are appropriate in the circumstances.

Answer (A) is incorrect because AU 410 construes the first reporting standard not to require a statement of fact by the auditor. Answer (C) is incorrect because the auditor's judgment about the fairness of the presentation of financial statements is applied within the framework of GAAP, not as an implied measure. Answer (D) is incorrect because, if an objective measure of compliance were available, the auditor could state a fact, not express an opinion.

37. Several sources of GAAP consulted by an auditor are in conflict as to the application of an accounting principle. Which of the following should the auditor consider the most authoritative?

A. FASB Technical Bulletins.

B. AICPA Accounting Interpretations.

C. FASB Statements of Financial Accounting Concepts.

D. AICPA Technical Practice Aids.

The correct answer is (A). *(CPA, adapted)*

REQUIRED: The most authoritative source of GAAP.

DISCUSSION: AU 411 establishes the GAAP hierarchy. FASB Technical Bulletins are in the second tier. The first tier of GAAP for nongovernmental entities consists of officially established accounting principles, which are principles contemplated by Conduct Rule 203. The next three tiers consist of other sources of established accounting principles. The fifth tier consists of other accounting literature.

Answer (B) is incorrect because AICPA Accounting Interpretations are in the fourth tier. Answers (C) and (D) are incorrect because FASB Statements of Financial Accounting Concepts and AICPA Technical Practice Aids are in the fifth tier.

38. Under the AICPA *Code of Professional Conduct*, a CPA may express an unqualified opinion on financial statements that contain a departure from promulgated GAAP if (s)he can demonstrate that because of unusual circumstances the financial statements would be misleading if the departure were not made. Which of the following is an example of unusual circumstances that could justify such a departure?

A. The evolution of a new form of business.

B. An unusual degree of materiality.

C. Conflicting industry practices.

D. A theoretical disagreement with a standard promulgated by the FASB.

The correct answer is (A). *(Publisher)*

REQUIRED: The circumstance that could justify a departure from promulgated GAAP.

DISCUSSION: According to an Interpretation of Conduct Rule 203, examples of unusual circumstances that would permit a departure from promulgated GAAP (SFASs and their Interpretations, ARBs, and APBs) are new legislation or the evolution of a new form of business transaction. What constitutes unusual circumstances is normally a matter of professional judgment.

Answer (B) is incorrect because an unusual degree of materiality is an event that is not so unusual as to justify departure from promulgated GAAP. Answer (C) is incorrect because the existence of conflicting industry practices is an example of an event cited in an Interpretation of Conduct Rule 203 that is not so unusual as to justify departure from promulgated GAAP. Answer (D) is incorrect because the client's or CPA's theoretical disagreement with a standard does not justify a departure therefrom.

39. An auditor should obtain sufficient knowledge of an entity's information system relevant to financial reporting to understand the

A. Safeguards used to limit access to computer facilities.

B. Process used to prepare significant accounting estimates.

C. Procedures used to assure proper authorization of transactions.

D. Policies used to detect the concealment of fraud.

The correct answer is (B). *(CPA, adapted)*

REQUIRED: The purpose of obtaining sufficient knowledge of an entity's information system relevant to financial reporting.

DISCUSSION: The auditor should obtain sufficient knowledge of the information system relevant to financial reporting to understand (1) the classes of significant transactions, (2) the ways those transactions are initiated, (3) the accounting records and supporting documents for those transactions, (4) the accounting processing involved, and (5) the financial reporting process used to prepare the entity's financial statements, including significant accounting estimates and disclosures (AU 319).

Answers (A), (C), and (D) are incorrect because limiting access, proper authorization of transactions, and detection of fraud involve policies and procedures outside the information system relevant to financial reporting.

1.5 Nature of the *Code of Professional Conduct*

40. Which of the following statements best explains why the CPA profession has found it essential to promulgate ethical standards and to establish means for ensuring their observance?

A. Vigorous enforcement of an established code of ethics is the best way to prevent unscrupulous acts.

B. Ethical standards that emphasize excellence in performance over material rewards establish a reputation for competence and character.

C. A distinguishing mark of a profession is its acceptance of responsibility to the public.

D. A requirement for a profession is to establish ethical standards that stress primarily a responsibility to clients and colleagues.

The correct answer is (C). *(CPA, adapted)*

REQUIRED: The reason for ethical standards.

DISCUSSION: Article II of the AICPA *Code of Professional Conduct* states, "Members should accept the obligation to act in a way that will serve the public interest, honor the public trust, and demonstrate commitment to professionalism." According to the accompanying explanation, "A distinguishing mark of a profession is acceptance of its responsibility to the public. The accounting profession's public consists of clients, credit grantors, governments, employers, investors, the business and financial community, and others who rely on the objectivity and integrity of CPAs to maintain the orderly functioning of commerce."

Answer (A) is incorrect because vigorous enforcement is significant but secondary to the creation of an environment in the profession that fosters voluntary adherence to ethical principles. Answer (B) is incorrect because excellence in performance is but one of the effects of accepting responsibility to the public. Answer (D) is incorrect because the responsibility of CPAs is to a public that is not limited to clients and colleagues but includes all those who rely on their objectivity and integrity.

41. The AICPA *Code of Professional Conduct* contains both general ethical principles that are aspirational in character and also a

A. List of violations that would cause the automatic suspension of a member's license.

B. Set of specific, mandatory rules describing minimum levels of conduct a member must maintain.

C. Description of a member's procedures for responding to an inquiry from a trial board.

D. List of specific acts discreditable to the profession.

The correct answer is (B). *(CPA, adapted)*

REQUIRED: The content of the *Code of Professional Conduct.*

DISCUSSION: The AICPA Code contains two sections: Principles and Rules. The principles are goal-oriented. The rules provide more specific guidance. The principles "call for an unswerving commitment to honorable behavior," but are not mandatory. Members who fail to comply with the rules, however, may face disciplinary action.

Answer (A) is incorrect because the bylaws (BL 730), not the Code, list violations resulting in an automatic suspension. Answer (C) is incorrect because the bylaws (BL 740R) describe trial board procedures. Answer (D) is incorrect because Conduct Rule 501 simply states that discreditable acts are prohibited. However, the related interpretations specify certain types of discreditable acts.

42. Which AICPA Conduct Rule applies only to members in the practice of public accounting?

A. *General Standards* (201).

B. *Accounting Principles* (203).

C. *Independence* (101).

D. *Compliance with Standards* (202).

The correct answer is (C). *(Publisher)*

REQUIRED: The AICPA Conduct Rule that applies only to members in public accounting.

DISCUSSION: Conduct Rule 101 states, "A member in public practice shall be independent in the performance of professional services as required by standards promulgated by bodies designated by Council." The scope of services comprehended by this rule is broader than the expression of opinions on financial statements. Hence, it applies to such professional services as reviews, reports on prospective financial information, and reports on other attestation engagements.

Answers (A), (B), and (D) are incorrect because Conduct Rules 201, 202, and 203 apply to all members, whether or not in public practice.

43. The AICPA *Code of Professional Conduct* does not include enforceable Conduct Rules on which of the following?

A. Independence and integrity and objectivity.

B. Professional competence and due professional care.

C. Accounting principles.

D. Responsibilities to colleagues.

The correct answer is (D). *(Publisher)*

REQUIRED: The subject on which the Code provides no enforceable Conduct Rules.

DISCUSSION: At one time the Code included two rules concerning colleagues, but they were deleted after threats of antitrust actions against the profession by both the Federal Trade Commission and the U.S. Justice Department. The principles express the profession's recognition of its responsibilities to colleagues as well as to the public and clients, but adherence to them is not mandatory.

Answer (A) is incorrect because independence and integrity and objectivity are covered by Conduct Rules 101 and 102, respectively. Answer (B) is incorrect because professional competence and due professional care are two of the general standards listed in Conduct Rule 201. Answer (C) is incorrect because Conduct Rule 203 covers accounting principles.

44. Conduct Rule 201, *General Standards*, does not require a member to

A. Complete all engagements with professional competence.

B. Plan and supervise adequately the performance of professional services.

C. Obtain sufficient relevant data to afford a reasonable basis for all conclusions.

D. Provide no assurance about prospective financial statements.

The correct answer is (D). *(Publisher)*

REQUIRED: The subject not encompassed by Conduct Rule 201.

DISCUSSION: The section on prospective financial statements was deleted from Conduct Rule 201 because guidance has been provided by the ASB in AT 200, *Financial Forecasts and Projections*.

Answer (A) is incorrect because Conduct Rule 201 requires compliance with the following standards: professional competence, due professional care, planning and supervision, and sufficient relevant data. A member should undertake only those professional services that can reasonably be expected to be completed with professional competence. Answer (B) is incorrect because Conduct Rule 201 requires that the performance of professional services be adequately planned and supervised. Answer (C) is incorrect because Conduct Rule 201 requires that a member obtain sufficient relevant data to afford a reasonable basis for all conclusions or recommendations related to any professional services performed.

45. CPAs are required to complete engagements competently. Competence embraces all of the following except

A. An unbiased mental attitude.

B. The technical qualifications of the CPA's staff.

C. The capacity to exercise judgment.

D. The ability to research subject matter and consult with others.

The correct answer is (A). *(Publisher)*

REQUIRED: The item not associated with competence.

DISCUSSION: Conduct Rule 101 requires the CPA to maintain an unbiased mental attitude. "A member in public practice shall be independent in the performance of professional services as required by standards promulgated by bodies designated by Council."

Answers (B) and (C) are incorrect because, according to an AICPA Interpretation of Conduct Rule 201, "Competence relates both to knowledge of the profession's standards, techniques, and the technical subject matter involved, and to the ability to exercise sound judgment in applying such knowledge in the performance of professional services." Answer (D) is incorrect because, in some cases, "additional research or consultation with others does not ordinarily represent a lack of competence, but rather is a normal part of the performance of professional services."

46. When management refuses to disclose material illegal acts that were identified by the independent auditor, the independent auditor may be charged with violating the AICPA *Code of Professional Conduct* for

A. Disclaiming an opinion.

B. Withdrawing from the engagement.

C. Failing to uncover the illegal activities during prior audits.

D. Reporting these activities to the audit committee.

The correct answer is (A). *(CPA, adapted)*

REQUIRED: The inappropriate auditor action relative to disclosure of illegal activities.

DISCUSSION: When the auditor concludes that an illegal act is material and that the act has not been appropriately disclosed or accounted for, a normal disclaimer of opinion is not suitable. The auditor should disclose the problem in a report that includes either a qualified or an adverse opinion or withdraw from the engagement. Moreover, the auditor may, in some circumstances, have a duty of disclosure outside the entity, e.g., in a report on Form 8-K or in a response to a subpoena. Furthermore, the Private Securities Litigation Reform Act of 1995 may also be applicable to reporting on illegal acts.

Answer (B) is incorrect because, under AU 317, *Illegal Acts by Clients*, withdrawal may be warranted in certain cases. Answer (C) is incorrect because audits in compliance with GAAS cannot assure detection of all illegal acts. Answer (D) is incorrect because the auditor may notify the client's audit committee of illegal acts.

47. The AICPA *Code of Professional Conduct*

A. Prohibits encroachment on the practice of another CPA.

B. Prohibits offers of employment to employees of another CPA without notice.

C. Encourages but does not require CPAs to cooperate with each other.

D. Encourages but does not require CPAs to refrain from advertising or engaging in other forms of solicitation.

The correct answer is (C). *(Publisher)*

REQUIRED: The true statement concerning the *Code of Professional Conduct*.

DISCUSSION: The nonbinding Principles state that members "have a continuing responsibility to cooperate with each other to improve the art of accounting, maintain the public's confidence, and carry out the profession's special responsibilities for self-governance."

Answers (A) and (B) are incorrect because, currently, no Conduct Rules govern responsibilities to colleagues. The two rules previously in force, *Encroachment* and *Offers of Employment*, were deleted as a result of threats of antitrust litigation from the FTC and the Justice Department. These rules prohibited encroachment on the practice of another CPA and the offer of employment to an employee of another CPA without prior notification. Answer (D) is incorrect because CPAs are not encouraged or required to refrain from solicitation unless it is false, misleading, or deceptive.

48. According to The IIA Standard 280, *Due Professional Care*, "Due care implies reasonable care and competence, not infallibility or extraordinary performance." This statement makes which of the following unnecessary?

A. The conduct of audits and verifications to a reasonable extent.

B. The conduct of detailed audits of all transactions.

C. The reasonable assurance that compliance does exist.

D. The consideration of the possibility of material fraud.

The correct answer is (B). *(CIA, adapted)*

REQUIRED: The item stating what is unnecessary under the due care standard.

DISCUSSION: Standard 280 states, "Due care requires the auditor to conduct audits and verifications to a reasonable extent but does not require detailed audits of all transactions."

Answer (A) is incorrect because due care requires the auditor to conduct audits and verifications to a reasonable extent. Answer (C) is incorrect because the internal auditor cannot give absolute assurance that noncompliance or irregularities do not exist. Answer (D) is incorrect because the possibility of material fraud or noncompliance should be considered.

49. Which of the following is required for a CPA firm to designate itself as "Members of the American Institute of Certified Public Accountants" on its letterhead?

A. All owners must be members.

B. The owners whose names appear in the firm name must be members.

C. At least one of the owners must be a member.

D. The firm must be a dues-paying member.

The correct answer is (A). *(CPA, adapted)*

REQUIRED: The requirement for a CPA firm to use the designation, "Members of the AICPA."

DISCUSSION: Conduct Rule 505, *Form of Organization and Name*, states that a firm may not use the quoted designation unless all of its owners are members of the Institute.

Answers (B) and (C) are incorrect because all owners, not just certain owners, must be AICPA members. Answer (D) is incorrect because the owners, not the firm, must be members of the AICPA.

50. Anyone inquiring about the professional reputation and standing of a CPA firm may contact the AICPA Division for CPA Firms and expect to receive

A. Copies of complaints against the CPA firm that are currently being adjudicated by the AICPA Joint Trial Board.

B. Copies of peer review reports on the CPA firm after the reports have been accepted.

C. Information regarding prima facie violations of the *Code of Professional Conduct* or AICPA bylaws not deemed of sufficient gravity to warrant further formal action.

D. Information regarding pending investigations of individuals within the CPA firm.

The correct answer is (B). *(CPA, adapted)*

REQUIRED: The information obtainable from the Division for CPA Firms.

DISCUSSION: Anyone inquiring about the professional reputation and standing of a CPA firm may contact the Division for CPA Firms and receive information on the firm's enrollment in an AICPA-approved practice monitoring program and, if the firm is enrolled in either the SEC Practice Section or Partnering for CPA Practice Success/The Alliance for CPA Firms (PCPS), copies of the firm's most recent peer review report after the report has been accepted by the relevant report acceptance body. The Division will provide copies of accepted peer review reports and information submitted by member firms on applications for membership and annual updates. There is no charge for this service.

Answers (A), (C), and (D) are incorrect because neither the Division for CPA Firms nor the Professional Ethics Division can respond to inquiries about complaints against CPA firms currently being adjudicated, violations not deemed of sufficient gravity to warrant further formal action, or pending investigations of individuals within the CPA firm. However, the Professional Ethics Division can respond to inquiries about disciplinary action taken by the Joint Trial Board or a sub-board thereof and published in a membership periodical of the AICPA.

1.6 Code -- Independence, Integrity, and Objectivity

51. An auditor strives to achieve independence in appearance to

A. Maintain public confidence in the profession.

B. Become independent in fact.

C. Comply with the generally accepted auditing standards of field work.

D. Maintain an unbiased mental attitude.

The correct answer is (A). *(CPA, adapted)*

REQUIRED: The reason the auditor strives to achieve independence in appearance.

DISCUSSION: Third parties depend on the CPA's report because (s)he is viewed as possessing the necessary impartiality. Public confidence would be impaired if such objectivity even appeared to be lacking. The auditor must guard against the presumption of a loss of independence in addition to maintaining independence in fact.

Answer (B) is incorrect because an auditor must be independent both in fact (an unbiased mental attitude) and in appearance. Answer (C) is incorrect because independence relates to the general standards, not to the standards of field work. Answer (D) is incorrect because an auditor must be independent both in fact (an unbiased mental attitude) and in appearance.

52. Which of the following most completely describes how independence has been defined by the CPA profession?

A. Performing an audit from the viewpoint of the public.

B. Avoiding the appearance of significant interests in the affairs of an audit client.

C. Possessing the ability to act with integrity and objectivity.

D. Accepting responsibility to act professionally and in accordance with a professional code of ethics.

The correct answer is (C). *(CPA, adapted)*

REQUIRED: The best description of the accounting profession's definition of independence.

DISCUSSION: Integrity, objectivity, and independence are overlapping concepts. Integrity requires honesty and candor within the limits of confidentiality. It also requires, among other things, observation of the principles of objectivity and independence. Objectivity is impartiality, intellectual honesty, and freedom from conflicts of interest. Independence precludes relationships that may appear to impair objectivity in rendering attestation services. In rendering services, a member in public practice should therefore be independent in appearance as well as in fact.

Answer (A) is incorrect because, although his/her performance of the attest function serves the public interest, an auditor's adoption of any viewpoint other than strict impartiality is inconsistent with professional standards. Answer (B) is incorrect because the auditor must be independent in fact as well as in appearance. Answer (D) is incorrect because one who accepts responsibility for acting in accordance with professional standards may not necessarily have the ability to act with integrity and objectivity.

53. The concept of materiality would be least important to an auditor when considering the

A. Effects of a direct financial interest in the client upon the CPA's independence.

B. Decision whether to use positive or negative confirmations of accounts receivable.

C. Adequacy of disclosure of a client's illegal act.

D. Discovery of weaknesses in a client's internal control.

The correct answer is (A). *(CPA, adapted)*

REQUIRED: The item with respect to which materiality is least important.

DISCUSSION: According to an Interpretation of Conduct Rule 101, independence is impaired if a CPA has any direct financial interest in a client. Whether this direct interest is material is irrelevant. The test of materiality is applied, however, if the financial interest is indirect.

Answer (B) is incorrect because negative confirmations may be used when the combined assessed level of inherent and control risk is low, many small balances are involved, and the auditor has no reason to believe that the recipients are unlikely to give them consideration. Answer (C) is incorrect because, in considering the effect of an illegal act, an auditor should evaluate its qualitative and quantitative materiality. Answer (D) is incorrect because an auditor who is considering internal control must make materiality judgments.

54. Jaye B. Honest, CPA, was offered the engagement to audit Wicket Corporation for the year ended June 30, 1999. She had served as a director of Wicket Corporation until June 30, 1997, and her spouse currently owns 10 of the 10,000 outstanding shares of Wicket Corporation. She should

A. Accept the engagement.

B. Let her partner accept and conduct the engagement.

C. Refuse the engagement because she had served as a director.

D. Refuse the engagement because of her spouse's stock ownership.

The correct answer is (D). *(Publisher)*

REQUIRED: The effect of a spouse's ownership of stock and the CPA's former position as a director.

DISCUSSION: Independence is impaired if a member has a direct financial interest in the client. According to an Interpretation of Conduct Rule 101, the term "member" includes spouses, whether or not dependent, and dependent persons, whether or not related. The interests or positions of nondependent close relatives may also impair independence, although the term "member" excludes such relatives. The CPA should refuse the engagement to audit the company because her spouse's stock ownership is directly ascribed to her. Materiality is not an issue.

Answer (A) is incorrect because she is not independent and should not accept the engagement. Answer (B) is incorrect because the term member includes the member's firm and its proprietors, partners, or shareholders. Answer (C) is incorrect because, if she has not served as a director during the period covered by the financial statements, during the period of the engagement, or at the time of expressing an opinion, independence is not impaired by reason of prior service.

55. Under the AICPA *Code of Professional Conduct*, a member may not

A. Have any direct financial interest in a client during the period covered by the financial statements.

B. Perform bookkeeping services for an audit client.

C. Perform advisory services for an audit client.

D. Have any joint, closely held investment with a principal shareholder of an audit client during the period of the audit engagement.

The correct answer is (D). *(D. Wells)*

REQUIRED: The situation impairing independence.

DISCUSSION: According to an Interpretation of Conduct Rule 101, a member may not have "any joint, closely held business investment with the enterprise or with any officer, director, or principal stockholders thereof that was material in relation to the member's net worth or to the net worth of the member's firm." The prohibited interests are those held during the period of the professional engagement or at the time of expressing an opinion.

Answer (A) is incorrect because a member may have a direct financial interest in a client during the period covered by the financial statements if that interest is disposed of prior to beginning the professional engagement. Answer (B) is incorrect because an Interpretation of Conduct Rule 101 describes the requirements that a member who performs accounting services for a client must meet to be considered independent. The client must make an informed acceptance of responsibility for the financial statements, the member must not serve as an employee or manager, and the member must comply with applicable standards for audits, reviews, or compilations if statements are prepared from books the member has maintained. Answer (C) is incorrect because an Ethics Ruling has stated that advisory services do not impair independence.

56. A CPA who has a direct financial interest in a nonclient having a material investment in the CPA's audit client would

A. Lack independence only if the CPA's investment in the nonclient is material.

B. Lack independence only if the CPA can exercise significant influence over the nonclient.

C. Lack independence.

D. Not lack independence.

The correct answer is (C). *(Publisher)*

REQUIRED: The effect on independence of a direct financial interest in an entity having a material investment in an audit client.

DISCUSSION: If the investment by the nonclient in the client is material, any direct or material indirect financial interest the CPA has in the nonclient will impair independence. Thus, given that the CPA has a direct financial interest, materiality is not an issue and the CPA lacks independence.

Answer (A) is incorrect because an immaterial direct interest impairs independence when the nonclient investor has a material interest in the client investee. Answer (B) is incorrect because the ability to exert significant influence is relevant only when the nonclient investor's interest in the client investee is immaterial. Answer (D) is incorrect because independence is impaired.

57. A CPA purchased stock in a client corporation and placed it in an educational trust for the CPA's minor child. The trust securities were not material to the CPA but were material to the child's personal net worth. Would the independence of the CPA be considered to be impaired with respect to the client?

A. Yes, because the stock would be considered a direct financial interest and, consequently, materiality is not a factor.

B. Yes, because the stock would be considered an indirect financial interest that is material to the CPA's child.

C. No, because the CPA would not be considered to have a direct financial interest in the client.

D. No, because the CPA would not be considered to have a material indirect financial interest in the client.

The correct answer is (A). *(CPA, adapted)*

REQUIRED: The effect on independence of a CPA's purchase of the client's stock and placing it in a trust for a minor child.

DISCUSSION: An Interpretation of Conduct Rule 101 states independence is impaired if "a member or a member's firm had or was committed to acquire any direct or material indirect financial interest in the enterprise." The term "member" includes spouses and dependents. Assuming the minor child is a dependent, his/her direct financial interest impairs the CPA's independence regardless of materiality. The same result would follow if the CPA were a trustee of the trust, even if (s)he had no other relationship to the beneficiary.

Answer (B) is incorrect because a dependent person's interest is ascribed to the CPA. The CPA therefore has the same direct interest as the child. Answer (C) is incorrect because the CPA is deemed to have a direct interest. Answer (D) is incorrect because materiality is irrelevant if the CPA is deemed to have a direct interest.

58. Conduct Rule 101, *Independence*, applies to

A. Proprietors, partners, and shareholders only of a CPA firm.

B. All clerical individuals participating in the engagement.

C. All individuals participating in the engagement, except those performing routine clerical functions, and individuals with managerial positions located in an office participating in a significant portion of the engagement.

D. All professional employees of the firm who were previously associated with the client.

The correct answer is (C). *(Publisher)*

REQUIRED: The personnel to whom Conduct Rule 101 applies.

DISCUSSION: According to an Interpretation of Conduct Rule 101, the expressions "a member" and "a member or a member's firm" include the member's firm and its proprietors, partners, or shareholders; all nonclerical individuals participating in the engagement; all individuals with a managerial position in an office with significant involvement in the engagement; or any entity that can be controlled by one of the foregoing (or by any two or more acting together).

Answer (A) is incorrect because nonclerical participants in the engagement, managerial personnel in offices significantly involved, entities that can be controlled by one of the foregoing, and others are also among those to whom Conduct Rule 101 applies. Answer (B) is incorrect because Conduct Rule 101 does not apply to persons performing routine clerical duties. Answer (D) is incorrect because Conduct Rule 101 does not apply to an individual who is disassociated from the client and does not participate in the engagement.

59. The appearance of independence of a CPA, or that CPA's firm, could be impaired if the CPA

A. Provides appraisal, valuation, or actuarial services for a client.

B. Joins a trade association, which is a client, and serves in a nonmanagement capacity.

C. Accepts a token gift from a client.

D. Serves as an executor and trustee of the estate of an individual who owned the majority of the stock of a closely held client corporation.

The correct answer is (D). *(CPA, adapted)*

REQUIRED: The basis for the impairment of the appearance of independence.

DISCUSSION: Independence is impaired with regard to an enterprise if, during the engagement or at the time of expressing an opinion, "a member or a member's firm was a trustee of any trust or executor or administrator of any estate if such trust or estate had or was committed to acquire any direct or material indirect financial interest in the enterprise." An Ethics Ruling states that mere designation as trustee or executor does not impair independence but that actual service does.

Answer (A) is incorrect because independence is not typically impaired if all significant matters of judgment involved with the results incorporated into the financial statements are determined or approved by the client. Answer (B) is incorrect because independence is not impaired, provided the CPA does not participate in management. Answer (C) is incorrect because a token gift will not impair independence. However, a CPA who accepts more than a token gift, even with the knowledge of the member's firm, will appear to lack independence.

60. Dickins & Co., CPAs, offers to maintain on its computer certain routine accounting records for its audit client, Lake. If Lake accepts the offer and Dickins & Co. continues to function as independent auditor, Dickins & Co. will violate the rules relating to auditor's independence of which organization(s)?

	SEC	AICPA
A.	Yes	No
B.	Yes	Yes
C.	No	Yes
D.	No	No

The correct answer is (A). *(Publisher)*

REQUIRED: The SEC and the AICPA positions on the independence of a CPA firm that provides computerized accounting services to its client.

DISCUSSION: The SEC position is that performing accounting services for the audit client impairs the independence of the audit firm. The AICPA view, however, is that the firm may retain its independence while keeping client accounting records, provided certain requirements are met. The application of these inconsistent positions seldom causes conflict because large clients, which are the most likely to report to the SEC, usually have their own accounting and computer systems and need not request these services from their auditors. Moreover, the SEC rules apply to publicly traded companies only.

Answers (B), (C), and (D) are incorrect because Dickins & Co. has violated SEC but not necessarily AICPA rules.

61. According to the profession's ethical standards, an auditor would be considered independent in which of the following instances?

A. The auditor's checking account, which is fully insured by a federal agency, is held at a client financial institution.

B. The auditor is also an attorney who serves the client as its general counsel.

C. A professional employee of the auditor is the treasurer of a charitable organization that is a client.

D. The client owes the auditor fees for two consecutive annual audits.

The correct answer is (A). *(CPA, adapted)*

REQUIRED: The instance in which an auditor would be considered independent.

DISCUSSION: The independence of a member or a member's firm is not impaired if the member's depository relationship (checking, savings, certificates of deposit, money market accounts) is fully insured by a state or federal deposit insurance agency. If the amounts involved are not fully insured by an appropriate governmental agency, independence is not impaired if the uninsured portion is not material to the member or the member's firm.

Answer (B) is incorrect because an auditor's independence is impaired if (s)he serves the client as its general counsel or the equivalent. Such service would constitute "acting in a management capacity." Answer (C) is incorrect because a treasurer is an officer who performs management functions. Answer (D) is incorrect because independence is impaired if billed or unbilled fees, or a note receivable arising from such fees, for professional services rendered more than 1 year prior to the report date remain unpaid when the current year's report is issued.

62. In which of the following instances would the independence of the CPA most likely not be considered to be impaired? The CPA has been retained as the auditor of a

A. Charitable organization in which the spouse of the CPA serves as treasurer.

B. Municipality in which the CPA owns $25,000 of the $2,500,000 indebtedness of the municipality.

C. Credit union of which the CPA is a member.

D. Company in which the CPA's investment club owns a 10% interest.

The correct answer is (C). *(CPA, adapted)*

REQUIRED: The situation that does not impair the CPA's independence.

DISCUSSION: According to an Ethics Ruling, membership in a credit union will not impair independence if the member and/or his/her partners or employees individually qualify for the membership other than as a result of the services rendered, the member has no significant influence over credit union policies, any loans to the member meet the requirements of Interpretation 101-5, and any deposits are fully insured or, if uninsured, amounts are not material.

Answer (A) is incorrect because the employment of the spouse is ascribed to the CPA. The treasurer is an officer and is therefore considered to be a member of management. Answer (B) is incorrect because independence is impaired if the member or the member's firm has any loan to the client. Answer (D) is incorrect because ownership of stock in a client through an investment club is a direct financial interest. It impairs independence regardless of materiality.

63. Which of the following legal situations would be considered to impair the auditor's independence?

A. Intention by current management to commence litigation against the auditor alleging deficiencies in audit work, although the auditor believes there is only a remote possibility that such a claim will be filed.

B. Actual litigation by the auditor against the client for an amount not material to the auditor or the client's financial statements arising out of billing disputes.

C. Actual litigation by the auditor against the current management alleging management fraud or deceit.

D. Probable litigation by the client against the auditor for an amount not material to the auditor or to the financial statements of the client arising out of disputes as to billings for tax services.

The correct answer is (C). *(CPA, adapted)*

REQUIRED: The actual or intended litigation that would impair the auditor's independence.

DISCUSSION: According to an AICPA Interpretation, the following are guidelines for determining when actual or threatened litigation would impair independence: litigation has begun alleging deficient audit work; litigation has begun alleging fraud or deceit by current management; and management has expressed an intention to commence litigation alleging deficient audit work, and the auditor concludes that it is probable that such a claim will be filed.

Answer (A) is incorrect because independence is impaired if the auditor concludes that it is probable that such a claim will be filed. Answers (B) and (D) are incorrect because, if the litigation is related to an engagement not requiring independence, such as tax or consulting services, impairment would not necessarily result unless the amount in controversy is material to one of the litigants.

64. In which of the following circumstances would a CPA who audits XM Corporation lack independence?

A. The CPA and XM's president are both on the Board of Directors of COD Corporation.

B. The CPA and XM's president each owns 25% of FOB Corporation, a closely held company.

C. The CPA has an automobile loan from XM, a financial institution. The loan is collateralized by the automobile.

D. The CPA reduced XM's usual audit fee by 40% prior to the audit because XM's financial condition was unfavorable.

The correct answer is (B). *(CPA, adapted)*

REQUIRED: The circumstance in which a CPA would lack independence.

DISCUSSION: According to Interpretation 101-1, independence is impaired with regard to an enterprise if, during the engagement or at the time of expressing an opinion, "a member or a member's firm had any joint, closely held business investment with the enterprise or with any officer, director, or stockholders thereof that was material" to the member or the member's firm.

Answer (A) is incorrect because joint service with an officer of the client on the board of an unrelated entity does not constitute a prohibited transaction, interest, or relationship. Answer (C) is incorrect because an automobile loan from a financial institution client is permitted. The only new loans permitted after January 1, 1992 from a financial institution client for which independence is required are automobile loans and leases collateralized by the automobile, loans fully collateralized by the cash surrender value of an insurance policy, loans fully collateralized by cash deposits at the same financial institution (e.g., passbook loans), and credit cards and cash advances if the aggregate outstanding balance on the current statement is reduced to $5,000 or less by the payment due date. The loans must have been made under normal lending procedures, terms, and requirements and must, at all times, be kept current as to all terms. Answer (D) is incorrect because the only ethical prohibition regarding fees is that contingent fees shall not be charged for certain services (see Conduct Rule 302). Otherwise, fees may vary with many factors as long as they are related to services rendered and not to the CPA's findings or the results of findings. Hence, a CPA's fee may be charged on an ability-to-pay basis.

65. AICPA Interpretation 101-1 prohibits loans to a CPA from a client financial institution for which independence is required except for certain permitted loans made under normal lending procedures, terms, and requirements. When making the comparison between the terms of the CPA's loan and those of other borrowers, which item(s) should be considered in the determination of normal lending procedures?

A. Repayment terms.

B. Interest rate including points.

C. Closing costs.

D. All of the answers are correct.

The correct answer is (D). *(Publisher)*

REQUIRED: The item(s) considered to determine whether normal lending procedures have been followed.

DISCUSSION: CPAs are permitted to obtain certain loans from client financial institutions for which independence is required if the loans are made under normal conditions. The procedures, terms, and requirements should be reasonably comparable with those of similar loans committed to other borrowers in the same period. Among the items to be considered in determining whether the loan was made under normal lending procedures, etc., are the amount in relation to the collateral and the credit standing of the borrower, repayment terms, interest rate including points, closing costs, and general availability of such loans to the public.

Answers (A), (B), and (C) are incorrect because the items to be considered include all those listed.

66. A CPA audits the financial statements of a local bank. According to the AICPA *Code of Professional Conduct*, the appearance of independence ordinarily would not be impaired if the CPA

A. Serves on the bank's committee that approves loans.

B. Owns several shares of the bank's common stock.

C. Obtains after January 1, 1992 a home mortgage from the bank.

D. Uses the bank's timesharing computer service to solve client-related problems.

The correct answer is (D). *(CPA, adapted)*

REQUIRED: The situation in which the CPA firm would retain the appearance of independence.

DISCUSSION: Using the bank's timesharing computer services to solve client-related problems is considered a normal incident of an audit, and the CPA's independence would not be impaired.

Answer (A) is incorrect because a CPA's independence is impaired if (s)he serves in any capacity equivalent to that of a member of management or of a decision-making employee. Answer (B) is incorrect because even an immaterial direct financial interest impairs independence. Answer (C) is incorrect because a home mortgage impairs independence unless it is a grandfathered loan in accordance with Interpretation 101-5. After January 1, 1992, obtaining a new loan of a type described as a grandfathered loan (home mortgages, other secured loans, and unsecured loans not material to the member's net worth) impairs independence if the lender is a client requiring independence at the date a loan commitment or line of credit is granted.

67. Jordan is the executive partner of Cain & Jordan, CPAs. One of its clients is a large nonprofit charitable organization. The organization has asked Jordan to be on its board of directors, which consists of a large number of the community's leaders. For Cain & Jordan to be considered independent, which of the following requirements must be met?

	Board Participation Purely Honorary	Audit Participation by Jordan Prohibited
A.	Yes	Yes
B.	No	Yes
C.	No	No
D.	Yes	No

The correct answer is (D). *(Publisher)*

REQUIRED: The best description of the effect of a CPA's position as a board member of a charitable organization.

DISCUSSION: According to an AICPA Interpretation, the member and the member's firm will be independent as long as the position is purely honorary, it is identified as such in all letterheads and externally circulated materials in which (s)he is named as a director or trustee, the member restricts participation to use of his/her name, and (s)he does not vote or participate in management functions. Jordan may directly participate in the audit even though (s)he serves as an honorary director.

Answers (A), (B), and (C) are incorrect because, as long as the CPA's position is purely honorary, the firm remains independent.

68. An audit independence issue might be raised by the auditor's participation in consulting services engagements. Which of the following statements is most consistent with the profession's attitude toward this issue?

A. Information obtained as a result of a consulting engagement is confidential to that engagement and should not influence performance of the attest function.

B. The decision as to loss of independence must be made by the client based upon the facts of the particular case.

C. The auditor should not make management decisions for an audit client.

D. The auditor who is asked to review management decisions is also competent to make these decisions and can do so without loss of independence.

The correct answer is (C). *(CPA, adapted)*

REQUIRED: The statement most consistent with the profession's attitude toward independence relative to consulting services.

DISCUSSION: The auditor cannot act in any capacity equivalent to that of a member of management or of an employee with respect to the client and maintain independence. Thus, the auditor should not make management decisions for an audit client because (s)he would lack independence.

Answer (A) is incorrect because the auditor should use all information available in assessing the fairness of the financial statements. Answer (B) is incorrect because the auditor, not the client, must determine if (s)he has been put in a position in which independence might be questioned. Answer (D) is incorrect because the auditor may review management decisions and make suggestions, but (s)he may not actually make those decisions without losing independence.

69. A CPA who performs primary actuarial services for a client would normally be precluded from expressing an opinion on the financial statements of that client if the

A. Fees for the actuarial services have not been paid.

B. Actuarial services are a major determinant of the pension expense.

C. Client does not determine all significant matters of judgment.

D. Actuarial assumptions used are not in accordance with GAAS.

The correct answer is (C). *(CPA, adapted)*

REQUIRED: The situation in which a CPA could not provide actuarial and auditing services.

DISCUSSION: According to an Ethics Ruling, the independence of a CPA who provides actuarial services is not impaired if the significant matters of judgment are determined or approved by the client and the client is in a position to have an informed judgment on the results. This ruling has been extended to appraisal and valuation services.

Answer (A) is incorrect because, unless the fees have been unpaid for over a year at the date of the current year's report and thus might be deemed to be a loan to the client, the CPA may accept the audit engagement. Answer (B) is incorrect because, even if the results of the actuarial services are incorporated into the financial statements, the auditor's independence is not impaired as long as significant matters of judgment are determined by the client. Answer (D) is incorrect because the assumptions should be in accordance with GAAP, not GAAS.

70. A violation of the profession's ethical standards most likely would have occurred when a CPA

A. Expressed an unqualified opinion on the 19X2 financial statements when fees for the 19X1 audit were unpaid.

B. Reviews business processes selected by the client for their operational efficiency and effectiveness.

C. Purchased a CPA firm's practice of monthly write-ups for a percentage of fees to be received over a 3-year period.

D. Made arrangements with a financial institution to collect notes issued by a client in payment of fees due for the current year's audit.

The correct answer is (A). *(CPA, adapted)*

REQUIRED: The ethical violation.

DISCUSSION: An Ethics Ruling considers independence to be impaired if billed or unbilled fees, or a note receivable arising from such fees, for professional services rendered more than 1 year prior to the report date remain unpaid when the current year's report is issued. However, this ruling is inapplicable to fees outstanding from a client in bankruptcy. Moreover, long overdue fees would not preclude the CPA from performing services not requiring independence.

Answer (B) is incorrect because a CPA will not impair independence by providing operational auditing services if (s)he does not act as a manager or an employee of the client. Answer (C) is incorrect because no pronouncement prohibits purchase of a bookkeeping firm for a percentage of fees. Answer (D) is incorrect because the AICPA has ruled that this practice does not violate the Code.

71. Which of the following does not impair a CPA's independence?

A. The CPA performs the duties of a transfer agent or a registrar for a client.

B. The CPA participates as the treasurer of a charitable organization who is a client.

C. The client is in bankruptcy and has not paid fees related to the previous year's audit.

D. The CPA is a university faculty member who audits the student senate fund.

The correct answer is (C). *(Publisher)*

REQUIRED: The situation that does not impair a CPA's independence.

DISCUSSION: An Ethics Ruling states that independence will be impaired if, when the current year's report is issued, billed or unbilled fees, or a note receivable arising from such fees, remain unpaid for any professional services provided more than 1 year prior to the report date. These unpaid fees are tantamount to a loan. However, this ruling does not apply to fees owed by a client in bankruptcy.

Answer (A) is incorrect because a CPA who does the work of a registrar or transfer agent is undertaking management and operational responsibilities that impair independence. Answer (B) is incorrect because a CPA's independence is impaired if (s)he is connected with the client as an officer or in another capacity equivalent to that of management. Answer (D) is incorrect because the CPA cannot become independent of his/her employer (the university), which administers the student senate fund.

72. Which of the following impairs a CPA's independence regarding the client?

A. The CPA serves as general counsel for a client.

B. The CPA initially screens candidates for controller of a client.

C. The CPA instructs and trains client personnel during the implementation of a new system.

D. A CPA has an immaterial interest in a limited partnership. A client also has an immaterial interest in the limited partnership.

The correct answer is (A). *(Publisher)*

REQUIRED: The situation that impairs independence.

DISCUSSION: According to an Ethics Ruling, a member "would not be considered independent with respect to the client because serving as general counsel or its equivalent would be acting in a management capacity."

Answer (B) is incorrect because the CPA may recommend a position description and candidate specifications, search for and screen candidates, and recommend qualified candidates. The CPA may not hire personnel. Answer (C) is incorrect because the CPA is independent provided that (s)he does not make any management decisions. Because the CPA should avoid direct supervision of the actual operation of the system, supervision should be restricted to instruction and training. Answer (D) is incorrect because, given that the nonclient investee is not material to the client investor, the CPA's investment in the nonclient investee would impair independence with respect to the client only if it were material.

73. Which of the following most likely impairs a CPA's independence?

A. Owning stock in a mutual investment fund that owns stock in the CPA's client.

B. Belonging to an investment club that holds stock in a client.

C. Serving as a cofiduciary with a client bank with respect to a trust.

D. Auditing the insurance company that invests and manages contributions to the firm's retirement plan. These amounts are in a pooled separate account.

The correct answer is (B). *(Publisher)*

REQUIRED: The situation that impairs independence.

DISCUSSION: Membership in an investment club that holds stock in a client impairs independence with respect to that client because the CPA is deemed to have a direct financial interest. Any direct financial interest impairs independence (Interpretation 101-1).

Answer (A) is incorrect because ownership through a mutual investment company is an indirect financial interest in the client. An indirect interest does not impair independence unless it is material or the CPA has significant influence over the fund. Answer (C) is incorrect because, unless the trust assets are material to the bank or its trust department, the CPA is independent. Answer (D) is incorrect because independence is not impaired as a result of investing in the pooled separate account, which is not part of the insurer's general assets.

74. In which of the following situations would a CPA's independence be considered to be impaired?

I. The CPA maintains a checking account that is fully insured by a government deposit insurance agency at an audit-client financial institution.

II. The CPA has a direct financial interest in an audit client, but the interest is maintained in a blind trust.

III. The CPA owns a commercial building and leases it to an audit client. The lease meets all the criteria of a capital lease.

A. I and II.

B. II and III.

C. I and III.

D. I, II, and III.

The correct answer is (B). *(CPA, adapted)*

REQUIRED: The situations in which independence is impaired.

DISCUSSION: Under an Ethics Ruling, when a member or member's firm leases property to or from a client, independence is not impaired if the lease meets the criteria of an operating lease, the terms and conditions of the agreement compare with those of similar leases and all amounts are paid in accordance with the lease. However, if the lease meets all the criteria of a capital lease and does not qualify as a grandfathered or permitted loan under Interpretation 101-5, it will impair the member's independence. The reason is that a capital lease is considered a loan to or from the client. Moreover, independence is impaired if a member has any direct financial interest in the client. An Ethics Ruling states that independence is impaired whether or not the financial interest is in a blind trust.

Answers (A), (C), and (D) are incorrect because no impairment occurs if the member's depository relationship is fully insured.

75. According to the profession's ethical standards, a CPA would be considered independent in which of the following instances?

A. The CPA agrees to indemnify the client against losses from client acts.

B. The CPA has a material direct financial interest in a client but transfers the interest into a blind trust.

C. The CPA owns an office building, and the mortgage on the building is guaranteed by a client.

D. The CPA belongs to a country club client in which membership requires the acquisition of a pro rata share of equity.

The correct answer is (D). *(CPA, adapted)*

REQUIRED: The circumstances in which a CPA would be considered independent.

DISCUSSION: If membership is essentially social, independence is not impaired because the equity (or debt) ownership is not a direct financial interest. But the CPA should not serve on the governing board or participate in management.

Answer (A) is incorrect because this agreement violates Interpretations 101-1-A and 101-1-B. Answer (B) is incorrect because independence is impaired if a member has any direct financial interest in the client. An Ethics Ruling states that independence is impaired whether or not the financial interest is in a blind trust. Answer (C) is incorrect because independence is impaired if the CPA has a loan from the client. A loan includes a guarantee of a loan.

76. The AICPA *Code of Professional Conduct* states, in part, that a CPA should maintain integrity and objectivity. Objectivity in the Code refers to a CPA's ability to

A. Be impartial, intellectually honest, and free of conflicts of interest.

B. Distinguish independently between accounting practices that are acceptable and those that are not.

C. Be unyielding in all matters dealing with auditing procedures.

D. Choose independently between alternate accounting principles and auditing standards.

The correct answer is (A). *(Publisher)*

REQUIRED: The definition of objectivity in the *Code of Professional Conduct*.

DISCUSSION: According to the Principles, "Objectivity is a state of mind, a quality that lends itself to a member's services. It is a distinguishing feature of the profession. The principle of objectivity imposes the obligation to be impartial, intellectually honest, and free of conflicts of interest."

Answer (B) is incorrect because the CPA uses both judgment and GAAP to evaluate whether a client's accounting practices are acceptable. Answer (C) is incorrect because the CPA is expected to use professional judgment, which may include flexibility, in applying audit procedures. Answer (D) is incorrect because auditing standards are concerned with the quality of the auditor's performance, whereas adherence to accounting principles by management is a prerequisite for fairly stated financial statements.

77. A CPA would not violate Conduct Rule 102, *Integrity and Objectivity*, if the CPA

A. Performs expert witness services for a client.

B. Subordinates his/her judgment to that of client personnel when performing consulting services.

C. Knowingly misrepresents facts.

D. Accepts the judgment of a client instead of his/her own when performing tax services.

The correct answer is (A). *(Publisher)*

REQUIRED: The situation in which the CPA would not violate Conduct Rule 102.

DISCUSSION: According to an Ethics Ruling, a CPA who serves as an expert witness is not an advocate as contemplated by Interpretation 102-6. Rather, an expert witness is someone with "specialized knowledge, training, and experience who should arrive at and present positions objectively."

Answers (B) and (D) are incorrect because, in the performance of any professional service, a member shall not subordinate his/her judgment to others, including the client (Conduct Rule 102). Answer (C) is incorrect because a member shall not knowingly misrepresent facts.

1.7 Code -- Responsibilities to Clients

78. Which of the following statements best describes the distinction between the auditor's and management's responsibilities?

A. Management has responsibility for maintaining and adopting sound accounting policies, and the auditor has responsibility for establishing and maintaining internal control.

B. Management has responsibility for the basic data underlying financial statements, and the auditor has responsibility for drafting the financial statements.

C. The auditor's responsibility is confined to the audited portion of the financial statements, and management's responsibility is confined to the unaudited portions.

D. The auditor's responsibility is confined to expressing an opinion, but the financial statements remain the responsibility of management.

The correct answer is (D). *(Publisher)*

REQUIRED: The statement that best distinguishes between the auditor's and management's responsibilities concerning audited financial statements.

DISCUSSION: AU 110, *Responsibilities and Functions of the Independent Auditor*, states that the auditor is responsible for the opinion on financial statements, whereas management is responsible for the representations made in the financial statements.

Answer (A) is incorrect because management has responsibility for establishing and maintaining internal control. Answer (B) is incorrect because management is responsible for preparing the financial statements. Answer (C) is incorrect because the auditor expresses an opinion on the financial statements taken as a whole, and management is responsible for all the assertions in the financial statements.

79. Which of the following statements concerning an accountant's disclosure of confidential client data is ordinarily correct?

A. Disclosure may be made to any state agency without subpoena.

B. Disclosure may be made to any party on consent of the client.

C. Disclosure may be made to comply with an IRS audit request.

D. Disclosure may be made to comply with generally accepted accounting principles.

The correct answer is (B). *(CPA, adapted)*

REQUIRED: The condition allowing disclosure of confidential client data.

DISCUSSION: Under Conduct Rule 301, an accountant may disclose any confidential client information with the specific consent of the client.

Answer (A) is incorrect because disclosure may be made to a state agency only pursuant to a subpoena or summons or with the client's consent. Answer (C) is incorrect because, without a client's consent, an accountant may disclose confidential information to the IRS only pursuant to a subpoena or summons. Answer (D) is incorrect because compliance with GAAP is a responsibility of clients who issue financial statements, not the accountants who report on them.

80. Thorp, CPA, was engaged to audit Ivor Co.'s financial statements. During the audit, Thorp discovered that Ivor's inventory contained stolen goods. Ivor was indicted and Thorp was subpoenaed to testify at the criminal trial in state court. Ivor claimed accountant-client privilege to prevent Thorp from testifying. Which of the following statements is correct regarding Ivor's claim?

A. Ivor can claim an accountant-client privilege only in states that have enacted a statute creating such a privilege.

B. Ivor can claim an accountant-client privilege in neither state courts nor federal courts.

C. The accountant-client privilege can be claimed only in civil suits.

D. The accountant-client privilege can be claimed only to limit testimony to audit subject matter.

The correct answer is (A). *(CPA, adapted)*

REQUIRED: The true statement concerning accountant-client privilege.

DISCUSSION: Although communication between lawyers and clients is privileged, no common-law concept extends this privilege to the accountant-client relationship. A minority of states have enacted statutes recognizing as privileged the confidential communication between an accountant and a client.

Answer (B) is incorrect because a minority of states recognize the privilege. Moreover, the federal law restructuring the IRS created a federal accountant-client privilege in tax cases. Answer (C) is incorrect because, in states where the privilege exists, it also applies to criminal actions. Answer (D) is incorrect because, in states where the privilege exists, it is not limited to audit matters.

81. An external auditor is not permitted to discuss confidential client information except with the specific consent of the client. This ethical proscription

A. Is unenforceable.

B. Will prevent the auditor from engaging another auditing firm to conduct a peer review.

C. Will not preclude the auditor from complying with a validly issued court subpoena.

D. Is often used by a client to blunt the auditor's efforts to modify the standard auditor's report.

The correct answer is (C). *(CMA, adapted)*

REQUIRED: The effect of prohibiting disclosure of confidential client information.

DISCUSSION: Conduct Rule 301 does not prohibit a CPA from disclosing confidential client information

1. In compliance with a validly issued and enforceable subpoena or summons,
2. In the proper discharge of his/her professional obligations under Conduct Rules 202, *Compliance with Standards*, and 203, *Accounting Principles*,
3. In a review of the CPA's professional practice under AICPA or state CPA society or board of accountancy authorization, or
4. During the initiation of a complaint with, or in response to any inquiry made by, the professional ethics division, trial board of the AICPA, or an investigative or disciplinary body of a state society or board of accountancy.

Answer (A) is incorrect because conduct rules are enforceable through the AICPA, state CPA societies, etc. Answer (B) is incorrect because an exception is made for peer reviews. Answer (D) is incorrect because the CPA is not independent if the client can dictate the content of the report. However, the auditor cannot ordinarily disclose, without the client's specific consent, information not required to be disclosed in financial statements to comply with GAAP (AU 431).

82. AICPA Conduct Rule 301, *Confidential Client Information*, is violated when a member in public practice

A. Provides client profit and loss percentages to a trade association without the client's consent.

B. Uses outside computer services to process tax returns.

C. Performs consulting services for similar clients.

D. Advises potential consulting services clients about previous problems on similar engagements.

The correct answer is (A). *(Publisher)*

REQUIRED: The activity violating Conduct Rule 301.

DISCUSSION: An Ethics Ruling states that, prior to disclosing confidential client profit and loss percentages to a trade association, the CPA must have specific client consent.

Answer (B) is incorrect because, according to an Ethics Ruling, using outside computer services to process tax returns is permissible as long as client confidentiality is maintained. Many CPAs use outside computer services for processing tax returns. Answer (C) is incorrect because most CPAs perform consulting services for clients in the same or related industries. Answer (D) is incorrect because, according to an Ethics Ruling, CPAs must make full disclosure about any reservations concerning the usefulness of potential consulting services, especially those based on past experience with similar engagements. However, client confidentiality must be preserved or waived.

83. To which of the following parties may a CPA partnership provide its working papers, without being lawfully subpoenaed or without the client's consent?

A. The IRS.

B. The FASB.

C. Any surviving partner(s) on the death of a partner.

D. A CPA before purchasing a partnership interest in the firm.

The correct answer is (C). *(CPA, adapted)*

REQUIRED: The party who can receive working papers from a CPA without a subpoena or client consent.

DISCUSSION: Working papers may be disclosed to another partner of the accounting firm without the client's consent because such information has not been communicated to outsiders. A partner of the CPA has a fiduciary obligation to the client not to disclose confidential information without consent.

Answer (A) is incorrect because the partnership may not provide the IRS with confidential client information without client permission, a subpoena, or a summons. Answer (B) is incorrect because the CPA or his/her firm may not disclose confidential information to the FASB without client consent. Answer (D) is incorrect because a CPA may not provide working papers to a prospective purchaser. However, an exception is made for a review of the practice in conjunction with a prospective purchase, sale, or merger.

84. A publicly held company that disagrees with the independent auditor on a significant matter affecting its financial statements has several courses of action. Which of the following courses of action would be inappropriate?

A. Appeal to the FASB to review the significant matter.

B. Modify the financial statements by expressing in the footnotes its viewpoint with regard to the significant matter.

C. Ask the auditor to refer in the auditor's report to a client footnote that discusses the client point of view with regard to the significant matter.

D. Engage another independent auditor.

The correct answer is (A). *(CPA, adapted)*

REQUIRED: The inappropriate action by a public company when a disagreement arises with its auditor.

DISCUSSION: The disagreement would not be considered by the FASB. The board does not provide services for the settlement of disputes between clients and CPAs.

Answers (B) and (C) are incorrect because the viewpoint may be communicated in the footnotes. Answer (D) is incorrect because one alternative of the client is to engage a new auditor. However, the SEC requires public companies to disclose the reason for an auditor change by filing Form 8-K, and the AICPA requires predecessor-successor communication.

85. An auditor has withdrawn from an audit engagement of a publicly held company after finding fraud that may materially affect the financial statements. The auditor should set forth the reasons and findings in correspondence to the

A. Securities and Exchange Commission.

B. Client's legal counsel.

C. Stock exchanges on which the company's stock is traded.

D. Board of directors.

The correct answer is (D). *(CPA, adapted)*

REQUIRED: The persons or agencies to be notified when an auditor withdraws after finding fraud.

DISCUSSION: When an audit indicates the presence of errors or fraud that require a modification of the opinion, and the client refuses to accept the auditor's report as modified, the auditor should withdraw and communicate the reasons for withdrawal to the audit committee of the board of directors (AU 317). Withdrawal may or may not be appropriate in other circumstances, depending on the diligence and cooperation of management and the board in investigating the matter and taking action (AU 316). Moreover, the Private Securities Litigation Reform Act of 1995, which applies to public companies, requires the auditor to report directly to the board these conclusions regarding lack of remedial action: that an illegal act materially affects the financial statements, that senior management has not taken appropriate remedial action, and that this failure will result in a modified report or the auditor's withdrawal. The company then has one business day to notify the SEC.

Answers (A) and (C) are incorrect because the auditor is usually under no obligation to report fraud to outside parties. The firm, however, is required to disclose the reason for a change in auditors on SEC Form 8-K. Answer (B) is incorrect because the auditor may wish to consult his/her legal counsel but not the client's counsel.

86. A CPA's retention of client records as a means of enforcing payment of an overdue audit fee is an action that is

A. Not addressed by the AICPA *Code of Professional Conduct*.

B. Acceptable if sanctioned by state law.

C. Prohibited under the AICPA *Code of Professional Conduct*.

D. A violation of GAAS.

The correct answer is (C). *(CPA, adapted)*

REQUIRED: The profession's policy concerning a CPA's retention of client records.

DISCUSSION: An Interpretation of Conduct Rule 501, *Acts Discreditable*, defines client records as "any accounting or other records belonging to the client that were provided to the member by or on behalf of the client." This interpretation prohibits the retention (after a demand is made for them) of client records to enforce payment or for any other purpose. Such an act is deemed to be discreditable to the profession.

Answer (A) is incorrect because Conduct Rule 501 prohibits retention of client records as a means of enforcing payment of an overdue audit fee. Answer (B) is incorrect because the profession may require CPAs to adhere to standards beyond the legal minimum. Answer (D) is incorrect because retention of client records as a means of enforcing payment of an overdue audit fee is prohibited by the *Code of Professional Conduct*, not by GAAS.

87. With respect to records in a CPA's possession, the *Code of Professional Conduct* provides that

A. An auditor may retain client records if fees due with respect to a completed engagement have not been paid.

B. Working papers that contain journal entries not reflected in the client's records need not be furnished to the client upon request.

C. Extensive schedules prepared by the client at the auditor's request are working papers that belong to the auditor and need not be furnished to the client upon request.

D. The auditor who returns client records must comply with any subsequent requests to again provide such information.

The correct answer is (C). *(Publisher)*

REQUIRED: The true statement regarding records in the CPA's possession.

DISCUSSION: According to an Interpretation of Conduct Rule 501, "A member's workpapers -- including, but not limited to, analyses and schedules prepared by the client at the request of the member -- are the member's property, not client records, and need not be made available."

Answer (A) is incorrect because client records must be returned even if fees have not been paid. Answer (B) is incorrect because working papers containing client financial information not reflected in the client's books must be returned to the client upon request if the engagement is complete. Answer (D) is incorrect because, once the member has complied with the requirements for the return of client records, (s)he has no further obligation to provide such information.

88. Conduct Rule 501 states that a member shall not commit an act discreditable to the profession. Which of the following would not be considered such an act?

A. Retention of a client's records after a demand is made for them.

B. Retention of a client's records after a demand is made for them in a state that specifically grants the CPA a lien on all client records.

C. Withholding as a result of nonpayment of fees for a completed engagement certain information already contained in the client's books.

D. Failure to provide the client with client records that are part of the working papers.

The correct answer is (C). *(Publisher)*

REQUIRED: The act not considered discreditable to the profession.

DISCUSSION: The member's duty to return such information is not absolute. If fees for a completed engagement have not been paid, it may be withheld. The member's duty is absolute with regard to client records. The duty is conditional upon payment of fees with respect to information such as adjusting, closing, combining, or consolidating entries or information normally found in books of original entry and general or subsidiary ledgers.

Answer (A) is incorrect because CPAs may not retain client records after their return has been demanded. Answer (B) is incorrect because an Interpretation of Conduct Rule 501 states that an auditor who retains client records after a demand is made for their return is in violation of the Code even if state law permits the lien. Answer (D) is incorrect because, even though client records are part of the audit working papers, the CPA has an obligation to provide the client with those records.

1.8 Code -- Other Responsibilities and Practices

89. When a CPA is associated with financial statements that do not comply with promulgated GAAP because the statements would be misleading without the departure, the CPA is not required to disclose

A. The departure.

B. The approximate effects of the departure in comparison to the application of GAAP.

C. The reason the departure does not have a material effect on the statements.

D. The reasons compliance would be misleading.

The correct answer is (C). *(Publisher)*

REQUIRED: The disclosure not required when application of promulgated GAAP would be misleading.

DISCUSSION: Under Conduct Rule 203, a CPA who performs services that require representations of conformity with promulgated GAAP is required to describe the departure, the approximate effects of the departure (if practicable), and the reasons compliance would result in misleading financial statements. But this requirement applies only if the effect on the statements or data is material.

Answer (A) is incorrect because the CPA is required to disclose the departure. Answer (B) is incorrect because the CPA is required to disclose the approximate effects of the departure in comparison with the application of GAAP. Answer (D) is incorrect because the CPA is required to disclose the reasons compliance would be misleading.

90. A CPA who is employed by a nonaccounting corporation performs services for the employer, including auditing the employer's financial statements. Reports issued with respect to such activities are distributed with the CPA's name and CPA designation appearing on the corporate letterhead. These reports should

A. Be restricted to internal use.

B. Make no reference to GAAS.

C. Be on plain paper (not on the corporate letterhead).

D. Refer to an audit.

The correct answer is (B). *(Publisher)*

REQUIRED: The true statement about reports issued on the financial statements of a CPA's employer.

DISCUSSION: A CPA not in public practice who uses the CPA designation in a manner to imply that (s)he is independent of the employer has made a knowing misrepresentation of fact violating Conduct Rule 102. Thus, it is advisable that the employment title be clearly indicated. Moreover, an auditor who is not independent may not express an opinion. A reference to GAAS would imply independence.

Answer (A) is incorrect because, if a report is made available to third parties, it may indicate the CPA's professional designation if no implication of independence is conveyed. Answer (C) is incorrect because, if the report is to outsiders, it must be on the corporate letterhead. Answer (D) is incorrect because no reference should be made to GAAS, an audit, or a review. Such a reference might imply independence.

91. According to an Ethics Ruling based on the *Code of Professional Conduct*, a CPA

A. May not, upon leaving a firm, take any of the firm's client files without permission.

B. Is not associated with unaudited interim reports issued by clients even if the CPA's name is listed in the report.

C. Cannot undertake the responsibility of supervising and evaluating the work of specialists.

D. May disclose May 1996 or later Uniform CPA Examination questions.

The correct answer is (A). *(Publisher)*

REQUIRED: The true statement concerning a CPA's responsibilities.

DISCUSSION: Unless permitted by contract, a CPA, upon leaving the firm, may not take any of the firm's client files or proprietary information. Such behavior would be an act discreditable. Providing client files, records, or working papers to another firm without specific consent would also violate the client's confidentiality.

Answer (B) is incorrect because a member is associated with financial statements of a public entity when (s)he has consented to the use of his/her name in a report, document, or written communication containing the statements (AU 504). Answer (C) is incorrect because CPAs must be able to define the tasks to be performed by specialists and evaluate the results. Answer (D) is incorrect because solicitation or knowing disclosure of May 1996 or later CPA examination questions is an act discreditable.

92. The AICPA *Code of Professional Conduct* would be violated if a CPA accepted a fee for services and the fee was

A. Fixed by a public authority.

B. Based on a price quotation submitted in competitive bidding.

C. Based on the results of judicial proceedings in a tax matter.

D. Payable after a specified finding was attained in a review of financial statements.

The correct answer is (D). *(CPA, adapted)*

REQUIRED: The fee arrangement that violates the *Code of Professional Conduct*.

DISCUSSION: A contingent fee is one that is dependent upon a specified finding. Conduct Rule 302 prohibits contingent fees (1) for the audit or review of a financial statement, (2) for a compilation if a third party is reasonably expected to use the financial statement and the report does not mention the member's lack of independence, (3) for an examination of prospective financial information, and (4) for the preparation of original or amended tax returns or claims for tax refunds. However, contingent fees may be accepted for other services.

Answer (A) is incorrect because Conduct Rule 302 states that fees fixed by courts or other public authorities are not contingent. Answer (B) is incorrect because competitive bidding is not prohibited. Answer (C) is incorrect because, in tax matters, fees determined based on the results of judicial proceedings or the findings of governmental agencies are not contingent.

93. Which service may be rendered under a contingent fee arrangement? A CPA

A. Audits the financial statements of a company that intends to issue securities for sale to the public, with the fee contingent upon the proceeds from the sale of the securities.

B. Compiles financial statements for a client seeking a loan, with the fee contingent upon the amount the client is able to borrow. The report does not disclose lack of independence.

C. Examines prospective financial statements for a client who intends to sell limited partnerships, with the CPA's fee contingent upon the proceeds.

D. Performs services for a client in bankruptcy, with the fee to be set by the court.

The correct answer is (D). *(Publisher)*

REQUIRED: The service that may be rendered under a contingent fee arrangement.

DISCUSSION: The fee arrangement is acceptable under Conduct Rule 302 because fees are not regarded as contingent if fixed by a court or other public authority.

Answer (A) is incorrect because a contingent fee is prohibited for an audit of financial statements. Answer (B) is incorrect because a contingent fee is prohibited for a compilation if the report does not disclose lack of independence and a third party is reasonably expected to use the financial statements. Answer (C) is incorrect because a contingent fee is prohibited for an examination of prospective financial statements.

94. According to Conduct Rule 502, advertising or other forms of solicitation that are false, misleading, or deceptive are not in the public interest, and AICPA members in public practice shall not seek to obtain clients in such a manner. Such activities include all the following except those that

A. Indicate the CPA's educational and professional attainments.

B. Imply the ability to influence a court.

C. Claim to be able to save the taxpayer 20% of a determined tax liability.

D. Create unjustified expectations of favorable results.

The correct answer is (A). *(Publisher)*

REQUIRED: The advertising activity not considered false, misleading, or deceptive.

DISCUSSION: Advertising and solicitation are acceptable as long as they do not involve falsehood or deception. Members may engage in self-laudatory, comparative, or endorsement advertising; in-person solicitation; and advertising that some may view as in bad taste. Thus, an accurate statement of educational and professional attainments is clearly permissible.

Answer (B) is incorrect because advertisement of influence over courts, tribunals, regulatory agencies, or a similar body or official is deceptive. Answer (C) is incorrect because a correct amount of tax liability exists and a claim to save a taxpayer part of that amount is deceptive. Answer (D) is incorrect because creating false and unjustified expectations of favorable results is misleading.

95. The profession's ethical standards most likely are violated when a CPA represents that specific consulting services will be performed for a stated fee and it is apparent at the time of the representation that the

A. Actual fee will be substantially higher.

B. Actual fee will be substantially lower than the fees charged by other CPAs for comparable services.

C. CPA will not be independent.

D. Fee is a competitive bid.

The correct answer is (A). *(CPA, adapted)*

REQUIRED: The action that violates ethical standards regarding fee representation.

DISCUSSION: An Interpretation of Conduct Rule 502 prohibits forms of solicitation that are false, misleading, or deceptive. A representation that specific services will be performed for a stated fee, when it is likely at the time that the actual fee will be substantially higher, is a prohibited form of solicitation.

Answer (B) is incorrect because a CPA is permitted to charge lower fees than other CPAs. Answer (C) is incorrect because independence is required in an audit, but not for consulting services. Answer (D) is incorrect because competitive bids for consulting services are allowed.

96. Inclusion of which of the following statements in a CPA's advertisement is not acceptable pursuant to the AICPA *Code of Professional Conduct*?

A. Paul Fall
Certified Public Accountant
Fluency in Spanish and French

B. Paul Fall
Certified Public Accountant
J.D., Evans Law School 1990

C. Paul Fall
Certified Public Accountant
Free Consultation

D. Paul Fall
Certified Public Accountant
Endorsed by AICPA

The correct answer is (D). *(CPA, adapted)*

REQUIRED: The advertisement not in accordance with the AICPA *Code of Professional Conduct*.

DISCUSSION: A CPA may not claim to be endorsed by the Institute. A member may, however, state that (s)he is a member.

Answer (A) is incorrect because an accurate statement about fluency in languages is acceptable. Answer (B) is incorrect because an accurate statement about educational attainments is acceptable. Answer (C) is incorrect because advertising free consultation is acceptable.

97. A violation of the profession's ethical standards most likely occurs when a CPA

A. Purchases another CPA's accounting practice and bases the price on a percentage of the fees accruing from clients over a 3-year period.

B. Receives as a commission a percentage of the amounts invested by the CPA's audit clients in a tax shelter with the client's knowledge and approval.

C. Has a public accounting practice and also is the owner of a business that offers data processing services to the public.

D. Practices in a commercial corporation, a form of organization permitted by state law.

The correct answer is (B). *(Publisher)*

REQUIRED: The most likely ethics violation.

DISCUSSION: Conduct Rule 503 states, "A member in public practice shall not for a commission recommend or refer to a client any product or service, or for a commission recommend or refer any product or service to be supplied by a client, or receive a commission, when the member or the member's firm also performs for that client" certain services. These include an audit or review of a financial statement, a compilation if a third party is reasonably expected to use the financial statement and the report does not indicate lack of independence, or an examination of prospective financial information.

Answer (A) is incorrect because a sales price based on expected future cash flows is appropriate. Answer (C) is incorrect because a CPA may own a business offering services of a type performed by public accountants. However, (s)he will be deemed to be in the practice of public accounting and must abide by the Rules of Conduct. Answer (D) is incorrect because the practice of public accounting may be any form permitted by law, provided the organization conforms to resolutions of the AICPA Council.

98. Which of the following is prohibited by the AICPA *Code of Professional Conduct*?

A. Practice of public accounting in the form of a professional corporation that uses a firm name indicating specialization.

B. Use of the partnership name for a limited period by one of the partners in a public accounting firm after the death or withdrawal of all other partners.

C. Failing to provide working papers to the client after a request has been made.

D. Prematurely expressing an opinion for an audit because of time pressures from the client.

The correct answer is (D). *(Publisher)*

REQUIRED: The action considered a violation of the *Code of Professional Conduct*.

DISCUSSION: The Code prohibits a member from subordinating his/her judgment to others. The auditor must complete the audit prior to signing the report.

Answer (A) is incorrect because the Code does not prohibit the use of a fictitious name or the indication of a specialization. However, the name or indication of specialization may not be misleading. In addition, the AICPA permits CPAs to use trade names (e.g., "Suburban Tax Services") that are not false or deceptive. A firm may be organized in any form allowed by state law. Answer (B) is incorrect because names of one or more past owners may be included in the firm name of a successor organization as long as the name is not misleading. Answer (C) is incorrect because the working papers are the property of the CPA.

99. Which of the following acts by a CPA who is not in public practice is most likely to be a violation of the ethical standards of the profession?

A. Using the CPA designation without disclosing employment status in connection with financial statements issued for external use by the CPA's employer.

B. Distributing business cards indicating the CPA designation and the CPA's title and employer.

C. Corresponding on the CPA's employer's letterhead, which contains the CPA designation and the CPA's employment status.

D. Compiling the CPA's employer's financial statements and making reference to the CPA's lack of independence.

The correct answer is (A). *(CPA, adapted)*

REQUIRED: The action violating ethical standards.

DISCUSSION: According to an Ethics Ruling, a member not in public practice who uses the CPA designation in a manner implying that (s)he is independent of the employer has committed a knowing misrepresentation of fact in violation of Conduct Rule 102.

Answer (B) is incorrect because, as long as the CPA's title and the employer's name are on the business cards, their use is permissible. Answer (C) is incorrect because, as long as the CPA's title and the employer's name are on the letterhead, its use is permissible. Answer (D) is incorrect because an accountant may compile a nonpublic entity's financial statements if (s)he issues the appropriate report. The lack of independence, but not the reason therefor, should be disclosed (AR 100). If an accountant who is not independent is associated with the financial statements of a public entity (except a compilation report) but has not audited or reviewed them, (s)he must issue a disclaimer of opinion that states his/her lack of independence (AU 504).

100. Susan, CPA, performs compilation services for Dalstar, a nonpublic entity. The compilation reports issued by Susan disclose lack of independence and are not used by third parties. Susan has accepted a commission from a software company for recommending its products to Dalstar. The commission agreement was disclosed to Dalstar. Susan also refers Dalstar to Thomas, CPA, who is more competent with respect to engagements involving the industry in which Dalstar operates. Thomas performs an audit of Dalstar's financial statements and subsequently remits to Susan a portion of the fee collected. The referral fee agreement was likewise disclosed to Dalstar. Susan accepts the fee. Who, if anyone, has violated the *Code of Professional Conduct*?

A. Only Susan.

B. Both Susan and Thomas.

C. Only Thomas.

D. Neither Susan nor Thomas.

The correct answer is (D). *(Publisher)*

REQUIRED: The violator(s) of the *Code of Professional Conduct* when a CPA pays a referral fee to another CPA.

DISCUSSION: A commission is "compensation, except a referral fee, for recommending or referring any product or service to be supplied by another person" (FTC Order dated August 3, 1990). Conduct Rule 503 prohibits receipt of a disclosed commission only if the CPA performs for the client an audit, a review, a compilation when the report will be used by third parties and the report does not disclose the CPA's lack of independence, or an examination of prospective financial information. A referral fee is "compensation for recommending or referring any service of a CPA to any person" (FTC Order cited above). Conduct Rule 503 permits referral fees if they are disclosed to the client. Consequently, Susan has not violated Conduct Rule 503 by accepting either the disclosed commission or the disclosed referral fee. Thomas has not violated the Code by paying the disclosed referral fee.

Answers (A), (B), and (C) are incorrect because neither Susan nor Thomas has violated the Code.

101. Ann Able, CPA, is considering forming a partnership with Jim Baker for the purpose of practicing public accounting. Which of the following is true?

A. The AICPA *Code of Professional Conduct* requires Baker to be a CPA.

B. Baker need not be a CPA if the partnership does not represent itself as a partnership of CPAs.

C. If Baker is not a CPA, he need not conform to the AICPA *Code of Professional Conduct*.

D. If Baker is not a CPA, he may not participate in the management of the partnership.

The correct answer is (B). *(Publisher)*

REQUIRED: The true statement concerning a partnership with a non-CPA.

DISCUSSION: According to an Ethics Ruling, although the partnership may be created and public accounting services performed, the partnership is not permitted to represent itself as a partnership of CPAs.

Answer (A) is incorrect because some state boards and CPA societies have rules prohibiting mixed partnerships, but the Code does not prohibit a member from forming a partnership with non-CPAs. Answer (C) is incorrect because all partners must conform to the Code. Answer (D) is incorrect because the non-CPA is not precluded from participating in management.

102. Under Conduct Rule 505, *Form of Organization and Name*, and the related resolution of the AICPA Council, which of the following is a characteristic of a form of organization in which a member may practice public accounting?

A. The name may be impersonal as long as it does not indicate a specialty.

B. The owners must be jointly and severally liable for the acts of the entity.

C. The entity must be a professional corporation.

D. A majority of the ownership of the firm must belong to CPAs.

The correct answer is (D). *(Publisher)*

REQUIRED: The characteristic of an organization in which an AICPA member may practice public accounting.

DISCUSSION: A member may practice public accounting only in a form of organization permitted by state law and only if such entity has specified characteristics. CPAs must own a majority of the firm in terms of voting rights and financial interests. A non-CPA owner, including an investor or commercial enterprise, must be actively engaged in providing services to clients as his/her principal occupation. A CPA must have ultimate responsibility for all the services provided. Any non-CPA owner must have a baccalaureate degree. Non-CPA owners cannot hold themselves out to be CPAs, must abide by the Code, and must complete the work-related CPE requirements. Owners must own their equity in their own right. Ownership must be transferred to the firm or to other qualified owners if the non-CPA ceases to be actively engaged in the firm.

Answer (A) is incorrect because the firm name may be impersonal or fictitious or indicate a specialty as long as it is not misleading. Answer (B) is incorrect because the relevant Council resolution does not address the question of liability. Answer (C) is incorrect because the entity may be in any form allowed under state law.

103. A violation of the profession's ethical standards most likely occurs when a CPA who

A. Has been admitted to the Bar represents on letterhead to be an attorney and a CPA.

B. Has not prepared a newsletter permits the publisher to attribute it to the CPA.

C. Is controller of a bank permits the bank to use the controller's CPA title in the listing of officers in its publications.

D. Maintains a separate, distinct practice but forms an association with other CPAs for joint advertising. The group practices public accounting under the association's name.

The correct answer is (D). *(Publisher)*

REQUIRED: The most likely ethics violation.

DISCUSSION: The practice of public accounting under the name of an association or group is not permitted. The public is likely to be confused about the actual relationship of the parties. Accordingly, each firm should practice in its own firm name, but it may indicate the name of the association elsewhere on its stationery.

Answer (A) is incorrect because, according to an Ethics Ruling, a single letterhead may be used. The Code does not prohibit the simultaneous practice of law and accounting. Answer (B) is incorrect because an Ethics Ruling permits attribution of a newsletter, tax booklet, or similar publication to a member if the member has a reasonable basis for concluding that information attributed to the member is not false, misleading, or deceptive. Answer (C) is incorrect because an Ethics Ruling permits the controller to be identified as a CPA in the listing of bank officers.

104. A violation of the profession's ethical standards most likely occurs when a CPA in public practice

A. Uses a records-retention agency to store the CPA's working papers and client records.

B. Serves as an expert witness in a damage suit and receives compensation based on the amount awarded to the plaintiff.

C. Refers life insurance prospects to the CPA's spouse, who is a life insurance agent.

D. Serves on a municipal board of income tax appeals, discloses that status to concerned parties and participates as a board member in a tax appeal involving a client but does not receive the client's consent for such action.

The correct answer is (D). *(CPA, adapted)*

REQUIRED: The most likely ethics violation.

DISCUSSION: Under Interpretation 102-2, if the significant relationship creating a conflict of interest is disclosed to, and consent is obtained from, all appropriate parties, Conduct Rule 102 does not prohibit performance of the professional service. Moreover, an Ethics Ruling has determined that service on a governmental body is within the Interpretation. (But disclosure and consent do not eliminate an impairment of independence.) The failure to secure the client's consent means that the arrangement could be viewed as impairing the CPA's objectivity.

Answer (A) is incorrect because an Ethics Ruling permits the use of such a records center. Nevertheless, the responsibility for safeguarding the confidentiality of the client's records still rests with the CPA. Answer (B) is incorrect because contingent fees are allowed except in certain cases. Answer (C) is incorrect because the benefit (commission) received by the spouse as a result of the referral is ascribed to the CPA, but receipt of disclosed commissions is permissible in certain circumstances.

105. Which action is not considered a discreditable act under the Interpretations of Conduct Rule 501, *Acts Discreditable*?

A. A CPA-defendant has lost a final appeal of an adverse verdict in a sexual harassment suit in state court.

B. A CPA-defendant has lost a final appeal of an adverse verdict in a racial discrimination suit in federal court.

C. A CPA has a bank collect notes received from a client in payment of fees.

D. A CPA fails to follow standards and procedures established by governmental agencies in audits of grants by those agencies.

The correct answer is (C). *(Publisher)*

REQUIRED: The action not a discreditable act.

DISCUSSION: An Ethics Ruling permits CPAs to assign client notes received in payment of fees to banks for collection.

Answers (A) and (B) are incorrect because a final adverse legal determination of culpability under antidiscrimination law creates a presumption that the member has committed an act discreditable. Answer (D) is incorrect because a member must follow established governmental standards and procedures in addition to GAAS in auditing governmental agencies, grantees, etc. Thus, failing to follow standards and procedures established by governmental agencies in audits of grants by those agencies is a discreditable act.

106. A CPA serving as a bank director should not be concerned with

A. A possible conflict of interest between the bank and the CPA's clients.

B. The compatibility of serving as a bank director and the possibility of soliciting clients.

C. The CPA's independence with respect to a client's receiving a large loan from the bank.

D. Disclosure of confidential client information to the bank.

The correct answer is (B). *(Publisher)*

REQUIRED: The situation not an ethics violation by a practicing CPA who is serving as director of a bank.

DISCUSSION: The *Code of Professional Conduct* does not prohibit solicitation of clients. Solicitation is permitted as long as it is not false, misleading, or deceptive.

Answer (A) is incorrect because the conflict between the bank's and the clients' interests may not be avoidable. As a result, the CPA's objectivity may be questioned. Answer (C) is incorrect because, if the CPA's client receives a material loan from the bank, the CPA's independence may be impaired with respect to that client. Answer (D) is incorrect because the CPA's responsibility to the client precludes the disclosure of confidential client information, but failure to disclose may breach the fiduciary duty owed to the bank.

107. Which of the following violates the *Code of Professional Conduct*?

A. A member not in public practice is a bank controller who is designated as a CPA on bank stationery and in bank advertisements listing officers of the bank.

B. A member who is also a licensed attorney simultaneously practices both professions. The member does not use separate letterheads.

C. A partner in a CPA firm is elected to public office. After his/her withdrawal from the firm, the remaining partners continue to use a firm name that includes his/her name.

D. A member shares offices with another member. Their joint letterhead implies that a partnership exists when each member is in fact practicing individually.

The correct answer is (D). *(Publisher)*

REQUIRED: The violation of the *Code of Professional Conduct*.

DISCUSSION: According to an Ethics Ruling, CPAs should not use a letterhead showing the names of two accountants when a partnership between them does not exist. Such a representation is misleading. Furthermore, some courts have held that such an arrangement may be a de facto partnership, and the individual CPAs may be liable for the obligations of the de facto partnership and of the de facto partners.

Answer (A) is incorrect because the bank controller's use of the CPA title is permitted by a specific Ethics Ruling. Answer (B) is incorrect because an Ethics Ruling states that a single letterhead may be used. Answer (C) is incorrect because the name of a past owner may be included in the firm name of a successor organization.

108. Which is most likely a violation of the AICPA *Code of Professional Conduct*?

A. A member firm buys computer time at wholesale prices from another CPA firm and sells it at retail prices to clients.

B. A member begins a public accounting firm with the trade name "Pay Less Tax Service."

C. A tax booklet is attributed to a member firm even though it was prepared by an outside author.

D. A member forms a partnership for the practice of public accounting with non-CPAs.

The correct answer is (B). *(Publisher)*

REQUIRED: The most likely ethics violation.

DISCUSSION: Members may use a trade name as long as it is not deceptive or misleading. "Pay Less" may be construed as misleading for a tax service.

Answer (A) is incorrect because a member may purchase a product from a third-party supplier and resell the product to a client. Answer (C) is incorrect because an Ethics Ruling permits a tax booklet to be attributed to the member in these circumstances given a reasonable basis for concluding that the information attributed to the member is not false, misleading, or deceptive. Answer (D) is incorrect because the partnership of a CPA with non-CPAs is not precluded by the Code even though it is prohibited by some states. All members of the partnership must conform to the Code, and the firm may not represent itself as a partnership of CPAs.

1.9 Legal Liability

109. Contract law is the basis for the legal liability at common law of an auditor to his/her client. From which of the following may the auditor's liability arise?

A. Only fraudulent actions by the auditor.

B. Only gross negligence or fraudulent actions by the auditor.

C. Negligence, gross negligence, or fraudulent actions by the auditor.

D. Neither negligence nor fraudulent actions by the auditor.

The correct answer is (C). *(Publisher)*

REQUIRED: The basis for an auditor's legal liability to a client at common law.

DISCUSSION: An auditor's liability to a client arises from their contract, which is usually documented in the audit engagement letter. The auditor is obligated to carry out the contract (perform the audit) by exercising reasonable care. (S)he will be liable to the client for any negligence or fraud.

Answer (A) is incorrect because the auditor will also be liable for negligence. Answer (B) is incorrect because the auditor will also be liable for failure to use reasonable care (ordinary negligence). Answer (D) is incorrect because both negligence and fraud will create a contractual liability. The contract implies a duty to exercise reasonable care.

110. Which of the following best describes litigation involving CPAs?

A. The Racketeer Influenced and Corrupt Organizations Act was specifically passed by Congress to address illegitimate actions by CPAs.

B. A CPA may successfully assert as a defense that the CPA had no motive to be part of a fraud.

C. A CPA may be exposed to criminal as well as civil liability.

D. A CPA is primarily responsible for a client's footnotes in an annual report filed with the SEC.

The correct answer is (C). *(Publisher)*

REQUIRED: The best description of litigation involving CPAs.

DISCUSSION: A CPA may be exposed to criminal as well as civil liability under the Securities Act of 1933, the Securities Exchange Act of 1934, and the RICO Act.

Answer (A) is incorrect because the RICO Act was enacted to curtail inroads of organized crime into legitimate business. Answer (B) is incorrect because, although absence of intent is a defense to fraud, motive is not relevant. Answer (D) is incorrect because management, not the CPA, is responsible for the financial statements, including the footnotes.

111. The prevailing legal view is that an auditor's liability to third parties at common law may be based on

A. Fraud only when such parties were in privity of contract with the auditor.

B. Gross negligence only if the auditor knew such parties were intended beneficiaries of the audit.

C. Ordinary negligence and that any third party who relied on the auditor's work may recover.

D. Ordinary negligence if such parties belonged to a specifically foreseen class but were not specifically known.

The correct answer is (D). *(Publisher)*

REQUIRED: The basis for an auditor's legal liability to a third party at common law.

DISCUSSION: An auditor has not contracted with third parties, so the potential responsibility to them is not as great as to the client. Auditors may be liable to any third parties for gross negligence and intentional acts of deceit (fraud). However, auditors may be liable at common law for ordinary negligence to third parties in certain circumstances. Indeed, courts have been steadily expanding these circumstances. Thus, the Restatement (Second) of Torts, a work published by the American Law Institute that reflects the trends in state law, provides for liability when a third party, although not specifically known at the time of the audit, belonged to a limited and foreseen class of financial statement users. For example, all banks would be included in the class if the audit report were intended to be used by the client to obtain a bank loan. Other creditors, however, would be excluded from the class of potential plaintiffs.

Answers (A) and (B) are incorrect because the auditor may be liable for fraud and gross negligence to all third parties. Answer (C) is incorrect because the majority view precludes recovery on the basis of ordinary negligence unless the plaintiff belonged to a specifically foreseen class of users (intended beneficiaries).

112. How does the Securities Act of 1933, which imposes civil liability on auditors for misrepresentations or omissions of material facts in a registration statement, expand auditors' liability to purchasers of securities beyond that of common law?

A. Purchasers only have to prove loss caused by reliance on audited financial statements.

B. Privity with purchasers is not a necessary element of proof.

C. Purchasers have to prove either fraud or gross negligence as a basis for recovery.

D. Auditors are held to a standard of care described as professional skepticism.

The correct answer is (B). *(CPA, adapted)*

REQUIRED: The expansion of auditor liability under the Securities Act of 1933.

DISCUSSION: Privity, i.e., being a party to the contract with the auditor, is not a required element of proof under Section 11, the most frequently invoked basis for recovery under the Securities Act of 1933. Privity is often the deciding factor in common law cases, however.

Answer (A) is incorrect because a plaintiff must simply prove that a loss occurred in a transaction involving the particular securities covered by the registration statement and that the registration statement contained a false statement or an omission of a material fact for which the auditors were responsible. If these elements are proven, the burden shifts to the auditors to prove that they exercised due diligence. Negligence, privity, and reliance are not elements of the plaintiff's case. Answer (C) is incorrect because the plaintiff need not prove fraud, gross negligence, negligence, privity, or reliance. Answer (D) is incorrect because auditors are held to the standard of due diligence, which may be satisfied by following GAAS in the conduct of the audit.

113. Which statement is correct concerning an auditor's statutory legal liability?

A. The Securities Act of 1933 broadened the auditor's liability and the Securities Exchange Act of 1934 narrowed it.

B. The auditor has a greater burden of defense under the Securities Act of 1933 than the Securities Exchange Act of 1934.

C. Criminal liability only arises under state law.

D. Statutes usually modify the auditor's liability to the client.

The correct answer is (B). *(Publisher)*

REQUIRED: The correct statement concerning an auditor's statutory liability.

DISCUSSION: In general, the Securities Act of 1933 regulates initial sales of securities to the public. The Securities Exchange Act of 1934 regulates subsequent sales and exchanges of securities. Under the 1933 act, a purchaser need only prove damages resulting from the purchase of securities covered by a registration statement containing a false statement or omission in a section audited or prepared by the auditor. The auditor must then prove that (s)he was not negligent (or fraudulent), usually by showing that (s)he made a reasonable investigation (the "due diligence" defense). Under the 1934 act, the purchaser must prove that (s)he did not know the statement was false, that (s)he relied on it, and, under the antifraud provisions, that the auditor acted with intent or reckless disregard for the truth. Thus, gross negligence is the minimum basis for liability, and the auditor need not prove due diligence.

Answer (A) is incorrect because both securities statutes imposed greater liability on auditors than had existed under the common law. However, the 1934 act places a greater burden of proof on the plaintiff than the 1933 act. Answer (C) is incorrect because criminal liability can also arise under federal securities law. Answer (D) is incorrect because statutes usually modify the auditor's liability to third parties. The auditor's liability to clients remains contractual.

114. When engaged to compile unaudited financial statements for a private company, the accountant's responsibility to detect errors, irregularities, and illegal acts

A. Does not exist unless the parties have a written agreement.

B. Arises from the accountant's obligation to apply normal auditing procedures.

C. Is to design procedures to provide reasonable assurance of detecting material misstatements.

D. Is limited to informing the client that the engagement cannot be relied upon to disclose fraud.

The correct answer is (D). *(Publisher)*

REQUIRED: The accountant's responsibility to detect errors and fraud when engaged to compile unaudited financial statements.

DISCUSSION: The accountant's understanding with the entity should provide that the engagement cannot be relied upon to detect errors and fraud and that (s)he will inform the entity of any such material matters that come to his/her attention.

Answer (A) is incorrect because a contract for services need not be in writing to be valid. Answer (B) is incorrect because the accountant need not apply auditing procedures to information gathered in the preparation of unaudited statements. Answer (C) is incorrect because AU 110 requires auditors "to plan and perform the audit to obtain reasonable assurance about whether the financial statements are free of material misstatement, whether caused by error or fraud."

115. The scope and nature of an auditor's contractual obligation to a client is ordinarily set forth in the

A. Management representation letter.

B. Scope paragraph of the auditor's report.

C. Engagement letter.

D. Introductory paragraph of the auditor's report.

The correct answer is (C). *(CPA, adapted)*

REQUIRED: The form of the contractual agreement with a client.

DISCUSSION: An auditor should establish an understanding with the client regarding the services to be performed. The variety of matters that are included in the understanding may be communicated in an engagement letter (AU 310). Thus, the audit scope, responsibilities of management and the auditor, arrangements regarding the conduct of the audit, additional services to be provided, fees, and other matters should be set forth in a contract evidenced by an engagement letter. An engagement letter should be prepared for prospective clients on each engagement, audit or otherwise. Such a letter is highly recommended although not specifically required by GAAS. If the client agrees to the contractual relationship by signing a copy of the letter, it represents a written contract.

Answer (A) is incorrect because an auditor obtains a written management representation letter to complement other procedures, but it is not part of the engagement letter. Answer (B) is incorrect because the scope paragraph (1) states that the audit was conducted in accordance with GAAS, (2) sets forth the requirements of GAAS, (3) describes the nature of an audit, and (4) states that the audit provides a reasonable basis for the opinion. Answer (D) is incorrect because the introductory paragraph (1) states that the financial statements were audited and (2) describes the responsibilities of management and the auditor.

116. DMO Enterprises, Inc. engaged the accounting firm of Martin, Seals, & Anderson to perform its annual audit. The firm performed the audit in a competent, nonnegligent manner and billed DMO for $16,000, the agreed fee. Shortly after delivery of the audited financial statements, Hightower, the assistant controller, disappeared, taking with him $28,000 of DMO's funds. It was then discovered that Hightower had been engaged in a highly sophisticated, novel defalcation scheme during the past year. He had previously embezzled $35,000 of DMO funds. DMO has refused to pay the accounting firm's fee and is seeking to recover the $63,000 that was stolen by Hightower. Which of the following is correct?

A. The accountants cannot recover their fee and are liable for $63,000.

B. The accountants are entitled to collect their fee and are not liable for $63,000.

C. DMO is entitled to rescind the audit contract and thus is not liable for the $16,000 fee, but it cannot recover damages.

D. DMO is entitled to recover the $28,000 defalcation and is not liable for the $16,000 fee.

The correct answer is (B). *(CPA, adapted)*

REQUIRED: The correct statement concerning the disputed fee of auditors who failed to uncover a sophisticated embezzlement scheme.

DISCUSSION: An audit cannot guarantee that fraud will be detected. The auditor's opinion reflects that the audit is intended to give only reasonable assurance that the financial statements are free of material misstatement. Thus, AU 110 requires auditors "to plan and perform the audit to obtain reasonable assurance about whether the financial statements are free of material misstatement, whether caused by error or fraud." If the auditors planned and performed the audit in accordance with GAAS, including AU 110, the accounting firm fulfilled its contract with the client. The auditors should not be held liable for the loss and are entitled to their fee.

Answer (A) is incorrect because the accountants are entitled to the $16,000 in unpaid fees and are not liable for either the current embezzlement of $28,000 or the past embezzlement of $35,000. Answer (C) is incorrect because the client is liable for the $16,000 fee. Answer (D) is incorrect because the client is liable for the $16,000 fee and may not recover the $28,000 defalcation from the accountants.

117. Ocean and Associates, CPAs, audited the financial statements of Drain Corporation. As a result of Ocean's negligence in conducting the audit, the financial statements included material misstatements. Ocean was unaware of this fact. The financial statements and Ocean's unqualified opinion were included in a registration statement and prospectus for an original public offering of stock by Drain. Sharp purchased shares in the offering. Sharp received a copy of the prospectus prior to the purchase but did not read it. The shares declined in value as a result of the misstatements in Drain's financial statements becoming known. Under which of the following acts is Sharp most likely to prevail in a lawsuit against Ocean?

	Securities Exchange Act of 1934, Section 10(b), Rule 10b-5	Securities Act of 1933, Section 11
A.	Yes	Yes
B.	Yes	No
C.	No	Yes
D.	No	No

The correct answer is (C). *(CPA, adapted)*

REQUIRED: The basis for recovery under securities law in a suit against negligent accountants.

DISCUSSION: Section 11 is the most frequently invoked basis for suit under the Securities Act of 1933. Under Section 11, the investor need prove only that (s)he suffered losses in a transaction involving the particular securities covered by the registration statement and that the registration statement contained a false statement or an omission of a material fact for which the CPAs were responsible, e.g., in the audited financial statements. Thus, under Section 11, Sharp need not prove reliance or negligence and will prevail if Ocean fails to prove due diligence. Sharp is unlikely to prevail under the antifraud provisions of the Securities Exchange Act of 1934 because of the absence of scienter.

Answers (A), (B), and (D) are incorrect because Sharp would most likely prevail under the 1933 act but not the 1934 act.

118. As a direct result of his failure to follow GAAS, Bob Smyth, CPA, did not detect an embezzlement by an employee of the client. To recover the losses from Smyth under common law, the client must

	Prove Negligence	Be in Privity of Contract
A.	Yes	No
B.	No	Yes
C.	Yes	Yes
D.	No	No

The correct answer is (A). *(Publisher)*

REQUIRED: The common law liability of a CPA who failed to adhere to GAAS and did not detect a material embezzlement.

DISCUSSION: Under common law, the CPA is liable to clients for losses attributable to the CPA's negligence. Failure to adhere to GAAS is evidence of negligence. A CPA and the audited company are in privity of contract; i.e., they are parties to the same contract. However, privity is not a requirement. Most courts extend the accountant's liability for negligence to primary beneficiaries, foreseen third parties, or even reasonably foreseeable third parties.

Answers (B), (C), and (D) are incorrect because the client must be a party to the contract and prove negligence on the part of the CPA.

119. Under Section 11 of the Securities Act of 1933, which of the following standards may a CPA use as a defense?

	Generally Accepted Accounting Principles	Generally Accepted Fraud Detection Standards
A.	Yes	Yes
B.	Yes	No
C.	No	Yes
D.	No	No

The correct answer is (B). *(CPA, adapted)*

REQUIRED: The standards a CPA may use as a defense under Section 11.

DISCUSSION: A CPA is strictly liable to investors under Section 11 but will not be liable if (s)he can prove due diligence. This defense requires proof that a reasonable investigation was conducted and that the CPA reasonably believed that the financial statements were accurate on the effective date of the registration statement. Proof of adherence to GAAP and GAAS is the usual basis for such a due diligence defense.

Answers (A), (C), and (D) are incorrect because adherence to GAAP and GAAS is a defense, but generally accepted fraud detection standards do not exist.

120. Martin Corporation orally engages Dawson, CPA, to audit its year-end financial statements. The engagement is to be completed within 2 months after the close of Martin's fiscal year for a fixed fee of $2,500. Under these circumstances what obligation is assumed by Dawson?

A. None. The contract is unenforceable because it is not in writing.

B. An implied promise to exercise reasonable standards of competence and care.

C. An implied obligation to take extraordinary steps to discover all defalcations.

D. The obligation of an insurer of its work who is liable without fault.

The correct answer is (B). *(CPA, adapted)*

REQUIRED: The obligation assumed by a CPA engaged to audit financial statements.

DISCUSSION: CPAs are required to adhere to reasonable standards of competence and care and perform an audit in accordance with GAAS. They are expected to complete the contract based upon the agreed terms.

Answer (A) is incorrect because an oral contract is enforceable (but subject to disagreement, which can be avoided with an engagement letter). Answer (C) is incorrect because an ordinary audit should be designed to provide reasonable assurance that material errors and irregularities will be detected. Hence, it need not include extraordinary procedures to uncover all fraud, whether or not material. Answer (D) is incorrect because auditors are not insurers. They do not undertake to guarantee the results of their work regardless of fault. Rather, they are required to use due professional care.

121. You are a CPA retained by the manager of a cooperative retirement village to do write-up work. You are expected to prepare unaudited financial statements with each page marked "unaudited" and accompanied by a disclaimer of opinion stating no audit was made. In performing the work, you discover that there are no invoices to support $25,000 of the manager's claimed disbursements. The manager informs you that all the disbursements are proper. What should you do?

A. Submit the expected statements but omit the $25,000 of unsupported disbursements.

B. Include the unsupported disbursements in the statements because you are not expected to make an audit.

C. Obtain from the manager a written statement that you informed him/her of the missing invoices and that (s)he gave his/her assurance that the disbursements were proper.

D. Notify the owners that some of the claimed disbursements are unsupported and withdraw if the situation is not satisfactorily resolved.

The correct answer is (D). *(CPA, adapted)*

REQUIRED: The appropriate action by a CPA who discovers a material irregularity while doing compilation work.

DISCUSSION: These facts are based on *1136 Tenants' Corp. v. Max Rothenburg & Co.* (1972), a case that imposed liability on a CPA doing compilation work for not pursuing an investigation of facts that appeared questionable on their face. Although the CPA need not audit the information, (s)he is responsible to take further action concerning information that is incorrect, incomplete, or otherwise unsatisfactory. Such action includes communication with the owners.

Answer (A) is incorrect because submitting the statements but omitting the unsupported disbursements is an inappropriate action on the part of the CPA. Answer (B) is incorrect because including the unsupported disbursements in the statements is an inappropriate action on the part of the CPA. Answer (C) is incorrect because obtaining the manager's statement is insufficient.

122. Under the antifraud provisions of Section 10(b) of the Securities Exchange Act of 1934, a CPA may be liable if the CPA acted

A. Negligently.

B. With independence.

C. Without due diligence.

D. Without good faith.

The correct answer is (D). *(CPA, adapted)*

REQUIRED: The basis for a CPA's liability under Section 10(b).

DISCUSSION: The distinguishing element of fraud is scienter, which is the intent to deceive or defraud. Acting in good faith indicates lack of scienter. Hence, a CPA who acted without good faith cannot assert the good faith defense.

Answer (A) is incorrect because fraud entails an intent to deceive or defraud, not mere negligence. Answer (B) is incorrect because a CPA who performs attest services must be independent. Answer (C) is incorrect because lack of due diligence, *per se*, does not signify the existence of scienter.

1.10 Quality Control and Peer Review for CPA Firms

123. A CPA firm is reasonably assured of meeting its responsibility to provide services that conform with professional standards by

A. Adhering to generally accepted auditing standards.

B. Having an appropriate system of quality control.

C. Joining professional societies that enforce ethical conduct.

D. Maintaining an attitude of independence in its engagements.

The correct answer is (B). *(CPA, adapted)*

REQUIRED: The means of reasonably assuring that a CPA firm's services meet professional standards.

DISCUSSION: A system of quality control should provide reasonable assurance that the firm's personnel comply with professional standards applicable to its audit and accounting practice (QC 20). GAAS apply to individual audit engagements. Quality control standards apply to the firm's practice as a whole (AU 161).

Answer (A) is incorrect because a firm must comply with all applicable standards, not merely GAAS. Answer (C) is incorrect because adhering to ethical standards is only one aspect of quality control. Answer (D) is incorrect because independence is included in the first of the five elements of quality control.

124. A firm of independent auditors must establish and follow quality control policies and procedures because these standards

A. Are necessary to meet increasing requirements of auditors' liability insurers.

B. Are required by the SEC for auditors of all firms.

C. Include formal filing of records of such policies and procedures.

D. Give reasonable assurance that the firm as a whole will conform with generally accepted auditing standards.

The correct answer is (D). *(Publisher)*

REQUIRED: The reason a firm of independent auditors establishes a quality control system.

DISCUSSION: The system of quality control includes the organizational structure and the policies adopted and procedures established to provide reasonable assurance that the firm as a whole will comply with GAAS and other applicable standards. Policies and procedures should be established with respect to the following elements: independence, integrity, and objectivity; personnel management; acceptance and continuance of clients and engagements; engagement performance; and monitoring (QC 20).

Answer (A) is incorrect because companies that insure CPAs against liability for malpractice establish their own requirements and insurance rates. Answer (B) is incorrect because all CPA firms are obligated to adhere to quality control standards issued by the ASB. The SEC has authority only over those firms that must report under the securities laws. Answer (C) is incorrect because quality control standards do not require formal records to be filed with the AICPA or any other body.

125. Quality control for a CPA firm, as referred to in Statements on Quality Control Standards (SQCS), applies to

A. Auditing services only.

B. Auditing and consulting services.

C. Auditing and tax services.

D. Auditing and accounting and review services.

The correct answer is (D). *(CPA, adapted)*

REQUIRED: The applicability of the quality control standards.

DISCUSSION: According to QC 20, quality control for a CPA firm applies to all audit, attest, accounting and review, and other services for which professional standards have been established by the ASB and the Accounting and Review Services Committee. The SQCSs therefore do not apply to compliance with standards for consulting services and tax services, which are issued by different senior technical committees.

Answers (A), (B), and (C) are incorrect because the SQCSs apply to auditing and accounting and review services but not to consulting and tax services.

126. Which of the following are elements of a CPA firm's quality control that should be considered in establishing its quality control policies and procedures?

	Personnel Management	Monitoring	Engagement Performance
A.	Yes	Yes	No
B.	Yes	Yes	Yes
C.	No	Yes	Yes
D.	Yes	No	Yes

The correct answer is (B). *(CPA, adapted)*

REQUIRED: The elements that should be considered in establishing quality control policies and procedures.

DISCUSSION: The quality control element of personnel management relates to assuring that employees have the skills needed for the responsibilities they are called upon to assume. The quality control element of monitoring is concerned with providing reasonable assurance that procedures related to the other elements are suitably designed and being effectively applied. The quality control element of engagement performance requires the firm to establish policies and procedures to ensure proper planning, performing, supervising, reviewing, documenting, and communicating the results of engagements (QC 20).

Answers (A), (C), and (D) are incorrect because each should be considered in establishing a firm's quality control policies and procedures.

127. The nature and extent of a CPA firm's quality control policies and procedures depend on

	The CPA Firm's Size	The Nature of the CPA Firm's Practice	Cost-Benefit Considerations
A.	Yes	Yes	Yes
B.	Yes	Yes	No
C.	Yes	No	Yes
D.	No	Yes	Yes

The correct answer is (A). *(CPA, adapted)*

REQUIRED: The factors affecting a CPA firm's quality control policies and procedures.

DISCUSSION: The nature and extent of a firm's quality control policies and procedures depend on a number of factors, such as the firm's size, the degree of operating autonomy allowed, its personnel policies, the nature of its practice and organization, and appropriate cost-benefit considerations (QC 20).

Answers (B), (C), and (D) are incorrect because the CPA firm's size, the nature of the CPA firm's practice, and cost-benefit considerations are factors that affect quality control policies and procedures.

128. Which of the following is an element of a CPA firm's quality control system that should be considered in establishing its quality control policies and procedures?

A. Complying with laws and regulations.

B. Using statistical sampling techniques.

C. Managing personnel.

D. Considering audit risk and materiality.

The correct answer is (C). *(CPA, adapted)*

REQUIRED: The element of a CPA firm's quality control system.

DISCUSSION: The quality control element of personnel management requires establishment of policies and procedures to provide reasonable assurance that only persons with the required training and proficiency perform the work (QC 20).

Answer (A) is incorrect because the auditor considers compliance with laws and regulations. However, this consideration is not an element of a CPA firm's quality control system. Answer (B) is incorrect because an auditing firm may use statistical or nonstatistical sampling techniques in performing audits. Answer (D) is incorrect because an auditor must consider audit risk and materiality in performing the audit, but this consideration is not an element of a quality control system.

129. The primary purpose of establishing quality control policies and procedures for deciding whether to accept a new client is to

A. Enable the CPA firm to attest to the reliability of the client.

B. Satisfy the CPA firm's duty to the public concerning the acceptance of new clients.

C. Minimize the likelihood of association with clients whose management lacks integrity.

D. Anticipate before performing any field work whether an unqualified opinion can be expressed.

The correct answer is (C). *(CPA, adapted)*

REQUIRED: The primary purpose of establishing quality control policies and procedures for deciding whether to accept a new client.

DISCUSSION: CPA firms should have policies and procedures to determine whether to accept or continue a new client or to perform a specific engagement for a client. The objective is to minimize the likelihood of association with clients whose managers may lack integrity (QC 20).

Answer (A) is incorrect because the CPA firm attests to the fairness of the financial statements, not to the reliability of the client. Answer (B) is incorrect because the CPA firm has a duty to the public with regard to its reporting responsibilities but not client acceptance. Answer (D) is incorrect because the field work will dictate whether an unqualified opinion can be expressed.

130. In connection with the element of personnel management, a CPA firm's system of quality control should ordinarily provide that all personnel

A. Have the knowledge required to enable them to fulfill responsibilities assigned.

B. Possess judgment, motivation, and adequate experience.

C. Seek assistance from persons having appropriate levels of knowledge, judgment, and authority.

D. Demonstrate compliance with peer review directives.

The correct answer is (A). *(CPA, adapted)*

REQUIRED: The requirement for all personnel.

DISCUSSION: According to QC 20, the firm's policies and procedures should provide reasonable assurance that personnel will have the knowledge required to meet assigned responsibilities. CPE and training activities fulfill this requirement and allow employees to progress within the firm.

Answer (B) is incorrect because motivation and judgment are often difficult to assess. Answer (C) is incorrect because seeking assistance from persons having appropriate levels of knowledge, judgment, and authority relates to the element of engagement performance. Answer (D) is incorrect because peer review directives may relate to any or all of the quality control elements.

131. In pursuing a CPA firm's quality control objectives, a CPA firm may maintain records indicating which partners or employees of the CPA firm were previously employed by the CPA firm's clients. Which quality control element would this be most likely to satisfy?

A. Professional relationship.

B. Experience requirements.

C. Independence, integrity, and objectivity.

D. Advancement.

The correct answer is (C). *(CPA, adapted)*

REQUIRED: The quality control element associated with records of employment of personnel by the firm's clients.

DISCUSSION: CPA firms should avoid situations in which third parties might question the firm's independence. Thus, they should adhere to the independence standards established by the *Code of Professional Conduct*, state board of accountancy, state CPA society, the SEC, and any other law or regulation (QC 20).

Answers (A) and (B) are incorrect because professional relationship and experience requirements are not quality control elements. Answer (D) is incorrect because advancement is an aspect of the element of personnel management. It relates to assuring that employees selected for advancement have the skills needed for the responsibilities they will be called upon to assume.

132. The audit work performed by each assistant should be reviewed to determine whether it was adequately performed and to evaluate whether the

A. Auditor's system of quality control has been maintained at a high level.

B. Results are consistent with the conclusions to be presented in the auditor's report.

C. Audit procedures performed are approved in the professional standards.

D. Audit has been performed by persons having adequate technical training and proficiency as auditors.

The correct answer is (B). *(CPA, adapted)*

REQUIRED: The reason for reviewing the audit work of each assistant.

DISCUSSION: The first standard of field work requires assistants to be properly supervised. Thus, the "work performed by each assistant should be reviewed to determine whether it was adequately performed and to evaluate whether the results are consistent with the conclusions to be presented in the auditor's report" (AU 311).

Answer (A) is incorrect because the review of the audit work of each assistant is only a part of quality control. Answer (C) is incorrect because determination of whether the procedures are in accordance with GAAS is necessary in the planning stage. Answer (D) is incorrect because the selection of assistants having adequate technical training and proficiency concerns planning, not supervision.

133. Quality control policies and procedures should provide the firm with reasonable assurance that the policies and procedures relating to the other elements of quality control are being effectively applied. This statement defines the quality control element of

A. Planning.

B. Supervision.

C. Independence, integrity, and objectivity.

D. Monitoring.

The correct answer is (D). *(Publisher)*

REQUIRED: The element concerned with effective application of all elements of quality control.

DISCUSSION: The quality control element of monitoring is concerned with providing reasonable assurance that policies and procedures related to the other elements are suitably designed and being effectively applied. Monitoring involves considering and evaluating the relevance and adequacy of policies and procedures, the appropriateness of guidance materials and practice aids, the effectiveness of professional development, and the compliance with policies and procedures (QC 20).

Answers (A) and (B) are incorrect because planning and supervision are aspects of the element of engagement performance. This element encompasses all phases of the design and execution of an engagement. Answer (C) is incorrect because the element of independence, integrity, and objectivity provides reasonable assurance that personnel at all levels remain independent in fact and appearance, perform all professional responsibilities with integrity, and maintain objectivity in discharging those responsibilities.

134. In connection with the element of monitoring, a CPA firm's system of quality control should ordinarily provide for the maintenance of

A. A file of minutes of staff meetings.

B. Updated personnel files.

C. Documentation to demonstrate compliance with its policies and procedures.

D. Documentation to demonstrate compliance with peer review directives.

The correct answer is (C). *(CPA, adapted)*

REQUIRED: The item maintained in connection with the quality control element of monitoring.

DISCUSSION: The quality control element of monitoring is concerned with providing reasonable assurance that policies and procedures related to the other elements are suitably designed and being effectively applied. "Documentation should be retained for a period of time sufficient to enable those performing monitoring procedures and a peer review to evaluate the extent of the firm's compliance with its quality control standards" (QC 20).

Answers (A), (B), and (D) are incorrect because a file of minutes of staff meetings, updated personnel files, and documentation to demonstrate compliance with peer review directives are examples of the documentation of compliance.

135. Williams & Co. is a CPA firm enrolled in Partnering for CPA Practice Success, the AICPA Alliance for CPA Firms (PCPS). The firm is to have a peer review. The review will most likely be performed by

A. Partners of Williams & Co. who are not associated with the particular audits being reviewed.

B. Audit review staff of the SEC.

C. Audit review staff of the AICPA.

D. Another CPA firm.

The correct answer is (D). *(CPA, adapted)*

REQUIRED: The parties most likely to perform a peer review of a CPA firm.

DISCUSSION: Peer review is a necessary part of the practice-monitoring requirement for AICPA membership. A peer review of a firm enrolled in the AICPA peer review program or of a member of the PCPS is administered by a state CPA society or sponsoring organization authorized by the AICPA Peer Review Board. A review team may be formed (1) by a firm engaged by the reviewed firm or (2) by a state CPA society. Also, an association of firms may be authorized to aid its members by organizing review teams for on-site and off-site reviews (PR 100). Furthermore, a PCPS firm need not perform the peer review of a PCPS firm, and the team captain need not be a PCPS member.

Answer (A) is incorrect because partners of the firm being reviewed are not considered independent for the purpose of peer review. Answer (B) is incorrect because the SEC does not perform peer reviews. Answer (C) is incorrect because the AICPA does not have professional staff to perform peer reviews.

136. In 1977, the AICPA established the Division for CPA Firms. The SEC Practice Section and the PCPS were created to provide an organization for self-regulation. What was the primary reason for creating the Division for CPA Firms?

A. To raise money through dues for lobbying efforts.

B. To promote peer review by the AICPA.

C. To provide the AICPA with a mechanism for monitoring the performance of firms and imposing sanctions against them.

D. To maintain a united front against Congress.

The correct answer is (C). *(Publisher)*

REQUIRED: The primary reason for the creation of the Division for CPA Firms.

DISCUSSION: Prior to the creation of the Division for CPA Firms, only individuals belonged to the AICPA. Hence, no mechanism for monitoring the performance of firms existed. The establishment of the two sections provided a vehicle for establishing standards and imposing sanctions for substandard performance. Membership in the Division for CPA Firms is one way to meet the requirement for participation in an approved practice monitoring program.

Answer (A) is incorrect because, although there is a fee for belonging to the sections, the money is primarily used for administering the programs. Answer (B) is incorrect because, prior to the establishment of the Division for CPA Firms, peer review was provided on a voluntary basis through other programs of the AICPA. Answer (D) is incorrect because, although pressures from Congress were important in the AICPA's self-regulatory efforts, the Division is not an adversary of Congress.

137. The AICPA's Division for CPA Firms has two separate but similar sections, the SEC Practice Section and the PCPS. Basic membership requirements for both sections include all the following except

A. A peer review at least once every 3 years.

B. Periodic rotation of the partner in charge on an audit.

C. Compliance with quality control standards.

D. Continuing education for professional staff.

The correct answer is (B). *(Publisher)*

REQUIRED: The requirement not necessary for membership in both sections of the Division for CPA Firms.

DISCUSSION: Small firms and proprietorships find it difficult to rotate partners in charge of audits. Thus, only the SEC Practice Section requires that partners in charge be rotated. The requirement is that a new audit partner be placed in charge of each SEC engagement if another partner has been in charge for 7 consecutive years. This requirement does not apply if the firm has fewer than five SEC clients or fewer than 10 partners. Moreover, a concurring review of the audit report and financial statements issued in an SEC engagement must be made by a partner other than the audit partner-in-charge.

Answer (A) is incorrect because a peer review at least once every 3 years is required for membership in both sections. Answer (C) is incorrect because compliance with quality control standards is required for membership in both sections. Answer (D) is incorrect because continuing education for professional staff is required for membership in both sections.

138. If a firm having an SEC client has joined both the SEC Practice Section and the PCPS of the AICPA's Division for CPA Firms, that firm must have

A. A peer review for each section.

B. No peer review because membership is evidence of effective quality control.

C. Only one peer review to satisfy both memberships.

D. A peer review performed by the AICPA.

The correct answer is (C). *(Publisher)*

REQUIRED: The true statement about peer review when a firm has membership in both the SEC Practice Section and the PCPS.

DISCUSSION: A firm having membership in both organizations needs only one peer review every 3 years to satisfy the requirement. However, peer reviews of members of the two organizations are subject to different standards. Standards for Performing and Reporting on Peer Reviews do not apply to reviews of members of the SEC Practice Section. The peer review committee of the SECPS issues standards applicable to its members.

Answer (A) is incorrect because one peer review suffices to meet the requirements of both organizations. Answer (B) is incorrect because all firms belonging to one of these organizations must have a peer review every 3 years. Answer (D) is incorrect because a peer review is usually performed by a firm selected by the firm being reviewed.

139. Which statement is true concerning membership in the SEC Practice Section or the PCPS?

A. A firm must have an SEC client to join the SEC Practice Section.

B. Firms with SEC clients may join the PCPS.

C. Only firms without SEC clients may join the PCPS.

D. All firms must join either the PCPS or the SEC Practice Section.

The correct answer is (B). *(Publisher)*

REQUIRED: The true statement concerning membership in the Division for CPA Firms.

DISCUSSION: The AICPA Bylaws state that members may not practice with a firm auditing one or more SEC clients if that firm is not a member of the SEC Practice Section. Thus, firms with SEC clients must join the SEC Practice Section. They may also join the PCPS.

Answer (A) is incorrect because firms without SEC clients may join the SEC Practice Section. Answer (C) is incorrect because firms with SEC clients may join both groups. Answer (D) is incorrect because the Bylaws indicate that a member of the AICPA may engage in the practice of public accounting only with a firm that is enrolled in an Institute-approved practice-monitoring program. However, the AICPA does not require that firms without SEC clients enroll in the PCPS. The implementing resolution related to the aforementioned bylaw establishes a peer review division within the AICPA to conduct in association with state CPA societies a practice-monitoring program for public practitioners. This program is an alternative to joining the Division for CPA Firms.

1.11 Responsibilities in Tax Practice

140. Statements on Responsibilities in Tax Practice (SRTP) have been issued by the Responsibilities in Tax Practice Committee and the Tax Executive Committee of the AICPA. Which of the following is the correct assertion about these statements?

A. They have also been approved by the Council of the AICPA.

B. Their authority depends on the general acceptability of the pronouncements.

C. Compliance is required by the AICPA *Code of Professional Conduct*.

D. The statements should be applied retroactively to all tax engagements.

The correct answer is (B). *(Publisher)*

REQUIRED: The true statement concerning Statements on Responsibilities in Tax Practice.

DISCUSSION: SRTP contain certain standards of responsibility that are more restrictive than those established by the Treasury Department or by the Institute's *Code of Professional Conduct*. They depend on the general acceptability of the opinions expressed for their authority.

Answer (A) is incorrect because the standards have been approved by at least two-thirds of the members of the Responsibilities in Tax Practice Committee and the Tax Executive Committee by formal vote. However, they have not been considered and acted upon by the Council of the Institute. Answer (C) is incorrect because the series of statements is intended to constitute a body of advisory opinion as to appropriate standards of tax practice. They delineate the extent of a CPA's responsibility to the client, the public, the government, and the profession (TX 102). Answer (D) is incorrect because the tax standards explicitly state that they are not intended to be retroactive.

141. When a CPA prepares a client's federal income tax return, the CPA has the responsibility to

A. Be an advocate for the entity's realistically sustainable position.

B. Verify the data to be used in preparing the return.

C. Take a position of independent neutrality.

D. Argue the position of the Internal Revenue Service.

The correct answer is (A). *(CPA, adapted)*

REQUIRED: The responsibility of a CPA who prepares a federal income tax return.

DISCUSSION: A CPA engaged in tax practice has the right and responsibility to be an advocate for the client. But a CPA should not recommend a tax return position absent "a good faith belief that the position has a realistic possibility of being sustained administratively or judicially on its merits if challenged." However, a CPA may recommend a position that is not frivolous if it is adequately disclosed (TX 112). Such action, by itself, does not impair the objectivity and integrity required by Conduct Rule 102.

Answer (B) is incorrect because the data need not be verified unless the information seems incomplete or incorrect. Answer (C) is incorrect because a CPA must be independent when performing attestation services, but not for tax return preparation. Answer (D) is incorrect because the CPA has the right and the responsibility to be an advocate of the client, not the IRS.

142. A CPA who is engaged to prepare an income tax return has a duty to prepare it in such a manner that the tax is

A. The legal minimum.

B. Computed in conformity with generally accepted accounting principles.

C. Supported by the client's audited financial statements.

D. Not subject to change upon audit.

The correct answer is (A). *(CPA, adapted)*

REQUIRED: The CPA's duty in preparing a client's income tax return.

DISCUSSION: A CPA should serve to the best of his/her ability and with professional concern for the client's best interests, consistent with responsibilities to the public. According to TX 112, "it is well established that the taxpayer has no obligation to pay more taxes than are legally owed, and the CPA has a duty to the client to assist in achieving that result." Within the limits of the law and ethical practice, the CPA should strive for the legal minimum tax, not for tax evasion.

Answer (B) is incorrect because the tax according to the tax return is computed based on the Internal Revenue Code, tax regulations, revenue rulings, etc. Answer (C) is incorrect because the tax expense according to the statements is based on GAAP. Moreover, the tax preparer need not audit the client's statements. Answer (D) is incorrect because discovery of errors may necessitate a change.

143. A CPA must sign the preparer's declaration on a federal income tax return

A. Only when the CPA prepares a tax return for compensation.

B. Only when the CPA can declare that a tax is based on information of which the CPA has personal knowledge.

C. Whenever the CPA prepares a tax return for others.

D. Only when the return is for an individual or corporation.

The correct answer is (A). *(CPA, adapted)*

REQUIRED: The condition for signing the preparer's declaration on a federal income tax return.

DISCUSSION: Treasury Regulations require preparers to sign all the returns they prepare and to include their identification numbers. However, a preparer is defined as a person who prepares (or employs persons to prepare) for compensation any tax return or claim for refund of tax imposed by Subtitle A of the Internal Revenue Code (which covers income taxes on all entities).

Answer (B) is incorrect because the CPA may prepare a return based on information provided by the client. Personal knowledge of the information is not required. Answer (C) is incorrect because the CPA must sign only when (s)he receives compensation. Answer (D) is incorrect because the signature requirement applies to returns and claims for refund by all income tax-paying entities.

144. Which of the following is implied when a CPA signs the preparer's declaration on a federal income tax return?

A. The tax return is not misleading based on all information of which the CPA has knowledge.

B. The tax return and supporting schedules were prepared in accordance with GAAP.

C. The tax return was examined in accordance with standards established by the AICPA's Federal Tax Division.

D. The tax return was prepared by a CPA who maintained an impartial attitude.

The correct answer is (A). *(CPA, adapted)*

REQUIRED: The implication when a CPA signs the preparer's declaration on a federal income tax return.

DISCUSSION: Conduct Rule 102 states, "In the performance of any professional service, a member shall not knowingly misrepresent facts or subordinate his/her judgment to others."

Answer (B) is incorrect because the tax return and supporting schedules should be prepared in accordance with federal tax law. Answer (C) is incorrect because the CPA is not required to examine or review documents or other evidence supporting the client's information. Answer (D) is incorrect because a CPA in tax practice should take a position of client advocacy, barring any wrongdoing.

145. The preparer of a federal income tax return signs a preparer's declaration that states,

> Under penalties of perjury, I declare that I have examined this return, including accompanying schedules and statements, and to the best of my knowledge and belief, it is true, correct, and complete. Declaration of preparer (other than the taxpayer) is based on all information of which the preparer has any knowledge.

A CPA who signs this declaration as preparer of a client's tax return warrants that

A. Information furnished by the client was relied upon in preparing the tax return unless it appeared incorrect or incomplete.

B. Information furnished by the client was audited in accordance with GAAS.

C. All available evidence in support of material assertions in the tax return was audited in accordance with GAAS.

D. All available evidence in support of material assertions in the tax return was documented in the CPA's working papers.

The correct answer is (A). *(CPA, adapted)*

REQUIRED: The warranty given by a CPA who signs the tax preparer's declaration on a federal income tax return.

DISCUSSION: The preparer's declaration should be understood to relate to information known by the CPA or made available to him/her in connection with the preparation of a return. The declaration should not imply an investigation in support of material furnished by the client. The CPA may ordinarily rely on the information furnished by the client unless, in light of his/her knowledge, the information presented appears to be "incorrect, incomplete, or inconsistent either on its face or on the basis of facts known to the CPA" (TX 132).

Answers (B) and (C) are incorrect because the CPA does not perform an audit in accordance with GAAS of the information used to prepare the return. Answer (D) is incorrect because the CPA need not examine or verify supporting data.

146. As part of your annual audit of a client, you prepare the federal income tax return. What modifications should you make to the preparer's declaration when signing the return?

	Modify to Conform to Audit Report	Modify to State That Information Was from Audited Financial Statements
A.	Yes	No
B.	No	No
C.	Yes	Yes
D.	No	Yes

The correct answer is (B). *(Publisher)*

REQUIRED: The modifications that the CPA should make to the preparer's declaration.

DISCUSSION: The CPA should make no modification of the preparer's declaration on a federal income tax return. Modification will not affect the signer's responsibilities as preparer. Unusual circumstances may be disclosed in a rider not constituting a modification.

Answers (A), (C), and (D) are incorrect because no modification should be made. Furthermore, the CPA neither audits the information in the tax return nor warrants by signing as preparer that an investigation has been made.

147. When a reasonable basis exists for omission of an answer to an applicable question on a tax return,

A. The CPA-preparer need not provide an explanation for the omission on the return.

B. A brief explanation of the reason for the omission must be provided on the return.

C. The question should be marked as nonapplicable.

D. A note on the return should state that the answer will be provided if the information is requested.

The correct answer is (A). *(CPA, adapted)*

REQUIRED: The proper action when a reasonable basis exists for omission of an answer on a tax return.

DISCUSSION: According to TX 122, *Answers to Questions on Returns*, the CPA should sign the preparer's declaration when a question has not been answered only if the CPA has made "a reasonable effort to obtain from the client, and provide, appropriate answers to all questions on a tax return." A possible disadvantage to the client does not justify omission of information or omission of an explanation for missing information. However, given reasonable grounds for the omission, the CPA is not required to provide an explanation on the return, although (s)he must consider whether the omission may cause the return to be incomplete.

Answers (B) and (D) are incorrect because, given reasonable grounds for the omission, the CPA is not required to provide an explanation on the return. Answer (C) is incorrect because an omission may be reasonable on grounds other than inapplicability.

148. According to the profession's standards, which of the following actions should be taken by a CPA tax preparer who discovers an error in a client's previously filed tax return?

A. Advise the IRS.

B. Correct the error.

C. Advise the client.

D. End the relationship with the client.

The correct answer is (C). *(CPA, adapted)*

REQUIRED: The proper action of a CPA who discovers an error in a previously filed tax return.

DISCUSSION: According to TX 162, a CPA should inform the client promptly upon becoming aware of an error in a previously filed return and "recommend the measures to be taken." In the case of a material understatement, an amended return should be filed by the client. A claim for refund is appropriate for a material overstatement. The advice may be given to the client orally.

Answer (A) is incorrect because a CPA should not inform the IRS without the client's permission, except if required by law. Answer (B) is incorrect because a CPA is not responsible for correcting a discovered error unless requested to do so by the client. Answer (D) is incorrect because a CPA need not end the relationship with the client over the discovery of a previous error.

149. Jones, CPA, prepared Smith's federal income tax return and appropriately signed the preparer's declaration. Several months later, Jones learned that Smith improperly altered several figures before mailing the tax return to the IRS. Jones should communicate disapproval of this action to Smith and

A. Take no further action with respect to the current year's tax return but consider the implications of Smith's actions for any future relationship.

B. Inform the IRS of the unauthorized alteration.

C. File an amended tax return.

D. Refund any fee collected, return all relevant documents, and refuse any further association with Smith.

The correct answer is (A). *(CPA, adapted)*

REQUIRED: The proper action of a tax preparer-CPA whose client improperly altered the return.

DISCUSSION: When the CPA discovers an error, (s)he must inform the client and recommend the measures to be taken. It is then the client's responsibility to correct the error. If the IRS is likely to bring criminal charges, the client should be advised to seek legal counsel. If the error is not corrected, "the CPA should consider whether to continue a professional relationship with the client" (TX 162).

Answer (B) is incorrect because the CPA may not inform the IRS, except if required by law. Answer (C) is incorrect because the CPA may not file an amended return without the client's permission. Answer (D) is incorrect because TX 162 does not mention refunding fees, returning documents, and refusing further association.

150. Kopel was engaged to prepare Raff's 1997 federal income tax return. During the tax preparation interview, Raff told Kopel that he paid $3,000 in property taxes in 1997. Actually, Raff's property taxes amounted to only $600. Based on Raff's word, Kopel deducted the $3,000 on Raff's return, resulting in an understatement of Raff's tax liability. Kopel had no reason to believe that the information was incorrect. Kopel did not request underlying documentation and was reasonably satisfied by Raff's representation that Raff had adequate records to support the deduction. Which of the following statements is correct?

A. To avoid the preparer penalty for willful understatement of tax liability, Kopel was obligated to examine the underlying documentation for the deduction.

B. To avoid the preparer penalty for willful understatement of tax liability, Kopel would be required to obtain Raff's representation in writing.

C. Kopel is not subject to the preparer penalty for willful understatement of tax liability because the deduction that was claimed was more than 25% of the actual amount that should have been deducted.

D. Kopel is not subject to the preparer penalty for willful understatement of tax liability because Kopel was justified in relying on Raff's representation.

The correct answer is (D). *(CPA, adapted)*

REQUIRED: The correct statement concerning tax return preparer liability.

DISCUSSION: A tax return preparer may rely, without verification, on information provided by the client when the preparer is reasonably justified in relying upon the client's representations. However, a preparer must make a reasonable inquiry if the information appears to be incorrect or incomplete.

Answer (A) is incorrect because the preparer is not subject to preparer penalties for willful understatement because (s)he is justified in relying on the data furnished by the taxpayer. The preparer is not a guarantor of the accuracy of the return. Answer (B) is incorrect because a preparer is not required to obtain a written representation from the client prior to preparing a client's return. Answer (C) is incorrect because preparer penalties are assessed only when the preparer has recommended a position that does not have a realistic possibility of success.

151. Elwyn, CPA, is preparing a federal tax return for Emma, who stated that she had made about $150 of cash donations to charitable organizations for which she had no receipts. These donations had been given to solicitors at supermarkets, airports, etc. What should Elwyn do with this information when preparing the tax return?

A. Ignore it because the information cannot be verified.

B. Identify $150 as "Other miscellaneous contributions."

C. Request that Emma obtain receipts from the charitable organizations.

D. Increase one of the other specifically named contributions by $150.

The correct answer is (B). *(Publisher)*

REQUIRED: The proper action by the CPA regarding the use of estimated tax data.

DISCUSSION: TX 142, *Use of Estimates*, permits the CPA to prepare tax returns involving the use of estimates if it is impracticable to obtain exact data and the amounts are reasonable. Estimates must not be presented so as to imply greater accuracy than exists. The CPA should therefore identify the approximate amount of the contribution as "Other miscellaneous contributions."

Answer (A) is incorrect because the use of estimates is not prohibited by the AICPA. Answer (C) is incorrect because the client is unable to obtain receipts. Answer (D) is incorrect because the information should not be presented in a manner implying greater accuracy than exists.

152. In tax practice, which of the following would not be considered a basis for a CPA's good faith belief that a tax return position is likely to be sustained?

A. A low probability that the return will be audited.

B. IRS General Counsel Memoranda.

C. Private letter rulings.

D. Well-reasoned articles by tax specialists.

The correct answer is (A). *(Publisher)*

REQUIRED: The authority not a basis for a CPA's good faith belief that a tax return position will be sustained.

DISCUSSION: A CPA may not recommend a tax return position absent a good faith belief that the position "has a realistic possibility of being sustained administratively or judicially on its merits if challenged." But a CPA may prepare and sign the preparer's declaration if this standard is not met provided that the position is not frivolous and is adequately disclosed. In no case, however, may a CPA recommend a position that "exploits the IRS audit selection process" or serves solely as a bargaining position in negotiations with the IRS.

Answers (B), (C), and (D) are incorrect because IRS General Counsel Memoranda, private letter rulings, and well-reasoned articles by tax specialists are bases for a good faith belief that a position is sustainable.

153. According to the profession's standards, which of the following statements is correct regarding the standards a CPA should follow when recommending tax return positions and preparing tax returns?

A. A CPA may recommend a position that the CPA concludes is frivolous as long as the position is adequately disclosed on the return.

B. A CPA may recommend a position in which the CPA has a good faith belief that the position has a realistic possibility of being sustained if challenged.

C. A CPA will usually not advise the client of the potential penalty consequences of the recommended tax return position.

D. A CPA may sign a tax return as preparer knowing that the return takes a position that will not be sustained if challenged.

The correct answer is (B). *(CPA, adapted)*

REQUIRED: The true statement about the standards followed in recommending tax return positions and preparing returns.

DISCUSSION: According to TX 112, a CPA in tax practice has the right and responsibility to be an advocate for the client. However, a CPA should not recommend a tax return position without "a good faith belief that the position has a realistic possibility of being sustained administratively or judicially on its merits if challenged." Nevertheless, a CPA may recommend a position that is not frivolous if it is adequately disclosed.

Answer (A) is incorrect because a CPA may not recommend a frivolous position, regardless of disclosure. Answer (C) is incorrect because a CPA should advise the client of the potential penalty consequences of an unrealistic position and the opportunity to avoid penalties through disclosure. Answer (D) is incorrect because a CPA should not sign a tax return if (s)he believes that a tax position taken does not have a realistic possibility of being upheld if challenged by the IRS.

154. CPAs often provide tax advice to their clients. When subsequent developments affect advice previously provided with respect to significant matters, the CPA

A. Must communicate this change whether or not (s)he is still employed by the client.

B. May not communicate this information to the client unless the client is a continuing client.

C. May communicate this information to the client whether or not (s)he is still engaged.

D. Should withdraw immediately.

The correct answer is (C). *(Publisher)*

REQUIRED: The proper action when previous tax advice may no longer be appropriate.

DISCUSSION: The CPA may communicate with the client when subsequent developments affect advice previously provided with respect to significant matters. But (s)he cannot be expected to have assumed responsibility for initiating such communication except while (s)he is assisting a client in implementing procedures or plans associated with the advice provided. Of course, the CPA may undertake this obligation by specific agreement with the client (TX 182).

Answer (A) is incorrect because the CPA is under no obligation to initiate the communication unless (s)he is assisting the client in implementing the procedures associated with the advice. Answer (B) is incorrect because a continuing client relationship is not a prerequisite of such communication. Answer (D) is incorrect because immediate withdrawal is a nonsense answer.

1.12 Consulting Services

155. Statements on Standards for Consulting Services are issued by the AICPA Management Consulting Services Executive Committee in connection with consulting services. Which statement concerning consulting services is false?

A. Consulting services differ fundamentally from the CPA's function of attesting to the assertions of other parties.

B. Consulting services ordinarily involve external reporting.

C. Most practitioners, including those who provide audit and tax services, also provide consulting services to their clients.

D. The performance of consulting services for attest clients does not, in and of itself, impair independence.

The correct answer is (B). *(Publisher)*
REQUIRED: The false statement about consulting services.
DISCUSSION: The nature and scope of a consulting service is determined solely by the agreement between the practitioner and the client. The work is usually performed for the sole use and benefit of the client.
Answer (A) is incorrect because, in an attest service, the practitioner expresses a conclusion about the reliability of a written assertion that is the responsibility of another party. Answer (C) is incorrect because consulting services have evolved from accounting-related matters to a broad array of services involving many technical disciplines, industry knowledge, and consulting skills. Answer (D) is incorrect because the CPA can maintain independence in fact and appearance for attestation clients while performing consulting services.

156. According to the profession's standards, which of the following are considered consulting services?

	Advisory Services	Implementation Services	Product Services
A.	Yes	Yes	Yes
B.	Yes	Yes	No
C.	Yes	No	Yes
D.	No	Yes	Yes

The correct answer is (A). *(CPA, adapted)*
REQUIRED: The services that are considered to be consulting services.
DISCUSSION: CS 100 specifically includes advisory services, implementation services, and product services as applicable consulting services. Other consulting services include consultations, transaction services, and staff and other support services.
Answers (B), (C), and (D) are incorrect because advisory services, implementation services, and product services are all consulting services.

157. A pervasive characteristic of a CPA's role in a consulting services engagement is that of being a(n)

A. Objective advisor.

B. Independent practitioner.

C. Computer specialist.

D. Confidential reviewer.

The correct answer is (A). *(CPA, adapted)*
REQUIRED: The pervasive characteristic of a CPA's role in a consulting services engagement.
DISCUSSION: A consulting services practitioner should serve the client's interest by seeking to accomplish the objectives established by the understanding with the client while maintaining integrity and objectivity.
Answer (B) is incorrect because independence is not a requirement for consulting services. Answer (C) is incorrect because a consultant need not be a computer specialist to develop findings and provide recommendations. Answer (D) is incorrect because a review is an attestation service.

158. Ann Covington, CPA, has been asked to perform a consulting services engagement concerning the analysis of a potential merger. She has little experience with the industry involved. What is her most appropriate action?

A. Accept the engagement and perform it in accordance with GAAS.

B. Accept the engagement and perform additional research or consult with others to obtain sufficient competence.

C. Accept the engagement and issue a report vouching for the achievability of the results of the merger.

D. Decline the engagement because she lacks sufficient knowledge.

The correct answer is (B). *(Publisher)*
REQUIRED: The appropriate action by a CPA who has been asked to provide consulting services concerning unfamiliar matters.
DISCUSSION: The CPA may accept the engagement but should conduct research or consult with others to obtain a sufficient level of knowledge concerning the subject of the engagement. Conduct Rule 201 requires an AICPA member to "undertake only those professional services that the member or the member's firm can reasonably expect to be completed with professional competence."
Answer (A) is incorrect because audits, not consulting services engagements, are performed in accordance with GAAS. Answer (C) is incorrect because an accountant's report on prospective financial information must always contain a caveat that the prospective results may not be achieved. Answer (D) is incorrect because the CPA need not decline the engagement if she does the research necessary to complete the engagement with professional competence.

159. Which of the following general standards apply to consulting services?

	Due Professional Care	Independence in Mental Attitude	Planning and Supervision
A.	No	Yes	No
B.	No	Yes	Yes
C.	Yes	No	Yes
D.	Yes	No	No

The correct answer is (C). *(CPA, adapted)*

REQUIRED: The general standard(s) applicable to consulting services.

DISCUSSION: The general standards for consulting services include the general standards for the profession given in the AICPA's Conduct Rule 201: professional competence, due professional care, planning and supervision, and sufficient relevant data. In addition, CS 100 requires the following general standards for all consulting services:

1. Serve the client interest by seeking to accomplish the objectives established by the understanding with the client while maintaining integrity and objectivity.
2. Establish with the client a written or oral understanding about the responsibilities of the parties and the nature, scope, and limitations of the services to be performed.
3. Inform the client of conflicts of interest, significant reservations concerning the scope or benefits of the engagement, and significant engagement findings or events.

Independence standards apply to attestation services, not to consulting services.

Answers (A), (B), and (D) are incorrect because the consulting services practitioner must observe the general standards of due care and planning and supervision. (S)he need not be independent.

160. The form of communication with a client in a consulting service should be

A. Either oral or written.

B. Oral with appropriate documentation in the work papers.

C. Written, and copies should be sent to both management and the board of directors.

D. Written, and a copy should be sent to management alone.

The correct answer is (A). *(CPA, adapted)*

REQUIRED: The form of communication with a client in a consulting service.

DISCUSSION: In a consulting service, reports may be written or oral depending on the understanding with the client, the need for a formal record, the intended use of results, the significance or sensitivity of material covered, and the degree results are communicated during the engagement.

Answers (B), (C), and (D) are incorrect because communications may be written or oral.

161. According to the standards of the profession, which of the following events would require a CPA performing a consulting services engagement for a nonaudit client to withdraw from the engagement?

I. The CPA has a conflict of interest that is disclosed to the client, and the client consents to the CPA's continuing the engagement.

II. The CPA fails to obtain a written understanding from the client concerning the scope of the engagement.

A. I only.

B. II only.

C. Both I and II.

D. Neither I nor II.

The correct answer is (D). *(CPA, adapted)*

REQUIRED: The event(s) that would force a CPA to withdraw from a consulting engagement for a nonaudit client.

DISCUSSION: The additional general standards for consulting services require serving the client interest with integrity and objectivity. If a conflict of interest is disclosed and consented to, objectivity is not deemed to be impaired, and the professional service may be performed. In addition, an accountant may establish either a written or an oral understanding with the client regarding the scope of the engagement. Thus, an accountant need not withdraw from an engagement when the understanding of the scope of the engagement is not in writing.

Answers (A), (B), and (C) are incorrect because neither a disclosed and consented to conflict of interest nor a lack of a written agreement concerning the scope of the engagement forces a CPA to withdraw from a consulting engagement for a nonaudit client.

162. Which of the following statements applies to consultation services engagements?

A. A practitioner should obtain an understanding of the internal control to assess control risk.

B. A practitioner is not permitted to compile a financial forecast.

C. A practitioner should obtain sufficient relevant data to complete the engagement.

D. A practitioner is to maintain an appearance of independence.

The correct answer is (C). *(CPA, adapted)*

REQUIRED: The statement applicable to consultation services engagements.

DISCUSSION: The general standards for consulting services include the general standards for the profession given in the AICPA's Conduct Rule 201: professional competence, due professional care, planning and supervision, and sufficient relevant data. Under Conduct Rule 201, a member should "obtain sufficient relevant data to afford a reasonable basis for conclusions or recommendations in relation to any professional services performed."

Answer (A) is incorrect because an assessment of control risk is irrelevant to many consulting services. Answer (B) is incorrect because a practitioner may perform a service regarding prospective financial information in conjunction with a consulting service. Answer (D) is incorrect because consulting services require integrity and objectivity but not independence.

1.13 Attestation Standards

163. In performing an attestation engagement, a CPA typically

A. Supplies litigation support services.

B. Assesses control risk at a low level.

C. Expresses a conclusion about an assertion.

D. Provides management consulting advice.

The correct answer is (C). *(CPA, adapted)*

REQUIRED: The usual CPA's task in an attestation engagement.

DISCUSSION: When a CPA in the practice of public accounting performs an attest engagement, the engagement is subject to the attestation standards. AT 100 states, "An attest engagement is one in which a practitioner is engaged to issue or does issue a written communication that expresses a conclusion about the reliability of a written assertion that is the responsibility of another party."

Answer (A) is incorrect because litigation support services are consulting services. Answer (B) is incorrect because the CPA assesses control risk in an audit but not necessarily in all attest engagements. Furthermore, the assessment may not be at a low level. Answer (D) is incorrect because an attest engagement results in a conclusion about an assertion.

164. AT 100 states five general standards, two standards of field work, and four standards of reporting. These standards

A. Supersede the 10 generally accepted auditing standards.

B. Apply only to the expression of a positive opinion on historical financial statements.

C. Apply only to attest services rendered by a CPA in the practice of public accounting.

D. Must be followed by a practitioner engaged to provide compilation services on prospective financial information.

The correct answer is (C). *(Publisher)*

REQUIRED: The proper application of the attestation standards.

DISCUSSION: A practitioner is a CPA in the practice of public accounting. The attestation standards apply only to attest engagements involving a practitioner. Thus, these standards apply only to attest services rendered by a CPA in the practice of public accounting.

Answer (A) is incorrect because the attestation standards do not supersede but are an extension of the 10 GAAS. Answer (B) is incorrect because the attestation standards were issued as a result of the growth in the types of attest services offered. CPAs now provide assurances regarding representations other than historical statements and in forms other than the positive opinion. Answer (D) is incorrect because AT 100 does not apply to compilations, which do not entail expression of a conclusion about the reliability of written assertions for which others are responsible. However, both AT 100 and other standards may apply to other services provided with respect to such information.

165. Which of the following professional services would be considered an attest engagement?

A. A consulting service engagement to provide computer processing advice to a client.

B. An engagement to report on compliance with statutory requirements.

C. An income tax engagement to prepare federal and state tax returns.

D. The compilation of financial statements from a client's accounting records.

The correct answer is (B). *(CPA, adapted)*

REQUIRED: The attest services offered by practitioners.

DISCUSSION: Attest services have traditionally been limited to expressing a positive opinion on historical financial statements on the basis of an audit in accordance with GAAS. But CPAs increasingly provide assurance on representations other than historical statements and in forms other than a positive opinion. AT 500, *Compliance Attestation*, provides guidance for engagements related to management's written assertions about statutory, regulatory, or contractual requirements.

Answer (A) is incorrect because consulting services in which the practitioner provides advice or recommendations to a client are not considered attest services. Answer (C) is incorrect because tax return preparation is not an attest service. Answer (D) is incorrect because a compilation of a financial statement is not an attest service according to AT 100.

166. Which of the following is not an attestation standard?

A. Sufficient evidence shall be obtained to provide a reasonable basis for the conclusion that is expressed in the report.

B. The report shall identify the assertion being reported on and state the character of the engagement.

C. The work shall be adequately planned and assistants, if any, shall be properly supervised.

D. A sufficient understanding of internal control shall be obtained to plan the engagement.

The correct answer is (D). *(CPA, adapted)*

REQUIRED: The item not an attestation standard.

DISCUSSION: The attestation standards of field work do not mention internal control (AT 100). However, the second standard of field work applicable to audits in accordance with GAAS states, "A sufficient understanding of internal control is to be obtained to plan the audit and to determine the nature, timing, and extent of tests to be performed."

Answer (A) is incorrect because the evidentiary requirement is contained in the second attestation standard of field work. Answer (B) is incorrect because the first attestation standard of reporting concerns the character of the engagement. Answer (C) is incorrect because the first attestation standard of field work concerns planning and supervision.

167. Which of the following field work or reporting standards included in GAAS explicitly corresponds to an attestation standard?

A. A sufficient understanding of internal control is to be obtained to plan the audit and to determine the nature, timing, and extent of tests to be performed.

B. The report shall identify those circumstances in which such principles (GAAP) have not been consistently observed in the current period in relation to the preceding period.

C. Informative disclosures in the financial statements are to be regarded as reasonably adequate unless otherwise stated in the report.

D. Sufficient competent evidential matter is to be obtained through inspection, observation, inquiries, and confirmations to afford a reasonable basis for an opinion regarding the financial statements under audit.

The correct answer is (D). *(Publisher)*

REQUIRED: The auditing standard that corresponds to an attestation standard.

DISCUSSION: The third standard of field work included in GAAS is paralleled by the second field work standard included in the attestation standards. AT 100 states, "Sufficient evidence shall be obtained to provide a reasonable basis for the conclusion that is expressed in the report."

Answer (A) is incorrect because the second auditing standard of field work has no explicit parallel in the attestation standards. One reason is that internal control may not be relevant to some assertions reported on by a practitioner. Answer (B) is incorrect because the second (consistency) and third (disclosure) auditing standards of reporting do not have analogues in the attestation standards. They are considered to be encompassed by the second attestation standard of reporting. It states, "The report shall state the practitioner's conclusion about whether the assertion is presented in conformity with the established or stated criteria against which it was measured." Thus, references to financial statements and GAAP are omitted from the attestation standards because they are intended to provide a framework for the attest function beyond historical financial statements. Answer (C) is incorrect because the third standard of field work has no analogue in the attestation standards.

168. Which of the following is the authoritative body designated to promulgate attestation standards?

A. Auditing Standards Board.

B. Governmental Accounting Standards Board.

C. Financial Accounting Standards Board.

D. General Accounting Office.

The correct answer is (A). *(CPA, adapted)*

REQUIRED: The authoritative body designated to promulgate attestation standards.

DISCUSSION: Statements on Standards for Attestation Engagements are issued by the Auditing Standards Board, Accounting and Review Services Committee, and the Management Consulting Services Executive Committee. The Council of the AICPA granted these bodies, which also promulgate SASs, SSARSs, and SSCSs, respectively, the authority to interpret Conduct Rules 201 and 202. The SSAEs are issued pursuant to that authority.

Answer (B) is incorrect because the GASB issues accounting and reporting standards for local and state governments. Answer (C) is incorrect because the FASB establishes GAAP. Answer (D) is incorrect because the GAO issues government auditing standards.

169. Which of the following is a conceptual difference between the attestation standards and generally accepted auditing standards?

A. The attestation standards provide a framework for the attest function beyond historical financial statements.

B. The requirement that the practitioner be independent in mental attitude is omitted from the attestation standards.

C. The attestation standards do not permit an attest engagement to be part of a business acquisition study or a feasibility study.

D. None of the standards of field work in generally accepted auditing standards are included in the attestation standards.

The correct answer is (A). *(CPA, adapted)*

REQUIRED: The conceptual difference between the attestation standards and GAAS.

DISCUSSION: "Two principal conceptual differences exist between the attestation standards and the 10 existing GAAS. First, the attestation standards provide a framework for the attest function beyond historical financial statements." Second, the attestation standards "accommodate the growing number of attest services in which the practitioner expresses assurance below the level that is expressed for the traditional audit ('positive opinion')" (AT 100).

Answer (B) is incorrect because, in any attest engagement, the practitioner must be independent in mental attitude. Answer (C) is incorrect because attestation services may be provided in conjunction with other services provided to clients. Answer (D) is incorrect because the attestation standards and GAAS require that the work be adequately planned and that assistants be properly supervised. Both also require sufficient evidence.

170. The expansion of the attest function has resulted in attestation standards of reporting that are organized differently from the standards of reporting included in GAAS. Consequently, the attestation standards of reporting

A. Cover one level and form of assurance.

B. Reflect the limitation of the use of certain reports to specified users.

C. Concern one basic presentation of assertions.

D. Are inapplicable when users have established the criteria against which assertions are measured.

The correct answer is (B). *(Publisher)*

REQUIRED: The effect of the expansion of the attest function on the attestation standards of reporting.

DISCUSSION: GAAS contemplate issuance of a general-distribution audit report. The attestation standards reflect the expansion of the attest function to include engagements tailored to the needs of specified parties who have participated in establishing either the nature and scope of the engagement or the specified criteria against which the assertions were measured. Thus, the fourth attestation standard of reporting states, "The report on an engagement to evaluate an assertion that has been prepared in conformity with agreed-upon criteria or on an engagement to apply agreed-upon procedures should contain a statement limiting its use to the parties who have agreed upon such criteria or procedures."

Answer (A) is incorrect because the attest function has expanded "to cover more than one level and form of assurance on a variety of presentations of assertions" (AT 100). The attest function is no longer limited to expressing a positive opinion on historical financial statements presented in accordance with GAAP. Answer (C) is incorrect because the attestation standards cover a variety of presentations of assertions. Answer (D) is incorrect because user participation in establishing measurement criteria is a conceptual difference between GAAS and the attestation standards.

171. In accordance with AT 700, ***Management's Discussion and Analysis***, the presentation of an MD&A constitutes a written assertion that

A. May be examined but not reviewed.

B. May be examined or reviewed.

C. A practitioner may attest to only if the entity is public.

D. A practitioner may attest to only if the entity is nonpublic.

The correct answer is (B). *(Publisher)*

REQUIRED: The true statement about an attest engagement performed upon the presentation of an MD&A.

DISCUSSION: Under AT 700, a practitioner may perform an attest engagement regarding an MD&A prepared pursuant to SEC rules and presented in an annual report or other document. This presentation constitutes a written assertion that may be examined or reviewed whether the entity is public or private. However, a report on a review cannot be filed with the SEC.

Answer (A) is incorrect because the MD&A may be reviewed. Answers (C) and (D) are incorrect because the entity presenting the MD&A may be public or private.

1.14 Assurance Services

172. Assurance services are best described as

A. Services designed for the improvement of operations, resulting in better outcomes.

B. Independent professional services that improve the quality of information, or its context, for decision makers.

C. The assembly of financial statements based on assumptions of a responsible party.

D. Services designed to express a positive opinion on historical financial statements based on the results of an audit.

The correct answer is (B). *(Publisher)*

REQUIRED: The description of assurance services.

DISCUSSION: The AICPA defines assurance services as "independent professional services that improve the quality of information, or its context, for decision makers." Assurance services encompass audit and other attestation services as well as other, nonstandard, services, but they do not include consulting services. Assurance services should result in better information for decision making, with the form of output consisting of some form of communication. A formal written report need not be required. The level of assurance is flexible. For example, it may be at the compilation level, or it may be explicit assurance about the usefulness of information for the intended purpose. The assurance may also arise simply from the CPA's involvement.

Answer (A) is incorrect because the objective of consulting services is better outcomes, whereas the objective of assurance services is better decision making. Answer (C) is incorrect because compilation services involve the assembly of financial statements based on assumptions of a responsible party. Answer (D) is incorrect because the traditional audit is an attestation service. Assurance services include but are not limited to attest engagements.

173. The objective of assurance services is best described as

A. Providing more reliable information.

B. Enhancing decision making.

C. Comparing internal information and policies with those of other firms.

D. Improving the firm's outcomes.

The correct answer is (B). *(Publisher)*

REQUIRED: The objective of assurance services.

DISCUSSION: The objective of assurance services, as stated by the AICPA, is to provide information that assists in better decision making. Assurance services encompass audit and other attestation services as well as other, nonstandard, services. Assurance services do not include consulting services.

Answer (A) is incorrect because providing more reliable information is the objective of attestation services. The objective of assurance services is broader. Answer (C) is incorrect because assurance services do not necessarily involve analysis of other organizations. Answer (D) is incorrect because providing information that results in better outcomes is an objective of consulting services.

174. Assurance services differ from consulting services in that they

	Focus on Outcomes	Involve Monitoring of One Party by Another
A.	Yes	Yes
B.	Yes	No
C.	No	Yes
D.	No	No

The correct answer is (C). *(Publisher)*

REQUIRED: The way(s) in which assurance services differ from consulting services.

DISCUSSION: Assurance services encompass attestation services but not consulting services. Assurance services differ from consulting services because (1) they focus on improving information and decision making rather than outcomes, and (2) they usually involve situations in which one party has oversight responsibility for another rather than the two-party arrangements common in consulting engagements.

Answers (A), (B), and (D) are incorrect because assurance services involve improving information and monitoring.

175. An AICPA special committee has developed business plans for assurance services covering which of the following?

A. Elder care, electronic commerce, and reporting on management's discussion and analysis.

B. Electronic commerce, development of financial forecasts, and risk assessment.

C. Information systems design, performance measurement, and health care delivery.

D. Assurances to underwriters, health care delivery, and elder care.

The correct answer is (C). *(Publisher)*

REQUIRED: The areas in which business plans for assurance services have been developed by the AICPA.

DISCUSSION: An AICPA special committee has developed business plans for six assurance services: (1) providing assurance about whether care delivery goals for the elderly are met; (2) providing assurance about the integrity and security of electronic transactions, documents, and supporting systems; (3) assessing whether an organization's performance measures are relevant and reliable; (4) assessing health care providers' performance; (5) improving risk information through assessment of the probability and magnitude of significant adverse events; and (6) providing assurance about the design and operation of information systems.

Answers (A), (B), and (D) are incorrect because reporting on an MD&A, developing forecasts, and providing comfort letters to underwriters are not among the newly identified assurance services. They are subject to existing SSAEs or SASs.

176. According to the AICPA, the CPA WebTrust service is needed

A. To manage growth in international commerce.

B. To certify that a web site is completely trustworthy.

C. To assure that web sites meet Internet protection standards.

D. To assure transaction integrity regarding electronic consumer commerce.

The correct answer is (D). *(Publisher)*

REQUIRED: The reason for WebTrust assurance.

DISCUSSION: CPAs licensed by the AICPA can issue the CPA WebTrust seal. This service provides Internet users with assurance about electronic business engagements. The seal indicates that the CPA has audited the organization and its web site in three areas: disclosure of business practices, transaction integrity, and protection of private customer information.

Answer (A) is incorrect because CPA WebTrust is needed due to the growth of commerce over the Internet. Answer (B) is incorrect because the service assures that a site bearing the seal is trustworthy and reliable with regard to the confidentiality of consumer information, disclosures, and transaction integrity, but the assurance given is not absolute. Answer (C) is incorrect because the service assures that a site meets standards of consumer information protection.

177. The AICPA committee on assurance services has identified a new professional service that it calls ElderCare-Plus. The fundamental purpose of this assurance service is to assist the elderly and their families by

A. Investing the funds of the elderly person.

B. Reporting whether specified objectives are being met by caregivers.

C. Choosing caregivers.

D. Performing operational audits of health care providers.

The correct answer is (B). *(Publisher)*

REQUIRED: The fundamental purpose of ElderCare-Plus.

DISCUSSION: The AICPA committee on assurance services has developed business plans for six assurance services, one of which involves elder care. The fundamental purpose of elder care services is to gather evidence and report to concerned parts (e.g., adult children of an elderly parent) as to whether agreed-upon objectives have been met with regard to care delivery, such as medical, household, and financial services. Related services provided directly to the elderly person or to the other concerned parties may include oversight of investments (but not investing funds), assistance in the choice of caregivers, accounting for the elderly person's income and expenses, and arranging for care and services, such as transportation, meal delivery, or placement in a retirement facility.

Answer (A) is incorrect because the CPA might oversee, but not make, investments. Answer (C) is incorrect because the CPA might help in the choice of caregivers but would not make the decision. Answer (D) is incorrect because an operational audit is far beyond the limits of an elder care service.

178. The AICPA's WebTrust requires from client management a

A. Written assertion.

B. Set of financial statements.

C. Third-party verification letter.

D. Letter of engagement.

The correct answer is (A). *(Publisher)*

REQUIRED: The requirement of management for WebTrust.

DISCUSSION: WebTrust was developed from the attestation standards and requires a written assertion by management. The written assertion must establish that the three principles relating to electronic commerce are met: (1) business practices disclosure, (2) transaction integrity, and (3) information protection. When a web site complies with these principles, it is granted the CPA WebTrust seal which is displayed on the entity's web page. Consumers can access the examination report and CPA WebTrust principles and criteria through the entity's web page.

Answers (B), (C), and (D) are incorrect because a written or an electronic assertion from management is required before a WebTrust seal is granted.

179. Under the AICPA's assurance service, WebTrust, the broad principles relating to web sites are business integrity and

A. Information disclosure.

B. Information disclosure and web site performance.

C. Business practices disclosure and information protection.

D. Business practices disclosure and transaction assurance.

The correct answer is (C). *(Publisher)*

REQUIRED: The principles relating to web sites which are addressed by WebTrust.

DISCUSSION: WebTrust is designed to help break down the obstacles to mainstream consumer acceptance of electronic commerce. WebTrust accomplishes this task by providing an examination level of assurance relating to three broad principles: (1) business practices disclosures: the web site operator discloses its business practices for electronic commerce transactions and executes transactions in accordance with those policies; (2) transaction integrity: the web site operator maintains effective controls to ensure that customers' orders placed using electronic commerce are completed and billed as agreed; (3) information protection: the web site operator maintains effective controls to ensure that private customer information is protected from uses not related to its business.

Answers (A), (B), and (D) are incorrect because business practices disclosure, transaction integrity, and information protection are the enumerated principles related to WebTrust.

CHAPTER TWO
AUDIT PLANNING AND RISK ASSESSMENT

This chapter addresses various fundamental questions about the conduct of audits. Whether to accept the engagement embraces such issues as the timing of the auditor's appointment, the evaluation of the client's integrity, and predecessor-successor communication. Audit planning is required by the first standard of field work. It involves developing an overall strategy for the audit, particularly obtaining and evaluating evidence. Audit risk must be considered in every audit. The auditor must assess inherent and control risk and establish the level to which (s)he wishes to restrict overall audit risk. The auditor uses these factors to determine the acceptable level of detection risk. The auditor must also plan and perform the audit to obtain reasonable assurance about whether the financial statements are free of material misstatement, whether caused by error or fraud (irregularities). The auditor's responsibility is the same for illegal acts having a material direct effect on the financial statements. However, an audit in accordance with GAAS provides no assurance that illegal acts having material but indirect effects will be detected. Furthermore, the auditor must specifically assess the risk of material misstatement due to fraud. Finally, every audit must be documented. Working papers provide the principal support for the audit. They show that the engagement was adequately planned and supervised, that the auditor considered internal control, and that the evidence obtained was competent and sufficient.

2.1 Engagement Acceptance

1. An auditor obtains knowledge about a new client's business and its industry to

A. Make constructive suggestions concerning improvements in the client's internal control.

B. Develop an attitude of professional skepticism concerning management's financial statement assertions.

C. Evaluate whether the aggregation of known misstatements causes the financial statements taken as a whole to be materially misstated.

D. Understand the events and transactions that may have an effect on the client's financial statements.

The correct answer is (D). *(CPA, adapted)*

REQUIRED: The reason to obtain knowledge of a new client's business and industry.

DISCUSSION: "The auditor should obtain a level of knowledge of the entity's business that will allow him/her to plan and perform the audit in accordance with GAAS. That level of knowledge should enable him/her to obtain an understanding of the events, transactions, and practices that, in his/her judgment, may have a significant effect on the financial statements" (AU 311).

Answer (A) is incorrect because communication of internal control related matters occurs during and after the audit. Obtaining knowledge of the client's business occurs prior to audit planning. Answer (B) is incorrect because the auditor should adopt an attitude of professional skepticism in all phases of an engagement. Answer (C) is incorrect because evaluating whether the financial statements are materially misstated is done after the collection of evidence.

2. Prior to beginning the field work on a new audit engagement in which a CPA does not possess expertise in the industry in which the client operates, the CPA should

A. Reduce audit risk by lowering the preliminary levels of materiality.

B. Design special substantive tests to compensate for the lack of industry expertise.

C. Engage financial experts familiar with the nature of the industry.

D. Obtain a knowledge of matters that relate to the nature of the entity's business.

The correct answer is (D). *(CPA, adapted)*

REQUIRED: The action taken by an auditor who lacks experience with the client's industry.

DISCUSSION: If the auditor lacks knowledge of the potential client's industry, (s)he should undertake procedures to gain the knowledge. An Interpretation under Conduct Rule 201 states that if a CPA does not have or is unable to gain sufficient competence, (s)he should suggest the engagement of someone competent to perform the service either independently or as an associate.

Answers (A) and (B) are incorrect because the auditor cannot make judgments about materiality levels and design substantive tests until (s)he has sufficient knowledge of the entity's business. Answer (C) is incorrect because engaging specialists is done only after the auditor has found that (s)he is not able to obtain sufficient knowledge through such normal procedures as inquiry of client personnel, review of previous working papers, and study of industry audit guides.

3. Which of the following factors most likely would cause an auditor not to accept a new audit engagement?

A. An inadequate understanding of the entity's internal control.

B. The close proximity to the end of the entity's fiscal year.

C. Concluding that the entity's management probably lacks integrity.

D. An inability to perform preliminary analytical procedures before assessing control risk.

The correct answer is (C). *(CPA, adapted)*

REQUIRED: The factor most likely to cause an auditor not to accept a new audit engagement.

DISCUSSION: During an audit, management makes many representations to the auditor. If management lacks integrity, the auditor's reliance on those representations would not be appropriate. Thus, the auditor should not accept an engagement if management lacks integrity.

Answer (A) is incorrect because the understanding of the entity's internal control is obtained subsequent to the acceptance of the engagement. Answer (B) is incorrect because, "although early appointment is preferable, an independent auditor may accept an engagement near or after the close of the fiscal year" (AU 310). Answer (D) is incorrect because analytical procedures are performed after the acceptance of the engagement.

4. Before accepting an engagement to audit a new client, an auditor is required to

A. Make inquiries of the predecessor auditor after obtaining the consent of the prospective client.

B. Obtain the prospective client's signature to the engagement letter.

C. Prepare a memorandum setting forth the staffing requirements and documenting the preliminary audit plan.

D. Discuss the management representation letter with the prospective client's audit committee.

The correct answer is (A). *(CPA, adapted)*

REQUIRED: The step required of an auditor before accepting an engagement to audit a new client.

DISCUSSION: AU 315, *Communications between Predecessor and Successor Auditors*, requires the successor auditor to take the initiative in communicating with the predecessor auditor. Communication should be made only after obtaining the client's permission, and the successor should request that the client authorize the predecessor to respond fully to the successor's inquiries.

Answer (B) is incorrect because, although recommended, an engagement letter is not required for the auditor to accept an engagement. However, the auditor should establish an understanding with the client and document it in the working papers (AU 310). Answer (C) is incorrect because planning the audit is not required to be performed prior to accepting an engagement. Answer (D) is incorrect because discussion of the management representation letter is not required prior to accepting an engagement.

5. Before accepting an audit engagement, a successor auditor should make specific inquiries of the predecessor auditor regarding the predecessor's

A. Opinion of any subsequent events occurring since the predecessor's audit report was issued.

B. Understanding as to the reasons for the change of auditors.

C. Awareness of the consistency in the application of GAAP between periods.

D. Evaluation of all matters of continuing accounting significance.

The correct answer is (B). *(CPA, adapted)*

REQUIRED: The specific inquiry that should be made by the successor to the predecessor auditor.

DISCUSSION: The successor auditor should inquire about reasons for the change in auditors, disagreements with management about accounting principles and auditing procedures, facts bearing on management's integrity, and communications to audit committees or others regarding fraud, illegal acts by clients, and internal-control-related matters.

Answer (A) is incorrect because the predecessor has no responsibility for events subsequent to the date of his/her report. Answer (C) is incorrect because the predecessor auditor would have considered consistency and reported lack of consistency in the previously issued reports. Answer (D) is incorrect because the question relates to the successor auditor's decision to accept the engagement, not the collection and evaluation of evidence.

6. Upon discovering material misstatements in a client's financial statements that the client would not revise, an auditor withdrew from the engagement. If asked by the successor auditor about the termination of the engagement, the predecessor auditor should

A. State that (s)he found material misstatements that the client would not revise.

B. Suggest that the successor ask the client.

C. Suggest that the successor obtain the client's permission to discuss the reasons.

D. Indicate that a misunderstanding occurred.

The correct answer is (C). *(Publisher)*

REQUIRED: The appropriate response by a predecessor auditor when asked by a successor about his/her relationship with the client.

DISCUSSION: The successor auditor must obtain the client's permission before the predecessor auditor may discuss the reasons for termination of the previous relationship (AU 315). Furthermore, a member of the AICPA in public practice must not disclose confidential client information without the specific consent of the client (Conduct Rule 301).

Answers (A) and (D) are incorrect because the predecessor auditor should say nothing concerning the relationship until client permission is obtained. Answer (B) is incorrect because the predecessor is usually expected to cooperate with the successor, provided that the client consents. In unusual circumstances, such as pending litigation, the predecessor auditor may not respond fully to inquiries, and the successor may decide, as a result, not to accept the engagement.

2.2 Audit Planning

7. AU 311, *Planning and Supervision*, states that the auditor should consider the nature, extent, and timing of the work to be performed and should prepare a written audit program for every audit. Which audit standard is most closely related to this requirement?

A. The audit is to be performed by a person or persons having adequate technical training and proficiency as an auditor.

B. In all matters relating to the assignment, an independent mental attitude is to be maintained by the auditor(s).

C. Due professional care is to be exercised in the planning and performance of the audit and preparation of the report.

D. The work is to be adequately planned and assistants, if any, are to be properly supervised.

The correct answer is (D). *(Publisher)*

REQUIRED: The standard most closely related to the requirement for a written audit program.

DISCUSSION: The first standard of field work requires adequate planning and proper supervision. Audit planning involves developing an overall strategy for the expected conduct and scope of the audit. An audit program, which aids in instructing assistants in the work to be done, should set forth in reasonable detail the audit procedures the auditor believes necessary to accomplish audit objectives.

Answer (A) is incorrect because proper education and experience in the field of auditing are needed to provide services to the public (the first general standard). Answer (B) is incorrect because auditors must be unbiased and maintain an attitude of judicial impartiality (the second general standard). Answer (C) is incorrect because each professional within the independent auditor's organization must observe the standards of field work and reporting (the third general standard).

8. Which of the following is required documentation in an audit in accordance with generally accepted auditing standards?

A. A flowchart or narrative of the information system describing the recording and classification of transactions for financial reporting.

B. An audit program setting forth in detail the procedures necessary to accomplish the engagement's objectives.

C. A planning memorandum establishing the timing of the audit procedures and coordinating the assistance of entity personnel.

D. An internal control questionnaire identifying policies and procedures that assure specific objectives will be achieved.

The correct answer is (B). *(CPA, adapted)*

REQUIRED: The required documentation in an audit.

DISCUSSION: According to AU 311, in planning the audit, the auditor should consider the nature, extent, and timing of the work to be performed and should prepare a written audit program (or a set of written audit programs) for every audit. It sets forth in reasonable detail the specific audit procedures the auditor believes are necessary to accomplish the audit objectives.

Answer (A) is incorrect because the auditor should document the understanding of internal control, but a flowchart or narrative of the information system for financial reporting is just one method. For example, the auditor may use a questionnaire to document the understanding. Answer (C) is incorrect because the auditor may request and receive assistance from entity personnel, but a planning memorandum establishing the timing is not required under GAAS. Answer (D) is incorrect because the auditor should document the understanding of internal control, but a questionnaire is only one method of accomplishing this objective. For example, flowcharts and narratives are other methods.

9. An auditor is planning an audit engagement for a new client in a business that is unfamiliar to the auditor. Which of the following is the least useful source of information for the auditor during the preliminary planning stage, when the auditor is trying to obtain a general understanding of audit problems that might be encountered?

A. Textbooks and periodicals related to the industry.

B. AICPA Audit and Accounting Guides.

C. Financial statements of other entities in the industry.

D. Results of performing substantive tests.

The correct answer is (D). *(CPA, adapted)*

REQUIRED: The least useful source of information for early planning of the audit.

DISCUSSION: The first standard of field work requires adequate planning of the audit. The auditor must acquire sufficient knowledge of the client's business to plan and perform the audit in accordance with GAAS. However, substantive tests are performed to collect evidence to test management's assertions embodied in the financial statements. Most are performed after the planning stage of the audit.

Answers (A), (B), and (C) are incorrect because textbooks and periodicals related to the industry, AICPA Audit and Accounting Guides, and financial statements of other entities in the industry are useful sources of information (AU 311).

10. Which of the following procedures is an auditor least likely to perform in planning a financial statement audit?

A. Coordinating the assistance of entity personnel in data preparation.

B. Discussing matters that may affect the audit with firm personnel responsible for non-audit services to the entity.

C. Selecting a sample of vendors' invoices for comparison with receiving reports.

D. Reading the current year's interim financial statements.

The correct answer is (C). *(CPA, adapted)*

REQUIRED: The procedure an auditor is least likely to perform in planning a financial statement audit.

DISCUSSION: Selecting a sample of vendors' invoices for comparison with receiving reports is a substantive test. Substantive testing is performed in the field work stage of a financial statement audit, not in the planning stage.

Answers (A), (B), and (D) are incorrect because coordinating the assistance of entity personnel, discussing matters that may affect the audit with firm personnel, and reading the current year's interim financial statements are examples of planning procedures identified in AU 311.

11. Which of the following is an effective audit planning and control procedure that helps prevent misunderstandings and inefficient use of audit personnel?

A. Make copies, for inclusion in the working papers, of those client supporting documents examined by the auditor.

B. Provide the client with copies of the audit programs to be used during the audit.

C. Arrange a preliminary conference with the client to discuss audit objectives, fees, timing, and other information.

D. Arrange to have the auditor prepare and post any necessary adjusting or reclassification entries prior to final closing.

The correct answer is (C). *(CPA, adapted)*

REQUIRED: The effective audit planning and control procedure to avoid misunderstandings and inefficient use of audit personnel.

DISCUSSION: A preliminary conference with the client to discuss various audit objectives, fees, timing, the reports to be prepared, the use of client personnel, etc., is an appropriate procedure to prevent misunderstandings during the audit. The arrangement should be documented in the engagement letter.

Answer (A) is incorrect because copies of client supporting documents are made during the audit itself, not during the planning stages. Also, not all documents need to be copied. Answer (B) is incorrect because the client should not be told which audit procedures are going to be used. Such information might be misused to circumvent the audit. Answer (D) is incorrect because the client (not the auditor) must prepare and post adjusting or reclassification entries.

12. Which of the following is most likely the first step an auditor will perform after accepting an initial audit engagement?

A. Prepare a rough draft of the financial statements and of the auditor's report.

B. Assess control risk for the assertions embodied in the financial statements.

C. Tour the client's facilities and review the general records.

D. Consult with and review the work of the predecessor auditor prior to discussing the engagement with the client management.

The correct answer is (C). *(CPA, adapted)*

REQUIRED: The auditor's first step after accepting an initial audit engagement.

DISCUSSION: The first step on an initial audit should be to tour the client's facilities and review the general records to obtain an overview of the client's business. This overview provides information about the physical facilities, the location of accounting records, the extent of segregation of functions, the documentation of activities, and the attitude of personnel as well as a starting point for understanding the client's internal control.

Answer (A) is incorrect because preparing the report is one of the last steps performed in the engagement. Answer (B) is incorrect because the auditor must obtain an understanding of internal control before assessing control risk. Answer (D) is incorrect because consulting with the predecessor auditor is required by AU 315, *Communications between Predecessor and Successor Auditors*, before accepting the engagement.

13. In planning the audit engagement, the auditor should consider each of the following except

A. Matters relating to the entity's business and the industry in which it operates.

B. The entity's accounting policies and procedures.

C. Anticipated levels of control risk and materiality.

D. The kind of opinion (unqualified, qualified, or adverse) that is likely to be expressed.

The correct answer is (D). *(Publisher)*

REQUIRED: The factor not considered in planning the audit engagement.

DISCUSSION: Although AU 311 states that the nature of the report expected to be rendered (e.g., a report on consolidated or consolidating financial statements or special reports such as those on compliance with contractual provisions) should be considered in the planning phase, determining the kind of opinion to be expressed occurs after the completion of audit procedures.

Answer (A) is incorrect because AU 311 states that matters relating to the entity's business and the industry in which it operates should be considered in planning the audit. Other matters to be considered are the financial statement items likely to require adjustment, the conditions that may require extension or modification of audit tests, and the methods used to process significant accounting information, including the use of service organizations, such as outside service centers. Answers (B) and (C) are incorrect because the entity's accounting policies and procedures and anticipated levels of control risk and materiality should be considered during audit planning.

14. In designing written audit programs, an auditor should establish specific audit objectives that relate primarily to the

A. Timing of audit procedures.

B. Cost-benefit of gathering evidence.

C. Selected audit techniques.

D. Financial statement assertions.

The correct answer is (D). *(CPA, adapted)*

REQUIRED: The item to which specific audit objectives primarily relate.

DISCUSSION: Most audit work consists of obtaining and evaluating evidence about financial statement assertions, which are management representations embodied in financial statement components. AU 326 states, "In obtaining evidential matter in support of financial statement assertions, the auditor develops specific audit objectives in light of those assertions."

Answer (A) is incorrect because timing is important in meeting the objectives of the audit but does not relate to the audit objectives themselves. Answer (B) is incorrect because the cost-benefit of gathering evidence is important to the auditor but is not the primary consideration in determining the objectives of the audit. Answer (C) is incorrect because audit objectives determine the specific audit techniques.

15. Audit programs are modified to suit the circumstances of particular engagements. A complete audit program usually should be developed

A. Prior to beginning the actual audit work.

B. After the auditor has obtained an understanding of internal control and assessed control risk.

C. After obtaining an understanding of the information and communication and control activities components of internal control.

D. When the engagement letter is prepared.

The correct answer is (B). *(Publisher)*

REQUIRED: The time at which a complete audit program should be developed.

DISCUSSION: Only after the understanding of internal control is obtained and control risk has been assessed can the auditor determine the nature, timing, and extent of substantive tests of financial statement assertions (AU 319). However, as the audit progresses, the auditor should consider necessary modifications in light of evidence collected.

Answer (A) is incorrect because the auditor cannot determine the necessary substantive tests until an understanding of internal control has been obtained and an assessment of control risk has been made. This process is part of the audit work. Answer (C) is incorrect because the auditor must also obtain an understanding of the control environment, risk assessment, and monitoring components of internal control before planning the audit. Answer (D) is incorrect because the auditor must obtain an understanding of internal control and assess control risk before preparing the audit program. This process follows the preparation of the engagement letter.

16. Which of the following ultimately determines the specific audit procedures necessary to provide an independent auditor with a reasonable basis for the expression of an opinion?

A. The audit program.

B. The auditor's judgment.

C. Generally accepted auditing standards.

D. The auditor's working papers.

The correct answer is (B). *(CPA, adapted)*

REQUIRED: The factor ultimately determining specific audit procedures.

DISCUSSION: The auditor's professional judgment must determine the necessary audit programs and the specific audit procedures that will gather sufficient competent evidence to afford a reasonable basis for an opinion.

Answer (A) is incorrect because audit programs are usually modified during the engagement to adapt to audit evidence as it is gathered. Answer (C) is incorrect because GAAS are general objectives, broad in scope, that are concerned with the quality of the auditor's performance. They do not specify the audit procedures to be applied. Answer (D) is incorrect because working papers document that the auditor has carried out the procedures (s)he has deemed necessary. They do not determine the procedures undertaken.

17. An audit program should be designed for each individual audit and should include audit steps and procedures to

A. Detect and eliminate all fraud.

B. Increase the amount of management information available.

C. Provide assurances that the objectives of the audit are met.

D. Insure that only material items are audited.

The correct answer is (C). *(CIA, adapted)*

REQUIRED: The true statement about an audit program.

DISCUSSION: A written audit program prescribes the nature, timing, and extent of work to be done. It sets forth in reasonable detail the specific audit procedures the auditor believes are necessary to accomplish the audit objectives. Accordingly, an audit program is a useful tool in scheduling and controlling the audit.

Answer (A) is incorrect because an external auditor must plan and perform the audit to provide reasonable, not absolute, assurance about whether the financial statements are free of material misstatement, whether caused by error or fraud. Answer (B) is incorrect because audit procedures are designed to gather audit evidence, not management information. Answer (D) is incorrect because items not individually material may be material in the aggregate.

18. Most of the independent auditor's work in formulating an opinion on financial statements consists of

A. Considering internal control.

B. Obtaining and examining evidential matter.

C. Examining cash transactions.

D. Comparing recorded accountability with assets.

The correct answer is (B). *(CPA, adapted)*

REQUIRED: The principal activity of an auditor in formulating an opinion.

DISCUSSION: According to AU 326, *Evidential Matter*, most of the independent auditor's work in formulating an opinion on financial statements consists of obtaining and examining evidence. Evidence is the underlying accounting data and all corroborating information available to the auditor.

Answer (A) is incorrect because considering internal control is a specific example of obtaining and examining evidence and is not as comprehensive as answer (B). Answers (C) and (D) are incorrect because examining cash transactions and comparing recorded accountability with assets are just two examples of obtaining and examining evidence.

19. Which of the following is the correct order of performing the steps A through C below?

A = Test of controls

B = Preparation of a flowchart documenting the understanding of the client's internal control

C = Substantive tests

A. ABC.

B. ACB.

C. BAC.

D. BCA.

The correct answer is (C). *(CPA, adapted)*

REQUIRED: The correct order of audit steps.

DISCUSSION: The auditor first obtains an understanding of the client's internal control policies and procedures that are relevant to audit planning. This understanding may include flowcharting the system. Next, the auditor must assess control risk. If control risk is to be assessed below the maximum level, this process will entail identifying specific control policies and procedures relevant to specific financial statement assertions and performing tests of controls to evaluate their effectiveness. The auditor uses the understanding obtained and the assessment of control risk to plan the nature, timing, and extent of substantive tests (AU 319).

Answers (A), (B), and (D) are incorrect because the appropriate order is BAC.

20. You have undertaken a preliminary survey of a manufacturing operation. Which of the following is the objective of a walk-through?

A. Determining the layout of the plant facilities and gathering information to prepare flowcharts.

B. Observing the physical flow of materials among production departments.

C. Obtaining an understanding of the process and control points by following the processing steps.

D. All of the answers are correct.

The correct answer is (D). *(CIA, adapted)*

REQUIRED: The objective of a walk-through of a manufacturing operation.

DISCUSSION: A walk-through is a physical inspection of an auditee's facilities and accounting records to gain an overall understanding of client operations. The term walk-through also describes tracing one or two transactions through all phases of the cycle, e.g., the processing of sales from credit approval to payment to verify that all steps are performed by the appropriate personnel in the correct order. A walk-through is part of obtaining an understanding of internal control, not a test of controls.

Answers (A), (B), and (C) are incorrect because determining the layout of the plant facilities and gathering information to prepare flowcharts, observing the physical flow of materials, and obtaining an understanding of the process and control points are objectives of a walk-through.

21. Which of the following is an aspect of scheduling and controlling the audit engagement?

A. Including in the audit program a column for estimated and actual time.

B. Performing audit work only after the client's books of account have been closed for the period under examination.

C. Writing a conclusion in individual working papers indicating how the results of the audit will affect the auditor's report.

D. Including in the engagement letter an estimate of the minimum and maximum audit fee.

The correct answer is (A). *(CPA, adapted)*

REQUIRED: The aspect of scheduling and controlling the audit engagement.

DISCUSSION: The audit program is a tool for scheduling and controlling the audit. It should contain a detailed set of procedures for accomplishing audit objectives, estimated times for each step, and the personnel required. Thus, it can be used to document the progress of the audit and the auditor's compliance with the first standard of field work (planning and supervision).

Answer (B) is incorrect because audit work may be done throughout the year before the books have been closed. Answer (C) is incorrect because writing a conclusion is an evaluation of the evidence rather than part of scheduling and controlling the audit. Answer (D) is incorrect because the engagement letter, describing the contractual agreement between the auditor and client, precedes the audit.

22. The element of the audit planning process most likely to be agreed upon with the client before implementation of the audit strategy is the determination of the

A. Timing of inventory observation procedures to be performed.

B. Evidence to be gathered to provide a sufficient basis for the auditor's opinion.

C. Procedures to be undertaken to discover litigation, claims, and assessments.

D. Pending legal matters to be included in the inquiry of the client's attorney.

The correct answer is (A). *(CPA, adapted)*

REQUIRED: The element of audit planning most likely to be agreed upon with the client before implementation.

DISCUSSION: GAAS require auditors to observe or make at least some physical counts of inventory and to become satisfied about the effectiveness of the methods of inventory-taking and the client's representations concerning quantities and condition (AU 331). Observation of inventory necessitates coordination of the efforts of the auditors and the client prior to performance of the procedure.

Answers (B) and (C) are incorrect because the evidence to be gathered and the procedures to be undertaken to discover litigation, claims, and assessments are not subject to the client's approval but to the auditor's professional judgment. Answer (D) is incorrect because determination of the specific legal issues to be raised in the inquiry letter is not appropriate in the planning phase. It should await a more complete understanding of the client's affairs.

23. In comparison with the detailed audit program of the independent auditor who is engaged to audit the financial statements of a large publicly held company, the comprehensive internal audit program is

A. More detailed and covers areas that normally are not considered by the independent auditor.

B. More detailed although it covers fewer areas than are normally covered by the independent auditor.

C. Substantially identical to the audit program used by the independent auditor because both consider substantially identical areas.

D. Less detailed and covers fewer areas than are normally considered by the independent auditor.

The correct answer is (A). *(CPA, adapted)*

REQUIRED: The best description of the difference between the independent auditor's audit program and an internal audit program.

DISCUSSION: The independent auditor's purpose is to express an opinion on the fairness of the financial statements, i.e., to evaluate the client's financial reporting system. The purposes of the internal auditor also extend to evaluating the efficiency of operations. The internal auditor's work is more comprehensive because (s)he must evaluate whether plans and policies have been complied with, objectives have been attained, and resources have been used economically.

Answer (B) is incorrect because the internal audit program covers more areas than that of the independent auditor. Answers (C) and (D) are incorrect because the internal audit program is more detailed and covers more areas.

2.3 Risk Assessment

24. The audit risk against which the auditor and those who rely on his/her opinion require reasonable protection is a combination of three separate risks at the account-balance or class-of-transactions level. The first risk is inherent risk. The second risk is that material misstatements will not be prevented or detected by internal control. The third risk is that

A. The auditor will reject a correct account balance as incorrect.

B. Material misstatements that occur will not be detected by the audit.

C. The auditor will apply an inappropriate audit procedure.

D. The auditor will apply an inappropriate measure of audit materiality.

The correct answer is (B). *(Publisher)*

REQUIRED: The component of audit risk in addition to inherent risk and control risk.

DISCUSSION: According to AU 312, one component of audit risk is detection risk, which is the risk that the auditor will not detect a material misstatement that exists in an assertion. Detection risk for a substantive test of details has two elements: (1) the risk that analytical procedures and other relevant substantive tests will fail to detect misstatements at least equal to tolerable misstatement and (2) the allowable risk of incorrect acceptance for the substantive test of details. The auditor assesses control risk (the second component) when considering the client's internal control. This assessment, the assessment of inherent risk, and the level to which the auditor wishes to restrict overall audit risk are the factors that the auditor uses to determine the acceptable level of detection risk.

Answers (A), (C), and (D) are incorrect because the components of audit risk are inherent risk, control risk, and detection risk.

25. Some account balances, such as those for pensions or leases, are the results of complex calculations. The susceptibility to material misstatements in these types of accounts is defined as

A. Audit risk.

B. Detection risk.

C. Sampling risk.

D. Inherent risk.

The correct answer is (D). *(CMA, adapted)*

REQUIRED: The susceptibility to material misstatements in account balances resulting from complex calculations.

DISCUSSION: Inherent risk is the susceptibility of an assertion to a material misstatement in the absence of related controls. This risk is greater for some assertions and related balances or classes than others. For example, complex calculations are more likely to be misstated than simple ones, and cash is more likely to be stolen than an inventory of coal. Inherent risk exists independently of the audit (AU 312).

Answer (A) is incorrect because audit risk is the risk that the auditor may unknowingly fail to appropriately modify an opinion on financial statements that are materially misstated. Answer (B) is incorrect because detection risk is the risk that the auditor will not detect a material misstatement that exists in an assertion. Answer (C) is incorrect because sampling risk is the risk that a particular sample may contain proportionately more or fewer monetary misstatements or deviations from controls than exist in the population as a whole (AU 350).

26. As the acceptable level of detection risk decreases, an auditor may change the

A. Timing of substantive tests by performing them at an interim date rather than at year-end.

B. Nature of substantive tests from a less effective to a more effective procedure.

C. Timing of tests of controls by performing them at several dates rather than at one time.

D. Assessed level of inherent risk to a higher amount.

The correct answer is (B). *(CPA, adapted)*

REQUIRED: The change resulting from a decrease in the acceptable level of detection risk.

DISCUSSION: The assurance provided by substantive tests must increase if the acceptable level of detection risk decreases. The auditor may (1) change from a less to a more effective procedure, for example, by directing tests toward independent parties outside the entity rather than toward client personnel; (2) change the timing of substantive tests, such as from an interim date to year-end; or (3) change the extent of testing, such as by using a larger sample (AU 319).

Answer (A) is incorrect because more assurance is provided by testing at year-end. Answer (C) is incorrect because the auditor tests controls when (s)he wishes to assess control risk at below the maximum level. The resulting assessment is then used in the determination of the acceptable level of detection risk. Answer (D) is incorrect because the assessed level of inherent risk affects the acceptable level of detection risk but not vice versa.

27. The risk that an auditor's procedures will lead to the conclusion that a material misstatement does not exist in an account balance when, in fact, such misstatement does exist is

A. Audit risk.

B. Inherent risk.

C. Control risk.

D. Detection risk.

The correct answer is (D). *(CPA, adapted)*

REQUIRED: The risk that audit procedures will fail to find a material misstatement.

DISCUSSION: Detection risk is "the risk that the auditor will not detect a material misstatement that exists in an assertion" (AU 312).

Answer (A) is incorrect because audit risk includes inherent risk and control risk, which are not affected by the auditor's procedures. Answer (B) is incorrect because inherent risk is the susceptibility of an assertion to material misstatement in the absence of related controls. Answer (C) is incorrect because control risk is the risk that a material misstatement in an assertion will not be prevented or detected on a timely basis by internal control.

28. Which of the following audit risk components may be assessed in nonquantitative terms?

	Control Risk	Detection Risk	Inherent Risk
A.	Yes	Yes	Yes
B.	No	Yes	Yes
C.	Yes	Yes	No
D.	Yes	No	Yes

The correct answer is (A). *(CPA, adapted)*

REQUIRED: The audit risk components that may be assessed in nonquantitative terms.

DISCUSSION: According to AU 312, the "components of audit risk may be assessed in quantitative terms such as percentages or in nonquantitative terms that range, for example, from a minimum to a maximum."

Answers (B), (C), and (D) are incorrect because all audit risk components may be assessed in nonquantitative terms.

29. Audit risk consists of inherent risk, control risk, and detection risk. Which of the following statements is true?

A. Cash is more susceptible to theft than an inventory of coal because it has a greater inherent risk.

B. The risk that material misstatement will not be prevented or detected on a timely basis by internal control can be reduced to zero by effective controls.

C. Detection risk is a function of the efficiency of an auditing procedure.

D. The existing levels of inherent risk, control risk, and detection risk can be changed at the discretion of the auditor.

The correct answer is (A). *(Publisher)*

REQUIRED: The true statement about audit risk.

DISCUSSION: Inherent risk is the susceptibility of an assertion to material misstatement in the absence of related controls. Some assertions and related balances or classes of transactions have greater inherent risk. Thus, cash has a greater inherent risk than less liquid assets.

Answer (B) is incorrect because some control risk will always exist. Internal control has inherent limitations. Answer (C) is incorrect because detection risk is a function of auditing effectiveness (achieving results), not efficiency. Answer (D) is incorrect because the actual levels of inherent risk and control risk are independent of the audit process. Acceptable detection risk is a function of the desired level of overall audit risk and the assessed levels of inherent risk and control risk. Hence, detection risk can be changed at the discretion of the auditor, but inherent risk and control risk cannot. However, the auditor's preliminary judgments about inherent risk and control risk may change as the audit progresses.

30. The acceptable level of detection risk is inversely related to the

A. Assurance provided by substantive tests.

B. Risk of misapplying auditing procedures.

C. Preliminary judgment about materiality levels.

D. Risk of failing to discover material misstatements.

The correct answer is (A). *(CPA, adapted)*

REQUIRED: The concept to which acceptable detection risk is inversely related.

DISCUSSION: An auditor considers internal control to assess control risk. The greater (lower) the assessed level of control risk, the lower (greater) the acceptable level of detection risk. In turn, the acceptable level of detection risk affects substantive testing. For example, as the acceptable level of detection risk decreases, the auditor changes the nature, timing, or extent of substantive tests to increase the assurance they provide. Hence, the relationship between substantive testing and acceptable detection risk is inverse.

Answer (B) is incorrect because the risk of misapplying auditing procedures is related to the auditor's training and experience. Answer (C) is incorrect because preliminary judgments about materiality levels are used by the auditor to determine the acceptable level of audit risk. Materiality and overall audit risk are inversely related. However, detection risk is just one component of audit risk (AU 312). Answer (D) is incorrect because the lower the level of detection risk acceptable to the auditor, the greater the assurance that should be provided by substantive testing. Given this additional assurance, the risk of failing to detect material misstatements (detection risk) should be decreased. Accordingly, the relationship of acceptable detection risk and the risk of failing to detect material misstatements is direct.

31. According to auditing standards, the auditor uses the assessed level of control risk (together with the assessed level of inherent risk) to determine the acceptable level of detection risk for financial statement assertions. As the acceptable level of detection risk decreases, the auditor may do one or more of the following except change the

A. Nature of substantive tests to more effective procedures.

B. Timing of substantive tests, such as performing them at year-end rather than at an interim date.

C. Extent of substantive tests, such as using larger sample sizes.

D. Assurances provided by substantive tests to a lower level.

The correct answer is (D). *(Publisher)*

REQUIRED: The improper action when the acceptable level of detection risk decreases.

DISCUSSION: The overall allowable audit risk of material misstatement in a financial statement assertion equals the product of inherent risk, control risk, and detection risk (expressed as probabilities). The audit risk formula in AU 350 further divides detection risk for a substantive test of details into (1) the risk that analytical procedures and other substantive tests will fail to detect misstatements equal to tolerable misstatement and (2) the allowable risk of incorrect acceptance for the substantive test of details. After determining the level to which (s)he wishes to restrict the risk of material misstatement and the assessed levels of control risk and inherent risk, the auditor performs substantive tests to restrict detection risk to the acceptable level. Accordingly, the level of detection risk that an auditor may accept is inversely related to control risk and inherent risk. If either increases, the acceptable level of detection risk decreases, and the auditor should change the nature, timing, or extent of substantive tests to increase the assurance they provide.

Answers (A), (B), and (C) are incorrect because use of more effective substantive tests, changing the timing of substantive tests, and changing the extent of testing are possible responses to a decrease in the acceptable level of detection risk.

32. According to AU 312, *Audit Risk and Materiality in Conducting an Audit*, the concepts of audit risk and materiality are interrelated and must be considered together by the auditor. Which of the following is true?

A. Audit risk is the risk that the auditor may unknowingly express a modified opinion when in fact the financial statements are fairly stated.

B. The phrase in the auditor's standard report "present fairly, in all material respects, in conformity with generally accepted accounting principles" indicates the auditor's belief that the financial statements taken as a whole are not materially misstated.

C. If misstatements are not important individually but are important in the aggregate, the concept of materiality does not apply.

D. Material fraud but not material errors cause financial statements to be materially misstated.

The correct answer is (B). *(Publisher)*

REQUIRED: The true statement about the significance of audit risk and materiality.

DISCUSSION: The opinion paragraph of the standard report explicitly refers to materiality. Hence, financial statements that are presented fairly, in all material respects, in conformity with GAAP are not materially misstated. Material misstatement can result from errors or fraud.

Answer (A) is incorrect because audit risk is the risk the auditor may unknowingly fail to appropriately modify the opinion on financial statements that are materially misstated. Answer (C) is incorrect because the concept of materiality recognizes that some misstatements, either individually or in the aggregate, are important for the fair presentation of financial statements. Qualitative as well as quantitative factors affect materiality judgments. Answer (D) is incorrect because both material errors and material fraud cause financial statements to be materially misstated.

33. AU 350 gives a formula for risk relationships. Overall allowable audit risk (AR) is the risk that monetary misstatements equal to tolerable misstatement may remain undetected. Control risk (CR) is the auditor's assessment of the risk that internal control may not prevent or detect material misstatements. Inherent risk (IR) is the susceptibility of an assertion to material misstatement given no related controls. In the audit risk formula, AP is the auditor's assessment of the risk that analytical procedures and other relevant substantive tests will fail to detect material misstatements not detected by the relevant controls. TD is the allowable risk of incorrect acceptance for a substantive test of details given that material misstatements occur in an assertion and are not detected by internal control or by analytical procedures and other substantive tests. Which model represents the overall allowable audit risk?

A. $AR = IR \times CR \times AP \times TD$.

B. $AR = IR + CR + AP + TD$.

C. $AR = IR + CR - (AP + TD)$.

D. $AR = IR + CR - (AP \times TD)$.

The correct answer is (A). *(Publisher)*

REQUIRED: The model associated with the overall allowable audit risk.

DISCUSSION: AU 350 states that the model for the overall allowable audit risk is not intended to be a mathematical formula including all factors that may influence the determination of individual risk components. However, the model is sometimes useful in considering and planning appropriate risk levels. AR is equal to the joint probability that material misstatements will occur in an assertion, that internal control will not prevent or detect material misstatements, and that subsequent procedures will also not detect them. Hence, AR is expressed as the product of IR, CR, AP, and TD.

Answers (B), (C), and (D) are incorrect because each is a nonsensical relationship.

34. The equation in AU 350 for the overall allowable audit risk (AR = IR x CR x AP x TD) is sometimes solved for TD (the allowable risk of incorrect acceptance associated with a test of details) because

A. The most important element is TD.

B. This version of the formula assists in planning a specific substantive test of details.

C. The overall allowable audit risk cannot be determined.

D. Auditors always consider tests of details first.

The correct answer is (B). *(Publisher)*

REQUIRED: The reason the allowable audit risk formula is solved for TD.

DISCUSSION: The auditor first establishes the overall allowable audit risk (AR) with respect to a particular balance or class of transactions. After considering internal control, (s)he can assess control risk (CR) as well as inherent risk (IR). After applying analytical procedures and considering the results of other substantive tests, (s)he can then assess the risk (AP) that those procedures and tests did not detect misstatements in an assertion equal to tolerable misstatement. The auditor can then calculate the allowable risk of incorrect acceptance (TD) for a particular substantive test. Determination of this level of risk is necessary for planning the nature, timing, and extent of the substantive test.

Answer (A) is incorrect because the overall allowable audit risk is the most important element in planning appropriate audit tests. Answer (C) is incorrect because the auditor's professional judgment and experience is used to determine overall allowable audit risk. Answer (D) is incorrect because overall audit risk should be established and some analytical procedures should be performed at an early stage. Also, the assessment of control risk should ordinarily be made before the planning of most tests of details.

35. Which of the following models expresses the general relationship of the auditor's assessments of control risk (CR) and inherent risk (IR), the detection risk associated with analytical procedures and other relevant substantive tests (AP), and overall allowable audit risk (AR) that would lead the auditor to conclude that a substantive test of details of an account balance is not necessary?

	AP	CR	AR	IR
A.	20%	40%	10%	100%
B.	20%	60%	5%	100%
C.	10%	70%	4.5%	100%
D.	30%	40%	5.5%	100%

The correct answer is (A). *(CPA, adapted)*

REQUIRED: The model expressing the relationship of risks not requiring an additional substantive test of details.

DISCUSSION: According to AU 350, the allowable risk of incorrect acceptance associated with a particular substantive test of details (TD) is equal to AR divided by the product of CR, AP, and IR. When the allowable level of AR exceeds the product of CR, AP, and IR, the planned substantive test of details may not be necessary because the relevant controls, analytical procedures, and other substantive tests may have reduced to an acceptable level the risk that monetary misstatements equal to tolerable misstatement will remain undetected. Thus, when AP is 20%, CR is 40%, and IR is 100%, risk is controlled at 8% (20% x 40% x 100%), which is less than a 10% AR.

Answer (B) is incorrect because, if AR is 5% and the product of AP, CR, and IR is 12% (20% x 60% x 100%), the additional substantive test will be necessary. Answer (C) is incorrect because, if AR is 4.5% and the product of AP, CR, and IR is 7% (10% x 70% x 100%), the additional substantive test will be necessary. Answer (D) is incorrect because, if AR is 5.5% and the product of AP, CR, and IR is 12% (30% x 40% x 100%), the additional substantive test will be necessary.

36. The concept of materiality with respect to the attest function

A. Applies only to publicly held firms.

B. Has greater application to the standards of reporting than the other generally accepted auditing standards.

C. Requires that relatively more effort be directed to those assertions that are more susceptible to misstatement.

D. Requires the auditor to make judgments as to whether misstatements affect the fairness of the financial statements.

The correct answer is (D). *(Publisher)*

REQUIRED: The meaning of materiality with respect to the attest function.

DISCUSSION: The concept of materiality recognizes that some, but not all, matters are important to the fairness of the financial statements. "Audit risk is the risk that the auditor may unknowingly fail to appropriately modify the opinion on financial statements that are materially misstated" (AU 312). A decrease either in the amount of misstatements deemed to be material or in the acceptable level of audit risk requires the auditor to select more effective procedures, perform procedures closer to the balance sheet date, or increase the extent of procedures.

Answer (A) is incorrect because the concept of materiality applies to all auditees. Answer (B) is incorrect because materiality applies to all GAAS. Answer (C) is incorrect because the degree of inherent risk is the reason that more effort must be directed to assertions (e.g., cash) that are more susceptible to misstatement.

37. In considering materiality for planning purposes, an auditor believes that misstatements aggregating $10,000 would have a material effect on an entity's income statement but that misstatements would have to aggregate $20,000 to materially affect the balance sheet. Ordinarily, it would be appropriate to design auditing procedures that would be expected to detect misstatements that aggregate

A. $10,000

B. $15,000

C. $20,000

D. $30,000

The correct answer is (A). *(CPA, adapted)*

REQUIRED: The materiality level used to design auditing procedures.

DISCUSSION: Because financial statements and the necessary audit tests are interrelated, as well as for reasons of efficiency, procedures should normally be designed to detect the smallest aggregate level of misstatements that could be material to any one statement. The smallest aggregate level of statements material to one statement is $10,000.

Answer (B) is incorrect because $15,000 is the average of the aggregate amounts material to the income statement and the balance sheet. Answer (C) is incorrect because $20,000 is the aggregate level of misstatements material to the balance sheet. Answer (D) is incorrect because $30,000 is the sum of the aggregate amounts material to the income statement and the balance sheet.

38. Madison Corporation has a few large accounts receivable that total $1,000,000. Nassau Corporation has a great number of small accounts receivable that also total $1,000,000. The importance of a misstatement in any one account is therefore greater for Madison than for Nassau. This is an example of the auditor's concept of

A. Materiality.

B. Comparative analysis.

C. Reasonable assurance.

D. Audit risk.

The correct answer is (A). *(CPA, adapted)*

REQUIRED: The concept applicable to the relative size of individual accounts receivable.

DISCUSSION: The concept of materiality requires the auditor to evaluate the relative importance of items to users of financial statements. In an entity with few but large accounts receivable, the individual accounts are relatively more important and the possibility of material misstatement is greater than in an entity with many small accounts.

Answer (B) is incorrect because comparative analysis is a term that is associated with analytical procedures. Answer (C) is incorrect because reasonable assurance is implicit in the third field work standard: Sufficient evidence should be gathered to afford a reasonable basis for an opinion. Moreover, reasonable assurance is mentioned in the auditor's standard report. Answer (D) is incorrect because "audit risk is the risk that the auditor may unknowingly fail to appropriately modify the opinion on financial statements that are materially misstated" (AU 312).

2.4 Errors, Fraud (Irregularities), and Illegal Acts

39. Due professional care requires the auditor to exercise

A. Objective judgment.

B. Independent integrity.

C. Professional skepticism.

D. Impartial conservatism.

The correct answer is (C). *(CPA, adapted)*

REQUIRED: The auditor's attitude in planning and performing an audit in accordance with GAAS.

DISCUSSION: According to AU 230, "Due professional care requires the auditor to exercise professional skepticism." The auditor should diligently perform the gathering and objective evaluation of evidence throughout the audit process. Moreover, the auditor neither assumes that management is dishonest nor assumes unquestioned honesty.

Answers (A), (B), and (D) are incorrect because, although objective judgment, independent integrity, and impartial conservatism are qualities appropriate for practitioners, none is required to be applied specifically in an audit.

40. Which of the following statements best describes an auditor's responsibility regarding misstatements?

A. An auditor should plan and perform an audit to provide reasonable assurance of detecting misstatements that are material to the financial statements.

B. An auditor is responsible to detect material errors but has no responsibility to detect material fraud (irregularities) that is concealed through employee collusion or management override of internal control.

C. An auditor has no responsibility to detect material misstatements unless analytical procedures or tests of transactions identify conditions causing a reasonably prudent auditor to suspect that the financial statements were materially misstated.

D. An auditor has no responsibility to detect material misstatements because an auditor is not an insurer and an audit does not constitute a guarantee.

The correct answer is (A). *(CPA, adapted)*

REQUIRED: The auditor's responsibility to detect errors and irregularities.

DISCUSSION: AU 110 states, "The auditor has a responsibility to plan and perform the audit to obtain reasonable assurance about whether the financial statements are free of material misstatements, whether caused by error or fraud."

Answers (B), (C), and (D) are incorrect because the audit should provide reasonable assurance about whether the financial statements are free of material misstatement.

41. Certain management characteristics may heighten the auditor's concern about the risk of material misstatements. The characteristic that is least likely to cause concern is that management

A. Operating and financing decisions are made by numerous individuals.

B. Commits to unduly aggressive forecasts.

C. Has an excessive interest in increasing the entity's stock price through use of unduly aggressive accounting practices.

D. Is interested in inappropriate methods of minimizing earnings for tax purposes.

The correct answer is (A). *(Publisher)*

REQUIRED: The management characteristic least likely to indicate increased risk.

DISCUSSION: The auditor would be concerned if the decision process were dominated by one individual or a small group. In that case, compensating controls, e.g., effective oversight by the audit committee, reduce risk.

Answer (B) is incorrect because one risk factor is management's commitment to third parties to achieve unduly aggressive or clearly unrealistic forecasts. Answer (C) is incorrect because another risk factor is display of an excessive interest in improving the entity's stock price or earnings trend through use of unusually aggressive accounting practices. Answer (D) is incorrect because still another risk factor pertaining to management's characteristics and influence over the control environment is an interest in inappropriate methods of minimizing earnings for tax purposes.

42. Which of the following circumstances is most likely to cause an auditor to suspect material misstatement of the client's financial statements as a result of fraud?

A. Property and equipment are usually sold at a loss before being fully depreciated.

B. Unusual discrepancies between the entity's records and confirmation replies.

C. Monthly bank reconciliations usually include several in-transit items.

D. Clerical errors are listed on a computer-generated exception report.

The correct answer is (B). *(CPA, adapted)*

REQUIRED: The circumstance most likely indicative of material fraud.

DISCUSSION: If a condition or circumstance differs adversely from the auditor's expectation, the auditor needs to consider the reason for such a difference. An example of such a condition is "unusual discrepancies between the entity's records and confirmation replies" (AU 316, *Consideration of Fraud in a Financial Statement Audit*).

Answer (A) is incorrect because sale at a loss before being fully depreciated suggests that the depreciation method is inadequate. Answer (C) is incorrect because in-transit items are normal. Answer (D) is incorrect because a listing of errors is an effective control.

43. Which of the following is least likely to suggest to an auditor that the client's management may have overridden internal control?

A. There are numerous delays in preparing timely internal financial reports.

B. Management does not correct material internal control weaknesses that it knows about.

C. Differences are always disclosed on a computer exception report.

D. There have been two new controllers this year.

The correct answer is (C). *(CPA, adapted)*

REQUIRED: The fact least likely to suggest management override of internal control.

DISCUSSION: The disclosure of differences on a computer exception report suggests that management is not overriding internal control (presumably, exceptions would not be listed if management were overriding the system).

Answer (A) is incorrect because delays in the preparation of timely internal financial reports may imply that management is hiding something. Answer (B) is incorrect because management reluctance to correct material weaknesses suggests that these conditions are being used to override internal control. Answer (D) is incorrect because replacing two controllers suggests that management may be trying to direct accounting methods, i.e., to override.

44. Which of the following circumstances is most likely to cause an auditor to consider whether a material misstatement exists?

A. Transactions selected for testing are not supported by proper documentation.

B. The turnover of senior management is low.

C. Management places little emphasis on meeting earnings projections.

D. Operating and financing decisions are dominated by several persons.

The correct answer is (A). *(CPA, adapted)*

REQUIRED: The circumstance most likely indicating a material misstatement.

DISCUSSION: Discrepancies in the accounting records suggest likely material misstatement. One condition that should raise doubt is an unsupported or unauthorized balance or transaction (AU 316).

Answer (B) is incorrect because the auditor would consider the risk of material misstatement to be greater if the turnover of senior management were high. Answer (C) is incorrect because the auditor would consider the risk of material misstatement to be greater if management placed undue emphasis on meeting earnings projections. Answer (D) is incorrect because the auditor would consider the risk of material misstatement to be greater if management were dominated by a single individual.

45. Which of the following is a true statement about an auditor's responsibility regarding consideration of fraud in a financial statement audit?

A. The auditor should consider the client's internal control, and plan and perform the audit to provide absolute assurance of detecting all material misstatements.

B. The auditor should assess the risk that errors may cause the financial statements to contain material misstatements, and determine whether the necessary controls are prescribed and are being followed satisfactorily.

C. The auditor should consider the types of misstatements that could occur, determine whether the necessary controls are prescribed and are being followed, but need not specifically assess the risk of fraud.

D. The auditor should specifically assess the risk of material misstatement due to fraud.

The correct answer is (D). *(Publisher)*

REQUIRED: The true statement about an auditor's responsibility regarding consideration of fraud in a financial statement audit.

DISCUSSION: AU 316 requires that the auditor specifically assess the risk of material misstatement due to fraud. This assessment is considered in the design of audit procedures. The fraud risk factors to be considered in this assessment relate to misstatements arising from (1) fraudulent reporting and (2) misappropriation of assets.

Answer (A) is incorrect because the audit should provide reasonable assurance about whether the financial statements are free of material misstatements. Answers (B) and (C) are incorrect because the risk of material misstatement due to fraud must be assessed.

46. Which of the following statements describes why a properly planned and performed audit may not detect a material misstatement resulting from fraud?

A. Audit procedures that are effective for detecting an unintentional misstatement may be ineffective for an intentional misstatement that is concealed through collusion.

B. An audit is planned and performed to provide reasonable assurance of detecting material misstatements caused by errors but not fraud.

C. The factors considered in assessing control risk indicated an increased risk of intentional misstatements but only a low risk of unintentional errors in the financial statements.

D. The auditor did not consider factors influencing audit risk for account balances that have effects pervasive to the financial statements taken as a whole.

The correct answer is (A). *(CPA, adapted)*

REQUIRED: The reason a properly planned and performed audit may not detect a material misstatement resulting from fraud.

DISCUSSION: Collusion involves collaboration by client personnel and third parties or by management or employees of the client to conceal fraud. Concealment is any attempt to reduce the likelihood of detection. The skillfulness of the perpetrator, the frequency and extent of manipulation, and the size of amounts involved affect the auditor's ability to detect a concealed irregularity.

Answer (B) is incorrect because the auditor's responsibility is the same for material fraud as for material errors. Answer (C) is incorrect because, if the risk of intentional misstatements is assessed to be high, the auditor would apply additional procedures and thereby increase the probability of uncovering the fraud. Answer (D) is incorrect because an audit that is properly planned and performed should consider audit risk factors for accounts having pervasive effects on the statements.

47. In connection with the audit of financial statements, an independent auditor could be responsible for failure to detect a material fraud if

A. Statistical sampling techniques were not used on the audit engagement.

B. The auditor planned the work in a hasty and inefficient manner.

C. The auditors performing important parts of the work failed to discover a personal relationship between the treasurer and the cashier.

D. The fraud was perpetrated by one of the client's employees, who circumvented existing internal control.

The correct answer is (B). *(CPA, adapted)*

REQUIRED: The situation in which the independent auditor could be responsible for failure to detect a material fraud.

DISCUSSION: If the auditor had planned the work in a hasty and inefficient manner, thus violating the first standard of field work (adequate planning and supervision) as well as the third general standard (due professional care), (s)he would be responsible for failure to detect a material fraud.

Answer (A) is incorrect because the auditor is not required to use statistical sampling techniques. Answer (C) is incorrect because discovery of a personal relationship between a treasurer and a cashier is not within the audit scope. Answer (D) is incorrect because, even if the auditor adequately planned the audit, an employee might still have been able to circumvent internal control.

48. In a financial statement audit, the auditor should consider categories of fraud risk factors relating to misstatements arising from (1) fraudulent financial reporting and (2) misappropriation of assets. Which of the following is a category of risk factors that should be considered in relation to misstatements arising from misappropriation of assets?

A. Industry conditions.

B. Operating characteristics.

C. Management's characteristics.

D. Controls.

The correct answer is (D). *(Publisher)*

REQUIRED: The category of risk factors that should be considered in relation to misstatements arising from misappropriation of assets.

DISCUSSION: The auditor must specifically assess the risk of material misstatement due to fraud, a risk that is part of audit risk. The assessment is considered in designing audit procedures. Accordingly, AU 316 states that the auditor should consider three categories of risk factors related to fraudulent reporting: management's characteristics and influence over the control environment, industry conditions, and operating characteristics and financial stability. The two categories of risk factors related to misappropriation of assets are controls and susceptibility of assets to misappropriation.

Answers (A), (B), and (C) are incorrect because industry conditions, operating characteristics, and management's characteristics relate to fraudulent reporting.

49. If an independent audit leading to an opinion on financial statements causes the auditor to believe that material fraud exists, (s)he should first

A. Consider the implications for other aspects of the audit and discuss the matter with appropriate levels of management.

B. Make the investigation necessary to determine whether fraud has in fact occurred.

C. Request that management investigate to determine whether fraud has in fact occurred.

D. Consider whether fraud was the result of a failure by employees to comply with existing controls.

The correct answer is (A). *(CPA, adapted)*

REQUIRED: The appropriate action when the auditor believes that material fraud exists.

DISCUSSION: When the audit leads the auditor to believe that material fraud exists, (s)he should first consider the implications for other aspects of the audit. (S)he should then discuss the matter with a level of management at least one level above those involved and with senior management, attempt to obtain sufficient evidence to determine whether fraud exists, and, if appropriate, suggest that the client consult legal counsel (AU 316).

Answer (B) is incorrect because making the investigation necessary to determine whether fraud has in fact occurred is not the first step to be taken when the auditor believes that material fraud exists. Answer (C) is incorrect because the auditor should not rely solely on management's investigation. Answer (D) is incorrect because considering whether fraud was the result of a failure by employees to comply with existing controls is not the first step to be taken.

50. Auditing standards require that auditors be aware of relevant factors relating to fraudulent reporting. Which of the following statements is false concerning fraudulent reporting?

A. Fraud frequently involves a pressure or an incentive to commit fraud and a perceived opportunity to do so.

B. Two types of fraud relevant to the auditor include material misstatements arising from fraudulent financial reporting and material misstatements arising from misappropriation of assets.

C. Fraud involves actions of management but excludes the actions of employees or third parties.

D. An audit rarely involves the authentication of documentation; thus, fraud may go undetected by the auditor.

The correct answer is (C). *(Publisher)*

REQUIRED: The false statement concerning fraudulent reporting.

DISCUSSION: Misappropriation of assets may be accompanied by false or misleading records and may involve one or more individuals among management, employees, or third parties.

Answer (A) is incorrect because the two conditions are ordinarily present in fraud. Answer (B) is incorrect because misstatements arising from fraudulent reporting are intentional misstatements or omissions to deceive financial statement users, and misstatements arising from misappropriation of assets involve theft the effect of which is nonconformity of the financial statements with GAAP. Answer (D) is incorrect because auditors are not trained or expected to be experts in authentication, and there is some risk that fraud may go undetected.

51. Moor, CPA, discovers a likely fraud during an audit but concludes that its effects, if any, could not be so material as to affect the opinion. Moor should

A. Perform additional audit procedures to determine whether fraud has occurred and, if so, the amount thereof.

B. Report the finding to the appropriate representatives of the client with the recommendation that it be pursued to a conclusion.

C. Confer with the client about the additional audit procedures necessary to determine whether fraud has occurred and, if so, the amount thereof.

D. Notify the proper external authorities.

The correct answer is (B). *(Publisher)*

REQUIRED: The auditor's proper action when suspected fraud is not so material as to affect the opinion.

DISCUSSION: The auditor should refer the matter of an immaterial fraud to an appropriate level of management. The appropriate level of management is at least one level above the highest level involved. The auditor should also be satisfied that, in view of the organizational position of the likely perpetrator, the likely fraud has no implications for other aspects of the audit or that those implications have been adequately considered.

Answers (A) and (C) are incorrect because the auditor is not required to pursue immaterial errors or fraud. Answer (D) is incorrect because the matter should be pursued with an appropriate level of management.

52. An auditor's consideration of the risk of material misstatement due to fraud and the results of audit tests indicate a significant risk of fraud. The auditor should

A. Express either a qualified or an adverse opinion.

B. Consider withdrawing from the engagement and communicating the reasons for withdrawal to the audit committee.

C. Express only an adverse opinion because of the strong possibility of fraud.

D. Inform proper authorities outside the entity.

The correct answer is (B). *(Publisher)*

REQUIRED: The appropriate action by an auditor who has identified a significant risk of fraud.

DISCUSSION: If, after the application of appropriate procedures, the auditor is unable to conclude whether possible fraud may materially affect the financial statements, the auditor should consider withdrawing from the engagement and communicating his/her reasons to the audit committee or others with equivalent authority and responsibility. Whether the auditor withdraws "may depend on the diligence and cooperation of senior management or the board of directors in investigating the circumstances and taking appropriate action" (AU 316).

Answers (A) and (C) are incorrect because an adverse opinion is appropriate only when the financial statements are not fairly presented. Answer (D) is incorrect because the auditor should communicate with an appropriate level of management and the audit committee.

53. Disclosure of possible fraud to parties other than the client's senior management and its audit committee ordinarily is not part of an auditor's responsibility. However, to which of the following outside parties may a duty to disclose possible fraud exist?

I. To the SEC when the client reports an auditor change
II. To a successor auditor when the successor makes appropriate inquiries
III. To a government funding agency from which the client receives financial assistance

A. I and II.

B. I and III.

C. II and III.

D. I, II, and III.

The correct answer is (D). *(CPA, adapted)*

REQUIRED: The outside parties to whom a duty to disclose irregularities exists.

DISCUSSION: A duty of disclosure to parties other than the client may exist when the entity reports an auditor change to the SEC on Form 8-K; for example, the auditor may have withdrawn because the client failed to take appropriate remedial action, and the failure may be a "reportable event" or the source of a "disagreement." Under AU 315, a predecessor auditor must respond to inquiries by a successor if the client gives its specific permission. An auditor must respond in accordance with the requirements of audits of recipients of government funds.

Answers (A), (B), and (C) are incorrect because a duty of disclosure to parties other than the client may exist when the entity reports an auditor change to the SEC on Form 8-K, the client gives its specific permission for a predecessor auditor to respond to the successor auditor's inquiries, and the client receives financial assistance from a government agency.

54. Which of the following statements concerning illegal acts by clients is correct?

A. An auditor's responsibility for material misstatements caused by illegal acts that have a direct and material effect on the financial statements is the same as that for errors and fraud.

B. An audit in accordance with generally accepted auditing standards normally includes audit procedures specifically designed to detect illegal acts that have an indirect but material effect on the financial statements.

C. An auditor considers illegal acts from the perspective of the reliability of management's representations rather than their relation to audit objectives derived from financial statement assertions.

D. An auditor has no responsibility to detect illegal acts by clients that have an indirect effect on the financial statements.

The correct answer is (A). *(CPA, adapted)*

REQUIRED: The true statement concerning illegal acts.

DISCUSSION: An auditor has the obligation to plan and perform the audit to provide reasonable assurance about whether the financial statements are free of material misstatements, whether caused by error or fraud (AU 316). This standard also applies to illegal acts that have a direct and material effect on the financial statements.

Answer (B) is incorrect because certain illegal acts "relate more to an entity's operating aspects than to its financial and accounting aspects, and their financial statement effect is indirect." An audit in accordance with GAAS is usually not specifically designed to detect illegal acts that have such indirect effects. Answer (C) is incorrect because the auditor considers illegal acts "from the perspective of their known relation to audit objectives derived from financial statement assertions rather than from the perspective of legality per se" (AU 317). Answer (D) is incorrect because, if illegal acts come to the auditor's attention, (s)he must undertake appropriate procedures. Absent such evidence, the auditor must make inquiries about compliance with laws and regulations and obtain written representations from management.

55. An auditor's document includes the following:

"Our audit is subject to the risk that errors, fraud, or illegal acts, including fraud or defalcations, if they exist, will not be detected. However, we will inform you of any such matters that come to our attention."

The above passage is most likely from

A. The explanatory paragraph of a "subject to" qualified auditor's report.

B. An engagement letter.

C. The explanatory paragraph of a compliance report on a government entity subject to GAO standards.

D. A comfort letter.

The correct answer is (B). *(CPA, adapted)*

REQUIRED: The likely source of the quoted language.

DISCUSSION: The primary purpose of an engagement letter is to provide a written record of the agreement with the client as to the services to be provided by the auditor. It sets forth the rights and obligations under the contract between the client and the auditor. An engagement letter should also state the nature of the audit. Although not required by GAAS, engagement letters are highly recommended.

Answer (A) is incorrect because "subject to" opinions may not be expressed (AU 508). Answer (C) is incorrect because an explanatory paragraph would contain specific information about compliance by the audited entity.
Answer (D) is incorrect because a comfort letter, for example, one addressed to underwriters, is based on a review, not an audit.

56. The most likely reason an audit cannot reasonably be expected to bring all illegal acts by the client to the auditor's attention is that

A. Illegal acts are perpetrated by management override of the information and communication component of internal control.

B. Illegal acts by clients often relate to operating aspects rather than accounting aspects.

C. The information and communication component of the client's internal control procedures may be so effective that the auditor performs only minimal substantive testing.

D. Illegal acts may be perpetrated by the only person in the client's organization with access to both assets and the accounting records.

The correct answer is (B). *(CPA, adapted)*

REQUIRED: The most likely reason an audit is not expected to detect all client illegal acts.

DISCUSSION: AU 317 states that some illegal acts, such as violations of tax law, have a direct and material effect on the financial statements. Other illegal acts, such as violations of environmental protection laws, "relate more to an entity's operating aspects than to its financial and accounting aspects, and their financial statement effect is indirect." An audit in accordance with GAAS usually does not include audit procedures specifically designed to detect illegal acts that have such indirect effects.

Answer (A) is incorrect because many illegal acts are not subject to internal control; e.g., violations of insider trading rules may result from transactions that are recorded appropriately. Answer (C) is incorrect because illegal acts may involve matters outside the information and communication component so that even extensive substantive tests would not detect them. Answer (D) is incorrect because illegal acts may not involve manipulation of records.

57. Jones, CPA, is auditing the financial statements of XYZ Retailing, Inc. What assurance does Jones provide that direct-effect illegal acts that are material to XYZ's financial statements, and illegal acts that have a material but indirect effect on the financial statements, will be detected?

	Direct-Effect Illegal Acts	Indirect-Effect Illegal Acts
A.	Reasonable	None
B.	Reasonable	Reasonable
C.	Limited	None
D.	Limited	Reasonable

The correct answer is (A). *(CPA, adapted)*

REQUIRED: The auditor assurance provided in connection with a client's potential illegal acts.

DISCUSSION: An auditor has the obligation to plan and perform the audit to provide reasonable assurance about whether the financial statements are free of material misstatements, whether caused by error or fraud (AU 316). This standard also applies to illegal acts that have a direct and material effect on the financial statements. However, because of the nature of illegal acts that have an indirect effect on the financial statements, "an audit made in accordance with GAAS provides no assurance that illegal acts will be detected or that any contingent liabilities that may result will be disclosed" (AU 317).

Answers (B), (C), and (D) are incorrect because the auditor provides reasonable assurance regarding direct-effect illegal acts but no assurance regarding indirect-effect illegal acts.

58. Some illegal acts (such as violations of the Occupational Safety and Health Act) relate to operating aspects of an entity more than to its financial or accounting aspects. In a financial statement audit,

A. Regular audit procedures can reasonably be expected to detect these acts.

B. The auditor should contact appropriate enforcement agencies.

C. The auditor should inquire of management about violations of laws and regulations.

D. Violations of laws having indirect effects on the financial statements are not of interest to the auditor.

The correct answer is (C). *(Publisher)*

REQUIRED: The auditor's responsibility for illegal acts relating to operating aspects of an entity.

DISCUSSION: In the absence of evidence concerning illegal acts that have a material but indirect effect on financial statements, an audit in accordance with GAAS will customarily not include procedures specifically designed to detect such acts. However, in an audit of financial statements presented in accordance with GAAP, the auditor should obtain specific written representations from management concerning "violations or possible violations of laws or regulations whose effects should be considered for disclosure in the financial statements or as a basis for recording a loss contingency" (AU 333).

Answer (A) is incorrect because the audit cannot be expected to detect all illegal acts. Answer (B) is incorrect because the auditor is customarily not responsible for contacting outside agencies either in search of or to disclose illegal acts. Answer (D) is incorrect because illegal acts relating to operating aspects of an entity are of interest to the auditor. They bear upon the integrity of management and may materially affect the financial statements.

59. When an auditor becomes aware of a possible client illegal act, the auditor should obtain an understanding of the nature of the act to

A. Consider whether other similar acts have occurred.

B. Recommend remedial actions to the audit committee.

C. Evaluate the effect on the financial statements.

D. Determine the reliability of management's representations.

The correct answer is (C). *(CPA, adapted)*

REQUIRED: The reason the auditor obtains an understanding of the nature of a possible illegal act.

DISCUSSION: AU 317 states that when the auditor becomes aware of information concerning a possible illegal act, the auditor should obtain an understanding of the nature of the act, the circumstances in which it occurred, and sufficient other information to evaluate the effect on the financial statements. The auditor's ultimate purpose is to form an opinion on the fairness of the financial statements.

Answer (A) is incorrect because the auditor may consider whether other similar acts have occurred when applying any additional procedures necessary to obtain further understanding of the nature of the act. Answer (B) is incorrect because the auditor should communicate with the audit committee with respect to a discovered illegal act, but this purpose is a secondary objective of the audit. Answer (D) is incorrect because, if the auditor determines that an illegal act has occurred, (s)he should assess the effects on the representations of management in other areas of the audit.

60. During the annual audit of Ajax Corp., a publicly held company, Jones, CPA, a continuing auditor, determined that illegal political contributions had been made during each of the past 7 years, including the year under audit. Jones notified the board of directors about the illegal contributions, but they refused to take any action because the amounts involved were immaterial to the financial statements. Jones should reconsider the intended degree of reliance to be placed on the

A. Letter of audit inquiry to the client's attorney.

B. Prior years' audit programs.

C. Management representation letter.

D. Preliminary judgment about materiality levels.

The correct answer is (C). *(CPA, adapted)*

REQUIRED: The effect on the auditor of the client's failure to take corrective action for an illegal act.

DISCUSSION: "The auditor should consider the implications of an illegal act in relation to other aspects of the audit, particularly the reliability of representations of management" (AU 317). Management's representations are documented by the auditor in the management representation letter.

Answer (A) is incorrect because the letter of audit inquiry to the client's attorney will be responded to by the client's attorney, not the client. Answer (B) is incorrect because the prior years' audit programs will not be relied upon in the current audit. Answer (D) is incorrect because the results of the acts have been judged immaterial to the financial statements, and no reconsideration is necessary.

61. An auditor concludes that a client has committed an illegal act that has not been properly accounted for or disclosed. The auditor should withdraw from the engagement if the

A. Auditor is precluded from obtaining sufficient competent evidence about the illegal act.

B. Illegal act has an effect on the financial statements that is both material and direct.

C. Auditor cannot reasonably estimate the effect of the illegal act on the financial statements.

D. Client refuses to accept the auditor's report as modified for the illegal act.

The correct answer is (D). *(CPA, adapted)*

REQUIRED: The situation in which the auditor should withdraw from the engagement.

DISCUSSION: When an auditor concludes that a client has committed an illegal act that has not been properly accounted for or disclosed and the client refuses to accept the auditor's report as modified, "the auditor should withdraw from the engagement and indicate the reasons for withdrawal in writing to the audit committee or board of directors" (AU 317).

Answer (A) is incorrect because, if the auditor is precluded from obtaining sufficient competent evidence about an illegal act, a disclaimer should be issued. Answer (B) is incorrect because the auditor should express a qualified or adverse opinion if financial statements are not fairly presented. Answer (C) is incorrect because, if an auditor cannot reasonably estimate the effect of an illegal act on the financial statements, but no scope limitation or departure from GAAP exists, (s)he should consider either disclaiming an opinion or including an explanatory paragraph in a report expressing an unqualified opinion.

62. If the auditor considers an illegal act to be sufficiently serious to warrant withdrawing from the engagement, the auditor will likely

A. Notify all parties who may rely upon the company's financial statements of the company's illegal act.

B. Consult with legal counsel as to what other action, if any, should be taken.

C. Return all incriminating evidence and working papers to the client's audit committee for follow-up.

D. Contact the successor auditor to make the successor aware of the possible consequences of relying on management's representations.

The correct answer is (B). *(CPA, adapted)*

REQUIRED: The action by an auditor who withdraws as a result of an illegal act.

DISCUSSION: According to AU 317, the auditor should consider consulting legal counsel in these circumstances. Such consultation may be necessary in assessing the effects of continued association with the client or determining whether the auditor may have a duty to notify parties outside the client that overrides his/her duty of confidentiality to the client.

Answer (A) is incorrect because notifying others is the responsibility of management. Answer (C) is incorrect because the auditor has no responsibility to return all incriminating evidence and working papers to the client's audit committee for follow-up. Answer (D) is incorrect because the successor auditor, with client approval, has the burden of initiating communication with the predecessor.

63. Usually, the decision to notify parties outside the client's organization regarding an illegal act is the responsibility of

A. The independent auditor.

B. Management.

C. Outside legal counsel.

D. The internal auditor.

The correct answer is (B). *(CPA, adapted)*

REQUIRED: The person(s) responsible for contacting outside parties about illegal acts.

DISCUSSION: Deciding whether to contact parties other than personnel within the client's organization about an illegal act is the responsibility of management. However, the auditor's responsibility to report externally may be expanded in special engagements. For example, in audits of governmental units, the auditor may be required to report on the unit's compliance with laws and regulations applicable to federal financial assistance programs (AU 317). Furthermore, to comply with certain legal or regulatory requirements, such as those stated by the Private Securities Litigation Reform Act of 1995, the auditor may be required to report illegalities to the SEC.

Answers (A), (C), and (D) are incorrect because the independent auditor, the outside legal counsel, and the internal auditor ordinarily are not responsible for contacting outside parties about illegal acts.

2.5 Working Papers and Documentation

64. The primary purpose of an auditor's working papers is to

A. Provide evidence of the planning and execution of audit procedures performed.

B. Serve as a means with which to prepare the financial statements.

C. Document deficiencies in internal control with recommendations to management for improvement.

D. Comply with the auditing standards of the profession.

The correct answer is (A). *(CIA, adapted)*

REQUIRED: The primary purpose of an auditor's working papers.

DISCUSSION: Audit working papers provide the principal evidence for the report; aid in planning, performing, and reviewing the audit; document whether audit objectives were achieved; facilitate third-party review; provide a basis for evaluating the quality assurance program; aid in the auditors' professional development; provide support in the event of fraud, litigation, insurance claims, etc.

Answer (B) is incorrect because working papers do not provide the means for preparation of the financial statements. Answer (C) is incorrect because documentation of control deficiencies is only one example of working paper content, not the primary purpose for them. Answer (D) is incorrect because the preparation of adequate working papers is a requirement of the standards but not the primary purpose for their existence.

65. Which of the following documentation is not required for an audit in accordance with generally accepted auditing standards?

A. A written audit program setting forth the procedures necessary to accomplish the audit's objectives.

B. An indication that the accounting records agree or reconcile with the financial statements.

C. A client engagement letter that summarizes the timing and details of the auditor's planned field work.

D. The basis for the auditor's conclusions when the assessed level of control risk is below the maximum level.

The correct answer is (C). *(CPA, adapted)*

REQUIRED: The documentation not required for an audit.

DISCUSSION: Although highly recommended, a client engagement letter is not required in an audit or any other engagement.

Answer (A) is incorrect because a written audit program is required by AU 311, *Planning and Supervision*. Answer (B) is incorrect because the working papers should demonstrate that the accounting records agree or reconcile with the financial statements. Answer (D) is incorrect because AU 319 requires the auditor to document the basis for the auditor's conclusions when the assessed level of control risk is below the maximum.

66. Working papers that record the procedures used by the auditor to gather evidence should be

A. Considered the primary support for the financial statements being audited.

B. Viewed as the connecting link between the books of account and the financial statements.

C. Designed to meet the circumstances of the particular engagement.

D. Destroyed when the audited entity ceases to be a client.

The correct answer is (C). *(CPA, adapted)*

REQUIRED: The correct statement concerning audit working papers.

DISCUSSION: AU 339 states that working papers should be designed to meet the circumstances of a particular engagement. "Working papers serve mainly to provide the principal support for the auditor's report, including the representation regarding observance of the standards of field work," which is implied by the reference to GAAS in the report.

Answer (A) is incorrect because the financial statements are primarily supported by the client's accounting records. Answer (B) is incorrect because working papers are not a part of, or a substitute for, the client's accounting records. Answer (D) is incorrect because the auditor should retain working papers "for a period sufficient to meet the needs of his/her practice and to satisfy any pertinent legal requirements of records retention" (AU 339).

67. Which of the following conditions constitutes inappropriate working paper preparation?

A. All forms and directives used by the auditee department are included in the working papers.

B. Flowcharts are included in the working papers.

C. Findings are cross-referenced to supporting documentation.

D. Tick marks are explained in working papers.

The correct answer is (A). *(CIA, adapted)*

REQUIRED: The inappropriate working paper preparation method.

DISCUSSION: Working papers should be confined to information that is material and relevant to the audit and audit findings. Hence, forms and directives used by the auditee should be included only to the extent they support the findings and recommendations and are consistent with audit objectives.

Answer (B) is incorrect because a graphic representation of the auditee's controls, document flows, and other activities is often vital for understanding operations and is therefore a proper part of the audit documentation. Answer (C) is incorrect because cross-referencing is essential to the orderly arrangement and understanding of working papers and reduces duplication. Answer (D) is incorrect because tick marks are audit verification symbols that should be standard throughout the audit and defined in the working papers.

68. An auditor's working papers will ordinarily be least likely to include documentation showing how the

A. Client's schedules were prepared.

B. Engagement was planned.

C. Understanding of the client's internal control was obtained and control risk was assessed.

D. Unusual matters were resolved.

The correct answer is (A). *(CPA, adapted)*

REQUIRED: The item least likely to be documented in the auditor's working papers.

DISCUSSION: AU 339 states that the working papers should contain documentation showing that (1) the engagement was adequately planned and supervised, (2) an understanding of internal control was obtained and control risk was assessed, and (3) sufficient competent evidence was obtained to afford a reasonable basis for an opinion. Documentation of the preparation of clients' schedules is not necessary because the schedules themselves represent how they were prepared.

Answers (B), (C), and (D) are incorrect because the working papers show how the engagement was planned, how the understanding of the client's internal control was obtained and control risk was assessed, and how unusual matters were resolved.

69. Which of the following is usually included or shown in the auditor's working papers?

A. The procedures used by the auditor to verify the personal financial status of members of the client's management team.

B. Analyses that are designed to be a part of, or a substitute for, the client's accounting records.

C. Excerpts from authoritative pronouncements that support the underlying generally accepted accounting principles used in preparing the financial statements.

D. The manner in which exceptions and unusual matters disclosed by the auditor's procedures were resolved or treated.

The correct answer is (D). *(CPA, adapted)*

REQUIRED: The component of working papers.

DISCUSSION: The audit working papers should include information showing that the audit was properly planned and supervised, that an understanding of internal control was obtained and control risk was assessed and that sufficient competent evidence was obtained to afford a reasonable basis for an opinion. All exceptions and unusual matters should be followed up, with the resolution and/or treatment included in the working papers.

Answer (A) is incorrect because the auditor seldom, if ever, verifies the personal financial status of the management. Answer (B) is incorrect because, as AU 339 notes, the auditor's working papers are not to be regarded as a part of, or a substitute for, the client's accounting records. Answer (C) is incorrect because management, not the auditor, must document and support the general acceptability of the accounting principles used by the client.

70. Although the quantity and content of audit working papers vary with each particular engagement, an auditor's permanent files most likely include

A. Schedules that support the current year's adjusting entries.

B. Prior years' accounts receivable confirmations that were classified as exceptions.

C. Documentation indicating that the audit work was adequately planned and supervised.

D. Analyses of capital stock and other owners' equity accounts.

The correct answer is (D). *(CPA, adapted)*

REQUIRED: The component of the permanent section of the auditor's working papers.

DISCUSSION: The permanent section of the auditor's working papers usually contains copies of important company documents. They may include the articles of incorporation, stock options, contracts, and bylaws; the engagement letter, which is the contract between the auditor and the client; analyses from previous audits of accounts of special importance to the auditor, such as long-term debt, PP&E, and shareholders' equity; and information concerning internal control, e.g., flowcharts, organization charts, and questionnaires.

Answers (A) and (B) are incorrect because the schedules and confirmations are included in the current files. Answer (C) is incorrect because documentation indicating that the audit work was adequately planned and supervised is always included in the current working papers files.

71. Which of the following factors would least likely affect the quantity and content of an auditor's working papers?

A. The condition of the client's records.

B. The assessed level of control risk.

C. The nature of the auditor's report.

D. The content of the representation letter.

The correct answer is (D). *(CPA, adapted)*

REQUIRED: The least likely factor affecting the quantity and content of an auditor's working papers.

DISCUSSION: The management representation letter reflects management's acceptance of the assertions made in the financial statements. It is used by the auditor to document that understanding.

Answers (A), (B), and (C) are incorrect because AU 339 states that the quantity, type, and content of working papers will depend on (1) the anticipated nature of the auditor's report, (2) the nature of the engagement, (3) the nature of the financial statements, schedules, or other information reported on, (4) the nature and condition of the client's records, (5) the assessed control risk, and (6) the needs for supervision and review of the audit work.

72. Audit working papers are indexed by means of reference numbers. The primary purpose of indexing is to

A. Permit cross-referencing and simplify supervisory review.

B. Support the audit report.

C. Eliminate the need for follow-up reviews.

D. Determine that working papers adequately support findings, conclusions, and reports.

The correct answer is (A). *(CIA, adapted)*

REQUIRED: The primary purpose of indexing.

DISCUSSION: Indexing permits cross-referencing, which is important because it simplifies supervisory review either during the audit or subsequently by creating an audit trail of related items through the working papers. It thus facilitates preparation of the final report, later audits of the same auditee, and peer review.

Answer (B) is incorrect because the working papers as a whole should support the audit report. Answer (C) is incorrect because follow-up is necessitated by the auditee conditions, not the state of working papers. Answer (D) is incorrect because determining that working papers adequately support findings, conclusions, and reports is the purpose of supervisory review.

73. The audit working paper that reflects the major components of an amount reported in the financial statements is the

A. Interbank transfer schedule.

B. Carryforward schedule.

C. Supporting schedule.

D. Lead schedule.

The correct answer is (D). *(CPA, adapted)*

REQUIRED: The working paper that reflects the major components of a financial statement amount.

DISCUSSION: Lead schedules help to eliminate detail from the auditor's working trial balance by classifying and summarizing similar or related items that are contained on the supporting schedules. A lead schedule contains the detailed accounts from the general ledger making up the line item total in the financial statements; e.g., the cash account might consist of petty cash, cash-general, cash-payroll, etc. Lead schedules and other elements of working papers should be cross-referenced.

Answer (A) is incorrect because an interbank transfer schedule is a working paper prepared for several days before and after the period under audit to determine that both parts of these transactions are recorded in the same period and in the appropriate period. Answer (B) is incorrect because a carryforward schedule is a continuing schedule of an account with a balance carried forward in the permanent file. Answer (C) is incorrect because supporting schedules provide details aggregated in the lead schedule.

74. An auditor ordinarily uses a working trial balance resembling the financial statements without footnotes, but containing columns for

A. Cash flow increases and decreases.

B. Audit objectives and assertions.

C. Reclassifications and adjustments.

D. Reconciliations and tickmarks.

The correct answer is (C). *(CPA, adapted)*

REQUIRED: The columns contained on a working trial balance in the auditor's working papers.

DISCUSSION: A working trial balance is ordinarily used to record the year-end ledger balances prior to audit in the auditor's working papers. Reclassifications and adjustments are accumulated on the trial balance to reflect the final audited balances.

Answer (A) is incorrect because cash flow increases or decreases are reflected on the client's statement of cash flows. Answer (B) is incorrect because the audit objectives and tests of management's assertions are determined in the planning stage of the audit and reflected in the working papers. Answer (D) is incorrect because the working trial balance has no column for reconciliations and tickmarks.

75. In the course of the audit of financial statements for the purpose of expressing an opinion thereon, the auditor will normally prepare a schedule of unadjusted differences for which (s)he did not propose adjustment when they were uncovered. The primary purpose served by this schedule is to

A. Point out to the responsible client officials the errors made by various company personnel.

B. Summarize the adjustments that must be made before the company can prepare and submit its federal tax return.

C. Identify the potential financial statement effects of errors or disputed items that were considered immaterial when discovered.

D. Summarize the errors made by the company so that corrections can be made after the audited financial statements are released.

The correct answer is (C). *(CPA, adapted)*

REQUIRED: The purpose of the schedule of unadjusted differences for which the auditor did not propose adjustments.

DISCUSSION: The schedule of unadjusted differences identifies for management and the auditor the potential cumulative financial statement effect of errors or disputed items that were considered immaterial when discovered. The individual unadjusted differences may become material when viewed collectively.

Answer (A) is incorrect because detection of errors by specific employees is not the primary purpose of the schedule. Answer (B) is incorrect because the unadjusted (immaterial) differences normally are not corrected for tax purposes. Answer (D) is incorrect because unadjusted items were judged immaterial and thus do not require correction. If corrections are necessary, i.e., if the collective unadjusted differences are material, the corrections should be made before the financial statements are released.

76. A difference of opinion concerning accounting and auditing matters relative to a particular phase of the audit arises between an assistant auditor and the auditor responsible for the engagement. After appropriate consultation, the assistant auditor asks to be dissociated from the resolution of the matter. The working papers would probably be

A. Silent on the matter because it is an internal matter of the auditing firm.

B. Expanded to note that the assistant auditor is completely dissociated from responsibility for the auditor's opinion.

C. Expanded to document the additional work required because all disagreements of this type will require expanded substantive testing.

D. Expanded to document the assistant auditor's position and the manner in which the difference of opinion was resolved.

The correct answer is (D). *(CPA, adapted)*

REQUIRED: The proper action when the auditor and an assistant have a difference of opinion.

DISCUSSION: AU 311 states that differences of opinion concerning accounting and auditing issues should be documented in the working papers, listing both the details of the disagreement and the basis for the resolution.

Answer (A) is incorrect because GAAS require documentation of the dispute and its resolution. Answer (B) is incorrect because the working papers should document the assistant's position. Answer (C) is incorrect because not all disagreements require expanded testing.

77. An auditor who has accepted an engagement to audit financial statements wishes to review the predecessor's working papers. Such a review is

A. Permitted if the client and the predecessor auditor consent.

B. Permitted if the successor auditor refers in the audit report to the predecessor auditor's report and work.

C. Required if the successor auditor is to express an unqualified opinion.

D. Not permitted because the successor auditor should be independent.

The correct answer is (A). *(Publisher)*

REQUIRED: The appropriate action concerning the review of a predecessor's working papers.

DISCUSSION: AU 315 states that the predecessor customarily makes him/herself available to the successor and makes available for review certain parts of the working papers. However, the successor should request that the client authorize such access to the predecessor's working papers, and the predecessor may want to request a consent and acknowledgment letter from the client to document this authorization. Moreover, the extent, if any, of the access allowed by the predecessor to the working papers is a matter of judgment.

Answer (B) is incorrect because referring to the work of the predecessor auditor as part of the basis for the successor auditor's opinion is an unacceptable practice. Answer (C) is incorrect because the successor is only required to inquire of the predecessor concerning information that will assist the successor in deciding whether to accept the engagement. Answer (D) is incorrect because reviewing the predecessor auditor's working papers is not considered to affect the successor auditor's independence.

78. Which of the following analyses appearing in a predecessor's working papers is the successor auditor least likely to be interested in reviewing?

A. Analysis of noncurrent balance sheet accounts.

B. Analysis of current balance sheet accounts.

C. Analysis of contingencies.

D. Analysis of income statement accounts.

The correct answer is (D). *(CPA, adapted)*

REQUIRED: The analysis from a predecessor's working papers in which a successor would be least interested.

DISCUSSION: The predecessor's analyses of balance sheet accounts, both current and noncurrent, and those relating to contingencies are of primary interest to the successor auditor because the successor must satisfy him/herself as to the reasonableness of the beginning balances. Analyses of income statement accounts are not needed because they have no beginning balances.

Answers (A), (B), and (C) are incorrect because analyses of noncurrent balance sheet accounts, current balance sheet accounts, and contingencies reflect concern about beginning balances.

79. Using microcomputers in auditing may affect the methods used to review the work of staff assistants because

A. The audit field work standards for supervision may differ.

B. Documenting the supervisory review may require assistance of consulting services personnel.

C. Supervisory personnel may not have an understanding of the capabilities and limitations of microcomputers.

D. Working paper documentation may not contain readily observable details of calculations.

The correct answer is (D). *(CPA, adapted)*

REQUIRED: The reason using microcomputers may affect the review of the work of staff assistants.

DISCUSSION: The first standard of field work requires assistants to be properly supervised. Thus, the "work performed by each assistant should be reviewed to determine whether it was adequately performed and to evaluate whether the results are consistent with the conclusions to be presented in the auditor's report" (AU 311). With the introduction of computers, accountants have been able to perform fewer manual calculations. Usually, the necessary numbers are entered into computer spreadsheets, and the answer is produced. Thus, the review of a staff assistant's work performed with a computer is different from that required when calculations are done manually.

Answer (A) is incorrect because the audit field work standards for supervision are the same whether or not a computer is used. Answer (B) is incorrect because audit staff typically have skills appropriate for the use of microcomputers in documenting the work product of the audit. Answer (C) is incorrect because supervisors of the audit staff typically have the skills to evaluate the appropriate use of microcomputers.

80. In an internal audit, the audit supervisor determines that working papers are complete

A. When satisfied that the audit objectives have been met and the working papers support the conclusions.

B. When working papers refer to the steps outlined in the audit program.

C. Only after the auditor who prepared the working papers has signed and dated them.

D. When proper cross-references to other working papers are noted.

The correct answer is (A). *(CIA, adapted)*

REQUIRED: The time when the audit supervisor determines that working papers are complete.

DISCUSSION: The IIA Standard 420 states that working papers "that document the audit should be prepared by the auditor and reviewed by management of the internal auditing department. These papers should record the information obtained and the analyses made and should support the bases for the findings and recommendations to be reported." Hence, they are complete when the audit objectives established at the outset of the planning process have been attained.

Answers (B), (C), and (D) are incorrect because working papers should refer to the steps outlined in the audit program, be signed and dated by the preparer, and be cross-referenced, but are not deemed complete until supervisory review determines that they support the audit report.

81. Standardized working papers are often used, chiefly because they allow working papers to be prepared more

A. Efficiently.

B. Professionally.

C. Neatly.

D. Accurately.

The correct answer is (A). *(CIA, adapted)*

REQUIRED: The reason for standardized working papers.

DISCUSSION: Use of standardized (pro forma) working papers improves audit efficiency by diminishing the time spent in their preparation. For example, standard forms may be developed for the audit program listing, records of the results of interviews, and worksheets.

Answers (B) and (D) are incorrect because standard forms do not necessarily result in greater professionalism or accuracy. Answer (C) is incorrect because standard forms clearly reduce time spent in working paper preparation but do not necessarily result in greater neatness.

82. After field work audit procedures are completed, a partner of the CPA firm who has not been involved in the audit performs a second or wrap-up working paper review. This second review usually focuses on

A. The fair presentation of the financial statements in conformity with GAAP.

B. Fraud involving the client's management and its employees.

C. The materiality of the adjusting entries proposed by the audit staff.

D. The communication of internal control weaknesses to the client's audit committee.

The correct answer is (A). *(CPA, adapted)*

REQUIRED: The purpose of a second review by an audit partner.

DISCUSSION: Analytical procedures are required in an overall review and are typically performed by an audit partner. The purpose of those procedures is to assist the auditor in assessing the conclusions reached and in the evaluation of the overall financial statement presentation (AU 329). If the firm is a member of the SEC Practice Section of the Division for CPA Firms, a concurring review of the audit report and the financial statements is required. The reviewer must be a partner other than the audit partner-in-charge of an SEC engagement.

Answers (B) and (C) are incorrect because fraud involving the client's management and its employees and the materiality of the adjusting entries proposed by the audit staff are matters to be resolved by the audit team. Answer (D) is incorrect because communication of reportable conditions is performed by the supervisor in charge of the audit.

CHAPTER THREE
INTERNAL CONTROL

The AICPA pronouncement on internal control is AU 319, *Consideration of Internal Control in a Financial Statement Audit*. This pronouncement defines concepts and terminology relevant to internal control and the assessment of control risk, including the second standard of field work:

> A sufficient understanding of internal control is to be obtained to plan the audit and to determine the nature, timing, and extent of tests to be performed.

AU 319 incorporates the management assertions model and the audit risk model developed in AU 326, *Evidential Matter*, and AU 312, *Audit Risk and Materiality*, respectively, into the standards on internal control.

AU 319 also incorporates the concepts in the report on internal control issued by the Committee of Sponsoring Organizations (COSO) of the Commission on Fraudulent Financial Reporting. This document, *Internal Control--Integrated Framework*, establishes the definitions of internal control and of the components of internal control that are the basis for those used by the sponsoring organizations (AICPA, The IIA, IMA, AAA, and FEI).

This chapter contains questions on the definitions of the components of internal control relevant to an audit of financial statements, the consideration of that internal control, and the controls relevant to the various accounting cycles.

3.1 Definition and Overview of Internal Control

1. Corporate directors, management, external auditors, and internal auditors all play important roles in creating a proper control environment. Top management is primarily responsible for

A. Establishing a proper environment and specifying overall internal control.

B. Reviewing the reliability and integrity of financial information and the means used to collect and report such information.

C. Ensuring that external and internal auditors adequately monitor the control environment.

D. Implementing and monitoring controls designed by the board of directors.

The correct answer is (A). *(CIA, adapted)*

REQUIRED: The best description of top management's responsibility.

DISCUSSION: According to The IIA's SIAS 1, "Management plans, organizes, and directs in such a fashion as to provide reasonable assurance that established goals and objectives will be achieved." Also, "Management establishes and maintains an environment that fosters control."

Answer (B) is incorrect because internal auditing is responsible for reviewing the reliability and integrity of financial information and the means used to collect and report such information. Answer (C) is incorrect because management cannot delegate its responsibilities for control to auditors. Answer (D) is incorrect because the board has oversight responsibilities but ordinarily does not become involved in the details of operations.

2. Which of the following best describe the interrelated components of internal control?

A. Organizational structure, management philosophy, and planning.

B. Control environment, risk assessment, control activities, information and communication systems, and monitoring.

C. Risk assessment, backup facilities, responsibility accounting, and natural laws.

D. Legal environment of the firm, management philosophy, and organizational structure.

The correct answer is (B). *(CMA, adapted)*

REQUIRED: The components of internal control.

DISCUSSION: Internal control includes five components: the control environment, risk assessment, control activities, information and communication, and monitoring. The control environment sets the tone of an organization, influences control consciousness, and provides a foundation for the other components. Risk assessment is the identification and analysis of relevant risks to achievement of objectives. Control activities help ensure that management directives are executed. Information and communication are the identification, capture, and exchange of information in a form and time frame that allow people to meet their responsibilities. Monitoring assesses the performance of internal control over time (AU 319).

Answer (A) is incorrect because planning is not a component of internal control. Organizational structure and management philosophy are factors in the control environment component. Answer (C) is incorrect because risk assessment is the only component listed. Answer (D) is incorrect because the legal environment of the firm, management philosophy, and organizational structure are factors in the control environment component.

3. As part of understanding internal control, an auditor is not required to

A. Consider factors that affect the risk of material misstatement.

B. Ascertain whether internal control policies and procedures have been placed in operation.

C. Identify the types of potential misstatements that can occur.

D. Obtain knowledge about the operating effectiveness of internal control.

The correct answer is (D). *(CPA, adapted)*

REQUIRED: The step not required in obtaining the understanding of internal control.

DISCUSSION: The understanding is the knowledge of the five components of internal control that the auditor believes is necessary to plan the audit. It should include knowledge about not only the design of relevant controls but also whether they have been placed in operation. The auditor need not obtain knowledge about operating effectiveness as part of the understanding. However, if (s)he wishes to assess control risk at below the maximum level, the auditor must identify controls relevant to specific assertions and perform tests of their effectiveness (AU 319).

Answers (A), (B), and (C) are incorrect because the understanding is used to identify types of potential misstatements, to consider factors affecting the risk of material misstatements, to design substantive tests, and to assure that controls have been placed in operation.

4. In an audit of financial statements, an auditor's primary consideration regarding a control is whether it

A. Reflects management's philosophy and operating style.

B. Affects management's financial statement assertions.

C. Provides adequate safeguards over access to assets.

D. Enhances management's decision-making processes.

The correct answer is (B). *(CPA, adapted)*

REQUIRED: The primary audit consideration regarding a control.

DISCUSSION: An auditor's primary concern is to gather sufficient competent evidence to afford a reasonable basis for expressing an opinion on the financial statements. Audit evidence is obtained by performing audit procedures. These procedures are selected to achieve specific audit objectives. In turn, the objectives are determined in the light of management's financial statement assertions. Thus, the auditor is primarily concerned with whether a control affects financial statement assertions.

Answers (A), (C), and (D) are incorrect because management's philosophy and operating style, adequate safeguards over access to assets, and management's decision-making processes are important but not primary considerations in an audit of financial statements.

5. According to AU 319, after obtaining a sufficient understanding of internal control, the auditor assesses

A. The need to apply GAAS.

B. Detection risk to determine the acceptable level of inherent risk.

C. Detection risk and inherent risk to determine the acceptable level of control risk.

D. Control risk to determine the acceptable level of detection risk.

The correct answer is (D). *(Publisher)*

REQUIRED: The step that follows obtaining the understanding.

DISCUSSION: The acceptable level of detection risk is a function of the assessed levels of inherent risk and control risk. Hence, as the latter increase, the acceptable level of detection risk decreases.

Answer (A) is incorrect because GAAS must be applied in all financial statement audits. Answer (B) is incorrect because inherent risk and control risk, which depend on the entity's unique circumstances and not the auditor's procedures, must both be assessed to calculate the acceptable detection risk. Answer (C) is incorrect because the acceptable detection risk is a function of the assessments of inherent risk and control risk.

6. Which of the following are considered control environment factors?

	Detection Risk	Personnel Policies and Practices
A.	Yes	Yes
B.	Yes	No
C.	No	Yes
D.	No	No

The correct answer is (C). *(CPA, adapted)*

REQUIRED: The factor(s), if any, considered to be part of the control environment.

DISCUSSION: Human resource policies and practices are part of the control environment. They relate to hiring, orientation, training, evaluating, counseling, promoting, compensating, and remedial actions. The control environment is the component that sets the tone of an organization, influencing the control consciousness of its people. It is the foundation for the other components.

Answers (A), (B), and (D) are incorrect because human resource policies and practices are part of the control environment, but detection risk is not. It is the risk that the audit procedures will fail to detect material misstatements. Thus, detection risk is a function of the effectiveness of the procedures used by the auditor.

7. Internal control cannot be designed to provide reasonable assurance regarding the achievement of objectives concerning

A. Reliability of financial reporting.

B. Elimination of all fraud.

C. Compliance with applicable laws and regulations.

D. Effectiveness and efficiency of operations.

The correct answer is (B). *(Publisher)*

REQUIRED: The objective internal control cannot achieve.

DISCUSSION: Internal control is a process designed to provide reasonable assurance regarding the achievement of organizational objectives. Because of inherent limitations, however, no system can be designed to eliminate all fraud.

Answers (A), (C), and (D) are incorrect because internal control can provide reasonable assurance regarding reliability of financial reporting, compliance with applicable laws and regulations, and effectiveness and efficiency of operations.

8. Control activities constitute one of the five components of internal control. Control activities do not encompass

A. Performance reviews.

B. Information processing.

C. Physical controls.

D. An internal auditing function.

The correct answer is (D). *(Publisher)*

REQUIRED: The item not belonging to the control activities component.

DISCUSSION: Control activities are policies and procedures that help ensure that management directives are carried out. They are intended to ensure that necessary actions are taken to address risks to achieve the entity's objectives. Control activities have various objectives and are applied at various organizational and functional levels. However, an internal auditing function is part of the monitoring component.

Answers (A), (B), and (C) are incorrect because performance reviews, information processing, and physical controls are categories of control activities.

9. Monitoring is an important component of internal control. Which of the following items would not be an example of monitoring?

A. Management regularly compares divisional performance with budgets for the division.

B. Data processing management regularly generates exception reports for unusual transactions or volumes of transactions and follows up with investigation as to causes.

C. Data processing management regularly reconciles batch control totals for items processed with batch controls for items submitted.

D. Management has asked internal auditing to perform regular audits of the controls over cash processing.

The correct answer is (C). *(CIA, adapted)*

REQUIRED: The item not an example of monitoring.

DISCUSSION: Monitoring assesses the quality of internal control over time. Management considers whether internal control is properly designed and operating as intended and modifies it to reflect changing conditions. Monitoring may be in the form of separate, periodic evaluations or of ongoing monitoring. Ongoing monitoring occurs as part of routine operations. It includes management and supervisory review, comparisons, reconciliations, and other actions by personnel as part of their regular activities. However, reconciling batch control totals is a processing control.

Answer (A) is incorrect because budgetary comparison is a typical example of a monitoring control. Answer (B) is incorrect because investigation of exceptions is a monitoring control used by lower-level management to determine when their operations may be out of control. Answer (D) is incorrect because internal auditing is a form of monitoring. It serves to evaluate management's other controls.

10. Effective internal control

A. Reduces the need for management to review exception reports on a day-to-day basis.

B. Eliminates risk and potential loss to the organization.

C. Cannot be circumvented by management.

D. Is unaffected by changing circumstances and conditions encountered by the organization.

The correct answer is (A). *(CIA, adapted)*

REQUIRED: The service provided by effective control.

DISCUSSION: The need for management to spend time on a day-to-day basis reviewing exception reports is reduced when internal control is working effectively. An effective internal control should prevent as well as detect exceptions.

Answer (B) is incorrect because some risks are unavoidable and others can be eliminated only at excessive costs. Answer (C) is incorrect because the potential for management override is a basic limitation of internal control. Answer (D) is incorrect because controls should be modified as appropriate for changes in conditions.

11. One of the auditor's major concerns is to ascertain whether internal control is designed to provide reasonable assurance that

A. Profit margins are maximized, and operational efficiency is optimized.

B. The chief accounting officer reviews all accounting transactions.

C. Corporate morale problems are addressed immediately and effectively.

D. Financial statements are fairly presented.

The correct answer is (D). *(CMA, adapted)*

REQUIRED: The objective of internal control.

DISCUSSION: Controls relevant to an audit ordinarily pertain to the objective of preparing external financial statements that are fairly presented in conformity with GAAP or another comprehensive basis of accounting (AU 319).

Answer (A) is incorrect because many factors beyond the purview of the auditor affect profits, and the controls related to operational efficiency are usually not directly relevant to an audit. Answer (B) is incorrect because the chief accounting officer need not review all accounting transactions. Answer (C) is incorrect because controls relevant to a financial statement audit do not concern the treatment of corporate morale problems.

12. A reason to establish internal control is to

A. Safeguard the resources of the organization.

B. Provide reasonable assurance that the objectives of the organization are achieved.

C. Encourage compliance with organizational objectives.

D. Ensure the accuracy, reliability, and timeliness of information.

The correct answer is (B). *(Publisher)*

REQUIRED: The reason to establish internal control.

DISCUSSION: According to AU 319, "Internal control is a process, effected by an entity's board of directors, management, and other personnel, designed to provide reasonable assurance regarding the achievement of objectives in the following categories: reliability of financial reporting, effectiveness and efficiency of operations, and compliance with applicable laws and regulations."

Answers (A), (C), and (D) are incorrect because safeguarding resources, encouraging compliance with management's intentions, and ensuring the accuracy, reliability, and timeliness of information are subsumed under the overall purpose of providing reasonable assurance that the objectives of the organization are achieved.

13. Internal control is a function of management, and effective control is based upon the concept of charge and discharge of responsibility and duty. Which of the following is one of the overriding principles of internal control?

A. Responsibility for accounting and financial duties should be assigned to one responsible officer.

B. Responsibility for the performance of each duty must be fixed.

C. Responsibility for the accounting duties must be borne by the audit committee.

D. Responsibility for accounting must be assigned only to bonded employees.

The correct answer is (B). *(CPA, adapted)*

REQUIRED: The principle of internal control.

DISCUSSION: Effective internal control may be obtained by decentralization of responsibilities and duties. Fixing the responsibility for each performance or duty makes it easier to trace problems to the person(s) responsible and hold them accountable for their actions.

Answer (A) is incorrect because accounting (record keeping) should be separated from finance (asset custody). Answer (C) is incorrect because the audit committee is responsible for overseeing the internal and external audits, not for accounting duties. Answer (D) is incorrect because bonding is not an overriding internal control principle. Employees having custodial, rather than accounting, responsibility are usually bonded.

14. When an organization has strong internal control, management can expect various benefits. The benefit least likely to occur is

A. Reduced cost of an external audit.

B. Elimination of employee fraud.

C. Availability of reliable data for decision-making purposes and protection of important documents and records.

D. Some assurance of compliance with the Foreign Corrupt Practices Act of 1977.

The correct answer is (B). *(CMA, adapted)*

REQUIRED: The least likely benefit of internal control.

DISCUSSION: Even the best internal control cannot guarantee the complete elimination of employee fraud. A strong system will reduce the risk of employee fraud and probably detect losses on a timely basis.

Answer (A) is incorrect because a lower level of control risk permits the auditor to accept a higher level of detection risk and thus to reduce substantive tests. Answer (C) is incorrect because a benefit of strong internal control is that management will have better data for decision-making purposes. The physical safety of important documents and records is also assured. Answer (D) is incorrect because strong internal control provides some assurance of compliance with the FCPA.

15. Which of the following is an example of a detective control in a management information system (MIS)?

A. Automated reports to management that specifically identify delinquent receivables.

B. A requirement for salaried employees to submit a separate request to work overtime.

C. Assurance to top management that computer centers are kept locked.

D. The employment of trustworthy, competent people to enter data into the data processing system.

The correct answer is (A). *(CIA, adapted)*

REQUIRED: The detective control within an MIS.

DISCUSSION: Detective controls measure the effectiveness of preventive controls. Review of delinquent receivables will aid management in detecting those accounts that should be investigated further.

Answer (B) is incorrect because a requirement for salaried employees to submit a separate request to work overtime is a preventive control, which is a precautionary step taken to avoid errors and other potential problems, including wrongdoing. Answer (C) is incorrect because assurance to top management that computer centers are kept locked is a preventive control. Answer (D) is incorrect because the employment of trustworthy, competent people to enter data into the data processing system is a preventive control.

16. Internal controls may be preventive, detective, or corrective. Which of the following is preventive?

A. Requiring two persons to open mail.

B. Reconciling the accounts receivable subsidiary file with the control account.

C. Using batch totals.

D. Preparing bank reconciliations.

The correct answer is (A). *(Publisher)*

REQUIRED: The internal control that is preventive.

DISCUSSION: Preventive controls are designed to prevent errors or fraud. Detective and corrective controls attempt to identify and correct errors or fraud that have already occurred. Preventive controls are usually more cost beneficial than detective or corrective controls. Assigning two individuals to open mail is an attempt to prevent misstatement of cash receipts.

Answer (B) is incorrect because reconciling the subsidiary file with the master file may detect and lead to the correction of errors, but the control does not prevent errors. Answer (C) is incorrect because the use of batch totals may detect a missing or lost document but will not necessarily prevent a document from becoming lost. Answer (D) is incorrect because bank reconciliations disclose errors in the accounts but have no preventive effect.

17. Which of the following statements about internal control is correct?

A. Properly maintained internal control reasonably ensures that collusion among employees cannot occur.

B. The establishment and maintenance of internal control are important responsibilities of the internal auditor.

C. Exceptionally strong internal control is enough for the auditor to eliminate substantive tests on a significant account balance.

D. The cost-benefit relationship is a primary criterion that should be considered in designing internal control.

The correct answer is (D). *(CPA, adapted)*

REQUIRED: The true statement about internal control.

DISCUSSION: The cost of a control should not exceed its benefits. Although the cost-benefit relationship is a primary criterion in designing internal control, precise measurement of costs and benefits is usually impossible, and management makes both quantitative and qualitative estimates and judgments in evaluating the relationship (AU 319).

Answer (A) is incorrect because collusion is an inherent limitation of internal control. Answer (B) is incorrect because establishment and maintenance of internal control are responsibilities of management. Answer (C) is incorrect because control risk ordinarily cannot be so low as to eliminate the need for substantive tests to restrict detection risk for all assertions related to significant account balances and classes of transactions.

18. Internal controls are designed to provide reasonable assurance that

A. Material errors or fraud will be prevented or detected and corrected within a timely period by employees in the course of performing their assigned duties.

B. Management's plans have not been circumvented by worker collusion.

C. The internal auditing department's guidance and oversight of management's performance is accomplished economically and efficiently.

D. Management's planning, organizing, and directing processes are properly evaluated.

The correct answer is (A). *(CIA, adapted)*

REQUIRED: The purpose of internal controls.

DISCUSSION: Cost-effective controls should restrict deviations to a tolerable rate. Thus, material errors and improper or illegal acts should be prevented or detected and corrected within a timely period by employees in the normal course of performing their assigned duties. Accordingly, the cost-benefit relationship is considered by management during the design of systems, and the potential loss associated with any exposure or risk is weighed against the cost to control it.

Answer (B) is incorrect because collusion is an inherent limitation of internal control. Answer (C) is incorrect because the board of directors or a similar body is responsible for the guidance and oversight of management. Answer (D) is incorrect because the examination and evaluation of management processes is a function of the internal auditing department.

3.2 Purpose of the Auditor's Consideration of Internal Control

19. The primary objective of procedures performed to obtain an understanding of internal control is to provide an auditor with

A. Evidence to use in reducing detection risk.

B. Knowledge necessary to plan the audit.

C. A basis for modifying tests of controls.

D. Information necessary to prepare flowcharts.

The correct answer is (B). *(CPA, adapted)*

REQUIRED: The primary objective of procedures to obtain an understanding of internal control.

DISCUSSION: The second standard of field work states, "A sufficient understanding of internal control is to be obtained to plan the audit and to determine the nature, timing, and extent of tests to be performed."

Answer (A) is incorrect because the understanding is primarily directed toward audit planning. Substantive testing is concerned with gathering evidence to reduce detection risk to an acceptable level. Answer (C) is incorrect because the understanding is the basis for determining the nature, timing, and extent of both substantive tests and tests of controls. Answer (D) is incorrect because flowcharts are but one part of the documentation of the understanding.

20. The ultimate purpose of assessing control risk is to contribute to the auditor's evaluation of the risk that

A. Tests of controls may fail to identify controls relevant to assertions.

B. Material misstatements may exist in the financial statements.

C. Specified controls requiring segregation of duties may be circumvented by collusion.

D. Entity policies may be overridden by senior management.

The correct answer is (B). *(CPA, adapted)*

REQUIRED: The purpose of assessing control risk.

DISCUSSION: "The ultimate purpose of assessing control risk is to contribute to the auditor's evaluation of the risk that material misstatements exist in the financial statements" (AU 319).

Answer (A) is incorrect because tests of controls are performed when the auditor wishes to assess control risk at below the maximum. An auditor must identify controls relevant to specific assertions before testing such controls. Answers (C) and (D) are incorrect because collusion and management override are inherent limitations of internal control.

21. Firms subject to the reporting requirements of the Securities Exchange Act of 1934 are required by the Foreign Corrupt Practices Act of 1977 to maintain satisfactory internal control. The role of the independent auditor relative to this act is to

A. Report clients with unsatisfactory internal control to the SEC.

B. Provide assurances to users as part of the traditional audit attest function that the client is in compliance with the present legislation.

C. Express an opinion on the sufficiency of the client's internal control to meet the requirements of the act.

D. Attest to the financial statements.

The correct answer is (D). *(Publisher)*

REQUIRED: The role of the independent auditor relative to the Foreign Corrupt Practices Act (FCPA).

DISCUSSION: Whether a client is in conformity with the FCPA is a legal question. Auditors cannot be expected to provide legal advice. The role of the auditor is to assess control risk in the course of an engagement to attest to the fair presentation of the financial statements.

Answer (A) is incorrect because there is no requirement that the auditor report violations of the act to the SEC, although a duty to disclose outside the client may exist in some circumstances; e.g., the client's failure to take remedial action regarding an illegal act may constitute a disagreement that it must report on Form 8-K (AU 317). Answer (B) is incorrect because the traditional attest function does not involve compliance auditing. Answer (C) is incorrect because the FCPA contains no requirement that an auditor express an opinion on internal control.

22. The requirement of the Foreign Corrupt Practices Act of 1977 to devise and maintain adequate internal control is assigned in the act to the

A. Chief financial officer.

B. Board of directors.

C. Director of internal auditing.

D. Company as a whole with no designation of specific persons or positions.

The correct answer is (D). *(CMA, adapted)*

REQUIRED: The person in a company responsible for compliance with the FCPA.

DISCUSSION: The accounting requirements apply to all public companies that must register under the Securities Exchange Act of 1934. The responsibility is thus placed on companies, not individuals.

Answers (A), (B), and (C) are incorrect because compliance with the FCPA is not the specific responsibility of the chief financial officer, the board of directors, or the director of internal auditing.

23. A CPA's consideration of internal control in a financial statement audit

A. Is usually more limited than that made in connection with an engagement to report on management's written assertion as to the effectiveness of internal control.

B. Is usually more extensive than that made in connection with an engagement to report on management's written assertion as to the effectiveness of internal control.

C. Will usually be identical to that made in connection with an engagement to report on management's written assertion as to the effectiveness of internal control.

D. Will usually result in a report on management's written assertion as to the effectiveness of internal control.

The correct answer is (A). *(CPA, adapted)*

REQUIRED: The scope of the consideration of internal control in an audit.

DISCUSSION: The scope of the consideration of internal control in an audit is usually less than that in an engagement to report on management's written assertion as to the effectiveness of internal control. The auditor must test controls in such an engagement. In the consideration of internal control during an audit, the auditor may not test controls if (s)he assesses control risk for the related assertions at the maximum level.

Answers (B) and (C) are incorrect because the evaluation procedures are more extensive in an engagement to report on management's written assertion as to the effectiveness of internal control. Answer (D) is incorrect because an audit does not result in a report on management's written assertion as to the effectiveness of internal control unless the requirements of an engagement for that purpose are also met.

24. A proper understanding of the client's internal control is an integral part of the audit planning process. The results of the understanding

A. Must be reported to the shareholders and the SEC.

B. Bear no relationship to the extent of substantive testing to be performed.

C. Are not reported to client management.

D. May be used as the basis for withdrawing from an audit engagement.

The correct answer is (D). *(CMA, adapted)*

REQUIRED: The true statement about the results of an understanding of a client's internal control.

DISCUSSION: The second standard of field work requires that the independent auditor obtain a sufficient understanding of internal control to plan the audit and determine the nature, timing, and extent of tests. This understanding may raise doubts about the auditability of the financial statements. Concerns about the nature and extent of the entity's records may cause the auditor to conclude that sufficient evidence for an opinion will not be available (AU 319).

Answer (A) is incorrect because the results are normally not required to be reported externally. Answer (B) is incorrect because the consideration of internal control determines the extent of audit testing. Answer (C) is incorrect because gaining an understanding may result in discovery of reportable conditions (AU 325).

25. A secondary result of the auditor's consideration of internal control is that the consideration may

A. Provide a basis for determining the nature, timing, and extent of audit tests.

B. Assure that management's procedures to detect irregularities are properly functioning.

C. Bring to the auditor's attention possible reportable conditions.

D. Develop evidence to support the assessed level of control risk.

The correct answer is (C). *(CPA, adapted)*

REQUIRED: The secondary result of considering internal control.

DISCUSSION: The auditor is not required to search for reportable conditions, which are significant deficiencies in the design or operation of internal control that could adversely affect the organization's ability to record, process, summarize, and report financial data consistent with the financial statement assertions. However, the auditor may become aware of reportable conditions during the audit. Reportable conditions must be communicated to the audit committee or its equivalent (AU 325).

Answer (A) is incorrect because the auditor is required to consider internal control to plan the audit. Answer (B) is incorrect because obtaining evidence to provide assurance about the proper functioning of the client's internal control is necessary to document an assessment of control risk below the maximum level. Answer (D) is incorrect because gathering evidence to support the assessed level of control risk is required during the consideration of internal control.

3.3 Concepts and Characteristics of Internal Control

26. Which of the following most likely would not be considered an inherent limitation of the potential effectiveness of an entity's internal control?

A. Incompatible duties.

B. Management override.

C. Mistakes in judgment.

D. Collusion among employees.

The correct answer is (A). *(CPA, adapted)*

REQUIRED: The item not considered an inherent limitation of internal control.

DISCUSSION: AU 319 lists the inherent limitations of internal control. The performance of incompatible functions, however, is a failure to separate duties properly, not an inevitable limitation on internal control. The segregation of functional responsibilities is an important category of control activities.

Answer (B) is incorrect because management establishes controls. Thus, it can override those policies and procedures. Answer (C) is incorrect because judgment in decision making can be faulty, and control may break down as a result of simple error or mistake. Answer (D) is incorrect because controls based on segregation of duties may be circumvented by collusion among employees.

27. Internal control can provide only reasonable assurance of achieving entity control objectives. One factor limiting the likelihood of achieving those objectives is that

A. The auditor's primary responsibility is the detection of fraud.

B. The board of directors is active and independent.

C. The cost of internal control should not exceed its benefits.

D. Management monitors internal control.

The correct answer is (C). *(Publisher)*

REQUIRED: The true statement about the limitation of internal control.

DISCUSSION: AU 319 states, "Another limiting factor is that the cost of an entity's internal control should not exceed the benefits that are expected to be derived. Although the cost-benefit relationship is a primary criterion that should be considered in designing internal control, the precise measurement of costs and benefits usually is not possible."

Answer (A) is incorrect because the auditor's responsibility is "to plan and perform the audit to obtain reasonable assurance about whether the financial statements are free of material misstatement, whether caused by error or fraud" (AU 110). Answer (B) is incorrect because an active and independent board strengthens the control environment. Answer (D) is incorrect because monitoring strengthens internal control.

28. An entity should consider the cost of a control in relationship to the risk. Which of the following controls best reflects this philosophy for a large dollar investment in heavy machine tools?

A. Conducting a weekly physical inventory.

B. Placing security guards at every entrance 24 hours a day.

C. Imprinting a controlled identification number on each tool.

D. Having all dispositions approved by the vice president of sales.

The correct answer is (C). *(Publisher)*

REQUIRED: The control appropriate for a large dollar investment in heavy machine tools.

DISCUSSION: A controlled identification number on each tool and periodic checking allow for an effective control at reasonable cost.

Answer (A) is incorrect because the cost of weekly inventories would likely outweigh the benefits derived. Answer (B) is incorrect because the cost of 24-hour guards would likely outweigh the benefits derived. Answer (D) is incorrect because, although the disposition of assets should be approved, the vice president of sales, who is not familiar with the heavy equipment, would not be the appropriate officer to provide the authorization.

29. The internal auditor recognizes that certain limitations are inherent in any internal control system. Which one of the following scenarios is the result of an inherent limitation of internal control?

A. The comptroller both makes and records cash deposits.

B. A security guard allows one of the warehouse employees to remove company assets from the premises without authorization.

C. The firm sells to customers on account, without credit approval.

D. An employee, who is unable to read, is assigned custody of the firm's computer tape library and run manuals that are used during the third shift.

The correct answer is (B). *(CIA, adapted)*

REQUIRED: The scenario that is the result of an inherent limitation of internal control.

DISCUSSION: Inherent limitations of internal control arise from faulty judgment in decision making, simple error or mistake, and the possibility of collusion and management override (AU 319). Thus, a control (use of security guards) based on segregation of functions may be overcome by collusion among two or more employees.

Answer (A) is incorrect because failure to segregate the functions of recording and asset custody is an avoidable condition. Answer (C) is incorrect because transactions can and should be authorized before execution. Answer (D) is incorrect because assignment of an unqualified employee is an avoidable, not an inherent, control weakness.

30. Regardless of the assessed level of control risk, an auditor would perform some

A. Tests of controls to determine their effectiveness.

B. Analytical procedures to verify the design of controls.

C. Substantive tests to restrict detection risk for significant transaction classes.

D. Dual-purpose tests to evaluate both the risk of monetary misstatement and preliminary control risk.

The correct answer is (C). *(CPA, adapted)*

REQUIRED: The procedures performed regardless of the assessed level of control risk.

DISCUSSION: AU 319 states, "Although the inverse relationship between control risk and detection risk may permit the auditor to change the nature or the timing of substantive tests or limit their extent, ordinarily the assessed level of control risk cannot be sufficiently low to eliminate the need to perform any substantive tests to restrict detection risk for all of the assertions relevant to significant account balances or transaction classes."

Answers (A), (B), and (D) are incorrect because, if control risk is assessed at the maximum, no tests of controls need be performed.

31. Control activities include procedures that pertain to physical controls over access to and use of assets and records. A departure from the purpose of such procedures is that

A. Access to the safe-deposit box requires two officers.

B. Only storeroom personnel and line supervisors have access to the raw materials storeroom.

C. The mail clerk compiles a list of the checks received in the incoming mail.

D. Only salespersons and sales supervisors use sales department vehicles.

The correct answer is (B). *(Publisher)*

REQUIRED: The departure from the purpose of control activities that limit access to assets.

DISCUSSION: Storeroom personnel have custody of assets, while supervisors are in charge of execution functions. To give supervisors access to the raw materials storeroom is a violation of the essential internal control principle of segregation of functions.

Answer (A) is incorrect because it is appropriate for two officers to be required to open the safe-deposit box. One supervises the other. Answer (C) is incorrect because mail room clerks typically compile a prelisting of cash. The list is sent to the accountant as a control for actual cash sent to the cashier. Answer (D) is incorrect because use of sales department vehicles should be limited to sales personnel unless proper authorization is obtained.

32. Basic to a proper control environment are the quality and integrity of personnel who must perform the prescribed procedures. Which is not a factor in providing for competent personnel?

A. Segregation of duties.

B. Hiring practices.

C. Training programs.

D. Performance evaluations.

The correct answer is (A). *(Publisher)*

REQUIRED: The factor not related to competence of personnel.

DISCUSSION: Human resource policies and practices are a factor in the control environment component of internal control. They affect the entity's ability to employ sufficient competent personnel to accomplish its objectives. Policies and practices include those for hiring, orientation, training, evaluating, promoting, compensating, and remedial actions. Although control activities based on the segregation of duties are important to internal control, they do not in themselves promote employee competence.

Answer (B) is incorrect because effective hiring practices result in selection of competent employees. Answer (C) is incorrect because effective training programs increase the competence of employees. Answer (D) is incorrect because performance evaluations improve competence by identifying substandard work and by serving as a basis for rewarding exceptional efforts.

33. Proper segregation of duties reduces the opportunities for persons to be in positions to both

A. Journalize entries and prepare financial statements.

B. Record cash receipts and cash disbursements.

C. Establish internal control and authorize transactions.

D. Perpetrate and conceal errors or fraud.

The correct answer is (D). *(CPA, adapted)*

REQUIRED: The effects of the segregation of duties and responsibilities.

DISCUSSION: Proper segregation of duties and responsibilities reduces the opportunity for an individual to both perpetrate and conceal an error or fraud in the normal course of his/her duties. Hence, different people should be assigned the responsibilities for authorizing transactions, record keeping, and asset custody.

Answer (A) is incorrect because accountants typically journalize entries and prepare financial statements. Answer (B) is incorrect because accountants may record both cash receipts and cash disbursements as long as they do not have custody of the cash. Answer (C) is incorrect because management establishes internal control and ultimately has the responsibility to authorize transactions.

34. Management's aggressive attitude toward financial reporting and its emphasis on meeting projected profit goals most likely would significantly influence an entity's control environment when

A. The audit committee is active in overseeing the entity's financial reporting policies.

B. External policies established by parties outside the entity affect its accounting practices.

C. Management is dominated by one individual who is also a shareholder.

D. Internal auditors have direct access to the board of directors and entity management.

The correct answer is (C). *(CPA, adapted)*

REQUIRED: The instance in which management's attitudes would most likely affect an entity's control environment.

DISCUSSION: Management philosophy and operating style is one factor affecting the control environment. Such characteristics as management's attitudes and actions toward financial reporting and its emphasis on meeting budget, profit, and other goals have a significant influence on the control environment, especially when management is dominated by one or a few individuals.

Answers (A), (B), and (D) are incorrect because an active audit committee, external influences, and an effective internal audit function serve to mitigate the risks associated with certain management attitudes.

35. Transaction authorization within an organization may be either specific or general. An example of specific transaction authorization is the

A. Setting of automatic reorder points for material or merchandise.

B. Approval of a detailed construction budget for a warehouse.

C. Establishment of requirements to be met in determining a customer's credit limits.

D. Establishment of sales prices for products to be sold to any customer.

The correct answer is (B). *(CPA, adapted)*

REQUIRED: The example of a specific transaction authorization.

DISCUSSION: A specific transaction authorization is applicable to a unique decision. A general authorization establishes criteria and authorizes the routine making of decisions subject to the criteria. Approving a detailed construction budget for a warehouse is a one-time decision.

Answer (A) is incorrect because setting of automatic reorder points for material or merchandise is a general transaction authorization. Answer (C) is incorrect because establishment of requirements to be met in determining a customer's credit limits is a general transaction authorization. Answer (D) is incorrect because establishment of sales prices for products to be sold to any customer is a general transaction authorization.

36. It is important for the auditor to consider the competence of the audit client's employees, because their competence bears directly and importantly upon the

A. Cost-benefit relationship of internal control.

B. Achievement of the objectives of internal control.

C. Comparison of recorded accountability with assets.

D. Timing of the tests to be performed.

The correct answer is (B). *(CPA, adapted)*

REQUIRED: The reason an auditor must consider the competence of employees.

DISCUSSION: Human resource policies and practices are a factor in the control environment component of internal control. For example, standards for hiring the most qualified individuals demonstrate a commitment to competent and trustworthy people. Human resource policies and practices concern hiring, orientation, training, evaluating, counseling, promoting, compensating, and remedial actions. Without sufficient competent employees, the auditee cannot achieve the objectives of internal control.

Answer (A) is incorrect because the cost-benefit relationship of the control system is a basic concept of internal control. Answer (C) is incorrect because comparison of recorded accountability with assets is an essential characteristic of internal control but is not directly related to the competence of employees. Answer (D) is incorrect because the timing of particular tests is dependent on such factors as the convenience of the auditor and client and the need for applying certain tests concurrently.

37. A proper segregation of duties requires

A. That an individual authorizing a transaction records it.

B. That an individual authorizing a transaction maintain custody of the asset that resulted from the transaction.

C. That an individual maintaining custody of an asset be entitled to access the accounting records for the asset.

D. That an individual recording a transaction not compare the accounting record of the asset with the asset itself.

The correct answer is (D). *(CMA, adapted)*

REQUIRED: The item required by proper segregation of duties.

DISCUSSION: One person should not be responsible for all phases of a transaction, i.e., for authorization, recording, and custodianship of the related assets. These duties should be performed by separate individuals to reduce the opportunities for any person to be in a position of both perpetrating and concealing errors or fraud in the normal course of his/her duties. For instance, an employee who receives and lists cash receipts should not be responsible for comparing the recorded accountability for cash with existing amounts.

Answer (A) is incorrect because authorization and record keeping should be separate. Answer (B) is incorrect because authorization and asset custody should be separate. Answer (C) is incorrect because record keeping and asset custody should be separate.

38. If internal control is properly designed, the same employee may be permitted to

A. Receive and deposit checks and also approve write-offs of customer accounts.

B. Approve vouchers for payment and also sign checks.

C. Reconcile the bank statements and also receive and deposit cash.

D. Sign checks and also cancel supporting documents.

The correct answer is (D). *(CPA, adapted)*

REQUIRED: The duties that are not incompatible with effective control.

DISCUSSION: Checks for disbursements should be signed by an officer, normally the treasurer, after necessary supporting evidence has been examined. The documentation typically consists of a voucher, a purchase order, a receiving report, and a vendor invoice. Canceling vouchers and supporting papers (with perforations, ink, etc.) upon payment of the voucher prevents the payment of a duplicate voucher. If the person signing the check cancels the documents, they cannot be recycled for duplicate payments.

Answer (A) is incorrect because authorization of transactions (write-offs of receivables) and custody of assets (checks) are incompatible duties. Answer (B) is incorrect because authorization (voucher approval) and custody of assets (checks) are incompatible functions. Answer (C) is incorrect because record keeping (reconciling the bank statements) and custody of cash are incompatible.

39. For effective internal control, which of the following functions should not be the responsibility of the treasurer's department?

A. Computer information processing.

B. Handling of cash.

C. Custody of securities.

D. Establishing credit policies.

The correct answer is (A). *(CPA, adapted)*

REQUIRED: The function that should not be the responsibility of the treasurer.

DISCUSSION: The treasurer performs the custodianship function. For a proper segregation of functions, the treasurer should not perform a recording function such as computer information processing.

Answer (B) is incorrect because the treasurer should have custody of liquid assets, such as cash. Answer (C) is incorrect because the treasurer should have custody of liquid assets, such as securities. Answer (D) is incorrect because the treasurer is responsible for maintaining an adequate level of funds to meet the organization's cash needs and should therefore participate in establishing credit policies.

40. A small entity may use less formal means to ensure that internal control objectives are achieved. For example, extensive accounting procedures, sophisticated accounting records, or formal controls are least likely to be needed if

A. Management is closely involved in operations.

B. The entity is involved in complex transactions.

C. The entity is subject to legal or regulatory requirements also found in larger entities.

D. Financial reporting objectives have been established.

The correct answer is (A). *(Publisher)*

REQUIRED: The situation in which less formal means of achieving control objectives are appropriate.

DISCUSSION: Effective management involvement may obviate the need for more formal means of ensuring that internal control objectives are met. Thus, a smaller entity may not have formal policies regarding credit approval, information security, or competitive bidding. It also may not have a written code of conduct. Instead, a smaller entity may develop a culture emphasizing integrity and ethical behavior through management example. Moreover, an effective control environment may not require outside members on the board. In a small company, less detailed controls are possible when management retains authority for specific authorization of transactions and oversees employees performing incompatible tasks.

Answers (B) and (C) are incorrect because complex transactions and legal or regulatory requirements may necessitate the more formal arrangements found in larger entities. Answer (D) is incorrect because all entities should establish financial reporting objectives. However, they may be recognized implicitly rather than explicitly in smaller entities. Management can assess the risks related to these objectives through direct personal involvement rather than a formal assessment process.

41. The situation most likely to be regarded as a strength in internal control by the external auditor is

A. The performance of financial audits by internal auditors.

B. The performance of operational audits by internal auditors.

C. The routine supervisory review of production planning.

D. The existence of a preventive maintenance program.

The correct answer is (A). *(CMA, adapted)*

REQUIRED: The activity most likely regarded as a strong internal control by the external auditor.

DISCUSSION: Internal auditing examines and evaluates the adequacy and effectiveness of an organization's controls. Its scope of work includes reviewing the reliability and integrity of financial data. The internal auditing function is part of the monitoring component of internal control and therefore may have an important effect on the entity's ability to record, process, summarize, and report financial data.

Answer (B) is incorrect because operational audits are concerned with operational efficiency and effectiveness. Answer (C) is incorrect because routine supervisory review of production planning is a concern of management but does not directly affect the fairness of the financial statements. Answer (D) is incorrect because the existence of a preventive maintenance program is not directly relevant to a financial statement audit.

42. The frequency of the comparison of recorded accountability with assets (for the purpose of safeguarding assets) should be determined by

A. The amount of assets independent of the cost of the comparison.

B. The nature and amount of the asset and the cost of making the comparison.

C. The cost of the comparison and whether the susceptibility to loss results from errors or fraud.

D. The auditor in consultation with client management.

The correct answer is (B). *(Publisher)*

REQUIRED: The factor(s) determining the frequency of comparing recorded accountability with assets.

DISCUSSION: Assets should be compared with the recorded accountability as frequently as the nature and amount of the assets require, within the limits of acceptable costs of comparison. The costs of safeguarding assets should not exceed the expected benefits.

Answer (A) is incorrect because the costs of controls should be considered when making the comparison. Answer (C) is incorrect because whether the susceptibility to loss arises from errors or fraud should have little bearing on the frequency of the comparison. Answer (D) is incorrect because management, not the auditor, has responsibility for internal control.

43. A company operates its own truck fleet. Rising operating costs have caused the company to reassess its internal control. Which one of the following controls may help to lower operating costs?

A. Preventive maintenance is performed independently of driver-requested maintenance.

B. Each driver has a control card for fuel use at the self-service diesel fuel dock.

C. Maintenance and repair part orders are determined and placed by using an EOQ system.

D. Parts and hand tools must be requisitioned from the parts department.

The correct answer is (B). *(CIA, adapted)*

REQUIRED: The best control to help lower operating costs.

DISCUSSION: Requiring each driver to use a control card will permit the matching of fuel used by each driver with the miles driven. This practice should lower or control fuel (operating) costs as well as create an audit trail as evidence of the incurrence of fuel costs.

Answer (A) is incorrect because a combination of preventive and driver-requested maintenance is more effective. Answer (C) is incorrect because use of an EOQ system for parts orders is an effective control over maintenance rather than operating costs. Answer (D) is incorrect because requiring requisitions for parts is an effective control over maintenance rather than operating costs.

44. An audit of a depository institution discloses the existence of a personal loan to the president of that institution. The loan is both sizable and below market rate. Which of the following is a cost-effective policy that will help prevent a recurrence of this questionable practice?

A. Loans above a nominal dollar level will not be extended to directors or to executives above a specified organizational level.

B. Loans above a nominal dollar level will not be extended to any director or employee.

C. Below-market-rate loans will not be extended to directors or to executives above a specified organizational level.

D. Below-market-rate loans will not be extended under any circumstances.

The correct answer is (A). *(CIA, adapted)*

REQUIRED: The policy that will help prevent a recurrence of an improper loan to an officer of a company.

DISCUSSION: High-ranking officials of an organization may be in a position to exercise undue influence over lower-level employees, for example, by bargaining for a reduced-rate loan in a negotiation that is clearly not at arm's length. A direct prohibition of any loans to high-ranking persons is a simple, cost-effective way of increasing the obstacles to self-serving behavior.

Answer (B) is incorrect because employees who are not in a position to bargain for below-market rates are appropriate institutional customers. Answer (C) is incorrect because not extending below-market-rate loans to directors or to executives above a specified organizational level leaves open the possibility of making loans at marginal rates that are favorable to the executive. Answer (D) is incorrect because not extending below-market-rate loans under any circumstances is neither cost effective nor prudent. Below-market-rate loans may be warranted, e.g., to prevent default.

3.4 Procedures for the Auditor's Consideration of Internal Control

45. When considering internal control in a financial statement audit, the independent external auditor is primarily concerned with

A. Detecting all errors.

B. Determining the effectiveness of operations.

C. Assessing the level of control risk.

D. Determining its efficiency.

The correct answer is (C). *(Publisher)*

REQUIRED: The independent auditor's primary concern in considering internal control.

DISCUSSION: In the consideration of internal control, the external auditor's primary concern is to plan the audit and determine the nature, timing, and extent of tests. This determination is in part dependent on the assessed level of control risk for specific financial statement assertions.

Answer (A) is incorrect because the auditor is concerned with the possibility of material errors and fraud. Answer (B) is incorrect because determining the effectiveness of operations relates to management objectives that normally do not affect the fairness of the financial statements. Answer (D) is incorrect because the assessment of control risk in a financial statement audit is concerned with the effectiveness rather than the efficiency of internal control.

46. The following are steps in the audit process:

I. Prepare flowchart
II. Gather exhibits of all documents
III. Interview personnel

The most logical sequence of steps is

A. I, II, III.

B. I, III, II.

C. III, II, I.

D. II, I, III.

The correct answer is (C). *(CPA, adapted)*

REQUIRED: The order of the steps in the consideration of internal control.

DISCUSSION: AU 319 requires the auditor to gain an understanding of internal control and to document that understanding. For example, after making inquiries (interviewing client personnel), the auditor might gather client documents and then prepare a flowchart reflecting the information obtained about their flow.

Answers (A), (B), and (D) are incorrect because the appropriate sequence is III, II, I.

47. Organizational charts are useful to an independent external auditor because they

A. Depict all lines of organizational communication.

B. Provide a starting point for assessing control risk.

C. Ensure the proper division of responsibilities.

D. Are essential to effective internal control.

The correct answer is (B). *(Publisher)*

REQUIRED: The reason organizational charts are useful.

DISCUSSION: AU 319 identifies the organizational structure as a control environment factor to be considered in understanding internal control. An organizational chart depicts the assignment of authority and responsibility within an organization and is a consideration in evaluating the effectiveness of the organizational structure.

Answer (A) is incorrect because only formal lines of communication are shown on an organizational chart. Answer (C) is incorrect because the organizational chart does not ensure a proper allocation and performance of responsibilities. Answer (D) is incorrect because an organizational chart pictorially describes an entity's purported organization, but it does not in itself provide internal control.

48. In gaining an understanding of internal control, the auditor may trace several transactions through the control process. The primary purpose of this task is to

A. Replace substantive tests.

B. Determine whether the controls have been placed in operation.

C. Determine the effectiveness of the control procedures.

D. Detect fraud.

The correct answer is (B). *(G. Fiebelkorn)*

REQUIRED: The reason an auditor traces several transactions through the control process.

DISCUSSION: The understanding should include knowledge about the design of relevant controls and whether they have been placed in operation. Tracing a few transactions through the control process should provide that evidence.

Answer (A) is incorrect because the auditor must perform at least some substantive testing for all material financial statement assertions. Answer (C) is incorrect because, in gaining the understanding, the auditor need not consider operating effectiveness. If the auditor wishes to assess control risk at below the maximum, (s)he will test controls and evaluate their effectiveness. Answer (D) is incorrect because tracing a few transactions is not likely to detect fraud.

49. Audit evidence concerning segregation of duties ordinarily is best obtained by

A. Performing tests of transactions that corroborate management's financial statement assertions.

B. Observing the employees as they apply specific controls.

C. Obtaining a flowchart of activities performed by available personnel.

D. Developing audit objectives that reduce control risk.

The correct answer is (B). *(CPA, adapted)*

REQUIRED: The best obtainable audit evidence concerning segregation of duties.

DISCUSSION: When documentary evidence does not exist, the auditor may rely on observation and inquiry about the effectiveness of the design or operation of a control, such as segregation of duties. Inquiry alone, however, will not ordinarily provide sufficient evidence to support the conclusion that the control significantly reduces the control risk for a specific assertion. Direct personal observation provides more assurance than inquiries.

Answer (A) is incorrect because tests of transactions to corroborate assertions are substantive tests, not tests of controls. Answer (C) is incorrect because a flowchart does not provide evidence that a control activity has been placed in operation or that it is effective. Answer (D) is incorrect because audit objectives are not audit evidence.

50. When obtaining an understanding of an entity's internal control, an auditor should concentrate on the substance of controls rather than their form because

A. The controls may be operating effectively but may not be documented.

B. Management may establish appropriate controls but not act on them.

C. The controls may be so inappropriate that no reliance is contemplated by the auditor.

D. Management may implement controls with costs in excess of benefits.

The correct answer is (B). *(CPA, adapted)*

REQUIRED: The reason an auditor should concentrate on the substance of controls, not their form.

DISCUSSION: The auditor must concentrate on the substance rather than the form of controls because management may establish controls but not act on them. For example, management may develop a code of conduct but condone violations of the code (AU 319).

Answer (A) is incorrect because an auditor should concentrate on the actual operating effectiveness of controls, not on a lack of evidence about form (documentation). Answer (C) is incorrect because, if controls are so inappropriate that the auditor assesses control risk at the maximum, their substance is irrelevant. Answer (D) is incorrect because, when considering internal control in a financial statement audit, the auditor is primarily concerned with the effectiveness of controls, not their cost-benefit relationship.

51. Which of the following is a step in an auditor's decision to assess control risk at below the maximum?

A. Apply analytical procedures to both financial data and nonfinancial information to detect conditions that may indicate weak controls.

B. Perform tests of details of transactions and account balances to identify potential errors and fraud.

C. Identify specific controls that are likely to detect or prevent material misstatements.

D. Document that the additional audit effort to perform tests of controls exceeds the potential reduction in substantive testing.

The correct answer is (C). *(CPA, adapted)*

REQUIRED: The step necessary to assess control risk at below the maximum.

DISCUSSION: Assessing control risk at below the maximum requires identifying specific controls relevant to specific assertions that are likely to prevent or detect material misstatements. It also entails performing tests of controls to evaluate the effectiveness of such controls (AU 319).

Answers (A) and (B) are incorrect because analytical procedures and tests of details are substantive tests. The auditor must perform tests of controls to assess control risk at below the maximum. Answer (D) is incorrect because, if the effort to perform tests of controls exceeds the potential reduction in substantive testing, assessing control risk at the maximum is justified.

52. Which of the following statements concerning control risk is correct?

A. Assessing control risk and obtaining an understanding of an entity's internal control may be performed concurrently.

B. When control risk is at the maximum level, an auditor is required to document the basis for that assessment.

C. Control risk may be assessed sufficiently low to eliminate substantive testing for significant transaction classes.

D. When assessing control risk, an auditor should not consider evidence obtained in prior audits about the operation of controls.

The correct answer is (A). *(CPA, adapted)*

REQUIRED: The true statement concerning control risk.

DISCUSSION: According to AU 319, assessing control risk and understanding internal control may be performed concurrently. Procedures performed to achieve one objective may also pertain to the other. Moreover, for efficiency reasons, the auditor may plan to test some controls when obtaining the understanding.

Answer (B) is incorrect because the auditor should document the conclusion but need not document the basis for the conclusion that control risk is assessed at the maximum. Answer (C) is incorrect because some substantive tests must always be applied to significant assertions about material account balances or classes of transactions. Answer (D) is incorrect because evidence from previous audits may be considered subject to certain limitations, e.g., evidence obtained currently about changes in internal control.

53. In obtaining an understanding of an entity's internal control in a financial statement audit, an auditor is not obligated to

A. Determine whether the controls have been placed in operation.

B. Perform procedures to understand the design of controls.

C. Document the understanding of the entity's internal control components.

D. Search for significant deficiencies in the operation of internal control.

The correct answer is (D). *(CPA, adapted)*

REQUIRED: The step an auditor need not take in obtaining an understanding of internal control.

DISCUSSION: The auditor should obtain a sufficient understanding of internal control to plan the audit. The understanding includes knowledge about the design of relevant controls and whether they have been placed in operation. In addition, the auditor should document the understanding of the entity's internal control. Though the auditor may become aware of deficiencies in the operation of internal control through gaining the understanding, (s)he is not obligated to search for such deficiencies.

Answers (A), (B), and (C) are incorrect because the auditor should understand the design of controls, determine whether they are in operation, and document the understanding.

54. According to SAS 55 (AU 319), *Consideration of Internal Control in a Financial Statement Audit*, an entity's internal control addresses objectives related to reliability of financial reporting, compliance with applicable laws and regulations, and effectiveness and efficiency of operations. However, not all of these objectives and the related controls are relevant to a financial statement audit. Which one of the following would most likely be considered in an audit?

A. Timely reporting and review of quality control results.

B. Maintenance of control over unused checks.

C. Marketing analysis of sales generated by advertising projects.

D. Maintenance of statistical production analyses.

The correct answer is (B). *(CMA, adapted)*

REQUIRED: The control most likely relevant to a financial statement audit.

DISCUSSION: Ordinarily, controls that are relevant to a financial statement audit pertain to the entity's objective of preparing financial statements for external purposes that are fairly presented in conformity with GAAP or another comprehensive basis of accounting. Maintenance of control over unused checks is an example of a relevant control because the objective is to provide assurance regarding the existence assertion for cash.

Answers (A), (C), and (D) are incorrect because timely reporting and review of quality control results, marketing analysis, and maintenance of statistical production analyses concern the effectiveness, economy, and efficiency of management decision processes that ordinarily do not relate to an entity's ability to present fair financial statements.

55. The information and communication component of internal control includes the methods and records established to record, process, summarize, and report transactions and to maintain accountability. For which of the following transactions would the auditor ordinarily have the greatest difficulty in obtaining assurance that internal control objectives are met?

A. Collection of interest and dividends by a retailer.

B. Acquisition of production equipment by a manufacturer.

C. Collection of contributions from the public by a nonprofit organization.

D. Collection of credit sales by a retailer.

The correct answer is (C). *(Publisher)*

REQUIRED: The transaction for which the auditor would have the greatest difficulty in gaining assurance that control objectives are met.

DISCUSSION: As part of the information and communication component, an accounting system should identify and record all valid transactions, permit their classification and recording at appropriately measured monetary values, determine the proper accounting period in which they should be recorded, and properly present them and related disclosures in the financial statements. Because corroborating documentation is often unavailable for contributions from the general public to a nonprofit organization, determining that these donations were properly accounted for is difficult.

Answers (A), (B), and (D) are incorrect because collection of interest and dividends by a retailer, acquisition of production equipment by a manufacturer, and collection of credit sales by a retailer are transactions for which corroborating evidence (documentation) should be available.

56. Based on a consideration of internal control completed at an interim date, the auditor assessed control risk at a low level and performed interim substantive tests. The records and procedures would most likely be tested again at year-end if

A. Tests of controls were not performed by the internal auditor during the remaining period.

B. Internal control provides a basis for limiting the extent of substantive testing.

C. The auditor used nonstatistical sampling during the interim period testing of controls.

D. Inquiries and observations lead the auditor to believe that conditions have changed.

The correct answer is (D). *(CPA, adapted)*

REQUIRED: The reason for retesting records and procedures at year-end.

DISCUSSION: Rapidly changing business conditions or other circumstances may predispose management to misstate financial statements in the remaining period. The auditor may then conclude that substantive tests covering the remaining period will be ineffective to control the incremental audit risk associated with testing at an interim date. In that case, the auditor should ordinarily decide to examine the relevant accounts as of the balance-sheet date (AU 313).

Answer (A) is incorrect because, by itself, the failure of the internal auditor to test controls during the remaining period does not require a change in audit strategy. Answer (B) is incorrect because a lower assessment of control risk increases the acceptable level of detection risk and decreases the necessary extent of tests. Answer (C) is incorrect because use of nonstatistical methods at the interim date does not necessitate retesting if sufficient competent evidence has been obtained.

57. An independent auditor might consider the procedures performed by the internal auditors because

A. They are employees whose work must be reviewed during substantive testing.

B. They are employees whose work may affect the nature, timing, and extent of audit procedures.

C. Their work affects the cost-benefit trade-off.

D. Their degree of independence may be inferred from the nature of their work.

The correct answer is (B). *(CPA, adapted)*

REQUIRED: The reason an independent auditor might consider the procedures performed by internal auditors.

DISCUSSION: The work of the internal auditors cannot be substituted for the work of the independent auditor; however, the internal auditing function is part of the monitoring component of internal control. Consequently, the independent auditor should obtain an understanding of internal auditing sufficient to identify activities relevant to the audit (AU 322).

Answer (A) is incorrect because the independent auditor should obtain an understanding of internal auditing sufficient to identify activities relevant to the audit during the consideration of internal control. Answer (C) is incorrect because management is responsible for evaluating the cost-benefit relationship. Answer (D) is incorrect because internal auditors are not independent of the entity in the sense required by the *Code of Professional Conduct*.

58. Although substantive tests may support the accuracy of underlying records, these tests frequently provide no affirmative evidence of segregation of duties because

A. Substantive tests rarely guarantee the accuracy of the records if only a sample of the transactions has been tested.

B. The records may be accurate even though they are maintained by a person who performs incompatible functions.

C. Substantive tests relate to the entire period under audit, but tests of controls ordinarily are confined to the period during which the auditor is on the client's premises.

D. Many computerized procedures leave no audit trail of who performed them, so substantive tests may necessarily be limited to inquiries and observation of office personnel.

The correct answer is (B). *(CPA, adapted)*

REQUIRED: The reason substantive tests may provide no affirmative evidence of segregation of duties.

DISCUSSION: Substantive tests, such as reconciliations or confirmations, may provide no affirmative evidence of segregation of duties because the records may be accurate even though maintained by a person who performs incompatible functions; that is, lack of segregation would not be revealed by substantive tests unless the detection of material inaccuracies resulted in performance of additional procedures.

Answer (A) is incorrect because properly applied sampling methods may provide reasonable assurance about the accuracy of records, including a quantification of the sampling risk. Answer (C) is incorrect because tests of the effectiveness of controls are concerned with the consistency of their application during the entire period under audit. Answer (D) is incorrect because, given computerized procedures, the auditor must perform substantive tests by auditing through the computer.

59. After obtaining an understanding of internal control and assessing control risk, an auditor decided not to perform additional tests of controls. The auditor most likely concluded that the

A. Additional evidence to support a further reduction in control risk was not cost-beneficial to obtain.

B. Assessed level of inherent risk exceeded the assessed level of control risk.

C. Internal control was properly designed and justifiably may be relied on.

D. Evidence obtainable through test of controls would not support an increased assessment of control risk.

The correct answer is (A). *(CPA, adapted)*

REQUIRED: The most likely reason the auditor decided not to perform additional tests of controls.

DISCUSSION: After obtaining the understanding of internal control and assessing control risk, the auditor may desire to seek a further reduction in the assessed level of control risk for certain assertions. In such cases, the auditor considers whether additional evidential matter sufficient to support a further reduction is likely to be available, and whether performing tests of controls to obtain that evidential matter is efficient (AU 319).

Answer (B) is incorrect because the assessment of inherent risk is independent of the assessment of control risk. Answer (C) is incorrect because gaining an understanding of internal control, i.e., obtaining knowledge about the design of controls and whether they have been placed in operation, is insufficient to assess control risk below the maximum. Answer (D) is incorrect because the issue is whether additional tests of controls will support a decreased assessment of control risk.

3.5 Tests of Controls

60. After gaining an understanding of internal control, the auditor may attempt to assess control risk at less than the maximum. For this purpose, the auditor should (1) identify specific controls that are likely to prevent or detect material misstatements in the relevant financial statement assertions and (2) perform tests of controls. The purpose of these tests is to

A. Assure that the auditor has an adequate understanding of internal control.

B. Evaluate the effectiveness of such controls.

C. Provide recommendations to management to improve internal control.

D. Evaluate inherent risk.

The correct answer is (B). *(Publisher)*

REQUIRED: The purpose of tests of controls.

DISCUSSION: The purpose of tests of controls is to evaluate the effectiveness of the design or operation of controls in preventing or detecting material misstatements. The auditor tests whether controls are suitably designed to prevent or detect material misstatements in specific assertions. The auditor also tests how a control was applied, by whom it was applied, and whether it was applied consistently during the audit period (AU 319).

Answer (A) is incorrect because the auditor gains an understanding of internal control primarily through previous experience with the entity, inquiries, inspection of documents and records, and observation of activities. Answer (C) is incorrect because the auditor is not obligated to search for reportable conditions but should communicate those of which (s)he becomes aware. Answer (D) is incorrect because inherent risk is the susceptibility of an assertion to a material misstatement in the absence of related controls.

61. Tests of controls are concerned primarily with each of the following questions except

A. How were the controls applied?

B. Why were the controls applied?

C. Were the necessary controls consistently performed?

D. By whom were the controls applied?

The correct answer is (B). *(CPA, adapted)*

REQUIRED: The question that is not directly relevant to tests of controls.

DISCUSSION: Tests of controls are undertaken when the auditor wishes to assess control risk at below the maximum level. Their purpose is to evaluate the effectiveness of the design or operation of controls. Determining why controls were applied is more closely associated with understanding internal control than with assessing control risk at below the maximum level.

Answers (A), (C), and (D) are incorrect because tests of controls directed toward operating effectiveness are concerned with how and by whom controls were applied and whether they were applied consistently during the audit period.

62. Tests of controls are least likely to be omitted with regard to

A. Accounts believed to be subject to ineffective controls.

B. Accounts representing few transactions.

C. Accounts representing many transactions.

D. Subsequent events.

The correct answer is (C). *(Publisher)*

REQUIRED: The circumstances in which tests of controls are least likely to be omitted.

DISCUSSION: For high-volume accounts, the auditor usually must test controls because cost-benefit considerations preclude the review of all transactions. If the control risk for such accounts can be assessed at less than the maximum, the effect will be to reduce the assurance required by substantive tests.

Answer (A) is incorrect because, if, as a result of obtaining the understanding of internal control, the auditor believes that controls are unlikely to be effective, (s)he may assess control risk at the maximum and omit tests of controls. Answer (B) is incorrect because, given few transactions, examining all transactions is more efficient than testing controls. Answer (D) is incorrect because each subsequent event that requires consideration by management and evaluation by the independent auditor should be examined. Hence, tests of relevant controls are likely to be omitted.

63. Which of the following procedures is not used in tests of controls over purchases?

A. Examine vouchers and supporting documents for authorization.

B. Trace vouchers to entries in the vouchers register.

C. Confirm inventory held in public warehouses.

D. Reperform calculations on some supporting documentation.

The correct answer is (C). *(D. Wells)*

REQUIRED: The procedure that is not a test of controls over purchases.

DISCUSSION: The confirmation of inventory held in public warehouses is a substantive test of an account balance in the purchasing cycle.

Answers (A), (B), and (D) are incorrect because examining vouchers and supporting documents for authorization, tracing vouchers to entries in the vouchers register, and reperforming calculations on some supporting documentation are typical tests of controls performed in testing purchases.

64. The objective of tests of details of transactions performed as tests of controls is to

A. Monitor the design and use of entity documents such as prenumbered shipping forms.

B. Determine whether controls have been placed in operation.

C. Detect material misstatements in the account balances of the financial statements.

D. Evaluate whether controls operated effectively.

The correct answer is (D). *(CPA, adapted)*

REQUIRED: The objective of the tests of the details of transactions performed as tests of controls.

DISCUSSION: Tests of controls are directed toward the design or operation of a control to assess its effectiveness in preventing or detecting material misstatements in a financial statement assertion.

Answer (A) is incorrect because the client's internal control should monitor the use of entity documents. Answer (B) is incorrect because determining whether controls have been placed in operation is part of obtaining the understanding of internal control. Answer (C) is incorrect because the purpose of substantive tests is to detect material misstatements in the account balances of the financial statements.

65. To obtain evidence about control risk, an auditor ordinarily selects tests from a variety of techniques, including

A. Analysis.

B. Confirmation.

C. Reperformance.

D. Comparison.

The correct answer is (C). *(CPA, adapted)*

REQUIRED: The procedure most closely associated with tests of controls.

DISCUSSION: According to AU 319, the auditor selects tests of controls "from a variety of techniques such as inquiry, observation, inspection, and reperformance of a control that pertains to an assertion. No one specific test of controls is always necessary, applicable, or equally effective in every circumstance."

Answers (A), (B), and (D) are incorrect because analysis, confirmation, and comparison are more closely associated with substantive testing.

66. An auditor wishes to perform tests of controls on a client's cash disbursements procedures. If the controls leave no audit trail of documentary evidence, the auditor most likely will test the procedures by

A. Confirmation and observation.

B. Observation and inquiry.

C. Analytical procedures and confirmation.

D. Inquiry and analytical procedures.

The correct answer is (B). *(CPA, adapted)*

REQUIRED: The tests of controls applied when controls leave no audit trail of documentary evidence.

DISCUSSION: Documentation of design or operation may not exist for some factors in the control environment, such as the assignment of authority and responsibility. In such circumstances, evidence about effectiveness of design or operation may be obtained through observation and inquiry.

Answers (A), (C), and (D) are incorrect because analytical procedures and confirmation are substantive tests, not tests of controls.

67. Which of the following types of evidence would an auditor most likely examine to determine whether controls are operating as designed?

A. Confirmations of receivables verifying account balances.

B. Letters of representations corroborating inventory pricing.

C. Attorneys' responses to the auditor's inquiries.

D. Client records documenting the use of computer programs.

The correct answer is (D). *(CPA, adapted)*

REQUIRED: The evidence most likely to provide assurance about the operating effectiveness of controls.

DISCUSSION: In testing controls over the computer processing function, the auditor should obtain evidence of proper authorization and recording of access to computer programs and files.

Answer (A) is incorrect because confirmations customarily request information regarding account balances. Thus, they are substantive tests, not tests of controls. Answer (B) is incorrect because representations about inventory pricing are obtained through substantive testing. Answer (C) is incorrect because inquiry of attorneys is a substantive test.

68. The likelihood of assessing control risk too high is the risk that the sample selected to test controls

A. Does not support the auditor's planned assessed level of control risk when the true operating effectiveness of the control justifies such an assessment.

B. Contains misstatements that could be material to the financial statements when aggregated with misstatements in other account balances or transactions classes.

C. Contains proportionately fewer deviations from prescribed controls than exist in the balance or class as a whole.

D. Does not support the tolerable misstatement for some or all of management's assertions.

The correct answer is (A). *(CPA, adapted)*

REQUIRED: The condition under which the auditor would assess control risk too high.

DISCUSSION: According to AU 350, one aspect of sampling risk in performing tests of controls is the risk of assessing control risk too high. It is the risk that the assessed level of control risk based on the sample is greater than the true operating effectiveness of the control.

Answers (B) and (D) are incorrect because substantive tests are directed towards misstatements in management's assertions. Answer (C) is incorrect because, if the sample deviation rate is lower than the population rate, the auditor may assess control risk too low.

69. Which of the following procedures concerning accounts receivable is an auditor most likely to perform to obtain evidential matter in support of an assessed level of control risk below the maximum level?

A. Observing an entity's employee prepare the schedule of past due accounts receivable.

B. Sending confirmation requests to an entity's principal customers to verify the existence of accounts receivable.

C. Inspecting an entity's analysis of accounts receivable for unusual balances.

D. Comparing an entity's uncollectible accounts expense to actual uncollectible accounts receivable.

The correct answer is (A). *(CPA, adapted)*

REQUIRED: The procedure used to obtain evidential matter in support of an assessed level of control risk below the maximum level.

DISCUSSION: To assess control risk below the maximum, an auditor must perform tests of controls. Tests of controls include inquiry, observation, inspection, and reperformance of a control by the auditor. Thus, observing an entity's employee prepare the schedule of past due accounts receivable provides evidence of the effectiveness of certain controls over accounts receivable.

Answer (B) is incorrect because sending confirmation requests to verify the existence of accounts receivable is a test of the details of balances, which is a substantive test. Answer (C) is incorrect because inspecting an entity's analysis of accounts receivable for unusual balances is a test of the details of balances, which is a substantive test. Answer (D) is incorrect because comparing uncollectible accounts expense to actual uncollectible accounts receivable is a form of analytical procedure, which is used to determine if the auditor's expectation is supported by client data.

70. An auditor is least likely to test controls that provide for

A. Approval of the purchase and sale of trading securities.

B. Classification of revenue and expense transactions by product line.

C. Segregation of the functions of recording disbursements and reconciling the bank account.

D. Comparison of receiving reports and vendors' invoices with purchase orders.

The correct answer is (B). *(CPA, adapted)*

REQUIRED: The controls least likely to be tested.

DISCUSSION: The independent auditor is primarily concerned with the fairness of external financial reporting. (S)he would be less likely to test controls over records used solely for internal management purposes. If items in financial statements are not classified by product line, the independent auditor would thus be unlikely to expend significant audit effort in testing such classifications.

Answer (A) is incorrect because a basic management objective of internal control is proper authorization of transactions. Answer (C) is incorrect because a basic management objective of establishing internal control is to provide for comparing recorded accountability with existing assets at reasonable intervals, such as by reconciling bank statements with the accounting records. Such reconciliations should be performed by an independent employee. Answer (D) is incorrect because comparison of receiving reports and vendors' invoices with purchase orders is a basic control over the purchasing function.

71. In performing tests of controls, the auditor will normally find that

A. The level of inherent risk is directly proportionate to the rate of error.

B. The rate of deviations in the sample exceeds the rate of error in the accounting records.

C. The rate of error in the sample exceeds the rate of deviations.

D. All unexamined items result in errors in the accounting records.

The correct answer is (B). *(CPA, adapted)*

REQUIRED: The normal finding by an auditor during tests of controls.

DISCUSSION: When testing controls, the auditor is directly concerned with deviations from specific controls. Failure to comply with a control does not necessarily result in an error in the records; e.g., the absence of an authorization signature does not necessarily mean that the transaction was improperly recorded. Accordingly, the rate of deviations from a control normally exceeds the error rate in the records.

Answer (A) is incorrect because inherent risk and the rate of error are not necessarily correlated. Effective controls may minimize the error rate even though inherent risk is high. Answer (C) is incorrect because the sample error rate should approximate the rate of total deviations from the control tested. Answer (D) is incorrect because unaudited items are not necessarily in error.

3.6 Internal Control of the Sales-Receivables-Cash Receipts Cycle

72. The internal control objectives of the revenue cycle include all of the following except

A. Revenue cycle transactions are properly executed.

B. Appropriate goods are ordered so that sales can be made.

C. Transactions relating to revenue are properly recorded.

D. Custody over assets resulting from the revenue cycle is properly maintained.

The correct answer is (B). *(Publisher)*

REQUIRED: The internal control objective not directly related to the revenue cycle.

DISCUSSION: The revenue cycle embraces the activities pertaining to exchanges with customers and the collection in cash of the amounts paid for the goods or services provided. Ordering appropriate goods, which is an objective of the purchases-payables cycle, is only indirectly related to the revenue cycle.

Answer (A) is incorrect because an internal control objective of the revenue cycle is that revenue-cycle transactions be properly executed. Answer (C) is incorrect because an internal control objective of the revenue cycle is that transactions relating to revenue be properly recorded. Answer (D) is incorrect because an internal control objective of the revenue cycle is that custody over assets resulting from the revenue cycle be properly maintained.

73. Which of the following are not directly involved in the revenue cycle?

A. Sales manager and the credit manager.

B. Treasurer and controller.

C. Billing clerk.

D. Receiving department clerk.

The correct answer is (D). *(Publisher)*

REQUIRED: The person(s) not directly involved in the revenue cycle.

DISCUSSION: The receiving department clerk is involved in the purchases-payables cycle. The clerk counts the goods and prepares receiving reports that provide partial authorization for invoice payment.

Answer (A) is incorrect because the sales manager is responsible for executing sales transactions, and the credit manager authorizes sales. Answer (B) is incorrect because the treasurer has custody of cash receipts from sales, and the controller maintains records for the sales and billing cycle. Answer (C) is incorrect because the billing clerk is responsible for the preparation of invoices and the billing process.

74. Which of the following should report to the treasurer?

A. Internal auditor.

B. Sales clerk.

C. Bookkeeper.

D. Credit manager.

The correct answer is (D). *(Publisher)*

REQUIRED: The person who should report to the treasurer.

DISCUSSION: The treasurer's primary responsibility is to safeguard assets. Although credit approval is an authorization process, assets are lost if credit is improperly granted. Thus, the credit manager should be responsible to one who has no vested interest in the granting of credit.

Answer (A) is incorrect because the internal auditor is part of internal control and should report to the audit committee. Answer (B) is incorrect because the sales clerk is involved with the execution of sales transactions and would more appropriately report to the sales manager. Answer (C) is incorrect because record keeping should be separated from authorization and asset custody.

75. An auditor tests an entity's policy of obtaining credit approval before shipping goods to customers in support of management's financial statement assertion of

A. Valuation or allocation.

B. Completeness.

C. Existence or occurrence.

D. Rights and obligations.

The correct answer is (A). *(CPA, adapted)*

REQUIRED: The assertion related to the credit policy.

DISCUSSION: The proper approval of credit provides assurance that the account receivable will be collectible; thus, it is related to the valuation assertion that accounts receivable are recorded at net realizable value.

Answer (B) is incorrect because completeness concerns whether all transactions and accounts have been presented. Answer (C) is incorrect because existence or occurrence concerns whether assets or liabilities exist and whether recorded transactions have occurred. Answer (D) is incorrect because rights and obligations assertions deal with whether assets are the rights of the entity and obligations are liabilities of the entity at a given date.

76. At which point in an ordinary sales transaction of a wholesaling business is a lack of specific authorization of least concern to the auditor in the conduct of an audit?

A. Granting of credit.

B. Shipment of goods.

C. Determination of discounts.

D. Selling of goods for cash.

The correct answer is (D). *(CPA, adapted)*

REQUIRED: The point in an ordinary sales transaction at which specific authorization is of least concern to an auditor.

DISCUSSION: Selling goods for cash is the consummation of a transaction that would likely be covered by a general authorization. Thus, the risk of loss arising from lack of specific authorization of cash sales is minimal.

Answer (A) is incorrect because granting of credit in a sales transaction may require specific authorization, i.e., special consideration before approval by the appropriate person. Answers (B) and (C) are incorrect because shipment of goods and determination of discounts in sales transactions may require specific authorization.

77. Which of the following most likely would be the result of ineffective controls in the revenue cycle?

A. Final authorization of credit memos by personnel in the sales department could permit an employee defalcation scheme.

B. Fictitious transactions could be recorded, causing an understatement of revenues and an overstatement of receivables.

C. Irregularities in recording transactions in the subsidiary accounts could result in a delay in goods shipped.

D. Omission of shipping documents could go undetected, causing an understatement of inventory.

The correct answer is (A). *(CPA, adapted)*

REQUIRED: The most likely result of ineffective controls in the revenue cycle.

DISCUSSION: Ineffective controls in the revenue cycle, such as inappropriate division of duties and responsibilities, inadequate supervision, or deficient authorization, may result in the ability of employees to perpetrate irregularities. Thus, sales personnel should approve sales returns and allowances but not the related credit memos. Moreover, no authorization for the return of goods, defective or otherwise, should be considered complete until the goods are returned as evidenced by a receiving report.

Answer (B) is incorrect because recording fictitious sales would overstate revenues. Answer (C) is incorrect because the customers' accounts are not posted until after goods are shipped. Answer (D) is incorrect because, if shipping documents are omitted, shipments of goods may not be credited to inventory, thereby overstating the account.

78. Which of the following credit approval procedures would be the basis for developing a deficiency finding for a wholesaler?

A. Trade-credit standards are reviewed and approved by the finance committee of the board of directors.

B. Customers not meeting trade-credit standards are shipped merchandise on a cash-on-delivery (C.O.D.) basis only.

C. Salespeople are responsible for evaluating and monitoring the financial condition of prospective and continuing customers.

D. An authorized signature from the credit department, denoting approval of the customer's credit, is to appear on all credit-sales orders.

The correct answer is (C). *(CIA, adapted)*

REQUIRED: The credit approval procedure justifying a deficiency finding.

DISCUSSION: Salespeople should be responsible for generating sales and providing service to customers. For effective control purposes, the credit department should be responsible for monitoring the financial condition of prospective and continuing customers in the credit approval process.

Answer (A) is incorrect because trade-credit standards may be evaluated and approved by a committee of the board or delegated to management. Answer (B) is incorrect because shipping merchandise on a cash-on-delivery (C.O.D.) basis only is customary if trade-credit standards are not met. Answer (D) is incorrect because the credit department should approve transactions based upon credit information before sales are processed.

79. The markup applied to a company's products has varied between customers. An audit procedure most likely to uncover this situation is

A. Checking to see if sales have been made to customers with inadequate credit ratings.

B. Checking to see if salespeople were able to set prices without clearance from the central office.

C. Determining if production costs have been excessive.

D. Analyzing selling costs for excessiveness.

The correct answer is (B). *(CIA, adapted)*

REQUIRED: The audit procedure most likely to uncover variations in markups among customers.

DISCUSSION: Markup is selling price minus cost of goods sold. The markup for a given product will vary among customers only if selling price varies. This situation can occur if salespeople set selling prices without proper authorization. The auditor should determine whether effective controls are in place over pricing. For example, if a standard price cannot be set, guidelines should be prepared for salespeople to follow.

Answer (A) is incorrect because creditworthiness does not have a necessary relationship to pricing. However, less reliable customers may sometimes be charged a higher price. Answer (C) is incorrect because excessive production costs relate to the efficiency of the production process, not to the markups applied to products. Answer (D) is incorrect because, unless excessive sales costs apply to some but not all customers, they do not explain the variation in markups.

80. Alpha Company uses its sales invoices for posting perpetual inventory records. Inadequate internal control over the invoicing function allows goods to be shipped that are not invoiced. The inadequate controls could cause an

A. Understatement of revenues, receivables, and inventory.

B. Overstatement of revenues and receivables, and an understatement of inventory.

C. Understatement of revenues and receivables, and an overstatement of inventory.

D. Overstatement of revenues, receivables, and inventory.

The correct answer is (C). *(CPA, adapted)*

REQUIRED: The result of shipping goods that are not invoiced.

DISCUSSION: If goods are shipped before the sales are invoiced, inventory will not be credited for the shipments, thus overstating inventory. Moreover, if the accounting function does not receive copies of the invoices, sales and receivables will not be recorded, with the consequent understatement of those accounts.

Answer (A) is incorrect because shipping goods that are not invoiced could cause an overstatement of inventory. Answer (B) is incorrect because shipping goods that are not invoiced could cause an overstatement of inventory and an understatement of revenues and receivables. Answer (D) is incorrect because shipping goods that are not invoiced could cause an understatement of revenues and receivables.

81. Which of the following controls most likely would help ensure that all credit sales transactions of an entity are recorded?

A. The billing department supervisor sends copies of approved sales orders to the credit department for comparison to authorized credit limits and current customer account balances.

B. The accounting department supervisor independently reconciles the accounts receivable subsidiary ledger to the accounts receivable control account monthly.

C. The accounting department supervisor controls the mailing of monthly statements to customers and investigates any differences reported by customers.

D. The billing department supervisor matches prenumbered shipping documents with entries in the sales journal.

The correct answer is (D). *(CPA, adapted)*

REQUIRED: The control to detect unrecorded sales.

DISCUSSION: The sequential numbering of documents provides a standard control over transactions. The numerical sequence should be accounted for by an independent party. A major objective is to detect unrecorded and unauthorized transactions. Moreover, comparing shipments with the sales journal also will detect unrecorded transactions.

Answer (A) is incorrect because credit approval does not ensure that sales have been recorded. Answer (B) is incorrect because the reconciliation will not detect sales that were never recorded. Answer (C) is incorrect because customers are unlikely to report understatement of their accounts.

82. Proper authorization of write-offs of uncollectible accounts should be approved in which of the following departments?

A. Accounts receivable.

B. Credit.

C. Accounts payable.

D. Treasurer.

The correct answer is (D). *(CPA, adapted)*

REQUIRED: The department authorizing write-offs of uncollectible accounts.

DISCUSSION: The write-off of uncollectible accounts requires strong controls. The initiation of the write-off is performed by the credit manager. However, approval should be made by an independent party, typically the treasurer. The credit manager will be evaluated, in part, on the amount of bad debt written off and should require significant evidence before initiating a write-off.

Answers (A) and (C) are incorrect because accounts receivable and accounts payable are accounting functions and should not be involved with the authorization of transactions. Answer (B) is incorrect because write-offs of uncollectible accounts should be approved by someone outside the credit department who does not have a record keeping function.

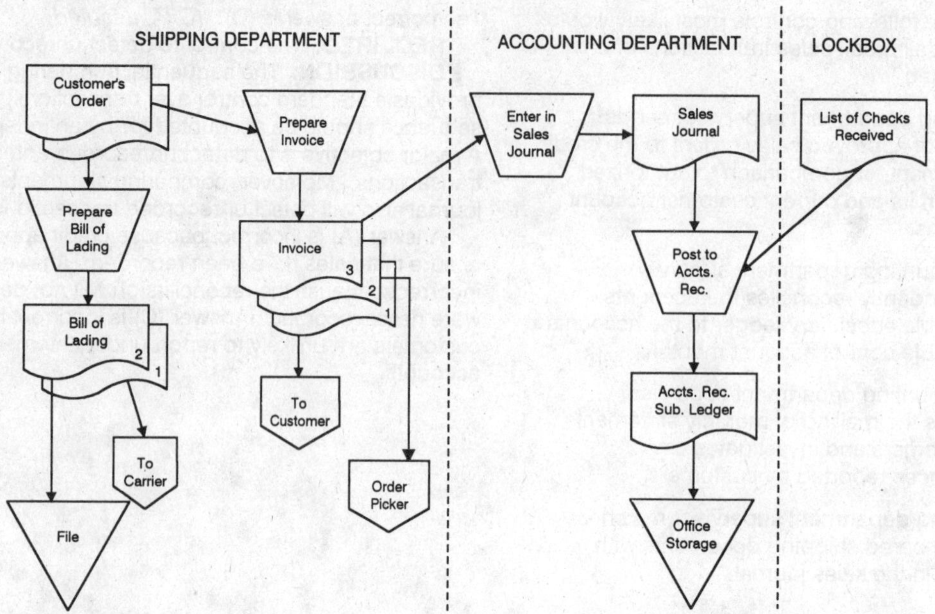

83. Examining the flowchart of the order processing cycle shown above yields a conclusion that this system could well result in

A. Loss of float in handling cash receipts.

B. Errors on invoices.

C. Cash loss.

D. Defalcation in shipping.

The correct answer is (D). *(CIA, adapted)*

REQUIRED: The internal control weakness in the order processing flowchart.

DISCUSSION: The shipping department has been charged with too much responsibility according to the flowchart. For example, the billing department should prepare the sales invoice from an approved sales order. Also, the shipping department should not take customer orders. When one department is given too many functions to perform, the possibility of defalcation and other errors is increased. Defalcation is the misappropriation (embezzlement) of money or property.

Answer (A) is incorrect because the lockbox minimizes the loss of float in handling cash receipts since it expedites cash receipts. Answer (B) is incorrect because the customer's order and the invoice copy presumably go to the accounting department to be rechecked. Answer (C) is incorrect because the cash custody function is not flowcharted.

Questions 84 through 87 are based on the following information. Sales procedures that were encountered during the regular annual audit of Marvel Wholesale Distributing Company are as follows:

Customer orders are received by the sales-order department. A clerk computes the dollar amount of the order and sends it to the credit department for approval. Credit approval is stamped on the order and returned to the sales-order department. An invoice is prepared in two copies, and the order is filed in the customer order file.

The customer copy of the invoice is sent to the billing department and held in the pending file awaiting notification that the order has been shipped.

The shipping copy of the invoice is routed through the warehouse and the shipping department as authority for the respective departments to release and ship the merchandise.

Shipping department personnel pack the order and prepare a three-copy bill of lading: the original copy is mailed to the customer, the second copy is sent with the shipment, and the other is filed in sequence in the bill of lading file. The invoice shipping copy is sent to the billing department.

The billing clerk matches the received shipping copy with the customer copy from the pending file. Both copies of the invoice are priced, extended, and footed. The customer copy is then mailed directly to the customer, and the shipping copy is sent to the accounts receivable clerk.

The accounts receivable clerk enters the invoice data in a sales-accounts receivable journal, posts the customer's account in the subsidiary customers' accounts ledger, and files the shipping copy in the sales invoice file. The invoices are numbered and filed in sequence.

84. To gather audit evidence concerning the proper credit approval of sales, the auditor would select a sample of transaction documents from the population represented by the

A. Customer order file.

B. Bill of lading file.

C. Subsidiary customers' accounts ledger.

D. Sales invoice file.

The correct answer is (A). *(CPA, adapted)*

REQUIRED: The file or ledger containing evidence of proper issuance of credit sale approvals.

DISCUSSION: The customer order is first sent to the credit department, and credit approval is stamped on it. It is then returned to the sales department and filed. The customer order file thus contains the only documentation for credit approvals.

Answer (B) is incorrect because the bill of lading file contains no evidence of credit approvals. Answer (C) is incorrect because the subsidiary customers' accounts ledger contains no evidence of credit approvals. Answer (D) is incorrect because the sales invoice file contains no evidence of credit approvals.

85. To determine whether internal control operated effectively to minimize errors of failure to post invoices to the customers' accounts ledger, the auditor should select a sample of transactions from the population represented by the

A. Customer order file.

B. Bill of lading file.

C. Subsidiary customers' accounts ledger.

D. Sales invoice file.

The correct answer is (D). *(CPA, adapted)*

REQUIRED: The source of data to ascertain whether internal control minimized accounts receivable posting errors.

DISCUSSION: The auditor should trace sales according to the sales invoices to the accounts receivable subsidiary ledger. Sales invoices in the sales invoice file without corresponding entries in the subsidiary ledger represent transactions not posted.

Answer (A) is incorrect because the customer order file does not necessarily contain sales information. Customer orders may not be accepted or shipped. Answer (B) is incorrect because the bill of lading file does not necessarily contain sales information. All shipments do not necessarily pertain to customer orders. Answer (C) is incorrect because the items in the subsidiary ledger represent those transactions that have been posted. The direction of the testing should be from sales invoice to subsidiary ledger, not subsidiary ledger to sales invoice.

86. To determine whether internal control operated effectively to minimize errors of failure to invoice a shipment, the auditor should select a sample of transactions from the population represented by the

A. Customer order file.

B. Bill of lading file.

C. Subsidiary customers' accounts ledger.

D. Sales invoice file.

The correct answer is (B). *(CPA, adapted)*

REQUIRED: The appropriate test to ascertain whether internal control minimized failures to invoice shipments.

DISCUSSION: The auditor should match bill of lading file copies relating to customer shipments to sales invoices (or possibly to the accounts receivable subsidiary ledger) to determine if shipments were not billed.

Answer (A) is incorrect because the customer order file may contain orders that were not approved and shipped. Answer (C) is incorrect because an inconsistency between a customer balance and an invoice may result from payment, not necessarily from failure to invoice a shipment. Answer (D) is incorrect because the direction of the testing is wrong. To test for failure to invoice, the auditor should not be sampling from a file containing only invoiced orders.

87. To gather audit evidence that uncollected items in customers' accounts represented valid trade receivables, the auditor should select a sample of items from the population represented by the

A. Customer order file.

B. Bill of lading file.

C. Subsidiary customers' accounts ledger.

D. Sales invoice file.

The correct answer is (C). *(CPA, adapted)*

REQUIRED: The test appropriate for determining the validity of accounts receivable.

DISCUSSION: The auditor should sample from records of open accounts receivable to determine if they represent valid assets. The open accounts receivable are maintained in the subsidiary customers' accounts ledger. Items would be confirmed directly with the debtors.

Answers (A), (B), and (D) are incorrect because the customer order file, the bill of lading file, and the sales invoice file are not updated for shipment or payment.

88. An auditor observes the mailing of monthly statements to a client's customers and reviews evidence of follow-up on errors reported by the customers. This test of controls most likely is performed to support management's financial statement assertion(s) of

	Presentation and Disclosure	Existence or Occurrence
A.	Yes	Yes
B.	Yes	No
C.	No	Yes
D.	No	No

The correct answer is (C). *(CPA, adapted)*

REQUIRED: The financial statement assertion(s), if any, related to observing the client's follow-up on errors reported.

DISCUSSION: The existence assertion concerns whether assets or liabilities exist at the balance sheet date. Observation of the mailing of monthly statements, as well as observing the correction of reported errors, provides evidence that controls may be effective in ensuring that the client's customers are bona fide.

Answers (A) and (B) are incorrect because the observation of client activities related to customer statements provides little evidence concerning presentation or disclosure in the financial statements. Answer (D) is incorrect because the mailing and follow-up procedures provide evidence that controls may be effective in ensuring that the client's customers are bona fide.

89. In a retail cash sales environment, which of the following controls is often absent?

A. Competent personnel.

B. Segregation of functions.

C. Supervision.

D. Asset access limited to authorized personnel.

The correct answer is (B). *(Publisher)*

REQUIRED: The control often absent in a cash sales environment.

DISCUSSION: In the usual retail cash sales situation, the sales clerk authorizes and records the transactions and takes custody of assets. However, management ordinarily employs other compensating controls to minimize the effects of the failure to segregate functions. The cash receipts function is closely supervised, cash registers provide limited access to assets, and an internal recording function maintains control over cash receipts.

Answers (A), (C), and (D) are incorrect because competent personnel, supervision, and limitation of access to assets are compensating controls normally found in a cash sales environment.

90. For effective internal control, the controller should direct the

A. Billing clerk.

B. Credit manager.

C. Sales clerk.

D. Cashier.

The correct answer is (A). *(Publisher)*

REQUIRED: The position that should be supervised by the controller.

DISCUSSION: To establish effective internal control, the billing department, which performs a recording function, should be under the direction of the controller who typically has responsibility for record keeping.

Answer (B) is incorrect because the credit manager has an authorization function and should not be under the direction of the controller. Answer (C) is incorrect because the sales clerk executes transactions and should not be under the direction of the controller. Answer (D) is incorrect because the cashier has an asset custody function and should not be under the direction of the controller.

91. An auditor noted that the accounts receivable department is separate from other accounting activities. Credit is approved by a separate credit department. Control accounts and subsidiary ledgers are balanced monthly. Similarly, accounts are aged monthly. The accounts receivable manager writes off delinquent accounts after 1 year, or sooner if a bankruptcy or other unusual circumstances are involved. Credit memoranda are prenumbered and must correlate with receiving reports. Which of the following areas could be viewed as an internal control weakness of the above organization?

A. Write-offs of delinquent accounts.

B. Credit approvals.

C. Monthly aging of receivables.

D. Handling of credit memos.

The correct answer is (A). *(CIA, adapted)*

REQUIRED: The area viewed as an internal control weakness of the organization.

DISCUSSION: The accounts receivable manager has the ability to perpetrate irregularities because (s)he performs incompatible functions. Authorization and recording of transactions should be separate. Thus, someone outside the accounts receivable department should authorize write-offs.

Answer (B) is incorrect because credit approval is an authorization function that is properly segregated from the record keeping function. Answer (C) is incorrect because monthly aging is appropriate. Answer (D) is incorrect because the procedures regarding credit memoranda are standard controls.

92. One of two office clerks in a small company prepares a sales invoice for $4,300; however, the invoice is incorrectly entered by the bookkeeper in the general ledger and the accounts receivable subsidiary ledger as $3,400. The customer subsequently remits $3,400, the amount on the monthly statement. Assuming there are only three employees in the department, the most effective control to prevent this type of error is

A. Assigning the second office clerk to independently check the sales invoice prices, discounts, extensions, and footings, and to account for the invoice serial number.

B. Requiring that monthly statements be prepared by the bookkeeper and verified by one of the other office clerks prior to mailing.

C. Using predetermined totals to control posting routines.

D. Requiring the bookkeeper to perform periodic reconciliations of the accounts receivable subsidiary ledger and the general ledger.

The correct answer is (C). *(CIA, adapted)*

REQUIRED: The most effective control to prevent posting errors.

DISCUSSION: A control total should be generated for the transactions to be posted. It should then be compared with the total of items posted to the individual accounts.

Answer (A) is incorrect because the misposting was an error that occurred subsequent to assigning the second office clerk to independently check the sales invoice prices, discounts, extensions, and footings, and to account for the invoice serial number. Answer (B) is incorrect because requiring that monthly statements be prepared by the bookkeeper and verified by one of the other office clerks prior to mailing would not detect an initial misposting. The statements are based on the misposted records. Answer (D) is incorrect because requiring the bookkeeper to perform periodic reconciliations of the accounts receivable subsidiary ledger and the general ledger would not detect an initial misposting. The reconciliations are based on the misposted records.

93. Which of the following would be the best protection for a company that wishes to prevent the lapping of trade accounts receivable?

A. Segregate duties so that the bookkeeper in charge of the general ledger has no access to incoming mail.

B. Segregate duties so that no employee has access to both checks from customers and currency from daily cash receipts.

C. Have customers send payments directly to the company's depository bank.

D. Request that customers' payment checks be made payable to the company and addressed to the treasurer.

The correct answer is (C). *(CPA, adapted)*

REQUIRED: The best protection from lapping of accounts receivable.

DISCUSSION: Lapping is the delayed recording of cash receipts to cover a cash shortage. Current receipts are posted to the accounts of customers who paid one or two days previously to avoid complaints (and discovery) when monthly statements are mailed. The best protection is for the customers to send payments directly to the company's depository bank. This procedure precludes client personnel from having access to the money.

Answers (A) and (D) are incorrect because having payments sent directly to the depository bank is the best protection. Cash receipts are not physically received by firm personnel. Answer (B) is incorrect because all monies should be entrusted to the treasurer for safekeeping.

94. To conceal defalcations involving receivables, an experienced bookkeeper would be expected to charge which of the following accounts?

A. Miscellaneous income.

B. Petty cash.

C. Miscellaneous expense.

D. Sales returns.

The correct answer is (D). *(CPA, adapted)*

REQUIRED: The account charged to conceal defalcations.

DISCUSSION: If monies have been abstracted from customers paying on account, a bookkeeper would debit sales returns and credit accounts receivable. If accounts receivable are not credited, the customer will continue to be billed and will complain.

Answers (A), (B), and (C) are incorrect because debiting miscellaneous income, petty cash, or miscellaneous expense and crediting accounts receivable results in an unusual entry that is likely to be reviewed and discovered.

95. Upon receipt of customers' checks in the mail room, a responsible employee should prepare a remittance listing that is forwarded to the cashier. A copy of the listing should be sent to the

A. Internal auditor to investigate the listing for unusual transactions.

B. Treasurer to compare the listing with the monthly bank statement.

C. Accounts receivable bookkeeper to update the subsidiary accounts receivable records.

D. Entity's bank to compare the listing with the cashier's deposit slip.

The correct answer is (C). *(CPA, adapted)*

REQUIRED: The use of the client's remittance listing.

DISCUSSION: Individuals with record-keeping responsibility should not have custody of cash. They should use either the remittance advices or a listing of remittances to make entries to the cash and accounts receivable control accounts and to the subsidiary accounts receivable records. Having different people make entries in the control accounts and subsidiary records is an effective control.

Answer (A) is incorrect because the internal auditors should have no ongoing control responsibilities. The investigation of unusual transactions is first conducted in the treasurer's department. Answer (B) is incorrect because the monthly bank statement should be reconciled by someone outside of the treasury function. Answer (D) is incorrect because the entity's bank will supply a validated deposit slip based on the deposit for the day.

96. Cash receipts from sales on account have been misappropriated. Which of the following acts would conceal this defalcation and be least likely to be detected by an auditor?

A. Understating the sales journal.

B. Overstating the accounts receivable control account.

C. Overstating the accounts receivable subsidiary ledger.

D. Understating the cash receipts journal.

The correct answer is (A). *(CPA, adapted)*

REQUIRED: The act that would conceal theft of cash receipts from credit sales and be least likely to be detected.

DISCUSSION: Not recording sales on account in the books of original entry is the most effective way to conceal a subsequent theft of cash receipts. The accounts will be incomplete but balanced, and procedures applied to the accounting records will not detect the defalcation. Moreover, customers are not likely to alert the auditor to the irregularity because an unrecorded sale will not be billed and an unrecorded receivable will not be confirmed.

Answers (B) and (C) are incorrect because the discrepancy between the accounts receivable control account and the accounts receivable subsidiary ledger would alert the auditor to the misstatement. Answer (D) is incorrect because understating the cash receipts journal will not conceal the defalcation. Cash receipts will not reconcile with the credits to accounts receivable. If accounts receivable are not credited, confirmation will detect the fraud.

97. For the purpose of proper accounting control, postdated checks remitted by customers should be

A. Restrictively endorsed.

B. Returned to customer.

C. Recorded as a cash sale.

D. Placed in the joint custody of two officers.

The correct answer is (A). *(CPA, adapted)*

REQUIRED: The appropriate procedure for handling postdated checks remitted by customers.

DISCUSSION: All checks remitted by customers should be restrictively endorsed with the phrase "For Deposit Only" in the company account regardless of their date. They should be physically safeguarded until deposit.

Answer (B) is incorrect because acceptance of a postdated check may be the firm's best (only) chance to collect cash from the customer. Answer (C) is incorrect because a postdated check does not represent cash. Answer (D) is incorrect because the postdated check should be kept by the treasurer and accounted for by the controller.

98. Which of the following controls is most likely to deter lapping of collections from customers?

A. Independent internal verification of dates of entry in the cash receipts journal with dates of daily cash summaries.

B. Authorization of write-offs of uncollectible accounts by a supervisor independent of credit approval.

C. Segregation of duties between receiving cash and posting the accounts receivable ledger.

D. Supervisory comparison of the daily cash summary with the sum of the cash receipts journal entries.

The correct answer is (C). *(CPA, adapted)*

REQUIRED: The best protection from lapping of collections from customers.

DISCUSSION: Lapping is the delayed recording of cash receipts to cover a cash shortage. Lapping is possible when an employee who maintains the accounts receivable ledger also has physical custody of the cash receipts. The best protection is to require customers to send payments directly to the company's depository bank. The next best procedure is to assure that the accounts receivable clerk has no access to cash received by the mail room. Thus, the duties of receiving cash and posting the accounts receivable ledger are segregated.

Answers (A) and (D) are incorrect because lapping delays recording cash receipts so that posting the cash receipts journal and recording in the cash summary occur on the same date and in the same amounts. Answer (B) is incorrect because lapping involves delayed posting of cash payments, not bad debt write-offs. Moreover, the credit manager should approve write-offs.

Questions 99 and 100 are based on the following information. Management discovers that a supervisor at one of their restaurant locations removes excess cash and resets sales totals throughout the day on the point of sale (POS) system. At closing, the supervisor deposits cash equal to the recorded sales on the POS system and keeps the rest.

The supervisor forwards the close-of-day POS reports from the POS system along with a copy of the bank deposit slip to the company's revenue accounting department. The revenue accounting department records the sales and the cash for the location in the general ledger and verifies the deposit slip to the bank statement. Any differences between sales and deposits are recorded in an over/short account and, if necessary, followed up with the location supervisor. The customer food order checks are serially numbered, and it is the supervisor's responsibility to see that they are accounted for at the end of each day. Customer checks and the transaction journal tapes from the POS system are kept by the supervisor for one week at the location and then destroyed.

99. Which of the following controls allowed the fraud to occur?

A. The accounting for customer food checks by the supervisor.

B. The deposit of cash receipts by the supervisor.

C. The matching of the bank deposit slips to the bank statement by revenue accounting.

D. The forwarding of the close-of-day POS reports to revenue accounting.

The correct answer is (A). *(CIA, adapted)*

REQUIRED: The control that allowed the fraud to occur.

DISCUSSION: An inappropriate segregation of duties existed because the supervisor was responsible for accounting for customer food checks and depositing receipts and had the ability to reset POS totals throughout the day.

Answer (B) is incorrect because the depositing of receipts by the supervisor is not the problem. The supervisor's access to cash and ability to reset POS totals throughout the day allowed the fraud. Answer (C) is incorrect because an independent verification of the deposits made by the supervisor is appropriate. Answer (D) is incorrect because the forwarding of the close-of-day POS reports to revenue accounting is a step in the process of independently verifying sales.

100. Which of the following audit procedures would have detected the fraud?

A. Flowcharting the controls over the verification of bank deposits.

B. Comparing a sample of the close-of-day POS reports to copies of the bank deposit slips.

C. On a test basis, verifying that the serial-numbered customer food checks are accounted for.

D. For selected days, reconciling the total of customer food checks to daily bank deposits.

The correct answer is (D). *(CIA, adapted)*

REQUIRED: The audit procedure that would have detected the fraud.

DISCUSSION: Using the total of the customer food checks as a confirmation of sales would have detected the shortage in the bank deposit.

Answer (A) is incorrect because the fraud involved receipts, not deposits. Answer (B) is incorrect because the fraud involved altering the amounts on the close-of-day POS reports by resetting the POS system totals to zero. Answer (C) is incorrect because the accounting for individual customer food checks would not have detected the fraud. It did not involve manipulation of these documents.

101. For effective internal control, employees maintaining the accounts receivable subsidiary ledger should not also approve

A. Employee overtime wages.

B. Credit granted to customers.

C. Write-offs of customer accounts.

D. Cash disbursements.

The correct answer is (C). *(CPA, adapted)*

REQUIRED: The activity incompatible with maintaining the accounts receivable subsidiary ledger.

DISCUSSION: An employee who authorizes a transaction, such as the write-off of a receivable, ordinarily should not be responsible for recording the same transaction. Segregating the functions of authorization, record keeping, and custody of assets reduces the possibility that an employee may be able to both perpetrate and conceal a fraud in the normal course of his/her duties.

Answers (A) and (D) are incorrect because authorization of cash disbursements, e.g., for overtime, is not related to receivables. Answer (B) is incorrect because, although credit approval effectively authorizes a debit to receivables, combining that function with keeping the receivables records is less likely to result in fraud than approving write-offs.

102. To safeguard the assets through proper internal control, accounts receivable that are written off should be transferred to

A. A separate ledger.

B. An attorney for evidence in collection proceedings.

C. A tax deductions file.

D. A credit manager, since customers may seek to reestablish credit by paying.

The correct answer is (A). *(CPA, adapted)*

REQUIRED: The proper disposition of accounts receivable that are written off.

DISCUSSION: Accounts receivable that are written off should be transferred to a separate ledger, which should be maintained by the accounting department and periodically reviewed to determine if accounts have become collectible.

Answer (B) is incorrect because, if collection proceedings are initiated, the expectation is that the accounts will be collected and therefore should not be written off. Answer (C) is incorrect because the tax effects of accounts receivable are reflected in bad debt expense. Answer (D) is incorrect because the credit manager should not control the accounts receivable. The credit manager's function is to authorize credit, not maintain custody of assets.

103. Sound internal control procedures dictate that defective merchandise returned by customers should be presented initially to the

A. Accounts receivable supervisor.

B. Receiving clerk.

C. Shipping department supervisor.

D. Sales clerk.

The correct answer is (B). *(CPA, adapted)*

REQUIRED: The individual to whom customers should return defective merchandise.

DISCUSSION: For control purposes, all receipts of goods or materials should be handled by the receiving clerk. Receiving reports should be prepared for all items received.

Answers (A), (C), and (D) are incorrect because all returns of goods should be handled by an independent receiving function.

104. When an office supply company is unable to fill an order completely, it marks the out-of-stock items as back ordered on the customer's order and enters these items in a back order file that management can view or print. Customers are becoming disgruntled with the company because it seems unable to keep track of and ship out-of-stock items as soon as they are available. The best approach for ensuring prompt delivery of out-of-stock items is to

A. Match the back order file to goods received daily.

B. Increase inventory levels to minimize the number of times that stockouts occur.

C. Implement electronic data interchange with supply vendors to decrease the time to replenish inventory.

D. Reconcile the sum of filled and back orders with the total of all orders placed daily.

The correct answer is (A). *(CIA, adapted)*

REQUIRED: The best approach for ensuring prompt delivery of out-of-stock items.

DISCUSSION: Reconciling the back order file to shipments received daily would identify unfilled orders for appropriate action.

Answer (B) is incorrect because increasing inventory levels might minimize the number of times that out-of-stock conditions occur but will not affect delivery of the items that are out of stock. Answer (C) is incorrect because implementing electronic data interchange with supply vendors may decrease the time to replenish inventory but will not affect delivery of the items that are out of stock. Answer (D) is incorrect because reconciling the sum of filled and back orders with the total of all orders placed daily ensures that orders are either filled or back ordered but will not affect delivery of the items that are out of stock.

105. Cash receipts should be deposited on the day of receipt or the following business day. Select the most appropriate audit procedure to determine that cash is promptly deposited.

A. Review cash register tapes prepared for each sale.

B. Review the functions of cash handling and maintaining accounting records for proper separation of duties.

C. Compare the daily cash receipts totals with the bank deposits.

D. Review the functions of cash receiving and disbursing for proper separation of duties.

The correct answer is (C). *(CIA, adapted)*

REQUIRED: The most appropriate audit procedure to determine that cash is promptly deposited.

DISCUSSION: A standard control over the cash receipts function is to require that daily cash receipts be deposited promptly and intact. Hence, the total of cash receipts for a day should equal the bank deposit because no cash disbursements are made from the daily receipts. To determine whether cash receipts are promptly deposited, the auditor should compare the daily cash receipts totals with bank deposits.

Answer (A) is incorrect because reviewing the cash register tapes will not ensure that cash is deposited. Answer (B) and (D) are incorrect because separating functions will not ensure that cash is deposited.

106. To establish illegal slush funds, corporations may divert cash received in normal business operations. An auditor would encounter the greatest difficulty in detecting the diversion of proceeds from

A. Scrap sales.

B. Dividends.

C. Purchase returns.

D. C.O.D. sales.

The correct answer is (A). *(CPA, adapted)*

REQUIRED: The transaction from which the diversion of proceeds is most difficult to detect.

DISCUSSION: Because scrap sales often provide little documentary evidence to corroborate cash receipts, it is difficult to detect abstraction of proceeds from unrecorded sales.

Answer (B) is incorrect because the auditor can ordinarily reconcile the expected dividends from securities held with the actual amounts received. Answers (C) and (D) are incorrect because purchase returns and C.O.D. sales are usually well documented and controlled.

3.7 Internal Control of the Purchases-Payables-Cash Disbursements Cycle

107. The primary audit objective regarding the purchasing of materials by the client is to

A. Ascertain that materials paid for are on hand.

B. Observe the annual physical count.

C. Investigate the recording of unusual transactions regarding materials.

D. Determine the reliability of financial reporting by the purchasing function.

The correct answer is (D). *(Publisher)*

REQUIRED: The auditor's primary objective in reviewing a client's materials purchasing cycle.

DISCUSSION: The auditor must obtain an understanding of the client's controls over the purchasing cycle and assess control risk to determine the nature, timing, and extent of substantive testing of details of purchasing cycle account balances and transactions.

Answer (A) is incorrect because materials not on hand may have been sold or used in production. Answer (B) is incorrect because this question relates to purchasing, not the inventory function. Answer (C) is incorrect because investigating the recording of unusual transactions is an audit procedure rather than an objective.

108. Which of the following questions would be inappropriate on an internal control questionnaire concerning purchase transactions?

A. Are an approved purchase requisition and a signed purchase order required for each purchase?

B. Are prenumbered purchase orders and receiving reports used and accounted for?

C. Are all goods received in a centralized receiving department and counted, inspected, and compared with purchase orders on receipt?

D. Are intact cash receipts deposited daily in the bank?

The correct answer is (D). *(Publisher)*

REQUIRED: The question not associated with purchase transactions.

DISCUSSION: The question concerning the daily deposit of intact cash receipts is related to the cash receipts cycle, not the purchases-payables-cash disbursements cycle.

Answer (A) is incorrect because a question concerning the requirement of an approved purchase requisition and a signed purchase order is appropriate relative to internal control over purchase transactions. Answer (B) is incorrect because a question concerning the use of prenumbered purchase orders and receiving reports is appropriate relative to internal control over purchase transactions. Answer (C) is incorrect because a question concerning activities of a centralized receiving department is appropriate relative to internal control over purchase transactions.

109. If internal control is well-designed, employees in the same department most likely would approve purchase orders and also

A. Reconcile the open invoice file.

B. Inspect goods upon receipt.

C. Authorize requisitions of goods.

D. Negotiate terms with vendors.

The correct answer is (D). *(CPA, adapted)*

REQUIRED: The task appropriately performed by employees who approve purchase orders.

DISCUSSION: To prevent or detect errors or fraud in the performance of assigned responsibilities, duties are often segregated. Approving purchase orders and negotiating terms with vendors are part of the authorization process performed by the purchasing department.

Answer (A) is incorrect because reconciling the open invoice file is the accounting department's function. Answer (B) is incorrect because inspection of goods upon receipt is the receiving department's function. Answer (C) is incorrect because authorization of the requisition is inventory control's function.

110. To minimize the risk that agents in the purchasing department will use their positions for personal gain, the organization should

A. Require competitive bidding.

B. Request internal auditors to confirm selected purchases and accounts payable.

C. Specify that all items purchased must pass value-per-unit-of-cost reviews.

D. Direct the purchasing department to maintain records on purchase prices paid, with review of such being required each 6 months.

The correct answer is (A). *(CIA, adapted)*

REQUIRED: The control that will minimize the risk that purchasing agents will use their positions for personal gain.

DISCUSSION: The primary function of a purchasing department is to ensure the authorized acquisition of goods of a specified quality on a timely basis at an economical price. Competitive bidding procedures should reduce both costs and the likelihood that a purchasing agent will show favoritism to a vendor.

Answer (B) is incorrect because confirmation establishes the existence of the liabilities but does not test the choice of vendor. Answer (C) is incorrect because specifying that all items purchased must pass value-per-unit-of-cost reviews is essentially a detective, not a preventive, control. Answer (D) is incorrect because directing the purchasing department to maintain records on purchase prices paid, with review of such being required each 6 months, is essentially a detective, not a preventive, control.

111. A university does not have a centralized receiving function for departmental purchases of books, supplies, and equipment. Which of the following controls would most effectively prevent payment for goods not received, if performed prior to invoice payment?

A. Vendor invoices should be matched with department purchase orders.

B. Names and addresses on vendor invoices should be compared to a list of department-authorized vendors.

C. Vendor invoices should be approved by a departmental supervisor other than the employee ordering the goods.

D. Invoices over a specified amount should be approved by the vice president of finance.

The correct answer is (C). *(CIA, adapted)*

REQUIRED: The control that would most effectively prevent payment for goods not received, if performed prior to invoice payment.

DISCUSSION: The departmental supervisors are the most likely to be aware of the goods received by their departments. Moreover, segregating ordering authority from payment authority will prevent unauthorized purchases.

Answer (A) is incorrect because purchase orders do not provide evidence that the goods were received. Answer (B) is incorrect because comparison with lists of authorized vendors does not provide evidence that goods were received. Answer (D) is incorrect because the vice president of finance is unlikely to have knowledge of goods received by the departments.

112. The principal function of a cash budget is to

A. Ensure that the accounting principles relevant to cash transactions are applied consistently from period to period.

B. Ensure that the accounting records are accurate.

C. Physically safeguard cash.

D. Implement asset and liability maturity matching.

The correct answer is (D). *(Publisher)*

REQUIRED: The principal function of a cash budget.

DISCUSSION: Financial management customarily matches asset and liability maturities. Hence, long-term assets are usually financed with long-term debt and equity, and short-term financing is matched with temporary current assets. The purpose of maturity matching is to reduce the risk that the entity will be unable to pay its obligations as they become due.

Answers (A) and (B) are incorrect because the budget is ordinarily considered a financial tool, not an accounting check. Answer (C) is incorrect because the cash budget plans for the sources and uses of cash, whereas safes and bank accounts physically safeguard cash.

113. Your objective is to determine that nonrecurring purchases, initiated by various user organizations, have been properly authorized. If all purchases are made through the purchasing department, to which of the following documents would you vouch purchases?

A. Purchase requisitions.

B. Purchase orders.

C. Invoices.

D. Receiving reports.

The correct answer is (A). *(CIA, adapted)*

REQUIRED: The document to which purchases should be vouched.

DISCUSSION: When the auditor tests for unauthorized nonrecurring purchases, (s)he should vouch purchases to the purchase requisitions. The initiating authorization by the user department is embodied in a properly authorized purchase requisition.

Answer (B) is incorrect because the purchase order does not contain the crucial initiating authorization. Answers (C) and (D) are incorrect because the authorization for a purchase is not contained in the vendor's invoice or the receiving report.

114. Effective controls relevant to purchasing of raw materials should usually include all of the following except

A. Systematic reporting of product changes that will affect raw materials.

B. Determining the need for the raw materials prior to preparing the purchase order.

C. Obtaining third-party written quality and quantity reports prior to payment for the raw materials.

D. Obtaining financial approval prior to making a commitment.

The correct answer is (C). *(CPA, adapted)*

REQUIRED: The procedure that is not an effective control over usual purchases.

DISCUSSION: Obtaining third-party written quality and quantity reports prior to payment for raw materials is unnecessary. Only in exceptional cases when client personnel are not sufficiently knowledgeable about the purchased goods would outside advice be necessary.

Answer (A) is incorrect because the latest product changes should be incorporated in the bill of materials records so that obsolete materials are not ordered. Answer (B) is incorrect because only needed items should be ordered. Answer (D) is incorrect because financial approval before making a commitment is important so that funds will be available when payment is required.

115. In assessing control risk for purchases, an auditor vouches a sample of entries in the voucher register to the supporting documents. Which assertion would this test of controls most likely support?

A. Completeness.

B. Existence or occurrence.

C. Valuation or allocation.

D. Rights and obligations.

The correct answer is (B). *(CPA, adapted)*

REQUIRED: The assertion tested by vouching.

DISCUSSION: A voucher signifies a liability. Its issuance is recorded in the voucher register after comparison of the vendor's invoice with the purchase requisition, purchase order, and receiving report. The direction of testing is an important consideration in meeting specific audit objectives. Selecting a sample of recorded entries in the voucher register and vouching them to the supporting documentation provides evidence that the transactions occurred.

Answer (A) is incorrect because this procedure does not test for unrecorded transactions. Answers (C) and (D) are incorrect because this procedure provides evidence regarding the amount owed and whether the entry reflects an obligation of the company, but it most strongly supports the assertion about existence.

116. In assessing control risk for the purchasing cycle, the auditor will be least influenced by

A. The effectiveness of controls in other cycles, e.g., the sales-receivables-cash receipts cycle.

B. The existence within the purchasing cycle of internal control strengths that offset weaknesses.

C. The audit work performed in the purchasing cycle by the company's internal auditor.

D. The availability of a company manual describing policies and procedures for the purchasing cycle.

The correct answer is (A). *(Publisher)*

REQUIRED: The least influential factor in the assessment of control risk for the purchasing cycle.

DISCUSSION: The auditor must obtain sufficient evidence to support the assessed level (if below the maximum) and document his/her conclusion and the basis therefor (AU 319). The effectiveness of internal control in other areas of an organization should not affect the assessment of control risk for the purchasing cycle. Each area should be judged upon its own merits.

Answers (B), (C), and (D) are incorrect because the availability of a company manual describing policies and procedures for the purchasing cycle, the scope and results of audit work by the company's internal auditor, and the existence of internal control strengths that offset weaknesses are important in the assessment of control risk.

117. Based on observations made during an audit, the independent auditor should discuss with management the effectiveness of the company's controls that protect against the purchase of

A. Required supplies provided by a vendor who offers no trade or cash discounts.

B. Inventory items acquired based on an economic order quantity (EOQ) inventory management concept.

C. New equipment that is needed but does not qualify for an accelerated write-off under the class life rules.

D. Supplies individually ordered, without considering possible volume discounts.

The correct answer is (D). *(CPA, adapted)*

REQUIRED: The potential weakness in the controls relevant to purchasing.

DISCUSSION: Because an auditor must communicate to the audit committee or its equivalent any reportable conditions observed during an audit (AU 325), (s)he should discuss procedures with management that permit the avoidable loss of assets. (S)he should therefore be concerned with whether the failure to consider possible volume discounts is attributable to an error or fraud.

Answer (A) is incorrect because the firm may consider other factors such as quality and service, not just whether a discount is offered on the required supplies. Answer (B) is incorrect because inventory management is appropriately based on EOQ concepts. It minimizes the sum of inventory ordering costs and inventory carrying costs. Answer (C) is incorrect because equipment acquisition should be based on need for the equipment, not on whether the purchase qualifies for preferential tax treatment.

118. Effective controls relevant to the economy and efficiency of purchases will result in proper evaluation of the time for ordering merchandise. When making this evaluation, the purchasing company should give primary consideration to

A. The price differences that exist among various vendors who can supply the merchandise at the required time.

B. The borrowing cost of money (interest) that the company must incur as a consequence of acquiring the merchandise.

C. The trade-off between the cost of owning and storing excess merchandise and the risk of loss by not having merchandise on hand.

D. The flow of funds within the company that indicates when money is available to pay for merchandise.

The correct answer is (C). *(CPA, adapted)*

REQUIRED: The primary consideration regarding the timing of purchase orders.

DISCUSSION: Effective purchasing departments should use the basic economic order quantity (EOQ) calculation that minimizes both the cost of owning and storing excess merchandise and the cost of ordering merchandise (and thus the timing of ordering). This model assumes the demand is constant and does not consider the cost of stockouts. Probabilistic models have been developed to incorporate the risk of loss (cost) by not having merchandise on hand.

Answer (A) is incorrect because the price differences that exist among various vendors does not address the question of when to order. Answer (B) is incorrect because the borrowing cost of money (interest) that the company must incur as a consequence of acquiring the merchandise does not address the question of when to order. Answer (D) is incorrect because, if the merchandise is needed, the treasurer is responsible for assuring that financing, which may be external, is arranged.

119. Which of the following constitutes the best evidence of the transfer of accountability for incoming material from the receiving department to other departments or activities?

A. The physical evidence of that type of material in other departments.

B. Oral evidence from personnel in both receiving and other departments.

C. An authorized signature on the prescribed transfer form.

D. Documentary evidence in the form of entries in journals and ledgers.

The correct answer is (C). *(CIA, adapted)*

REQUIRED: The best evidence of the transfer of accountability for incoming material.

DISCUSSION: Internal control must maintain effective accountability for assets. The signature on a prescribed form documents the transfer of accountability for assets and thus permits the recorded accountability to be compared with the existing assets when necessary.

Answer (A) is incorrect because the physical evidence of that type of material in other departments provides evidence of the physical transfer of material, not of accountability. Answer (B) is incorrect because a paper trail is preferable to oral evidence. Answer (D) is incorrect because the entries must be supported by documentation.

120. An internal control questionnaire indicates that an approved receiving report is required to accompany every check request for payment of merchandise. Which of the following procedures provides the greatest assurance that this control is operating effectively?

A. Select and examine receiving reports and ascertain that the related canceled checks are dated no earlier than the receiving reports.

B. Select and examine receiving reports and ascertain that the related canceled checks are dated no later than the receiving reports.

C. Select and examine canceled checks and ascertain that the related receiving reports are dated no earlier than the checks.

D. Select and examine canceled checks and ascertain that the related receiving reports are dated no later than the checks.

The correct answer is (D). *(CPA, adapted)*

REQUIRED: The procedure providing assurance that an approved receiving report is required to accompany every check request for payment of merchandise.

DISCUSSION: The best procedure is to test whether any checks have been issued without receiving reports. An appropriate sample of canceled checks and the related supporting documentation should be examined. The checks should not have been written before the dates on the receiving reports.

Answer (A) is incorrect because selecting and examining receiving reports and ascertaining that the related canceled checks are dated no earlier than the receiving reports tests in the wrong direction. This procedure determines whether receiving reports resulted in issuance of checks. Answer (B) is incorrect because selecting and examining receiving reports and ascertaining that the related canceled checks are dated no later than the receiving reports tests in the wrong direction. This procedure determines whether receiving reports resulted in issuance of checks. Answer (C) is incorrect because the dates on the checks should be later than the dates on the receiving reports.

121. A receiving department receives copies of purchase orders for use in identifying and recording inventory receipts. The purchase orders list the name of the vendor and the quantities of the materials ordered. A possible error that this system could allow is

A. Payment to unauthorized vendors.

B. Payment for unauthorized purchases.

C. Overpayment for partial deliveries.

D. Delay in recording purchases.

The correct answer is (C). *(CIA, adapted)*

REQUIRED: The error that may occur in a purchasing system.

DISCUSSION: To ensure a fair count, the copy of the purchase order sent to the receiving clerk should not include quantities. The receiving clerk should count the items in the shipment and prepare a receiving report. Copies are sent to inventory control and accounts payable.

Answer (A) is incorrect because comparing receipts with purchase orders will help detect unauthorized vendors. Answer (B) is incorrect because comparing receipts with purchase orders will help detect unauthorized purchases. Answer (D) is incorrect because using purchase orders to identify receipts will not delay recording purchases.

122. Which of the following controls is most effective in assuring that recorded purchases are free of material errors?

A. The receiving department compares the quantity ordered on purchase orders with the quantity received on receiving reports.

B. Vendors' invoices are compared with purchase orders by an employee who is independent of the receiving department.

C. Receiving reports require the signature of the individual who authorized the purchase.

D. Purchase orders, receiving reports, and vendors' invoices are independently matched in preparing vouchers.

The correct answer is (D). *(CPA, adapted)*

REQUIRED: The control most effective in assuring that recorded purchases are free of material errors.

DISCUSSION: A voucher should not be prepared for payment until the vendor's invoice has been matched against the corresponding purchase order and receiving report. This procedure provides assurance that a valid transaction has occurred and that the parties have agreed on the terms, such as price and quantity.

Answer (A) is incorrect because the receiving department should receive a blind copy of the purchase order. Answer (B) is incorrect because, although independent comparison of vendors' invoices with purchase orders is a reasonable control, it is not as comprehensive as (D). Answer (C) is incorrect because the receiving report is prepared by the receiving department, not by those initiating requisitions.

123. Which of the following observations, made during the preliminary survey of a local department store's disbursement cycle, reflects a control strength?

A. Individual department managers use prenumbered forms to order merchandise from vendors.

B. The receiving department is given a copy of the purchase order complete with a description of goods, quantity ordered, and extended price for all merchandise ordered.

C. The treasurer's office prepares checks for suppliers based on vouchers prepared by the accounts payable department.

D. Individual department managers are responsible for the movement of merchandise from the receiving dock to storage or sales areas as appropriate.

The correct answer is (C). *(CIA, adapted)*

REQUIRED: The observation about the disbursement cycle indicative of a control strength.

DISCUSSION: Accounting for payables is a recording function. The matching of the supplier's invoice, the purchase order, and the receiving report (and usually the purchase requisition) should be the responsibility of the accounting department. These are the primary supporting documents for the payment voucher prepared by the accounts payable section that will be relied upon by the treasurer in making payment.

Answer (A) is incorrect because the managers should submit purchase requisitions to the purchasing department. The purchasing function should be separate from operations. Answer (B) is incorrect because, to encourage a fair count, the receiving department should receive a copy of the purchase order from which the quantity has been omitted. Answer (D) is incorrect because the receiving department should transfer goods directly to the storeroom to maintain security. A copy of the receiving report should accompany the goods to the storeroom so that the amount stored can be compared with the amount in the report.

124. During the audit of a construction contract, it was discovered that the contractor was being paid for each ton of dirt removed. The contract called for payment based on cubic yards removed. Which internal control might have prevented this error?

A. Comparison of invoices with purchase orders or contracts.

B. Comparison of invoices with receiving reports.

C. Comparison of actual costs with budgeted costs.

D. Extension checks of invoice amounts.

The correct answer is (A). *(CIA, adapted)*

REQUIRED: The internal control that might have prevented use of an incorrect measure of work done.

DISCUSSION: The contractor's invoice would have stated a unit of measure different from that in the contract. Thus, a comparison of the invoice with the original contract would have disclosed the error.

Answer (B) is incorrect because the dirt removed would not have been received by the company; hence no receiving reports would have existed. Answer (C) is incorrect because this comparison would not have directly detected the specific reason for a variance. However, the cost comparison would have detected the variance and prompted an investigation of its cause. Answer (D) is incorrect because the problem was not a mathematical error but an erroneous basis for payment.

125. The procedure that would best discourage the resubmission of vendor invoices after they have been paid is

A. A requirement for double endorsement of checks.

B. The cancellation of vouchers by accounting personnel.

C. The cancelation of vouchers by treasurer personnel.

D. The mailing of payments directly to payees by accounting personnel.

The correct answer is (C). *(CMA, adapted)*

REQUIRED: The procedure best discouraging resubmission of vendor invoices after payment.

DISCUSSION: Canceling vouchers and supporting papers (with perforations, ink, etc.) upon payment prevents the payment of a duplicate voucher. If the person signing the check does the canceling, the documents cannot be recycled for duplicate payments. Securing the paid-voucher file from access by the accounts payable clerk is another effective control.

Answer (A) is incorrect because a single endorsement is not a control weakness if the person who signs does not have incompatible functions and if proper documentation is required before signing. Answer (B) is incorrect because the vouchers should not be canceled before payment. Answer (D) is incorrect because mailing payments directly to payees does not prevent a second use of invoices by unethical personnel. Also, record keepers should not have access to signed checks.

126. Which of the following controls is not usually performed with regard to vouchers payable in the accounting department?

A. Determining the mathematical accuracy of the vendor's invoice.

B. Having an authorized person approve the voucher.

C. Controlling the mailing of the check and remittance advice.

D. Matching the receiving report with the purchase order.

The correct answer is (C). *(CPA, adapted)*

REQUIRED: The control not usually applied to vouchers payable by the accounting department.

DISCUSSION: The treasurer has an asset custody function that should be segregated from the recording function of the accounting department. Consequently, checks for disbursements should be signed by an officer, normally the treasurer, after necessary supporting evidence has been examined. The treasurer should also be responsible for canceling the supporting documentation and mailing the signed checks and remittance advices. The documentation typically consists of a payment voucher, a purchase order, a receiving report, and a vendor invoice.

Answer (A) is incorrect because the accounting department determines the mathematical accuracy of the vendor's invoice. Answer (B) is incorrect because the accounting department has an authorized person approve the voucher. Answer (D) is incorrect because the accounting department matches the receiving report with the purchase order.

127. Which of the following controls is not usually performed in the vouchers payable department?

A. Matching the vendor's invoice with the related receiving report.

B. Approving vouchers for payment by having an authorized employee sign the vouchers.

C. Indicating the asset and expense accounts to be debited.

D. Accounting for unused prenumbered purchase orders and receiving reports.

The correct answer is (D). *(CPA, adapted)*

REQUIRED: The control not usually performed in the vouchers payable department.

DISCUSSION: Employees in the vouchers payable department should have no responsibilities related to purchasing or receiving goods. The purchasing department accounts for unused prenumbered purchase orders. The receiving department accounts for unused prenumbered receiving reports.

Answers (A), (B), and (C) are incorrect because matching the vendor's invoice with the related receiving report, purchase requisition, and purchase order, signing of vouchers by an authorized employee to signify that information has been verified, and indicating the affected accounts on the voucher are functions of the vouchers payable department.

128. Propex Corporation uses a voucher register and does not record invoices in a subsidiary ledger. Propex will probably benefit most from the additional cost of maintaining an accounts payable subsidiary ledger if

A. There are usually invoices in an unmatched invoice file.

B. Vendors' requests for confirmation of receivables often go unanswered for several months until paid invoices can be reviewed.

C. Partial payments to vendors are continuously made in the ordinary course of business.

D. It is difficult to reconcile vendors' monthly statements.

The correct answer is (C). *(CPA, adapted)*

REQUIRED: The situation in which an accounts payable subsidiary ledger is useful.

DISCUSSION: If a firm makes partial payments to vendors, it may be difficult to keep track of the amounts still due on vouchers. An accounts payable subsidiary ledger provides a continuous record of amounts due to vendors.

Answer (A) is incorrect because some unmatched invoices will usually be awaiting appropriate receiving reports in any organization. Answer (B) is incorrect because Propex will benefit only to the extent of good vendor relations if it promptly answers confirmation requests. This benefit is less significant than knowing continuously how much is owed to each vendor. Answer (D) is incorrect because, under a voucher system, there is no need to reconcile vendors' monthly statements unless problems arise.

129. Fraudulent use of corporate credit cards would be minimized by which of the following controls?

A. Establishing a corporate policy on the issuance of credit cards to authorized employees.

B. Periodically reviewing the validity of the need for credit cards at executive and operating levels.

C. Reconciling the monthly statement from the credit card company with the submitted copies of the cardholders' charge slips.

D. Subjecting credit card charges to the same expense controls as those used on regular company expense forms.

The correct answer is (D). *(CIA, adapted)*

REQUIRED: The control minimizing fraudulent use of corporate credit cards.

DISCUSSION: Credit card charges should be controlled in much the same manner as expense accounts and other expense reports, including use of limitations on specific kinds of expenditures. These charges should be compared with supporting documentation, such as receiving reports and invoices.

Answer (A) is incorrect because establishing a corporate policy on the issuance of credit cards to authorized employees concerns the question of credit card availability, not credit card use. Answer (B) is incorrect because periodically reviewing the validity of the need for credit cards at executive and operating levels concerns the question of credit card availability, not credit card use. Answer (C) is incorrect because reconciling the monthly statement from the credit card company with the submitted copies of the cardholders' charge slips is a check on the billing of charges.

130. Which of the following questions would not appear in an internal control questionnaire relating to cash disbursements?

A. Are all disbursements except for petty cash made by check?

B. Are imprinted and prenumbered checks used and is a check protection device used in printing the check amount?

C. Is each check supported by an approved voucher?

D. Are prelistings made of all cash receipts?

The correct answer is (D). *(Publisher)*

REQUIRED: The question not appearing in a questionnaire about cash disbursements.

DISCUSSION: Prelisting of cash receipts is performed in the mail room as part of the sales-receivables-cash receipts cycle. This question would be inappropriate in a questionnaire relating to cash disbursements. The questionnaire should list inquiries as to whether supporting documentation is mutilated upon signing; issuing a check to cash or bearer is prohibited; signing blank checks is prohibited; unused checks are controlled; voided checks are retained and accounted for; and the check signer is responsible for mailing signed checks.

Answers (A), (B), and (C) are incorrect because whether all disbursements except for petty cash are made by check, whether imprinted and prenumbered checks and a check protection device are used, and whether each check is supported by an approved voucher are appropriate questions.

131. Which of the following controls is not usually performed in the treasurer's department?

A. Verifying the accuracy of checks and vouchers.

B. Controlling the mailing of checks to vendors.

C. Approving vendors' invoices for payment.

D. Canceling payment vouchers when paid.

The correct answer is (C). *(CPA, adapted)*

REQUIRED: The control not usually performed in the treasurer's department.

DISCUSSION: The accounts payable department is responsible for compiling documentation to support an account payable. This approval process is performed in the accounting department.

Answers (A), (B), and (D) are incorrect because verifying the accuracy of checks and vouchers, controlling the mailing of checks to vendors, and canceling payment vouchers when paid are procedures typically performed in the treasurer's department.

132. If internal control is well-designed, the same employee may be permitted to

A. Mail signed checks and also cancel supporting documents.

B. Prepare receiving reports and also approve purchase orders.

C. Approve vouchers for payment and also have access to unused purchase orders.

D. Mail signed checks and also prepare bank reconciliations.

The correct answer is (A). *(CPA, adapted)*

REQUIRED: The functions the same employee may be permitted to perform.

DISCUSSION: The cash disbursements department has an asset custody function. Consequently, this department is responsible for signing checks after verification by reference to the supporting documents. The supporting documents should then be canceled and the checks mailed. Cancellation prevents the documentation from being used to support duplicate payments. Moreover, having the party who signs the checks place them in the mail reduces the risk that they will be altered or diverted.

Answer (B) is incorrect because receiving should not know how many units have been ordered. Answer (C) is incorrect because accounts payable is responsible for approving vouchers, and purchasing should be the only department with access to purchase orders. Answer (D) is incorrect because the bank reconciliation is performed by someone with no asset custody function, e.g., an accounting department employee.

133. Which of the following is a standard control over cash disbursements?

A. Checks should be signed by the controller and at least one other employee of the company.

B. Checks should be sequentially numbered and the numerical sequence should be accounted for by the person preparing bank reconciliations.

C. Checks and supporting documents should be marked "Paid" immediately after the check is returned with the bank statement.

D. Checks should be sent directly to the payee by the employee who prepares documents that authorize check preparation.

The correct answer is (B). *(CPA, adapted)*

REQUIRED: The standard control over cash disbursements.

DISCUSSION: The sequential numbering of checks provides a standard control over cash disbursements. The numerical sequence of canceled checks should be accounted for by the person preparing bank reconciliations. Physical control over blank checks should be maintained by the treasurer.

Answer (A) is incorrect because to separate custody of and accounting for cash, the controller should not have the authority to sign checks. Answer (C) is incorrect because supporting documents (but not the check) should be marked "Paid" immediately upon signing the check to preclude resubmission with a duplicate invoice. Answer (D) is incorrect because the check signer (not the check preparer) should oversee the mailing of the checks.

134. Operating control of the check-signing machine normally should be the responsibility of the

A. General accounting function.

B. Treasury function.

C. Legal counsel.

D. Internal audit function.

The correct answer is (B). *(CPA, adapted)*

REQUIRED: The department that should have operating control of the check-signing machine.

DISCUSSION: The operating control of a check-signing machine normally should be the responsibility of the treasurer. (S)he maintains custody of assets.

Answer (A) is incorrect because cash custody should not be assigned to a department that maintains accounting records. Answer (C) is incorrect because legal counsel should not have access to the check-signing machine. (S)he performs a staff function without operational authority. Answer (D) is incorrect because, to maintain its objectivity, the internal audit department should not have any responsibility for operations.

135. Which of the following items in a communication about reportable conditions in internal control over cash receipts and disbursements is least significant?

A. Cash receipts are not deposited intact daily.

B. Treasurer fails to verify the names and addresses of check payees.

C. Signed checks are distributed by the controller to approved payees.

D. Checks are signed by one person.

The correct answer is (D). *(Publisher)*

REQUIRED: The reportable condition concerning cash transactions that is of least significance.

DISCUSSION: The auditor should be least concerned that the checks are signed by only one person as long as that person is not assigned other incompatible functions and proper documentation is required before signing.

Answer (A) is incorrect because cash receipts should be deposited intact daily. Answer (B) is incorrect because the treasurer should sign checks based on proper documentation. The accounting function, which prepares the voucher (authorization for payment), should verify the payees' names and addresses. Answer (C) is incorrect because the controller, who is responsible for accounting for cash, should not have access to signed checks.

136. Which of the following questions would an auditor most likely include on an internal control questionnaire for notes payable?

A. Are assets that collateralize notes payable critically needed for the entity's continued existence?

B. Are two or more authorized signatures required on checks that repay notes payable?

C. Are the proceeds from notes payable used for the purchase of noncurrent assets?

D. Are direct borrowings on notes payable authorized by the board of directors?

The correct answer is (D). *(CPA, adapted)*

REQUIRED: The question most likely included on an internal control questionnaire for notes payable.

DISCUSSION: Control is enhanced when different persons or departments authorize, record, and maintain custody of assets for a class of transactions. Authorization of notes payable is best done by the board of directors.

Answer (A) is incorrect because the importance of specific assets to the entity is an operational matter and not a primary concern of an auditor in the consideration of internal control. Answer (B) is incorrect because questions about the payment function are likely to be included on the questionnaire relating to cash disbursements. Answer (C) is incorrect because the use of funds is an operating decision made by management and is not a primary concern of the auditor in the consideration of internal control.

137. Under which of the following circumstances would an auditor be most likely to intensify an audit of a $500 imprest petty cash fund?

A. Reimbursement vouchers are not prenumbered.

B. Reimbursement occurs twice each week.

C. The custodian occasionally uses the cash fund to cash employee checks.

D. The custodian endorses reimbursement checks.

The correct answer is (B). *(CPA, adapted)*

REQUIRED: The circumstance in which the auditor would intensify an audit of a petty cash fund.

DISCUSSION: If the auditor determines that reimbursement occurs twice each week, (s)he would intensify the audit of the imprest cash fund. The frequent need for reimbursement suggests that the fund is not functioning as planned.

Answer (A) is incorrect because, although failure to prenumber vouchers is not a preferable practice, it does not suggest errors or fraud. Answer (C) is incorrect because use of the cash fund to cash employee checks is not a preferable practice, but it does not suggest errors or fraud. Answer (D) is incorrect because the custodian's endorsement of reimbursement checks is an appropriate procedure to obtain cash for the fund.

3.8 Internal Control of Personnel and Payroll

138. Which of the following is an operating control over the staffing function?

A. Making background checks on all new hires.

B. Maintaining records of the department's accomplishments.

C. Encouraging new hires to participate in professional organizations.

D. Encouraging personnel to participate in firm-sponsored external activities.

The correct answer is (A). *(CIA, adapted)*

REQUIRED: The operating control over staffing.

DISCUSSION: Staffing concerns providing the necessary personnel to achieve organizational objectives economically. Because honest and capable personnel also help create an environment conducive to effective internal control, hiring policies and procedures are crucial. Background checks, for example, may screen out potential hirees of questionable character.

Answer (B) is incorrect because maintaining records is an accounting control. Answers (C) and (D) are incorrect because professional development activities concern the directing function, that is, motivating people in an organization to contribute effectively to achieve goals.

139. Effective controls over the payroll function may include

A. Reconciliation of totals on job time tickets with job reports by employees responsible for those specific jobs.

B. Verification of agreement of job time tickets with employee clock card hours by a payroll department employee.

C. Preparation of payroll transaction journal entries by an employee who reports to the supervisor of the personnel department.

D. Custody of rate authorization records by the supervisor of the payroll department.

The correct answer is (B). *(CPA, adapted)*

REQUIRED: The effective control over payroll.

DISCUSSION: The total time spent on jobs should closely approximate the total time indicated on time cards. Comparing these records should therefore provide an independent check of the accuracy of time reported on the time cards.

Answer (A) is incorrect because an independent party should perform the review function; employees should not review themselves. Answer (C) is incorrect because the functions of authorization, custody of assets, and record keeping should not be performed (or controlled) by the same parties. The payroll department should prepare the payroll transaction journal entries. If the personnel department performed this task, authorization and record keeping would be combined. Answer (D) is incorrect because personnel authorizes the pay rates used in the payroll calculation.

140. In manufacturing environments, employees are often required to use time cards and job time tickets. Which is the false statement related to the use of these documents?

A. Job time tickets are completed by employees for each job worked on, and an employee may have one or many job time tickets in a day.

B. Only one time card should exist for each employee.

C. Time reported on job time tickets should be reconciled to time cards.

D. Payroll should be prepared from job time tickets.

The correct answer is (D). *(Publisher)*

REQUIRED: The false statement about job time tickets and time cards.

DISCUSSION: The payroll should be prepared from the time cards, which are the official records of time worked. The allocation of direct labor to the various jobs and the identification of indirect labor that should be charged to overhead is determined from the job time tickets.

Answer (A) is incorrect because a different job time ticket should be prepared for each employee task, and an employee may work on one or many jobs in a day. Answer (B) is incorrect because each employee should have only one time card, which is the official record of hours worked. Answer (C) is incorrect because the time reported on the time tickets should be reconciled to the time cards.

141. Organizational independence in the processing of payroll is achieved by functional separations that are built into the system. Which one of the following functional separations is not required for internal control purposes?

A. Separation of timekeeping from payroll preparation.

B. Separation of personnel function from payroll preparation.

C. Separation of payroll preparation and paycheck distribution.

D. Separation of payroll preparation and maintenance of year-to-date records.

The correct answer is (D). *(CMA, adapted)*

REQUIRED: The functional separation that is not required for internal control purposes.

DISCUSSION: Most companies have their payrolls prepared by the same individuals who maintain the year-to-date records. There is no need for this functional separation because both duties involve record keeping.

Answer (A) is incorrect because separating timekeeping and payroll preparation is an effective control. It prevents one person from claiming that an employee worked certain hours and then writing a check to that employee. Payment to an absent or fictitious employee would therefore require collusion between two employees. Answer (B) is incorrect because personnel should be separate from payroll. The former authorizes the calculation of the payroll by the latter. Answer (C) is incorrect because separating paycheck preparation from distribution makes it more difficult for fictitious employees to receive checks.

142. Which of the following controls is most effective in providing reasonable assurance that salary, wage, and benefit expenses are incurred only for work performed?

A. All time cards and reports are reviewed and approved in writing by immediate line supervisors having no responsibilities for paycheck distribution.

B. The accuracy of extensions of hours worked and pay rates is rechecked by an independent party, and pay rate and other key payroll information is changed only upon the receipt of a written authorization from the personnel department.

C. Actual payroll amounts are regularly compared against budgeted amounts by management, with all material budget variances being investigated.

D. The payroll register is used as the source document for posting employment-related expenses to the general ledger.

The correct answer is (A). *(CIA, adapted)*

REQUIRED: The most effective control providing reasonable assurance that salary, wage, and benefit expenses are incurred only for work performed.

DISCUSSION: Review and approval of time cards by line supervisors is appropriate because they should know whether work has been performed. Also, they do not distribute paychecks, so they are not in a position to divert falsely authorized checks.

Answer (B) is incorrect because an arithmetic check of payroll calculations provides no control over the actual hours reported, which is the basis for compensating work performed. Also, proper authority for pay rate changes controls the level of pay, not the reporting of hours of work performed. Answer (C) is incorrect because comparisons between actual and budgeted labor expense may reveal overall inefficient labor use, but probably not particular improprieties. Answer (D) is incorrect because posting to the general ledger from the payroll register controls recording of the expense, not the propriety of the labor hours reported.

143. In the audit of which of the following types of profit-oriented enterprises is the auditor most likely to place special emphasis on testing the controls over proper classification of payroll transactions?

A. A manufacturing organization.

B. A retailing organization.

C. A wholesaling organization.

D. A service organization.

The correct answer is (A). *(CPA, adapted)*

REQUIRED: The organization in which payroll transaction classifications are most important to the auditor.

DISCUSSION: A manufacturing organization is characteristically labor intensive with a high frequency and volume of payroll transactions requiring classification into direct labor and overhead. Payroll information is important in the costing of work-in-process, finished goods inventory, and cost of goods sold.

Answers (B), (C), and (D) are incorrect because retailing, wholesaling, and service organizations are normally not as labor intensive and do not require as many payroll transactions as a manufacturer. Furthermore, their labor costs are typically expensed rather than capitalized as part of inventory.

144. Which of the following departments most likely approves changes in pay rates and deductions from employee salaries?

A. Personnel.

B. Treasurer.

C. Controller.

D. Payroll.

The correct answer is (A). *(CPA, adapted)*

REQUIRED: The department that most likely approves changes in pay rates and deductions.

DISCUSSION: The personnel department provides the authorization for payroll-related transactions, e.g., hiring, termination, and changes in pay rates and deductions.

Answer (B) is incorrect because the treasurer performs a custody function for payroll-related transactions. Answers (C) and (D) are incorrect because the payroll department, which is overseen by the controller, has a record keeping function for payroll-related transactions.

145. Which of the following controls is most likely to prevent direct labor hours from being charged to manufacturing overhead?

A. Periodic independent counts of work-in-process for comparison with recorded amounts.

B. Comparison of daily journal entries with approved production orders.

C. Use of time tickets to record actual labor worked on production orders.

D. Reconciliation of work-in-process inventory with periodic cost budgets.

The correct answer is (C). *(CPA, adapted)*

REQUIRED: The control to prevent direct labor hours from being charged to manufacturing overhead.

DISCUSSION: Time tickets should specifically identify labor hours as direct or indirect.

Answer (A) is incorrect because independent counts of work-in-process for comparison with recorded amounts provide assurance that all inventories are accounted for but do not assure proper classification of the costs within the account. Answer (B) is incorrect because comparison of daily journal entries with approved production orders only provides assurance that costs are being assigned to production orders. Answer (D) is incorrect because reconciliation of work-in-process inventory with periodic cost budgets is an analytical procedure that might detect, but would not prevent, the problem.

146. The purpose of segregating the duties of hiring personnel and distributing payroll checks is to separate the

A. Human resources function from the controllership function.

B. Administrative controls from the internal accounting controls.

C. Authorization of transactions from the custody of related assets.

D. Operational responsibility from the record keeping responsibility.

The correct answer is (C). *(CPA, adapted)*

REQUIRED: The purpose of segregating the duties of hiring personnel and distributing payroll checks.

DISCUSSION: In principle, the payroll function should be divided into its authorization, recording, and custody functions. Authorization of hiring, wage rates, and deductions is provided by personnel. Authorization of hours worked is provided by production. Based upon these authorizations, accounting calculates and records the payroll. Based on the calculated amounts, the treasurer prepares and distributes payroll checks.

Answer (A) is incorrect because neither the controller (accounting function) nor the personnel department (human resources function) should distribute checks. Answer (B) is incorrect because the professional standards no longer recognize the distinction between administrative controls and internal accounting controls. Answer (D) is incorrect because neither hiring personnel (authorization) nor distributing checks (asset custody) is a record keeping activity.

147. Which of the following situations represents an internal control weakness in the payroll department?

A. Payroll department personnel are rotated in their duties.

B. Paychecks are distributed by the employees' immediate supervisor.

C. Payroll records are reconciled with quarterly tax reports.

D. The timekeeping function is independent of the payroll department.

The correct answer is (B). *(CMA, adapted)*

REQUIRED: The internal control weakness in the payroll department.

DISCUSSION: A supervisor who distributes payroll checks is in a position to divert paychecks of fictitious employees if (s)he also has access to personnel records. This opportunity results from being assigned the incompatible functions of authorization, record keeping, and custodianship. A person unrelated to either payroll record keeping or the operating department should distribute checks.

Answer (A) is incorrect because periodic rotation of payroll personnel inhibits the perpetration and concealment of fraud. Answer (C) is incorrect because reconciling payroll records with quarterly tax reports is an analytical procedure that may detect a discrepancy. Answer (D) is incorrect because timekeeping should be independent of employee records.

148. Which of the following personnel department procedures reduces the risk of payroll fraud and represents an appropriate responsibility for the department?

A. Distributing paychecks.

B. Authorizing overtime hours.

C. Authorizing the addition or deletion of employees from the payroll.

D. Collection and retention of unclaimed paychecks.

The correct answer is (C). *(CIA, adapted)*

REQUIRED: The procedure reducing the risk of fraud that is the responsibility of the personnel department.

DISCUSSION: The payroll department is responsible for assembling payroll information (record keeping). The personnel department is responsible for authorizing employee transactions such as hiring, firing, and changes in pay rates and deductions. Segregating the recording and authorization functions helps prevent fraud.

Answer (A) is incorrect because the treasurer should perform the asset custody function regarding payroll. Answer (B) is incorrect because authorizing overtime is a responsibility of operating management. Answer (D) is incorrect because unclaimed checks should be in the custody of the treasurer until they can be deposited in a special bank account.

149. Which of the following procedures most likely would be considered a weakness in an entity's internal control over payroll?

A. A voucher for the amount of the payroll is prepared in the general accounting department based on the payroll department's payroll summary.

B. Payroll checks are prepared by the payroll department and signed by the treasurer.

C. The employee who distributes payroll checks returns unclaimed payroll checks to the payroll department.

D. The personnel department sends employees' termination notices to the payroll department.

The correct answer is (C). *(CPA, adapted)*

REQUIRED: The ineffective control over payroll.

DISCUSSION: The payroll department assembles payroll information, which is a recording function. Custody of assets, such as unclaimed payroll checks, is incompatible with record keeping.

Answer (A) is incorrect because preparation of a voucher is appropriately performed by the accounting department, which has a record keeping function. Answer (B) is incorrect because the treasurer's signing of checks is consistent with the asset custody function. Answer (D) is incorrect because the personnel department properly performs the authorization function regarding employment transactions.

150. Each Friday afternoon payroll checks are distributed by the shift superintendent. The plant is so large and the turnover is so great that the superintendent does not know many of the workers. Undelivered checks are returned to the payroll clerk, from whom the workers can obtain them at some later time. The payroll clerk routinely continues the payroll record for workers one week after their departure from the firm, ultimately cashes the unclaimed checks, and keeps the money. Which of the following is a control designed to prevent this misappropriation?

A. Require the shift superintendent to know all the workers by name.

B. Require the timekeeper to compute the weekly pay of each worker and to make distribution of the checks received from the treasurer's office.

C. Require the treasurer's office to prepare checks only on the basis of supporting documentation from both the timekeeper and payroll office.

D. Periodically rotate the shift superintendent.

The correct answer is (C). *(CIA, adapted)*

REQUIRED: The control designed to prevent a misappropriation by a payroll clerk.

DISCUSSION: The payroll should be prepared from the time cards, which are the official records of time worked, and the authorized pay rates and deductions. After the payroll is prepared, it should be independently verified. Also, the payroll department has a recording function and should not be charged with custody of related assets (undelivered paychecks) even temporarily. Undelivered checks should be sent to the treasurer for deposit in a bank account after a reasonable period of time.

Answer (A) is incorrect because requiring the shift superintendent to know all workers by name is a control that would be difficult to execute. Answer (B) is incorrect because the timekeeper should not perform these incompatible functions. (S)he should neither compute weekly pay nor have custody of assets. Answer (D) is incorrect because the payroll clerk's fraud does not depend on the identity of the shift superintendent.

151. Proper internal control over the cash payroll function mandates which of the following?

A. The payroll clerk should fill the envelopes with cash and a computation of the net wages.

B. Unclaimed pay envelopes should be retained by the paymaster.

C. Each employee should be asked to sign a receipt.

D. A separate checking account for payroll should be maintained.

The correct answer is (C). *(CPA, adapted)*

REQUIRED: The most appropriate control over cash payroll.

DISCUSSION: Under a cash payroll system, the receipt signed by the employee, which is the only document in support of payment, is essential to verify proper payment.

Answer (A) is incorrect because a person (e.g., a cashier) other than the one computing net wages should put the cash in the envelope. Answer (B) is incorrect because unclaimed cash payroll should be deposited in a special bank account for safekeeping. Answer (D) is incorrect because effective internal control does not require that a separate account be maintained. Only a limited number of checks is necessary for a cash payroll.

152. A large retail enterprise has established a policy that requires the paymaster to deliver all unclaimed payroll checks to the internal auditing department at the end of each payroll distribution day. This policy was most likely adopted to

A. Assure that employees who were absent on a payroll distribution day are not paid for that day.

B. Prevent the paymaster from cashing checks that are unclaimed for several weeks.

C. Prevent a bona fide employee's check from being claimed by another employee.

D. Detect any fictitious employee who may have been placed on the payroll.

The correct answer is (D). *(CPA, adapted)*

REQUIRED: The reason for delivering unclaimed payroll checks to the internal auditing department.

DISCUSSION: A follow-up of unclaimed checks may result in identification of fictitious or terminated employees, thus eliminating an employee's opportunity to claim a paycheck belonging to a terminated employee. The unclaimed checks should then be turned over to a custodian so the internal auditing function does not assume operating responsibilities.

Answer (A) is incorrect because assuring that employees are not paid for absences is an operating responsibility, which should not be undertaken by the internal auditing department. Answer (B) is incorrect because preventing the paymaster from cashing checks can be achieved by immediately turning the unclaimed checks over to a custodian. Answer (C) is incorrect because preventing a bona fide employee's check from being claimed by another employee is a control that applies only to unclaimed checks and thus would not identify checks claimed by the wrong employees.

153. Employers bond employees who handle cash receipts because fidelity bonds reduce the possibility of employing dishonest individuals and

A. Protect employees who make unintentional errors from possible monetary damages resulting from their errors.

B. Deter dishonesty by making employees aware that insurance companies may investigate and prosecute dishonest acts.

C. Facilitate an independent monitoring of the receiving and depositing of cash receipts.

D. Force employees in positions of trust to take periodic vacations and rotate their assigned duties.

The correct answer is (B). *(CPA, adapted)*

REQUIRED: The purpose of bonding employees.

DISCUSSION: Effective internal control, including personnel practices that stress the hiring of trustworthy people, does not guarantee against losses from embezzlement and other fraudulent acts committed by employees. Accordingly, an employer may obtain a fidelity bond to insure against losses arising from illegal acts by the covered employees. Blanket policies that cover groups of employees are often obtained by larger employers. Prior to issuing this form of insurance, the underwriters investigate the individuals to be covered, a practice that prevents the hiring of employees whose past misdeeds can be uncovered in this way. Also, employees should be informed that bonding companies are diligent in prosecuting bonded individuals who commit fraud.

Answer (A) is incorrect because bonding insures employers against intentional wrongdoing. Answers (C) and (D) are incorrect because bonding is irrelevant to an independent monitoring of the receiving and depositing of cash receipts or to forcing trusted employees to take periodic vacations and rotate their assigned duties.

154. An auditor will ordinarily ascertain whether payroll checks are properly endorsed during the audit of

A. Time cards.

B. The voucher system.

C. Cash in bank.

D. Accrued payroll.

The correct answer is (A). *(CPA, adapted)*

REQUIRED: The phase in the audit when payroll check endorsements are audited.

DISCUSSION: Ordinarily, the auditor examines the endorsements on payroll checks while obtaining an understanding of and testing the payroll cycle, which includes consideration of time cards.

Answers (B) and (C) are incorrect because the voucher system and cash in bank are usually not integral to the payroll cycle. Answer (D) is incorrect because accrued payroll implies that payroll checks were not issued, e.g., for a partial payroll period just prior to year-end.

3.9 Internal Control of Securities

155. Each of the following is a proper control over securities and investments except

A. Proper authorization of transactions.

B. Custodian bonded and separate from investment records.

C. Storage in a safe-deposit box.

D. Custodian separate from treasury function.

The correct answer is (D). *(Publisher)*

REQUIRED: The improper control over securities and investments.

DISCUSSION: The custody of cash and securities should be placed with the treasury function. The treasurer should therefore not be separated from custody of securities and investments.

Answers (A) and (C) are incorrect because proper authorization of transactions and storage in a safe-deposit box are proper controls over securities and investments. Answer (B) is incorrect because the custodian should be bonded and should not have access to records.

156. Which of the following controls would an entity most likely use to assist in satisfying the completeness assertion related to long-term investments?

A. Senior management verifies that securities in the bank safe-deposit box are registered in the entity's name.

B. The internal auditor compares the securities in the bank safe-deposit box with recorded investments.

C. The treasurer vouches the acquisition of securities by comparing brokers' advices with canceled checks.

D. The controller compares the current market prices of recorded investments with the brokers' advices on file.

The correct answer is (B). *(CPA, adapted)*

REQUIRED: The control to test the completeness assertion for long-term investments.

DISCUSSION: An interpretation of AU 326 states, "Substantive tests designed primarily to obtain evidence about the completeness assertion include analytical procedures and tests of details of related populations." The related population consists of the assets in the safe-deposit box. This population should be compared with the records of the investments to provide assurance that the balance is complete, that is, contains all long-term investments.

Answer (A) is incorrect because verification that securities are registered in the entity's name relates to the rights assertion. Answer (C) is incorrect because comparing canceled checks with brokers' advices pertains to the rights assertion. Answer (D) is incorrect because comparing market prices with brokers' advices relates most directly to the valuation assertion.

157. Which of the following questions is not appropriate for an internal control questionnaire concerning securities?

A. Is there a periodic reconciliation of the detail of securities with the security control account?

B. Is there a record of all identification numbers of securities, and are securities held in the name of the company?

C. Do the internal auditors periodically test controls over securities?

D. All of the questions are appropriate.

The correct answer is (D). *(Publisher)*

REQUIRED: The question not appropriate for an control questionnaire on securities.

DISCUSSION: Each item listed is an important control regarding securities.

Answer (A) is incorrect because there should be a periodic reconciliation of the individual securities with the control account in the general ledger. Answer (B) is incorrect because all aspects of the securities, including the identification numbers, should be recorded, and the securities should be in the name of the firm rather than held in bearer form or in the name of an individual. Answer (C) is incorrect because the internal auditors should periodically test the controls over securities.

158. An internal auditor is reviewing the company's policy regarding investing in financial derivatives. The auditor would normally expect to find all of the following in the policy except

A. A statement indicating whether derivatives are to be used for hedging or speculative purposes.

B. A specific authorization limit for the amount and types of derivatives that can be used by the organization.

C. A specific limit on the amount authorized for any single trader.

D. A statement requiring board review of each transaction because of the risk involved in such transactions.

The correct answer is (D). *(CIA, adapted)*

REQUIRED: The item not normally expected to be found in a policy regarding investing in financial derivatives.

DISCUSSION: Policies are general statements that guide managers' decision making. They are developed by the board of directors to provide guidelines for achieving objectives. Management is responsible for daily operations and should abide by the policies. Consequently, the board would not review each transaction.

Answers (A), (B), and (C) are incorrect because, whether the derivatives are to be used for hedging or speculating, authorization limits are appropriate guidelines to be included in the policy.

159. When considering internal control over securities, the auditor is especially concerned about

A. Access to stock certificates by the corporate controller.

B. Access to stock certificates by the corporate treasurer.

C. Preparation of accrual adjustments on bonds by the corporate controller.

D. Approval of temporary stock investment purchases by the corporate treasurer or company president.

The correct answer is (A). *(CMA, adapted)*

REQUIRED: The major concern of an auditor considering internal control over securities.

DISCUSSION: Access to stock certificates by the controller is a breakdown of the fundamental segregation of duties needed for effective internal control. The controller, who performs the accounting function, should not have access to the assets.

Answer (B) is incorrect because the treasurer, in the normal performance of the custodianship function, rightly has access to stock certificates. Answer (C) is incorrect because the controller prepares accrual adjustments on bonds, e.g., interest and discount (premium) amortization. Answer (D) is incorrect because the approval of temporary stock purchases by the treasurer or the president is a typical delegation of authority by the board. However, the directors should periodically review this activity.

160. When an entity uses a trust company as custodian of its trading securities, the possibility of concealing fraud most likely would be reduced if the

A. Trust company has no direct contact with the entity employees responsible for maintaining investment accounting records.

B. Securities are registered in the name of the trust company rather than the entity itself.

C. Interest and dividend checks are mailed directly to an entity employee who is authorized to sell securities.

D. Trust company places the securities in a bank safe-deposit vault under the custodian's exclusive control.

The correct answer is (A). *(CPA, adapted)*

REQUIRED: The condition that would reduce the possibility of the concealment of fraud.

DISCUSSION: To conceal fraud related to trading securities, collusion between those responsible for record keeping and custody would be required. The possibility of collusion is reduced if no direct contact between responsible parties exists.

Answer (B) is incorrect because the securities should be registered in the name of the owner. Answer (C) is incorrect because interest and dividends should be sent to the trust company custodian. Answer (D) is incorrect because use of a bank safe-deposit vault under the custodian's exclusive control is an appropriate control but does not minimize the possibility of collusion.

161. An employee should not be able to visit the corporate safe-deposit box containing investment securities without being accompanied by another corporate employee. What would be a possible consequence of an employee's being able to visit the safe-deposit box unaccompanied?

A. The employee could pledge corporate investments as security for a short-term personal bank loan.

B. The employee could steal securities, and the theft would never be discovered.

C. It would be impossible to obtain a fidelity bond on the employee.

D. There would be no record of when company personnel visited the safe-deposit box.

The correct answer is (A). *(CIA, adapted)*

REQUIRED: The possible result of an unaccompanied visit to the safe-deposit box.

DISCUSSION: The bank should maintain a record, which can be inspected by company personnel, of all safe-deposit box visits. Access should be limited to authorized officers. Firms typically require the presence of two authorized persons for access to the box. This precaution provides supervisory control over, for example, the temporary removal of the securities to serve as a pledge for a loan (hypothecation of securities).

Answer (B) is incorrect because an audit would eventually uncover an outright theft assuming no alteration of the asset records. Answer (C) is incorrect because obtaining a fidelity bond is contingent upon the character of the employee, not the presence of a specific control. Answer (D) is incorrect because the bank maintains a record of visits.

162. Which of the following procedures is most likely to give the greatest assurance that securities held as investments are safeguarded?

A. There is no access to securities between year-end and the date of the auditor's security count.

B. Proceeds from the sale of investments are received by an employee who does not have access to securities.

C. Investment acquisitions are authorized by a member of the board of directors before execution.

D. Access to securities requires the signatures and presence of two designated officials.

The correct answer is (D). *(CPA, adapted)*

REQUIRED: The control procedure that best safeguards securities held as investments.

DISCUSSION: The presence of two authorized individuals is usually required for access to securities, especially those held in safe-deposit boxes. This precaution provides supervisory control.

Answer (A) is incorrect because denying access to authorized officials is not conducive to successful financial management. Moreover, the procedure is effective for a short period only. Answer (B) is incorrect because other employees may have improper access. Answer (C) is incorrect because the issue is the physical safety of assets already held, not authorization of acquisitions.

3.10 Internal Control of Inventory

163. Internal control over inventories is important for all of the following reasons except

A. Inventories are often the largest current asset.

B. Inventories directly affect the results of operations.

C. Inventories are the most liquid asset.

D. Inventories are a material component of total assets.

The correct answer is (C). *(Publisher)*

REQUIRED: The statement not a reason internal control over inventories is important.

DISCUSSION: Cash is considered the most liquid asset and most subject to inherent risk.

Answer (A) is incorrect because inventories typically represent an extremely large component of current assets. Answer (B) is incorrect because inventories, once sold, become cost of goods sold, and therefore are an important component of the results of operations. Answer (D) is incorrect because inventories typically represent a large portion of the total assets of a firm.

164. Which of the following questions would not be appropriate for an internal control questionnaire concerning inventory?

A. Are goods stored in locked storage areas?

B. Are disbursement vouchers approved before payment?

C. Is access to the storeroom limited to authorized personnel?

D. Are there independent, periodic comparisons of inventory records with goods on hand?

The correct answer is (B). *(Publisher)*

REQUIRED: The question inappropriate for an internal control questionnaire on inventory.

DISCUSSION: Disbursement vouchers should be prepared for all types of expenditures, not just inventory. Thus, a question about vouchers would be more appropriately asked in the cash disbursements questionnaire.

Answer (A) is incorrect because goods in locked storage areas relates directly to the internal controls over the inventory function. Answer (C) is incorrect because limitation of access to the storeroom to authorized personnel relates directly to the internal controls over the inventory function. Answer (D) is incorrect because independent, periodic comparisons of inventory records with goods on hand relates directly to the controls over the inventory function.

165. An essential procedural control to ensure the accuracy of the recorded inventory quantities is

A. Performing a gross profit test.

B. Testing inventory extensions.

C. Calculating unit costs and valuing obsolete or damaged inventory items in accordance with inventory policy.

D. Establishing a cutoff for goods received and shipped.

The correct answer is (D). *(CIA, adapted)*

REQUIRED: The control over recorded inventory quantities.

DISCUSSION: A proper cutoff point for goods received and shipped assures that only goods owned by the client are included in inventory.

Answers (A), (B), and (C) are incorrect because performing a gross profit test, testing inventory extensions, calculating unit costs, and valuing obsolete or damaged inventory items are primarily concerned with the dollar valuation of inventory rather than with the quantity of items in inventory.

166. Apex Manufacturing Corporation mass produces eight different products. The controller who is interested in strengthening internal control over the accounting for materials used in production is most likely to implement

A. An economic order quantity (EOQ) system.

B. A job-order cost accounting system.

C. A perpetual inventory system.

D. A separation of duties among production personnel.

The correct answer is (C). *(CPA, adapted)*

REQUIRED: The best system to strengthen internal control over accounting for materials.

DISCUSSION: A perpetual inventory system provides for continuous updating of inventory records and thus accounting for materials used. Close and continuous attention must be paid to materials usage to keep a perpetual system up to date.

Answer (A) is incorrect because EOQ makes reordering more cost effective but does not strengthen the control over accounting for materials used. Answer (B) is incorrect because a job-order cost system determines the cost of special order products. Also, a process-cost system, not a job-order system, is applicable to mass production. Answer (D) is incorrect because separation of duties among production workers does not improve control over accounting for materials unless the functions of authorization, asset custody, and recording are also separated.

167. An internal auditor is examining inventory control in a merchandising division with annual sales of $3,000,000 and a 40% gross profit rate. Tests show that 2% of the dollar amount of purchases do not get into inventory because of breakage and employee theft. Adding certain controls costing $35,000 annually could reduce these losses to .5% of purchases. Should the controls be recommended?

A. Yes, because the projected saving exceeds the cost of the added controls.

B. No, because the cost of the added controls exceeds the projected savings.

C. Yes, because the ideal system of internal control is the most extensive one.

D. Yes, regardless of cost-benefit considerations, because the situation involves employee theft.

The correct answer is (B). *(CIA, adapted)*

REQUIRED: The correct decision as to whether to add inventory controls and the reason.

DISCUSSION: Controls must be subject to the cost-benefit criterion. The annual cost of these inventory controls is $35,000, but the cost saving is only $27,000 {(2% – .5%) x [$3,000,000 sales x (100% – 40% gross profit rate)]}. Hence, the cost exceeds the benefit, and the controls should not be recommended.

Answer (A) is incorrect because cost exceeds the benefit. Answer (C) is incorrect because the ideal system is not likely to be feasible on account of its cost. Answer (D) is incorrect because cost-benefit considerations apply even to employee theft.

168. The objectives of internal control for a production cycle are to provide assurance that transactions are properly executed and recorded, and that

A. Independent internal verification of activity reports is established.

B. Transfers to finished goods are documented by a completed production report and a quality control report.

C. Production orders are prenumbered and signed by a supervisor.

D. Custody of work-in-process and of finished goods is properly maintained.

The correct answer is (D). *(CPA, adapted)*

REQUIRED: The objectives of internal control for a production cycle.

DISCUSSION: A principal objective of internal control is to safeguard assets. In the production cycle, control procedures must be in place to ensure that inventory is protected from misuse and theft. Accordingly, inventories should be in the custody of a storekeeper, and transfers should be properly documented and recorded to establish accountability.

Answers (A), (B), and (C) are incorrect because independent internal verification of activity reports, documenting transfers to finished goods, and the use of prenumbered production orders signed by a supervisor are control procedures, not objectives.

169. To determine if an organization is purchasing excess raw materials, an internal auditor should

A. Be sure that standards are established for quality, quantity, and sourcing for raw materials.

B. Ascertain that production budgets and economic order quantities are integrated and have been used in determining quantities purchased.

C. Obtain assurance that purchasing agent assignments are rotated periodically.

D. Determine that the purchasing department has a written charter with a set of procedures and guidelines covering purchasing operations.

The correct answer is (B). *(CIA, adapted)*

REQUIRED: The procedure to determine if an organization is purchasing excess raw materials.

DISCUSSION: An economic order quantity (EOQ) model can be used to determine the order quantity (or production run) that minimizes the sum or order costs (or setup costs for production) and carrying costs, given annual demand. Production needs and the EOQ model should be coordinated to ascertain the optimal levels of raw materials purchases.

Answer (A) is incorrect because these standards are beneficial, but excess inventory will still result if production, EOQs, and purchasing are not coordinated. Answer (C) is incorrect because rotation of purchasing agents is a control intended to prevent conflicts of interest, not excessive purchasing. Answer (D) is incorrect because the existence of procedures and guidelines is not proof that they are being followed.

170. A purchasing agent places an order for inventory whenever a requisition is received from the warehouse. The warehouse clerk issues requisitions based on periodic physical counts because no perpetual records are maintained. Numerous duplicate orders have been placed for goods previously ordered but not received. To prevent this excess ordering, the firm should

A. Keep an adequate record of open purchase orders and review it before ordering.

B. Count goods in the warehouse less often.

C. Use prenumbered purchase orders.

D. Not use purchase requisitions.

The correct answer is (A). *(Publisher)*

REQUIRED: The procedure by which a company using a monthly physical inventory as a basis for purchase orders can prevent excess ordering.

DISCUSSION: A well-kept open purchase order file will provide information on outstanding orders and, if reviewed prior to ordering, will prevent duplicate orders.

Answer (B) is incorrect because, to requisition needed goods on a timely basis, goods must be counted often. Answer (C) is incorrect because prenumbered purchase orders fail to provide information on purchase orders placed but not received. Answer (D) is incorrect because purchase requisitions are authorizations for purchases and should be the basis for a purchase order.

171. A company uses an MRP (materials requirement planning) system to control inventory. One objective is to minimize raw material inventories while avoiding production shutdowns. One way to achieve this objective using MRP is to

A. Regularly update the authorized master production schedule.

B. Use an EOQ (economic order quantity) model.

C. Take a physical inventory monthly instead of annually.

D. Use a second-order exponential smoothing model with seasonality factors.

The correct answer is (A). *(CIA, adapted)*

REQUIRED: The means of minimizing raw material inventories.

DISCUSSION: MRP is a computer-based information system designed to plan and control materials used in production. It determines the quantity of finished goods that will be required and the point when they will be needed. The system requires prompt notice of changes in production schedules.

Answer (B) is incorrect because an EOQ system is a general inventory management model that attempts to balance ordering and carrying costs. Answer (C) is incorrect because taking inventory does not reduce the amount on hand. Answer (D) is incorrect because an MRP system must be concerned with very short-term rather than seasonal variations in production requirements.

172. For several years a client's physical inventory count has been lower than the books have shown at the time of the count, and downward adjustments of the inventory account have been required. Contributing to the inventory problem could be weaknesses in internal control that led to the failure to record some

A. Purchases returned to vendors.

B. Sales returns received.

C. Sales discounts allowed.

D. Cash purchases.

The correct answer is (A). *(CPA, adapted)*

REQUIRED: The transaction that results in an overstatement of inventory.

DISCUSSION: Purchases returned to the vendor but not recorded overstate inventory records. The goods are reflected in inventory but are not on hand.

Answer (B) is incorrect because unrecorded sales returns are included in the physical count but do not appear on the books, resulting in an understatement (not overstatement) of inventory. Answer (C) is incorrect because failure to record sales discounts overstates sales figures but has no effect on inventory. Answer (D) is incorrect because unrecorded cash purchases are included in the physical count but do not appear on the books, resulting in an understatement (not overstatement) of inventory.

173. A firm's inventory consisted of 1,000 different items, 20 of which accounted for 70% of the dollar value. The most recent regular quarterly manual count revealed an unnecessary 2 years' supply of several of the more expensive items. The control that would best help to correct this oversupply problem is

A. Use of a control total over the number of unique inventory items.

B. Limit check on the total dollar value of the inventory.

C. Use of authorizing signatures on requisitions for inventory requested by production.

D. Perpetual inventory of the larger dollar value items in the inventory.

The correct answer is (D). *(CIA, adapted)*

REQUIRED: The control to prevent oversupply.

DISCUSSION: In a perpetual system, purchases (or transfers from work-in-process) are recorded directly in the inventory account when they are made. Inventory is correspondingly reduced as sales occur. Thus, a running total of inventory can be monitored throughout the period.

Answer (A) is incorrect because a control total would verify that no inventory records were lost or that no new ones were added. It would not aid in the solution of the inventory acquisition problem. Answer (B) is incorrect because a limit test on the total inventory value would provide information as to when the inventory dollar level reached a certain point but not on the makeup of the inventory. Answer (C) is incorrect because use of authorizing signatures would provide control over requisitions but not over the rest of the inventory acquisition process.

174. Which of the following controls most likely would be used to maintain accurate inventory records?

A. Perpetual inventory records are periodically compared with the current cost of individual inventory items.

B. A just-in-time inventory ordering system keeps inventory levels to a desired minimum.

C. Requisitions, receiving reports, and purchase orders are independently matched before payment is approved.

D. Periodic inventory counts are used to adjust the perpetual inventory records.

The correct answer is (D). *(CPA, adapted)*

REQUIRED: The control most useful in maintaining accurate inventory records.

DISCUSSION: The recorded accountability for assets should be compared with existing assets at reasonable intervals. If assets are susceptible to loss through errors and fraud, the comparison should be made independently. Thus, periodic inventory counts should be reconciled to the perpetual inventory records to provide assurance that the inventory records properly reflect the inventory on hand.

Answer (A) is incorrect because periodic comparison of inventory records with current cost information may provide assurance that inventories are maintained at lower of cost or market but does not assure the accuracy of the records. Answer (B) is incorrect because a JIT system may provide assurance that inventory levels are maintained at the desired minimum but does not assure the accuracy of records. Answer (C) is incorrect because matching documents provides assurance that only goods that are authorized and received are paid for but does not assure the accuracy of records.

175. EOQ formulas, ABC analysis, and two-bin systems are commonly used elements of the control cycle for the stores process. These controls primarily relate to what part of the cycle?

A. Determination of need.

B. Acceptance of materials.

C. Storage of materials.

D. Release of materials.

The correct answer is (A). *(CIA, adapted)*

REQUIRED: The part of the control cycle for stores in which the listed techniques are used.

DISCUSSION: ABC analysis divides inventory into high-, medium-, and low-value items for purposes of frequency of review and reordering. EOQ models determine the economic order quantity that minimizes order and carrying costs. Once the reorder point is established, a two-bin system may be used to signal the time to reorder when perpetual records are not kept: an inventory item is divided into two groups; when the first is depleted, the order is placed and the second protects against stockout until replenishment. Thus, each technique is concerned with determination of need.

Answers (B), (C), and (D) are incorrect because EOQ formulas, ABC analysis, and two-bin systems relate to determination of need, not acceptance, storage, or release of materials.

176. Appropriate control over obsolete materials requires that they be

A. Carried at cost in the accounting records until the actual disposition takes place.

B. Sorted, treated, and packaged before disposition in order to obtain the best selling price.

C. Determined by an approved authority to be unusable for their normal purposes.

D. Retained within the regular storage area.

The correct answer is (C). *(CIA, adapted)*

REQUIRED: The appropriate control over obsolete materials.

DISCUSSION: Because auditors, storekeepers, etc., may not have the requisite expertise to determine whether materials are usable, that decision must often be made by a designated independent authority. To provide effective control of materials, this determination, asset custody, and authorization for disposal are functions that should be segregated.

Answer (A) is incorrect because obsolete materials should be carried at net realizable value. Answer (B) is incorrect because costs of sorting, etc., may be greater than disposal value. Answer (D) is incorrect because obsolete materials frequently should be segregated.

177. Which of the following organizational controls related to the processing of scrap would you recommend?

A. Separate the responsibility for processing scrap materials from the operational activities that produce the scrap materials.

B. Define each manager's responsibility for processing scrap and authorize one person in each production department to perform this function.

C. Specify detailed procedures for each manager to follow in determining the quantity, grade, and packaging of scrap.

D. Give the managers the authority to obtain competitive bids for the disposal of scrap.

The correct answer is (A). *(CIA, adapted)*

REQUIRED: The most appropriate organizational control relating to processing scrap.

DISCUSSION: Organizational controls concern the separation of functional responsibilities: custodianship, record keeping, authorization, and execution. Thus, those who generate the scrap should not subsequently process it.

Answers (B) and (C) are incorrect because managers with operational responsibility over scrap should not also have the authority to process it. Answer (D) is incorrect because managers with operational responsibility over scrap should not also have the authority to dispose of it.

3.11 Internal Control of Property, Plant, and Equipment

178. Which of the following questions would an auditor least likely include on an internal control questionnaire concerning the initiation and execution of equipment transactions?

A. Are requests for major repairs approved at a higher level than the department initiating the request?

B. Are prenumbered purchase orders used for equipment and periodically accounted for?

C. Are requests for purchases of equipment reviewed for consideration of soliciting competitive bids?

D. Are procedures in place to monitor and properly restrict access to equipment?

The correct answer is (D). *(CPA, adapted)*

REQUIRED: The question least likely to be included on an internal control questionnaire concerning initiation and execution of equipment transactions.

DISCUSSION: Although access to equipment should be restricted to authorized personnel only, the issue is the initiation and execution of equipment transactions, not custody of the assets.

Answers (A), (B), and (C) are incorrect because approval of major repairs, use of prenumbered purchase orders, and competitive bidding are related to the issue of transaction initiation and execution.

179. Which control is not appropriate for property, plant, and equipment?

A. Disposal of fully depreciated assets.

B. Proper authority for acquisition and retirement of assets.

C. Detailed property records and physical controls over assets.

D. Written policies for capitalization and expenditure and review of application of depreciation methods.

The correct answer is (A). *(Publisher)*

REQUIRED: The improper control over property, plant, and equipment.

DISCUSSION: No control should require disposal of fully depreciated assets. Such assets may still be productive and used in the business and should remain on the books until disposal.

Answer (B) is incorrect because proper authority for acquisition and retirement of assets is a proper control over property, plant, and equipment. Answer (C) is incorrect because detailed property records and physical controls over assets are proper controls over property, plant, and equipment. Answer (D) is incorrect because written policies for capitalization and expenditure and review of application of depreciation methods are proper controls over property, plant, and equipment.

180. Equipment acquisitions that are misclassified as maintenance expense most likely would be detected by a control that provides for

A. Segregation of duties of employees in the accounts payable department.

B. Independent verification of invoices for disbursements recorded as equipment acquisitions.

C. Investigation of variances within a formal budgeting system.

D. Authorization by the board of directors of significant equipment acquisitions.

The correct answer is (C). *(CPA, adapted)*

REQUIRED: The control to detect misclassification of equipment acquisitions as maintenance expense.

DISCUSSION: A formal planning and budgeting system that estimates maintenance expense at a certain level will report a significant variance if capital expenditures are charged to the account. Investigation of the variance is likely to disclose the misclassification.

Answer (A) is incorrect because accounts payable assembles the required payment documentation but is unlikely to question the classification of the expenditure. Answer (B) is incorrect because testing the population of recorded equipment acquisitions will not detect items misclassified as maintenance expense. Answer (D) is incorrect because the misclassification would occur subsequent to authorization.

181. One objective of internal control is to record property, plant, and equipment (PPE) additions correctly as to account, amount, and period. Which of the following environmental considerations indicates that the risk of material misstatement of these additions is high?

A. Most construction is performed in-house.

B. All material additions are required to be approved by the board of directors.

C. Recently acquired loans preclude further plant acquisition for 3 years.

D. Gross property, plant, and equipment increased 36% during the current period.

The correct answer is (A). *(K.M. Macur)*

REQUIRED: The environmental consideration indicating a high risk of material misstatement.

DISCUSSION: The inherent risk of misstatement for in-house construction is high. For example, the company must allocate overhead, allocate labor costs between regular and construction labor, and estimate the interest cost to be capitalized. An outside construction company would send an invoice, and determining the amount to record would therefore be relatively easy.

Answer (B) is incorrect because approval of all material additions by the board of directors is a control consideration relating to authorization, not recording. Answer (C) is incorrect because reducing the amount of construction is most likely to decrease risk. Answer (D) is incorrect because the increase in PPE does not necessarily significantly increase the risk of misstatement, especially if valuation is based on vendors' prices rather than the entity's own estimates of the costs of in-house construction.

182. Which of the following is an internal control weakness related to factory equipment?

A. Checks issued in payment of purchases of equipment are not signed by the controller.

B. All purchases of factory equipment are required to be made by the department in need of the equipment.

C. Factory equipment replacements are usually made when estimated useful lives, as indicated in depreciation schedules, have expired.

D. Proceeds from sales of fully depreciated equipment are credited to other income.

The correct answer is (B). *(CPA, adapted)*

REQUIRED: The internal control weakness related to factory equipment.

DISCUSSION: Making purchases of factory equipment is a function incompatible with the production activities of user departments. Satisfactory internal control requires separation of incompatible functions, so purchases of factory equipment should be made by a separate purchasing department.

Answer (A) is incorrect because controllers, who perform a record-keeping function, should not sign checks. Answer (C) is incorrect because, if estimated useful lives are accurate, replacing equipment at the end of those lives is a reasonable policy, not a control weakness. Answer (D) is incorrect because gains (all proceeds of fully depreciated equipment) from sales other than of inventory should be credited to other income or gain on sale of equipment.

183. Which of the following controls most likely would justify a reduced assessed level of control risk concerning plant and equipment acquisitions?

A. Periodic physical inspection of plant and equipment by the internal audit staff.

B. Comparison of current-year plant and equipment account balances with prior-year actual balances.

C. The review of prenumbered purchase orders to detect unrecorded trade-ins.

D. Approval of periodic depreciation entries by a supervisor independent of the accounting department.

The correct answer is (A). *(CPA, adapted)*

REQUIRED: The control that would justify reducing an assessed level of control risk.

DISCUSSION: A periodic physical inspection by the internal audit staff is the best procedure for verifying the existence of plant and equipment. Direct observation by an independent, competent, and objective internal audit staff helps to reduce the potential for fictitious acquisitions or other fraudulent activities. The result is a lower assessed level of control risk.

Answer (B) is incorrect because comparing records of assets may not detect nonexistent assets. Answer (C) is incorrect because reviewing purchase orders is less effective than direct verification. Answer (D) is incorrect because depreciation is based on recorded amounts. If they are misstated, depreciation will also be misstated.

184. Which of the following procedures is most likely to prevent the improper disposition of equipment?

A. A separation of duties between those authorized to dispose of equipment and those authorized to approve removal work orders.

B. The use of serial numbers to identify equipment that could be sold.

C. Periodic comparison of removal work orders with authorizing documentation.

D. A periodic analysis of the scrap sales and the repairs and maintenance accounts.

The correct answer is (A). *(CPA, adapted)*

REQUIRED: The procedure most likely to prevent the improper disposition of equipment.

DISCUSSION: Segregation of duties reduces the opportunity for an individual to both perpetrate and conceal errors or fraud. Accordingly, the authorization, recording, and asset custody functions should be separated. Thus, the same individual should not approve removal work orders (authorization) and dispose of equipment (asset custody).

Answers (B), (C), and (D) are incorrect because the use of serial numbers to identify equipment that could be sold, periodic comparison of removal work orders with authorizing documentation, and a periodic analysis of the scrap sales and the repairs and maintenance accounts may detect but will not prevent improper dispositions.

185. An auditor notes year-to-year increases of over $200,000 for small tool expense at a manufacturing facility that has produced the same amount of identical product for the last 3 years. Production inventory is kept in a controlled staging area adjacent to the receiving dock, but the supply of small tools is kept in an unsupervised area near the exit to the plant employees' parking lot. After determining that all of the following alternatives are equal in cost and are also feasible for local management, the auditor can best address the security issue by recommending that plant management

A. Move the small tools inventory to the custody of the production inventory staging superintendent and implement the use of a special requisition to issue small tools.

B. Initiate a full physical inventory of small tools on a monthly basis.

C. Place supply of small tools in a secured area, install a key-access card system for all employees, and record each key-access transaction on a report for the production superintendent.

D. Close the exit to the employee parking lot and require all plant employees to use a doorway by the receiving dock that also provides access to the plant employees' parking area.

The correct answer is (A). *(CIA, adapted)*

REQUIRED: The best preventive control to reduce the risk of loss of small tools.

DISCUSSION: Physical control of assets is a preventive control that reduces the likelihood of theft or other loss. Giving responsibility for custody of small tools to one individual establishes accountability. Requiring that requisitions be submitted ensures that tool use is properly authorized.

Answer (B) is incorrect because a full physical inventory is a periodic, detective control that would only be effective in determining the amount of losses. Answer (C) is incorrect because recording each key-access transaction is a preventive and detective control that does not record the number or type of tools removed from the inventory. Answer (D) is incorrect because requiring all plant employees to use a doorway by the receiving dock is a preventive control that does not limit access to the small tools inventory.

186. Which of the following controls would most likely allow for a reduction in the scope of the auditor's tests of depreciation expense?

A. Review and approval of the periodic equipment depreciation entry by a supervisor who does not actively participate in its preparation.

B. Comparison of equipment account balances for the current year with the current-year budget and prior-year actual balances.

C. Review of the miscellaneous income account for salvage credits and scrap sales of partially depreciated equipment.

D. Authorization of payment of vendors' invoices by a designated employee who is independent of the equipment receiving function.

The correct answer is (A). *(CPA, adapted)*

REQUIRED: The control permitting reduction in tests of depreciation.

DISCUSSION: A reduction in control risk and the consequent increase in the acceptable level of detection risk may permit the auditor to alter the nature, timing, or extent of substantive tests. An independent check on the validity and accuracy of depreciation expense clearly enhances the effectiveness of internal control and is thus likely to reduce the external auditor's assessment of control risk.

Answer (B) is incorrect because comparison of equipment account balances for the current year with the current-year budget and prior-year actual balances is an auditor's analytical procedure to test the completeness of the current-year equipment balance. Answer (C) is incorrect because review of the miscellaneous income account for salvage credits and scrap sales of partially depreciated equipment is an audit procedure to detect unrecorded fixed asset disposals. Answer (D) is incorrect because authorization of payment of invoices by a designated employee independent of the receiving function relates to authorization of cash disbursements.

<u>3.12 Communication with Audit Committees</u> (See also Module 8.5)

187. Reportable conditions are matters that come to an auditor's attention that should be communicated to an entity's audit committee because they represent

A. Disclosures of information that significantly contradict the auditor's going concern assumption.

B. Material fraud or illegal acts perpetrated by high-level management.

C. Significant deficiencies in the design or operation of internal control.

D. Manipulation or falsification of accounting records or documents from which financial statements are prepared.

The correct answer is (C). *(CPA, adapted)*

REQUIRED: The definition of a reportable condition.

DISCUSSION: Reportable conditions are matters coming to the auditor's attention that represent significant deficiencies in the design or operation of internal control that, in the auditor's judgment, could adversely affect the organization's ability to record, process, summarize, and report financial data consistent with the assertions of management in the financial statements (AU 325).

Answer (A) is incorrect because disclosures indicating a substantial doubt about the going concern assumption pertain not to internal control but to such conditions and events as operating losses, loan defaults, and labor difficulties. Answers (B) and (D) are incorrect because reportable conditions include more than fraud or illegal acts.

188. Which of the following best describes the auditor's responsibility with respect to reportable conditions under AU 325?

A. The auditor must report the conditions whether or not the audit committee knows of them.

B. The auditor must exercise due diligence in searching for reportable conditions.

C. The auditor may report the conditions orally, but reporting in writing is preferable.

D. The auditor's report is a general purpose report and may be distributed to the stockholders.

The correct answer is (C). *(D. Finkbiner)*

REQUIRED: The correct statement concerning the auditor's responsibility for reportable conditions.

DISCUSSION: The report should preferably be in writing. If it is oral, the auditor should document the communication by appropriate memoranda or notations in the working papers.

Answer (A) is incorrect because, if the audit committee has acknowledged its understanding and consideration of such deficiencies and the associated risks, the auditor may decide the matters do not need to be reported. Answer (B) is incorrect because the auditor is not obligated to search for reportable conditions; however, (s)he may become aware of conditions through the application of audit procedures or otherwise. Answer (D) is incorrect because the report is intended solely for the information and use of the audit committee, management, and others within the organization.

189. Which of the following statements is correct concerning an auditor's communication of internal control related matters (reportable conditions) noted in an audit?

A. The auditor may issue a written report to the audit committee representing that no reportable conditions were noted.

B. Reportable conditions should be recommunicated each year even if the audit committee has acknowledged its understanding of such deficiencies.

C. Reportable conditions may not be communicated in a document that contains suggestions regarding activities that concern other topics such as business strategies or administrative efficiencies.

D. The auditor may choose to communicate significant internal control related matters either during the course of the audit or after the audit is concluded.

The correct answer is (D). *(CPA, adapted)*

REQUIRED: The true statement concerning an auditor's communication of reportable conditions noted in an audit.

DISCUSSION: Timely communication of reportable conditions may be desirable. Hence, the auditor has the option of making an interim communication before conclusion of the engagement. The timing of the communication is determined by the significance of the matters noted and the urgency of corrective action.

Answer (A) is incorrect because AU 325 prohibits issuance of a report declaring that no reportable conditions were noted. The limited assurance that would be provided could easily be misinterpreted. Answer (B) is incorrect because reportable conditions may be known to management, and their existence may reflect a decision to accept the risk because of cost or other considerations. If the audit committee has acknowledged the deficiencies and their risks, the auditor may choose not to report such matters. Answer (C) is incorrect because items beneficial to the client may be communicated even though they are not control related.

190. When communicating internal control related matters noted in an audit, an auditor's report issued on reportable conditions should indicate that

A. Errors or fraud may occur and not be detected because of the inherent limitations of internal control.

B. The expression of an unqualified opinion on the financial statements may be dependent on corrective follow-up action.

C. The deficiencies noted were not detected within a timely period by employees in the normal course of performing their assigned functions.

D. The purpose of the audit was to report on the financial statements and not to provide assurance on internal control.

The correct answer is (D). *(CPA, adapted)*

REQUIRED: The content of an auditor's report issued on reportable conditions.

DISCUSSION: AU 325 states, "Any report issued on reportable conditions should indicate that the purpose of the audit was to report on the financial statements and not to provide assurance on internal control."

Answers (A) and (C) are incorrect because the report on reportable conditions identifies significant deficiencies in the design or operation of internal control, not errors or fraud. Answer (B) is incorrect because the opinion on the financial statements should be supported by evidence collected by the auditor, not subsequent corrective actions by management.

191. Which of the following statements concerning material weaknesses and reportable conditions is correct?

A. An auditor should identify and communicate material weaknesses separately from reportable conditions.

B. All material weaknesses are reportable conditions.

C. An auditor should report immediately material weaknesses and reportable conditions discovered during an audit.

D. All reportable conditions are material weaknesses.

The correct answer is (B). *(CPA, adapted)*

REQUIRED: The true statement concerning reportable conditions.

DISCUSSION: A material weakness is a reportable condition "in which the design or operation of one or more of the internal control components does not reduce to a relatively low level the risk that errors or fraud in amounts that would be material in relation to the financial statements being audited may occur and not be detected within a timely period by employees in the normal course of performing their assigned functions" (AU 325). Reportable conditions include but are not limited to material weaknesses.

Answer (A) is incorrect because an auditor may, but is not required to, identify material weaknesses separately. Answer (C) is incorrect because whether an interim communication is made depends on the relative significance of the matters noted and the urgency of corrective action. Answer (D) is incorrect because not all reportable conditions are material weaknesses.

192. Which of the following representations should not be included in a report on internal control related matters noted in an audit?

A. Reportable conditions related to the design of internal control exist, but none is deemed to be a material weakness.

B. There are no significant deficiencies in the design or operation of internal control.

C. Corrective follow-up action is recommended due to the relative significance of material weaknesses discovered during the audit.

D. The auditor's consideration of internal control would not necessarily disclose all reportable conditions that exist.

The correct answer is (B). *(CPA, adapted)*

REQUIRED: The item not included in a report on internal control related matters.

DISCUSSION: No report should be issued if no reportable conditions were noted. The potential for misinterpretation would exist if the auditor issued a report representing that no reportable conditions were found (AU 325).

Answer (A) is incorrect because the report may state that the reportable conditions noted are not material weaknesses. Answer (C) is incorrect because an interim communication may be the appropriate means for recommending corrective follow-up action on significant matters noted. Answer (D) is incorrect because the language in the report may state that the consideration of internal control might not disclose all reportable conditions.

193. Which of the following statements is correct concerning an auditor's required communication of reportable conditions?

A. A reportable condition previously communicated during the prior year's audit that remains uncorrected causes a scope limitation.

B. An auditor should perform tests of controls on reportable conditions before communicating them to the client.

C. An auditor's report on reportable conditions should include a restriction on the distribution of the report.

D. An auditor should communicate reportable conditions after tests of controls but before commencing substantive tests.

The correct answer is (C). *(CPA, adapted)*

REQUIRED: The true statement concerning the auditor's required communication of reportable conditions.

DISCUSSION: A report on reportable conditions should (1) state that the purpose of the audit was to report on the financial statements, not to provide assurance on internal control; (2) give the definition of reportable conditions; and (3) state that report distribution is restricted to management, the audit committee, and others within the organization (or a specified regulatory agency or other third party).

Answer (A) is incorrect because, although a reportable condition previously communicated may require continued communication in the following year, it does not necessarily cause a limitation on the scope of the audit. Answer (B) is incorrect because tests of controls are performed on internal control, not on reportable conditions. Answer (D) is incorrect because reportable conditions are typically reported at the conclusion of the audit. However, they may be communicated during the audit if such information is considered useful to the client.

194. A CPA had previously communicated a reportable condition in connection with an audit of prior financial statements. As of the current audit date, the condition has not been corrected, and the audit committee has not acknowledged its understanding and consideration of the risks involved. What communication should be made by the CPA?

A. None, because management has been previously put on notice and now has sole responsibility.

B. A new communication is required only if it involves an area in which the auditor has assessed control risk at below the maximum level.

C. A new communication is required only if the auditor has assessed control risk at the maximum level.

D. The condition should be reported.

The correct answer is (D). *(Publisher)*

REQUIRED: The effect on the auditor of a previously communicated reportable condition.

DISCUSSION: AU 325 requires communication about reportable conditions and makes no exception solely for previous reporting of a condition. But "provided the audit committee has acknowledged its understanding and consideration of such deficiencies and the associated risks, the auditor may decide the matter does not need to be reported."

Answer (A) is incorrect because, even though internal control is the responsibility of management, the auditor has the responsibility to report the condition to the audit committee. Answers (B) and (C) are incorrect because the auditor should report the condition regardless of the assessment of control risk.

195. Which of the following matters is an auditor required to communicate to an entity's audit committee?

I. Disagreements with management about matters significant to the entity's financial statements that have been satisfactorily resolved

II. Initial selection of significant accounting policies in emerging areas that lack authoritative guidance

A. I only.

B. II only.

C. Both I and II.

D. Neither I nor II.

The correct answer is (C). *(CPA, adapted)*

REQUIRED: The matter(s), if any, to be communicated to the audit committee.

DISCUSSION: AU 380, *Communication with Audit Committees*, states that the matters to be discussed with the audit committee include the auditors' responsibility under GAAS; significant accounting policies; sensitive accounting estimates; significant audit adjustments; auditor disagreements with management, whether or not satisfactorily resolved; management's consultations with other accountants; issues discussed with management prior to the auditors' retention; and any serious difficulties the auditors may have had with management during the audit.

Answers (A), (B), and (D) are incorrect because significant accounting policies and all disagreements with management should be discussed.

196. In identifying matters for communication with an entity's audit committee, an auditor is most likely to ask management whether

A. The turnover in the accounting department was unusually high.

B. It consulted with another CPA firm about accounting matters.

C. There were any subsequent events of which the auditor was unaware.

D. It agreed with the auditor's assessed level of control risk.

The correct answer is (B). *(CPA, adapted)*

REQUIRED: The matter communicated to the audit committee.

DISCUSSION: The auditor may, but is not required to, inquire of management concerning any consultations with other accountants. However, if the auditor becomes aware that management has consulted with other accountants, the auditor should discuss with the audit committee his/her views about significant matters involved in that consultation (AU 380).

Answer (A) is incorrect because a high turnover of employees may increase the assessed control risk but does not require communication with the audit committee. Answer (C) is incorrect because the subsequent events discovered by the auditor need not be communicated to the audit committee. Answer (D) is incorrect because the assessed level of control risk is a matter of auditor judgment and is not negotiated with the client.

197. Which of the following matters is an auditor required to communicate to an entity's audit committee?

A. The basis for assessing control risk below the maximum.

B. The process used by management in formulating sensitive accounting estimates.

C. The auditor's preliminary judgments about materiality levels.

D. The justification for performing substantive procedures at interim dates.

The correct answer is (B). *(CPA, adapted)*

REQUIRED: The required communication to an entity's audit committee.

DISCUSSION: Certain management estimates are particularly sensitive because they are significant to the financial statements, and future events affecting them may differ from current judgments. The audit committee should be informed about the process used in formulating sensitive estimates and the basis for the auditor's conclusions concerning their reasonableness (AU 380).

Answers (A), (C), and (D) are incorrect because the basis for assessing control risk, preliminary judgments about materiality, and the reasons for interim procedures need not be communicated to the audit committee.

198. An auditor is obligated to communicate a proposed audit adjustment to an entity's audit committee only if the adjustment

A. Has not been recorded before the end of the auditor's field work.

B. Has a significant effect on the entity's financial reporting process.

C. Is a recurring matter that was proposed to management the prior year.

D. Results from the correction of a prior period's departure from GAAP.

The correct answer is (B). *(CPA, adapted)*

REQUIRED: The circumstances in which a proposed audit adjustment must be communicated to the audit committee.

DISCUSSION: The auditor should inform the audit committee about adjustments arising from the audit that could in his/her judgment have a significant effect on the entity's financial reporting process, either individually or in the aggregate (AU 380).

Answer (A) is incorrect because the entries affecting the year-end financial statement balances can be made subsequent to year-end. Answers (C) and (D) are incorrect because the significance of the matter is the important consideration.

3.13 External Auditors' Relations with Internal Auditors

199. The independent auditor should understand the internal audit function as it relates to internal control because

A. The audit programs, working papers, and reports of internal auditors may often be used as a substitute for the work of the independent auditor's staff.

B. The procedures performed by the internal audit staff may eliminate the independent auditor's need for considering internal control.

C. The work performed by internal auditors may be a factor in determining the nature, timing, and extent of the independent auditor's procedures.

D. The understanding of the internal audit function is an important substantive test to be performed by the independent auditor.

The correct answer is (C). *(CPA, adapted)*

REQUIRED: The reason the independent auditor must understand the internal audit function.

DISCUSSION: AU 322, *The Auditor's Consideration of the Internal Audit Function in an Audit of Financial Statements*, states that the independent auditor should obtain an understanding of the internal audit function when obtaining an understanding of a client's internal control. The understanding should be sufficient to identify internal audit activities relevant to audit planning. Thus, an internal audit function is one of many factors to be considered in determining the nature, timing, and extent of audit procedures.

Answer (A) is incorrect because programs, working papers, and reports of internal auditors may never be used to substitute for the work of the independent auditor's staff. Answer (B) is incorrect because AU 319 requires the independent auditor to obtain an understanding of internal control and to assess control risk. Answer (D) is incorrect because the understanding of the internal audit function is part of the independent auditor's consideration of internal control, not a substantive test.

200. If the independent auditors decide that it is efficient to consider how the work performed by the internal auditors may affect the nature, timing, and extent of audit procedures, they should assess the internal auditors'

A. Competence and objectivity.

B. Efficiency and experience.

C. Independence and review skills.

D. Training and supervisory skills.

The correct answer is (A). *(CPA, adapted)*

REQUIRED: The internal auditors' traits that the independent auditors should consider.

DISCUSSION: If the external auditors decide that it is efficient to consider how the internal auditors' work may affect the nature, timing, and extent of audit procedures, the competence and objectivity of the internal auditors should be assessed. Assessing competence entails obtaining information about education and experience; professional certification and CPE; audit policies, programs, and procedures; assignment of internal auditors; supervision and review of their activities; quality of working papers, reports, and recommendations; and evaluation of internal auditors' performance. Assessing objectivity includes obtaining information about organizational status (the level to which the internal auditors report; access to the board, audit committee, or the owner-manager; and whether these individuals oversee employment decisions related to the internal auditors) and about policies to maintain internal auditors' objectivity concerning the areas audited (AU 322).

Answers (B) and (D) are incorrect because competence encompasses the traits of efficiency, experience, training, and supervisory skills. Moreover, objectivity must also be assessed. Answer (C) is incorrect because internal auditors are not independent in the sense intended by the *Code of Professional Conduct* and GAAS.

201. In assessing the competence and objectivity of an entity's internal auditor, an independent auditor is least likely to consider information obtained from

A. Discussions with management personnel.

B. External peer reviews of the internal auditor's activities.

C. Previous experience with the internal auditor.

D. The results of analytical procedures.

The correct answer is (D). *(CPA, adapted)*

REQUIRED: The least likely procedure in assessing the competence and objectivity of an entity's internal auditor.

DISCUSSION: Analytical procedures are evaluations of financial information made by a study of plausible relationships among both financial and nonfinancial data, using models that range from simple to complex. They are substantive tests used by the auditor to gather evidence about the fairness of the financial statements.

Answers (A), (B), and (C) are incorrect because, in "assessing competence and objectivity, the auditor usually considers information obtained from previous experience with the internal audit function, from discussions with management personnel, and from a recent external quality review, if performed" (AU 322).

202. For which of the following judgments may an independent auditor share responsibility with an entity's internal auditor who is assessed to be both competent and objective?

	Materiality of Misstatements	Evaluation of Accounting Estimates
A.	Yes	No
B.	No	Yes
C.	No	No
D.	Yes	Yes

The correct answer is (C). *(CPA, adapted)*

REQUIRED: The judgment(s), if any, for which an independent auditor may share responsibility with an internal auditor.

DISCUSSION: The responsibility to report on the financial statements rests solely with the independent auditor and cannot be shared with the internal auditors. Because the auditor has the ultimate responsibility to express an opinion on the financial statements, judgments about assessments of inherent and control risk, the materiality of misstatements, the sufficiency of tests performed, the evaluation of significant accounting estimates, and other matters affecting the auditor's report should always be those of the external auditor.

Answers (A), (B), and (D) are incorrect because the independent auditor cannot share responsibility with the internal auditor for judgments about materiality or accounting estimates.

203. Internal auditing can affect the scope of the external auditor's audit of financial statements by

A. Decreasing the external auditor's need to perform detailed tests.

B. Allowing the external auditor to limit his/her audit to substantive testing.

C. Limiting direct testing by the external auditor to assertions not directly tested by internal auditing.

D. Eliminating the need to be on hand during the physical count of inventory.

The correct answer is (A). *(CIA, adapted)*

REQUIRED: The effect of internal auditing on the scope of the external audit.

DISCUSSION: The work of the internal auditors may affect the nature, timing, and extent of the audit procedures, which include those for understanding internal control, assessing control risk, and conducting substantive tests.

Answer (B) is incorrect because the external auditor must always obtain an understanding of internal control and assess control risk. Answer (C) is incorrect because the auditor must perform direct tests of assertions related to material financial statement amounts if the risk of material misstatement or the subjectivity involved in the evaluation of audit evidence is high. Answer (D) is incorrect because the external auditor must observe the client's physical inventory.

204. When assessing an internal auditor's competence, a CPA ordinarily obtains information about all of the following except

A. Quality of working paper documentation.

B. Educational level and professional experience.

C. Audit programs and procedures.

D. Access to information about related parties.

The correct answer is (D). *(CPA, adapted)*

REQUIRED: The information a CPA ordinarily does not obtain when assessing an internal auditor's competence.

DISCUSSION: If the external auditors decide that it is efficient to consider how the internal auditors' work may affect the nature, timing, and extent of audit procedures, the competence and objectivity of the internal auditors should be assessed. Assessing competence entails obtaining information about education and experience; professional certification and CPE; audit policies, programs, and procedures; assignment of internal auditors; supervision and review of their activities; quality of working papers, reports, and recommendations; and evaluation of internal auditors' performance. An internal auditor's access to information is related to objectivity.

Answers (A), (B), and (C) are incorrect because quality of working paper documentation, educational level and professional experience, and audit programs and procedures provide information about competence.

205. Which of the following is a false statement about the relationship of the internal auditor and the scope of the external audit of a company's financial statements?

A. The nature, timing, and extent of the external auditor's substantive tests may be affected by the work of the internal auditors.

B. The internal auditors may assist the external auditor in performing substantive tests and tests of controls under certain circumstances.

C. The external auditor is not required to give consideration to the internal audit function beyond obtaining an understanding sufficient to identify activities relevant to planning the audit.

D. The internal auditors may determine the extent to which audit procedures should be employed by the external auditor.

The correct answer is (D). *(CMA, adapted)*

REQUIRED: The false statement about the relationship between the internal auditor and external auditor.

DISCUSSION: According to AU 322, the independent external auditor is required to obtain an understanding of the internal audit function to identify activities relevant to the audit. If internal audit activities are relevant, (s)he should then determine whether it is efficient to consider the internal auditors' work further. If it is efficient, the auditor should assess the competence and objectivity of the internal auditors. If they are sufficiently competent and objective, the auditor may then consider how (not whether) their work will affect the audit.

Answer (A) is incorrect because the work of the internal auditors may affect the substantive procedures performed by the external auditor. Answer (B) is incorrect because internal auditors may directly assist in substantive tests and tests of controls if their competence and objectivity are assessed and their work is properly supervised, reviewed, evaluated, and tested. Answer (C) is incorrect because the auditor must obtain an understanding of the internal audit function but may conclude that the activities of the internal auditors are not relevant to the audit. The auditor may also conclude that further consideration of their activities is not efficient or that they lack sufficient competence and objectivity.

206. During an audit, an internal auditor may provide direct assistance to an independent CPA in

	Obtaining an Understanding of Internal Control	Performing Tests of Controls	Performing Substantive Tests
A.	No	No	No
B.	Yes	No	No
C.	Yes	Yes	No
D.	Yes	Yes	Yes

The correct answer is (D). *(CPA, adapted)*

REQUIRED: The types of direct assistance an internal auditor may provide to an independent CPA.

DISCUSSION: The auditor may request direct assistance from the internal auditor when performing the audit. Thus, the auditor may appropriately request the internal auditor's assistance in obtaining the understanding of internal control, performing tests of controls, or performing substantive tests (AU 322).

Answers (A), (B), and (C) are incorrect because the internal auditor may provide assistance in all phases of the audit as long as the internal auditor's competence and objectivity have been tested and the independent auditor supervises, reviews, evaluates, and tests the work performed by the internal auditor to the extent appropriate.

207. The coordination of activities between internal and external auditors

A. Results in no duplication of audit efforts.

B. Includes the exchange of audit reports and management letters.

C. Prohibits internal auditors from using the same audit techniques as external auditors, and vice versa.

D. Prevents external auditors from having access to the programs used by internal auditors.

The correct answer is (B). *(CIA, adapted)*

REQUIRED: The true statement about coordination of internal and external audit activities.

DISCUSSION: The IIA's Standard 550, *External Auditors*, requires the director of internal auditing to coordinate internal and external audit efforts "to ensure adequate audit coverage and to minimize duplicate efforts. Coordination involves periodic meetings to discuss matters of mutual interest, access to each other's audit programs and working papers, exchange of audit reports and management letters, and common understanding of audit techniques, methods, and terminology."

Answer (A) is incorrect because some duplication is unavoidable. Answer (C) is incorrect because common techniques should often be used. Answer (D) is incorrect because internal auditors often make their programs and working papers available to the external auditor.

3.14 Internal Control Documentation

208. The auditor's consideration of the client's internal control is documented in order to substantiate

A. Conformity of the accounting records with generally accepted accounting principles.

B. Compliance with generally accepted auditing standards.

C. Adherence to procedures for economic, effective, and efficient management decision making.

D. The fairness of the financial statement presentation.

The correct answer is (B). *(CPA, adapted)*

REQUIRED: The reason for the auditor's documentation of the consideration of the client's internal control.

DISCUSSION: The auditor should document the understanding of internal control and the conclusions about the assessed level of control risk for specific assertions. If the assessed level is below the maximum, the basis for the conclusion must also be documented.

Answers (A) and (D) are incorrect because the entire audit process, not just the consideration of internal control, establishes the fairness of the financial statement presentation, including conformity with GAAP. Answer (C) is incorrect because adherence to procedures for certain decision-making processes, such as those relating to product pricing, may not be relevant to a financial statement audit.

209. Which of the following statements regarding auditor documentation of the client's internal control is correct?

A. Documentation must include flowcharts.

B. Documentation must include procedural write-ups.

C. No documentation is necessary although it is desirable.

D. No one particular form of documentation is necessary, and the extent of documentation may vary.

The correct answer is (D). *(CPA, adapted)*

REQUIRED: The true statement about the auditor's documentation of the client's internal control.

DISCUSSION: The auditor may document his/her understanding of internal control in the form of answers to a questionnaire, narrative memoranda, flowcharts, decision tables, or any other form that the auditor considers appropriate in the circumstances.

Answers (A) and (B) are incorrect because flowcharts and procedural write-ups are not required. Answer (C) is incorrect because documentation is required but not in any specific form.

210. When an auditor assesses control risk below the maximum level, the auditor is required to document the auditor's

	Basis for Concluding That Control Risk Is Below the Maximum Level	Understanding of the Entity's Internal Control Components
A.	No	No
B.	Yes	Yes
C.	Yes	No
D.	No	Yes

The correct answer is (B). *(CPA, adapted)*

REQUIRED: The item(s) that should be documented when assessed control risk is below the maximum level.

DISCUSSION: The auditor should document his/her understanding of internal control and the conclusions about the assessed level of control risk for specific assertions. If the assessed level is below the maximum, the basis for the conclusion must also be documented.

Answers (A), (C), and (D) are incorrect because the basis for concluding that control risk is below the maximum level and the understanding should be documented.

211. Which of the following is not a medium that can normally be used by an auditor to record information concerning a client's internal control?

A. Narrative memorandum.

B. Procedures manual.

C. Flowchart.

D. Decision table.

The correct answer is (B). *(CPA, adapted)*

REQUIRED: The medium not used by an auditor to record information concerning a client's internal control.

DISCUSSION: A procedures manual is one source of information about the client's internal control. However, the auditor normally does not prepare this manual and record information in it. The accounting procedures manual is a client document that explains the client's accounting system and how to implement it.

Answers (A), (C), and (D) are incorrect because memoranda, flowcharts, and decision tables are means of documenting the understanding of internal control (AU 319).

212. When documenting the understanding of a client's internal control, the independent auditor sometimes uses a systems flowchart, which can best be described as a

A. Pictorial presentation of the flow of instructions in a client's internal computer system.

B. Diagram that clearly indicates an organization's internal reporting structure.

C. Graphic illustration of the flow of operations that is used to replace the auditor's internal control questionnaire.

D. Symbolic representation of a system or series of sequential processes.

The correct answer is (D). *(CPA, adapted)*

REQUIRED: The best description of a systems flowchart.

DISCUSSION: A systems flowchart is a symbolic representation of the flow of documents and procedures through a series of steps in the accounting process of the client's organization.

Answer (A) is incorrect because a pictorial presentation of the flow of instructions in a client's internal computer system is a computer program flowchart. Answer (B) is incorrect because the organizational chart depicts the client's internal reporting structure. Answer (C) is incorrect because a flowchart does not necessarily replace the auditor's internal control questionnaire. Controls beyond those depicted on the systems flowchart must also be considered by the auditor, and information obtained from the questionnaire may be used to develop the flowchart.

213. The normal sequence of documents and operations on a well-prepared systems flowchart is

A. Top to bottom and left to right.

B. Bottom to top and left to right.

C. Top to bottom and right to left.

D. Bottom to top and right to left.

The correct answer is (A). *(CPA, adapted)*

REQUIRED: The normal sequence of documents and operations on a well-prepared systems flowchart.

DISCUSSION: The direction of flow in the normal sequence of documents and operations on a well-prepared systems flowchart is from top to bottom and from left to right.

Answer (B) is incorrect because the normal vertical movement is top to bottom. Answer (C) is incorrect because the normal horizontal movement is left to right. Answer (D) is incorrect because the normal sequence is top to bottom and left to right.

214. An advantage of using systems flowcharts to document information about internal control instead of using internal control questionnaires is that systems flowcharts

A. Identify internal control weaknesses more prominently.

B. Provide a visual depiction of clients' activities.

C. Indicate whether control procedures are operating effectively.

D. Reduce the need to observe clients' employees performing routine tasks.

The correct answer is (B). *(CPA, adapted)*

REQUIRED: The advantage of systems flowcharts over internal control questionnaires.

DISCUSSION: Systems flowcharts provide a visual representation of a series of sequential processes, that is, of a flow of documents, data, and operations. In many instances a flowchart is preferable to a questionnaire because a picture is usually more easily comprehended.

Answer (A) is incorrect because a systems flowchart can present the flow of information and documents in a system, but does not specifically identify the weaknesses. Answer (C) is incorrect because the flowchart does not provide evidence of how effectively the procedures are actually operating. Answer (D) is incorrect because the flowchart is useful in documenting the understanding of control, but it does not reduce the need for observation of employees performing tasks if those tests of controls are deemed necessary.

215. The diamond-shaped symbol is commonly used in flowcharting to show or represent a

A. Process or a single step in a procedure or program.

B. Terminal output display.

C. Decision point, conditional testing, or branching.

D. Predefined process.

The correct answer is (C). *(CIA, adapted)*

REQUIRED: The meaning of the diamond-shaped symbol used in flowcharting.

DISCUSSION: Flowcharts illustrate in pictorial fashion the flow of data, documents, and/or operations in a system. Flowcharts may summarize a system or present great detail, e.g., as found in program flowcharts. According to the American National Standards Institute, the diamond-shaped symbol represents a decision point or test of a condition in a program flowchart, that is, the point at which a determination must be made as to which logic path (branch) to follow. The diamond is also sometimes used in systems flowcharts.

Answer (A) is incorrect because the rectangle is the appropriate symbol for a process or a single step in a procedure or program. Answer (B) is incorrect because a terminal display is signified by a symbol similar to the shape of a cathode ray tube. Answer (D) is incorrect because a predefined processing step is represented by a rectangle with double lines on either side.

216. In connection with the consideration of internal control, an auditor encounters the following flowcharting symbols:

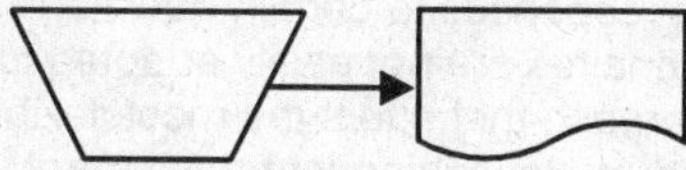

The auditor should conclude that a

A. Master file has been created by a manual operation.

B. Master file has been created by a computer operation.

C. Document has been generated by a computer operation.

D. Document has been generated by a manual operation.

The correct answer is (D). *(CPA, adapted)*

REQUIRED: The meaning of the flowcharting symbols shown.

DISCUSSION: The symbol on the left represents a manual operation and the symbol on the right a document. The arrow's direction suggests that a document is prepared through a manual operation.

Answer (A) is incorrect because a master file is depicted by a parallelogram (input/output), or a symbol for the type of storage device used (e.g., magnetic tape or disk). Answers (B) and (C) are incorrect because a computer operation is depicted by a rectangle.

217. The following is a section of a system flowchart for a payroll application.

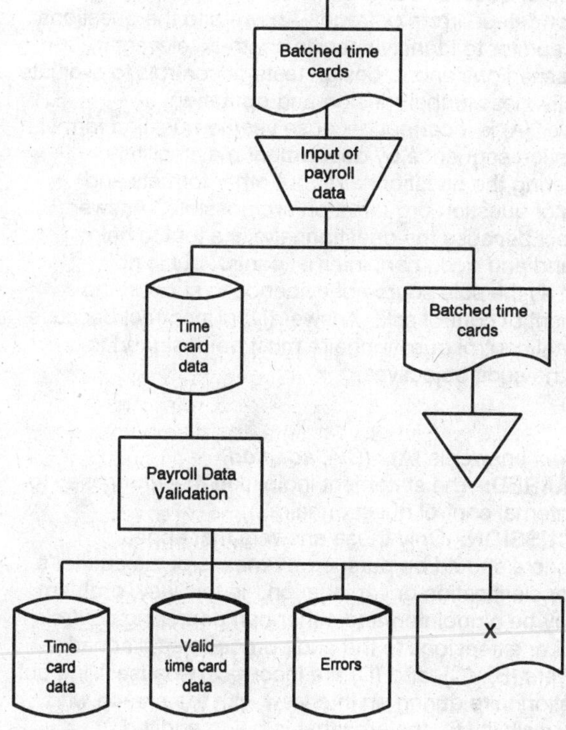

Symbol X could represent

A. Erroneous time cards.

B. An error report.

C. Batched time cards.

D. Unclaimed payroll checks.

The correct answer is (B). *(CPA, adapted)*

REQUIRED: The item represented by Symbol X.

DISCUSSION: Symbol X is a document, that is, hard copy output of the validation routine shown. The time card data, the validated data, and the errors are recorded on magnetic disk after the validation process. Thus, either an error report or the valid time card information is represented by Symbol X.

Answers (A) and (C) are incorrect because time cards were stored offline before the validation process. Answer (D) is incorrect because no payroll checks are shown.

218. A questionnaire consists of a series of questions relating to controls normally required to prevent or detect errors and fraud that may occur for each type of transaction. Which of the following is not an advantage of a questionnaire?

A. A questionnaire provides a framework that minimizes the possibility of overlooking aspects of internal control.

B. A questionnaire can be easily completed.

C. A questionnaire is flexible in design and application.

D. The completed questionnaire provides documentation that the auditor understands internal control for planning purposes.

The correct answer is (C). *(Publisher)*

REQUIRED: The statement not considered an advantage of a questionnaire.

DISCUSSION: Questionnaires are designed to be inflexible in that the responses to certain questions are expected. Questionnaires are not easily adapted to unique situations. The approach that offers the most flexibility is a narrative memorandum describing internal control. The next most flexible approach is a flowchart.

Answer (A) is incorrect because a questionnaire provides a framework to assure that control concerns are not overlooked. Answer (B) is incorrect because a questionnaire is relatively easy to complete. For the most part, only yes/no responses are elicited from management and employees. Answer (D) is incorrect because the completed questionnaire can become part of the working papers to document the auditor's understanding of internal control.

219. A well-designed internal control questionnaire should

A. Elicit "yes" or "no" responses rather than narrative responses and be organized by department.

B. Be a sufficient source of data for assessment of control risk.

C. Help evaluate the effectiveness of internal control.

D. Be independent of the objectives of the audit.

The correct answer is (C). *(CIA, adapted)*

REQUIRED: The function of a well-designed internal control questionnaire.

DISCUSSION: An internal control questionnaire consists of a series of questions about the firm's controls designed to prevent or detect errors or fraud. Answers to the questions help the auditor to identify specific controls relevant to specific assertions and to design tests of controls to evaluate the effectiveness of their design and operation.

Answer (A) is incorrect because yes/no question formats and question sequence by department may facilitate administering the questionnaire, but other formats and methods of question organization are possible. Answer (B) is incorrect because the questionnaire is a tool to help understand and document internal control but is not sufficient as the sole source of evidence to support the assessment of control risk. Answer (D) is incorrect because the internal control questionnaire must be designed to achieve the audit objectives.

220. Which of the following statements indicates the wrong way to use an internal control questionnaire?

A. Clarifying all answers with written remarks and explanations.

B. Filling out the questionnaire during an interview with the person who has responsibility for the area that is being audited.

C. Constructing the questionnaire so that a no response requires attention.

D. Supplementing the completed questionnaire with a narrative description or flowchart.

The correct answer is (A). *(CIA, adapted)*

REQUIRED: The statement indicating the wrong way to use an internal control questionnaire.

DISCUSSION: Only those answers that appear inappropriate should be pursued by means of the auditor's asking for clarification or explanation. In this way, problem areas may be pinpointed and either compensating controls identified or extensions to the audit procedures planned.

Answers (B), (C), and (D) are incorrect because filling out the questionnaire during an interview with the person who has responsibility for the area that is being audited, constructing the questionnaire so that a no response requires attention, and supplementing the completed questionnaire with a narrative description or flowchart are appropriate uses of an internal control questionnaire.

CHAPTER FOUR
AUDIT EVIDENCE AND PROCEDURES

This chapter concerns auditing procedures, the resulting audit evidence, and related matters. The emphasis is on financial audits as performed by both internal and external auditors. Questions on audit procedures and audit evidence unique to internal auditing, especially efficiency, compliance, operational, and other audits, are found in Chapter 9, Internal Auditing.

4.1 Nature, Competence, and Sufficiency

1. Which of the following is a false statement about audit objectives?

A. There should be a one-to-one relationship between audit objectives and procedures.

B. Audit objectives should be developed in light of management assertions about the financial statement components.

C. Selection of tests to meet audit objectives should depend upon the understanding of internal control.

D. The auditor should resolve any substantial doubt about any of management's material financial statement assertions.

The correct answer is (A). *(Publisher)*

REQUIRED: The false statement concerning audit objectives.

DISCUSSION: AU 326, *Evidential Matter*, states, "There is not necessarily a one-to-one relationship between audit objectives and procedures. Some auditing procedures may relate to more than one objective. On the other hand, a combination of auditing procedures may be needed to achieve a single objective."

Answer (B) is incorrect because the assertions made by management should be considered when the auditor develops audit objectives. Answer (C) is incorrect because the understanding of internal control and the assessed control risk affect the nature, timing, and extent of the auditor's substantive tests (AU 319, *Consideration of Internal Control in a Financial Statement Audit*). Answer (D) is incorrect because the auditor must consider whether specific audit objectives have been achieved; all substantial doubts about material assertions by management should be resolved before an opinion is formed.

2. AU 326 states that management makes certain assertions that are embodied in financial statement components; for example, two such categories of assertions are completeness and valuation or allocation. Which of the following is not a broad category of management assertions according to AU 326?

A. Rights and obligations.

B. Presentation and disclosure.

C. Existence or occurrence.

D. Errors or fraud.

The correct answer is (D). *(Publisher)*

REQUIRED: The category of assertions not explicitly listed in AU 326.

DISCUSSION: Management implicitly represents that the financial statements are free from material misstatements. But this representation is not explicitly noted in AU 326 as a category of assertions. AU 326 describes five categories of assertions. Assertions about completeness address whether all transactions and accounts that should be represented in the financial statements are so included. Assertions about valuation or allocation address whether asset, liability, revenue, and expense components have been included in the financial statements at appropriate amounts. Assertions about rights and obligations address whether assets are the rights of the entity and liabilities are the obligations of the entity at the balance sheet date. Assertions about presentation and disclosure address whether particular components of the financial statements are properly classified, described, and disclosed. Assertions about existence or occurrence address whether assets or liabilities of the entity exist at a given date and whether recorded transactions have occurred during a given period.

Answers (A), (B), and (C) are incorrect because rights and obligations, presentation and disclosure, and existence or occurrence are categories of management assertions.

3. The third standard of field work requires the auditor to collect sufficient competent evidence in support of the opinion. Which procedure is not listed in this standard?

A. Inspection.

B. Inquiries.

C. Observation.

D. Reconciliation.

The correct answer is (D). *(Publisher)*

REQUIRED: The procedure not listed in the third standard of field work.

DISCUSSION: The third standard of field work lists the following procedures: inspection, observation, inquiries, and confirmations. Although reconciliations are often made by the auditor in collecting evidence, the procedure is not explicitly mentioned in the third standard of field work.

Answers (A), (B), and (C) are incorrect because inspection, inquiries, and observation are listed in the third standard of field work.

4. Which of the following statements concerning audit evidence is correct?

A. To be competent, audit evidence should be either persuasive or relevant, but need not be both.

B. The measure of the validity of audit evidence lies in the auditor's judgment.

C. The difficulty and expense of obtaining audit evidence concerning an account balance is a valid basis for omitting the test.

D. A client's accounting data can be sufficient audit evidence to support the financial statements.

The correct answer is (B). *(CPA, adapted)*

REQUIRED: The true statement about audit evidence.

DISCUSSION: AU 326 states, "The measure of the validity of such evidence for audit purposes lies in the judgment of the auditor." Unlike legal evidence, audit evidence is not circumscribed by rigid rules. In determining whether evidence is competent and sufficient, the auditor must make many judgments about relevance, objectivity, timeliness, the existence of corroboration, etc.

Answer (A) is incorrect because, to be competent, audit evidence must be both valid and relevant. Moreover, an auditor usually must rely on evidence that is persuasive rather than convincing. Answer (C) is incorrect because, although the cost of obtaining evidence and its usefulness should be rationally related, the matter of difficulty and expense is not itself a valid basis for omitting a test. Answer (D) is incorrect because accounting data must be supported by corroborating information.

5. Which of the following factors is most important in determining the competence of audit evidence?

A. The reliability of the evidence in meeting the audit objective.

B. The objectivity of the auditor gathering the evidence.

C. The quantity of the evidence obtained.

D. The independence of the source of evidence.

The correct answer is (A). *(CIA, adapted)*

REQUIRED: The most important factor in determining the competence of audit evidence.

DISCUSSION: Information is competent if it is reliable and the best obtainable through appropriate audit techniques. AU 326 states that competent evidence is both valid and relevant. Accordingly, reliable evidence that meets the audit objective is competent.

Answer (B) is incorrect because the objectivity of the auditor is important, but the issue is whether the evidence obtained is competent. Answer (C) is incorrect because the quality of competence is not determined by the quantity of the evidence. Answer (D) is incorrect because the independence of the source is only one factor in determining whether the evidence is sufficiently reliable.

6. Which of the following is the best explanation of the difference, if any, between audit objectives and audit procedures?

A. Audit procedures establish broad general goals; audit objectives specify the detailed work to be performed.

B. Audit objectives are tailor-made for each assignment; audit procedures are generic in application.

C. Audit objectives define specific desired accomplishments; audit procedures provide the means of achieving audit objectives.

D. Audit procedures and audit objectives are essentially the same.

The correct answer is (C). *(CIA, adapted)*

REQUIRED: The best explanation of the difference between objectives and procedures.

DISCUSSION: The first step in planning the audit is to establish the audit objectives and the scope of work. After obtaining background information, determining what resources are necessary, communicating with those who need to know about the audit, and performing a preliminary survey, the auditors prepare the audit program, a list of the detailed procedures necessary to gather evidence to achieve the audit objectives. These procedures are specific audit steps developed in light of the objectives of the audit.

Answers (A) and (D) are incorrect because objectives are specific goals and procedures are detailed steps to achieve these goals. Answer (B) is incorrect because both objectives and procedures must be defined specifically for each assignment.

7. Substantive auditing tests are performed by the auditor to substantiate that

A. An understanding of internal control has been obtained.

B. Management has effectively designed controls and that they are operating effectively.

C. The rate of deviations found in tests of controls did not exceed the auditor's tolerable rate.

D. Account balances are not materially misstated.

The correct answer is (D). *(CMA, adapted)*

REQUIRED: The reason for substantive tests.

DISCUSSION: Substantive tests are auditing procedures designed to detect material misstatements in the financial statement assertions. They consist of tests of details of transactions and balances, and analytical procedures. The auditor performs substantive tests to restrict detection risk to an acceptable level (AU 319).

Answer (A) is incorrect because the auditor substantiates the understanding of internal control by means of documentation. Answer (B) is incorrect because procedures directed toward the effectiveness of the design or operation of a control are tests of controls. Answer (C) is incorrect because most substantive tests are performed after the assessment of control risk has been made. This assessment is necessary to determine the degree of audit effort applied to substantive tests. Substantive tests are not performed to verify the results of tests of controls.

8. In gathering evidence in the performance of substantive tests, the auditor

A. Should use the test month approach.

B. Relies on persuasive rather than convincing evidence in the majority of cases.

C. Would consider the client's documentary evidence more competent than evidence gathered from observation and physical inspection.

D. Would express an adverse opinion if (s)he has substantial doubt as to any assertion of material significance.

The correct answer is (B). *(Publisher)*

REQUIRED: The correct assumption about the performance of substantive tests.

DISCUSSION: Given the limits of time and cost to which evidence gathering is subject, even an experienced auditor is rarely convinced beyond all doubt regarding all aspects of the financial statements. Hence, the auditor must usually rely on persuasive rather than convincing evidence.

Answer (A) is incorrect because there is no requirement to select specific months for detail testing. "Test month approach" is a nonexistent term. Answer (C) is incorrect because evidence from physical inspection or observation is usually judged more competent than documentary evidence for the existence assertion. Answer (D) is incorrect because the auditor must be convinced that the financial statements, taken as a whole, are not presented fairly before (s)he expresses an adverse opinion.

9. JP Industries has significant information that is transmitted, processed, maintained, and accessed electronically. The auditor has concluded that it is not possible to reduce detection risk to an acceptable level by performing only substantive tests for a number of financial statement assertions. The auditor's alternative strategy is to

A. Increase the acceptable audit risk.

B. Focus audit tests on other assertions for which substantive tests prove to be effective.

C. Require management to change its information system to provide appropriate evidence.

D. Perform tests of controls to gather evidential matter to use in assessing control risk related to those assertions.

The correct answer is (D). *(Publisher)*

REQUIRED: The appropriate audit strategy when the client processes significant information electronically.

DISCUSSION: When significant information is transmitted, processed, maintained, or accessed electronically, reducing detection risk to an acceptable level by performing substantive tests alone may not be feasible. For example, the risk of improper initiation or alteration of information is increased when information is produced, maintained, or accessed only in electronic form. Thus, in such cases, the auditor should perform tests of controls or consider the consequences for the report (AU 326).

Answer (A) is incorrect because the auditor has already established an acceptable level of audit risk. Answer (B) is incorrect because the auditor cannot express an unqualified opinion if (s)he remains in substantial doubt about any material assertion. Answer (C) is incorrect because the auditor should not expect management to change its information system solely to accommodate the audit.

10. The primary difference between an audit of the balance sheet and an audit of the income statement is that the audit of the income statement addresses the verification of

A. Transactions.

B. Authorizations.

C. Costs.

D. Cutoffs.

The correct answer is (A). *(CPA, adapted)*

REQUIRED: The difference between the audit of the income statement and the balance sheet.

DISCUSSION: The audit of the income statement focuses on the propriety of handling transactions because most income statement accounts represent large volumes of transactions. The audit of the balance sheet concentrates on verification of account balances.

Answer (B) is incorrect because all transactions must be authorized. Answer (C) is incorrect because the auditor is equally concerned with the costs reflected in the income statement and the balance sheet. Answer (D) is incorrect because cutoffs to verify that only current period transactions are reflected apply to both statements.

11. Which of the following statements concerning evidence is correct?

A. Competent evidence supporting management's assertions should be convincing rather than merely persuasive.

B. Effective internal control contributes little to the reliability of the evidence created within the entity.

C. The cost of obtaining evidence is not an important consideration to an auditor in deciding what evidence should be obtained.

D. A client's accounting data cannot be considered sufficient audit evidence to support the financial statements.

The correct answer is (D). *(CPA, adapted)*

REQUIRED: The true statement concerning evidence.

DISCUSSION: Evidence supporting the financial statements consists of underlying accounting data (books of original entry, ledgers, accounting manuals, spreadsheets, etc.) and corroborating information (written and electronic checks, EFT records, confirmations, information obtained by inquiry, etc.). AU 326 states, "Accounting data alone cannot be considered sufficient support for financial statements; on the other hand, without adequate attention to the propriety and accuracy of the underlying accounting data, an opinion on financial statements would not be warranted."

Answer (A) is incorrect because the auditor must usually rely on evidence that is merely persuasive. Answer (B) is incorrect because the more effective internal control, the more assurance it provides about the reliability of the accounting data and financial statements. Answer (C) is incorrect because the auditor will consider the cost of evidence relative to its usefulness. If the auditor deems necessary evidence too costly, a scope limitation results.

12. The competence of evidence available to an auditor is least likely to be affected by

A. The relevance of such evidence to the financial statement assertion being investigated.

B. The relationship of the preparer of such evidence to the entity being audited.

C. The timeliness of such audit evidence.

D. The sampling method employed by the auditor to obtain a sample of such evidence.

The correct answer is (D). *(Publisher)*

REQUIRED: The factor that does not affect the competence of audit evidence.

DISCUSSION: Competent evidence is both valid and relevant. Ordinarily, evidence obtained from independent sources, developed under effective control, or generated through the auditor's personal experience is presumed to be the most competent (AU 326). The sample selection method does not affect the competence of evidence as long as the sample is representative of the population.

Answer (A) is incorrect because competent evidence must be valid and relevant. Answer (B) is incorrect because the independence of the source (or preparer) of the evidence from the auditee provides greater assurance of its reliability. Answer (C) is incorrect because timeliness is an aspect of relevance. Competent evidence must be relevant.

13. Which of the following procedures would provide the most reliable audit evidence?

A. Inquiries of the client's internal audit staff held in private.

B. Inspection of prenumbered client purchase orders filed in the vouchers payable department.

C. Analytical procedures performed by the auditor on the entity's trial balance.

D. Inspection of bank statements obtained directly from the client's financial institution.

The correct answer is (D). *(CPA, adapted)*

REQUIRED: The procedure that provides the most reliable audit evidence.

DISCUSSION: When documentation is prepared solely by client personnel, its persuasiveness will be less than that prepared by the auditor or an independent party. Ordinarily, the most reliable documentation is created outside the entity and has never been within the client's control, e.g., statements obtained from the bank, letters from attorneys, and letters from insurance brokers.

Answer (A) is incorrect because the internal audit staff is not independent. Answer (B) is incorrect because the purchase orders are internally generated. Answer (C) is incorrect because analytical procedures are based on the entity's internal records.

14. An auditor is least likely to use confirmations in connection with the audit of

A. Inventories.

B. Refundable income taxes.

C. Long-term debt.

D. Shareholders' equity.

The correct answer is (B). *(CPA, adapted)*

REQUIRED: The item for which confirmations are least likely to be used.

DISCUSSION: Income taxes are paid to governmental entities, which are in a better position to state what amounts have been paid than what amounts are refundable based on a tax return that may not yet have been filed. The U.S. government does not usually respond to confirmations.

Answer (A) is incorrect because inventories held on consignment or in public warehouses may be confirmed. Answer (C) is incorrect because a bank confirmation includes information about long-term debt owed to the bank. Confirmations may also be sent to other long-term creditors. Answer (D) is incorrect because shares outstanding are confirmed with the independent registrar and stock transfer agent. If the company acts as its own registrar and stock transfer agent, the auditor may send confirmations to shareholders.

15. The most reliable forms of documentary evidence are those documents that are

A. Prenumbered.

B. Internally generated.

C. Easily duplicated.

D. Authorized by a responsible official.

The correct answer is (D). *(CMA, adapted)*

REQUIRED: The most reliable forms of documentary evidence.

DISCUSSION: Externally generated documents are deemed to be more reliable than those produced by the auditee. However, the evidentiary value of the latter is enhanced if they are subject to effective control. Accordingly, authorization by an appropriate party lends credibility to a document because it increases the probability that the underlying transaction is valid.

Answer (A) is incorrect because the use of prenumbered and sequentially issued documents is an effective control, but such documents may be accessible to an employee who is perpetrating fraud. Answers (B) and (C) are incorrect because internally generated and easily duplicated documents are readily available to those attempting to commit fraud.

16. Which of the following presumptions does not relate to the competence of audit evidence?

A. The more effective internal control, the more assurance it provides about the accounting data and financial statements.

B. An auditor's opinion, to be economically useful, is formed within a reasonable time and based on evidence obtained at a reasonable cost.

C. Evidence obtained from independent sources outside the entity is more reliable than evidence secured solely within the entity.

D. The independent auditor's direct personal knowledge, obtained through observation and inspection, is more persuasive than information obtained indirectly.

The correct answer is (B). *(CPA, adapted)*

REQUIRED: The presumption not relating to the competence of audit evidence.

DISCUSSION: Competent evidence is both valid and relevant. Ordinarily, evidence obtained from independent sources, developed under effective internal control, or generated through the auditor's personal experience is presumed to be the most competent (AU 326). However, cost-benefit considerations relate to the sufficiency, not the competence, of evidence.

Answer (A) is incorrect because, the more effective internal control, the more assurance it provides about the reliability of the accounting data and financial statements. Answer (C) is incorrect because evidence obtained from independent sources outside an entity provides greater assurance of reliability than evidence secured solely within the entity. Answer (D) is incorrect because the independent auditor's direct personal knowledge, obtained through physical examination, observation, computation, and inspection, is more persuasive than information obtained indirectly.

17. AU 326 describes three presumptions concerning the validity of evidence. The situations given below indicate the relative degrees of assurance provided by two types of evidence obtained in different situations. Which describes an exception to one of the general presumptions?

A. The auditor has obtained greater assurance about the balance of sales at Plant A where (s)he has made limited tests of transactions because of effective internal control than at Plant B where (s)he has made extensive tests of transactions because of ineffective internal control.

B. The auditor's computation of interest payable on outstanding bonds provides greater assurance than reliance on the client's calculation.

C. The report of an expert regarding the valuation of a collection of paintings held as an investment provides greater assurance than the auditor's physical observation of the paintings.

D. The schedule of insurance coverage obtained from the company's insurance agent provides greater assurance than one prepared by the internal audit staff.

The correct answer is (C). *(Publisher)*

REQUIRED: The exception to the presumptions concerning validity of audit evidence.

DISCUSSION: AU 326 describes three presumptions concerning the validity of evidence. Evidence is usually more valid when (1) it is obtained from independent sources, (2) accounting data and financial statements are developed under effective internal control, and (3) it consists of the auditor's direct knowledge obtained by examination, observation, computation, or inspection. Preference for the report of a specialist over the auditor's physical observation of works of art is acceptable because the auditor is not expected to have such expertise. Physical observation provides evidence of the existence of assets but often does not verify their value, ownership, cost, or condition. Consequently, the presumption in favor of the auditor's direct knowledge is overcome in this case.

Answer (A) is incorrect because control risk should be lower when control is effective, and judging that greater assurance has been provided about sales at Plant A is consistent with the second presumption stated above. Answer (B) is incorrect because the auditor's direct knowledge should be preferred to indirect knowledge. Answer (D) is incorrect because information obtained from independent sources is more valid than that prepared by the client's staff.

18. Observation is considered a reliable audit procedure, but one that is limited in usefulness. However, it is used in a number of different audit situations. Which of the following statements is true regarding observation as an audit technique?

A. It is the most effective audit methodology to use in filling out internal control questionnaires.

B. It is the most persuasive methodology to learn how transactions are really processed during the period under audit.

C. It is rarely sufficient to satisfy any audit assertion other than existence.

D. It is the most persuasive audit technique for determining if fraud has occurred.

The correct answer is (C). *(CIA, adapted)*

REQUIRED: The true statement about the audit technique of observation.

DISCUSSION: Observation is effective for verifying whether particular assets such as inventory or equipment exist at a given date. However, it is of limited use in addressing other assertions. Thus, it provides less persuasive evidence about the assertions of completeness, rights, valuation, and presentation and disclosure. For example, merely observing inventory does not determine whether the auditee has rights in it.

Answer (A) is incorrect because interviews are the most effective method to fill out questionnaires. The interview results should be supplemented with observations. Answer (B) is incorrect because observation provides information on how transactions are processed at one moment in time, not how they are processed throughout the period under audit investigation. Answer (D) is incorrect because the auditor will very seldom be able to observe a fraud.

19. To test for unsupported entries in the ledger, the direction of audit testing should be from the

A. Journal entries.

B. Ledger entries.

C. Original source documents.

D. Externally generated documents.

The correct answer is (B). *(CPA, adapted)*

REQUIRED: The direction of testing for unsupported entries in the ledger.

DISCUSSION: To discover unsupported entries in the ledger, a sample of entries should be selected to determine whether any entry lacks proper support. The direction of testing is from the ledger entries to the books of original entry to the source documents.

Answer (A) is incorrect because entries could have been made in the ledger without an entry in the journal. Answers (C) and (D) are incorrect because the auditor would select documents and trace them to the records to search for unrecorded, not unsupported, entries.

20. Assuming a low assessed level of control risk, which of the following audit procedures is least likely to be performed?

A. Physical inspection of a sample of inventory.

B. Search for unrecorded cash receipts.

C. Obtainment of a client representation letter.

D. Confirmation of accounts receivable.

The correct answer is (B). *(CPA, adapted)*

REQUIRED: The procedure least necessary when control risk is low.

DISCUSSION: GAAS do not specifically require a search for unrecorded cash receipts. Given a low assessed level of control risk, the auditor might decide to reduce the audit effort devoted to substantive tests of assertions about cash and omit the procedure.

Answer (A) is incorrect because AU 331, *Inventories*, states that observation of inventories is a generally accepted auditing procedure. An auditor who expresses an opinion when inventories have not been observed must justify the opinion expressed. Answer (C) is incorrect because AU 333, *Client Representations*, requires written representations from management. Answer (D) is incorrect because, according to AU 330, *The Confirmation Process*, confirmation of accounts receivable is a generally accepted auditing procedure. There is a presumption in favor of confirmation.

21. You have been assigned to audit the maintenance department of an organization. Which of the following is likely to produce the least reliable audit evidence?

A. Notes on discussions with mechanics in the maintenance operation.

B. A schedule comparing actual maintenance expenses with budgeted expenses and those of the prior period and disclosing important differences.

C. A narrative covering review of user reports on maintenance service.

D. An analysis of changes in certain maintenance department ratios.

The correct answer is (A). *(CIA, adapted)*

REQUIRED: The procedure that is likely to produce the least reliable evidence in an audit of a maintenance department.

DISCUSSION: Although representations by personnel of the auditee are evidence, auditor observation and analysis of documents provide more reliable evidence.

Answer (B) is incorrect because the comparison provides more reliable evidence relative to the maintenance department's operations. Such documentary evidence is presumably prepared independently of the audited department. Answer (C) is incorrect because reports by users of maintenance services are likewise independent evidence. They are of interest to internal auditors because they bear on the quality of performance. Answer (D) is incorrect because analytical procedures are typically considered more reliable than representations by client personnel.

22. Each of the following might, by itself, form a valid basis for an auditor to decide to omit a test except for the

A. Difficulty and expense involved in testing a particular item.

B. Assessment of control risk at a low level.

C. Inherent risk involved.

D. Relationship between the cost of obtaining evidence and its usefulness.

The correct answer is (A). *(CPA, adapted)*

REQUIRED: The consideration that is not a valid reason for omission of an audit test.

DISCUSSION: The costs and benefits of obtaining evidence should have a rational relationship. However, the difficulty and expense of performing a test are not in themselves considered valid reasons for omitting it if the test is necessary to obtain sufficient competent evidence to afford a reasonable basis for an opinion (AU 326).

Answer (B) is incorrect because the lower the control risk, the higher the acceptable detection risk, and the greater the justification for omitting a substantive test. Answer (C) is incorrect because a test might be omitted if the susceptibility to errors and fraud is slight. Answer (D) is incorrect because the cost of obtaining evidence and its usefulness should have a rational relationship.

23. Which of the following auditing procedures is ordinarily performed last?

A. Reading of the minutes of the directors' meetings.

B. Confirming accounts payable.

C. Obtaining a management representation letter.

D. Testing of the purchasing function.

The correct answer is (C). *(CPA, adapted)*

REQUIRED: The auditing procedure ordinarily performed last.

DISCUSSION: Written representations by management should be dated no earlier than the date of the report because the auditor is concerned with events occurring through that date that may require adjustment to or disclosure in the financial statements (AU 333).

Answer (A) is incorrect because reading the minutes is customarily done in the preliminary or planning phase of the audit. Answer (B) is incorrect because confirming accounts payable is done at interim dates or year-end. Answer (D) is incorrect because testing of the purchasing function is done at interim dates or year-end.

24. Before applying substantive tests to the details of asset accounts at an interim date, an auditor should assess

A. Control risk at below the maximum level.

B. Inherent risk at the maximum level.

C. The difficulty in controlling the incremental audit risk.

D. Materiality for the accounts tested as insignificant.

The correct answer is (C). *(CPA, adapted)*

REQUIRED: The assessment made prior to applying substantive tests at an interim date.

DISCUSSION: Before substantive tests of details are performed at interim dates, the auditor should assess the difficulty of controlling the incremental audit risk. Factors to be considered include the cost of substantive tests to cover the remaining period; the possible impairment of the effectiveness of those tests, if the auditor assesses control risk at the maximum; the existence of rapidly changing business conditions or circumstances that might lead management to misstate the financial statements; the predictability of year-end balances; the propriety of the auditee's procedures for adjusting accounts and establishing cutoffs; and the question of whether the financial reporting information system permits investigation of unusual transactions or entries, other causes of significant fluctuations, and changes in the composition of balances (AU 313, *Substantive Tests prior to the Balance Sheet Date*).

Answers (A) and (B) are incorrect because assessing control risk or inherent risk at or below the maximum is not required. Answer (D) is incorrect because the accounts need not be tested if they are not material.

25. Before applying principal substantive tests to the details of accounts at an interim date prior to the balance sheet date, an auditor should

A. Assess control risk as below the maximum for the assertions embodied in the accounts selected for interim testing.

B. Determine that the accounts selected for interim testing are not material to the financial statements taken as a whole.

C. Consider whether the amounts of the year-end balances selected for interim testing are reasonably predictable.

D. Obtain written representations from management that all financial records and related data will be made available.

The correct answer is (C). *(CPA, adapted)*

REQUIRED: The auditor action prior to applying principal substantive tests at an interim date.

DISCUSSION: Among the auditor's considerations is whether the year-end balances of accounts selected for interim examination are reasonably predictable as to amount, relative significance, and composition.

Answer (A) is incorrect because assessing control risk at below the maximum is not required. However, if the auditor assesses control risk at the maximum for the remaining period, (s)he should consider whether the effectiveness of certain substantive tests to cover that period will be impaired. Answer (B) is incorrect because the accounts selected for interim testing are likely to be material. Answer (D) is incorrect because written representations will be obtained from the client regardless of when testing is done.

26. If an auditor conducts an audit of financial statements in accordance with generally accepted auditing standards, which of the following will the auditor most likely detect?

A. Misposting of recorded transactions.

B. Unrecorded transactions.

C. Forgery.

D. Collusive fraud.

The correct answer is (A). *(Publisher)*

REQUIRED: The error or fraud most likely to be detected by the auditor.

DISCUSSION: Until a transaction is recorded, leaving an audit trail, standard audit procedures are often ineffective. A misposting of previously recorded transactions is therefore the most likely item to be detected.

Answer (B) is incorrect because unrecorded transactions leave no audit trail. Answer (C) is incorrect because auditors usually are not qualified to detect forgery. Answer (D) is incorrect because the possibility of collusion is an inherent limitation of internal control. The purpose of segregation of duties can be circumvented if two or more persons agree to commit an irregularity.

27. In evaluating an entity's accounting estimates, one of an auditor's objectives is to determine whether the estimates are

A. Not subject to bias.

B. Consistent with industry guidelines.

C. Based on objective assumptions.

D. Reasonable in the circumstances.

The correct answer is (D). *(CPA, adapted)*

REQUIRED: The objective of evaluating an entity's accounting estimates.

DISCUSSION: "The auditor is responsible for evaluating the reasonableness of accounting estimates made by management in the context of the financial statements taken as a whole" (AU 342, *Auditing Accounting Estimates*).

Answer (A) is incorrect because accounting estimates are based on subjective as well as objective factors and may be subject to bias. Answer (B) is incorrect because there are few industry guidelines relative to accounting estimates. Answer (C) is incorrect because estimates may be based on subjective factors.

28. In evaluating the reasonableness of an accounting estimate, an auditor is most likely to concentrate on key factors and assumptions that are

A. Consistent with prior periods.

B. Similar to industry guidelines.

C. Objective and not susceptible to bias.

D. Deviations from historical patterns.

The correct answer is (D). *(CPA, adapted)*

REQUIRED: The focus of an auditor when evaluating the reasonableness of an accounting estimate.

DISCUSSION: "In evaluating the reasonableness of an accounting estimate, an auditor normally concentrates on key factors and assumptions that are (1) significant to the accounting estimate, (2) sensitive to variations, (3) deviations from historical patterns, and (4) subjective and susceptible to misstatement and bias" (AU 342).

Answer (A) is incorrect because the auditor would concentrate on estimates that are deviations from historical patterns. Answer (B) is incorrect because key factors and assumptions similar to industry guidelines would not help evaluate the reasonableness of an accounting estimate. Answer (C) is incorrect because the auditor would concentrate on key factors and assumptions that are subjective and susceptible to misstatement and bias.

4.2 Analytical Procedures

29. Analytical procedures can best be categorized as

A. Substantive tests.

B. Tests of controls.

C. Qualitative tests.

D. Budget comparisons.

The correct answer is (A). *(CIA, adapted)*

REQUIRED: The best classification of analytical procedures.

DISCUSSION: According to AU 329, *Analytical Procedures*, analytical procedures "consist of evaluations of financial information made by a study of plausible relationships among both financial and nonfinancial data." They "involve comparisons of recorded amounts, or ratios developed from recorded amounts, to expectations developed by the auditor."

Answer (B) is incorrect because tests of controls are used to evaluate the effectiveness of control activities. Answer (C) is incorrect because analytical procedures tend to be quantitative even when nonfinancial information is considered. Answer (D) is incorrect because budget comparisons are only one of many types of analytical procedures.

30. Analytical procedures enable the auditor to predict the balance or quantity of an item under audit. Information to develop this estimate can be obtained from all of the following except

A. Tracing transactions through the system to determine whether procedures are being applied as prescribed.

B. Comparison of financial data with data for comparable prior periods, anticipated results (e.g., budgets and forecasts), and similar data for the industry in which the entity operates.

C. Study of the relationships of elements of financial data that would be expected to conform to a predictable pattern based upon the entity's experience.

D. Study of the relationships of financial data with relevant nonfinancial data.

The correct answer is (A). *(Publisher)*

REQUIRED: The procedure not a source of information for analytical procedures.

DISCUSSION: Tracing transactions through the system is a test of controls directed toward the operating effectiveness of internal control, not an analytical procedure.

Answer (B) is incorrect because the basic premise of analytical procedures is that plausible relationships among data may be reasonably expected to exist and continue in the absence of known conditions to the contrary. Well-drafted budgets and forecasts prepared at the beginning of the year should therefore be compared with actual results, and client information should be compared with data for the industry in which the client operates. Answer (C) is incorrect because the auditor should expect financial ratios and relationships to exist and to remain relatively stable in the absence of reasons for variation. Answer (D) is incorrect because financial information is related to nonfinancial information; e.g., salary expense should be related to the number of hours worked.

31. The objective of performing analytical procedures in planning an audit is to identify the existence of

A. Unusual transactions and events.

B. Illegal acts that went undetected because of internal control weaknesses.

C. Related party transactions.

D. Recorded transactions that were not properly authorized.

The correct answer is (A). *(CPA, adapted)*

REQUIRED: The objective of analytical procedures.

DISCUSSION: The objective of analytical procedures "is to identify such things as the existence of unusual transactions and events, and amounts, ratios, and trends that might indicate matters that have financial statement and audit planning ramifications" (AU 329).

Answer (B) is incorrect because the objective of performing analytical procedures to plan the audit is to identify areas of specific risk, not specific illegal acts. Answer (C) is incorrect because, although the auditor should evaluate disclosures about related party transactions, analytical procedures performed to plan the audit would not necessarily detect such transactions. Answer (D) is incorrect because tests of controls would be necessary to determine whether transactions were properly authorized.

32. Analytical procedures used in planning an audit should focus on

A. Evaluating the adequacy of evidence gathered concerning unusual balances.

B. Testing individual account balances that depend on accounting estimates.

C. Enhancing the auditor's understanding of the client's business.

D. Identifying material weaknesses in internal control.

The correct answer is (C). *(CPA, adapted)*

REQUIRED: The focus of analytical procedures used in planning.

DISCUSSION: When used in planning an audit, analytical procedures should focus on enhancing the auditor's understanding of the client's business and identifying unusual relationships and unexpected fluctuations in data that may indicate areas of greater risk of misstatement (AU 329).

Answer (A) is incorrect because evaluation of evidence is done in the final stage of the audit. Answer (B) is incorrect because analytical procedures are predictions or expectations of account balances or ratios but are not specifically designed to test estimates. Answer (D) is incorrect because the auditor's understanding of internal control and tests of controls may identify material weaknesses.

33. For all audits of financial statements made in accordance with generally accepted auditing standards, the use of analytical procedures is required to some extent

	In the Planning Stage	As a Substantive Test	In the Review Stage
A.	Yes	No	Yes
B.	No	Yes	No
C.	No	Yes	Yes
D.	Yes	No	No

The correct answer is (A). *(CPA, adapted)*

REQUIRED: The required use(s) of analytical procedures.

DISCUSSION: The auditor is required to apply analytical procedures in planning the nature, timing, and extent of other auditing procedures. However, analytical procedures may be, but are not required to be, used as substantive tests to provide competent evidence about specific financial statement assertions. Analytical procedures give supervisors and reviewers an overall perspective on the financial information being audited and are required in the final review.

Answers (B), (C), and (D) are incorrect because analytical procedures are required in the planning and overall review stages but not as substantive tests.

34. Which of the following statements is true concerning analytical procedures?

A. Analytical procedures usually involve comparisons of ratios developed from recorded amounts with assertions developed by management.

B. Analytical procedures used in planning an audit ordinarily use data aggregated at a high level.

C. Analytical procedures can replace tests of controls in gathering evidence to support the assessed level of control risk.

D. Analytical procedures are more efficient, but not more effective, than tests of details and transactions.

The correct answer is (B). *(CPA, adapted)*

REQUIRED: The true statement concerning analytical procedures.

DISCUSSION: Analytical procedures applied in planning the audit focus on enhancing the understanding of the business and the transactions and events since the last audit, identify areas that may represent specific audit risks, and ordinarily use data aggregated at a high level.

Answer (A) is incorrect because analytical procedures involve comparisons of recorded amounts, or ratios developed therefrom, with expectations developed by the auditor. Answer (C) is incorrect because tests of controls are required if control risk is to be assessed at below the maximum. Analytical procedures are used as substantive tests but not as tests of controls. Answer (D) is incorrect because, for many assertions, analytical procedures may not be as effective or efficient as tests of details in providing the desired level of assurance.

35. According to professional standards, analytical procedures are least likely to be applied to

A. Test disclosures about reportable operating segments.

B. Review financial statements or interim financial information.

C. Compile financial statements.

D. Plan an audit and assist in the final review.

The correct answer is (C). *(Publisher)*

REQUIRED: The inappropriate use of analytical procedures.

DISCUSSION: AR 100, *Compilation and Review of Financial Statements*, states that no audit procedures need be applied in a compilation of financial statements. The accountant is only required to read the financial statements to identify obvious errors.

Answer (A) is incorrect because an Interpretation of AU 326 states that an auditor should consider applying analytical procedures consisting of comparisons of information about segments with comparable information for the prior year and with budgeted information. Answer (B) is incorrect because analytical procedures ordinarily should be applied in a review of interim financial information (AU 722, *Interim Financial Information*) and in a review of financial statements of a private entity (AR 100). Answer (D) is incorrect because AU 329 requires analytical procedures to be applied in the planning and final review stages of an audit.

36. Analytical procedures performed in the overall review stage of an audit suggest that several accounts have unexpected relationships. The results of these procedures most likely indicate that

A. Irregularities exist among the relevant account balances.

B. Internal control activities are not operating effectively.

C. Additional tests of details are required.

D. The communication with the audit committee should be revised.

The correct answer is (C). *(CPA, adapted)*

REQUIRED: The implication when analytical procedures applied in the overall review stage of the audit have unexpected results.

DISCUSSION: Analytical procedures are required to be performed in the final review stage of the audit. They assist in assessing the conclusions reached and in evaluating the overall financial presentation. When analytical procedures have unexpected results, the auditor should investigate the causes. Thus, additional tests of details should be performed to gather additional evidence (AU 329).

Answer (A) is incorrect because analytical procedures can identify unexpected relationships but not their causes. Answer (B) is incorrect because tests of controls are conducted to determine the effectiveness of their design and operation. Answer (D) is incorrect because, until the auditor determines the cause of the unexpected relationships, the auditor does not know whether the communication with the audit committee should be revised.

37. A basic premise underlying analytical procedures is that

A. These procedures cannot replace tests of balances and transactions.

B. Statistical tests of financial information may lead to the discovery of material misstatements in the financial statements.

C. The study of financial ratios is an acceptable alternative to the investigation of unusual fluctuations.

D. Plausible relationships among data may reasonably be expected to exist and continue in the absence of known conditions to the contrary.

The correct answer is (D). *(CPA, adapted)*

REQUIRED: The premise underlying analytical procedures.

DISCUSSION: AU 329 states, "A basic premise underlying the application of analytical procedures is that plausible relationships among data may reasonably be expected to exist and continue in the absence of known conditions to the contrary." Variability in these relationships can be explained by, for example, unusual events or transactions, business or accounting changes, misstatements, or random fluctuations.

Answer (A) is incorrect because, for some assertions, analytical procedures alone may provide the auditor with the level of assurance (s)he desires. Answer (B) is incorrect because analytical procedures, such as simple comparisons, do not necessarily require statistical testing. Answer (C) is incorrect because the objective of analytical procedures, such as ratio analysis, is to identify significant differences for evaluation and possible investigation.

38. As a result of analytical procedures, the independent auditor determines that the gross profit percentage has declined from 30% in the preceding year to 20% in the current year. The auditor should

A. Document management's intentions with respect to plans for reversing this trend.

B. Evaluate management's performance in causing this decline.

C. Require footnote disclosure.

D. Consider the possibility of a misstatement in the financial statements.

The correct answer is (D). *(CPA, adapted)*

REQUIRED: The appropriate action when the auditor has identified a decline in the gross profit rate.

DISCUSSION: AU 329 indicates that the auditor should consider the possibility of a misstatement when (s)he has identified unexpected differences between recorded amounts and expectations. Because a change of 10% is likely to be judged significant, the auditor should reconsider the expectations used and make inquiries of management. If the difference still cannot be explained, additional procedures should be performed.

Answer (A) is incorrect because an auditor appropriately considers management's plans for dealing with adverse conditions that create a substantial doubt about the ability of the entity to continue as a going concern (AU 341, *The Auditor's Consideration of an Entity's Ability to Continue as a Going Concern*). In the absence of this doubt, however, the auditor's scope of work does not include consideration of management's plans to reverse the trend. Answer (B) is incorrect because the auditor typically does not evaluate management's performance. Answer (C) is incorrect because requiring disclosure is premature. The auditor must first determine the cause of the decline.

39. An auditor testing long-term investments ordinarily uses analytical procedures to ascertain the reasonableness of the

A. Completeness of recorded investment income.

B. Classification as available-for-sale or trading securities.

C. Valuation of trading securities.

D. Existence of unrealized gains or losses.

The correct answer is (A). *(CPA, adapted)*

REQUIRED: The use of analytical procedures when an auditor tests long-term investments.

DISCUSSION: The auditor may develop expectations regarding the completeness assertion for recorded investment income from stocks by using dividend records published by standard investment advisory services to recompute dividends received. Interest income from bond investments can be calculated from interest rates and payment dates noted on the certificates. Income from equity-based investments can be estimated from audited financial statements of the investees.

Answer (B) is incorrect because the classification depends on management's objectives regarding the specific investments, not relationships among the data. Answer (C) is incorrect because valuation is a function of fair values. Answer (D) is incorrect because unrealized gains or losses are dependent on the fair values of specific securities and cannot be calculated based on plausible relationships among the data.

40. Which of the following ratios is the least useful in reviewing the overall profitability of a manufacturing company?

A. Net income to net worth.

B. Net income to working capital.

C. Net income to sales.

D. Net income to total assets.

The correct answer is (B). *(CPA, adapted)*

REQUIRED: The least useful ratio in reviewing the overall profitability of a manufacturing company.

DISCUSSION: The ratio of net income to working capital is not typically considered in evaluating overall profitability. It does not give a broad measure of how effectively the firm is managed because it does not consider long-term assets and liabilities.

Answer (A) is incorrect because net income to net worth is a ratio that offers meaningful information concerning profitability. It measures the return on resources provided by owners (shareholders' equity). Answer (C) is incorrect because net income to sales (profit margin) is a useful index of operational earning capacity, including levels of prices and costs, but has the weakness of ignoring the assets that produce the sales. Answer (D) is incorrect because net income to total assets is an indicator of the earnings on all resources of the entity.

41. Which of the following is the most reliable analytical approach to verification of the year-end financial statement balances of a wholesale business?

A. Verify depreciation expense by multiplying the depreciable asset balances by one divided by the depreciation rate.

B. Verify commission expense by multiplying sales revenue by the company's standard commission rate.

C. Verify interest expense, which includes imputed interest, by multiplying long-term debt balances by the year-end prevailing interest rate.

D. Verify FICA tax liability by multiplying total payroll costs by the FICA contribution rate in effect during the year.

The correct answer is (B). *(CPA, adapted)*

REQUIRED: The reliable analytical procedure to verify balances of a wholesale business.

DISCUSSION: If the wholesaler uses a standard commission rate, commission expense should be related to sales revenue. The auditor should also compare actual with budgeted and prior year amounts.

Answer (A) is incorrect because one divided by the life of the asset is the formula for the straight-line depreciation rate. The client may also use other depreciation methods. Answer (C) is incorrect because interest expense is not related to the prevailing rate but to contracted and imputed rates. Answer (D) is incorrect because FICA tax is withheld from individual wages up to a ceiling amount. No tax liability exists for amounts above the ceiling, so the test will probably overstate the liability.

42. An auditor's decision either to apply analytical procedures as substantive tests or to perform tests of transactions and account balances usually is determined by the

A. Availability of data aggregated at a high level.

B. Relative effectiveness and efficiency of the tests.

C. Timing of tests performed after the balance sheet date.

D. Auditor's familiarity with industry trends.

The correct answer is (B). *(CPA, adapted)*

REQUIRED: The basis for choosing between analytical procedures and tests of details.

DISCUSSION: The decision is based on the auditor's judgment about the expected effectiveness and efficiency of the available procedures. The auditor considers the level of assurance required to be provided by substantive testing for a particular audit objective related to a particular assertion. (S)he must then decide which procedure or combination of procedures can provide that level of assurance. "For some assertions, analytical procedures are effective in providing the appropriate level of assurance" (AU 329).

Answers (A), (C), and (D) are incorrect because availability of data, timing of tests, and familiarity with industry trends are among the factors in evaluating effectiveness and efficiency.

43. Which result of an analytical procedure suggests the existence of obsolete merchandise?

A. Decrease in the inventory turnover rate.

B. Decrease in the ratio of gross profit to sales.

C. Decrease in the ratio of inventory to accounts payable.

D. Decrease in the ratio of inventory to accounts receivable.

The correct answer is (A). *(CIA, adapted)*

REQUIRED: The analytical procedure that might uncover obsolete merchandise.

DISCUSSION: Inventory turnover is equal to cost of sales divided by average inventory. If inventory is increasing at a faster rate than sales, the turnover rate decreases and suggests a buildup of unsalable inventory.

Answers (B), (C), and (D) are incorrect because the ratios of gross profit to sales, inventory to accounts payable, and inventory to accounts receivable do not necessarily change when obsolete merchandise is on hand.

44. An auditor's preliminary analysis of accounts receivable turnover revealed the following rates:

19X2	19X1	19X0
4.3	6.2	7.3

Which of the following is the most likely cause of the decrease in accounts receivable turnover?

A. Increase in the cash discount offered.

B. Liberalization of credit policy.

C. Shortening of due date terms.

D. Increased cash sales.

The correct answer is (B). *(CIA, adapted)*

REQUIRED: The most likely cause of a decrease in accounts receivable turnover.

DISCUSSION: The accounts receivable turnover ratio equals net credit sales over average accounts receivable. Accounts receivable turnover will decrease if net credit sales decrease or average accounts receivable increase. Liberalization of credit policy will increase receivables.

Answer (A) is incorrect because an increase in cash sales that reduces credit sales as a result of an increased cash discount has an indeterminate effect on the turnover ratio. Both the numerator and denominator are decreased but not necessarily by the same amount. An increase in cash sales not affecting credit sales has no effect on the ratio.

Answer (C) is incorrect because shortening due dates decreases the average accounts receivable outstanding and increases the ratio if other factors are held constant.

Answer (D) is incorrect because increased cash sales have an indeterminate effect on the turnover ratio.

45. Which of the following is least likely to be comparable between similar corporations in the same industry line of business?

A. Earnings per share.

B. Return on total assets before interest and taxes.

C. Accounts receivable turnover.

D. Operating cycle.

The correct answer is (A). *(CPA, adapted)*

REQUIRED: The measure least likely to be comparable between similar firms.

DISCUSSION: Similar companies in the same industry that are equally profitable may have quite different earnings per share because of differences in shares outstanding and in other aspects of their capital structures.

Answers (B), (C), and (D) are incorrect because similar companies should have comparable returns on total assets, accounts receivable turnover, and operating cycles.

46. Auditors sometimes use comparison of ratios as audit evidence. For example, an unexplained decrease in the ratio of gross profit to sales suggests which of the following possibilities?

A. Unrecorded purchases.

B. Unrecorded sales.

C. Merchandise purchases being charged to selling and general expense.

D. Fictitious sales.

The correct answer is (B). *(CPA, adapted)*

REQUIRED: The reason for a decrease in the gross profit ratio.

DISCUSSION: Error or fraud that decreases gross profit relative to sales (or increases sales relative to gross profit) causes the ratio to decline. Unrecorded sales cause inventory to decrease and cost of sales to increase with no increase in sales, thereby decreasing gross profit relative to sales and lowering the ratio.

Answers (A) and (C) are incorrect because unrecorded or misrecorded purchases result in a lower recorded cost of sales, a greater gross profit, and an increase in the ratio.

Answer (D) is incorrect because fictitious sales increase sales with no associated cost, hence gross profit is inflated and the ratio increases.

47. If accounts receivable turned over 7.1 times in 1997 as compared to only 5.6 times in 1998, it is possible that there were

A. Unrecorded credit sales in 1998.

B. Unrecorded cash receipts in 1997.

C. More thorough credit investigations made by the company late in 1997.

D. Fictitious sales in 1998.

The correct answer is (D). *(CPA, adapted)*

REQUIRED: The reason accounts receivable turnover might decrease.

DISCUSSION: The accounts receivable turnover is the ratio of sales to average receivables. Fictitious sales would increase both the numerator and denominator. Adding an equal amount to both the numerator and denominator decreases a fraction greater than 1.0. For example, adding 1 to both parts of the fraction 3/2 decreases it to 4/3. The turnover ratio would decrease still more in the next period because the fictitious items would continue to increase receivables (which are cumulative) but not sales (which are closed periodically).

Answer (A) is incorrect because unrecorded sales in 1998 would increase the ratio, not decrease it. Both the numerator and denominator would be reduced by the same amount. Answer (B) is incorrect because unrecorded cash receipts in 1997 would decrease the 1997 ratio because the denominator would be larger. Answer (C) is incorrect because more thorough credit investigations would normally have resulted in a better quality but lower amount of receivables, thus increasing the turnover ratio.

48. An auditor compares this year's revenues and expenses with those of the prior year and investigates all changes exceeding 10%. By this procedure the auditor is most likely to learn that

A. An increase in property tax rates has not been recognized in the client's accrual.

B. This year's provision for uncollectible accounts is inadequate because of worsening economic conditions.

C. Fourth quarter payroll taxes were not paid.

D. The client changed its capitalization policy for small tools year before last.

The correct answer is (D). *(CPA, adapted)*

REQUIRED: The event likely to be discovered by comparing current and prior year revenues and expenses.

DISCUSSION: Investigating changes in revenues and expenses should detect unusual events, transactions, etc., that have an impact on the income statement accounts. A change in the capitalization policy for tools year before last would probably have a significant effect on small tools expense.

Answer (A) is incorrect because this year's reported property tax expense is probably similar to last year's, so the auditor would find no indication of a tax expense understatement. Answer (B) is incorrect because, in such circumstances, a constant provision (which would not be investigated) would be more likely to be inadequate than a material change. Answer (C) is incorrect because payroll taxes payable is a balance sheet account. Nonpayment would not be discovered by analysis of revenues and expenses.

49. Zee Company sells two products, X and Y. In the current year, unit sales volume decreased compared with the prior year by 20% and 5% for X and Y, respectively, after their prices were increased by 10%. Dollar sales of X and Y were $200,000 and $100,000, respectively, in the prior year. Accordingly, Zee company's total current-year dollar sales were

A. $330,000

B. $280,500

C. $271,000

D. $255,000

The correct answer is (B). *(Publisher)*

REQUIRED: The amount of total sales for two products given volume and price changes.

DISCUSSION: First, calculate the change in volume while holding prices constant. Next, calculate the effects of the price changes.

	Product X	Product Y	Total
Sales	$200,000	$100,000	
Volume change	(40,000)(20%)	(5,000)(5%)	
Before price change	$160,000	$ 95,000	
Price change	16,000 (10%)	9,500 (10%)	
Total	$176,000	$104,500	$280,500

Answer (A) is incorrect because $330,000 equals total sales assuming no change in volume. Answer (C) is incorrect because $271,000 equals total sales with no adjustment for the increase in the price of Y. Answer (D) is incorrect because $255,000 reflects the decline in volume but not the price change.

50. A not-for-profit organization published a monthly magazine that had 15,000 subscribers on January 1. The number of subscribers increased steadily throughout the year, and at December 31 there were 16,200 subscribers. The annual magazine subscription cost was $10 on January 1 and was increased to $12 for new members on April 1. An auditor would expect the receipts from subscriptions for the year ended December 31 to be approximately

A. $194,400

B. $179,400

C. $164,400

D. $163,800

The correct answer is (D). *(CPA, adapted)*

REQUIRED: The expected receipts from subscriptions given a steady increase in subscribers and a price increase.

DISCUSSION: If all original and new subscribers paid $10 up to April 1, and new subscribers after April 1 paid $12, the total receipts would be $163,800, assuming 100 new subscribers per month [(16,200 – 15,000) ÷ 12].

	Number	Rate	Revenue
Original subscribers	15,000	$10	$150,000
New until April 1 (1/4 x 1,200)	300	10	3,000
New after April 1 (3/4 x 1,200)	900	12	10,800
Total expected			$163,800

Answer (A) is incorrect because $194,400 assumes that all subscribers paid the $12 rate ($12 x 16,200). Answer (B) is incorrect because $179,400 assumes that all new subscribers paid the $12 rate and that the old subscribers paid an $11 rate [($12 x 1,200) + ($11 x 15,000)]. Answer (C) is incorrect because $164,400 assumes that all 1,200 new subscribers paid the $12 rate [$150,000 + ($12 x 1,200)].

51. The auditor is evaluating the effectiveness of a sales commission plan adopted 12 months earlier. An audit procedure likely to provide strong evidence of the plan's effectiveness is to

A. Calculate the percentage change in monthly sales by product line for the last 3 years.

B. Compare monthly selling costs of this year with those of the 2 preceding years.

C. Regress monthly indices of external economic conditions against sales for the 2 preceding years and compare predictions with reported sales.

D. Compare the ratio of selling costs per dollar of sales each month for the past year with that of other companies in the industry.

The correct answer is (C). *(CIA, adapted)*

REQUIRED: The technique to determine the effectiveness of a newly installed sales commission plan.

DISCUSSION: The auditor requires evidence as to whether sales have increased more than could be expected from changes in external economic conditions. Regression analysis is a statistical tool to generate predictions based on projections of current economic conditions. It provides benchmarks whereby current sales may be compared with expected sales to evaluate the effect of the sales commission variable.

Answer (A) is incorrect because simple comparison of month-to-month sales figures does not take into account changes in external economic factors. Answers (B) and (D) are incorrect because the effectiveness of the sales commission plan should be measured by the sales generated, not by costs.

52. Analytical procedures used in the overall review stage of an audit generally include

A. Considering unusual or unexpected account balances that were not previously identified.

B. Performing tests of transactions to corroborate management's financial statement assertions.

C. Gathering evidence concerning account balances that have not changed from the prior year.

D. Retesting controls that appeared to be ineffective during the assessment of control risk.

The correct answer is (A). *(CPA, adapted)*

REQUIRED: The analytical procedure used in the final review stage.

DISCUSSION: Analytical procedures are required to be used as an overall review in the final review stage of the audit. They are useful in assessing the conclusions reached by the auditor and in evaluating financial statement presentation. Procedures ordinarily should include reading the statements and notes and considering (1) the adequacy of evidence regarding previously identified unusual or unexpected balances and (2) unusual or unexpected balances or relationships not previously noted (AU 329).

Answer (B) is incorrect because analytical procedures are not tests of transactions. Answer (C) is incorrect because the lack of change from the prior year may not be unusual or unexpected. Answer (D) is incorrect because analytical procedures are substantive tests, not tests of controls.

4.3 Sales-Receivables Cycle

53. Which of the following is not a principal objective of the auditor in the audit of revenues?

A. To verify cash deposited during the year.

B. To obtain an understanding of internal control and assess control risk, with particular emphasis on the use of accrual accounting to record revenue.

C. To verify that earned revenue has been recorded and recorded revenue has been earned.

D. To identify and interpret significant trends and variations in the amounts of various categories of revenue.

The correct answer is (A). *(CPA, adapted)*

REQUIRED: The statement not a principal objective of an auditor when auditing revenues.

DISCUSSION: The verification of cash deposits during the year is not part of the audit of revenues. Verification of cash and marketable securities is undertaken as a separate part of the audit program.

Answer (B) is incorrect because the auditor must obtain an understanding of internal control sufficient to plan the audit. (S)he must also assess control risk to determine the acceptable detection risk. Answer (C) is incorrect because proper verification that accrual accounting has been properly applied is an important objective of the audit of revenues. Answer (D) is incorrect because the heavy volume of transactions in revenue accounts may result in substantial audit risk, which may be reduced by use of analytical procedures.

54. In the audit of which of the following general ledger accounts will tests of controls be particularly appropriate?

A. Equipment.

B. Bonds payable.

C. Bank charges.

D. Sales.

The correct answer is (D). *(CPA, adapted)*

REQUIRED: The account for which tests of controls are most appropriate.

DISCUSSION: In auditing the sales or revenue account, tests of controls are particularly appropriate, provided the auditor believes that control risk can be assessed at less than the maximum. Because of the large number of transactions, examining all items will seldom be cost-effective.

Answer (A) is incorrect because the ease of verifying the physical existence of equipment and computing depreciation may make it inefficient to evaluate the effectiveness of controls. Answer (B) is incorrect because the ready availability of evidence in the contractual agreements and the infrequency of transactions make tests of controls less necessary for bonds payable. Answer (C) is incorrect because evidence of bank charges is easily obtainable from an independent source. Bank charges are usually reported as a single amount on each monthly bank statement.

55. Auditors are often concerned with the possibility of overstatement of sales and receivables. However, management may also have reasons for understating these balances. Which of the following would explain understatement of sales and receivables?

A. To windowdress the financial statements.

B. To avoid paying taxes.

C. To meet budgets and forecasts.

D. All of the answers are correct.

The correct answer is (B). *(Publisher)*

REQUIRED: The reason(s) for understating sales and receivables.

DISCUSSION: State sales taxes and federal and state income taxes are based upon sales or profits, respectively. Management may attempt to reduce or avoid tax liability by not recording and reporting all sales and receivables.

Answer (A) is incorrect because sales and receivables would be overstated to windowdress the statements. Answer (C) is incorrect because management may attempt to overstate sales to achieve forecasts or to meet budgets. Answer (D) is incorrect because one of the choices is correct.

56. Tracing bills of lading to sales invoices provides evidence that

A. Shipments to customers were invoiced.

B. Shipments to customers were recorded as sales.

C. Recorded sales were shipped.

D. Invoiced sales were shipped.

The correct answer is (A). *(CPA, adapted)*

REQUIRED: The evidence provided by tracing bills of lading to sales invoices.

DISCUSSION: Comparing the seller's copies of shipping documents (such as bills of lading) with billing documents (sales invoices) provides evidence that the amounts shipped were billed to customers. The absence of invoices for goods shipped suggests that the related sales were unrecorded at the balance sheet date.

Answer (B) is incorrect because the shipping documents would have to be traced to the sales records, not the sales invoices, to obtain direct proof that shipments were recorded as sales. Answers (C) and (D) are incorrect because the proper direction of testing to determine whether invoiced and recorded sales were shipped is from the sales records to the bills of lading. A sales record without a related shipping document might indicate a fictitious sale or an improper sales cutoff.

57. An auditor most likely would review an entity's periodic accounting for the numerical sequence of shipping documents and invoices to support management's financial statement assertion of

A. Existence or occurrence.

B. Rights and obligations.

C. Valuation or allocation.

D. Completeness.

The correct answer is (D). *(CPA, adapted)*

REQUIRED: The assertion supported by reviewing the numerical sequence of shipping documents and invoices.

DISCUSSION: The completeness assertion concerns whether all transactions and accounts that should be presented in the financial statements are included. Testing the numerical sequence of shipping documents and invoices may detect omitted items.

Answer (A) is incorrect because the existence or occurrence assertion addresses whether assets or liabilities exist at a given date and whether recorded transactions have occurred. Answer (B) is incorrect because the rights and obligations assertion concerns whether assets are rights of the entity and liabilities are obligations at a given date. Answer (C) is incorrect because the valuation or allocation assertion concerns whether assets, liabilities, revenues, and expenses have been included at appropriate amounts.

58. Which of the following might be detected by an auditor's review of the client's sales cutoff?

A. Excessive goods returned for credit.

B. Unrecorded sales discounts.

C. Lapping of year-end accounts receivable.

D. Inflated sales for the year.

The correct answer is (D). *(CPA, adapted)*

REQUIRED: The condition that might be detected by review of the client's sales cutoff.

DISCUSSION: A cutoff review of sales is designed to detect the client's manipulation of sales for the period under audit. By examining recorded sales for several days before and after the balance sheet date and comparing them with sales invoices and shipping documents, the auditor may detect the recording of a sale in a period other than that in which title passed. The completeness assertion is the primary focus of the cutoff tests.

Answer (A) is incorrect because sales returns are not recorded in the sales journal and thus are not examined in the sales cutoff test. Answer (B) is incorrect because examination of cash receipts would reveal unrecorded discounts. Answer (C) is incorrect because lapping may be detected by the confirmation of customer balances and tracing amounts received according to duplicate deposit slips to the accounts receivable subsidiary ledger. Lapping is the concealment of a cash shortage by a delayed recording of cash receipts.

59. A cutoff test of sales complements the verification of

A. Sales returns.

B. Cash.

C. Accounts receivable.

D. Sales allowances.

The correct answer is (C). *(CPA, adapted)*

REQUIRED: The account verification complemented by a sales cutoff test.

DISCUSSION: A purpose of a sales cutoff test is to obtain assurance that receivables are recorded in the appropriate period. The auditor should examine sales and receivables recorded several days before and after the cutoff date and compare them with the sales invoices and shipping documents to assure they have been recorded in the proper period.

Answer (A) is incorrect because sales returns are not recorded in the sales journal and thus are not examined in the sales cutoff test. Answer (B) is incorrect because cash collections of accounts receivable are totally unrelated to the sales cutoff test. Answer (D) is incorrect because sales allowances are not recorded in the sales journal and thus are not examined in the sales cutoff test.

60. A company's sales cutoff is December 31. All goods sold are shipped FOB destination, and the company records sales 3 days after shipment. The following sales were recorded as indicated:

Date Shipped	Month Recorded	Selling Price (Amounts in Thousands)	Cost (Amounts in Thousands)
December 28	December	$182	$190
December 29	December	60	50
December 30	January	144	145
January 2	December	230	215
January 5	January	182	174

Ignoring tax effects, the net effect on income for the month ended December 31 of any failures to observe a proper cutoff was

A. $(1,000)

B. $15,000

C. $24,000

D. $25,000

The correct answer is (D). *(Publisher)*

REQUIRED: The net effect on income of the failure to observe a proper cutoff.

DISCUSSION: FOB destination means that title and risk of loss do not pass to the buyer until the goods are tendered at the specified place. The December 29 shipment (which resulted in a $10,000 gain) should have been recorded in January because the company records sales 3 days after shipment. Because the selling price of this shipment was greater than its cost, the effect of the error was to overstate income for December by the $10,000 difference. The January 2 shipment (which resulted in a $15,000 gain) was also erroneously recorded in December. Because its selling price was more than cost, the effect of the error was to overstate income for December by the $15,000 gain. The net effect of these errors is that income for the month ended December 31 was overstated by $25,000.

Answers (A), (B), and (C) are incorrect because an overstatement of $25,000 occurred.

61. An auditor observed the auditee's annual physical inventory on December 15. The auditee adjusted the inventory balance and detailed perpetual inventory records to agree with the count. Goods are shipped FOB shipping point. Listed below are four material items discovered when the auditor tested the sales cutoff as of the client's fiscal year-end at December 31. Which item does not require an adjusting entry on the auditee's books?

	Shipped	Recorded as Sale	Credited to Inventory
A.	1/1	12/31	12/31
B.	12/31	1/3	12/31
C.	12/14	12/16	12/16
D.	12/9	12/20	12/12

The correct answer is (D). *(Publisher)*

REQUIRED: The item not requiring an adjusting entry.

DISCUSSION: Goods shipped on 12/9 would have been properly recorded as a sale on 12/20, a date within the same accounting period. Moreover, the credit to inventory on 12/12 preceded the physical count on 12/15. No adjustment is necessary.

Answer (A) is incorrect because the 1/1 shipment should have been recorded as a sale in the same period or year. Answer (B) is incorrect because the 12/31 shipment should have been recorded as a sale in the same period or year. Answer (C) is incorrect because items shipped on 12/14 should have been excluded from the 12/15 inventory, and no credit would have been necessary on 12/16.

62. In verifying a November 30, 1998 sales cutoff date, an auditor would be most concerned with comparing records of

A. November 1998 cash receipts with December 1998 bank deposits.

B. November 1998 purchases with December 1998 shipments.

C. November 1998 accounts receivable with November 1998 sales.

D. November 1998 sales with November 1998 shipping documents.

The correct answer is (D). *(CMA, adapted)*

REQUIRED: The greatest concern of an auditor verifying a sales cutoff date.

DISCUSSION: When the auditor analyzes transactions that occurred within a few days before and after the end of the month, (s)he can determine if they have been recorded in the proper accounting periods. The sales cutoff test compares sales records with sales invoices, customer orders, and shipping documents. Thus, a comparison of November sales with November shipping documents should help assure that goods recorded as sold were actually shipped.

Answer (A) is incorrect because a cash cutoff is not at issue. Answer (B) is incorrect because purchases do not necessarily correspond to sales. Answer (C) is incorrect because the accounts receivable do not include cash sales or accounts already settled.

63. The auditor finds a situation in which one person has the ability to collect receivables, make deposits, issue credit memos, and record receipt of payments. The auditor suspects the individual may be stealing from cash receipts. Which of the following audit procedures would be most effective in discovering fraud in this scenario?

A. Send positive confirmations to a random selection of customers.

B. Send negative confirmations to all outstanding accounts receivable customers.

C. Perform a detailed review of debits to customer discounts, sales returns, or other debit accounts, excluding cash posted to the cash receipts journal.

D. Take a sample of bank deposits and trace the detail in each bank deposit back to the entry in the cash receipts journal.

The correct answer is (C). *(CIA, adapted)*

REQUIRED: The audit procedure most effective in detecting theft from cash receipts.

DISCUSSION: The most effective procedure is to perform a detailed review of debits to customer discounts, sales returns, etc. These accounts could be used to conceal a theft of cash payments without alerting customers.

Answers (A) and (B) are incorrect because an employee who performs asset custody, authorization, and recording functions can conceal the theft by debiting customer discounts or sales returns. Customers would be unaware of the activity because their balances would reflect their expectations. Answer (D) is incorrect because bank deposits will agree with journal entries. The stolen amounts are never recorded.

64. A large university has relatively ineffective internal control. The university's auditor seeks assurance that all tuition revenue has been recorded. The auditor could best obtain the desired assurance by

A. Confirming a sample of tuition payments with the students.

B. Observing tuition payment procedures on a surprise basis.

C. Comparing business office revenue records with registrar's office records of students enrolled.

D. Preparing a year-end bank reconciliation.

The correct answer is (C). *(CIA, adapted)*

REQUIRED: The best procedure for testing whether all tuition revenue has been recorded.

DISCUSSION: To be assured that all tuition revenue is being recorded, the auditor must perform substantive tests, which are tests of details and analytical procedures to detect misstatements in an account balance, transaction class, or disclosure component. Comparing business office revenue records with registrar's office records of students enrolled provides analytical evidence based on independently generated records.

Answer (A) is incorrect because confirmations of payments do not detect unrecorded receipts. Answer (B) is incorrect because observation is a test of controls, not a substantive test of the completeness assertion for the revenue balance. Answer (D) is incorrect because preparing a year-end bank reconciliation would only detect an unrecorded deposit or other cash accounting error.

65. If the objective of a test of details of transactions is to detect overstatements of sales, the auditor's direction of testing should be from the

A. Cash receipts journal to the sales journal.

B. Sales journal to the cash receipts journal.

C. Source documents to the accounting records.

D. Accounting records to the source documents.

The correct answer is (D). *(CPA, adapted)*

REQUIRED: The appropriate test to detect an overstatement of sales.

DISCUSSION: Overstatements of sales likely result from entries in sales with no supporting documentation. The proper direction of sampling is to select entries in the sales account and vouch them to the shipping documents. The source documents represent the valid sales.

Answers (A) and (B) are incorrect because the cash receipts journal and the sales journal are books of original entry, not source documents. Answer (C) is incorrect because the proper direction of testing is from the accounting records to the source documents.

66. One objective of an audit of a water utility for a small city is to determine whether all customers are being billed. The best direction of testing is from the

A. Meter department records to the sales register.

B. Sales register to the meter department records.

C. Accounts receivable ledger to the sales register.

D. Sales register to the accounts receivable ledger.

The correct answer is (A). *(Publisher)*

REQUIRED: The best direction of testing to determine whether all customers are being billed.

DISCUSSION: The best direction of testing is to proceed from the meter department records, which indicate those customers who have received service, to the sales register. Comparing services rendered with billings is the best way to detect omitted billings.

Answer (B) is incorrect because comparing the sales register with the meter records is useful for verifying the amounts billed for which service was not provided. Answers (C) and (D) are incorrect because comparisons between the accounts receivable ledger and the sales register are useful for verifying the accuracy of the posting of accounts receivable.

67. An inappropriate audit objective relative to accounts receivable is to determine that

A. The accounts exist and are properly valued.

B. The accounts represent the complete transaction process.

C. The accounts are collected by the balance sheet date.

D. The client has rights in the accounts receivable.

The correct answer is (C). *(Publisher)*

REQUIRED: The determination that is not an audit objective relative to accounts receivable.

DISCUSSION: Accounts receivable represent the amounts due the client at the balance sheet date. The auditor should not expect the accounts to be collected at the balance sheet date.

Answer (A) is incorrect because the determination that accounts exist and are properly valued is an appropriate audit objective relating to management assertions or representations (existence and valuation) made in financial statement components (AU 326). The auditor's responsibility is to obtain and evaluate evidence concerning the assertions made by management. Answer (B) is incorrect because an audit objective may appropriately relate to the completeness assertion. Answer (D) is incorrect because an audit objective may be developed in the light of an assertion about rights.

68. An auditor's purpose in reviewing credit ratings of customers with delinquent accounts receivable most likely is to obtain evidence concerning management's assertions about

A. Valuation or allocation.

B. Presentation and disclosure.

C. Existence or occurrence.

D. Rights and obligations.

The correct answer is (A). *(CPA, adapted)*

REQUIRED: The auditor's purpose in reviewing credit ratings of customers with delinquent accounts receivable.

DISCUSSION: Reviewing delinquent customer credit ratings provides evidence for assessing the likelihood of collection. The collectibility of an account receivable is related to the valuation assertion.

Answers (B), (C), and (D) are incorrect because the primary purpose of the auditor's consideration of the credit ratings of customers is to determine whether accounts are reported at net collectible value, which is a valuation consideration.

69. In evaluating the adequacy of the allowance for doubtful accounts, an auditor most likely reviews the entity's aging of receivables to support management's financial statement assertion of

A. Existence or occurrence.

B. Valuation or allocation.

C. Completeness.

D. Rights and obligations.

The correct answer is (B). *(CPA, adapted)*

REQUIRED: The assertion tested by reviewing the entity's aging of receivables.

DISCUSSION: Assertions about valuation or allocation concern whether financial statement components have been included at appropriate amounts in accordance with GAAP. For example, management asserts that trade accounts receivable are stated at net realizable value (gross accounts receivable minus allowance for uncollectible accounts). Aging the receivables is a procedure for assessing the reasonableness of the allowance.

Answer (A) is incorrect because the existence or occurrence assertion addresses whether assets or liabilities exist at a given date and whether recorded transactions have occurred. Answer (C) is incorrect because the completeness assertion concerns whether all transactions that should be presented are included. Answer (D) is incorrect because the rights and obligations assertion concerns whether assets are rights of the entity and liabilities are obligations at a given date.

70. AU 330 defines confirmation as "the process of obtaining and evaluating a direct communication from a third party in response to a request for information about a particular item affecting financial statement assertions." Two assertions for which confirmation of accounts receivable balances provides primary evidence are

A. Completeness and valuation.

B. Valuation and rights and obligations.

C. Rights and obligations and existence.

D. Existence and completeness.

The correct answer is (C). *(CPA, adapted)*

REQUIRED: The assertions tested by confirming receivables.

DISCUSSION: Confirmation by means of direct (independent) communication with debtors is the generally accepted auditing procedure for accounts receivable. Confirmations are most likely to be effective for the existence and rights-and-obligations assertions. Thus, confirmation provides evidence that receivables are valid and that the client has the right of collection.

Answers (A), (B), and (D) are incorrect because the valuation assertion concerns whether items have been included in the financial statements at appropriate amounts. For receivables, net realizable values are appropriate. The completeness assertion concerns whether all items that should be presented are so included, for example, whether all receivables have been recorded. Unrecorded receivables are usually not discovered by confirmation. Thus, confirmation provides insufficient evidence about both the valuation assertion and the completeness assertion.

71. Auditors may use positive or negative forms of confirmation requests for accounts receivable. An auditor most likely will use

A. The positive form to confirm all balances regardless of size.

B. A combination of the two forms, with the positive form used for large balances and the negative form for the small balances.

C. A combination of the two forms, with the positive form used for trade receivables and the negative form for other receivables.

D. The positive form when the combined assessed level of inherent and control risk for assertions related to receivables is acceptably low, and the negative form when it is unacceptably high.

The correct answer is (B). *(CPA, adapted)*

REQUIRED: The true statement about the use of positive and negative confirmations.

DISCUSSION: A positive confirmation asks the debtor for a reply. It may ask the respondent to state whether (s)he agrees with the information given or request that the recipient fill in the account balance or provide other information. The latter type of positive confirmation is called a blank form. The negative confirmation asks for a response only when the debtor disagrees. A combination of the two forms is often used.

Answer (A) is incorrect because the negative form is often used, especially when many small balances are involved. Answer (C) is incorrect because the choice of confirmation does not depend on the nature of the receivable. Answer (D) is incorrect because the positive form is used when control risk is high.

72. In the confirmation of accounts receivable, the auditor would most likely

A. Request confirmation of a sample of the inactive accounts.

B. Seek to obtain positive confirmations for at least 50% of the total dollar amount of the receivables.

C. Require confirmation of all receivables from agencies of the federal government.

D. Require that confirmation requests be sent within 1 month of the fiscal year-end.

The correct answer is (A). *(CPA, adapted)*

REQUIRED: The most likely auditor action regarding confirmation of receivables.

DISCUSSION: When the combined assessed level of inherent and control risk is at an acceptably low level, the auditor will confirm only a sample of receivables. The sample should include inactive or past due accounts. If such accounts are to be regarded as assets, acknowledgment of the debts must be obtained. Confirming inactive accounts may also detect lapping or establish what amounts are in dispute.

Answer (B) is incorrect because GAAS do not establish a percentage dollar amount to be confirmed. Confirming all large balances, however, may account for a substantial dollar value of the receivables. Answer (C) is incorrect because the record systems and operating procedures of governmental agencies may not permit confirmation. Answer (D) is incorrect because, when internal control is effective, confirmations may be sent more than 1 month before year-end.

73. The negative request form of accounts receivable confirmation may be used when the

	Combined Assessed Level of Inherent and Control Risk Is	Number of Small Balances Is	Consideration by the Recipient Is
A.	Low	Many	Likely
B.	Low	Few	Unlikely
C.	High	Few	Likely
D.	High	Many	Likely

The correct answer is (A). *(CPA, adapted)*

REQUIRED: The conditions appropriate for use of negative accounts receivable confirmation.

DISCUSSION: AU 330 states, "Negative confirmation requests may be used to reduce audit risk to an acceptable level when (1) the combined assessed level of inherent and control risk is low, (2) a large number of small balances is involved, and (3) the auditor has no reason to believe that the recipients of the requests are unlikely to give them consideration." Returned negative confirmations provide evidence about assertions in the financial statements, but unreturned negative confirmation requests rarely provide significant evidence about assertions other than some aspects of existence.

Answers (B), (C), and (D) are incorrect because negative confirmations should not be used when the combined assessed level of control risk and inherent risk is high, small balances are few, or consideration by recipients is unlikely.

74. Negative confirmation of accounts receivable is less effective than positive confirmation of accounts receivable because

A. A majority of recipients usually lack the willingness to respond objectively.

B. Some recipients may report incorrect balances that require extensive follow-up.

C. The auditor cannot infer that all nonrespondents have verified their account information.

D. Negative confirmations do not produce evidence that is statistically quantifiable.

The correct answer is (C). *(CPA, adapted)*

REQUIRED: The reason negative confirmations are less effective than positive confirmations.

DISCUSSION: Because a failure to reply is assumed to indicate the debtor's agreement when negative confirmations are used, no auditor follow-up occurs, and no explicit evidence is provided that the intended parties received their requests and verified the information. Thus, unreturned negative confirmation requests rarely provide significant evidence about assertions other than existence. Positive confirmations require a reply, whether or not the debtor agrees with the balance. Alternative procedures are applied to the nonresponses to obtain the evidence necessary to reduce audit risk to an acceptable level (AU 330).

Answer (A) is incorrect because the assumed lack of objectivity to which this answer refers would affect both forms of confirmation. Answer (B) is incorrect because inaccurate reporting would affect positive and negative confirmations. Answer (D) is incorrect because both forms of confirmation produce evidence that is quantifiable.

75. To reduce the risks associated with accepting fax responses to requests for confirmations of accounts receivable, an auditor most likely would

A. Examine the shipping documents that provide evidence for the existence assertion.

B. Verify the sources and contents of the faxes in telephone calls to the senders.

C. Consider the faxes to be nonresponses and evaluate them as unadjusted differences.

D. Inspect the faxes for forgeries or alterations and consider them to be acceptable if none are noted.

The correct answer is (B). *(CPA, adapted)*

REQUIRED: The procedure to reduce the risk of accepting false confirmations by fax.

DISCUSSION: Because establishing the source of a fax is often difficult, the auditor should ensure that the confirmations returned by fax are genuine. One way is to verify the sources by following up with telephone calls to the senders.

Answer (A) is incorrect because the purpose of the confirmation is to test the existence of the receivable by direct communication with the debtor. Answer (C) is incorrect because a fax is considered a valid response if the source can be verified. Answer (D) is incorrect because faxes may not be signed. Furthermore, the auditor is unlikely to be qualified to recognize forgeries.

76. An auditor confirms a representative number of open accounts receivable as of December 31 and investigates respondents' exceptions and comments. By this procedure, the auditor is most likely to learn of which of the following?

A. One of the cashiers has been covering a personal embezzlement by lapping.

B. One of the sales clerks has not been preparing charge slips for credit sales to family and friends.

C. One of the computer processing control clerks has been removing all sales invoices applicable to his account from the data file.

D. The credit manager has misappropriated remittances from customers whose accounts have been written off.

The correct answer is (A). *(CPA, adapted)*

REQUIRED: The fraud most likely to be detected by confirming receivables.

DISCUSSION: Lapping is the theft of a cash payment from one customer concealed by crediting that customer's account when a second customer makes a payment. When lapping exists at the balance sheet date, the confirmation of customer balances will probably detect the fraud because the customers' and company's records of lapped accounts will differ.

Answer (B) is incorrect because, if a charge slip has not been prepared, no accounts receivable balance will exist to be confirmed. Answer (C) is incorrect because, if a sales invoice is not processed, no account balance will appear in the records. Answer (D) is incorrect because, once the account has been written off, the account is no longer open.

77. An auditor who has confirmed accounts receivable may discover that the sales journal was held open past year-end if

A. Positive confirmations sent to debtors are not returned.

B. Negative confirmations sent to debtors are not returned.

C. Most of the returned negative confirmations indicate that the debtor owes a larger balance than the amount being confirmed.

D. Most of the returned positive confirmations indicate that the debtor owes a smaller balance than the amount being confirmed.

The correct answer is (D). *(Publisher)*

REQUIRED: The result of confirmation indicating that the sales journal was held open past year-end.

DISCUSSION: When the majority of the returned positive confirmations indicate smaller balances at year-end than those in the client's records, the client may have held open the sales journal after year-end and debited customers' accounts for the period under audit rather than for the subsequent period. The effect would be to overstate sales and receivables.

Answer (A) is incorrect because the failure to receive replies to positive confirmations may cause the auditor concern about the existence assertion. Answer (B) is incorrect because the failure to return negative confirmations provides some evidence about the existence assertion. Answer (C) is incorrect because replies indicating balances larger than those confirmed suggest that the sales journal was closed prior to year-end.

78. During the process of confirming receivables as of December 31, 1998, a positive confirmation was returned indicating the "balance owed as of December 31 was paid on January 9, 1999." The auditor would most likely

A. Determine whether there were any changes in the account between January 1 and January 9, 1999.

B. Determine whether a customary trade discount was taken by the customer.

C. Reconfirm the zero balance as of January 10, 1999.

D. Verify that the amount was received.

The correct answer is (D). *(CPA, adapted)*

REQUIRED: The auditor action when a confirmation response states that the year-end balance was paid.

DISCUSSION: Responses to confirmations that involve significant differences are investigated by the auditor. Others are delegated to client employees with a request that explanations be given to the auditor. Such differences often arise because of recent cash payments. In that event, the auditor should trace remittances to verify that stated amounts were received.

Answer (A) is incorrect because the auditor wishes to confirm a year-end balance, not transactions in the subsequent period. Also, the reply does not suggest a discrepancy in the account. Answer (B) is incorrect because the auditor is more concerned with confirming the balance due at year-end than with whether a customer took a discount. Answer (C) is incorrect because reconfirmation is not required.

79. Confirmation of accounts receivable is a generally accepted auditing procedure. The presumption that an auditor will confirm accounts receivable is not overcome if

A. Based on prior years' audit experience, response rates will be inadequate.

B. Based on experience with similar engagements, responses are expected to be unreliable.

C. The combined assessed level of inherent and control risk is high.

D. The accounts receivable are immaterial.

The correct answer is (C). *(Publisher)*

REQUIRED: The condition not sufficient to overcome the presumption that an auditor will confirm accounts receivable.

DISCUSSION: The presumption may be overcome if the combined assessed level of inherent and control risk is low, and the assessed level, together with the evidence expected to be obtained from performance of other procedures, is sufficient to reduce audit risk to an acceptably low level for the applicable assertions. An auditor who has decided not to request confirmations must document how the presumption was overcome.

Answers (A) and (B) are incorrect because the presumption may be overcome if confirmations would be ineffective. Answer (D) is incorrect because confirmations are not required if accounts receivable are not material to the financial statements.

80. A company has computerized sales and cash receipts journals. The computer programs for these journals have been properly debugged. The auditor discovered that the total of the accounts receivable subsidiary accounts differs materially from the accounts receivable control account. This discrepancy could indicate

A. Credit memoranda being improperly recorded.

B. Lapping of receivables.

C. Receivables not being properly aged.

D. Statements being intercepted prior to mailing.

The correct answer is (A). *(CIA, adapted)*

REQUIRED: The reason the accounts receivable subsidiary ledger may differ from the control account.

DISCUSSION: Sales returns and allowances require the crediting of accounts receivable. The recording of unauthorized credit memoranda is one explanation for the discrepancy if sales and cash receipts are properly recorded.

Answer (B) is incorrect because lapping entails the theft of cash receipts and the use of subsequent receipts to conceal the theft. The effect is to overstate receivables, but no difference between the control total and the total of subsidiary accounts would arise. Answer (C) is incorrect because aging does not involve accounting entries. Answer (D) is incorrect because interception of customer statements might indicate fraudulent receivables but would not cause the subsidiary ledger discrepancy.

81. Which of the following is the greatest drawback of using subsequent collections evidenced only by a deposit slip as an alternative procedure when responses to positive accounts receivable confirmations are not received?

A. Checking of subsequent collections can never be used as an alternative auditing procedure.

B. By examining a deposit slip only, the auditor does not know whether the payment is for the receivable at the balance sheet date or a subsequent transaction.

C. A deposit slip is not received directly by the auditor.

D. A customer may not have made a payment on a timely basis.

The correct answer is (B). *(Publisher)*

REQUIRED: The greatest drawback of using subsequent collections as an alternative to confirmation.

DISCUSSION: The deposit slip does not indicate which receivables are being paid. The deposits may not be from the collection of accounts receivable, or the receipts may be for sales made after year-end.

Answer (A) is incorrect because the auditor may use alternative procedures. Indeed, the alternative procedures may be omitted when no unusual qualitative factors or systematic characteristics are related to the nonresponses and when treating the nonresponses as 100% misstatements does not affect the auditor's decision about whether the financial statements are materially misstated (AU 330). If an account receivable is paid, an account receivable presumably existed. Answer (C) is incorrect because copies of the deposit slips can be provided to the auditor by the bank. Also, the bank proofs the original of the deposit slip when received. Answer (D) is incorrect because, although late payment may cause a problem, the auditor typically performs field work 45 to 60 days after year-end.

82. Which of the following procedures would an auditor most likely perform for year-end accounts receivable confirmations when the auditor did not receive replies to second requests?

A. Review the cash receipts journal for the month prior to year-end.

B. Intensify the study of internal control concerning the revenue cycle.

C. Increase the assessed level of detection risk for the existence assertion.

D. Inspect the shipping records documenting the merchandise sold to the debtors.

The correct answer is (D). *(CPA, adapted)*

REQUIRED: The most appropriate audit procedure when customers fail to reply to second requests.

DISCUSSION: When customers fail to answer a second request for a positive confirmation, the accounts may be disputed, uncollectible, or fictitious. The auditor should then use alternative procedures (examination of subsequent cash receipts, shipping documents, or other client documentation of existence) to obtain evidence about the validity of nonresponding accounts.

Answer (A) is incorrect because previous collections cannot substantiate year-end balances. Answer (B) is incorrect because nonresponse to a confirmation request is not proof of ineffective control. Nonresponses do occur and are expected. Answer (C) is incorrect because control risk and inherent risk are assessed, but detection risk is not. However, the acceptable level of detection risk may be decreased if the assessment of inherent risk or control risk is increased as a result of reassessment of risks.

83. The CPA learns that collections of accounts receivable during the last 10 days of December were not recorded. The effect will be to

A. Leave both working capital and the current ratio unchanged at December 31.

B. Overstate both working capital and the current ratio at December 31.

C. Overstate working capital with no effect on the current ratio at December 31.

D. Overstate the current ratio with no effect on working capital at December 31.

The correct answer is (A). *(Publisher)*

REQUIRED: The effect of failing to record year-end collections.

DISCUSSION: Working capital is equal to current assets minus current liabilities, and the current ratio is equal to current assets divided by current liabilities. Because cash and accounts receivable are both current assets, the error has no effect on working capital and the current ratio at December 31 because it did not change total current assets.

Answer (B) is incorrect because neither working capital nor the current ratio is affected by failing to record cash collections. The only effects are that cash is understated and accounts receivable overstated. Answer (C) is incorrect because working capital is not affected. Answer (D) is incorrect because the current ratio is not affected.

84. The most effective audit procedure for determining the collectibility of an account receivable is the

A. Confirmation of the account.

B. Examination of the related sales invoice(s).

C. Review of the subsequent cash collections.

D. Review of authorization of credit sales to the customer and the previous history of collections.

The correct answer is (C). *(CMA, adapted)*

REQUIRED: The most effective audit procedure for determining collectibility.

DISCUSSION: Collectibility pertains to the assertion of valuation. It is the principal issue with regard to the adequacy of the allowance for doubtful accounts. The best way to determine collectibility is to learn whether the receivable was subsequently collected. A confirmation provides evidence that a contract exists and that the debtor acknowledges the debt, but the subsequent collection of the receivable is the only means of gaining complete assurance that the amount will be paid.

Answer (A) is incorrect because confirmation tends to be more effective in providing evidence about the existence than the valuation (collectibility) assertion. Answer (B) is incorrect because examination of the related sales invoice(s) is a test of the validity, not the collectibility, of a receivable. Answer (D) is incorrect because experience is a good indicator of collectibility but is not as good as collection.

85. All of the following are examples of substantive tests to verify the valuation of net accounts receivable except the

A. Recomputation of the allowance for bad debts.

B. Inspection of accounts for current versus noncurrent status in the statement of financial position.

C. Inspection of the aging schedule and credit records of past due accounts.

D. Comparison of the allowance for bad debts with past records.

The correct answer is (B). *(CMA, adapted)*

REQUIRED: The item that is not an example of a test of valuation.

DISCUSSION: The inspection of accounts for current versus noncurrent status is a test of management's assertion relating to statement presentation and disclosure, not valuation.

Answer (A) is incorrect because recomputation of the allowance for bad debts tests the valuation of the account balance. Answer (C) is incorrect because inspection of the aging schedule and credit records of past due accounts tests the valuation of the account balance. Answer (D) is incorrect because comparison of the allowance for bad debts with past records tests the valuation of the account balance.

86. Once a CPA has determined that accounts receivable have increased because of slow collections in a tight money environment, the CPA is likely to

A. Increase the balance in the allowance for bad debts account.

B. Review the going concern ramifications.

C. Review the credit and collection policy.

D. Expand tests of collectibility.

The correct answer is (D). *(CPA, adapted)*

REQUIRED: The appropriate audit response when receivables have increased because of slow collections.

DISCUSSION: Whenever collections of receivables have slowed, the auditor should determine the effects on the allowance for doubtful accounts. (S)he should therefore expand tests of collectibility, e.g., with a review of collections subsequent to the balance sheet date and investigation of credit ratings.

Answer (A) is incorrect because an increase in the allowance account may not be required if the accounts are collectible as in the past. Answer (B) is incorrect because questioning whether the client is a going concern is necessary only if the client is on the verge of bankruptcy or some other form of cessation. Answer (C) is incorrect because a review of credit and collection policy is only one part of the expansion of tests of collectibility.

87. An auditor reconciles the total of the accounts receivable subsidiary ledger to the general ledger control account as of October 31. By this procedure, the auditor is most likely to learn of which of the following?

A. An October invoice was improperly computed.

B. An October check from a customer was posted in error to the account of another customer with a similar name.

C. An opening balance in a subsidiary ledger account was improperly carried forward from the previous accounting period.

D. An account balance is past due and should be written off.

The correct answer is (C). *(CPA, adapted)*

REQUIRED: The error detected by reconciling the subsidiary ledger to the general ledger.

DISCUSSION: By reconciling the accounts receivable ledger to the general ledger control account, transfer errors will be identified.

Answer (A) is incorrect because reconciliation of the subsidiary ledger and control account will not detect an error if entries to both are based on the same erroneous document. Only recalculation of invoices will detect this error. Answer (B) is incorrect because posting to the wrong account will most likely be detected by confirmation. The trial balance total and the control account are not affected by such an error. Answer (D) is incorrect because uncollectibility will most probably be detected through aging receivables.

88. You are preparing the audit program for testing the sales tax revenues of your state government. Which of the following procedures is most effective in ascertaining that reporting taxpayers are properly disclosing their sales taxes?

A. Test selected sales tax returns for proper computation of sales tax remitted.

B. Confirm sales tax receipts with a sample of companies that file returns.

C. Compare the list of licensed business firms to the list of business firms filing sales tax returns.

D. Undertake field examinations of selected taxpayers.

The correct answer is (D). *(CIA, adapted)*

REQUIRED: The procedure most effective in determining that taxpayers are properly disclosing their sales taxes.

DISCUSSION: Field examinations of a sample drawn from the population of all licensed businesses would probably be effective in identifying taxpayers not properly reporting sales taxes. This procedure would detect both improper reporting and failure to report.

Answer (A) is incorrect because the computation described would provide evidence as to the correctness of the returns, but not as to whether taxes were being properly reported. Answer (B) is incorrect because sampling only from the population of companies that file returns excludes those that have not filed. Answer (C) is incorrect because, although the comparison might discover firms that do not file, it would exclude from the examination those that filed improperly.

89. An auditor suspects that a client's customer, whose accounts receivable balance represents a material proportion of the client's total receivables, is fictitious. The evidence that would provide the strongest proof that the auditor's suspicion is unfounded, given the existence of weaknesses in the client's internal control over accounts receivable, is

A. Receipt of a positive confirmation response.

B. Subsequent posting of the collection of the account balance.

C. Nonresponse to a negative confirmation request.

D. Location of the customer's name and address in a published industry directory.

The correct answer is (D). *(Publisher)*

REQUIRED: The best evidence that a client's customer is not fictitious.

DISCUSSION: Verifying that the debtor exists and has the same address as appears in the client's records provides evidence that the customer is not fictitious. A published industry directory is an independent source of evidence of the customer's existence. Together with the return of a positive confirmation, the industry directory provides strong proof of the validity of the account.

Answer (A) is incorrect because confirmation responses can be falsified to conceal fraud. A false address may be given at which the confirmation request will be intercepted by a participant in the fraud. Answer (B) is incorrect because the payment may be either entirely fictitious or the posting of another customer's payment (lapping). Answer (C) is incorrect because a negative confirmation request may be intercepted by a party to fraud.

4.4 Purchases-Payables Cycle

90. In auditing accounts payable, an auditor's procedures most likely will focus primarily on management's assertion of

A. Existence or occurrence.

B. Presentation and disclosure.

C. Completeness.

D. Valuation or allocation.

The correct answer is (C). *(CPA, adapted)*

REQUIRED: The assertion that is the focus of an audit of accounts payable.

DISCUSSION: The primary audit risk for accounts payable is the potential for understatement of the liability. Thus, the auditor will most likely focus on the completeness assertion.

Answer (A) is incorrect because the existence or occurrence assertion concerns whether liabilities exist at a given date and whether transactions occurred during the period. The audit risk for accounts payable is not great for that assertion. Answer (B) is incorrect because the risk of inappropriate presentation and disclosure on the financial statements is not as great as the risk that some items are not included. Answer (D) is incorrect because the risk that accounts payable are not valued in accordance with GAAP is less than the risk that the balance may not be complete.

91. To determine whether accounts payable are complete, an auditor performs a test to verify that all merchandise received is recorded. The population of documents for this test consists of all

A. Payment vouchers.

B. Receiving reports.

C. Purchase requisitions.

D. Vendor's invoices.

The correct answer is (B). *(CPA, adapted)*

REQUIRED: The population of documents for a test to verify that all merchandise received is recorded.

DISCUSSION: The population to be tested consists of receiving reports. An account payable should have been recorded for each receiving report.

Answer (A) is incorrect because a payment voucher is prepared for each account payable. A payment voucher would not exist for an unrecorded payable. Answer (C) is incorrect because the goods requisitioned may not have been ordered. If ordered, they may not have been received. Hence, a payable may not exist for each requisition. Answer (D) is incorrect because a vendor's invoice does not prove receipt of goods and incurrence of a liability.

92. The primary audit test to determine if accounts payable are valued properly is

A. A confirmation of accounts payable.

B. Vouching accounts payable to supporting documentation.

C. An analytical procedure.

D. Verification that accounts payable are reported as a current liability in the balance sheet.

The correct answer is (B). *(Publisher)*

REQUIRED: The audit test to determine if accounts payable are properly valued.

DISCUSSION: Relatively few problems are encountered by the auditor in meeting the objective of determining the proper valuation of accounts payable. The auditor vouches the recorded accounts payable to the supporting documentation, the invoice and purchase order, to determine if the accounts are accurately valued.

Answer (A) is incorrect because the confirmation of accounts payable cannot be relied on to reveal unrecorded liabilities. Answer (C) is incorrect because analytical procedures provide an overall review of the payables, but they are not specifically directed at valuation of individual accounts. Answer (D) is incorrect because whether accounts payable are reported as a current liability is related to the audit objective concerning statement presentation and disclosure rather than proper valuation.

93. Which of the following procedures is least likely to be performed before the balance sheet date?

A. Observation of inventory.

B. Testing internal control over cash.

C. Search for unrecorded liabilities.

D. Confirmation of receivables.

The correct answer is (C). *(CPA, adapted)*

REQUIRED: The procedure least likely to be performed before the balance sheet date.

DISCUSSION: The search for unrecorded liabilities will probably be performed after the balance sheet date. The auditor will review cash disbursements made subsequent to year-end to determine if payments are for previously unrecorded liabilities.

Answer (A) is incorrect because, if control is effective and the client maintains well-kept perpetual records, the auditor's observation procedures usually can be performed during or at the end of the period under audit (AU 331). Answer (B) is incorrect because the understanding of internal control is customarily obtained prior to the balance sheet date to permit the auditor to plan the audit and determine the nature, extent, and timing of tests. Answer (D) is incorrect because receivables confirmation may be made either during (if control is effective), at the end of, or after the period.

94. An audit assistant found a purchase order for a regular supplier in the amount of $5,500. The purchase order was dated after receipt of the goods. The purchasing agent had forgotten to issue the purchase order. Also, a disbursement of $450 for materials did not have a receiving report. The assistant wanted to select additional purchase orders for investigation but was unconcerned about the lack of a receiving report. The audit director should

A. Agree with the assistant because the amount of the purchase order exception was considerably larger than the receiving report exception.

B. Agree with the assistant because the cash disbursement clerk had been assured by the receiving clerk that the failure to fill out a report didn't happen very often.

C. Disagree with the assistant because the two problems have an equal risk of loss associated with them.

D. Disagree with the assistant because the lack of a receiving report has a greater risk of loss associated with it.

The correct answer is (D). *(CIA, adapted)*

REQUIRED: The implications of a missing purchase order and a missing receiving report.

DISCUSSION: The risk of a material fraud is greater for the missing receiving report than for the postdated purchase order. In the latter case, the goods were received, and the company has obtained what it paid for. Because the goods come from a regular supplier, the likelihood is that the purchase was in fact authorized. However, the lack of a receiving report in support of a disbursement is a much more serious matter. It suggests potential fraud because an approved payment voucher should be accompanied by a purchase order, supplier's invoice, and a receiving report. One possibility is that duplicate payments are being made.

Answer (A) is incorrect because the potential for fraud and heightened control risk made the absence of a receiving report a material matter despite its dollar amount. Answer (B) is incorrect because the hearsay testimony of the cash disbursement clerk has very little evidentiary value. Answer (C) is incorrect because the missing receiving report indicates a much greater risk than the postdated purchase order.

95. When using confirmations to provide evidence about the completeness assertion for accounts payable, the appropriate population most likely is

A. Vendors with whom the entity has previously done business.

B. Amounts recorded in the accounts payable subsidiary ledger.

C. Payees of checks drawn in the month after the year end.

D. Invoices filed in the entity's open invoice file.

The correct answer is (A). *(CPA, adapted)*

REQUIRED: The appropriate population when confirmations of accounts payable are used to test the completeness assertion.

DISCUSSION: When sending confirmations for accounts payable, the population of accounts should include small and zero balances as well as large tested balances. The auditor should use the activity in the account as a gauge for selection. That is, if orders are placed with a vendor on a consistent basis, the confirmation should be sent to that vendor regardless of the recorded balance due.

Answers (B) and (D) are incorrect because the auditor, in testing the completeness assertion, is concerned with balances that have not been recorded or invoices that have not been filed. Answer (C) is incorrect because, although this is an auditing concern, this would not be the population for the confirmation process.

96. Which of the following is a substantive test that an auditor is most likely to perform to verify the existence and valuation of recorded accounts payable?

A. Investigating the open purchase order file to ascertain that prenumbered purchase orders are used and accounted for.

B. Receiving the client's mail, unopened, for a reasonable period of time after year-end to search for unrecorded vendor's invoices.

C. Vouching selected entries in the accounts payable subsidiary ledger to purchase orders and receiving reports.

D. Confirming accounts payable balances with known suppliers who have zero balances.

The correct answer is (C). *(CPA, adapted)*

REQUIRED: The substantive test for the existence and valuation of recorded accounts payable.

DISCUSSION: Vouching a sample of recorded accounts payable to purchase orders and receiving reports provides evidence that the obligations exist at a given date. The purchase orders evidence the initiation of the transactions, and the receiving reports indicate that goods were received and that liabilities were thereby incurred. Thus, these documents provide evidence that amounts are owed to others, that the transactions occurred, and that the liabilities have been included at appropriate amounts.

Answer (A) is incorrect because ascertaining that prenumbered documents are used and accounted for relates most directly to the completeness assertion. Answer (B) is incorrect because searching for unrecorded liabilities relates most directly to completeness. Answer (D) is incorrect because confirming payables with known suppliers having zero balances is a procedure for detecting unrecorded liabilities. Thus, it relates most directly to completeness.

97. Only one of the following four statements, which compare confirmation of accounts payable with suppliers and confirmation of accounts receivable with debtors, is false. The false statement is that

A. Confirmation of accounts receivable with debtors is a more widely accepted auditing procedure than is confirmation of accounts payable with suppliers.

B. Statistical sampling techniques are more widely accepted in the confirmation of accounts payable than in the confirmation of accounts receivable.

C. As compared with the confirmation of accounts receivable, the confirmation of accounts payable will tend to emphasize accounts with zero balances at the balance sheet date.

D. It is less likely that the confirmation request sent to the supplier will show the amount owed than that the request sent to the debtor will show the amount due.

The correct answer is (B). *(Publisher)*

REQUIRED: The false statement concerning confirmation of accounts payable and receivable.

DISCUSSION: In both cases, the use of statistical sampling is appropriate for relatively large populations with common characteristics.

Answer (A) is incorrect because externally generated evidence usually obviates the need for the confirmation of accounts payable. The self-interest of creditors protects against understatement of client liabilities. Also, confirming payables does not detect unrecorded liabilities, whereas confirming receivables may detect fictitious or overstated accounts. Answer (C) is incorrect because the audit of accounts payable, not accounts receivable, may focus attention on accounts with zero balances to discover understatements of payables. Answer (D) is incorrect because the creditor may be in the process of billing a client for current shipments, the amounts in the client's records may not reflect all liabilities. Hence, the auditor may refrain from stating an amount in the confirmation request so that all purchases may be confirmed. For receivables, only payments in transit will need to be reconciled by the auditor.

98. The confirmation of accounts payable

A. Is always appropriate by internal auditors, but never appropriate by external auditors.

B. Contributes little to determining whether unrecorded accounts payable exist.

C. Is an important method of establishing the existence of unrecorded accounts payable.

D. Is often used by external auditors in connection with their audit of inventories.

The correct answer is (B). *(CMA, adapted)*

REQUIRED: The true statement regarding the confirmation of accounts payable.

DISCUSSION: The auditor's primary concern in auditing accounts payable is that unrecorded liabilities may exist. Confirmation of accounts payable may not be effective for eliciting evidence relevant to the completeness assertion, but confirming the accounts of vendors with zero balances may sometimes reveal unrecorded liabilities.

Answer (A) is incorrect because, even though confirmation is not required, it might be used in both internal and external audits when the combined assessed level of inherent and control risk increases. Answer (C) is incorrect because confirmation is most useful for verifying amounts recorded in the books. Answer (D) is incorrect because the audit of inventories is primarily conducted through physical observation, although confirmation of inventories may be used for goods held by others.

99. Confirmation of accounts payable with creditors is most appropriate when

A. The majority of accounts payable balances are owed to related parties.

B. Creditor statements are not available, and internal control over accounts payable is unsatisfactory.

C. Accounts payable balances are immaterial.

D. Internal control over accounts payable is effective, and sufficient evidence exists to minimize the risk of a material misstatement.

The correct answer is (B). *(Publisher)*

REQUIRED: The reason for confirming accounts payable.

DISCUSSION: When internal control relevant to assertions about accounts payable is ineffective, control risk is increased. The auditor may need to change the nature, timing, or extent of substantive tests and consider the use of confirmations. The auditor should also confirm accounts payable when documentary evidence is lacking, individual creditors have relatively large balances, the client has made a major purchase from the creditor regardless of the size of the balance, unusual transactions are involved, or the account is secured.

Answer (A) is incorrect because the auditor only needs to give particular consideration to confirming the accounts with related parties in the presence of other indications that the payables should be confirmed. Answer (C) is incorrect because confirmation of accounts payable is usually unnecessary when the payables are immaterial. Answer (D) is incorrect because the confirmation of accounts payable is usually not considered when internal control is effective.

100. Purchase cutoff procedures test the completeness assertion. A company should include goods in its inventory if it

A. Has sold the goods.

B. Holds legal title to the goods.

C. Has physical possession of the goods.

D. Has paid for the goods.

The correct answer is (B). *(Publisher)*

REQUIRED: The purpose of a purchase cutoff.

DISCUSSION: In general, a cutoff ensures that transactions are recorded in the appropriate period. A proper purchase cutoff is intended to assure inclusion of the goods in inventory and the recognition of a liability in the period in which the client acquired title to the goods.

Answer (A) is incorrect because sold goods should be removed from inventory. Answer (C) is incorrect because title can pass without actual possession (e.g., shipments to the client FOB shipping point). Answer (D) is incorrect because the goods may be purchased on credit and need not be paid for by the cutoff date.

101. A firm has recently converted its purchasing cycle from a manual to an online computer system. The internal auditor in charge of the first post-implementation audit of the new system has access to a generalized audit software package. One audit objective is to determine whether all material liabilities for trade accounts payable have been recorded. Which of the following would most help achieve this objective?

A. A listing of all purchase transactions processed after the cutoff date.

B. A listing of all accounts payable ledger accounts with a post office box given as the vendor mailing address.

C. A listing of all duplicate (1) purchase orders, (2) receiving reports, and (3) vendor invoices.

D. A listing of all vendors with a debit balance in the accounts payable ledgers.

The correct answer is (A). *(CIA, adapted)*

REQUIRED: The procedure for determining whether all liabilities for trade accounts payable have been recorded.

DISCUSSION: Examining a listing of all purchase transactions processed after the cutoff date tests the completeness of accounts payable. It investigates the possibility that accounts payable have been recorded in the wrong period.

Answer (B) is incorrect because listing payables with post office boxes is useful in the detection of fraud, but has little efficacy in the determination of the completeness of accounts payable. Answer (C) is incorrect because listing duplicate documents is not helpful in the search for all legitimate accounts payable. Answer (D) is incorrect because liability accounts typically have a credit balance. An account payable with a debit balance is often the result of the misclassification of a receivable. The result of such an error is the overstatement of accounts payable. The internal auditor is testing for an understatement of accounts payable.

102. When title to merchandise in transit has passed to the audit client, the auditor engaged in the performance of a purchase cutoff will encounter the greatest difficulty in gaining assurance with respect to the

A. Quantity.

B. Quality.

C. Price.

D. Terms.

The correct answer is (B). *(CPA, adapted)*

REQUIRED: The greatest audit concern when title to merchandise in transit passes to the client.

DISCUSSION: The purpose of the cutoff is to ensure that the asset and related liability are recognized in the correct period. Accordingly, merchandise that is included in ending inventory but has not yet arrived may not be available for inspection. The quality of such merchandise cannot be assured until the inspection has been conducted after the goods are received.

Answers (A), (C), and (D) are incorrect because the auditor should be able to determine the quantity, the price, and the terms of the agreement from supporting documentation.

103. The most important procedure to employ in ascertaining the existence of improper payments usually is

A. Inquiring of the treasurer's office personnel as to the existence of duplicate payments.

B. Reviewing payment voucher supporting documents for receiving reports, invoices, purchase orders, and approval-to-pay initials.

C. Observing of payment procedures in the treasurer's office for conformance to policies and procedures manual specifications.

D. Comparing total payments by type this year with those of prior years.

The correct answer is (B). *(CIA, adapted)*

REQUIRED: The most important procedure in ascertaining the existence of improper payments.

DISCUSSION: Payment vouchers bearing the required approvals should be supported by a properly authorized purchase requisition, a purchase order executing the transaction, a receiving report indicating all goods ordered have been received in good condition, and a vendor invoice confirming the amount owed. The absence of supporting documents or the presence of duplicates, forgeries, or improperly executed items may indicate errors or fraud.

Answer (A) is incorrect because inquiry is not effective when addressed to persons who may have perpetrated a fraud. Answer (C) is incorrect because observation is not effective if possible guilty parties are aware of the auditor's presence. Answer (D) is incorrect because an analytical procedure might disclose large-scale fraud, but, if the problem existed in the prior year, the procedure may not detect the improper payments in the current year.

104. Which of the following audit procedures is least likely to detect an unrecorded liability?

A. Analysis and recomputation of interest expense.

B. Analysis and recomputation of depreciation expense.

C. Mailing of standard bank confirmation forms.

D. Reading of the minutes of meetings of the board of directors.

The correct answer is (B). *(CPA, adapted)*

REQUIRED: The procedure least likely to detect an unrecorded liability.

DISCUSSION: The analysis and recomputation of depreciation expense is useful in determining whether the expense and asset accounts have been properly stated. Liabilities are not part of the depreciation recording process, so analysis and recomputation of depreciation would not detect unrecorded liabilities.

Answer (A) is incorrect because the recomputation of interest expense may reveal greater interest expense than expected based upon the recorded debt of the organization. Answer (C) is incorrect because the standard bank confirmation form requests information about other accounts not listed on the form that may come to the attention of the bank. Answer (D) is incorrect because a significant liability often requires approval by the board of directors.

105. Unrecorded liabilities are most likely to be found during the review of which of the following documents?

A. Unpaid bills.

B. Shipping records.

C. Bills of lading.

D. Unmatched sales invoices.

The correct answer is (A). *(CPA, adapted)*

REQUIRED: The documents that should be reviewed to detect unrecorded liabilities.

DISCUSSION: The auditor examines unvouchered invoices (unpaid bills) because they could represent payables that should have been recorded prior to year-end. This procedure should be carried out through the last day of field work.

Answers (B), (C), and (D) are incorrect because shipping records, bills of lading, and unmatched sales invoices relate to the client's sales.

106. In a payables application, checks are authorized and paid based on matching purchase orders, receiving reports, and vendor invoices. Partial payments are common. An appropriate audit procedure for verifying that a purchase order has not been paid twice is to sort the

A. Receiving report file by purchase order, compute total amounts received by purchase order, compare total amounts received with purchase order amounts, and investigate any discrepancies between the total amounts received and purchase order amounts.

B. Vendor invoice file by purchase order, compute total amounts invoiced by purchase order, compare total amounts invoiced with purchase order amounts, and investigate any discrepancies between the total amounts invoiced and purchase order amounts.

C. Receiving report file by vendor invoice amounts and investigate any discrepancies between the total amounts received and vendor invoice amounts.

D. Check register file by purchase order, compute total amounts paid by purchase order, compare total amounts paid with purchase order amounts, and investigate any discrepancies between the total amounts paid and purchase order amounts.

The correct answer is (D). *(CIA, adapted)*

REQUIRED: The appropriate audit procedure for verifying that a purchase order has not been paid twice.

DISCUSSION: The audit objectives for payables include the discovery of unrecorded liabilities and overpayments. Effective internal control over payments avoids these problems by matching supporting documents, using proper check preparation methods, and providing for stringent authorization procedures. The audit process described tests the effectiveness of internal control over payments in a way that merely tracing a sample of checks to purchase orders could not.

Answer (A) is incorrect because the procedure described compares goods received with goods ordered. Answer (B) is incorrect because the procedure described compares goods invoiced by the vendor and goods ordered. Answer (C) is incorrect because the procedure described compares goods received and goods invoiced.

107. Which of the following audit procedures is best for identifying unrecorded trade accounts payable?

A. Reviewing cash disbursements recorded subsequent to the balance sheet date to determine whether the related payables apply to the prior period.

B. Investigating payables recorded just prior to and just subsequent to the balance sheet date to determine whether they are supported by receiving reports.

C. Examining unusual relationships between monthly accounts payable balances and recorded cash payments.

D. Reconciling vendors' statements to the file of receiving reports to identify items received just prior to the balance sheet date.

The correct answer is (A). *(CPA, adapted)*

REQUIRED: The procedure most likely to reveal unrecorded liabilities.

DISCUSSION: The greatest risk in the audit of payables is that unrecorded liabilities exist. Omission of an entry to record a payable is an irregularity more difficult to detect than an inaccurate or false entry. The search for unrecorded payables should include examining cash disbursements made after the balance sheet date and comparing them with the accounts payable trial balance, sending confirmations to vendors with zero balances, and reconciling payable balances with vendors' documentation.

Answer (B) is incorrect because investigating recorded payables to determine whether they are supported by receiving reports tests only the amounts that have been recorded. Answer (C) is incorrect because examining unusual relationships between monthly accounts payable balances and recorded cash payments tests only the amounts that have been recorded. Answer (D) is incorrect because reconciling vendors' statements to the file of receiving reports to identify items received just prior to the balance sheet date does not determine whether these items are recorded.

108. In an audit of a public warehouse, which of the following is the most important audit procedure with respect to disclosing unrecorded liabilities?

A. Confirmation of negotiable receipts with holders.

B. Review of outstanding receipts.

C. Inspection of receiving and issuing procedures.

D. Observation of inventory.

The correct answer is (C). *(CPA, adapted)*

REQUIRED: The most important audit procedure to disclose unrecorded liabilities of a public warehouse.

DISCUSSION: When auditing a public warehouse, the inspection of receiving and issuing procedures is the most important procedure for disclosing unrecorded liabilities. Shipping orders and receiving reports that are not reflected in the records suggest that transactions are not being properly recorded.

Answer (A) is incorrect because the auditor is not likely to know the names of the holders when receipts are negotiable. Answer (B) is incorrect because a review of outstanding receipts only furnishes audit evidence concerning recorded receipts, not whether the liabilities have been recorded. Answer (D) is incorrect because observation of inventory provides evidence that the inventory exists but not that the related liabilities are unrecorded.

109. One objective of an audit of the purchasing function is to determine the cost of late payment of invoices containing trade discounts. The appropriate population from which a sample would be drawn is the file of

A. Receiving reports.

B. Purchase orders.

C. Canceled checks.

D. Paid vendor invoices.

The correct answer is (D). *(CIA, adapted)*

REQUIRED: The sample to determine the cost of late payment of invoices containing trade discounts.

DISCUSSION: A vendor invoice shows both the amount and terms of payment for purchase. Failure to pay within the discount period is normally not advantageous. Hence, lost discounts may signify inefficiency in the purchases-payables-cash disbursements function or a shortage of cash.

Answer (A) is incorrect because receiving reports indicate the date and quantity received but not whether discounts were offered or taken. Answer (B) is incorrect because purchase orders show only the quantity and expected price of a purchase. Answer (C) is incorrect because canceled checks show only the total paid, not whether a discount was offered or taken.

110. In verifying debits to perpetual inventory records of a nonmanufacturing firm, the auditor is most interested in examining the purchase

A. Journal.

B. Requisitions.

C. Orders.

D. Invoices.

The correct answer is (D). *(CPA, adapted)*

REQUIRED: The document(s) most useful to the auditor when verifying debits to perpetual inventory records.

DISCUSSION: Vendor invoices, which state the items purchased, the amount due, and the payment terms, document inventory cost when compared with purchase orders and receiving reports.

Answer (A) is incorrect because the purchase journal is created from the information on the vendor invoices. Answer (B) is incorrect because purchase requisitions, which are requests by authorized personnel to order goods, other assets, or services, do not authoritatively state vendor prices. Answer (C) is incorrect because, although the purchase order is a formal written offer to buy specified goods and serves as a purchase authorization, it may not state the price the vendor ultimately charges.

111. In an audit of a purchasing department, which of the following usually is considered a risk factor?

A. Purchase specifications are developed by the department requesting the material.

B. Purchases are made against blanket or open purchase orders for certain types of items.

C. Purchases are made from parties related to buyers or other company officials.

D. Purchases are not rotated among suppliers included on an approved vendor list.

The correct answer is (C). *(CIA, adapted)*

REQUIRED: The item considered to be a risk factor.

DISCUSSION: Purchasing from parties related to buyers or other company officials is a risk factor because it suggests the possibility of fraud. Such conflicts of interest may result in transactions unfavorable to the company.

Answer (A) is incorrect because the requesting department normally develops specifications. Answer (B) is incorrect because open purchase orders are customary for high-use items. Answer (D) is incorrect because an approved vendor list is often maintained as a control to help ensure that purchases are made only from reliable vendors. However, rotation is not usually appropriate.

112. Which of the following procedures relating to the examination of accounts payable could the auditor delegate entirely to the client's employees?

A. Test footings in the accounts payable ledger.

B. Reconcile unpaid invoices to vendors' statements.

C. Prepare a schedule of accounts payable.

D. Mail confirmations for selected account balances.

The correct answer is (C). *(CPA, adapted)*

REQUIRED: The procedure that could be delegated entirely to the client's employees.

DISCUSSION: Preparation of schedules is usually delegated to the client's employees. The auditor should review and test the schedules prepared by the client, however.

Answer (A) is incorrect because the auditor should perform test footings in the accounts payable ledger to assure proper addition. Answer (B) is incorrect because reconciliation of unpaid invoices to vendors' statements might disclose unrecorded liabilities and should be performed by the auditor. Answer (D) is incorrect because the auditor should mail all confirmations to the creditors.

4.5 Cash

113. Which of the following is not an audit objective related to cash?

A. Reported cash exists.

B. The client has ownership rights in the reported cash.

C. Compensating cash balances are reported as other current assets.

D. The reported cash balance includes all cash transactions that should have been recorded.

The correct answer is (C). *(Publisher)*

REQUIRED: The item not considered an objective of the audit of cash.

DISCUSSION: Normally, cash should be identified as a current asset. When compensating balances exist, however, any cash balances legally restricted under loan or line of credit agreements should be segregated on the balance sheet and classified according to the appropriate classification of the related debt, either current or noncurrent.

Answer (A) is incorrect because one objective is to verify management's assertion that cash exists. Answer (B) is incorrect because the auditor should establish that the client has ownership rights in the cash balances. Answer (D) is incorrect because the completeness objective requires the auditor to gather evidence that the reported cash balance includes all cash transactions that should have been recorded.

114. Normally, the audit objective of valuation is of minimum concern during the audit of cash. However, the auditor's concern about the valuation objective would most likely increase when

A. Both currency and negotiable securities are on hand.

B. The client uses a demand deposit account.

C. The proof of cash cannot be reconciled.

D. The client has foreign currency accounts.

The correct answer is (D). *(Publisher)*

REQUIRED: The most likely reason for the auditor to be concerned about the valuation of cash.

DISCUSSION: Foreign currency accounts must be converted to U.S. dollars based upon the current exchange rate. Changes in the conversion rate and restrictions on the movement of foreign currency create problems of valuation for the auditor.

Answer (A) is incorrect because the auditor is more concerned about the existence than the valuation of cash. The latter is ordinarily easily determined once the former is established. Thus, currency can usually be valued at its face amount, and negotiable securities normally have readily ascertainable market values. Answer (B) is incorrect because a demand deposit account, which is simply a checking account, is used by most organizations for cash disbursements. Answer (C) is incorrect because the inability to reconcile a proof of cash affects the auditor's concern about the existence, not the valuation, of cash.

115. When counting cash on hand, the auditor must exercise control over all cash and other negotiable assets to prevent

A. Theft.

B. Irregular endorsement.

C. Substitution.

D. Deposits in transit.

The correct answer is (C). *(CPA, adapted)*

REQUIRED: The reason for controlling cash and negotiable assets.

DISCUSSION: Simultaneous verification of cash and cash equivalents, such as trading securities, avoids the possibility of conversion of negotiable assets to cash to conceal a cash shortage. The auditor should control and verify all liquid assets at one time (AU 313).

Answers (A) and (B) are incorrect because simultaneous verification does not directly prevent theft or irregular endorsement except during the time the auditor controls the assets. Rather, it helps to uncover a fraud that has already occurred by making its concealment more difficult.

Answer (D) is incorrect because deposits in transit (those recorded on the client's but not the bank's books) are a normal result of business activity.

116. An auditor ordinarily sends a standard confirmation request to all banks with which the client has done business during the year under audit, regardless of the year-end balance. A purpose of this procedure is to

A. Provide the data necessary to prepare a proof of cash.

B. Request that a cutoff bank statement and related checks be sent to the auditor.

C. Detect kiting activities that may otherwise not be discovered.

D. Seek information about other deposit and loan amounts that come to the attention of the institution in the process of completing the confirmation.

The correct answer is (D). *(CPA, adapted)*

REQUIRED: The reason confirmations are sent to all banks used by the client.

DISCUSSION: The AICPA Standard Form to Confirm Account Balance Information with Financial Institutions is used to confirm certain basic information about deposits and direct liabilities on loans. To confirm other matters, such as contingent liabilities and security agreements, auditors send a separate letter, signed by the client, to a responsible official. The standard form is designed to substantiate only the information that is stated on the confirmation request. It is not designed to provide assurance about accounts not listed on the form and does not provide significant evidence about the completeness assertion. Nevertheless, the standard form contains this language: "Although we do not request or expect you to conduct a comprehensive, detailed search of your records, if during the process of completing this confirmation, additional information about other deposit and loan accounts we may have with you comes to your attention, please include such information below."

Answer (A) is incorrect because the data for a proof of cash are in the month-end bank statement. Answer (B) is incorrect because the client must sign a letter requesting the bank to send a cutoff bank statement directly to the auditor shortly after year-end. Answer (C) is incorrect because the auditor should prepare a bank transfer schedule for a few days before and after the balance sheet date to determine whether transfers among the client's accounts have been recorded in the proper periods.

117. The AICPA Standard Form to Confirm Account Balance Information with Financial Institutions requests all of the following except

A. Due date of a direct liability.

B. The principal amount paid on a direct liability.

C. Description of collateral for a direct liability.

D. The interest rate of a direct liability.

The correct answer is (B). *(Publisher)*

REQUIRED: The item not requested on a standard bank account balance confirmation form.

DISCUSSION: The principal amount paid on a direct liability is not listed on the AICPA standard form. The auditor is not concerned with the amount of a liability already paid. The form confirms account number/description, balance, due date, interest rate, date through which interest is paid, and description of collateral.

Answers (A), (C), and (D) are incorrect because the due date, a description of the collateral, and the interest rate are requested on a standard bank cash confirmation form to obtain third-party evidence concerning the client's liability.

118. Bank teller supervisors might manipulate accounts using their privileged computer access codes. They could withdraw money for their own use and move money among accounts when depositors complain to the bank about errors. The audit procedure most likely to detect this is

A. Reviewing transactions on privileged access codes.

B. Reviewing transactions for employees' accounts.

C. Verifying proof records for teller access codes.

D. Testing the accuracy of account posting programs.

The correct answer is (A). *(CIA, adapted)*

REQUIRED: The audit procedure most likely to detect the fraud.

DISCUSSION: A basic control problem in a computer system is the absence of the separation of functions found in manual systems. Thus, the supervisors' possession of privileged codes allows access to both deposits and related records. Controls must be implemented to compensate for this lack of segregation. Reviewing the system access log for transactions involving the supervisors' codes is one such control.

Answer (B) is incorrect because reviewing transactions for employees' accounts will not detect transfers to accounts not in the employees' names. Answer (C) is incorrect because verifying proof records for teller access codes determines whether daily transactions balance. Answer (D) is incorrect because the issue is whether transactions are authorized, not whether the postings are accurate.

119. Which of the following audit tests or procedures is performed during year-end field work?

A. Examination of employee authorizations for medical insurance withholdings.

B. Count of petty cash.

C. Comparison of data on purchase orders and payment vouchers.

D. Analysis of cutoff bank statement.

The correct answer is (D). *(CMA, adapted)*

REQUIRED: The test performed at year-end.

DISCUSSION: Analysis of a cutoff bank statement is a procedure that entails consideration of a bank statement for part of a month that includes canceled checks and other debit/credit memos. The statement is requested by the client to be sent directly to the auditor. The cutoff bank statement covers at least 7 business days following the client's year-end, thus permitting the auditor to verify that deposits in transit and checks outstanding listed on the client's year-end bank reconciliation have been recorded by the bank. The cutoff statement also may help the auditor to detect outstanding but unrecorded checks at year-end.

Answers (A), (B), and (C) are incorrect because, whereas analysis of the cutoff bank statement can only be performed at year-end, employee authorizations for medical insurance withholdings, the count of petty cash, and comparison of data on purchase orders and payment vouchers may be performed at an interim date.

120. During the examination of a cutoff bank statement, an auditor noticed that the majority of checks listed as outstanding at the preceding December 31 had not cleared the bank. Which of the following is not a likely explanation of this finding?

A. Checks were written prior to year-end but were not mailed on a timely basis.

B. Kiting was used to cover a shortage of cash.

C. The cash disbursements journal had been held open past year-end.

D. The cutoff bank statement was requested too soon after year-end.

The correct answer is (B). *(Publisher)*

REQUIRED: The unwarranted conclusion when the majority of checks outstanding at year-end have not cleared.

DISCUSSION: Kiting is an attempt to conceal a cash shortage by recording a deposit in the current period from an interbank transfer but failing to record the disbursement until the following period. The check would be returned in the cutoff bank statement with no record in the cash disbursements journal or on the bank reconciliation.

Answer (A) is incorrect because, if the checks were held after year-end, they would not likely have cleared the bank prior to receipt of the cutoff bank statement. Answer (C) is incorrect because the cash disbursements journal could have been held open, thus permitting disbursements actually made in the subsequent period to be predated and recorded in the period under audit. Answer (D) is incorrect because, if the cutoff bank statement is requested too soon after year-end, the checks mailed at year-end may not have had time to clear the bank and be returned.

121. A proof of cash used by an auditor

A. Proves that the client's year-end balance of cash is fairly stated.

B. Confirms that the client has properly separated the custody function from the recording function with respect to cash.

C. Validates that the client's bank did not make an error during the period being examined.

D. Determines whether any unauthorized disbursements or unrecorded deposits were made for the given time period.

The correct answer is (D). *(CMA, adapted)*

REQUIRED: The purpose of a proof of cash.

DISCUSSION: A proof of cash consists of a four-column worksheet, with bank reconciliations in the first and fourth columns for the beginning and end of the period and reconciliations of cash receipts and disbursements in the middle columns. The amounts per books and per bank should reconcile both horizontally and vertically. The proof of cash thus detects unauthorized disbursements or unrecorded deposits for the period. It is useful when internal control over cash transactions is ineffective.

Answer (A) is incorrect because a proof of cash only reconciles one bank account. Other procedures are necessary to provide evidence concerning the fairness of the cash balance, e.g., examination of cash on hand and cash in foreign countries. Answer (B) is incorrect because the auditor must obtain an understanding of internal control relevant to cash to determine whether the custody function is properly separated from the recording function. Answer (C) is incorrect because a proof of cash may detect an error made by the client's bank, but that is not the reason the auditor performs the proof.

122. A bank cutoff statement is least likely to detect

A. Including a nonexistent deposit in transit on the bank reconciliation.

B. Omitting checks, which were written prior to year-end, from the outstanding check list on the bank reconciliation.

C. Writing and dating of checks prior to year-end but not releasing the checks until after year-end.

D. Applying cash receipts from one customer to another customer's account (lapping).

The correct answer is (D). *(D. Wells)*

REQUIRED: The purpose not served by a bank cutoff statement.

DISCUSSION: Lapping is detected through confirmation of accounts receivable and comparing information on remittance advices and deposit slips with the cash receipts journal.

Answer (A) is incorrect because the cutoff bank statement would not show the nonexistent deposit. Answer (B) is incorrect because some checks returned with the cutoff bank statement dated prior to year-end would not appear on the year-end bank reconciliation. Answer (C) is incorrect because few, if any, of the checks that appear as outstanding on the bank reconciliation at year-end would have cleared the bank and be included in the cutoff bank statement.

123. Which of the following cash transfers results in a misstatement of cash at December 31, 1998?

Bank Transfer Schedule

	Disbursement		Receipt	
	Recorded in Books	Paid by Bank	Recorded in Books	Received by Bank
A.	12/31/98	1/4/99	12/31/98	12/31/98
B.	1/4/99	1/5/99	12/31/98	1/4/99
C.	12/31/98	1/5/99	12/31/98	1/4/99
D.	1/4/99	1/11/99	1/4/99	1/4/99

The correct answer is (B). *(CPA, adapted)*

REQUIRED: The interbank cash transfer that indicates an error in cash cutoff.

DISCUSSION: An error in cash cutoff occurs if one-half of the transaction is recorded in the current period and one-half in the subsequent period. Transfer B was recorded as a receipt on 12/31/98 but not as a disbursement until 1/4/99. This discrepancy is an error in cutoff called kiting. It overstates the cash balance because the amount of the transfer is included in both bank accounts at year-end.

Answers (A), (C), and (D) are incorrect because the disbursement and the receipt are recorded in the books in the same month.

Questions 124 and 125 are based on the following information. Raughley Co. prepared a bank reconciliation as of March 31 for the month of March. The following disbursements were made from an account in First National Bank and paid to an account in Second National Bank. The timing of the recording of the payments and receipts by the banks and on the books of Raughley Co. is shown in the next column.

	First National Bank Payment Date		Second National Bank Receipt Date	
	Bank	Books	Bank	Books
$1,000	3/31	3/30	3/31	3/30
5,000	4/2	3/30	3/31	3/31
2,500	4/3	3/31	4/2	4/2
4,000	4/3	3/31	4/2	3/31

124. Which transaction is a deposit in transit on the bank reconciliation?

A. $4,000
B. $2,500
C. $5,000
D. $1,000

The correct answer is (A). *(Publisher)*
REQUIRED: The deposit in transit.
DISCUSSION: A deposit in transit is one recorded in the books as a receipt by the balance sheet date but is not recorded as a deposit by the bank until the next period. The $4,000 item is a deposit in transit because it was recorded as a receipt in the books on 3/31 but not as a deposit by the bank until 4/2.

Answer (B) is incorrect because the receipt was recorded in the books and by the bank in the same period (April). Answers (C) and (D) are incorrect because the receipt was recorded in the books and by the bank in the same period (March).

125. Which transaction is not an outstanding check on the bank reconciliation?

A. $4,000
B. $2,500
C. $5,000
D. $1,000

The correct answer is (D). *(Publisher)*
REQUIRED: The outstanding check.
DISCUSSION: An outstanding check is written on the payor bank in the current period but does not clear the bank until the subsequent period. The $1,000 item does not reflect an outstanding check because the disbursement was recorded in the books on 3/30 and by the bank on 3/31.

Answers (A), (B), and (C) are incorrect because the payment was recorded on the books in March and by the bank in April.

Questions 126 and 127 are based on the following information.

Miles Company
Bank Transfer Schedule
December 31

Check Number	Bank Accounts From	Bank Accounts To	Amount	Date Disbursed per Books	Date Disbursed per Bank	Date Deposited per Books	Date Deposited per Bank
2020	1st Natl.	Suburban	$32,000	12/31	1/5♦	12/31	1/3▲
2021	1st Natl.	Capital	21,000	12/31	1/4♦	12/31	1/3▲
3217	2nd State	Suburban	6,700	1/3	1/5	1/3	1/6
0659	Midtown	Suburban	5,500	12/30	1/5♦	12/30	1/3▲

126. The tick mark ♦ most likely indicates that the amount was traced to the

A. December cash disbursements journal.

B. Outstanding check list of the applicable bank reconciliation.

C. January cash disbursements journal.

D. Year-end bank confirmations.

The correct answer is (B). *(CPA, adapted)*

REQUIRED: The meaning of the tick mark ♦ in the bank transfer schedule.

DISCUSSION: The tick marks indicate the dates that amounts were disbursed according to the bank. In each case, the amount was recorded in the books at the end of the preceding period. Because the checks traced had not cleared at December 31, they were not included in the December bank statement. Thus, these outstanding checks are reconciling items (differences between the books and the December bank statements for the respective drawee banks).

Answer (A) is incorrect because the transfer schedule already indicates that the marked transactions were recorded in the December cash disbursements journal. Tracing to the bank reconciliation serves the more useful purpose of determining whether these checks were included as reconciling items. Answer (C) is incorrect because the marked disbursements were recorded in December. Answer (D) is incorrect because the bank confirmation requests information about the year-end balance, which would not include the outstanding checks.

127. The tick mark ▲ most likely indicates that the amount was traced to the

A. Deposits in transit of the applicable bank reconciliation.

B. December cash receipts journal.

C. January cash receipts journal.

D. Year-end bank confirmations.

The correct answer is (A). *(CPA, adapted)*

REQUIRED: The meaning of the tick mark ▲ in the bank transfer schedule.

DISCUSSION: The tick marks indicate transfers recorded by the depository banks in January that were recorded in the books in December. Accordingly, these transactions were deposits in transit at December 31 and should have been included in the appropriate bank reconciliations.

Answer (B) is incorrect because the marked amounts were known to be recorded in the books. Answer (C) is incorrect because the December cash receipts journal includes the marked transactions. Answer (D) is incorrect because the bank confirmation at year-end would not include items recorded by the bank in January.

128. On the last day of the fiscal year, the cash disbursements clerk drew a company check on Bank A and deposited the check in the company account at Bank B to cover a previous theft of cash. The disbursement has not been recorded. The auditor will best detect this form of kiting by

A. Comparing the detail of cash receipts as shown by the cash receipts records with the detail on the confirmed duplicate deposit tickets for 3 days prior to and subsequent to year-end.

B. Preparing from the cash disbursements book a summary of bank transfers for one week prior to and subsequent to year-end.

C. Examining the composition of deposits in both Bank A and B subsequent to year-end.

D. Examining paid checks returned with the bank statement of the next accounting period after year-end.

The correct answer is (D). *(CPA, adapted)*

REQUIRED: The best audit procedure to detect kiting.

DISCUSSION: Because the check used to make the bank transfer is not recorded in the current period, the check is not listed as outstanding on the reconciliation of the bank account on which it was drawn. The auditor detects kiting by comparing paid checks, returned in the next period and dated prior to year-end, with the checks listed as outstanding on the related bank reconciliation. In other words, the auditor searches for checks that should have been listed as outstanding but were not.

Answer (A) is incorrect because the deposits and receipts records are accounted for correctly in kiting. Answer (B) is incorrect because the cash disbursements book would not contain this disbursement at year-end. Answer (C) is incorrect because the deposit records are accounted for correctly in kiting.

129. An internal auditor would be concerned about the possibility of fraud if

A. Cash receipts, net of the amounts used to pay petty cash-type expenditures, are deposited in the bank daily.

B. The monthly bank statement reconciliation is performed by the same employee who maintains the perpetual inventory records.

C. The accounts receivable subsidiary ledger and accounts payable subsidiary ledger are maintained by the same person.

D. One person, acting alone, has sole access to the petty cash fund (except for a provision for occasional surprise counts by a supervisor or auditor).

The correct answer is (A). *(CIA, adapted)*

REQUIRED: The reason an internal auditor would be concerned about the possibility of fraud.

DISCUSSION: Paying petty cash expenditures from cash receipts facilitates the unauthorized removal of cash before deposit. All cash receipts should be deposited intact daily. Petty cash expenditures should be handled through an imprest fund.

Answer (B) is incorrect because the monthly bank reconciliation should not be performed by a person who makes deposits or writes checks, but the inventory clerk does not have these responsibilities. Answer (C) is incorrect because there is no direct relationship between the transactions posted to the accounts receivable and accounts payable subsidiary ledgers. Having the same person maintain both ledgers does not create a control weakness. Answer (D) is incorrect because, to establish accountability for petty cash, only one person should have access to the fund.

130. Using a wide variety of solicitation techniques, a large public charity raises funds for medical research from the general public. In an audit of donations, the internal auditor is least likely to use which of the following audit procedures?

A. Written confirmation of a sample of direct mail pledges.

B. Reconciliation of depository bank accounts.

C. Surprise observation of door-to-door solicitation teams.

D. Reconciliation of raffle tickets sold to amounts deposited in the bank.

The correct answer is (C). *(CIA, adapted)*

REQUIRED: The least likely audit procedure in an audit of donations.

DISCUSSION: An analysis of the instructions given to door-to-door solicitation teams is more appropriate than a surprise observation. The lack of materiality of individual donations, the presence of other controls, and the inability to sample enough teams all make direct observation an inefficient audit procedure.

Answer (A) is incorrect because written confirmation of mail pledges provides evidence of existence. Answer (B) is incorrect because reconciliation of depository bank accounts provides evidence of the completeness of cash. Answer (D) is incorrect because reconciliation of raffle tickets sold to amounts deposited in the bank tests completeness of the raffle revenues.

4.6 Inventories

131. Observation of inventories is a generally accepted auditing procedure. Which of the following statements concerning this accepted auditing procedure is not correct?

A. Regardless of the inventory system maintained by the client, an annual physical count must be made of each item in the inventory, and test counts must be made by the auditor.

B. The independent auditor, when asked to audit financial statements covering the current period and one or more periods for which (s)he had not observed or made some physical counts, may be able to become satisfied as to such prior inventories through appropriate alternative procedures.

C. When the well-kept perpetual inventory records are checked by the client periodically by comparisons with physical counts, the auditor's observation procedures usually can be performed either during or after the end of the period under audit.

D. Inventories, which in the ordinary course of business are physically located in public warehouses, may be verified by direct confirmation in writing from the custodians, provided that, when the amount involved is a significant portion of the current assets or the total assets, additional procedures are applied as deemed necessary.

The correct answer is (A). *(Publisher)*

REQUIRED: The invalid statement pertaining to observation of inventory.

DISCUSSION: Firms may use methods of determining inventories, such as statistical sampling, that are highly effective and sufficiently reliable to make an annual physical count of each item in inventory unnecessary. The auditor should, however, be present to observe such counts as (s)he deems necessary to become satisfied as to the effectiveness of the procedures (AU 331).

Answer (B) is incorrect because, if the auditor is able to become satisfied as to the fairness of the current year's inventory, (s)he may be able to apply tests of prior transactions, review records of prior counts, and employ other procedures to become satisfied as to the prior year's inventory. Answer (C) is incorrect because, if the client's controls are effective, the physical count and auditor observation may take place before, at, or after year-end. Answer (D) is incorrect because AU 331 and AU 901, *Public Warehouses -- Controls and Auditing Procedures for Goods Held*, indicate that direct confirmation of goods held in public warehouses is appropriate. However, other procedures should be applied when such inventories represent a significant proportion of the client's current or total assets. These may include (1) obtaining an understanding of the client's internal control and testing the controls relevant to investigating the warehouseman and evaluating its performance, (2) obtaining an independent accountant's report on the warehouseman's relevant controls or applying alternative procedures to gain reasonable assurance that information received from the warehouseman is reliable, (3) observing physical counts whenever practicable, and (4) securing confirmations from lenders when warehouse receipts have been pledged as collateral.

132. In an audit of inventories, an auditor is least likely to verify that

A. The financial statement presentation of inventories is appropriate.

B. Damaged goods and obsolete items have been properly accounted for.

C. All inventory owned by the client is on hand at the time of the count.

D. The client has used proper inventory pricing.

The correct answer is (C). *(CPA, adapted)*

REQUIRED: The item that is not an objective of an audit of inventories.

DISCUSSION: An auditor does not expect all inventory to which the auditee has title to be on hand at the date of the count. Some purchased goods may still be in transit at that time. Also, some inventory may be away from the premises on consignment but still properly included in the count.

Answer (A) is incorrect because the auditor should test management's assertions about presentation. Answers (B) and (D) are incorrect because the auditor should test assertions about valuation.

133. Which of the following audit procedures probably provides the most reliable evidence concerning the entity's assertion of rights and obligations related to inventories?

A. Trace test counts noted during the entity's physical count to the entity's summarization of quantities.

B. Inspect agreements to determine whether any inventory is pledged as collateral or subject to any liens.

C. Select the last few shipping advices used before the physical count and determine whether the shipments were recorded as sales.

D. Inspect the open purchase order file for significant commitments that should be considered for disclosure.

The correct answer is (B). *(CPA, adapted)*

REQUIRED: The procedure providing the most reliable evidence concerning rights and obligations related to inventories.

DISCUSSION: The major audit objective of testing the assertion of rights and obligations for inventories is to determine that the entity has legal title or similar rights of ownership to the inventories. Typically, the auditor will examine paid vendors' invoices, consignment agreements, and contracts.

Answer (A) is incorrect because tracing test counts to the summarization of quantities tests the assertion of completeness. Answer (C) is incorrect because examining cutoff procedures tests the assertion of completeness. Answer (D) is incorrect because determining whether commitments should be disclosed in the footnotes deals with the assertion of statement presentation and disclosure.

134. An auditor is most likely to inspect loan agreements under which an entity's inventories are pledged to support management's financial statement assertion of

A. Existence or occurrence.

B. Completeness.

C. Presentation and disclosure.

D. Valuation or allocation.

The correct answer is (C). *(CPA, adapted)*

REQUIRED: The assertion tested by inspection of loan agreements under which inventories are pledged.

DISCUSSION: According to AU 326, "Assertions about presentation and disclosure address whether particular components of the financial statements are properly classified, described, and disclosed." Determining that the pledge or assignment of inventories is appropriately disclosed is an audit objective related to the presentation and disclosure assertion.

Answer (A) is incorrect because inspection of loan agreements does not determine whether inventories physically exist. Answer (B) is incorrect because inspection of loan agreements does not determine whether the inventory includes all items owned by the company. Answer (D) is incorrect because inspection of loan agreements does not determine whether inventory is included at proper amounts, e.g., at LCM.

135. An auditor selected items for test counts while observing a client's physical inventory. The auditor then traced the test counts to the client's inventory listing. This procedure most likely obtained evidence concerning management's assertion of

A. Rights and obligations.

B. Completeness.

C. Existence or occurrence.

D. Valuation.

The correct answer is (B). *(CPA, adapted)*

REQUIRED: The assertion relevant to tracing test counts to the client's inventory listing.

DISCUSSION: Tracing the details of test counts to the final inventory schedule assures the auditor that items in the observed physical inventory are included in the inventory records. The auditor should compare the inventory tag sequence numbers in the final inventory schedule with those in the records of his/her test counts made during the client's physical inventory.

Answer (A) is incorrect because the reconciliation of the test counts with the inventory listing does not provide assurance that the inventory is owned by the client. Answer (C) is incorrect because, although the observation of inventory provides evidence as to existence, specifically tracing test counts to the inventory listing provides assurance of completeness. Answer (D) is incorrect because the valuation assertion is tested by determining whether items are included in inventory at LCM.

136. Periodic or cycle counts of selected inventory items are made at various times during the year rather than a single inventory count at year-end. Which of the following is necessary if the auditor plans to observe inventories at interim dates?

A. Complete recounts by independent teams are performed.

B. Perpetual inventory records are maintained.

C. Unit cost records are integrated with production accounting records.

D. Inventory balances are rarely at low levels.

The correct answer is (B). *(CPA, adapted)*

REQUIRED: The precondition for observing inventories at interim dates.

DISCUSSION: "When the well-kept perpetual inventory records are checked by the client periodically by comparisons with physical counts, the auditor's observation procedures usually can be performed either during or after the end of the period under audit" (AU 331). If substantive tests are applied at an interim date, the audit risk that misstatements existing at the balance sheet date will not be detected is increased. The incremental risk may be reduced if substantive tests can be designed both to cover the remaining period and to permit the extension to year-end of audit conclusions made at the interim date (AU 313).

Answer (A) is incorrect because complete recounts of inventory by independent teams is rarely necessary. Answer (C) is incorrect because, although integrating cost records into the production records may provide for increased coordination, the process is not necessary to rely on cycle counts of inventory. Answer (D) is incorrect because inventory counts are typically easier when inventory balances are at low levels.

137. A client maintains perpetual inventory records in both quantities and dollars. If the assessed level of control risk is high, an auditor will probably

A. Apply gross profit tests to ascertain the reasonableness of the physical counts.

B. Increase the extent of tests of controls relevant to the inventory cycle.

C. Request the client to schedule the physical inventory count at the end of the year.

D. Insist that the client perform physical counts of inventory items several times during the year.

The correct answer is (C). *(CPA, adapted)*

REQUIRED: The auditor's action if control risk for inventory is high.

DISCUSSION: If control risk is high, extending work done on an interim basis to year-end might be inappropriate. Thus, observation of inventory at year-end provides the best evidence as to existence.

Answer (A) is incorrect because comparing the gross profit test results with the prior year's results provides evidence about sales and cost of goods sold but not inventory. Answer (B) is incorrect because, if the auditor believes controls are unlikely to be effective, tests of controls would not be performed. Answer (D) is incorrect because the risk is that year-end inventory would be misstated.

138. When outside firms of nonaccountants specializing in the taking of physical inventories are used to count, list, price, and subsequently compute the total dollar amount of inventory on hand at the date of the physical count, the auditor will ordinarily

A. Consider the report of the outside inventory-taking firm to be an acceptable alternative procedure to the observation of physical inventories.

B. Make or observe some physical counts of the inventory, recompute certain inventory calculations, and test certain inventory transactions.

C. Not reduce the extent of work on the physical count of inventory.

D. Consider the reduced audit effort with respect to the physical count of inventory as a scope limitation.

The correct answer is (B). *(CPA, adapted)*

REQUIRED: The auditor's responsibility when an outside firm has taken the inventory.

DISCUSSION: The taking of inventory by an outside firm of nonaccountants does not substitute for the auditor's own observation or performing some test counts. The extent of his/her procedures may be reduced, but only after a proper evaluation of the outside firm's work, including examining its program, observing its procedures and controls, recomputing calculations, and applying tests to subsequent transactions.

Answer (A) is incorrect because the use of experts to count the inventory may reduce the extent of the auditor's other work on the inventory, but it cannot be a complete substitute. Answer (C) is incorrect because the independent auditor may be able to reduce the extent of his/her procedures but only after a proper evaluation of the outside firm's work. Answer (D) is incorrect because a scope limitation should not be reported unless the auditor's judgment concerning the extent of contact with the inventory is restricted; i.e., the client limits the CPA's involvement in the observation and review of the inventory count.

139. After accounting for a sequence of inventory tags, an auditor traces a sample of tags to the physical inventory listing to obtain evidence that all items

A. Included in the listing have been counted.

B. Represented by inventory tags are included in the listing.

C. Included in the listing are represented by inventory tags.

D. Represented by inventory tags are bona fide.

The correct answer is (B). *(CPA, adapted)*

REQUIRED: The reason for tracing a sample to the physical inventory listing.

DISCUSSION: The auditor should observe the counting process, determine that proper procedures are followed, and make selected test counts. Because the auditor does not make a complete count, not every misstatement will be detected, but (s)he should be able to determine that no large block of inventory has been omitted. Having accounted for a sequence of inventory tags, the auditor should trace a sample of the tags to the physical inventory sheets. The purpose is to test the completeness assertion: all inventory listed on a tag should be reflected in the sheets.

Answer (A) is incorrect because the direction of testing must be from the listing to the tags to obtain evidence that all items included in the listing have been counted. Answer (C) is incorrect because the direction of testing must be from the listing to the tags to obtain evidence that all items included in the listing are represented by inventory tags. Answer (D) is incorrect because the validity of the tags is determined by examining the inventory itself.

140. If the perpetual inventory records show lower quantities of inventory than the physical count, an explanation of the difference might be unrecorded

A. Sales.

B. Sales discounts.

C. Purchases.

D. Purchase discounts.

The correct answer is (C). *(CPA, adapted)*

REQUIRED: The reason the physical count might exceed the perpetual inventory amount.

DISCUSSION: In a perpetual system, purchases are debited directly to inventory at the time of the transaction rather than to a purchases account. A sale requires an immediate credit to inventory. Hence, failure to record a purchase would understate inventory.

Answer (A) is incorrect because an unrecorded sale would overstate inventory. Answer (B) is incorrect because sales discounts affect neither the quantity nor the valuation of inventory. Answer (D) is incorrect because unrecorded purchase discounts affect the valuation but not the quantity of inventory.

141. An independent auditor may accept a client's sampling method for the performance of physical inventory only if

A. The client is willing to accept a qualification of the auditor's opinion because of a scope limitation.

B. Control risk is assessed at the maximum.

C. The sampling plan has statistical validity.

D. Over half of the dollar value of the inventory is counted.

The correct answer is (C). *(Publisher)*

REQUIRED: The basis for an auditor's acceptance of a sampling method for inventory.

DISCUSSION: According to AU 331, "If statistical sampling methods are used by the client in the taking of the physical inventory, the auditor must be satisfied that the sampling plan is reasonable and statistically valid, that it has been properly applied, and that the results are reasonable in the circumstances." But the auditor still should be present to observe such counts as (s)he deems necessary to assure that the inventory exists.

Answer (A) is incorrect because a scope limitation does not exist unless the auditor is precluded from evaluating the client's sampling plan or observing the counts. Answer (B) is incorrect because the auditor is more likely to accept the method when controls are effective and control risk is assessed at less than the maximum. Answer (D) is incorrect because the extent of the counts depends on the circumstances and the auditor's judgment. No fixed percentage of the inventory must be counted.

142. The physical count of inventory of a retailer was higher than shown by the perpetual records. Which of the following could explain the difference?

A. Inventory items had been counted but the tags placed on the items had not been taken off the items and added to the inventory accumulation sheets.

B. Credit memos for several items returned by customers had not been recorded.

C. No journal entry had been made on the retailer's books for several items returned to its suppliers.

D. An item purchased "FOB shipping point" had not arrived at the date of the inventory count and had not been reflected in the perpetual records.

The correct answer is (B). *(CPA, adapted)*

REQUIRED: The reason that the physical count exceeded the amount in the perpetual records.

DISCUSSION: If credit memos for items returned by customers have not been prepared and recorded, the returned items will be reflected in the physical inventory but not in the perpetual records.

Answer (A) is incorrect because items counted but not added to the inventory accumulation sheets will understate the physical count. Answer (C) is incorrect because, if no journal entry has been made for items returned to vendors, the perpetual records will be overstated. Answer (D) is incorrect because, if an entry has not been made in the perpetual records and the item has not been received, both the records and physical inventory will be understated by the same amount. FOB shipping point means that title passes when the items are shipped, and they should be included in both inventory and accounts payable at that time.

143. An auditor is most likely to learn of slow-moving inventory through

A. Inquiry of sales personnel.

B. Inquiry of warehouse personnel.

C. Physical observation of inventory.

D. Review of perpetual inventory records.

The correct answer is (D). *(CPA, adapted)*

REQUIRED: The procedure most likely to detect slow-moving inventory.

DISCUSSION: In a perpetual inventory system, receipts and issuances of goods are recorded as the transactions occur, both as to quantities and prices. By comparing the dates of receipt and issuance, the auditor is readily able to identify slow-moving and possibly obsolete inventory.

Answers (A) and (B) are incorrect because inquiries are less reliable and comprehensive than a review of perpetual inventory records. Answer (C) is incorrect because observation will prove useful only if the appearance of the items suggested the length of time they were held.

144. Which of the following procedures will best detect the theft of valuable items from an inventory that consists of hundreds of different items selling for $1 to $10 and a few items selling for hundreds of dollars?

A. Maintain a perpetual inventory of only the more valuable items with frequent periodic verification of the validity of the perpetual inventory record.

B. Have an independent auditing firm examine and report on management's assertion about the design and operating effectiveness of the control activities relevant to inventory.

C. Have separate warehouse space for the more valuable items with sequentially numbered tags.

D. Require an authorized officer's signature on all requisitions for the more valuable items.

The correct answer is (A). *(CPA, adapted)*

REQUIRED: The best procedure to detect the theft of valuable items from an inventory.

DISCUSSION: The costs of maintaining perpetual records for a large volume of inexpensive items are likely to exceed the benefits of more accurate and timely information and better safeguards against theft. For high value items, maintaining such records, with frequent reconciliations to physical counts, may prove cost beneficial.

Answer (B) is incorrect because the engagement would not necessarily result in detection of theft, although it might identify material weaknesses or other reportable conditions that encourage theft. Answer (C) is incorrect because separate warehouse space for the more valuable items with sequentially numbered tags is helpful but not as effective in detecting (as opposed to preventing) theft as a system whereby the quantity that should be on hand is known with reasonable accuracy at all times. Answer (D) is incorrect because requiring an authorized officer's signature on all requisitions for the more valuable items is useful but less effective than maintaining perpetual inventory records.

145. Which of the following is the best audit test to evaluate the accuracy of the inventory records for materials inventory in a production operation?

A. Trace selected inventory receipts to perpetual inventory records.

B. Vouch selected postings in the perpetual inventory records to source documents.

C. Perform turnover tests for materials inventory.

D. Reconcile quantities on hand per physical counts of selected items with perpetual inventory records and verify pricing.

The correct answer is (D). *(CIA, adapted)*

REQUIRED: The best audit test for evaluating the accuracy of the inventory records for materials inventory.

DISCUSSION: The objectives in designing an audit test should be to verify both the quantity on hand and the dollar value of inventory. By reconciling the quantities on hand determined by the physical count with the perpetual inventory records and verifying pricing, both objectives are met. The auditor's observation of the physical count is an indispensable audit procedure.

Answer (A) is incorrect because tracing selected inventory receipts to perpetual inventory records provides less reliable evidence than observation of the physical count. Answer (B) is incorrect because vouching selected postings in the perpetual inventory records to source documents provides less reliable evidence than observation of the physical count. Answer (C) is incorrect because analytical procedures do not provide direct evidence of inventory amounts.

146. Purchase cutoff procedures should be designed to test whether all inventory

A. Purchased and received before year-end was paid for.

B. Ordered before year-end was received.

C. Purchased and received before year-end was recorded.

D. Owned by the company is in the possession of the company at year-end.

The correct answer is (C). *(CPA, adapted)*

REQUIRED: The purpose of a purchase cutoff.

DISCUSSION: A purchase cutoff is an audit procedure related to the audit objective of testing the completeness assertion about inventories. It is performed to obtain evidence that all goods owned by the client at the balance sheet date are included in inventory and that the related liability is recorded. Legal title to goods in transit is determined by whether the shipping terms are FOB shipping point or destination.

Answer (A) is incorrect because items may be included in inventory although not yet paid for. Answer (B) is incorrect because the company may not have title to goods on order. Answer (D) is incorrect because the company may have title to goods in transit or held on consignment.

147. For the week before Moore Company's physical count, all receiving reports include a notation that they have been prepared prior to the count. For the week after the physical count, all receiving reports indicate that they have been prepared after the count. The receiving department continues to receive goods after the cutoff time while the physical count is in process. To determine the accuracy of the cutoff, the auditor should

A. Trace a sample of receiving reports issued after the last receiving report to the physical items to see that they have been included in the physical count.

B. Trace a sample of receiving reports issued before the last receiving report to the physical items to see that they have not been included in the physical count.

C. Observe that the receiving clerk is stamping the receiving reports properly.

D. List the number of the last receiving report for items included in the physical count.

The correct answer is (D). *(Publisher)*

REQUIRED: The procedure for testing the inventory cutoff.

DISCUSSION: The numbers of the last receiving and shipping reports should be recorded so that the auditor may determine whether an accurate cutoff was made. For example, merchandise represented by receiving reports numbered after the cutoff should not be included in inventory.

Answer (A) is incorrect because receiving reports prepared after the cutoff should be traced on a test basis to the inventory records to determine that the items have not been included. Answer (B) is incorrect because receiving reports prepared before the cutoff should be traced on a test basis to the inventory records to determine that the items have been included. Answer (C) is incorrect because the least effective method of checking the accuracy of the cutoff of inventory is to observe that the receiving clerk is stamping the receiving reports properly. The auditor is primarily concerned with the dates on the receiving reports in order to verify that goods received or shipped near year-end are accounted for in the proper reporting period.

148. The audit of year-end physical inventories should include steps to verify that the client's purchases and sales cutoffs were adequate. The audit steps should be designed to detect whether merchandise included in the physical count at year-end was not recorded as a

A. Sale in the subsequent period.

B. Purchase in the current period.

C. Sale in the current period.

D. Purchase return in the subsequent period.

The correct answer is (C). *(CPA, adapted)*

REQUIRED: The error detected by the audit of purchases and sales cutoffs.

DISCUSSION: Goods on hand and counted in the year-end inventory should not also have been recorded as sold during the current audit period. If they were sold, they could not have been owned by the client at year-end. Cutoff tests include comparison of the records of sales and purchases for several days before and after the balance sheet date with duplicate sales invoices and shipping records.

Answer (A) is incorrect because year-end inventory most likely will be sold in the subsequent period. Answer (B) is incorrect because year-end inventory most likely was purchased in the current period. Answer (D) is incorrect because unreturned items are owned by the client and should be in ending inventory.

149. An auditor's observation of physical inventories at the main plant at year-end provides direct evidence to support which of the following objectives?

A. Accuracy of the priced-out inventory.

B. Evaluation of lower of cost or market test.

C. Identification of obsolete or damaged merchandise to evaluate allowance (reserve) for obsolescence.

D. Determination of goods on consignment at another location.

The correct answer is (C). *(CIA, adapted)*

REQUIRED: The objective supported by observation of inventory.

DISCUSSION: One way to discover damaged or obsolete merchandise is to observe the client's physical inventory count and inspect the merchandise during the inventory process. The auditor should check for dusty packages, rusted metal, physical damage to the merchandise, etc. The auditor may also need to consult a specialist regarding the quality or condition of merchandise.

Answers (A) and (B) are incorrect because observation verifies physical existence and condition, not price or cost accuracy. Answer (D) is incorrect because observation at the main plant is not evidence of the existence of goods at another site.

150. An auditor concluded that no excessive costs for an idle plant were charged to inventory. This conclusion most likely related to the auditor's objective to obtain evidence about the financial statement assertions regarding inventory, including presentation and disclosure and

A. Valuation and allocation.

B. Completeness.

C. Existence or occurrence.

D. Rights and obligations.

The correct answer is (A). *(CPA, adapted)*

REQUIRED: The assertion related to the conclusion that no excessive costs for an idle plant were inventoried.

DISCUSSION: Inventory should properly include the costs of direct labor, direct materials, and manufacturing overhead. Thus, to be properly valued, an appropriate amount of manufacturing overhead should be charged to inventory. Costs of an idle plant should not be included in manufacturing overhead.

Answers (B), (C), and (D) are incorrect because excessive costs for an idle plant do not affect the completeness, existence or occurrence, and rights and obligations assertions.

151. Some firms that dispose of only a small part of their total output by consignment shipments fail to make any distinction between consignment shipments and regular sales. Which of the following suggests to the auditor that the client's goods have been shipped on consignment?

A. Numerous shipments of small quantities.

B. Numerous shipments of large quantities and few returns.

C. Large debits to accounts receivable and small periodic credits.

D. Large debits to accounts receivable and large periodic credits.

The correct answer is (C). *(CPA, adapted)*

REQUIRED: The condition indicative of goods shipped on consignment.

DISCUSSION: A consignment is a shipment of inventory by the owner to a sales agent (the consignee), who sells the goods and then pays the consignor. Goods on consignment are owned by the consignor. Large debits to accounts receivable and small periodic credits suggest that large quantities have been "sold," but smaller quantities are being "paid for." Typically, consignment payments are remitted periodically as the consignee makes sales. Failing to distinguish sales and consignments overstates net income and understates inventory.

Answers (A) and (B) are incorrect because fewer but larger shipments with many returns indicate consignments. Answer (D) is incorrect because consigned goods are normally paid for in small amounts as they are sold.

152. During an investigation of unexplained inventory shrinkage, an internal auditor is testing inventory additions as recorded in the perpetual inventory records. Because of internal control weaknesses, the information recorded on receiving reports may not be reliable. Under these circumstances, which of the following documents provide the best evidence of additions to inventory?

A. Purchase orders.

B. Purchase requisitions.

C. Vendors' invoices.

D. Vendors' statements.

The correct answer is (C). *(CIA, adapted)*

REQUIRED: The best evidence of additions to inventory when receiving reports are unreliable.

DISCUSSION: Vendors' invoices state the quantities and costs of goods shipped. Thus, they provide an external source of evidence of additions to inventory. However, an adjustment must be made for purchase returns.

Answer (A) is incorrect because the quantity ordered may not equal the quantity shipped by the vendor. Answer (B) is incorrect because the quantity requested in a purchase requisition may not equal the quantity actually ordered or the quantity shipped by the vendor. Answer (D) is incorrect because vendors' statements normally list only the invoice number, date, and total. They do not list invoice detail such as quantities shipped.

153. To obtain evidence as to the reasonableness and completeness of inventory balances, auditors often perform analytical procedures. Which of the following quantitative relationships is not applicable to inventory balances?

A. The gross profit percentage.

B. Debt-to-equity ratio.

C. Inventory turnover ratios.

D. Number of days' sales in inventory.

The correct answer is (B). *(Publisher)*

REQUIRED: The quantitative relationship not applicable to inventory balances.

DISCUSSION: The debt-to-equity ratio, a measure of leverage, relates to corporate financing, not inventory. It equals total debt divided by total equity.

Answer (A) is incorrect because the gross profit percentage (gross profit ÷ net sales) provides information about inventories. Gross profit is equal to net sales minus cost of goods sold, and inventories affect cost of goods sold. Any significant unexplained variance in the percentage may be the result of an inventory misstatement. Answer (C) is incorrect because inventory ratios, such as cost of goods sold divided by average inventory, should remain relatively constant in the absence of known conditions to the contrary. Answer (D) is incorrect because the number of days' sales in inventory (360 ÷ inventory turnover) is a measure that can be monitored by the auditor. The number of days' sales in inventories should be relatively constant.

154. During the preliminary survey phase of an audit of the organization's production cycle, management stated that the sale of scrap was well controlled. Evidence to verify that assertion can best be gained by

A. Comparing current revenue from scrap sales with that of prior periods.

B. Interviewing persons responsible for collecting and storing the scrap.

C. Comparing the quantities of scrap expected from the production process with the quantities sold.

D. Comparing the results of a physical inventory of scrap on hand with perpetual inventory records.

The correct answer is (C). *(CIA, adapted)*

REQUIRED: The best procedure to verify the assertion that the sale of scrap is well controlled.

DISCUSSION: If the sale of scrap is well controlled, a large amount will not be on hand. Most scrap will be sold when produced. Hence, if the quantities sold are approximately the same as those expected, an auditor can assume that the controls over the sale of scrap are effective.

Answer (A) is incorrect because comparing current revenue from scrap sales with that of prior periods presumes that prior periods' amounts were correct and that no change has occurred in quantity produced. Answer (B) is incorrect because the persons responsible for collecting and storing the scrap can only describe the safeguards in place to handle scrap before its sale. Answer (D) is incorrect because comparing the physical count with perpetual inventory records verifies only the accuracy of perpetual inventory records.

4.7 Property, Plant, and Equipment

155. Property, plant, and equipment (PPE) is typically judged to be one of the accounts least susceptible to fraud because

A. The amounts recorded on the balance sheet for most companies are immaterial.

B. The inherent risk is usually low.

C. The depreciated values are always smaller than cost.

D. Internal control is inherently effective regarding this account.

The correct answer is (B). *(Publisher)*

REQUIRED: The reason PPE is not susceptible to fraud.

DISCUSSION: Property, plant, and equipment is one of the accounts least susceptible to material misstatement in the absence of related controls. Inherent risk is low because of the infrequency of transactions in the account, the relative ease with which the existence of these assets can be verified, the slow turnover, and the simplicity of cutoff procedures.

Answer (A) is incorrect because PPE amounts are often quite large. Answer (C) is incorrect because some PPE items (e.g., land) are not depreciated. Answer (D) is incorrect because the susceptibility to misstatement is a matter of inherent risk, not control risk.

156. Which is the best audit procedure to obtain evidence to support the legal ownership of real property?

A. Examination of corporate minutes and board resolutions with regard to approvals to acquire real property.

B. Examination of closing documents, deeds, and ownership documents registered and on file at the county courthouse.

C. Discussion with corporate legal counsel concerning the acquisition of a specific piece of property.

D. Confirmation with the title company that handled the escrow account and disbursement of proceeds for the closing of the property.

The correct answer is (B). *(CIA, adapted)*

REQUIRED: The best audit procedure for obtaining evidence to support the legal ownership of real property.

DISCUSSION: Examination of title documents, the deed, and any other supporting documents, such as closing documents, will be helpful in verifying ownership. But these are not conclusive. An inspection of public records will determine if there are any interests in the property (e.g., mortgages, judgment liens, or claims to the title) that do not appear in the auditee's records.

Answer (A) is incorrect because an examination of corporate minutes and board resolutions will not provide evidence of actual ownership, only approval to acquire the property. Answer (C) is incorrect because the testimony of corporate legal counsel provides only corroborating evidence. Answer (D) is incorrect because confirmation with an escrow agent is evidence only of the closing. It does not provide evidence regarding subsequent transactions, such as a mortgage liability not recorded in the company books.

157. When few property and equipment transactions occur during the year, the continuing auditor usually obtains an understanding of internal control and performs

A. Tests of controls.

B. Analytical procedures to verify current year additions to property and equipment.

C. A thorough examination of the balances at the beginning of the year.

D. Extensive tests of current year property and equipment transactions.

The correct answer is (D). *(CPA, adapted)*

REQUIRED: The PPE procedures performed by a continuing auditor.

DISCUSSION: Testing the details of transactions is the preferable procedure for property and equipment because the beginning balance would have been subjected to audit procedures and the number of subsequent transactions in the account is normally minimal. The auditor may choose to assess control risk at the maximum level after obtaining the understanding of internal control because (s)he believes that evaluating the effectiveness of the relevant controls would be inefficient.

Answer (A) is incorrect because tests of controls are unnecessary if the auditor does extensive testing of details. Answer (B) is incorrect because analytical procedures are unnecessary as substantive tests if the auditor does extensive testing of details. Answer (C) is incorrect because a continuing auditor would already have examined the beginning balances.

158. In the audit of property, plant, and equipment, the auditor tries to do all of the following except to

A. Obtain an understanding of internal control.

B. Determine the extent of property abandoned during the year.

C. Assess the adequacy of replacement funds.

D. Judge the reasonableness of the depreciation.

The correct answer is (C). *(CPA, adapted)*

REQUIRED: The determination not made during an audit of PPE.

DISCUSSION: In performing the attest function, the external auditor is not directly concerned with evaluating the soundness of the client's business practices or financial prospects. Whether replacement funds are adequate does not bear on the question of whether the financial statements are fairly presented in conformity with GAAP.

Answer (A) is incorrect because, in all audits, GAAS require the auditor to obtain an understanding sufficient to plan the audit and to determine the nature, timing, and extent of tests. Answer (B) is incorrect because the auditor should determine whether abandonments of property were properly recorded so as to avoid overstatement of assets. Answer (D) is incorrect because depreciation affects both asset valuation and income.

159. Which of the following combinations of procedures is an auditor most likely to perform to obtain evidence about fixed asset additions?

A. Inspecting documents and physically examining assets.

B. Recomputing calculations and obtaining written management representations.

C. Observing operating activities and comparing balances to prior period balances.

D. Confirming ownership and corroborating transactions through inquiries of client personnel.

The correct answer is (A). *(CPA, adapted)*

REQUIRED: The combination of procedures most likely to obtain evidence about fixed asset additions.

DISCUSSION: The auditor's direct observation of fixed assets is one means of determining whether additions have been made. Tracing to the detailed records determines whether additions have been recorded. Inspection of such documents as deeds, lease agreements, insurance policies, invoices, canceled checks, and tax notices may also reveal additions.

Answer (B) is incorrect because recomputations are based on book amounts and will not reveal unrecorded additions. Management representations may also be incomplete. Answer (C) is incorrect because analytical procedures may not detect additions offset by disposals. Answer (D) is incorrect because the auditor must become aware of additions before confirming ownership or corroborating transactions.

160. If an auditor tours a production facility, which of the misstatements or questionable practices is most likely to be detected by the audit procedure specified?

A. Depreciation expense on fully depreciated machinery has been recognized.

B. Overhead has been overapplied.

C. Necessary facility maintenance has not been performed.

D. Insurance coverage on the facility has lapsed.

The correct answer is (C). *(CIA, adapted)*

REQUIRED: The misstatement or questionable practice uncovered by touring the client's plant.

DISCUSSION: The auditor is likely to discover that necessary plant maintenance was not performed during the year through direct observation of asset condition.

Answer (A) is incorrect because only inspection of depreciation records will reveal depreciation recorded for fully depreciated machines. Answer (B) is incorrect because the auditor compares actual overhead incurred with overhead applied to determine whether overhead was underapplied. Answer (D) is incorrect because the auditor inspects the insurance contracts to detect lapsed insurance coverage.

161. Treetop Corporation acquired a building and arranged mortgage financing during the year. Verification of the related mortgage acquisition costs would be least likely to include an examination of the related

A. Deed.

B. Canceled checks.

C. Closing statement.

D. Interest expense.

The correct answer is (A). *(CPA, adapted)*

REQUIRED: The item that the auditor would least likely inspect to verify mortgage acquisition costs.

DISCUSSION: A deed provides evidence concerning ownership rights and obligations relative to mortgaged property. However, it typically does not contain information about costs of mortgages.

Answers (B), (C), and (D) are incorrect because canceled checks, a closing statement, and interest expense provide evidence concerning the cost of a mortgage.

162. In testing for unrecorded retirements of equipment, an auditor is most likely to

A. Select items of equipment from the accounting records and then locate them during the plant tour.

B. Compare depreciation journal entries with similar prior-year entries in search of fully depreciated equipment.

C. Inspect items of equipment observed during the plant tour and then trace them to the equipment subsidiary ledger.

D. Scan the general journal for unusual equipment additions and excessive debits to repairs and maintenance expense.

The correct answer is (A). *(CPA, adapted)*

REQUIRED: The procedure most useful in detecting unrecorded retirements of equipment.

DISCUSSION: The completeness assertion is that all transactions and accounts that should be presented are so included. Thus, the equipment account should reflect all retirement transactions as well as all additions. To test for unrecorded retirements, the auditor inspects selected items chosen from the records. However, unlike confirmation of receivables or observation of inventories, inspection of equipment, especially a complete physical inventory, is not a generally accepted auditing procedure. But a high assessment of control risk may induce the auditor to inspect a sample of items.

Answer (B) is incorrect because fully depreciated equipment may not be physically retired. Answer (C) is incorrect because, to detect unrecorded retirements, the direction of testing should be from the records to the physical assets. Answer (D) is incorrect because the concern is with retirements of equipment, not additions.

163. One audit procedure for an audit of facilities and equipment is to test the accuracy of recorded depreciation. Which of the following is the best source of evidence that the equipment in question is in service?

A. A review of depreciation policies and procedures.

B. A comparison of depreciation schedules with a listing of insurance appraisals for the same equipment.

C. A comparison of depreciation schedules with the maintenance and repair logs for the same equipment.

D. A review of inventory documentation for the equipment.

The correct answer is (C). *(CIA, adapted)*

REQUIRED: The best source of evidence that the equipment in question is in service.

DISCUSSION: The maintenance and repair records provide evidence that equipment exists and is in use. Equipment in service is more likely to require maintenance than retired equipment. However, the best evidence is the auditor's direct observation.

Answer (A) is incorrect because a review of policies and procedures provides no evidence about the existence assertion for specific assets. Answer (B) is incorrect because a comparison with current insurance records would be inconclusive. Retired equipment could still be insured. Answer (D) is incorrect because retired equipment could still be in the inventory.

164. The auditor is least likely to learn of retirements of equipment through which of the following?

A. Review of the purchase return and allowance account.

B. Review of depreciation.

C. Analysis of the debits to the accumulated depreciation account.

D. Review of insurance policy riders.

The correct answer is (A). *(CPA, adapted)*

REQUIRED: The procedure least likely to provide evidence about retirements of equipment.

DISCUSSION: Review of the purchase return and allowance account offers no information about the retirement of equipment. This account is used to record the return of purchased inventory and is unaffected by the entries to record the acquisition, depreciation, and disposition of fixed assets.

Answers (B) and (C) are incorrect because review of depreciation may reveal equipment retirements. Answer (D) is incorrect because reduction in insurance coverage may indicate a retirement of equipment.

165. Determining that proper amounts of depreciation are expensed provides assurance about management's assertions of valuation or allocation and

A. Presentation and disclosure.

B. Completeness.

C. Rights and obligations.

D. Existence or occurrence.

The correct answer is (A). *(CPA, adapted)*

REQUIRED: The assertion tested by consideration of the amounts of depreciation that are expensed.

DISCUSSION: The presentation and disclosure assertion concerns whether particular components of the financial statements are properly classified, described, and disclosed. For example, if cost of sales includes depreciation, the auditor should determine that this classification is appropriate and that it is properly disclosed.

Answers (B), (C), and (D) are incorrect because expressing of proper amounts of depreciation relates to the valuation and presentation and disclosure assertions.

166. The auditor may conclude that depreciation charges are insufficient by noting

A. Insured values greatly in excess of book values.

B. Large numbers of fully depreciated assets.

C. Continuous trade-ins of relatively new assets.

D. Excessive recurring losses on assets retired.

The correct answer is (D). *(CPA, adapted)*

REQUIRED: The condition indicating insufficient depreciation charges.

DISCUSSION: Excessive recurring losses on assets retired indicate excess book values at the dates of disposition. The implication is that the method of cost allocation has not been sufficient. The effect of such understating of depreciation in prior periods would have been to overstate income in those periods and understate income in the period of retirement.

Answer (A) is incorrect because the insured values of assets should reflect market values. Book values reflect historical cost. Answer (B) is incorrect because large numbers of fully depreciated assets indicate excessive, not insufficient, depreciation charges. Answer (C) is incorrect because trade-ins of relatively new assets suggest rapid technological change in the client's industry.

167. The most appropriate reason for changes to accumulated depreciation is that

A. Depreciation for prior periods was understated.

B. Major repairs have lengthened the life of an asset.

C. A depreciable asset has been recorded at current cost.

D. Retained earnings have been appropriated for a possible loss on retirement.

The correct answer is (B). *(Publisher)*

REQUIRED: The reason for a decrease in accumulated depreciation.

DISCUSSION: If major repairs have lengthened the life of an asset, the company should reduce the amount of accumulated depreciation to increase the book value of the asset. This practice is acceptable for representing the increased life of an asset.

Answer (A) is incorrect because an adjustment for understated depreciation requires a credit, not a debit, to accumulated depreciation. Answer (C) is incorrect because depreciable assets ordinarily should be recorded at historical cost. Answer (D) is incorrect because an appropriation affects retained earnings accounts only.

168. An auditor analyzes repairs and maintenance accounts primarily to obtain evidence in support of the audit assertion that all

A. Noncapitalizable expenditures for repairs and maintenance have been recorded in the proper period.

B. Expenditures for property and equipment have been recorded in the proper period.

C. Noncapitalizable expenditures for repairs and maintenance have been properly charged to expense.

D. Expenditures for property and equipment have not been charged to expense.

The correct answer is (D). *(CPA, adapted)*

REQUIRED: The reason an auditor analyzes repairs and maintenance expense.

DISCUSSION: The auditor should vouch significant debits from the repairs and maintenance expense account to determine whether any should have been capitalized.

Answer (A) is incorrect because an improper cutoff of repairs and maintenance expenses is not a major risk. Answer (B) is incorrect because the repairs and maintenance expense accounts are not the appropriate sources of evidence regarding the cutoff of expenditures for property and equipment. Answer (C) is incorrect because vouching additions to plant, property, and equipment provides evidence of whether any expense has been inappropriately charged as a capital item.

169. In violation of a company policy, Lowell Company erroneously capitalized the cost of painting its warehouse. The auditor examining Lowell's financial statements will most likely detect this misstatement when

A. Discussing capitalization policies with Lowell's controller.

B. Examining maintenance expense accounts.

C. Observing, during the physical inventory observation, that the warehouse had been painted.

D. Examining the construction work orders supporting items capitalized during the year.

The correct answer is (D). *(CPA, adapted)*

REQUIRED: The procedure to detect the capitalization of a maintenance expense.

DISCUSSION: The audit program for PPE includes verification of additions by vouching them to the original documents. The entries in the journals are supported by authorizations, vendors' invoices, contracts, deeds, and construction work orders. Inspection of the work order for painting the warehouse would alert the auditor that an expense had been incorrectly capitalized.

Answer (A) is incorrect because, given that the policy of the firm is to expense painting costs, discussion with the controller will not uncover the misstatement. Answer (B) is incorrect because items capitalized will not be reflected in maintenance accounts. Answer (C) is incorrect because the auditor will not detect improper accounting for the cost by observing the painted warehouse.

170. Which of the following costs should not be capitalized?

A. Major reconditioning of a delivery truck.

B. Machine operator's wages during a period of testing and adjusting new machinery.

C. Fencing the plant parking lot.

D. Maintenance of an unused stand-by plant.

The correct answer is (D). *(Publisher)*

REQUIRED: The cost that should not be capitalized.

DISCUSSION: That the plant is on stand-by for current operations suggests that maintenance should be reflected in current costs. The plant, even though unused, is not the same as a nonproductive asset. If the idle plant is not expected to be used, however, it should be written down to net realizable value and excluded from the fixed assets accounts. Maintenance costs might then be considered as costs of disposal.

Answer (A) is incorrect because the costs of a major reconditioning of a delivery truck should be capitalized. Improvements, additions, and replacements benefit several periods by extending the useful life of an asset or by increasing future service potential. Answer (B) is incorrect because costs of putting a capital asset into service are capitalized according to GAAP. Answer (C) is incorrect because the costs of fencing the plant parking lot should be capitalized and depreciated as land improvements.

171. An audit client has leased an asset and appropriately recorded a capital lease. Because of the existence of a bargain purchase option, the auditor should determine

A. Whether the sum of the minimum lease payments equals the fair value of the property.

B. That the leased property is being depreciated over the life of the lease.

C. Whether the interest rate used in discounting the minimum lease payments is the client's incremental borrowing rate or the lessor's implicit rate.

D. That the cost of the property to the lessor is the cost recorded by the client.

The correct answer is (C). *(Publisher)*

REQUIRED: The appropriate audit procedure relative to a capital lease.

DISCUSSION: A leased asset should be capitalized at the sum of the discounted minimum lease payments. Thus, the interest rate used in the discounting process is an important consideration in determining whether the asset is fairly presented in the balance sheet. The interest rate is the client's incremental borrowing rate, unless the lessor's implicit rate is known and is less than the client's incremental rate.

Answer (A) is incorrect because the total amount of lease payments represents both the cost of the asset and interest expense. Answer (B) is incorrect because the asset should be depreciated over its estimated life, which is not necessarily the life of the lease (given that the lease is capitalized or a result of a bargain purchase option). Answer (D) is incorrect because the lessee does not capitalize the asset at the cost to the lessor.

4.8 Other Assets

172. The primary audit objectives for other assets include all of the following except to

A. Determine that the asset is written off on a periodic basis.

B. Become satisfied that the asset does in fact exist.

C. Determine the basis of the carrying amount of the asset.

D. Determine whether the asset is fairly presented in the financial statements.

The correct answer is (A). *(Publisher)*

REQUIRED: The item not considered an audit objective for other assets.

DISCUSSION: The auditor should be concerned that each asset is presented fairly in accordance with GAAP. If GAAP require periodic allocation of costs, determining that the asset is written off on a periodic basis is an appropriate audit objective. However, for nondepreciable assets, e.g., land, verification of the write-off is not an audit objective.

Answers (B), (C), and (D) are incorrect because becoming satisfied that the asset does in fact exist, determining the basis of the carrying amount of the asset, and determining whether the asset is fairly presented in the financial statements are appropriate audit objectives for other assets.

173. A client has a large and active investment portfolio that is kept in a bank safe-deposit box. If the auditor is unable to count the securities at the balance sheet date, the auditor most likely will

A. Request the bank to confirm to the auditor the contents of the safe-deposit box at the balance sheet date.

B. Examine supporting evidence for transactions occurring during the year.

C. Count the securities at a subsequent date and confirm with the bank whether securities were added or removed since the balance sheet date.

D. Request the client to have the bank seal the safe-deposit box until the auditor can count the securities at a subsequent date.

The correct answer is (D). *(CPA, adapted)*

REQUIRED: The procedure most likely performed if the auditor cannot count securities at the balance sheet date.

DISCUSSION: Securities should be inspected simultaneously with the verification of cash and the count of other liquid assets to prevent transfers among asset categories for the purpose of concealing a shortage. If this procedure is not possible but the securities are kept by a custodian in a bank safe-deposit box, the client may instruct the custodian that no one is to have access to the securities unless in the presence of the auditor. Thus, when the auditor finally inspects the securities, (s)he may conclude that they represent what was on hand at the balance sheet date.

Answers (A) and (C) are incorrect because the bank does not have access to the contents of the client's safe-deposit box. Answer (B) is incorrect because supporting evidence for transactions occurring during the year is not a substitute for inspection of the securities.

174. Which of the following is not one of the auditor's primary objectives in an audit of trading securities?

A. To determine whether securities are authentic.

B. To determine whether securities are the property of the client.

C. To determine whether securities actually exist.

D. To determine whether securities are properly classified on the balance sheet.

The correct answer is (A). *(CPA, adapted)*

REQUIRED: The item that is not one of the auditor's primary objectives in examining trading securities.

DISCUSSION: The objectives of the audit of trading securities are to determine whether (1) the controls relevant to the securities and the revenue therefrom are effective, (2) the securities actually exist and are owned by the client, (3) all transactions and accounts that should be presented are included in the financial statements, (4) the securities are properly accounted for in conformity with GAAP, and (5) their balance sheet classification is accurate. The auditor is not expected, however, to have the expertise to evaluate the authenticity of securities. If forgery is suspected, (s)he should engage a specialist.

Answers (B), (C), and (D) are incorrect because primary objectives of the audit of trading securities are to determine whether they are the property of the client (rights and obligations assertion), whether they exist (existence assertion), and whether they are properly classified on the balance sheet (presentation and disclosure assertion).

175. Ann Melton, CPA, observes the count of securities on December 31. She records the serial numbers of the securities and reconciles them and the number of shares with company records. Which fraud should be detected by this procedure?

A. An investee company declared and paid a stock dividend on December 15. The stock certificate for the additional shares was received directly by the treasurer who made no record of the receipt and embezzled the shares.

B. The treasurer embezzled and sold securities on April 4. She speculated successfully with the proceeds and replaced the securities on December 29.

C. The treasurer borrowed securities on July 15 to use as collateral for a personal loan. He repaid the loan and returned the securities on December 2.

D. The treasurer embezzled interest receipts from bonds by having the payments mailed directly to him.

The correct answer is (B). *(Publisher)*

REQUIRED: The fraud likely to be detected by reconciling the serial numbers of securities and the number of shares with company records.

DISCUSSION: The auditor would be most likely to discover that the company's securities had been misappropriated and then later replaced by using this procedure. The company records would indicate securities with serial numbers different from those counted by the auditor.

Answer (A) is incorrect because information concerning stock splits, stock dividends, and cash dividends from publications such as the *Wall Street Journal* or other similar sources would have to be consulted to determine the client's holdings. Answer (C) is incorrect because a surprise interim count or joint control of securities would be necessary to detect or prevent the temporary misappropriation of the securities. Answer (D) is incorrect because tests of interest income accounts, not serial numbers of securities, would show whether interest had been misappropriated.

176. Which of the following statements regarding the audit of negotiable notes receivable is not correct?

A. Confirmation from the debtor is an acceptable alternative to inspection.

B. Materiality of the amount involved is a factor considered when selecting the accounts to be confirmed.

C. Physical inspection of a note by the auditor does not provide conclusive evidence.

D. Notes receivable discounted with recourse need to be confirmed.

The correct answer is (A). *(CPA, adapted)*

REQUIRED: The false statement about the audit of negotiable notes receivable.

DISCUSSION: While notes receivable should be confirmed, negotiable notes are akin to stocks and bonds in that they must also be inspected to determine whether the client has custody. Confirmation also does not establish collectibility. For this purpose, the auditor should examine cash receipts records to determine promptness of interest and principal payments.

Answer (B) is incorrect because the auditor should usually attempt to confirm a substantial amount of the dollar value of receivables. Answer (C) is incorrect because inspection by auditors may not detect forgery or establish ownership. Answer (D) is incorrect because receivables discounted with recourse should be confirmed. Those discounted without recourse need not be because the client then has no contingent liability.

177. Which of the following is the least effective audit procedure regarding the existence assertion for the securities held by the auditee?

A. Examination of paid checks issued in payment of securities purchased.

B. Vouching all changes during the year to supporting documents.

C. Simultaneous count of liquid assets.

D. Confirmation from the custodian.

The correct answer is (A). *(Publisher)*

REQUIRED: The audit procedure giving the least assurance of the existence of securities.

DISCUSSION: Paid checks issued in payment for securities do not assure that the investments are in existence and still owned by the client at the balance sheet date.

Answer (B) is incorrect because vouching changes in the account to supporting documents provides evidence of both purchases and sales. Answer (C) is incorrect because a simultaneous count of securities, cash, and other liquid assets is the ideal way to verify the investment balance. Answer (D) is incorrect because a confirmation request sent by the auditor directly to a bank, broker, or other holder is a means of independently identifying which securities are in existence and owned by the client.

178. A company makes a practice of investing excess short-term cash in trading securities that are traded regularly on national exchanges. A reliable test of the valuation of those securities is

A. Consideration of current market quotations.

B. Confirmation of securities held by the broker.

C. Recalculation of investment value using a valuation model.

D. Calculation of premium or discount amortization.

The correct answer is (A). *(CIA, adapted)*

REQUIRED: The reliable test of the valuation of trading securities.

DISCUSSION: The objectives of the audit of securities are to determine whether (1) the controls relevant to securities and revenue therefrom are adequate, (2) the securities exist and are owned by the auditee, (3) all transactions and accounts that should be presented are included in the financial statements, (4) the balance sheet classification of securities is appropriate, and (5) they are properly accounted for in conformity with GAAP. Trading and available-for-sale securities should be measured on the statement of financial position at fair value. If market quotations are based on sufficient market activity, they usually provide sufficient competent evidence regarding valuation (AU 332, *Auditing Investments*).

Answer (B) is incorrect because, although confirmation of securities held by the broker addresses the existence and rights and obligations assertions, it does not determine the valuation of the securities. Answer (C) is incorrect because valuation models may be used for certain securities when no quoted market prices exist. In that case, the auditor should assess the reasonableness and appropriateness of the model. Answer (D) is incorrect because any discount or premium on trading securities is not amortized.

179. An auditee is holding equity securities as collateral for a debt. The auditor should

A. Determine from data published in the financial press that the auditee has recorded dividend income from the collateral.

B. Ascertain the value of the securities.

C. Ascertain that the amount recorded for the collateral in the investment account is equal to its fair value at the balance sheet date.

D. Verify that the client has taken title to the securities.

The correct answer is (B). *(Publisher)*

REQUIRED: The proper audit procedure for securities held as collateral.

DISCUSSION: A client may hold an asset of another company as security for an outstanding debt. If the asset is important for evaluating the fair value and collectibility of the investment (the debt), the auditor should obtain evidence about the client's rights and the existence, fair value, and transferability of the collateral. Current market quotations from financial publications or from national exchanges and NASDAQ usually provide sufficient evidence of the value of regularly traded securities.

Answer (A) is incorrect because the client (creditor) has no dividend income from the collateral. The debtor still owns the securities and earns the income, although the client may apply cash dividends to reduce the debt. Answer (C) is incorrect because the collateral is not recorded as a client investment until the debtor defaults and the client obtains title. Answer (D) is incorrect because the client will take title from the debtor only if the debt is not paid.

180. Which of the following is the most effective audit procedure for verification of dividends earned on investments in equity securities?

A. Tracing deposited dividend checks to the cash receipts book.

B. Reconciling amounts received with published dividend records.

C. Comparing the amounts received with preceding year dividends received.

D. Recomputing selected extensions and footings of dividend schedules and comparing totals to the general ledger.

The correct answer is (B). *(CPA, adapted)*

REQUIRED: The most effective audit procedure for verification of dividends earned.

DISCUSSION: Standard investment advisory services publish dividend records for all listed stocks. They show amounts and payment dates for dividend declarations and permit the auditor to independently recompute the client's reported dividend income.

Answer (A) is incorrect because tracing deposited checks does not test whether all checks were deposited. Answer (C) is incorrect because dividends may vary from period to period. Answer (D) is incorrect because recomputation tests the arithmetic accuracy of the records, not their validity.

181. In establishing the existence and ownership of an investment held by a corporation in the form of publicly traded stock, an auditor should inspect the securities or

A. Obtain written representations from management confirming that the securities are properly classified as trading securities.

B. Inspect the audited financial statements of the investee company.

C. Confirm the number of shares owned that are held by an independent custodian.

D. Determine that the investment is carried at the lower of cost or market.

The correct answer is (C). *(CPA, adapted)*

REQUIRED: The procedure to establish the existence and ownership of an investment in stock.

DISCUSSION: To test the existence assertion and the rights and obligations (ownership) assertion, the auditor should perform one or more of the following procedures, depending on the nature of the investments and the assessment of audit risk: inspection; confirmation with the issuer, custodian, or counterparty; confirmation of unsettled transactions with the broker-dealer; or reading partnership or similar agreements (AU 332). Thus, brokers, banks, agents, or others holding securities for the client should be requested by the client to respond directly to the auditor's confirmation requests.

Answer (A) is incorrect because the classification of securities relates to the presentation and disclosure assertion. Furthermore, equity securities held for long-term investment purposes are classified as available-for-sale, not trading. Answer (B) is incorrect because an investment accounted for using the equity method might require the auditor to inspect audited financial statements of the investee to test the assertion about valuation. Answer (D) is incorrect because determining the carrying value does not test the existence and rights and obligations assertions. Furthermore, equity securities with readily determinable fair values accounted for under SFAS 115, *Accounting for Certain Investments in Debt and Equity Securities*, are recorded at fair value.

182. Apex Incorporated issued common stock to acquire another company in an acquisition that was accounted for as a pooling of interests. The auditor examining this transaction would be least interested in ascertaining

A. The net book value of the acquired company.

B. The par value of the stock that was issued.

C. Whether the acquisition was approved by the board of directors of Apex Incorporated.

D. Whether the fair value of the acquired assets was independently appraised.

The correct answer is (D). *(CPA, adapted)*

REQUIRED: The information regarding a pooling of least concern to an auditor.

DISCUSSION: In a pooling of interests, assets and liabilities are recorded at their carrying (book) values. An independent appraisal of the fair values of the assets is of greater interest in a transaction accounted for by the purchase method (APB 16, *Business Combinations*).

Answer (A) is incorrect because the net book value of the acquired company is of interest in a pooling. Assets and liabilities are recorded at their carrying (book) values. Answer (B) is incorrect because the shareholders' equities of the companies are combined in a pooling. However, the capital stock of the surviving entity must equal the par or stated value of outstanding shares following the combination. Thus, an adjustment to the combined other contributed capital and retained earnings accounts may be needed. Answer (C) is incorrect because the auditor should verify that the transaction was properly authorized.

183. In connection with an audit of the prepaid insurance account, which of the following procedures is usually not performed by the auditor?

A. Recompute the portion of the premium that expired during the year.

B. Prepare excerpts of insurance policies for audit working papers.

C. Confirm premium rates with an independent insurance broker.

D. Examine support for premium payments.

The correct answer is (C). *(CPA, adapted)*

REQUIRED: The procedure not usually performed when auditing prepaid insurance.

DISCUSSION: The objectives of the audit of prepayments include determining that amounts shown reflect all prepayments, are properly valued according to GAAP, apply to future periods, are expected to be realized (to provide future benefits), and are accurately classified. Ascertaining that a prepayment is properly valued involves verifying the amount of the expenditure by examining invoices from insurers, canceled checks, and the insurance policy. But the auditor does not usually confirm premium rates with an independent insurance broker. Paid checks and other documents are sufficient evidence of the amounts paid.

Answers (A), (B), and (D) are incorrect because recomputing the portion of the premium that expired during the year, preparing excerpts of insurance policies for audit working papers, and examining support for premium payments are appropriate procedures.

184. When auditing prepaid insurance, an auditor discovers that the original insurance policy on plant equipment is not available for inspection. The policy's absence most likely indicates the possibility of a(n)

A. Insurance premium due but not recorded.

B. Deficiency in the coinsurance provision.

C. Lien on the plant equipment.

D. Understatement of insurance expense.

The correct answer is (C). *(CPA, adapted)*

REQUIRED: The likely reason an insurance policy is not available for inspection.

DISCUSSION: When liens are placed on equipment or property, the lienholder often requires that the assets be insured and that the lienholder be named as the beneficiary of the insurance. Hence, the policy would likely be held by the lienholder even though the client is required to pay the premiums.

Answer (A) is incorrect because the premium has been paid and recorded as prepaid insurance. Answer (B) is incorrect because coinsurance provisions require that the policy holder maintain coverage of a certain percentage of the value of the property (often 80-90%). Answer (D) is incorrect because the issue is not the recording of insurance, but the physical existence of the policy.

185. An auditor is most likely to verify the interest earned on bond investments by

A. Verifying the receipt and deposit of interest checks.

B. Confirming the bond interest rate with the issuer of the bonds.

C. Recomputing the interest earned on the basis of face amount, interest rate, and period held.

D. Testing controls relevant to cash receipts.

The correct answer is (C). *(CPA, adapted)*

REQUIRED: The method most likely used to verify bond interest earned.

DISCUSSION: The audit program for investments includes making an independent computation of revenue (such as dividends and interest). For example, bond certificates contain information about interest rates, payment dates, issue date, and face amount that the auditor can use to recalculâte bond interest earned, including amounts accrued but not collected, during the period the auditee has held the investment.

Answer (A) is incorrect because verifying the receipt and deposit of interest checks does not consider accrued interest. Answer (B) is incorrect because confirming the bond interest rate does not, by itself, verify interest earned; the interest earned must be recomputed. Answer (D) is incorrect because verification of interest earned requires substantive testing, not tests of controls.

186. Which of the following provides the best form of evidence pertaining to the annual valuation of an investment in which the independent auditor's client owns a 30% voting interest?

A. Market quotations of the investee company's stock.

B. Current fair value of the investee company's assets.

C. Historical cost of the investee company's assets.

D. Audited financial statements of the investee company.

The correct answer is (D). *(CPA, adapted)*

REQUIRED: The best evidence for valuation of a 30% voting interest.

DISCUSSION: Because a 30% voting interest creates a presumption that the investor is able to exercise significant influence over the investee, the equity method of accounting for the investment must be used. This method requires the investor to recognize the appropriate percentage of the investee's earnings as a debit to the investment and a credit to income. Dividends reduce the investment. Audited financial statements of the investee are usually sufficient evidence regarding the investor's equity.

Answer (A) is incorrect because market quotations may provide sufficient evidence regarding the fair value of the securities but not the equity in net assets and results of operations of the investee. Answer (B) is incorrect because the relevant valuation is of the equity in net assets and results of operations. Answer (C) is incorrect because an equity method investment is not carried at historical cost.

187. The auditor, in determining whether the client has adopted the appropriate accounting method for an investment in the voting stock of an investee, should obtain evidence primarily by

A. Inquiries to the client as to whether the client can exercise significant influence over the investee.

B. Direct confirmation with the investee concerning the control or influence that can be exercised by the client.

C. Comparison of the number of shares held by the investor with the investee's number of shares outstanding according to the written confirmation.

D. An independent, third party's opinion concerning the potential influence or control that can be exercised by the client over the investee.

The correct answer is (A). *(Publisher)*

REQUIRED: The procedure to be used in assessing whether the client has properly accounted for investments.

DISCUSSION: The auditor should inquire of the investor's management concerning the client's ability to exercise significant influence over the investee (APB 18, *Equity Method for Investments in Common Stock*). The auditor should also inquire as to the circumstances serving as a basis for management's conclusions. The investment should be accounted for under the equity method rather than the fair value method if the investor can exercise significant influence. Such influence is rebuttably presumed if the investor holds 20% or more of the voting stock.

Answer (B) is incorrect because inquiry should be made of the client. The investee might not want to disclose that the client has such influence. Answer (C) is incorrect because significant influence may depend more upon the diversity of ownership of the investee than the number of shares held by the client. Answer (D) is incorrect because the auditor normally considers management's responses to inquiries in conjunction with the attendant circumstances as a basis for the conclusion.

188. A corporate balance sheet indicates that one of the corporate assets is a patent. An auditor will most likely obtain evidence regarding the continuing validity and existence of this patent by obtaining a written representation from

A. A patent attorney.

B. A regional state patent office.

C. The patent inventor.

D. The patent owner.

The correct answer is (A). *(CPA, adapted)*

REQUIRED: The appropriate source of evidence of the validity and existence of a patent.

DISCUSSION: A patent is an intangible asset representing a governmental grant of rights to an invention for a specified time. Its lack of physical substance makes it hard to verify its existence and ownership. To obtain evidence regarding the continuing validity and existence of a patent, the auditor should obtain a written representation from a patent attorney, an independent specialist who has expertise not normally possessed by auditors. The attorney can perform the necessary research and express an opinion on which the auditor may reasonably rely.

Answer (B) is incorrect because patents are obtained from the Patent and Trademark Office of the Department of Commerce. Answer (C) is incorrect because the inventor may have no current knowledge of the status of the patent. Answer (D) is incorrect because the owner is usually the client. The auditor needs independent evidence to corroborate client representations.

189. Deferred charges, such as issue cost of debt or cost of factory rearrangement, should usually be

A. Disallowed by the auditor.

B. Reported on the balance sheet as a noncurrent asset.

C. Written off immediately as a current operating expense.

D. Converted to deferred credits by periodic transactions.

The correct answer is (B). *(Publisher)*

REQUIRED: The proper disposition of deferred charges.

DISCUSSION: Deferred charges that are allocable to the operations of several years should be classified separately as noncurrent assets. The auditor's objective in examining deferred charges is to determine that they are proper charges to future operations and that their amounts and allocation are reported fairly in accordance with GAAP.

Answer (A) is incorrect because deferred charges established in accordance with GAAP are proper assets and may be presented in the balance sheet. Answer (C) is incorrect because deferred charges are assets. They provide probable future economic benefits controllable by the entity that arise from past transactions or events. Answer (D) is incorrect because deferred charges cannot be converted into deferred credits.

190. In verifying the amount of goodwill recorded by a client, the most convincing evidence an auditor can obtain is by comparing the recorded value of assets acquired with the

A. Assessed value as evidenced by tax bills.

B. Seller's book value as evidenced by financial statements.

C. Insured value as evidenced by insurance policies.

D. Appraised value as evidenced by independent appraisals.

The correct answer is (D). *(CPA, adapted)*

REQUIRED: The most convincing evidence concerning goodwill recorded by a client.

DISCUSSION: Goodwill is recorded in a business combination accounted for as a purchase when the price paid for the identifiable net assets of the acquired company exceeds the sum of their fair values (APB 16). If the carrying amount of an investment reflects (1) factors, such as goodwill, not recognized by the investee or (2) fair values materially different from the investee's carrying amounts, the auditor should consider obtaining current evaluations of these amounts. Evaluations by persons independent of the investor and investee usually provide greater assurance of reliability than those by persons associated with those companies, although evaluations by such parties may be acceptable.

Answer (A) is incorrect because a tax bill is an assessment on physical asset value only, not on the entity's going concern value. Answer (B) is incorrect because the seller's financial statements reflect the historical cost to the acquired company, not current fair value. Answer (C) is incorrect because the client may not even have insured the full value of the physical assets, much less the presumably greater going concern value of the business.

191. The auditor can best verify a client's bond sinking-fund transactions and year-end balance by

A. Confirmation with individual holders of retired bonds.

B. Confirmation with the bond trustee.

C. Recomputation of interest expense, interest payable, and amortization of bond discount or premium.

D. Examination and count of the bonds retired during the year.

The correct answer is (B). *(CPA, adapted)*

REQUIRED: The best way to verify a client's bond sinking-fund transactions.

DISCUSSION: The bond trustee is an outside, independent agent responsible for maintaining subsidiary ledgers and paying dividends. (S)he also often keeps the sinking-fund accounts. Consequently, the auditor should verify bond sinking-fund transactions with this trustee.

Answer (A) is incorrect because confirmation with individual holders of retired bonds provides some evidence relative to the retirement process, but not of the balance in the sinking fund or of the transactions during the year. Answer (C) is incorrect because it is only part of the overall procedure of which trustee confirmation is the most important step. Answer (D) is incorrect because examination and count of the bonds retired during the year provides some evidence relative to the retirement process, but not of the balance in the sinking fund or of the transactions during the year.

192. The best audit procedure for determining the existence of open commodity futures contracts at year-end is the review of

A. Canceled checks in the subsequent period.

B. Available broker trade advices.

C. The replies to the standard confirmation requests sent to financial institutions.

D. Direct confirmations with the client's commodity traders.

The correct answer is (D). *(CPA, adapted)*

REQUIRED: The best audit procedure for determining the existence of open commodity futures contracts.

DISCUSSION: Direct confirmation with the client's commodity traders provides independent verification of open commodity futures contracts and may reveal undisclosed liabilities.

Answer (A) is incorrect because payment for futures would have been made when the contract was made. Answer (B) is incorrect because the auditor is concerned that obligations be fairly represented. It is possible to lose or destroy trade advices. Answer (C) is incorrect because the standard form inquires specifically about deposit balances and direct liabilities to the financial institution. The client's bank or other financial institution would not likely have information relative to open commodity futures contracts. The client's broker is the independent party with first-hand knowledge.

4.9 Long-Term Debt and Other Liabilities

193. An auditor's program to audit long-term debt should include steps that require

A. Examining bond trust indentures.

B. Inspecting the accounts payable subsidiary ledger.

C. Investigating credits to the bond interest income account.

D. Verifying the existence of the bondholders.

The correct answer is (A). *(CPA, adapted)*

REQUIRED: The procedure to be included in the audit program for long-term debt.

DISCUSSION: The bond trust indenture contains information concerning contractual arrangements made with bondholders, such as the face amount of the bonds, interest rates, payment dates, descriptions of collateral, provisions for conversion or retirement, trustee duties, and sinking-fund requirements. The auditor should examine any bond trust indenture to determine that the client is complying with its terms and with the law.

Answer (B) is incorrect because accounts payable are current liabilities, not long-term debt. Answer (C) is incorrect because credits to bond interest income do not pertain to long-term debt (income relates to investments, not debt). Answer (D) is incorrect because the existence of bondholders is implied by the reporting of bonded debt.

194. In an audit of bonds payable, an auditor expects the trust indenture to include the

A. Auditee's debt-to-equity ratio at the time of issuance.

B. Effective yield of the bonds issued.

C. Subscription list.

D. Description of the collateral.

The correct answer is (D). *(Publisher)*

REQUIRED: The information in a bond trust indenture.

DISCUSSION: A bond trust indenture is the contractual agreement between the bondholders and the bond issuer. It contains the date of issue and the date of maturity of the bond issue as well as the amount of the bonds, interest rates, payment dates, descriptions of collateral, provisions for conversion or retirement, trustee duties, sinking-fund requirements, and restrictions on the borrower.

Answer (A) is incorrect because current financial ratios are usually not included, but restrictive ratios may be; e.g., the debt-to-equity ratio might not be permitted to exceed 2 to 1. Answer (B) is incorrect because the effective yield to maturity of the bonds issued may be calculated from the premium or discount and the stated interest rate, but is not included in the trust indenture. Answer (C) is incorrect because the subscriptions list contains the names of the original subscribers, but these names are not normally included in the trust indenture.

195. During an audit of a publicly held company, the auditor should obtain written confirmation regarding debenture transactions from the

A. Debenture holders.

B. Client's attorney.

C. Internal auditors.

D. Trustee.

The correct answer is (D). *(CPA, adapted)*

REQUIRED: The source of confirmation of debenture transactions.

DISCUSSION: Debentures are bonds backed by the general credit of the issuer and not secured by specific assets. A bond issuer normally employs the services of an independent financial institution as trustee. The bond trustee is responsible for executing bond transactions, e.g., distributing or paying interest, and protecting the interests of bondholders. Accordingly, the auditor should confirm transactions with the trustee.

Answer (A) is incorrect because direct communication with bondholders is unnecessary when a trustee is used. Answer (B) is incorrect because the client's attorney does not have the information necessary to furnish independent evidence regarding bond transactions. Answer (C) is incorrect because internal auditors are not knowledgeable about bond transaction details or independent.

196. With respect to bonds issued during the period under audit, the independent external auditor should

A. Inspect the records maintained by the bond trustee.

B. Determine that the net cash received equaled the face amount of the bonds payable.

C. Determine that the amount sold does not exceed the amount authorized.

D. Confirm the existence of the bondholders.

The correct answer is (C). *(Publisher)*

REQUIRED: The proper audit procedure for a new issue of bonds.

DISCUSSION: Bonds issued during the year under audit should be traced to the minutes of the shareholders' or board of directors' meetings to check for proper authorization. The amount sold should be no greater than the amount authorized in the minutes.

Answer (A) is incorrect because an auditor usually can rely on the confirmation of information with the bond trustee (who is usually an independent third party). Answer (B) is incorrect because the credit to the bonds payable account should be for the face value of the bonds. The debit to cash will not ordinarily equal face value because bonds are usually issued at a premium or a discount. Answer (D) is incorrect because bondholder rights exist on the basis of the sale of bonds; a liability for interest and principal exists irrespective of who and where the bondholders are.

197. With respect to bonds issued during the period under audit, the auditor should

A. Review proper presentation and disclosure in the financial statements.

B. Consider whether the bond issue complied with applicable laws and regulations.

C. Calculate the effective interest rate to see if it is substantially the same as the rates for similar issues.

D. Determine that bonds are not owned by directors or officers of the company.

The correct answer is (A). *(Publisher)*

REQUIRED: The audit procedure relevant to the audit of bonds payable currently being issued.

DISCUSSION: The objectives of the audit of long-term debt are to obtain an understanding of the relevant controls and to assess control risk; ascertain that all long-term debt has been recorded and constitutes bona fide liabilities; verify that federal and state laws relative to financial reporting have been complied with; determine that premium, discount, interest payable, and interest expense are accurately recorded; monitor compliance with debt contracts; and review proper presentation and disclosure in the financial statements.

Answer (B) is incorrect because the opinion of counsel on the legality of the issue should address these matters. Answer (C) is incorrect because the effective interest rate for similar issues changes with the overall interest rate. Answer (D) is incorrect because directors or officers of a company may invest in company bonds.

198. During the year under audit, a company has completed a private placement of a substantial amount of bonds. Which of the following is the most important step in the auditor's program for the audit of bonds payable?

A. Confirming the amount issued with the bond trustee.

B. Tracing the cash received from the issue to the accounting records.

C. Examining the bond records maintained by the transfer agent.

D. Recomputing the annual interest cost and the effective yield.

The correct answer is (B). *(CPA, adapted)*

REQUIRED: The most important step in auditing a private placement of bonds.

DISCUSSION: In a private placement of bonds, one not involving the use of an independent trustee, the auditor is most concerned that the cash received from the issue is accurately recorded. The auditor is also concerned that the cash is adequately safeguarded by the treasurer's department. Failure to employ a trustee substantially increases control risk for all aspects of bond issues.

Answer (A) is incorrect because a bond trustee is not apt to be used by the issuer if bonds are privately placed. Answer (C) is incorrect because a transfer agent is not apt to be used by the issuer if bonds are privately placed. Answer (D) is incorrect because the mathematical check of the accuracy of the annual interest cost and the effective yield is not as important as the auditor's verification that cash received is properly accounted for.

199. During an audit, Wicks learns that the audit client was granted a 3-month waiver of the repayment of principal on the installment loan with Blank Bank without an extension of the maturity date. With respect to this loan, the audit program used by Wicks is least likely to include a verification of the

A. Interest expense for the year.

B. Balloon payment.

C. Total liability at year-end.

D. Installment loan payments.

The correct answer is (B). *(CPA, adapted)*

REQUIRED: The item least likely to be verified in the audit of an installment loan.

DISCUSSION: The auditor's primary concern is that the liability is reported correctly in the financial statements. The amount of the balloon payment falling due in a future period as a result of the waiver is of less importance.

Answer (A) is incorrect because the auditor should verify interest expense to determine that it is recorded properly and determine the applicability of SFAS 15, *Accounting by Debtors and Creditors for Troubled Debt Restructurings*. Answer (C) is incorrect because becoming satisfied as to the total liability at year-end is a primary objective of the auditor. Answer (D) is incorrect because the amount of installment loan payments determines the amount of the current liability at year-end.

200. An auditor's purpose in reviewing the renewal of a note payable shortly after the balance sheet date most likely is to obtain evidence concerning management's assertions about

A. Existence or occurrence.

B. Presentation and disclosure.

C. Completeness.

D. Valuation or allocation.

The correct answer is (B). *(CPA, adapted)*

REQUIRED: The purpose in reviewing the renewal of a note payable shortly after the balance sheet date.

DISCUSSION: The auditor should be aware of transactions occurring shortly after year-end to determine the impact on the year-end balances and disclosures. Subsequent events provide information about conditions that did or did not exist at the balance sheet date. Events of the second type, such as the renewal of the note payable, do not require adjustment of the financial statements but may require disclosure (AU 560, *Subsequent Events*). Accordingly, the auditor should determine that the note payable renewal had essentially the same terms and conditions as the recorded debt at year-end. A significant change may affect the presentation of notes payable, the interpretation of the year-end financial statements, and the required disclosures in the notes.

Answers (A), (C), and (D) are incorrect because the renewal does not significantly affect the other noted assertions about existence or occurrence, completeness, and valuation or allocation.

201. Several years ago Conway, Inc. secured a conventional real estate mortgage loan. Which of the following audit procedures is least likely to be performed by an auditor auditing the mortgage balance?

A. Examine the current year's canceled checks.

B. Review the mortgage amortization schedule.

C. Inspect public records of lien balances.

D. Recompute mortgage interest expense.

The correct answer is (C). *(CPA, adapted)*

REQUIRED: The audit procedure least likely to be performed regarding a mortgage loan.

DISCUSSION: Public real estate records would not disclose the current balance. They only disclose the original amount of the mortgage. Other evidence is normally available, such as receipts for payments to the mortgagee, confirmations with payees, etc.

Answer (A) is incorrect because canceled checks represent the decrease in the mortgage balance and should be inspected by the auditor. Answer (B) is incorrect because the mortgage amortization schedule is evidence of the amount that should have been paid during the period as well as the principal balance at year-end. Answer (D) is incorrect because the recomputation of interest expense and interest payable is an important means of verifying the amount of outstanding liabilities.

202. In auditing long-term bonds payable, an auditor most likely will

A. Perform analytical procedures on the bond premium and discount accounts.

B. Examine documentation of assets purchased with bond proceeds for liens.

C. Compare interest expense with the bond payable amount for reasonableness.

D. Confirm the existence of individual bondholders at year-end.

The correct answer is (C). *(CPA, adapted)*

REQUIRED: The appropriate procedure for testing long-term bonds payable.

DISCUSSION: The recorded interest expense should reconcile with the outstanding bonds payable. If interest expense appears excessive relative to the recorded bonds payable, unrecorded liabilities may exist.

Answer (A) is incorrect because analytical procedures on the bond premium and discount accounts are not likely to be effective in uncovering potential unrecorded payables. Answer (B) is incorrect because the examination of documentation related to assets is considered in the audit of assets, not bonds payable. Answer (D) is incorrect because a confirmation tests existence, but the greatest audit risk is that the bonds payable balance is not complete.

203. The audit procedures used to verify accrued liabilities differ from those employed for the verification of accounts payable because

A. Accrued liabilities usually pertain to services of a continuing nature while accounts payable are the result of completed transactions.

B. Accrued liability balances are less material than accounts payable balances.

C. Evidence supporting accrued liabilities is nonexistent while evidence supporting accounts payable is readily available.

D. Accrued liabilities at year-end will become accounts payable during the following year.

The correct answer is (A). *(CPA, adapted)*

REQUIRED: The difference between audit procedures used to verify accrued liabilities and those used to verify accounts payable.

DISCUSSION: The procedures differ because the balances result from different transactional processes. Liabilities are accrued for such continuing transactions as rent, salaries, and interest. Accounts payable are short-term obligations arising from the purchase of goods and services in the ordinary course of business.

Answer (B) is incorrect because one balance is not inherently more or less material than the other. Answer (C) is incorrect because supporting documentary evidence exists for both. Answer (D) is incorrect because once accrued liabilities become accounts payable (not necessarily at year-end), the audit procedures do not differ.

204. The auditor is most likely to verify accrued commissions payable in conjunction with the

A. Sales cutoff test.

B. Verification of contingent liabilities.

C. Review of post balance sheet date disbursements.

D. Examination of trade accounts payable.

The correct answer is (A). *(CPA, adapted)*

REQUIRED: The audit step performed concurrently with verifying accrued commissions payable.

DISCUSSION: Sales commissions and accrued sales commissions payable are based upon sales of the period. The auditor verifies accrued commissions payable in conjunction with procedures applied to the sales cutoff test. The purpose is to obtain reasonable assurance that revenues and related liabilities are recorded in the same period in accordance with the matching principle.

Answer (B) is incorrect because the auditor would review the minutes of board meetings, send an inquiry letter to the client's legal counsel, send bank confirmations, obtain a representation letter from the client, and review correspondence with financial institutions to verify or detect contingent liabilities. Answer (C) is incorrect because the review of disbursements in the subsequent period is performed to detect unrecorded liabilities. Answer (D) is incorrect because the examination of trade accounts payable is performed in conjunction with the audit of inventories, purchases, and cash disbursements.

205. SFAS 5, *Accounting for Contingencies*, defines a loss contingency and states the requirements for recognition as a charge to income and a credit to an accrued liability. An accrual could not be made as a result of

A. Guarantees of indebtedness incurred by others.

B. Repurchase commitments.

C. Pending litigation or threats of expropriation.

D. General business risks.

The correct answer is (D). *(Publisher)*

REQUIRED: The impermissible basis for accruing a contingent liability and recognizing a loss.

DISCUSSION: General business risks do not provide a possible basis for accrual of a contingent liability because "not all uncertainties inherent in the accounting process give rise to contingencies" (SFAS 5). General or unspecified business risks cannot meet the conditions for accrual: the loss is probable at the balance sheet date, and it can be reasonably estimated.

Answer (A) is incorrect because guarantees of indebtedness incurred by others are listed in SFAS 5 as loss contingencies. Answer (B) is incorrect because repurchase commitments are listed in SFAS 5 as loss contingencies. Answer (C) is incorrect because pending litigation or threats of expropriation are listed in SFAS 5 as loss contingencies.

206. In an audit for the fiscal year ended on December 31, 1998, the auditor discovered that a debit had been made on January 15, 1999, to a notes receivable account from the cash disbursements journal. This entry may indicate that a

A. Receivable has been established from a party for whom the client has guaranteed a debt.

B. Provision for contingencies is required.

C. Contingent liability was created in 1999.

D. Contingent asset has been recognized.

The correct answer is (A). *(Publisher)*

REQUIRED: The implication of a debit made to notes receivable and a credit made to cash.

DISCUSSION: The entry suggests that a contingent liability has become a real liability and has been settled. The payment of the debt upon default of the party would be recognized in the accounts by a debit to notes receivable and a credit to cash.

Answer (B) is incorrect because no provision for contingencies is needed if the liability has been paid. Answer (C) is incorrect because the entry suggests that a contingent liability became an actual liability and has been paid. Answer (D) is incorrect because contingent assets are never recognized in the accounts until realized. Contingent liabilities are recognized when they are probable and they are subject to reasonable estimation.

4.10 Owners' Equity

207. In an examination of shareholders' equity, an auditor is most concerned that

A. Capital stock transactions are properly authorized.

B. Stock splits are capitalized at par or stated value on the dividend declaration date.

C. Dividends during the year under audit were approved by the shareholders.

D. Changes in the accounts are verified by a bank serving as a registrar and stock transfer agent.

The correct answer is (A). *(Publisher)*

REQUIRED: The most important consideration when examining the owners' equity section.

DISCUSSION: A primary concern of the auditor is that all capital stock transactions are properly authorized. Accordingly, all entries in the capital stock account should be vouched to the minutes of the board of directors' meetings. The articles of incorporation, by-laws, and minutes of shareholders' meetings should also be reviewed. The auditor requires information about the number and rights of shares authorized and issued, the par or stated value, conversion and call features, stock dividends, and stock splits. The auditor also determines whether transactions are properly accounted for and shareholders' equity items are presented in accordance with GAAP.

Answer (B) is incorrect because stock splits require no transfer from retained earnings. Answer (C) is incorrect because the board of directors usually approves dividends. Answer (D) is incorrect because the registrar and transfer agent, who is responsible for increases and exchanges of stock, is not responsible for monitoring all changes in the accounts.

208. In the audit of a medium-sized manufacturing concern, which one of the following areas can be expected to require the least amount of audit time?

A. Owners' equity.

B. Revenue.

C. Assets.

D. Liabilities.

The correct answer is (A). *(CPA, adapted)*

REQUIRED: The area requiring the least audit time for a medium-sized company.

DISCUSSION: Transactions affecting owners' equity are usually few even though they may be significant in amount. Consequently, the audit time required will probably be small compared to that needed for active accounts. Owners' equity will ordinarily be affected only by stock issuance, treasury stock transactions, dividends, and closing entries.

Answers (B), (C), and (D) are incorrect because the auditor will usually spend more time on revenues, assets, and liabilities than on owners' equity.

209. Mayer, CPA, is auditing owners' equity. Tests typically include all the following except

A. Reviewing the bank reconciliation for the imprest dividend account.

B. Tracing individual dividend payments to the capital stock records.

C. Verifying the authorization of dividends by inspecting the directors' minutes.

D. Determining that dividend declarations comply with debt agreements.

The correct answer is (B). *(Publisher)*

REQUIRED: The procedure not normally performed in an audit of owners' equity.

DISCUSSION: An auditor does not normally trace individual dividend payments to the capital stock records. (S)he may test certain large dividend payments but, because the amount of each dividend is usually small, detail checking is minimal. The need for extensive checking is reduced when the client uses an independent financial institution as its agent for dividend payments. The stock transfer agent often performs this function because it maintains detailed records of shareholders.

Answers (A), (C), and (D) are incorrect because determining that dividend declarations comply with debt agreements, verifying the authorization of dividends, and reviewing the bank reconciliation for the imprest dividend account are appropriate auditing procedures.

210. When a corporate client maintains its own stock records, the auditor primarily will rely upon

A. Confirmation with the company secretary of shares outstanding at year-end.

B. Review of the corporate minutes for data as to shares outstanding.

C. Confirmation of the number of shares outstanding at year-end with the appropriate state official.

D. Inspection of the stock book at year-end and accounting for all certificate numbers.

The correct answer is (D). *(Publisher)*

REQUIRED: The appropriate procedure when a company is its own registrar and transfer agent.

DISCUSSION: When an independent registrar and a stock transfer agent are employed by the client, the auditor may simply confirm the shares issued and outstanding at year-end. But when the client acts as its own registrar and transfer agent, the auditor should perform procedures equivalent to independent confirmations. (S)he should account for stock certificate numbers, examine all canceled certificates, and reconcile the subsidiary shareholder ledger with the general ledger.

Answer (A) is incorrect because confirmations are usually sent to independent parties. Answer (B) is incorrect because the minutes indicate the number of shares authorized, not the number outstanding. Answer (C) is incorrect because state officials and officers do not maintain records as to the number of a corporation's outstanding shares.

211. When a client company does not maintain its own stock records, the auditor should obtain written confirmation from the transfer agent and registrar concerning

A. Restrictions on the payment of dividends.

B. The number of shares issued and outstanding.

C. Guarantees of preferred stock liquidation value.

D. The number of shares subject to agreements to repurchase.

The correct answer is (B). *(CPA, adapted)*

REQUIRED: The information confirmed by the transfer agent and registrar.

DISCUSSION: The independent stock registrar is a financial institution employed to prevent improper issuances of stock, especially over-issuances. It verifies that each issue is properly authorized by the articles of incorporation and properly issued by the stock transfer agent. New stock certificates are examined and registered by the registrar before being issued. The stock transfer agent maintains detailed shareholder records and facilitates transfer of shares. Both are independent and reliable sources of evidence concerning total shares issued and outstanding at year-end. The trend has been to combine their functions.

Answer (A) is incorrect because the articles of incorporation, bylaws, and minutes of directors' and shareholders' meetings are potential sources of this information. Answer (C) is incorrect because guarantees of preferred stock liquidation value are beyond the purview of the transfer agent and registrar. Answer (D) is incorrect because the number of shares subject to agreements to repurchase is approved by the board of directors.

212. A company declared and paid a stock dividend. Its independent external auditor should determine that

A. The officers authorized the issuance of the stock dividend.

B. The stock dividend was properly recorded by means of a memorandum entry only.

C. Shareholders received their additional shares by confirming year-end holdings with them.

D. Appropriate amounts were transferred from retained earnings to capital stock and additional paid-in capital.

The correct answer is (D). *(Publisher)*

REQUIRED: The appropriate audit procedure when a company has declared a stock dividend.

DISCUSSION: The auditor should gather evidence that the stock dividend was properly authorized by the board of directors and does not result in the issuance of shares in excess of the number permitted by the articles of incorporation. The auditor must also verify the amounts transferred from retained earnings to capital stock and additional paid-in capital.

Answer (A) is incorrect because usually only the board of directors authorizes stock and cash dividends. Answer (B) is incorrect because large stock dividends (issuances in excess of 20-25% of the shares outstanding) are capitalized at an amount specified by the applicable state statute, which is usually the par value. Small stock dividends are recorded at fair value. Answer (C) is incorrect because the auditor does not usually confirm holdings with shareholders. Instead, the auditor confirms the total shares issued and outstanding with the independent registrar and stock transfer agent.

213. The auditor is concerned with establishing that dividends are paid to client corporation shareholders owning stock as of the

A. Issue date.

B. Declaration date.

C. Record date.

D. Payment date.

The correct answer is (C). *(CPA, adapted)*

REQUIRED: The date that establishes the right to receive a declared dividend.

DISCUSSION: Persons who hold stock in the corporation as of the record date are entitled to payment of the dividend. The auditor should test the dividend payment list to gather evidence that dividends were paid to the appropriate shareholders. The integrity of the dividend payment process is enhanced when an independent agent (usually a financial institution) is used to disburse dividends.

Answer (A) is incorrect because the issue date is the date the stock was issued. Answer (B) is incorrect because the declaration date is the date the company declares the amount of a dividend and specifies the date of record. Answer (D) is incorrect because, on the payment date, the dividends are paid to those shareholders who owned stock as of the record date.

214. The auditor would not expect the client to debit retained earnings for which of the following transactions?

A. A 10% stock dividend.

B. A 60% stock dividend.

C. A 4-for-1 stock split.

D. An appropriation of retained earnings for treasury stock.

The correct answer is (C). *(Publisher)*

REQUIRED: The transaction not requiring a debit to retained earnings.

DISCUSSION: A 4-for-1 stock split results in an increase in the number of shares and a proportionate decrease in the par or stated value per share. No entry is recorded for a stock split. A memo entry, however, is made indicating that the par value has been changed.

Answer (A) is incorrect because a small stock dividend should be capitalized at fair value. Answer (B) is incorrect because a large stock dividend is normally capitalized at par value. Answer (D) is incorrect because crediting appropriations for treasury stock and debiting retained earnings is a necessary entry.

215. An audit program for the retained earnings account should include a step that requires verification of the

A. Fair value used to charge retained earnings to account for a two-for-one stock split.

B. Approval of the adjustment to the beginning balance as a result of a write-down of an account receivable.

C. Authorization for both cash and stock dividends.

D. Gain or loss resulting from disposition of treasury shares.

The correct answer is (C). *(CPA, adapted)*

REQUIRED: The step that should be performed in the audit of retained earnings.

DISCUSSION: The auditor should determine from the minutes of the board of directors' meetings that proper authorization has been made for both cash and stock dividends. All dividends require transfers from (debits to) retained earnings. Thus, dividends should be audited in conjunction with retained earnings.

Answer (A) is incorrect because no change is made in retained earnings for stock splits. Answer (B) is incorrect because a write-down of accounts receivable is taken through the income statement, not directly to retained earnings. Answer (D) is incorrect because only losses on treasury stock transactions can be charged to retained earnings. Gains and some losses are taken to additional paid-in-capital accounts.

216. During an audit of an entity's shareholders' equity accounts, the auditor determines whether there are restrictions on retained earnings resulting from loans, agreements, or state law. This audit procedure most likely is intended to verify management's assertion of

A. Existence or occurrence.

B. Completeness.

C. Valuation or allocation.

D. Presentation and disclosure.

The correct answer is (D). *(CPA, adapted)*

REQUIRED: The assertion that the auditor tests relative to restrictions on retained earnings.

DISCUSSION: The presentation and disclosure assertion concerns the classification, description, and disclosure of financial statement components (AU 326). Hence, when restrictions have been placed on retained earnings, the auditor should determine that they are properly disclosed in the notes to the financial statements.

Answers (A), (B), and (C) are incorrect because restrictions on retained earnings have little relevance to the other assertions.

217. With respect to treasury stock, the auditor should not object to which of the following?

A. Restrictions on retained earnings have not been met.

B. Dividends have been paid on treasury stock.

C. The treasury stock certificates have been destroyed.

D. Treasury stock is recorded at cost rather than par value.

The correct answer is (D). *(Publisher)*

REQUIRED: The appropriate treatment of treasury stock.

DISCUSSION: Treasury stock may be valued at cost or at par value according to GAAP.

Answer (A) is incorrect because certain states restrict retained earnings relative to treasury stock. The auditor should take exception to the failure to comply with the restriction. Answer (B) is incorrect because dividends are only paid on shares issued and outstanding. Answer (C) is incorrect because the auditor should inspect the treasury stock or confirm the stock with the custodian or registrar. Even after retirement, the certificates should be kept to provide evidence that they have not been reissued.

218. If the auditee has a material amount of treasury stock on hand at year-end, the auditor should

A. Count the certificates at the same time other securities are counted.

B. Count the certificates only if the company had treasury stock transactions during the year.

C. Not count the certificates if treasury stock is a deduction from shareholders' equity.

D. Count the certificates only if the company classifies treasury stock with other assets.

The correct answer is (A). *(Publisher)*

REQUIRED: The true statement about the audit of treasury stock.

DISCUSSION: All capital transactions should be verified. Thus, the auditor must count the certificates of treasury stock on hand at year-end at the same time the other securities are counted. This procedure provides direct evidence that the treasury stock exists and is in the possession of the client. Any treasury stock certificates not on hand are confirmed with the holders.

Answers (B) and (C) are incorrect because the auditor should inspect treasury stock certificates at year-end. Answer (D) is incorrect because treasury stock is never classified as an asset.

219. In performing tests concerning the granting of stock options, an auditor should

A. Confirm the transaction with the Secretary of State in the state of incorporation.

B. Verify the existence of option holders in the entity's payroll records or stock ledgers.

C. Determine that sufficient treasury stock is available to cover any new stock issued.

D. Trace the authorization for the transaction to a vote of the board of directors.

The correct answer is (D). *(CPA, adapted)*

REQUIRED: The tests performed by the auditor concerning the granting of stock options.

DISCUSSION: Shareholders' equity transactions, for example, issuances of stock, purchases of treasury stock, declarations of dividends, and the issuance of stock options to employees or others require authorization by the board of directors. Hence, the auditor should inspect minutes of board meetings to verify that stock options were granted.

Answer (A) is incorrect because the Secretary of State is not likely to have knowledge of the granting of stock options within a particular entity. Answer (B) is incorrect because the existence of option holders is not a major risk concerning the audit of stock options. Answer (C) is incorrect because the firm need not hold treasury stock at the time of granting stock options if the shares are publicly traded and can be acquired as needed or if the firm has the ability to issue new shares.

220. In an examination of shareholders' equity, the auditor should determine that the enterprise reports accumulated other comprehensive income in the balance sheet in the

A. Liabilities section.

B. Equity section as a component separate from retained earnings and additional paid-in capital.

C. Retained earnings section.

D. Other assets section.

The correct answer is (B). *(Publisher)*

REQUIRED: The treatment of accumulated other comprehensive income.

DISCUSSION: According to SFAS 130, *Reporting Comprehensive Income*, if an enterprise that reports a full set of financial statements has items of other comprehensive income, it must display comprehensive income and its components in a financial statement having the same prominence as the other statements included in the full set. No particular format is required, but net income must be shown as a component of comprehensive income in that statement. However, absent items of other comprehensive income, e.g., foreign currency items, minimum pension liability adjustments, or unrealized gains and losses on certain securities, an enterprise need not report comprehensive income. Furthermore, the total of other comprehensive income for a period is transferred to a component of equity in the balance sheet separate from retained earnings and additional paid-in capital.

Answers (A), (C), and (D) are incorrect because accumulated other comprehensive income is reported in a separate component of shareholders' equity.

4.11 Personnel and Payroll

221. In an audit of payroll, an auditor is primarily concerned about

A. Excess FICA and income tax withholding.

B. Errors in employee time records.

C. Misposted payroll amounts.

D. Errors or fraud in the amount of payments.

The correct answer is (D). *(Publisher)*

REQUIRED: The auditor's primary concern in an audit of payroll.

DISCUSSION: The auditor is primarily concerned about the possibility of errors or fraud in the amount of payment when auditing payroll transactions. Employee compensation is a major item of expense and is especially susceptible to fraud unless internal control is effective. The inherent risk for payroll transactions is increased by the need for rapid processing of a large amount of information.

Answers (A), (B), and (C) are incorrect because excess FICA and income tax withholding, errors in employee time records, and misposted payroll amounts are important, but secondary, considerations.

222. In auditing payroll, an auditor most likely would

A. Verify that checks representing unclaimed wages are mailed.

B. Trace individual employee deductions to entity journal entries.

C. Observe entity employees during a payroll distribution.

D. Compare payroll costs with entity standards or budgets.

The correct answer is (D). *(CPA, adapted)*

REQUIRED: The procedure used in the audit of payroll.

DISCUSSION: Comparing payroll costs with budgeted amounts is a standard analytical procedure that would be performed in any audit of the payroll function.

Answer (A) is incorrect because checks representing unclaimed wages should be maintained by the treasurer until claimed by the appropriate employees. Answer (B) is incorrect because the individual employee deductions would not result in entity journal entries, but the sum of the payroll would result in cumulative journal entries. Answer (C) is incorrect because observation of payroll distribution is a standard procedure but one that might not be necessary when assessed control risk is low.

223. Which of the following audit procedures would provide the least relevant evidence in determining that payroll payments were made to bona fide employees?

A. Reconcile time cards in use to employees on the job.

B. Examine canceled checks for proper endorsement and compare with personnel records.

C. Test for segregation of the authorization for payment from the hire/fire authorization.

D. Test the payroll account bank reconciliation by tracing outstanding checks to the payroll register.

The correct answer is (D). *(CIA, adapted)*

REQUIRED: The procedure that provides the least relevant evidence that payroll payments were made to bona fide employees.

DISCUSSION: A payroll account proof tests for completeness of the recorded transactions, not for their validity.

Answer (A) is incorrect because verification that an employee is actually working is a common procedure to test for nonexistent employees. Answer (B) is incorrect because examining for proper endorsements and comparing with records may detect improper payments. Answer (C) is incorrect because segregation of payroll authorization from employment decisions helps to eliminate the conditions in which one person can arrange payment to fictitious employees.

224. An auditor is most likely to perform substantive tests of details on payroll transactions and balances when

A. Cutoff tests indicate a substantial amount of accrued payroll expense.

B. The assessed level of control risk relative to payroll transactions is low.

C. Analytical procedures indicate unusual fluctuations in recurring payroll entries.

D. Accrued payroll expense consists primarily of unpaid commissions.

The correct answer is (C). *(CPA, adapted)*

REQUIRED: The best reason for substantive tests of details on payroll.

DISCUSSION: The auditor should evaluate significant unexpected differences revealed by analytical procedures. The first step is to reconsider the methods and factors used in developing the expectations and to make inquiries of management. If a suitable explanation is not received, additional procedures to investigate the differences are necessary.

Answer (A) is incorrect because a substantial amount of accrued payroll expense is not an abnormal condition. Answer (B) is incorrect because a low assessed level of control risk may permit the auditor to devote less effort to substantive tests. Answer (D) is incorrect because the existence of unpaid earned commissions provides no indication of a misstatement.

225. To check the accuracy of hours worked, an auditor would ordinarily compare clock cards with

A. Personnel records.

B. Shop job time tickets.

C. Labor variance reports.

D. Time recorded in the payroll register.

The correct answer is (B). *(CPA, adapted)*

REQUIRED: The item with which the auditor compares clock cards to verify hours worked.

DISCUSSION: The auditor should compare shop job time tickets with the clock cards to determine the accuracy of the hours worked. The job tickets, which contain the total hours worked on each job, should not vary significantly from the employee time cards used to compute payroll.

Answer (A) is incorrect because the personnel department is responsible for authorizing employment, pay rates, and employee reclassifications. The timekeeping function should be performed separately. Answer (C) is incorrect because labor variance reports only show the difference between the time budgeted and the time charged to certain jobs. Answer (D) is incorrect because the time recorded in the payroll register is taken from clock time cards.

226. Analytical procedures may be applied to payroll to detect unusual items. Which of the following is an appropriate analytical procedure for payroll?

A. Compare the relationship of hours worked to payroll with that of the preceding year.

B. Inspect authorizations on time cards.

C. Compare rates authorized under a union contract with payroll records.

D. Review payroll bank account reconciliation.

The correct answer is (A). *(Publisher)*

REQUIRED: The analytical procedure for payroll.

DISCUSSION: Analytical procedures involve comparisons of recorded amounts with expectations developed by the auditor. Sources of information for developing these expectations include financial information for comparable prior periods; anticipated results, e.g., budgets and forecasts; relationships of elements of financial information within the period; industry information; and relationships of financial information with relevant nonfinancial information (AU 329). Evaluating the relationship of hours worked and payroll for the current and preceding years involves comparing financial information with relevant nonfinancial information in the light of an expectation developed based on data from a comparable prior period.

Answer (B) is incorrect because inspecting authorizations on time cards is a test of controls. Answers (C) and (D) are incorrect because comparing rates authorized under a union contract with payroll records and reviewing the payroll bank account reconciliation directly test the validity of payroll.

227. One payroll audit objective is to determine whether the employees received pay in amounts recorded in the payroll journal. To satisfy this objective, the auditor should

A. Reconcile the payroll bank account.

B. Request that a company official distribute all paychecks.

C. Determine whether a proper segregation of duties exists between recording payroll and reconciling the payroll bank account.

D. Compare canceled payroll checks with the payroll journal.

The correct answer is (D). *(CIA, adapted)*

REQUIRED: The procedure to verify that employees received pay in amounts recorded in the payroll journal.

DISCUSSION: To test the accuracy of the payroll journal, the auditor should vouch a sample of the entries to supporting documents, i.e., the canceled checks, timekeeping information, and records of wage rates and authorized deductions.

Answers (A) and (C) are incorrect because reconciling the payroll bank account and determining whether a proper segregation of duties exists should be part of the audit program for payroll, but neither procedure tests the agreement of amounts received by employees with the payroll journal entries. Answer (B) is incorrect because a company official should distribute all paychecks, but this procedure does not assure the agreement of amounts received by employees with the payroll journal entries.

228. An auditor found that employee time cards in one department are not properly approved by the supervisor. Which of the following could result?

A. Duplicate paychecks might be issued.

B. The wrong hourly rate could be used to calculate gross pay.

C. Employees might be paid for hours they did not work.

D. Payroll checks might not be distributed to the appropriate payees.

The correct answer is (C). *(CIA, adapted)*

REQUIRED: The misstatement that could occur if time cards are not approved by a supervisor.

DISCUSSION: The time cards report the number of hours worked. Failure to approve the time worked could result in an amount of pay inconsistent with actual hours worked.

Answer (A) is incorrect because each employee would have one time card and be issued one check based on the time card. Answer (B) is incorrect because the authorized pay rates should be provided by the personnel department. Answer (D) is incorrect because the paymaster should assure that only authorized employees receive a paycheck.

229. An internal auditor wishes to determine whether salaried employees in the division being audited are taking more paid vacation time than they have earned. Which of the following audit procedures would be most effective?

A. Observing which employees were absent because of vacations and tracing those absences through the payroll records to subtractions from accumulated vacation time.

B. Comparing total vacation time taken by selected employees in the most recent 12 months per payroll records to the time taken by the same employees in the preceding 12 months.

C. Sending confirmations to selected employees, asking them to verify the accuracy of the number of days of vacation used during the year and the number of remaining unused days as obtained from the payroll records.

D. Comparing the accrued vacation pay liability as computed for the firm's most recent balance sheet with the corresponding amount for 1 year earlier and investigating any significant change.

The correct answer is (A). *(CIA, adapted)*

REQUIRED: The audit procedure to test for excessive vacation time.

DISCUSSION: Salaried employees do not punch a clock to create a record of their presence, so observation by the auditor may be necessary to determine whether they are present. The time such an employee is absent may be compared with vacation pay and the payroll charged to vacation time to determine whether an excessive amount is being taken.

Answer (B) is incorrect because many reasons may justify the year-to-year change; for example, increased employee seniority or use of time accumulated from the previous year. Also, comparison of payroll records tests recorded amounts only. Answer (C) is incorrect because a confirmation sent to a wrongdoer is not likely to elicit an incriminating reply. Answer (D) is incorrect because comparing the accrued vacation pay liability with the corresponding amount for 1 year earlier tests recorded amounts only.

230. The client's bookkeeper perpetrated a theft by preparing erroneous W-2 forms. The bookkeeper's FICA withholding was overstated by $500 and the FICA withholding from all other employees was understated. Which of the following is an audit procedure that would detect such a fraud?

A. Multiplication of the applicable rate by the individual gross taxable earnings.

B. Using Form W-4 and withholding charts to determine whether deductions authorized per pay period agree with amounts deducted per pay period.

C. Footing and crossfooting of the payroll register followed by tracing postings to the general ledger.

D. Vouching canceled checks to federal tax Form 941.

The correct answer is (A). *(CPA, adapted)*

REQUIRED: The audit procedure that would detect a manipulation of withholding taxes.

DISCUSSION: One objective of the audit of payroll is to verify the client's compliance with various legal requirements, e.g., income tax withholding, Social Security taxes, workers' compensation, unemployment insurance, and wage and hour laws. The auditor should perform tests of controls by sampling payroll transactions. The deductions authorized by employees or required by law should be compared with those actually made. By comparing the recorded amounts withheld on individual employees' W-2 forms with those independently calculated by the auditor, (s)he should detect any misstatement of FICA withholding.

Answer (B) is incorrect because the irregularity was not in the records for each pay period but in the year-end summaries of withholding (W-2). Answer (C) is incorrect because the total amount of FICA taxes is correct, so the records will foot and crossfoot correctly. Answer (D) is incorrect because the total amount of FICA taxes remitted with the Form 941 was correct.

4.12 Management Representations

231. A purpose of a management representation letter is to reduce

A. Audit risk to an aggregate level of misstatement that could be considered material.

B. An auditor's responsibility to detect material misstatements only to the extent that the letter is relied on.

C. The possibility of a misunderstanding concerning management's responsibility for the financial statements.

D. The scope of an auditor's procedures concerning related party transactions and subsequent events.

The correct answer is (C). *(CPA, adapted)*

REQUIRED: The purpose of a management representation letter.

DISCUSSION: Management's written representations confirm oral representations given to the auditor, indicate and document their continuing appropriateness, and reduce the possibility of misunderstanding about the subject matter of the representations. That subject matter includes management's acknowledgment of responsibility for the financial statements.

Answers (A), (B), and (D) are incorrect because a letter of representations is not a substitute for the procedures necessary to afford a reasonable basis for an opinion.

232. When an audit is made in accordance with generally accepted auditing standards, the auditor should always

A. Document the understanding of the client's internal control and the basis for all conclusions about the assessed level of control risk for financial statement assertions.

B. Employ analytical procedures as substantive tests to obtain evidence about specific assertions related to account balances.

C. Obtain certain written representations from management.

D. Observe the taking of physical inventory on the balance sheet date.

The correct answer is (C). *(CPA, adapted)*

REQUIRED: The requirement of an audit made in accordance with GAAS.

DISCUSSION: AU 333 requires that the auditor obtain certain written representations from management. They corroborate information received orally from management but do not substitute for the procedures necessary to afford a reasonable basis for the opinion.

Answer (A) is incorrect because, if control risk is assessed at the maximum level for some assertions, the auditor should document that conclusion but need not document its basis (AU 319). Answer (B) is incorrect because analytical procedures are required to be applied in the planning and final review stages of an audit but not as a substitute for tests of details. Answer (D) is incorrect because, when well-kept perpetual inventory records are checked by the client periodically through comparisons with physical counts, the auditor's observation procedures usually can be performed either during or after the end of the period under audit.

233. Which of the following statements ordinarily is included among the written management representations obtained by the auditor?

A. Compensating balances and other arrangements involving restrictions on cash balances have been disclosed.

B. Management acknowledges responsibility for illegal actions committed by employees.

C. Sufficient evidence has been made available to permit the expression of an unqualified opinion.

D. Management acknowledges that there are no material weaknesses in internal control.

The correct answer is (A). *(CPA, adapted)*

REQUIRED: The statement included among written management representations.

DISCUSSION: AU 333 lists the issues ordinarily addressed in representation letters, if applicable. One illustrative representation given in AU 333 states, "Arrangements with financial institutions involving compensating balances or other arrangements involving restrictions on cash balances, line of credit, or similar arrangements have been properly disclosed."

Answer (B) is incorrect because, assuming illegal acts have occurred, management will rarely acknowledge responsibility for employees' behavior. However, the subject of fraud is one that is ordinarily included in the letter. Answer (C) is incorrect because the auditor judges the sufficiency of evidence. Answer (D) is incorrect because representations about internal control are not among those listed in AU 333.

234. When considering the use of management's written representations as audit evidence about the completeness assertion, an auditor should understand that such representations

A. Complement, but do not replace, substantive tests designed to support the assertion.

B. Constitute sufficient evidence to support the assertion when considered in combination with a sufficiently low assessed level of control risk.

C. Are not part of the evidence considered to support the assertion.

D. Replace a low assessed level of control risk as evidence to support the assertion.

The correct answer is (A). *(CPA, adapted)*

REQUIRED: The use of management representations.

DISCUSSION: AU 333 states that management's representations are audit evidence but do not substitute for procedures necessary to afford a reasonable basis for the opinion. Thus, they complement other audit procedures.

Answer (B) is incorrect because, regardless of the assessed level of control risk, some substantive testing of significant account balances, transaction classes, and disclosure components of financial statements is required. Management representations do not substitute for such testing even in combination with a low level of control risk. Answer (C) is incorrect because management's written representations are audit evidence. Answer (D) is incorrect because, although substantive tests may vary with control risk, representations cannot substitute for the substantive tests that are required in light of the assessed levels of inherent risk and control risk and the resulting acceptable level of detection risk.

235. A written management representation letter is most likely to be an auditor's best source of corroborative information of a client's intention to

A. Terminate an employee pension plan.

B. Make a public offering of its common stock.

C. Settle an outstanding lawsuit for an amount less than the accrued loss contingency.

D. Discontinue a line of business.

The correct answer is (D). *(CPA, adapted)*

REQUIRED: The client's intention that is best corroborated by a management representation letter.

DISCUSSION: Written management representations are audit evidence but do not ordinarily substitute for other auditing procedures. However, the client's plan for discontinuing a line of business is an example of a matter about which other procedures may provide little evidence. Accordingly, the written representation will be necessary as confirmation of management's intent.

Answers (A) and (B) are incorrect because minutes of directors' meetings document a client's intention to terminate an employee pension plan or to make a public offering of its common stock. Answer (C) is incorrect because an inquiry of the client's lawyer provides more reliable evidence about litigation.

236. A written representation from a client's management that, among other matters, acknowledges responsibility for the fair presentation of financial statements, should normally be signed by the

A. Chief executive officer and the chief financial officer.

B. Chief financial officer and the chair of the board of directors.

C. Chair of the audit committee of the board of directors.

D. Chief executive officer, the chair of the board of directors, and the client's lawyer.

The correct answer is (A). *(CPA, adapted)*

REQUIRED: The persons who normally should sign the management representation letter.

DISCUSSION: The management representation letter should be signed by members of management with overall responsibility for financial and operating matters who, the auditor believes, are responsible for and knowledgeable about the areas covered in the representations. AU 333 states that these members are normally the chief executive officer and the chief financial officer.

Answers (B), (C), and (D) are incorrect because, although others may hold high positions in the firm, they are not ultimately responsible or do not have as broad a knowledge as the chief executive officer and chief financial officer. The auditor is not precluded from obtaining representations from others in the firm, however.

237. Hall accepted an engagement to audit the 1998 financial statements of XYZ Company. XYZ completed the preparation of the 1998 financial statements on February 13, 1999, and Hall began the field work on February 17, 1999. Hall completed the field work on March 24, 1999, and completed the report on March 28, 1999. The management representation letter normally would be dated

A. February 13, 1999.

B. February 17, 1999.

C. March 24, 1999.

D. March 28, 1999.

The correct answer is (C). *(CPA, adapted)*

REQUIRED: The appropriate date of the management representation letter.

DISCUSSION: AU 333 states that the representation letter should be dated no earlier than the date of the auditor's report, which is usually the date of completion of field work (March 24). This date is chosen because the auditor is concerned with events occurring through the date of the report that may require adjustment to or disclosure in the financial statements.

Answer (A) is incorrect because February 13, 1999 is the date preparation of the statements was completed. Answer (B) is incorrect because February 17, 1999 is the date field work began. Answer (D) is incorrect because March 28, 1999 is the date the audit report was completed.

Questions 238 and 239 are based on the following information. During the annual audit of BCD Corp., a publicly held company, Smith, CPA, a continuing auditor, determined that illegal political contributions had been made during each of the past 7 years, including the year under audit. Smith notified the directors of BCD Corp. of the illegal contributions, but they refused to take any action because the amounts involved were immaterial to the financial statements.

238. Smith should reconsider the intended degree of reliability of the

A. Management representation letter.

B. Preliminary judgment about materiality levels.

C. Letter of audit inquiry to the client's attorney.

D. Prior years' audit programs.

The correct answer is (A). *(CPA, adapted)*

REQUIRED: The item that may be of questionable reliability.

DISCUSSION: The auditor should consider the implications of an illegal act in relation to the other representations of management. If management cannot be trusted in this matter, serious doubts arise about the other representations. The auditor must also consider the possible effects of continuing association with the client (AU 317, *Illegal Acts by Clients*).

Answer (B) is incorrect because the detection of the illegal act does not affect the preliminary judgment about materiality made at the planning stage of the audit. However, this information could influence the auditor's judgment about materiality in evaluating the audit findings at the completion of the audit (AU 312, *Audit Risk and Materiality in Conducting an Audit*). Answer (C) is incorrect because the illegal act by the client does not raise an issue about the attorney's integrity and the reliability of the response to the letter of inquiry. Answer (D) is incorrect because prior years' programs are considered in preparing the current year's program, but they are not used in the current audit. Moreover, the current year's procedures are apparently effective because the illegal act was detected.

239. Because management took no action, Smith should

A. Report the illegal contributions to the Securities and Exchange Commission.

B. Express a qualified opinion or an adverse opinion.

C. Disregard the political contributions because the board of directors was notified and the amounts involved were immaterial.

D. Consider withdrawing from the engagement.

The correct answer is (D). *(CPA, adapted)*

REQUIRED: The effect of management's failure to take action regarding an illegality.

DISCUSSION: Under AU 317, if the client does not take the remedial action considered necessary by the auditor, the auditor should consider withdrawal from the engagement even when the illegal act is not material. (S)he should weigh the effects on his/her ability to rely on management's representations and the possible results of continued association with the client. The auditor may also wish to seek legal advice.

Answer (A) is incorrect because notifying others is ordinarily management's responsibility. However, when the auditor withdraws because of the client's failure to take remedial action, the entity may be required to report the auditor change on Form 8-K. The Private Securities Litigation Reform Act of 1995 will also apply if the auditor determines that the effects of the illegal act were material. Thus, after the auditor's conclusions are reported to the board, the directors have one business day to inform the SEC. Answer (B) is incorrect because, if the effects of the illegal act are not material, a modified opinion may not be necessary. Answer (C) is incorrect because the auditor must consider withdrawal.

240. If management refuses to furnish certain written representations that the auditor believes are essential, which of the following is appropriate?

A. The auditor can rely on oral evidence relating to the matter as a basis for an unqualified opinion.

B. The client's refusal does not constitute a scope limitation that may lead to a modification of the opinion.

C. The client's refusal may have an effect on the auditor's ability to rely on other representations of management.

D. The auditor should express an adverse opinion because of management's refusal.

The correct answer is (C). *(CPA, adapted)*

REQUIRED: The effect of management's refusal to furnish essential written representations.

DISCUSSION: The refusal constitutes a scope limitation sufficient to preclude an unqualified opinion and is ordinarily sufficient to support a disclaimer of an opinion or a withdrawal from the engagement. The auditor must also consider the effects of the refusal on his/her ability to rely on management's other representations (AU 333).

Answer (A) is incorrect because oral representations must be confirmed in writing. Answer (B) is incorrect because the auditor must modify the opinion, disclaim an opinion, or withdraw from the engagement. Answer (D) is incorrect because a qualified opinion or a disclaimer is more appropriate than an adverse opinion unless the auditor knows that the financial statements are not fairly presented.

241. An auditor frequently asks client personnel questions about the accounts under audit. Although such evidence may be useful, it is weak and should be corroborated by the auditor. Which of the following replies is most useful to the auditor?

A. "Yes, that's how we record that item."

B. "No, I always perform that procedure."

C. "No, we don't always require authorization."

D. "Yes, all inventory is counted."

The correct answer is (C). *(Publisher)*

REQUIRED: The response most likely to be useful.

DISCUSSION: Although oral evidence furnished by client personnel should not be relied upon exclusively, the results of inquiries may help the auditor to identify areas that require additional audit attention. For example, the reply to the question about authorization indicates that the client may not be complying with authorization requirements.

Answers (A), (B), and (D) are incorrect because assurances by client personnel that procedures have been performed provide audit evidence of limited value.

242. An auditor should obtain written representations from management concerning litigation, claims, and assessments. These representations may be limited to matters that are considered either individually or collectively material provided an understanding on the limits of materiality for this purpose has been reached by

A. The auditor and the client's lawyer.

B. Management and the auditor.

C. Management, the client's lawyer, and the auditor.

D. The auditor independently of management.

The correct answer is (B). *(CPA, adapted)*

REQUIRED: The materiality limitation on the scope of management's representations.

DISCUSSION: Management's representations may be limited to matters that are considered individually or collectively material on the condition that management and the auditor have reached an understanding concerning the limits of materiality. Such limitations do not apply to certain representations not directly related to amounts in the financial statements, e.g., acknowledgment of responsibility for fair presentation, availability of records, and fraud involving management and persons with significant roles in internal control (AU 333).

Answers (A) and (C) are incorrect because the lawyer and the auditor (not the client) jointly determine the limits of materiality for purposes of the lawyer's response, not management's. This question, however, relates to representations by management. Answer (D) is incorrect because the auditor and management must reach an understanding.

243. A client requests that a predecessor auditor reissue the report on financial statements of a prior period to be presented comparatively with the financial statements of a subsequent period. If no filings with the SEC are contemplated, the auditor

A. May reissue the report without performing additional procedures.

B. Should obtain an updating management representation letter before reissuing the report.

C. Should refuse to reissue the report because (s)he is not a continuing auditor.

D. May reissue the report only if it refers to the successor auditor's work.

The correct answer is (B). *(Publisher)*

REQUIRED: The true statement about reissuance of an audit report.

DISCUSSION: When a predecessor auditor is requested to reissue, or consent to the reuse of, the report on prior-period financial statements to be presented comparatively with the audited statements of a subsequent period, (s)he must obtain an updating representation letter from the former client's management. This requirement applies even if no SEC filings are necessary. The letter should state whether any information has come to management's attention requiring modification of prior representations and whether subsequent events have occurred that necessitate adjustment to or disclosure in the current financial statements (AU 333). The predecessor auditor should also obtain a representation letter from the successor auditor.

Answer (A) is incorrect because various procedures must be performed (AU 508). For example, updating representations must be obtained (AU 333). Answer (C) is incorrect because a predecessor auditor may reissue a report. Answer (D) is incorrect because no reference should be made to the successor auditor's report or work (AU 508).

4.13 Litigation Involving the Client

244. The primary source of information to be reported about litigation, claims, and assessments is the

A. Client's lawyer.

B. Court records.

C. Client's management.

D. Independent auditor.

The correct answer is (C). *(CPA, adapted)*

REQUIRED: The primary source of information to be reported about litigation, claims, and assessments.

DISCUSSION: "Management is responsible for adopting policies and procedures to identify, evaluate, and account for litigation, claims, and assessments as a basis for the preparation of financial statements in conformity with generally accepted accounting principles" (AU 337, *Inquiry of a Client's Lawyer Concerning Litigation, Claims, and Assessments*).

Answer (A) is incorrect because the client's lawyer is the auditor's primary source of evidence to corroborate the information furnished by management. Answer (B) is incorrect because the auditor does not ordinarily examine court records. Answer (D) is incorrect because the auditor collects evidence to support management's assertions concerning litigation, claims, and assessments.

245. The primary reason an auditor requests that letters of inquiry be sent to a client's attorneys is to provide the auditor with

A. The probable outcome of asserted claims and pending or threatened litigation.

B. Corroboration of the information furnished by management about litigation, claims, and assessments.

C. The attorneys' opinions of the client's historical experiences in recent similar litigation.

D. A description and evaluation of litigation, claims, and assessments that existed at the balance sheet date.

The correct answer is (B). *(CPA, adapted)*

REQUIRED: The primary reason that letters of audit inquiry are sent to a client's attorneys.

DISCUSSION: A letter of audit inquiry to a client's lawyer is the auditor's primary means of corroborating information furnished by management concerning litigation, claims, and assessments. Evidence obtained from the client's legal department may provide the needed corroboration, but it does not substitute for information that outside counsel refuses to furnish (AU 337).

Answers (A) and (D) are incorrect because management provides a description and evaluation of litigation, claims, and assessments that existed at the balance sheet date. The letter of audit inquiry corroborates that information. Answer (C) is incorrect because the auditor is concerned with current litigation, not recent similar litigation.

246. The letter of audit inquiry addressed to the client's lawyer will not ordinarily be

A. Sent to a lawyer who was engaged by the audit client during the year and soon thereafter resigned the engagement.

B. Used to corroborate the information originally obtained from management concerning litigation, claims, and assessments.

C. Limited to references concerning only pending or threatened litigation with respect to which the lawyer has been engaged.

D. Needed during the audit of clients whose securities are not registered with the SEC.

The correct answer is (C). *(CPA, adapted)*

REQUIRED: The false statement about the letter of audit inquiry to the client's lawyer.

DISCUSSION: A letter of audit inquiry to a client's lawyer includes, but is not limited to, management-prepared lists of unasserted claims and assessments as well as pending or threatened litigation, claims, and assessments with respect to which the lawyer has been engaged. The lawyer is expected to respond appropriately (within the limits of materiality) if (s)he has given substantive attention to any of these matters on behalf of the company in the form of legal consultation or representation.

Answer (A) is incorrect because the auditor should communicate with all lawyers engaged by the client during the year. Answer (B) is incorrect because management is the auditor's primary source of information concerning litigation, claims, and assessments. The inquiry letter is the primary means of corroboration. Answer (D) is incorrect because the lawyer's letter is customary in all audits.

247. Which of the following is not an audit procedure that the independent auditor performs with respect to litigation, claims, and assessments?

A. Inquire of and discuss with management the policies and procedures adopted for litigation, claims, and assessments.

B. Obtain from management a description and evaluation of litigation, claims, and assessments that existed at the balance sheet date.

C. Obtain assurance from management that it has disclosed all unasserted claims that the lawyer has advised are probable of assertion and must be disclosed.

D. Confirm directly with the client's lawyer that all claims have been recorded in the financial statements.

The correct answer is (D). *(CPA, adapted)*

REQUIRED: The procedure that is not performed regarding litigation.

DISCUSSION: Under SFAS 5, a loss contingency is recorded in the financial statements only if it is probable and its amount can be reasonably estimated. Hence, many contingent claims will not be recorded.

Answer (A) is incorrect because inquiring of, and discussing with, management the policies and procedures adopted for litigation, claims, and assessments is a procedure required by AU 337. Answer (B) is incorrect because obtaining from management a description and evaluation of litigation, claims, and assessments that existed at the balance sheet date is a procedure required by AU 337. Answer (C) is incorrect because obtaining assurance from management that it has disclosed all unasserted claims that the lawyer has advised are probable of assertion is a procedure required by AU 337.

248. A CPA has received a lawyer's letter in which no significant disagreements with the client's assessments of contingent liabilities were noted. The resignation of the client's lawyer shortly after receipt of the letter should alert the auditor that

A. Undisclosed unasserted claims may have arisen.

B. The lawyer was unable to form a conclusion with respect to the significance of litigation, claims, and assessments.

C. The auditor must begin a completely new examination of contingent liabilities.

D. An adverse opinion will be necessary.

The correct answer is (A). *(CPA, adapted)*

REQUIRED: The implication of the resignation of the client's lawyer soon after responding to the inquiry letter.

DISCUSSION: A lawyer may be required to resign an engagement (under his/her code of professional responsibility) if the client disregards advice concerning financial accounting and reporting for litigation, claims, and assessments. Given that the response to the letter of audit inquiry stated that the client's assessment of contingent liabilities was satisfactory, the source of disagreement may be undisclosed, unasserted claims.

Answer (B) is incorrect because inability to form a legal conclusion does not ordinarily cause an ethical conflict with the client sufficient to cause the lawyer's resignation. Answer (C) is incorrect because much of the auditor's work, particularly that performed on client records, may still be valid. Answer (D) is incorrect because an adverse opinion is expressed only when the financial statements or related disclosures (including omissions thereof) are not presented fairly.

249. Which of the following statements concerning litigation, claims, and assessments, which were extracted from a letter from a client's lawyer, is most likely to cause the auditor to request clarification?

A. "I believe that the possible liability to the company is nominal in amount."

B. "I believe that the action can be settled for less than the damages claimed."

C. "I believe that the plaintiff's case against the company is without merit."

D. "I believe that the company will be able to defend this action successfully."

The correct answer is (B). *(CPA, adapted)*

REQUIRED: The lawyer's statement most likely causing an auditor's request for clarification.

DISCUSSION: The letter of audit inquiry requests, among other things, that the lawyer evaluate the likelihood of unfavorable outcomes of pending or threatened litigation, claims, and assessments. It also requests that the lawyer estimate, if possible, the amount or range of potential loss (AU 337). Thus, the auditor is concerned about the amount of the expected settlement as well as the likelihood of the outcome.

Answer (A) is incorrect because the lawyer's statement that the amount of possible liability will not be material states an amount or range of loss. Answers (C) and (D) are incorrect because the lawyer has stated that no liability is expected.

250. A lawyer's response to an auditor's request for information concerning litigation, claims, and assessments will ordinarily contain which of the following?

A. An explanation regarding limitations on the scope of the response.

B. A statement of concurrence with the client's determination of which unasserted possible claims warrant specification.

C. Confidential information that would be prejudicial to the client's defense if publicized.

D. An assertion that the unasserted possible claims identified by the client represent all such claims of which the lawyer may be aware.

The correct answer is (A). *(CPA, adapted)*

REQUIRED: The statement ordinarily contained in the lawyer's response to an audit inquiry.

DISCUSSION: The letter of audit inquiry requests a statement about the nature of, and reasons for, any limitation on the lawyer's response. The lawyer may limit the response to matters to which (s)he has given substantive attention in the form of legal consultation or representation and to matters that are material, provided the lawyer and auditor agree on the limits of materiality for this purpose. These limitations are not limitations on the audit scope.

Answers (B) and (D) are incorrect because the lawyer is only required to comment on those matters on which his/her views differ from those stated by management. Answer (C) is incorrect because the lawyer's response will not ordinarily contain sensitive information. Information prejudicial to the client may be disclosed, but the auditor has the responsibility to keep it confidential.

251. The scope of an audit is not restricted when an attorney's response to an auditor as a result of a client's letter of audit inquiry limits the response to

A. Matters to which the attorney has given substantive attention in the form of legal representation.

B. An evaluation of the likelihood of an unfavorable outcome of the matters disclosed by the entity.

C. The attorney's opinion of the entity's historical experience in recent similar litigation.

D. The probable outcome of asserted claims and pending or threatened litigation.

The correct answer is (A). *(CPA, adapted)*

REQUIRED: The appropriate limitations on the lawyer's response to the auditor's inquiry.

DISCUSSION: AU 337 states that two limitations on the lawyer's response will not be considered scope limitations. The response may be limited to matters to which the lawyer has given substantive attention on behalf of the client in the form of legal consultation or representation. Also, if the lawyer and auditor have reached an understanding as to the limits of materiality, the response may be limited to matters that are individually or collectively material.

Answer (B) is incorrect because an evaluation of the likelihood of an unfavorable outcome of the matters disclosed by the entity is just one matter covered in a letter of audit inquiry. Answer (C) is incorrect because a response should be made regarding all material litigation, claims, and assessments to which the lawyer has given substantive attention. Answer (D) is incorrect because the probable outcome of asserted claims and pending or threatened litigation is just one matter covered.

252. An auditor should obtain evidence relevant to all the following factors concerning third-party litigation against a client except the

A. Period in which the underlying cause for legal action occurred.

B. Probability of an unfavorable outcome.

C. Jurisdiction in which the matter will be resolved.

D. Existence of a situation indicating an uncertainty as to the possible loss.

The correct answer is (C). *(CPA, adapted)*

REQUIRED: The least important audit consideration when obtaining evidence regarding litigation.

DISCUSSION: When performing audit procedures after year-end, the auditor is least interested in determining where the particular matter in litigation will be resolved. The major concern is the impact of the event on the fair presentation of the year-end financial statements. Accordingly, the auditor should obtain evidence of the existence, amount, degree of probability, and timing of the cause of the litigation.

Answers (A), (B), and (D) are incorrect because the period in which the underlying cause for legal action occurred, the probability of an unfavorable outcome, and uncertainty as to the possible loss are factors about which evidence should be gathered to determine the effect of litigation on the financial statements.

253. The appropriate date for the client to specify as the effective date in the audit inquiry to a lawyer is

A. The balance sheet date.

B. Seven working days after the request is received by the lawyer.

C. The date of the audit inquiry itself.

D. The expected date of the completion of audit field work.

The correct answer is (D). *(Publisher)*

REQUIRED: The appropriate effective date of the letter of inquiry to a lawyer.

DISCUSSION: According to an interpretation of AU 337, the date of the lawyer's response "should be as close to the completion of the field work as practicable." The auditor is concerned with events occurring through the date of the report that may require adjustment to, or disclosure in, the financial statements.

Answers (A), (B), and (C) are incorrect because the balance sheet date, 7 working days after the request is received by the lawyer, and the date of the audit inquiry itself are not ordinarily as close as practicable to the completion of field work.

254. The refusal of a client's lawyer to provide a representation on the legality of a particular act committed by the client is ordinarily

A. Sufficient reason to issue a "subject to" opinion.

B. Considered to be a scope limitation.

C. Insufficient reason to modify the auditor's report because of the lawyer's obligation of confidentiality.

D. Proper grounds to withdraw from the engagement.

The correct answer is (B). *(CPA, adapted)*

REQUIRED: The auditor's conclusion when the client's lawyer refuses to corroborate information.

DISCUSSION: The lawyer's refusal either orally or in writing to provide the requested information is a scope limitation sufficient to preclude an unqualified opinion because the letter of audit inquiry to the client's lawyer is the primary means of corroborating management's representations about litigation, claims, and assessments. However, a statement in the letter, for example, "It would be inappropriate for this firm to respond to a general inquiry relating to the existence of unasserted possible claims and assessments," is not considered a scope limitation.

Answer (A) is incorrect because "subject to" is an unacceptable phrase in an audit opinion. Answer (C) is incorrect because an unqualified opinion cannot be expressed when a material scope limitation has been imposed. Answer (D) is incorrect because the failure could preclude an unqualified opinion but would not likely be grounds for withdrawal.

4.14 Use of Specialists

255. Which of the following statements is correct about the auditor's use of the work of a specialist?

A. The specialist should not have an understanding of the auditor's corroborative use of the specialist's findings.

B. The auditor is required to perform substantive procedures to verify the specialist's assumptions and findings.

C. The client should not have an understanding of the nature of the work to be performed by the specialist.

D. The auditor should obtain an understanding of the methods and assumptions used by the specialist.

The correct answer is (D). *(CPA, adapted)*

REQUIRED: The true statement about the auditor's use of the work of a specialist.

DISCUSSION: AU 336, *Using the Work of a Specialist*, states that the auditor should obtain an understanding of the methods and assumptions used to determine whether the findings are suitable for corroborative purposes. The auditor should consider whether the specialist's findings support the assertions and should test the accounting data provided by the client to the specialist.

Answers (A) and (C) are incorrect because the auditor, the client, and the specialist should have an understanding about the nature of the work to be performed. Answer (B) is incorrect because, if the specialist's findings support the assertions, the auditor may reasonably conclude that sufficient, competent evidence has been obtained.

256. Which of the following statements concerning the auditor's use of the work of a specialist is true?

A. If the auditor believes that the determinations made by the specialist are unreasonable, only a qualified opinion may be expressed.

B. If the specialist is related to the client, the auditor is still permitted to use the specialist's findings as corroborative evidence.

C. The specialist may not be related to the client.

D. The specialist is identified in the auditor's report when the auditor expresses an unqualified opinion.

The correct answer is (B). *(CPA, adapted)*

REQUIRED: The true statement about use of a specialist.

DISCUSSION: A related specialist may be acceptable under certain circumstances. The auditor should assess the risk that the specialist's objectivity may be impaired. If the auditor believes that objectivity might be impaired, the auditor should perform additional audit procedures or hire another specialist (AU 336).

Answer (A) is incorrect because, if the findings are unreasonable, additional procedures should be applied. If they do not resolve the matter, the opinion of another specialist should be sought. If the issue is still not resolved, a qualified opinion or a disclaimer should ordinarily be expressed. An adverse opinion should be expressed only when the auditor concludes the financial statements are materially misstated. Answer (C) is incorrect because a related specialist may be acceptable under certain circumstances. Answer (D) is incorrect because the specialist may be identified whenever the auditor modifies the standard report as a result of the work of a specialist.

257. Which of the following is not a specialist upon whose work an auditor may rely?

A. Actuary.

B. Appraiser.

C. Internal auditor.

D. Engineer.

The correct answer is (C). *(CPA, adapted)*

REQUIRED: The individual not considered a specialist.

DISCUSSION: For the purposes of AU 336, a specialist is a person or firm possessing special skill or knowledge in a particular field other than accounting or auditing. The external auditor should consider the work of internal auditors but should not deem them to be specialists in the sense contemplated by AU 336.

Answers (A), (B), and (D) are incorrect because specialists include, but are not limited to, actuaries, appraisers, engineers, environmental consultants, geologists, and attorneys (if not engaged to provide services to the client regarding litigation, claims, or assessments).

258. In using the work of a specialist, an auditor referred to the specialist's findings in the auditor's report. This is an appropriate reporting practice if the

A. Auditor is not familiar with the professional certification, personal reputation, or particular competence of the specialist.

B. Auditor, as a result of the specialist's findings, adds an explanatory paragraph emphasizing a matter regarding the financial statements.

C. Specialist is aware that his/her work will be used to evaluate the assertions in the financial statements.

D. Auditor, as a result of the specialist's findings, decides to indicate a division of responsibility with the specialist.

The correct answer is (B). *(CPA, adapted)*

REQUIRED: The instance in which an auditor may refer to a specialist's findings.

DISCUSSION: An auditor ordinarily should not refer to the work or findings of a specialist. However, "The auditor may, as a result of the report or findings of the specialist, decide to add explanatory language to his/her standard report or depart from an unqualified opinion." The specialist may be identified "if the auditor believes the reference will facilitate an understanding of the reason for the explanatory paragraph or the departure from the unqualified opinion" (AU 336). Emphasizing a matter is a basis for adding an explanatory paragraph that may justify referring to a specialist.

Answer (A) is incorrect because the auditor is required to evaluate the professional qualifications of the specialist. Answer (C) is incorrect because the specialist's awareness of the use of his/her work is independent of the decision to refer to the specialist. Answer (D) is incorrect because a division of responsibility with the specialist is inappropriate.

259. If a material difference exists between a specialist's findings and the assertions in the financial statements, or if the auditor believes that the findings of the specialist are unreasonable, the auditor should

A. Refer to the work of the specialist in the scope paragraph of the report.

B. Refer to the work of the specialist in a separate explanatory paragraph of the report.

C. Apply additional auditing procedures.

D. Describe the basic findings of the specialist in a separate explanatory paragraph but omit any reference to the specialist's procedure or name.

The correct answer is (C). *(Publisher)*

REQUIRED: The effect of the specialist's work when the findings are at variance with the financial statements.

DISCUSSION: AU 336 states that the auditor should apply additional auditing procedures if the specialist's findings are unreasonable or materially different from the assertions in the financial statements. If the matter is still unresolved after applying these procedures and obtaining the opinion of another specialist, the audit opinion may have to be qualified or disclaimed.

Answer (A) is incorrect because the auditor should never refer to the specialist in the scope paragraph. Answer (B) is incorrect because the auditor may refer to the specialist only if (s)he departs from an unqualified opinion or adds an explanatory paragraph to the standard report. Answer (D) is incorrect because the auditor may refer to and identify the specialist in certain circumstances.

260. When an outside specialist has assumed full responsibility for taking the client's physical inventory, reliance on the specialist's report is acceptable if

A. The auditor is satisfied through application of appropriate procedures as to the reputation and competence of the specialist.

B. Circumstances made it impracticable or impossible for the auditor to either do the work personally or observe the work done by the inventory firm.

C. The auditor conducted the same audit tests and procedures as would have been applicable if the client employees took the physical inventory.

D. The auditor's report contains a reference to the assumption of full responsibility.

The correct answer is (C). *(CPA, adapted)*

REQUIRED: The basis for relying on the work of an outside inventory specialist.

DISCUSSION: AU 331 charges the auditor with responsibility for the observation of inventories. The auditor must perform this procedure whether the client or an outside specialist takes the physical inventory. The auditor must still examine the outside firm's program, observe its procedures and controls, make or observe some physical counts, recompute calculations, and test intervening transactions.

Answer (A) is incorrect because, although the auditor is concerned with the reputation and competence of the specialist, (s)he still must become satisfied as to the existence of the inventory. Answer (B) is incorrect because the auditor usually cannot express an unqualified opinion unless (s)he has made or observed some physical counts. Answer (D) is incorrect because the auditor cannot assign responsibility to a specialist.

4.15 Subsequent Events (See also Module 7.11.)

261. Which of the following procedures can be performed only in the subsequent period?

A. Examination of data to determine that a proper cutoff has been made.

B. Tests of the details of balances.

C. Tests of the details of transactions.

D. Reading of the minutes of the board of directors' meetings.

The correct answer is (A). *(Publisher)*

REQUIRED: The procedure that can be performed only in the subsequent period.

DISCUSSION: The objective of a cutoff test is to determine that transactions are reported in the correct period. A cutoff test can be performed only after year-end when all transactions for the year can be identified.

Answers (B), (C), and (D) are incorrect because the tests of the details of transactions and balances and most other audit procedures can be performed during the year. However, minutes of meetings during the subsequent period through the date of the audit report should be considered.

262. Which of the following procedures would an auditor most likely perform to obtain evidence about the occurrence of subsequent events?

A. Confirming a sample of material accounts receivable established after year-end.

B. Comparing the financial statements being reported on with those of the prior period.

C. Investigating personnel changes in the accounting department occurring after year-end.

D. Inquiring as to whether any unusual adjustments were made after year-end.

The correct answer is (D). *(CPA, adapted)*

REQUIRED: The subsequent events procedure.

DISCUSSION: Procedures performed at or near the completion of field work normally include inquiring of management as to (1) whether the interim statements were prepared on the same basis as the statements being reported on, (2) whether any substantial contingent liabilities or commitments existed at the date of the balance sheet, (3) whether any significant change had occurred in equity, (4) whether any unusual adjustments had been made during the subsequent period, and (5) the current status of items that were accounted for on a basis of tentative, preliminary, or inconclusive data.

Answer (A) is incorrect because the auditor confirms receivables before year-end. Answer (B) is incorrect because this analytical procedure is performed at the beginning of the audit. Answer (C) is incorrect because personnel changes after year-end do not typically relate to the recording of subsequent events.

263. An auditor is concerned with completing various phases of the audit after the balance sheet date. This subsequent period extends to the date of the

A. Auditor's report.

B. Final review of the audit working papers.

C. Public issuance of the financial statements.

D. Delivery of the auditor's report to the client.

The correct answer is (A). *(CPA, adapted)*

REQUIRED: The date to which subsequent events work should be extended.

DISCUSSION: Subsequent events work should be performed at or near the completion of the field work (AU 560), and the audit report is normally dated as of the last day of the field work (AU 530, *Dating of the Independent Auditor's Report*).

Answer (B) is incorrect because subsequent events work should be extended to the date of the report. Answer (C) is incorrect because the date of the public issuance of the financial statements is later than the date of the report. Answer (D) is incorrect because the delivery of the auditor's report to the client occurs after the date of the report.

264. Which of the following statements best expresses the auditor's responsibility with respect to events occurring in the subsequent events period?

A. The auditor has no responsibility for events occurring in the subsequent period unless these events affect transactions recorded on or before the balance sheet date.

B. The auditor's responsibility is to determine that transactions recorded on or before the balance sheet date actually occurred.

C. The auditor is fully responsible for events occurring in the subsequent period and should extend all detailed procedures through the last day of field work.

D. The auditor is responsible for determining that a proper cutoff has been made and for performing a general review of events occurring in the subsequent period.

The correct answer is (D). *(Publisher)*

REQUIRED: The best description of the auditor's subsequent events responsibility.

DISCUSSION: AU 560 states, "Events and transactions sometimes occur subsequent to the balance sheet date, but prior to the issuance of the financial statements and the auditor's report, that have a material effect on the financial statements and therefore require adjustment or disclosure in the statements." Certain specific procedures such as the determination that proper cutoffs have been made and the examination of data to aid in evaluating assets and liabilities as of the balance sheet date are normally applied in the subsequent events period. Other phases of the audit, however, will have been substantially completed by year-end. The auditor is responsible for performing a general subsequent events review but not for continuously reviewing matters about which (s)he has already become satisfied.

Answer (A) is incorrect because the auditor is responsible for conditions not existing at year-end that must be disclosed to prevent the statements from being misleading. Answer (B) is incorrect because transactions occurring prior to year-end are not subsequent events. Answer (C) is incorrect because the auditor is only expected to apply the subsequent events procedures (not all audit procedures) described in AU 560.

265. Which of the following procedures should an auditor ordinarily perform regarding subsequent events?

A. Compare the latest available interim financial statements with the financial statements being audited.

B. Send second requests to the client's customers who failed to respond to initial accounts receivable confirmation requests.

C. Communicate material weaknesses in internal control to the client's audit committee.

D. Review the cutoff bank statements for several months after the year-end.

The correct answer is (A). *(CPA, adapted)*

REQUIRED: The subsequent events procedure.

DISCUSSION: Subsequent events procedures include reading the latest interim statements and comparing them with the statements being reported on; inquiring about and discussing with management various financial and accounting matters; reading the minutes of directors', shareholders', and committee meetings; obtaining a letter of representations from management; inquiring of client's legal counsel; and performing any further procedures deemed necessary.

Answer (B) is incorrect because second confirmation requests would not disclose subsequent events. Answer (C) is incorrect because communication of material weaknesses is not a subsequent events procedure. Answer (D) is incorrect because cutoff bank statements are requested from banks 7 to 10 days after year-end. They are used to verify the client's bank reconciliations and detect kiting.

266. Which of the following events occurring after the issuance of an auditor's report most likely would cause the auditor to make further inquiries about the previously issued financial statements?

A. A technological development that could affect the entity's future ability to continue as a going concern.

B. The discovery of information regarding a contingency that existed before the financial statements were issued.

C. The entity's sale of a subsidiary that accounts for 30% of the entity's consolidated sales.

D. The final resolution of a lawsuit explained in a separate paragraph of the auditor's report.

The correct answer is (B). *(CPA, adapted)*

REQUIRED: The event occurring after the issuance of an auditor's report most likely resulting in further inquiries.

DISCUSSION: When the auditor becomes aware of information that relates to prior financial statements but that was not known to him/her at the date of the report and that (s)he would have investigated if it had been discovered during the audit, the auditor should undertake to determine whether the information is reliable and whether the facts existed at the report date.

Answers (A) and (C) are incorrect because an event occurring after issuance of the report need not be considered by the auditor if it would not affect the report. Answer (D) is incorrect because the auditor need not consider final determinations or resolutions of contingencies that were disclosed in the financial statements or that resulted in a departure from the auditor's standard report.

267. After issuing a report, an auditor has no obligation to make continuing inquiries or perform other procedures concerning the audited financial statements, unless

A. Information, which existed at the report date and may affect the report, comes to the auditor's attention.

B. The control environment changes after issuance of the report.

C. Information about an event that occurred after the end of field work comes to the auditor's attention.

D. Final determinations or resolutions are made of contingencies that had been disclosed in the financial statements.

The correct answer is (A). *(CPA, adapted)*

REQUIRED: The basis for the obligation to perform procedures after the report is issued.

DISCUSSION: Although the auditor may need to extend subsequent events procedures when public companies make filings under the Securities Act of 1933 (AU 711, *Filings under Federal Securities Statutes*), (s)he ordinarily need not apply any procedures after the issuance of the report. But, if the auditor becomes aware of information that relates to the financial statements previously reported on, that (s)he did not know at the date of the report, and that is of such a nature and from such a source that (s)he would have investigated it had it come to light during the course of the audit, (s)he should, as soon as practicable, determine whether the information is reliable and whether the facts existed at the date of the report (AU 561, *Subsequent Discovery of Facts Existing at the Date of the Auditor's Report*).

Answers (B) and (D) are incorrect because the auditor has no responsibility to consider changes in controls or monitor disclosed contingencies after the report is issued. Answer (C) is incorrect because the subsequent event must have occurred prior to the date of the auditor's report for the auditor to have reporting responsibility.

268. Subsequent to the issuance of the auditor's report, the auditor became aware of facts existing at the report date that would have affected the report had the auditor then been aware of such facts. After determining that the information is reliable, the auditor should next

A. Notify the board of directors that the auditor's report must no longer be associated with the financial statements.

B. Determine whether there are persons relying or likely to rely on the financial statements who would attach importance to the information.

C. Request that management disclose the effects of the newly discovered information by adding a footnote to subsequently issued financial statements.

D. Issue revised pro forma financial statements taking into consideration the newly discovered information.

The correct answer is (B). *(CPA, adapted)*

REQUIRED: The next step after determining the reliability of a subsequently discovered fact.

DISCUSSION: When new information that existed at the report date has been found to be reliable, appropriate action must be taken if the matter would have affected the report and was not reflected in the financial statements, provided the auditor "believes there are persons currently relying or likely to rely on the financial statements who would attach importance to the information" (AU 561). The time elapsed since issuance is a factor to be weighed.

Answer (A) is incorrect because notifying the board of directors that the auditor's report must no longer be associated with the financial statements is only necessary when the client refuses to make necessary disclosures. Answer (C) is incorrect because the appropriate action will depend on such factors as whether the effects of the new information can be promptly determined and whether issuance of statements for a subsequent period is imminent. Answer (D) is incorrect because the appropriate action will depend on such factors as whether the effects of the new information can be promptly determined and whether issuance of statements for a subsequent period is imminent.

269. After an audit report containing an unqualified opinion on a nonpublic client's financial statements was issued, the client decided to sell the shares of a subsidiary that accounts for 30% of its revenue and 25% of its net income. The auditor should

A. Determine whether the information is reliable and, if determined to be reliable, request that revised financial statements be issued.

B. Notify the entity that the auditor's report may no longer be associated with the financial statements.

C. Describe the effects of this subsequently discovered information in a communication with persons known to be relying on the financial statements.

D. Take no action because the auditor has no obligation to make any further inquiries.

The correct answer is (D). *(CPA, adapted)*

REQUIRED: The auditor's responsibility after the report date when the client sells shares of its subsidiary.

DISCUSSION: AU 561 states, "After (s)he has issued the report, the auditor has no obligation to make any further or continuing inquiry or perform any other auditing procedures with respect to the audited financial statements covered by that report, unless new information that may affect the report comes to his/her attention."

Answers (A), (B), and (C) are incorrect because each is an action that might be appropriate if (s)he had subsequently discovered facts that existed at the date of the report.

270. An auditor concludes that the omission of a substantive procedure considered necessary at the time of the audit may impair the auditor's current ability to support the previously expressed opinion. The auditor need not apply the omitted procedure if

A. The risk of adverse publicity or litigation is low.

B. The results of other procedures that were applied tend to compensate for the procedure omitted.

C. The auditor's opinion was qualified because of a departure from generally accepted accounting principles.

D. The results of the subsequent period's tests of controls make the omitted procedure less important.

The correct answer is (B). *(CPA, adapted)*

REQUIRED: The circumstances in which an auditor need not apply an omitted procedure.

DISCUSSION: According to AU 390, *Consideration of Omitted Procedures after the Report Date*, the results of other procedures applied or audit evidence obtained in a later audit (possibly at an interim date) may compensate for an omitted procedure. Furthermore, the auditor should assess the importance of the omitted procedure to the support of the audit opinion in relation to the overall engagement and the circumstances of the audit.

Answer (A) is incorrect because a low risk of adverse consequences to the auditor does not justify failing to apply the omitted procedure. Answer (C) is incorrect because the omission may have resulted in an inappropriate report or affected a matter not the basis for the qualification. Thus, the nature of the opinion does not justify failure to correct the omission. Answer (D) is incorrect because the results of the tests of controls in a subsequent period do not necessarily apply to the earlier period.

271. On March 15, 1999, Kent, CPA, expressed an unqualified opinion on a client's audited financial statements for the year ended December 31, 1998. On May 4, 1999, Kent's internal inspection program disclosed that engagement personnel failed to observe the client's physical inventory. Omission of this procedure impairs Kent's current ability to support the unqualified opinion. If the shareholders are currently relying on the opinion, Kent should first

A. Advise management to disclose to the shareholders that Kent's unqualified opinion should not be relied on.

B. Undertake to apply alternative procedures that would provide a satisfactory basis for the unqualified opinion.

C. Reissue the auditor's report and add an explanatory paragraph describing the departure from GAAS.

D. Compensate for the omitted procedure by performing tests of controls to reduce audit risk to a sufficiently low level.

The correct answer is (B). *(CPA, adapted)*

REQUIRED: The appropriate action when an auditor discovers that a necessary audit procedure was not performed during the previous audit.

DISCUSSION: If the auditor determines that the omission impairs his/her current ability to support the opinion and (s)he believes persons are currently relying or are likely to rely on the report, the auditor should promptly undertake to apply the omitted procedure or alternative procedures that would provide a satisfactory basis for the opinion (AU 390).

Answer (A) is incorrect because notification of users would only be necessary if the auditor could not become satisfied upon applying the procedure. Answer (C) is incorrect because the auditor has followed generally accepted auditing standards in becoming satisfied with the application of the procedure. Answer (D) is incorrect because tests of controls do not substitute for required substantive tests.

4.16 Related Party Transactions

272. When auditing related party transactions, an auditor places primary emphasis on

A. Confirming the existence of the related parties.

B. Verifying the valuation of the related party transactions.

C. Evaluating the disclosure of the related party transactions.

D. Ascertaining the rights and obligations of the related parties.

The correct answer is (C). *(CPA, adapted)*

REQUIRED: The primary concern of the auditor about related party transactions.

DISCUSSION: The auditor's primary emphasis with regard to related party transactions should be on the presentation and disclosure assertions with respect to their nature and their effect on the financial statements. However, the FASB requires that transactions with related parties be accounted for on the same basis as would be appropriate if the parties were not related.

Answers (A), (B), and (D) are incorrect because, in an audit of related party transactions, the auditor places no special emphasis on the existence, valuation, and rights and obligations assertions.

273. After determining that a related party transaction has, in fact, occurred, an auditor should

A. Add a separate paragraph to the auditor's standard report to explain the transaction.

B. Perform analytical procedures to verify whether similar transactions occurred, but were not recorded.

C. Obtain an understanding of the business purpose of the transaction.

D. Substantiate that the transaction was consummated on terms equivalent to an arm's-length transaction.

The correct answer is (C). *(CPA, adapted)*

REQUIRED: The procedure performed after determining that a related party transaction has occurred.

DISCUSSION: After identifying related party transactions, the auditor should become satisfied about their purpose, nature, extent, and effect. Among other things, the auditor should obtain an understanding of the business purpose of the transaction (AU 334, *Related Parties*).

Answer (A) is incorrect because, if the related party transaction has been accounted for properly, no modification of the standard report is necessary. However, in some cases, the auditor may wish to add a separate paragraph emphasizing that the entity has had significant related party transactions (AU 508). Answer (B) is incorrect because the auditor is not responsible for undisclosed, unrecorded related party transactions. Answer (D) is incorrect because the auditor normally cannot determine whether a transaction was consummated on terms equivalent to an arm's-length transaction. The auditor's primary concern is with disclosure of related party transactions.

274. Which of the following is most likely to indicate the existence of related parties?

A. Writing down obsolete inventory just before year-end.

B. Failing to correct previously identified internal control deficiencies.

C. Depending on a single product for the success of the entity.

D. Borrowing money at an interest rate significantly below the market rate.

The correct answer is (D). *(CPA, adapted)*

REQUIRED: The item that most likely indicates the existence of related parties.

DISCUSSION: Exchanging property for similar property in a nonmonetary transaction, borrowing or lending at rates significantly above or below market rates, selling realty at a price materially different from its appraised value, and making loans with no scheduled repayment terms are possible related party transactions (AU 334).

Answer (A) is incorrect because inventory is customarily written down to lower of cost or market at year-end. Answer (B) is incorrect because the cost of correction may exceed the benefits. Answer (C) is incorrect because dependence on one product is not a transaction that by its nature suggests the existence of related parties. However, AU 334 cites it as a possible condition motivating related party transactions.

275. An auditor searching for related party transactions should obtain an understanding of each subsidiary's relationship to the total entity because

A. This may permit the audit of intercompany account balances to be performed as of concurrent dates.

B. Intercompany transactions may have been consummated on terms equivalent to arm's-length transactions.

C. This may reveal whether particular transactions would have taken place if the parties had not been related.

D. The business structure may be deliberately designed to obscure related party transactions.

The correct answer is (D). *(CPA, adapted)*

REQUIRED: The reason for understanding parent-subsidiary relationships.

DISCUSSION: AU 334 states that "the auditor should obtain an understanding of management responsibilities and the relationship of each component to the total entity." The auditor should also consider internal control and the business purpose of each component of the entity. The auditor should be aware that sometimes "business structure and operating style are occasionally deliberately designed to obscure related party transactions."

Answer (A) is incorrect because a concurrent audit is not required. Answer (B) is incorrect because the auditor's concern is that related party transactions were not at arm's-length. Answer (C) is incorrect because, except for routine transactions, determining whether a transaction would have occurred and what the terms would have been if the parties were unrelated is ordinarily not possible.

276. Which of the following would not necessarily be a related party transaction?

A. A sale to another corporation with a similar name.

B. A purchase from another corporation that is controlled by the corporation's chief shareholder.

C. A loan from the corporation to a major shareholder.

D. Sale of land to the corporation by the spouse of a director.

The correct answer is (A). *(CPA, adapted)*

REQUIRED: The transaction not necessarily with a related party.

DISCUSSION: Principal owners, management, and members of their immediate families are parties related to the enterprise. Other parties with which the enterprise may deal are related if one party can control or significantly influence the management or operating policies of the other to the extent that one of the parties might be prevented from fully pursuing its own interests. A corporation that merely has a similar name is not necessarily related.

Answers (B), (C), and (D) are incorrect because a purchase from another corporation that is controlled by the corporation's chief shareholder, a loan from the corporation to a major shareholder, and sale of land to the corporation by the spouse of a director are related party transactions.

277. The existence of a related party transaction may be indicated when another entity

A. Sells real estate to the corporation at a price that is comparable to its appraised value.

B. Absorbs expenses of the corporation.

C. Borrows from the corporation at a rate of interest equal to the current market rate.

D. Lends to the corporation at a rate of interest equal to the current market rate.

The correct answer is (B). *(CPA, adapted)*

REQUIRED: The indicator of the existence of a related party transaction.

DISCUSSION: Typical related party transactions include interest-free or low interest loans, real estate sales at prices different from appraisal values, nonmonetary exchanges of similar property, and loans with no scheduled terms (AU 334). Thus, when another entity absorbs the interest cost for a loan or otherwise provides an advantage that would not be characteristic of an arm's-length transaction, the existence of related parties may be indicated.

Answers (A), (C), and (D) are incorrect because a purchase of realty at appraised value and lending or borrowing at the current market rate are indications of arm's-length transactions between unrelated parties.

278. In the absence of evidence to the contrary, transactions with related parties should not be assumed to be outside the ordinary course of business. The auditor should, however, be aware of the possibility that transactions with related parties may have been motivated solely or in large part by extraordinary conditions. Which of the following is not normally a condition motivating a transaction outside of the ordinary course of business?

A. Lack of sufficient working capital or credit to continue business.

B. An urgent desire for a continued favorable earnings record in the hope of supporting the price of the company's stock.

C. Dependence on a single or relatively few products, customers, or transactions for the ongoing success of the venture.

D. Mutual benefit to both parties.

The correct answer is (D). *(Publisher)*

REQUIRED: The condition not considered a motive for a transaction outside the ordinary course of business.

DISCUSSION: Parties customarily execute transactions that are mutually beneficial. These are considered within the ordinary course of business. The absence of mutual benefit is an indication that the transaction is not at arm's-length and that special disclosure is required to prevent the statements from being misleading.

Answer (A) is incorrect because lack of sufficient working capital or credit to continue business is a condition suggesting that transactions resulting from related party activities are in substance different from their form. Other such conditions include an overly optimistic earnings forecast; a declining industry characterized by a large number of business failures; excess capacity; significant litigation, especially litigation between shareholders and management; and significant danger of obsolescence because the company is in a high-technology industry. Answers (B) and (C) are incorrect because each is a condition motivating a transaction outside of the ordinary course.

279. Which of the following auditing procedures is most likely to assist an auditor in identifying related party transactions?

A. Retesting ineffective controls previously reported to the audit committee.

B. Sending second requests for unanswered positive confirmations of accounts receivable.

C. Reviewing accounting records for nonrecurring transactions recognized near the balance sheet date.

D. Inspecting communications with law firms for evidence of unreported contingent liabilities.

The correct answer is (C). *(CPA, adapted)*

REQUIRED: The procedure that is most likely to assist the auditor in identifying related party transactions.

DISCUSSION: AU 334 identifies a number of procedures intended to provide guidance for identifying material transactions with parties known to be related and for identifying material transactions that may be indicative of the existence of previously undetermined relationships. One of those procedures is reviewing accounting records for large, unusual, or nonrecurring transactions or balances, paying particular attention to transactions recognized at or near the end of the reporting period.

Answer (A) is incorrect because retesting ineffective controls is not an effective use of audit resources. Answer (B) is incorrect because confirmations typically do not provide effective evidence as to related party transactions. Answer (D) is incorrect because inspecting communications with law firms for evidence of unreported contingent liabilities is for the purpose of identifying potential litigations, claims, and assessments requiring disclosure in the financial statements.

280. Which of the following is an unusual procedure that may be deemed necessary to discover the effect of a related party transaction?

A. Examine invoices and other pertinent documents such as receiving or shipping reports.

B. Confirm or discuss significant information with intermediaries, such as banks, guarantors, or agents.

C. Determine whether the transaction has been approved by the board of directors or other appropriate officials.

D. Inspect or confirm the transferability and value of collateral.

The correct answer is (B). *(Publisher)*

REQUIRED: The unusual procedure to discover the effect of a related party transaction.

DISCUSSION: AU 334 suggests that, to understand fully a related party transaction, certain procedures not otherwise required to comply with GAAS should be considered. The confirmation or discussion of significant information with intermediaries, such as banks, guarantors, attorneys, or agents, is an unusual procedure that might be applied when necessary to understand a related party transaction.

Answers (A), (C), and (D) are incorrect because each is a normal procedure that may be performed by an auditor to obtain satisfaction as to the purpose, nature, and extent of related party transactions and their effects.

281. Disclosure in financial statements of a reporting entity that has participated in related party transactions that are material, individually or in the aggregate, should include all of the following except

A. The nature of the relationship.

B. A description of the transactions for the period reported upon including amounts, if any, and such other information necessary to an understanding of the effects on the financial statements.

C. A statement that the transactions would have taken place regardless of whether the parties were related.

D. The dollar volume of the transactions, amounts due from or to related parties and, if not otherwise apparent, the terms and manner of settlement.

The correct answer is (C). *(Publisher)*

REQUIRED: The item concerning related party transactions not required to be disclosed.

DISCUSSION: It is ordinarily not possible to determine whether a particular transaction would have taken place if the parties had not been related or, assuming it would have taken place, what the terms and the manner of settlement would have been. Accordingly, representations to the effect that "a transaction was consummated on terms equivalent to those that prevail in arm's-length transactions" are difficult to substantiate and should not be included in the disclosures.

Answer (A) is incorrect because the nature of the relationship is information that is of interest to readers of the financial statements in determining the effects of related party transactions on those statements (SFAS 57, *Related Party Disclosures*). Answer (B) is incorrect because a description of the transactions for the period reported upon including amounts, if any, and such other information necessary to an understanding of the effects on the financial statements require disclosure. Answer (D) is incorrect because the dollar volume of the transactions, amounts due from or to related parties and, if not otherwise apparent, the terms and manner of settlement require disclosure.

282. Ajax, Inc. is an affiliate of the audit client and is audited by another firm of auditors. Which of the following is most likely to be used by the auditor of the client to obtain assurance that all guarantees of the affiliate's indebtedness have been detected?

A. Send the standard bank confirmation request to all of the client's lender banks.

B. Review client minutes and obtain a representation letter.

C. Examine supporting documents for all entries in intercompany accounts.

D. Obtain written confirmation of indebtedness from the auditor of the affiliate.

The correct answer is (B). *(CPA, adapted)*

REQUIRED: The procedure used to determine that all guarantees of indebtedness have been detected.

DISCUSSION: The client's independent auditor should review minutes of board of directors and relevant committee meetings and obtain a representation letter to gain assurance that all guarantees of the affiliate's indebtedness have been detected.

Answer (A) is incorrect because bank confirmations sent to the client's lender banks would not detect guarantees of indebtedness to nonbank creditors. Answer (C) is incorrect because guarantees are not reflected in the accounts. Answer (D) is incorrect because confirmations, per se, are not typically obtained from other auditors.

4.17 Statement of Cash Flows

283. When auditing a client's statement of cash flows, an auditor will rely primarily upon

A. Determination of the amount of cash at year-end.

B. Cross-referencing to balances and transactions considered in connection with the audit of the other financial statements.

C. Analysis of significant ratios of prior years as compared to the current year.

D. The audit guidance provided by SFAS 95, *Statement of Cash Flows*.

The correct answer is (B). *(CPA, adapted)*

REQUIRED: The evidence on which the auditor will primarily rely when auditing a statement of cash flows.

DISCUSSION: The statement of cash flows represents balances taken from the other statements as well as analysis of changes in those balances. Consequently, this statement is audited in conjunction with the balance sheet and income statement accounts.

Answer (A) is incorrect because the statement reflects the changes in the cash balance rather than the balance in the account at year-end. Answer (C) is incorrect because analysis of ratios (an analytical procedure) used as a substantive test may be effective and efficient for testing some assertions but not all of those encompassed by a statement of cash flows. Answer (D) is incorrect because SFAS 95 prescribes GAAP for the statement of cash flows, not audit guidance.

284. An auditor is reviewing a corporate client's statement of cash flows. The auditor should expect the cash flows to be classified according to

A. Fund inflows and fund outflows.

B. Cash inflows and cash outflows.

C. Operating activities, sources, and uses.

D. Investing, financing, and operating activities.

The correct answer is (D). *(Publisher)*

REQUIRED: The activities into which cash receipts and cash payments should be classified.

DISCUSSION: To provide the most useful information about cash receipts and cash payments to investors, creditors, and others, a statement of cash flows should report the cash effects of an entity's operations, its investing transactions, and its financing transactions during the period. In addition, the related disclosures should report the effects of investing and financing transactions that do not directly affect cash.

Answer (A) is incorrect because a statement of cash flows is based on cash. Answer (B) is incorrect because the cash flows must be classified according to investing, financing, and operating activities. Answer (C) is incorrect because sources and uses were used in the now-superseded statement of changes in financial position.

285. When auditing a corporate client's statement of cash flows, an auditor expects to find interest revenue classified as a cash inflow from

A. Financing or investing activities.

B. Investing activities.

C. Financing activities.

D. Operating activities.

The correct answer is (D). *(Publisher)*

REQUIRED: The classification of interest revenue.

DISCUSSION: Operating activities include all transactions and other events that are not classified as investing and financing activities. In general, the cash effects of transactions and other events that enter into the determination of income are to be classified as operating activities. Cash receipts from the sale of goods or services and from interest on loans and dividends on equity securities are ordinarily classified as cash inflows from operating activities. The cash outflows from operating activities include cash payments to suppliers for inventory, to employees for wages, to governments for taxes, to lenders for interest, and to other suppliers for other expenses.

Answer (A) is incorrect because financing activities include the issuance of stock, the payment of dividends, treasury stock transactions, the issuance of debt, the repayment or other settlement of debt obligations, and receipt of donor-restricted resources. Investing activities include the lending of money and the collecting of those loans (but not the receipt of interest thereon), and the acquisition, sale, or other disposal of (1) securities that are not cash equivalents and (2) productive assets that are expected to generate revenue over a long period of time. Answers (B) and (C) are incorrect because interest revenue is classified as a cash inflow from operating activities.

286. Many of the Granada Corporation's convertible bondholders have converted their bonds into stock during the year under audit. The independent auditor should review the Granada Corporation's statement of cash flows and related disclosures to ascertain that they show

A. Only the cash used to reduce the convertible debt.

B. Only the cash provided by the issuance of stock.

C. The issuance of the stock and reduction in convertible debt.

D. Nothing relating to the conversion because it does not affect cash.

The correct answer is (C). *(CPA, adapted)*

REQUIRED: The proper reporting of the conversion of bonds to stock.

DISCUSSION: Information about noncash financing and investing activities must be reported in related disclosures but not on the face of the statement of cash flows. Exclusion of such transactions from the statement avoids complicating it and emphasizes the entity's cash receipts and payments (SFAS 95). The issuance of stock and the reduction of convertible debt should therefore be disclosed in a related but separate schedule. All financing (and investing) activities during the period should be reported, including those that do not directly affect cash.

Answers (A) and (B) are incorrect because, although both parts of the financing activity should be reported, neither involves a cash flow. Answer (D) is incorrect because all financing and investing activities should be reported.

CHAPTER FIVE
INFORMATION SYSTEMS

This chapter covers computers, computer operations, computer systems, and the auditing of computer operations and systems. The first six modules are definitional. Module 5.1 is an introduction, and Modules 5.2 through 5.6 relate to computer system attributes, development, and design. Modules 5.7 through 5.10 concern computer processing control and their evaluation. Module 5.11 defines the auditor's understanding and testing of a client's computer processing internal control. Module 5.12 involves the use of the computer to assist the auditor in gathering evidence. Module 5.13 presents specific Certified Information Systems Auditor (CISA) concepts. The following discussion provides an overview of computer processing controls.

COMPUTER PROCESSING CONTROLS

A variety of controls may be performed to assure the accuracy, completeness, and authorization of transactions. The two broad groupings of information systems control activities are general and application controls.

General controls include controls over data center operations, system software acquisition and maintenance, applications system development and maintenance, and access security. These controls apply to mainframe, minicomputer, and end-user environments (AU 319).

1. **Data center operation controls** include the plan of the organization and the operation of the computer processing activity. They are concerned with the proper segregation of duties and responsibilities within the computer processing environment. The responsibilities of systems analysts, programmers, operators, file librarians, and the control group should be performed by different individuals, and proper supervision should be provided. Operating controls insure efficient and effective operation within the computer processing department. These controls also assure proper procedures in case of data loss because of error or disaster. Typical operating controls include the proper labeling of all files both internally and externally, halt and error procedures, duplicate files, and reconstruction procedures for files. We term these **operating and organizational controls**, and they are considered in Module 5.7.

2. **System software acquisition and maintenance controls** and **application system development and maintenance controls** are concerned with the proper planning, procurement, testing, and documentation of systems. These controls also provide for security and virus protection of software including operating systems, utility programs, and application software. Maintenance controls include authorizations and documentation including proper use of flowcharts. We term these **program development and documentation controls**, and they are covered in Module 5.8.
3. **Access security controls** provide assurance that only authorized individuals have access to computer equipment and data files. Such controls include physical safeguards of equipment, proper library security, and passwords. These controls are considered in Module 5.9.

Application controls apply to the processing of individual applications. These controls help ensure that transactions are valid, properly authorized, and completely and accurately processed. They can be classified into input, processing, and output controls. They are considered in Module 5.10.

1. **Input controls** are designed to provide reasonable assurance that data received for computer processing have been properly authorized and are in a form suitable for processing. Input controls also include those that relate to rejection, correction, and resubmission of data that were initially incorrect.
2. **Processing controls** are designed to provide reasonable assurance that data submitted for processing have been processed appropriately, i.e., that all transactions are processed as authorized, no authorized transactions are omitted, and no unauthorized transactions are added.
3. **Output controls** are designed to assure that the processing results are accurate and that only authorized personnel receive the output.

5.1 Introduction to the Information Systems Environment

1. A management information system

A. Can exist only with computers.
B. Primarily processes data and produces reports.
C. Supports the operations, management, and decision-making functions in an organization.
D. Is a single large system in an organization.

The correct answer is (C). *(CIA, adapted)*

REQUIRED: The description of a management information system.

DISCUSSION: A management information system (MIS) is a system of resources within the organization that processes data to generate information useful in operations and management. It provides the most comprehensive support for decision making involving structured tasks.

Answer (A) is incorrect because an MIS rarely exists without computers except in small businesses. Answer (B) is incorrect because the data processing cycle (processing of data and production of reports) generates information for use in the MIS. Answer (D) is incorrect because the MIS consists of many subsystems, including the accounting information system.

2. Early decision models used with structured decisions, such as inventory reordering and production scheduling, emphasized finding the structure of the decision and programming as much of it as possible. More recent models have been developed to support unstructured decision processes. Models of the latter type are called

A. Decision support systems.

B. Management information systems.

C. Systems analysis techniques.

D. Rational decision models.

The correct answer is (A). *(CIA, adapted)*

REQUIRED: The term for models developed to support unstructured decision processes.

DISCUSSION: A decision support system (DSS) assists middle- and upper-level managers in long-term, nonroutine, and often unstructured decision making. The system combines data, decision models, and user-friendly software to provide end users with capabilities for analysis rather than specified information flows. It is an aid to decision making, not the automation of a decision process.

Answer (B) is incorrect because an MIS does not normally include subsystems that provide support for unstructured decisions. Answer (C) is incorrect because systems analysis techniques are used to design the DSS. Answer (D) is incorrect because all decision models are rational.

3. Which of the following is not a benefit of using information technology in solving audit problems?

A. It helps reduce audit risk.

B. It improves the timeliness of the audit.

C. It increases audit opportunities.

D. It improves the auditor's judgment.

The correct answer is (D). *(CIA, adapted)*

REQUIRED: The item not a benefit of using information technology in solving audit problems.

DISCUSSION: Judgment is the fruit of an auditor's formal education, professional experience, and personal qualities. Information technology is merely a tool for achieving audit objectives. It does not improve the auditor's judgment.

Answer (A) is incorrect because information technology allows more data to be reviewed and reduces audit risk. Answer (B) is incorrect because information technology can expedite the audit. Answer (C) is incorrect because information technology can be used to implement a new approach to the audit of an application or function.

4. The first phase in the evolutionary development of information systems occurs when

A. Management discovers it is losing money.

B. Resources permit the hiring of a system staff.

C. The decision is made to acquire a computer system.

D. The growth of an enterprise brings about the need for improved administrative planning and control.

The correct answer is (D). *(CDP, adapted)*

REQUIRED: The first phase in the evolutionary development of an information system.

DISCUSSION: As its information needs change, an organization requires improved methods of processing data to provide information for managerial decisions and to control the implementation of those decisions. When this need is recognized, firms begin systems development activities.

Answer (A) is incorrect because management may lose money for many reasons other than the lack of systems development. Answer (B) is incorrect because the need for improved processing should be the deciding criterion, not whether resources permit the hiring of additional staff. Answer (C) is incorrect because the need should precede the decision to acquire a computer system.

5. Management activities can be classified in three levels: strategic planning, management control, and operational control. Information requirements vary with the level of management activity. Which of the following best describes the information requirements for strategic planning?

A. Frequent use, external, aggregate information.

B. Future-oriented, outdated, detailed information.

C. Highly current, accurate, largely internal information.

D. Wide scope, aggregate, future-oriented information.

The correct answer is (D). *(CIA, adapted)*

REQUIRED: The best description of the information requirements for strategic planning.

DISCUSSION: Strategic planning concerns development of the entity's long-range mission and objectives and the means for accomplishing them. Such plans are often stated in general terms and exclude operational detail because of uncertainty about future conditions. Strategic planning is commonly defined as having a planning horizon of 1 to 10 years. The information needed for strategic planning tends to come from external sources, to be very wide in scope, and to be highly aggregated (not detailed). Moreover, this information is future oriented, much less current than that needed for operational or management control, relatively less accurate, and infrequently used.

Answer (A) is incorrect because information needed for strategic planning is not frequently used. Answer (B) is incorrect because information needed for strategic planning is not detailed or necessarily outdated. Answer (C) is incorrect because information needed for operational control needs to be highly current and accurate and is largely internal.

6. Who is ultimately responsible for the implementation of cost-effective controls in an automated system?

A. The director of internal auditing.

B. Operating management.

C. The computer processing audit manager.

D. The control group in the computer processing department.

The correct answer is (B). *(CIA, adapted)*

REQUIRED: The party or parties primarily responsible for the implementation of cost-effective controls.

DISCUSSION: Operating management should assure that effective controls are implemented in all parts of an organization. Management is ultimately responsible for establishing systems to provide reasonable assurance of achieving organizational objectives and goals.

Answer (A) is incorrect because internal auditing is responsible for evaluating, but not establishing, internal controls. Answer (C) is incorrect because the computer processing audit manager is only one member of operating management. Answer (D) is incorrect because the control group acts as a liaison between system users and the computer department and implements many controls on an operational basis, but it is not responsible for the development of controls.

7. Regardless of the nature of the client's information processing system, the auditor must consider internal control. In a computer environment, the auditor must, at a minimum, have

A. A basic familiarity with the computer's operating system.

B. A sufficient understanding of the entire computer system.

C. An expertise in computer systems analysis.

D. A background in programming procedures.

The correct answer is (B). *(Publisher)*

REQUIRED: The degree of understanding an auditor must have of a client's computer processing system.

DISCUSSION: The first general standard (GAAS) requires the audit to be performed by a person having adequate technical training and proficiency as an auditor. The second standard of field work requires that a sufficient understanding of internal control be obtained to plan the audit and determine the nature, timing, and extent of substantive tests. Hence, the auditor should have the training and proficiency that are necessary to understand control activities relevant to the computer processing system. This understanding must be sufficient for audit planning and testing.

Answer (A) is incorrect because familiarity with the computer's operating system is less important than understanding the entire processing system. Answers (C) and (D) are incorrect because auditors usually do not need to be experts in computer systems analysis or programming, although certain audit procedures may require special expertise.

8. Which of the following statements most likely represents a disadvantage for an entity that keeps microcomputer-prepared data files rather than manually prepared files?

A. Attention is focused on the accuracy of the programming process rather than errors in individual transactions.

B. It is usually easier for unauthorized persons to access and alter the files.

C. Random error associated with processing similar transactions in different ways is usually greater.

D. It is usually more difficult to compare recorded accountability with the physical count of assets.

The correct answer is (B). *(CPA, adapted)*

REQUIRED: The disadvantage of microcomputer-prepared data files.

DISCUSSION: In a manual system, one individual is usually assigned responsibility for maintaining and safeguarding the records. However, in a microcomputer environment, the data files may be subject to change by others without documentation or an indication of who made the changes.

Answer (A) is incorrect because the focus on programming is an advantage of using the computer. A program allows transactions to be processed uniformly. Answer (C) is incorrect because an advantage of the computer is that it processes similar transactions in the same way. Answer (D) is incorrect because the method of maintaining the files is independent of the ability to compare this information in the file with the physical count of assets.

9. The most common computer-related problem confronting organizations is

A. Hardware malfunction.

B. Input errors and omissions.

C. Disruption to computer processing caused by natural disasters.

D. Fraud.

The correct answer is (B). *(CIA, adapted)*

REQUIRED: The most common problem confronting an organization using computers.

DISCUSSION: The most common problem confronting an organization in its use of computers is erroneous or incomplete input. Input is especially susceptible to errors and omissions because of the substantial human intervention required. Comprehensive and effective input controls are necessary to ensure that data stored in files or used in processing are not contaminated.

Answer (A) is incorrect because hardware malfunction is not considered a major problem once the development and testing phase is complete. Answer (C) is incorrect because the second most common problem is the disruption to processing caused by natural disasters such as fire or power failures. Answer (D) is incorrect because the third most common problem is computer abuse, e.g., fraud.

10. Which one of the following statements about an accounting information system (AIS) is incorrect?

A. AIS supports day-to-day operations by collecting and sorting data about an organization's transactions.

B. The information produced by AIS is made available to all levels of management for use in planning and controlling an organization's activities.

C. AIS is best suited to solve problems where there is great uncertainty and ill-defined reporting requirements.

D. AIS is often referred to as a transaction processing system.

The correct answer is (C). *(CMA, adapted)*

REQUIRED: The incorrect statement about an accounting information system (AIS).

DISCUSSION: An AIS is a subsystem of a management information system that processes financial and transactional data relevant to managerial and financial accounting. The AIS supports operations by collecting and sorting data about an organization's transactions. An AIS is concerned not only with external parties, but also with the internal activities needed for management decision making at all levels. An AIS is best suited to solve problems when reporting requirements are well defined. A decision support system is a better choice for problems in which decision making is less structured.

Answers (A), (B), and (D) are incorrect because they are attributes of an AIS.

11. The two broad groupings of information systems control activities are general controls and application controls. General controls include controls

A. Designed to assure that only authorized users receive output from processing.

B. For developing, modifying, and maintaining computer programs.

C. That relate to the correction and resubmission of faulty data.

D. Designed to ensure that all data submitted for processing have been properly authorized.

The correct answer is (B). *(Publisher)*

REQUIRED: The general controls.

DISCUSSION: General controls relate to all or many computerized activities and often include control over the development, modification, and maintenance of computer programs and control over the use of and changes to data maintained on computer files. They include such controls as (1) operating and organizational controls, (2) systems acquisition and maintenance controls, (3) application system development and maintenance controls, and (4) access security controls.

Answers (A), (C), and (D) are incorrect because controls over report distribution (output), correction of input errors, and authorization of input are application controls.

12. Which of the following risks are greater in computerized systems than in manual systems?

I. Erroneous data conversion
II. Erroneous source document preparation
III. Repetition of errors
IV. Concentration of data

A. I and II.

B. II and III.

C. I, III, and IV.

D. I, II, III, and IV.

The correct answer is (C). *(CISA, adapted)*

REQUIRED: The risks that are greater in a computer system than a manual system.

DISCUSSION: Unlike a manual system, a computer system converts data to machine-readable form so that transactions can be processed. This additional step increases the risk of input error. Moreover, if an error exists in the program, systematic, repetitive errors will occur in processing transactions. Finally, data are typically stored magnetically on tapes or disks. This concentration of data increases the risk of loss from natural and other disasters.

Answers (A), (B), and (D) are incorrect because source document preparation either precedes processing or is eliminated altogether in a computerized system. Thus, the risk of erroneous source document preparation in computerized systems is the same as or less than the equivalent risk in manual systems.

13. Compared with closed systems, open systems are characterized by

A. Less expensive components.

B. Decreased interoperability.

C. More dependence on particular vendors.

D. More restricted portability.

The correct answer is (A). *(CIA, adapted)*

REQUIRED: The item that characterizes open systems.

DISCUSSION: According to Module 11 of the Systems Auditability and Control Report, "Open systèms are information systems assembled from parts manufactured to public standards." Since the 1980s, government agencies have demanded that suppliers provide components with interfaces defined by public standards. These standards apply especially to operating systems and telecommunications protocols. Thus, they permit systems from different suppliers to work together (interoperability). Moreover, open systems can be sized to an entity's needs (scalability), and relocated to new platforms (portability), and used for years to come (compatibility). Another result of product interchangeability is the formation of a commodity market and a decline in prices. Less product differentiation means that competition is increasingly based solely on price.

Answer (B) is incorrect because open systems have increased interoperability. Answer (C) is incorrect because users of open systems have a wider range of vendors available. Answer (D) is incorrect because open systems are more portable.

14. Prudent managers will recognize the limits within which expert systems can be effectively applied. An expert system would be most appropriate to

A. Compensate for the lack of certain technical knowledge within the organization.

B. Help make customer-service jobs easier to perform.

C. Automate daily managerial problem-solving.

D. Emulate human expertise for strategic planning.

The correct answer is (B). *(CIA, adapted)*

REQUIRED: The most appropriate use for an expert system.

DISCUSSION: Expert systems are systems that allow a computer to make decisions in a human way. Expert systems allow even small companies to perform activities and provide services previously only available from larger firms. The use of expert systems has helped to improve the quality of customer service in applications such as maintenance and scheduling by automating them and making them easy to perform.

Answer (A) is incorrect because expert systems codify and apply existing knowledge, but they do not create knowledge that is lacking. Answer (C) is incorrect because expert systems do best in automating lower-level clerical functions. Answer (D) is incorrect because expert systems concern problems with relatively few possible outcomes that are all known in advance.

5.2 Basic Hardware Concepts

15. Which of the following is not an element of hardware?

A. Monitors.

B. Application programs.

C. Magnetic tape readers.

D. Scanners.

The correct answer is (B). *(Publisher)*

REQUIRED: The item that is not considered hardware.

DISCUSSION: Computer hardware consists of the configuration of physical equipment. Application software consists of programs written for or by users to perform certain ultimate tasks specified by the users.

Answer (A) is incorrect because monitors are output devices for display of data or graphics. Answer (C) is incorrect because a magnetic tape reader senses information recorded as magnetic spots on a magnetic tape and reads them into the central processing unit (CPU). Answer (D) is incorrect because scanners are devices that digitize documents and graphics.

16. Today organizations are using microcomputers for data presentation because microcomputer use, compared to mainframe use, is more

A. Controllable.

B. Conductive to data integrity.

C. Reliable.

D. Cost effective.

The correct answer is (D). *(CIA, adapted)*

REQUIRED: The reason for using microcomputers for data presentation.

DISCUSSION: In cooperative processing, microcomputers are more cost effective than mainframes for data entry and presentation. They are better suited to frequent screen updating and graphical user interfaces.

Answer (A) is incorrect because microcomputer use is less controllable than mainframe use. Answer (B) is incorrect because the difficulty of control in a microcomputer environment threatens data integrity. Answer (C) is incorrect because, given their decades of refinement and the use of redundant hardware components, mainframes are usually more reliable than microcomputers.

17. Which of the following is a hardware device not usually associated with input?

A. Printer.

B. Optical scanner.

C. Cassette tape device.

D. CRT terminal.

The correct answer is (A). *(Publisher)*

REQUIRED: The hardware device not usually associated with input.

DISCUSSION: A printer is used to produce a hard copy of information output. Printers may print one character, one line, or one page at a time. They also vary with respect to speed and quality.

Answer (B) is incorrect because an optical scanner reads characters directly from source documents based upon the shapes of the characters. Answer (C) is incorrect because a cassette device performs both input and output functions. Answer (D) is incorrect because a CRT or cathode-ray tube terminal is an input or output device.

18. Which of the following computer hardware devices allows for an immediate update of merchandise inventory in a retail environment?

A. Inventory control terminal.

B. Cathode ray tube (CRT) terminal.

C. Video display terminal.

D. Point-of-sale terminal.

The correct answer is (D). *(CIA, adapted)*

REQUIRED: The computer hardware device that allows for an immediate update of merchandise inventory.

DISCUSSION: Point-of-sale terminals are replacing cash registers in retail stores. They capture data by optical scanning or by keying. The data are then transmitted to a CPU. The system permits collection of sales data, updating and ordering of inventory, pricing at the point of sale, and checking of customer credit cards.

Answer (A) is incorrect because the term inventory control terminal is not meaningful in this context. Answer (B) is incorrect because a CRT terminal is a video display device that is the most common device used for human-computer interaction. Answer (C) is incorrect because video display terminal is a generic term for any device with a keyboard and a visual display that interacts with a computer.

19. Some taxpayers complete the tax return forms by handwriting block style letters and numbers in designated areas on the forms. The characters will most likely be translated into machine-readable form by

A. Keydisk.

B. MICR.

C. OCR.

D. POS.

The correct answer is (C). *(CIA, adapted)*

REQUIRED: The method of translating handwritten characters on a tax form into machine-readable form.

DISCUSSION: OCR is optical character recognition, which permits typed or handwritten characters to be recognized by an optical scanner if they are printed carefully in a single style. The advantage of OCR devices is the elimination of the time, effort, cost, and errors of additional data preparation.

Answer (A) is incorrect because keydisk means operator keying of data at a data entry workstation. Data for keydisk entry are not normally prepared this carefully. Answer (B) is incorrect because MICR is magnetic ink character recognition. Taxpayers typically use ordinary writing instruments. Answer (D) is incorrect because POS is point-of-sale capture of sale transaction data.

20. Banks are required to process many transactions from paper documents (e.g., checks, deposit slips) during the course of an average business day. This requires a reliable, yet economical form of input. The most common source automation device used by banks is

A. A disk pack.

B. Magnetic tape.

C. Bar coding.

D. Magnetic ink character recognition.

The correct answer is (D). *(CMA, adapted)*

REQUIRED: The most common source automation device used by banks.

DISCUSSION: Magnetic ink character recognition (MICR) is used by banks to read the magnetic ink on checks and deposit slips. MICR is a form of data entry device.

Answer (A) is incorrect because a disk pack is a storage device. Answer (B) is incorrect because magnetic tape is a storage device. Answer (C) is incorrect because bar coding is a data entry technique often used by manufacturers, wholesalers, and retailers, but is rarely used by banks.

21. The principal advantage of magnetic tape as a storage medium is that it

A. Permits random access.

B. Uses variable length records.

C. Is a low-cost medium.

D. Requires less labor-intensive intervention.

The correct answer is (C). *(CIA, adapted)*

REQUIRED: The principal advantage of magnetic tape.

DISCUSSION: The principal advantage of magnetic tape is its low cost relative to disk storage for the same volume of data. It is a relatively stable and reliable medium that can store a large volume of data. Moreover, it can be reused.

Answer (A) is incorrect because magnetic tape uses sequential access. Answer (B) is incorrect because disk devices can also use variable length records. Answer (D) is incorrect because magnetic tape is labor-intensive to mount and dismount.

22. Which of the following statements about microcomputers, minicomputers, and mainframe computers is true?

A. Microcomputers usually cost more than minicomputers but less than mainframes.

B. Because of the increased use of microcomputers, there will be little need for mainframes in the near future.

C. Minicomputers must be programmed directly in machine language while mainframes use higher-level language.

D. The cost per transaction to process on each type of computer has decreased in recent years.

The correct answer is (D). *(Publisher)*

REQUIRED: The true statement concerning micro, mini, and mainframe computers.

DISCUSSION: Advances in technology have resulted in less expensive computers and increased computing power. The cost to process transactions on all kinds of computers has therefore decreased.

Answer (A) is incorrect because microcomputers (personal computers) may cost less than $1,000. Relative to microcomputers, minicomputers are more costly, more powerful, have more memory, and are able to interface with more peripheral equipment. Mainframes are large computers with many peripheral devices and large memories. There is virtually no upper limit on the cost of a mainframe. Answer (B) is incorrect because, although microcomputers have become extremely popular, e.g., for word processing, databases, and other business-related activities, large mainframes are still necessary for simulations and processing not possible on other smaller computers. Minicomputers fill the gap between micro and mainframe computers, and a relatively strong demand also exists for these types of processors. Answer (C) is incorrect because all three computers ordinarily may be programmed in higher-level languages.

23. Internal auditors often encounter different microcomputer platforms in separate operating divisions or geographic locations. Which of the following statements is true?

I. Most data and programs from one microcomputer platform are transferable to another environment only through translation and emulation programs.

II. Neither data nor programs are transferable when the hardware is not identical.

III. Neither data nor programs are transferable when the operating systems are not identical.

IV. Most data and many programs are transferable among environments through shareware programs.

A. I.

B. I, IV.

C. III.

D. II, III.

The correct answer is (A). *(CIA, adapted)*

REQUIRED: The true statement(s) about microcomputer platforms.

DISCUSSION: An emulator is a hardware device that permits one system to imitate another, that is, to use the same data and programs and obtain the same results as the other system. A translator is a program that translates from one programming language into another.

Answer (B) is incorrect because shareware is not available to meet most conversion needs. Shareware is a program that can be freely copied and tested before purchase. If the party obtaining the shareware continues to use it, there is an obligation to send payment to the author. Shareware typically is found on bulletin boards and online information systems. Answers (C) and (D) are incorrect because there are facilities to transfer data and programs between some environments.

24. A piece of hardware that takes the computer's digital information and transforms it into signals that can be sent over ordinary telephone lines is called a(n)

A. Terminal emulator.

B. Communications control unit.

C. Intelligent terminal.

D. Modem.

The correct answer is (D). *(CIA, adapted)*

REQUIRED: The hardware that transforms digital information into analog signals.

DISCUSSION: Modems are used to communicate between terminals and a CPU, usually across telephone lines. The modem (modulator-demodulator) converts the digital form of data storage in a computer into analog or sound waves that can be communicated across telephone lines. The modem at the receiving end converts the analog signal back to the digital form used by the terminal or CPU.

Answer (A) is incorrect because a terminal emulator permits a microcomputer to interface with a mainframe. Answer (B) is incorrect because communications control units include communications processors (front-end processors), multiplexors, and concentrators. Communications processors are small computers that perform communications tasks (storing and moving data, editing, message switching, etc.) Multiplexors combine signals from different terminals into one signal to be sent to the CPU or other point. A concentrator is essentially a more advanced multiplexor. Answer (C) is incorrect because an intelligent terminal is hardware that has processing ability.

25. Most microcomputers (PCs) have both a floppy disk drive and a hard disk drive. The major difference between the two types of storage is that a hard disk

A. Has a much larger storage capacity than a floppy disk and can also access information much more quickly.

B. Is a direct-access storage medium, whereas a floppy disk is a sequential-access storage medium.

C. Provides an automatic audit trail, whereas a floppy disk does not.

D. Is suitable for an online system, whereas a floppy disk is not.

The correct answer is (A). *(CIA, adapted)*

REQUIRED: The difference between floppy disk and hard disk storage.

DISCUSSION: Floppy disks were developed by IBM out of plastic film that rotates the desired stored data to an opening in its cover where it is accessed by the computer's read-write device. Hard disks are used in larger systems as well as in microcomputers. They require much less power and maintenance than floppies and can store far more data. Also, the read-write operations and disk rotation are much faster with hard disks.

Answer (B) is incorrect because both floppy disk and hard disk are direct-access storage media. Answer (C) is incorrect because neither hard disk nor floppy disk provides an automatic audit trail. Answer (D) is incorrect because both floppy disk and hard disk are suited for an online system.

26. A manufacturer of complex electronic equipment such as oscilloscopes and microscopes has been shipping its products with thick paper manuals but wants to reduce the cost of producing and shipping this documentation. Of the following, the best medium for the manufacturer to use to accomplish this result is

A. VCR tape.

B. Digital audiotape (DAT).

C. Compact disk/read-only memory (CD-ROM).

D. Computer output to microfilm (COM).

The correct answer is (C). *(CIA, adapted)*

REQUIRED: The best way to reduce the cost of producing and shipping documentation.

DISCUSSION: CD-ROM is cheaper to produce and ship than the existing paper, yet it permits large volumes of text and images to be reproduced. Users of the electronic equipment are likely to have access to CD-ROM readers on PCs for using such documentation.

Answer (A) is incorrect because a VCR tape is useful for watching video, not storing manuals. Answer (B) is incorrect because DAT is primarily used as a backup medium in imaging systems and as a master for CD-ROM. Answer (D) is incorrect because COM is used for frequent access to archived documents, such as canceled checks in banking applications.

27. In the accounting department of a large organization, the most likely use of a CD-ROM would be to

A. Create permanent audit trails of EDI transactions.

B. Store images of documents received in the department.

C. Record the front and back of checks returned from the bank.

D. Provide a way to look up accounting standards and guidelines.

The correct answer is (D). *(CIA, adapted)*

REQUIRED: The most likely use of a CD-ROM in an accounting department.

DISCUSSION: CD-ROM (compact disk, read-only memory) is a fixed optical medium appropriate for storage of very large quantities of unchanging information. Researching standards is the best use of CD-ROM technology for an accounting department because the data are static enough for periodic updates to remain sufficiently current. CD-ROMs commonly use indexing and searching facilities that make reference works usable.

Answer (A) is incorrect because creating permanent audit trails of EDI transaction sequences is likely to be accomplished with write once, read many times (WORM) devices. Answer (B) is incorrect because maintaining images of documents with graphical components is likely to be done with redundant arrays of inexpensive disks (RAID). This technology is a magnetic medium that provides a primary storage method for imaging systems. Answer (C) is incorrect because recording the front and back of checks in banking applications is likely to be done with a microform such as microfilm.

28. Uninterruptible power supplies are used in computer centers to reduce the likelihood of

A. Failing to control concurrent access to data.

B. Losing data stored in main memory.

C. Dropping bits in data transmission.

D. Crashing disk drive read-write heads.

The correct answer is (B). *(CIA, adapted)*

REQUIRED: The reason for uninterruptible power supplies in computer centers.

DISCUSSION: Fully protected systems have generator or battery backup to prevent data destruction and downtime from electrical power disturbances. Loss of electrical power or voltage fluctuations need not disturb the vulnerable contents of main memory if an uninterruptible system is in place.

Answer (A) is incorrect because concurrency controls serve this purpose. Answer (C) is incorrect because hardware controls built into the system avoid errors in transmission. Answer (D) is incorrect because disk drives are currently designed to protect against crashing read-write heads.

29. When evaluating the downsizing of the plant materials inventory system, data center personnel considered redundant array of inexpensive disks (RAID) for the inventory database. One reason to use RAID is to ensure that

A. If one drive fails, all data can still be reconstructed.

B. All data are split evenly across pairs of drives.

C. Before-and-after images are stored for all transactions.

D. Write time is minimized to avoid concurrency conflicts.

The correct answer is (A). *(CIA, adapted)*

REQUIRED: The reason to use RAID.

DISCUSSION: A disk array expedites data transfer and provides fault tolerance. It combines two or more drives with special controller circuitry and software to execute reads and writes as if only one disk drive existed. When files are stored on RAID, data can be reconstructed even if one drive fails because a second copy of the data is on another drive.

Answer (B) is incorrect because splitting data evenly across pairs of drives (data striping) results in faster reads and writes but reduced reliability. The failure of one drive causes loss of all data. Answer (C) is incorrect because writing before-and-after images is a means of creating a transaction log for database transactions, which can be implemented with or without RAID. Answer (D) is incorrect because minimizing write time is not an advantage of RAID.

30. In a microcomputer system, the place where parts of the operating system program and language translator program are permanently stored is

A. Read only memory (ROM).

B. Magnetic disk drive.

C. Random access memory (RAM).

D. Magnetic tape drive.

The correct answer is (A). *(CMA, adapted)*

REQUIRED: The place where parts of the operating system and language translator are stored.

DISCUSSION: ROM consists of semiconductor chips that come from the manufacturer with programs already stored in them. These chips can be read from but not written to and therefore constitute permanent storage. Start up instructions are permanently stored in ROM in a microcomputer to initiate processing and prevent users from accidentally erasing or changing the system. Some microcomputers, however, have erasable, programmable ROM (EPROM). EPROM may be erased by an ultraviolet technique (but not by the microcomputer) after which new instructions may be entered.

Answers (B), (C), and (D) are incorrect because magnetic disk, RAM, and magnetic tape are temporary storage devices.

31. Access time in relation to computer processing is the amount of time it takes to

A. Transmit data from a remote terminal to a central computer.

B. Complete a transaction from initial input to output.

C. Perform a computer instruction.

D. Retrieve data from memory.

The correct answer is (D). *(CMA, adapted)*

REQUIRED: The definition of access time.

DISCUSSION: Access time is the interval between the moment at which an instruction control unit initiates a call for data and the moment at which delivery of the data is completed. For example, direct access memory is faster than sequential access memory.

Answer (A) is incorrect because access time refers to the speed of data retrieval not data transmittal. Answer (B) is incorrect because throughput time is the time to complete a transaction from initial input to output. Answer (C) is incorrect because access time is much slower than the time required to execute an instruction.

32. Which of the following measures would indicate the computational power of a microprocessor?

A. Capacity of the hard disk.

B. Main memory storage capacity.

C. Number of bits processed per second.

D. Read only memory.

The correct answer is (C). *(CIA, adapted)*

REQUIRED: The measure indicating the computational power of a microprocessor.

DISCUSSION: Processing speed is commonly calculated in terms of arithmetic-logic operations performed per second. Another method of performance measurement is word size, that is, the number of bits that can be manipulated in one operation by the processing unit.

Answers (A) and (B) are incorrect because capacity of the hard disk and main memory storage capacity are measures of memory. Answer (D) is incorrect because read only memory is main memory that ordinarily cannot be modified by the user. It is not a performance measure.

33. The significance of hardware controls is that they

A. Ensure correct programming of operating system functions.

B. Assure the correct execution of machine instructions.

C. Reduce the incidence of user input errors in online systems.

D. Ensure that run-to-run totals in application systems are consistent.

The correct answer is (B). *(CIA, adapted)*

REQUIRED: The significance of hardware controls.

DISCUSSION: Hardware controls are built into the equipment by the manufacturer to detect and control errors arising from the use of the equipment. Examples include parity checks, read-after-write checks, and echo checks.

Answer (A) is incorrect because programmers and/or analysts must correct errors in computer programs. Answer (C) is incorrect because use of input screens, limit tests, self-checking digits, and other input controls can reduce the incidence of input errors in online systems. Answer (D) is incorrect because run-to-run totals ensure the completeness of update in an online system by accumulating separate totals for all transactions processed throughout a period. This total is compared with the total of items accepted for processing.

34. In a data center, many hardware controls assure the accuracy of data processed. One hardware control used to evaluate stored data by counting the number of on bits in each character and then determining whether the total obtained is odd or even is a

A. Programmed check.

B. Header label check.

C. Check digit routine.

D. Parity check.

The correct answer is (D). *(CIA, adapted)*

REQUIRED: The hardware control that counts on bits.

DISCUSSION: Hardware controls are built into the computer by the manufacturer. A parity check adds the on bits in a byte and determines whether the sum is odd or even, depending on whether the computer has odd or even parity, respectively. This check verifies that all data have been transferred without loss. For example, if the computer has even parity, an on bit will be added to a byte that contains an odd number of on bits. An off bit is added if a byte has an even number of on bits.

Answer (A) is incorrect because a programmed check is an edit test performed by a program (software). Answer (B) is incorrect because a header label identifies a file on a tape or disk. Software makes this check. Answer (C) is incorrect because a self-checking digit is a suffix digit related algorithmically to the preceding digit(s) of an identification number. It is an application control to verify that the number has been transferred correctly from one medium or device to another.

35. Payroll master file updates are sent from a remote terminal to a mainframe program on a real-time system. A control that works to ensure accuracy of the transmission is a(n)

A. Echo check.

B. Protection ring.

C. Hash total.

D. Integrated test facility.

The correct answer is (A). *(CIA, adapted)*

REQUIRED: The control that works to ensure accuracy of the transmission.

DISCUSSION: An echo check is a hardware control that provides for a peripheral device to return (echo) a signal sent by the CPU. For example, the CPU sends a signal to the printer, and the printer, just prior to printing, sends a signal back to the CPU verifying that the proper print codes have been received.

Answer (B) is incorrect because a protection ring prevents accidental writing on a tape file. A real-time system would not use tape files. Answer (C) is incorrect because hash totals are used to control data sent to a batch system, not a real-time system. Answer (D) is incorrect because integrated test facilities are useful in testing real-time systems but cannot be used to ensure completeness of data transmissions.

36. A manufacturer is considering using bar-code identification for recording information on parts used by the manufacturer. A reason to use bar codes rather than other means of identification is to ensure that

A. The movement of all parts is recorded.

B. The movement of parts is easily and quickly recorded.

C. Vendors use the same part numbers.

D. Vendors use the same identification methods.

The correct answer is (B). *(CIA, adapted)*

REQUIRED: The reason to use bar codes.

DISCUSSION: Bar-code scanning is a form of optical character recognition. Bar codes are a series of bars of different widths that represent critical information about the item. They can be read and the information can be instantly recorded using a scanner. Thus, bar coding records the movement of parts with minimal labor costs.

Answer (A) is incorrect because any identification method may fail to record the movement of some parts. Answer (C) is incorrect because each vendor has its own part-numbering scheme. Answer (D) is incorrect because each vendor has its own identification method, although vendors in the same industry often cooperate to minimize the number of bar-code systems they use.

5.3 Basic Software and Data Organization Concepts

37. All of the following are examples of computer software except a(n)

A. Operating system.

B. Word processing package.

C. Language translator.

D. Telephone modem.

The correct answer is (D). *(CMA, adapted)*

REQUIRED: The item that is not computer software.

DISCUSSION: Software consists of programmed instructions to computer equipment (hardware). A modem is hardware. The term modem is an acronym for modulator-demodulator. This device converts digital signals to analog signals, e.g., sounds necessary for transmission by telephone lines. Another modem at the receiving end reconverts the analog signals back to the digital signals used by the computer.

Answer (A) is incorrect because an operating system is software that controls the overall functioning of the CPU and its peripheral devices. Answer (B) is incorrect because word processing software permits a microcomputer to display text on a screen, to edit that text, to store it on a disk, and to print it. Answer (C) is incorrect because a language translator is software that converts programs into machine-readable instructions.

38. A highly confidential file needs to be properly deleted from a microcomputer. The best way to accomplish this would be to use a(n)

A. Security card.

B. Encryption routine.

C. Disk utility.

D. Multiplexor.

The correct answer is (C). *(CIA, adapted)*

REQUIRED: The best way to delete a confidential file.

DISCUSSION: Unknown copies of sensitive data may exist in the hard drive or in memory. Most delete utilities erase file pointers but not underlying data. However, some utilities are available for this purpose.

Answer (A) is incorrect because security cards are used during logons. Answer (B) is incorrect because encryption routines are mathematical algorithms and keys used to encode sensitive information so that it is unintelligible until decrypted. Answer (D) is incorrect because a multiplexor is used to control multiple transmissions from linked terminals and modems.

39. In an overall description of a database, the names of data elements, their characteristics, and their relationship to each other are defined by using a

A. Data definition language.

B. Data control language.

C. Data manipulation language.

D. Data command interpreter language.

The correct answer is (A). *(CIA, adapted)*

REQUIRED: The language used to define a database.

DISCUSSION: The data definition language defines the database structure and content, especially the schema (the description of the entire database) and subschema (logical views of the database). The schema specifies characteristics such as the names of the data elements contained in the database and their relationship to each other. The subschema defines the logical data views required for applications. Thus, it limits the data elements and functions available to each application.

Answer (B) is incorrect because the data control language specifies the privileges and security rules governing database users. Answer (C) is incorrect because data manipulation language provides application programs with a means of interacting with the database to add, retrieve, modify, or delete data or relationships. Answer (D) is incorrect because data command interpreter languages are symbolic character strings used to control the current state of database management system operations.

40. Computer manufacturers install software programs permanently inside the computer as part of its main memory to provide protection from erasure or loss if electrical power is interrupted. This concept is known as

A. File integrity.

B. Software control.

C. Firmware.

D. Random access memory (RAM).

The correct answer is (C). *(CMA, adapted)*

REQUIRED: The term for software installed permanently in the computer.

DISCUSSION: Firmware consists of software programs permanently installed in the computer hardware. Firmware can be used to monitor internal conditions, e.g., by making signal counts (such as accesses to the computer) or taking snapshots of indicators. Thus, ROM (read only memory) is firmware.

Answer (A) is incorrect because file integrity is achieved by implementing controls that protect the completeness, accuracy, and physical security of files. Answer (B) is incorrect because software control refers to library control of programs. Answer (D) is incorrect because RAM is a computer's main memory.

41. A program that edits a group of source language statements for syntax errors and translates the statements into an object program is a(n)

A. Interpreter.

B. Compiler.

C. Debugger.

D. Encrypter.

The correct answer is (B). *(CIA, adapted)*

REQUIRED: The program that edits and translates source language statements into an object program.

DISCUSSION: A compiler is a form of software that performs language translation. It translates higher-level language (source code) programs into machine language object programs. The instructions in object code are grouped into modules. Prior to execution, the modules are joined by the linkage editor to form the load module. The load module is what the computer actually executes.

Answer (A) is incorrect because an interpreter translates and executes source language statements one at a time. Answer (C) is incorrect because a debugger is a program that traces program execution or captures variable values for the purpose of helping the developer find program errors. Answer (D) is incorrect because an encrypter is a program that converts ordinary text to encoded text that cannot be deciphered without access to the encryption key and procedure.

42. Specialized programs that perform generalized functions such as sorting and data comparison are called

A. Utility programs.

B. Communication programs.

C. Object programs.

D. Source programs.

The correct answer is (A). *(CISA, adapted)*

REQUIRED: The term describing programs that perform generalized functions such as sorting.

DISCUSSION: Utility programs are standardized subroutines that can be incorporated into other programs, e.g., to alphabetize or to find square roots. These routines are ordinarily supplied by the manufacturer and are part of the operating system.

Answer (B) is incorrect because communication programs provide interface between remote computer sites. Answers (C) and (D) are incorrect because object and source programs are not limited to utility functions. Programmers write programs in source languages to be converted into object programs that can be processed by the computer. Source languages include assembly languages that use symbols and codes dependent on the specific computer and compiler languages (e.g., COBOL and FORTRAN) consisting of English-like statements that are machine independent.

43. A computer program produces periodic payrolls and reports. The program is a(n)

A. Operating system.

B. Application program.

C. Report generator.

D. Utility program.

The correct answer is (B). *(CIA, adapted)*

REQUIRED: The term associated with a program used to produce user reports.

DISCUSSION: Application programs are written to solve specific user problems; that is, they perform the ultimate computer functions required by system users. Thus, a program designed to process payroll is an application program.

Answer (A) is incorrect because an operating system is a set of programs used by the CPU to control operations. Answer (C) is incorrect because a report generator is a component of a database management system that produces customized reports using data stored in the database. Answer (D) is incorrect because utility programs are standardized subroutines that can be incorporated into other programs.

44. An integrated set of computer programs that facilitate the creation, manipulation, and querying of integrated files is called a(n)

A. Compiler.

B. Operating system.

C. Assembly language.

D. Database management system.

The correct answer is (D). *(CIA, adapted)*

REQUIRED: The term for the programs that serve the stated purpose.

DISCUSSION: A database management system (DBMS) is an integrated set of computer programs that create the database, maintain the elements, safeguard the data from loss or destruction, and make the data available to application programs and inquiries. Examples include relational database systems such as Access and Paradox.

Answer (A) is incorrect because a compiler translates source code written in a higher-level language into machine-readable instructions. Answer (B) is incorrect because an operating system is a set of programs and routines used by the CPU to control the operations of the computer and its peripheral equipment. Answer (C) is incorrect because assembly languages correlate programmer commands on a one-to-one basis with machine instructions but employ mnemonic symbols, not the binary code used in machine languages.

45. Structured Query Language (SQL) is best defined as a

A. Programming language in which UNIX is written.

B. Report generator used to produce customized business reports.

C. Programming language in which most business applications are written.

D. Data manipulation language used in conjunction with a database management system (DBMS).

The correct answer is (D). *(Publisher)*

REQUIRED: The definition of SQL.

DISCUSSION: SQL is the most common standard data manipulation language for relational DBMSs. A data manipulation language is used for accessing and processing data from a database to satisfy requests for data and to create applications.

Answer (A) is incorrect because C is the language used in much of the UNIX operating system. Answer (B) is incorrect because a report generator has a greater emphasis on data formats, organization, and display than a query language. Answer (C) is incorrect because COBOL is the programming language in which most business applications are written.

46. Regardless of the language in which an application program is written, its execution by a microcomputer, minicomputer, or mainframe requires that primary memory contain

A. A utility program.

B. An operating system.

C. Compiler.

D. Assembly.

The correct answer is (B). *(D. Payne)*

REQUIRED: The item necessary to execute an application program.

DISCUSSION: An operating system (e.g., MS-DOS or Windows) is required in all computerized systems to oversee the elements of the CPU and the interaction of the hardware components.

Answer (A) is incorrect because utility programs are application programs that are usually attached to larger programs. They perform various activities, such as sorting data, merging files, converting data from one medium to another, and printing. Answer (C) is incorrect because a compiler converts (compiles) a program written in a source language, such as FORTRAN, into machine language. Answer (D) is incorrect because an assembler translates an assembly language program into machine language. Assembly language uses mnemonic codes for each machine language instruction.

47. BASIC, FORTRAN, and COBOL are all examples of

A. Application programs.

B. Machine languages.

C. High-level languages.

D. Operating systems.

The correct answer is (C). *(CIA, adapted)*

REQUIRED: The proper classification of BASIC, FORTRAN, and COBOL.

DISCUSSION: A procedure-oriented or higher-level language allows specification of processing steps in terms of highly aggregated operations. They are ordinarily user-friendly. Translation to an object program is performed by a compiler program. COBOL (COmmon Business Oriented Language) consists of a series of English-like statements. FORTRAN (FORmula TRANslation) is very effective for solving mathematics and engineering problems but is less so for business applications. BASIC (Beginner's All-purpose Symbolic Instruction Code) is a widely used language for microcomputers but is not widely used in large business application processing.

Answer (A) is incorrect because BASIC, etc., are languages, not application programs. Answer (B) is incorrect because machine language is a programming language made up of instructions that a computer can directly recognize and execute. Answer (D) is incorrect because an operating system is a set of programs and routines used by the CPU to control the operations of the computer and its peripheral equipment.

48. Structured programming is best described as a technique that

A. Makes the order of the coding reflect as closely as possible the dynamic execution of the program.

B. Reduces the maintenance time of programs by the use of small-scale program modules.

C. Provides knowledge of program functions to other programmers via peer reviews.

D. Controls the coding and testing of the high-level functions of the program in the development process.

The correct answer is (B). *(CISA, adapted)*

REQUIRED: The best description of structured programming.

DISCUSSION: Structured programming is an approach for creating a series of standardized, interrelated subroutines or modules. Guidelines are followed by programmers to create programs that are easy to read, maintain, and modify because changes in one module do not affect others.

Answer (A) is incorrect because the instructions coded by programmers do not necessarily reflect the actual order of the processing steps performed during execution by the computer. Answer (C) is incorrect because structured programming does allow other programmers to understand the coding but not via peer reviews. Answer (D) is incorrect because structured programming does not provide for testing during the development process.

49. An advantage of object-oriented approaches in software design is that they promote

A. Well-documented programs.

B. Simple control paths.

C. Clear decision logic.

D. Reusable code.

The correct answer is (D). *(CIA, adapted)*

REQUIRED: The advantage of object-oriented software design.

DISCUSSION: Object-oriented programming combines data and the related procedures into an object. Thus, an object's data can be manipulated only within the object. If the procedures (called methods) for manipulating the data in an object are changed, no other parts of the program are affected. The basic concepts of object-oriented programming are class and inheritance. Programs are written not for objects but for categories of similar objects. One class of objects inherits the characteristics of a more general class. An object-oriented approach is intended to produce reusable code. Because code segments can be reused in other programs, the time and cost of writing software should be reduced.

Answers (A) and (B) are incorrect because structured programming also produces well-documented programs and simple control paths. Answer (C) is incorrect because flowcharting and decision tables promote understandable decision logic.

50. The primary purpose of a macro program in an electronic spreadsheet application is to allow the end user to

A. Reduce keystrokes.

B. Merge files with two different formats.

C. Delete redundant files from the root directory.

D. Rearrange data elements.

The correct answer is (A). *(CIA, adapted)*

REQUIRED: The purpose of a macro program.

DISCUSSION: A macro program records keystrokes and commands used in repetitious jobs, which reduces the necessary keystrokes.

Answer (B) is incorrect because a merge file is a system software utility. Answer (C) is incorrect because deleting files is a system software utility. Answer (D) is incorrect because rearranging data elements is a possible macro application but is not the primary purpose of macros.

51. Computers understand codes that represent letters of the alphabet, numbers, or special characters. These codes require that data be converted into predefined groups of binary digits. Such chains of digits are referred to as

A. Registers.

B. ASCII code.

C. Input.

D. Bytes.

The correct answer is (D). *(CIA, adapted)*

REQUIRED: The term for the chains of digits that a computer is capable of understanding.

DISCUSSION: A byte is a grouping of bits required to define one unit of data, such as a letter or an integer.

Answer (A) is incorrect because a register is a location within the CPU where data and instructions are temporarily stored. Answer (B) is incorrect because ASCII (American Standard Code for Information Interchange) refers to the coding convention itself. Answer (C) is incorrect because input is the data placed into processing (noun) or the act of placing the data in processing (verb).

52. In an inventory system on a database management system (DBMS), one stored record contains part number, part name, part color, and part weight. These individual items are called

A. Fields.

B. Stored files.

C. Bytes.

D. Occurrences.

The correct answer is (A). *(CIA, adapted)*

REQUIRED: The term for the data elements in a record.

DISCUSSION: A record is a collection of related data items (fields). A field (data item) is a group of characters representing one unit of information.

Answer (B) is incorrect because a file is a group or set of related records ordered to facilitate processing. Answer (C) is incorrect because a byte is a group of bits (binary digits). It represents one character. Answer (D) is incorrect because occurrences is not a meaningful term in this context.

53. An inventory clerk, using a computer terminal, views the following on screen: part number, part description, quantity on-hand, quantity on-order, order quantity and reorder point for a particular inventory item. Collectively, these data make up a

A. Field.

B. File.

C. Database.

D. Record.

The correct answer is (D). *(CIA, adapted)*

REQUIRED: The term for the collection of data described.

DISCUSSION: A record is a collection of related data items (fields). A field (data item) is a group of characters representing one unit of information. The part number, part description, etc., are represented by fields.

Answer (A) is incorrect because field refers to a single data item. Answer (B) is incorrect because file refers to multiple records. Answer (C) is incorrect because database refers to multiple files.

54. Block codes

A. Are generally used to identify missing items from a set of documents or records.

B. Allow a user to number items sequentially.

C. Allow a user to assign meaning to particular segments of a coding scheme.

D. Are randomly calculated groups of numbers used as a control check.

The correct answer is (C). *(CMA, adapted)*

REQUIRED: The true statement about block codes.

DISCUSSION: Coding of data is the assignment of alphanumeric symbols consistent with a classification scheme. Block coding assigns blocks of numbers in a sequence to classes of items. For example, in a chart of accounts, assets may be assigned numbers 100-199, liabilities the numbers 200-299, etc.

Answers (A) and (B) are incorrect because some items in a block code may be unassigned to allow for flexibility. Answer (D) is incorrect because block codes are assigned judgmentally, not at random.

55. A file containing relatively permanent information used as a source of reference and periodically updated with detail is termed a

A. Transaction file.

B. Record layout.

C. Master file.

D. Dump.

The correct answer is (C). *(Publisher)*

REQUIRED: The file containing relatively permanent information.

DISCUSSION: A master file containing relatively permanent information, such as an inventory file listing the part number, description, quantities on hand, quantities on order, etc., is used in a file processing run. Transactions are processed against the master file, thus periodically updating it.

Answer (A) is incorrect because a transaction file (detail file) contains current transaction information used to update the master file, such as the number of items shipped to be removed from inventory. Answer (B) is incorrect because a record layout is a representation of the format of the records on the file. It would show the position and length of the fields in the file. The layout of every record in the file is the same. Answer (D) is incorrect because a dump is a listing of the contents of memory.

56. An internal auditor encounters a batch-processed payroll in which each record contains the same type of data elements, in the same order, with each data element needing the same number of storage spaces. Which file structure would most appropriately be used to support this set of records?

A. Single flat file structure.

B. Hierarchical structure.

C. Network structure.

D. Relational structure.

The correct answer is (A). *(CIA, adapted)*

REQUIRED: The file structure in which each record has the same type and order of data elements and the same storage requirements.

DISCUSSION: In a single flat file structure, all attributes and field lengths in a record are identical to those in the other records. The structure is typically a table with records for rows and attributes for columns.

Answer (B) is incorrect because a hierarchical or tree structure is used to express relationships in which one attribute or item is related to many others in layers of subordinate records. Answer (C) is incorrect because a network structure expresses complex relationships in which many attributes are related to many others. Answer (D) is incorrect because a relational structure is not unlike the flat structure but is far more sophisticated. It gives the system the ability to handle many data relationships that were not anticipated by the designers. It uses a series of tables in which each table defines a relationship.

57. With two letters (upper case only) or digits followed by three digits, how many codes can be created if the letters O, Q, and I are not to be used to avoid confusion errors with 0 and 1?

A. 66,000

B. 100,000

C. 1,089,000

D. 1,296,000

The correct answer is (C). *(CDP, adapted)*

REQUIRED: The number of unique codes possible in the situation given.

DISCUSSION: The first two items in the code may consist of any combination of 23 letters (26 characters in the alphabet minus O, Q, and I) and 10 numbers. Each of the next three positions can contain only one of 10 digits (0 to 9). The maximum number of unique codes is therefore 1,089,000 (33 x 33 x 10 x 10 x 10).

Answers (A), (B), and (D) are incorrect because the maximum number of unique codes is 1,089,000.

5.4 File Structures and Modes of Processing

58. A payroll system's master file is stored on tape. The payroll is processed at night once every 2 weeks. There is relatively little file maintenance required. Which of the following is most likely to be the appropriate processing method under the circumstances?

A. Parallel.

B. Online, real-time.

C. Network.

D. Batch.

The correct answer is (D). *(CIA, adapted)*

REQUIRED: The appropriate processing method.

DISCUSSION: Batch processing is the accumulation and grouping of transactions for processing on a delayed basis. The batch approach is suitable for applications that can be processed at intervals and involve large volumes of similar items, e.g., payroll, sales, inventory, and billing.

Answer (A) is incorrect because parallel means that two or more processes are executed concurrently. Answer (B) is incorrect because online means simply that data entry is performed via a terminal to a computer, and real-time means that transactions are processed when captured. The payroll operations need not be online or real-time. Answer (C) is incorrect because a network of computers may employ any mode of processing but is most likely to be used for online, real-time applications.

59. Misstatements in a batch computer system caused by incorrect programs or data may not be detected immediately because

A. Errors in some transactions may cause rejection of other transactions in the batch.

B. The identification of errors in input data typically is not part of the program.

C. There are time delays in processing transactions in a batch system.

D. The processing of transactions in a batch system is not uniform.

The correct answer is (C). *(CPA, adapted)*

REQUIRED: The reason errors may not be detected immediately in a batch computer system.

DISCUSSION: Transactions in a batch computer system are grouped together, or batched, prior to processing. Batches may be processed either daily, weekly, or even monthly. Thus, considerable time may elapse between the initiation of the transaction and the discovery of an error.

Answer (A) is incorrect because the transactions within the batch are typically not contingent upon one another. Answer (B) is incorrect because edit checks can be incorporated into batch processing environments. However, the edit checks are used to test the transactions in batches. Answer (D) is incorrect because a batch of transactions is typically processed uniformly.

60. Sequential access means that

A. Data are stored on magnetic tape.

B. The address of the location of data is found through the use of either an algorithm or an index.

C. Each record can be accessed in the same amount of time.

D. To read record 500, records 1 through 499 must be read first.

The correct answer is (D). *(CIA, adapted)*

REQUIRED: The characteristic of sequential access.

DISCUSSION: Sequential access means that records are stored in logical or physical order, and the only way to retrieve a record is to read the preceding records. Records may be sequentially ordered despite being physically separate. Thus, they may be linked via pointers.

Answer (A) is incorrect because magnetic tape is not the only medium on which data are stored sequentially. For instance, data storage on disk drives may also be sequential. Answer (B) is incorrect because locating data through a hashing function or index is a characteristic of direct or random file access. Answer (C) is incorrect because given sequential access storage, less time is needed to retrieve the first record than subsequent records.

61. A new purchasing system for just-in-time production requirements has been proposed. Users want access to current master file information at all times. To satisfy user needs, master file changes should be implemented with

A. Periodic entry with subsequent batch processing.

B. Periodic entry with immediate batch processing.

C. Online entry with subsequent batch processing.

D. Online entry with immediate processing.

The correct answer is (D). *(CIA, adapted)*

REQUIRED: The appropriate system for JIT production.

DISCUSSION: JIT production attempts to minimize inventory by more closely coordinating deliveries of needed materials and production. Thus, inventory data must be current. Online entry with immediate (real-time) processing gives users current master file information because changes are entered and applied to the master file as they occur.

Answers (A), (B), and (C) are incorrect because batch processing does not provide the timely information necessary to monitor production.

62. Which of the following features is least likely to be found in a real-time application?

A. User manuals.

B. Preformatted screens.

C. Automatic error correction.

D. Turnaround documents.

The correct answer is (D). *(CISA, adapted)*

REQUIRED: The feature not likely to be used in a real-time application.

DISCUSSION: Turnaround documents are source documents typically printed by the computer system as output and then later returned for use as machine-readable input. Real-time systems normally do not use source documents.

Answer (A) is incorrect because user manuals are an important component of a real-time system. They explain how to use the system properly. Answer (B) is incorrect because preformatted screens are usually the means by which users interact with real-time systems. Answer (C) is incorrect because automatic error correction is a prime advantage of real-time systems. It allows immediate error detection and correction.

63. The relationship between online, real-time database systems and batch processing systems is that

A. A firm will have only one processing mode because a single computer cannot do both.

B. A firm will not use batch processing if it has a large computer.

C. A firm may use both processing modes concurrently.

D. A firm will always prefer an online, real-time processing system because batch processing is slow.

The correct answer is (C). *(Publisher)*

REQUIRED: The relationship between online, real-time systems and batch processing systems.

DISCUSSION: Firms may find it beneficial to incorporate both processing modes into one system. A database may be established for information that must be obtained quickly, for instance, a sales processing system in which credit information must be available to sales personnel on an ongoing basis. However, other processing requirements may take advantage of the speed and control provided in a batch processing system. For example, payroll transactions may be processed quickly and efficiently in a batch mode.

Answer (A) is incorrect because one computer can operate in both modes. Answer (B) is incorrect because firms with large computers find it both cost effective and efficient to group transactions and process them periodically. Answer (D) is incorrect because a firm will not automatically prefer an online, real-time system. When transactions, e.g., payroll, can be conveniently grouped, processing is extremely fast and efficient in a batch mode.

64. Of the following, the greatest advantage of a database architecture is

A. Data redundancy can be reduced.

B. Conversion to a database system is inexpensive and can be accomplished quickly.

C. Multiple occurrences of data items are useful for consistency checking.

D. Backup and recovery procedures are minimized.

The correct answer is (A). *(CIA, adapted)*

REQUIRED: The greatest advantage of a database architecture.

DISCUSSION: Data organized in files and used by the organization's various applications programs are collectively known as a database. In a database system, storage structures are created that render the applications programs independent of the physical or logical arrangement of the data. Each data item has a standard definition, name, and format, and related items are linked by a system of pointers. The programs therefore need only to specify data items by name, not by location. A database management system handles retrieval and storage. Because separate files for different applications programs are unnecessary, data redundancy can be substantially reduced.

Answer (B) is incorrect because conversion to a database is often costly and time consuming. Answer (C) is incorrect because a traditional flat-file system, not a database, has multiple occurrences of data items. Answer (D) is incorrect because, given the absence of data redundancy and the quick propagation of data errors throughout applications, backup and recovery procedures are just as critical in a database as in a flat-file system.

65. Which of the following can be used for sequential but not direct access?

A. CD-ROM.

B. Magnetic disk.

C. Floppy disks.

D. Magnetic tape.

The correct answer is (D). *(Publisher)*

REQUIRED: The sequential access storage medium.

DISCUSSION: Magnetic tape is a sequential access medium. It contains records that must be processed in their physical order on the medium. Magnetic tape for computer storage is similar to sound recording tape.

Answers (A), (B), and (C) are incorrect because CD-ROM, magnetic disk, and floppy disk can be used as either sequential or random access media.

66. One advantage of a database management system (DBMS) is

A. That each organizational unit takes responsibility and control for its own data.

B. The cost of the data processing department decreases as users are now responsible for establishing their own data handing techniques.

C. A decreased vulnerability as the database management system has numerous security controls to prevent disasters.

D. The independence of the data from the application programs, which allows the programs to be developed for the user's specific needs without concern for data capture problems.

The correct answer is (D). *(CMA, adapted)*

REQUIRED: The advantage of a DBMS.

DISCUSSION: A fundamental characteristic of databases is that applications are independent of the database structure; when writing programs or designing applications to use the database, only the name of the desired item is necessary. Programs can be developed for the user's specific needs without concern for data capture problems. Reference can be made to the items using the data manipulation language, after which the DBMS takes care of locating and retrieving the desired items. The physical or logical structure of the database can be completely altered without having to change any of the programs using the data items; only the schema requires alteration.

Answer (A) is incorrect because each organizational unit develops programs to make use of elements of a broad database. Answer (B) is incorrect because data handling techniques are still the responsibility of the data processing department; it is the use of the data that is departmentalized. Answer (C) is incorrect because the DBMS is no safer than any other database system.

67. Which of the following is a false statement about a database management system application environment?

A. Data are used concurrently by multiple users.

B. Data are shared by passing files between programs or systems.

C. The physical structure of the data is independent of user needs.

D. Data definition is independent of any one program.

The correct answer is (B). *(CISA, adapted)*

REQUIRED: The false statement about data in a DBMS environment.

DISCUSSION: In this kind of system, applications use the same database. There is no need to pass files between applications.

Answer (A) is incorrect because the advantage of a DBMS is that data can be used concurrently by multiple users. Answer (C) is incorrect because, when a DBMS is used, the physical structure of the data is independent of user needs. Answer (D) is incorrect because, when a DBMS is used, the data are defined independently of the needs of any one program.

68. A flat file structure is used in database management systems (DBMS) when

A. A complex network structure is employed.

B. A network based structure is used and a complex database schema is developed.

C. A simple network structure is employed.

D. A relational database model is selected for use.

The correct answer is (D). *(CMA, adapted)*

REQUIRED: The situation in which a flat file structure is used with a DBMS.

DISCUSSION: A flat file structure is used with a relational database model. A relational structure organizes data in conceptual tables. One relation (table or file) can be joined together or related to another without pointers or linked lists if each contains one or more of the same fields (also known as columns or attributes). The relational structure has become popular because it is relatively easy to construct.

Answer (A) is incorrect because a complex network structure requires something more intricate than a flat file structure. Answers (B) and (C) are incorrect because a network structure reduces redundancy by arranging data through development of many-to-many relationships; that is, each item may have multiple antecedent as well as successive relationships, which would preclude a flat file structure.

69. The system that permits the computers in a distributed processing network to share the use of another end user's application program is

A. Electronic data interchange.

B. Interactive processing.

C. Executive support system.

D. Cooperative processing.

The correct answer is (D). *(CMA, adapted)*

REQUIRED: The system that permits the computers in a distributed processing network to share the use of another end user's application program.

DISCUSSION: Cooperative processing is a system in which computers in a distributed processing network can share the use of application programs belonging to another end user. The system assigns different machines the functions they perform best in executing a transaction-based application program. For example, a microcomputer might be used to enter and validate data for the application, and a mainframe might handle file input and output.

Answer (A) is incorrect because EDI is the communication of electronic documents directly from a computer in one entity to a computer in another entity. Answer (B) is incorrect because interactive processing does not allow for the use of another end user's application programs. Answer (C) is incorrect because an executive support system focuses on strategic objectives and gives immediate information about an organization's critical success factors.

70. To trace data through several application programs, an auditor needs to know what programs use the data, which files contain the data, and which printed reports display the data. If data exist only in a database system, the auditor could probably find all of this information in a

A. Data dictionary.

B. Database schema.

C. Data encryptor.

D. Decision table.

The correct answer is (A). *(CIA, adapted)*

REQUIRED: The information source in a database needed to trace data through several application programs.

DISCUSSION: The data dictionary is a file (possibly manual but usually computerized) in which the records relate to specified data items. It contains definitions of data items, the list of programs used to process them, and the reports in which data are found. Only certain persons or entities are permitted to retrieve data or to modify data items. Accordingly, these access limitations are also found in the data dictionary.

Answer (B) is incorrect because the schema describes the structure of the database. Answer (C) is incorrect because an encryptor encodes data. Answer (D) is incorrect because a decision table is a type of logic diagram that presents in matrix form the decision points and related actions reflected in a computer program.

71. Which of the following would not normally be considered a typical file structure for a database management system?

A. Relational structure.

B. Hierarchical structure.

C. Network structure.

D. Batched sequential structure.

The correct answer is (D). *(CIA, adapted)*

REQUIRED: The file structure that would not typically be used for a DBMS.

DISCUSSION: A DBMS is used to create and manage a database that combines related files for processing and access by users. A batched sequential structure precludes random access, which is contrary to the concept of a database.

Answer (A) is incorrect because a relational structure gives the DBMS the ability to handle many data relationships that were not anticipated when the database was organized. Answer (B) is incorrect because a hierarchical or tree structure is used in the DBMS to express relationships in which one attribute or item is related to many others. Answer (C) is incorrect because a network structure expresses complex relationships in which many attributes are related to many others.

72. All of the following are methods for distributing a relational database across multiple servers except

A. Snapshot (making a copy of the database for distribution).

B. Replication (creating and maintaining replica copies at multiple locations).

C. Normalization (separating the database into logical tables for easier user processing).

D. Fragmentation (separating the database into parts and distributing where they are needed).

The correct answer is (C). *(CIA, adapted)*

REQUIRED: The item not a method for distributing a relational database across multiple servers.

DISCUSSION: A distributed database is stored in two or more physical sites. However, normalization is a process of database design, not distribution. Normalization is the term for determining how groups of data items in a relational structure are arranged in records in a database. This process relies on "normal forms," that is, conceptual definitions of data records and specified design rules. Normalization is intended to prevent inconsistent updating of data items. It is a process of breaking down a complex data structure by creating smaller, more efficient relations, thereby minimizing or eliminating the repeating groups in each relation.

Answers (A) and (B) are incorrect because the replication or snapshot technique makes duplicates to be stored at multiple locations. Changes are periodically copied and sent to each location. If a database is small, storing multiple copies may be cheaper than retrieving records from a central site. Answer (D) is incorrect because fragmentation or partitioning stores specific records where they are most needed. For example, a financial institution may store a particular customer's data at the branch where (s)he usually transacts his/her business. If the customer executes a transaction at another branch, the pertinent data are retrieved via communications lines.

73. The indexed-sequential-access method (ISAM) is an approach to file organization

A. In which each data record has a pointer field containing the address of the next record in the list.

B. Uses an algorithm to convert a record key into a storage address to assist with later retrieval.

C. That allows sequential but not direct access to information as the transaction is processed.

D. In which records are stored sequentially in a direct access file and organized by a primary key stored in an index record.

The correct answer is (D). *(CMA, adapted)*

REQUIRED: The true statement about indexed-sequential-access file organization.

DISCUSSION: ISAM is a system in which records are stored sequentially in a direct access file and organized by a primary key stored in an index record. It does not use pointers. A pointer is a data element attached to a record that gives the address of the next logically related record. The virtue of an ISAM system is that it permits sequential processing of large numbers of records while providing for occasional direct access.

Answer (A) is incorrect because a linked list is a file organization in which each data record has a pointer field containing the address of the next record in the list. Answer (B) is incorrect because, in a direct file organization, a randomizing formula or hashing scheme (a transform algorithm) converts a record key into a storage address. This method permits direct access without an index. Answer (C) is incorrect because ISAM is both a direct and a sequential access method.

74. Which of the following database models is considered to be the most versatile?

A. The hierarchical model.

B. The tree model.

C. The network model.

D. The relational model.

The correct answer is (D). *(CIA, adapted)*

REQUIRED: The most versatile database model.

DISCUSSION: Because data are organized in two-dimensional tables, the relational database models are easier to construct than the complex architectures that result when using the hierarchical and network models. The tables (relations) provide flexibility because they can be combined (joined) in many ways to permit a wide variety of inquiries. They also permit data to be more readily added to or omitted from the data structures.

Answers (A) and (B) are incorrect because the tree or hierarchical model organizes data through the development of relationships that are strictly one to many. Construction of this model is difficult because the data are hard coded. When data are added to the database, the index must be completely redefined. In the relational model, however, new relations can be created by joining tables. Answer (C) is incorrect because the network model organizes data through the development of relationships that are many to many. Construction is therefore difficult.

75. The real-time feature normally would be most useful when applied to accounting for a firm's

A. Retained earnings.

B. Property records.

C. Depreciation records.

D. Merchandise inventory.

The correct answer is (D). *(Publisher)*

REQUIRED: The purpose for which real-time processing would be most useful.

DISCUSSION: Real-time processing accesses or updates files at the time input is made. Access to up-to-date inventory records is often important to answer inquiries and process sales orders.

Answer (A) is incorrect because information related to retained earnings is not often necessary on an immediate basis. Answer (B) is incorrect because property records are normally processed on a cycle basis. Immediate update of the files is not necessary. Answer (C) is incorrect because depreciation records are normally processed on a cycle basis.

76. Which of the following is usually not a consideration in real-time computer systems implementation?

A. Queues.

B. Interrupts.

C. Priority allocation.

D. Hardware diagnostics.

The correct answer is (D). *(CDP, adapted)*

REQUIRED: The item irrelevant to real-time computer systems implementation.

DISCUSSION: Hardware diagnostic routines are used to identify hardware problems. They are applicable to all computer systems and not relevant solely to real-time systems. An example of a hardware diagnostic is a parity check to test data for validity each time data are transmitted internally in the system.

Answers (A) and (C) are incorrect because deciding which jobs have priority in processing (queuing) is an important factor in real-time systems when the CPU must decide which transaction updates are most important. Answer (B) is incorrect because interrupts permit high-priority jobs entering the system to obtain immediate action. In multiprogramming, work on one program is interrupted so the processor may attend to another.

77. A business has decided to use magnetic disks to store accounts receivable information. What data file concepts should be used to provide the ability to answer customer inquiries as they are received?

A. Sequential storage and chains.

B. Sequential storage and indexes.

C. Record keys, indexes, and pointers.

D. Inverted file structure, indexes, and internal labels.

The correct answer is (C). *(CIA, adapted)*

REQUIRED: The data file concepts needed to answer customer inquiries as they are received.

DISCUSSION: A record key is an attribute that uniquely identifies or distinguishes each record from the others. An index is a table listing storage locations for attributes, often including those other than the unique record key attribute. A pointer is a data item that indicates the physical address of the next logically related record.

Answers (A) and (B) are incorrect because the ability to respond immediately to customers requires direct access. Answer (D) is incorrect because internal labels are used to indicate various things to the computer, such as the contents of various types of data storage media, the beginning of each file (with identification information), and the end of each file. However, they do not provide information for locating specific records in a file. An inverted file structure (inverted list) is an index based on a secondary key, for example, years of experience rather than an employee number (the primary key).

78. Coding in data processing assigns a unique identification number or key to each data record. Which one of the following statements about coding is false?

A. A primary key is the main code used to store and locate records within a file.

B. Records can be sorted, and temporary files created, using codes other than their primary keys.

C. Secondary keys are used when the primary keys cannot be found.

D. Secondary keys are used for alternative purposes, including inverted files, and a given data record may have more than one secondary key.

The correct answer is (C). *(CMA, adapted)*

REQUIRED: The statement about coding that is false.

DISCUSSION: A primary key is the main code used to store and locate records within a file. However, records can be sorted, and temporary files created, using codes other than the primary keys. Secondary keys are used for other purposes, including inverted files. An inverted file allows access to records by means of a key other than the primary key. A given data record can have more than one secondary key. Secondary keys are not substituted by the computer when primary keys cannot be found.

Answer (A) is incorrect because a primary key is the main code used to store and locate records within a file. Answer (B) is incorrect because records can be sorted, and temporary files created, using codes other than their primary keys. Answer (D) is incorrect because secondary keys are used for alternative purposes, including inverted files, and a given data record may have more than one secondary key.

79. A system in which the master files are updated in batch mode overnight and duplicated copies of the files are updated and queried during the day best describes which of the following online systems?

A. Memo updating.

B. Online updating.

C. Remote job entry.

D. Inquiry.

The correct answer is (A). *(CISA, adapted)*

REQUIRED: The term associated with the description given.

DISCUSSION: Memo updating minimizes the risk of damage to the database during processing transactions. A copy of the database is updated upon data entry, but a log of each transaction is also stored. Periodically, the transaction log is used to update the actual database and a new "memo" copy is established.

Answer (B) is incorrect because online updating requires master files to be updated a short time after the transaction is entered. Answer (C) is incorrect because remote job entry is the initiation of an application program from a remote terminal. Answer (D) is incorrect because inquiry provides users with a response to a request in a timely manner with no file update.

80. Which of the following is most likely characteristic of a direct access file that uses indexes or dictionaries as its addressing technique when processing randomly?

A. A randomizing formula is used.

B. Two accesses are required to retrieve each record.

C. Synonyms will be generated that will result in extra accesses.

D. There will be a high incidence of gaps or unassigned physical records within the file.

The correct answer is (B). *(CDP, adapted)*

REQUIRED: The most likely characteristic of a direct access file using indexes.

DISCUSSION: Typically, indexed files will use tables or indexes for locating the address of a record. For example, in accessing an alphabetic record, first the index must be accessed and searched (in much the same way as finding a telephone number in a directory) to locate the pointer or address of the record. Next, the record must be accessed at the address location.

Answer (A) is incorrect because a randomizing formula or hashing scheme is used to obtain direct access without consulting an index (direct access method). The procedure determines the address of a record by transforming the primary key of the record into a random number (the desired address). Answer (C) is incorrect because synonyms may be generated when access is obtained without indexation. If the randomizing formula generates the same address for two different keys (a synonym), the record is placed in the next higher available address. Answer (D) is incorrect because indexing permits elimination of most gaps. The direct access method leaves gaps because the randomizing procedure may not generate the numbers corresponding to many storage addresses.

5.5 Networks and Data Communication

81. A local area network (LAN) is best described as a(n)

A. Computer system that connects computers of all sizes, workstations, terminals, and other devices within a limited proximity.

B. System to allow computer users to meet and share ideas and information.

C. Electronic library containing millions of items of data that can be reviewed, retrieved, and analyzed.

D. Method to offer specialized software, hardware, and data handling techniques that improve effectiveness and reduce costs.

The correct answer is (A). *(CMA, adapted)*

REQUIRED: The best description of a local area network (LAN).

DISCUSSION: A LAN is a local distributed computer system, often housed within a single building. Computers, communication devices, and other equipment are linked by cable. Special software facilitates efficient data communication among the hardware devices.

Answer (B) is incorrect because a LAN is more than a system to allow computer users to share information; it is an interconnection of a computer system. Answer (C) is incorrect because a LAN is not a library. Answer (D) is incorrect because a LAN does not require specialized hardware.

82. In distributed data processing, a ring network

A. Has all computers linked to a host computer, and each linked computer routes all data through the host computer.

B. Links all communication channels to form a loop, and each link passes communications through its neighbor to the appropriate location.

C. Attaches all channel messages along one common line with communication to the appropriate location via direct access.

D. Organizes itself along hierarchical lines of communication usually to a central host computer.

The correct answer is (B). *(CMA, adapted)*

REQUIRED: The true statement about a ring network in a distributed data processing system.

DISCUSSION: In a distributed system, an organization's processing needs are examined in their totality. The decision is not whether an application should be done centrally or locally, but rather which parts are better performed by small local computers as intelligent terminals, and which parts are better performed at some other, possibly centralized, site. The key distinction between decentralized and distributed systems is the interconnection among the nodes in the network. A ring network links all communication channels to form a loop and each link passes communications through its neighbor to the appropriate location.

Answer (A) is incorrect because a star network routes all data through the host computer. Answer (C) is incorrect because a bus network attaches all channel messages along one common line with communication to the appropriate location via direct access. Answer (D) is incorrect because a tree configuration is organized along hierarchical lines to a host computer.

83. To identify those components of a telecommunications system that present the greatest risk, the internal auditor should first

A. Review the open systems interconnect (OSI) network model.

B. Identify the network operating costs.

C. Determine the business purpose of the network.

D. Map the network software and hardware products into their respective layers.

The correct answer is (C). *(CIA, adapted)*

REQUIRED: The procedure to identify the greatest risk of a telecommunications system.

DISCUSSION: The first step in an auditor's risk assessment for a telecommunications network should be to determine its business purpose. This step enables the auditor to isolate the components that have the greatest risk exposures. Major business purposes may include customer service, internal communication, direct revenue generation, process management, and financial reporting.

Answer (A) is incorrect because OSI is a seven-layer reference model developed by the International Standards Organization to permit different types of computers to communicate. Answer (B) is incorrect because the auditor may identify the network operating costs in a subsequent audit step. Answer (D) is incorrect because the auditor may map the network software and hardware products into their respective layers in a subsequent audit step.

84. When two devices in a data communications system are communicating, there must be agreement as to how both data and control information are to be packaged and interpreted. Which of the following terms is commonly used to describe this type of agreement?

A. Asynchronous communication.

B. Synchronous communication.

C. Communication channel.

D. Communication protocol.

The correct answer is (D). *(CIA, adapted)*

REQUIRED: The agreement as to how both data and control information are to be packaged and interpreted.

DISCUSSION: A protocol is the set of formal rules or conventions governing communication between a sending and a receiving device. It prescribes the manner by which data are transmitted between these communications devices. In essence, a protocol is the envelope within which each message is transmitted throughout a data communications network.

Answer (A) is incorrect because asynchronous communication is a mode of transmission. Communication is in disjointed segments, typically character by character, preceded by a start code and ended by a stop code. Answer (B) is incorrect because synchronous communication is a mode of transmission in which a continuous stream of blocks of characters result in faster communications. Answer (C) is incorrect because a communication channel is a transmission link between devices in a network. The term is also used for a small processor that controls input-output devices.

85. Large organizations often have their own telecommunications networks for transmitting and receiving voice, data, and images. Very small organizations, however, are unlikely to be able to make the investment required for their own networks and are more likely to use

A. Public switched lines.

B. Fast-packet switches.

C. Standard electronic mail systems.

D. A WAN.

The correct answer is (A). *(CIA, adapted)*

REQUIRED: The telecommunications networks likely to be used by small organizations.

DISCUSSION: Companies can use public switched lines (phone lines) on a per-transmission basis. This option is the most cost-effective way for low-volume users to conduct telecommunications.

Answer (B) is incorrect because fast-packet switches receive transmissions from various devices, break the data into packets, and route them over a network to their destination. They are typically installed by telecommunication utility companies and other large companies that have their own networks. Answer (C) is incorrect because electronic mail systems do not allow for voice transmissions. Answer (D) is incorrect because large organizations would use a wide area network.

86. Distributed computing provides several advantages over a centralized computer. Which of the following is not an advantage?

A. Communications costs are usually lower.

B. Alternate processing locations are available in case one site's computer is not functioning.

C. Security measures are easier to provide.

D. Investment in hardware is smaller for each site than for a central site.

The correct answer is (C). *(CIA, adapted)*

REQUIRED: The response that is not an advantage of distributed computing.

DISCUSSION: In a distributed system, a determination is made as to which parts of an application are best performed by small computers (e.g., intelligent terminals) and which should be performed at some other, possibly centralized, site. In other words, the best distribution of processing tasks among the interconnected nodes of the system is sought. Security therefore becomes more difficult when there are more sites to secure.

Answer (A) is incorrect because lower communications costs are an advantage of distributed computing. Answer (B) is incorrect because the availability of alternate processing locations is an advantage of distributed computing. Answer (D) is incorrect because, given smaller, less complex hardware requirements, the cost for each site would be less than for a central site.

87. An insurance firm uses a wide area network (WAN) to allow agents away from the home office to obtain current rates and client information and to submit approved claims using notebook computers and dial-in modems. In this situation, which of the following methods would provide the best data security?

A. Dedicated phone lines.

B. Call-back features.

C. Frequent changes of user IDs and passwords.

D. End-to-end data encryption.

The correct answer is (D). *(CIA, adapted)*

REQUIRED: The best data security method for a wide area network.

DISCUSSION: Encryption of data is a security procedure in which a program encodes data prior to transmission and another program decodes the data after transmission. Encoding is important when confidential data that can be electronically monitored are transmitted between geographically separated locations.

Answer (A) is incorrect because dedicated phone lines are not available to agents in the field. Answers (B) and (C) are incorrect because call-back features and frequent changes of user IDs and passwords are used to authenticate the user but do not otherwise protect the transmitted data.

88. Advantages of using fiber optics are that

I. The signal is attenuated.
II. Data is transmitted rapidly.
III. Fiber optic cable is small and flexible.
IV. They are unaffected by electrical interference.

A. I and III.

B. I and IV.

C. I, II, and III.

D. II, III, and IV.

The correct answer is (D). *(CISA, adapted)*

REQUIRED: The advantages of fiber optics.

DISCUSSION: A fiber optic cable uses light impulses that travel through clear flexible tubing half the size of a human hair. Fiber optic cables are not subject to electrical interference and are highly reliable. They provide for extremely flexible and fast data transmission. The signal remains strong across long distances; i.e., it does not tend to weaken (attenuate).

Answers (A), (B), and (C) are incorrect because attenuation of the signal is not an advantage of using fiber optics.

89. A real estate brokerage firm is moving into a building that is already equipped with extensive telephone wiring. The firm is considering the installation of a digital private branch exchange (PBX) to connect computers and other office devices such as copying machines, printers, and facsimile machines. A limitation of using a PBX-based system for this network is that

A. The firm would be dependent on others for system maintenance.

B. The system cannot easily handle large volumes of data.

C. Coaxial cabling would have to be installed throughout the building.

D. Relocating devices in the office would be difficult and expensive.

The correct answer is (B). *(CIA, adapted)*

REQUIRED: The limitation of a PBX system.

DISCUSSION: A PBX has the advantage of using existing telephone lines and therefore not needing special wiring. Moreover, equipment can be moved without necessitating rewiring. However, because PBX-based systems use telephone wiring (most often copper wire), they cannot easily handle large volumes of data.

Answer (A) is incorrect because the company would be responsible for all maintenance of the equipment, although it could contract for service. Answer (C) is incorrect because PBXs use telephone wiring. LANs typically require their own coaxial cabling. Answer (D) is incorrect because PBX-based systems do not require rewiring when devices are moved.

90. Which of the following risks is not greater in an electronic funds transfer (EFT) environment than in a manual system using paper transactions?

A. Unauthorized access and activity.

B. Duplicate transaction processing.

C. Higher cost per transaction.

D. Inadequate backup and recovery capabilities.

The correct answer is (C). *(CIA, adapted)*

REQUIRED: The risk not greater in an EFT environment than in a manual system using paper transactions.

DISCUSSION: EFT is a service provided by financial institutions worldwide that is based on EDI technology. EFT transaction costs are lower than for manual systems because documents and human intervention are eliminated from the transactions process.

Answers (A), (B), and (D) are incorrect because unauthorized access and activity, inaccurate transaction processing (including duplication), and inadequate backup and recovery capabilities are risks specific to EFT.

91. Which of the following is likely to be a benefit of electronic data interchange (EDI)?

A. Increased transmission speed of actual documents.

B. Improved business relationships with trading partners.

C. Decreased liability related to protection of proprietary business data.

D. Decreased requirements for backup and contingency planning.

The correct answer is (B). *(CIA, adapted)*

REQUIRED: The benefit of EDI.

DISCUSSION: Electronic data interchange is the electronic transfer of documents between businesses. EDI was developed to enhance just-in-time (JIT) inventory management. Advantages include speed, reduction of clerical errors, and elimination of repetitive clerical tasks and their costs. Improved business relationships result because of the mutual benefits conferred by EDI. Accordingly, some organizations require EDI.

Answer (A) is incorrect because EDI transmits document data, not the actual document. Answer (C) is incorrect because liability for protection of a trading partner's proprietary business data is a major risk that must be addressed by control procedures. Answer (D) is incorrect because backup and contingency planning requirements are not diminished by use of EDI.

92. As organizations move to implement EDI, more of them are turning to the use of value-added networks (VANs). Which of the following would not normally be performed by a VAN?

A. Store electronic purchase orders of one organization to be accessed by another organization.

B. Provide common interfaces across organizations thereby eliminating the need for one organization to establish direct computer communication with a trading partner.

C. Maintain a log of all transactions of an organization with its trading partner.

D. Provide translations from clients' computer applications to a standard protocol used for EDI communication.

The correct answer is (D). *(CIA, adapted)*

REQUIRED: The function not performed by a VAN.

DISCUSSION: Companies must purchase their own software to translate their data to a national standard protocol for EDI purposes, either ANSI X.12 in the U.S. or EDIFACT in Europe and most of the rest of the world. Once the data are in the standard format, the VAN handles all aspects of the communication. VANs are privately owned telecommunications carriers that sell capacity to outside users. Among other things, a VAN provides a mailbox service permitting EDI messages to be sent, sorted, and held until needed in the recipient's computer system.

Answers (A), (B), and (C) are incorrect because VANs normally provide mailbox services, common communication interfaces, and logs of transactions.

93. The Internet is made up of a series of networks that include

A. Gateways to allow personal computers to connect to mainframe computers.

B. Bridges to direct messages through the optimum data path.

C. Repeaters to physically connect separate local area networks (LANs).

D. Routers to strengthen data signals between distant computers.

The correct answer is (A). *(CIA, adapted)*

REQUIRED: The composition of the Internet.

DISCUSSION: The Internet facilitates information transfer between computers. Gateways are hardware or software products that allow translation between two different protocol families. For example, a gateway can be used to exchange messages between different e-mail systems.

Answer (B) is incorrect because routers are used to determine the best path for data. Answer (C) is incorrect because bridges connect LANs. Answer (D) is incorrect because repeaters strengthen signals.

94. Which of the following statements is(are) correct regarding the Internet as a commercially viable network?

I. Organizations must use firewalls if they wish to maintain security over internal data.

II. Companies must apply to the Internet to gain permission to create a home page to engage in electronic commerce.

III. Companies that wish to engage in electronic commerce on the Internet must meet required security standards established by the coalition of Internet providers.

A. I only.

B. II only.

C. III only.

D. I and III.

The correct answer is (A). *(CIA, adapted)*

REQUIRED: The true statement(s) about the Internet.

DISCUSSION: Companies that wish to maintain adequate security must use firewalls to protect data from being accessed by unauthorized users. A network firewall is a device that separates a network segment from the rest of the network. This machine maintains a connection between the networks but does not pass network traffic.

Answers (B), (C), and (D) are incorrect because anyone can establish a home page on the Internet, and no coalition of Internet providers dictates security standards. The lack of such standards is a major problem with the Internet.

95. The most difficult aspect of using Internet resources is

A. Making a physical connection.

B. Locating the best information source.

C. Obtaining the equipment required.

D. Getting authorization for access.

The correct answer is (B). *(CIA, adapted)*

REQUIRED: The most difficult aspect of using Internet resources.

DISCUSSION: The Internet is a series of networks throughout the world that facilitates information transfer between computers. Gateways allow mainframe computers to interface with personal computers. The graphics-rich environment of the World Wide Web (WWW) has been largely responsible for bringing the Internet out of the static realm of e-mail and text-only documents. The WWW continues to grow faster than any other segment of the Internet. Businesses, schools, government, and nonprofit organizations (in addition to millions of individuals) are gravitating to the Internet to promote themselves and their products to an audience spanning the entire planet. Accordingly, given the vast scope of the Internet, the most difficult aspect of its use is locating the best information sources. One solution has been the development of programs called browsers for accessing the WWW.

Answer (A) is incorrect because there is no limitation on the number of access ports. Answer (C) is incorrect because the only requirements for accessing Internet resources are a computer, a modem, a telephone line, and basic communications software. Answer (D) is incorrect because organizations routinely provide Internet access to their employees, and individuals can obtain access through individual subscriptions to commercial information service providers.

96. A company has a very large, widely dispersed internal auditing department. Management wants to implement a computerized system to facilitate communications among auditors. The specifications require that auditors have the ability to place messages in a central electronic repository where all auditors can access them. The system should facilitate finding information on a particular topic. Which type of system would best meet these specifications?

A. Electronic data interchange (EDI).

B. Electronic bulletin board system (BBS).

C. Fax/modem software.

D. Private branch exchange (PBX).

The correct answer is (B). *(CIA, adapted)*

REQUIRED: The best system to facilitate communications among auditors.

DISCUSSION: Bulletin board systems function as a centralized information source and message switching system for a particular interest group. Users review and leave messages for other users, and communicate with other users on the system at the same time.

Answer (A) is incorrect because EDI is for the electronic transmission of business information and electronic mail, but it does not offer central repositories that store messages for many parties to read. Answer (C) is incorrect because, although fax/modem software can store images of faxes received, it does not meet the criterion of ease of access to information on a particular topic. Answer (D) is incorrect because a PBX is a telecommunications system that routes calls to particular extensions within an organization.

5.6 System Planning and Design

97. The proper sequence of activities in the systems development life cycle is

A. Design, analysis, implementation, and operation.

B. Design, implementation, analysis, and operation.

C. Analysis, design, implementation, and operation.

D. Programming, analysis, implementation, and operation.

The correct answer is (C). *(CMA, adapted)*

REQUIRED: The sequential steps in a systems development life cycle.

DISCUSSION: The first step in systems development is identification and definition of a need relative to organizational objectives. The next step is to determine the scope of the required study and to proceed with a thorough analysis of the existing system. These steps lead to the general design of a new system. If the new system proves to be justified, the decision is then made to proceed with its implementation. Detailed systems design, including development and design of data files, is part of the implementation phase. Following implementation and operation, systems maintenance must be undertaken by analysts and programmers throughout the life of a system. Maintenance is the redesign of the system and programs to meet new needs or to correct design flaws.

Answers (A), (B), and (D) are incorrect because analysis precedes design.

98. An MIS manager has only enough resources to install either a new payroll system or a new data security system, but not both. Which of the following actions is most appropriate?

A. Giving priority to the security system.

B. Leaving the decision to the MIS manager.

C. Increasing MIS staff output in order for both systems to be installed.

D. Having the information systems steering committee set the priority.

The correct answer is (D). *(CISA, adapted)*

REQUIRED: The appropriate action given inadequate resources.

DISCUSSION: The needs assessment and cost-benefit analysis should be conducted by those responsible for making the decision. In this case, the information systems steering committee is the appropriate decision maker.

Answer (A) is incorrect because not enough information is given to conclude that priority should be given to the security system. Answer (B) is incorrect because the MIS manager should not be the only decision maker. Answer (C) is incorrect because the question indicates that development of both systems is not possible.

99. The analysis tool for the systems analyst and steering committee to use in selecting the best systems alternative is

A. Cost-benefit analysis.

B. Systems design.

C. Decision tree analysis.

D. User selection.

The correct answer is (A). *(CMA, adapted)*

REQUIRED: The analysis tool to be used in selecting the best systems alternative.

DISCUSSION: In any systems decision, there must be an evaluation of the relative costs and benefits of each alternative. Cost-benefit analysis is a simple test for possible solutions. Costs should be less than the benefits realized.

Answer (B) is incorrect because systems design is the process of matching user needs to applications. Answer (C) is incorrect because decision tree analysis maps out possible actions given probabilistic events. Probabilities are assigned, and the expected value for each decision choice and the events that might follow from that choice are calculated. Answer (D) is incorrect because user selection may ignore the cost of the new system.

100. Which one of the following is not considered a typical risk associated with outsourcing (the practice of hiring an outside company to handle all or part of the data processing)?

A. Inflexibility.

B. Loss of control.

C. Loss of confidentiality.

D. Less availability of expertise.

The correct answer is (D). *(CMA, adapted)*

REQUIRED: The item that is not considered a typical risk associated with outsourcing.

DISCUSSION: Some companies have outsourced their data processing function because of the economies provided, superior service quality, avoidance of changes in the organization's IS infrastructure, cost predictability, the freeing up of human and financial capital, avoidance of fixed costs, and the greater expertise offered by outside vendors. The risks of outsourcing include the inflexibility of the relationship, the loss of control, the vulnerability of important information, and often dependency on a single vendor.

Answers (A), (B), and (C) are incorrect because they are risks associated with outsourcing the data processing function.

101. The strengths of the bottom-up approach to systems development are that it

1. Supports evolutionary growth of organizational functions
2. Minimizes the cost of systems development and maintenance
3. Incorporates the existing organizational systems
4. Identifies the factors crucial to organizational success

A. 1 and 3.

B. 1 and 4.

C. 2 and 3.

D. 2 and 4.

The correct answer is (A). *(CIA, adapted)*

REQUIRED: The strengths of the bottom-up approach to systems development.

DISCUSSION: The bottom-up approach begins at the operational level, designs each functional unit, and then ties these units together at each management level of the organization. This approach builds on existing capabilities and allows for evolutionary growth of organizational functions.

Answer (B) is incorrect because identifying crucial factors at the organizational level is a strength of the top-down approach. It begins with organizational objectives and goals, then breaks them into functional requirements to be implemented at lower levels of the organization. Answers (C) and (D) are incorrect because the bottom-up approach may not be the least costly in all circumstances.

102. The process of learning how the current system functions, determining the needs of users, and developing the logical requirements of a proposed system is referred to as systems

A. Analysis.

B. Feasibility study.

C. Maintenance.

D. Implementation.

The correct answer is (A). *(CMA, adapted)*

REQUIRED: The term for the described process.

DISCUSSION: A systems analysis requires a survey of the existing system, the organization itself, and the organization's environment to determine whether a new system is needed. The survey results determine not only what, where, how, and by whom activities are performed but also why, how well, and whether they should be done at all. Ascertaining the problems and informational needs of decision makers is the next step. The systems analyst must consider the entity's key success variables, the decisions currently being made and those that should be made, the factors important in decision making, the information needed for decisions, and how well the current system makes those decisions. The systems analysis then establishes the requirements of a system that will meet user needs.

Answers (B), (C), and (D) are incorrect because feasibility study, maintenance, and implementation are steps subsequent to systems analysis.

103. Which of the following should be emphasized before designing any system elements in a top-down approach to new systems development?

A. Types of processing systems being used by competitors.

B. Computer equipment to be used by the system.

C. Information needs of managers for planning and control.

D. Controls in place over the current system.

The correct answer is (C). *(CIA, adapted)*

REQUIRED: The matter to be emphasized before designing a new system.

DISCUSSION: The top-down method begins with analysis of broad organizational goals, objectives, and policies as a basis for the design process. This step requires an understanding of the entity's environment and significant activities. The next step is to determine the decisions made by managers and the information required to make them. The necessary reports, databases, inputs, processing methods, and equipment specifications can then be defined. The weakness of the top-down approach is that it tends to concentrate on managers' information needs at the expense of the design of efficient transaction processing at the operational level.

Answer (A) is incorrect because the needs of the organization, not what competitors use, should be the overriding factor in systems development. Answer (B) is incorrect because the equipment selection should be a function of the processing needs, not vice versa. Answer (D) is incorrect because functional controls should be designed for the new system.

104. Which of the following is the most appropriate activity for an internal auditor to perform during a review of systems development activity?

A. Serve on the MIS steering committee that determines what new systems are to be developed.

B. Review the methodology used to monitor and control the system development function.

C. Recommend specific automated procedures to be incorporated into new systems that will provide reasonable assurance that all data submitted to an application are converted to machine-readable form.

D. Recommend specific operational procedures that will ensure that all data submitted for processing are converted to machine-readable form.

The correct answer is (B). *(CIA, adapted)*

REQUIRED: The procedure to perform during a review of systems development activity.

DISCUSSION: Auditor objectivity is not impaired when (s)he recommends standards of control for systems or reviews procedures before implementation. However, drafting procedures for systems and designing, installing, and operating systems are not audit functions. Thus, reviewing the methodology used by an organization is an appropriate activity that enables the internal auditor to determine whether (s)he can rely on the systems development activity to design and implement appropriate automated controls within applications.

Answer (A) is incorrect because service on a management decision-making committee is an operating responsibility and would impair audit objectivity. Answers (C) and (D) are incorrect because making recommendations for specific procedures is an operating responsibility.

105. Even though an organization is committed to using its mainframe for its manufacturing plant operations, it has been looking for ways to downsize other applications. The purpose of downsizing is to

A. Improve reliability.

B. Improve security.

C. Reduce complexity.

D. Decrease costs.

The correct answer is (D). *(CIA, adapted)*

REQUIRED: The purpose of downsizing.

DISCUSSION: The purpose of downsizing is to reduce costs of applications by abandoning larger, more expensive systems in favor of smaller, less expensive systems that are more versatile. However, downsized applications are less reliable than their mainframe predecessors because they are new and have not been used extensively. Typically, downsized client-server implementations lack the monitoring and control features that permit recovery from minor processing interruptions.

Answer (A) is incorrect because client-server technology used in downsizing is less reliable. Answer (B) is incorrect because security is usually better on a mainframe. Answer (C) is incorrect because downsizing applications often increases their complexity. The data files become fragmented across multiple systems.

106. Object technology provides a new and better way of enabling developers and users to build and tailor applications. In light of this technology, what action should management take with respect to its older (legacy) systems?

A. Plan for rapid migration of legacy systems to object-based applications.

B. Consider the more stable legacy systems as initial candidates for conversion.

C. Investigate the integration of object-based capabilities with legacy systems.

D. Defer the use of object technology until the legacy systems need replacement.

The correct answer is (C). *(CIA, adapted)*

REQUIRED: The approach to introducing object technology.

DISCUSSION: Object technology is an approach to writing computer programs that expedites development. Objects are self-contained, reusable parts that are especially helpful for developing interactive and graphical programs. A legacy system is an older system that has been operating for years. Legacy systems represent a significant investment and may still provide adequate service. To balance the need for meeting changes in the corporate and technical environments with the economic imperative represented by the investment in legacy systems, information systems departments should seek opportunities to add object-oriented capabilities to existing systems. However, issues such as the "year 2000" problem need to be considered when evaluating the usefulness of legacy systems.

Answer (A) is incorrect because the costs of migrating legacy systems and retraining the personnel who would develop and maintain them preclude rapid transition. Answer (B) is incorrect because legacy systems that are difficult to modify and maintain are better candidates for conversion to object technology. Answer (D) is incorrect because object technology should be explored as a better approach for implementing business applications.

107. Which of the following risks is more likely to be encountered in an end-user computing (EUC) environment as compared with a mainframe computer system?

A. Inability to afford adequate uninterruptible power supply systems.

B. User input screens without a graphical user interface (GUI).

C. Applications that are difficult to integrate with other information systems.

D. Lack of adequate utility programs.

The correct answer is (C). *(CIA, adapted)*

REQUIRED: The risk more likely to be encountered in an EUC environment.

DISCUSSION: The risk of allowing end users to develop their own applications is decentralization of control. End-user developed applications may not be subject to an independent outside review by systems analysts and are not created in the context of a formal development methodology. These applications may lack appropriate standards, controls, and quality assurance procedures. Moreover, when end users create their own applications and files, private information systems may proliferate in which data are largely uncontrolled. These systems may contain the same information, but end-user applications may update and define the data in different ways. Thus, determining the location of data and ensuring data consistency become more difficult because the applications are difficult to integrate.

Answers (A), (B), and (D) are incorrect because inability to afford adequate uninterruptible power supply systems, lack of a GUI, and lack of adequate utility programs are risks in all computing environments.

108. As the internal auditor reviewing microcomputer operations, your first step should be to determine the existence of

A. Procedures for training accounting department personnel in the uses of microcomputers, including the use of modems.

B. Backup procedures for computer processing when equipment is down or software is not operational.

C. Physical security for hardware and software.

D. Standards, policies, and procedures for acquiring, operating, and replacing hardware and software.

The correct answer is (D). *(CIA, adapted)*

REQUIRED: The primary first step in reviewing microcomputer operations.

DISCUSSION: A primary purpose of an operational audit is to determine whether standards are being met and policies and procedures are being complied with. A fundamental first step is to ascertain whether management has met its responsibility of establishing these policies (general guides to decision making), procedures (specific ways to accomplish work), and operating standards (defined performance measures).

Answers (A), (B), and (C) are incorrect because training procedures, backup procedures, and physical security are encompassed by standards, policies, and procedures for acquiring, operating, and replacing hardware and software to achieve the primary objective.

Questions 109 and 110 are based on the following information. Five brand managers in a consumer food products company met regularly to figure out what price points were being lowered by their competitors and how well coupon promotions did. The data they needed to analyze consisted of about 50 gigabytes of daily point-of-sale (POS) data from major grocery chains for each month. The brand managers are competent users of spreadsheet and database software on microcomputers. They considered several alternative software options to access and manipulate data to answer their questions.

109. The selected option is unlikely to use a hierarchical database system because

A. A hierarchical database system requires multiple joins.

B. Programming queries for it are too costly and time consuming.

C. Point-of-sale data are too sensitive for routine access.

D. Summarization of point-of-sale data would not answer the questions.

The correct answer is (B). *(CIA, adapted)*

REQUIRED: The reason the selected option is unlikely to use a hierarchical database system.

DISCUSSION: A hierarchical structure is tree-like. A record is divided into segments that are connected in one-to-many relationships. Because all of the paths through the data must be prespecified, a hierarchical structure is inflexible and does not support ad hoc queries. Thus, programming queries for a hierarchical database are costly and time consuming. Even if the programs can be written, machine resources are likely to be inadequate to execute them in a production environment.

Answer (A) is incorrect because hierarchical database systems do not have commands for joins, which are standard features in relational systems. Answer (C) is incorrect because the point-of-sale information is clearly proprietary, but brand managers must use it to manage the business. Answer (D) is incorrect because point-of-sale data contain precisely the information that, if summarized appropriately, would answer questions about product sales and coupon use.

110. The organization's senior management was pleased that its brand managers were taking the initiative to use sales data creatively. The information systems director, however, was concerned that the brand managers might be creating standard queries that would provide erroneous results for decision making. The best approach for ensuring the correctness of the brand managers' queries is

A. A source code review of the queries.

B. A code comparison audit.

C. A transaction retrieval and analysis.

D. An input/output analysis.

The correct answer is (A). *(CIA, adapted)*

REQUIRED: The best approach for ensuring correctness of queries.

DISCUSSION: A source code review, that is, a review of the programs written in a high-level language, would detect erroneous queries written by the managers, which then would be corrected.

Answer (B) is incorrect because a code comparison audit is used to compare two versions of the same program to verify that only authorized code is executed. Answer (C) is incorrect because a transaction retrieval and analysis is a sampling approach to collecting data about transactions to verify correct processing. Answer (D) is incorrect because an input-output analysis traces transactions from input to output.

111. Two major retail companies, both publicly traded and operating in the same geographic area, have recently merged. The companies are approximately the same size and have audit departments. Company A has little EDI experience. Company B has invested heavily in information technology and has EDI connections with its major vendors. Which of the following would be the least important risk factor when considering the ability to integrate the two companies' computer systems?

A. The number of programmers and systems analysts employed by each company.

B. The extent of EDI connections with vendors.

C. The compatibility of existing operating systems and database structures.

D. The size of company databases and the number of database servers used.

The correct answer is (A). *(CIA, adapted)*

REQUIRED: The least important risk factor when integrating two companies' computer systems.

DISCUSSION: The number of systems personnel employed may reflect differences in operating philosophy (outsourcing vs. in-house development of applications). However, the compatibility of personnel is a less serious concern than the compatibility of hardware and software.

Answer (B) is incorrect because Company A has little EDI experience. Hence, the greater the number of vendors that must be connected with Company A, the greater the risk exposure. Answer (C) is incorrect because the difficulty and expense of conversion will be increased if the computer systems have significant compatibility problems. Answer (D) is incorrect because the greater the complexity of the systems to be integrated, the greater the risk exposure.

112. A systems development approach used to quickly produce a model of user interfaces, user interactions with the system, and process logic is called

A. Neural networking.

B. Prototyping.

C. Reengineering.

D. Application generation.

The correct answer is (B). *(CIA, adapted)*

REQUIRED: The approach used to produce a model of user interfaces, user interactions with the system, and process logic.

DISCUSSION: Prototyping produces the first model(s) of a new system. This technique usually employs a software tool for quick development of a model of the user interface (such as by report or screen), interaction of users with the system (for example, a menu-screen approach or data entry), and processing logic (the executable module). Prototyping stimulates user participation because the model allows quick exploration of concepts and development of solutions with quick results.

Answer (A) is incorrect because neural networking involves hardware or software that imitates the processing activities of the human brain. Answer (C) is incorrect because reengineering salvages reusable components of existing systems and restructures them to develop new systems or to improve the old systems. Answer (D) is incorrect because an application generator is software that can be used to develop an application simply by describing its requirements to the computer rather than by writing a procedural program.

113. Which of the following is not an audit objective in the review of hardware acquisition?

A. Ensuring that adequate information for sound management decision making is available prior to contracting for the purchase, rent, or lease of new equipment.

B. Ensuring that vendors are provided with appropriate and uniform data for submission of bids according to management approved specifications and guidelines.

C. Ensuring that appropriate hardware is selected, installed, and tested in accordance with management approved specifications.

D. Ensuring that provisions are made to minimize damage or abuse to hardware and to maintain the hardware in good operating condition.

The correct answer is (D). *(CISA, adapted)*

REQUIRED: The audit objective not related to the review of hardware acquisition.

DISCUSSION: Determining whether controls are in place to minimize damage or abuse to equipment is considered in the evaluation of the firm's operating environment. This step occurs subsequent to the acquisition of the equipment.

Answer (A) is incorrect because ensuring that adequate information for sound management decision making is available is an objective of a hardware acquisition review. Answer (B) is incorrect because ensuring that vendors are provided with appropriate and uniform data is an objective of a hardware acquisition review. Answer (C) is incorrect because ensuring that appropriate hardware is selected, installed, and tested is an objective of a hardware acquisition review.

114. All of the following are included in the systems implementation process except

A. Training.

B. Documentation.

C. Systems design.

D. Testing and conversion.

The correct answer is (C). *(CMA, adapted)*

REQUIRED: The item not included in the systems implementation process.

DISCUSSION: Systems implementation includes training and educating users, documenting the systems, testing the systems' programs and procedures, systems conversion (including final testing and switchover), and systems follow-up. General systems design is not a part of the implementation stage of the life cycle, but the detailed systems design, such as the line-by-line coding of computer programs, is accomplished at this stage.

Answers (A), (B), and (D) are incorrect because training, documentation, and testing and conversion are parts of the implementation stage.

115. Which of the following is not an important element in deciding whether to lease or purchase computer equipment?

A. Cost of money.

B. Tax considerations.

C. Maintenance expense.

D. Parallel operations cost.

The correct answer is (D). *(CDP, adapted)*

REQUIRED: The unimportant element in deciding whether to lease or purchase computer equipment.

DISCUSSION: Any cost that is not affected by the decision need not be considered. Parallel operations costs (costs of operating both the old and new systems during the checkout period of the new system) are incurred whether the firm leases or purchases the equipment.

Answer (A) is incorrect because high interest rates may favor the lease option. Answer (B) is incorrect because the amount and availability of the investment tax credit, deductions for interest and depreciation, and other tax-planning factors will vary depending on the option chosen. Answer (C) is incorrect because maintenance expense will vary depending on the terms of the lease or purchase.

116. Which of the following would be considered an advantage in contracting for computer systems applications work?

A. Avoids maintaining a permanent staff larger than is required over the long term.

B. Avoids maintaining a large staff of systems programming people and reduces overhead.

C. Eliminates the need for the organization to take the time to gain knowledge and experience.

D. Provides a contractor with the opportunity to acquire knowledge about the company that can be used in the future as an alternate source for make or buy opportunities.

The correct answer is (A). *(CDP, adapted)*

REQUIRED: The advantage of contracting for computer systems applications work.

DISCUSSION: Firms contract for computer applications work (software development) for cost-benefit reasons. Resources need not be expended to provide for service capacities (i.e., applications or uses of computer systems) required only intermittently.

Answer (B) is incorrect because a systems programming staff does not normally perform applications programming work. They are used to maintain and develop operating systems. Answer (C) is incorrect because the organization should still understand the computer applications even though they are developed externally. Answer (D) is incorrect because a cost-effective computer system, not increasing contractor knowledge, is the advantage of purchasing outside applications work.

117. The cost-effectiveness of information technology is affected by how efficiently it is used. One procedure designed to help ensure efficiency is to

A. Control access to sensitive output.

B. Provide for backup and disaster recovery.

C. Monitor the change environment for software in use.

D. Delete copies of data files when the information is no longer needed.

The correct answer is (D). *(CIA, adapted)*

REQUIRED: The procedure designed to ensure the cost-effectiveness of information technology.

DISCUSSION: Efficiency is not achieved when facilities are underused, work is nonproductive, or procedures are uneconomical. Efficiency will be improved by freeing media and disk space for other uses, thus reducing data storage costs.

Answer (A) is incorrect because access to sensitive output is a security concern. Answer (B) is incorrect because backup and disaster recovery is an operational integrity issue. Answer (C) is incorrect because the change environment is a security and independence concern.

118. CASE (computer-aided software engineering) is the use of the computer to aid in the development of computer-based information systems. Which of the following could not be automatically generated with CASE tools and techniques?

A. Information requirements determination.

B. Program logic design.

C. Computer program code.

D. Program documentation.

The correct answer is (A). *(CIA, adapted)*

REQUIRED: The item not automatically generated by CASE.

DISCUSSION: CASE applies the computer to software design and development. It maintains on the computer a library of standard program modules and all of the system documentation, e.g., data flow diagrams, data dictionaries, and pseudocode (structured English); permits development of executable input and output screens; and generates program code in at least skeletal form. Thus, CASE facilitates the creation, organization, and maintenance of documentation and permits some automation of the coding process. However, information requirements must be determined prior to using CASE.

Answers (B), (C), and (D) are incorrect because CASE may generate program logic design, computer program code, and program documentation.

119. Which of the following steps should be included in an action plan covering privacy concerns?

I. Preparation of a plan to ensure that necessary privacy controls are integrated into the design of computer systems

II. Training of employees in the awareness of privacy and company policies

III. Preparation of a plan to inform customers of the organization's privacy policies

IV. Preparation of an analysis of the potential impact that privacy would have on the computer system

A. IV.

B. I and III.

C. II and IV.

D. I, II, III, and IV.

The correct answer is (D). *(CISA, adapted)*

REQUIRED: The step(s) that should be included in a privacy-related action plan.

DISCUSSION: Privacy considerations are among the many reasons for developing effective computer security. Failure to safeguard the privacy of confidential client information may result in both loss of business and litigation. Other information, such as trade secrets, must be shielded from disclosure to competitors. Moreover, some firms, e.g., defense contractors, may have access to information affecting national security. Accordingly, each of the listed steps is appropriate. Establishing a company code of ethics and a strong internal audit function are among the other aspects of a control environment that stresses concern for privacy issues.

Answer (A) is incorrect because steps I, II, and III should also be included. Answer (B) is incorrect because steps II and IV should also be included. Answer (C) is incorrect because steps I and III should also be included.

120. Management's enthusiasm for computer security seems to vary with changes in the environment, particularly the occurrence of other computer disasters. Which of the following concepts should be addressed when making a comprehensive recommendation regarding the costs and benefits of computer security?

I. Potential loss if security is not implemented

II. Probability of occurrences

III. Cost and effectiveness of the implementation and operation of computer security

A. I only.

B. I and II only.

C. III only.

D. I, II, and III.

The correct answer is (D). *(CIA, adapted)*

REQUIRED: The concept(s) that should be addressed in an analysis of cost-benefit considerations.

DISCUSSION: Potential loss is the amount of dollar damages associated with a security problem or loss of assets. Potential loss times the probability of occurrence is an estimate (expected value) of the exposure associated with lack of security. It represents a potential benefit associated with the implementation of security measures. To perform a cost-benefit analysis, the costs should be considered. Thus, all three items need to be addressed.

Answers (A), (B), and (C) are incorrect because potential loss, the probability thereof, and the cost and effectiveness of security measures are important elements of the analysis.

Questions 121 through 123 are based on the following information. The state administration has just appointed a new director of the Department of Information Systems (DIS). DIS is responsible for information systems for state functions and maintains large computers located in the state capital and distributed facilities in each county. In cooperation with staff in other state departments and agencies, DIS oversees the contracting process for outside contractors who develop major systems. After major systems have been installed and accepted, DIS is responsible for their maintenance.

One major system installed just as the new director of DIS was being appointed was the Integrated Public Assistance System (IPAS), which integrated record keeping, collections, and disbursements for food stamps, welfare, and child support for over one million recipients. At the time this system was developed, most of the costs for information systems for public assistance were paid by the federal government if a state's system met federal requirements. IPAS was designed for online entry of case information in county offices and overnight batch generation of checks to recipients.

Initially, when only a few counties had been converted to the system, response time on terminals in county offices was about 3 seconds. Now, with about half the counties converted, response time is at least 30 seconds and sometimes as long as 10 minutes. All data records appear to be correct despite the response time, and transmission errors have been negligible. The same computer also supports other online application systems that have been operating normally.

The long response times have delayed conversion of existing cases to the new system. During the conversion period, any new cases for public assistance were to be entered into the new system, but the lengthening response time has caused many new applicants to wait several months before their cases were entered, thus delaying the start of their authorized benefits.

The governor of the state is aware of the status of IPAS and has asked the new director of DIS to propose remedies for the situation. Realizing the need for assessing the system, the director of DIS has asked the state's internal auditing department to investigate the system configuration and recommend ways to improve online response.

121. If the response time were caused by application software, the most likely cause would be application programs that

A. Make erroneous updates of transactions to the master files.

B. Require more printing than the installed printers can accommodate.

C. Invoke more input-output operations than are necessary for the specified functions.

D. Contain infinite loops that degrade response time.

The correct answer is (C). *(CIA, adapted)*

REQUIRED: The most likely cause of slow response time if application software is to blame.

DISCUSSION: Processing is relatively more rapid than input and output. Thus, invoking more input-output operations than are necessary for the specified functions is the most likely application software cause of lengthening response time.

Answer (A) is incorrect because, despite the response time, all data records appear to be correct, so the programs are not likely to make erroneous updates of transactions to the master files. Answer (B) is incorrect because requiring more printing than the installed printers can accommodate does not appear to be the problem. Online terminal response is independent of printer use. Answer (D) is incorrect because the presence of infinite loops in application programs would cause the program to stop rather than just run more slowly.

122. If the response time is caused by central site hardware, the most likely cause is

A. A malfunctioning CPU.

B. Inadequate disk access.

C. Defective disk volumes.

D. Failing disk channels.

The correct answer is (B). *(CIA, adapted)*

REQUIRED: The most likely cause of slow response time if central site hardware is to blame.

DISCUSSION: As more records are added to the system, the disk space becomes saturated and degrades the system. Overhead time related to management of disk space takes more and more computer cycles and can degrade response time.

Answer (A) is incorrect because the symptom of a malfunctioning CPU would be complete failure or unusual results, neither of which is present here. Answer (C) is incorrect because a symptom of defective disk volumes would be unrecoverable or erroneous data on disk files, neither of which occurred here. Answer (D) is incorrect because a symptom of failing disk channels would be unrecoverable or erroneous data on disk files, neither of which occurred here.

123. If the response time is a function of the communications network, the most likely cause is

A. Defective terminals in county offices.

B. Insufficient transmission capacity.

C. A malfunctioning front-end controller.

D. Transient errors in transmission lines.

The correct answer is (B). *(CIA, adapted)*

REQUIRED: The most likely cause if the response time is a function of the communications network.

DISCUSSION: As more and more sites (counties) are added to the network, the transmission capacity may be overloaded. Transmission capacity is based on the technology used, e.g., telephone lines, microwave, and satellite. Directly tied to the technology is the communication equipment, e.g., the use of concentrators and front-end processors (controllers).

Answer (A) is incorrect because a symptom of defective terminals in county offices would be transmission errors, which are not present. Answer (C) is incorrect because a symptom of a malfunctioning front-end controller would be transmission or data errors, which are not present. Answer (D) is incorrect because a symptom of transient errors in transmission lines would be transmission errors, which are not present.

5.7 Operating and Organizational Controls

124. An auditor anticipates assessing control risk at a low level in a computerized environment. Under these circumstances, on which of the following procedures would the auditor initially focus?

A. Programmed control procedures.

B. Application control procedures.

C. Output control procedures.

D. General control procedures.

The correct answer is (D). *(CPA, adapted)*

REQUIRED: The initial concern when the auditor anticipates assessing control risk at less than the maximum in a computer environment.

DISCUSSION: Some computer controls relate to all computer activities (general controls), and some relate to specific tasks (application controls). Because general controls are pervasive in their effect, they should be tested before application controls. If the general controls are ineffective, tests of the application controls over input, processing, and output will be unlikely to permit the auditor to assess control risk at less than the maximum.

Answer (A) is incorrect because programmed procedures relate to application controls, which should be tested for effectiveness once the general controls prove to be effective. Answer (B) is incorrect because general controls are tested before application controls. Answer (C) is incorrect because output controls are application controls, which are tested after general controls.

125. In the organization of the information systems function, the most important separation of duties is

A. Not allowing the data librarian to assist in data processing operations.

B. Assuring that those responsible for programming the system do not have access to data processing operations.

C. Having a separate information officer at the top level of the organization outside of the accounting function.

D. Using different programming personnel to maintain utility programs from those who maintain the application programs.

The correct answer is (B). *(CMA, adapted)*

REQUIRED: The most important separation of duties in the information systems function.

DISCUSSION: Separation of duties is a general control that is vital in a computerized environment. Some separation of duties common in noncomputerized environments may not be feasible in a computer environment. However, certain tasks should not be combined. Systems analysts and programmers should be separate from computer operators. Both programmers and analysts may be able to modify programs, files, and controls, and should therefore have no access to those programs or to computer equipment. Operators should not be assigned programming duties or responsibility for systems design, and should have no opportunity to make changes in programs and systems.

Answer (A) is incorrect because librarians maintain control over documentation, programs, and data files; they should have no access to equipment, but they can assist in data processing operations. Answer (C) is incorrect because a separate information officer outside of the accounting function would not be as critical a separation of duties as that between programmers and processors. Answer (D) is incorrect because programmers usually handle all types of programs.

126. Your firm has recently converted its purchasing cycle from a manual process to an online computer system. Which of the following is a probable result associated with conversion to the new automatic system?

A. Processing errors are increased.

B. The firm's risk exposures are reduced.

C. Processing time is increased.

D. Traditional duties are less segregated.

The correct answer is (D). *(CIA, adapted)*

REQUIRED: The probable result associated with conversion to the new automatic system.

DISCUSSION: In a manual system with appropriate internal control, separate individuals are responsible for authorizing transactions, recording transactions, and custody of assets. These checks and balances prevent fraud and detect inaccurate or incomplete transactions. In a computer environment, however, this segregation of duties is not always feasible. For example, a computer may print checks, record disbursements, and generate information for reconciling the account balance.

Answer (A) is incorrect because a computer system decreases processing errors. Answer (B) is incorrect because the conversion to a new system does not reduce the number of risk exposures. Answer (C) is incorrect because processing time is decreased.

127. Within a computer processing activity, which control procedure typically leaves no visible or machine-readable evidence that the procedure was performed?

A. Proper segregation of functions.

B. Program changes for a computer application.

C. Approval of the program changes.

D. Computer-generated exception reports.

The correct answer is (A). *(Publisher)*

REQUIRED: The control procedure that typically leaves no visible or machine-readable evidence.

DISCUSSION: Although the formal segregation of functions may be documented in job descriptions, the actual segregation may be difficult to establish because it leaves no visible or machine-readable evidence. To obtain evidence that this control is working, the auditor must make corroborative inquiries and observe the auditee's personnel.

Answer (B) is incorrect because program changes for a computer application produce reports or other documents to provide visible evidence that controls were in operation. Answer (C) is incorrect because approval of the program changes should be documented. Answer (D) is incorrect because computer-generated exception reports provide visible evidence.

128. The organization chart is a graphic representation of the

A. Power structure.

B. Communications channels.

C. Locus of decision making.

D. Formal authority structure.

The correct answer is (D). *(CDP, adapted)*

REQUIRED: The relationship graphically represented by an organization chart.

DISCUSSION: An organization chart represents pictorially the formal lines of authority within an organization. It depicts the organizational structure and the hierarchical relationships of the functional units in the organization.

Answer (A) is incorrect because the power structure concerns personalities more than assigned responsibilities. Answer (B) is incorrect because, although the organization chart customarily shows communication lines, it does not represent the informal channels that operate within an organization. Answer (C) is incorrect because the organization chart depicts responsibility and authority, which includes more than the loci of decision making.

129. It is important to maintain proper segregation of duties in a computer environment. Which of the following access setups is appropriate?

	Update Access for Production Data		Update Access for Production Programs	
	Users Have?	Application Programmers Have?	Users Have?	Application Programmers Have?
A.	Yes	No	No	No
B.	Yes	No	No	Yes
C.	No	Yes	Yes	No
D.	No	Yes	Yes	Yes

The correct answer is (A). *(CIA, adapted)*

REQUIRED: The appropriate access setup.

DISCUSSION: Incompatible duties should be separated for effective control. End users need access to applications data and functions but not to systems software, applications programs, and most computer equipment. Application programmers should be segregated from computer operations, technical support staff, computer equipment, systems software, production versions of programs, and production data.

Answers (B), (C), and (D) are incorrect because users need access to data but not programs. Programmers do not need access to production programs or data.

130. A systems analyst should have access to each of the following except

A. Source code.

B. Password identification tables.

C. User procedures.

D. Edit criteria.

The correct answer is (B). *(CISA, adapted)*

REQUIRED: The item to which a systems analyst should not have access.

DISCUSSION: If the systems analyst has access to password identification tables, (s)he is in a position to access and change application programs and files without proper authorization.

Answer (A) is incorrect because the analyst needs access to source code for approved projects in progress. Answer (C) is incorrect because the analyst needs access to user procedures to determine how input is entered and output is used. Answer (D) is incorrect because the analyst needs access to edit criteria to obtain assurance that the system design criteria and objectives are incorporated in applications.

131. For a specific computer application jobstream, an explanation of the purpose, identification of computer components used, identification of input-output forms and media, and identification of programmed terminations and prescribed restart instructions would be found in the

A. Systems flowchart.

B. Program documentation.

C. Console log.

D. Computer run book.

The correct answer is (D). *(CIA, adapted)*

REQUIRED: The document meeting the given definition.

DISCUSSION: Documentation is a general control. All programs, procedures, and operating instructions should be documented before final approval. The computer (or console) run book provides operations documentation regarding the matters described in the question.

Answer (A) is incorrect because a systems flowchart shows the flow of information through the system, not the detailed operating instructions found in the computer run book. Answer (B) is incorrect because program documentation includes a statement of the purpose of the program, flowcharts and listings for the program, decision tables, controls, formats for records, inputs and outputs, program operating instructions, and program changes. It should be part of the computer run book. Answer (C) is incorrect because computer console logs typically contain information about jobs processed, job start and stop times, and problems encountered.

132. One of the major problems in a computer system is that incompatible functions may be performed by the same individual. One compensating control is the use of

A. Echo checks.

B. A self-checking digit system.

C. Computer-generated hash totals.

D. A computer log.

The correct answer is (D). *(CPA, adapted)*

REQUIRED: The control compensating for inadequate segregation of duties in a computer system.

DISCUSSION: A computer (console) log is a record of computer and software usage usually produced by the operating system. Proper monitoring of the log is a compensating control for the lack of segregation of duties. For instance, the log should contain a list of interventions by the operators.

Answer (A) is incorrect because echo checks are hardware controls used to determine if the correct message was received by an output device. Answer (B) is incorrect because a self-checking digit system is an input control that tests identification numbers. Answer (C) is incorrect because hash totals are control totals used to check for losses or inaccuracies arising during data movement.

133. Which of the following would represent an internal control weakness in a computer-based system?

A. Computer programmers write and revise programs designed by analysts.

B. The data control group is solely responsible for distributing reports and other output.

C. The computer librarian maintains custody and record keeping for computer application programs.

D. Computer operators have access to operator instructions and the authority to change programs.

The correct answer is (D). *(CIA, adapted)*

REQUIRED: The control weakness in a computer-based system.

DISCUSSION: Computer operators need access to operator instructions. Otherwise, they could not perform their duties. Operators, however, should not have the authority to change computer programs.

Answer (A) is incorrect because writing and revising computer programs are appropriate functions for programmers. Answer (B) is incorrect because distributing computer reports is an appropriate function of the control group. Answer (C) is incorrect because maintaining custody and related record keeping for computer programs is appropriate for a computer librarian.

134. The manager of computer operations prepares a weekly schedule of planned computer processing and distributes a copy of this schedule to the tape librarian. The control purpose this serves is to

A. Keep improper transactions from entering the computer facility.

B. Specify file retention and backup policies.

C. Authorize the release of data files to computer operators.

D. Specify the distribution of printed outputs.

The correct answer is (C). *(CIA, adapted)*

REQUIRED: The control purpose served by giving a copy of the processing schedule to the tape librarian.

DISCUSSION: An important operating control is to establish a library to preclude misplacement, misuse, or theft of data files, programs, and documentation. A librarian should perform this custodianship function and be appropriately accountable. The schedule of data processing activity provides authorization for release of files to operators and a consequent transfer of accountability.

Answer (A) is incorrect because the control group keeps improper transactions from entering the computer facility. Answer (B) is incorrect because file retention and backup policies are specified in the backup and recovery plan. Answer (D) is incorrect because the control group specifies the distribution of printed outputs.

135. In a large organization, the biggest risk in not having an adequately staffed information center help desk is

A. Increased difficulty in performing application audits.

B. Inadequate documentation for application systems.

C. Increased likelihood of use of unauthorized program code.

D. Persistent errors in user interaction with systems.

The correct answer is (D). *(CIA, adapted)*

REQUIRED: The biggest risk in not having an adequately staffed information center help desk.

DISCUSSION: Help desk personnel should be properly trained to log problems, resolve minor problems, and forward more difficult problems to appropriate individuals. An effective help desk minimizes user frustration and delays in processing, continuation of errors in user interaction with the information systems, processing mistakes necessitating later correction or reruns, and failures to log errors and analysis of their causes.

Answer (A) is incorrect because application audits are largely unaffected by help desk staffing. Answer (B) is incorrect because preparation of documentation is a development function. Answer (C) is incorrect because prevention of use of unauthorized program code is a function of change control.

136. Which of the following is the primary reason for conducting performance reviews of staff personnel?

A. To measure activity of a staff member.

B. To measure the progress of a staff member.

C. To determine staff promotions.

D. To determine the amount of raise.

The correct answer is (B). *(CISA, adapted)*

REQUIRED: The primary reason for conducting performance reviews.

DISCUSSION: A primary purpose of performance reviews is to evaluate the progress or performance of staff personnel. Staff personnel need this feedback to meet the objectives established by management.

Answer (A) is incorrect because the primary concern is the progress, not the activity, of a staff member. Answer (C) is incorrect because, although the outcome of a performance review may be a promotion, the primary purpose is to evaluate staff progress. Answer (D) is incorrect because, although the outcome of a performance review may be a raise, the primary purpose is to evaluate staff progress.

137. If complete separation of duties cannot be achieved in an online system, each of the following functions could be performed by the same individual without causing a major control violation except transaction

A. Origination.

B. Authorization.

C. Recording.

D. Correction.

The correct answer is (B). *(CISA, adapted)*

REQUIRED: The procedure that should be performed by a different person if segregation of duties is not possible.

DISCUSSION: Ideally, the duties of transaction authorization, recording, and asset custody are divided among separate employees. Correction of errors should be done by those responsible for making the error. The most important division is between asset custody and recording (accountability), and often those responsible for authorization have de facto custody because they may authorize the release or shipment of assets.

Answers (A), (C), and (D) are incorrect because correction could be performed by the same person who originates and records a transaction, provided the transactions are authorized by a person independent of record keeping.

138. In today's business environment, a company without a computer may be considered backward. But an IPF (information processing facility) is typically a large expense. In planning the physical location of the computer facility, the primary consideration for selecting a site is that it should

A. Maximize the visibility of the computer.

B. Minimize the distance that data control personnel must travel to deliver data and reports and be easily accessible by a majority of company personnel.

C. Be in the basement or on the ground floor.

D. Provide security.

The correct answer is (D). *(J. Brooks)*

REQUIRED: The primary consideration in selecting a site for a computer.

DISCUSSION: The primary criterion for selecting a site should be the security of the environment of the computer. The computer must be protected from disasters such as fire, windstorm, sabotage, and improper access.

Answer (A) is incorrect because a highly visible site is usually not physically secure. Answer (B) is incorrect because, although minimizing travel distance is important, it is not the primary consideration. Additionally, only authorized personnel should be allowed in the computer site; thus, easy access by a majority of company personnel is not necessary. Answer (C) is incorrect because the basement or the ground floor is not always the best location. In certain geographic areas, these locations would be subject to flooding.

139. Some companies have been the target of terrorist attacks in recent years. The best approach to avoid selection as a terrorist's target is to

A. Ensure that the disaster recovery plans are fully tested.

B. Harden the electrical and communications systems against attack.

C. Maintain as low a profile as possible for the data center.

D. Monitor the locations and activities of known terrorists.

The correct answer is (C). *(CIA, adapted)*

REQUIRED: The best approach to avoid terrorist attack.

DISCUSSION: The best approach to avoid becoming a terrorist's target is to refrain from (1) identifying the building on the outside as a data center, (2) showcasing the data center through glass windows, or (3) advertising the important role the data center plays in operations.

Answers (A) and (B) are incorrect because ensuring that the disaster recovery plans are fully tested and hardening systems are not preventive measures. Answer (D) is incorrect because monitoring the locations and activities of known terrorists is unlikely to be feasible.

140. Which of the following statements regarding security concerns for laptop computers is true?

A. The primary methods of control usually involve general controls.

B. Centralized control over the selection and acquisition of hardware and software is not a major concern.

C. Some traditional controls such as segregation of duties become more important.

D. As their use becomes more sophisticated, the degree of concern regarding physical security decreases.

The correct answer is (A). *(CIA, adapted)*

REQUIRED: The true statement about security concerns for laptop computers.

DISCUSSION: General controls apply to all computer activities. General controls to prevent theft of equipment and data and to restrict access to the use of equipment and data are the primary consideration, given the nature of laptop personal computers.

Answer (B) is incorrect because, to assure compatibility with other computers, files, and databases, and to control expenditures, it is necessary to have centralized control over the selection and acquisition of hardware and software. Answer (C) is incorrect because, given the nature and uses of laptop computers, segregation of duties may not be feasible. Answer (D) is incorrect because, as the use of laptop computers becomes more sophisticated, the degree of concern regarding physical security increases.

141. Which of the following should not be the responsibility of a database administrator?

A. Design the content and organization of the database.

B. Develop applications to access the database.

C. Protect the database and its software.

D. Monitor and improve the efficiency of the database.

The correct answer is (B). *(CIA, adapted)*

REQUIRED: The item not the responsibility of a database administrator.

DISCUSSION: The database administrator (DBA) is the person who has overall responsibility for developing and maintaining the database. One primary responsibility is for designing the content of the database. Another responsibility of the DBA is to protect and control the database. A third responsibility is to monitor and improve the efficiency of the database. The responsibility of developing applications to access the database belongs to systems analysts and programmers.

Answer (A) is incorrect because designing the content and organization of the database is a responsibility of the database administrator. Answer (C) is incorrect because protecting the database and its software is a responsibility of the database administrator. Answer (D) is incorrect because monitoring and improving the efficiency of the database is a responsibility of the database administrator.

142. The operational responsibility for the accuracy and completeness of computer-based information should be placed on which of the following groups?

A. Top management.

B. External auditors.

C. Internal auditors.

D. Users.

The correct answer is (D). *(CIA, adapted)*

REQUIRED: The group operationally responsible for the accuracy and completeness of computer-based information.

DISCUSSION: The operational responsibility for the accuracy and completeness of computer-based information should be placed on users. They are in the best position to review output in relation to the input provided and determine whether the results of processing are reasonable.

Answer (A) is incorrect because top management is charged with the overall control of computer-based information systems. Operational control resides in the users. Answer (B) is incorrect because external auditing is an independent appraisal function. Its principal purpose is the expression of an opinion about financial statements. Answer (C) is incorrect because internal auditing is an independent appraisal function. Internal auditors should not have operational responsibility.

143. Operating controls include all of the following except

A. Halt and error controls.

B. Batch controls.

C. Library security and use of proper file labels.

D. Duplicate files and backup procedures.

The correct answer is (B). *(Publisher)*

REQUIRED: The control not an operating control.

DISCUSSION: A batch total is the sum of information that results from adding a field from each record in a batch or group. It provides for control over the movement or processing of the batch and is considered an application control.

Answer (A) is incorrect because halt and error condition controls include explicit instructions that should appear in run manuals for handling halts and error messages for programs. Answer (C) is incorrect because library security controls include the organization and operation of a library to preclude misplacement or theft of tapes, programs, and other file media. In addition, internal and external labels should be used so that the proper files are processed. Answer (D) is incorrect because operating controls also include provisions for backup and reconstruction of files if data are lost as a result of processing errors or catastrophes.

144. In planning the audit of a disaster recovery plan for a minicomputer installation, the auditor should consider which of the following features of the plan as important to the minicomputer installation as to a mainframe installation?

I. Offsite storage facilities
II. Backup procedures
III. Hardware replacement provisions
IV. Training of system personnel

A. I and III.

B. II and IV.

C. I, II, and III.

D. I, II, III, and IV.

The correct answer is (D). *(CISA, adapted)*

REQUIRED: The features considered as important for minicomputers as for mainframes.

DISCUSSION: The nature of the computer facility does not alter the need for proper controls. Each of the items listed is an important feature of control that should be present, regardless of the type of computer system.

Answers (A), (B), and (C) are incorrect because all of the items listed are equally important in a minicomputer or mainframe environment.

145. Which of the following is most important when there is a lack of adequate fire detection and control equipment in the computer areas?

A. Adequate fire insurance.

B. Regular hardware maintenance.

C. Offsite storage of transaction and master files.

D. Fully tested backup processing facilities.

The correct answer is (C). *(CISA, adapted)*

REQUIRED: The most important control given a lack of fire detection and control equipment.

DISCUSSION: One of the primary risks against which a computer operation must be protected is the loss of programs and files. Backup procedures, including offsite storage of backup copies, are necessary to protect against loss.

Answer (A) is incorrect because, whereas adequate fire insurance is an important element for recovery, offsite storage of transaction and master files is essential to recovery. Answer (B) is incorrect because regular hardware maintenance does not relate to recovery. Answer (D) is incorrect because, whereas a fully tested backup processing facility is an important element for recovery, without offsite storage, recovery is ordinarily not feasible.

146. Because of a power surge, a read-write head damaged the surface of the disk volume containing the savings account master file used by an online savings account update and inquiry program. At the time of the failure, there were 20 active teller terminals connected to the program. The disk damage was the only physical damage resulting from the power fluctuation. Possible recovery steps are

1. Restart the online update and inquiry program.
2. Restore the savings account master file from the good records on the original disk.
3. Restore the savings account master file from the most recent file backup.
4. Display each teller's last transaction and prompt each teller to reenter any subsequent transactions.
5. Apply transactions occurring since the last complete file backup to the master file.
6. Prompt tellers to reenter their last transaction.

The best recovery procedure consists of which sequence of steps?

A. 2, 5, 1, 6

B. 2, 5, 1, 4

C. 3, 5, 1, 4

D. 3, 5, 1, 6

The correct answer is (C). *(CIA, adapted)*

REQUIRED: The sequence of steps in the best recovery procedure.

DISCUSSION: The use of restart and recovery procedures eliminates the need to reprocess all data in the event of a processing failure. If checkpoints are established during a processing run (e.g., by periodically copying necessary data and program indicators onto a storage medium), the run may be restarted from the checkpoint. Restart and recovery procedures can also be used in an online system. Accordingly, the recovery procedure should begin with updating the most recent copy of the damaged master file from the transactions log. The online update and inquiry program can then be activated and each teller told to reenter transactions after the last recorded transaction.

Answer (A) is incorrect because the original disk was damaged, thus preventing a full update from that source. Also, each teller should begin with the transaction following the last one logged before the power surge. Answer (B) is incorrect because the original disk was damaged, thus preventing a full update from that source. Answer (D) is incorrect because each teller should begin with the transaction following the last one logged before the power surge.

147. The most effective test of a disaster recovery plan is to

A. Have the IS auditor review the plan in detail.

B. Have the external auditor review the plan in detail.

C. Conduct a mock disaster and carry out disaster recovery procedures.

D. Conduct a structured walkthrough of the plan by all key individuals.

The correct answer is (C). *(CISA, adapted)*

REQUIRED: The most effective test of a disaster recovery plan.

DISCUSSION: The best method to test the effectiveness of a disaster plan is to simulate a disaster and evaluate the application of the recovery procedures.

Answers (A) and (B) are incorrect because having the IS auditor or the external auditor review the disaster recovery plan would not test the effectiveness of the plan. Answer (D) is incorrect because conducting a structured walkthrough would not be as effective as simulating a disaster.

148. Reciprocal agreements for alternative processing sites can have which of the following drawbacks?

I. They are expensive to maintain.

II. Incompatibilities in the operating software may occur.

III. The reciprocal data center may not be available during normal business hours.

IV. The reciprocal data center may not have adequate capacity.

V. Users ordinarily don't like reciprocal agreements.

A. I and II.

B. II, III, and IV.

C. III and V.

D. IV and V.

The correct answer is (B). *(CISA, adapted)*

REQUIRED: The drawbacks of reciprocal agreements for alternative processing.

DISCUSSION: The cost of maintaining a duplicate set of backup equipment is cost prohibitive. An alternative is to agree with other entities to provide share facilities in case of a disaster. Because those facilities may not be duplicates of existing systems, incompatibilities and lack of adequate capacity may exist. In addition, the agreeing facility must continue in operation for its own processing, and computer time may not be made available at convenient times.

Answer (A) is incorrect because reciprocal agreements are very inexpensive. Answer (C) is incorrect because users may not be aware of a reciprocal agreement or understand its ramifications. They may also be grateful for the existence of arrangements for backup facilities. Answer (D) is incorrect because users do not necessarily dislike reciprocal agreements.

149. Which two of the following would be part of a review to ensure that machine malfunctions, error recovery, and stop/restart procedures are clearly documented and periodically reviewed as a security precaution?

I. Reviewing for completeness the list of abnormal operations that require documented records

II. Reviewing the adequacy of procedures for processing on backup hardware

III. Interviewing management responsible for reviewing the records of abnormal operations and determining the adequacy of steps taken to assure the credibility and continuity of processing

IV. Interviewing the operations supervisor to determine the extent of rotation of personnel between shifts

A. I and III.

B. I and IV.

C. II and III.

D. II and IV.

The correct answer is (A). *(CISA, adapted)*

REQUIRED: The two procedures that would be part of a review to ensure that machine malfunctions, error recovery, and stop/restart procedures are clearly documented and reviewed.

DISCUSSION: The auditor should review the completeness of the list of typical abnormal operations for which documented records are required. But the mere existence of documentation does not assure that the described procedures would be carried out. Hence, the auditor should interview management to determine the adequacy of the procedures employed in case of malfunctions.

Answer (B) is incorrect because rotation of personnel is not a procedure to aid recovery from either a malfunction or an outright catastrophe. Answer (C) is incorrect because auxiliary processing is part of a disaster (e.g., a flood, fire or other interrupting regular operations) plan rather than a restart procedure (needed because of human errors or machine breakdowns). Answer (D) is incorrect because rotation of personnel is not a procedure to aid recovery from either a malfunction or an outright catastrophe. Moreover, auxiliary processing is part of a disaster plan rather than a restart procedure.

150. All of the following are examples of corrective controls except

A. Transaction trails.

B. Passwords.

C. Upstream resubmission.

D. Automatic error correction.

The correct answer is (B). *(CISA, adapted)*

REQUIRED: The item not a corrective control.

DISCUSSION: Passwords are controls over unauthorized access to the computer or to data files. They are a preventive, not a corrective, control.

Answer (A) is incorrect because a transaction trail is primarily a corrective rather than a detective control in computer systems given to the difficulty of manual review of a large volume of transactions. The transaction trail (an audit trail) is principally used to follow up and correct exceptions. Answer (C) is incorrect because upstream resubmission is the input of error corrections under more stringent controls than those over the original transactions. Error corrections are especially error prone. Answer (D) is incorrect because automatic error correction is a nonsense term.

151. A company updates its accounts receivable master file weekly and retains the master files and corresponding update transactions for the most recent 2-week period. The purpose of this practice is to

A. Verify run-to-run control totals for receivables.

B. Match internal labels to avoid writing on the wrong volume.

C. Permit reconstruction of the master file if needed.

D. Validate groups of update transactions for each version.

The correct answer is (C). *(CIA, adapted)*

REQUIRED: The purpose of periodic retention of master files and transaction data.

DISCUSSION: The grandfather-father-son approach normally employs magnetic tapes to furnish backup in a batch processing system. The procedure involves creation and retention of three generations of master files so that lost or destroyed data may be regenerated from the remaining master files and transaction data. In this case, a master file (the grandfather) and the first week's transactions are used to generate a second master file (the father). This file and the second week's transactions are the basis for the current master file (the son). Online systems employ rollback and recovery procedures; i.e., the master file is periodically dumped onto a storage medium. Reconstruction is then possible using the backup copy and the transactions log.

Answer (A) is incorrect because comparison of batch totals is a control over the completeness of processing, not a recovery procedure. Answer (B) is incorrect because internal labels may avoid destruction of data but do not aid in recovery. Answer (D) is incorrect because validation may avoid destruction of data but does not aid in recovery.

152. A company's management has expressed concern over the varied system architectures that the organization uses. Potential security and control concerns would include all of the following except

A. Users may have different user ID codes and passwords to remember for the several systems that they use.

B. There are difficulties in developing uniform security standards for the various platforms.

C. Backup file storage administration is often decentralized.

D. Having data distributed across many computers throughout the organization increases the risk that a single disaster would destroy large portions of the organization's data.

The correct answer is (D). *(CIA, adapted)*

REQUIRED: The item not a security and control risk resulting from use of varied system architectures.

DISCUSSION: The use of distributed systems with different architectures throughout the organization decreases the risk that a single disaster will destroy large portions of data. Centralization of data in a single mainframe environment would pose greater risk of data loss.

Answer (A) is incorrect because password proliferation is a considerable security concern. Users may be tempted to record their passwords or make them overly simple. Answer (B) is incorrect because consistent security across varied platforms is challenging as a result of the different features of various systems and the decentralization of security administration. Answer (C) is incorrect because decentralization of backup file storage administration may lead to lack of consistency and difficulty in monitoring compliance.

153. Good planning will help an organization restore computer operations after a processing outage. Good recovery planning should ensure that

A. Backup/restart procedures have been built into job streams and programs.

B. Change control procedures cannot be bypassed by operating personnel.

C. Planned changes in equipment capacities are compatible with projected workloads.

D. Service level agreements with owners of applications are documented.

The correct answer is (A). *(CIA, adapted)*

REQUIRED: The condition ensured by good recovery planning.

DISCUSSION: The disaster plan should embrace data center recovery, critical application recovery, and network recovery. It should be updated and current with regard to recent test results and new applications, equipment, and network configurations. The plan should also ensure that backup facilities are still able to process critical applications and that end-user responsibility is established. Another essential component of a disaster recovery plan is that backup/restart procedures have been anticipated and provided for in the application systems.

Answer (B) is incorrect because whether change control procedures can be bypassed is not usually a consideration in disaster recovery planning. Answer (C) is incorrect because planned rather than actual changes in equipment capacities are not relevant in disaster recovery planning. Answer (D) is incorrect because ensuring that service level agreements with owners of critical applications are adequate is not a function of disaster recovery planning.

154. Each day, after all processing is finished, a bank performs a backup of its online deposit files and retains it for 7 days. Copies of each day's transaction files are not retained. This approach is

A. Valid, in that having a week's worth of backups permits recovery even if one backup is unreadable.

B. Risky, in that restoring from the most recent backup file would omit subsequent transactions.

C. Valid, in that it minimizes the complexity of backup/recovery procedures if the online file has to be restored.

D. Risky, in that no checkpoint/restart information is kept with the backup files.

The correct answer is (B). *(CIA, adapted)*

REQUIRED: The true statement about retention of backup files but not each day's transaction files.

DISCUSSION: At appropriate intervals, the disk files should be copied on magnetic tape so that restart procedures can begin at those points if data are lost or destroyed. However, not retaining each day's transaction files is risky because information processed since the last backup file was created will be lost.

Answer (A) is incorrect because the practice of not retaining daily transaction data is unsound in that the bank loses a day's transactions for each backup that is unreadable. Answer (C) is incorrect because the practice of not retaining daily transaction data certainly minimizes complexity but at the expense of losing transaction data if the online file must be restored from the backup. Answer (D) is incorrect because checkpoint/restart information is not needed. The backups are created after all processing is finished for the day.

155. An inexperienced computer operator mounted an incorrect version of the accounts receivable master file on a tape drive during processing. Because of this error, the entire processing run had to be repeated at a significant cost. Which of the following software controls would be most effective in preventing this type of operator error from affecting the processing of files?

A. Data transmission check.

B. File header label check.

C. Memory isolation protection.

D. Unauthorized access protection.

The correct answer is (B). *(CIA, adapted)*

REQUIRED: The software control for preventing use of an incorrect version of a master file.

DISCUSSION: The use of external, header, and trailer labels should be enforced to ensure the proper access and protection of files. A header label is a machine-readable record at the beginning of a file that identifies the file. Software makes this check. A trailer label is a machine-readable label at the end of a file containing record counts and control totals. An external label is a human-readable identifying label affixed to the outside of a file holder, such as a magnetic tape file.

Answer (A) is incorrect because a data transmission check verifies only the accuracy of the communication. Answer (C) is incorrect because memory isolation protection (boundary protection) protects programs or data from interference (unauthorized reading and/or writing) caused by activity related to other programs or data stored on the same medium. Answer (D) is incorrect because access controls (passwords, etc.) prevent unauthorized access from remote locations, not authorized use by an operator.

156. The use of external labels with floppy disks is least likely to prevent which of the following?

A. Formatting a disk that was used for a backup of hard disk files.

B. Using a version of a file that has been subsequently revised.

C. Erasing an important file on a disk.

D. Spilling liquid on a disk and losing the files.

The correct answer is (D). *(Publisher)*

REQUIRED: The error or problem not likely prevented by external labels on floppy disks.

DISCUSSION: Proper handling of magnetic media requires safeguards from excessive heat, accidental magnetic contact, and physical abuse such as liquid spills. External labels do not prevent such occurrences.

Answer (A) is incorrect because all external file media, e.g., magnetic tapes and disks, should be properly labeled so that the user can determine the proper use of the files. Formatting the wrong disk and thereby erasing its contents could therefore be prevented by use of external labels. Answer (B) is incorrect because use of the wrong version of a file can be prevented by use of external labels. Answer (C) is incorrect because erasing an important file on a disk can be prevented by use of external labels.

157. In traditional information systems, computer operators are generally responsible for backing up software and data files on a regular basis. In distributed or cooperative systems, ensuring that adequate backups are taken is the responsibility of

A. User management.

B. Systems programmers.

C. Data entry clerks.

D. Tape librarians.

The correct answer is (A). *(CIA, adapted)*

REQUIRED: The persons responsible for ensuring that adequate backups are taken in distributed or cooperative systems.

DISCUSSION: In distributed or cooperative systems, the responsibility for ensuring that adequate backups are taken is the responsibility of user management. The systems are under the control of users, not a central information processing department.

Answer (B) is incorrect because distributed environments have no systems programmers comparable to those at central sites for traditional systems. Answer (C) is incorrect because distributed environments may not have data entry clerks. Users typically perform their own data entry. Answer (D) is incorrect because, in distributed environments, there are no tape librarians.

5.8 System and Application Software Acquisition and Maintenance

158. In the computer program development process, a problem will most likely result when

A. Programmers take a longer amount of time to perform programming tasks than expected.

B. Written specifications from the user are used to develop detail program code.

C. Programmers use specialized application tools to simulate the system being programmed.

D. User specifications are inadvertently misunderstood.

The correct answer is (D). *(CMA, adapted)*

REQUIRED: The most likely cause of a problem during computer program development.

DISCUSSION: Program development entails coding programs in accordance with the specifications established in the physical design phase of the systems development life cycle. The physical system design includes creating specifications for, among other things, work flow and programs (but not coding) that are consistent with the general or conceptual design. The general design incorporates user descriptions of the applications. Accordingly, a misunderstanding about user specifications can have fundamental and far-reaching consequences.

Answer (A) is incorrect because, although a programming delay is undesirable, it does not necessarily impair the achievement of objectives. Answer (B) is incorrect because user specifications are the foundation of the program development process. Answer (C) is incorrect because using specialized application tools should avert problems.

159. Each of the following would help ensure development of an effective application system except

A. Active participation by user departments in the development stage.

B. Management involvement in the development stage.

C. Prioritization of applications to be developed.

D. Postimplementation reviews.

The correct answer is (C). *(CISA, adapted)*

REQUIRED: The step that would not help ensure the development of an effective system.

DISCUSSION: Effectiveness relates to the ability to meet the objectives set forth by the organization. The nature of the applications themselves, not necessarily the order in which they are implemented, would influence their effectiveness.

Answer (A) is incorrect because active participation by user departments in the development stage helps assure that the objectives of the system are identified. Answer (B) is incorrect because management involvement helps assure that proper resources are directed to development. Answer (D) is incorrect because post implementation reviews are important for ensuring that a newly developed application includes the appropriate controls and effectively meets management's needs. If the system is not controlled or effective, the post implementation review should identify the weaknesses for further correction.

160. Program documentation is a control designed primarily to ensure that

A. Programmers have access to the tape library or information on disk files.

B. Programs do not make mathematical errors.

C. Programs are kept up to date and perform as intended.

D. No one has made use of the computer hardware for personal reasons.

The correct answer is (C). *(CMA, adapted)*

REQUIRED: The purpose of program documentation.

DISCUSSION: Complete, up-to-date documentation of all programs and associated operating procedures is necessary for efficient operation of a computer installation. Maintenance of programs is important to provide for continuity and consistency of data processing services to users. Program documentation (the program run manual) consists of problem statements, systems flowcharts, operating instructions, record layouts, program flowcharts, program listings, test data, and approval and change sheets.

Answer (A) is incorrect because programmers should not have access to operational materials. Answer (B) is incorrect because editing routines check for arithmetic errors prior to processing, and debugging should uncover errors in programs. Answer (D) is incorrect because documentation cannot ensure computer security.

161. The process of monitoring, evaluating, and modifying a system as needed is referred to as systems

A. Analysis.

B. Feasibility study.

C. Maintenance.

D. Implementation.

The correct answer is (C). *(CMA, adapted)*

REQUIRED: The term for the process of monitoring, evaluating, and modifying a system.

DISCUSSION: Systems maintenance must be undertaken by systems analysts and applications programmers continually throughout the life of a system. Maintenance is the redesign of the system and programs to meet new needs or to correct design flaws. These changes should be part of a regular program of preventive maintenance.

Answer (A) is incorrect because systems analysis is the process of determining user problems and needs, surveying the organization's present system, and analyzing the facts. Answer (B) is incorrect because a feasibility study determines whether a proposed system is technically, operationally, and economically feasible. Answer (D) is incorrect because implementation involves training and educating users, testing, conversion, and follow-up.

162. In the development of a large batch or online system, user management should approve all of the following except

A. Control activities.

B. Systems test plans.

C. Conversion processing.

D. Operating instructions.

The correct answer is (D). *(CISA, adapted)*

REQUIRED: The step in the development of a large computer system not requiring user management approval.

DISCUSSION: Management should approve those steps that affect its use of the system. Operating instructions involve technical tasks that computer personnel must accomplish to meet the objectives of the user group and need not be approved by management.

Answer (A) is incorrect because the control activities affect user management and therefore require approval. Answer (B) is incorrect because the testing of the system may involve adjustments by management and should be subject to approval. Answer (C) is incorrect because the conversion of the system may involve adjustments by management and should be subject to approval.

163. Effective internal control for application development should provide for which of the following?

I. A project steering committee to initiate and oversee the system

II. A technical systems programmer to evaluate systems software

III. Feasibility studies to evaluate existing systems

IV. The establishment of standards for systems design and programming

A. I and III.

B. I, II, and IV.

C. I, III, and IV.

D. II, III, and IV.

The correct answer is (C). *(CISA, adapted)*

REQUIRED: The components of effective internal control for application development.

DISCUSSION: Effective systems development requires participation by top management. This can be achieved through a steering committee composed of higher-level representatives of system users. The committee approves or recommends projects and reviews their progress. Studies of the economic, operational, and technical feasibility of new applications necessarily entail evaluations of existing systems. Another necessary control is the establishment of standards for system design and programming. Standards represent user and system requirements determined during systems analysis.

Answer (A) is incorrect because standards must be established. Answer (B) is incorrect because a technical systems programmer has a role in the development and modification of the operating system but not necessarily in applications development. The technical support in this area would be provided by systems analysts rather than programmers. Answer (D) is incorrect because a technical systems programmer has a role in the development and modification of the operating system but not necessarily in applications development.

164. Use of unlicensed software in an organization

I. Increases the risk of introducing viruses into the organization

II. Is not a serious exposure if only low-cost software is involved

III. Can be detected by software checking routines that run from a network server

A. I only.

B. I and II only.

C. I, II, and III.

D. I and III only.

The correct answer is (D). *(CIA, adapted)*

REQUIRED: The true statement(s) about use of unlicensed software.

DISCUSSION: Antivirus measures should include strict adherence to software acquisition policies. Unlicensed software is less likely to have come from reputable vendors and to have been carefully tested. Special software is available to test software in use to determine whether it has been authorized.

Answers (A), (B), and (C) are incorrect because use of unlicensed software increases the risk of viral infection, and its use can be detected by software checking routines. Moreover, the cost of the software is not relevant. Any software may contain a virus.

165. An insurance company is planning to implement new standard software in all its local offices. The new software has a fast response time, is very user friendly, and was developed with extensive user involvement. The new software captures, consolidates, edits, validates, and finally transfers standardized transaction data to the headquarters mainframe. Local managers, who were satisfied with existing locally written microcomputer applications, opposed the new approach because they anticipated

A. Increased workloads.

B. Lengthy retraining.

C. More accountability.

D. Less computer equipment.

The correct answer is (C). *(CIA, adapted)*

REQUIRED: The reason for opposing introduction of new software.

DISCUSSION: Cooperative processing implies a tighter coupling than previously existed between the microcomputers and the mainframe. The result may threaten the managers' perceived autonomy by increasing the control exercised by headquarters and therefore the accountability of local managers.

Answer (A) is incorrect because, given that only existing systems would be converted, the transaction volume would likely remain relatively constant. Answer (B) is incorrect because retraining would probably be needed, but PC-based transaction capture applications with graphical interfaces are often easy to learn with minimal training. Answer (D) is incorrect because, compared with mainframe-only processing, cooperative processing typically requires more computer equipment at distributed locations.

166. A benefit of using computer-aided software engineering (CASE) technology is that it can ensure that

A. No obsolete data fields occur in files.

B. Users become committed to new systems.

C. All programs are optimized for efficiency.

D. Data integrity rules are applied consistently.

The correct answer is (D). *(CIA, adapted)*

REQUIRED: The benefit of CASE.

DISCUSSION: CASE is an automated technology (at least in part) for developing and maintaining software and managing projects. A benefit of using CASE technology is that it can ensure that data integrity rules, including those for validation and access, are applied consistently across all files.

Answer (A) is incorrect because obsolete data fields must be recognized by developers or users. Once recognized, obsolete data fields can be treated consistently in CASE procedures. Answer (B) is incorrect because using CASE will not ensure user commitment to new systems if they are poorly designed or otherwise do not meet users' needs. Answer (C) is incorrect because, although it has the potential to accelerate system development, CASE cannot ensure that all programs are optimized for efficiency. In fact, some CASE-developed modules may need to be optimized by hand to achieve acceptable performance.

Questions 167 through 169 are based on the following information. Baker Manufacturing Co. has the following nine master files:

- Accounts payable
- Accounts receivable
- Bill of materials (material requirements for producing a product)
- Finished goods inventory
- Open production orders
- Open purchase orders
- Raw materials inventory
- Work-in-process inventory
- Production operations list (labor operations and machine requirements)

167. Master files maintained as part of the sales order processing system are

A. Accounts receivable, bill of materials.

B. Accounts payable, accounts receivable, finished goods inventory.

C. Accounts receivable, sales summary, production operations list.

D. Accounts receivable, finished goods inventory.

The correct answer is (D). *(Publisher)*

REQUIRED: The master files maintained as part of the sales order processing system.

DISCUSSION: A sales order processing cycle involves taking customers' orders and updating amounts owed by customers (accounts receivable) and the amount of inventory left after shipment (finished goods inventory).

Answer (A) is incorrect because the bill of materials file is used in production planning. Answer (B) is incorrect because the accounts payable files are used to process purchases. Answer (C) is incorrect because the production operations list file is used in production planning.

168. Master files maintained as part of the processing of purchase transactions are

A. Accounts payable, bill of materials, finished goods inventory, and open purchase orders.

B. Accounts payable, open purchase orders, raw materials inventory, and work-in-process inventory.

C. Accounts payable, bill of materials, and open purchase orders.

D. Accounts payable, open purchase orders, and raw materials inventory.

The correct answer is (D). *(Publisher)*

REQUIRED: The master files maintained as part of the processing of purchases.

DISCUSSION: The processing of purchase transactions involves preparing purchase orders and updating raw materials inventory on order (raw materials inventory) and purchase orders not yet received (open purchase orders). Upon receipt of the purchased item, updating is required for the amount on hand (raw material inventory), open purchase orders since the item was received (open purchase orders), and the amount owed to the vendor (accounts payable).

Answer (A) is incorrect because the bill of materials file is used in production planning, and finished goods inventory is part of the sales order processing cycle. Answer (B) is incorrect because the work-in-process inventory file is used in production planning. Answer (C) is incorrect because the bill of materials file is used in production planning.

169. Master files used to plan and report on the resources required for the coming period include

A. Bill of materials, open production orders, work-in-process inventory, and production operations list.

B. Finished goods inventory, open production orders, open purchase orders, and work-in-process inventory.

C. Finished goods inventory, open purchase orders, raw materials inventory, and work-in-process.

D. Bill of materials, open production orders, accounts payable, and production operations list.

The correct answer is (A). *(Publisher)*

REQUIRED: The master files used to plan and report on resources required for the coming period.

DISCUSSION: Production planning involves determining what needs to be produced (open production orders and finished goods inventory), what materials are required (bill of materials), what labor and machine operations are needed (production operations list), what resources are tied up in production (work-in-process), and what raw materials are available (raw materials inventory). Based on this evaluation, new production orders (open production orders) are issued.

Answers (B) and (C) are incorrect because the open purchase orders file is used in the processing of purchases. Answer (D) is incorrect because the accounts payable file is used in the processing of purchases.

170. The installation of a database management system (DBMS) is not likely to have any direct impact on

A. Data redundancy within files.

B. Sharing of common data.

C. The logic needed to solve a problem in an application program.

D. The internal control of data accuracy and access and inconsistencies within common data fields.

The correct answer is (C). *(CMA, adapted)*

REQUIRED: The item not likely to be affected by the installation of a DBMS.

DISCUSSION: A database is a set of related files arranged so that data usually need to be stored only once. A DBMS is an integrated set of computer programs that create the database, maintain the elements, safeguard the data from loss or destruction, and make the data available to application programs and inquiries. The physical and logical structure of the database is independent of the applications. Programs only need to specify the name of a data item because the DBMS will handle retrieval and storage. Moreover, program logic does not change.

Answers (A), (B), and (D) are incorrect because the installation of a DBMS is likely to reduce data redundancy, promote sharing of data, eliminate inconsistencies within data fields, and provide more sophisticated internal control over data accuracy and access.

171. The accountant who prepared a spreadsheet model for workload forecasting left the company, and the person's successor was unable to understand how to use the spreadsheet. The best control for preventing such situations from occurring is to ensure that

A. Use of end-user computing resources is monitored.

B. End-user computing efforts are consistent with strategic plans.

C. Documentation standards exist and are followed.

D. Adequate backups are made for spreadsheet models.

The correct answer is (C). *(CIA, adapted)*

REQUIRED: The best control to permit new employees to understand internally developed programs.

DISCUSSION: The accountant's successor could not use the forecasting model because of inadequate documentation. By requiring that documentation standards exist and are followed, the company will enable new employees to understand internally developed programs when the developer leaves the organization.

Answer (A) is incorrect because monitoring concerns controlling the use of resources. Answer (B) is incorrect because consistency with strategic plans concern evaluation of the system. Answer (D) is incorrect because maintaining adequate backups for spreadsheet models is necessary, but lack of adequate backup is not the reason the accountant's successor could not use the forecasting model.

172. Which of the following controls would best protect production programs from unauthorized modification?

A. Requiring two operators to be present during equipment operation.

B. Implementing management review of daily run logs.

C. Limiting program access solely to operators.

D. Restricting programmer access to the computer room.

The correct answer is (C). *(CISA, adapted)*

REQUIRED: The best control to provide protection against unauthorized changes in production programs.

DISCUSSION: Operators require access to production programs in order to run the programs. However, systems programmers and others should be denied access to the resident production programs to limit the risk of unauthorized changes.

Answer (A) is incorrect because unauthorized modifications can be made by programmers at terminals regardless of whether two operators are present during operation. Answer (B) is incorrect because an effective control would be a management review of console logs, not run logs. Answer (D) is incorrect because unauthorized modifications can be made by programmers at terminals regardless of whether programmers are denied access to the computer room.

173. Managers at a consumer products company purchased microcomputer software only from recognized vendors and prohibited employees from installing nonauthorized software on their microcomputers. To minimize the likelihood of computer viruses infecting any of its systems, the company should also

A. Restore infected systems with authorized versions.

B. Recompile infected programs from source code backups.

C. Institute program change control procedures.

D. Test all new software on a stand-alone microcomputer.

The correct answer is (D). *(CIA, adapted)*

REQUIRED: The best protection against viruses.

DISCUSSION: Software from recognized sources should be tested in quarantine (for example, in a test/development machine or a stand-alone microcomputer) because even vendor-supplied software may be infected with viruses. The software should be run with a vaccine program and tested for the existence of logic bombs, etc.

Answer (A) is incorrect because, if viruses infect a system, the company should restore the system with authorized software, but this procedure does not minimize the likelihood of initial infection. Answer (B) is incorrect because, if viruses infect programs that the company wrote, it should recompile the programs from source code backups, but this procedure does not minimize the likelihood of initial infection. Answer (C) is incorrect because instituting program change control procedures is good practice but does not minimize the likelihood of the system's being infected initially.

174. An audit test to substantiate that a company is complying with software copyright requirements is to

A. Review the corporate policy on copyrights.

B. Compare the software on a sample of microcomputers with the purchase documentation.

C. Inventory all the software that is being run on microcomputers.

D. Review the minutes of the MIS Steering Committee or similar body.

The correct answer is (B). *(CIA, adapted)*

REQUIRED: The audit test to substantiate that a company is complying with copyright requirements.

DISCUSSION: Software is customarily licensed to be used on particular machines. Consequently, unauthorized use and copying are persistent problems. A compliance audit may therefore entail sampling the software being used and comparing the related purchase agreements.

Answer (A) is incorrect because reviewing the policy will not determine compliance with copyright limitations. Answer (C) is incorrect because an inventory of software alone cannot determine compliance without comparing it with supporting purchase documentation. Answer (D) is incorrect because reviewing the minutes may determine the intent to comply with copyright laws, not compliance.

175. Which of the following is an indication that a computer virus of this category is present?

A. Frequent power surges that harm computer equipment.

B. Unexplainable losses of or changes to data.

C. Inadequate backup, recovery, and contingency plans.

D. Numerous copyright violations due to unauthorized use of purchased software.

The correct answer is (B). *(CIA, adapted)*

REQUIRED: The indicator of a computer virus.

DISCUSSION: The effects of computer viruses range from harmless messages to complete destruction of all data within the system. A symptom of a virus would be the unexplained loss of or change to data.

Answer (A) is incorrect because power surges are caused by hardware or power supply problems. Answer (C) is incorrect because inadequate back-up, recovery, and contingency plans are operating policy weaknesses. Answer (D) is incorrect because copyright violations represent policy or compliance problems.

176. Which of the following operating procedures increases an organization's exposure to computer viruses?

A. Encryption of data files.

B. Frequent backup of files.

C. Downloading public-domain software from electronic bulletin boards.

D. Installing original copies of purchased software on hard disk drives.

The correct answer is (C). *(CIA, adapted)*

REQUIRED: The procedure that increases exposure to viruses.

DISCUSSION: Viruses are spread through shared data. Downloading public-domain software carries a risk that contaminated data may enter the computer.

Answer (A) is incorrect because viruses are spread through the distribution of contaminated programs. Answer (B) is incorrect because backing up files does not increase the chances of a virus entering the computer system. Answer (D) is incorrect because original copies of purchased software on hard disk drives should be free of viruses.

177. The graphic portrayal of the flow of data and the information processing of a system, including computer hardware, is best displayed in a

A. Data-flow diagram.

B. System flowchart.

C. Gantt chart.

D. Program flowchart.

The correct answer is (B). *(CMA, adapted)*

REQUIRED: The best method of displaying the flow of data and the information processing of a system.

DISCUSSION: A system flowchart is a graphic analysis of a data processing application, usually prepared by a systems analyst. The system flowchart is general and stresses flows of data, not computer program logic. A program flowchart is a graphic representation of the detailed steps and logic of an individual computer program.

Answer (A) is incorrect because a data-flow diagram would show only the flow of data, not the total system. Answer (C) is incorrect because a Gantt chart is a bar chart used to monitor the progress of large projects. Answer (D) is incorrect because a program flowchart shows only the details of a single program, not the entire computer system.

178. Decision tables differ from program flowcharts in that decision tables emphasize

A. Ease of manageability for complex programs.

B. Logical relationships among conditions and actions.

C. Cost-benefit factors justifying the program.

D. The sequence in which operations are performed.

The correct answer is (B). *(CPA, adapted)*

REQUIRED: The distinction between decision tables and flowcharts.

DISCUSSION: A decision table identifies the contingencies considered in the description of a problem and the appropriate actions to be taken relative to those contingencies. Decision tables are logic diagrams presented in matrix form. Unlike flowcharts, they do not present the sequence of the actions described.

Answer (A) is incorrect because neither flowcharts nor decision tables emphasize ease of manageability. Answer (C) is incorrect because neither flowcharts nor decision tables emphasize cost-benefit factors. Answer (D) is incorrect because, unlike flowcharts, decision tables do not present the sequence of the actions described.

179. Which one of the following best reflects the basic elements of a data flow diagram?

A. Data sources, data flows, computer configurations, flowchart, and data storage.

B. Data source, data destination, data flows, transformation processes, and data storage.

C. Data flows, data storage, and program flowchart.

D. Data flows, program flowchart, and data destination.

The correct answer is (B). *(CMA, adapted)*

REQUIRED: The best description of the basic elements of a data flow diagram.

DISCUSSION: Structured analysis is a graphical method of defining the inputs, processes, and outputs of a system and dividing it into subsystems. It is a top down approach that specifies the interfaces between modules and the transformations occurring within each. Data flow diagrams are used in structured analysis. The basic elements of a data flow diagram include data source, data destination, data flows, transformation processes, and data storage.

Answer (A) is incorrect because computer configuration is not an element of a data flow diagram. Answers (C) and (D) are incorrect because a program flowchart is not an element of a data flow diagram.

180. A document flowchart represents

A. The sequence of logical operations performed during the execution of a computer program.

B. The possible combinations of alternative logic conditions and corresponding courses of action for each condition in a computer program.

C. The flow of data through a series of operations in an automated data processing system.

D. The flow of forms that relate to a particular transaction through an organization.

The correct answer is (D). *(CMA, adapted)*

REQUIRED: The definition of a document flowchart.

DISCUSSION: A document flowchart graphically presents the flow of forms (documents) through a system that relate to a given transaction, e.g., the processing of a customer's order. It shows the source, flow, processing, and final disposition of the various copies of all related documents.

Answer (A) is incorrect because a program flowchart represents the sequence of logical operations performed during the execution of a computer program. Answer (B) is incorrect because a decision table consists of the possible combinations of alternative logic conditions and corresponding courses of action for each condition in a computer program. Answer (C) is incorrect because a system flowchart is used to represent the flow of data through an automated data processing system.

181. An internal auditor is reviewing the following computer logic diagram:

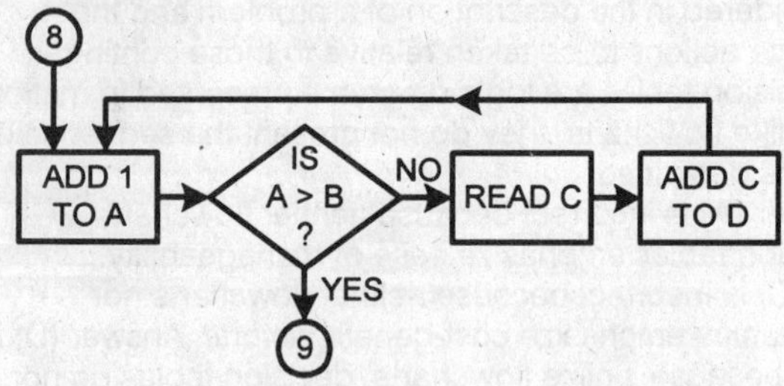

This diagram represents which of the following?

A. Program loop step.

B. Data validity check.

C. Balance test.

D. Limit test.

The correct answer is (A). *(CIA, adapted)*

REQUIRED: The operation described by the computer logic diagram.

DISCUSSION: Variable A will be increased by 1 and C will be added to D repetitively until A exceeds B. The diagram illustrates a program loop, a technique for performing repeated iterations of an instruction a specified number of times.

Answer (B) is incorrect because a data validity check compares the bits of each transmitted character with the valid combinations of bits. Answer (C) is incorrect because a balance test compares a gross amount with its components. Answer (D) is incorrect because a limit test ascertains whether a number falls within a predetermined range of reasonable values.

182. Which of the following types of evidence would an auditor most likely examine to determine whether internal controls are operating as designed?

A. Gross margin information from online data sources regarding the client's industry.

B. Confirmations of receivables verifying account balances.

C. Client records documenting the use of computer programs.

D. Anticipated results documented in budgets or forecasts.

The correct answer is (C). *(CPA, adapted)*

REQUIRED: The items tested to determine the operating effectiveness of internal control.

DISCUSSION: In testing controls over the computer processing function, the auditor should obtain evidence of proper authorization of access to computer programs and files.

Answers (A) and (D) are incorrect because analytical procedures are applied as substantive tests to gross margin information and anticipated results. Answer (B) is incorrect because confirmations customarily request information regarding account balances and are substantive tests, not tests of controls.

183. What benefit would an auditor derive from using an object code compare program to test program change controls?

A. It would show that the object program in production agrees with its related source version.

B. It would show when an object program was last put into production.

C. It would identify the lines of source code that have been changed since the control copy of the program was made.

D. It would identify program inefficiencies.

The correct answer is (A). *(CISA, adapted)*

REQUIRED: The benefits of using an object code compare program.

DISCUSSION: Comparing the production object code with the object code obtained from recompiling the production source code could identify any differences. These may be the result of unauthorized program changes and should be investigated.

Answer (B) is incorrect because using an object code compare program to test program change controls does not provide information concerning the implementation date. Answer (C) is incorrect because object code cannot be directly compared with source code to detect which lines of source code have been changed. Answer (D) is incorrect because a comparison of object modules does not analyze the processing performed by the program.

184. The correct labeling, in order, for the following flowchart symbols is

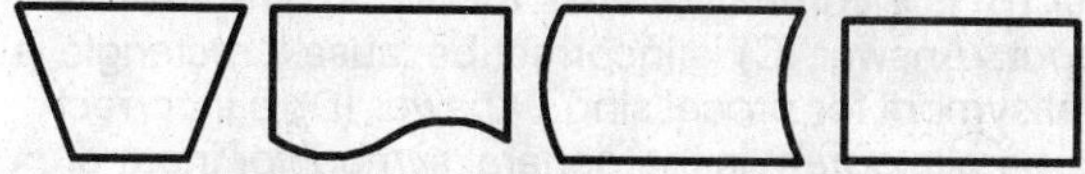

A. Document, display, online storage, and entry operation.

B. Manual operation, processing, offline storage, and input-output activity.

C. Display, document, online storage, and entry operation.

D. Manual operation, document, online storage, and entry operation.

The correct answer is (D). *(CMA, adapted)*

REQUIRED: The correct sequence of labels of four flowchart symbols.

DISCUSSION: The first symbol indicates a manual operation, which is an offline process. The second symbol represents a document, while the third symbol indicates online storage (e.g., a disk drive). The final symbol represents an operation. An operation is defined as a process resulting in a change in the information or the flow direction. In other words, it can be an entry operation.

Answer (A) is incorrect because the first symbol, a trapezoid, is for a manual operation. Answer (B) is incorrect because the third symbol is for online storage. Answer (C) is incorrect because the first symbol does not represent display.

185. The symbol employed to determine if an employee's wages are above or below the maximum limit for FICA taxes is

A.

B.

C.

D.

The correct answer is (B). *(CMA, adapted)*

REQUIRED: The symbol to determine if an employee's wages are within a limit.

DISCUSSION: The question implies a decision, for which a diamond is the flowcharting symbol.

Answer (A) is incorrect because a rectangle is the general symbol for a process or operation. Answer (C) is incorrect because a trapezoid symbolizes a manual operation. Answer (D) is incorrect because a square represents an auxiliary operation performed by a machine other than a computer.

186. The symbol employed to represent the printing of the employees' paychecks by the computer is

A.

B.

C.

D.

The correct answer is (C). *(CMA, adapted)*

REQUIRED: The flowchart symbol for the printing of paychecks by a computer.

DISCUSSION: The printing of paychecks by the computer is an operation depicted by the general processing symbol, which is a rectangle.

Answer (A) is incorrect because a trapezoid depicts a manual operation. Answer (B) is incorrect because a square is an auxiliary operation performed by a machine other than a computer. Answer (D) is incorrect because this symbol indicates manual input, e.g., entry of a proper code through a computer console.

187. The symbol employed to represent the employees' checks printed by the computer is

A. 

B. 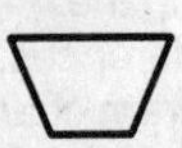

C. 

D. 

The correct answer is (D). *(CMA, adapted)*

REQUIRED: The symbol used to represent employee checks printed by a computer.

DISCUSSION: Employee checks printed by the computer are depicted by the document symbol, which resembles the top of a grand piano.

Answer (A) is incorrect because a parallelogram is the general symbol for input or output. Answer (B) is incorrect because a trapezoid indicates a manual operation. Answer (C) is incorrect because this symbol indicates manual input.

188. The symbol used to represent the physical act of collecting employees' time cards for processing is

A. 

B. 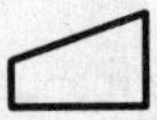

C. 

D. 

The correct answer is (A). *(CMA, adapted)*

REQUIRED: The symbol used to represent the physical act of collecting employees' time cards for processing.

DISCUSSION: Collecting employees' time cards is a manual operation represented by a trapezoid with equal nonparallel sides.

Answer (B) is incorrect because this symbol represents manual input. Answer (C) is incorrect because a rectangle is the general symbol for processing. Answer (D) is incorrect because a parallelogram is the general symbol for input or output.

189. The symbol used to represent the employees' payroll records stored on magnetic tape is

A. 

B. 

C. 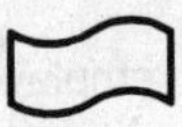

D. 

The correct answer is (D). *(CMA, adapted)*

REQUIRED: The symbol representing employees' payroll records stored on magnetic tape.

DISCUSSION: The magnetic tape symbol (a circle with a tangent at its base) indicates storage on magnetic tape.

Answer (A) is incorrect because a triangle with a mid-line parallel to its base depicts offline storage. Answer (B) is incorrect because this symbol represents online storage. Answer (C) is incorrect because this symbol represents punched paper tape.

190. The symbol used to represent the weekly payroll register generated by the computer is

A.

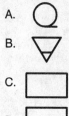

B.

C.

D.

The correct answer is (D). *(CMA, adapted)*

REQUIRED: The symbol used to represent a weekly payroll register printed by a computer.

DISCUSSION: The weekly payroll register on a computer printout is represented by a document symbol, which resembles the top of a grand piano.

Answer (A) is incorrect because a circle with a tangent at its base represents magnetic tape input-output or storage. Answer (B) is incorrect because a triangle with a mid-line parallel to its base depicts offline storage. Answer (C) is incorrect because a rectangle is the general symbol for a process.

191. The symbol used to represent the file of hard-copy, computer-generated payroll reports kept for future reference is

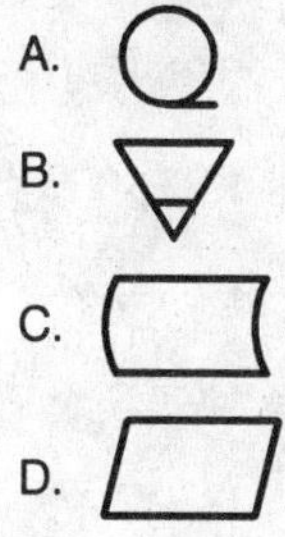

A.

B.

C.

D.

The correct answer is (B). *(CMA, adapted)*

REQUIRED: The symbol used to represent the kept file of hard-copy, computer-generated payroll reports.

DISCUSSION: Hard-copy, computer-generated payroll reports are kept in offline storage, which is symbolized by a triangle with a mid-line parallel to its base.

Answer (A) is incorrect because a circle with a tangent at its base represents a magnetic tape. Answer (C) is incorrect because this symbol represents online storage. Answer (D) is incorrect because a parallelogram is the general symbol for input or output.

192. Which of the following symbolic representations indicates that a sales invoice has been filed?

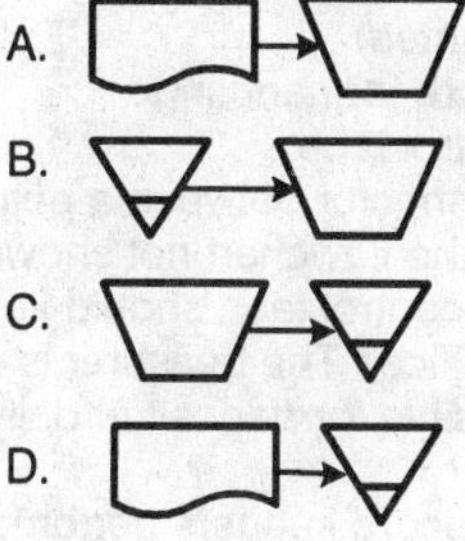

A.

B.

C.

D.

The correct answer is (D). *(CPA, adapted)*

REQUIRED: The symbols indicating filing of a document.

DISCUSSION: The arrow from the document symbol to the triangle with the mid-line parallel to its base indicates that a document has been stored in an offline file.

Answer (A) is incorrect because the arrow from the document symbol to the trapezoid indicates manual (offline) processing of the document. Answer (B) is incorrect because the arrow from offline storage to the manual operation symbol signifies manual (offline) processing of an offline file. Answer (C) is incorrect because the arrow from the trapezoid to the triangle with a mid-line indicates that manual (offline) processing is followed by offline file storage of the result.

Questions 193 through 197 are based on the following information. This flowchart depicts the processing of daily cash receipts for Rockmart Manufacturing.

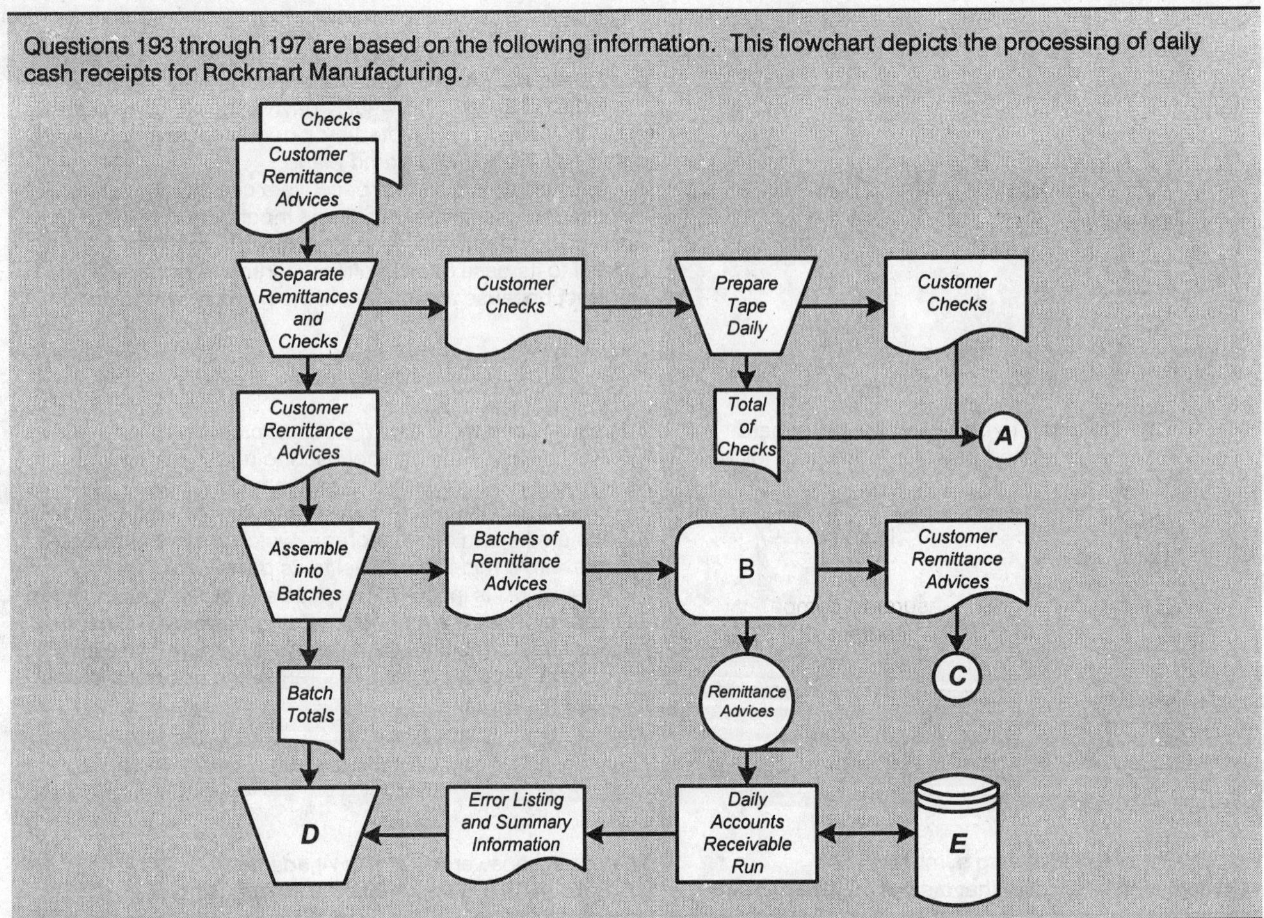

193. The customer checks accompanied by the control tape (refer to symbol A) would be

A. Forwarded daily to the billing department for deposit.

B. Taken by the mail clerk to the bank for deposit daily.

C. Forwarded to the treasurer for deposit daily.

D. Accumulated for a week and then forwarded to the treasurer for deposit weekly.

The correct answer is (C). *(CMA, adapted)*

REQUIRED: The proper procedure for handling customer checks and the related control tape.

DISCUSSION: Symbol A is a connector between a point on this flowchart and another part of the flowchart not shown. The checks and the adding machine control tape should flow through symbol A to the treasurer's office. The treasurer is the custodian of funds and is responsible for deposit of daily receipts.

Answer (A) is incorrect because record keepers perform functions that should be separate from custody of assets. Answer (B) is incorrect because the mail clerk should prepare a list of checks received before they are forwarded to the treasurer for deposit. Answer (D) is incorrect because daily receipts should be deposited intact daily and then reconciled with the bank deposit records.

194. The appropriate description that should be placed in symbol B would be

A. Keying and verifying.

B. Error correction.

C. Collation of remittance advices.

D. Batch processing.

The correct answer is (A). *(CMA, adapted)*

REQUIRED: The appropriate description for symbol B.

DISCUSSION: Since the figure below symbol B signifies magnetic tape, the operation represented by symbol B must be keying the information onto the tape. Verifying the keyed data would also occur at this step.

Answer (B) is incorrect because error correction would occur subsequently except for keying errors. Answer (C) is incorrect because collation has already occurred. Answer (D) is incorrect because batch processing describes the entire system.

195. The next action to take with the customer remittance advices (refer to symbol C) would be to

A. Discard them immediately.

B. File them daily by batch number.

C. Forward them to the internal audit department for internal review.

D. Forward them to the treasurer to compare with the monthly bank statement.

The correct answer is (B). *(CMA, adapted)*

REQUIRED: The action taken at symbol C.

DISCUSSION: All activity with respect to the paper documents most likely ceases at symbol C. Therefore, the batched documents must be filed.

Answer (A) is incorrect because the documents should be kept for reference and audit. Answer (C) is incorrect because internal auditors cannot feasibly review all documents regarding transactions even in an audit. Answer (D) is incorrect because comparison by the treasurer would be inappropriate. (S)he has custody of cash.

196. The appropriate description that should be placed in symbol D would be

A. Attach batch total to report and file.

B. Reconcile cash balances.

C. Compare batch total and correct as necessary.

D. Proof report.

The correct answer is (C). *(CMA, adapted)*

REQUIRED: The appropriate description for symbol D.

DISCUSSION: This flowcharting symbol indicates a manual operation or offline process. Since the input to this operation consists of an adding machine tape containing batch totals and a document containing summary information about the accounts receivable update and an error listing, the operation apparently involves comparing these items.

Answer (A) is incorrect because no filing symbol is given. Answer (B) is incorrect because the flowchart concerns daily receipts, not the reconciliation of cash balances. Answer (D) is incorrect because symbol D indicates a comparison, not output in the form of a report.

197. The appropriate description that should be placed in symbol E would be

A. Accounts receivable master file.

B. Bad debts master file.

C. Remittance advice master file.

D. Cash projection file.

The correct answer is (A). *(CMA, adapted)*

REQUIRED: The appropriate description of symbol E.

DISCUSSION: The flowcharting figure at symbol E indicates magnetic disk storage. Since it is an input and output for the daily computer processing of accounts receivable, it must be the accounts receivable master file.

Answer (B) is incorrect because bad debts are not a part of processing daily receipts. Answer (C) is incorrect because the remittance advice master file was not used for the daily accounts receivable run. Answer (D) is incorrect because the cash projection file was not used for the daily accounts receivable run.

198. An auditor should review the procedures within a program change control group to determine whether it does which of the following?

A. Makes programs available to programmers for change only on receiving written authorization.

B. Reviews user documentation for any necessary changes resulting from a program change.

C. Codes the necessary program changes.

D. Estimates the time and cost involved in a program change.

The correct answer is (A). *(CISA, adapted)*

REQUIRED: The function of a program change control group.

DISCUSSION: A program change control group is responsible for determining that proper procedures are carried out relative to controlling programming changes. This includes assuring that written authorizations are received for changes. To avoid fraud and to ensure compatibility with other programs, programmers should not be able to make unauthorized changes.

Answer (B) is incorrect because the systems analyst has the operational responsibility to assure that documentation is changed to reflect the modification. Answer (C) is incorrect because programmers, not the control group, should code the necessary changes. Answer (D) is incorrect because the systems analyst in conjunction with management should estimate the time and cost involved in a program change.

5.9 Access Security Controls

199. The primary objective of security software is to

A. Control access to information system resources.

B. Restrict access to prevent installation of unauthorized utility software.

C. Detect the presence of viruses.

D. Monitor the separation of duties within applications.

The correct answer is (A). *(CIA, adapted)*

REQUIRED: The primary objective of security software.

DISCUSSION: The objective of security software is to control access to information system resources, such as program libraries, data files, and proprietary software. Security software identifies and authenticates users, controls access to information, and records and investigates security related events and data.

Answer (B) is incorrect because security software will control the use of utilities, not their installation. Answer (C) is incorrect because antivirus software detects the presence of viruses. Answer (D) is incorrect because security software may be a tool to establish, but does not monitor, separation of duties.

200. Assigning passwords to computer users is a control to prevent unauthorized access. Because a password does not conclusively identify a specific individual, it must be safeguarded from theft. A method used to protect passwords is to

A. Require that they be displayed on computer screens but not printed on hard copy output.

B. Set maximum character lengths.

C. Require a minimum retention period.

D. Eliminate all records of old passwords.

The correct answer is (C). *(Publisher)*

REQUIRED: The password security technique.

DISCUSSION: Security measures include changing passwords frequently, that is, establishing a relatively short maximum retention period; not displaying or printing passwords; setting minimum lengths; prohibiting the use of certain words, character strings, or names; mandating a minimum retention period, so users cannot promptly change passwords back to their old and convenient values; and retaining old passwords to prevent their use.

Answer (A) is incorrect because a password should not be displayed. Answer (B) is incorrect because a minimum length requirement is more likely. Answer (D) is incorrect because retention of old passwords prevents their reuse.

201. To increase the security of application software, the internal audit director recommended that programmers be given diskless workstations. Using diskless workstations would increase security by

A. Making theft of programs more difficult.

B. Reducing workstation maintenance expense.

C. Imposing a stricter level of access control.

D. Prompting programmers to work more closely together.

The correct answer is (A). *(CIA, adapted)*

REQUIRED: The way in which diskless workstations increase security.

DISCUSSION: Diskless workstations increase security by preventing the copying of software to a floppy disk from a programmer's workstation. This control not only protects the company's interests in its data and proprietary programs but also guards against theft of software licensed to the company by vendors.

Answer (B) is incorrect because decreasing maintenance expense does not affect security of programs. Answer (C) is incorrect because access control is programmatic and is not ordinarily affected by switching to diskless workstations. Answer (D) is incorrect because switching to diskless workstations may or may not prompt programmers to work more closely together.

202. Which new issues, associated with rapidly advancing computer technology, create new risk exposures for organizations?

A. Changes in organizational reporting requirements and controls over computer abuse.

B. Controls over library tape procedures.

C. Complexity of operating systems and controls over privacy of data.

D. Changes in organizational behavior.

The correct answer is (C). *(CIA, adapted)*

REQUIRED: The circumstance that creates new risk exposures for organizations.

DISCUSSION: Advancing computer technology presents more complex audit environments. With the advent of systems that permit remote access, the risk that unauthorized parties may obtain or tamper with important information is increased.

Answer (A) is incorrect because changes in organizational reporting requirements are not new issues related to advancing computer technology. Answer (B) is incorrect because controls over library tape procedures have not been materially changed by advancing computer technology. Answer (D) is incorrect because changes in organizational behavior are not directly associated with auditor responsibilities in advancing technology.

203. An equipment manufacturer maintains dial-up ports into its order-entry system for the convenience of its customers worldwide so they may order parts as they need them. The manufacturer promises 48-hour delivery anywhere in the world for 95% of these parts orders. Because of the cost and sensitive nature of certain electronic parts, the manufacturer needs to maintain secure access to its order-entry system. The best technique for monitoring the security of access is

A. Integrated test facility for the order-entry system.

B. Tracing of transactions through the order-entry system.

C. Transaction selection of order-entry transactions.

D. Logging of unsuccessful access attempts.

The correct answer is (D). *(CIA, adapted)*

REQUIRED: The best technique for monitoring the security of access.

DISCUSSION: An access log should be used to record all attempts to use the system. The date and time, codes used, mode of access, and data involved are recorded. The system should monitor unsuccessful attempts because repeated attempts could suggest that someone is trying random or patterned character sequences in order to identify a password.

Answer (A) is incorrect because an integrated test facility (ITF) is a technique by which an auditor selects transactions and processing functions and applies the transactions to a fictitious entity during a normal processing cycle along with regular transactions. Answer (B) is incorrect because tracing follows the path of a transaction during processing. Answer (C) is incorrect because transaction selection uses an independent computer program to monitor and select transactions for internal audit review. Like tracing, it fails to determine whether a transaction is legitimate. It would be an appropriate technique to apply to transactions suspected to be illegitimate.

204. Data access security related to applications may be enforced through all the following except

A. User identification and authentication functions incorporated in the application.

B. Utility software functions.

C. User identification and authentication functions in access control software.

D. Security functions provided by a database management system.

The correct answer is (B). *(CIA, adapted)*

REQUIRED: The functions through which data access security cannot be enforced.

DISCUSSION: Utility programs perform routine functions (e.g., sorting and copying), are available to all users, and are promptly available for many different applications. Utility programs can actually be a serious weakness in data access security because some can bypass normal access controls.

Answer (A) is incorrect because, although the trend is for this type of control function to be performed by other software, most such controls still reside in application software. Answer (C) is incorrect because access control software has as one of its primary objectives improving data access security for all data on the system. Answer (D) is incorrect because most database management systems provide for improved data access security while they are running.

205. The duties properly assigned to an information security officer could include all of the following except

A. Developing an information security policy for the organization.

B. Maintaining and updating the list of user passwords.

C. Commenting on security controls in new applications.

D. Monitoring and investigating unsuccessful access attempts.

The correct answer is (B). *(CIA, adapted)*

REQUIRED: The duty not properly assigned to an information security office.

DISCUSSION: The information security officer should not know user passwords. They are normally stored on a computer in encrypted format, and users change them directly.

Answers (A), (C), and (D) are incorrect because developing an information security policy for the organization, commenting on security controls in new applications, and monitoring and investigating unsuccessful access attempts are appropriate duties of the information security officer.

206. All administrative and professional staff in a corporate legal department prepare documents on terminals connected to a host LAN file server. The best control over unauthorized access to sensitive documents in the system is

A. Required entry of passwords for access to the system.

B. Physical security for all disks containing document files.

C. Periodic server backup and storage in a secure area.

D. Required entry of passwords for access to individual documents.

The correct answer is (D). *(CIA, adapted)*

REQUIRED: The best control over unauthorized access to sensitive documents in a local area network.

DISCUSSION: Different passwords may be required to access the system, to read certain files, and to perform certain other functions. Required entry of passwords for access to individual documents is the best single control over unauthorized access to sensitive documents.

Answer (A) is incorrect because password security for access to the system permits all departmental employees access to all documents in the system. Answer (B) is incorrect because this system uses no floppy disks. Answer (C) is incorrect because periodic server backup and storage in a secure area is a good security/backup procedure, but it would not prevent access to sensitive documents online.

207. An auditor has just completed a physical security audit of a data center. Because the center engages in top-secret defense contract work, the auditor has chosen to recommend biometric authentication for workers entering the building. The recommendation might include devices that verify all of the following except

A. Fingerprints.

B. Retina patterns.

C. Speech patterns.

D. Password patterns.

The correct answer is (D). *(CIA, adapted)*

REQUIRED: The method that does not provide biometric authentication.

DISCUSSION: Biometric technologies are automated methods of establishing an individual's identity using physiological or behavioral traits. These characteristics include fingerprints, retina patterns, hand geometry, signature dynamics, speech, and keystroke dynamics.

Answers (A), (B), and (C) are incorrect because fingerprints, retina patterns, and speech patterns are biometrics measures.

208. As organizations become more computer integrated, management is becoming increasingly concerned with the quality of access controls to the computer system. Which of the following provides the most accountability?

	Option I	Option II	Option III	Option IV
Restrict access by:	Individuals	Groups	Individuals	Departments
Identify computer data at:	Field level	Workstation	Workstation	Individual record level
Restrict access:	Need to know	Right to know	Normal processing by employee type	Items identified as processed by department
Identify users by:	Password	Password	Key access to workstation, or password on workstation	Departmental password
Limit ability to:	Delete, add, or modify data	Add or delete files	Add, delete, or modify data stored at workstation	Add, delete, or modify data normally processed by department

A. Option I.

B. Option II.

C. Option III.

D. Option IV.

The correct answer is (A). *(CIA, adapted)*

REQUIRED: The access control option providing the most accountability.

DISCUSSION: Access should be limited to those whose activities necessitate access to the computer system. Moreover, the degree of access allowed should be consistent with an individual's responsibilities. Restricting access to particular individuals rather than groups or departments clearly establishes specific accountability. Not everyone in a group will need access or the same degree of access. Thus, passwords assigned to individuals should be required for identification of users by the system. Furthermore, data should be restricted at the field level, not the workstation level. It may be possible to limit access to a workstation, but most workstations are connected to larger mainframe or network databases. Thus, the security at the workstation level only would be insufficient.

Answers (B), (C), and (D) are incorrect because access should be restricted to particular individuals on a need-to-know basis, data should be restricted at the field level, and use should be limited to necessary functions performed by the accountable individual.

209. Authentication is the process by which the

A. System verifies that the user is entitled to enter the transaction requested.

B. System verifies the identity of the user.

C. User identifies him/herself to the system.

D. User indicates to the system that the transaction was processed correctly.

The correct answer is (B). *(CISA, adapted)*

REQUIRED: The definition of authentication.

DISCUSSION: Identification is the process of uniquely distinguishing one user from all others. Authentication is the process of determining that individuals are who they say they are. For example, a password may identify but not authenticate its user if it is known by more than one individual.

Answer (A) is incorrect because authentication involves verifying the identity of the user. This process does not necessarily confirm the functions the user is authorized to perform. Answer (C) is incorrect because user identification to the system does not imply that the system has verified the identity of the user. Answer (D) is incorrect because this procedure is an application control for accuracy of the transaction.

210. Scavenging for residual information in the main memory of a computer can be best prevented by

A. Resetting the values of memory locations to zero.

B. Requiring passwords for memory access.

C. Setting memory access for asynchronous control.

D. Setting memory access for synchronous control.

The correct answer is (A). *(CISA, adapted)*

REQUIRED: The control to prohibit scavenging for residual information in computer memory.

DISCUSSION: Individuals may attempt to gain access to sensitive information by accessing computer memory after a program has been run. Resetting values of memory locations to zero after each application makes it useless for individuals to scavenge memory.

Answer (B) is incorrect because passwords are intended to prevent unauthorized access. Once access is gained, however, they do not prevent access to computer memory. Answers (C) and (D) are incorrect because whether data transmission is synchronous or asynchronous does not prevent scavenging from memory. In asynchronous transmission, a single character formed by control bits is sent at a time. In synchronous transmission, a timing device is used to transmit blocks of characters at fixed intervals.

211. Which of the following is a control that will prevent accessing the accounts receivable files from a hardwired terminal located in a manufacturing department?

A. An echo check.

B. A device authorization table.

C. Providing only dial-up terminals.

D. Using data encryption.

The correct answer is (B). *(J. Brooks)*

REQUIRED: The control that will prevent access via a hardwired terminal.

DISCUSSION: A device authorization table restricts file access to those physical devices that logically need access. Because it is illogical for anyone to access the accounts receivable file from a manufacturing terminal, the device authorization table will deny access even when a valid password is used.

Answer (A) is incorrect because an echo check relates to the accuracy of signals sent from or to a terminal. Answer (C) is incorrect because dial-up terminals provide less security than hardwired terminals. Any terminal may dial into the communications port using public telephones. Answer (D) is incorrect because, although data encryption (transmitting data in code form) might make the data unusable, it would not prevent access.

212. An organization could incur material losses if a competitor gains access to sensitive operating information contained in computer files. The controls most likely to prevent such losses are

A. Controlled disposal of documents and encryption of data files.

B. Encryption of data files and frequent changing of passwords.

C. Primary and secondary key integrity checks and encryption of data files.

D. Primary and secondary key integrity checks and frequent changing of passwords.

The correct answer is (B). *(CIA, adapted)*

REQUIRED: The controls most likely to prevent competitors from gaining access to sensitive information.

DISCUSSION: Encryption is a typical security measure. A program encodes data so that it is more difficult for an intruder to understand or use the data. Also, frequent changing of passwords limits unauthorized access to files.

Answer (A) is incorrect because controlled disposal of documents is not limited to computer files. Answers (C) and (D) are incorrect because key integrity checks are not access controls. Key integrity checks prevent the updating process from creating inaccuracies in keys.

213. The telecommunication control of dial-up/disconnect/dial-back can be circumvented by using

A. Dedicated line technology.

B. Automatic call forwarding.

C. Encryption algorithms.

D. High baud rate lines.

The correct answer is (B). *(CISA, adapted)*

REQUIRED: The technique that would circumvent callback control procedures.

DISCUSSION: Automatic call forwarding can circumvent the control if the authorized user has this telephone service and the computer callback is forwarded to an unauthorized user.

Answer (A) is incorrect because dedicated line technology strengthens controls, not circumvents them. Answer (C) is incorrect because encryption algorithms strengthen controls, not circumvent them. Answer (D) is incorrect because the speed of the lines does not directly contribute to the strength or weakness of telecommunication controls.

5.10 Application Controls

214. While general controls relate to all client computer activities, application controls

A. Relate to all client non-computer activities.

B. Relate to specific tasks or programs performed by a computer.

C. Relate to the assignment and supervision of personnel.

D. Relate only to systems with database environments.

The correct answer is (B). *(Publisher)*

REQUIRED: The definition of application controls.

DISCUSSION: Application controls provide reasonable assurance that the recording, processing, and reporting of data are properly performed. These are termed input, processing, and output controls and relate to specific tasks or programs performed by the computer function.

Answer (A) is incorrect because application controls are computer processing controls. Answer (C) is incorrect because the assignment and supervision of personnel are general controls. They concern all or many computerized activities in the organization. Answer (D) is incorrect because application controls are appropriate for all computer systems.

215. Application control objectives do not normally include assurance that

A. Authorized transactions are completely processed once and only once.

B. Transaction data are complete and accurate.

C. Review and approval procedures for new systems are set by policy and adhered to.

D. Processing results are received by the intended user.

The correct answer is (C). *(CISA, adapted)*

REQUIRED: The assurance not provided by an application control.

DISCUSSION: Review and approval procedures for new systems are among the general controls known as system software acquisition and maintenance controls. A life cycle analysis should be conducted for the development of new systems.

Answers (A), (B), and (D) are incorrect because the objectives of application controls are authorized transactions are completely processed once and only once, transaction data are complete and accurate, and processing results are received by the intended user.

216. Data processing activities may be classified in terms of three stages or processes -- input, processing, and output. An activity that is not normally associated with the input stage is

A. Batching.

B. Recording.

C. Verifying.

D. Reporting.

The correct answer is (D). *(CMA, adapted)*

REQUIRED: The process not associated with input.

DISCUSSION: Reporting is normally associated with output, not input. Output is the processing result, e.g., account listings or displays, reports, magnetic files, invoices, or checks.

Answers (A), (B), and (C) are incorrect because batching, recording, and verifying are closely associated with input.

217. The purpose of input controls is to ensure the

A. Authorization of access to data files.

B. Authorization of access to program files.

C. Completeness, accuracy, and validity of updating.

D. Completeness, accuracy, and validity of input.

The correct answer is (D). *(CIA, adapted)*

REQUIRED: The purpose of input controls.

DISCUSSION: Input controls provide reasonable assurance that data received for computer processing have been properly authorized and are in a form suitable for processing, i.e., complete, accurate, and valid. Input controls also relate to rejection, correction, and resubmission of data that were initially incorrect.

Answers (A) and (B) are incorrect because access controls authorize access to data and program files. Answer (C) is incorrect because processing controls ensure the completeness, accuracy, and validity of updating.

218. Many customers, managers, employees, and suppliers have blamed the computer for making errors. In reality, computers make very few mechanical errors. The most likely source of errors in a fully operational computer-based system is

A. Operator error.

B. Systems analysis and programming.

C. Processing.

D. Input.

The correct answer is (D). *(CMA, adapted)*

REQUIRED: The most common cause of error.

DISCUSSION: GIGO is the acronym for garbage-in, garbage-out. Inappropriate input results in inappropriate output.

Answer (A) is incorrect because, although there is a chance of operator error, operators are typically guided by run manuals. Answer (B) is incorrect because, if programs are properly designed and tested before implementation, most bugs (errors) can be removed. Answer (C) is incorrect because, once programs are operationally tested, the processing usually does not result in errors.

219. Mill Co. uses a batch processing method to process its sales transactions. Data on Mill's sales transaction tape are electronically sorted by customer number and are subjected to programmed edit checks in preparing its invoices, sales journals, and updated customer account balances. One of the direct outputs of the creation of this tape most likely would be a

A. Report showing exceptions and control totals.

B. Printout of the updated inventory records.

C. Report showing overdue accounts receivable.

D. Printout of the sales price master file.

The correct answer is (A). *(CPA, adapted)*

REQUIRED: The most likely direct output of the creation of a sales transaction tape.

DISCUSSION: Batch processing is useful for processing large volumes of data. Editing (validation) of data should produce a cumulative automated error listing that includes not only errors found in the current processing run but also uncorrected errors from earlier runs. The creation of the tape will also generate various totals that will serve as controls over the completeness and accuracy of the processing.

Answer (B) is incorrect because an online database system is more appropriate for printing records that require up-to-date information. Answer (C) is incorrect because testing for overdue accounts receivable should be done prior to approving current sales orders. Answer (D) is incorrect because a complete listing of sales prices would not be found in a sales transactions file.

220. A mail-order retailer of low-cost novelty items is receiving an increasing number of complaints from customers about the wrong merchandise being shipped. The order code for items has the format *wwxxyyzz*. The major category is *ww*, *xx* is the minor category, *yy* identifies the item, and *zz* identifies the catalog. In many cases, the wrong merchandise was sent because adjacent characters in the order code had been transposed. The best control for decreasing the number of orders with the wrong merchandise is to

A. Require customers to specify the name for each item they order.

B. Add check-digits to the order codes and verify them for each order.

C. Separate the parts of the order code with hyphens to make the characters easier to read.

D. Use a master file reference for all order codes to verify the existence of items.

The correct answer is (B). *(CIA, adapted)*

REQUIRED: The control that prevents input of erroneous identification numbers.

DISCUSSION: Self-checking digits may be used to detect incorrect codes. The digit is generated by applying an algorithm to the code. During the input process, the check digit is recomputed by applying the same algorithm to the code actually entered.

Answer (A) is incorrect because having customers specify the name for each item they order would let the company correct erroneous order codes once they had been detected, but would not, in general, detect erroneous codes. Answer (C) is incorrect because separating the parts of the order code with hyphens would make the characters easier to read, but would not cure the problem of transposed characters. Answer (D) is incorrect because using a master file reference for all order codes would verify the existence of items, but would not detect erroneous order codes in which transposed characters in an order code match other items.

221. Data conversion is the translation of data into a form the computer can accept. What method of data conversion is most difficult to audit?

A. Keying data to disk for online processing.

B. Keying data to disk for batch processing.

C. Keying data to source documents for magnetic-ink character recognition.

D. Reading source data using optical-character recognition.

The correct answer is (A). *(CIA, adapted)*

REQUIRED: The type of data conversion that is most difficult to audit.

DISCUSSION: Data conversion in an online environment is difficult to audit because the audit trail is often invisible. Hard-copy source documents are often lacking.

Answer (B) is incorrect because keying to disk creates records readily available for testing. Answer (C) is incorrect because magnetic-ink character recognition provides batch control capability and hard-copy source documents. Answer (D) is incorrect because optical-character recognition retains hard-copy source documents and reduces the risks associated with the manual data conversion process.

222. The most valuable information for detecting unauthorized input from a terminal is provided by the

A. Console log printout.

B. Transaction journal.

C. Automated suspense file listing.

D. User error report.

The correct answer is (B). *(CISA, adapted)*

REQUIRED: The control to detect unauthorized input from a terminal.

DISCUSSION: A transaction log records all transactions received by the computer processing facility. The log can be subsequently compared with authorized transactions (e.g., authorized source documents) to assure validity of the transactions.

Answer (A) is incorrect because a console log does not record the individual transactions transmitted from a terminal. Answer (C) is incorrect because the suspense file only lists transaction activity if an edit error occurs. Answer (D) is incorrect because a user error report only lists input that results in an edit error.

223. Data input validation routines include

A. Terminal logs.

B. Passwords.

C. Hash totals.

D. Backup controls.

The correct answer is (C). *(CMA, adapted)*

REQUIRED: The example of a data input validation routine.

DISCUSSION: Application controls, including input controls, are designed to assure the accuracy and completeness of data entered into the computer. Input controls provide assurance that data have not been lost, suppressed, added, duplicated, or otherwise improperly changed. A hash total is an example of a data input validation routine. A hash total is a control total without a defined meaning, such as the total of employee numbers or invoice numbers, that is used to verify the completeness of data. Thus, the hash total for the employee listing by the personnel department could be compared with the total generated during the processing run.

Answers (A) and (B) are incorrect because terminal logs and passwords are access controls. Answer (D) is incorrect because backup controls are general controls.

224. Check digits, entry verification, and batch totals are examples of controls designed to provide reasonable assurance that

A. Data processing has been performed as intended without omission or double counting of transactions.

B. Only authorized persons have access to files.

C. Data received for processing have been properly converted.

D. Coding of data internal to the computer did not change when the data were moved from one internal storage location to another.

The correct answer is (C). *(CIA, adapted)*

REQUIRED: The purpose of check digits, entry verification, and batch totals.

DISCUSSION: These controls are input controls. They help determine that information was not miscoded or lost during the conversion from source documents to machine-readable form.

Answer (A) is incorrect because processing controls, not input controls, provide assurance that operations on data have been performed as intended. Answer (B) is incorrect because access controls are general controls. Answer (D) is incorrect because the hardware control known as a parity check determines that coding of data internal to the computer did not change when the data were moved from one internal storage location to another.

225. An internal auditor downloads the invoices, payments, and payables for goods received for the prior month to an audit workstation. The best approach for verifying the completeness of the data is for the auditor to use audit software on the workstation to

A. Match invoices with payments; match payments with invoices.

B. Match invoices with payables; match payables with invoices.

C. Match invoices with payments and payables; match payments and payables with invoices.

D. Match invoices with payments; match payments and payables with invoices.

The correct answer is (C). *(CIA, adapted)*

REQUIRED: The best software approach for verifying the completeness of the data downloaded to a workstation.

DISCUSSION: To evaluate completeness, the best approach is to audit in both directions. Matching invoices with payments and payables and payments and payables with invoices ensures that a valid invoice exists for each payment or payable.

Answers (A) and (B) are incorrect because matching invoices with payments or payables alone does not ensure that a payment or payable exists for each valid invoice; matching payments or payables alone with invoices does not ensure that an invoice exists for each payment or payable. Answer (D) is incorrect because matching invoices with payments alone does not ensure that a payment or payable exists for each valid invoice.

226. A wholesaling firm has a computerized billing system. Because of a clerical error while entering information from the sales order, one of its customers was billed for only three of the four items ordered and received. Which of the following controls could have prevented or resulted in prompt detection of this situation?

A. Matching line control counts produced by the computer with predetermined line control counts.

B. Periodic comparison of total accounts receivable per accounts receivable master file with total accounts receivable per accounts receivable control account.

C. A completeness check that does not allow a sales invoice to be processed if key fields are blank.

D. Prenumbered shipping documents together with a procedure for follow-up any time there is not a one-to-one relationship between shipping documents and sales invoices.

The correct answer is (A). *(CIA, adapted)*

REQUIRED: The control to prevent or promptly detect the clerical error.

DISCUSSION: Detective controls, such as a line control count, identify undesirable events as they occur. A line control count counts individual line items on documents. These counts are compared to predetermined line control counts for each document to detect missing lines.

Answer (B) is incorrect because a comparison of the accounts receivable master file and the control account would show no discrepancy. Both would be based on the three-item invoice. Answer (C) is incorrect because a completeness check could not be used to catch the billing error. Many invoices would properly include three or fewer items. Answer (D) is incorrect because all four items were included in the same shipment, so a sales invoice corresponding to the shipping document would exist.

227. If a control total were to be computed on each of the following data items, which would best be identified as a hash total for a payroll computer application?

A. Hours worked.

B. Total debits and total credits.

C. Net pay.

D. Department numbers.

The correct answer is (D). *(CPA, adapted)*

REQUIRED: The example of a hash total.

DISCUSSION: The three types of control totals are record counts, financial (amount) totals, and hash totals. Record counts establish the number of source documents and reconcile it to the number of output records. Financial (amount) totals compute dollar or amount totals from source documents (e.g., the total dollar amount of invoices processed) and reconcile them with the output records. Hash totals add numbers on input documents that are not normally added (e.g., department numbers for payroll processing) and reconcile them with output records.

Answers (A), (B), and (C) are incorrect because hours worked, total debits and total credits, and net pay are financial totals.

228. If, in reviewing an applications system, it is noted that batch controls are not used, which of the following statements by the user of the system is acceptable as a compensating control?

A. "The supervisor must approve all inputs."

B. "We do a 100% key verification of all data input."

C. "We do a 100% physical review of the input document to the output document."

D. "The volume of transactions prohibits batching."

The correct answer is (C). *(CISA, adapted)*

REQUIRED: The control that compensates for the lack of batch controls.

DISCUSSION: If the application provides for matching each input document with an output document, the need for batch totals is minimized. The physical review provides evidence that all records were processed.

Answer (A) is incorrect because approval of input does not assure that all input records are processed. Answer (B) is incorrect because key verification does not assure that the initial keypunching was done for all records. Answer (D) is incorrect because the greater the volume, the more appropriate batch totals become.

229. A company's labor distribution report requires extensive corrections each month because of labor hours charged to inactive jobs. Which of the following data processing input controls appears to be missing?

A. Completeness test.

B. Validity test.

C. Limit test.

D. Control total.

The correct answer is (B). *(CIA, adapted)*

REQUIRED: The data processing input control not met when labor hours are charged to inactive jobs.

DISCUSSION: Validity tests are used to ensure that transactions contain valid transaction codes, valid characters, and valid field size. If the jobs are checked first for validity, hours are not mistakenly assigned to them.

Answer (A) is incorrect because completeness tests are used to ensure that the input has the prescribed amount of data in all data fields. Answer (C) is incorrect because limit tests are used to determine whether the data exceed certain predetermined limits. Answer (D) is incorrect because control totals are used to reconcile computer input to the source document totals.

230. An online bank teller system permitted withdrawals from inactive accounts. The best control for denying such withdrawals is a

A. Proof calculation.

B. Check-digit verification.

C. Master file lookup.

D. Duplicate record check.

The correct answer is (C). *(CIA, adapted)*

REQUIRED: The best control for denying withdrawals from inactive accounts.

DISCUSSION: The master file will contain information about the status of bank accounts (i.e., active or inactive). By looking up the account numbers in the master file, the teller can verify that the account is active.

Answer (A) is incorrect because a proof calculation is the use of a predefined algorithm to be performed on the information in a telecommunications transmission to verify that no transmission errors occurred. Answer (B) is incorrect because a check-digit verification is used to control the accuracy of input of reference numbers but does not deny access to an inactive but valid account. Answer (D) is incorrect because a duplicate record check ensures that duplicate records are not processed.

231. Omen Company is a manufacturer of men's shirts and distributes weekly sales reports to each sales manager. The quantity 2R5 appeared in the quantity sold column for one of the items on the weekly sales report for one of the sales managers. The most likely explanation for what has occurred is that

A. The output quantity has been stated in hexadecimal numbers.

B. The computer has malfunctioned during execution.

C. The printer has malfunctioned and the "R" should have been a decimal point.

D. The program did not contain a data checking routine for input data.

The correct answer is (D). *(CMA, adapted)*

REQUIRED: The probable reason for reporting a quantity item using an alphabetic character.

DISCUSSION: The probable explanation for reporting a quantity using a character other than a digit is that the data were incorrectly encoded and the computer program did not perform a field check, which would have detected the error. A field check tests whether a field consists of the proper characters, whether alphabetic, numeric, special, or combinations thereof.

Answer (A) is incorrect because R is not a hexadecimal character. Hexadecimal characters are 0-9 and A-F representing 0 to 15 in decimal. Answer (B) is incorrect because the probability of a computer malfunction's resulting in the printing of an R is slight. Answer (C) is incorrect because 2.5 would not be appropriate for a quantity of shirts sold.

Questions 232 and 233 are based on the following information. A payroll transaction record was designed to contain the information presented as follows:

Column	Information
1-9	Employee SSN
10-30	Employee name
31-36	Department number
37-39	Hours worked

232. If the first letter of an employee's name is entered in column 9, the test most likely to detect the error during an input edit run is a

A. Self-checking number.

B. Field check.

C. Limit check.

D. Validity check.

The correct answer is (B). *(Publisher)*

REQUIRED: The test to detect an alphabetic character in a numeric field.

DISCUSSION: An inappropriate character in a field is discovered by a field check, which would detect an alphabetic character in a field that should contain only numeric characters.

Answer (A) is incorrect because the recalculation of a self-checking digit is used to verify identification codes. Answer (C) is incorrect because a limit check determines if a value is outside a prescribed range. Answer (D) is incorrect because a validity check tests the relationships among input items and other parts of the system.

233. If a record is rejected during computer processing because the employee does not work in the department indicated by the numbers in columns 31 through 36, the error was probably detected by a

A. Limit check.

B. Field check.

C. Validity check.

D. Self-checking number.

The correct answer is (C). *(Publisher)*

REQUIRED: The control to detect that an employee does not work in the department indicated on the record.

DISCUSSION: A validity check can be employed to determine the consistency of one field with another. A lookup on the personnel file would detect the error.

Answer (A) is incorrect because a limit check determines if a value is outside a prescribed range. Answer (B) is incorrect because a field check determines whether an improper character type appears in a field. Answer (D) is incorrect because a self-checking number tests identification numbers by recomputing a check digit.

234. An employee in the receiving department keyed in a shipment from a remote terminal and inadvertently omitted the purchase order number. The best systems control to detect this error is

A. Completeness test.

B. Sequence check.

C. Reasonableness test.

D. Compatibility test.

The correct answer is (A). *(CMA, adapted)*

REQUIRED: The control to detect the omission of a purchase order number keyed in from a remote terminal.

DISCUSSION: A completeness test checks that all data elements are entered before processing. An interactive system can be programmed to notify the user to enter the number before accepting the receiving report.

Answer (B) is incorrect because a sequence check tests for the ordering, not omission, of records. Answer (C) is incorrect because a limit or reasonableness test checks the values of data items against established limits. Answer (D) is incorrect because a compatibility test (field check) determines whether characters are appropriate to a field.

235. Which one of the following input controls or edit checks would catch certain types of errors within the payment amount field of a transaction?

A. Record count.

B. Echo check.

C. Check digit.

D. Limit check.

The correct answer is (D). *(CIA, adapted)*

REQUIRED: The input control or edit check that detects errors within the payment amount field of a transaction.

DISCUSSION: A limit, reasonableness, or range test determines whether an amount is within a predetermined limit for given information. It can only detect certain errors (i.e., those that exceed the acceptable limit).

Answer (A) is incorrect because a record count determines the number of documents entered into a process. Answer (B) is incorrect because an echo check tests the reliability of computer hardware. For example, the CPU sends a signal to a printer that is echoed just prior to printing. The signal verifies that the proper print position has been activated. Answer (C) is incorrect because a self-checking number is generated by applying an algorithm to an identification number.

236. Which one of the following input validation routines is not likely to be appropriate in a real-time operation?

A. Sign check.

B. Reasonableness check.

C. Sequence check.

D. Redundant data check.

The correct answer is (C). *(CMA, adapted)*

REQUIRED: The input validation routine not appropriate in a real-time operation.

DISCUSSION: The program controls listed prescreen or edit data prior to processing, but the sequence check is most likely to be used only in batch processing. A sequence check tests to determine that records are in proper order. For example, a payroll input file can be sorted into Social Security number order. A sequence check can then be performed to verify record order. This control would not apply in a real-time operation because records are not processed sequentially.

Answer (A) is incorrect because sign checks test data for the appropriate arithmetic sign. For instance, hours worked in a payroll should always be a positive number. Answer (B) is incorrect because reasonableness tests verify that amounts fall within predetermined limits. Answer (D) is incorrect because a redundancy check requires sending additional data items to serve as a check on the other transmitted data; for example, part of a customer name can be matched against the name associated with the transmitted customer number.

237. As part of an audit, the auditor was studying a computer flowchart containing the logic diagram shown below. Which of the following controls is represented by this diagram?

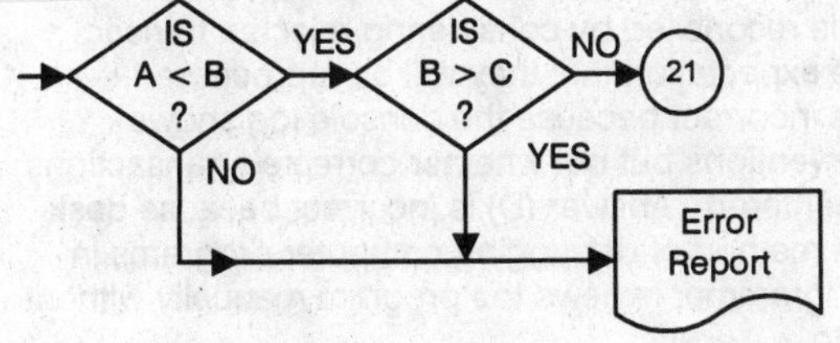

A. Field check.

B. Limit check.

C. Control total.

D. Password check.

The correct answer is (B). *(CIA, adapted)*

REQUIRED: The control represented by the flowchart.

DISCUSSION: The flowchart illustrates two decision blocks. The first block asks if A, the lower limit, is less than B, the value of interest. The second block asks if B is greater than the upper limit. The purpose of this test is to determine if B is within an acceptable or reasonable range. If it is not, an error report is generated.

Answer (A) is incorrect because a field check (valid character check) examines a field to test whether it contains an improper kind of character. Answer (C) is incorrect because a control total is used to control the completeness and accuracy of processing, not to evaluate the reasonableness of results. Answer (D) is incorrect because passwords restrict unauthorized access to the computer.

238. The online data entry control called preformatting is

A. A program initiated prior to regular input to discover errors in data before entry so that the errors can be corrected.

B. A check to determine if all data items for a transaction have been entered by the terminal operator.

C. A series of requests for required input data that requires an acceptable response to each request before a subsequent request is made.

D. The display of a document with blanks for data items to be entered by the terminal operator.

The correct answer is (D). *(CMA, adapted)*

REQUIRED: The definition of preformatting.

DISCUSSION: To avoid data entry errors in online systems, a preformatted screen approach may be used. It is a screen prompting approach that involves the display on a monitor of a set of boxes for entry of specified data items. The format may even be in the form of a copy of a transaction document. This technique is best suited to conversion of data from a source document.

Answer (A) is incorrect because an edit routine is a program initiated prior to regular input to discover errors in data before entry so that the errors can be corrected. Answer (B) is incorrect because a completeness check tests whether all data items for a transaction have been entered by the terminal operator. Answer (C) is incorrect because the dialogue approach is another screen prompting method for data entry. It is most appropriate when information is received orally, e.g., by phone.

239. When erroneous data are detected by computer program controls, such data may be excluded from processing and printed on an error report. This error report should be reviewed and followed up by the

A. Computer operator.

B. Systems analyst.

C. Data control group.

D. Computer programmer.

The correct answer is (C). *(CPA, adapted)*

REQUIRED: The individual or group responsible for reviewing and following up an error report.

DISCUSSION: Some entities use a data control group that acts as liaison between the users and the processing center. This group records input data in a control log, follows the progress of processing, distributes output, and establishes control totals. It is also responsible for following up error reports and assuring that erroneous records are reprocessed. The data control group must be organizationally independent of computer operations within the data processing function to allow for proper control.

Answers (A), (B), and (D) are incorrect because computer operators, systems analysts, and computer programmers are not independent of the computer processing operation.

240. Transactions that were erroneous and had been previously rejected by the computer system apparently were not being reentered and reprocessed once they had been corrected. This erroneous condition is best controlled by

A. Comparing a record count of transactions entered into the system.

B. Scanning the error control log.

C. Scanning the console log.

D. Desk checking.

The correct answer is (B). *(CMA, adapted)*

REQUIRED: The best control to assure that corrected transactions are resubmitted.

DISCUSSION: The erroneous transactions rejected by the system should be returned to the user departments for correction. The corrected transactions should then be resubmitted by the control group with some notation being made in the error control log. An error listing without a notation in this log indicates a corrected transaction that has not been reentered and reprocessed.

Answer (A) is incorrect because the record count of transactions is reconciled by considering rejected transactions with the expectation that they will be reprocessed. Answer (C) is incorrect because the console log shows operator interventions but not whether corrected transactions have been reentered. Answer (D) is incorrect because desk checking is a method of debugging computer programs in which the programmer reviews the program manually without computer help.

241. In the accounting system of Acme Company, the amounts of cash disbursements entered at a computer terminal are transmitted to the computer, which immediately transmits the amounts back to the terminal for display on the terminal screen. This display enables the operator to

A. Establish the validity of the account number.

B. Verify the amount was entered accurately.

C. Verify the authorization of the disbursement.

D. Prevent the overpayment of the account.

The correct answer is (B). *(CPA, adapted)*

REQUIRED: The effect of displaying the amounts entered at a terminal.

DISCUSSION: The display of the amounts entered is an input control that permits visual verification of the accuracy of the input by the operator. This procedure is closed-loop verification.

Answer (A) is incorrect because displaying the amounts entered at a terminal does not establish the validity of the account number. Answer (C) is incorrect because displaying the amounts entered at a terminal does not verify the authorization of the disbursement. Answer (D) is incorrect because displaying the amounts entered at a terminal does not prevent the overpayment of the account.

242. The key verification process associated with keying computer records for input to a computer system is

A. Effectively used to detect the erroneous recording of data on source documents.

B. Inexpensive and therefore widely used.

C. Used to detect errors introduced by the keying process.

D. Ordinarily used with a computer program written to check the data.

The correct answer is (C). *(CIA, adapted)*

REQUIRED: The purpose of key verification in a computer system.

DISCUSSION: Key verification is a procedure to determine if the keying process was performed properly. Information from source documents is rekeyed on a special keyboard by another operator and compared with that previously recorded. If there is a discrepancy, the error is corrected.

Answer (A) is incorrect because key verification does not detect errors in the source documents. Answer (B) is incorrect because, although widely used, key verification effectively doubles the work and is expensive. Answer (D) is incorrect because key verification is a manual process.

243. If a payroll system continues to pay employees who have been terminated, control weaknesses most likely exist because

A. Procedures were not implemented to verify and control the receipt by the computer processing department of all transactions prior to processing.

B. There were inadequate manual controls maintained outside the computer system.

C. Programmed controls such as limit checks should have been built into the system.

D. Input file label checking routines built into the programs were ignored by the operator.

The correct answer is (B). *(CISA, adapted)*

REQUIRED: The control weakness allowing terminated employees to continue being paid.

DISCUSSION: The authorization to pay employees comes from outside the computer department. Thus, inadequate controls external to the computer processing department are likely to allow the payments to terminated employees to continue without detection.

Answer (A) is incorrect because batch totals constitute adequate controls over properly authorized transactions but provide no control over unauthorized transactions. Answer (C) is incorrect because a limit check tests the reasonableness of a particular transaction but not whether it was authorized. Answer (D) is incorrect because paying proper attention to input file labels (header labels) will not detect unauthorized transactions.

244. The best approach for ensuring that only authorized employees receive computer output is

A. Place the output in bins early in the day rather than late in the day.

B. Load the output in a file to print at local workstations.

C. Hold the output in a secure area until it is picked up by authorized employees.

D. Make printouts available only at specified times.

The correct answer is (C). *(CIA, adapted)*

REQUIRED: The best approach for ensuring that only authorized employees receive computer output.

DISCUSSION: An independent data control group should receive user input, log it, transfer it to the computer center, monitor processing, review error messages, compare control totals, log and distribute output, and determine whether error corrections have been made. This group is therefore responsible for maintaining lists of authorized recipients in a distribution log and holding the output in a secure area until it is picked up.

Answer (A) is incorrect because placing output in bins does not ensure that unauthorized persons are denied access. Answer (B) is incorrect because output loaded in a file is available to anyone with access to the file. Answer (D) is incorrect because making printouts available at specified times does not control access.

245. The computerized property, plant, and equipment records of a manufacturing firm included a number of assets with negative book values. The reason is that the program used did not stop depreciation calculations when the book value reached salvage value or zero. Which of the following controls could have prevented or resulted in prompt detection of this situation?

A. Appropriate checks for alphanumeric characters in key numeric fields.

B. Appropriate completeness checks in application programs to ensure that records will not be processed if key fields are blank.

C. Periodic user review of computer-generated reports for unusual or abnormal items.

D. Reconciliation of control totals produced by computers with predetermined batch totals.

The correct answer is (C). *(CIA, adapted)*

REQUIRED: The control to detect nonsensical computer data output.

DISCUSSION: User review or review by the control group should detect erroneous output. A mere glance by a knowledgeable user would be sufficient to note negative book values of fixed assets, which are obviously incorrect.

Answer (A) is incorrect because the problem is not necessarily that inappropriate characters appeared in the field but that an unreasonable value was calculated. Thus, a limit or reasonableness test would have detected the error. Answer (B) is incorrect because nothing in the question indicates that key fields are blank. A salvage value field either does not exist or was not properly used in writing the program. Answer (D) is incorrect because periodic depreciation updating is done at regular time intervals, e.g., monthly. It would not be based on the submission of a batch of documents.

5.11 The Auditor's Understanding and Testing of Controls

246. The major purpose of the auditor's study and evaluation of the company's computer processing operations is to

A. Evaluate the competence of computer processing operating personnel.

B. Ensure the exercise of due professional care.

C. Evaluate the reliability and integrity of financial information.

D. Become familiar with the company's means of identifying, measuring, classifying, and reporting information.

The correct answer is (C). *(CIA, adapted)*

REQUIRED: The major purpose of the auditor's study and evaluation of the company's computer operations.

DISCUSSION: Information systems provide data for decision making, control, and compliance with external requirements. Thus, auditors should examine information systems and, as appropriate, ascertain whether financial records and reports contain accurate, reliable, timely, complete, and useful information, and controls over record keeping and reporting are adequate and effective.

Answer (A) is incorrect because determining the competence of computer processing operating personnel is not the major purpose of the evaluation. Answer (B) is incorrect because due professional care should be exercised in all audits. Answer (D) is incorrect because becoming familiar with the company's information system is a means to an end.

247. The auditor's consideration of computer processing internal control must include obtaining an understanding sufficient to plan the audit. Assuming procedures to assess control risk at less than the maximum level are not performed while obtaining the understanding, which of the following normally would not be done during the understanding phase?

A. Inquiring about processing.

B. Identifying the flow of transactions.

C. Testing the effectiveness of control.

D. Inspecting documents and observing client personnel.

The correct answer is (C). *(Publisher)*

REQUIRED: The procedure not normally performed in gaining an understanding of computer processing controls.

DISCUSSION: Testing controls should provide evidence as to the effectiveness of their design and operation. Although controls may be tested concurrently with obtaining the understanding of internal control, an auditor is not required to obtain knowledge about the effectiveness of controls as part of gaining the understanding. The understanding is concerned with whether particular policies or procedures have been placed in operation. Tests of controls must ultimately be performed, however, if control risk is assessed at less than the maximum (AU 319).

Answers (A), (B), and (D) are incorrect because inquiring about processing, identifying the flow of transactions, and inspecting documents and observing client personnel are customary means of obtaining the understanding.

248. Which of the following statements concerning the assessment of control risk in a client's computer environment is true?

A. The auditor's objectives with respect to the assessment of control risk are the same as in a manual system.

B. The auditor must obtain an understanding of the internal control and test controls in computer environments.

C. If the general controls are ineffective the auditor ordinarily can assess control risk at a low level if the application controls are effective.

D. The auditor usually can ignore the computer system if (s)he can obtain an understanding of the controls outside the computer system.

The correct answer is (A). *(Publisher)*

REQUIRED: The true statement about the auditor's assessment of control risk in a computer environment.

DISCUSSION: The auditor is required to obtain an understanding of internal control and assess control risk to plan the audit. Whether the control system is manual or computerized does not affect this objective.

Answer (B) is incorrect because the auditor need not test the effectiveness of the controls if control risk is assessed at the maximum. Answer (C) is incorrect because, if general controls are weak, the auditor is unlikely to assess control risk at a low level, no matter how effective the application controls appear to be. Answer (D) is incorrect because, when computer applications are significant, the auditor must consider the relevant control activities as an integral part of the assessment of control risk.

249. After reviewing terminal security controls, the auditor has concluded that the controls are insufficient. Which of the following audit techniques could the auditor have used to reach this conclusion?

I. Observation
II. Generalized audit software
III. Internal control questionnaires
IV. Control flowcharting

A. I.

B. II and III.

C. I, III, and IV.

D. I, II, III, and IV.

The correct answer is (C). *(CISA, adapted)*

REQUIRED: The audit techniques that could be the basis for concluding that security controls are insufficient.

DISCUSSION: An auditor reads documentation, observes the actions of employees, makes inquiries, prepares questionnaires, and develops flowcharts to gain an understanding of the controls. (S)he may then conclude that controls are inappropriate or insufficient, even without testing their effectiveness.

Answer (A) is incorrect because observation alone will not provide sufficient evidence for an audit conclusion about terminal security. Answers (B) and (D) are incorrect because generalized audit software is typically used to perform substantive tests but is not appropriate for testing terminal security.

250. The auditor's primary concern with an auditee programmer's writing a program to age inventory is

A. The auditor's programming expertise.

B. Loss of independence.

C. Saving valuable audit time.

D. The programmer's access to confidential information.

The correct answer is (B). *(CIA, adapted)*

REQUIRED: The auditor's primary concern with an auditee programmer's writing a program to age inventory.

DISCUSSION: If the auditor uses a program written by the auditee's programmer to perform an audit function (aging receivables), the independence of the auditor may be questioned. The auditor must therefore take appropriate steps to evaluate the program and control its use.

Answer (A) is incorrect because the auditor is concerned with the programmer's expertise and integrity. The auditor does not necessarily need programming ability. Answer (C) is incorrect because saving audit time is secondary to the need for objectivity in conducting the audit. Answer (D) is incorrect because the development of an inventory aging program typically does not involve access to confidential input information.

251. The auditor plans to select a sample of transactions to assess the extent that purchase discounts may have been lost by the company. After assessing the risks associated with lost purchase discounts, the auditor was most likely to select a sample from which one of the following populations?

A. Open purchase orders.

B. Paid EDI invoices.

C. Paid non-EDI invoices.

D. Paid EDI and non-EDI invoices.

The correct answer is (C). *(CIA, adapted)*

REQUIRED: The population sampled to assess the extent of lost purchase discounts.

DISCUSSION: Manual input and processing increase the risk of delayed payments and loss of purchase discounts. Furthermore, an EDI system is unlikely to offer cash discounts. Thus, the proper population from which to sample consists of paid invoices not processed through the EDI system.

Answer (A) is incorrect because open purchase orders have not yet been invoiced or paid. Answers (B) and (D) are incorrect because an EDI system is unlikely to offer cash discounts. In addition, the auditor was involved in the design and testing of the EDI system and presumably has knowledge of the EDI system's procedures.

252. For audit reliance to be placed on the results of processing in an application system, the auditor should be reasonably satisfied that

A. The system was tested before implementation.

B. An audit trail exists.

C. The system is well documented.

D. The system is functioning properly.

The correct answer is (D). *(CISA, adapted)*

REQUIRED: The assurance the auditor should obtain.

DISCUSSION: The most important element of assurance that the auditor should obtain is that the system is functioning properly. If this is the case, reliance can be placed upon the results of processing.

Answer (A) is incorrect because, although testing before implementation is an important consideration, even well-tested systems may not be functioning properly. Answer (B) is incorrect because audit trails are desirable but not absolutely necessary to place reliance on a system. Answer (C) is incorrect because full documentation is desirable but not absolutely necessary.

253. The most common techniques for auditing the manual procedures of a system include

I. Completion of a checklist
II. Review of user manuals
III. Use of generalized audit software
IV. Observation

A. II and III.

B. I, II, and IV.

C. I, III, and IV.

D. II, III, and IV.

The correct answer is (B). *(CISA, adapted)*

REQUIRED: The most common techniques for auditing the manual procedures of a system.

DISCUSSION: Completion of checklists and questionnaires, review of user manuals and other documentation, and observation and inquiries are typical techniques used by the auditor in auditing manual procedures. Generalized audit software is used in auditing computer systems.

Answers (A), (C), and (D) are incorrect because generalized audit software is used in auditing computer systems.

254. When an accounting application is processed by computer, an auditor cannot verify the reliable operation of programmed controls by

A. Manually comparing detail transaction files used by an edit program with the program's generated error listings to determine that errors were properly identified by the edit program.

B. Constructing a processing system for accounting applications and processing actual data from throughout the period through both the client's program and the auditor's program.

C. Manually reperforming, as of a moment in time, the processing of input data and comparing the simulated results with the actual results.

D. Periodically submitting auditor-prepared test data to the same computer process and evaluating the results.

The correct answer is (C). *(CPA, adapted)*

REQUIRED: The procedure by which an auditor cannot verify the reliable operation of programmed controls.

DISCUSSION: This procedure describes auditing around the computer. The computer is treated as a black box, and only the inputs and outputs are evaluated. Because the actual controls may not be understood or tested, the technique is ordinarily inappropriate if the effectiveness of programmed controls is an important component of internal control and the assessment of control risk.

Answer (A) is incorrect because a manual comparison of the computer-generated output of an auditor-controlled edit program with the error listings generated by the client's program would provide evidence that the client's programmed controls were operating as planned. Answer (B) is incorrect because parallel simulation can be an effective method of testing the reliability of controls. Answer (D) is incorrect because submitting auditor-prepared test data to the client's computer process is an effective method of evaluating the reliability of control procedures.

255. Which of the following could the auditor examine only in online systems?

A. Results of test decks.

B. Resolution of errors.

C. Levels of terminal access.

D. Tests of transactions.

The correct answer is (C). *(CIA, adapted)*

REQUIRED: The item an auditor could examine only in an online system.

DISCUSSION: Online operation implies direct communication with the CPU, and this typically requires computer terminals. Thus, only in online systems could the auditor examine levels of terminal access.

Answers (A), (B), and (D) are incorrect because the auditor could examine results of test decks, resolution of errors in offline systems, and tests of transactions in offline systems.

256. Which of the following is necessary to audit balances in an online computer system in an environment of destructive updating?

A. Periodic dumping of transaction files.

B. Year-end use of audit hooks.

C. An integrated test facility (ITF).

D. A well-documented audit trail.

The correct answer is (D). *(CPA, adapted)*

REQUIRED: The condition necessary to audit balances in an online computer system.

DISCUSSION: The processing of input records in an online, real-time computer system typically destroys the previous master file entry in an environment of destructive updating. Thus, a well-documented audit trail is especially important for the auditor.

Answer (A) is incorrect because periodic dumping of transaction files may be a way of monitoring transactions, but the auditor would not find it beneficial in the audit. Answer (B) is incorrect because the term audit hooks is a nonsense answer in this context. Answer (C) is incorrect because an ITF is a possible but unnecessary approach to auditing computer systems.

257. Which of the following is likely to be least important to an auditor who is considering internal control for the automated data processing function?

A. Ancillary program functions.

B. Disposition of source documents.

C. Operator competence.

D. Bit storage capacity.

The correct answer is (D). *(CPA, adapted)*

REQUIRED: The least important item in the consideration of internal control.

DISCUSSION: Bit storage capacity relates to the number of characters the system can store. This is of little or no concern to an auditor considering internal control.

Answer (A) is incorrect because ancillary or auxiliary program functions affect internal control. Answer (B) is incorrect because the auditor should inspect source documents. Answer (C) is incorrect because an entity must employ sufficient competent personnel to accomplish its goals and objectives. Thus, human resource policies and practices are a factor in the control environment that should be considered.

258. In a distributed database (DDB) environment, which of the following is a test of control for access control administration?

A. Reconciliation of batch control totals.

B. Examination of logged activity.

C. Prohibition of random access.

D. Analysis of system-generated core dumps.

The correct answer is (B). *(CIA, adapted)*

REQUIRED: The access control in a distributed database (DDB) environment.

DISCUSSION: A computer log could provide information concerning users who have accessed the system, the files accessed, the processing accomplished, the time of access, and the amount of time the processing took. The log thus provides data allowing an auditor to evaluate the effectiveness of the system's access controls.

Answer (A) is incorrect because batch totals are unlikely to be calculated in a DDB environment, which is characterized by online processing. Answer (C) is incorrect because DDB systems must provide for random access so that users can obtain information from the files as needed. Answer (D) is incorrect because core dumps, which represent information stored in the memory of the computer, provide little information for access control analysis.

259. After gaining an understanding of a client's computer processing internal control, an auditor may decide not to test the effectiveness of the computer processing control procedures. Which of the following is not a valid reason for choosing to omit tests of controls?

A. The controls duplicate operative controls existing elsewhere in the system.

B. There appear to be major weaknesses that would preclude assessing control risk at less than the maximum level.

C. The time and dollar costs of testing exceed the time and dollar savings in substantive testing if the tests of controls show the controls to be operative.

D. The controls appear effective enough to support a reduced level of control risk.

The correct answer is (D). *(CPA, adapted)*

REQUIRED: The invalid reason for omitting tests of controls.

DISCUSSION: Although controls appear to be effective based on the understanding of internal control, the auditor must perform tests of controls for those control activities for which control risk is to be assessed at less than the maximum level. Control risk affects the acceptable level of detection risk used in determining the nature, timing, and extent of substantive tests.

Answer (A) is incorrect because compensating controls may appropriately limit control risk. Answer (B) is incorrect because, if the auditor intends to assess control risk at the maximum level, tests of controls are unnecessary. Answer (C) is incorrect because, if tests of controls are not cost effective, the auditor should expand substantive testing.

260. Tests of controls in an advanced computer system

A. Can be performed using only actual transactions because testing of simulated transactions is of no consequence.

B. Can be performed using actual transactions or simulated transactions.

C. Is impracticable because many procedures within the computer processing activity leave no visible evidence of having been performed.

D. Is inadvisable because it may distort the evidence in live online files.

The correct answer is (B). *(CPA, adapted)*

REQUIRED: The correct statement about tests of controls in an advanced computer system.

DISCUSSION: Tests of controls determine the effectiveness of the design and operation of internal controls. They can be performed using either actual or simulated transactions. For example, the integrated test facility (ITF) method uses both actual and simulated transactions.

Answer (A) is incorrect because the auditor is concerned with the effectiveness of a control, not the processing of a particular transaction. Answer (C) is incorrect because many procedures that leave no visible evidence may leave machine-readable evidence. Answer (D) is incorrect because master files can be protected during tests of controls. An ITF, for example, uses dummy records so that test transactions will not contaminate live online files.

261. Auditing through the computer must be used when

A. Input transactions are batched and system logic is straightforward.

B. Processing primarily consists of sorting the input data and updating the master file sequentially.

C. Processing is primarily online and updating is real-time.

D. Generalized audit software is not available.

The correct answer is (C). *(CIA, adapted)*

REQUIRED: The condition requiring auditing through the computer.

DISCUSSION: When the computer plays a significant role in processing, storing, and reporting the information being audited, the auditor should audit through the computer. When processing is done in an online, real-time environment, the auditor is unlikely to obtain sufficient evidence outside the system to audit around the computer successfully.

Answer (A) is incorrect because, in a straightforward batch system, printouts and other documentation may be sufficient for adequate testing outside the computer. Answer (B) is incorrect because, when files are stored sequentially and processed in that manner, printouts and other documentation may be sufficient for adequate testing outside the computer. Answer (D) is incorrect because, whether or not generalized audit software is available, the auditor should consider the consequences of auditing around, rather than through, the computer.

262. Which of the following is an appropriate audit procedure that may be used to test the adequacy of application controls over computer-based accounts payable?

A. Observing computer library and operations area to obtain evidence to support an opinion about the security of accounts payable data files.

B. Manually comparing vendor invoice numbers with those listed on computer-generated lists of accounts payable to assess the effectiveness of computer-based sequence checks.

C. Testing purchase transactions using a test data approach.

D. Using a computer-generated questionnaire to obtain reliable information about the accuracy and completeness of input and update of accounts payable data from the organization's computer management personnel.

The correct answer is (C). *(CIA, adapted)*

REQUIRED: The audit procedure to test the application controls over accounts payable.

DISCUSSION: Using the test data approach, the auditor may develop and process a set of valid and invalid purchases transactions using the client's application programs. Based on the understanding of the programmed controls, the auditor has an expectation of the results of the processing. The auditor can determine whether the client's application controls are working effectively to reject and report invalid and questionable transactions.

Answer (A) is incorrect because data file security is a general control concern. Answer (B) is incorrect because the document numbers on vendor invoices are generated by the vendors. Hence, the purchasing firm has no access to a sequencing of such invoices. Answer (D) is incorrect because an auditor should never rely solely on the representations of an auditee.

263. When an auditor tests a computerized accounting system, which of the following is true of the test data approach?

A. Test data must consist of all possible valid and invalid conditions.

B. The program tested is different from the program used throughout the year by the client.

C. Several transactions of each type must be tested.

D. Test data are processed by the client's computer programs under the auditor's control.

The correct answer is (D). *(CPA, adapted)*

REQUIRED: The true statement concerning the test data approach.

DISCUSSION: Using the test data approach, the auditor develops and processes a set of valid and invalid transactions using the client's application programs. Based on the understanding of the programmed controls, the auditor has an expectation of the results of the processing. The auditor can determine if the client's controls are working effectively to reject and report invalid and questionable transactions.

Answer (A) is incorrect because the auditor should test those controls that must be evaluated to assess control risk below the maximum level. Answer (B) is incorrect because the program tested should be the same one used by management throughout the year; otherwise the auditor has no assurance concerning the effectiveness of the controls that were actually in place. Answer (C) is incorrect because only one of each type of transaction needs to be tested. The computer can be expected to test all similar transactions in the same manner.

264. The following flowchart depicts

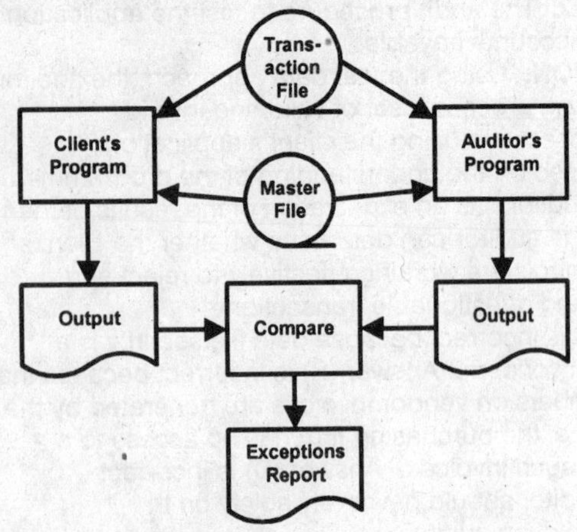

A. Program code checking.

B. Parallel simulation.

C. Integrated test facility.

D. Controlled reprocessing.

The correct answer is (B). *(CPA, adapted)*

REQUIRED: The audit technique depicted by the flowchart.

DISCUSSION: Parallel simulation is a test of the controls in a client's application program. An auditor-developed program is used to process actual client data and compare the output and the exceptions report with those of the client's application program. If the client's programmed controls are operating effectively, the two sets of results should be reconcilable.

Answer (A) is incorrect because program code checking refers to desk checking the client's application program code to determine if it contains the appropriate controls. Answer (C) is incorrect because an ITF introduces dummy records into the client's files and then processes dummy transactions to update the records. The auditor can test the controls by including various types of transactions to be processed. Answer (D) is incorrect because controlled reprocessing is a variant of parallel simulation that uses an authenticated copy of the auditee's program. The flowchart indicates that the auditor's program is being used.

265. Parallel simulation (the audit model technique) is an appropriate audit approach for

A. Testing for the presence of authorized signatures on documents.

B. Summarizing the results of accounts receivable confirmation work.

C. Calculating amounts for declining-balance depreciation charges.

D. Scanning the general ledger file for unusual transactions.

The correct answer is (C). *(CIA, adapted)*

REQUIRED: The proper use of parallel simulation.

DISCUSSION: Parallel simulation involves duplicate processing of the client's data using a program developed by the auditor. The auditor's program simulates the logic of the client's application program. The auditor may thus enter data and compare simulated test results with those from the auditee's program. Parallel simulation is appropriate for auditing depreciation because controls such as limit or reasonableness tests can be tested by the auditor.

Answer (A) is incorrect because testing for the presence of authorized signatures on documents is a test of controls that cannot be done by a program. Answer (B) is incorrect because confirmations provide auditor-developed data from sources external to the auditee. Parallel simulation seeks to duplicate auditee processing. Answer (D) is incorrect because scanning the general ledger file for unusual transactions does not replicate auditee processing.

266. When auditing computer security, the internal auditor usually does not

A. Perform tests of the effectiveness of controls.

B. Review contingency procedures and documentation standards.

C. Perform substantive tests.

D. Review personnel practices and policies.

The correct answer is (C). *(CIA, adapted)*

REQUIRED: The procedure not performed when auditing computer security.

DISCUSSION: Substantive tests are tests of details and analytical procedures to detect material misstatements in the account balance, transaction class, and disclosure components of financial statements (AU 319). The internal auditor usually does not perform substantive tests in auditing computer security. The internal auditor conducts a review of the adequacy and effectiveness of internal controls (IIA Standard 300).

Answers (A), (B), and (D) are incorrect because the internal auditor might perform tests of the effectiveness of controls, review contingency procedures and documentation standards, and review personnel practices and policies when auditing computer security.

267. A mail-order retailer has just modified its processing programs to charge each customer the appropriate sales tax. The best approach for detecting whether sales taxes are applied correctly is to

A. Move the program code that computes sales taxes to a single program and make this program part of the processing sequence.

B. Change the operator input screens to show the computation of sales taxes so the operator can verify the computation.

C. Modify the program code to prompt the operator to ask customers whether their areas have sales taxes and enter the appropriate rates.

D. Add the program code that will sort orders by area, compute taxes in the aggregate, and compare the amount with the sum of individual taxes charged for each area.

The correct answer is (D). *(CIA, adapted)*

REQUIRED: The best approach for detecting whether sales taxes are applied correctly.

DISCUSSION: Sales taxes vary from one jurisdiction to another. Hence, the program should sort orders by area. Verification of the accuracy of the tax charges can then be obtained by calculating the total taxes for each area in two ways: applying the tax rate to the aggregate sales and summing the taxes charged on individual sales.

Answer (A) is incorrect because moving the program code that computes sales taxes to a single program is a good system design approach, but it does not guarantee that sales tax processing is complete. Answer (B) is incorrect because changing the operator input screens does not ensure correct application of sales taxes. The operator may not know what the appropriate computation is. Answer (C) is incorrect because customers may not know the proper rates or may deny that their areas impose the taxes.

268. To determine whether any unauthorized program changes have been made since the last authorized program update, the best computer audit technique is for the auditor to conduct a(n)

A. Code comparison.

B. Code review.

C. Test data run.

D. Analytical review.

The correct answer is (A). *(CIA, adapted)*

REQUIRED: The best technique to determine whether unauthorized program changes have been made.

DISCUSSION: Code comparison is the process of comparing two versions of the same program to determine whether the two correspond. It is an efficient technique because it is performed by software.

Answer (B) is incorrect because code review is the process of reading program source code listings to determine whether the code contains potential errors or inefficient statements. Code review can be used as a means of code comparison but is inefficient. Answer (C) is incorrect because test data runs permit the auditor to verify the processing of preselected transactions. They provide no evidence about unexecuted portions of the program. Answer (D) is incorrect because analytical review is the process of creating and evaluating ratios between numbers, often in the context of financial statements.

269. To obtain evidence that online access controls are properly functioning, an auditor is most likely to

A. Create checkpoints at periodic intervals after live data processing to test for unauthorized use of the system.

B. Examine the transaction log to discover whether any transactions were lost or entered twice because of a system malfunction.

C. Enter invalid identification numbers or passwords to ascertain whether the system rejects them.

D. Vouch a random sample of processed transactions to assure proper authorization.

The correct answer is (C). *(CPA, adapted)*

REQUIRED: The procedure to obtain evidence that user online access controls are functioning.

DISCUSSION: Employees with access authority to process transactions that change records should not also have asset custody or program modification responsibilities. The auditor should determine that password authority is consistent with other assigned responsibilities. The auditor can directly test whether password controls are working by attempting entry into the system by using invalid identifications and passwords.

Answer (A) is incorrect because checkpoints are used as a recovery procedure in batch processing applications. Answer (B) is incorrect because testing for missing or duplicate transactions would not determine whether online access controls were functioning effectively. Answer (D) is incorrect because unauthorized transactions may be entered by anyone who knows valid passwords, etc.

270. Which of the following computer-assisted auditing techniques allows fictitious and real transactions to be processed together without the knowledge of client operating personnel?

A. Integrated test facility (ITF).

B. Input controls matrix.

C. Parallel simulation.

D. Data entry monitor.

The correct answer is (A). *(CPA, adapted)*

REQUIRED: The technique that processes fictitious and real transactions without the knowledge of client personnel.

DISCUSSION: Using an ITF, the auditor creates a test record within the client's actual system. Fictitious transactions affecting the test record along with actual transactions are processed. Client operating personnel need not be aware of the testing process.

Answers (B) and (D) are incorrect because input controls matrix and data entry monitor are not methods typically used by auditors to test a client's computer systems. Answer (C) is incorrect because parallel simulation reprocesses only real, not fictitious, transactions.

271. A primary reason auditors are reluctant to use an ITF (minicompany technique) is that it requires them to

A. Reserve specific master file records and process them at regular intervals.

B. Collect transaction and master file records in a separate file.

C. Notify user personnel so they can make manual adjustments to output.

D. Identify and reverse the fictitious entries to avoid contamination of control totals.

The correct answer is (D). *(CIA, adapted)*

REQUIRED: The reason for not using an ITF.

DISCUSSION: An ITF permits dummy transactions to be processed with live transactions but requires additional programming to ensure that programs will recognize the specially coded test data. Also, dummy files must be established (the test facility or dummy entity). Nevertheless, output (for example, control totals) is affected by the existence of the ITF transactions. One way to avoid the problem is to use immaterial transactions. However, the resulting differences between control totals may be troublesome, and the inability to use large numbers may preclude auditing limit tests. An alternative is to submit reversing entries. However, reversals (1) threaten data integrity if they are inaccurate, (2) must be submitted in the same run, and (3) may allow users to obtain contaminated data before the entries are made.

Answer (A) is incorrect because reserving specific master file records and processing them at regular intervals is typical of the base case system of evaluation. Answer (B) is incorrect because the embedded audit module technique involves selection of items of audit interest by the audit module included in an application program. These items are recorded in a separate audit log. Answer (C) is incorrect because making manual adjustments to output does not reverse the fictitious entries in the master file.

272. In auditing an online perpetual inventory system, an auditor selected certain file-updating transactions for detailed testing. The audit technique that will provide a computer trail of all relevant processing steps applied to a specific transaction is described as

A. Simulation.

B. Snapshot.

C. Code comparison.

D. Tagging and tracing.

The correct answer is (D). *(CIA, adapted)*

REQUIRED: The audit technique that provides a computer trail for processing a specific transaction.

DISCUSSION: Tagging and tracing describes selection of specific transactions and tags them with an indicator at input. A computer trail of all relevant processing steps of these tagged transactions in the application system can be printed or stored in a computer file for auditor evaluation.

Answer (A) is incorrect because simulation permits comparisons of live data but does not produce a trail of all relevant processing steps. Answer (B) is incorrect because a snapshot is a technique for recording the content of computer memory to aid in verifying a decision process. Answer (C) is incorrect because a code comparison is used to verify that program changes and computer maintenance procedures are correctly followed.

273. A small client recently put its cash disbursements system on a microcomputer. About which of the following is an auditor most likely to be concerned?

A. Programming of this microcomputer is in BASIC, although COBOL is the dominant, standard language for business processing.

B. This microcomputer is operated by employees who have other, noncomputer-processing job responsibilities.

C. Backup files are stored in another location away from the microcomputer.

D. There are restrictions on the amount of data that can be stored and on the length of time that data can be stored.

The correct answer is (B). *(CPA, adapted)*

REQUIRED: The issue of most concern to an auditor.

DISCUSSION: Segregation of duties is a basic category of control activities (AU 319). Functions are incompatible if a person is in a position both to perpetrate and conceal errors or irregularities. Hence, the duties of authorizing transactions, recording transactions, and having custody of assets should be assigned to different people. If the non-computer responsibilities are incompatible with use of the computer, for example, because an employee has access to assets, an auditor would be justifiably concerned.

Answer (A) is incorrect because the choice of language has little effect on internal control. Answer (C) is incorrect because storing backup files at a remote location is a control strength. Answer (D) is incorrect because restrictions on the amount and duration of data storage do not constitute a control weakness.

274. Different audit procedures may be required because a microcomputer may not be subject to the same degree of control as larger computers. The best audit approach in a microcomputer environment is to increase?

A. Tests of controls.

B. Substantive testing.

C. Attribute sampling.

D. Documentation review.

The correct answer is (B). *(CIA, adapted)*

REQUIRED: The best audit approach when a microcomputer environment lacks effective controls.

DISCUSSION: When control risk increases, the level of acceptable detection risk decreases. As the acceptable level of detection risk decreases, the assurance to be provided by substantive tests should increase.

Answer (A) is incorrect because microcomputers suffer from a lack of control owing to inadequately separated duties. Thus, increased tests of controls would not be effective. Answer (C) is incorrect because attribute sampling is ordinarily used in tests of controls to estimate error rates in the processing of transactions. When controls are absent, testing the effectiveness of controls serves no purpose. Answer (D) is incorrect because further review of documentation might improve the auditor's understanding of the system but would not decrease control risk.

275. The audit effort most likely to yield relevant evidence in determining the adequacy of an organization's disaster-recovery plan should focus on

A. The completeness of the plan as to facilities, operations, communications, security, and data processing.

B. The sufficiency of the list of replacement equipment needed in event of a disaster.

C. The question of whether the plan is in the planning or developmental stage.

D. The role of the internal auditing department in developing and testing the plan.

The correct answer is (A). *(CIA, adapted)*

REQUIRED: The focus of the audit effort regarding a disaster recovery plan.

DISCUSSION: A computer center should have a comprehensive (complete) reconstruction and recovery plan that will allow it to regenerate important programs and data files and continue operations in the event of disasters, equipment failures, or errors. The center should create backup (duplicate) copies of data files, databases, programs, and documentation, store backup copies off-site, and plan for auxiliary processing at another site.

Answers (B) and (C) are incorrect because consideration of the adequacy of the plan must extend to numerous factors other than the sufficiency of the list of replacement equipment and the question of whether the plan is in the planning or development stage. Answer (D) is incorrect because the involvement of internal auditing does not assure adequacy.

276. In order to decrease overall inventory costs, a manufacturer has implemented a distributed database system for maintaining all inventory records at each plant. Each plant can requisition inventory from other plants. Management believes, however, that materials requisitions that require inventory from multiple plants are not being entered in the database correctly; i.e., the inventory is shipped but the counts remain the same. The best approach for investigating the situation is

A. An embedded audit module.

B. An audit hook.

C. A snapshot.

D. Mapping.

The correct answer is (C). *(CIA, adapted)*

REQUIRED: The best approach for investigating a database system in which data are not processed correctly.

DISCUSSION: To determine why the inventory count has not changed, the processing must be tested. The best approach is to use the snapshot technique. It involves capturing the data used in processing at a specific point in the stream of processing. The snapshot technique will permit analysis of all data pertinent to a complex database update so that the correctness or deficiencies of updating can be determined.

Answer (A) is incorrect because an embedded audit module selects transactions meeting specific criteria. It permits continuous monitoring of the system but is not helpful in debugging this potential updating error. Answer (B) is incorrect because an audit hook is useful in calling audit routines to perform processing for audit activity but is not helpful in debugging this potential updating error. Answer (D) is incorrect because mapping is a procedure for reporting code usage within a program, not a procedure for verifying proper operation of a program.

277. What information would the auditor expect to find in the data dictionary that would assist in a payroll application audit?

A. Programs that access the data.

B. Type of operating system.

C. Online user identification.

D. System network architecture and flowcharts.

The correct answer is (A). *(CIA, adapted)*

REQUIRED: The information found in the data dictionary that would assist in the payroll audit.

DISCUSSION: The data dictionary is a file (possibly manual but usually computerized) in which the records relate to specified data items. It contains definitions of data records and files and the list of programs used to process them. Only certain persons or entities are permitted to retrieve data or to modify data items. Accordingly, these access limitations are also found in the data dictionary.

Answers (B), (C), and (D) are incorrect because the type of operating system, online user identification, and system network architecture and flowcharts are not customarily part of the data dictionary.

278. Matthews Corp. has changed from a system of recording time worked on clock cards to a computerized payroll system in which employees record time in and out with magnetic cards. The computer system automatically updates all payroll records. Because of this change

A. A generalized computer audit program must be used.

B. Part of the audit trail is altered.

C. The potential for payroll-related fraud is diminished.

D. Transactions must be processed in batches.

The correct answer is (B). *(CPA, adapted)*

REQUIRED: The effect of computerization of a payroll system.

DISCUSSION: In a manual payroll system, a paper trail of documents is created to provide audit evidence that controls over each step in processing are in place and functioning. One element of a computer system that differentiates it from a manual system is that a transaction trail useful for auditing purposes might exist only for a brief time or only in computer-readable form.

Answer (A) is incorrect because use of generalized audit software is only one of many ways of auditing through a computer. Answer (C) is incorrect because conversion to a computer system may actually increase the chance of fraud by eliminating segregation of incompatible functions and other controls. Answer (D) is incorrect because automatic updating indicates that processing is not in batch mode.

279. A service organization processes payroll data having a material effect on the financial statements of an audit client. The client has established certain internal control activities over input and output data. If the auditor wishes to assess control risk at less than the maximum, which of the following statements is false?

A. The auditor may decide that obtaining evidence of the operating effectiveness of the service organization's activities is not necessary or efficient and still be able to assess control risk at less than the maximum.

B. The auditor may need to perform tests of the service organization's processing controls that would provide a basis for assessing control risk below the maximum.

C. If certain relevant controls exist only at the service organization, the client's auditor must evaluate the operating effectiveness of those controls to assess control risk as less than the maximum.

D. If certain relevant controls exist only at the service organization and a service auditor issues a report on activities placed in operation, the client's auditor may use the report to assess control risk at below the maximum.

The correct answer is (D). *(Publisher)*

REQUIRED: The false statement about assessing control risk at less than the maximum when a service organization processes transactions for an audit client.

DISCUSSION: The use of a computer service organization reduces control risk through increased segregation of functions. If the client's controls over the data are effective, the auditor may be able to audit around the service organization's computer. The arrangement usually provides an adequate audit trail for this purpose. If controls necessary to achieve specific entity objectives are located at the service organization, the user auditor must either apply appropriate procedures at the service organization or obtain a report by a service auditor for the purpose of assessing control risk at below the maximum. The service auditor's report must report on activities placed in operation and on tests of operating effectiveness (AU 324).

Answer (A) is incorrect because the client's auditor may be able to assess control risk at less than the maximum after testing the relevant client controls over the service organization's activities. Answer (B) is incorrect because, if the relevant controls are at the service organization and an appropriate service auditor's report is not available or is not used, the auditor must test controls at the service organization if control risk is to be assessed at below the maximum. Answer (C) is incorrect because the evaluation of operating effectiveness must be based on the auditor's tests of controls at the service organization or on an appropriate service auditor's report if control risk is to be assessed at below the maximum level.

280. An audit of the electronic data interchange (EDI) area of a banking group revealed the facts listed below. Which one indicates the need for improved internal control?

A. Employees may only access the computer system via an ID and an encrypted password.

B. The system employs message sequencing as a way to monitor data transmissions.

C. Certain types of transactions may only be made at specific terminals.

D. Branch office employees may access the mainframe with a single call via modem.

The correct answer is (D). *(CIA, adapted)*

REQUIRED: The condition that indicates the need for improved internal control.

DISCUSSION: The system should employ automatic dial-back to prevent intrusion by unauthorized parties. This procedure accepts an incoming modem call, disconnects, and automatically dials back a prearranged number to establish a permanent connection for data transfer or inquiry.

Answer (A) is incorrect because employee access to the computer system via an ID and an encrypted password is considered acceptable. Encrypted passwords further decrease the likelihood of unauthorized access. Answer (B) is incorrect because message sequencing detects unauthorized access by numbering each message and incrementing each message by one more than the last one sent. This procedure will detect a gap or duplicate. Answer (C) is incorrect because allowing certain types of transactions (such as payroll transactions) to be made only at specific terminals minimizes the likelihood of unauthorized access.

5.12 Computer-Assisted Auditing

281. The auditor typically has two roles to play in computer environments. First, (s)he may be responsible for evaluating the client's computer system controls in the course of an audit. Second, (s)he may be able to

A. Use the computer as a tool to perform the audit more efficiently or effectively.

B. Earn additional revenue by selling hardware systems to audit clients.

C. Provide the IRS with computer files of audit clients.

D. Earn additional revenue by selling software systems to audit clients.

The correct answer is (A). *(Publisher)*

REQUIRED: The two roles of auditors in computer systems.

DISCUSSION: The computer has provided the auditor with a powerful tool to permit performance of the audit more efficiently and effectively. Computers may be used to test the client's records more intensely and in greater detail than would be possible manually.

Answer (B) is incorrect because providing clients with hardware directly would affect the auditor's integrity and objectivity. Members of the AICPA must be free of conflicts of interest in performing attestation functions (Conduct Rule 102). Answer (C) is incorrect because the auditor should not provide the IRS with information concerning the client without the client's permission. Answer (D) is incorrect because providing clients with software directly would affect the auditor's integrity and objectivity.

282. Modern computer technology makes it possible to perform paperless audits. For example, in an audit of computer-processed customer accounts receivable balances, an auditor might use a microcomputer to access the accounts receivable files directly and copy selected customer records into the microcomputer for audit analysis. Which of the following is an advantage of this type of paperless audit of accounts receivable balances?

A. It reduces the amount of substantive testing required.

B. It allows immediate processing of audit data on a spreadsheet working paper.

C. It increases the amount of technical skill required of the auditor.

D. It allows direct confirmation of customer account balances.

The correct answer is (B). *(CIA, adapted)*

REQUIRED: The advantage of a paperless audit of accounts receivable balances.

DISCUSSION: Electronic spreadsheets are software packages that display multicolumn worksheets, e.g., automated audit working papers. A major advantage of this type of auditing is the ability to process data immediately using microcomputer software without first having to enter the data manually into the microcomputer.

Answer (A) is incorrect because audit technology has no direct effect on the amount of substantive testing required. Answer (C) is incorrect because the need for increased expertise is not an advantage. Answer (D) is incorrect because processing computer files does not in itself provide confirmation of customer account balances, although software may assist in preparing confirmation requests.

283. A primary advantage of using generalized audit software (GAS) packages in auditing the financial statements of a client that uses a computer system is that the auditor may

A. Substantiate the accuracy of data through self-checking digits and hash totals.

B. Reduce the level of required tests of controls to a relatively small amount.

C. Access information stored on computer files without a complete understanding of the client's hardware and software features.

D. Consider increasing the use of substantive tests of transactions in place of analytical procedures.

The correct answer is (C). *(CPA, adapted)*

REQUIRED: The advantage of using GAS.

DISCUSSION: The primary use of GAS is to select and summarize a client's records for additional testing. These packages permit the auditor to audit through the computer; to extract, compare, analyze, and summarize data; and to generate output for use in the audit. They allow the auditor to exploit the computer to examine many more records than otherwise possible with far greater speed and accuracy. Although GAS requires the auditor to provide certain specifications about the particular client's records, computer equipment, and file formats, a detailed knowledge of the client's system may be unnecessary because the audit package is designed to be used in many environments.

Answer (A) is incorrect because self-checking digits and hash totals are application controls used by clients. Answer (B) is incorrect because GAS may permit far more comprehensive tests of controls than in a manual audit. Answer (D) is incorrect because the auditor is required to apply analytical procedures in the planning and overall review phases of the audit.

284. Which of the following statements is not true concerning the tasks that generalized audit software (GAS) is able to perform?

A. Provide totals of unusual items.

B. Check for duplications, missing information, or ranges of values.

C. Specify which data elements will be tested and the criteria to be used.

D. Verify calculation totals and analyses produced.

The correct answer is (C). *(CIA, adapted)*

REQUIRED: The false statement about GAS.

DISCUSSION: The primary use of GAS is to select and summarize a client's records for additional testing. However, GAS requires the auditor to provide certain specifications about the particular client's records, computer equipment, and file formats.

Answer (A) is incorrect because providing totals of unusual items is a function that can be performed by GAS. Answer (B) is incorrect because checking for duplications, missing information, or ranges of values is a function that can be performed by GAS. Answer (D) is incorrect because verifying calculation totals and analyses produced is a function that can be performed by GAS.

285. Which of the following represents a limitation on the use of generalized audit software (GAS)?

A. It requires lengthy detailed instructions in order to accomplish specific tasks.

B. It has limited application without significant modification.

C. It requires significant programming knowledge to be used effectively.

D. It can only be used on hardware with compatible operating systems.

The correct answer is (D). *(CIA, adapted)*

REQUIRED: The disadvantage of using GAS.

DISCUSSION: Diversity of programming languages, computers, systems designs, and differing data structures makes generalized audit software impossible to apply in certain situations.

Answer (A) is incorrect because the use of GAS is normally more efficient. Less time is required to write instructions to accomplish a function than to manually select and examine items. Answer (B) is incorrect because the program is generalized, i.e., designed to be used on a variety of systems without significant modifications. Answer (C) is incorrect because an advantage is that GAS requires minimal knowledge of computer technology.

286. An auditor is least likely to use computer software to

A. Construct parallel simulations.

B. Access client data files.

C. Prepare spreadsheets.

D. Assess computer control risk.

The correct answer is (D). *(CPA, adapted)*

REQUIRED: The task least likely to be done with computer software.

DISCUSSION: The auditor is required to obtain an understanding of internal control and assess control risk to plan the audit. This assessment is a matter of professional judgment that cannot be accomplished by a computer.

Answer (A) is incorrect because parallel simulation involves using an auditor's program to reproduce the logic of the client's program. Answer (B) is incorrect because computer software makes accessing client files much faster and easier. Answer (C) is incorrect because many audit spreadsheet programs are available.

287. The two requirements crucial to achieving audit efficiency and effectiveness with a microcomputer are selecting

A. The appropriate audit tasks for microcomputer applications and the appropriate software to perform the selected audit tasks.

B. The appropriate software to perform the selected audit tasks and client data that can be accessed by the auditor's microcomputer.

C. Client data that can be accessed by the auditor's microcomputer and audit procedures that are generally applicable to several clients in a specific industry.

D. Audit procedures that are generally applicable to several clients in a specific industry and the appropriate audit tasks for microcomputer applications.

The correct answer is (A). *(CPA, adapted)*

REQUIRED: The two requirements for audit efficiency and effectiveness using a microcomputer.

DISCUSSION: The question relates to using the computer as an audit tool. To use a microcomputer for this purpose effectively and efficiently, the auditor must have the appropriate hardware and software.

Answer (B) is incorrect because access to client data does not relate directly to the efficient and effective use of a microcomputer. Answer (C) is incorrect because access to the client's records and selection of standardized audit procedures pertain more to using generalized audit software to perform substantive tests than to using the microcomputer as an audit tool. Answer (D) is incorrect because selection of standardized procedures for the industry does not relate directly to the efficient and effective use of a microcomputer.

288. Which of the following audit procedures would an auditor be least likely to perform using generalized audit software (GAS)?

A. Searching records of accounts receivable balances for credit balances.

B. Evaluating proper segregation of duties.

C. Selecting accounts receivable for positive and negative confirmation.

D. Listing of unusually large inventory balances.

The correct answer is (B). *(CPA, adapted)*

REQUIRED: The least likely use of GAS.

DISCUSSION: GAS allows auditors access to data files without the need to write specialized computer programs. They extract records, test extensions and footings, and summarize file data. Because evaluating proper segregation of duties is a matter of judgment, GAS would not be useful.

Answer (A) is incorrect because searching records of accounts receivable balances for credit balances is a function for which GAS is well suited. Answer (C) is incorrect because selecting accounts receivable for positive and negative confirmation is a function for which GAS is well suited. Answer (D) is incorrect because listing of unusually large inventory balances is a function for which GAS is well suited.

289. Smith Corporation has numerous customers. A customer file is kept on disk storage. Each customer record contains the name, address, credit limit, and account balance. The auditor wishes to test this file to determine whether credit limits are being exceeded. The best procedure for the auditor to follow is to

A. Develop test data that would cause some account balances to exceed the credit limit and determine if the system properly detects such situations.

B. Develop a program to compare credit limits with account balances and print out the details of any account with a balance exceeding its credit limit.

C. Request a printout of all account balances so they can be manually checked against the credit limits.

D. Request a printout of a sample of account balances so they can be individually checked against the credit limits.

The correct answer is (B). *(CPA, adapted)*

REQUIRED: The best technique to test a customer computer file to determine whether credit limits are being exceeded.

DISCUSSION: The auditor should consider developing a program to compare the balances with the credit limits and to print out the exceptions. The auditor can then focus on those customers whose credit limits may have been exceeded.

Answer (A) is incorrect because the auditor only needs to abstract information already available in the client's files. Answer (C) is incorrect because requesting a printout of all account balances so they can be manually checked against the credit limits would entail extensive manual work that could be done far more quickly and accurately by the computer. Answer (D) is incorrect because, although a sample may be useful, the information is available and the speed and power of the computer allows the auditor to identify all customers exceeding the credit limit.

290. An auditor using audit software probably would be least interested in which of the following fields in a computerized perpetual inventory file?

A. Economic order quantity.

B. Warehouse location.

C. Date of last purchase.

D. Quantity sold.

The correct answer is (A). *(CPA, adapted)*

REQUIRED: The field from an inventory record that would be least interesting to an auditor.

DISCUSSION: The economic order quantity, which is based on the most cost-effective combination of ordering and carrying costs, is a management decision with little impact on the fairness of the inventory balance on the financial statements.

Answer (B) is incorrect because the auditor would be interested in the storage location of the inventory item for test-count purposes. Answer (C) is incorrect because the auditor would be interested in the date of last purchase for various reasons. For example, if the date is not relatively recent, the item may be slow-moving or obsolete, with consequent implications for its lower-of-cost-or-market valuation. On the other hand, a date of purchase near year-end suggests the need for cutoff tests. Answer (D) is incorrect because the quantity sold is obviously significant for determining the accuracy of the inventory balance, sales, cost of sales, and related accounts.

291. When an auditor performs tests on a computerized inventory file containing over 20,000 line items, that auditor can maintain independence and perform most efficiently by

A. Asking the console operator to print every item that cost more than $100.

B. Using a generalized audit software package.

C. Obtaining a printout of the entire file and then selecting each nth item.

D. Using the systems department's programmer to write an extraction program.

The correct answer is (B). *(CIA, adapted)*

REQUIRED: The method to maintain independence and perform efficiently in testing an inventory file.

DISCUSSION: Independence can be preserved when the auditor acquires general audit software (GAS) from an external source rather than relying on auditee-developed audit software. Also, efficiency is enhanced to the extent GAS can be used (as compared to manual auditing or writing special audit programs).

Answer (A) is incorrect because independence is jeopardized when an operator is involved in the process. Answer (C) is incorrect because printing out the entire file is both unnecessary and inefficient. Answer (D) is incorrect because overreliance on an auditee's programmer impairs independence.

292. Which of the following is not an advantage of using a generalized computer audit program? Such use

A. Requires the auditor to have only a minimal knowledge of computer technology while providing the auditor with a high level of programming independence.

B. Assures compatibility with database management systems.

C. Eliminates the requirement to develop custom audit software for each type of audit.

D. Permits greater reliance to be placed on the audit results than could be obtained from manual techniques.

The correct answer is (B). *(CIA, adapted)*

REQUIRED: The item that is not an advantage of a generalized computer audit program.

DISCUSSION: Although generalized computer audit programs are compatible with many systems, they do not assure compatibility with database management systems.

Answer (A) is incorrect because the auditor need not be an expert in computer technology to use audit packages effectively. Answer (C) is incorrect because the use of generalized packages typically eliminates the requirement to develop custom software for each engagement. Answer (D) is incorrect because more items can be tested using a computer package than can be examined manually. Thus, greater reliance can be placed on the procedure.

293. Auditors often make use of computer programs that perform routine processing functions, such as sorting and merging. These programs are made available by computer companies and others and are specifically referred to as

A. Compiler programs.

B. Supervisory programs.

C. Utility programs.

D. User programs.

The correct answer is (C). *(CPA, adapted)*

REQUIRED: The term for programs used to perform routine functions.

DISCUSSION: Utility programs are provided by manufacturers of equipment to perform routine processing tasks required by both clients and auditors, such as extracting data, sorting, merging, and copying. Utility programs are pretested, are independent of the client's own programming efforts, and furnish useful information without the trouble of writing special programs for the engagement.

Answer (A) is incorrect because compiler programs convert source programs written in a higher-level language into computer-readable object programs, i.e., into machine language. Answer (B) is incorrect because supervisory programs, also termed operating systems, are master programs responsible for controlling operations within a computer system. Answer (D) is incorrect because user programs are those prepared for a particular application.

294. Which of the following concepts distinguishes the retention of computerized audit working papers from the traditional hard copy form?

A. Analyses, conclusions, and recommendations are filed on electronic media and are therefore subject to computer system controls and security procedures.

B. Evidential support for all findings is copied and provided to local management during the closing conference and to each person receiving the final report.

C. Computerized data files can be used in computer audit procedures.

D. Audit programs can be standardized to eliminate the need for a preliminary survey at each location.

The correct answer is (A). *(CIA, adapted)*

REQUIRED: The distinction between computerized audit working papers and the traditional hard copy.

DISCUSSION: The only difference between the computerized and hard copy form is how the working papers are stored. Electronic working papers would be saved either on disks or hard drive, whereas hard copy would be stored in a file cabinet. Unlike computerized working papers, hard copies are not subject to computer controls and security procedures.

Answer (B) is incorrect because evidential support would be retained and provided on the basis of the nature of the finding and not the media used for storing working papers. Answer (C) is incorrect because this capability is not an exclusive function of computerized working papers. Answer (D) is incorrect because, though the nature of the preliminary survey may change in some cases, the requirement for this phase of the audit is not eliminated by computerized working papers.

5.13 CISA Concepts

295. Which of the following are typical responsibilities of a Certified Information Systems Auditor?

I. Analyze systems strategy, policies, and procedures

II. Analyze systems development acquisition and maintenance

III. Evaluate logical, physical, environmental, and data validation controls

A. I and III.

B. I and II.

C. II and III.

D. I, II, and III.

The correct answer is (D). *(CISA, adapted)*

REQUIRED: The responsibilities of an information systems audit unit.

DISCUSSION: According to the Information Systems Audit and Control Association (ISACA), the job content of IS auditors is organized into the following five domains:

Information Systems Audit Standards and Practices and Information Systems Security and Control Practices
Information Systems Organization and Management
Information Systems Process
Information Systems Integrity, Confidentiality, and Availability
Information Systems Development, Acquisition, and Maintenance

Thus, the scope of an IS audit unit is broad and encompasses all of those items listed in the question.

Answers (A), (B), and (C) are incorrect because all are typical responsibilities of a CISA.

296. Which of the following statements best describes the data processing technical requirements for IS auditors? IS auditors should

A. Be as technically proficient as the people they audit.

B. Be able to understand the systems they are auditing.

C. Only possess a limited amount of technical knowledge, mainly in the area of current buzzwords.

D. Only possess a knowledge of auditing and controls.

The correct answer is (B). *(CISA, adapted)*

REQUIRED: The statement that best describes the technical requirements of IS auditors.

DISCUSSION: According to the description of ISACA Job Domain 2, *Information Systems Organization and Management*, IS auditors should analyze and evaluate the information systems (IS) strategy, policies and procedures, management practices, and organization structures.

Answer (A) is incorrect because IS auditors can rely on the work of technical specialists in those areas in which they are not as proficient as the people they are auditing. Answer (C) is incorrect because IS auditors need more than a limited amount of data processing knowledge. IS auditors should understand the systems they are auditing. Answer (D) is incorrect because IS auditors need more than knowledge of auditing and controls. They should understand the data processing systems they are auditing.

297. The first step the IS audit manager should take when preparing the annual IS audit plan is to

A. Meet with the audit committee members to discuss the IS audit plan for the upcoming year.

B. Ensure that the IS audit staff is competent in areas that are likely to appear on the plan and provide training as necessary.

C. Assess the overall risks and develop objectives.

D. Begin with the prior year's IS audit plan and carry over any IS audit steps that have not been completed.

The correct answer is (C). *(CISA, adapted)*

REQUIRED: The first step in the annual audit plan.

DISCUSSION: Domain 1, *Information Systems Audit Standards and Information Systems Security and Control Practices*, describes performing an IS audit. The first step is to "assess the overall risks and then develop an audit program which consists of control objectives and audit procedures which should satisfy those objectives."

Answer (A) is incorrect because the IS audit manager would not meet with the audit committee until a risk analysis of areas of exposure has been completed. Answer (B) is incorrect because the IS audit manager does not know what areas are to appear on the IS audit plan until a risk analysis is completed and discussions are held with the audit committee members. Answer (D) is incorrect because a risk analysis would be the first step before any IS audit effort is expended.

298. In which of the following areas would an internal IS auditor expect to draw upon the work of an external auditor?

A. Safeguarding of company assets.

B. Accuracy and reliability of accounting records.

C. Promotion of operational efficiency.

D. Adherence to company policies and legal obligations.

The correct answer is (B). *(CISA, adapted)*

REQUIRED: The area in which the IS auditor would draw on the work of the external auditor.

DISCUSSION: External auditors express opinions on the fairness of the financial statements. Thus, the internal IS auditor would most likely draw on the work of the external auditor for assurances about the reliability of the accounting records.

Answer (A) is incorrect because an external auditor would not be relied upon to safeguard company assets. Answer (C) is incorrect because external auditors typically do not evaluate operational efficiencies unless specifically engaged to do so. External auditors' procedures are limited to those considered necessary to form an opinion on the fairness of the financial statements. Answer (D) is incorrect because, whereas external auditors may review adherence to company policies and legal obligations in specific situations, their review is limited to those procedures considered necessary to express an audit opinion.

299. Quality assurance includes which of the following activities?

I. Verify that system changes are authorized.

II. Oversee the maintenance of programs.

III. Ensure the appropriate participation by all relevant parties in the revision, evaluation, and dissemination of standards.

IV. Report to management on systems not performing as designed.

A. I and IV.

B. II and III.

C. II, III, and IV.

D. I, II, III, and IV.

The correct answer is (D). *(CISA, adapted)*

REQUIRED: The activities related to quality assurance.

DISCUSSION: Domain 3, *Information Systems Process*, describes the activities of quality assurance personnel to include all those listed.

Answer (A) is incorrect because quality assurance includes oversight of program maintenance and affirmation of the participation of the appropriate personnel in the process of revision, evaluation, and dissemination of standards. Answer (B) is incorrect because quality assurance includes verification that system changes are authorized and that system deviations are reported to management. Answer (C) is incorrect because quality assurance includes verification that system changes are authorized.

300. The audit objective of an IS resource management review is to provide assurance that

A. The IS manager practices effective, efficient, and economic support to the organization's business objectives.

B. Organizational resources of time and money are used in the most economical manner during the acquisition of hardware and software.

C. Appropriate control features are included in systems hardware and software.

D. All tasks have been computerized.

The correct answer is (A). *(CISA, adapted)*

REQUIRED: The audit objective of an IS resource management review.

DISCUSSION: According to Domain 2, *Information Systems Organization and Management*, the objective is to "analyze and evaluate the information systems (IS) strategy, policies and procedures, management practices, and organization structures." Management review includes evaluation of management's actions relating to the use of resources.

Answer (B) is incorrect because the audit objective of an IS resource management review is not limited to acquisition of hardware and software. Answer (C) is incorrect because whether appropriate control features are included in systems hardware and software does not relate to resource management but to control issues. Answer (D) is incorrect because proper processing methods should be evaluated using cost and benefit criteria.

301. A primary purpose of an input-output control module in an operating system is to assure that

A. Read and write requests are properly executed.

B. A record is maintained of all file accesses.

C. Control modules are held to near size.

D. Hardware errors are recorded promptly.

The correct answer is (A). *(CISA, adapted)*

REQUIRED: The purpose of an input-output control module in an operating system.

DISCUSSION: Input-output controls are concerned with the reading and writing of data. They should be used to determine if read and write requests are properly executed.

Answer (B) is incorrect because a console log is used to record file accesses and processing. Answer (C) is incorrect because holding control modules to near size is nonsensical in this context. Answer (D) is incorrect because hardware errors are detected by hardware controls, not by input-output controls.

302. In a public key encryption system, knowledge of which of the following keys would be required to decode the received message?

I. Private II. Public

A. I.

B. II.

C. Both I and II.

D. Neither I nor II.

The correct answer is (A). *(CISA, adapted)*

REQUIRED: The key(s) required to decode messages in a public key system.

DISCUSSION: In a public key system, the public key is used to encrypt the message prior to transmission, whereas the private key is needed to decrypt (decode) the message.

Answer (B) is incorrect because the private key, not the public key, is needed to decrypt (decode) the message. Answer (C) is incorrect because the public key is not needed. Answer (D) is incorrect because the private key is needed to decrypt (decode) the message.

303. Which of the following types of transmission media are most secure against unauthorized access or tapping?

A. Copper wire.

B. Twisted pair.

C. Fiber-optic cables.

D. Coaxial cables.

The correct answer is (C). *(CISA, adapted)*

REQUIRED: The most secure transmission medium.

DISCUSSION: Fiber-optic cables have been proven to be more tamper resistant than the other media listed. Optical transmissions cannot be wiretapped.

Answers (A), (B), and (D) are incorrect because copper wire, twisted pair, and coaxial cables can be tapped easily with inexpensive equipment.

304. Each of the following statements about distributed data processing (DDP) systems is true except

A. From the IS auditor's perspective, it is a desirable trend in DDP systems design to off-load operating system and communication functions from software into hardware or microcode.

B. DDP systems are essentially unauditable because of the complexity of network software.

C. DDP systems increase the need for effective risk analysis.

D. An important design goal of DDP systems is to provide more power and flexibility to the end users even though inadequate controls may exist in some of the end-user software.

The correct answer is (B). *(CISA, adapted)*

REQUIRED: The false statement concerning DDP systems.

DISCUSSION: Technical complexity is not a valid reason for failing to audit a processing system. The IS auditor should have sufficient technical knowledge and training to audit complex networks.

Answer (A) is incorrect because hardware or microcode functions have the advantage of being less prone to unauthorized modification than software. Answer (C) is incorrect because processing may be distributed to numerous user areas, each with varied risk levels and degrees of control, requiring an effective risk analysis methodology to ensure adequate audit coverage for critical functions. Answer (D) is incorrect because end-user software is usually designed for rapid development and ease of modification. It could be susceptible to errors in the hands of an inexperienced user.

305. An IS auditor is called as an expert witness by the plaintiff in litigation involving the misuses of a service bureau's computer by an unauthorized individual who used another's password to manipulate data. The IS auditor's testimony regarding security issues should include descriptions of each of the following except the

A. Access control.

B. Method of assignment of passwords.

C. Methods that could prevent similar misuse.

D. Controls that were overridden to gain access.

The correct answer is (C). *(CISA, adapted)*

REQUIRED: The inappropriate testimony by an IS auditor in a case involving unauthorized access to a plaintiff's files.

DISCUSSION: The IS auditor is not likely to be able to provide testimony that another method of control would have prevented the unauthorized action. Such testimony would be mere speculation by the auditor.

Answer (A) is incorrect because access control concerns procedures germane to the litigation. The auditor's assessments will be important to the plaintiff's case. Answer (B) is incorrect because the method of assignment of passwords is germane to the litigation. Answer (D) is incorrect because controls that were overridden to gain access are germane to the litigation.

306. A data center with online communications, a database management system, access control software, and a sophisticated network installed is planning its first test at the hotsite. The first test should include recovery of

A. All systems and application software.

B. Only the operating system.

C. All system software and the network.

D. Only the access control software.

The correct answer is (B). *(CISA, adapted)*

REQUIRED: The purpose of an initial test at a data center's hotsite.

DISCUSSION: A hotsite is the service bureau where a data center will obtain processing services in case of a disaster. The more common commercial hotsites limit the amount of time a subscriber can be present to perform testing. Thus, an organization's best approach is to first attempt to recover the operating system because it is the nucleus of all processing.

Answers (A), (C), and (D) are incorrect because the operating system should be recovered before other software, the network, and the access control software.

307. Which of the following is of most concern when contracting for a hotsite as the alternative processing facility?

A. The number of other subscribers to the hotsite.

B. Possession by the hotsite of the most current version of the operating software.

C. Location of the hotsite's offsite storage facility.

D. Number of years the hotsite has been in operation.

The correct answer is (A). *(CISA, adapted)*

REQUIRED: The item of most concern when contracting for a hotsite.

DISCUSSION: The number of other subscribers would affect the availability of facilities at the hotsite. The computer resources provided should be adequate to perform necessary processing.

Answer (B) is incorrect because, if the last update to the operating system is very recent, the hotsite may not have upgraded to it. Hence, the company would not want to deal with upgrading the operating system during recovery. Answer (C) is incorrect because assurance as to adequate protection of files, rather than the location of the hotsite's offsite storage facility, would be of concern. Answer (D) is incorrect because capabilities of a hotsite would be of greater concern.

308. The critical recovery time period is the length of time

A. The company will process at the alternative site before returning to the data center.

B. The company can do without IS services before business is significantly affected.

C. Covered by the offsite rotation cycle for backup files.

D. The recovery team will need to work together in a disaster condition.

The correct answer is (B). *(CISA, adapted)*

REQUIRED: The definition of critical recovery time.

DISCUSSION: The critical recovery time period is the time in which the company must recover IS services before the disaster has a significant negative effect on its ability to continue in existence.

Answer (A) is incorrect because the time the company will process at the alternative site before returning to the data center is less critical than the time the company can do without IS services before business is significantly affected. Answer (C) is incorrect because the time covered by the offsite rotation cycle for backup files is less critical than the time the company can do without IS services before business is significantly affected. Answer (D) is incorrect because the time the recovery team will need to work together in a disaster condition is less critical than the time the company can do without IS services before business is significantly affected.

309. Which of the following are features of security software packages?

I. Provision of an audit trail
II. Backup of critical files
III. Establishment of various levels of protection
IV. Monitoring of accesses to protected resources

A. I and IV.

B. II and III.

C. I, III, and IV.

D. I, II, III, and IV.

The correct answer is (C). *(CISA, adapted)*

REQUIRED: The control features included in security software packages.

DISCUSSION: Security software packages typically provide safeguards over unauthorized access and use of hardware and software. Passwords, console logs, dial-up/callback are techniques used to protect an installation.

Answer (A) is incorrect because establishment of various levels of protection is also a feature of security software packages. Answer (B) is incorrect because security software packages do not provide for backing up critical files. However, there may be a feature for backing up the security software files. Answer (D) is incorrect because security software packages do not provide for backing up critical files.

310. The IS auditor finds that data communications are subject to message encryption and that effective controls have been designed for the encryption and decryption processes. Based on this finding, tests of controls should be carried out to ensure that

A. The network has an effective mechanism for determining whether all parts of a message sent are received.

B. The X.25 interface standard is being correctly applied during encryption and decryption.

C. Authorized encryption and decryption procedures are being adhered to in practice.

D. Messages sent by way of satellite transmissions are not dispersed over too wide a receiving area.

The correct answer is (C). *(CISA, adapted)*

REQUIRED: The purpose of compliance tests (tests of controls).

DISCUSSION: Tests of controls evaluate the effectiveness of the design or operation of controls. The auditor has concluded that the encryption controls have been adequately designed, but tests must be conducted to see if they are being applied as intended.

Answer (A) is incorrect because testing to ensure that the network has an effective mechanism for determining whether all parts of a message sent are received can be performed during the evaluation of the design of the controls. Answer (B) is incorrect because the X.25 interface standard is only one of many controls that should be tested for effectiveness. Answer (D) is incorrect because determining that messages sent by way of satellite transmissions are not dispersed over too wide a receiving area is only one of many tests of effectiveness that should be performed.

311. An appropriate control technique for a data communications security review is to ensure that

A. Messages transmitted over secure media are always encrypted.

B. User authentication mechanisms are used with stand-alone microcomputer installations.

C. Telecommunication system commands can be entered only from the master console.

D. Sensitive messages are always transmitted bit by bit, enclosed between a start bit and a stop bit.

The correct answer is (C). *(CISA, adapted)*

REQUIRED: The appropriate technique for a data communications security review.

DISCUSSION: To assure security, systems commands should be made only from the master control console. In addition, a computer-generated log should be maintained of all systems modifications.

Answer (A) is incorrect because encryption may not be cost beneficial for nonsensitive data. Answer (B) is incorrect because user authentication mechanisms should be used on all systems, not just microcomputer installations. Answer (D) is incorrect because transmissions are usually in packets of data rather than bit by bit.

312. As transactions to update an online sales order system are processed, the transactions are copied to tape file. At the end of the day, the sales order entry disk files are copied to a backup tape. During the backup procedure, the disk file containing the sales order system failed, and the file was lost. Which, if any, of the following are required to restore the online sales order system?

I. The previous day's backup file
II. The previous day's transaction file
III. The current day's transaction file
IV. None. The system cannot be restored.

A. IV only.

B. I and III.

C. I and II.

D. I, II, and III.

The correct answer is (B). *(CISA, adapted)*

REQUIRED: The file(s) required to restore the online sales order system.

DISCUSSION: The previous day's backup will be the most current backup of the result of processing up until that time. The current day's transaction file will contain all of the activity since that time. The combination of those two files will allow restoration of the system.

Answer (A) is incorrect because restoration is possible. Answers (C) and (D) are incorrect because the previous day's transaction file includes the activity that has been included on the previous day's system backup file.

313. Why would the IS auditor of a company that is considering contracting its data processing needs to a service bureau request a copy of each candidate bureau's financial statements?

A. To evaluate the fairness of each service bureau's charges on the basis of relative profit margins.

B. To determine whether each service bureau is affiliated with a company that might represent a conflict of interests.

C. To evaluate each service bureau's financial stability and ability to fulfill the contract.

D. To obtain an understanding of the processing performed by each service bureau and the controls within the system.

The correct answer is (C). *(CISA, adapted)*

REQUIRED: The purpose of requesting financial statements from a service bureau.

DISCUSSION: A primary concern of a company contracting for its data processing needs is whether the service bureau has the financial stability to perform its contract. One means of assessing financial stability is to analyze the bureau's financial statements.

Answer (A) is incorrect because the financial statements do not disclose the relative profit margins by types of service provided. Answer (B) is incorrect because the financial statements are not the best source of such information. Answer (D) is incorrect because marketing literature of the service bureau provides a description of the services offered.

314. The results of a generalized audit software simulation of the aging of accounts receivable revealed substantial differences in the aging distribution although grand totals reconciled. Which of the following should the IS auditor do first to resolve the discrepancy?

A. Recreate the test, using different software.

B. List a sample of actual data to verify the accuracy of the test program.

C. Ignore the discrepancy because the grand totals reconcile and instruct the controller to correct the program.

D. Create test transactions and run test data on both the production and simulation programs.

The correct answer is (B). *(CISA, adapted)*

REQUIRED: The first step an IS auditor should take when illogical results are obtained from a GAS package.

DISCUSSION: Actual data are easily obtained and can be compared with the aging schedule to assess the integrity of the simulation program's logic.

Answer (A) is incorrect because only if it were determined that the program was corrupted would substitute software be required. Answer (C) is incorrect because the auditor has reason to believe that errors may exist and should determine the reasons for the discrepancy. Answer (D) is incorrect because this expensive procedure will not be justified until the data from the simulation have been checked.

CHAPTER SIX
STATISTICAL SAMPLING

This chapter covers statistical sampling applications to auditing. Statistical sampling permits auditors to measure and control the risk associated with examining only a part (a sample) of the items (the population) under audit.

Consider the following when performing a **test of controls** involving sampling:

1. Planning the sample requires consideration of the
   a. Relation of the sample to the objective of the test
   b. Tolerable rate of deviations that would support the assessed level of control risk
   c. Allowable risk of assessing control risk too low
   d. Characteristics of the population
2. Sample selection should be representative, and all items should have an opportunity to be selected.
3. Performance and Evaluation
   a. The effects of limitations on tests of controls should be considered.
   b. The sample deviation rate is the best estimate of the population deviation rate.
   c. If the sample does not support the planned assessed level of control risk for an assertion, the nature, timing, and extent of substantive tests may need to be reevaluated.

Consider the following when performing a **substantive test** involving sampling:

1. Planning the sample requires consideration of
   a. The relevant audit objectives and characteristics of the population
   b. Preliminary materiality judgments as to tolerable misstatement
   c. Allowable risk of incorrect acceptance for the substantive test of details
2. Sample selection should be conducted so that the sample represents the population. Consequently, all items should have an opportunity to be chosen.
3. Performance and Evaluation
   a. Appropriate audit procedures are applied to each sample item.
   b. The auditor must project the quantitative misstatement results of the sample to the population and compare it with tolerable misstatement.
   c. Projected misstatements, known misstatements detected by nonsampling tests, and other audit evidence should be considered in the aggregate in determining whether the financial statements are materially misstated.

NOTE ON TERMINOLOGY

Textbooks, firm literature, and auditing standards often use different vocabulary for the same concept. Also, professional exams and accounting professors have not been consistent in their use of terminology. However, if you study the questions and answer explanations in this chapter, you should be able to cope effectively with differences among terms you encounter. The two terms defined below cause considerable misunderstanding.

Confidence level or reliability is the estimated percentage of repeated simple random samples of size n that will adequately represent a normally distributed population. Thus, a confidence level of 90% means that samples should adequately represent the population about 90% of the time. Confidence level is related to audit risk because the auditor is accepting a risk of 10% (100% – 90%) that the sample will not represent the population.

In sampling for variables (substantive testing), the primary concern is "the risk of incorrect acceptance," or "the risk that the sample supports the conclusion that the recorded account balance is not materially misstated when it is materially misstated" (AU 350, *Audit Sampling*). In sampling for attributes (tests of controls), the primary concern is "the risk of assessing control risk too low," or "the risk that the assessed level of control risk based on the sample is less than the true operating effectiveness of the control." These wrong conclusions relate to effectiveness issues. They are termed Type II or beta errors.

Precision or confidence interval (allowance for sampling risk) is an interval around the sample statistic (for example, the mean) that is expected to contain the true value of the population. In principle, given repeated sampling and a normally distributed population, the confidence level is the percentage of all the precision intervals that may be constructed from simple random samples of size n that will include the population value. In practice, the confidence level is regarded as the probability that a precision interval will contain the population value.

The estimated size of the precision interval is based upon the tolerable deviation rate for a test of controls. In sampling for attributes (tests of controls), precision may be estimated by subtracting the expected deviation rate from the tolerable rate in the population.

In sampling for variables (substantive testing), planned precision is determined by considering tolerable misstatement in conjunction with the risks of incorrect acceptance and incorrect rejection. Tolerable misstatement should not exceed the auditor's preliminary judgments about materiality. The risk of incorrect acceptance is defined above. The risk of incorrect rejection is defined as "the risk that the sample supports the conclusion that the recorded account balance is materially misstated when it is not materially misstated" (a Type I or alpha error). The risk of incorrect rejection relates to efficiency issues because the auditor will likely continue auditing until the balance is finally supported. A table is typically consulted to determine the appropriate precision as a percentage of tolerable misstatement.

The following symbols and abbreviations are used in this chapter:

P	-- required precision interval	$\bar{x}$	-- mean of a sample
C	-- confidence coefficient	FPC	-- finite population correction factor
σ	-- (sigma) population standard deviation	Σ	-- summation symbol
s	-- sample standard deviation	AR	-- allowable audit risk
p	-- deviation rate	CR	-- control risk
q	-- 100% minus p	TD	-- allowable risk of incorrect acceptance for a test of details
n	-- sample size	AP	-- detection risk for analytical procedures and other relevant substantive tests of details
N	-- population size	IR	-- inherent risk
μ	-- population mean or average		
x	-- an observed value		

6.1 Purpose and Rationale of Statistical Sampling

1. AU 350, *Audit Sampling*, identifies two general approaches to audit sampling. They are

A. Random and nonrandom.

B. Statistical and nonstatistical.

C. Precision and reliability.

D. Risk and nonrisk.

The correct answer is (B). *(Publisher)*

REQUIRED: The two approaches to audit sampling.

DISCUSSION: Statistical sampling allows the auditor to control and measure risk associated with observing only a portion of a population. However, the choice of nonstatistical or statistical sampling does not directly affect the auditor's decisions about the auditing procedures to be applied, the competence of the evidence obtained with respect to sample items, or the actions that might be taken given the nature and causes of particular misstatements. Either approach, properly applied, can provide sufficient competent evidence.

Answer (A) is incorrect because random selection is necessary in statistical sampling so that the sample will represent the population. Answer (C) is incorrect because precision is the allowance for sampling risk, and reliability is the degree to which the sample is expected to be representative. Answer (D) is incorrect because all sampling involves risk.

2. In a sampling application, the group of items about which the auditor wants to estimate some characteristic is called the

A. Population.

B. Attribute of interest.

C. Sample.

D. Sampling unit.

The correct answer is (A). *(CIA, adapted)*

REQUIRED: The group of items about which an auditor wants to draw conclusions.

DISCUSSION: The population is the group of items about which an auditor wishes to draw conclusions. However, the difference between the targeted population (the population about which information is desired) and the sampled population (the population from which the sample is actually drawn) should be understood.

Answer (B) is incorrect because the attribute is the characteristic of the population the auditor wants to estimate. Answer (C) is incorrect because the sample is a subset of the population used to estimate the characteristic. Answer (D) is incorrect because a sampling unit is the item that is actually selected for examination. It is a subset of the population.

3. An advantage of statistical sampling over non-statistical sampling is that statistical sampling helps an auditor to

A. Minimize the failure to detect errors and fraud.

B. Eliminate nonsampling risk.

C. Reduce the level of audit risk and materiality to a relatively low amount.

D. Measure the sufficiency of the evidential matter obtained.

The correct answer is (D). *(CPA, adapted)*

REQUIRED: The advantage of statistical sampling.

DISCUSSION: Statistical sampling helps the auditor to design an efficient sample, to measure the sufficiency of the evidence obtained, and to evaluate the sample results. The third standard of field work requires auditors to obtain sufficient competent evidence. Sufficiency relates to the design and size of the sample. Statistical sampling permits the auditors to measure sampling risk and therefore to design more efficient samples, that is, samples of a size necessary to provide sufficient evidence.

Answer (A) is incorrect because, in some circumstances, professional judgment may indicate that nonstatistical methods are preferable to minimize the failure to detect errors and fraud. Answer (B) is incorrect because statistical sampling is irrelevant to nonsampling risk. Answer (C) is incorrect because statistical sampling does not reduce materiality.

4. When using sampling for substantive tests of details, the auditor must do all but which of the following?

A. Determine the tolerable misstatement.

B. Project sample misstatement results to the population.

C. Compute the sample standard deviation.

D. Select a representative sample.

The correct answer is (C). *(J. Swearingen)*

REQUIRED: The procedure not required in sampling.

DISCUSSION: AU 350 does not require that the sample standard deviation be calculated. The computation would be necessary if parametric statistical sampling were used, but statistical sampling is not required by AU 350.

Answer (A) is incorrect because evaluation in monetary terms of the sample results is related to the auditor's judgments. The maximum monetary misstatement that does not cause the financial statements to be materially misstated is the tolerable misstatement. An estimate of tolerable misstatement is vital to planning the audit. Answer (B) is incorrect because AU 350 requires that misstatement projected from the sample be compared with tolerable misstatement, with appropriate consideration given to sampling risk. Answer (D) is incorrect because AU 350 also requires that samples be representative. Thus, all population items should have an opportunity to be chosen.

5. The application of statistical sampling techniques is least related to which of the following generally accepted auditing standards?

A. The work is to be adequately planned and assistants, if any, are to be properly supervised.

B. In all matters relating to the assignment, an independence in mental attitude is to be maintained by the auditor.

C. A sufficient understanding of internal control is to be obtained to plan the audit and to determine the nature, timing, and extent of tests to be performed.

D. Sufficient competent evidential matter is to be obtained through inspection, observation, inquiries, and confirmations to afford a reasonable basis for an opinion regarding the financial statements under audit.

The correct answer is (B). *(CPA, adapted)*

REQUIRED: The standard to which statistical sampling is least related.

DISCUSSION: The second general standard (independence) concerns the mental attitude to be maintained by an auditor in all matters pertaining to the assignment. The application of statistical sampling techniques is more closely related to the standards of field work.

Answer (A) is incorrect because auditors should plan to use statistical sampling and supervise its implementation. Answer (C) is incorrect because statistical methods may be used for tests of controls as well as substantive tests. Answer (D) is incorrect because GAAS contemplate the use of statistical techniques in gathering evidential matter.

6. An auditor suspects that the invoices from a small number of vendors contain serious misstatements and therefore limits the sample to those vendors only. A major disadvantage of selecting such a directed sample of items to examine is the

A. Difficulty in obtaining sample items.

B. Inability to quantify the sampling error related to the total population of vendor invoices.

C. Absence of a normal distribution.

D. Tendency to sample a greater number of units.

The correct answer is (B). *(CIA, adapted)*

REQUIRED: The disadvantage of a directed sample.

DISCUSSION: Judgment sampling uses the auditor's subjective judgment to determine the sample size (number of items examined) and sample selection (which items to examine). This subjectivity is not always a weakness. The auditor, based on other audit work, may be able to test the most material and risky transactions and to emphasize the types of transactions subject to high control risk. Probability (random) sampling provides an objective method of determining sample size and selecting the items to be examined. Unlike judgment sampling, it also provides a means of quantitatively assessing precision and reliability.

Answer (A) is incorrect because obtaining invoices for a small number of vendors should be simple. Answer (C) is incorrect because the sampling distribution is expected to be normal even if the population distribution is not. Answer (D) is incorrect because judgment sampling provides no objective means for determining the appropriate sample size. Thus, it has no tendency to sample a greater number of units.

6.2 Sampling Concepts

7. If the size of the sample to be used in a particular test of attributes has not been determined by using statistical concepts, but the sample has been chosen in accordance with random selection procedures,

A. No inferences can be drawn from the sample.

B. The auditor has caused nonsampling risk to increase.

C. The auditor may or may not achieve desired precision at the desired level of confidence.

D. The auditor will have to evaluate the results by reference to the principles of discovery sampling.

The correct answer is (C). *(CPA, adapted)*

REQUIRED: The significance of choosing sample size without regard to statistical concepts.

DISCUSSION: According to the sample size formula for attribute sampling, the size of an attribute sample is a function of the auditor's desired precision, his/her desired level of confidence, the expected deviation rate, and the size of the population. When the auditor does not use these criteria to determine sample size, (s)he runs a risk of not meeting the audit objectives.

Answer (A) is incorrect because inferences can be drawn from both statistical and nonstatistical samples. Answer (B) is incorrect because nonsampling risk includes all aspects of audit risk not arising from sampling, e.g., misapplying a procedure or choosing an inappropriate procedure. Answer (D) is incorrect because discovery sampling is a special form of attribute sampling used to discover critical deviations.

8. An auditee uses statistical sampling in the taking of its physical inventory. The independent external auditor should

A. Either observe a statistical inventory count each year or qualify or disclaim an opinion.

B. Either observe a complete inventory count sometime during the year and become satisfied that the statistical procedures are valid or qualify or disclaim an opinion.

C. Observe such test counts as (s)he deems necessary and become satisfied with the statistical validity of the sample, the precision, and the confidence level.

D. Insist that the company take a complete physical inventory annually and observe the count.

The correct answer is (C). *(Publisher)*

REQUIRED: The responsibility of an auditor regarding statistical sampling in the taking of physical inventory.

DISCUSSION: Statistical methods for determining inventory quantities are sufficiently reliable to make a complete annual physical count unnecessary. However, "the auditor must be satisfied that the sampling plan is reasonable and statistically valid, that it has been properly applied, and that the results are reasonable in the circumstances." The auditor should still make or observe test counts as (s)he deems necessary (AU 331, *Inventories*).

Answer (A) is incorrect because the auditor must be present only to observe such test counts as (s)he deems necessary and must be satisfied as to the effectiveness of the counting procedures used. Answer (B) is incorrect because observation of a complete count may not be necessary. Answer (D) is incorrect because, if the auditor determines the statistical plan to be valid, etc., (s)he will not insist that the client take a complete annual physical inventory.

9. To quantify the risk that sample evidence leads to erroneous conclusions about the sampled population,

A. Each item in the sampled population must have an equal chance of being selected.

B. Each item in the sampled population must have a chance of being selected that is proportional to its book value.

C. Each item in the sampled population must have an equal or known probability of being selected.

D. The precise number of items in the population must be known.

The correct answer is (C). *(CIA, adapted)*

REQUIRED: The requirement for quantifying sampling risk.

DISCUSSION: Probability (random) sampling is used in any sampling plan in which every item in the population has an equal (or known) and nonzero probability of being chosen. A probability sample permits the use of statistical methods based on the laws of probability to quantify an estimate of sampling risk.

Answer (A) is incorrect because sampling risk can be quantified when purely random sampling is not used if the probability of selection is known and nonzero. Stratified random sampling is an example. Answer (B) is incorrect because each item in the sampled population must have a chance of being selected that is proportional to its book value in dollar-unit sampling, but this characteristic does not apply to other methods. Answer (D) is incorrect because sampling risk for an infinite population is quantifiable.

10. Each time an auditor draws a conclusion based on evidence from a sample, an additional risk, sampling risk, is introduced. An example of sampling risk is

A. Projecting the results of sampling beyond the population tested.

B. Properly applying an improper audit procedure to sample data.

C. Improperly applying a proper audit procedure to sample data.

D. Drawing an erroneous conclusion from sample data.

The correct answer is (D). *(CIA, adapted)*

REQUIRED: The example of sampling risk.

DISCUSSION: Sampling risk arises from the possibility that the conclusion drawn may differ from that reached if the test had been applied to all items in the population. It is the risk that a particular sample may contain proportionately more or fewer monetary misstatements or deviations from prescribed controls than exist in the balance or class as a whole (AU 350).

Answer (A) is incorrect because sample results are relevant only to the population tested. Improper projection of results is a nonsampling risk. Answers (B) and (C) are incorrect because sampling risk arises even though the proper procedure is correctly applied and the results are evaluated appropriately. Thus, choice of the wrong procedure and improper application of the right procedure are nonsampling risks.

11. Several risks are inherent in the evaluation of audit evidence that has been obtained through the use of statistical sampling. An example of a beta or Type II error related to sampling risk is the failure to

A. Properly define the population to be sampled.

B. Draw a random sample from the population.

C. Reject the statistical hypothesis that a book value is not materially misstated when the true book value is materially misstated.

D. Accept the statistical hypothesis that a book value is not materially misstated when the true book value is not materially misstated.

The correct answer is (C). *(CIA, adapted)*

REQUIRED: The example of beta or Type II error.

DISCUSSION: In hypothesis testing, the rejection of a true hypothesis is an alpha or Type I error. Failure to reject a false hypothesis is a beta or Type II error. Both kinds of errors are aspects of sampling risk. Incorrect acceptance, for example, is a beta or Type II error. If an account balance is erroneously accepted as fairly stated based upon a sample, additional audit work and the chances of exposing the mistake will probably be minimal. Hence, a beta error is more serious than an alpha (Type I) error (incorrect rejection leading to further audit work).

Answer (A) is incorrect because sampling risk is defined narrowly as the risk that audit conclusions based on a sample may differ from those based on testing all items in a population. Nonsampling risk consists of all other aspects of audit risk. Thus, the risk of mistakes in taking a sample is an aspect of nonsampling risk. Answer (B) is incorrect because failure to draw a random sample is related to nonsampling risk. Answer (D) is incorrect because incorrect rejection of a value is an alpha error.

12. A confidence level of 90% means that

A. The expected deviation rate is equal to 10%.

B. The point estimate obtained is within 10% of the true population value.

C. The probability is 90% that the sample results will not vary from the true characteristics of the population by more than a specified amount.

D. A larger sample size is required than if the desired confidence level were equal to 95%.

The correct answer is (C). *(CIA, adapted)*

REQUIRED: The meaning of a 90% confidence level.

DISCUSSION: A 90% confidence level signifies that, in repeated sampling from a normally distributed population, the precision intervals constructed around the results of simple random samples of size n will contain the true population value approximately 90% of the time.

Answers (A) and (B) are incorrect because the confidence level is a probability, not a deviation rate or a range of values. For attribute sampling (used in tests of controls), the complement of a 90% confidence level is a 10% risk of assessing control risk too low. For variables sampling (used in substantive testing), the complement of a 90% confidence level is a 10% risk of incorrect rejection. Answer (D) is incorrect because a smaller sample is required if the desired confidence level is 90% rather than 95%.

13. When planning a sample for a substantive test of details, an auditor should consider tolerable misstatement for the sample. This consideration should

A. Be related to the auditor's business risk.

B. Not be adjusted for qualitative factors.

C. Be related to preliminary judgments about materiality levels.

D. Not be changed during the audit process.

The correct answer is (C). *(CPA, adapted)*

REQUIRED: The true statement about tolerable misstatement.

DISCUSSION: When planning a sample for substantive tests, the auditor should consider how much monetary misstatement in the related account balance or class of transactions may exist without causing the financial statements to be materially misstated. This maximum monetary misstatement is the tolerable misstatement for the sample. It is used in audit planning to determine the necessary precision and sample size. Tolerable misstatement, combined for the entire audit plan, should not exceed the auditor's preliminary judgments about materiality (AU 350).

Answer (A) is incorrect because the auditor's business risk is irrelevant. Answer (B) is incorrect because qualitative factors should be considered; for example, the nature and cause of misstatements and their relationship to other phases of the audit. Answer (D) is incorrect because, if sample results suggest that planning assumptions were unsound, the auditor should take appropriate action.

14. As lower acceptable levels of both audit risk and materiality are established, the auditor should plan more work on individual accounts to

A. Find smaller misstatements.

B. Find larger misstatements.

C. Increase the tolerable misstatement in the accounts.

D. Decrease the risk of assessing control risk too low.

The correct answer is (A). *(CPA, adapted)*

REQUIRED: The result of lowering acceptable audit risk and materiality.

DISCUSSION: A lower acceptable level of materiality means that the tolerable misstatement in an account is smaller. As a result, the auditor must plan for a larger sample size and therefore more audit work on the accounts to discover smaller misstatements. Moreover, the lower the allowable audit risk that tolerable misstatement will be undetected after the auditor has completed all procedures deemed necessary, the lower the allowable risk of incorrect acceptance, and the greater the required sample size.

Answer (B) is incorrect because the auditor should plan to find smaller misstatements. Answer (C) is incorrect because, as the size of a material misstatement decreases, the level of tolerable misstatement decreases. Answer (D) is incorrect because, during substantive testing of an account balance, the auditor is ultimately concerned with decreasing the risk of incorrectly accepting the balance. Tests of controls, not substantive tests, are designed to decrease the risk of assessing control risk too low.

15. In statistical sampling for variables, setting the appropriate confidence level and desired sample precision are decisions made by the auditor that will affect sample size for a substantive test. Which of the following should not be a factor in the choice of desired precision?

A. The sampling risk.

B. The size of an account balance misstatement considered material.

C. The audit resources available for execution of the sampling plan.

D. The objectives of the audit test being conducted.

The correct answer is (C). *(CIA, adapted)*

REQUIRED: The factor not considered when selecting desired precision.

DISCUSSION: The basic sample size equation for variables sampling is

$$n = \frac{C^2\sigma^2}{P^2}$$

P is the average precision (per item in the population), C is the confidence coefficient, σ is the population standard deviation, and n is the sample size. C is the number of standard deviations in the standard normal distribution that corresponds to the specified confidence level. Thus, it controls sampling risk. The tolerable misstatement is related to materiality judgments. It determines the estimated precision. A table is ordinarily consulted to determine precision as a percentage of tolerable misstatement. The objective of the audit sample affects both sampling risk and precision. The audit resources available determine whether the test will be undertaken but should not affect the process once the audit procedure is undertaken.

Answers (A), (B), and (D) are incorrect because sampling risk, materiality, and the objectives of the audit test are factors in calculating desired precision.

16. An auditor's statistical sample drawn from a population of invoices indicates a mean value of $150 and sampling precision of ± $30 at a 95% confidence level. Which of the following statements correctly interprets these sample data?

A. In repeated sampling, the point estimate of the true population mean will be $150 about 95% of the time.

B. The probability is 95% that the true population mean is $150.

C. In repeated sampling, intervals with precision ± $30 around the sample mean will always contain the true population mean.

D. The probability is 95% that the range $120 to $180 contains the true population mean.

The correct answer is (D). *(CIA, adapted)*

REQUIRED: The interpretation of the sample data.

DISCUSSION: The relationship between the estimated mean, the precision interval, and the confidence level is that the auditor can state, at the desired confidence level given a simple random sample of size n taken from a normally distributed population, that the precision interval (the sample mean ± the precision amount) contains the true population mean. Here, the auditor is 95% confident that the interval $120 to $180 ($150 ± $30) contains the true population mean.

Answer (A) is incorrect because repeated samples will result in many different point estimates. Answer (B) is incorrect because the probability is 95% that the range $120 to $180 contains the true population value, not that this value is equal to the point estimate of $150. Answer (C) is incorrect because the probability is 95%, not 100%.

17. Which one of the following statements is true regarding two random samples drawn in the same way from the same population, one of size 30 and one of size 300?

A. The two samples would have the same expected value.

B. The larger sample is more likely to produce a large sample mean.

C. The smaller sample will have a smaller 95% confidence interval for the mean.

D. The smaller sample will, on the average, produce a lower estimate of the variance of the population.

The correct answer is (A). *(CIA, adapted)*

REQUIRED: The true statement about random samples of different size.

DISCUSSION: The expected value of a random sample of any size is equal to the population mean.

Answer (B) is incorrect because the larger sample is more reliable but both samples will produce an unbiased estimate of the population mean. Answer (C) is incorrect because the smaller sample is less reliable and therefore will have a wider 95% confidence interval. Answer (D) is incorrect because the variance is also a population parameter, and the expected value of the sample variance does not change with sample size.

18. The accounting department reports the accounts payable balance as $175,000. You are willing to accept that balance if it is within $15,000 of the actual balance. Using a variables sampling plan, you compute a 95% confidence interval of $173,000 to $190,000. You would therefore

A. Find it impossible to determine the acceptability of the balance.

B. Accept the balance but with a lower level of confidence.

C. Take a larger sample before totally rejecting the balance and requiring adjustments.

D. Accept the $175,000 balance because the confidence interval is within the materiality limits.

The correct answer is (D). *(CIA, adapted)*

REQUIRED: The conclusion regarding a balance that is within the computed confidence interval.

DISCUSSION: The auditor is willing to accept the book value if it is within $15,000 (the tolerable misstatement) of the population value. The sample mean used to estimate the population value must be $181,500 [($173,000 + $190,000) ÷ 2] because it is at the midpoint of the computed (achieved) confidence interval (precision). This interval is based on a precision (± $8,500) that is well within the tolerable misstatement (materiality limits) of ± $15,000. Thus, the auditor should accept the $175,000 value. The interval based on tolerable misstatement and the narrower achieved precision limits contain this value.

Answers (A) and (B) are incorrect because the achieved confidence interval ($173,000 to $190,000) contains the accounts payable balance at the 95% confidence level. Answer (C) is incorrect because the auditor does not need to take a larger sample. The book value is acceptable based on the initial sample.

19. The measure of variability of a statistical sample that serves as an estimate of the population variability is the

A. Basic precision.

B. Range.

C. Standard deviation.

D. Confidence interval.

The correct answer is (C). *(CIA, adapted)*

REQUIRED: The measure of population variability.

DISCUSSION: Variability (dispersion) is measured by the variance, standard deviation, quartile deviations, range, etc., of a sample or population. The population standard deviation (σ) is a measure of the degree of compactness of values. It is used to determine appropriate sample sizes. Given that N equals population size, μ is the population mean, and x_i is an observed value of a population item, the formula is

$$\sigma = \sqrt{\frac{\sum (x_i - \mu)^2}{N}}$$

Answer (A) is incorrect because basic precision is the range around the sample value that is expected to contain the true population value. Answer (B) is incorrect because the range is the difference between the largest and smallest values in a sample. It is a crude measure of variability but is not used to estimate population variability. Answer (D) is incorrect because confidence interval is a synonym for precision.

20. The variability of a population, as measured by the standard deviation, is the

A. Extent to which the individual values of the items in the population are spread about the mean.

B. Degree of asymmetry of a distribution.

C. Tendency of the means of large samples (at least 30 items) to be normally distributed.

D. Measure of the closeness of a sample estimate to a corresponding population characteristic.

The correct answer is (A). *(CIA, adapted)*

REQUIRED: The definition of standard deviation.

DISCUSSION: Standard deviation is a mathematical measure (denoted by σ) of the dispersion of items in a population about its mean.

Answer (B) is incorrect because skewness or asymmetry means that extreme values at one end of the distribution are not balanced by large values at the other end. Answer (C) is incorrect because the central limit theorem states that the distribution of sample means for large samples should be normally distributed even if the underlying population is not. Answer (D) is incorrect because precision is the interval about the sample value that is expected to contain the true value of the population.

21. The concept of standard deviation is significant in statistical sampling because

A. The central limit theorem states that repeated samples from a population will produce sample standard deviations that cluster around the actual standard deviation of the population.

B. The sample size for variables estimation is directly related to the magnitude of the population standard deviation.

C. The magnitude of the finite population correction factor is directly related to the magnitude of the standard deviation of the population.

D. Statistical sampling is inappropriate if the standard deviation is very small relative to the mean of the population.

The correct answer is (B). *(CIA, adapted)*

REQUIRED: The significance of the standard deviation.

DISCUSSION: The standard deviation is used in the formula for the calculation of sample size in variables sampling applications. The formula is

$$n = \frac{C^2\sigma^2}{P^2}$$

n is the sample size, C is the confidence coefficient, σ is the standard deviation of the population, and P is the average precision (per item in the population) specified by the auditor. As the population dispersion increases, so does the required sample size.

Answer (A) is incorrect because the central limit theorem relates to means, not standard deviations, of samples. Answer (C) is incorrect because the finite population correction factor is used to adjust the sample size for small populations. Answer (D) is incorrect because, if the standard deviation of the population is small, the result is very accurate estimation.

22. The standard deviation of the population is required in the sample size determination formula. However, the true value for the standard deviation of the population is not likely to be known. The auditor usually employs an estimate of this value based upon all the following except

A. A pre-sample.

B. The prior year's audit.

C. The available book values.

D. Inquiries of management.

The correct answer is (D). *(Publisher)*

REQUIRED: The item not involved in estimating the standard deviation of the population.

DISCUSSION: Although inquiries of management are important, management is unlikely to be able to estimate the standard deviation of the population under audit.

Answer (A) is incorrect because one acceptable approach is to determine an estimated population standard deviation from testing a pre-sample of 30-50 items. Once the total sample required is calculated, the pre-sample items can be included as part of the sample. Answer (B) is incorrect because the prior year's audit may provide evidence that might be used as an estimate for the current period. Answer (C) is incorrect because the available book values (e.g., the accounts receivable balances) may be used to determine the standard deviation of the book values, which in turn may be employed as a surrogate for the actual but unknown population standard deviation.

23. An auditor has taken a large sample from an audit population that is skewed in the sense that it contains a large number of small dollar balances and a small number of large dollar balances. The auditor can conclude

A. The sampling distribution is not normal; thus, PPS sampling based on the Poisson distribution more accurately defines the nature of the population.

B. The sampling distribution is normal; thus, the Z value can be used in evaluating the sample results.

C. The sampling distribution is not normal; thus, attribute sampling is the only alternative statistical tool that can appropriately be used.

D. None of the answers are correct.

The correct answer is (B). *(CIA, adapted)*

REQUIRED: The auditor's conclusion about a skewed population.

DISCUSSION: The central limit theorem states that, regardless of the distribution of the population from which random samples are taken, the shape of the sampling distribution of the means approaches the normal distribution as the sample size increases. Hence, Z values (the number of standard deviations in the standard normal distribution needed to provide specified levels of confidence) can be used. Z (sometimes designated as C in the sample-size formula) values represent areas under the curve for the standard normal distribution.

Answer (A) is incorrect because the sampling distribution is deemed to be normal (a continuous distribution). The Poisson distribution approaches the binomial distribution (a discrete distribution) for large samples and thus is related to attribute sampling. Answer (C) is incorrect because the sampling distribution can be normally distributed if a large enough sample size is taken. Moreover, attribute sampling is not appropriate for estimating population values. Answer (D) is incorrect because the sampling distribution is normal.

24. In a sampling application, the standard deviation represents a measure of the

A. Expected deviation rate.

B. Level of confidence desired.

C. Degree of data variability.

D. Extent of precision achieved.

The correct answer is (C). *(CIA, adapted)*

REQUIRED: The definition of standard deviation.

DISCUSSION: The standard deviation is a measure of data variability. The population standard deviation is a parameter that equals the square root of the population variance, which equals (for a finite population) the sum of the squared deviations from the mean, divided by the number of items in the population.

Answer (A) is incorrect because the expected deviation rate is associated with attribute sampling. The standard deviation is calculated for variables sampling. Answer (B) is incorrect because the confidence level is determined by auditor judgment. Answer (D) is incorrect because achieved precision in variables sampling is computed using the standard deviation.

25. Using the following results from a variables sample, compute the standard error of the mean.

Population size = 10,000
Sample size = 144
Sample standard deviation = \$24.00
Confidence level = 90% (C = 1.65)
Mean = \$84.00

A. \$60.00

B. \$7.00

C. \$3.30

D. \$2.00

The correct answer is (D). *(CIA, adapted)*

REQUIRED: The standard error of the mean given results from a variables sample.

DISCUSSION: The standard error of the mean equals the population standard deviation divided by the square root of the sample size. To determine achieved precision, the standard error of the mean is multiplied by the confidence coefficient. If the sample standard deviation is used as an estimate of the population standard deviation, the standard error of the mean is

$$\frac{\$24.00}{\sqrt{144}} = \$2.00$$

Answer (A) is incorrect because \$60 is a nonsensical number in this context. Answer (B) is incorrect because \$7.00 equals the mean (\$84) divided by the square root of the sample size ($\sqrt{144}$). Answer (C) is incorrect because \$3.30 is the estimated precision [(1.65 x \$24) ÷ $\sqrt{144}$].

26. In performing substantive tests, the auditor is concerned with two risks or errors of sampling:

1. The risk of incorrect rejection (an alpha or Type I error)
2. The risk of incorrect acceptance (a beta or Type II error)

Which of the following is true about alpha and beta errors?

A. The alpha error is of greater concern to the auditor than the beta error.

B. The beta error is of greater concern to the auditor than the alpha error.

C. The beta error and the alpha error are of equal importance to the auditor.

D. Neither the alpha error nor the beta error need be considered by the auditor.

The correct answer is (B). *(Publisher)*

REQUIRED: The relative importance of alpha and beta errors.

DISCUSSION: The risk of beta error, for example, the risk of incorrect acceptance, relates directly to the ability to detect material misstatements and is therefore of primary concern to the auditor. The risk of incorrect rejection (an alpha error) is that an account balance will be rejected as not fairly presented even though it is not materially misstated. Because the auditor will require additional audit evidence regarding a misstatement, an alpha error is not as serious as a beta error. Conversely, if an account balance is incorrectly accepted as fairly presented based upon a sample (a beta error), additional audit work will probably be minimal, and the chances of detecting the misstatement will be correspondingly reduced.

Answers (A), (C), and (D) are incorrect because an alpha error is not as serious as a beta error.

27. While performing a substantive test of details during an audit, the auditor determined that the sample results supported the conclusion that the recorded account balance was materially misstated. It was, in fact, not materially misstated. This situation illustrates the risk of

A. Assessing control risk too low.

B. Assessing control risk too high.

C. Incorrect rejection.

D. Incorrect acceptance.

The correct answer is (C). *(CPA, adapted)*

REQUIRED: The risk of erroneously concluding that a balance is materially misstated.

DISCUSSION: The two aspects of sampling risk for a substantive test of details are the risk of incorrect acceptance and the risk of incorrect rejection. The latter "is the risk that the sample supports the conclusion that the recorded account balance is materially misstated when it is not materially misstated" (AU 350).

Answers (A) and (B) are incorrect because the risk of assessing control risk too low and the risk of assessing control risk too high are aspects of sampling risk for tests of controls. Answer (D) is incorrect because the risk of incorrect acceptance is the risk that an auditor will erroneously conclude that a balance is not materially misstated.

28. In conducting a substantive test of an account balance, an auditor hypothesizes that no material misstatement exists. The risk that sample results will support the hypothesis when a material misstatement actually does exist is the risk of

A. Incorrect rejection.

B. Alpha error.

C. Incorrect acceptance.

D. Type I error.

The correct answer is (C). *(CIA, adapted)*

REQUIRED: The risk that sample results will support a false hypothesis.

DISCUSSION: For a substantive test, the two aspects of sampling risk are the risk of incorrect rejection (alpha or Type I error) and the risk of incorrect acceptance (beta or Type II error). The latter "is the risk that the sample supports the conclusion that the recorded account balance is not materially misstated when it is materially misstated" (AU 350).

Answers (A), (B), and (D) are incorrect because incorrect rejection (an alpha or Type I error) is the risk that a hypothesis will be rejected when no material misstatement exists.

29. The auditor failed to recognize a deviation included in a sample intended to test controls related to a transaction process. This failure best reflects

A. Statistical risk.

B. Sampling risk.

C. Audit risk.

D. Nonsampling risk.

The correct answer is (D). *(Publisher)*

REQUIRED: The term for the failure to recognize a control deviation.

DISCUSSION: Nonsampling risk includes the possibility of the auditor's failure to recognize a misstatement or deviation. Sampling risk results from the application of statistical sampling techniques. Sampling risk arises because fewer than 100% of the items are evaluated. Nonsampling risk includes all the aspects of audit risk that are not caused by sampling (AU 350).

Answers (A) and (B) are incorrect because, without examining every item, the exact population parameter cannot be determined, and a sampling or statistical risk will result. Answer (C) is incorrect because audit risk is the risk of concluding that the financial statements are fairly stated when they are not.

30. An auditor of a manufacturing company analyzes cost variances incurred in the manufacturing process to determine their statistical significance. Which of the following techniques is most likely to be used for this purpose?

A. Markov chains.

B. Monte Carlo method.

C. Application of probability theory.

D. Sensitivity analysis.

The correct answer is (C). *(CIA, adapted)*

REQUIRED: The technique used to determine the statistical significance of cost variances.

DISCUSSION: An auditor may use statistical control charts to determine the significance of variances in a cost accounting system. Control limits are established using probability theory to determine the likelihood that an observed variance indicates the system is out of control. If an observation falls outside the limits, an investigation should be made to determine the cause of the deviation.

Answer (A) is incorrect because Markov chains relate to a decision process. Answer (B) is incorrect because the Monte Carlo method is used in simulation models. Answer (D) is incorrect because sensitivity analysis studies the effect of changing a variable or parameter in a decision process.

31. In appraising the results of a statistical sample, the finite population correction (FPC) factor

A. Can be greater than one.

B. Has less effect as the sample becomes a larger proportion of the population.

C. Is needed when sampling is performed with replacement.

D. Is applied to reduce the size of the sample.

The correct answer is (D). *(CIA, adapted)*

REQUIRED: The use of the FPC factor.

DISCUSSION: The FPC factor reduces the sample size when it is large relative to the population size (N). The larger the sample size, the greater the probability that extreme values (which greatly affect the sample result) will be included in the sample. Hence, a somewhat smaller sample size is needed than if the population were infinite. An approximation of the FPC formula is

$$\sqrt{\frac{N - n}{N}}$$

Answer (A) is incorrect because the FPC factor can never be greater than one, as evidenced by its formula. Answer (B) is incorrect because the FPC factor has a greater (not lesser) effect as the sample becomes a larger proportion of the population. Answer (C) is incorrect because the use of the FPC factor is independent of whether sampling is performed with replacement.

6.3 Sampling Methods

32. Which of the following sampling methods is used to estimate a numerical measurement of a population, such as a dollar value?

A. Attribute sampling.

B. Stop-or-go sampling.

C. Variables sampling.

D. Random-number sampling.

The correct answer is (C). *(CPA, adapted)*

REQUIRED: The sampling method used to estimate a numerical measurement of a population.

DISCUSSION: Variables sampling samples dollar values or other quantities. The purpose of variables sampling is to estimate the value of a population.

Answers (A) and (B) are incorrect because attribute sampling and stop-or-go sampling are methods to test the control structure. Answer (D) is incorrect because random number sampling is a generic term relating to the selection of the sampling units.

33. The auditor uses variables and attribute sampling to make accounting estimates. These methods estimate, respectively

A. Deviation rate and quantities.

B. Quantities and deviation rate.

C. Constants and dollars.

D. Dollars and constants.

The correct answer is (B). *(Publisher)*

REQUIRED: The use of variables and attribute sampling.

DISCUSSION: Variables sampling is used by auditors to estimate quantities or dollar amounts in substantive testing. Attribute sampling applies to tests of controls and is used to estimate a deviation rate (occurrence rate) for a population.

Answer (A) is incorrect because the proper order is reversed. Answers (C) and (D) are incorrect because the terms are nonsense in this context.

34. The appropriate sampling plan to use to identify at least one deviation, assuming some number of such deviations exist in a population, and then to discontinue sampling when one irregularity is observed is

A. Stop-or-go sampling.

B. Discovery sampling.

C. Variables sampling.

D. Attribute sampling.

The correct answer is (B). *(CIA, adapted)*

REQUIRED: The sampling plan that should be used.

DISCUSSION: Discovery sampling is a form of attribute sampling applied when a control is critical and a single deviation is important, for example, commission of a material fraud. The expected deviation rate should be at or near zero, and the sample size is calculated so that the sample will include at least one example of a deviation if it occurs in the population at a given rate.

Answer (A) is incorrect because stop-or-go sampling is a variant of attribute sampling intended to reduce sample sizes when the population is relatively deviation free. It allows for discontinuing sampling when few or no deviations are found or for expanding the sample if the initial sample does not provide sufficient assurance. Answer (C) is incorrect because variables sampling estimates the value of a population. Answer (D) is incorrect because most attribute sampling applications are not discontinued when a single deviation is found.

35. In performing tests of controls over authorization of cash disbursements, which of the following statistical sampling methods is most appropriate?

A. Variables.

B. Stratified.

C. Ratio.

D. Attribute.

The correct answer is (D). *(CPA, adapted)*

REQUIRED: The sampling method most appropriate for tests of controls.

DISCUSSION: The auditor uses attribute sampling to test the effectiveness of controls. The auditor is concerned with the occurrence rate of procedural deviations in the population. Attribute sampling enables the auditor to estimate the occurrence rates and to determine whether the estimated rates are within an acceptable range.

Answer (A) is incorrect because variables sampling is concerned with quantities and dollar values (population totals). Answer (B) is incorrect because stratified sampling relates to variables estimation. Answer (C) is incorrect because ratio estimation is a method of variables sampling.

36. An auditor for the state highway and safety department needs to estimate the average highway weight of tractor-trailer trucks using the state's highway system. Which estimation method must be used?

A. Mean-per-unit (MPU).

B. Difference.

C. Ratio.

D. Probability-proportional-to-size.

The correct answer is (A). *(CIA, adapted)*

REQUIRED: The best sampling estimation method to estimate an average weight.

DISCUSSION: MPU estimation estimates the average value of population items. MPU averages the audit values of the sample items and multiplies the result by the number of items in the population.

Answers (B) and (C) are incorrect because difference and ratio estimation are techniques that compare book with audit values. Answer (D) is incorrect because PPS sampling selects items denominated in dollars using individual dollars as sampling units.

37. Which sampling method is most appropriate for the audit of the parts inventory of a wholesale electronic supply house when many small over- and understatements are expected?

A. Dollar-unit sampling.

B. Ratio or difference estimation.

C. Mean-per-unit sampling.

D. Stratified mean-per-unit sampling.

The correct answer is (B). *(J. Heian)*

REQUIRED: The appropriate sampling method when many small over- and understatements are expected.

DISCUSSION: Difference estimation of population misstatement entails determining the differences between the audit and book values for items in the sample, adding the differences, calculating the mean difference, and multiplying the mean by the number of items in the population. An allowance for sampling risk is also calculated. Ratio estimation is similar except that it estimates the population misstatement by multiplying the book value of the population by the ratio of the total audit value of the sample items to their total book value. Both methods are reliable and efficient when misstatements are relatively frequent, small misstatements predominate, and they do not tend to be in one direction (they are not skewed).

Answer (A) is incorrect because dollar-unit sampling is not appropriate when many misstatements are expected or the population contains understatements. Answers (C) and (D) are incorrect because MPU is considered less efficient than either ratio or difference estimation when many misstatements are present.

38. When would difference estimation or ratio estimation sampling methods be inappropriate?

A. If differences between the book values and audit values of a population are rare.

B. If the average difference between the audit value and book value of a population is small.

C. If differences between the book value and audit value of a population are numerous.

D. If the average difference between the audit value and book value of a population is large.

The correct answer is (A). *(CIA, adapted)*

REQUIRED: The circumstances in which difference or ratio estimation is inappropriate.

DISCUSSION: Difference estimation approximates total misstatement in the population by calculating the mean difference between the audited and book values in the sample and then multiplying by the number of population items. Ratio estimation approximates the total population misstatement by multiplying the proportion of the sample misstatement times the population book value. These methods are not reliable when misstatements are few or tend to be in one direction.

Answers (B) and (D) are incorrect because the frequency and direction of misstatements rather than their size determine whether difference and ratio estimation are reliable. However, difference estimation is preferable when the size of misstatements is independent of the recorded values. Answer (C) is incorrect because difference and ratio estimation are more reliable when misstatement rates are high.

39. The major reason that the difference and ratio estimation methods are expected to produce audit efficiency is that the

A. Number of members of the populations of differences or ratios is smaller than the number of members of the population of book values.

B. Beta risk may be completely ignored.

C. Calculations required in using difference or ratio estimation are less arduous and fewer than those required when using direct estimation.

D. Variability of the populations of differences or ratios is less than that of the populations of book values or audited values.

The correct answer is (D). *(CPA, adapted)*

REQUIRED: The reason for increased audit efficiency when using difference or ratio estimation sampling methods.

DISCUSSION: Difference estimation approximates total misstatement in the population by calculating the mean difference between the audited and book values in the sample and then multiplying by the number of population items. Ratio estimation approximates the total population misstatement by multiplying the proportion of the sample misstatement times the population book value. The variability in both of these estimates will likely be smaller than the variability within the population. Because the sample size varies directly with the variability of the population, the use of differences or ratios will usually allow for smaller sample sizes and greater efficiency in sampling.

Answer (A) is incorrect because the number of members in the population does not change if the sampling method changes. Answer (B) is incorrect because beta risk, the risk of accepting the book value when it is materially misstated, is present in any sampling method. Answer (C) is incorrect because the sample size must be calculated using basically the same formula for any sampling method employed.

40. An auditor is preparing to sample accounts receivable for overstatement. A statistical sampling method that automatically provides stratification when using systematic selection is

A. Attribute sampling.

B. Ratio-estimation sampling.

C. Dollar-unit sampling.

D. Mean-per-unit (MPU) sampling.

The correct answer is (C). *(CIA, adapted)*

REQUIRED: The sampling method that automatically stratifies accounts receivable.

DISCUSSION: Dollar-unit or probability-proportional-to-size (PPS) sampling uses attribute sampling concepts to estimate dollar amounts. It is a procedure for selecting items from a population using each dollar as a sampling unit. The procedure is applied by selecting every nth dollar in the population (the population consists of dollars in ascending value from $1 to the total value of the population). The item that contains the dollar selected is included in the sample. It effectively stratifies the population because the larger the account balance, the greater the chance of selection. Moreover, PPS sampling is not designed to address understatements or negative values without special modifications.

Answer (A) is incorrect because attribute sampling estimates deviation rates, not dollar amounts. Answer (B) is incorrect because ratio-estimation sampling uses the ratio of audited amounts to recorded amounts and does not automatically stratify. Answer (D) is incorrect because MPU averages the audit values of sample items and multiplies by the number in the population to estimate the population value. It does not automatically stratify.

41. Which of the following best describes an inherent limitation of the probability-proportional-to-size (PPS) sampling method?

A. It can only be used for substantive testing of asset accounts.

B. It is complicated and always requires the use of a computer system to perform the calculations.

C. Misstatement rates must be large and the misstatements must be overstatements.

D. Misstatement rates must be small and the misstatements must be overstatements.

The correct answer is (D). *(CIA, adapted)*

REQUIRED: The inherent limitation of PPS sampling.

DISCUSSION: PPS sampling uses attribute sampling concepts to estimate dollar amounts. Efficient use of PPS sampling requires misstatement rates to be small. The PPS sample size increases with the expected misstatement. Hence, the PPS sample size may be greater than that for classical variables sampling. Moreover, PPS sampling is not designed to address understatements or negative values without special modifications. Another disadvantage of PPS sampling is that misstatement estimates may be overly conservative, thereby increasing the risk of incorrect rejection.

Answer (A) is incorrect because PPS sampling is appropriate for substantive testing of most accounts when overstatement is of concern. Answer (B) is incorrect because PPS sampling is relatively simple and can be used with a table of the Poisson distribution. Answer (C) is incorrect because misstatement rates should be small.

42. Using statistical sampling to assist in verifying the year-end accounts payable balance, an auditor has accumulated the following data:

	Number of Accounts	Book Balance	Balance Determined by the Auditor
Population	4,100	$5,000,000	?
Sample	200	$ 250,000	$300,000

Using the ratio estimation technique, the auditor's estimate of year-end accounts payable balance is

A. $6,150,000

B. $6,000,000

C. $5,125,000

D. $5,050,000

The correct answer is (B). *(CPA, adapted)*

REQUIRED: The estimated balance using ratio estimation.

DISCUSSION: Ratio estimation estimates the total population misstatement by multiplying the proportion of the sample misstatement times the population book value. Here, the proportion of the sample misstatement is 20% [($300,000 – $250,000) ÷ $250,000]. The estimated population misstatement is $1,000,000 (.2 x $5,000,000). The estimated year-end balance is therefore $6,000,000 ($5,000,000 book balance + $1,000,000 estimated misstatement).

Answer (A) is incorrect because $6,150,000 assumes that the ratio is 23% [($6,150,000 – $5,000,000) ÷ $5,000,000]. Answer (C) is incorrect because $5,125,000 assumes that the ratio is 2.5% [($5,125,000 – $5,000,000) ÷ $5,000,000]. Answer (D) is incorrect because $5,050,000 equals the book value of the population ($5,000,000) plus the understatement error of the sample ($50,000).

43. In which sampling method is the probability of selection of an item proportional to the size or the value of the item (e.g., a $1,000 item is 10 times more likely to be selected than a $100 item)?

A. Discovery sampling.

B. Ratio estimation.

C. Dollar-unit sampling.

D. Stratified sampling.

The correct answer is (C). *(Publisher)*

REQUIRED: The sampling method in which the probability of selection of an item is proportional to its size.

DISCUSSION: Dollar-unit or probability-proportional-to-size (PPS) sampling defines individual dollars within an item or balance as the sampling units. Thus, an item containing 1,000 sampling units ($1,000) has a 10 times greater chance of being selected for audit than a balance with 100 sampling units ($100).

Answer (A) is incorrect because discovery sampling is a sampling plan to search for critical deviations. Answer (B) is incorrect because ratio estimation estimates the population misstatement by multiplying the proportion of sample misstatement times the population book value. Answer (D) is incorrect because stratification divides a population into subpopulations so that variability can be minimized and a more efficient sample can be drawn.

44. An internal auditor plans to test the accuracy of recorded quantities-on-hand in an inventory file against the actual quantities-on-hand. Under which of the following conditions would the auditor be least likely to use a stop-or-go sampling plan?

A. The population to be sampled is very large.

B. The auditor expects the population to contain a high rate of deviations.

C. The auditor plans to draw a relatively small sample size.

D. The auditor plans to determine an upper precision limit for the estimated percentage of deviations contained in the population.

The correct answer is (B). *(CIA, adapted)*

REQUIRED: The condition in which stop-or-go sampling is least likely to be used.

DISCUSSION: Stop-or-go sampling is an attribute sampling model that helps prevent oversampling by allowing the auditor to halt an audit test at the earliest possible moment. It is used when the auditor believes that the population contains relatively few deviations.

Answer (A) is incorrect because stop-or-go sampling is appropriate for populations of any size. Answer (C) is incorrect because stop-or-go sampling is designed to reduce sample size. Answer (D) is incorrect because the purpose of stop-or-go sampling is to state that a deviation rate is below a prespecified rate (upper precision limit) with a prespecified level of confidence.

45. A statistical sampling technique that will minimize sample size whenever a low deviation rate is expected is

A. Ratio-estimation sampling.

B. Difference-estimation sampling.

C. Stratified mean-per-unit sampling.

D. Stop-or-go sampling.

The correct answer is (D). *(CIA, adapted)*

REQUIRED: The technique that minimizes sample size.

DISCUSSION: Stop-or-go sampling is typically used when a low deviation rate is expected. It is a version of acceptance sampling, which, like other attribute sampling methods, is used to test the effectiveness of controls. Stop-or-go sampling is unlike acceptance sampling in that it does not rely on a fixed sample size. Thus, it may reduce the sample size because sample items are examined only until enough evidence has been gathered to reach the desired conclusion.

Answers (A), (B), and (C) are incorrect because deviation rate is irrelevant to such variables sampling methods as ratio estimation, difference estimation, and MPU.

6.4 Sample Selection

46. A distinguishing characteristic of random number sample selection is that each

A. Item is selected from a stratum having minimum variability.

B. Item's chance for selection is proportional to its dollar value.

C. Item in the population has a known and nonzero chance of being selected.

D. Stratum in the population has an equal number of items selected.

The correct answer is (C). *(CIA, adapted)*

REQUIRED: The distinguishing characteristic of random number sample selection.

DISCUSSION: Probability sampling is possible if every item in the population has a known and nonzero chance of being drawn. Simple random sampling is a special case of probability sampling in which every possible sample of a given size has the same probability of being chosen, and every item in the population has an equal probability of being chosen. Random selection can be used for stratified and other samples in which items do not have an equal chance of being selected.

Answers (A) and (D) are incorrect because stratifying the population is not required for random selection. Answer (B) is incorrect because dollar values are not used in random selection.

47. An auditor wishes to sample 200 sales receipts from a population of 5,000 receipts issued during the last year. The receipts have preprinted serial numbers and are arranged in chronological (and thus serial number) order. The auditor randomly chooses a receipt from the first 25 receipts and then selects every 25th receipt thereafter. The sampling procedure described here is called

A. Systematic random sampling.

B. Dollar-unit sampling.

C. Judgment interval sampling.

D. Variables sampling.

The correct answer is (A). *(CIA, adapted)*

REQUIRED: The sampling plan that selects a random start and then chooses each nth item.

DISCUSSION: Systematic (interval) sampling is accomplished by selecting a random start and taking every nth item in the population. The value of n is computed by dividing the population by the size of the sample. The random start should be in the first interval. An advantage of systematic sampling is its relative ease. It requires merely counting items in the population, not assigning a random number to each item. However, a systematic sampling plan assumes the items are arranged randomly in the population. If the auditor discovers that this condition does not exist, a random selection method should be used.

Answer (B) is incorrect because dollar-unit sampling selects individual dollars within an item or balance as the sampling units. Answer (C) is incorrect because judgment sampling uses the auditor's subjective judgment to determine the sample size (number of items examined) and sample selection (which items to examine). Answer (D) is incorrect because the sampling procedure described can be used for attribute as well as variables sampling.

48. To test compliance with a policy regarding sales returns recorded during the most recent year, an auditor systematically selected 5% of the actual returns recorded in March and April. Returns during these two busiest months of the year represented about 25% of total annual returns. Projections of deviation rates from this sample have limited usefulness because

A. The small size of the sample relative to the population makes sampling risk unacceptable.

B. The failure to stratify the population according to sales volume results in bias.

C. The systematic selection of returns during the 2 months is not sufficiently random.

D. The deviation rates during the 2 busiest months may not be representative of the whole year.

The correct answer is (D). *(CIA, adapted)*

REQUIRED: The reason for the limited usefulness of projections of deviation rates.

DISCUSSION: By selecting a sample from only 2 months, the auditor may be able to draw conclusions about the overall deviation rate during those months, but the sample does not provide sufficient information to draw conclusions about the overall rate for the year.

Answer (A) is incorrect because, although sampling risk is related to sample size, it is not related to the ratio of sample size to the population size. In addition, this problem does not contain sufficient information to evaluate the acceptability of sampling risk. Answer (B) is incorrect because the objective of stratifying a population is to decrease the sampling risk, not bias. This problem does not give enough information to decide whether stratification might have enabled the auditor to use a smaller sample. Answer (C) is incorrect because systematic selection with a random start is unbiased if the population is randomly organized.

49. Which of the following sample planning factors would influence the sample size for a substantive test of details for a specific account?

	Expected Amount of Misstatements	Measure of Tolerable Misstatement
A.	No	No
B.	Yes	Yes
C.	No	Yes
D.	Yes	No

The correct answer is (B). *(CPA, adapted)*

REQUIRED: The factors that would influence the sample size for a substantive test of details.

DISCUSSION: Certain variables sampling plans, for example, probability-proportional-to-size sampling, specifically consider the expected amount of misstatement and the measure of tolerable misstatement or materiality in the determination of sample size.

Answers (A), (C), and (D) are incorrect because certain sampling plans explicitly consider the expected amount of misstatements and tolerable misstatement.

50. Internal auditing is conducting an operational audit of the organization's mailroom activities to determine whether the use of express mail service is limited to cases of necessity. To test cost-effectiveness, the auditor selects the 100 most recent express-mail transactions for review. A major limitation of such a sampling technique is that it

A. Does not allow a statistical generalization about all express-mail transactions.

B. Results in a sample size that is too small to project to the population.

C. Does not evaluate existing controls in this area.

D. Does not describe the population from which it was drawn.

The correct answer is (A). *(CIA, adapted)*

REQUIRED: The major limitation of selecting a sample of the most recent transactions for review.

DISCUSSION: The last 100 express-mail transactions may not be representative of all express-mail transactions. The sample is a judgment rather than a statistical (probability or random) sample. Every item in the population (all express-mail transactions of the organization) does not have an equal (or known) and nonzero probability of being chosen. Thus, sampling risk cannot be quantified.

Answer (B) is incorrect because a sample of 100 may be sufficient. Answer (C) is incorrect because the auditor is testing for cost effectiveness. Answer (D) is incorrect because the last 100 transactions may describe the population from which they were drawn.

51. An auditor is conducting a survey of perceptions and beliefs of employees concerning an organization health care plan. The best approach to selecting a sample is to

A. Focus on people who are likely to respond so that a larger sample can be obtained.

B. Focus on managers and supervisors because they can also reflect the opinions of the people in their departments.

C. Use stratified sampling when the strata are defined by marital and family status, age, and salaried/hourly status.

D. Use monetary-unit sampling according to employee salaries.

The correct answer is (C). *(CIA, adapted)*

REQUIRED: The best way to sample employee beliefs.

DISCUSSION: Stratified sampling divides a population into subpopulations, thereby permitting the application of different techniques to each stratum. This approach reduces the effect of high variability if the strata are selected so that variability among the strata is greater than variability within each stratum. For example, one expects to find greater similarities among married people than between married people and unmarried people.

Answer (A) is incorrect because this convenience sample is likely to emphasize people with the time to respond. It tends to omit employees who are too busy to respond. Answer (B) is incorrect because managers and supervisors often do not have the same needs and perceptions as their subordinates and also often misperceive the views of employees. Answer (D) is incorrect because the survey tests perceptions and beliefs, not monetary amounts.

52. An entity wishes to determine inventory value by counting a sample of inventory items. If a stratified random sample is to be drawn, the strata should be identified in such a way that

A. The overall population is divided into subpopulations of equal size so that each subpopulation can be given equal weight when estimates are made.

B. Each stratum differs as much as possible with respect to unit costs, but the unit costs for items within each stratum are as similar as possible.

C. The sample means and standard deviation of each individual stratum will be equal to the means and standard deviations of all other strata.

D. The items in each stratum will follow a normal distribution so that probability theory can be used in making inferences from the sample data.

The correct answer is (B). *(Publisher)*

REQUIRED: The proper way to stratify a population of inventory items.

DISCUSSION: When the items in a population are heterogeneous, stratifying the population into homogeneous subpopulations may be advantageous. Each stratum should differ from the others, but the items within each stratum should be similar.

Answer (A) is incorrect because the purpose of stratification is to divide the population so that homogeneous items are grouped together, not to create subpopulations of equal size. Answer (C) is incorrect because the individual strata should be as different from each other as possible. Thus, the means and standard deviations of the strata should differ. Answer (D) is incorrect because whether an item should be included in a stratum is based upon the characteristic used for stratifying, not upon the distribution of the items within the stratum.

53. To use stratified sampling to evaluate a large, heterogeneous inventory, which of the following would least likely be used as a criterion to classify inventory items into strata?

A. Dollar value.

B. Number of items.

C. Turnover volume.

D. Storage locations.

The correct answer is (B). *(CIA, adapted)*

REQUIRED: The least likely criterion to classify inventory items into strata.

DISCUSSION: Stratifying a population means dividing it into subpopulations, thereby permitting application of different sampling techniques to each subpopulation or stratum. Stratifying allows for greater emphasis on larger or more important items. When the items in a population are heterogeneous, stratifying the population into homogeneous subpopulations may be advantageous. Each stratum should differ from the others, but the items within each stratum should be similar. Number of items is not usually associated with the risk of misstatement.

Answers (A), (C), and (D) are incorrect because the risk of misstatement is correlated with such factors as dollar value, turnover, and location.

54. Stratified mean-per-unit (MPU) sampling is a statistical technique that may be more efficient than unstratified MPU because it usually

A. May be applied to populations in which many monetary misstatements are expected to occur.

B. Produces an estimate having a desired level of precision with a smaller sample size.

C. Increases the variability among items in a stratum by grouping sampling units with similar characteristics.

D. Yields a weighted sum of the strata standard deviations that is greater than the standard deviation of the population.

The correct answer is (B). *(CPA, adapted)*

REQUIRED: The reason for using stratification.

DISCUSSION: The primary objective of stratification is to reduce the effect of high variability by dividing the population into subpopulations. Reducing the variance within each subpopulation allows the auditor to sample a smaller number of items while holding precision and confidence level constant.

Answer (A) is incorrect because the number of misstatements in the population is independent of the advantages of stratification. Answer (C) is incorrect because stratification is used to decrease the effects of variation within the strata. Answer (D) is incorrect because the standard deviation, which measures variation, should be less within the strata than for the population as a whole.

55. Which of the following is not a criterion for a good stratified random sampling plan?

A. Every item must belong to one and only one stratum.

B. The original population of items must be normally distributed.

C. An identifiable means of subdividing a heterogeneous population into groups with more homogeneous characteristics must be available.

D. The number of items in each group must be known or determinable.

The correct answer is (B). *(CIA, adapted)*

REQUIRED: The condition not a criterion for stratified sampling.

DISCUSSION: The population need not be normally distributed. Indeed, the purpose of stratification is to overcome skewness of distribution in the original population by defining subpopulations that are as nearly homogeneous as possible.

Answer (A) is incorrect because a necessary condition for stratification is that every item belong to one and only one stratum. Answer (C) is incorrect because a necessary condition for stratification is that an identifiable means of subdividing a heterogeneous population into groups with more homogeneous characteristics be available. Answer (D) is incorrect because a necessary condition for stratification is that the number of items in each group be known or determinable.

56. In a regional survey of suburban households to obtain data on television viewing habits, a statistical sample of suburban areas is first selected. Within the chosen areas, statistical samples of whole blocks are selected, and within the selected blocks, random samples of households are selected. This type of sample selection can best be described as

A. Attribute sampling.

B. Stratified sampling.

C. Cluster sampling.

D. Interval sampling.

The correct answer is (C). *(CIA, adapted)*

REQUIRED: The sampling method used to select random samples from statistically selected groups.

DISCUSSION: Block (cluster) sampling selects groups of items rather than individual items. For this plan to be effective, dispersion within clusters should be greater than dispersion among clusters. If blocks of homogeneous items are selected, the sample will be biased. Cluster sampling is most appropriate when each group is representative of the entire population.

Answer (A) is incorrect because attribute sampling is not a selection technique. Answer (B) is incorrect because stratified sampling separates the population into several strata, with the elements in each stratum possessing some common attribute. The sample is then chosen using a statistical sampling approach. Answer (D) is incorrect because interval sampling selects every nth item for sampling with a randomized starting point.

57. An auditor is designing a sampling plan to test the accuracy of daily production reports over the past 3 years. All of the reports contain the same information except that Friday reports also contain weekly totals and are prepared by managers rather than by supervisors. Production normally peaks near the end of a month. If the auditor wants to select two reports per month using an interval sampling plan, which of the following techniques reduces the likelihood of bias in the sample?

A. Estimating the rate of misstatements in the population.

B. Using multiple random starts.

C. Increasing the confidence level.

D. Increasing the precision.

The correct answer is (B). *(CIA, adapted)*

REQUIRED: The technique that reduces the chance of bias in the sample.

DISCUSSION: Systematic (interval) sample entails choosing a random start and then selecting subsequent items at fixed intervals. However, if the population is not random, for example, because it exhibits cyclical variation, the results will be biased. This bias may be overcome by taking repeated systematic samples, each with a random start. In effect, each possible systematic sample in the population is a cluster. Thus, the repeated systematic samples, each with a random start, constitute a random sample of clusters.

Answer (A) is incorrect because estimating the rate of misstatements in the population has no effect on bias. Bias is related to the selection method. Answers (C) and (D) are incorrect because increasing the confidence level or the precision has no effect on bias.

58. The advantage of selecting a sample by cluster is that this method

A. Increases the precision and confidence level of the sample.

B. Reduces the time required to locate the individual items chosen for examination.

C. Decreases the standard deviation of the sample.

D. Decreases sample size.

The correct answer is (B). *(Publisher)*

REQUIRED: The advantage of cluster sampling.

DISCUSSION: The use of cluster or block sampling may allow the auditor to select on a random basis a large set of data (a block) to be examined. Because the auditor need not establish a correspondence between random numbers and items in the population, time may be saved.

Answers (A), (C), and (D) are incorrect because sample size, the standard deviation of the sample, and the precision and confidence level of the sample are independent of the sample selection method.

59. Which of the following is a false statement about cluster sample selection?

A. Every item in the sample must correspond to a random number.

B. Sample groups of items rather than individual items are selected.

C. Cluster sampling is normally used when the sampling units (documents) are filed sequentially.

D. Dispersion within clusters should be greater than between clusters.

The correct answer is (A). *(Publisher)*

REQUIRED: The false statement.

DISCUSSION: Because cluster sampling entails selection of groups rather than individual items from a population, random numbers are not assigned to individual items within the population. Rather, clusters or blocks are randomly selected for audit.

Answer (B) is incorrect because cluster sampling selects blocks or clusters of items rather than individual items for audit. Answer (C) is incorrect because, when documents are sequentially filed, time can be saved by selecting blocks rather than individual items from the population. Answer (D) is incorrect because dispersion within the clusters should be large and dispersion among the clusters should be small.

60. An accounts receivable aging schedule was prepared on 300 pages with each page containing the aging data for 50 accounts. The pages were numbered from 1 to 300, and the accounts listed on each were numbered from 1 to 50. An auditor selected accounts receivable for confirmation using a table of numbers as illustrated:

Select Column from Table of Numbers	Separate Five Digits: First Three Digits Last Two Digits	
02011	020-11	x
85393	853-93	*
97265	972-65	*
61680	616-80	*
16656	166-56	*
42751	427-51	*
69994	699-94	*
07942	079-42	y
10231	102-31	z
53988	539-88	*

x Mailed confirmation to account 11 listed on p. 20.
y Mailed confirmation to account 42 listed on p. 79.
z Mailed confirmation to account 31 listed on p. 102.
* Rejected.

This procedure is an example of

A. Acceptance sampling.

B. Systematic sampling.

C. Sequential sampling.

D. Random sampling.

The correct answer is (D). *(CPA, adapted)*

REQUIRED: The appropriate term associated with the sampling method illustrated.

DISCUSSION: This sampling method is random. When random sampling is used, each item in the population has an equal or known and nonzero chance of being selected for inclusion in the sample. The auditor in this instance selected a random sample using a random number table. Before this approach can be used, a correspondence between the random numbers and the items in the population must be established. In this example, the relationship was established by designating the first three digits from the random number table as corresponding to the page number and the last two digits as corresponding to the item number. The number 85393 is rejected because (1) the page number (853) does not lie between 1 and 300, and (2) the item number (93) does not lie between 1 and 50. If either of these conditions occurs, the random number is rejected. If the random number falls within both ranges (e.g., 02011), the item corresponding to the random number is included in the sample. The eleventh item on page 20 is therefore chosen for confirmation.

Answer (A) is incorrect because acceptance sampling is a form of attribute sampling. The described plan is concerned with the value of the account and is therefore an example of variables sampling. Answer (B) is incorrect because systematic sampling is a special type of random sampling that needs no correspondence between random numbers and items in the population. Answer (C) is incorrect because sequential (stop-or-go) sampling needs no correspondence between random numbers and items in the population.

61. An auditor desires to use a table of random digits to select a sample from a population of documents that have the following broken number sequences: 0001-1000, 2000-5000, and 8000-11000. Which of the following is the most efficient approach to overcome the problem of the broken number sequences?

A. Deduct four-digit constant values from the second and third sequences, choose the appropriate random numbers, and add the constants back to the individual numbers.

B. Skip through the entire random number tables until large blocks of digits appear that will fit within the three different number sequences.

C. Choose appropriate random numbers from the tables without modifying the approach and recognize that a large selection of unusable numbers will occur.

D. Select three different starting points in the random tables and vary the selection pattern to obtain needed numbers in the three different sequences.

The correct answer is (A). *(CIA, adapted)*

REQUIRED: The most efficient approach to overcoming the problem of broken number sequences when using a random digits table.

DISCUSSION: Efficient use of random digits tables often requires that constants be subtracted from the items in the population so that it more closely matches the numbers in the table. After an acceptable number is found in the table, the constant is added back to determine which item is selected. Randomness of selection is not impaired by this technique.

Answer (B) is incorrect because random digits tables do not contain large blocks of usable numbers. Answer (C) is incorrect because selecting many unusable numbers is inefficient. Answer (D) is incorrect because use of random digits tables requires a single starting point and a consistent selection pattern.

6.5 Attribute Sampling

62. Statistical sampling may be used to test the effectiveness of controls. The auditor's procedures should result in a statistical conclusion concerning

A. Population characteristics occurring at least once in the population.

B. The population value not being misstated by more than a fixed amount.

C. Monetary precision exceeding a certain predetermined amount.

D. The relation of the population deviation rate to the tolerable rate.

The correct answer is (D). *(Publisher)*

REQUIRED: The conclusion that can be drawn from statistical tests of controls.

DISCUSSION: The auditor uses attribute sampling to test the effectiveness of controls. The auditor is concerned with the occurrence rate of procedural deviations in the population. Attribute sampling enables the auditor to estimate the occurrence rate of deviations and to determine the relation of the estimated rate to the tolerable rate.

Answer (A) is incorrect because the only way to be certain that a characteristic occurs at least once is to examine items until one is located. Answer (B) is incorrect because variables sampling is concerned with quantities (e.g., population totals). Answer (C) is incorrect because variables sampling is concerned with dollar values (e.g., monetary precision), whereas attribute sampling is concerned with deviation rates.

63. An auditor planning an attribute sample from a large number of invoices intends to estimate the actual rate of deviations. Which factor below is the most important for the auditor to consider?

A. Audit objective.

B. Population size.

C. Desired confidence level.

D. Population variance.

The correct answer is (A). *(CIA, adapted)*

REQUIRED: The most important factor in planning an attribute sample.

DISCUSSION: Attribute sampling enables the auditor to estimate the occurrence rate in a population and to determine the relation of the estimated rate to the tolerable rate. However, the audit objective must be known before audit procedures can be designed and their results evaluated.

Answer (B) is incorrect because knowing the population is large is sufficient. Answer (C) is incorrect because the desired confidence level is a function of the purposes to be served by the audit. Answer (D) is incorrect because the variance is calculated in variables, not attribute, sampling applications.

64. Statistical sampling usually may be applied in tests of controls when the client's controls

A. Permit detection of material misstatements in the accounting records.

B. Leave an audit trail.

C. Are described in accounting manuals.

D. Depend primarily on segregation of duties.

The correct answer is (B). *(Publisher)*

REQUIRED: The condition permitting use of statistical sampling in tests of controls.

DISCUSSION: Sampling techniques are useful when a population can be identified from which to sample. When attribute sampling is applied in tests of controls, an audit trail of documents and notations thereon (such as signatures) must exist to provide evidence of the effectiveness of the control.

Answer (A) is incorrect because the client's controls, if appropriate, are always expected to detect material misstatements. Answer (C) is incorrect because the auditor is more concerned with the existence and effectiveness of controls rather than with their documentation. Answer (D) is incorrect because segregation of duties is tested through inquiry and observation rather than through sampling.

65. An auditor plans to examine a sample of 20 purchase orders for proper approvals as prescribed by the client's internal control. One of the purchase orders in the chosen sample of 20 cannot be found, and the auditor is unable to use alternative procedures to test whether that purchase order was properly approved. The auditor should

A. Choose another purchase order to replace the missing purchase order in the sample.

B. Consider this test of controls invalid and proceed with substantive tests because internal control is ineffective.

C. Treat the missing purchase order as a deviation for the purpose of evaluating the sample.

D. Select a completely new set of 20 purchase orders.

The correct answer is (C). *(CPA, adapted)*

REQUIRED: The effect of failure to locate a sample item.

DISCUSSION: According to AU 350, "If the auditor is not able to apply the planned audit procedures or appropriate alternative procedures to selected items, (s)he should consider the reasons for this limitation, and (s)he should ordinarily consider those selected items to be deviations from the procedures for the purpose of evaluating the sample."

Answer (A) is incorrect because the auditor would choose another purchase order only if an item in the sample were not used, e.g., if it were properly voided. Answer (B) is incorrect because the sampling plan could be completed by counting the missing purchase order as a deviation. Answer (D) is incorrect because selecting a new sample is unnecessary.

66. For which of the following audit tests would an auditor most likely use attribute sampling?

A. Making an independent estimate of the amount of a LIFO inventory.

B. Examining invoices in support of the valuation of fixed asset additions.

C. Selecting accounts receivable for confirmation of account balances.

D. Inspecting employee time cards for proper approval by supervisors.

The correct answer is (D). *(CPA, adapted)*

REQUIRED: The appropriate use of attribute sampling.

DISCUSSION: The approvals represent the application of a control. Attribute sampling enables the auditor to estimate the occurrence rate of control deviations and to determine its relation to the tolerable rate. Thus, a control such as proper approval of time cards by supervisors can be tested for effectiveness using attribute sampling.

Answer (A) is incorrect because variables sampling is useful in estimating the amount of inventory. Answer (B) is incorrect because examining invoices in support of the valuation of fixed asset additions is a substantive test for which variables sampling is appropriate. Answer (C) is incorrect because the selection of accounts receivable for confirmation is a substantive test.

67. In testing payroll transactions, an auditor discovers that four out of a statistical sample of 100 selected time cards were not signed by the appropriate supervisor. To evaluate the materiality or significance of this control deficiency, the auditor should

A. Compare the tolerable deviation rate with the expected deviation rate.

B. Compute an upper precision limit and compare with the tolerable deviation rate.

C. Evaluate the dollar amount of the four time cards in relation to the financial statements.

D. Report the deviations and let management assess the significance because they are in the best position to know.

The correct answer is (B). *(CIA, adapted)*

REQUIRED: The procedure applied to evaluate the materiality of the control deficiency.

DISCUSSION: After specifying the confidence level and tolerable rate of deviations, the auditor determines the sample size and precision. The tolerable rate is the rate the auditor is willing to accept without altering the assessed level of control risk. The achieved precision is the range of values constructed based on a statistic derived from a random sample. At the stated confidence level, the auditor expects this range to contain the true population value. In this attribute sampling application, the upper, but not the lower, precision limit is of interest. This limit should be compared with the maximum tolerable rate.

Answer (A) is incorrect because both the expected deviation rate and the tolerable rate are known before sampling. Answer (C) is incorrect because any monetary misstatement in the sample must first be extrapolated to the population before the significance can be assessed. Answer (D) is incorrect because the auditor should determine the significance of detected deviations.

68. In addition to evaluating the frequency of deviations in tests of controls, an auditor also considers certain qualitative aspects of the deviations. The auditor most likely will give broader consideration to the implications of a deviation if it is

A. The only deviation discovered in the sample.

B. Identical to a deviation discovered during the prior year's audit.

C. Caused by an employee's misunderstanding of instructions.

D. Initially concealed by a forged document.

The correct answer is (D). *(CPA, adapted)*

REQUIRED: The aspect of a deviation requiring broader consideration.

DISCUSSION: The discovery of fraud ordinarily requires broader consideration than the discovery of an unintentional deviation. The discovery of an initially concealed forged document raises concerns because it indicates that the integrity of employees may be in doubt.

Answer (A) is incorrect because a single deviation discovered in a sample may not cause major concern. Answer (B) is incorrect because deviations are often repetitive. Discovery of an identical deviation in a subsequent year is not unusual. Answer (C) is incorrect because a misunderstanding is not fraud and does not necessarily arouse concern.

69. The tolerable rate for a test of controls depends primarily on which of the following?

A. The cause of the deviations.

B. The effect on substantive tests of assessing control risk at a certain level.

C. The amount of any substantive misstatement.

D. The limit used in audits of similar clients.

The correct answer is (B). *(L.M. Bailey)*

REQUIRED: The determinant of the tolerable rate.

DISCUSSION: The tolerable rate is the maximum rate of deviations from a prescribed control that the auditor is willing to accept without altering the assessment of control risk for the assertions related to the activity. The tolerable rate is determined based on two considerations: the planned assessed level of control risk and the assurance desired to be provided by the evidence in the sample (AU 350). The lower the assessed control risk, the higher the acceptable level of detection risk. Because substantive tests are performed to reduce detection risk to the acceptable level, the nature, timing, and extent of such tests will be affected if audit evidence indicates that a higher assessed level of control risk and thus a lower acceptable level of detection risk are necessary.

Answer (A) is incorrect because the cause of the deviations is unknown prior to testing. The auditor sets the tolerable rate prior to such tests. Answer (C) is incorrect because the misstatement is unknown prior to testing. Answer (D) is incorrect because audit clients are unlikely to be so similar that the same tolerable rate can be used.

70. Which of the following statements is correct concerning statistical sampling in tests of controls?

A. As the population size increases, the sample size should increase proportionately.

B. Deviations from specific controls at a given rate ordinarily result in misstatements at a lower rate.

C. The relationship between the expected population deviation rate and the sample size is inverse.

D. In determining the tolerable rate, an auditor considers detection risk and the sample size.

The correct answer is (B). *(CPA, adapted)*

REQUIRED: The true statement concerning statistical sampling and tests of controls.

DISCUSSION: Deviations from a specific control increase the risk of misstatements in the accounting records. However, deviations do not always result in misstatements. Thus, deviations from a specific control at a given rate ordinarily result in misstatements at the financial statement level at a lower rate (AU 350).

Answer (A) is incorrect because, as population size increases, the required sample size increases at a decreasing rate. Answer (C) is incorrect because the relationship between the expected population deviation rate and the required sample size is direct. Answer (D) is incorrect because the tolerable rate depends on the planned assessed level of control risk and the assurance to be provided by the evidence in the sample.

71. The diagram below depicts the auditor's estimated maximum deviation rate compared with the tolerable rate, and also depicts the true population deviation rate compared with the tolerable rate.

Auditor's Estimate Based on Sample Results	True State of Population: Deviation Rate Exceeds Tolerable Rate	True State of Population: Deviation Rate Is Less Than Tolerable Rate
Maximum Deviation Rate Exceeds Tolerable Rate	I.	III.
Maximum Deviation Rate Is Less Than Tolerable Rate	II.	IV.

As a result of testing controls, the auditor assesses control risk too high and thereby increases substantive testing. This is illustrated by situation

A. I.

B. II.

C. III.

D. IV.

The correct answer is (C). *(CPA, adapted)*

REQUIRED: The situation that involves assessing control risk too high.

DISCUSSION: The risk of assessing control risk too high is one aspect of sampling risk in testing controls. According to AU 350, it "is the risk that the assessed level of control risk based on the sample is greater than the true operating effectiveness of the control." Like the risk of incorrect rejection in substantive testing, the risk of assessing control risk too high is a form of alpha (Type I) error. Alpha error concerns the efficiency, not the effectiveness, of the audit because it ordinarily leads to application of further audit procedures and ultimate arrival at the correct conclusion.

Answer (A) is incorrect because, in situation I, the auditor would properly assess control risk at a high level. Answer (B) is incorrect because, in situation II, the sample might lead to assessing control risk too low. Answer (D) is incorrect because, in situation IV, the auditor would properly assess control risk at less than the maximum level.

72. As a result of sampling procedures applied as tests of controls, an auditor incorrectly assesses control risk lower than appropriate. The most likely explanation for this situation is that

A. The deviation rates of both the auditor's sample and the population exceed the tolerable rate.

B. The deviation rates of both the auditor's sample and the population are less than the tolerable rate.

C. The deviation rate in the auditor's sample is less than the tolerable rate, but the deviation rate in the population exceeds the tolerable rate.

D. The deviation rate in the auditor's sample exceeds the tolerable rate, but the deviation rate in the population is less than the tolerable rate.

The correct answer is (C). *(CPA, adapted)*

REQUIRED: The most likely explanation for assessing control risk lower than appropriate.

DISCUSSION: When the deviation rate in the sample is less than the tolerable rate, the auditor concludes that the controls tested are effective. If, in fact, the true deviation rate in the population is greater than the tolerable rate, the auditor would assess control risk too low.

Answers (A) and (B) are incorrect because, if the sample rate and the population rate are both greater or less than the tolerable rate, the auditor's conclusion should be accurate. Answer (D) is incorrect because, if the sample rate exceeds the population rate, the auditor is likely to assess control risk too high.

73. In evaluating an attribute sample, the estimated range that is expected to contain the population characteristic is the

A. Confidence level.

B. Precision.

C. Upper deviation limit.

D. Expected deviation rate.

The correct answer is (B). *(CIA, adapted)*

REQUIRED: The range within which the estimate of the population characteristic is expected to fall.

DISCUSSION: Precision, or the confidence interval, is an interval around the sample statistic that is expected to contain the true population value. Precision for an attribute sample is based upon the tolerable rate of deviation. The upper limit of the interval is of greatest interest in attribute sampling applications.

Answer (A) is incorrect because the confidence level is the specified measure of how reliable the auditor wants the sample results to be. Answer (C) is incorrect because precision is the range between the lower and upper deviation limits. Answer (D) is incorrect because the expected deviation rate is a measure of how frequently the auditor expects the characteristic of interest to exist in the population prior to selecting and evaluating the sample.

74. A test of 200 invoices randomly selected by the auditor revealed that 35 had not been approved for payment. At the 95% confidence level, what precision can be assigned?

A. 6.9%

B. 5.3%

C. 9.1%

D. 3.5%

The correct answer is (B). *(CIA, adapted)*

REQUIRED: The achieved precision.

DISCUSSION: The following sample size formula for an attribute sampling application can be solved for precision:

$$n = \frac{C^2pq}{P^2}$$

C is the confidence coefficient, p is the expected deviation rate, q is 1 – p, P is the specified precision rate, and n is the sample size.

$$P^2 = \frac{(1.96)^2 \times (35 \div 200) \times [1 - (35 \div 200)]}{200}$$

$$P^2 = .0028$$

$$P = .053 \text{ or } 5.3\%$$

Answers (A), (C), and (D) are incorrect because the above formula determines the precision.

Questions 75 through 78 are based on the following information.

Confidence Level	Deviation Rate	Field Size	Sample Sizes for Precision of +1%	+2%	+3%	+4%	+5%	+6%	+8%	+10%
95%	10%	200					82	65		
		400			196	140	103	77		
		500			217	151	108	81		
		1,000		464	278	178	121	88	51	50
		2,000		604	322	195	129	92	53	51
99%	10%	200						91	64	
		400				193	149	117	76	52
		500				214	162	124	79	53
		1,000			399	272	193	142	85	56
		2,000		854	498	314	213	153	89	58

75. You are using attribute sampling to test the effectiveness of a control over a file of 1,000 purchase orders. You expect a 10% deviation rate in the population and would like to select a sample sufficiently large to provide a precision of 10% with a 99% level of confidence. What sample size is needed?

A. 50

B. 56

C. 121

D. 193

The correct answer is (B). *(CIA, adapted)*

REQUIRED: The determined sample size.

DISCUSSION: For a population of 1,000, an expected deviation rate of 10%, a confidence level of 99%, and a precision of 10%, the attribute sampling table specifies a minimum sample size of 56.

Answer (A) is incorrect because 50 is the minimum sample size for a confidence level of 95%. Answer (C) is incorrect because 121 is the minimum sample size for a confidence level of 95% and a precision of 5%. Answer (D) is incorrect because 193 is the minimum sample size for a population of 400 and a precision of 4%.

76. You are using attribute sampling to test the effectiveness of a control over a file of 1,000 purchase orders. You expect a 10% deviation rate in the population and would like your sample results to vary by no more than 40 purchase orders. If you selected a sample size of 178, how reliable would you conclude your sample results to be?

A. 90%

B. 95%

C. 96%

D. 99%

The correct answer is (B). *(CIA, adapted)*

REQUIRED: The determined reliability.

DISCUSSION: For a population of 1,000, an expected deviation rate of 10%, a precision of 4% (40 ÷ 1,000), and a sample size of 178, the attribute sampling table specifies a 95% confidence level or reliability.

Answer (A) is incorrect because the table gives no values for a confidence level of 90%. Answer (C) is incorrect because the table gives no values for a confidence level of 96%. Answer (D) is incorrect because 272 is the sample size for a population of 1,000, precision of 4%, and a 10% deviation rate.

77. You used attribute sampling to test a population of 1,000 purchase orders, and the results showed a deviation rate of 9%. If your sample size was 85 and your confidence level was 99%, what was the upper occurrence limit?

A. 17%

B. 9%

C. 8%

D. 1%

The correct answer is (A). *(CIA, adapted)*

REQUIRED: The determined upper occurrence limit.

DISCUSSION: For a population size of 1,000, a confidence level of 99%, and a sample size of 85, the precision is +8%. Given the deviation rate of 9%, the upper occurrence limit is 17% (8% + 9%).

Answer (B) is incorrect because 9% is the deviation rate. Answer (C) is incorrect because 8% is the precision. Answer (D) is incorrect because 1% is the difference between the precision and the deviation rate, which has no relevance.

78. You used attribute sampling to test a population of 2,000 purchase orders. Using a reliability level of 99%, an expected deviation rate of 10%, and a sample size of 195, the precision is

A. More than 5%.

B. More than 3% but less than 5%.

C. More than 6% but less than 8%.

D. Indeterminable from the data given.

The correct answer is (A). *(CIA, adapted)*

REQUIRED: The determined precision.

DISCUSSION: At the 99% confidence level and population size of 2,000, the attribute sampling table shows that a sample size of 195 has a precision of between 5% and 6%.

Answer (B) is incorrect because, at the 95% confidence level and a population size of 2,000, a sample size of 195 has a precision of 4%. Answer (C) is incorrect because a sample of 195 has a precision of less than 6% for all values in the table. Answer (D) is incorrect because the precision is determinable from the data given.

79. What is an auditor's evaluation of a statistical sample for attributes when a test of 50 documents results in three deviations if the tolerable rate is 7%, the expected population deviation rate is 5%, and the allowance for sampling risk is 2%?

A. Modify the planned assessed level of control risk because the tolerable rate plus the allowance for sampling risk exceeds the expected population deviation rate.

B. Accept the sample results as support for the planned assessed level of control risk because the sample deviation rate plus the allowance for sampling risk exceeds the tolerable rate.

C. Accept the sample results as support for the planned assessed level of control risk because the tolerable rate minus the allowance for sampling risk equals the expected population deviation rate.

D. Modify the planned assessed level of control risk because the sample deviation rate plus the allowance for sampling risk exceeds the tolerable rate.

The correct answer is (D). *(CPA, adapted)*

REQUIRED: The evaluation of an attribute sample given the sample deviation, sampling risk, tolerable rate, and expected rate.

DISCUSSION: The sample has a 6% (3 ÷ 50) deviation rate. The auditor's upper precision limit is 8% (6% + the 2% allowance for sampling risk, which is the difference between the tolerable rate of 7% and the expected rate of 5%). Thus, the true deviation rate could be as large as 8% and exceed the tolerable rate. Accordingly, the auditor should revise his/her consideration of the planned assessed level of control risk for the relevant assertions and possibly alter the nature, timing, and extent of substantive tests (AU 350).

Answer (A) is incorrect because precision (allowance for sampling risk) is the difference between the tolerable rate and the expected rate, and the precision interval is constructed around the sample rate, not the tolerable rate. Answer (B) is incorrect because a deviation rate that may be as large as 8% is a reason for revising the consideration of the planned assessed level of control risk. Answer (C) is incorrect because the sample deviation rate, which is the best estimate of the true rate, must not be ignored.

6.6 Variables Sampling

80. Very small random samples (fewer than 30) should normally be avoided when using a variables sampling plan because

A. The estimated standard deviation of the population will increase disproportionately.

B. The skew of the distribution of sample means cannot be determined.

C. The estimated population mean value will increase disproportionately.

D. The size of the sampling risk will increase disproportionately.

The correct answer is (D). *(CIA, adapted)*

REQUIRED: The reason to avoid small sample sizes.

DISCUSSION: When small samples are selected from a population, the chance is greater that the sample will not adequately represent the population. Small samples (fewer than 30) should therefore be avoided because of the increase in sampling risk.

Answers (A) and (C) are incorrect because, if the sample is too small and is therefore not representative, the misstatement may lie in either direction depending on the sample. Answer (B) is incorrect because the results of a small sample can be statistically evaluated, but they are usually not as precise or reliable as those achieved when the sample is larger. Thus, the mean, standard error, skewness, etc., are less useful for very small samples.

81. In applying variables sampling, an auditor attempts to

A. Estimate a qualitative characteristic of interest.

B. Determine various rates of occurrence for specified attributes.

C. Discover at least one instance of a critical deviation.

D. Predict a monetary population value within a range of precision.

The correct answer is (D). *(CIA, adapted)*

REQUIRED: The purpose of variables sampling.

DISCUSSION: Variables sampling is used to estimate the value of a population. In auditing, this process entails estimating the monetary value of an account balance or other accounting total. The result is often stated in terms of a point estimate plus or minus a stated dollar value (the range of precision at the desired level of confidence).

Answer (A) is incorrect because the estimate is quantitative. Answer (B) is incorrect because determining various rates of occurrence for specified attributes applies to attribute sampling. Answer (C) is incorrect because discovering at least one instance of a critical deviation is the purpose of discovery sampling.

82. In estimation sampling for variables, which of the following must be known in order to estimate the appropriate sample size required to meet the auditor's needs in a given situation?

A. The qualitative aspects of misstatements.

B. The total dollar amount of the population.

C. The acceptable level of risk.

D. The estimated deviation rate in the population.

The correct answer is (C). *(CPA, adapted)*

REQUIRED: The factor that must be known to estimate sample size.

DISCUSSION: Variables sampling is employed in substantive testing because it may be used to estimate the amount of a variable, such as an account balance, and to quantify the risk that the estimate may not approximate the true value. AU 350 states, "When planning a particular sample for a substantive test of details, the auditor should consider the relationship of the sample to the audit objective, preliminary estimates of materiality levels, the auditor's allowable risk of incorrect acceptance, and characteristics of the population."

Answer (A) is incorrect because qualitative aspects of misstatements are a matter for sample evaluation, not sample size selection. Answer (B) is incorrect because estimating the population value is the objective of the sample. Also, some sampling methods, e.g., mean-per-unit sampling, ignore the book values of individual sample items. Answer (D) is incorrect because attribute sampling is concerned with deviation rates.

83. An auditor used a mean-per-unit sampling plan to estimate the average cost of repairing photocopy machines. The sample size was 50, and population size was 2,000. The mean of the sample was $75. The standard deviation was $14, and the standard error of the mean was $2. What is the confidence interval at a 95% confidence level (Z = 2)?

A. $47 to $103.

B. $71 to $79.

C. $61 to $89.

D. $73 to $75.

The correct answer is (B). *(CIA, adapted)*

REQUIRED: The confidence interval for a given confidence level.

DISCUSSION: If C is the confidence coefficient, n is the sample size, and σ is the standard deviation, the following is the basic variables sampling formula solved for precision (P):

$$P = \frac{C\sigma}{\sqrt{n}}$$

If C is given as 2 (Z = 2), the confidence interval equals the mean plus or minus two times the standard error of the mean ($\sigma \div \sqrt{n}$ = $2). Thus, the confidence interval equals $75 ± $4, or $71 to $79.

Answer (A) is incorrect because $47 to $103 equals two standard deviations above and below the mean. Answer (C) is incorrect because $61 to $89 equals one standard deviation above and below the mean. Answer (D) is incorrect because $73 to $75 equals one standard error below the mean.

84. In an application of mean-per-unit sampling, the following information has been obtained:

Reported book value	$600,000
Point estimate (estimated total value)	591,000
Allowance for sampling risk (precision)	± 22,000
Tolerable misstatement	± 45,000

The appropriate conclusion is that the reported book value is

A. Acceptable only if the risk of incorrect rejection is at least twice the risk of incorrect acceptance.

B. Acceptable.

C. Not acceptable.

D. Acceptable only if the risk of incorrect acceptance is at least twice the risk of incorrect rejection.

The correct answer is (B). *(CIA, adapted)*

REQUIRED: The correct conclusion given an application of mean-per-unit sampling.

DISCUSSION: In mean-per-unit sampling, the audit estimate of the population value is obtained by multiplying the number of items in the population by the average value of the audited sample items. The precision interval is constructed around the audited value of the sample items. When the point estimate of the audited population value is $591,000 with a precision interval of plus or minus $22,000, a book value of $600,000 is acceptable because it falls within the allowance for sampling risk (precision). The precision is determined by considering the tolerable misstatement in conjunction with the allowable risk of incorrect acceptance (an issue related to audit effectiveness) and allowable risk of incorrect rejection (an efficiency issue). A table is typically consulted that gives the ratio of the precision to tolerable misstatement for the specified risks of incorrect rejection and incorrect acceptance. For example, the table sets precision at 50% of tolerable misstatement, or approximately $22,000, when the specified risk of incorrect acceptance is 50% of the risk of incorrect rejection.

Answers (A) and (D) are incorrect because the allowable risks of incorrect acceptance and incorrect rejection are separately determined by the auditor based on professional judgment. Answer (C) is incorrect because the reported value is acceptable.

85. An auditor selected a random sample of 100 items from a population of 2,000 items. The total dollars in the sample were $10,000, and the standard deviation was $10. If the achieved precision based on this sample was plus or minus $4,000, the minimum acceptable value of the population would be

A. $204,000

B. $196,000

C. $199,000

D. $199,800

The correct answer is (B). *(CIA, adapted)*

REQUIRED: The minimum acceptable value of the population.

DISCUSSION: The mean value of a sample item is $100 ($10,000 ÷ 100), so the estimated population value is $200,000. Given achieved precision of $4,000, the minimum acceptable value of the population is $196,000 ($200,000 – $4,000).

Answer (A) is incorrect because $204,000 results from adding $4,000. Answer (C) is incorrect because $199,000 subtracts the total standard deviation of the sample, assuming $10 is the standard deviation per sample item. Answer (D) is incorrect because $199,800 subtracts the standard deviation of the population, assuming $10 is the total standard deviation of the 100-item sample.

86. In a variables sampling application, an auditor draws random samples from two equal-sized groups of inventory items. The mean value of the inventory in the first group was calculated to be $3,000, with a standard deviation of $500. The mean value of inventory in the second group was estimated to be $1,000, with a standard deviation of $90. If the auditor had drawn an unstratified sample from the entire population, the expected mean value of inventory would be $2,000, and the expected standard deviation would be

A. Between $90 and $500, but not $295.

B. Less than $90.

C. Greater than $500.

D. $295.

The correct answer is (C). *(Publisher)*

REQUIRED: The standard deviation given an unstratified sample.

DISCUSSION: The standard deviation is a measure of variability within a population. That the population was stratified indicates that each stratum has a smaller standard deviation than the population as a whole. If the two diverse populations are combined, the resulting standard deviation is likely to be larger than that of either of the separate strata. Because the standard deviations of the two strata were $500 and $90, the expected standard deviation is likely to be greater than $500.

Answers (A) and (B) are incorrect because the resulting standard deviation is likely to be larger than that of either of the separate strata. Answer (D) is incorrect because $295 is the simple average of the standard deviations of the two strata. The resulting standard deviation is likely to be larger than that of either of the separate strata.

87. An auditor's finding was stated as follows: "Twenty of one hundred randomly selected items tested revealed that $200 of cash discounts on purchases were lost." This variables sampling finding is deficient because the

A. Recommendation specifies no action.

B. Sampling methodology is not defined.

C. Amount is not material.

D. Probable effect on the entire population is not provided.

The correct answer is (D). *(CIA, adapted)*

REQUIRED: The reason the variables sampling finding is deficient.

DISCUSSION: The finding states the number of population items selected and the total amount of purchase discounts lost but does not extend the sample results to the population.

Answer (A) is incorrect because no action may be necessary if there is a reason for the loss of purchase discounts or if the amount is immaterial. Answer (B) is incorrect because the methodology was stated to be random sampling. Answer (C) is incorrect because the amount may or may not be material.

6.7 Dollar-Unit (PPS) Sampling

88. An auditor is planning to use monetary-unit sampling for testing the dollar value of a large accounts receivable population. The advantages of using monetary-unit sampling (MUS) include all of the following except

A. It is an efficient model for establishing that a low error rate population is not materially misstated.

B. It does not require the normal distribution approximation required by variables sampling.

C. It can be applied to a group of accounts because the sampling units are homogenous.

D. It results in a smaller sample size than classical variables sampling for larger numbers of misstatements.

The correct answer is (D). *(CIA, adapted)*

REQUIRED: The item not an advantage of MUS.

DISCUSSION: MUS is also known as probability-proportional-to-size (PPS) sampling or dollar-unit sampling. It is a modified version of attribute sampling that relates deviation rates to dollar amounts. It uses the dollar as the sampling unit. MUS is appropriate for testing account balances, such as those for inventory and receivables, in which some items may be far larger than others in the population. In effect, it stratifies the population because the larger account balances have a greater chance of being selected. MUS is most useful if few misstatements are expected. Moreover, it is designed to detect overstatements. It is not effective for estimating understatements because, the greater the understatement, the less likely the item will be selected. Furthermore, as the number of expected misstatements increases, MUS requires a larger sample size than classical variables sampling.

Answer (A) is incorrect because MUS is efficient when few misstatements are expected. Answer (B) is incorrect because MUS does not assume normally distributed populations. Answer (C) is incorrect because MUS uses dollars as sampling units.

89. When an auditor uses dollar-unit statistical sampling to examine the total value of invoices, each invoice

A. Has an equal probability of being selected.

B. Can be represented by no more than one dollar unit.

C. Has an unknown probability of being selected.

D. Has a probability proportional to its dollar value of being selected.

The correct answer is (D). *(CIA, adapted)*

REQUIRED: The effect of using dollar-unit sampling to examine invoices.

DISCUSSION: Dollar-unit sampling results in the selection of every nth dollar; thus, a $1,000 item is 1,000 times more likely to be selected than a $1 item. The probability of selection of a sampled item is directly proportional to the size of the item.

Answer (A) is incorrect because each dollar, but not each invoice, has an equal probability of being selected unless all invoices are for the same amount. Answer (B) is incorrect because it is possible for two or more dollars to be selected from the same item; e.g., a $4,500 item will be represented by four dollars if every 1,000th dollar is selected. Answer (C) is incorrect because the probability of selection can be calculated using the dollar value of the item and the dollar value of the population.

90. Monetary-unit sampling (MUS) is most useful when the auditor

A. Is testing the accounts payable balance.

B. Cannot cumulatively arrange the population items.

C. Expects to find several material misstatements in the sample.

D. Is concerned with overstatements.

The correct answer is (D). *(CIA, adapted)*

REQUIRED: The best use of MUS.

DISCUSSION: MUS is also known as probability-proportional-to-size (PPS) sampling or dollar-unit sampling. It is a modified version of attribute sampling that relates deviation rates to dollar amounts. It uses the dollar as the sampling unit. MUS sampling is appropriate for testing account balances, such as those for inventory and receivables, in which some items may be far larger than others in the population. In effect, it stratifies the population because the larger account balances have a greater chance of being selected. MUS is most useful if few misstatements are expected. Moreover, it is designed to detect overstatements. It is not effective for estimating understatements because, the greater the understatement, the less likely the item will be selected. Special design considerations are required if the auditor anticipates understatements or zero or negative balances.

Answer (A) is incorrect because an audit of accounts payable is primarily concerned with understatements. Answer (B) is incorrect because the items in the population must be arranged by cumulative dollar total. The first dollar is chosen randomly, the second equals the random start plus the sample interval in dollars, etc. Answer (C) is incorrect because, as the expected amount of misstatement increases, the MUS sample size increases. MUS may also overstate the upper misstatement limit when misstatements are found. The result might be rejection of an acceptable balance.

91. Which of the following most likely would be an advantage in using classical variables sampling rather than probability-proportional-to-size (PPS) sampling?

A. An estimate of the standard deviation of the population's recorded amounts is not required.

B. The auditor rarely needs the assistance of a computer program to design an efficient sample.

C. Inclusion of zero and negative balances usually does not require special design considerations.

D. Any amount that is individually significant is automatically identified and selected.

The correct answer is (C). *(CPA, adapted)*

REQUIRED: The advantage of using classical variables sampling rather than PPS sampling.

DISCUSSION: PPS is most useful if few misstatements are expected and if overstatement is the most likely kind of misstatement. One disadvantage of PPS sampling is that it is designed to detect overstatements. It is not effective for estimating understatements. The smaller the item, the less likely it will be selected in the sample, but the more likely the item is understated.

Answer (A) is incorrect because the sample size formula for estimation of variables includes the standard deviation of the population. Answer (B) is incorrect because a computer program is helpful in many sampling applications. Answer (D) is incorrect because, in classical variables sampling, every item has an equal and nonzero probability of selection.

92. Which of the following would be an improper technique when using dollar-unit statistical sampling in an audit of accounts receivable?

A. Combining negative and positive dollar misstatements in the appraisal of a sample.

B. Using a sampling technique in which the same account balance could be selected more than once.

C. Selecting a random starting point and then sampling every nth dollar unit (systematic sampling).

D. Defining the sampling unit in the population as an individual dollar and not as an individual account balance.

The correct answer is (A). *(CIA, adapted)*

REQUIRED: The improper technique when using dollar-unit sampling in an audit of receivables.

DISCUSSION: When using dollar-unit sampling, the auditor may calculate the gross projected likely misstatement (GPLM) and the gross upper misstatement limit (GUML) for overstatements, ignoring understatements. (S)he then calculates these values for understatements, ignoring overstatements. The net upper misstatement limits are then determined by subtracting the GPLM for one kind of misstatement from the GUML for the other. The resulting net upper misstatement limits for over- and understatements define the precision interval. However, more complicated computations may be appropriate in certain extreme cases. The GUMLs may not be netted, and individual positive and negative misstatements also cannot be netted.

Answer (B) is incorrect because two or more dollars may be selected from the same item; e.g., a $10,000 item will be represented twice if every 5,000th dollar is selected. Answer (C) is incorrect because dollar-unit sampling consists of selecting a random start and then sampling every nth dollar unit. Answer (D) is incorrect because dollar-unit sampling defines the sampling unit in the population as an individual dollar and not as an individual account balance.

93. The use of probability-proportional-to-size sampling is inefficient if

A. Bank accounts are being audited.

B. Statistical inferences are to be made.

C. Each account is of equal importance.

D. The number of sampling units is large.

The correct answer is (C). *(CIA, adapted)*

REQUIRED: The inefficient use of probability-proportional-to-size (PPS) sampling.

DISCUSSION: Probability-proportional-to-size sampling gives greater weight to larger, more significant items. If all items are of the same importance, PPS is inappropriate.

Answer (A) is incorrect because PPS sampling could be appropriate in an audit of bank accounts if larger items are more important than smaller items (which is usually true in variables sampling). Answer (B) is incorrect because PPS sampling permits statistical inferences to be made. Answer (D) is incorrect because PPS sampling could be appropriate with a large number of sampling units if larger items are more important than smaller items.

94. In selecting a sample using dollar-unit sampling, the dollar is the sampling unit. Thus, if the 300th dollar of invoices is selected,

A. Only that dollar is audited.

B. Only an invoice with exactly $300 is audited.

C. An invoice of less than $300 cannot be selected.

D. The invoice containing the 300th dollar is audited.

The correct answer is (D). *(Publisher)*

REQUIRED: The item sampled.

DISCUSSION: The dollar selected is a basis for choosing the sales invoice to be audited. Thus, the 300th dollar identifies an invoice on which all dollars will be audited.

Answer (A) is incorrect because, not only is the 300th dollar audited, but also all other dollars on the invoice selected. Answer (B) is incorrect because an invoice with any amount may be selected by the technique, not just those for exactly $300. Answer (C) is incorrect because an invoice with any amount may be selected by the technique, not just those for $300 or more.

Questions 95 and 96 are based on the following information. The work of an auditor has been assigned to take a dollar-unit sample of a population of vouchers in the purchasing department. The population has a total book value of $300,000. The auditor believes that a maximum misstatement of $900 is acceptable and would like to have 95% confidence in the results. (The reliability factor at 95% and zero misstatements = 3.00).

Table of First 10 Vouchers in Population

Voucher #	Balance	Cumulative Balance
1	$100	$ 100
2	150	250
3	40	290
4	200	490
5	10	500
6	290	790
7	50	840
8	190	1,030
9	20	1,050
10	180	1,230

95. Given a random start of $50 as the first dollar amount, what is the number of the fourth voucher to be selected, assuming that the sample size will be 1,000?

A. 4

B. 6

C. 7

D. 8

The correct answer is (D). *(CIA, adapted)*

REQUIRED: The number of the fourth voucher selected using dollar-unit sampling.

DISCUSSION: The vouchers have a book value of $300,000 and 1,000 items are to be sampled, so every 300th dollar will be chosen. Given a random start of $50, the vouchers containing the 50th, 350th, 650th, and 950th dollars will be selected. The cumulative amount of the first eight vouchers is $1,030. Accordingly, voucher 8 is the fourth voucher audited. It contains the 950th dollar.

Answer (A) is incorrect because voucher 4 contains the 350th dollar and is the second voucher selected. Answer (B) is incorrect because voucher 6 contains the 650th dollar and is the third voucher selected. Answer (C) is incorrect because voucher 7 is not selected.

96. In examining the sample, one overstatement was detected causing an extension of $270 to the tolerable misstatement. Assuming that the sample size was 1,000 and that the maximum dollar amount of overstatement if no misstatements were found was established to be $900 before the sampling analysis, what conclusion can the auditor now make from the sampling evidence?

A. (S)he is 95% confident that the dollar amount of overstatement in the population of vouchers is between $900 and $1,170.

B. (S)he is 95% confident that the dollar amount of overstatement in the population of vouchers exceeds $1,170.

C. (S)he is 95% confident that the dollar amount of overstatement in the population of vouchers is less than $1,170.

D. An insufficient number of misstatements was detected to warrant a conclusion.

The correct answer is (C). *(CIA, adapted)*

REQUIRED: The conclusion from the audit evidence given an extension of tolerable misstatement.

DISCUSSION: Had the internal auditor detected no misstatements in the sample, (s)he could have been 95% confident that the dollar amount of overstatement in the balance was less than $900. Given discovery of an overstatement causing an extension to the tolerable misstatement of $270, the auditor could conclude with 95% confidence that the overstatement is less than $1,170 ($900 + $270).

Answers (A) and (B) are incorrect because the auditor is 95% confident that the overstatement is less than $1,170. Answer (D) is incorrect because a conclusion would have been warranted even if no misstatements had been found.

Questions 97 through 100 are based on the following information. Edwards has decided to use probability-proportional-to-size (PPS) sampling in the audit of a client's accounts receivable balance. Few, if any, account balance overstatements are expected. Edwards plans to use the following PPS sampling table:

Reliability Factors for Overstatements

Number of Overstatements	Risk of Incorrect Acceptance 1%	5%	10%	15%	20%
0	4.61	3.00	2.31	1.90	1.61
1	6.64	4.75	3.89	3.38	3.00
2	8.41	6.30	5.33	4.72	4.28

The following information was also available:

Tolerable misstatement	$15,000
Risk of incorrect acceptance	5%
Recorded amount of accounts receivable	$300,000

Three overstatements were discovered in a PPS sample:

	Recorded Amount	Audit Amount
1st	$ 400	$ 320
2nd	500	0
3rd	3,000	2,500

97. Edwards should use a sampling interval of

A. $20,000

B. $15,000

C. $10,000

D. $5,000

The correct answer is (D). *(Publisher)*

REQUIRED: The sampling interval for a PPS sample.

DISCUSSION: Because the dollar amount of anticipated misstatement is not given, it must be assumed to be zero. In that case, the PPS sample size formula is

$$n = \frac{BV \times RF}{TM}$$

n is the sample size, BV the book value, RF the reliability factor (always from the zero line of the table), and TM the tolerable misstatement. The sampling interval equals BV divided by n. Solving the formula for this value establishes that the interval also equals TM divided by RF, or $5,000 ($15,000 ÷ 3.00 at 5% risk of incorrect acceptance and zero overstatements).

Answer (A) is incorrect because $20,000 equals the $15,000 TM divided into the $300,000 BV. Answer (B) is incorrect because $15,000 is the tolerable misstatement. Answer (C) is incorrect because the derivation of $10,000 cannot be readily determined.

98. Based on the sampling interval calculated in the preceding question, Edwards should use a sample size of

A. 60

B. 50

C. 40

D. 30

The correct answer is (A). *(Publisher)*

REQUIRED: The sample size for a PPS sample.

DISCUSSION: The sample size equals the book value divided by the sampling interval, or 60 ($300,000 ÷ $5,000).

Answer (B) is incorrect because a sample size of 50 assumes an interval of $6,000, not $5,000. Answer (C) is incorrect because a sample size of 40 assumes an interval of $7,500. Answer (D) is incorrect because a sample size of 30 assumes an interval of $10,000.

99. Without prejudice to the answers in the preceding questions, assume that the sampling interval is $1,000. What is the total projected misstatement given the three misstatements discovered?

A. $1,750

B. $1,700

C. $1,200

D. $1,000

The correct answer is (B). *(Publisher)*

REQUIRED: The total projected misstatement.

DISCUSSION: The total projected misstatement is the sum of the misstatements projected based on the respective logical sampling units (accounts receivable) containing misstatements. If a logical unit has a book value less than the sampling interval, a tainting percentage [(book value – audit value) ÷ book value] is calculated for that misstatement and then multiplied by the sampling interval. The percentage taint in the logical unit is extended to all dollars in the sampling interval it represents. If the book value is equal to or greater than the sampling interval, the misstatement in the logical unit is the projected misstatement.

Book Value	Audit Value	Tainting %	Sampling Interval	Projected Misstatement
$ 400	$ 320	20%	$1,000	$ 200
500	0	100%	1,000	1,000
3,000	2,500	--	--	500
				$1,700

Answer (A) is incorrect because the derivation of $1,750 cannot be readily determined. Answer (C) is incorrect because $1,200 is the total projected misstatement for the first two items. Answer (D) is incorrect because $1,000 is the projected misstatement for item two.

100. Assuming a sampling interval of $1,000, what is the upper misstatement limit (UML) based on this sample?

A. $1,700

B. $3,000

C. $5,560

D. $5,790

The correct answer is (C). *(Publisher)*

REQUIRED: The upper misstatement limit (UML).

DISCUSSION: The first component of the UML is basic precision: the product of the sampling interval ($1,000) and the risk factor (3.00) for zero misstatements at the specified risk of incorrect acceptance (5%). The second component is the total projected misstatement ($1,700). The third component is an allowance for widening the precision gap as a result of finding more than zero misstatements. This allowance is determined only with respect to logical sampling units with book values less than the sampling interval. If a sample item is equal to or greater than the sampling interval, the degree of taint for that interval is certain, and no further allowance is necessary. The first step in calculating this allowance is to determine the adjusted incremental changes in the reliability factors (these factors increase, and precision widens, as the number of misstatements increases). The factors are from the 5% column in the table. To prevent double counting of amounts already included in basic precision, in projected misstatement, and in the adjustments for higher-ranked misstatements, the preceding reliability factor plus 1.0 is subtracted from each factor. The projected misstatements are then ranked from highest to lowest, each adjusted incremental reliability factor is multiplied by the related projected misstatement, and the products are summed.

Basic precision ($1,000 × 3.00)		$3,000
Total projected misstatement (see Q. 99)		1,700
Allowance for precision gap widening:		
(4.75 – 3.00 – 1.00) × $1,000 =	$750	
(6.30 – 4.75 – 1.00) × $200 =	110	860
UML		$5,560

Answer (A) is incorrect because $1,700 is the total projected misstatement given the three misstatements discovered. Answer (B) is incorrect because $3,000 is the basic precision. Answer (D) is incorrect because $5,790 {$5,560 + [(7.76 – 6.30 – 1.00) x $500]} improperly includes an allowance for precision gap widening for a third misstatement.

101. Which of the following statements is true concerning probability-proportional-to-size (PPS) sampling, also known as dollar-unit sampling?

A. The sampling distribution should approximate the normal distribution.

B. Overstated units have a lower probability of sample selection than units that are understated.

C. The auditor controls the risk of incorrect acceptance by specifying that risk level for the sampling plan.

D. The sampling interval is calculated by dividing the number of physical units in the population by the sample size.

The correct answer is (C). *(CPA, adapted)*

REQUIRED: The true statement about PPS sampling.

DISCUSSION: AU 350 considers PPS sampling to be an appropriate random-based method. Thus, it is a technique whereby the auditor can measure and control the risks associated with observing fewer than 100% of the population. The auditor can quantify and measure beta risk, i.e., the risk of accepting a client's book value as fair when it is materially misstated.

Answer (A) is incorrect because PPS requires no assumptions about the population or sampling distribution. Answer (B) is incorrect because, as the size of the units in the population increases, so does the probability of selection. Answer (D) is incorrect because the sampling interval is calculated by dividing the total dollars, not units, in the population by the sample size. Every nth dollar is then selected after a random start.

6.8 Relationships -- Sample Size Determinants

102. A number of factors influence the sample size for a substantive test of details of an account balance. All other factors being equal, which of the following would lead to a larger sample size?

A. A lower assessed level of control risk.

B. Increased use of analytical procedures to obtain evidence about particular assertions.

C. Smaller expected frequency of deviations.

D. Smaller measure of tolerable misstatement.

The correct answer is (D). *(CPA, adapted)*

REQUIRED: The factor increasing sample size.

DISCUSSION: Holding the risk of incorrect acceptance constant, a reduction in acceptable tolerable misstatement requires the auditor to select a larger sample. The larger sample reduces the allowance for sampling risk.

Answer (A) is incorrect because, as control risk decreases, the acceptable level of detection risk increases. Substantive tests are applied to reduce detection risk to the acceptable level. As that level rises, the assurance that must be provided by substantive tests declines. Smaller samples may therefore be appropriate when acceptable detection risk increases. Answer (B) is incorrect because "the auditor's reliance on substantive tests to achieve an audit objective related to a particular assertion may be derived from tests of details, from analytical procedures, or from a combination of both" (AU 329, *Analytical Procedures*). Thus, use of analytical procedures might reduce or eliminate the need for tests of details. Answer (C) is incorrect because frequency of deviations concerns sampling for attributes, not for variables. Moreover, a smaller expected deviation rate permits a smaller sample.

103. The size of a sample designed for dual-purpose testing should be

A. The larger of the samples that would otherwise have been designed for the two separate purposes.

B. The smaller of the samples that would otherwise have been designed for the two separate purposes.

C. The combined total of the samples that would otherwise have been designed for the two separate purposes.

D. More than the larger of the samples that would otherwise have been designated for the two separate purposes, but less than the combined total of the samples that would otherwise have been designed for the two separate purposes.

The correct answer is (A). *(CPA, adapted)*

REQUIRED: The true statement about sample size for dual-purpose testing.

DISCUSSION: According to AU 350, dual-purpose testing is the use of a sample for both tests of controls and substantive testing. It is customarily employed when the auditor believes that "there is an acceptably low risk that the rate of deviations from the prescribed control in the population exceeds the tolerable rate." Hence, a related substantive test might be planned at a level of risk that anticipates an assessed level of control risk below the maximum. The sample size "should be the larger of the samples that would otherwise have been designed for the two separate purposes."

Answers (B), (C), and (D) are incorrect because the larger of the two samples should be chosen.

104. Which of the following combinations results in a decrease in sample size in an attribute sample?

	Allowable Risk of Assessing Control Risk Too Low	Tolerable Rate	Expected Population Deviation Rate
A.	Increase	Decrease	Increase
B.	Decrease	Increase	Decrease
C.	Increase	Increase	Decrease
D.	Increase	Increase	Increase

The correct answer is (C). *(CPA, adapted)*

REQUIRED: The combination that results in a decrease in the size of an attribute sample.

DISCUSSION: To determine the sample size for a test of controls, the auditor considers (1) the tolerable rate of deviations, (2) the expected actual rate of deviations, and (3) the allowable risk of assessing control risk too low. An increase in the allowable risk of assessing control risk too low, an increase in the tolerable rate, and a decrease in the expected rate have the effect of diminishing the degree of assurance to be provided by the sample. Thus, each factor is a basis for reducing sample size.

Answers (A), (B), and (D) are incorrect because an increase in the allowable risk of assessing control risk too low, an increase in the tolerable rate, and a decrease in the expected rate are reasons for decreasing sample size.

105. You seek to determine the misstatements made in recording sales invoices. Which of the following factors will usually be most significant in determining the number of sales invoices to select for testing?

A. The total number of invoices for the period.

B. The estimated loss being incurred by the division.

C. The dollars of sales considered to be material.

D. The precision desired.

The correct answer is (D). *(CIA, adapted)*

REQUIRED: The factor most significant in determining the required sample size.

DISCUSSION: The auditor's precision is usually the most important factor in determining the number of sales invoices to be selected. The precision is squared before it is used in the sample size formula. Accordingly, relatively small changes in the desired precision have a great effect on the required sample size.

Answer (A) is incorrect because the population size has a relatively small effect on the required sample size. The finite population correction factor reduces the required sample size for samples that are large relative to the population. Answer (B) is incorrect because the estimated loss being incurred by the division is not a factor used in calculating sample size. Answer (C) is incorrect because the amount of sales considered to be material is not a factor used in calculating sample size.

106. In an audit of a governmental agency, you are searching for expenditures that are improperly classified. Assuming a statistical sampling plan is adopted, which of the factors listed below most directly affects the number of items that you seek to review?

A. Magnitude of the dollar budget for the agency.

B. Number of items you found misclassified in last year's audit.

C. Quality of internal control.

D. Estimated deviation rate.

The correct answer is (D). *(CIA, adapted)*

REQUIRED: The most significant factor used in determining the size of the sample.

DISCUSSION: In the attribute sample size formula, the estimated deviation rate, its complement, and the square of the confidence coefficient are factors appearing in the numerator. The square of the precision is in the denominator.

Answer (A) is incorrect because attribute sampling is concerned with deviation rates, not quantities or dollar values. Answer (B) is incorrect because, although the number of items misclassified in the previous period may be helpful, the auditor still must calculate the estimated deviation rate for the current period. Answer (C) is incorrect because the quality of internal control is not explicitly recognized in the sample size formula. However, the estimation of the deviation rate may be influenced by the auditor's understanding of internal control.

Questions 107 through 111 are based on the following information. The following table shows comparative population characteristics and audit specifications of two populations:

	Characteristics of Population 1 Relative to Population 2		Audit Specifications as to a Sample from Population 1 Relative to a Sample from Population 2	
	Size	Variability	Specified Precision	Specified Confidence Level
Case 1	Equal	Equal	Equal	Higher
Case 2	Equal	Larger	Wider	Equal
Case 3	Larger	Equal	Tighter	Lower
Case 4	Smaller	Smaller	Equal	Lower
Case 5	Larger	Equal	Equal	Higher

For each question (each case), you are to indicate the required sample size to be selected from population 1 relative to the sample from population 2. Your answer choice should be selected from the following responses:

A. Larger than the required sample size from Population 2.

B. Equal to the required sample size from Population 2.

C. Smaller than the required sample size from Population 2.

D. Indeterminate relative to the required sample size from Population 2.

REQUIRED: The effects on sample size of changing the characteristics and specifications of two populations.

DISCUSSION: In general, four factors affect sample size for a variables sampling application: population size, variability of the population, specified precision (allowance for sampling risk), and specified confidence level (reliability). Increases in population size, variability, and specified confidence level cause sample sizes to become larger. Increases in specified precision cause sample sizes to become smaller.

107. In Case 1, the required sample size from Population 1 is

The correct answer is (A). *(CPA, adapted)*

In Case 1, all other attributes are the same except that Population 1 will have a higher specified confidence level. A higher confidence level has a higher confidence coefficient, which varies directly with sample size. Thus, the auditor must take a larger sample size from Population 1 than from Population 2.

108. In Case 2, the required sample size from Population 1 is

The correct answer is (D). *(CPA, adapted)*

In Case 2, variability in Population 1 is larger and the specified precision is wider. Larger variability (a larger σ) requires a larger sample size, but the wider precision decreases the sample size. The magnitudes are unknown, so the relative required sample size is not determinable.

109. In Case 3, the required sample size from Population 1 is

The correct answer is (D). *(CPA, adapted)*

Case 3 specifies a larger population size, a tighter specified precision, and a lower confidence level. The larger size of Population 1 and the tighter precision require a larger sample size; however, the lower specified confidence level requires a smaller sample size. Because the magnitudes are unknown, the effect on sample size is not determinable.

110. In Case 4, the required sample size from Population 1 is

The correct answer is (C). *(CPA, adapted)*

In Case 4, Population 1 is smaller than Population 2, the variability is smaller, and the required specified confidence level is lower. Smaller population size indicates a smaller sample size. The smaller variability and lower confidence level also decrease the sample size. Thus, the sample required from Population 1 is smaller than that from Population 2.

111. In Case 5, the required sample size from Population 1 is

The correct answer is (A). *(CPA, adapted)*

In Case 5, Population 1 is larger and has a higher specified confidence level. Both attributes are directly related to sample size. Thus, the sample from Population 1 will be larger than that from Population 2.

112. An auditor is considering a sample size of 50 to estimate the average amount per invoice in a large trucking company. How will the precision of the sample results be affected if the sample size is increased to 200?

A. The larger sample will be about two times as precise as the smaller sample.

B. The larger sample will be about four times as precise as the smaller sample.

C. Although precision will not be increased that much, a possible downward bias in the estimate of the average per invoice would be corrected.

D. Both sample sizes are larger than 30, so the increase will not have that much of an effect on precision.

The correct answer is (A). *(CIA, adapted)*

REQUIRED: The effect on precision of increasing the sample size.

DISCUSSION: The precision of sample results is inversely proportional to the square root of the sample size. Thus, increasing the sample by a factor of four decreases (tightens) the precision by a factor of two.

Answer (B) is incorrect because the precision of sample results does not increase at the same rate as sample size. Answer (C) is incorrect because the expected value of the sample mean is the same regardless of sample size. Answer (D) is incorrect because precision will tighten by a factor of two.

113. In attribute sampling, a 10% change in which of the following factors normally will have the least effect on the size of a statistical sample?

A. Population size.

B. Precision (confidence interval).

C. Reliability (confidence level).

D. Standard deviation.

The correct answer is (A). *(CPA, adapted)*

REQUIRED: The factor having the least effect on sample sizes in attribute sampling.

DISCUSSION: A change in the size of the population has a very small effect on the required sample size when the population is large. This conclusion can be shown by analyzing the finite population correction factor sometimes applied to the standard sample size formula. An approximation of the FPC formula is

$$n = n' \sqrt{\frac{N - n'}{N}}$$

n' equals the preliminary sample size, n equals the determined sample size, and N is the population size. Changes in N cause very little change in the expression; e.g., a reduction in the population such that the former sample size now constitutes about 20% of the reduced population only decreases the required sample size by about 10%.

Answer (B) is incorrect because precision (confidence interval) has a major effect on sample size. Answer (C) is incorrect because reliability (confidence level) has a major effect on sample size. Answer (D) is incorrect because standard deviation has a major effect on sample size.

114. In testing a control, an auditor established an upper precision limit of 6% and a confidence level of 95%. The expected deviation rate was 4%. If the auditor expects a deviation rate of only 2% but wishes to retain the same upper precision limit and confidence level, the sample size should approximate

A. 518

B. 412

C. 369

D. 47

The correct answer is (D). *(Publisher)*

REQUIRED: The effect of a change in occurrence rate on sample size.

DISCUSSION: In attribute sampling, the expected deviation rate varies directly with sample size. Thus, a reduction in the deviation rate should cause a reduction in the required sample size. Based on the attribute sampling formula below, the sample size should be the number calculated with the formula for sample size.

$$n = \frac{C^2pq}{P^2} = \frac{1.96^2 \times .02 \times .98}{.04^2} = 47$$

C is the confidence coefficient, p is the deviation rate, q is 100% – p, P is the specified precision interval (tolerable rate minus the expected occurrence rate), and n is the sample size. The specified precision is equal to the desired upper precision limit minus the occurrence rate. In this example, P increases from 2% to 4%.

Answers (A), (B), and (C) are incorrect because 47 is the sample size.

115. If all other sample size planning factors were exactly the same in attribute sampling, changing the confidence level from 95% to 90% and changing the desired precision from 2% to 5% would result in a revised sample size that is

A. Larger.

B. Smaller.

C. Unchanged.

D. Indeterminate.

The correct answer is (B). *(CIA, adapted)*

REQUIRED: The sample size effect of decreasing the confidence level and widening the desired precision interval.

DISCUSSION: If C is the confidence coefficient, p is the expected deviation rate, q is 100% minus p, and P is the desired precision, the basic sample-size formula for attribute sampling is

$$n = \frac{C^2pq}{P^2}$$

Thus, if the confidence level is reduced (the numerator item C is lower) and precision is widened (the denominator item P is greater), sample size will be smaller.

Answer (A) is incorrect because increasing C and narrowing P would result in a larger sample size.
Answers (C) and (D) are incorrect because decreasing C and widening P decreases the sample size.

116. An auditor is testing inventory at two locations. Site I has 50,000 items and Site II has 25,000 items. The auditor will sample without replacement to test for an expected deviation rate of 4%. The sampling plan is based on a confidence level of 95% and a tolerable rate of 6% for both locations. The ratio of the sample for Site I to the sample for Site II is

A. Greater than two-to-one.

B. Two-to-one.

C. More than one-to-one but less than two-to-one.

D. One-to-one.

The correct answer is (C). *(Publisher)*

REQUIRED: The effect of population size on the sample size.

DISCUSSION: The relationship between population size and sample size is direct. As the population size increases, so does the necessary sample size, although not proportionally. In fact, as populations become extremely large, i.e., approaching infinity, the required sample approaches a constant. Thus, more items would have to be sampled from Site I than Site II, but not twice as many.

Answers (A), (B), and (D) are incorrect because the ratio is less than 2:1 but greater than 1:1.

117. Hill has decided to use probability-proportional-to-size (PPS) sampling, sometimes called dollar-unit sampling, in the audit of a client's accounts receivable balances. Hill plans to use the following PPS sampling table:

TABLE 1
Reliability Factors for Overstatements

Number of Overstatements	Risk of Incorrect Acceptance 1%	5%	10%	15%	20%
0	4.61	3.00	2.31	1.90	1.61
1	6.64	4.75	3.89	3.38	3.00
2	8.41	6.30	5.33	4.72	4.28

TABLE 2
Expansion Factors for Expected Errors

	Risk of Incorrect Acceptance 1%	5%	10%	15%	20%
Factor	1.9	1.6	1.5	1.4	1.3

Additional Information

Tolerable misstatement	$ 24,000
Anticipated misstatement	$ 5,000
Risk of incorrect acceptance	5%
Recorded amount of accounts receivable	$240,000
Number of accounts	360

What sample size should Hill use?

A. 120

B. 108

C. 45

D. 30

The correct answer is (C). *(Publisher)*

REQUIRED: The size of the PPS sample.

DISCUSSION: PPS sampling is appropriate for account balances that may include a few overstated items, such as inventory and receivables. PPS sampling relies on an attribute sampling approach (Poisson distribution) to reach a conclusion regarding the probability of overstating an account balance by a specified amount of dollars. The PPS sample size formula is

$$n = \frac{BV \times RF}{TM - (AM \times EF)}$$

n equals sample size, BV is the book value of the account, RF is the appropriate risk factor (always the zero line of Table 1), TM is tolerable misstatement, AM is the anticipated misstatement, and EF is the expansion factor (from Table 2):

$$n = \frac{\$240{,}000 \times 3.00}{\$24{,}000 - (\$5{,}000 \times 1.6)}$$

Answers (A), (B), and (D) are incorrect because the sample size formula determines that 45 is the appropriate sample size.

118. What effect does an increase in the standard deviation have on the required sample size of mean-per-unit estimation and dollar-unit sampling? Assume no change in any of the other characteristics of the population and no change in desired precision and confidence.

	Mean-per-Unit Estimation	Dollar-Unit Sampling
A.	Decrease in sample size	No change in sample size
B.	No change in sample size	Decrease in sample size
C.	Increase in sample size	No change in sample size
D.	No change in sample size	Increase in sample size

The correct answer is (C). *(CIA, adapted)*

REQUIRED: The effect of an increase in the standard deviation on the required sample size.

DISCUSSION: An increase in the standard deviation represents an increase in the variability of the population. It therefore requires increasing the sample size when MPU is used. A sample for an MPU application is determined from the standard variables sampling sample size formula. The DUS sample size formula does not include the population standard deviation or other measure of variability. The sampling units consist of individual dollars. Hence, they are homogeneous, and no measure of their variability is necessary.

Answers (A), (B), and (D) are incorrect because the MPU sample increases, but the DUS sample is not affected.

119. An auditor initially planned to use unrestricted random sampling with replacement in the audit of accounts receivable. Later, the auditor decided to use unrestricted random sampling without replacement. As a result of this decision, the sample size should

A. Increase.

B. Remain the same.

C. Decrease.

D. Be indeterminate.

The correct answer is (C). *(CPA, adapted)*

REQUIRED: The effect of sampling without replacement on the sample size.

DISCUSSION: Unrestricted random sampling means each item in the population has an equal and nonzero chance of being selected. Sampling with replacement means an item may be included more than once in the sample. Sampling without replacement removes an item from the population after selection. Sampling without replacement uses information about the population more efficiently. It results in a smaller sample, if other things are held constant, because the sample size formula for sampling without replacement is multiplied by the finite population correction factor (always less than 1.0).

Answers (A), (B), and (D) are incorrect because the sample size should decrease.

Questions 120 through 124 are based on the following information. Robert Lambert is a CPA of Rainbow Manufacturing Corporation. Rainbow manufactures two products: Product A and Product B. Product A requires raw materials that have a very low per-item cost, and Product B requires raw materials that have a very high per-item cost. Raw materials for both products are stored in a single warehouse. In 1998, Rainbow established the total value of raw materials stored in the warehouse by physically inventorying an unrestricted random sample of items selected without replacement. Mr. Lambert is evaluating the statistical validity of alternative sampling plans Rainbow is considering for 1999. Lambert knows the size of the 1998 sample and that Rainbow did not use stratified sampling in 1998. Assumptions about the population, variability, specified precision (confidence interval), and specified reliability (confidence level) for a possible 1999 sample are given in each of the following five questions. You are to indicate in each case the effect upon the size of the 1999 sample as compared to the 1998 sample. Each of the five cases is independent of the other four and is to be considered separately.

Your answer choice for each question should be selected from the following responses:

A. Larger than the 1998 sample size.

B. Equal to the 1998 sample size.

C. Smaller than the 1998 sample size.

D. Of a size that is indeterminate based upon the information given.

REQUIRED: The effects of changing population size, variability of population, specified precision, specified reliability, and sample selection methods on sample size.

DISCUSSION: The size of the population, the population variability (standard deviation), and the specified reliability all vary directly with the required sample size. Specified precision varies inversely with sample size; the smaller or tighter the precision, the larger the sample size necessary and vice versa. Alternative sample selection methods can also affect the size of the sample.

---

120. Rainbow wants to use stratified sampling in 1999 (the total population will be divided into two strata, one each for the raw materials for Product A and Product B). Compared with 1998, the population size of the raw materials inventory is approximately the same, and the variability of the items in the inventory is approximately the same. The specified precision and specified reliability are to remain the same. Under these assumptions, the required sample size for 1999 should be

The correct answer is (C). *(CPA, adapted)*

DISCUSSION: In this case, all factors are held constant except that the population is to be stratified. One subpopulation will contain materials with a very low per-item cost, while the other subpopulation will include raw materials that have a high per-item cost. By dividing the population into two strata, the variability within each subpopulation will probably be greatly reduced compared to that of the single population sampled in 1998. Because the variability is less, the sample sizes will be smaller. The sum of the two samples will likely be less than the prior year's sample size.

121. Rainbow wants to use stratified sampling in 1999. Compared with 1998, the population size of the raw materials inventory is approximately the same, and the variability of the items in the inventory is approximately the same. Rainbow specified the same precision but desires to change the specified reliability from 90% to 95%. Under these assumptions, the required sample size for 1999 should be

The correct answer is (D). *(CPA, adapted)*

DISCUSSION: Stratification allows smaller sample sizes when the total population contains a high amount of variability. The purpose of stratification is to create strata each of which has less variability than the total population. However, the effect of increasing the specified reliability from 90% to 95% is to increase sample size. Because the magnitude of the variability change is unknown, the effect on the sample size is not determinable.

122. Rainbow wants to use unrestricted random sampling without replacement in 1999. Compared with 1998, the population size of the raw materials inventory is approximately the same, and the variability of the items in the inventory is approximately the same. Rainbow specifies the same precision but desires to change the specified reliability from 90% to 95%. Under these assumptions, the required sample size for 1999 should be

The correct answer is (A). *(CPA, adapted)*

DISCUSSION: The only change from 1998 to 1999 is that the specified reliability (confidence level) will increase from 90% to 95%. Because reliability varies directly with sample size, a larger sample will be required for 1999.

123. Rainbow wants to use unrestricted random sampling without replacement in 1999. Compared with 1998, the population size of the raw materials inventory has increased, and the variability of the items in the inventory has increased. The specified precision and specified reliability are to remain the same. Under these assumptions, the required sample size for 1999 should be

The correct answer is (A). *(CPA, adapted)*

DISCUSSION: The increase in population size and in variability are directly related to sample size. Because both changes increase the necessary sample size, the sample for 1999 will be larger than that for 1998.

124. Rainbow wants to use unrestricted random sampling without replacement in 1999. Compared with 1998, the population size of the raw materials inventory has increased, but the variability of the items in the inventory has decreased. The specified precision and specified reliability are to remain the same. Under these assumptions, the required sample size for 1999 should be

The correct answer is (D). *(CPA, adapted)*

DISCUSSION: Population size and variability are directly related to sample size. The increase in population dictates an increase in sample size, while the decrease in variability requires a decrease in sample size. Because the magnitudes of the changes are not given, the change in the size of the sample is indeterminate.

Questions 125 and 126 are based on the following information.

Determination of Sample Size
RISK LEVEL -- 10% (90% RELIABILITY)

Sample Size	Occurrence Rate (%)				
	1.0	2.0	3.0	4.0	5.0
	Upper Precision Limit (%)				
100	3.3	5.2	6.6	7.8	9.1
200	2.6	4.0	5.2	6.4	7.6
300	2.2	3.5	4.7	5.9	7.0
350		3.3		5.7	
400	2.0	3.2	4.4	5.6	6.7
450		3.1		5.5	
500	1.8	3.1	4.2	5.4	6.5
550		3.0		5.3	
600	1.7	2.9	4.1	5.2	6.3
700	1.7	2.9	4.0	5.1	6.2

125. If 10% risk (90% reliability) is acceptable with an expected occurrence rate of 3% and an upper precision limit (tolerable rate) of 5%, the minimum sample size should be

A. 117

B. 240

C. 300

D. 550

The correct answer is (B). *(CIA, adapted)*

REQUIRED: The minimum sample size given risk, expected occurrence rate, and an upper precision limit.

DISCUSSION: At an occurrence rate of 3%, the sample size for an upper precision limit of 5.2% is 200. For a limit of 4.7%, the sample size is 300. For a limit of 5%, interpolation yields a sample size of 240.

$$\left[\frac{(5.2\ -\ 5.0)}{(5.2\ -\ 4.7)} \times (300\ -\ 200)\right] + 200\ =\ 240$$

Answer (A) is incorrect because a sample size of 117 signifies an upper precision limit between 6.6% and 5.2%. Answer (C) is incorrect because a sample size of 300 corresponds to an upper precision limit of 4.7%. Answer (D) is incorrect because a sample size of 550 relates to an upper precision limit between 4.2% and 4.1%.

126. At 10% risk (90% reliability), a sample of 200 items has been drawn and tested. The upper precision limit (tolerable rate) is 3%. Which of the following statements is true?

A. If four deviations were found, the population would be acceptable.

B. If two deviations were found, the population would be acceptable.

C. A tolerable rate of 3% indicates a high planned assessed level of control risk for the control tested.

D. The auditor should assume that each deviation results in a misstatement in the accounting records.

The correct answer is (B). *(CIA, adapted)*

REQUIRED: The true statement given risk, sample size, and the tolerable rate.

DISCUSSION: If the sample consists of 200 items and two deviations are found, the occurrence rate is 1%. At 90% reliability, the upper precision limit for an occurrence rate of 1% is 2.6%. The population is acceptable because one can state with 90% reliability that the true occurrence rate is 2.6% or less, which is less than the tolerable rate of 3%.

Answer (A) is incorrect because at an occurrence rate of 2% (four deviations in a sample of 200), the upper precision limit (4%) exceeds the tolerable rate (3%). Answer (C) is incorrect because a low tolerable rate suggests that the planned assessed level of control risk is low (that is, the auditor expects internal control to be effective). Answer (D) is incorrect because a deviation does not signify a misstatement in the records.

CHAPTER SEVEN
AUDIT REPORTS

This chapter includes questions on audit reports covering most of AU Sections 400 and 500. Chapter 8, Special Reports and Other Reporting Issues, addresses the remaining matters relevant to external auditing, and internal audit reports are covered in Chapter 9.

Thus, Chapter 7 concerns reports issued on the results of audits performed in accordance with GAAS by independent, external auditors. The language of these audit reports is determined by the four generally accepted auditing standards of reporting (given below) and the related Statements on Auditing Standards. The SASs interpret GAAS but are themselves considered to be GAAS.

1. The report shall state whether the financial statements are presented in accordance with generally accepted accounting principles.
2. The report shall identify those circumstances in which such principles have not been consistently observed in the current period in relation to the preceding period.
3. Informative disclosures in the financial statements are to be regarded as reasonably adequate unless otherwise stated in the report.
4. The report shall contain either an expression of opinion regarding the financial statements, taken as a whole, or an assertion to the effect that an opinion cannot be expressed. When an overall opinion cannot be expressed, the reasons therefor should be stated. In all cases in which an auditor's name is associated with financial statements, the report should contain a clear-cut indication of the character of the auditor's work, if any, and the degree of responsibility the auditor is taking.

7.1 Purposes

1. GAAS encompass four reporting standards. They include all but which of the following?

A. The report shall state whether the financial statements are presented in accordance with GAAP.

B. The report shall state that GAAS have been followed in the conduct of the audit.

C. The report should identify those circumstances in which GAAP have not been consistently applied.

D. Informative disclosures in the financial statements are to be regarded as reasonably adequate unless otherwise stated in the report.

The correct answer is (B). *(Publisher)*

REQUIRED: The item not a reporting standard.

DISCUSSION: Although the auditor's standard report must state in the scope paragraph that GAAS have been followed, the four generally accepted reporting standards do not explicitly require such a statement. All the other answers state reporting standards.

Answer (A) is incorrect because the first standard of reporting requires a statement as to whether the financial statements are in accordance with GAAP. Answer (C) is incorrect because the requirement to identify lack of consistency is contained in the second reporting standard. Answer (D) is incorrect because the requirement to report on lack of adequate disclosure is stated in the third reporting standard.

2. The objective of the traditional audit of financial statements is

A. To make suggestions as to the form or content of the financial statements or to draft them in whole or in part.

B. To express an opinion on the fairness with which the statements present financial position, results of operations, and cash flows in accordance with generally accepted accounting principles.

C. To assure adoption of sound accounting policies and the establishment and maintenance of internal control.

D. To express an opinion on the accuracy with which the statements present financial position, results of operations, and cash flows in accordance with generally accepted accounting principles.

The correct answer is (B). *(Publisher)*

REQUIRED: The objective of an audit.

DISCUSSION: Based on a traditional audit, the independent auditor expresses an opinion on the fairness, in all material respects, of the presentation of financial statements, i.e., on whether they will be misleading to users. The report is the medium through which the auditor expresses an opinion or a disclaimer of opinion. The report should state whether the audit was in accordance with GAAS and whether, in the auditor's opinion, the statements are presented in conformity with GAAP (AU 110, *Responsibilities and Functions of the Independent Auditor*).

Answer (A) is incorrect because the auditor may make suggestions concerning the statements or help prepare them, but (s)he is responsible only for expressing an opinion as to their fairness. The statements remain the representations of management. Answer (C) is incorrect because management is responsible for adopting sound accounting policies and establishing and maintaining internal control. Answer (D) is incorrect because the auditor expresses an opinion on the fairness of financial statements, not their accuracy.

3. Which of the following best describes why an independent auditor is asked to express an opinion on the fair presentation of financial statements?

A. It is difficult to prepare financial statements that fairly present a company's financial position, results of operations, and cash flows without the expertise of an independent auditor.

B. It is management's responsibility to seek available independent aid in the appraisal of the financial information shown in its financial statements.

C. The opinion of an independent party is needed because a company may not be objective with respect to its own financial statements.

D. It is a customary courtesy that all shareholders receive an independent report on management's stewardship in managing the affairs of the business.

The correct answer is (C). *(CPA, adapted)*

REQUIRED: The best reason for an independent auditor's opinion.

DISCUSSION: The opinion of a suitably qualified, independent, outside party lends credibility to the financial statements. The opinion contained in the audit report, which accompanies the audited financial statements, is the result of the auditor's performance of the attest function: the gathering of evidence during the audit and the expression of an opinion on the fairness of the statements.

Answer (A) is incorrect because the auditor's independence is vital to the performance of the attest function, not his/her preparation of financial statements. For purposes of SEC reporting, preparing the financial statements may be considered an impairment of independence. Also, the assertions in the statements are the sole responsibility of management. Answer (B) is incorrect because management does not seek an appraisal of the financial statements, only an opinion as to whether they are presented fairly.
Answer (D) is incorrect because, although the distribution of information to shareholders is customary, it is not the primary reason for an auditor's report.

4. The fourth standard of reporting requires the auditor's report to contain either an expression of opinion regarding the financial statements taken as a whole or an assertion to the effect that an opinion cannot be expressed. The objective of the fourth standard is to prevent

A. Misinterpretations regarding the degree of responsibility the auditor is assuming.

B. An auditor from reporting on one basic financial statement and not the others.

C. An auditor from expressing different opinions on each of the basic financial statements.

D. Restrictions on the scope of the audit, whether imposed by the client or by the inability to obtain evidence.

The correct answer is (A). *(CPA, adapted)*

REQUIRED: The purpose of the fourth reporting standard.

DISCUSSION: The overall purpose of the fourth standard of reporting is to prevent misinterpretation of the degree of responsibility assumed by the auditor when his/her name is associated with financial statements (AU 508 and AU 504). "In all cases in which the auditor's name is associated with financial statements, the report should contain a clear-cut indication of the character of the auditor's work, if any, and the degree of responsibility the auditor is taking" (AU 150, *Generally Accepted Auditing Standards*).

Answer (B) is incorrect because limited reporting engagements are permissible. Answer (C) is incorrect because the requirement to report on the financial statements "taken as a whole" applies equally to a complete set and to a single statement. Thus, an unqualified opinion may be expressed on one statement and a qualified or adverse opinion or a disclaimer may be expressed on another if warranted. Answer (D) is incorrect because, if the scope is restricted, for whatever reason, the auditor should appropriately reflect the restriction in the report.

5. Which of the following best describes the reference to the expression "taken as a whole" in the fourth generally accepted auditing standard of reporting?

A. It applies equally to a complete set of financial statements and to an individual financial statement.

B. It applies only to a complete set of financial statements.

C. It applies equally to each item in each financial statement.

D. It applies equally to each material item in each financial statement.

The correct answer is (A). *(CPA, adapted)*

REQUIRED: The definition of "taken as a whole" in the fourth reporting standard.

DISCUSSION: The phrase "taken as a whole" applies equally to a set of financial statements and to an individual financial statement, e.g., to a balance sheet. The auditor may express an unqualified opinion on one of the financial statements and express a qualified or adverse opinion or disclaim an opinion on another if the circumstances warrant such treatment (AU 508, *Reports on Audited Financial Statements*).

Answer (B) is incorrect because "taken as a whole" also applies to each financial statement. Answers (C) and (D) are incorrect because "taken as a whole" refers to the financial statements, not to specific items in the statements.

6. A major purpose of the auditor's report on financial statements is to

A. Assure investors of the complete accuracy of the financial statements.

B. Clarify for the public the nature of the auditor's responsibility and performance.

C. Deter creditors from extending loans in high-risk situations.

D. Describe the specific auditing procedures undertaken to gather evidence for the opinion.

The correct answer is (B). *(N. Schmukler)*

REQUIRED: The purpose of the auditor's report.

DISCUSSION: One of the highest priorities of the AICPA has been to reduce the gap between the nature of the auditor's responsibility and performance and the public's perception of the audit function. The auditor's report promulgated by AU 508 clarifies the role of the auditor with the intention of diminishing the gap.

Answer (A) is incorrect because an auditor's opinion provides no assurance of complete accuracy. The report explicitly states that evidence is examined on a "test basis." Answer (C) is incorrect because the sole purpose of the auditor's report is to express an opinion on the fairness of presentation of the financial statements. The report provides some of the information upon which users of the statements may make informed decisions, but it does not substitute for the judgment of users or accept responsibility for the assertions contained in the statements. Answer (D) is incorrect because the scope paragraph provides only a brief, general explanation of what an audit entails.

7. How are management's responsibility and the auditor's responsibility represented in the standard auditor's report?

	Management's Responsibility	Auditor's Responsibility
A.	Explicitly	Explicitly
B.	Implicitly	Implicitly
C.	Implicitly	Explicitly
D.	Explicitly	Implicitly

The correct answer is (A). *(CPA, adapted)*

REQUIRED: The representation of the responsibilities of management and the auditor in the standard audit report.

DISCUSSION: The introductory paragraph of the independent auditor's report explicitly states, "These financial statements are the responsibility of the Company's management. Our responsibility is to express an opinion on these financial statements based on our audit" (AU 508).

Answers (B), (C), and (D) are incorrect because the representation of management's and the auditor's responsibilities is explicit in the standard auditor's report.

8. If a company's external auditor expresses an unqualified opinion as a result of the audit of the company's financial statements, readers of the audit report can assume that

A. The external auditor found no fraud.

B. The company is financially sound and the financial statements are accurate.

C. Internal control is effective.

D. All material disagreements between the company and the external auditor about the application of accounting principles were resolved to the satisfaction of the external auditor.

The correct answer is (D). *(CMA, adapted)*

REQUIRED: The assumption made about an external auditor's unqualified opinion.

DISCUSSION: The first standard of reporting requires the auditor to state whether the financial statements are presented in conformity with GAAP (AU 150). GAAP are the conventions, rules, and procedures necessary to define accepted accounting practice at a given time. They provide the uniform standard for judging whether statements are fairly presented (AU 411, *The Meaning of "Present Fairly in Conformity with GAAP" in the Independent Auditor's Report*). When the statements are materially affected by what the auditor believes to be an unjustified departure from GAAP, and management has declined to rectify the matter, the auditor should express a qualified or adverse opinion (AU 508).

Answer (A) is incorrect because the reader may only assume that any fraud found did not, in the auditor's opinion, prevent the statements from being fairly presented. Answer (B) is incorrect because the auditor is not an appraiser of the company, and an opinion offers no prediction about the performance of the auditee. Also, an unqualified opinion provides reasonable assurance that the statements are not materially misstated, not that they are accurate. Answer (C) is incorrect because an unqualified opinion may be expressed even though control risk was assessed at the maximum level.

9. The securities of Ralph Corporation are listed on a regional stock exchange and registered with the Securities and Exchange Commission (SEC). The management of Ralph engages a CPA to perform an independent audit of Ralph's financial statements. The primary objective of this audit is to provide assurance to the

A. Regional stock exchange.

B. Board of directors of Ralph Corporation.

C. SEC.

D. Investors in Ralph securities.

The correct answer is (D). *(CPA, adapted)*

REQUIRED: The primary users of a public company audit.

DISCUSSION: The opinion of a suitably qualified, independent, outside party lends credibility to the financial statements and provides some protection to third parties who may rely upon them when making investment decisions. Some users have the authority to obtain any information desired, but investors do not.

Answers (A), (B), and (C) are incorrect because, although an audit by an independent CPA may provide information useful to stock exchanges, directors, and regulators, the primary objective is to lend credibility to the financial statements available to investors.

7.2 Generally Accepted Accounting Principles

10. The auditor's judgment concerning the overall fairness of the presentation of financial position, results of operations, and cash flows is applied within the framework of

A. Quality control.

B. Generally accepted auditing standards, which include the concept of materiality.

C. The auditor's assessment of control risk.

D. Generally accepted accounting principles.

The correct answer is (D). *(CPA, adapted)*

REQUIRED: The framework within which the auditor judges the financial statements.

DISCUSSION: The first standard of reporting requires the auditor to state whether the audited entity's financial statements are presented in conformity with GAAP (AU 150). Without this framework, the auditor would have no uniform standard for judging fairness of presentation (AU 411).

Answer (A) is incorrect because quality control standards relate to the conduct of a CPA firm's audit practice as a whole. Adequate quality control provides reasonable assurance of the independent auditor's compliance with GAAS. Answer (B) is incorrect because, although the auditor must comply with GAAS, (s)he must specifically judge whether the statements are presented fairly in accordance with GAAP. Answer (C) is incorrect because the assessment of control risk is but one step in an audit. The ultimate purpose is to express an opinion on the fair presentation of the statements in conformity with GAAP.

11. For an entity's financial statements to be presented fairly in conformity with generally accepted accounting principles, the principles selected should

A. Be applied on a basis consistent with those followed in the prior year.

B. Be approved by the Auditing Standards Board or the appropriate industry subcommittee.

C. Reflect transactions in a manner that presents the financial statements within a range of acceptable limits.

D. Match the principles used by most other entities within the entity's particular industry.

The correct answer is (C). *(CPA, adapted)*

REQUIRED: The requirement for an entity's financial statements to be presented fairly in conformity with GAAP.

DISCUSSION: The auditor's judgments about GAAP include "whether the financial statements reflect the underlying transactions and events in a manner that presents the financial position, results of operations, and cash flows stated within a range of acceptable limits, that is, limits that are reasonable and practicable to attain in financial statements" (AU 411).

Answer (A) is incorrect because lack of consistency does not necessarily preclude fair presentation in accordance with GAAP. Answer (B) is incorrect because the ASB promulgates auditing standards, not GAAP. Answer (D) is incorrect because the accounting principles selected and applied should have general acceptance but need not be the most prevalent used in the industry.

12. The auditor's opinion refers to generally accepted accounting principles (GAAP). Which of the following best describes GAAP?

A. The interpretations of accounting rules and procedures by certified public accountants on audit engagements.

B. The pronouncements of the Financial Accounting Standards Board and its predecessor, the Accounting Principles Board.

C. The guidelines set forth by various governmental agencies that derive their authority from Congress.

D. The conventions, rules, and procedures that are necessary to define accepted accounting practice at a particular time.

The correct answer is (D). *(CPA, adapted)*

REQUIRED: The statement that best describes GAAP.

DISCUSSION: GAAP are the "conventions, rules, and procedures necessary to define accepted accounting practice at a particular time." They include both the broad guidelines and the detailed practices and procedures promulgated by the profession that provide uniform standards to measure financial presentations (AU 411).

Answer (A) is incorrect because interpretations of GAAP made by CPAs on audit engagements are judgments about the application of GAAP to particular circumstances. Answer (B) is incorrect because GAAP include but are not limited to pronouncements of the APB and FASB. Answer (C) is incorrect because, although the federal government can require disclosures by public companies, for example, through regulations of the SEC, GAAP are much broader. They apply to all entities, whether public or private and regardless of size.

13. Which of the following is a source of officially established accounting principles for nongovernmental entities?

A. International Accounting Standards.

B. FASB Concepts Statements.

C. FASB Interpretations.

D. AICPA Issues Papers.

The correct answer is (C). *(Publisher)*

REQUIRED: The source of GAAP as designated by the AICPA for nongovernmental entities.

DISCUSSION: AU 411 presents a GAAP hierarchy for both nongovernmental entities and state and local governments. The nongovernmental hierarchy has five tiers. The first tier [category (a)] consists of sources of officially established accounting principles (FASB Statements and Interpretations, APB Opinions, and AICPA Accounting Research Bulletins). The next three tiers [categories (b), (c), and (d)] contain other sources of established accounting principles. The fifth tier includes other accounting literature.

Answers (A), (B), and (D) are incorrect because International Accounting Standards, FASB Concepts Statements, and AICPA Issues Papers are considered other accounting literature rather than established accounting principles.

14. The auditing standards provide separate GAAP hierarchies for nongovernmental entities and state and local governments. Which of the following is true concerning the GAAP hierarchy for state and local governments?

A. Not all FASB Statements and Interpretations are at the top of the hierarchy.

B. GASB Concepts Statements are considered established accounting principles.

C. Not all GASB Statements and Interpretations are at the top of the hierarchy.

D. All AICPA Industry Audit and Accounting Guides are considered established accounting principles.

The correct answer is (A). *(Publisher)*

REQUIRED: The true statement about the GAAP hierarchy for state and local governments.

DISCUSSION: The GAAP hierarchy for state and local governments has five tiers. The first tier [category (a)] consists of sources of officially established accounting principles (GASB Statements and Interpretations, plus AICPA and FASB pronouncements if made applicable to state and local governments by a GASB Statement or Interpretation). The next three tiers [categories (b), (c), and (d)] contain other sources of established accounting principles. The fifth tier includes other accounting literature. If a FASB or AICPA pronouncement is not specifically made applicable to state and local governments by the GASB, widely recognized and prevalent industry practice prevails as GAAP for state and local governments. Prior to this change in the hierarchy, the GASB was compelled to issue statements allowing state and local governments to avoid following certain FASB Statements.

Answers (B) and (D) are incorrect because GASB Concepts Statements and AICPA Industry Audit and Accounting Guides not specifically made applicable to state and local governments are considered other accounting literature. Answer (C) is incorrect because all GASB Statements and Interpretations are in the top tier.

15. When the financial statements contain a departure from generally accepted accounting principles, the effect of which is material, the auditor should

A. Qualify the opinion and explain the effect of the departure from GAAP in a separate paragraph.

B. Qualify the opinion and describe the departure from GAAP within the opinion paragraph.

C. Disclaim an opinion and explain the effect of the departure from GAAP in a separate paragraph.

D. Disclaim an opinion and describe the departure from GAAP within the opinion paragraph.

The correct answer is (A). *(CPA, adapted)*

REQUIRED: The auditor's report when the statements contain a material departure from GAAP.

DISCUSSION: When the financial statements are materially affected by a departure from GAAP, the auditor should express a qualified or adverse opinion. The opinion will contain a separate explanatory paragraph(s) preceding the opinion paragraph. The explanation should state the auditor's substantive reasons for the conclusions about the departure and disclose the principal effects of the subject matter of the qualification or adverse opinion, if practicable. If the effects are not reasonably determinable, the report should so state. The opinion paragraph should refer to the separate explanation (AU 508).

Answer (B) is incorrect because a separate explanatory paragraph(s) is required. Answers (C) and (D) are incorrect because a material departure from GAAP justifies expression of a qualified or adverse opinion. A disclaimer of opinion is appropriate when the audit scope is insufficient to permit the auditor to form an opinion.

16. When criteria to select among alternative accounting principles have not been established to relate accounting methods to circumstances, the auditor

A. Must treat all alternative principles as acceptable.

B. May concur with management's selection of an accounting principle that appears appropriate when applied in a manner similar to the application of an established principle to a similar event.

C. Is required by current authoritative literature to obtain a ruling from the AICPA.

D. Is required by the SEC to seek advice from the FASB about the proper accounting method.

The correct answer is (B). *(Publisher)*

REQUIRED: The auditor's responsibility absent criteria for selection from alternative accounting principles.

DISCUSSION: Specifying the circumstances in which one principle should be selected from alternatives is the function of authoritative bodies. But criteria may not yet exist to provide guidance in certain situations. In these cases, management may be able to select an accounting principle that appears appropriate when applied in a manner similar to the application of an established principle to an analogous transaction or event (AU 411).

Answer (A) is incorrect because alternative accounting principles may be applicable, but a principle is unacceptable if it does not result in fair reporting. Answer (C) is incorrect because a ruling from the AICPA is not required. Answer (D) is incorrect because advice from the FASB is not required.

17. A CPA engaged to audit financial statements observes that the accounting for a certain material item is not in conformity with GAAP, although the departure is prominently disclosed in a footnote to the financial statements. The CPA should

A. Express an unqualified opinion but insert a separate paragraph emphasizing the matter by reference to the footnote.

B. Disclaim an opinion.

C. Not allow the accounting treatment for this item to affect the type of opinion because the departure from GAAP was disclosed.

D. Qualify the opinion because of the departure from GAAP.

The correct answer is (D). *(CPA, adapted)*

REQUIRED: The effect on the audit opinion of a material departure from GAAP.

DISCUSSION: When financial statements are materially affected by a departure from GAAP and the audit has been in accordance with GAAS, the auditor should express a qualified or an adverse opinion, stating the basis for the opinion in the report, even though full and prominent footnote disclosure has been made.

Answer (A) is incorrect because an unqualified opinion cannot be expressed when the statements are materially affected by a departure from GAAP. Answer (B) is incorrect because a disclaimer is appropriate when the audit scope was insufficient to form an opinion. Answer (C) is incorrect because footnote disclosure of the departure from GAAP does not overcome the need for a modified opinion.

18. Eagle Company's financial statements contain a departure from generally accepted accounting principles because, due to unusual circumstances, the statements would otherwise be misleading. The auditor should express an opinion that is

A. Qualified and describe the departure in a separate paragraph.

B. Unqualified but not mention the departure in the auditor's report.

C. Qualified or adverse, depending on materiality, and describe the departure in a separate paragraph.

D. Unqualified and describe the departure in a separate paragraph.

The correct answer is (D). *(CPA, adapted)*

REQUIRED: The opinion expressed when a departure from GAAP results in fairly presented financial statements.

DISCUSSION: Conduct Rule 203, *Accounting Principles*, prohibits expression of an opinion that financial statements are in conformity with GAAP if they contain a material departure from GAAP. However, an exception is permitted when the auditor can demonstrate that because of unusual circumstances the statements would otherwise be misleading. Given these circumstances, and if no other basis for modifying the opinion exists, the CPA may express an unqualified opinion, with a separate paragraph that describes the departure, its effects, and the reasons compliance with GAAP would be misleading.

Answers (A) and (C) are incorrect because an adverse or qualified opinion is not expressed when the statements are fairly presented. Answer (B) is incorrect because an explanatory paragraph must be added even though the opinion is unqualified.

19. According to the profession's ethical standards, which of the following events may justify a departure from a Statement of Financial Accounting Standards?

	New Legislation	Evolution of a New Form of Business Transaction
A.	No	Yes
B.	Yes	No
C.	Yes	Yes
D.	No	No

The correct answer is (C). *(CPA, adapted)*

REQUIRED: The event(s), if any, that may justify departure from an SFAS.

DISCUSSION: In general, strict compliance with accounting principles is required. However, Conduct Rule 203 recognizes that, due to unusual circumstances, adhering to GAAP may cause financial statements to be misleading. An Interpretation under Conduct Rule 203 lists new legislation and the evolution of a new form of business transaction as events that may justify departure from an SFAS and other officially established accounting principles.

Answers (A), (B), and (D) are incorrect because new legislation and the evolution of a new form of business transaction may justify departure from an SFAS.

20. Patentex developed a new secret formula that is of great value because it has resulted in a virtual monopoly. Patentex has capitalized all research and development costs associated with this formula. Greene, CPA, who is auditing this account, will probably

A. Confer with management regarding transfer of the amount from the balance sheet to the income statement.

B. Confirm that the secret formula is registered and on file with the county clerk's office.

C. Confer with management regarding a change in the title of the account to goodwill.

D. Confer with management regarding ownership of the secret formula.

The correct answer is (A). *(CPA, adapted)*

REQUIRED: The auditor's proper response upon discovering the capitalization of R&D costs.

DISCUSSION: SFAS 2, *Accounting for Research and Development Costs*, requires that R&D costs be expensed "when incurred." The auditor should confer with management about this departure from GAAP. If management refuses to adopt the accepted principle, the auditor will express a qualified or an adverse opinion if the departure has a material effect on the statements taken as a whole. The correction is to expense the amounts capitalized.

Answer (B) is incorrect because confirming that the formula is registered is relevant to the existence, rights, and valuation assertions but not to the choice of accounting principle. Answer (C) is incorrect because reclassifying R&D costs as goodwill would be misleading. The costs must be expensed. Answer (D) is incorrect because conferring with management about ownership of the formula is relevant to the rights assertion, not to the choice of accounting principle.

21. To which of the following material asset accounts would an auditor object?

A. Franchise fees paid.

B. Goodwill resulting from revaluation based on an objective appraisal by an expert.

C. Excess cost over the fair value of the net identifiable assets of a significant subsidiary.

D. Research and development costs that will be billed to a customer at a subsequent date.

The correct answer is (B). *(CPA, adapted)*

REQUIRED: The material asset account that is not in accordance with GAAP.

DISCUSSION: The recording of goodwill from revaluation based on an objective appraisal by an expert is not in accordance with GAAP. Only goodwill resulting from the purchase of another company may be recorded.

Answer (A) is incorrect because the cost of a franchise should be capitalized and amortized over the life of the franchise, but not to exceed 40 years. Answer (C) is incorrect because the excess of cost over the fair value of the net identifiable assets acquired is recorded as goodwill. Answer (D) is incorrect because costs incurred in conducting R&D activities under contractual arrangements are not covered by SFAS 2 and may be capitalized.

22. When an auditor expresses an opinion stating that financial statements intended for distribution to the general public are in accordance with prescribed accounting regulations of a regulatory authority, the auditor

A. Is expressing a piecemeal opinion.

B. Should issue a standard report except for substitution of "prescribed accounting regulations of ... regulatory body" in place of generally accepted accounting principles.

C. Should also express a qualified or adverse opinion as to material variances from generally accepted accounting principles as appropriate.

D. Need only observe the general and field work standards in expressing an opinion.

The correct answer is (C). *(Publisher)*

REQUIRED: The reporting when statements are based on regulations prescribed by a regulatory body.

DISCUSSION: GAAP also apply to companies whose accounting practices are prescribed by governmental regulations, e.g., utilities, insurance companies, and financial institutions. The first standard of reporting is thus applicable to opinions on the statements of such companies presented for purposes other than filings with their respective supervisory agencies. Consequently, the auditor should express a qualified or an adverse opinion if the statements contain a material departure from GAAP (AU 544, *Lack of Conformity with GAAP*). But if the statements are prepared only for filing with the regulatory agency, AU 623, *Special Reports*, applies, and an unqualified opinion based on the prescribed methods is a possibility.

Answer (A) is incorrect because piecemeal opinions are prohibited (AU 508). Answer (B) is incorrect because, if financial statements are prepared in accordance with a basis of accounting prescribed by a regulatory body, they are not intended solely for filing with that body, and no AICPA pronouncement permits additional distribution of reports thereon, the auditor must use the standard form of report modified for departures from GAAP (AU 544). Answer (D) is incorrect because the reporting standards also apply.

23. The following appeared in an audit report: "As described in Note 4, these financial statements were prepared on the basis of accounting that the partnership used for income tax purposes, which is a comprehensive basis of accounting other than generally accepted accounting principles." This sentence is

A. Unacceptable in any audit report.

B. Acceptable in a special report.

C. An indication that the partnership is in liquidation.

D. In a report that must be approved by the IRS.

The correct answer is (B). *(Publisher)*

REQUIRED: The true statement about the quoted language.

DISCUSSION: When financial statements are prepared on a comprehensive basis other than GAAP, a paragraph should be included in the auditor's report referring to a footnote describing the basis and indicating that it departs from GAAP. The auditor's opinion should indicate whether the statements are presented fairly in the context of the comprehensive basis described (AU 623).

Answer (A) is incorrect because the quoted wording is standard in a special report. Answer (C) is incorrect because an entity in liquidation would likely record assets at net realizable value. Answer (D) is incorrect because the IRS need not be consulted about audit reports.

24. On January 2, 1999, the Retail Auto Parts Co. received a notice from its primary suppliers that effective immediately all wholesale prices would be increased 10%. On the basis of the notice, Retail Auto Parts Co. revalued its December 31, 1998 inventory to reflect the higher costs. The inventory constituted a material proportion of total assets; however, the effect of the revaluation was material to current assets but not to total assets or net income. In reporting on the company's financial statements for the year ended December 31, 1998, in which inventory is valued at the adjusted amounts, the auditor would most likely

A. Express an unqualified opinion provided the nature of the adjustment and the amounts involved are disclosed in footnotes.

B. Express a qualified opinion.

C. Disclaim an opinion.

D. Express an adverse opinion.

The correct answer is (B). *(CPA, adapted)*

REQUIRED: The effect on the opinion of the client's revaluation of inventory.

DISCUSSION: The auditor should express a qualified opinion and disclose that the financial statements have not been presented in conformity with GAAP. Inventory should be recorded at lower of cost or market. Holding gains should not be recognized until realized, i.e., when inventory is sold.

Answer (A) is incorrect because Conduct Rule 203 prohibits expression of an unqualified opinion in these circumstances even though full disclosure is made. Answer (C) is incorrect because a disclaimer is proper only when evidence is insufficient to form an opinion. Answer (D) is incorrect because an adverse opinion is probably not appropriate. The effect of revaluation was not material to total assets or net income.

25. The client includes in the determination of net income certain material items properly classifiable as other comprehensive income. In this situation, the auditor must express a(n)

A. Unqualified opinion.

B. Qualified opinion.

C. Adverse opinion.

D. Qualified or adverse opinion.

The correct answer is (D). *(Publisher)*

REQUIRED: The opinion when a client includes other comprehensive income items in the determination of net income.

DISCUSSION: Other comprehensive income items (foreign currency translation adjustments, minimum pension liability adjustments, unrealized gains and losses on available-for-sale securities, and net gain or loss on derivatives designated and qualifying as cash flow hedges) are excluded from the determination of net income. The total of other comprehensive income for a period is transferred to a component of shareholders' equity that is displayed separately from retained earnings and additional paid-in capital in the balance sheet (SFAS 130, *Reporting Comprehensive Income*). Given that the departure from GAAP is material, the auditor should express either a qualified or an adverse opinion (AU 508).

Answer (A) is incorrect because the report must be modified for the failure to apply GAAP. Answer (B) is incorrect because, if the auditor concludes that the financial statements taken as a whole are not presented fairly, an adverse opinion is justified. Answer (C) is incorrect because the auditor may conclude that, except for the effects of the departure from GAAP, the financial statements are presented fairly. In that case, a qualified opinion is justified.

26. Garden Apartments, Inc. completed construction and began to rent a 250-unit apartment complex on November 25, 1997. During December, 75 units were leased, and an additional 125 units were leased in January 1998.

During the month of November 1997, the company charged to expense $23,000 for the cost of advertising, a grand opening party, and the advertising agency fee for planning the campaign. As a part of the promotional campaign, all tenants signing leases were given expensive gifts. At June 30, 1998, the balance sheet reflected $15,200 of deferred costs associated with these gifts, and a footnote stated that the costs were being amortized over the life of the related lease.

During your audit of the financial statements of Garden Apartments, Inc. for the year ended June 30, 1998 (made in accordance with GAAS), no facts other than those above came to your attention that would cause your opinion to be other than that the statements were fairly presented in accordance with GAAP. Your report on the financial statements should contain

A. An adverse opinion.

B. An unqualified opinion.

C. A "subject to" opinion.

D. A disclaimer of opinion.

The correct answer is (B). *(Publisher)*

REQUIRED: The effect of the accounting treatment of certain costs on the auditor's opinion.

DISCUSSION: Advertising and promotion costs should properly be expensed, and the direct costs of leasing the apartments may be capitalized and expensed over the lives of the leases. These transactions were accounted for in conformity with GAAP, and an unqualified opinion is appropriate.

Answer (A) is incorrect because an adverse opinion states that the financial statements are not presented fairly in accordance with GAAP. Answer (C) is incorrect because AU 508 states, "Phrases such as 'subject to' are not clear or forceful enough and should not be used." Answer (D) is incorrect because a disclaimer is appropriate only when the auditor has collected insufficient evidence to express an opinion.

27. A client that owns 18% of the voting stock of an investee has accounted for the investment under the equity method. The effect of using the equity method rather than the cost method is material. In this instance,

A. The client is definitely in violation of GAAP.

B. A decision as to whether an 18% interest provides an ability to exercise significant influence rests with management, and the auditor should consider the equity method to be the appropriate valuation method.

C. Because an interest of less than 20% implies that the investor cannot exercise significant influence over the investee, the auditor will need to obtain evidence to support a claim to the contrary.

D. If the equity method is used in the published financial statements, and the auditor agrees that this method is appropriate, no disclosure that the 20% presumption was set aside is required.

The correct answer is (C). *(Publisher)*

REQUIRED: The true statement about accounting for an 18% ownership interest under the equity method.

DISCUSSION: Accounting for a less than 20% investment under the equity method is a violation of GAAP unless the client can exercise significant influence over the investee. APB 18, *The Equity Method of Accounting for Investments in Common Stock*, establishes a rebuttable presumption of no significant influence when less than 20% of the investee's voting stock is held. If the client cannot demonstrate significant influence, given the material effect of using the equity rather than the cost method, the auditor should express a qualified or an adverse opinion.

Answer (A) is incorrect because the equity method is appropriate if the client exercises significant influence over the investee. Answer (B) is incorrect because the auditor is responsible for determining whether the client has demonstrated that it exercises significant influence. Answer (D) is incorrect because GAAP require disclosure of the accounting method used and, in this case, the reason the equity method was chosen.

28. The client's generally distributed financial statements do not reflect a provision for a deferred income tax liability because this accounting procedure is not required by the regulatory commission that prescribes uniform accounting procedures for the industry in which this company operates. A footnote accompanying the financial statements correctly discloses the amount of the deferred tax liability at the statement date as $2,200,000, an amount material to the financial statements taken as a whole. What is the effect of these circumstances on the auditor's opinion?

A. They will not affect the auditor's opinion because the client's accounting procedures conform to the uniform accounting procedures applicable to the industry of which the client is a part.

B. The auditor should express either an adverse opinion or a qualified opinion depending on his/her judgment as to the effects of the departure from GAAP on the overall fairness of the financial statements.

C. They will not affect the auditor's opinion because the footnote disclosure provides the reader with the information necessary for a proper interpretation of the client's financial position and results of operations.

D. They will affect the auditor's opinion only if (s)he believes the content of the footnote is insufficient to meet the requirements of adequate disclosure.

The correct answer is (B). *(Publisher)*

REQUIRED: The effect of a material departure from GAAP resulting from the client's adherence to uniform procedures prescribed by a regulatory agency.

DISCUSSION: AU 623 defines the elements of the auditor's report when (s)he is reporting on financial statements prepared in accordance with a comprehensive basis of accounting other than GAAP. This form of reporting does not include an opinion concerning adherence to GAAP. But when reporting on statements prepared in accordance with the requirements of a regulatory body, the auditor must use the standard form of report, unless the statements are intended solely for filing with a regulatory agency (AU 544). Thus, given that the statements are for general distribution, the standard form of report should be used, and the auditor should express either an adverse or a qualified opinion, depending on the effects of the departure from GAAP and the fairness with which the financial statements are presented, because a provision for a deferred tax liability is required by SFAS 109.

Answer (A) is incorrect because, given that a general-distribution report based on the requirements of a regulatory body is to be issued, the auditor may not express an opinion solely on conformity with the other comprehensive basis of accounting. (S)he must state whether the statements are in accordance with GAAP. An opinion on conformity with the prescribed basis of accounting should be expressed in an additional paragraph. Answers (C) and (D) are incorrect because failure to adhere to GAAP is not remedied by footnote disclosure.

29. An auditor's client is a nonprofit organization. GAAP for this type of nonprofit organization have been clearly defined, and the client has followed such practices. The preferred method of reporting on the client's adherence to such practices is to

A. Use the phrase "In conformity with generally accepted accounting principles" in the opinion paragraph.

B. Use the phrase "In conformity with generally accepted accounting practices for a nonprofit organization in the ... field" in the opinion paragraph.

C. Describe the accounting practices in a separate paragraph, with appropriate reference thereto in the opinion paragraph.

D. Make no reference because accounting practices differ for each nonprofit organization.

The correct answer is (A). *(Publisher)*

REQUIRED: The preferred method of stating that a nonprofit organization uses GAAP.

DISCUSSION: Because the auditee uses GAAP, the language in the standard audit report is appropriate.

Answer (B) is incorrect because the standard opinion paragraph does not require modification for the type of organization being reported on. Answer (C) is incorrect because the client should describe the accounting principles employed in a summary of significant accounting policies preceding the footnotes or as the first note to the statements. Answer (D) is incorrect because GAAS, including the first standard of reporting, must be adhered to when an auditor reports on any statement. The auditor must therefore indicate whether the statements are presented in conformity with GAAP.

30. AU 625, *Reports on the Application of Accounting Principles*, provides guidance to a reporting accountant who

A. Has been engaged to report on financial statements.

B. Is preparing a written report on the application of accounting principles to hypothetical as well as specific transactions.

C. Intends to give oral advice in the form of a position paper not related to specific transactions or financial statements.

D. Is requested to provide expert testimony in litigation involving accounting matters.

The correct answer is (B). *(Publisher)*

REQUIRED: The applicability of AU 625.

DISCUSSION: Management, accountants, and intermediaries may consult others about the applicability of accounting principles. AU 625 guides the reporting accountant when (s)he (1) prepares a written report on the application of accounting principles to specified transactions (completed or proposed), (2) is requested to prepare a written report on the type of opinion that may be expressed on a specific entity's financial statements, or (3) reports in writing to intermediaries on the application of accounting principles to hypothetical transactions (those not involving a specific principle).

Answers (A) and (D) are incorrect because AU 625 does not apply to engagements to report on financial statements, to assistance in litigation or expert testimony therein, or to advice to other public accountants. Answer (C) is incorrect because AU 625 is not applicable to position papers, e.g., articles or speeches, unless they are intended to provide guidance on specific transactions or on the opinion to be expressed on a specific entity's statements.

31. Before reporting on the financial statements of a U.S. entity that have been prepared in conformity with another country's accounting principles, an auditor practicing in the U.S. should

A. Understand the accounting principles generally accepted in the other country.

B. Be certified by the appropriate auditing or accountancy board of the other country.

C. Notify management that the auditor is required to disclaim an opinion on the financial statements.

D. Receive a waiver from the auditor's state board of accountancy to perform the engagement.

The correct answer is (A). *(CPA, adapted)*

REQUIRED: The requirement for reporting on financial statements of a U.S. entity prepared in conformity with another country's accounting principles.

DISCUSSION: AU 534, *Reporting on Financial Statements Prepared for Use in Other Countries*, states that an independent auditor practicing in the U.S. may report on the financial statements of a U.S. entity prepared in conformity with accounting principles generally accepted in another country. However, the auditor must clearly understand, and obtain written representations from management about, the purpose and uses of the statements. (S)he must also comply with the general and field work standards of GAAS.

Answer (B) is incorrect because the accountant needs to be a CPA in the U.S. Answer (C) is incorrect because the accountant can express an opinion on the fairness of the financial statements. Answer (D) is incorrect because no waiver is required to perform this service.

7.3 Consistency Issues

32. The objective of the consistency standard is to provide assurance that

A. There are no variations in the format and presentation of financial statements.

B. Substantially different transactions and events are not accounted for on an identical basis.

C. The auditor is consulted before material changes are made in the application of accounting principles.

D. The comparability of financial statements between periods is not materially affected by changes in accounting principles without disclosure.

The correct answer is (D). *(CPA, adapted)*

REQUIRED: The objective of the standard of reporting relating to consistency.

DISCUSSION: The second standard of reporting concerns the consistency of application of GAAP: "The report shall identify those circumstances in which such principles have not been consistently observed in the current period in relation to the preceding period" (AU 508). The objective is to assure that the comparability of financial statements has not been materially affected by changes in accounting principles or, if comparability has been affected, to require proper reporting. Implicit in the objective is that principles are consistently observed within each period (AU 420, *Consistency of Application of GAAP*).

Answer (A) is incorrect because variations in the format and presentation of financial statements (e.g., changes in classification) are not considered to be changes affecting consistency within the meaning of AU 420. Answer (B) is incorrect because the auditor reports on whether accounting practices were consistent, not identical. Answer (C) is incorrect because consultation is not required.

33. Seripak Corporation made a material change in accounting principle with which the auditor concurs. The auditor should express

A. An unqualified opinion with a separate explanatory paragraph.

B. A "subject to" opinion with a separate explanatory paragraph.

C. A "subject to" opinion without a separate explanatory paragraph.

D. An "except for" opinion without a separate explanatory paragraph.

The correct answer is (A). *(K.J. Plucinski)*

REQUIRED: The appropriate report when the auditor concurs with a change in accounting principle.

DISCUSSION: A material change in accounting principle raises a consistency issue. Thus, a report with a separate explanatory paragraph is required. Unless the change is unjustified, it does not require a modification of the opinion.

Answers (B) and (C) are incorrect because the phrase "subject to" is not acceptable in any report. Such language is not clear or forceful enough. Answer (D) is incorrect because the report should contain a separate explanatory paragraph but no qualification. If the auditor does not concur with the change, the opinion should be modified because of the departure from GAAP.

34. If management fails to provide adequate justification for a change from one generally accepted accounting principle to another, the auditor should

A. Add an explanatory paragraph and express a qualified or an adverse opinion for lack of conformity with generally accepted accounting principles.

B. Disclaim an opinion because of uncertainty.

C. Disclose the matter in a separate explanatory paragraph(s) but not modify the opinion paragraph.

D. Neither modify the opinion nor disclose the matter because both principles are generally accepted.

The correct answer is (A). *(Publisher)*

REQUIRED: The effect of management's failure to justify a change in accounting principle.

DISCUSSION: If management has not provided reasonable justification for a change, the new principle is not generally accepted, or the method of accounting for the effect of the change does not conform with GAAP, the auditor should express a qualified or an adverse opinion in the report for the year of change and add (an) explanatory paragraph(s) preceding the opinion paragraph (AU 508). The presumption that an entity should not change an accounting principle is overcome only when it justifies use of an acceptable alternative as preferable (APB 20, *Accounting Changes*).

Answer (B) is incorrect because a disclaimer may be issued for a scope limitation but not for failure to justify a change in GAAP. Answers (C) and (D) are incorrect because a modified opinion must be expressed.

35. The following explanatory paragraph was included in an auditor's report to indicate a lack of consistency:

> As discussed in note T to the financial statements, the company changed its method of computing depreciation in 1998.

How should the auditor report on this matter if the auditor concurred with the change?

	Type of Opinion	Location of Explanatory Paragraph
A.	Unqualified	Before opinion paragraph
B.	Unqualified	After opinion paragraph
C.	Qualified	Before opinion paragraph
D.	Qualified	After opinion paragraph

The correct answer is (B). *(CPA, adapted)*

REQUIRED: The reporting of a lack of consistency.

DISCUSSION: AU 508 states that a change in accounting principles or in the method of their application having a material effect on comparability requires the auditor to refer to the change in an explanatory paragraph of the report. This paragraph should follow the opinion paragraph and identify the nature of the change and refer to a footnote that discusses the change.

Answers (A), (C), and (D) are incorrect because the opinion should be unqualified and the explanatory paragraph should follow the opinion paragraph.

36. Below are lists of accounting changes affecting consistency and comparability. All items are material. Which list does not contain a change requiring recognition in the audit report?

A. Correction of an error in an accounting principle; change in accounting estimate; a reclassification.

B. Reclassification; a substantially different transaction; an accounting change having no material effect on the financial statements in the current year but having a substantial effect in subsequent years.

C. Substantially different transactions; certain changes in the presentation of cash flows; a change in reporting entity.

D. Correction of an error not involving an accounting principle; change in accounting estimate; a change in reporting entity.

The correct answer is (B). *(Publisher)*

REQUIRED: The set of items requiring no reference in the auditor's report as to consistency.

DISCUSSION: Six accounting changes affect consistency and require an additional paragraph in the auditor's report (AU 420): (1) changes in accounting principle, (2) changes in the reporting entity, (3) failure to restate prior year statements after a pooling of interests, (4) correction of an error in principle, (5) changes in principle inseparable from a change in estimate, and (6) changes in the presentation of cash flows that involve determination of the items treated as cash equivalents. Five changes affect comparability but not consistency and require no modification of the report: (1) changes in accounting estimate, (2) error corrections not involving a principle, (3) changes in classification and reclassification, (4) substantially different transactions or events, and (5) changes having no material effect in the current year but expected to have a material future effect.

Answers (A), (C), and (D) are incorrect because a correction of an error in an accounting principle, a change in the determination of items treated as cash equivalents, and a change in the reporting entity require modification of the report.

37. APB 20 indicates that a number of accounting changes should be handled on a retroactive or restatement basis. These exceptions are typically comprehensive and substantially affect reported net income. Which of the following is not an exception requiring restatement of prior financial statements for comparative purposes in the year of an accounting change?

A. A change in the useful lives of depreciable assets.

B. A change from the LIFO inventory valuation method to another method.

C. A change in the method of accounting for long-term construction-type contracts.

D. Issuance of financial statements by a company for the first time to obtain additional equity capital to effect a business combination or to register securities.

The correct answer is (A). *(Publisher)*

REQUIRED: The accounting change not applied retroactively to the statements of prior years.

DISCUSSION: A change in the useful lives of depreciable assets is a change in estimate that does not affect consistency and should be accounted for prospectively.

Answer (B) is incorrect because the change from LIFO by a firm that has used the method for a number of years would have a significant effect on the current year's income. LIFO cost of goods sold would likely reflect low inventory values. A change to LIFO from any other method, however, would not require restatement. Answer (C) is incorrect because a change from the completed-contract method to the percentage-of-completion method, or vice versa, has a significant effect on the comparability of the financial statements. Answer (D) is incorrect because private companies selling equity securities for the first time should make their prior financial statements as meaningful as possible.

38. Under APB 20, which of the following is not a requirement for ordinary accounting changes?

A. The cumulative effect of the adjustment should be reported in income between extraordinary items and net income.

B. The items should be reported on a net of tax basis.

C. The adjustment to retained earnings should be clearly marked in the balance sheet as "adjustment for the cumulative effect on prior years of retroactively applying the new method of accounting."

D. Income before extraordinary items and net income computed on a pro forma basis should be shown on the face of the income statement for all periods presented as if the newly adopted principle had been applied during all periods affected.

The correct answer is (C). *(Publisher)*

REQUIRED: The requirement not established for ordinary accounting changes by APB 20.

DISCUSSION: No adjustments are necessary to the retained earnings account because the cumulative effect of the change on net income is reported in the income statement of the current year, and no prior period financial statements are restated. Restatement and direct adjustment of retained earnings would be appropriate if one of the exceptions to APB 20 requiring retroactive treatment of accounting changes is applicable, e.g., a change in the method of accounting for long-term construction contracts or a change from LIFO to another inventory method.

Answer (A) is incorrect because the cumulative effect of the adjustment should be reported in the income statement between extraordinary items and net income. Answer (B) is incorrect because items should be reported on a net of tax basis in a manner similar to that used for an extraordinary item. Answer (D) is incorrect because income before extraordinary items and net income computed on a pro forma basis should be shown on the face of the income statement. Related earnings per share data should also be reported.

39. Tread Corp. accounts for the effect of a material accounting change prospectively when the inclusion of the cumulative effect of the change is required in the current year. The auditor should choose between expressing a(n)

A. Qualified opinion or a disclaimer of opinion.

B. Disclaimer of opinion or an unqualified opinion with an explanatory paragraph.

C. Unqualified opinion with an explanatory paragraph and an adverse opinion.

D. Adverse opinion and a qualified opinion.

The correct answer is (D). *(CPA, adapted)*

REQUIRED: The auditor's reporting options when a client fails to comply with GAAP.

DISCUSSION: APB 20 defines accounting changes and GAAP for reporting an accounting change. When an audit client's financial statements contain a material departure from GAAP, the auditor should express a qualified or an adverse opinion.

Answer (A) is incorrect because a disclaimer is expressed only when the audit scope is insufficient to form an opinion. Answer (B) is incorrect because a disclaimer or an unqualified opinion is inappropriate for a GAAP violation. Answer (C) is incorrect because an unqualified opinion can be expressed only if the financial statements contain no material departure from GAAP.

40. When there has been a change in accounting principles, but the effect of the change on the comparability of the financial statements is not material, the auditor should

A. Refer to the change in an explanatory paragraph.

B. Explicitly concur that the change is preferred.

C. Not refer to consistency in the auditor's report.

D. Refer to the change in the opinion paragraph.

The correct answer is (C). *(CPA, adapted)*

REQUIRED: The reference, if any, in the auditor's report to a change in accounting principle not considered material.

DISCUSSION: The standard report implies that comparability between or among periods has not been materially affected by changes in accounting principles because either no change has occurred or there has been a change in principles or in the method of their application, but its effect on comparability is not material (AU 508).

Answer (A) is incorrect because an additional paragraph is added following the opinion paragraph only if the change is material. Answer (B) is incorrect because the auditor should not refer to consistency when the effect on comparability is immaterial. Answer (D) is incorrect because the auditor should refer to the change in the opinion paragraph only if (s)he takes exception to it in expressing the opinion.

41. If the auditor is reporting on several periods and a change in accounting principle from straight-line to declining-balance depreciation occurred in the earliest period reported upon, the auditor should

A. Refer to the change in the report even though there is no inconsistency subsequent to the change.

B. Qualify the opinion for the first year reported on but express an unqualified opinion for the subsequent years.

C. Not refer to the change.

D. Require restatement of the financial statements for the period immediately preceding the period of change in addition to referring to the change in the report.

The correct answer is (A). *(Publisher)*

REQUIRED: The effect on the report when a change in principle occurs in the earliest period reported upon.

DISCUSSION: The auditor must add a separate explanatory paragraph following the opinion paragraph to reflect the inconsistency. This paragraph is required in reports on financial statements of subsequent years as long as the year of change is presented and reported on. The paragraph is necessary although the year of the change is the earliest year reported on and there is no inconsistency in the application of principles in years subsequent to the change. However, the paragraph may be omitted when a change not requiring a cumulative-effect type adjustment is made at the beginning of the earliest year presented and reported on (AU 508).

Answers (B) and (C) are incorrect because the auditor must add an explanatory paragraph, but, if (s)he concurs with the change, it will not be a basis for departing from an unqualified opinion. Answer (D) is incorrect because cumulative-effect type changes do not require restatement of prior periods' financial statements.

42. If an accounting change has no material effect on the financial statements in the current year, but the change is reasonably certain to have a material effect in later years, the change should be

A. Treated as a consistency modification in the auditor's report for the current year.

B. Disclosed in the notes to the financial statements of the current year.

C. Disclosed in the notes to the financial statements and referred to in the auditor's report for the current year.

D. Treated as a subsequent event.

The correct answer is (B). *(CPA, adapted)*

REQUIRED: The treatment of a change with no material current effect.

DISCUSSION: AU 420 states, "If an accounting change has no material effect on the financial statements in the current year, but the change is reasonably certain to have substantial effects in later years, the change should be disclosed in the notes to the financial statements whenever the statements of the period of change are presented, but the independent auditor need not recognize the change in the report as to consistency."

Answer (A) is incorrect because the auditor should modify the opinion for lack of adequate disclosure if the change is not included in the footnotes by the client. By itself, however, lack of consistency does not necessitate modification of the opinion paragraph. Answer (C) is incorrect because the auditor need not recognize the change in the audit report. Answer (D) is incorrect because changes in accounting methods are not subsequent events.

43. The ABC Manufacturing Co. in 1996 and 1997 included certain factory administrative expenses in the general and administrative expense category. For the year ended December 31, 1998, ABC has decided that these expenses should be allocated to units produced as part of factory overhead. The amount involved is material. The auditor should regard this change as

A. A classification change that does not require special treatment or comment.

B. A change in an accounting principle that requires management justification.

C. A change in an accounting estimate that requires footnote explanation.

D. A change from the absorption costing inventory method to the direct costing inventory method.

The correct answer is (B). *(Publisher)*

REQUIRED: The auditor's treatment of a change in accounting for certain expenses.

DISCUSSION: The change in the treatment of these expenses is a change in accounting principle, that is, a change in a convention, rule, or procedure applied in accounting practice. A change in accounting principle requires reasonable justification by the client and a separate explanatory paragraph in the auditor's report. The auditor must also become satisfied that the new principle is generally accepted and that the method of accounting for the effect of the change conforms with GAAP (AU 508).

Answer (A) is incorrect because classification changes result from changes in account titles or items included within account classifications. Answer (C) is incorrect because changes in estimates require no modification of the auditor's report unless they are inseparable from a change in principle. However, a material change in estimate may require footnote disclosure. Answer (D) is incorrect because a change to direct costing would entail treating fixed manufacturing costs as period costs (immediate expenses), not as product (inventoriable) costs.

44. A company has changed its method of inventory valuation from an unacceptable one to one in conformity with generally accepted accounting principles. The auditor's report on the financial statements of the year of the change should include

A. No reference to consistency.

B. A reference to a prior-period adjustment.

C. A footnote explaining the change.

D. Justification for the change and the impact of the change on reported net income.

The correct answer is (B). *(CPA, adapted)*

REQUIRED: The effect on the report when a change is made from an unacceptable to an acceptable principle.

DISCUSSION: Such a change is a correction of an error in accounting principle, but it also requires recognition in the auditor's report as to consistency (AU 420). An error correction requires a prior-period adjustment, and the change is identified in a separate paragraph of the auditor's report following the opinion paragraph.

Answer (A) is incorrect because a reference should be made in a separate explanatory paragraph. Answer (C) is incorrect because an auditor's report should not contain footnotes. Answer (D) is incorrect because justification for the change in principle is the responsibility of management, and the impact of those changes should be reflected in management's financial statements.

45. An entity changed from the straight-line method to the declining-balance method of depreciation for all newly acquired assets. This change has no material effect on the current year's financial statements but is reasonably certain to have a substantial effect in later years. If the change is disclosed in the notes to the financial statements, the auditor should issue a report with a(n)

A. Qualified opinion.

B. Explanatory paragraph.

C. Unqualified opinion.

D. Consistency modification.

The correct answer is (C). *(CPA, adapted)*

REQUIRED: The report issued when a change in accounting principle has no material current effect.

DISCUSSION: If a change in accounting principle has no material effect on the current financial statements, but is reasonably certain to have a substantial effect in future years, the change should be disclosed but need not be recognized in the report (AU 420).

Answer (A) is incorrect because a justified change in accounting principle does not result in a qualified opinion. Answers (B) and (D) are incorrect because, if an accounting change has no material effect on the current financial statements but is likely to affect future financial statements, the auditor need not modify the report.

46. Green Company uses the first-in, first-out method of costing for its international subsidiary's inventory and the last-in, first-out method of costing for its domestic inventory. The different costing methods would cause Green's auditor to issue a report with a(n)

A. Explanatory paragraph as to consistency.

B. Qualified opinion.

C. Opinion modified as to consistency.

D. Unqualified opinion.

The correct answer is (D). *(CPA, adapted)*

REQUIRED: The audit report when two business segments use different inventory methods.

DISCUSSION: A difference between the accounting principles used by two segments of an entity does not raise a consistency issue. The second standard of reporting concerns the consistent observation of principles in the current period in relation to the preceding period, that is, between periods. Thus, the use of two different cost flow assumptions does not, by itself, affect the comparability of the entity's financial statements between periods if no accounting changes have occurred.

Answer (A) is incorrect because no explanatory paragraph as to consistency is necessary. Answer (B) is incorrect because an unqualified opinion is possible even in the event of a lack of consistency. Answer (C) is incorrect because an opinion modified as to consistency is required only for a change in accounting principle.

47. A change in the method of determining the items to be treated as cash equivalents in the statement of cash flows

A. Is treated as a reclassification for both disclosure and reporting purposes and ordinarily requires no reference in the auditor's report.

B. Requires disclosure in the financial statements and reference in the auditor's report.

C. Must be disclosed in the notes to the financial statements and usually is not referred to in the auditor's report.

D. Is considered an accounting change not affecting consistency.

The correct answer is (B). *(Publisher)*

REQUIRED: The correct treatment of a change in the policy regarding determination of cash equivalents.

DISCUSSION: SFAS 95, *Statement of Cash Flows*, requires disclosure of the enterprise's policy regarding determination of the items to be treated as cash equivalents. A change in that policy is a change in principle requiring retroactive restatement. AU 420 states that this type of change in presentation of cash flows requires an explanatory paragraph in the audit report.

Answer (A) is incorrect because a change in policy determining cash equivalents is a change in principle, not a reclassification. Answers (C) and (D) are incorrect because the change affects consistency and requires an explanatory paragraph.

48. Which of the following requires recognition in the auditor's report as to consistency?

A. Changing the salvage value of an asset.

B. Changing the presentation of prepaid insurance from inclusion in other assets to disclosure as a separate line item.

C. Dividing a consolidated subsidiary into two subsidiaries that are both consolidated.

D. Changing from consolidating a subsidiary to carrying it on the equity basis.

The correct answer is (D). *(CPA, adapted)*

REQUIRED: The change requiring recognition in the auditor's report as to consistency.

DISCUSSION: Accounting changes affecting consistency require recognition in the auditor's report. A change in the reporting entity is an accounting change that affects consistency. Changing among the cost, equity, and consolidation methods of accounting for a subsidiary is a change in the reporting entity and therefore requires recognition in the report (AU 420).

Answer (A) is incorrect because a change in estimate does not require a reference to consistency. Answer (B) is incorrect because changing the presentation of account balances is a change in classification or reclassification and does not affect consistency. Answer (C) is incorrect because no change in the reporting entity affecting consistency has occurred. The original consolidated entity remains the same.

49. In which of the following situations concerning consistency would the auditor appropriately issue the standard report?

A. A change in the method of accounting for specific subsidiaries included in the group of companies for which consolidated statements are presented.

B. A change from an accounting principle that is not generally accepted to one that is generally accepted.

C. A change in the percentage used to calculate the provision for warranty expense.

D. The correction of a mistake in the application of a generally accepted accounting principle.

The correct answer is (C). *(CPA, adapted)*

REQUIRED: The situation in which the standard report is appropriate.

DISCUSSION: A change in the calculation of warranty expense is a change in accounting estimate. Changes that affect comparability but not the consistent application of accounting principles do not require recognition in the auditor's report (AU 508).

Answer (A) is incorrect because a change in the reporting entity affects consistency. Answer (B) is incorrect because a change from an accounting principle that is not generally accepted to one that is generally accepted is a correction of an error in principle and requires recognition in the report. Answer (D) is incorrect because correction of a mistake in the application of GAAP is an error correction requiring recognition in the report.

50. An accounting change may result in financial statements that are actually those of a different reporting entity. The change should be reported by restating the financial statements of all prior periods presented. Which of the following is not a change in the reporting entity?

A. Presenting consolidated statements in place of statements of individual companies or accounting for a business combination using the pooling of interests method.

B. Changing specific subsidiaries included in the group of companies for which consolidated financial statements are presented or changing the companies included in combined financial statements.

C. Creating, terminating, purchasing, or disposing of a subsidiary or other business unit.

D. Changing among the cost, equity, or consolidation methods of accounting for subsidiaries and investments.

The correct answer is (C). *(Publisher)*

REQUIRED: The accounting change not considered a change in reporting entity for the purposes of APB 20.

DISCUSSION: The users of financial statements have a right to expect that changes in account balances are the results of transactions. If changes in account balances arise from changes in accounting principles, the auditor has a responsibility to report accordingly. A change in an account caused by the creation, termination, purchase, or disposition of a subsidiary or business unit is considered to result from a transaction, and the auditor need not recognize it in his/her report as an accounting change (AU 420).

Answers (A), (B), and (D) are incorrect because consolidation or pooling, changing the constituents of a consolidated entity, and changing the method of accounting for subsidiaries and investments result from a management decision (rather than a transaction) that changes the reporting entity and requires recognition in the auditor's report as to consistency.

51. If a change in accounting principle is inseparable from the effect of a change in estimate, this material event should be accounted for as a change in

A. Estimate, and the auditor should report on consistency.

B. Principle, and the auditor should report on consistency.

C. Estimate, and the auditor should not recognize the change in the report.

D. Principle, and the auditor should not recognize the change in the report.

The correct answer is (A). *(CPA, adapted)*

REQUIRED: The true statement about a change in principle inseparable from a change in estimate.

DISCUSSION: When the effect of a change in accounting principle is inseparable from the effect of a change in estimate, APB 20 requires that it be accounted for in the same manner as a change in estimate only. However, because a change in principle is involved, this type of change requires recognition in the independent auditor's report as to consistency (AU 420). An example is the change from deferring and amortizing a cost to recording it as an expense when incurred because its future benefits are doubtful. Because the new method recognizes a change in estimated future benefits, the effect of the change in principle is inseparable from the change in estimate.

Answers (B), (C), and (D) are incorrect because the change should be accounted for as an estimate, and the auditor should refer to the change in the report.

7.4 Disclosure Considerations

52. Footnotes that are included with financial statements are the responsibility of the

A. Securities and Exchange Commission.

B. Company's management.

C. Independent auditor.

D. Internal auditor.

The correct answer is (B). *(Publisher)*

REQUIRED: The person(s) primarily responsible for the accuracy of footnotes.

DISCUSSION: The footnotes are considered part of the basic financial statements (AU 551, *Reporting on Information Accompanying the Basic Financial Statements in Auditor-Submitted Documents*). Because management has the primary responsibility for the financial statements, it also has the primary responsibility for the fairness of information included in footnotes.

Answer (A) is incorrect because the SEC is responsible for assuring that firms comply with federal securities laws. Answer (C) is incorrect because the independent external auditor is responsible for expressing an opinion on the fairness of the financial statements. Answer (D) is incorrect because the internal auditor advises management.

53. When an auditor qualifies an opinion because of inadequate disclosure, the auditor should describe the nature of the omission in a separate explanatory paragraph and modify the

	Introductory Paragraph	Scope Paragraph	Opinion Paragraph
A.	Yes	No	No
B.	Yes	Yes	No
C.	No	Yes	Yes
D.	No	No	Yes

The correct answer is (D). *(CPA, adapted)*

REQUIRED: The effect(s) on the auditor's report of inadequate disclosure.

DISCUSSION: If management fails to disclose information required by GAAP, the auditor should express a qualified opinion or an adverse opinion because of the departure from GAAP. (S)he should also provide the information in the report, if practicable, unless omission is appropriate under a specific SAS. If the opinion is qualified, the opinion paragraph should include the appropriate qualifying language and refer to the explanatory paragraph(s) preceding the opinion paragraph.

Answers (A), (B), and (C) are incorrect because the auditor should modify only the opinion paragraph.

54. The standard independent auditor's report names the basic financial statements in the introductory paragraph. They include the statements of financial position,

A. Income, and cash flows.

B. Income, changes in retained earnings, and cash flows.

C. Income, retained earnings, and cash flows.

D. Income, and retained earnings.

The correct answer is (C). *(Publisher)*

REQUIRED: The basic financial statements.

DISCUSSION: The statements of financial position, income, retained earnings, and cash flows are the basic financial statements upon which the auditor reports (AU 508). When both financial position and results of operations are presented, disclosure of changes in shareholders' equity accounts (other than retained earnings) and in the number of shares of equity securities is required to be made in the basic financial statements, the notes thereto, or in a separate statement of changes in shareholders' equity (APB 12, *Omnibus Opinion–1967*). Furthermore, SFAS 130 requires an enterprise that has items of other comprehensive income and that reports financial position, results of operations, and cash flows to display comprehensive income and its components. This display should be in a financial statement given the same prominence as the other statements constituting the full set. However, no specific format is required for this statement as long as net income is displayed as a component of comprehensive income.

Answers (A), (B), and (D) are incorrect because the basic financial statements include the statements of financial position, income, cash flows, and retained earnings.

55. If financial statements are to meet the requirements of adequate disclosure,

A. All information pertaining to the company must be disclosed in the statements or related footnotes, even though some of the disclosures are potentially detrimental to the company or its shareholders.

B. All information believed by the auditor to be essential to the fair presentation of the financial statements must be disclosed, no matter how confidential management believes the data to be.

C. Statement footnotes should be written in very technical language to avoid misinterpretation by the reader.

D. A statement footnote must clearly detail any deficiencies contained in the financial statements themselves.

The correct answer is (B). *(Publisher)*

REQUIRED: The true statement about the requirements of adequate disclosure.

DISCUSSION: In considering the adequacy of disclosure, the auditor necessarily uses confidential client information. Otherwise, forming an opinion on the statements would be difficult. To the extent required by GAAP, such information must be disclosed (AU 431, *Adequacy of Disclosure in Financial Statements*). But beyond these requirements, the auditor who discloses confidential information without specific consent violates Conduct Rule 301, *Confidential Client Information*.

Answer (A) is incorrect because only the information required by GAAP must be disclosed. Answer (C) is incorrect because footnotes need only be written so that the informative disclosures are reasonably adequate. Answer (D) is incorrect because footnotes do not list deficiencies contained in the financial statements. The financial statements must conform with GAAP.

56. If the basic financial statements are accompanied by a separate statement of changes in shareholders' equity, this statement should

A. Not be identified in the introductory paragraph but should be reported on separately in the opinion paragraph.

B. Be excluded from both the introductory and opinion paragraphs.

C. Be identified in the introductory paragraph of the report but need not be reported on separately in the opinion paragraph.

D. Be identified in the introductory paragraph of the report and must be reported on separately in the opinion paragraph.

The correct answer is (C). *(CPA, adapted)*

REQUIRED: The effect on the report of presenting a separate statement of changes in shareholders' equity.

DISCUSSION: If the basic statements are accompanied by a separate statement of changes in shareholders' equity, it should be identified in the introductory paragraph. It need not be reported on separately in the opinion paragraph, however, because such changes are included in the presentation of financial position, results of operations, and cash flows (AU 508).

Answers (A), (B), and (D) are incorrect because the statement of changes in shareholders' equity, if presented, should be identified in the introductory paragraph, but it need not be reported on separately in the opinion paragraph.

57. Adequate disclosure means that sufficient information is presented so that financial statements are not misleading. The decisions concerning adequate disclosure should reflect the needs of

A. Reasonably prudent investors.

B. Any and all readers of the financial statements.

C. Experts in accounting and finance.

D. Governmental regulatory agencies.

The correct answer is (A). *(Publisher)*

REQUIRED: The parties toward whom the adequate disclosure requirement is directed.

DISCUSSION: The definition of a reasonably prudent investor is a difficult matter. Nevertheless, adequate disclosure is usually deemed to encompass the amount and quality of information necessary for a reasonably well-informed individual to make investment decisions.

Answer (B) is incorrect because, even if financial statements are general-purpose, they are not expected to meet the needs of any and all readers. Answer (C) is incorrect because the disclosure should be such that expertise in accounting or finance is not required to interpret the statements. Answer (D) is incorrect because regulatory bodies exist to protect the public, who are the ultimate beneficiaries of the disclosure requirements.

58. Which of the following statements is false regarding disclosure in a client's financial statements?

A. Information essential for a fair presentation should be set forth in the financial statements.

B. Omission of a statement of cash flows is considered inadequate disclosure.

C. Inadequate disclosure normally results in the auditor including the required information in the report.

D. The auditor should never disclose information in the report that the client has not shown in the financial statements.

The correct answer is (D). *(Publisher)*

REQUIRED: The false statement regarding disclosure in the financial statements.

DISCUSSION: AU 431 states, "If management omits from the financial statements, including the accompanying notes, information that is required by generally accepted accounting principles, the auditor should express a qualified or an adverse opinion and should provide the information in the report, if practicable."

Answer (A) is incorrect because information essential for a fair presentation should be set forth in the financial statements. Answer (B) is incorrect because omission of a statement of cash flows is considered inadequate disclosure. Answer (C) is incorrect because inadequate disclosure normally results in the auditor's including the required information in the report.

59. If a publicly held company issues financial statements that purport to present its financial position and results of operations but omits the statement of cash flows, the auditor ordinarily will express a(n)

A. Disclaimer of opinion.

B. Qualified opinion.

C. Review report.

D. Unqualified opinion with a separate explanatory paragraph.

The correct answer is (B). *(CPA, adapted)*

REQUIRED: The opinion expressed when a client fails to present a statement of cash flows.

DISCUSSION: Under SFAS 95, an entity that reports financial position and results of operations must provide a statement of cash flows. Thus, the omission of the cash flow statement is normally a basis for qualifying the opinion. If the statements fail to disclose information required by GAAP, the auditor should provide the information in the report, if practicable. However, the auditor is not required to prepare a basic financial statement. Accordingly, (s)he should qualify the opinion and explain the reason in a separate paragraph (AU 508).

Answer (A) is incorrect because the question concerns disclosure rather than a scope limitation. Answer (C) is incorrect because the engagement is an audit. Answer (D) is incorrect because the lack of disclosure normally requires qualification of the opinion.

60. Footnotes to financial statements may be used to

A. Describe the nature and type of auditing procedures applied to the financial statements.

B. Make an unsubstantiated claim that related party transactions were consummated on terms equivalent to those that prevail in arm's-length transactions.

C. Correct an improper financial statement presentation.

D. Indicate bases for valuing assets.

The correct answer is (D). *(Publisher)*

REQUIRED: The purpose of footnotes.

DISCUSSION: Footnotes should be used to describe the valuation bases for the assets on the balance sheet. For example, it should be stated that property is recorded at historical cost and that such cost is systematically allocated to appropriate accounting periods.

Answer (A) is incorrect because the financial statements should not refer to the audit or the work of the auditor. Answer (B) is incorrect because SFAS 57, *Related Party Disclosures*, states that the representations "shall not imply that related party transactions were consummated on terms equivalent to those that prevail in arm's-length transactions unless such representations can be substantiated." Answer (C) is incorrect because footnotes are not a substitute for recognition in financial statements of items that meet recognition criteria.

61. A closely held manufacturing company must disclose all of the following information in audited financial statements except

A. Replacement cost of inventory.

B. Pledged inventory.

C. LIFO reserves.

D. Changes in methods of accounting for inventory.

The correct answer is (A). *(CPA, adapted)*

REQUIRED: The disclosure not required of a closely held manufacturing company.

DISCUSSION: A manufacturing company should report inventory at full absorption cost unless the fair value is less than cost. Whether they are closely or publicly held, companies need not report replacement cost of inventory.

Answer (B) is incorrect because pledged inventory is a disclosure required of all companies. Answer (C) is incorrect because LIFO reserves are disclosures required of all companies using LIFO. Answer (D) is incorrect because changes in methods of accounting for inventory are disclosures required of all companies.

62. Your client and Company B combined during the current fiscal period. All the requirements of APB 16 for a pooling of interests were met. However, only the current-year financial statements of the new entity are being presented. A footnote discloses that a pooling was consummated, but it does not contain any prior financial data for either of the two companies. Assuming that the client refuses to modify the information to be reported, the opinion should be qualified as to

	Consistency	Disclosure
A.	Yes	No
B.	Yes	Yes
C.	No	Yes
D.	No	No

The correct answer is (C). *(Publisher)*

REQUIRED: The effect of the client's refusal to provide prior year financial data after a pooling of interests.

DISCUSSION: If single-year statements only are presented for the year of the pooling, a footnote should adequately disclose the transaction and the revenues, extraordinary items, and net income of the pooled entities for the preceding year on a combined basis. Omission of these disclosures requires qualification of the opinion as to the lack of disclosure and may also require a separate paragraph explaining the effect on the consistency of application of GAAP caused by this change (AU 420). Because the middle paragraph added as a result of the inadequacy of disclosure should contain all the necessary information regarding the inconsistency, a separate paragraph following the opinion paragraph is not necessary. Moreover, audit opinions are no longer qualified for lack of consistency (AU 508).

Answers (A), (B), and (D) are incorrect because the report must be qualified as to disclosure, not consistency.

63. Which of the following concepts is not encompassed by the phrase "present fairly in all material respects, in conformity with generally accepted accounting principles"?

A. The appropriateness of the principles.

B. The adequacy of informative disclosures.

C. The reflection of changes in the purchasing power of the monetary unit.

D. The form and content of the financial statements.

The correct answer is (C). *(Publisher)*

REQUIRED: The concept not encompassed by the phrase "present fairly in conformity with GAAP."

DISCUSSION: Enterprises are encouraged but not required to disclose supplemental information on the effects of changing prices (SFAS 89, *Financial Reporting and Changing Prices*).

Answer (A) is incorrect because the auditor's opinion concerning the fairness of presentation in conformity with GAAP is based on certain judgments, e.g., about whether the accounting principles selected and applied are appropriate in the circumstances (AU 411). Answer (B) is incorrect because GAAP require adequate disclosure of material matters related to the form, content, and arrangement of the financial statements and their footnotes (AU 431). Answer (D) is incorrect because the form and content of the financial statements are encompassed by the phrase "present fairly in conformity with GAAP."

64. In which of the following situations would an auditor ordinarily choose between expressing a qualified opinion or an adverse opinion?

A. The auditor did not observe the entity's physical inventory and is unable to become satisfied as to its balance by other auditing procedures.

B. The financial statements fail to disclose information that is required by generally accepted accounting principles.

C. The auditor is asked to report only on the entity's balance sheet and not on the other basic financial statements.

D. Events disclosed in the financial statements cause the auditor to have substantial doubt about the entity's ability to continue as a going concern.

The correct answer is (B). *(CPA, adapted)*

REQUIRED: The situation in which a qualified or an adverse opinion is expressed.

DISCUSSION: Departures from GAAP, including inadequate disclosures, may result in either a qualified or an adverse opinion. The auditor must exercise judgment as to the materiality of the departure, weighing factors such as dollar magnitude, significance to the entity, pervasiveness of misstatements, and impact on the statements taken as a whole (AU 508). If the departure from GAAP is not sufficiently material to require an adverse opinion, the auditor should express a qualified opinion.

Answer (A) is incorrect because a scope limitation is not a basis for an adverse opinion. Answer (C) is incorrect because a limited reporting engagement may result in the expression of an unqualified opinion. Answer (D) is incorrect because substantial doubt about the entity's ability to continue as a going concern normally results in the addition of a paragraph to the end of the report.

65. On January 15, 1999, before the Mapleview Co. released its financial statements for the year ended December 31, 1998, it settled a long-standing lawsuit. A material loss resulted and no prior liability had been recorded. How should this loss be disclosed or recognized?

A. The loss should be disclosed in footnotes to the financial statements, but the financial statements themselves need not be adjusted.

B. The loss should be disclosed in an explanatory paragraph in the auditor's report.

C. No disclosure or recognition is required.

D. The financial statements should be adjusted to recognize the loss.

The correct answer is (D). *(Publisher)*

REQUIRED: The proper disclosure of a material loss on an existing lawsuit after year-end.

DISCUSSION: Subsequent events that provide additional evidence with respect to conditions that existed at the balance sheet date and that affect the estimates inherent in the process of preparing the financial statements should be reflected in the current financial statements. Settlement of a lawsuit is indicative of conditions existing at year-end and calls for adjustment of the statements (AU 560, *Subsequent Events*).

Answer (A) is incorrect because the financial statements should be adjusted to reflect the loss. Answer (B) is incorrect because the audit report need not be modified. Answer (C) is incorrect because failure to adjust the statements for a material loss on an asset that existed at year-end would be misleading.

66. A major customer of an audit client suffers a fire just prior to completion of year-end field work. The audit client believes that this event could have a significant direct effect on the financial statements. The auditor should

A. Advise management to disclose the event in notes to the financial statements.

B. Disclose the event in the auditor's report.

C. Withhold submission of the auditor's report until the extent of the direct effect on the financial statements is known.

D. Advise management to adjust the financial statements.

The correct answer is (A). *(CPA, adapted)*

REQUIRED: The appropriate action by the auditor concerning a subsequent event.

DISCUSSION: Subsequent events, such as a fire or other casualty, that provide evidence with respect to conditions that did not exist at the balance sheet date should not result in adjustment of the financial statements, but such events should be disclosed in the notes if necessary to keep the statements from being misleading (AU 560).

Answer (B) is incorrect because subsequent events, such as a fire or other casualty, that provide evidence with respect to conditions that did not exist at the balance sheet date are rarely disclosed in the audit report. Answer (C) is incorrect because an unreasonable amount of time may elapse before all the effects are known. Answer (D) is incorrect because adjustment of the financial statements is inappropriate. The fire damage did not exist at the balance sheet date.

67. Green, CPA, concludes that there is substantial doubt about JKL Co.'s ability to continue as a going concern. If JKL's financial statements adequately disclose its financial difficulties, Green's auditor's report should

	Include an Explanatory Paragraph Following the Opinion Paragraph	Specifically Use the Words "Going Concern"	Specifically Use the Words "Substantial Doubt"
A.	Yes	Yes	Yes
B.	Yes	Yes	No
C.	Yes	No	Yes
D.	No	Yes	Yes

The correct answer is (A). *(CPA, adapted)*

REQUIRED: The effect of a substantial doubt about the going concern assumption.

DISCUSSION: According to AU 341, *The Auditor's Consideration of an Entity's Ability to Continue as a Going Concern*, an evaluation must be made as to whether substantial doubt exists "about the entity's ability to continue as a going concern for a reasonable period of time, not to exceed 1 year beyond the date of the financial statements." If the auditor reaches this conclusion after identifying conditions and events that create such doubt and after evaluating management's plans to mitigate their effects, (s)he should consider the adequacy of disclosure and include an explanatory paragraph (after the opinion paragraph) in the report. The auditor must use language in the explanatory paragraph that includes the phrases "substantial doubt" and "going concern." Also, the explanatory paragraph should not use conditional language in expressing its conclusion about the existence of a substantial doubt. The substantial doubt is not a basis for a qualified or an adverse opinion, but a disclaimer is not precluded in the case of such a material uncertainty.

Answers (B), (C), and (D) are incorrect because the words "substantial doubt" and "going concern" must be included and the auditor should include an explanatory paragraph after the opinion paragraph.

68. Which of the following conditions or events most likely would cause an auditor to have substantial doubt about an entity's ability to continue as a going concern?

A. Cash flows from operating activities are negative.

B. Research and development projects are postponed.

C. Significant related party transactions are pervasive.

D. Stock dividends replace annual cash dividends.

The correct answer is (A). *(CPA, adapted)*

REQUIRED: The basis for substantial doubt about the going concern assumption.

DISCUSSION: The significance of conditions or events depends on circumstances, and some conditions or events may be significant only in conjunction with others. Such conditions and events include negative trends, financial difficulties, internal matters, and external matters. Negative cash flows from operating activities provide evidence of negative trends and financial difficulties.

Answer (B) is incorrect because an entity may postpone R&D and not raise doubts about its ability to continue as a going concern. Answer (C) is incorrect because the auditor's concern is with the adequacy of disclosure for related party transactions. Answer (D) is incorrect because stock dividends preserve cash and are not indicative of going concern problems.

69. Grant Company's financial statements adequately disclose uncertainties that concern future events, the outcome of which are not susceptible to reasonable estimation. The auditor's report should include

A. An unqualified opinion.

B. A "subject to" qualified opinion.

C. An "except for" qualified opinion.

D. An adverse opinion.

The correct answer is (A). *(CPA, adapted)*

REQUIRED: The opinion when financial statements adequately disclose uncertainties.

DISCUSSION: In the absence of a scope limitation or a departure from GAAP, an uncertainty does not require modification of the report.

Answer (B) is incorrect because a "subject to" qualified opinion is never permissible. Answer (C) is incorrect because a qualified opinion related to an uncertainty is appropriate given a scope limitation or a departure from GAAP. Answer (D) is incorrect because, absent a departure from GAAP, an uncertainty does not result in an adverse opinion.

70. Zero Corp. suffered a loss having a material effect on its financial statements as a result of a customer's bankruptcy that rendered a trade receivable uncollectible. This bankruptcy occurred suddenly because of a natural disaster 10 days after Zero's balance sheet date, but one month before the issuance of the financial statements and the auditor's report. Under these circumstances, the

	Financial Statements Should Be Adjusted	Event Requires Financial Statement Disclosure, but No Adjustment	Auditor's Report Should Be Modified for a Lack of Consistency
A.	Yes	No	No
B.	Yes	No	Yes
C.	No	Yes	Yes
D.	No	Yes	No

The correct answer is (D). *(CPA, adapted)*

REQUIRED: The effect on the financial statements and the auditor's report of a subsequent event.

DISCUSSION: Certain subsequent events may provide additional evidence about conditions at the date of the balance sheet and affect estimates inherent in the preparation of the statements. These events require adjustment by the client in the financial statements at year-end. Other subsequent events provide evidence about conditions not existing at the date of the balance sheet but arising subsequent to that date and affecting the interpretation of the year-end financial statements. These events may require disclosure in footnotes to the financial statements but do not require adjustment of the financial statement balances. Thus, in this case, the financial statements should not be adjusted, but disclosure should be made in the notes. The auditor's report is unaffected.

Answers (A), (B), and (C) are incorrect because the financial statements are not adjusted, the matter is disclosed, and the auditor's report is not affected.

71. Which of the following phrases would an auditor most likely include in the auditor's report when expressing a qualified opinion because of inadequate disclosure?

A. Subject to the departure from generally accepted accounting principles, as described above.

B. With the foregoing explanation of these omitted disclosures.

C. Except for the omission of the information discussed in the preceding paragraph.

D. Does not present fairly in all material respects.

The correct answer is (C). *(CPA, adapted)*

REQUIRED: The phrase included when the opinion is qualified because of inadequate disclosure.

DISCUSSION: A report qualified for inadequate disclosure includes a separate paragraph preceding the opinion paragraph. The opinion paragraph states, "In our opinion, except for the omission of information discussed in the preceding paragraph, the financial statements referred to above present fairly. . . ."

Answer (A) is incorrect because a "subject to" opinion should not be expressed in any circumstance. Answer (B) is incorrect because the phrase "with the foregoing explanation" is not forceful enough, lacks clarity, and should not be used. Answer (D) is incorrect because the phrase "does not present fairly" indicates an adverse opinion.

72. If the auditor discovers that the fair value of a client's investments in trading securities has increased, the auditor should insist that the

A. Investments be reported at lower of cost or market.

B. Investments be classified as long-term for balance sheet purposes with full disclosure in the footnotes.

C. Holding gain be recognized in the financial statements of the client.

D. Equity section of the balance sheet separately show a credit equal to the amount of the gain.

The correct answer is (C). *(Publisher)*

REQUIRED: The auditor's action when (s)he discovers that the fair value of trading securities has increased.

DISCUSSION: According to SFAS 115, *Accounting for Certain Investments in Debt and Equity Securities*, unrealized holding gains and losses on trading securities are included in earnings. Failure of the client to adhere to SFAS 115 is a departure from GAAP and requires a qualified or adverse opinion if the gain is material.

Answer (A) is incorrect because the gain must be recognized in the income statement and the investment reported at fair value. Answer (B) is incorrect because no reclassification is necessary for a change in fair value of an investment. Answer (D) is incorrect because an unrealized gain or loss on available-for-sale securities is reported as a separate component of shareholders' equity until realized.

73. An auditor most likely would modify an unqualified opinion if the entity's financial statements include a footnote on related party transactions

A. Disclosing loans to related parties at interest rates significantly below prevailing market rates.

B. Describing an exchange of real estate for similar property in a nonmonetary related party transaction.

C. Stating that a particular related party transaction occurred on terms equivalent to those that would have prevailed in an arm's-length transaction.

D. Presenting the dollar volume of related party transactions and the effects of any change from prior periods in the method of establishing the terms.

The correct answer is (C). *(CPA, adapted)*

REQUIRED: The footnote on related party transactions that would most likely result in a modified opinion.

DISCUSSION: The auditor's primary concern regarding related party transactions is for adequate disclosure because the accounting treatment of these transactions is ordinarily the same as for other transactions. It is difficult to substantiate representations that the related party transactions were consummated on terms equivalent to those that prevail in arm's-length transactions. An auditor who believes the representations to be unsubstantiated should express a qualified or an adverse opinion (AU 334, *Related Parties*).

Answers (A) and (B) are incorrect because loans and exchanges of real estate are common related party transactions that do not require an opinion modification. However, the auditor may wish to include an explanatory paragraph to emphasize such matters. Answer (D) is incorrect because the dollar amount of related party transactions and the effects of changes in the method of establishing the terms should be disclosed.

74. When an independent auditor wishes to include in the report additional explanatory matter (not required for adequate disclosure) to highlight certain circumstances or to aid in the interpretation of the financial statements, this additional disclosure should be referred to in

A. The scope paragraph only.

B. Neither the scope paragraph nor the opinion paragraph.

C. The introductory paragraph and the opinion paragraph.

D. The opinion paragraph only.

The correct answer is (B). *(Publisher)*

REQUIRED: The proper treatment in the audit report of additional information not required for adequate disclosure.

DISCUSSION: An auditor may wish to emphasize a matter affecting the statements even though (s)he intends to express an unqualified opinion. This information should be contained in a separate explanatory paragraph (AU 508).

Answer (A) is incorrect because the scope paragraph should remain unchanged. Answer (C) is incorrect because the introductory and opinion paragraphs should remain unchanged. Answer (D) is incorrect because the opinion paragraph should remain unchanged.

75. An auditor's standard report expresses an unqualified opinion and includes an explanatory paragraph that emphasizes a matter included in the notes to the financial statements. The auditor's report is deficient if the explanatory paragraph states that the entity

A. Is a component of a larger business enterprise.

B. Has omitted a statement of cash flows.

C. Has had a significant subsequent event.

D. Has accounting reclassifications that enhance the comparability between years.

The correct answer is (B). *(CPA, adapted)*

REQUIRED: The statement in an explanatory paragraph indicating a deficiency in the report.

DISCUSSION: The statement of cash flows is a basic financial statement. Its omission when financial position and results of operations are presented is a departure from GAAP that requires the auditor to modify the opinion paragraph.

Answers (A), (C), and (D) are incorrect because matters that may be emphasized in an explanatory paragraph of a report expressing an unqualified opinion include the entity's position as a component of a larger business enterprise, a significant subsequent event, and accounting reclassifications that enhance the comparability between years.

76. When a publicly held company refuses to include in its audited financial statements any of the segment disclosures that the auditor believes are required, the auditor should express

A. An unqualified opinion with a separate explanatory paragraph emphasizing the matter.

B. A qualified opinion because of inadequate disclosure.

C. An adverse opinion because of a significant uncertainty.

D. A disclaimer of opinion because of the significant scope limitation.

The correct answer is (B). *(CPA, adapted)*

REQUIRED: The effect on the report of the client's failure to include required segment disclosures.

DISCUSSION: According to an Interpretation of AU 326 that addresses segment disclosures, the auditor's standard report on financial statements prepared in conformity with GAAP implicitly applies to segment information included in those statements. The auditor should not refer to segment information unless the audit reveals a related material misstatement or omission, or unless the audit was subject to a scope limitation. In accordance with AU 508, if material information is not included that the auditor believes should be disclosed, the auditor should modify the opinion for inadequate disclosure and describe the information omitted. The auditor should include this information in the report, if practicable, unless a specific SAS allows its omission from the report (no currently effective SAS provides for this exemption). Furthermore, the auditor need not assume the position of a preparer of financial information.

Note: The FASB has issued SFAS 131, *Disclosures about Segments of an Enterprise and Related Information*, a pronouncement that adopts an operating-segment approach to disclosure. The change to an operating-segment approach is similar to a reclassification of prior-period information made for comparative purposes. Thus, given full disclosure in the statements, the auditor need not refer to the change in the report.

Answer (A) is incorrect because inadequate disclosure requires an opinion modification if it is material. Answer (C) is incorrect because the issue is disclosure, not an uncertainty. Moreover, by itself, an uncertainty does not result in a required report modification. Answer (D) is incorrect because inadequate disclosure is not a scope limitation.

7.5 Unqualified, Qualified, and Adverse Opinions

77. Which paragraphs of an auditor's standard report on financial statements should refer to generally accepted auditing standards (GAAS) and generally accepted accounting principles (GAAP)?

	GAAS	GAAP
A.	Opening	Scope
B.	Scope	Scope
C.	Scope	Opinion
D.	Opening	Opinion

The correct answer is (C). *(CPA, adapted)*

REQUIRED: The paragraphs of the standard report that refer to GAAS and GAAP.

DISCUSSION: The auditor's report should contain a clear-cut indication of the character of the auditor's work, if any, and state the degree of responsibility assumed (AU 150). GAAS are referred to only in the scope paragraph because they relate to the nature of the audit. The opinion paragraph contains an opinion as to whether the statements as a whole are fairly presented, in all material respects, in conformity with GAAP. Neither GAAS nor GAAP are mentioned in the introductory paragraph, which identifies the financial statements audited and describes the responsibilities of management and of the auditor (AU 508).

Answers (A), (B), and (D) are incorrect because the scope paragraph refers to GAAS and the opinion paragraph to GAAP.

78. Which of the following circumstances is not considered a departure from the auditor's standard report?

A. The auditor wishes to emphasize a particular matter regarding the financial statements.

B. The auditor's opinion is based in part on the report of another auditor.

C. The financial statements are affected by a departure from a generally accepted accounting principle.

D. The auditor is asked to report only on the balance sheet but has unlimited access to information underlying all the basic financial statements.

The correct answer is (D). *(CPA, adapted)*

REQUIRED: The circumstance not resulting in a departure from the auditor's standard report.

DISCUSSION: When the auditor is asked to report only on the balance sheet, has unlimited access to information underlying all the basic financial statements, and applies all the procedures (s)he considers necessary, only the reporting objectives are limited, and the report is not considered a departure from the standard report.

Answer (A) is incorrect because emphasis of a matter requires an additional paragraph but not a modified opinion. Answer (B) is incorrect because, if the principal auditor does not assume responsibility for the other auditor's work, (s)he should make the appropriate disclosure in the introductory and scope paragraphs and refer to it in the opinion paragraph. If the CPA accepts responsibility for the work of the other CPA, no report modification is necessary. Answer (C) is incorrect because a material departure from GAAP requires a modified opinion.

79. An auditor includes a separate paragraph in an otherwise unmodified report to emphasize that the entity being reported on had significant transactions with related parties. The inclusion of this separate paragraph

A. Is considered a qualification of the opinion.

B. Violates generally accepted auditing standards if this information is already disclosed in footnotes to the financial statements.

C. Necessitates a revision of the opinion paragraph to include the phrase "with the foregoing explanation."

D. Is appropriate and would not negate the unqualified opinion.

The correct answer is (D). *(CPA, adapted)*

REQUIRED: The effect of a separate paragraph in an otherwise unmodified report.

DISCUSSION: An auditor may emphasize a matter in an explanatory paragraph and express an unqualified opinion. Matters to be emphasized might include that the entity is a component of a larger enterprise or that it has had significant related party transactions. Subsequent events and accounting matters affecting comparability (e.g., a divestiture) are other matters suitable for this treatment.

Answer (A) is incorrect because emphasis of a matter in a separate paragraph is not inconsistent with an unqualified opinion. Answer (B) is incorrect because the auditor can emphasize a matter without violating GAAS. Answer (C) is incorrect because "with the foregoing explanation" creates doubt as to whether the report was intended to be qualified.

80. Without affecting the CPA's willingness to express an unqualified opinion on the client's financial statements, corporate management may refuse a request to

A. Authorize its attorney to confirm that a list of pending or threatened litigation prepared by management includes all items known to the attorney.

B. Change its basis of accounting for inventories from FIFO to LIFO because, in the opinion of the CPA, the FIFO method fails to give adequate recognition to the extraordinary increases in prices of merchandise acquired and held by the company.

C. Write down to salvage value certain equipment that is no longer useful.

D. Allow the CPA to examine tax returns for years prior to that of the financial statements being audited.

The correct answer is (B). *(CMA, adapted)*

REQUIRED: The request from an auditor that the client could refuse without jeopardizing an unqualified opinion.

DISCUSSION: FIFO (first-in, first-out) and LIFO (last-in, first-out) are both generally accepted methods of accounting for inventories. LIFO has the advantage during periods of inflation of matching current costs with current revenues. An independent auditor who has requested a change from FIFO to LIFO is likely to express an unqualified opinion even if management refuses to do so because the financial statements would still conform with GAAP.

Answer (A) is incorrect because a lawyer's refusal to furnish the information requested in the inquiry letter is a scope limitation sufficient to preclude an unqualified opinion (AU 337, *Inquiry of a Client's Lawyer Concerning Litigation, Claims, and Assessments*). Answer (C) is incorrect because refusal to write down obsolete equipment is a departure from GAAP that will result in modification of the opinion if the resulting misstatement is material. Answer (D) is incorrect because a scope limitation concerning tax liabilities may require qualifying or disclaiming an opinion depending on the importance of the omitted procedures to the auditor's ability to form an opinion.

81. Which of the following phrases should be included in the opinion paragraph when an auditor expresses a qualified opinion?

	When Read in Conjunction with Note X	With the Foregoing Explanation
A.	Yes	No
B.	No	Yes
C.	Yes	Yes
D.	No	No

The correct answer is (D). *(CPA, adapted)*

REQUIRED: The phrase(s) used in a qualified opinion.

DISCUSSION: The auditor should use a phrase such as "with the exception of" or "except for" to qualify an opinion, followed by the basis for the qualification and a reference to the explanatory paragraph(s) preceding the opinion paragraph. The explanatory paragraph(s) should state the substantive reasons for the qualification and disclose the principal effects of the subject matter of the qualification, if practicable, or refer to a footnote including such disclosures. However, the notes are part of the financial statements, and a phrase such as "when read in conjunction with the footnotes" in the opinion paragraph is likely to be misunderstood. Moreover, wording such as "with the foregoing explanation" is neither clear nor forceful enough.

Answers (A), (B), and (C) are incorrect because the phrases "when read in conjunction with the footnotes" and "with the foregoing explanation" are unacceptable.

82. An auditor's report includes an additional paragraph disclosing a difference of opinion between the auditor and the client for which the auditor believes an adjustment to the financial statements should be made. The opinion paragraph of the auditor's report most likely expresses

A. An unqualified opinion.

B. A qualified opinion.

C. A "subject to" opinion.

D. A disclaimer of opinion.

The correct answer is (B). *(CPA, adapted)*

REQUIRED: The opinion most likely expressed given a dispute between the auditor and the client.

DISCUSSION: The most likely reason for a separate paragraph disclosing a difference of opinion with the client is a departure from GAAP. Such a disagreement is usually the basis for a qualified opinion. If the departure from GAAP causes the statements, taken as a whole, not to be fairly presented, an adverse opinion expressed.

Answer (A) is incorrect because the auditor cannot express an unqualified opinion if (s)he believes the statements contain a material departure from GAAP. Answer (C) is incorrect because the wording "subject to" is unacceptable in any report. Answer (D) is incorrect because an opinion must be expressed if one is formed by the auditor.

83. An auditor may not express a qualified opinion when

A. A scope limitation prevents the auditor from completing an important audit procedure.

B. The auditor's report refers to the work of a specialist.

C. An accounting principle at variance with generally accepted accounting principles is used.

D. The auditor lacks independence with respect to the audited entity.

The correct answer is (D). *(CPA, adapted)*

REQUIRED: The situation in which an auditor may not express a qualified opinion.

DISCUSSION: A CPA may not express an opinion when not independent. (S)he should disclaim an opinion and state that (s)he is not independent (AU 504, *Association with Financial Statements*).

Answer (A) is incorrect because a scope limitation is the basis for a qualified opinion or a disclaimer depending upon the auditor's assessment of the importance of the omitted procedure(s) (AU 508). Answer (B) is incorrect because the report may refer to and identify a specialist if the auditor departs from an unqualified opinion or adds an explanatory paragraph as a result of the specialist's report or findings (AU 336, *Using the Work of a Specialist*). Answer (C) is incorrect because a material departure from GAAP requires a modified opinion.

84. An auditor will express an adverse opinion if

A. A severe scope limitation has been imposed by the client.

B. A violation of GAAP is sufficiently material that a qualified opinion is not justified.

C. A qualified opinion cannot be expressed because the auditor lacks independence.

D. The company's ability to continue as a going concern is subject to substantial doubt.

The correct answer is (B). *(K.J. Plucinski)*

REQUIRED: The circumstances in which the auditor will express an adverse opinion.

DISCUSSION: The auditor will express a qualified opinion when the statements are fairly presented in accordance with GAAP except for the effects of the matter to which the qualification relates. When the statements as a whole are not fairly presented in conformity with GAAP, a qualified opinion will be inappropriate, and an adverse opinion must be expressed (AU 508).

Answer (A) is incorrect because a severe client-imposed scope limitation will result in a disclaimer of opinion. Answer (C) is incorrect because a lack of independence will result in a disclaimer of opinion. Answer (D) is incorrect because such a doubt will result in a separate explanatory paragraph or a disclaimer of opinion.

85. An auditor's report includes the following statement: "The financial statements do not present fairly the financial position, results of operations, or cash flows in conformity with generally accepted accounting principles." This auditor's report was most likely issued in connection with financial statements that are

A. Inconsistent.

B. Based on prospective financial information.

C. Misleading.

D. Affected by a material uncertainty.

The correct answer is (C). *(CPA, adapted)*

REQUIRED: The nature of the financial statements on which the quoted report was issued.

DISCUSSION: The language quoted states an adverse opinion. The essence of an adverse opinion is that the statements reported on, taken as a whole, are not fairly presented in accordance with GAAP (AU 508). The financial statements should be based on principles having general acceptance that are appropriate in the circumstances. They should also be (1) informative about matters affecting their use, understanding, and interpretation; (2) neither too detailed nor too condensed; and (3) presented to reflect the underlying transactions and events within a range of acceptable limits (AU 411). If financial statements fail to meet these standards, they are misleading.

Answer (A) is incorrect because an inconsistency, by itself, results in no modification of the opinion but in an explanatory paragraph. Answer (B) is incorrect because the standard examination report on a financial forecast or projection refers to guidelines established by the AICPA, not to GAAP (AT 200). Answer (D) is incorrect because a material uncertainty does not, by itself, result in a required report modification.

86. When financial statements are presented that are not in conformity with generally accepted accounting principles, an auditor may express a

	Qualified Opinion	Disclaimer of an Opinion
A.	Yes	No
B.	Yes	Yes
C.	No	Yes
D.	No	No

The correct answer is (A). *(CPA, adapted)*

REQUIRED: The proper report when statements do not conform with GAAP.

DISCUSSION: Departures from GAAP may result in either a qualified or an adverse opinion. The auditor must exercise judgment as to the materiality of the departure, weighing factors such as dollar magnitude, significance to the entity, pervasiveness of misstatements, and impact on the statements taken as a whole (AU 508). If the departure from GAAP is not sufficiently material to require an adverse opinion, the auditor should express a qualified opinion.

Answers (B), (C), and (D) are incorrect because departures from GAAP may result in either a qualified or an adverse opinion, but a disclaimer is appropriate only when the auditor cannot form an opinion.

87. When an auditor expresses an adverse opinion, the opinion paragraph should include

A. The principal effects of the departure from generally accepted accounting principles.

B. A direct reference to a separate paragraph disclosing the basis for the opinion.

C. The substantive reasons for the financial statements being misleading.

D. A description of the uncertainty or scope limitation that prevents an unqualified opinion.

The correct answer is (B). *(CPA, adapted)*

REQUIRED: The matter included in the opinion paragraph when an adverse opinion is expressed.

DISCUSSION: An adverse opinion states that the financial statements are not fairly presented in accordance with GAAP. When an adverse opinion is expressed, the opinion paragraph should include a direct reference to a separate paragraph that discloses the basis for the adverse opinion. This paragraph should precede the opinion paragraph and state (1) all the substantive reasons for the adverse opinion and (2) the principal effects of the subject matter of the adverse opinion, if practicable (AU 508).

Answers (A) and (C) are incorrect because the principal effects of the subject matter of the adverse opinion, if practicable, and all the substantive reasons for the adverse opinion should be stated in the explanatory paragraph. Answer (D) is incorrect because an adverse opinion is not expressed as a result of an uncertainty or scope limitation.

88. An auditor may reasonably express a "subject to" qualified opinion for

	Lack of Consistency	Departure from Generally Accepted Accounting Principles
A.	Yes	Yes
B.	Yes	No
C.	No	Yes
D.	No	No

The correct answer is (D). *(CPA, adapted)*

REQUIRED: The type of opinion that uses the phrase "subject to."

DISCUSSION: The phrase "subject to" should not be used in any report. It is not clear or forceful enough (AU 508).

Answers (A), (B), and (C) are incorrect because the phrase "subject to" should not be used in any report.

89. The opinion paragraph of an independent auditor's report begins, "In our opinion, based upon our audit and the report of other auditors, the financial statements referred to above present fairly, in all material respects, the financial position . . ." This language states

A. A disclaimer of opinion.

B. An unqualified opinion.

C. An "except for" opinion.

D. A qualified opinion.

The correct answer is (B). *(Publisher)*

REQUIRED: The opinion expressed when the report refers to the report of another auditor.

DISCUSSION: When the auditor refers to the report of another auditor as a basis, in part, for his/her opinion, (s)he must clearly indicate the division of responsibility by disclosure in the introductory paragraph and by reference to the report of the other auditor in the scope and opinion paragraphs (AU 508 and AU 543, *Part of Audit Performed by Other Independent Auditors*). These references do not in themselves constitute a disclaimer or a modification of the opinion expressed. This is an unqualified opinion even though it varies from the standard report.

Answer (A) is incorrect because an opinion is being expressed. Answers (C) and (D) are incorrect because the quotation contains no qualifying language.

90. An auditor is in compliance with the fourth standard of reporting when (s)he issues a report containing

A. A piecemeal opinion and a disclaimer on the statements as a whole.

B. An unqualified opinion in which (s)he explains that, to a limited extent, (s)he is not fully independent of the client.

C. A qualified opinion with respect to the income statement and the statement of cash flows and an unqualified opinion with respect to the statement of financial position.

D. An opinion qualified with respect to the degree of responsibility accepted for the accompanying financial statements.

The correct answer is (C). *(Publisher)*

REQUIRED: The report in compliance with the fourth standard of reporting.

DISCUSSION: The fourth standard of reporting requires an expression of opinion regarding the statements taken as a whole or an assertion to the effect that an opinion cannot be expressed. The phrase "taken as a whole" applies equally to a complete set of statements and to an individual statement. The auditor may thus express different opinions on different statements (AU 508).

Answer (A) is incorrect because opinions on identified items in the statements (piecemeal opinions) are inappropriate when the auditor has expressed a disclaimer of opinion or an adverse opinion on the statements taken as a whole. Piecemeal opinions tend to overshadow or contradict a disclaimer or an adverse opinion. Answer (B) is incorrect because the auditor must be independent to express any opinion. Answer (D) is incorrect because an auditor may not qualify an opinion with respect to responsibility. Opinions are qualified as to the fairness of financial presentation.

91. An auditor may express a qualified opinion under which of the following circumstances?

	Lack of Sufficient Competent Evidential Matter	Restrictions on the Scope of the Audit
A.	Yes	Yes
B.	Yes	No
C.	No	Yes
D.	No	No

The correct answer is (A). *(CPA, adapted)*

REQUIRED: The circumstances in which the auditor may express a qualified opinion.

DISCUSSION: A qualified opinion is expressed because of a departure from GAAP, a lack of sufficient competent evidence, or a restriction on the scope of the audit. The auditor may be required to qualify the opinion or disclaim an opinion because of scope restrictions, "whether imposed by the client or by circumstances, such as the timing of the work, the inability to obtain sufficient competent evidential matter, or an inadequacy in the records" (AU 508).

Answers (B), (C), and (D) are incorrect because lack of sufficient competent evidence and other scope restrictions may result in a qualified opinion.

92. If the independent auditor has not become satisfied by means of other auditing procedures with respect to opening inventories, (s)he should

A. Disclaim an opinion or qualify the opinion on the statements taken as a whole.

B. Either disclaim an opinion on the statement of income or qualify the opinion thereon, depending on the degree of materiality of the amounts involved.

C. Either disclaim an opinion on the statement of income or qualify the opinion thereon, regardless of the degree of materiality of the amounts involved.

D. Express an adverse opinion on the statements taken as a whole when the amount in question is material.

The correct answer is (B). *(Publisher)*

REQUIRED: The opinion expressed when the auditor is not satisfied as to opening inventories.

DISCUSSION: An unqualified opinion is possible only if the audit has been conducted in accordance with GAAS and if the auditor has applied all procedures (s)he deems necessary. A scope restriction, e.g., on the observation of inventories, may prevent the auditor from obtaining the evidence required to support an unqualified opinion. If (s)he has become satisfied as to current inventory, the auditor may use alternate procedures to become satisfied as to opening inventories (AU 331, *Inventories*). But if (s)he cannot become satisfied regarding inventories, a qualified opinion or a disclaimer of opinion must be expressed, depending on the importance of the omitted procedure. Because cost of goods sold is dependent on opening inventories, an unqualified opinion on the income statement is not possible.

Answer (A) is incorrect because the restriction may apply only to the income statement. Answer (C) is incorrect because the materiality of the amounts involved determines the opinion expressed. Answer (D) is incorrect because an adverse opinion is inappropriate for a scope limitation.

93. A separate paragraph of an auditor's report describes an uncertainty as follows:

> As discussed in Note X to the financial statements, the Company is a defendant in a lawsuit alleging infringement of certain patent rights and claiming damages. Discovery proceedings are in progress.

What type of opinion should the auditor express under these circumstances?

A. Unqualified.

B. "Subject to" qualified.

C. "Except for" qualified.

D. Disclaimer.

The correct answer is (A). *(CPA, adapted)*

REQUIRED: The opinion that should be expressed because of an uncertainty.

DISCUSSION: AU 508 does not require the addition of an uncertainties paragraph. However, standards provide the auditor with the option of emphasizing a matter regarding the financial statements by adding a separate paragraph to the report. This separate paragraph does not affect the opinion expressed on the financial statements.

Answer (B) is incorrect because the phrase "subject to" is not permitted in any report. Answer (C) is incorrect because, by itself, an uncertainty does not result in an opinion modification. Answer (D) is incorrect because a disclaimer is less likely than an unqualified opinion on these facts. Moreover, an auditor's report containing a disclaimer would give all the substantive reasons for the disclaimer.

94. In which of the following circumstances would an auditor most likely add an explanatory paragraph to the standard report while expressing an unqualified opinion?

A. The auditor is asked to report on the balance sheet but not on the other basic financial statements.

B. There is substantial doubt about the entity's ability to continue as a going concern.

C. Management's estimates of the effects of future events are unreasonable.

D. Certain transactions cannot be tested because of management's records retention policy.

The correct answer is (B). *(CPA, adapted)*

REQUIRED: The situation most likely resulting in an explanatory paragraph and an unqualified opinion.

DISCUSSION: If the auditor reaches this conclusion after identifying conditions and events that create such doubt and after evaluating management's plans to mitigate their effects, (s)he should consider the adequacy of disclosure and include an explanatory paragraph (after the opinion paragraph) in the report. The auditor must use language in the explanatory paragraph that includes the words "substantial doubt" and "going concern."

Answer (A) is incorrect because an auditor may be asked to report on one financial statement. In that event, (s)he may appropriately express an unqualified opinion without adding an explanatory paragraph. Answer (C) is incorrect because the statements are not fairly presented if the estimates included in them are unreasonable. An unqualified opinion could not be expressed. Answer (D) is incorrect because a qualification or disclaimer of opinion is appropriate when the scope of the audit is limited.

95. If an auditor is satisfied that sufficient evidence supports management's assertions about an uncertainty and its presentation or disclosure, the auditor should

A. Express an unqualified opinion.

B. Express an unqualified opinion with a separate explanatory paragraph.

C. Disclaim an opinion.

D. Express a qualified opinion or disclaim an opinion, depending upon the materiality of the loss.

The correct answer is (A). *(CPA, adapted)*

REQUIRED: The opinion expressed when the likelihood is remote that an uncertainty will have a material effect.

DISCUSSION: In the absence of a departure from GAAP, for example, because of inadequate disclosure, or a scope limitation, an uncertainty does not require modification of the report.

Answer (B) is incorrect because a separate paragraph is not required. Answers (C) and (D) are incorrect because a disclaimer is appropriate only when the scope of the audit was too limited to warrant expression of an opinion. Moreover, an uncertainty does not, by itself, require any report modification.

Questions 96 through 101 are based on the following information. An audit was performed by Leo Gonzales, CPA, of the financial statements of Lectronic Leasing Company for the year ended December 31.

A cash advance to Computer Credit Corporation is material to the presentation of Lectronic's financial position. Computer Credit's unaudited financial statements show negative working capital, negative shareholders' equity, and losses in each of the 5 preceding years. Mr. Gonzales has suggested an allowance for the uncollectibility of the advance to Computer Credit.

All of the capital stock of both Lectronic and Computer Credit is owned by Paul McRae and his family. Mr. McRae adamantly refuses to consider an allowance for uncollectibility. He insists that Computer Credit eventually will be profitable and be able to repay the advance. Mr. McRae proposes the following footnote to Lectronic's statements:

Footnote 1 to Financial Statements

At December 31, the Company had advanced $500,000 to Computer Credit Corporation. We obtained written confirmation of this debt from Computer Credit Corporation and reviewed unaudited financial statements of Computer Credit Corporation. Computer Credit Corporation is not in a position to repay this advance at this time, but the Company has informed us that it is optimistic as to the future of Computer Credit Corporation. Computer Credit Corporation's capital stock is wholly owned by Lectronic Leasing Company's common shareholders.

96. With respect to Lectronic's advance to Computer Credit, Mr. Gonzales

A. Needs no disclosure in his auditor's report because the common ownership of the two companies has been adequately disclosed.

B. Needs no disclosure in his auditor's report because the auditor is not expected to be an expert appraiser of property values.

C. Should be concerned in formulating his auditor's opinion primarily with the issue of collectibility from Lectronic's viewpoint.

D. Should be concerned in formulating his auditor's opinion primarily with the consolidated financial position of the two companies.

The correct answer is (C). *(CPA, adapted)*

REQUIRED: The treatment in the report of a material advance to a related party, collectibility of which is doubtful.

DISCUSSION: The auditor has apparently concluded that a material receivable is uncollectible. Management refuses to create an allowance for the bad debt; thus the auditor may conclude that Lectronic's statements are misleading, requiring a modification of the opinion. The debt also represents a material transaction with a related party. The auditor will expect the client to disclose (1) the nature of the relationship, (2) a description of the transaction, (3) the amounts due, and (4) the terms and manner of settlement of the debt (AU 334).

Answer (A) is incorrect because both the related party transaction and uncollectibility of the receivable must be mentioned in the audit report. The basis for the modification of the opinion must be explained. Answer (B) is incorrect because, although not expected to be an appraiser of property values, the auditor must modify the opinion unless convinced that the financial statements are fairly presented. Answer (D) is incorrect because the scope of the engagement extends only to Lectronic's statements.

97. A deficiency in the given footnote is that it

A. Does not identify the auditor.

B. Is worded as a representation of the auditor.

C. Does not state the auditor's conclusion or opinion.

D. Includes the client's representation as to collectibility.

The correct answer is (B). *(CPA, adapted)*

REQUIRED: The deficiency in the given footnote.

DISCUSSION: The financial statements and footnotes are the representations of management. The assertions of the auditor are made in the audit report, although the report may refer to the footnotes in certain cases.

Answers (A) and (C) are incorrect because footnotes should not identify the auditor or restate his/her conclusions. Answer (D) is incorrect because the client may properly include a representation as to the collectibility of a debt in the footnotes.

98. Assume that Mr. Gonzales concludes, based upon appropriate audit procedures, that the advance to Computer Credit will not be repaid. His report will include a

A. Disclaimer of opinion.

B. Qualified opinion or disclaimer of opinion.

C. "Subject to" opinion or adverse opinion.

D. Qualified opinion or adverse opinion.

The correct answer is (D). *(CPA, adapted)*

REQUIRED: The type of report if the auditor concludes that the advance will not be repaid.

DISCUSSION: If the advance is treated as uncollectible, the financial statements are not in accordance with GAAP because management has refused to establish an allowance account. The auditor should express a qualified opinion or an adverse opinion depending on the materiality of the debt (AU 508).

Answers (A) and (B) are incorrect because a disclaimer of opinion is appropriate only when the auditor is unable to form an opinion. Answer (C) is incorrect because a "subject to" opinion is not an acceptable form of reporting.

99. Assume that Mr. Gonzales concludes, based upon appropriate audit procedures, that Mr. McRae's optimism concerning Computer Credit can be neither substantiated nor disproved and that evidence to form an opinion is not available because of the auditee's record retention policies. His report will include a(n)

A. Disclaimer of opinion.

B. Qualified opinion for the failure to follow GAAP.

C. Separate explanatory paragraph based on the uncertainty or an adverse opinion.

D. Adverse opinion only.

The correct answer is (A). *(CPA, adapted)*

REQUIRED: The report issued given an uncertainty.

DISCUSSION: If the auditor has not obtained sufficient evidential matter to support management's assertions concerning an uncertainty, an unqualified opinion is not appropriate. A qualification or disclaimer of opinion because of a scope limitation is appropriate when sufficient evidential matter related to an uncertainty does or did exist but was not available for reasons such as management's record retention policies or a restriction imposed by management.

Answer (B) is incorrect because no departure from GAAP is described. Answers (C) and (D) are incorrect because an adverse opinion is expressed only when the auditor believes the statements are not fairly presented in conformity with GAAP.

100. Assume that Mr. Gonzales introduces the opinion paragraph of his report as follows: "With the explanation given in Footnote 1, in our opinion the aforementioned financial statements present fairly..." This is a(n)

A. Unqualified opinion.

B. Adverse opinion.

C. Qualified opinion.

D. Improper type of reporting.

The correct answer is (D). *(CPA, adapted)*

REQUIRED: The proper characterization of the phrase "With the explanation given in Footnote 1."

DISCUSSION: Because the footnotes are part of the financial statements, reporting that those statements are fairly presented when read in conjunction with a cited footnote is likely to be misunderstood and accordingly should not be done. But a separate explanatory paragraph may be shortened by a reference to a footnote (AU 508).

Answers (A), (B), and (C) are incorrect because the quoted phrase is not used in any report.

101. Assume that subsequent to the completion of field work (but prior to issuance of Mr. Gonzales' report) Mr. McRae and his family sell all of their stock in Computer Credit and the new owners repay the advance from Lectronic. Mr. Gonzales' opinion as to Lectronic's financial statements will be

A. Unaffected because the sale of Computer Credit stock occurred subsequent to the audit date.

B. Unaffected because the sale of Computer Credit stock occurred subsequent to the completion of field work.

C. Qualified unless the repayment of the advance is recorded by Lectronic as a December 31 transaction.

D. Unqualified because the issue of collectibility is now settled.

The correct answer is (D). *(CPA, adapted)*

REQUIRED: The effect on the report of a subsequent event that resolves a material uncertainty.

DISCUSSION: The subsequent event provides additional evidence with respect to conditions existing at the balance sheet date. Such an event may require adjustment of the financial statements and consequently may affect the audit report (AU 560). Here, the auditor can now express an unqualified opinion, assuming no other basis exists for modifying the opinion. The subsequent event has eliminated the uncertainty as to collectibility of the receivable.

Answers (A) and (B) are incorrect because the auditor is responsible for subsequent events occurring prior to the issuance of the report. Answer (C) is incorrect because no qualification as to collectibility of the receivable is necessary. The best evidence of collectibility is payment.

102. An external auditor discovers that a payroll supervisor of the firm being audited has misappropriated $10,000. The firm's total assets and before-tax net income are $14 million and $3 million, respectively. Assuming no other issues affect the report, the external auditor's report will most likely contain a(n)

A. Disclaimer of opinion.

B. Adverse opinion.

C. Scope qualification.

D. Unqualified opinion.

The correct answer is (D). *(CMA, adapted)*

REQUIRED: The audit report issued after detection of an irregularity.

DISCUSSION: The auditor is likely to express an unqualified opinion for two reasons. First, the misappropriated amount is immaterial relative to assets and income. Second, as long as the misappropriation is accounted for properly, the financial statements will be fairly presented in accordance with GAAP.

Answer (A) is incorrect because a disclaimer is appropriate when the audit is insufficient to permit formation of an opinion. Answer (B) is incorrect because an adverse opinion states that the statements are not fairly presented. An immaterial item, properly accounted for, does not impair the fairness of presentation. Answer (C) is incorrect because the audit scope has not been limited.

103. During the year ended December 31, 1998, Price Corporation reported its fixed assets at lower of cost or market (LCM) because their fair value had declined. The loss has been included as an extraordinary item in the income statement and the adjustment has been fully disclosed in the footnotes. If a CPA believes that the values reported in the financial statements are reasonable, what opinion should be expressed?

A. An unqualified opinion.

B. A "subject to" qualified opinion.

C. An adverse opinion.

D. A disclaimer of opinion.

The correct answer is (C). *(Publisher)*

REQUIRED: The opinion expressed when fixed assets are reported at LCM.

DISCUSSION: The fixed assets of a company should be recorded at historical cost minus accumulated depreciation. Recording them at LCM is therefore a departure from GAAP. The CPA should express either a qualified opinion or an adverse opinion, assuming that the effects of the departure are material (AU 508).

Answer (A) is incorrect because a material departure from GAAP precludes an unqualified opinion. Answer (B) is incorrect because a "subject to" qualified opinion is an unacceptable form of reporting. Answer (D) is incorrect because a disclaimer is proper when the audit is not sufficient in scope to permit formation of an opinion.

104. If a company is experiencing financial difficulty that raises substantial doubt about its ability to continue as a going concern, GAAS require the auditor to

A. Withdraw from the engagement.

B. Value the assets on a liquidation basis.

C. Plan to conduct a complete audit rather than perform procedures on a test basis.

D. Include in the report a paragraph describing the nature of the difficulties.

The correct answer is (D). *(N. Schmukler)*

REQUIRED: The auditor's responsibility when the entity may not be able to continue as a going concern.

DISCUSSION: Auditing standards require the auditor to alert financial statement users to the existence of doubt about the ability of an auditee to continue in existence. AU 341 is intended to reduce the instances when, shortly after the expression of an unqualified opinion, the auditee becomes bankrupt. Hence, the auditor's substantial doubt requires inclusion of an explanatory paragraph in the report. This paragraph should include the words "substantial doubt" and "going concern."

Answer (A) is incorrect because the auditor need not withdraw. Answer (B) is incorrect because the existence of a substantial doubt does not require that assets be presented on a liquidation basis; they may continue to be presented on a going concern basis unless liquidation is imminent. Answer (C) is incorrect because, even when the entity may not be able to continue as a going concern, the audit will normally be performed on a test basis.

105. During the year, the research staff of Dermoplex, Inc. devoted its entire efforts toward developing a skin cancer ointment. All costs that could be attributed directly to the project were accounted for as deferred charges and classified on the balance sheet as an asset. If the amounts involved are material, the auditor should

A. Express an unqualified opinion with a separate paragraph explaining the uncertainty of cost recovery.

B. Disclaim an opinion.

C. Express an adverse opinion.

D. Express an unqualified opinion provided that the uncertainty about ultimate realization of the deferred charges is disclosed in the footnotes.

The correct answer is (C). *(Publisher)*

REQUIRED: The appropriate opinion when the client has capitalized R&D costs.

DISCUSSION: Capitalizing R&D costs is not permitted according to GAAP. Ordinarily, they must be expensed in the period in which they were incurred (SFAS 2). Because capitalizing R&D costs is a departure from GAAP and the amounts involved are material, the auditor should express an adverse opinion if the statements as a whole are not fairly presented in conformity with GAAP. A qualified opinion might be appropriate, however, depending on the materiality of the exception.

Answers (A) and (D) are incorrect because the issue is not uncertainty but the departure from GAAP. Answer (B) is incorrect because the auditor has sufficient evidence to express an opinion that the financial statements are materially misstated.

106. In which circumstance would the auditor not consider the need to modify the report?

A. The client's legal counsel is requested to advise whether a material act is legal or illegal but refuses to do so.

B. The auditor concludes that the effect of an illegal act creates substantial doubt about the entity's ability to continue as a going concern.

C. The auditor concludes that the effect of an illegal act, taken alone or with similar acts, is material in amount and has not been properly accounted for or disclosed in the financial statements.

D. None of the answers are correct.

The correct answer is (D). *(Publisher)*

REQUIRED: The circumstance in which the auditor would not consider modifying the report.

DISCUSSION: All of the answer choices given describe circumstances in which the report should be modified.

Answer (A) is incorrect because the auditor may be unable to determine the legality of certain acts or the amounts associated with them as a result of an inability to gather sufficient competent evidence; e.g., the client's legal counsel may have refused to give advice. In these circumstances, the scope limitation may require a qualified opinion or a disclaimer. Answer (B) is incorrect because, if the effects of an illegal act create substantial doubt about the entity's ability to continue as a going concern, a separate explanatory paragraph is required. Answer (C) is incorrect because, if the effects of an illegal act are material but have not been properly accounted for or disclosed, the departure from GAAP may result in a qualified or an adverse opinion (AU 317, *Illegal Acts by Clients*).

107. The federal government alleges that your client has overcharged on certain contracts and is demanding a material refund. If the company is compelled to return this sum, the current ratio of 2:1 in the present financial statements would be reduced to 1.2:1, and a substantial reduction in retained earnings would occur. No decision has been reached at the end of field work, and a footnote adequately describing the event and negotiations has been written by the client. The auditor should most likely

A. Express an adverse opinion because of the material uncertainty.

B. Issue an unmodified report because adequate disclosure of the uncertainty has been made in the footnotes.

C. Express a qualified opinion because of the material uncertainty.

D. Express a piecemeal opinion.

The correct answer is (B). *(Publisher)*

REQUIRED: The appropriate report when a properly disclosed loss contingency exists.

DISCUSSION: When a material uncertainty exists, the auditor need only modify the report when a scope limitation exists or the financial statements depart from GAAP. Given that disclosure is in conformity with GAAP and that no indication is given of a scope limitation, the auditor need not modify the report.

Answer (A) is incorrect because an adverse opinion is not appropriate if the financial statements are presented fairly. Answer (C) is incorrect because a qualified opinion is not expressed solely on the basis of an uncertainty. Answer (D) is incorrect because a piecemeal opinion is never appropriate.

108. The introductory paragraph of an auditor's report is not modified when the

A. Entity declines to include in the financial statements segment information that the auditor believes is required to be disclosed.

B. Financial statements of a prior period that are presented for comparative purposes have been audited by a predecessor auditor whose report is not given.

C. Principal auditor indicates the division of responsibility by making reference to the audit of a consolidated subsidiary by another auditor.

D. Auditor was engaged to express an opinion on the balance sheet only.

The correct answer is (A). *(C.J. Skender)*

REQUIRED: The situation in which the introductory paragraph is not modified.

DISCUSSION: Failure to include segment information is a departure from GAAP because of inadequate disclosure. The auditor should modify the opinion and provide the information in the report, if practicable, unless a specific SAS allows its omission from the report (AU 508). However, no currently effective pronouncement addresses the issue of whether omitted segment disclosures must be included in the audit report. Accordingly, at a minimum, the auditor will include an explanatory paragraph describing the omitted matter and will also modify the opinion paragraph but not the introductory paragraph.

Answer (B) is incorrect because, if the predecessor auditor's report is not presented, the successor auditor should indicate in the introductory paragraph that the financial statements were audited by another auditor, the date of his/her report, the type of report issued, and, if the opinion was not unqualified, the substantive reasons therefor (AU 508). Answer (C) is incorrect because an opinion based in part on the report of another auditor requires modification of the introductory, scope, and opinion paragraphs of the report to indicate the division of responsibility. Answer (D) is incorrect because only the statements audited are identified in the introductory paragraph.

109. During the course of an audit of the financial statements of Excellent Corporation, Smart, CPA, discovered that the company vice-president had misrepresented one of the company's products before the Food and Drug Administration by falsifying test results. Unasserted claims, material in amount, loom in the near future. Management refuses to permit the inclusion of a liability for such claims even though it is probable that they will be asserted and the amount of loss can be reasonably estimated. Smart should issue a report with a(n)

A. Explanatory paragraph and either an adverse opinion or a qualified opinion.

B. Qualified opinion and an explanatory paragraph but should not consider expressing an adverse opinion.

C. Qualified opinion and no explanatory paragraph.

D. Unqualified opinion and an explanatory paragraph.

The correct answer is (A). *(Publisher)*

REQUIRED: The opinion that should be expressed when the client improperly refuses to provide for a material loss contingency.

DISCUSSION: According to SFAS 5, *Accounting for Contingencies*, a loss contingency should be recognized in the accounts if its occurrence is probable and its amount can be reasonably estimated. The client's refusal to do so is a departure from GAAP. Given that the amount involved is material, the auditor should express a qualified opinion or an adverse opinion. The report should also include a separate paragraph disclosing the substantive reasons for the modified opinion and the principal effects of the subject matter of the opinion, if determinable (AU 508).

Answer (B) is incorrect because the matter may be sufficiently material to require an adverse rather than a qualified opinion. Answer (C) is incorrect because a separate explanatory paragraph will be necessary. Answer (D) is incorrect because a material departure from GAAP requires a qualified or an adverse opinion.

110. A client makes test counts on the basis of a statistical plan. The auditor observes such counts as are deemed necessary and is able to become satisfied as to the reliability of the client's procedures. In reporting on the results of the audit, the auditor

A. Can express an unqualified opinion.

B. Must comment in the scope paragraph as to the inability to observe year-end inventories.

C. Is required to disclaim an opinion if the inventories were material.

D. Must qualify the opinion if the inventories were material.

The correct answer is (A). *(Publisher)*

REQUIRED: The report when a client uses statistical sampling to count inventory.

DISCUSSION: When the client uses statistical sampling to determine inventory quantities, the auditor must become satisfied that the procedures are reliable. The auditor must observe at least some counts and must be satisfied that the sampling plan is reasonable and statistically valid, that it has been properly applied, and that its results are reasonable (AU 331). Given no significant scope limitation, the report need not refer to failure to observe a year-end physical count or to the alternative procedures employed. The auditor may express an unqualified opinion (AU 508).

Answer (B) is incorrect because comment in the scope paragraph on the omission of a procedure is unnecessary if the auditor has become satisfied by applying alternative procedures. Answer (C) is incorrect because no significant scope limitation existed. Answer (D) is incorrect because the auditor need not qualify the opinion if the financial statements are fairly stated.

111. When a scope limitation has precluded the auditor from obtaining sufficient competent evidential matter to determine whether certain client acts are illegal, (s)he would most likely express

A. An unqualified opinion with a separate explanatory paragraph.

B. Either a qualified opinion or an adverse opinion.

C. Either a disclaimer of opinion or a qualified opinion.

D. Either an adverse opinion or a disclaimer of opinion.

The correct answer is (C). *(CPA, adapted)*

REQUIRED: The report issued when evidence about illegal client acts is insufficient.

DISCUSSION: The auditor may be unable to determine the legality of certain acts or the amounts associated with them because of an inability to gather sufficient competent evidence; e.g., internal control may have been circumvented, resulting in failure to record or properly document the acts, or client's legal counsel may have refused to give advice. In these circumstances, the scope limitation requires a qualified opinion or a disclaimer, although a client-imposed scope limitation ordinarily results in a disclaimer.

Answer (A) is incorrect because a material scope limitation results in a qualified opinion or a disclaimer. Answers (B) and (D) are incorrect because an adverse opinion is only appropriate when the statements as a whole are not fairly presented.

112. Late in December, Tech Products Company sold available-for-sale securities that had appreciated in value and then repurchased them the same day. The sale and purchase transactions resulted in a large gain. Without the gain, the company would have reported a loss for the year. Which statement with respect to the auditor is correct?

A. If the sale and repurchase are disclosed, an unqualified opinion should be expressed.

B. The repurchase transaction is a sham and the auditor should insist upon a reversal or express an adverse opinion.

C. The auditor should withdraw from the engagement and refuse to be associated with the company.

D. A disclaimer of opinion should be expressed.

The correct answer is (A). *(CPA, adapted)*

REQUIRED: The auditor's proper reaction to a sale and repurchase of appreciated securities.

DISCUSSION: Unrealized holding gains and losses on available-for-sale securities are recorded in other comprehensive income. Thus, to include the appreciation in the determination of net income, the company had to sell the securities. Because a transaction occurred, the proper accounting is to record the gain realized on the sale. Although management has indulged in obvious window-dressing, an unqualified opinion may still be expressed if disclosure is adequate to prevent the financial statements from being misleading.

Answer (B) is incorrect because the transactions should be recorded. Answer (C) is incorrect because no legal or ethical principle requires the auditor to withdraw. Answer (D) is incorrect because the transactions do not preclude forming an opinion on the statements and accompanying notes.

113. A note to the financial statements of the First Security Bank indicates that all of the records relating to the bank's business operations are stored on magnetic disks, and that no emergency backup systems or duplicate disks are stored because the bank and its auditors consider the occurrence of a catastrophe to be remote. Based upon this note, the auditor's report should express

A. A "subject to" opinion.

B. A qualified opinion.

C. An unqualified opinion.

D. An adverse opinion.

The correct answer is (C). *(CPA, adapted)*

REQUIRED: The opinion the auditor should render when a client fails to provide for backup records.

DISCUSSION: Failure to provide for backup records does not affect the fairness of the financial statements, regardless of the negative implications for the client's internal control. The auditor should therefore express an unqualified opinion in the absence of other indications to the contrary.

Answer (A) is incorrect because the wording "subject to" is not acceptable in any report. Answers (B) and (D) are incorrect because the absence of backup records is not a basis for expressing a qualified or an adverse opinion if the financial statements are fairly presented in conformity with GAAP.

114. An auditor who uses the work of a specialist may refer to and identify the specialist in the auditor's report if the

A. Specialist is also considered to be a related party.

B. Auditor indicates a division of responsibility related to the work of the specialist.

C. Specialist's work provides the auditor greater assurance of reliability.

D. Auditor expresses a qualified opinion or an adverse opinion related to the work of the specialist.

The correct answer is (D). *(CPA, adapted)*

REQUIRED: The circumstance in which an auditor may refer to a specialist.

DISCUSSION: The report or findings of the specialist may cause the auditor to add an explanatory paragraph to the standard report or to depart from an unqualified opinion. In these cases, the report may refer to and identify the specialist to facilitate understanding of the reason for the paragraph or departure (AU 336).

Answer (A) is incorrect because the work of an unrelated specialist ordinarily provides greater assurance of reliability, but a related specialist may be acceptable in some circumstances. However, whether the specialist is a related party is irrelevant to the decision to refer to him/her in the report. Answer (B) is incorrect because an auditor can divide responsibility with another auditor who performed part of the audit but not with a specialist. Answer (C) is incorrect because the auditor's use of a specialist is intended to provide greater assurance regarding the conclusions in the audit report, but reference to his/her work is justified only in certain circumstances.

115. When would the auditor refer to the work of an appraiser in the auditor's report?

A. An unqualified opinion is expressed and no explanatory paragraph is added, but the auditor wishes to disclose the use of a specialist.

B. A qualified opinion is expressed because of a matter unrelated to the work of the appraiser.

C. An adverse opinion is expressed based on a difference of opinion between the client and the outside appraiser as to the value of certain assets.

D. A disclaimer of opinion is expressed because of a scope limitation imposed on the auditor by the appraiser.

The correct answer is (C). *(CPA, adapted)*

REQUIRED: The basis for reference to an appraiser.

DISCUSSION: Given a material difference between the specialist's findings and the assertions in the statements, the auditor should apply additional procedures, possibly including obtaining the opinion of another specialist. If the auditor concludes that the client's assertions are not in conformity with GAAP, a qualified or an adverse opinion should be expressed. The report may refer to and identify the specialist to facilitate understanding of the reason for the modification (AU 336).

Answer (A) is incorrect because the auditor should not refer to a specialist when an unqualified opinion is expressed unless an explanatory paragraph is added. Answer (B) is incorrect because the qualification must be related to the work of the specialist. Answer (D) is incorrect because an appraiser cannot impose a scope limitation on the auditor. The auditor can consult another appraiser.

7.6 Disclaimers of Opinion

116. Statements on Auditing Standards (SASs) describe the CPA's reporting responsibility for unaudited financial statements of public companies, while Statements on Standards for Accounting and Review Services (SSARSs) describe the CPA's reporting responsibilities for unaudited financial statements of nonpublic entities. Which of the following is a false statement about the responsibilities of a CPA when associated with unaudited financial statements?

A. Unaudited financial statements of nonpublic entities should include either a compilation report or review report.

B. Unaudited financial statements of public entities should include a disclaimer.

C. The CPA must be independent to issue disclaimers, compilation reports, or review reports.

D. Whatever the report form, the primary concern should be to indicate the degree of responsibility the CPA is assuming.

The correct answer is (C). *(Publisher)*

REQUIRED: The false statement about the CPA's association with unaudited financial statements.

DISCUSSION: When a CPA is associated with the financial statements of a public entity and either lacks independence or fails to collect sufficient competent evidential matter, (s)he should disclaim an opinion on the financial statements (AU 504 and AU 508). When associated with the unaudited statements of a private entity, a CPA who lacks independence may be asked to compile financial statements. A compilation report may be issued despite the lack of independence because no assurance is being offered and, in effect, a disclaimer is being presented in the report. The CPA must be independent, however, when (s)he issues a review report because it provides limited assurances to users (AR 100, *Compilation and Review of Financial Statements*).

Answer (A) is incorrect because, when a CPA is associated with the financial statements of a private entity, (s)he should issue either a compilation report or, if a review is performed, a review report. Answer (B) is incorrect because the CPA should issue a disclaimer when (s)he is associated with the financial statements of a public entity for which (s)he has not performed an audit or a review. Answer (D) is incorrect because part of the CPA's obligation to the users of the report is to indicate the degree of responsibility assumed.

117. A disclaimer of opinion on the financial statements that was issued because of a scope limitation on an audit differs from a compilation report on the unaudited statements of a nonpublic entity in that

A. A compilation report offers some assurances. A disclaimer offers none.

B. A compilation relates only to income statements and balance sheets. A disclaimer pertains to all financial statements presented.

C. Any procedures applied in a compilation should be described in the report, but procedures applied when a disclaimer is issued should not be described.

D. A compilation report states what service was performed. A disclaimer states what service was to be performed.

The correct answer is (D). *(Publisher)*

REQUIRED: The difference between a disclaimer and a compilation report.

DISCUSSION: The standard disclaimer of opinion issued because of a scope limitation on an audit begins, "We were engaged to audit the accompanying" financial statements (AU 508). A standard compilation report begins, "I(we) have compiled the accompanying" financial statements (AR 100).

Answer (A) is incorrect because neither report offers any form of assurance. Answer (B) is incorrect because both reports refer to all financial statements presented. Answer (C) is incorrect because the procedures performed should not be described in either report.

118. In which of the following circumstances would an auditor usually choose between expressing a qualified opinion and disclaiming an opinion?

A. Departure from generally accepted accounting principles.

B. Inadequate disclosure of accounting policies.

C. Inability to obtain sufficient competent evidential matter.

D. Unreasonable justification for a change in accounting principle.

The correct answer is (C). *(CPA, adapted)*

REQUIRED: The circumstance in which the auditor chooses between a disclaimer and a qualified opinion.

DISCUSSION: Scope restrictions, whether client-imposed or the result of circumstances such as the timing of the work, the inability to obtain sufficient competent evidence, or inadequate accounting records, may require a qualification of the opinion or a disclaimer. The choice depends on the assessment of the importance of the omitted procedure(s).

Answers (A), (B), and (D) are incorrect because a departure from GAAP, inadequate disclosure, and an unreasonable justification for a change in accounting principle usually require a choice between a qualified and an adverse opinion.

119. Under which of the following circumstances might an auditor disclaim an opinion?

A. The financial statements contain a departure from generally accepted accounting principles, the effect of which is material.

B. The principal auditor decides to refer to the report of another auditor who audited a subsidiary.

C. There has been a material change between periods in the method of application of accounting principles.

D. The auditor is unable to obtain sufficient evidence to support management's assertions concerning an uncertainty.

The correct answer is (D). *(CPA, adapted)*

REQUIRED: The reason for a disclaimer.

DISCUSSION: AU 508 states that a qualification or disclaimer of opinion is appropriate for a scope limitation relating to an uncertainty if sufficient evidence does or did exist but was not available to the auditor for reasons such as management's record retention policies or a restriction imposed by management.

Answer (A) is incorrect because the auditor should express a qualified or an adverse opinion when the statements contain a material departure from GAAP. Answer (B) is incorrect because reference to the report of another auditor as a partial basis for the opinion is not even a qualification of the opinion, much less a disclaimer. It is a sharing of responsibility. Answer (C) is incorrect because, if the auditor concurs in the change, lack of consistency requires only an explanatory paragraph.

120. A CPA is associated with client-prepared financial statements but is not independent. With respect to the CPA's lack of independence, which of the following actions by the CPA might confuse a reader of such financial statements?

A. Stamping the word unaudited on each page of the financial statements.

B. Disclaiming an opinion and stating that independence is lacking.

C. Issuing a modified auditor's report explaining the reason for the auditor's lack of independence.

D. Preparing an accountant's report that includes essential data that are not disclosed in the financial statements.

The correct answer is (C). *(CPA, adapted)*

REQUIRED: The confusing action by a CPA who is not independent and is associated with financial statements.

DISCUSSION: When a CPA lacks independence, (s)he should disclaim an opinion and state specifically that (s)he is not independent. The reasons for lack of independence and any procedures performed should not be described. Issuing a modified report improperly implies that an audit was performed (AU 504).

Answer (A) is incorrect because marking each page of unaudited financial statements clearly and conspicuously as unaudited would not confuse a reader. Answer (B) is incorrect because, when an auditor is not independent, a disclaimer is appropriate. Answer (D) is incorrect because, if management omits data required by GAAP, the accountant must urge the client to revise the presentation. If the client refuses, a CPA who is not independent should modify the disclaimer to disclose the departure and, if practicable, its effect on the financial statements.

121. A CPA is concerned about association with unaudited financial statements because

A. Users may be misled regarding the degree of responsibility the CPA is accepting.

B. A fee cannot be charged unless the CPA is associated with financial statements.

C. Association is necessary for compliance with the requirement of due professional care.

D. An audit must be performed if the CPA is associated with financial statements.

The correct answer is (A). *(Publisher)*

REQUIRED: The reason for concern about association with unaudited financial statements.

DISCUSSION: The association of a CPA with financial statements may lead users to attribute undeserved credibility to them. When the statements are unaudited or unreviewed, the CPA should make clear the degree of responsibility assumed by including a disclaimer of opinion in the report (AU 504).

Answer (B) is incorrect because fees should be based on the extent and degree of difficulty of the services performed, not on whether the CPA is associated with statements. Answer (C) is incorrect because a member of the AICPA must perform all services with due care. Answer (D) is incorrect because a CPA may be associated with financial statements without auditing or reviewing them if (s)he disclaims an opinion.

122. Under which of the following circumstances is a disclaimer of opinion inappropriate?

A. The auditor is engaged after fiscal year-end and is unable to observe physical inventories or apply alternative procedures to verify their balances.

B. The auditor is unable to determine the amounts associated with fraud committed by the client's management.

C. The financial statements fail to contain adequate disclosure concerning related party transactions.

D. The client refuses to permit its attorney to furnish information requested in a letter of audit inquiry.

The correct answer is (C). *(CPA, adapted)*

REQUIRED: The circumstances in which a disclaimer is inappropriate.

DISCUSSION: A disclaimer is inappropriate when the auditor believes that the financial statements contain material departures from GAAP. Inadequacy of the disclosures required by GAAP is such a departure. Because SFAS 57 requires certain disclosures about related party transactions, the inadequacy of such disclosures is a basis for expressing a qualified or an adverse opinion and providing the information in the report, if practicable, unless omission from the report is recognized as appropriate by a specific SAS (AU 431 and AU 508).

Answer (A) is incorrect because a significant scope limitation, such as a failure to perform a generally accepted auditing procedure (observing inventory) and not becoming satisfied by alternative procedures, may result in a qualified opinion or in a disclaimer. Answer (B) is incorrect because a disclaimer or qualified opinion (and communication with the audit committee or the board) should be expressed in these circumstances (AU 316, *The Auditor's Responsibility to Detect and Report Errors and Irregularities*). Answer (D) is incorrect because a client-imposed scope limitation ordinarily results in a disclaimer.

123. When Auditee Company was formed, Bill Larson, CPA, performed professional services for which he accepted common stock as a portion of his compensation. Currently, he owns 2% of Auditee's outstanding common stock, an amount that is immaterial to both his firm's and his personal net worth. What is Larson's reporting responsibility in these circumstances?

A. If Larson is satisfied as to the fairness of the financial statements, he may express an unqualified opinion because his financial interest in the client is immaterial.

B. It is not possible for Larson's audit to meet the requirements of GAAS. He must disclaim an opinion and state that he is not independent.

C. Larson must disclaim an opinion and state his lack of independence and the reason for his lack of independence so that the reader will be able to evaluate all of the relevant facts of the case.

D. If Larson is satisfied as to the fairness of the financial statements, he may express an unqualified opinion, but he should note in a separate paragraph that he holds a nominal interest in the client's common stock.

The correct answer is (B). *(Publisher)*

REQUIRED: The reporting responsibility of a CPA who has an immaterial financial interest in a client.

DISCUSSION: According to Interpretation 101-1 of Conduct Rule 101, *Independence*, independence is considered to be impaired if "during the period of a professional engagement or at the time of expressing an opinion, a member or a member's firm had or was committed to acquire any direct or material indirect financial interest in the enterprise" (see also the second general auditing standard). Larson's interest in the client is immaterial but direct; hence, he is not independent. When a CPA lacks independence, (s)he must disclaim and explicitly state his/her lack of independence but not the reasons for it (AU 504).

Answer (A) is incorrect because any direct financial interest in the client, regardless of its materiality, prevents an auditor from being independent. Lack of independence precludes the expression of any opinion. Answer (C) is incorrect because the CPA should not state the reasons for lack of independence. They might mislead the reader concerning the importance of the impairment of independence. Answer (D) is incorrect because any direct financial interest in the client, regardless of its materiality, prevents an auditor from being independent.

124. Which of the following is an example of a CPA's being associated with unaudited financial statements?

A. A client of a CPA consults with the CPA on a data processing matter prior to preparing and submitting input data to an independent computer service company for preparation of unaudited financial statements.

B. Computer input data are prepared by the CPA's client and are submitted to an independent computer service company that was recommended by the CPA. The resulting unaudited financial statements are returned to the client.

C. The CPA analyzes the client's input data before sending the data to an independent computer service company, and the processed financial statements are returned directly to the client.

D. A CPA recommends that a client use the client's computer to process data that generate unaudited financial statements.

The correct answer is (C). *(CPA, adapted)*

REQUIRED: The example of an association of a CPA with unaudited financial statements.

DISCUSSION: According to AU 504, if a CPA helps prepare or consents to the use of his/her name with unaudited financial statements, (s)he is associated with them. A CPA who reviews the client's input data has assisted in the preparation of the statements and is deemed to be associated with them.

Answer (A) is incorrect because consulting with the client does not constitute preparation of the financial statements by the CPA. Answer (B) is incorrect because recommending a computer service company does not constitute preparation of the financial statements by the CPA. Answer (D) is incorrect because recommending that a client use its own computer does not constitute preparation of the financial statements by the CPA.

125. When an independent CPA assists in preparing the financial statements of a publicly held entity but has not audited or reviewed them, the CPA should issue a disclaimer of opinion. In such situations, the CPA has no responsibility to apply any procedures beyond

A. Documenting that internal control is not being relied on.

B. Reading the financial statements for obvious material misstatements.

C. Ascertaining whether the financial statements are in conformity with GAAP.

D. Determining whether management has elected to omit substantially all required disclosures.

The correct answer is (B). *(CPA, adapted)*

REQUIRED: The CPA's responsibility for unaudited financial statements.

DISCUSSION: According to AU 504, if a CPA helps prepare or consents to the use of his/her name with unaudited financial statements, (s)he is associated with them. In this situation, the CPA's responsibility is to issue a disclaimer stating that (s)he has not audited the statements and expresses no opinion on them. The CPA has no responsibility to apply any procedures beyond reading the financial statements for obvious material misstatements.

Answer (A) is incorrect because the CPA need not document procedures either applied or not applied. Answer (C) is incorrect because the CPA does not ascertain whether the financial statements are in conformity with GAAP. Answer (D) is incorrect because the CPA must read the financial statements for obvious material misstatements, which include, but are not limited to, inadequate disclosure.

126. Because of a scope limitation, an auditor disclaimed an opinion on the financial statements taken as a whole, but the auditor's report included a statement that the current asset portion of the entity's balance sheet was fairly stated. The inclusion of this statement is

A. Not appropriate because it may tend to overshadow the auditor's disclaimer of opinion.

B. Not appropriate because the auditor is prohibited from reporting on only one basic financial statement.

C. Appropriate provided the auditor's scope paragraph adequately describes the scope limitation.

D. Appropriate provided the statement is in a separate paragraph preceding the disclaimer of opinion paragraph.

The correct answer is (A). *(CPA, adapted)*

REQUIRED: The suitability of a statement in an auditor's disclaimer concerning whether an element of the balance sheet was stated fairly.

DISCUSSION: "Piecemeal opinions (expressions of opinion as to certain identified items in financial statements) should not be expressed when the auditor has disclaimed an opinion or has expressed an adverse opinion on the financial statements taken as a whole because piecemeal opinions tend to overshadow or contradict a disclaimer of opinion or an adverse opinion" (AU 508).

Answer (B) is incorrect because the auditor can report on one basic financial statement and not on others. Such a limited reporting engagement is acceptable. Answers (C) and (D) are incorrect because a piecemeal opinion is inappropriate in these circumstances.

127. If an accountant concludes that unaudited financial statements of a public entity on which the accountant is disclaiming an opinion also lack adequate disclosure, the accountant should suggest appropriate revision. If the client does not accept the accountant's suggestion, the accountant should

A. Express an adverse opinion and describe the appropriate revision in the report.

B. Refer to the appropriate revision and issue a modified report expressing limited assurance.

C. Describe the appropriate revision to the financial statements in the accountant's disclaimer of opinion.

D. Accept the client's inaction because the statements are unaudited and the accountant has disclaimed an opinion.

The correct answer is (C). *(CPA, adapted)*

REQUIRED: The action when the client refuses to revise unaudited statements to provide adequate disclosure.

DISCUSSION: Inadequate disclosure is a departure from GAAP. When an accountant who is associated with the unaudited statements of a public entity suggests revision because of such a departure and the client refuses, the disclaimer should be modified to describe the departure. The "description should refer specifically to the nature of the departure and, if practicable, state the effects on the financial statements or include the necessary information for adequate disclosure" (AU 504).

Answer (A) is incorrect because an opinion may be expressed only if an audit has been performed. Answer (B) is incorrect because a disclaimer expresses no assurance. Answer (D) is incorrect because the accountant must modify the disclaimer if the client does not act. If the client will not accept the modified disclaimer, the accountant should refuse to be associated with the statements and, if necessary, withdraw from the engagement (AU 504).

128. Harris, CPA, performed the audit of the 1998 financial statements of Lanco, Inc. The unaudited 1997 financial statements were to be presented with the 1998 financial statements for comparative purposes. Harris prepared a report to accompany both sets of financial statements. The statements are not to be presented in documents filed with the SEC. The presentation should not include

A. Marking the 1997 columns as unaudited.

B. A separate paragraph.

C. The language "except for" in the scope paragraph.

D. A statement in the report that the 1997 financial statements were not audited by Harris.

The correct answer is (C). *(L.M. Bailey)*

REQUIRED: The improper aspect of a report on audited and unaudited statements presented in comparative form.

DISCUSSION: The phrase "except for" is used to qualify an opinion on audited financial statements. It appears in the opinion, not the scope, paragraph.

Answer (A) is incorrect because the unaudited statements should be clearly marked to identify their status. Answer (B) is incorrect because the prior period's report should be reissued, or the current period's report should include a separate paragraph describing the responsibility assumed for the prior period's statements. However, when unaudited statements are presented in comparative form with audited statements in an SEC filing, the unaudited statements need not be referred to in the auditor's report (AU 504). Answer (D) is incorrect because, if the 1997 report is reissued, it should contain a statement that the 1997 financial statements were not audited by Harris.

7.7 Scope Limitations

129. Limitation on the scope of the audit may require the auditor to express a qualified opinion or to disclaim an opinion. Which of the following would usually be a limitation on the scope of the audit?

A. The unavailability of sufficient competent evidential matter.

B. The engagement of the auditor to report on only one basic financial statement.

C. The audit of a subsidiary's financial statements by an auditor other than the one who audits and reports on the consolidated financial statements.

D. The engagement of the auditor after year-end.

The correct answer is (A). *(CPA, adapted)*

REQUIRED: The limitation on the scope of the audit.

DISCUSSION: Restrictions on the audit may be imposed by the client or by circumstances, such as the timing of the work, inadequacy of the accounting records, or an inability to obtain sufficient competent evidence. Scope limitations prevent the auditor from applying all procedures deemed necessary and result in either a qualified opinion or a disclaimer. The auditor's decision depends on the importance of the omitted procedure(s).

Answer (B) is incorrect because reports on one financial statement do not involve scope limitations if the auditor's access to information is not limited and if (s)he applies all the procedures deemed necessary. Answer (C) is incorrect because reference to another auditor's report as a partial basis for an opinion is not a qualification or a scope limitation. Answer (D) is incorrect because the auditor engaged after year-end may be able to become satisfied as to the fairness of the financial statements through the use of alternative procedures.

130. An auditor decides to express a qualified opinion on an entity's financial statements because a major inadequacy in its computerized accounting records prevents the auditor from applying necessary procedures. The opinion paragraph of the auditor's report should state that the qualification pertains to

A. A client-imposed scope limitation.

B. A departure from generally accepted auditing standards.

C. The possible effects on the financial statements.

D. Inadequate disclosure of necessary information.

The correct answer is (C). *(CPA, adapted)*

REQUIRED: The wording in the opinion paragraph when the opinion is qualified because of a scope limitation.

DISCUSSION: AU 508 states that, when an auditor qualifies the opinion because of a scope limitation, the wording in the opinion paragraph should indicate that the qualification pertains to the possible effects on the financial statements and not to the scope limitation itself.

Answer (A) is incorrect because the qualification should not pertain to the scope limitation. Answer (B) is incorrect because the auditor apparently has followed GAAS in the conduct of the audit. Answer (D) is incorrect because the lack of sufficient competent evidence does not constitute inadequate disclosure.

131. An auditor's opinion reads as follows: "In our opinion, except for the above-mentioned limitation on the scope of our audit...." This is an example of an

A. Acceptable review opinion.

B. Acceptable emphasis of a matter.

C. Acceptable qualified opinion.

D. Unacceptable reporting practice.

The correct answer is (D). *(CPA, adapted)*

REQUIRED: The true statement about combining the phrases "except for" and "limitation on the scope."

DISCUSSION: When an opinion is qualified because of a scope limitation, the opinion paragraph should indicate that the qualification pertains to the possible effects on the statements (AU 508). The language given in the question bases the qualification on the restriction itself and is unacceptable.

Answer (A) is incorrect because the standard review report states that no opinion is expressed. Answer (B) is incorrect because a matter is emphasized in a separate explanatory paragraph. Emphasis of a matter is consistent with an unqualified opinion. Answer (C) is incorrect because a qualified opinion should include language similar to the following: "In our opinion, except for the effects of such adjustments, if any, as might have been determined to be necessary had we been able to examine evidence...."

132. Which action should be taken by a CPA who has been asked to audit the financial statements of a company whose fiscal year has ended?

A. Discuss with the client the possibility of an adverse opinion because of the late engagement date.

B. Ascertain whether circumstances are likely to permit an adequate audit and expression of an unqualified opinion.

C. Inform the client of the need to issue a qualified opinion if the physical inventory has already been taken.

D. Ascertain whether an understanding of internal control can be obtained and control risk can be assessed after completion of the field work.

The correct answer is (B). *(CPA, adapted)*

REQUIRED: The proper action when the CPA is engaged after the end of the fiscal year.

DISCUSSION: According to AU 310, *Appointment of the Independent Auditor*, the auditor should ascertain whether circumstances are likely to permit an adequate audit. If they do not, the auditor should discuss with the client the possible necessity for a qualified opinion or disclaimer of opinion.

Answer (A) is incorrect because a scope limitation, by itself, cannot result in an adverse opinion. Answer (C) is incorrect because a qualified opinion is not inevitable. The auditor may consider the application of alternative procedures if observing the physical inventory is impracticable. Answer (D) is incorrect because the consideration of internal control should precede other aspects of the field work.

133. Park, CPA, was engaged to audit the financial statements of Tech Co., a new client, for the year ended December 31, 1998. Park obtained sufficient audit evidence for all of Tech's financial statement items except Tech's opening inventory. Due to inadequate financial records, Park could not verify Tech's January 1, 1998 inventory balances. Park's opinion on Tech's 1998 financial statements most likely will be

	Balance Sheet	Income Statement
A.	Disclaimer	Disclaimer
B.	Unqualified	Disclaimer
C.	Disclaimer	Adverse
D.	Unqualified	Adverse

The correct answer is (B). *(CPA, adapted)*

REQUIRED: The appropriate opinion on each financial statement when the auditor cannot verify opening inventory.

DISCUSSION: Because the balance sheet presents information as of a specific moment in time, the auditor should be able to become satisfied regarding the balances presented at year-end. However, beginning inventory enters materially into the determination of the statements of income, retained earnings, and cash flows. Thus, the auditor will probably not be able to form an opinion as to the fairness of these statements and should issue a disclaimer on them.

Answers (A), (C), and (D) are incorrect because the opinion on the balance sheet should be unqualified, but an opinion on the income statement should be disclaimed.

134. Green, CPA, was engaged to audit the financial statements of Essex Co. after its fiscal year had ended. The timing of Green's appointment as auditor and the start of field work made confirmation of accounts receivable by direct communication with the debtors ineffective. However, Green applied other procedures and was satisfied as to the reasonableness of the account balances. Green's auditor's report most likely contained a(n)

A. Unqualified opinion.

B. Unqualified opinion with an explanatory paragraph.

C. Qualified opinion because of a scope limitation.

D. Qualified opinion because of a departure from GAAS.

The correct answer is (A). *(CPA, adapted)*

REQUIRED: The opinion expressed when an auditor becomes satisfied as to receivables by using alternate procedures.

DISCUSSION: Because the CPA is satisfied as to the amounts of receivables, no scope limitation exists. Accordingly, the report need not refer to the omission of the procedures or the use of alternative procedures, and the CPA may express an unqualified opinion (AU 508).

Answer (B) is incorrect because no basis is given for including an explanatory paragraph. Answer (C) is incorrect because no scope limitation exists. Answer (D) is incorrect because the auditor has not departed from GAAS. The presumption that confirmation requests will be made is overcome if the use of confirmations would be ineffective (AU 330, *The Confirmation Process*).

135. When disclaiming an opinion because of a client-imposed scope limitation, an auditor should indicate in a separate paragraph why the audit did not comply with generally accepted auditing standards. The auditor should also omit the

	Scope Paragraph	Opinion Paragraph
A.	No	Yes
B.	Yes	Yes
C.	No	No
D.	Yes	No

The correct answer is (D). *(CPA, adapted)*

REQUIRED: The paragraph(s), if any, omitted from a disclaimer.

DISCUSSION: When a scope limitation exists, the auditor may express a qualified opinion or disclaim an opinion, depending on the materiality of the scope limitation. If an opinion is disclaimed, the introductory and opinion paragraphs are modified, and the scope paragraph is omitted.

Answers (A), (B), and (C) are incorrect because the scope paragraph is omitted, but the report contains an opinion paragraph.

136. If the auditor obtains satisfaction with respect to the accounts receivable balance by alternative procedures because it is impracticable to confirm accounts receivable, the auditor's report should be unqualified and could be expected to

A. Disclose that alternative procedures were used because of a client-imposed scope limitation.

B. Disclose in the opinion paragraph that confirmation of accounts receivable was impracticable.

C. Not mention the alternative procedures.

D. Refer to a footnote that discloses the alternative procedures.

The correct answer is (C). *(CPA, adapted)*

REQUIRED: The proper reference in the report to alternative means of obtaining satisfaction about receivables.

DISCUSSION: If the auditor cannot confirm receivables but is able to become satisfied by applying alternative procedures, there is no significant scope limitation, and the report need not refer to the omission of the procedures or the use of alternative procedures.

Answer (A) is incorrect because the report need not refer to the alternative procedures. Answer (B) is incorrect because reference to the omitted procedure is not necessary. Answer (D) is incorrect because reference to a footnote that discloses the alternative procedures is not appropriate.

137. A limitation on the scope of an audit sufficient to preclude an unqualified opinion will always result when management

A. Engages the auditor after the year-end physical inventory count is completed.

B. Fails to correct a material internal control weakness that had been identified during the prior year's audit.

C. Refuses to furnish a management representation letter to the auditor.

D. Prevents the auditor from reviewing the working papers of the predecessor auditor.

The correct answer is (C). *(CPA, adapted)*

REQUIRED: The scope limitation that is always sufficient to preclude an unqualified opinion.

DISCUSSION: According to AU 333, *Management Representations*, "Management's refusal to furnish written representations constitutes a limitation on the scope of the audit sufficient to preclude an unqualified opinion and is ordinarily sufficient to cause an auditor to disclaim an opinion or withdraw from the engagement." However, the circumstances may permit a qualified opinion. Furthermore, the auditor should consider the effects of management's refusal on his/her ability to rely on other management representations.

Answer (A) is incorrect because a limitation sufficient to preclude an unqualified opinion will not arise if the auditor becomes satisfied as to inventory by other procedures. Answer (B) is incorrect because failure to correct a previously identified material internal control weakness is not a limitation on the auditor's ability to apply necessary procedures. Answer (D) is incorrect because review of the predecessor's working papers may not be necessary to the audit.

138. Morris, CPA, suspects that a pervasive scheme of illegal bribes exists throughout the operations of Worldwide Import-Export, Inc., a new audit client. Morris notified the audit committee and Worldwide's legal counsel, but neither could assist Morris in determining whether the amounts involved were material to the financial statements or whether senior management was involved in the scheme. Under these circumstances, Morris should

A. Express an unqualified opinion with a separate explanatory paragraph.

B. Disclaim an opinion on the financial statements.

C. Express an adverse opinion on the financial statements.

D. Issue a special report regarding the illegal bribes.

The correct answer is (B). *(CPA, adapted)*

REQUIRED: The auditor action when (s)he cannot determine the amounts involved in illegal acts or the extent of management's involvement.

DISCUSSION: Bribery is an illegal act within the meaning of AU 317, that is, a violation of laws or governmental regulations. Under AU 317, if the auditor is precluded by the client from obtaining sufficient evidence to evaluate whether an illegal act has occurred, the auditor ordinarily should disclaim an opinion.

Answer (A) is incorrect because an unqualified opinion is not justified. Answer (C) is incorrect because an adverse opinion is expressed only when the financial statements are not presented fairly. Answer (D) is incorrect because special reports as defined in AU 623 are not issued on such topics.

139. The auditor would most likely disclaim an opinion because of

A. The client's failure to present supplementary information required by the FASB.

B. Inadequate disclosure of material information.

C. A client-imposed scope limitation.

D. The qualification of an opinion by the other auditor of a subsidiary when responsibility has been divided.

The correct answer is (C). *(CPA, adapted)*

REQUIRED: The most likely basis for a disclaimer.

DISCUSSION: Restrictions on the audit may be imposed by the client or by circumstances, such as the timing of the work, inadequacy of the accounting records, or an inability to obtain sufficient competent evidence. They result in either a qualified opinion or a disclaimer. When restrictions that significantly limit the scope of the audit are imposed by the client, the auditor normally should disclaim an opinion (AU 508).

Answer (A) is incorrect because the omission does not affect the opinion. The required information does not change accounting and reporting standards for preparing basic financial statements (AU 558, *Required Supplementary Information*). But the auditor should include an explanatory paragraph. Answer (B) is incorrect because inadequate disclosure of material matters is a departure from GAAP requiring a qualified or an adverse opinion. Answer (D) is incorrect because the nature and significance of the subject of the qualification may vary substantially. Thus, the principal auditor may have no need to modify the report because of such a qualification.

140. A limitation on the scope of an audit sufficient to preclude an unqualified opinion will usually result when management

A. Presents financial statements that are prepared in accordance with the cash receipts and disbursements basis of accounting.

B. States that the financial statements are not intended to be presented in conformity with generally accepted accounting principles.

C. Does not make the minutes of the board of directors' meetings available to the auditor.

D. Asks the auditor to report on the balance sheet and not on the other basic financial statements.

The correct answer is (C). *(CPA, adapted)*

REQUIRED: The basis for a scope limitation sufficient to preclude an unqualified opinion.

DISCUSSION: According to AU 508, an auditor should ordinarily disclaim an opinion because of a client-imposed scope limitation.

Answer (A) is incorrect because, if the auditor is issuing a special report on financial statements prepared on a comprehensive basis of accounting other than GAAP, for example, the cash basis, an unqualified opinion may be expressed (AU 623). Answer (B) is incorrect because stating that the financial statements are not intended to be presented in conformity with GAAP does not constitute a scope limitation. Answer (D) is incorrect because a limitation on the reporting engagement is not a scope limitation if the auditor is able to apply necessary procedures and his/her access to information is not limited.

141. A limitation on the scope of the audit sufficient to preclude an unqualified opinion will always result when management

A. Asks the auditor to report on the balance sheet and not on the other basic financial statements.

B. Refuses to permit its lawyer to respond to the letter of audit inquiry.

C. Discloses material related party transactions in the footnotes to the financial statements.

D. Knows that confirmation of accounts receivable is not feasible.

The correct answer is (B). *(CPA, adapted)*

REQUIRED: The limitation on the scope of the audit sufficient to preclude an unqualified opinion.

DISCUSSION: Inquiry of a client's lawyer is a necessary audit procedure. The refusal to permit the lawyer to furnish the information requested in an inquiry letter, either in writing or orally, would be a limitation on the scope of the audit sufficient to preclude an unqualified opinion (AU 337).

Answer (A) is incorrect because a limited reporting engagement is not considered a scope limitation if the auditor's access to information is not limited and (s)he applies the procedures (s)he considers necessary. Answer (C) is incorrect because disclosure of material related party transactions is required by SFAS 57. Answer (D) is incorrect because, when circumstances other than a client-imposed limitation preclude confirmation of receivables, the auditor need not qualify the opinion or disclaim an opinion if (s)he can become satisfied about receivables by applying alternative procedures.

142. A limitation on the scope of an audit sufficient to preclude an unqualified opinion will usually result when management

A. Is unable to obtain audited financial statements supporting the entity's investment in a foreign subsidiary.

B. Refuses to disclose in the notes to the financial statements related party transactions authorized by the board of directors.

C. Does not sign an engagement letter specifying the responsibilities of both the entity and the auditor.

D. Fails to correct a reportable condition communicated to the audit committee after the prior year's audit.

The correct answer is (A). *(CPA, adapted)*

REQUIRED: The scope limitation sufficient to preclude an unqualified opinion.

DISCUSSION: A common scope restriction is the inability to obtain audited financial statements of an investee. A restriction on the application of procedures to important financial statement elements requires the auditor to determine whether (s)he has examined sufficient competent evidence to permit expression of an unqualified or a qualified opinion or whether (s)he should disclaim an opinion.

Answer (B) is incorrect because refusal to make related party disclosures is a departure from GAAP, not a scope limitation. Answer (C) is incorrect because failure to sign an engagement letter is not sufficient to preclude an unqualified opinion. Answer (D) is incorrect because failure to correct a reportable condition is not a limitation of scope.

7.8 Addressing and Dating the Report

143. The auditor's report may be addressed to the company whose financial statements are being audited or to that company's

A. Chief operating officer.

B. President.

C. Board of directors.

D. Chief financial officer.

The correct answer is (C). *(CPA, adapted)*

REQUIRED: The addressee of the auditor's report.

DISCUSSION: The auditor's report should be addressed to the company whose statements are being audited or to its board of directors or shareholders. If the client is an unincorporated entity, the report should be addressed as circumstances dictate, e.g., to the partners or the proprietor. If the statements audited are not those of the client, the client is the proper addressee (AU 508).

Answers (A), (B), and (D) are incorrect because the auditor's report should not be addressed to the chief operating officer, the president, or the chief financial officer.

144. An auditor has been engaged by the State Bank to audit the XYZ Corporation in conjunction with a loan commitment. The report would most likely be addressed to

A. The shareholders, XYZ Corporation.

B. The State Bank.

C. The board of directors, XYZ Corporation.

D. To whom it may concern.

The correct answer is (B). *(Publisher)*

REQUIRED: The proper addressee of the report when the auditee is not the client.

DISCUSSION: AU 508 states that occasionally an auditor is retained to audit the financial statements of a company that is not his/her client. In such a case, the report customarily is addressed to the client and not to the board of directors or shareholders of the company whose financial statements are being audited.

Answers (A) and (C) are incorrect because the State Bank is the CPA's client and the report should be addressed to it. Answer (D) is incorrect because an audit report should not be addressed to whom it may concern.

145. The date of the audit report is important because

A. The user has a right to expect that the auditor has performed certain procedures to detect subsequent events that would materially affect the financial statements through the date of the report.

B. The auditor bills time to the client up to and including the audit report date, and the statement to the client should reflect this date.

C. GAAS require all audits to be performed on a timely basis.

D. It should coincide with the date of the financial statements.

The correct answer is (A). *(Publisher)*

REQUIRED: The importance of the audit report date.

DISCUSSION: AU 560 states that the auditor should perform certain procedures at or near the date of the completion of field work, which usually is the date of the auditor's report. These procedures include (1) reading the latest available interim financial statements and comparing them with the year-end statements; (2) inquiring of and discussing with officers and other executives a) whether any substantial contingent liabilities or commitments existed at the balance sheet date, b) whether there was any significant change in capital stock, long-term debt, or working capital, c) the current status of items in the financial statements being reported upon that were accounted for on a basis of tentative, preliminary, or inconclusive data, and d) whether any unusual adjustments had been made during the period from the balance sheet date to the date of inquiry; (3) reading the available minutes of meetings of shareholders, directors, and appropriate committees; (4) inquiring of the client's legal counsel concerning litigation, claims, and assessments; and (5) obtaining a letter of representations from the officers.

Answer (B) is incorrect because the auditor may bill the client for services after the report date. Answer (C) is incorrect because the auditor must use due care, but no standard requires the audit to be performed on a timely basis. Answer (D) is incorrect because the report should usually be dated as of the end of field work.

146. On February 13, 1998, Fox, CPA, met with the audit committee of the Gem Corporation to review the draft of Fox's report on the company's financial statements as of and for the year ended December 31, 1997. On February 16, 1998, Fox completed all remaining field work at the Gem Corporation's headquarters. On February 17, 1998, Fox typed and signed the final version of the auditor's report. On February 18, 1998, the final report was mailed to Gem's audit committee. What date should have been used on Fox's report?

A. February 13, 1998

B. February 16, 1998

C. February 17, 1998

D. February 18, 1998

The correct answer is (B). *(CPA, adapted)*

REQUIRED: The date that should be used on the auditor's report.

DISCUSSION: February 16, 1998 is the date that all field work was completed. This date is usually the date of the report according to AU 530, *Dating of the Independent Auditor's Report*. The auditor is not responsible for making any inquiries or carrying out any audit procedures for the period after the date of the report (but see AU 711, *Filings under Federal Securities Statutes*, regarding filings under the Securities Act of 1933).

Answers (A), (C), and (D) are incorrect because the report should be dated upon completion of the field work.

147. An auditor's report on comparative financial statements should be dated as of the date of the

A. Issuance of the report.

B. Completion of the auditor's recent field work.

C. Latest financial statements being reported on.

D. Last subsequent event disclosed in the statements.

The correct answer is (B). *(CPA, adapted)*

REQUIRED: The date of the report on comparative financial statements.

DISCUSSION: According to AU 508, "Ordinarily, the auditor's report on comparative financial statements should be dated as of the date of completion of his/her most recent audit."

Answer (A) is incorrect because using the date of issuance implies that the auditor performed audit procedures up to that date. Answer (C) is incorrect because the report should be dated as of the last day of the latest field work so as to encompass the subsequent events period, not the end of the period under audit. Answer (D) is incorrect because, if an event requiring disclosure occurs after the completion of field work, the auditor may dual date the report, i.e., date the report as of the completion of field work except for the footnote disclosing the subsequent event, which would be dated as of its occurrence.

148. An auditor's decision concerning whether to dual date the audit report is based upon the auditor's willingness to

A. Extend auditing procedures.

B. Accept responsibility for subsequent events.

C. Permit inclusion of a footnote captioned: Event (Unaudited) Subsequent to the Date of the Auditor's Report.

D. Assume responsibility for events subsequent to the issuance of the auditor's report.

The correct answer is (A). *(CPA, adapted)*

REQUIRED: The factor upon which the decision to dual date the audit report is based.

DISCUSSION: When a subsequent event disclosed in the financial statements occurs after the completion of field work but before the issuance of the report, the auditor may use dual dating. (S)he may date the report as of the completion of field work except for the matters affected by the subsequent event, which would be assigned the appropriate later date. In that case, the auditor's responsibility for events after the completion of field work would be limited to the specific event. If the auditor is willing to accept responsibility to the later date and accordingly extends subsequent events procedures to that date, the auditor may choose the later date as the date for the entire report (AU 530 and AU 560).

Answer (B) is incorrect because the auditor must assume responsibility for subsequent events occurring between the balance sheet date and the date of the report. Answer (C) is incorrect because a caption regarding an unaudited event subsequent to the date of the auditor's report is appropriate for a reissuance of an auditor's report, not for the original report (AU 530). Answer (D) is incorrect because the auditor does not assume responsibility for events subsequent to the date of the report (but see AU 711 regarding filings under the Securities Act of 1933).

149. An auditor issued an audit report that was dual dated for a subsequent event occurring after the completion of field work but before issuance of the auditor's report. The auditor's responsibility for events occurring subsequent to the completion of field work was

A. Limited to include only events occurring before the date of the last subsequent event referred to.

B. Limited to the specific event referred to.

C. Extended to subsequent events occurring through the date of issuance of the report.

D. Extended to include all events occurring since the completion of field work.

The correct answer is (B). *(CPA, adapted)*

REQUIRED: The auditor's responsibility for events occurring subsequent to the completion of field work when the report is dual dated.

DISCUSSION: Subsequent to the completion of field work, the auditor is responsible only for the specific subsequent event. (S)he is responsible for other subsequent events only up to the date of the completion of field work (AU 530).

Answers (A) and (D) are incorrect because the auditor's post-field-work responsibility extends only to the specified subsequent event. Answer (C) is incorrect because the date(s) of the report determine(s) the auditor's responsibility.

150. Normally, an independent accountant's responsibility for subsequent events work ends at the date of the report. However, when registration filings with the SEC contain audited financial statements, the accountant must extend subsequent events work to

A. The prospectus date.

B. The filing date.

C. The effective date.

D. The date the final security is sold.

The correct answer is (C). *(Publisher)*

REQUIRED: The date to which the auditor should extend subsequent events work for a registration statement.

DISCUSSION: The auditor should extend procedures to the effective date or as close thereto as reasonable and practicable. In addition to the subsequent-events procedures outlined in AU 560, the accountant should also (1) read the entire prospectus and other pertinent portions of the registration statement and (2) inquire of and obtain written representations from officers and other executives responsible for financial and accounting matters about whether any significant events have occurred other than those reflected or disclosed in the registration statement (AU 711).

Answers (A), (B), and (D) are incorrect because the registration statement speaks as of the effective date, which differs from the prospectus date (the date the document is prepared for first submission to the SEC), the filing date (the date the prospectus and other documents are submitted to the SEC), and the date the last security is sold.

151. In May 1998, an auditor reissues the auditor's report on the 1996 financial statements at a continuing client's request. The 1996 financial statements are not restated and the auditor does not revise the wording of the report. The auditor should

A. Dual date the reissued report.

B. Use the release date of the reissued report.

C. Use the original report date on the reissued report.

D. Use the current-period auditor's report date on the reissued report.

The correct answer is (C). *(CPA, adapted)*

REQUIRED: The date of a reissued report.

DISCUSSION: Under AU 530, use of the original date in a reissued report removes any implication that records, transactions, or events after such date have been audited or reviewed. The auditor will thus have no responsibility to carry out procedures relating to the period between original issuance and reissuance (but see AU 711 regarding filings under the Securities Act of 1933).

Answer (A) is incorrect because the report is dual dated only if it has been revised since the original reissue date. Answer (B) is incorrect because the release date of the reissued report implies that additional audit procedures have been applied. Answer (D) is incorrect because use of the current report date implies that the report has been updated for additional audit procedures applied between the original issue date and the current auditor's report date.

152. On September 30, 1998, Miller was asked to reissue an auditor's report, dated March 31, 1998, on a client's financial statements for the year ended December 31, 1997. Miller will submit the reissued report to the client in a document that contains information in addition to the client's basic financial statements. However, Miller discovered that the client suffered substantial losses on receivables resulting from conditions that occurred since March 31, 1998. Miller should

A. Request the client to disclose the event in a separate, appropriately labeled note to the financial statements and reissue the original report with its original date.

B. Request the client to restate the financial statements and reissue the original report with a dual date.

C. Reissue the original report with its original date without regard to whether the event is disclosed in a separate footnote.

D. Not reissue the original report but express a "subject to" qualified opinion that discloses the event in a separate paragraph.

The correct answer is (A). *(CPA, adapted)*

REQUIRED: The auditor action regarding reissuance of a report and a disclosable subsequent event.

DISCUSSION: The subsequent event concerned conditions that arose after the balance sheet date and thus required disclosure only (AU 560). If an event of this kind occurs between the date of the report and the date of its reissuance, and it comes to the auditor's attention, it may be disclosed in a footnote. The caption may be as follows: Event (Unaudited) Subsequent to the Date of the Independent Auditor's Report. In this case, the auditor's report would have the same date as the original report (AU 530).

Answer (B) is incorrect because restatement is not necessary. The conditions arose after the balance sheet date. Also, the auditor is not assuming responsibility for the subsequent event and thus should not dual date the report. Answer (C) is incorrect because, when financial statements are reissued, a footnote is required if disclosure of the subsequent event is necessary to prevent the statements from being misleading (AU 560). Answer (D) is incorrect because a "subject to" opinion is never permissible.

7.9 Comparative Financial Statements

153. When comparative financial statements are presented, the fourth standard of reporting, which refers to financial statements "taken as a whole," should be considered to apply to the financial statements of the

A. Periods presented plus one preceding period.

B. Current period only.

C. Current period and those of the other periods presented.

D. Current and immediately preceding period only.

The correct answer is (C). *(CPA, adapted)*

REQUIRED: The periods to which the fourth standard of reporting applies.

DISCUSSION: The fourth standard of reporting requires expression of an opinion on the statements taken as a whole or an assertion that an opinion cannot be expressed. The phrase "taken as a whole" applies not only to the current period's statements but also to those of prior periods presented on a comparative basis (AU 508).

Answers (A), (B), and (D) are incorrect because the phrase "taken as a whole" applies not only to the current period's statements but also to those of prior periods presented on a comparative basis.

154. When financial statements of a prior period are presented on a comparative basis with financial statements of the current period, the continuing auditor is responsible for

A. Expressing dual dated opinions.

B. Updating the report on the previous financial statements only if there has not been a change in the opinion.

C. Updating the report on the previous financial statements only if the previous opinion was qualified and the reasons for the qualification no longer exist.

D. Updating the report on the previous financial statements regardless of the opinion previously expressed.

The correct answer is (D). *(CPA, adapted)*

REQUIRED: The responsibility of a continuing auditor relative to comparative statements.

DISCUSSION: The reference in the fourth reporting standard to expression of an opinion on the financial statements taken as a whole should be considered to apply not only to the statements of the current period but also to those of one or more prior periods being presented comparatively with those of the current period. Thus, a continuing auditor should update the report on the individual statements of one or more prior periods presented on a comparative basis. Hence, the auditor's report on comparative statements should usually be dated as of the completion of the most recent audit (AU 508).

Answer (A) is incorrect because dual dated reports relate to events that occur between the last day of field work (the normal date of the auditor's report) and the report's release date. Answers (B) and (C) are incorrect because the report must be updated regardless of whether the opinion has changed.

155. Which of the following is a true statement concerning the auditor's report on comparative financial statements?

A. A continuing auditor may under certain circumstances express an opinion different from the previous opinion.

B. The report should not express an opinion different from that previously expressed on the statements of a prior period because the differences would lessen the public's confidence in the integrity of the auditor's report.

C. A predecessor auditor may reissue the report on the financial statements of a prior period provided (s)he performs certain procedures, including obtaining representation letters from the successor auditor and from management, and provided (s)he refers in the reissued report to the work of the successor auditor.

D. If the financial statements of the prior period have been audited, but those of the current period have not, the auditor should update the report on the prior period and include as a separate paragraph in the report a disclaimer of opinion on the unaudited financial statements.

The correct answer is (A). *(Publisher)*

REQUIRED: The true statement about reports on comparative financial statements.

DISCUSSION: A continuing auditor should update the report on the statements of one or more prior periods presented comparatively with the statements of the current period. A continuing auditor is one who has audited the current period's statements and those of one or more consecutive periods immediately preceding the current period. An updated report is distinguishable from the reissuance of a prior report because the continuing auditor considers information acquired during the audit of the current period's statements and issues the updated report in conjunction with the report on the current period statements. An updated report may contain an opinion different from that expressed in the previous report because the auditor may have become aware during the current audit of circumstances or events affecting a prior period's statements, e.g., restatement in the current period to correct a prior departure from GAAP (AU 508).

Answer (B) is incorrect because the auditor is required to be alert during the current audit for circumstances and events that affect the prior period statements presented or the adequacy of disclosures therein. Answer (C) is incorrect because the predecessor auditor should perform certain procedures, including obtaining representation letters from the successor auditor and from management, but should not refer to the report or work of the successor auditor. Answer (D) is incorrect because updating implies that the auditor has considered information obtained during the current year's audit.

156. When reporting on comparative financial statements, which of the following circumstances ordinarily should cause the auditor to change the previously expressed opinion on the prior year's financial statements?

A. The prior year's financial statements are restated following a pooling of interests in the current year.

B. A departure from generally accepted accounting principles caused an adverse opinion on the prior year's financial statements and those statements have been properly restated.

C. A change in accounting principle caused the auditor to make a consistency modification in the current year's auditor's report.

D. A scope limitation caused a qualified opinion on the prior year's financial statements but the current year's opinion was properly unqualified.

The correct answer is (B). *(CPA, adapted)*

REQUIRED: The event that causes an auditor to change a previously expressed opinion.

DISCUSSION: AU 508 states that, if an opinion in an updated report is different from the one previously expressed, the auditor should disclose all the substantive reasons for the different opinion in a separate paragraph preceding the opinion paragraph of the report. The explanatory paragraph should include (1) the date of the auditor's previous report, (2) the type of opinion previously expressed, (3) the circumstances or events that caused the auditor to express a different opinion, and (4) a statement that the auditor's updated opinion on the statements of the prior period is different from the previous opinion.

Answer (A) is incorrect because a pooling of interests is a change in the reporting entity accounted for by restating the financial statements of all prior periods presented to show information for the new entity for all periods. Answer (C) is incorrect because a change in accounting principle in the current period has no effect on the opinion on the prior year's statements. The auditor should add a paragraph at the end of the current year's report identifying the change. Answer (D) is incorrect because the scope limitation from the prior year requires the auditor to express a qualified opinion on the prior year's financial statements.

157. An auditor expressed a qualified opinion on the prior year's financial statements because of a lack of adequate disclosure. These financial statements are properly restated in the current year and presented in comparative form with the current year's financial statements. The auditor's updated report on the prior year's financial statements should

A. Be accompanied by the auditor's original report on the prior year's financial statements.

B. Continue to express a qualified opinion on the prior year's financial statements.

C. Make no reference to the type of opinion expressed on the prior year's financial statements.

D. Express an unqualified opinion on the restated financial statements of the prior year.

The correct answer is (D). *(CPA, adapted)*

REQUIRED: The effect on the auditor's updated report when the opinion has changed from the previous year.

DISCUSSION: During the audit, an auditor may become aware of circumstances or events affecting the statements of a prior period and should consider them when updating the report. For example, if the opinion was modified because of a departure from GAAP and the statements are restated in the current period to conform with GAAP, the updated report should indicate the restatement and express an unqualified opinion. The opinion should contain an explanatory paragraph preceding the opinion paragraph to describe the previous report and the reasons for the change in opinion.

Answer (A) is incorrect because the original report should not be reissued. Answer (B) is incorrect because the opinion has changed and the auditor should not continue to express the previous opinion. Answer (C) is incorrect because an explanatory paragraph should be added to the current audit report explaining the reason for the change and the type of opinion previously expressed.

158. Which of the following portions of a continuing auditor's standard report on comparative financial statements is incorrect?

A. "In our opinion, the financial statements referred to above present fairly, in all material respects, the financial position."

B. "Of XYZ Company as of December 31, 1998 and 1997 and the results of its operations and its cash flows."

C. "For the years then ended in conformity with generally accepted accounting principles."

D. "Applied on a basis consistent with that of the preceding year."

The correct answer is (D). *(CPA, adapted)*

REQUIRED: The improper portion of a continuing auditor's standard report on comparative statements.

DISCUSSION: The auditor's standard three-paragraph report is silent as to consistency. If the comparability of the financial statements has been materially affected by a change in accounting principles or in the method of their application, the change should be referred to in an explanatory paragraph following the opinion paragraph. Agreement with the change is implied unless the auditor takes exception to it (AU 508).

Answers (A), (B), and (C) are incorrect because the opinion paragraph in a standard report on comparative statements states an opinion, identifies the auditee and statements presented, and mentions GAAP.

159. When single-year financial statements are presented, an auditor ordinarily would express an unqualified opinion in an unmodified report if the

A. Auditor is unable to obtain audited financial statements supporting the entity's investment in a foreign affiliate.

B. Entity declines to present a statement of cash flows with its balance sheet and related statements of income and retained earnings.

C. Auditor wishes to emphasize an accounting matter affecting the comparability of the financial statements with those of the prior year.

D. Prior year's financial statements were audited by another CPA whose report, which expressed an unqualified opinion, is not presented.

The correct answer is (D). *(CPA, adapted)*

REQUIRED: The conditions under which an unqualified opinion would be expressed in an unmodified report.

DISCUSSION: When single-year financial statements are presented, the auditor's reporting responsibility is limited to those statements. If the prior year's financial statements are not presented for comparative purposes, the current-year auditor should not refer to the prior year's statements and the report thereon. Furthermore, the failure to present comparative statements is not a basis for modifying the opinion or the report.

Answer (A) is incorrect because an inability to obtain audited financial statements supporting an entity's investment in a foreign affiliate is a scope limitation requiring either a qualified opinion or a disclaimer of opinion. Answer (B) is incorrect because, if the entity declines to present a statement of cash flows, the auditor should express a qualified opinion. Answer (C) is incorrect because adding an additional paragraph to emphasize a matter results in a modified report.

160. Unaudited financial statements for the prior year presented in comparative form with audited financial statements for the current year should be clearly marked to indicate their status and

I. The report on the prior period should be reissued to accompany the current period report.

II. The report on the current period should include as a separate paragraph a description of the responsibility assumed for the prior period's financial statements.

A. I only.

B. II only.

C. Both I and II.

D. Either I or II.

The correct answer is (D). *(CPA, adapted)*

REQUIRED: The true statement(s) about comparative presentation of unaudited prior year's statements with audited current year's statements.

DISCUSSION: In these circumstances, the audit report on comparative statements presented in documents filed with the SEC would not refer to the unaudited statements, and these statements should be clearly marked as unaudited. In all other cases, the unaudited statements (that may have been reviewed or compiled) should also be clearly marked to indicate their status, and either the report on the prior period should be reissued (AU 530) or the report on the current period should include as a separate paragraph a description of the responsibility assumed for the prior period's statements (AU 504).

Answers (A), (B), and (C) are incorrect because either a separate paragraph in the current report or a reissued prior report may be used.

161. Gole, CPA, is engaged to review the 1998 financial statements of North Co., a nonpublic entity. Previously, Gole audited North's 1997 financial statements and expressed an unqualified opinion. Gole decides to include a separate paragraph in the 1998 review report because North plans to present comparative financial statements for 1998 and 1997. This separate paragraph should indicate that

A. The 1998 review report is intended solely for the information of management and the board of directors.

B. The 1997 auditor's report may no longer be relied on.

C. No auditing procedures were performed after the date of the 1997 auditor's report.

D. There are justifiable reasons for changing the level of service from an audit to a review.

The correct answer is (C). *(CPA, adapted)*

REQUIRED: The reference in a separate paragraph in a review report when comparative statements are presented and an audit was performed in the previous year.

DISCUSSION: A continuing accountant who performs a lower level of service should include a separate paragraph describing the responsibility assumed for the financial statements of the prior period or reissue the previous report. The paragraph included in the review report should indicate that no auditing procedures were performed after the date of the auditor's report.

Answer (A) is incorrect because a review report may be distributed to any user. Answer (B) is incorrect because the previous auditor's report may still be relied upon. Answer (D) is incorrect because no mention of the reasons for the change of service should be made in the review report.

162. Audited financial statements of the prior period are presented comparatively with unaudited statements of the current period in a document not filed with the SEC, and the report on the current period is to contain a separate paragraph describing the responsibility assumed for the financial statements of the prior period. The report on the current period should not indicate

A. That the financial statements of the prior period were audited previously and no auditing procedures were performed after the previous report date.

B. The date of the previous report and the type of opinion expressed previously.

C. The substantive reasons for any modification of the opinion on the prior-period statements.

D. That nothing has come to the auditors' attention to lead them to believe that material changes have taken place since that date.

The correct answer is (D). *(Publisher)*

REQUIRED: The disclosure not required in the report when audited prior-period statements are presented with unaudited current-period statements.

DISCUSSION: When unaudited financial statements are presented in comparative form with audited financial statements, the financial statements that have not been audited should be clearly marked to indicate their status. In an SEC filing, the unaudited statements should not be referred to in the auditor's report. But in any other document, either (1) the report on the prior period should be reissued or (2) the report on the current period should include a separate paragraph describing the responsibility assumed for the financial statements of the prior period. When the statements of the prior period have been audited and the report on the current period is to contain a separate paragraph, it should include all of the information specified in answers (A) through (C) (AU 504). Negative assurances are not permissible in general-distribution attest reports except in certain contexts, e.g., in letters for underwriters (AU 634) or in other attest engagements in which attestation risk is reduced only to a moderate level, e.g., a review of a private company's financial statements (AT 100, *Attestation Standards*).

Answers (A), (B), and (C) are incorrect because the report should state that the financial statements of the prior period were audited previously, the date of the previous report and the type of opinion expressed, and the substantive reasons for any modification of the opinion.

163. When management does not provide reasonable justification that a change in accounting principle is preferable and it presents comparative financial statements, the auditor should express a qualified opinion

A. Only in the year of the accounting principle change.

B. Each year that the financial statements initially reflecting the change are presented.

C. Each year until management changes back to the accounting principle formerly used.

D. Only if the change is to an accounting principle that is not generally accepted.

The correct answer is (B). *(CPA, adapted)*

REQUIRED: The year(s) or circumstance in which an unjustified accounting change requires a qualified opinion.

DISCUSSION: If management has not provided reasonable justification for a change, the new principle is not generally accepted, or the method of accounting for the effect of the change does not conform with GAAP, the auditor should express a qualified or an adverse opinion in the report for the year of change and add (an) explanatory paragraph(s) preceding the opinion paragraph. Also, "the auditor should continue to express the exception with respect to the financial statements for the year of change as long as they are presented and reported on" (AU 508).

Answers (A) and (C) are incorrect because the qualified opinion should be expressed each year the statements for the year of change are presented and reported on regardless of any future change in principle. Answer (D) is incorrect because a qualified opinion may be appropriate if the auditor determines that the change to an acceptable principle is unjustified.

164. When reporting on comparative financial statements, the auditor's report should include an additional explanatory paragraph concerning consistency when the financial statements of the current year include a change

A. From the cost method to the equity method of accounting for a subsidiary.

B. In the estimated salvage value of several assets.

C. In the income statement classification of an expense account from other expenses to selling expenses.

D. In inventory pricing to correct a mathematical error in the total value of the opening inventory.

The correct answer is (A). *(CPA, adapted)*

REQUIRED: The reason for modifying the report on comparative statements for consistency.

DISCUSSION: Changes in accounting principle or in the method of their application that have a material effect on comparability require the auditor to refer to consistency by including a separate explanatory paragraph identifying the change and referring to the footnote that describes the change in detail (AU 508). A change in the reporting entity, such as changing among the cost, equity, or consolidation methods of accounting for subsidiaries, is a special type of change in accounting principle.

Answers (B), (C), and (D) are incorrect because a change in estimate, a reclassification, or an error correction not involving an accounting principle affects comparability but not consistency and requires no report modification.

165. Comparative financial statements include the prior year's statements that were audited by a predecessor auditor whose report is not presented. If the predecessor's report was unqualified, the successor should

A. Express an opinion on the current year's statements alone and make no reference to the prior year's statements.

B. Indicate in the auditor's report that the predecessor auditor expressed an unqualified opinion.

C. Obtain a letter of representations from the predecessor concerning any matters that might affect the successor's opinion.

D. Request the predecessor auditor to reissue the prior year's report.

The correct answer is (B). *(CPA, adapted)*

REQUIRED: The successor auditor's disclosure about the report of a predecessor.

DISCUSSION: The successor auditor should state in the introductory paragraph that the prior year's financial statements were audited by another auditor. (S)he should give the date and the type of report and, if the report was modified, the reasons for modification. If the predecessor auditor expressed an unqualified opinion but included an explanatory paragraph, the nature of and reasons for such paragraph should be described (AU 508).

Answer (A) is incorrect because the prior year's financial statements presented comparatively must be considered in an auditor's report. Answer (C) is incorrect because the successor should communicate with the predecessor prior to accepting the engagement. Answer (D) is incorrect because the predecessor's report may be reissued and the successor's report would then be silent as to the predecessor. However, the question indicates that the predecessor's report is not presented.

166. Comparative financial statements include the financial statements of the prior year that were audited by a predecessor auditor whose report is not presented. If the predecessor's report was qualified, the successor should

A. Indicate the substantive reasons for the qualification in the predecessor auditor's opinion.

B. Request the client to reissue the predecessor's report on the prior year's statements.

C. Issue an updated comparative audit report indicating the division of responsibility.

D. Express an opinion only on the current year's statements and make no reference to the prior year's statements.

The correct answer is (A). *(CPA, adapted)*

REQUIRED: The successor auditor's action if the predecessor's qualified report is not presented.

DISCUSSION: When the predecessor's report is not presented, the successor's report should include in the introductory paragraph (1) a statement that the financial statements of the prior period were audited by another auditor, (2) the date of the report, (3) the type of report issued, and (4), if the report was other than a standard report, the substantive reasons therefor.

Answer (B) is incorrect because, although the report may be reissued, the question states that the report is not presented. Answer (C) is incorrect because division of responsibility is only appropriate when other auditors have audited a portion of the current statements being reported on. Answer (D) is incorrect because the statements presented in comparative form must be reported on or a disclaimer must be presented.

167. After properly communicating with the predecessor auditor, Seal & Co., CPAs, accepted the engagement to audit Mass Company's annual financial statements. Mass desires that comparative statements from years audited by the predecessor auditor be presented in the annual report. The predecessor auditor's report will not be presented. In its report, Seal should

A. Not refer to the report of the predecessor auditor in the introductory paragraph.

B. Refer to the report of the predecessor auditor in both the introductory and opinion paragraphs.

C. Refer to the report of the predecessor auditor in the opinion paragraph only.

D. Not refer to the report of the predecessor auditor in the opinion paragraph.

The correct answer is (D). *(CPA, adapted)*

REQUIRED: The auditor action when the previous year's financial statements were audited by another auditor.

DISCUSSION: According to AU 508, when the prior period's statements have been audited by a predecessor auditor whose report is not presented, the introductory paragraph of the successor's report should include (1) a statement that other auditors audited the prior period's statements, (2) the date of their report, (3) the type of report issued, and (4) the substantive reasons if the report was other than a standard report. Also, "The successor auditor should not name the predecessor auditor in the report; however, the successor auditor may name the predecessor auditor if the predecessor auditor's practice was acquired by, or merged with, that of the successor auditor."

Answers (A), (B), and (C) are incorrect because reference to the predecessor's report should be made in, and only in, the introductory paragraph.

168. When unaudited financial statements are presented in comparative form with audited financial statements in a document filed with the Securities and Exchange Commission, such statements should be

	Marked as "Unaudited"	Withheld until Audited	Referred to in the Auditor's Report
A.	Yes	No	No
B.	Yes	No	Yes
C.	No	Yes	Yes
D.	No	Yes	No

The correct answer is (A). *(CPA, adapted)*

REQUIRED: The treatment of unaudited statements presented comparatively with audited statements in a document filed with the SEC.

DISCUSSION: AU 504 states, "When unaudited financial statements are presented in comparative form with audited statements in documents filed with the Securities and Exchange Commission, such statements should be clearly marked as 'unaudited' but should not be referred to in the auditor's report."

Answers (B), (C), and (D) are incorrect because the statements should neither be withheld until audited nor referred to in the auditor's report.

169. The predecessor auditor, who is satisfied after properly communicating with the successor auditor, has reissued a report because the audit client desires comparative financial statements. The predecessor auditor's report should

A. Refer to the report of the successor auditor only in the scope paragraph.

B. Refer to the work of the successor auditor in the scope and opinion paragraphs.

C. Refer to both the work and the report of the successor auditor only in the opinion paragraph.

D. Not refer to the report or the work of the successor auditor.

The correct answer is (D). *(CPA, adapted)*

REQUIRED: The true statement about reference to the successor auditor in a reissued report.

DISCUSSION: A predecessor auditor who has been asked to reissue his/her report should (1) read the current-period statements, (2) compare the statements (s)he reported on with other statements to be presented comparatively, (3) obtain a representation letter from the successor auditor, and (4) obtain an updating representation letter from the management of the former client. The predecessor auditor may also wish to consider the professional reputation and standing of the successor auditor and other matters discussed in AU 543, but the reissued report should not refer to the report or work of the successor auditor.

Answers (A), (B), and (C) are incorrect because the reissued report should not refer to the report or the work of the successor auditor.

170. When a predecessor auditor reissues the report on the prior period's financial statements at the request of the former client, the predecessor auditor should

A. Indicate in the introductory paragraph of the reissued report that the financial statements of the subsequent period were audited by another CPA.

B. Read the current period's statements and compare them with those for the prior period.

C. Obtain a representation letter from the client's lawyer.

D. Add an explanatory paragraph to the reissued report stating that the predecessor has not performed additional auditing procedures concerning the prior period's financial statements.

The correct answer is (B). *(CPA, adapted)*

REQUIRED: The procedure performed by the predecessor auditor before reissuing a report.

DISCUSSION: AU 508 requires performance of certain procedures by the predecessor auditor before reissuing a report on prior-period financial statements. (S)he should (1) read the current period's financial statements, (2) compare the prior and current financial statements, (3) obtain a representation letter from the successor auditor, and (4) obtain an updating representation letter from the management of the former client.

Answer (A) is incorrect because the reissued report should not refer to the successor auditor. Answer (C) is incorrect because the predecessor auditor should obtain representation letters from the successor auditor and management but not from the client's lawyer. However, the successor auditor must inquire of the client's outside counsel to corroborate management's representations about litigation, claims, and assessments (AU 337). Answer (D) is incorrect because the report should not be modified unless the auditor's previous conclusions have changed since the prior report was issued.

7.10 Related Party Transactions

171. An audit in accordance with GAAS cannot be expected to provide assurance that all related party transactions will be discovered. Nevertheless, during the course of the audit, the auditor should be aware of the possible existence of material related party transactions that could affect the financial statements. The primary concern of the auditor regarding related party transactions is that

A. They are accounted for using the standards set forth by the FASB for related party transactions.

B. Their existence and significance be adequately disclosed.

C. They are reported to the SEC because they are illegal.

D. Their form be emphasized rather than their economic substance.

The correct answer is (B). *(Publisher)*

REQUIRED: The auditor's responsibility with regard to related party transactions.

DISCUSSION: Established accounting principles ordinarily do not require transactions with related parties to be accounted for on a basis different from what would be appropriate if the parties were not related. Until applicable accounting standards are established by authoritative bodies, the auditor should view related party transactions within the framework of existing pronouncements, with emphasis on the adequacy of disclosure (AU 334).

Answer (A) is incorrect because GAAP ordinarily do not establish specific requirements for the recording of related party transactions. Answer (C) is incorrect because related party transactions, per se, are not illegal. Answer (D) is incorrect because the substance of the transactions should be emphasized, not their form.

172. When one party has the ability to significantly influence the management or operating policies of the other to the extent that one of the transacting parties might be prevented from fully pursuing its separate interests, the parties are related for purposes of AU 334. Which of the following is not usually regarded as a party related to a firm?

A. Affiliates, principal owners, and entities for which investments are accounted for by the equity method.

B. Third parties that can significantly influence the operating policies of the transacting parties.

C. Management and members of their immediate families.

D. The U.S. government.

The correct answer is (D). *(Publisher)*

REQUIRED: The party not considered a related party.

DISCUSSION: Although the U.S. government regulates certain aspects of business activity, it is not considered a related party when dealing with a firm.

Answer (A) is incorrect because affiliates, owners, and those related through investment interests may exercise influence to the extent that one (or more) of the transacting parties might be prevented from pursuing its separate interests (AU 334). Answer (B) is incorrect because parties that can significantly influence the operating policies of the transacting parties by definition are related parties. Answer (C) is incorrect because management and members of their immediate families may exercise influence to the extent that one (or more) of the transacting parties might be prevented from pursuing its separate interests.

173. The auditor should be aware of the possibility of related party transactions. Examples of transactions that raise questions as to their substance and may be indicative of the existence of related party transactions include all of the following except

A. Borrowing or lending on an interest-free basis or at a rate of interest significantly above or below current market rates.

B. Selling real estate at a price that differs significantly from its appraised value or exchanging property for similar property in a nonmonetary transaction.

C. The purchase of particularly small quantities of an item based upon current market price.

D. Making loans with no scheduled terms as to when or how the funds will be repaid.

The correct answer is (C). *(Publisher)*

REQUIRED: The item not indicative of the existence of related party transactions.

DISCUSSION: The purchase of very large quantities at market prices might be indicative of related party transactions because the related party may influence the purchaser to buy large quantities of its excess production. However, the purchase of small quantities at regular prices does not indicate the existence of a related party transaction.

Answer (A) is incorrect because borrowing or lending on an interest-free basis or at a rate of interest significantly above or below current market rates may be indicative of related parties (AU 334). Answer (B) is incorrect because selling real estate at a price that differs significantly from its appraised value or exchanging property for similar property in a nonmonetary transaction may be indicative of related parties. Answer (D) is incorrect because making loans with no scheduled terms may be indicative of related parties.

174. For a reporting entity that has participated in related party transactions that are material, disclosure in the financial statements should include

A. The nature of the relationship and the terms and manner of settlement.

B. Details of the transactions within major classifications.

C. A statement to the effect that a transaction was consummated on terms equivalent to those that prevail in arm's-length transactions.

D. A reference to deficiencies in the entity's internal control.

The correct answer is (A). *(CPA, adapted)*

REQUIRED: The financial statement disclosures required for related party transactions.

DISCUSSION: Disclosure in financial statements of a reporting entity that has participated in material related party transactions should include (1) the nature of the relationship, (2) a description of the transactions, (3) the dollar value of the transactions, (4) the amounts due from or to related parties, and (5), if not otherwise apparent, the terms and manner of settlement (SFAS 57).

Answer (B) is incorrect because the client need not separate the transactions into major classifications. Answer (C) is incorrect because a statement that transactions approximated those at arm's-length is not required. If such a representation is made, the auditor must reach a conclusion as to its propriety. Answer (D) is incorrect because the client is not obligated to provide disclosures about its internal control.

175. Current authoritative literature ordinarily requires material related party transactions to be

A. Accounted for differently from transactions between unrelated parties but not separately disclosed.

B. Accounted for on the same basis as transactions between unrelated parties and not separately disclosed.

C. Separately disclosed but not accounted for differently from transactions between unrelated parties.

D. Separately disclosed and accounted for differently from transactions between unrelated parties.

The correct answer is (C). *(Publisher)*

REQUIRED: The accounting treatment of material related party transactions.

DISCUSSION: AU 334 states, "Certain accounting pronouncements prescribe accounting treatment when related parties are involved. However, established accounting principles ordinarily do not require transactions with related parties to be accounted for on a basis different from what would be appropriate if the parties were not related."

Answers (A), (B), and (D) are incorrect because related party transactions are separately disclosed but are usually accounted for in the same way as other transactions.

176. In the absence of evidence to the contrary, transactions with related parties should not be assumed to be outside the ordinary course of business. The auditor should, however, be aware of the possibility that transactions with related parties may have been motivated solely, or in a large measure, by certain conditions. The auditor should evaluate these conditions to identify related parties and related party transactions. Which of the following is not one of those conditions?

A. A lack of sufficient working capital or credit to continue business.

B. An urgent desire for a continued favorable earnings record to support the price of the company stock.

C. Dependence upon a single or relatively few products, customers, or transactions.

D. Reduction in number and dollar value of accounts receivable.

The correct answer is (D). *(Publisher)*

REQUIRED: The item not a likely motivation for related party transactions.

DISCUSSION: A reduction in accounts receivable does not necessarily have negative implications for a business. It may simply reflect improved collection procedures or tighter credit policies. Hence, the reduction is not, per se, a condition likely to motivate related party transactions. In addition to those cited in the question, conditions indicative of related party transactions include an overly optimistic earnings forecast; a declining industry characterized by a large number of business failures; excess capacity; significant litigation, especially between shareholders and management; and significant risk of obsolescence, e.g., in a high-technology industry.

Answers (A), (B), and (C) are incorrect because a lack of sufficient working capital or credit, a desire for a continued favorable earnings record, or a dependence upon a single or relatively few products, customers, or transactions may motivate a related party transaction.

177. While expressing an unqualified opinion, an auditor includes a separate paragraph in the report to emphasize that the entity being reported upon had significant transactions with related parties. This inclusion

A. Violates GAAS if this information is already disclosed in footnotes to the financial statements.

B. Necessitates a revision of the opinion paragraph to include the phrase "with the foregoing explanation."

C. Is appropriate and would not negate the unqualified opinion.

D. Is considered a qualification of the opinion.

The correct answer is (C). *(CPA, adapted)*

REQUIRED: The effect of emphasizing related party transactions in a separate paragraph of the report.

DISCUSSION: An auditor may emphasize a matter in a separate paragraph while expressing an unqualified opinion. Significant related party transactions, the status of the entity as a component of a larger enterprise, an accounting matter affecting comparability, and an unusually important subsequent event are examples of matters that might be emphasized (AU 508).

Answers (A) and (D) are incorrect because GAAS permit emphasis of a matter without qualifying the opinion. Answer (B) is incorrect because the opinion paragraph should not refer to the separate paragraph.

178. An auditor refers to significant related party transactions in a separate paragraph of the report. If the ensuing opinion paragraph contains the words "with the foregoing explanation," the auditor is considered to have

A. Expressed an unqualified opinion with appropriate reference to the separate paragraph.

B. Expressed an adverse opinion.

C. Expressed a negative assurance opinion.

D. Reported inappropriately.

The correct answer is (D). *(CPA, adapted)*

REQUIRED: The true statement about use of the phrase "with the foregoing explanation."

DISCUSSION: A separate explanatory paragraph is used when the auditor wishes to emphasize a matter, to describe uncertainties, to identify lack of consistency in applying GAAP, to express a qualified opinion, etc. The phrase "with the foregoing explanation" should never be used because it may be misunderstood as an attempt to qualify the opinion or, when a qualified opinion is expressed, because it is not clear or forceful enough (AU 508).

Answers (A), (B), and (C) are incorrect because no opinion should use a phrase such as "with the foregoing explanation."

179. An auditor would be most likely to consider modifying an otherwise unqualified opinion if the client's financial statements include a footnote on related party transactions

A. Representing that certain related party transactions were consummated on terms equivalent to those obtainable in transactions with unrelated parties.

B. Presenting the dollar volume of related party transactions and the effects of any change in the method of establishing terms from that used in the prior period.

C. Explaining the business purpose of the sale of real property to a related party.

D. Disclosing compensating balance arrangements maintained for the benefit of related parties.

The correct answer is (A). *(CPA, adapted)*

REQUIRED: The most likely basis for expressing a qualified opinion.

DISCUSSION: According to AU 334, "Except for routine transactions, it will ordinarily not be possible to determine whether a particular transaction would have taken place if the parties had not been related, or, assuming it would have taken place, what the terms and manner of settlement would have been." Accordingly, representations concerning such matters are difficult to substantiate. If the auditor is unable to reach a conclusion as to their propriety, (s)he should consider including in the report a comment to that effect and expressing a qualified opinion or a disclaimer.

Answers (B), (C), and (D) are incorrect because the dollar volume of related party transactions and the effects of any change in the method of establishing terms, the business purpose of the sale of real property to a related party, and compensating balance arrangements maintained for the benefit of related parties are required disclosures.

7.11 Subsequent Events and Subsequently Discovered Facts (See also Module 4.15.)

180. Subsequent events for reporting purposes are defined as events that occur subsequent to the

A. Balance sheet date.

B. Date of the auditor's report.

C. Balance sheet date but prior to the date of the auditor's report.

D. Date of the auditor's report and concern contingencies that are not reflected in the financial statements.

The correct answer is (C). *(CPA, adapted)*

REQUIRED: The definition of subsequent events.

DISCUSSION: Subsequent events are those that "occur subsequent to the balance sheet date, but prior to the issuance of the financial statements and auditor's report, that have a material effect on the financial statements and therefore require adjustment or disclosure in the statements" (AU 560). If the balance sheet date is 12/31/97, and the auditor's report is dated 3/1/98, the subsequent events period is from 12/31/97 to 3/1/98.

Answers (A), (B), and (D) are incorrect because subsequent events occur subsequent to the balance sheet date but prior to the issuance of the financial statements and auditor's report.

181. Two types of subsequent events require consideration by management and evaluation by the auditor. One type consists of those events that provide additional evidence with respect to conditions that existed at the date of the balance sheet and affect the estimates inherent in the process of preparing financial statements. The financial statements should be adjusted for any changes in estimates resulting from the use of such evidence. The second type of subsequent event consists of those events that provide evidence with respect to conditions that did not exist at the date of the balance sheet but arose subsequent to that date. These events

A. Are also used in adjusting the financial statements.

B. Should not be considered for any purposes.

C. Should ordinarily be disclosed in the auditor's report.

D. May require disclosure in footnotes to the financial statements.

The correct answer is (D). *(Publisher)*

REQUIRED: The extent to which subsequent events relevant to conditions arising after the balance sheet date should be reflected in the statements or in the audit report.

DISCUSSION: These events should not result in adjustment of the financial statements, although they may require disclosure to keep the financial statements from being misleading. Disclosure may be made in the footnotes and occasionally by presentation of pro forma data giving effect to the subsequent event as if it had occurred at the balance sheet date. If the event has a sufficiently material impact, the auditor may wish to refer to it in an explanatory paragraph in the report (AU 560).

Answer (A) is incorrect because only the subsequent events that provide additional evidence of conditions existing at year-end (first type) should result in adjustment. Answer (B) is incorrect because subsequent events that provide evidence with respect to conditions that did not exist at the balance sheet date (second type) should be disclosed. Answer (C) is incorrect because the second type of subsequent event is only occasionally noted in the audit report.

182. Which of the following procedures would an auditor most likely perform to obtain evidence about the occurrence of subsequent events?

A. Recomputing a sample of large-dollar transactions occurring after year-end for arithmetic accuracy.

B. Investigating changes in shareholders' equity occurring after year-end.

C. Inquiring of the entity's legal counsel concerning litigation, claims, and assessments arising after year-end.

D. Confirming bank accounts established after year-end.

The correct answer is (C). *(CPA, adapted)*

REQUIRED: The auditing procedure for the subsequent events period.

DISCUSSION: Procedures applied after the balance sheet date should include the examination of data to determine that proper cutoffs have been made and to evaluate assets and liabilities as of the balance sheet date. Additional procedures include (1) reading the latest available interim statements; (2) inquiries of and discussion with officers and other executives as to whether substantial contingent liabilities or commitments exist, whether there was any significant change in equities or long-term debt, the current status of items that were accounted for on the basis of tentative, preliminary, or inconclusive data, and whether any adjustments had been made during the period from the balance sheet date to the date of inquiry; (3) reading the available minutes of meetings of shareholders, directors, and other committees; (4) inquiring of the client's legal counsel; (5) obtaining a representation letter; and (6) making additional necessary inquiries (AU 560).

Answer (A) is incorrect because testing arithmetic accuracy does not obtain evidence about the occurrence of a subsequent event. Answer (B) is incorrect because the auditor should inquire of officers and other executives as to significant changes in shareholders' equity, but an investigation of such changes is less likely than the inquiry of legal counsel. Answer (D) is incorrect because a bank account established after year-end is not an asset that existed at the balance sheet date.

183. Some subsequent events provide evidence of conditions not in existence at the balance sheet date. Some of these events are of such a nature that disclosure is required to keep the financial statements from being misleading. Adequate disclosure of these events may include

A. Adjustment of the financial statements.

B. Pro forma financial statement presentation.

C. Footnotes to the auditor's report.

D. Restatement of prior-period financial statements.

The correct answer is (B). *(Publisher)*

REQUIRED: The proper disclosure of a subsequent event related to a condition not existing at year-end.

DISCUSSION: Subsequent events related to conditions that did not exist at the date of the balance sheet should not result in adjustments of the financial statements. These events are usually disclosed in statement footnotes. Occasionally, such an event may be significant and have such pervasive effects that disclosure can best be made by supplementing the historical statements with pro forma financial data giving effect to the event as if it had occurred on the date of the balance sheet. AU 560 suggests presentation of pro forma statements, usually a balance sheet only, in columnar form on the face of the historical statements. But firms usually incorporate the pro forma balance sheets in footnotes.

Answers (A) and (D) are incorrect because only subsequent events that relate to conditions existing at the balance sheet date require adjustment of the financial statements. Answer (C) is incorrect because footnotes are attached to financial statements, not auditors' reports.

184. Subsequent events affecting the realization of assets ordinarily will require adjustment of the financial statements under audit because such events typically represent the

A. Culmination of conditions that existed at the balance sheet date.

B. Final estimates of losses relating to casualties occurring in the subsequent events period.

C. Discovery of new conditions occurring in the subsequent events period.

D. Preliminary estimate of losses relating to new events that occurred subsequent to the balance sheet date.

The correct answer is (A). *(CPA, adapted)*

REQUIRED: The reason subsequent events affecting asset realization require adjustment of the statements.

DISCUSSION: All information that becomes available prior to the issuance of the financial statements should be used by management in its evaluation of the conditions on which the estimates underlying the statements were based. The financial statements should be adjusted for events in the subsequent events period that provide additional evidence concerning conditions that existed at the balance sheet date. Subsequent events affecting the realization of assets typically represent the culmination of conditions that existed at year-end (AU 560).

Answers (B), (C), and (D) are incorrect because conditions that did not exist at the balance sheet date, if material, require footnote disclosure or even pro forma presentation but not adjustment of the statements.

185. Wilson, CPA, completed the field work of the audit of Abco's December 31, 1997 financial statements on March 6, 1998. A subsequent event requiring adjustment of the 1997 financial statements occurred on April 10, 1998, and came to Wilson's attention on April 24, 1998. If the adjustment is made without disclosure of the event, Wilson's report ordinarily should be dated

A. March 6, 1998.

B. April 10, 1998.

C. April 24, 1998.

D. Using dual dating.

The correct answer is (A). *(CPA, adapted)*

REQUIRED: The date of the report if the statements are adjusted for a subsequent event without disclosure.

DISCUSSION: If a subsequent event requiring adjustment occurs prior to the issuance of the report and the event comes to the auditor's attention, the statements should be adjusted. If the statements are not adjusted, the opinion should be qualified. In some cases, a disclaimer of opinion or an adverse opinion may be appropriate. When the adjustment is made without disclosure, the report should usually be dated as of the completion of field work (AU 530).

Answers (B) and (C) are incorrect because, when a subsequent event of the type requiring adjustment is not disclosed, the report should usually be dated as of the completion of field work. Answer (D) is incorrect because dual dating is not permitted when the subsequent event is not disclosed.

186. Which of the following material events occurring subsequent to the December 31, 1997 balance sheet would not ordinarily result in an adjustment of the financial statements before they are issued on March 2, 1998?

A. Write-off of a receivable from a debtor who had suffered from a deteriorating financial condition for the past 6 years. The debtor filed for bankruptcy on January 23, 1998.

B. Acquisition of a subsidiary on January 23, 1998. Negotiations had begun in December of 1997.

C. Settlement of extended litigation on January 23, 1998 in excess of the recorded year-end liability.

D. A 3-for-5 reverse stock split consummated on January 23, 1998.

The correct answer is (B). *(CPA, adapted)*

REQUIRED: The material subsequent event not requiring adjustment of the statements.

DISCUSSION: The financial statements should be adjusted for material subsequent events that provide information relative to conditions existing at the balance sheet date. The acquisition of the subsidiary did not occur until after year-end; hence, the purchase required only footnote disclosure, not adjustment of the statements.

Answer (A) is incorrect because the poor financial condition of the debtor existed at year-end. Answer (C) is incorrect because the litigation was pending at year-end. Answer (D) is incorrect because retroactive effect should be given to stock splits according to SFAS 128, *Earnings per Share*.

187. Creditor Co. had a large account receivable that was considered fully collectible at its year end. However, the debtor's plant was destroyed during the subsequent events period. Because the debtor was uninsured, it is unlikely that the account will be paid. What is the effect of this event on the year-end statements?

A. Disclosure by means of supplemental, pro forma financial data.

B. Adjustment of the financial statements.

C. Disclosure in a footnote to the financial statements.

D. No financial statement disclosure necessary.

The correct answer is (C). *(Publisher)*

REQUIRED: The proper treatment of a debtor's major casualty subsequent to year end.

DISCUSSION: A debtor's major casualty subsequent to year-end rendering a major receivable uncollectible is not indicative of conditions existing at the balance sheet date, so adjustment of the financial statements is not appropriate. Because the event could influence the users of the financial statements, disclosure in a footnote should be made (AU 560).

Answer (A) is incorrect because disclosure by means of supplemental, pro forma financial data would be inappropriate. Answer (B) is incorrect because adjustment of the financial statements would be inappropriate. Answer (D) is incorrect because financial statement disclosure is necessary.

188. The U.S. Tax Court ruled in favor of Defendant Co. after year-end but before completion of the audit. Litigation involved deductions claimed on prior years' tax returns. The company had credited accrued taxes payable at year-end for the full amount sought by the IRS. The IRS will not appeal the ruling. What is the effect of this event on the year-end statements?

A. Disclosure by means of supplemental, pro forma financial data.

B. Adjustment of the financial statements.

C. Disclosure in a footnote to the financial statements.

D. No financial statement disclosure necessary.

The correct answer is (B). *(Publisher)*

REQUIRED: The proper treatment of the settlement of litigation subsequent to year-end.

DISCUSSION: The ruling of the Tax Court provides additional evidence with respect to conditions that existed at the date of the financial statements and affects the estimates used in their preparation. Consequently, the settlement in the subsequent events period for an amount different from that recorded requires the client to adjust the statements.

Answer (A) is incorrect because disclosure by means of supplemental, pro forma financial data would be inappropriate. Answer (C) is incorrect because disclosure in a footnote to the financial statements would be inappropriate. Answer (D) is incorrect because financial statement disclosure is necessary.

189. After year-end but before completion of the audit, a major investment adviser issued a pessimistic report on Investee Co.'s long-term prospects. The market price for its common stock subsequently declined significantly. What is the effect of this event on the year-end statements?

A. Disclosure by means of supplemental, pro forma financial data.

B. Adjustment of the financial statements.

C. Disclosure in a footnote to the financial statements.

D. No financial statement disclosure necessary.

The correct answer is (D). *(Publisher)*

REQUIRED: The proper treatment of a major decline in the price of stock subsequent to year-end.

DISCUSSION: The market price of common stock is not a financial event that affects the fairness or interpretation of the financial statements. Accordingly, no disclosure is necessary for changes in the market price of the securities.

Answer (A) is incorrect because disclosure by means of supplemental, pro forma financial data would be inappropriate. Answer (B) is incorrect because adjustment of the financial statements would be inappropriate. Answer (C) is incorrect because disclosure in a footnote to the financial statements would be inappropriate.

190. Parent Co. sold a major division during the subsequent events period. The new owner assumed the bonded indebtedness associated with this property. What is the effect of this event on the year-end statements?

A. Disclosure by means of supplemental, pro forma financial data.

B. Adjustment of the financial statements.

C. Presentation of a narrative description in a footnote to the financial statements.

D. No required financial statement disclosure.

The correct answer is (A). *(Publisher)*

REQUIRED: The proper treatment of the sale of a division after the balance sheet date.

DISCUSSION: The sale of a major division in the subsequent events period provides evidence of conditions not existing at the balance sheet date and thus does not require adjustment of the statements. Disclosure must be made, however, because the event is of such a nature that nondisclosure would make the statements misleading. The form of the disclosure depends upon the significance of the event. In this case, many accounts are affected, and pro forma statements presented on the face of the historical statements are the best method. However, the pro forma statements are sometimes presented in a footnote.

Answer (B) is incorrect because adjustment of the financial statements would be inappropriate. Answer (C) is incorrect because a narrative disclosure in a footnote to the financial statements would be insufficient. Answer (D) is incorrect because financial statement disclosure is necessary.

191. Advertiser Co.'s directors voted immediately after year-end to double the advertising budget for the coming year and authorized a change in advertising agencies. What is the effect of this event on the year-end statements?

A. Disclosure by means of supplemental, pro forma financial data.

B. Adjustment of the financial statements.

C. Disclosure in a footnote to the financial statements.

D. No financial statement disclosure necessary.

The correct answer is (D). *(Publisher)*

REQUIRED: The proper treatment of an increase in the advertising budget subsequent to the balance sheet date.

DISCUSSION: Changing of budgets and other managerial decisions made by the directors or management are not significant subsequent events. Hence, no financial statement disclosure or adjustment is necessary.

Answer (A) is incorrect because disclosure by means of supplemental, pro forma financial data would be inappropriate. Answer (B) is incorrect because adjustment of the financial statements would be inappropriate. Answer (C) is incorrect because disclosure in a footnote to the financial statements would be inappropriate.

192. If a subsequent event requiring only disclosure occurs after completion of field work but prior to issuance of the audit report, the auditor should

A. Modify the opinion and dual date the audit report. No additional field work is required.

B. Date the audit report as of the last day of field work and caption the footnote disclosing the subsequent event as being subsequent to the completion of the field work.

C. Not modify the audit opinion if the event is properly disclosed and date the audit report as of the time of completion of the field work.

D. Either dual date the audit report or date the audit report as of the time of the completion of the extended field work.

The correct answer is (D). *(Publisher)*

REQUIRED: The correct action when a subsequent event requiring only disclosure occurs after completion of field work but prior to issuance of the report.

DISCUSSION: The auditor may use dual dating or date the entire report as of the date of the subsequent event occurring after completion of field work. If the report is dual dated, the auditor's responsibility for events subsequent to the completion of field work is limited to the specific event. If the date of the report is the date of that event, responsibility extends to that date, and, accordingly, the auditor should perform the necessary additional subsequent events procedures through the new date of the report (AU 530).

Answer (A) is incorrect because, if the client properly footnotes or otherwise discloses the item, no opinion modification is necessary. Answer (B) is incorrect because captioning the footnote is insufficient. Answer (C) is incorrect because the occurrence of the event must be acknowledged in dating the report.

193. Toby Hooper, CPA, had drafted an unqualified opinion on the audit of Chem Waste Disposal when she received a letter from the client's independent counsel. The letter indicated that the state Department of Environmental Protection may prohibit Chem Waste from accepting any further waste for processing because of irregularities in its operating practices. Counsel intends to take all appropriate action to keep the firm in business, but the outcome is highly uncertain. Based on this information, Hopper should

A. Express an unqualified opinion with disclosure of the event in a separate explanatory paragraph of her report.

B. Issue a standard report because the event happened after year-end.

C. Express an adverse opinion on the financial statements and disclose all reasons therefor.

D. Add a footnote to the audit report explaining the event.

The correct answer is (A). *(Publisher)*

REQUIRED: The appropriate action when the CPA has obtained new information affecting the audit report.

DISCUSSION: According to AU 341, an evaluation must be made as to whether substantial doubt exists "about the entity's ability to continue as a going concern for a reasonable period of time, not to exceed 1 year beyond the date of the financial statements." If the auditor reaches this conclusion after identifying conditions and events that create such doubt and after evaluating management's plans to mitigate their effects, (s)he should consider the adequacy of disclosure and include an explanatory paragraph (after the opinion paragraph) in the report. This paragraph must use the phrases "substantial doubt" and "going concern." If disclosure is inadequate, the departure from GAAP requires modification of the opinion. If the uncertainty is sufficiently material, a disclaimer may be appropriate.

Answer (B) is incorrect because, if a material uncertainty exists as to whether the client is a going concern, a standard report cannot be issued. Answer (C) is incorrect because grounds do not exist for an opinion that the statements are not fairly presented. Answer (D) is incorrect because a footnote is not appropriate for an audit report.

194. Subsequent to the issuance of an auditor's report, the auditor became aware of facts existing at the report date that would have affected the report had the auditor then been aware of such facts. After determining that the information is reliable, the auditor should next

A. Determine whether there are persons relying or likely to rely on the financial statements who would attach importance to the information.

B. Request that management disclose the newly discovered information by issuing revised financial statements.

C. Issue revised pro forma financial statements taking into consideration the newly discovered information.

D. Give public notice that the auditor is no longer associated with financial statements.

The correct answer is (A). *(CPA, adapted)*

REQUIRED: The step performed by an auditor who becomes aware of facts existing at the report date that would have affected the report.

DISCUSSION: AU 561, *Subsequent Discovery of Facts Existing at the Date of the Auditor's Report*, states that, if an auditor decides that action should be taken to prevent future reliance on the report, (s)he should advise the client to make appropriate disclosures to persons who are known to be relying or who are likely to rely on the financial statements and the related report.

Answer (B) is incorrect because, although requesting that management issue revised statements would be appropriate, it should not be the first step taken by the auditor. Answer (C) is incorrect because management is responsible for the financial statements, not the auditor. Answer (D) is incorrect because the auditor may continue association with the client as long as appropriate measures are taken.

195. When a contingency is resolved immediately subsequent to the issuance of a report that included a paragraph emphasizing the contingency, the auditor should

A. Insist that the client issue revised financial statements.

B. Inform the audit committee that the report cannot be relied upon.

C. Take no action regarding the event.

D. Inform the appropriate authorities that the report cannot be relied upon.

The correct answer is (C). *(CPA, adapted)*

REQUIRED: The proper auditor action for resolutions of contingencies after the issuance of the audit report.

DISCUSSION: The auditor is under no obligation to make any further or continuing inquiry or perform any other auditing procedures with respect to the audited financial statements covered by the report, unless new information that may affect the report comes to his/her attention. The resolution of a contingency is not deemed to be new information for this purpose (AU 561).

Answers (A), (B), and (D) are incorrect because the auditor has no obligation with regard to the resolution of contingencies after the report has been issued.

196. When the effect of subsequently discovered facts that existed at the date of the auditor's report can be promptly determined, the client should issue, to those relying on the statements and related auditor's report,

A. Revised statements with the revision described in a footnote to the statements. The original audit report should accompany the revised statements.

B. Revised statements with the revision described in a footnote to the statements. No auditor's report should accompany the statements.

C. A narrative explanation of the effect of the subsequent discovery of facts existing at the date of the report.

D. Revised statements and a revised audit report with the revision described in a footnote to the statements and referred to in the revised report.

The correct answer is (D). *(Publisher)*

REQUIRED: The client action when the effects of subsequently discovered facts existing at the date of the audit report can be readily determined.

DISCUSSION: AU 561 states, "If the effect on the financial statements or auditor's report of the subsequently discovered information can promptly be determined, disclosure should consist of issuing, as soon as practicable, revised financial statements and auditor's report. The reasons for the revision usually should be described in a note to the financial statements and referred to in the auditor's report."

Answers (A) and (B) are incorrect because the auditor's report, appropriately modified, should be included with the revised financial statements. Answer (C) is incorrect because the client will normally include the reason for the change in a footnote to the revised financial statements.

197. The auditor learned of the following situations after issuing the audit report on February 6. Each is important to users of the financial statements. For which one does the auditor have responsibility for disclosure of the newly discovered facts?

A. A major lawsuit against the company, which was the basis for a modified report, was settled on unfavorable terms on March 1.

B. The client undertook merger negotiations on March 16, and concluded a merger agreement on April 1.

C. On February 16, a fire destroyed the principal manufacturing plant.

D. A conflict of interest involving credit officers and a principal company supplier was discovered on March 3.

The correct answer is (D). *(CPA, adapted)*

REQUIRED: The situation for which the auditor has a responsibility for disclosure of newly discovered facts.

DISCUSSION: The auditor has a responsibility after the issuance of the report for events that come to his/her attention for which (s)he would have extended procedures or modified the report. A conflict of interest situation would have been examined by the auditor had (s)he known about it during the audit process. Consequently, the auditor has a responsibility to determine the nature of the event and whether it might affect the fairness of the financial statements and the propriety of the report (AU 561).

Answer (A) is incorrect because the auditor has no responsibility to update the report for resolutions of contingencies that were properly disclosed. Answers (B) and (C) are incorrect because the auditor need not apply any other audit procedures or update the report for occurrences after the subsequent events period.

198. An auditor has found that the notes to the financial statements do not mention that, 15 days after the balance sheet date, the company issued a substantial amount of debentures. According to the company's attorney, the debenture agreement restricts the payment of future cash dividends. The client has declined to include the matter of the debentures in the notes because the issuance occurred after the balance sheet date. The auditor should

A. Add the note to the financial statements.

B. Provide the missing information in the report and express an adverse opinion.

C. Provide the missing information in the report and express a qualified opinion.

D. Provide the missing information in the report and disclaim an opinion.

The correct answer is (C). *(Publisher)*

REQUIRED: The proper action by an auditor when the client refuses to disclose a material subsequent event.

DISCUSSION: A subsequent event not providing evidence as to conditions existing at the balance sheet date does not result in adjustment of the statements. However, it may require disclosure to keep the statements from being misleading. AU 560 cites the sale of a bond issue as an example of a subsequent event requiring disclosure but not adjustment. When such an event occurs between the report date and the issue date, it should be disclosed in a footnote or the auditor should modify the opinion (AU 530).

Answer (A) is incorrect because the auditor has no authority to add a footnote to the financial statements. All assertions therein are the representations of management. Answers (B) and (D) are incorrect because the auditor should usually express a qualified opinion if the client refuses to make a necessary disclosure about subsequent events. However, an adverse opinion may be justified in some cases.

199. Soon after Boyd's audit report was issued, Boyd learned of certain related party transactions that occurred during the year under audit. These transactions were not disclosed in the notes to the financial statements. Boyd should

A. Plan to audit the transactions during the next engagement.

B. Recall all copies of the audited financial statements.

C. Determine whether the lack of disclosure would affect the auditor's report.

D. Ask the client to disclose the transactions in subsequent interim statements.

The correct answer is (C). *(CPA, adapted)*

REQUIRED: The step the auditor should take when (s)he becomes aware of previously unknown information.

DISCUSSION: An auditor may become aware of information related to the financial statements previously reported on that was not known at the date of the report. If the nature and source of the information are such that (s)he would have investigated it had it been discovered during the audit, the auditor should, as soon as practicable, determine whether the information is reliable and whether the facts existed at the date of the report. If these criteria are met, the auditor must take appropriate action if the report would have been affected and if (s)he believes persons who are currently relying or likely to rely on the statements would consider the information important (AU 561).

Answer (A) is incorrect because the auditor must take more immediate action if the lack of disclosure affects the report. Answer (B) is incorrect because recall of the audited financial statements is not feasible. Answer (D) is incorrect because issuance of revised statements and notice to appropriate parties may be necessary, but only if the auditor has determined that the original statements would be affected by the lack of disclosure.

200. Bill Blake, CPA, as a result of newly discovered facts, has concluded that action should be taken to prevent future reliance on the report. He should

A. Advise the client to make appropriate disclosure of the facts to persons who are known to be currently relying on the financial statements.

B. Recall the financial statements.

C. Make appropriate disclosure of the correction in the statements of a subsequent period.

D. Issue a disclaimer of opinion that should usually be followed by revised statements and a qualified opinion.

The correct answer is (A). *(Publisher)*

REQUIRED: The proper action to prevent future reliance on the auditor's report.

DISCUSSION: If the auditor has concluded that the report should no longer be relied upon, (s)he should advise the client to make appropriate disclosure of the newly discovered facts. When the client undertakes to make such disclosures, the method used and the disclosure made will depend on the circumstances. If the effect on the financial statements or auditor's report can promptly be determined, however, disclosure should consist of issuing, as soon as practicable, revised financial statements and a revised auditor's report (AU 561).

Answer (B) is incorrect because the client should issue appropriate revised financial statements but need not recall the original statements. Answer (C) is incorrect because the client should make appropriate disclosures to third parties relying upon the financial statements in revised statements for the current period. Answer (D) is incorrect because a disclaimer of opinion should not be issued prior to issuing the appropriate report with the revised financial statements.

201. What is the first step the auditor should take when a client refuses to disclose the effects of newly discovered facts existing at the date of the auditor's report, assuming the effects are material and persons are still relying on the statements and related audit report?

A. Notification to each member of the board of directors of the refusal.

B. Notification of regulatory agencies having jurisdiction over the client that the audit report should no longer be relied on.

C. Notification to the client that the audit report is not to be associated with the financial statements.

D. Resignation as auditor of the client.

The correct answer is (A). *(Publisher)*

REQUIRED: The first step the auditor should take when a client has refused to disclose newly discovered facts.

DISCUSSION: If the client refuses to make required disclosures, the auditor should notify each member of the board of directors of such refusal and of his/her intent, in the absence of disclosure by the client, to take the steps outlined in AU 561 to prevent future reliance on the report. The steps that can appropriately be taken will depend upon (1) the degree of certainty of the auditor's knowledge that persons are currently relying or will rely on the financial statements and will attach importance to the information and (2) the auditor's ability as a practical matter to communicate with them.

Answers (B), (C), and (D) are incorrect because, although appropriate, notification of regulatory agencies, notification to the client that the audit report is not to be associated with the financial statements, and resignation as auditor are not the first steps that should be taken when the client refuses to cooperate with the disclosure process.

202. An auditor completed field work for a client on February 15 and issued a report on March 10. On April 8 the client suffered the loss of a significant portion of its plant facilities by fire. The client requested additional copies of the previously issued report on May 5. Assuming no additional audit work has been or will be performed, the auditor should

A. Disregard the casualty and reissue the original report with no change in date.

B. Have the client disclose the event in a separate note to the statements identified as "Event (Unaudited) Subsequent to the Date of the Report of the Independent Auditor."

C. Use dual dating.

D. Choose between (B) or (C).

The correct answer is (B). *(Publisher)*

REQUIRED: The treatment in a reissued report of a material event that occurred after the original report date.

DISCUSSION: A major casualty occurring after the date of the original report requires disclosure in the financial statements covered by the reissued report. The reissuance of a report for purposes of AU 530 includes furnishing additional copies of a previously issued report. If the auditor performs procedures with respect to the casualty, (s)he may use dual dating. If no audit work is performed relative to this event, it should be marked unaudited in a footnote to the financial statements captioned as described.

Answer (A) is incorrect because the auditor cannot disregard the casualty. It must be disclosed in the financial statements. Answers (C) and (D) are incorrect because dual dating is inappropriate when the subsequent event is unaudited.

203. Under which of the following circumstances may audited financial statements contain a note disclosing an event occurring after the balance sheet date that is labeled unaudited?

A. When the subsequent event requires adjustment of the financial statements.

B. When the event occurs after completion of field work and before issuance of the auditor's report.

C. When audit procedures with respect to the event were not performed by the auditor.

D. When the event occurs between the date of the auditor's original report and the date of the reissuance of the report.

The correct answer is (D). *(CPA, adapted)*

REQUIRED: The basis for including a note disclosing an unaudited event.

DISCUSSION: When an event of the type requiring only disclosure occurs between the date of the independent auditor's original report and the date of the reissuance of such a report, the event may be disclosed in a separate note to the financial statements captioned as follows: "Event (Unaudited) Subsequent to the Date of the Report of the Independent Auditor" (AU 530).

Answer (A) is incorrect because the note may pertain only to an event that requires disclosure but not adjustment. Answer (B) is incorrect because the auditor's report must cover a disclosable event occurring prior to the issuance of the report. Answer (C) is incorrect because a note disclosing an unaudited event may refer only to an event occurring after the report date that requires disclosure in, but not adjustment of, the statements. The note is not appropriate for any unaudited event occurring after the balance sheet date.

204. Karr has audited the financial statements of Lurch Corporation for the year ended December 31, 1997. Although Karr's field work was completed on February 17, 1998, Karr's report was dated February 28, 1998 and was received by the management of Lurch on March 5, 1998. On April 4, 1998, the management of Lurch asked that Karr approve inclusion of this report in its annual report to shareholders that will include unaudited financial statements for the first quarter ended March 31, 1998. Karr approved the inclusion. Under the circumstances, Karr is responsible for inquiring as to events occurring through

A. February 17, 1998.

B. February 28, 1998.

C. March 31, 1998.

D. April 4, 1998.

The correct answer is (B). *(CPA, adapted)*

REQUIRED: The date through which the auditor assumes responsibility.

DISCUSSION: Normally, the date of the completion of field work is the date of the report, and the auditor has no responsibility to make any inquiry or carry out any procedures for the period after the date of the report (but see AU 711 regarding SEC filings). An independent auditor may also reissue the report. Use of the original report date in the reissued report removes any implication that records, transactions, or events after that date have been audited or reviewed. The auditor has no responsibility in such cases to make further investigation or inquiry as to events after the original report date (AU 530).

Answer (A) is incorrect because, in this situation, the auditor assumed responsibility up to 2/28/98, not the date of completion of field work, 2/17/98. Answers (C) and (D) are incorrect because the auditor assumed responsibility for events only up to the date of the report.

205. A registration statement filed with the Securities and Exchange Commission may contain the reports of two or more independent auditors on their audits of the financial statements for different periods. What responsibility does the auditor who has not audited the most recent financial statements have relative to events occurring after the date of his/her report that may affect the financial statements on which (s)he reported?

A. The auditor has responsibility for events up to the subsequent fiscal year-end.

B. The auditor has responsibility for events up to the date of the subsequent audit report.

C. The auditor has responsibility for events up to the effective date of the registration statement.

D. The auditor has no responsibility beyond the date of the original report.

The correct answer is (C). *(CPA, adapted)*

REQUIRED: The responsibility of the predecessor auditor for comparative statements filed with the SEC.

DISCUSSION: An auditor of financial statements for a prior period but not for the most recent audited period has a responsibility for events occurring after the date of the prior period financial statements and up to the effective date of the registration statement. The predecessor auditor should (1) read pertinent portions of the prospectus and of the registration statement and (2) obtain a representation letter from the successor auditor regarding whether the audit revealed any matters that might have a material effect on the financial statements reported on by the predecessor. The predecessor auditor should make inquiries and perform other procedures regarding the appropriateness of any adjustment or disclosure affecting the prior-period statements (AU 711).

Answers (A), (B), and (D) are incorrect because, although the auditor ordinarily has no responsibility beyond the date of the original report, the filing of a registration statement extends the responsibility to the effective date of the registration statement.

206. A continuing auditor should update the report on prior financial statements by issuing a report modified for the

A. Resolution of an uncertainty related to and discovered in the current period.

B. Removal in the current period of doubt about the entity's ability to continue as a going concern.

C. Determination in the current period that a substantial doubt exists about the entity's ability to continue as a going concern for a reasonable time.

D. Inconsistency involved in restating prior-period statements to correct an error discovered in the prior years' inventory count.

The correct answer is (B). *(Publisher)*

REQUIRED: The reason a continuing auditor should update the report on prior statements.

DISCUSSION: A continuing auditor should update the report on prior-period statements presented comparatively with those of the current period (AU 508). If the auditor determines that, in the current period, a substantial doubt has been removed about the reporting entity's ability to continue as a going concern for a reasonable period, the related explanatory paragraph in the report on the prior-period statements need not be repeated (AU 341).

Answer (A) is incorrect because resolution of an uncertainty discovered in the current period does not affect prior-period statements. Answer (C) is incorrect because determination that a going concern issue exists in the current period typically does not affect prior-period statements. Answer (D) is incorrect because restatement based on correction of an error not involving an accounting principle does not require recognition as to consistency (AU 420).

<u>7.12 Other Auditors</u> (See also Module 7.9 relative to predecessor auditors.)

207. When two or more auditing firms participate in an audit, one firm should be the principal auditor. If the principal auditor makes reference to another auditor in an audit that would otherwise result in an unqualified opinion, the type of audit report issued should be

A. An unqualified opinion.

B. A qualified opinion.

C. An adverse opinion.

D. A disclaimer of opinion.

The correct answer is (A). *(CMA, adapted)*

REQUIRED: The audit opinion expressed when the principal auditor refers to the work of another auditor.

DISCUSSION: The principal auditor must decide whether to accept responsibility for the work of the other CPAs. If the principal auditor does not accept responsibility for their work, the division of responsibility should be stated in the report. However, this division of responsibility does not influence the nature of the opinion expressed.

Answers (B), (C), and (D) are incorrect because, if the statements are fairly presented, in all material respects, in accordance with GAAP, an unqualified opinion is indicated.

208. Hal Halsey is auditing the consolidated financial statements of Rex, Inc., a publicly held corporation. Lincoln is the auditor who has audited and reported on the financial statements of a wholly owned subsidiary of Rex, Inc. Halsey's first concern with respect to the Rex financial statements is to decide whether he

A. May serve as the principal auditor and report as such on the consolidated financial statements of Rex, Inc.

B. May refer to the work of Lincoln in his report on the consolidated financial statements.

C. Should review the working papers of Lincoln with respect to the audit of the subsidiary's financial statements.

D. Should resign from the engagement because an unqualified opinion cannot be expressed on the consolidated financial statements.

The correct answer is (A). *(CPA, adapted)*

REQUIRED: The first concern of an auditor when a subsidiary has been audited by another auditor.

DISCUSSION: The auditor must decide whether his/her participation is sufficient to justify serving as the principal auditor and reporting as such on the financial statements. Thus, the auditor must consider the extent of his/her knowledge of the overall financial statements, the importance of the components (s)he audited in relation to the enterprise as a whole, and the materiality of the portion audited by the other auditor (AU 543).

Answer (B) is incorrect because the decision whether to refer to the other auditor is made only after the decision to serve as the principal auditor. Answer (C) is incorrect because the decision to review the working papers of the other auditor is made after the decision to serve as principal auditor. It is a procedure that may be performed when deciding whether to refer to the other auditor's work. Answer (D) is incorrect because performance of part of the audit by another auditor does not preclude expressing an unqualified opinion.

209. When a principal auditor decides to refer to another auditor's audit, the principal auditor's report should always indicate clearly, in the introductory, scope, and opinion paragraphs, the

A. Magnitude of the portion of the financial statements examined by the other auditor.

B. Disclaimer of responsibility concerning the portion of the financial statements examined by the other auditor.

C. Name of the other auditor.

D. Division of responsibility.

The correct answer is (D). *(CPA, adapted)*

REQUIRED: The disclosure requirement when reference to another auditor is made.

DISCUSSION: The division of responsibility between the portion of the financial statements covered by the principal auditor's own audit and that covered by the other auditor should be clearly defined in the introductory, scope, and opinion paragraphs (AU 543).

Answer (A) is incorrect because the portion of the financial statements audited by the other auditor should be disclosed by stating the dollar amounts of total assets, total revenues, or other appropriate criteria in the introductory paragraph. Answer (B) is incorrect because a division of responsibility, not a disclaimer, is indicated. Answer (C) is incorrect because naming the other auditor is not required; (s)he may be named only if (s)he gives express permission and if his/her report is presented together with that of the principal auditor.

210. If the principal auditor decides to refer in the report to the audit made by another auditor,

A. The principal auditor assumes responsibility for the report of the other auditor.

B. The other auditor is relieved of responsibility for his/her report but not his/her work.

C. The other auditor is responsible for both his/her report and his/her work.

D. The other auditor is relieved of responsibility for his/her work but not his/her report.

The correct answer is (C). *(Publisher)*

REQUIRED: The effect of referring to another auditor's audit.

DISCUSSION: Whether or not the principal auditor refers in the report to the audit made by the other auditor, the other auditor remains responsible for the performance of his/her work and for his/her report (AU 543).

Answer (A) is incorrect because the principal auditor assumes responsibility for the other auditor's work insofar as it relates to the principal auditor's expression of an opinion on the financial statements taken as a whole only when (s)he does not refer to the work of the other auditor. Answers (B) and (D) are incorrect because the other auditor is not relieved of the responsibility for his/her work or report.

211. Pell, CPA decides to serve as principal auditor in the audit of the financial statements of Tech Consolidated, Inc. Smith, CPA audits one of Tech's subsidiaries. In which situation(s) should Pell refer to Smith's audit?

I. Pell reviews Smith's working papers and assumes responsibility for Smith's work but expresses a qualified opinion on Tech's financial statements.

II. Pell is unable to review Smith's working papers; however, Pell's inquiries indicate that Smith has an excellent reputation for professional competence and integrity.

A. I only.

B. II only.

C. Both I and II.

D. Neither I nor II.

The correct answer is (B). *(CPA, adapted)*

REQUIRED: The situation in which a principal auditor should refer to another auditor's audit.

DISCUSSION: Once the principal auditor becomes satisfied as to the independence and professional reputation of the other auditor, (s)he may decide to refer to the other auditor's audit because it may be impracticable for the principal auditor to review the other auditor's work or to use other procedures that (s)he deems necessary to obtain satisfaction as to the other auditor's audit. Such a reference indicates a division of responsibility between the auditors. The reference to the other auditor does not prohibit an unqualified opinion (AU 543).

Answers (A) and (C) are incorrect because, if the principal auditor accepts responsibility for the other auditor's audit, (s)he should not state in the report that another auditor performed part of the audit. Such a reference might lead to misinterpretation of the degree of responsibility assumed. The type of opinion expressed is not relevant to the decision to make reference. Answer (D) is incorrect because the principal auditor may refer to the other auditor's audit when (s)he wishes to divide responsibility.

212. An auditor's report contains the following: "We did not audit the financial statements of JK Company, a wholly owned subsidiary, which statements reflect total assets and revenues constituting 17% and 19%, respectively, of the related consolidated totals. Those statements were audited by other auditors whose report has been furnished to us, and our opinion, insofar as it relates to the amounts included for JK Company, is based solely on the report of the other auditors." These sentences

A. Disclaim an opinion.

B. Qualify the opinion.

C. Divide responsibility.

D. Are an improper form of reporting.

The correct answer is (C). *(CPA, adapted)*

REQUIRED: The effect of the given sentences in an auditor's report.

DISCUSSION: The given sentences are part of an introductory paragraph provided as an example in AU 543 of appropriately reporting the decision to refer to the work of another auditor. They meet the requirement that such reference indicate clearly the division of responsibility.

Answer (A) is incorrect because the last sentence refers to the expression of an opinion. Answer (B) is incorrect because the language cited does not preclude an unqualified or an adverse opinion. Answer (D) is incorrect because the wording is standard.

213. Regarding the magnitude of financial statements audited by the other auditor relative to the overall statements upon which the principal auditor expresses an opinion,

A. The dollar amounts or percentages of total assets, total revenues, or other appropriate criteria should be disclosed in the principal auditor's report.

B. The dollar amounts and percentages of at least total revenues and total assets must be disclosed in the principal auditor's report.

C. No mention is necessary unless approximately 50% or more of the assets or revenues are audited by the other auditor. Disclosure, if necessary, should be according to the appropriate criteria and reveal the portion of the financial statements audited by the other auditor.

D. No mention is necessary unless the audit report of the other auditor is not presented. Disclosure, if necessary, should be according to the appropriate criteria and reveal the portion of the financial statements audited by the other auditor.

The correct answer is (A). *(Publisher)*

REQUIRED: The true statement about disclosure of the portion of the statements audited by another auditor.

DISCUSSION: When the principal auditor decides to refer to the work of another auditor, the report should indicate clearly, in the introductory, scope, and opinion paragraphs, the division of responsibility between that portion of the statements covered by his/her audit and that covered by the other auditor. The introductory paragraph of the report should disclose the magnitude of the portion audited by the other auditor by stating the dollar amounts or the percentages. A representation in the scope paragraph is also made that states, "We believe that our audits and the report of other auditors provide a reasonable basis for our opinion." The opinion paragraph states, "In our opinion, based on our audits, and the report of other auditors" (AU 508).

Answer (B) is incorrect because the magnitude of the other auditor's work may be stated either in dollar amounts or in percentages of total assets, total revenues, or other appropriate criteria. Answers (C) and (D) are incorrect because a principal auditor who refers to the audit of another auditor must disclose the portion of the statements audited by the other auditor.

214. An auditor may issue the standard audit report when the

A. Auditor refers to the findings of a specialist.

B. Financial statements are derived and condensed from complete audited financial statements that are filed with a regulatory agency.

C. Financial statements are prepared on the cash receipts and disbursements basis of accounting.

D. Principal auditor assumes responsibility for the work of another auditor.

The correct answer is (D). *(CPA, adapted)*

REQUIRED: The situation in which an auditor may issue the standard audit report.

DISCUSSION: If the principal auditor can become satisfied regarding the independence, professional reputation, and the audit performed by the other auditor, (s)he may be able to express an opinion on the financial statements taken as a whole without referring to the audit of the other auditor. If (s)he assumes responsibility for the work of the other auditor, the report should not state that part of the audit was performed by another auditor. This reference could be misleading about the degree of responsibility assumed. In these circumstances, therefore, a standard report is appropriate (AU 543).

Answer (A) is incorrect because the auditor does not refer to a specialist unless (s)he departs from an unqualified opinion or adds an explanatory paragraph (AU 336). Answer (B) is incorrect because the report on condensed statements indicates that the auditor has audited and expressed an opinion on the complete statements, the date of that report, the type of opinion expressed therein, and "whether, in the auditor's opinion, the information set forth in the condensed financial statements is fairly stated in all material respects in relation to the complete financial statements from which it has been derived" (AU 552, *Reporting on Condensed Financial Statements and Selected Financial Data*). Answer (C) is incorrect because a special report may be appropriate.

215. In which of the following situations would a principal auditor least likely make reference to another auditor who audited a subsidiary of the entity?

A. The other auditor was retained by the principal auditor and the work was performed under the principal auditor's guidance and control.

B. The principal auditor finds it impracticable to review the other auditor's work or otherwise be satisfied as to the other auditor's work.

C. The financial statements audited by the other auditor are material to the consolidated financial statements covered by the principal auditor's opinion.

D. The principal auditor is unable to be satisfied as to the independence and professional reputation of the other auditor.

The correct answer is (A). *(CPA, adapted)*

REQUIRED: The situation in which a principal auditor is least likely to refer to another auditor.

DISCUSSION: The principal auditor normally does not refer to another auditor when the other auditor is an associate or correspondent firm whose work is acceptable to the principal auditor or when the other auditor was retained by the principal auditor and the work was performed under the principal auditor's guidance and control (AU 543).

Answer (B) is incorrect because, if the principal finds it impracticable to review the work of the other auditor, it is likely that the other auditor will be mentioned in the principal auditor's report. Answer (C) is incorrect because the more material the items audited by the other auditor, the more likely reference will be made in the principal auditor's report. Answer (D) is incorrect because, when the auditor cannot become satisfied as to the independence and professional reputation of the other auditor, the opinion should be qualified or an opinion should be disclaimed with respect to the financial statements taken as a whole.

216. Investor Co. has a material investment in Investee Co. that was accounted for by the equity method. Moore & Marr, CPAs, audit Investor but not Investee. Moore & Marr may express an unqualified opinion on Investor's financial statements if it

A. Reviews the working papers of Investee's auditor.

B. Obtains Investee's audited financial statements and make inquiries concerning the professional reputation and independence of Investee's auditor.

C. Obtains only Investee's audited financial statements.

D. Obtains only Investee's unaudited financial statements.

The correct answer is (B). *(Publisher)*

REQUIRED: The requirement for the principal auditor to express an unqualified opinion when (s)he has not audited an equity investee.

DISCUSSION: With respect to investments accounted for under the equity method, the auditor who uses another auditor's report to report on the client's equity and share of earnings or losses is in the position of a principal auditor. But whether or not the principal auditor wishes to refer to the work of the other auditor, (s)he must make inquiries as to the professional reputation and independence of the other auditor (AU 543). Furthermore, the principal auditor may not express an unqualified opinion when an investment is material unless (s)he has acquired sufficient competent evidence about assertions relevant to the investment. The inability to obtain audited statements of the investee is a common scope limitation that would preclude an unqualified opinion (AU 508).

Answer (A) is incorrect because the principal auditor typically reviews the other auditor's working papers only if (s)he decides not to refer to the audit performed by the other auditor. The decision to refer is likely in this case because the investment is material, and Investor's auditor has not audited the investee. Answers (C) and (D) are incorrect because the principal auditor must inquire as to the reputation and professional standing of the other auditor as well as obtain audited statements.

217. Thomas, CPA, has audited the consolidated financial statements of Kass Corporation. Jones, CPA, has audited the financial statements of its sole subsidiary, which is material in relation to the total audited by Thomas. It would be appropriate for Thomas to serve as the principal auditor, but it is impracticable for Thomas to review the work of Jones. Assuming an unqualified opinion is expressed by Jones, one would expect Thomas to

A. Refuse to express an opinion on the consolidated financial statements.

B. Express an unqualified opinion on the consolidated financial statements and not refer to the work of Jones.

C. Express an unqualified opinion on the consolidated financial statements and refer to the work of Jones.

D. Express a qualified opinion on the consolidated financial statements as a result of referring to the work of Jones.

The correct answer is (C). *(CPA, adapted)*

REQUIRED: The correct action by the principal auditor when (s)he cannot review the work of another auditor.

DISCUSSION: Once the principal auditor is able to become satisfied as to the independence and professional reputation of the other auditor, (s)he may decide to refer to the other auditor's audit because it may be impracticable for the principal auditor to review the other auditor's work or to use other procedures that (s)he deems necessary to obtain satisfaction as to the other auditor's audit. Such a reference indicates a division of responsibility between the auditors. The reference to the other auditor does not prohibit an unqualified opinion (AU 543).

Answer (A) is incorrect because the principal auditor should not refuse to express an opinion; part of an audit may be made by other independent auditors. Answer (B) is incorrect because the principal auditor must refer to the other auditor unless (s)he takes steps (s)he deems appropriate to become satisfied as to the other auditor's audit. Answer (D) is incorrect because the reference to another auditor is not a qualification.

218. When the report of a principal auditor refers to the audit by another auditor, the other auditor may be named if express permission to do so is given and if the

A. Report of the principal auditor names the other auditor in both the introductory and opinion paragraphs.

B. Principal auditor accepts responsibility for the work of the other auditor.

C. Report of the other auditor is presented together with the report of the principal auditor.

D. Other auditor is not an associate or correspondent firm whose work is done at the request of the principal auditor.

The correct answer is (C). *(CPA, adapted)*

REQUIRED: The circumstances in which a principal auditor may name the other auditor.

DISCUSSION: The other auditor may be named but only with his/her express permission and provided his/her report is presented together with that of the principal auditor (AU 543).

Answer (A) is incorrect because the principal auditor may divide responsibility but should refer to other auditors in the report instead of naming them unless certain conditions are met. Answer (B) is incorrect because, if the principal auditor accepts responsibility for the work of the other auditor, no mention should be made of the other auditor. Answer (D) is incorrect because the other auditor named by the principal auditor may be an associate or a correspondent firm. However, the principal auditor is more likely not to refer to the other auditor in such a case.

219. The principal auditor of consolidated financial statements has become satisfied about the independence and professional reputation of an auditor who has audited a subsidiary included in the consolidated group. The principal auditor has also become satisfied about the audit performed by the other auditor. The report of the other auditor expressed a qualified opinion, but the principal auditor believes the qualification to be immaterial in regard to the consolidated financial statements. Accordingly, the principal auditor

A. May express an unqualified opinion but must include a separate paragraph describing the other auditor's report.

B. Must express a qualified opinion but need not refer to the audit of the other auditor.

C. Must express a qualified opinion and refer to the audit of the other auditor.

D. Need not refer to the audit of the other auditor.

The correct answer is (D). *(Publisher)*

REQUIRED: The recognition given by the principal auditor to an immaterial qualification by another auditor.

DISCUSSION: The principal auditor need not refer to the audit of the other auditor if (s)he is willing to accept responsibility for the other auditor's work. Because the qualification stated by the other auditor is immaterial to the consolidated financial statements, it need not cause a qualification of the opinion.

Answers (A), (B), and (C) are incorrect because, given that the other auditor's qualification is not material to the consolidated statements, the principal auditor need not refer to the other auditor's audit or qualify the opinion.

220. AU 543 gives guidance to a principal auditor on making inquiries of the other auditor. That pronouncement also states that the other auditor remains responsible for the performance of his/her work and report. To fulfill that responsibility, the other auditor

A. May make inquiries of the principal auditor.

B. Must make inquiries of the principal auditor.

C. May not make inquiries of the principal auditor.

D. May make inquiries but only if the principal auditor has initiated the communication.

The correct answer is (A). *(Publisher)*

REQUIRED: The correct statement about inquiries made by other auditors of the principal auditor.

DISCUSSION: Before issuing the report, the other auditor should consider whether (s)he should inquire of the principal auditor as to matters that may be significant to his/her audit. The other auditor's consideration of whether to make the inquiry may be based on various factors. One such factor might be the existence of unusual or complex transactions or relationships between the component (s)he is auditing and the component the principal auditor is auditing. Another factor to be considered is the knowledge that, in the past, matters relating to his/her audit have arisen that were known to the principal auditor but not to him/her (AU 543).

Answers (B), (C), and (D) are incorrect because inquiries by other auditors of principal auditors are allowed but not required.

CHAPTER EIGHT
SPECIAL REPORTS AND OTHER REPORTING ISSUES

This chapter includes questions on miscellaneous reporting issues. These include special reports, compilations, reviews, reports on internal control, letters to underwriters, and governmental auditing.

8.1 Definition and Purpose of Special Reports

1. Auditors may issue a special report for all of the following except an audit of financial presentations

A. That are prepared on a basis of accounting that the entity uses to file its tax return.

B. Of specified elements or accounts.

C. Of an organization that has limited the scope of the audit.

D. To comply with contractual agreements.

The correct answer is (C). *(Publisher)*

REQUIRED: The report not considered a special report.

DISCUSSION: Special reports are issued in connection with (1) statements prepared in accordance with a comprehensive basis of accounting other than GAAP; (2) specified elements, accounts, or items of a statement; (3) compliance with aspects of contractual agreements or regulatory requirements related to audited statements; (4) financial presentations to comply with contractual agreements or regulatory provisions; and (5) financial information presented in prescribed forms that require a prescribed form of auditor's report (AU 623, *Special Reports*). A limitation imposed by the client on the scope of the audit is therefore not a proper basis for issuing a special report.

Answer (A) is incorrect because the tax basis is a comprehensive basis other than GAAP. Answer (B) is incorrect because special reports include those on specified elements, accounts, or items. Answer (D) is incorrect because special reports include those on financial presentations to comply with contractual agreements.

2. For reporting purposes, the independent auditor should consider each of the following types of financial presentation to be a financial statement, except the statement of

A. Changes in owners' equity.

B. Operations by product lines.

C. Changes in the elements of working capital.

D. Cash receipts and disbursements.

The correct answer is (C). *(CPA, adapted)*

REQUIRED: The presentation not a financial statement.

DISCUSSION: AU 623 defines a financial statement as a "presentation of financial data, including accompanying notes, derived from accounting records and intended to communicate an entity's economic resources or obligations at a moment in time or the changes therein for a period of time in accordance with a comprehensive basis of accounting." AU 623 lists ten types of financial statements but excludes the statement of changes in working capital.

Answers (A), (B), and (D) are incorrect because statements of changes in owners' equity, operations by product lines, and cash receipts and disbursements are financial statements.

3. An auditor's report would be designated a special report when it is issued in connection with

A. Interim financial information of a publicly held company that is subject to a limited review.

B. Compliance with aspects of regulatory requirements related to audited financial statements.

C. Application of accounting principles to specified transactions.

D. Limited use prospective financial statements such as financial projection.

The correct answer is (B). *(CPA, adapted)*

REQUIRED: The service resulting in a special report.

DISCUSSION: Entities may be required by contractual agreements, such as bond indentures, or by regulatory agencies to furnish compliance reports by independent auditors. Reports based upon compliance with aspects of contractual agreements or regulatory provisions should be provided in conjunction with an ordinary audit of financial statements. The report envisioned provides negative assurance that may be given in the report on the financial statements or in a separate report. But this assurance should not extend to any covenants relating to matters that have not been subjected to audit procedures (AU 623).

Answer (A) is incorrect because AU 722, *Interim Financial Information*, applies to reviews of interim financial information. Answer (C) is incorrect because a report on the application of accounting principles is governed by AU 625, *Reports on the Application of Accounting Principles*. Answer (D) is incorrect because AT 200, *Financial Forecasts and Projections*, applies to projections.

4. Auditors' reports issued in connection with which of the following are not considered to be special reports?

A. Specified elements, accounts, or items of a financial statement.

B. Compliance with aspects of contractual agreements related to audited financial statements.

C. Financial statements prepared in conformity with the price-level basis of accounting.

D. Compiled financial statements prepared in accordance with appraised liquidation values.

The correct answer is (D). *(CPA, adapted)*

REQUIRED: The improper basis for a special report.

DISCUSSION: Special reports relate to (1) statements prepared in accordance with a comprehensive basis of accounting other than GAAP; (2) specified elements, accounts, or items of a statement; (3) compliance with aspects of contractual agreements or regulatory requirements related to audited statements; (4) financial presentations to comply with contractual agreements or regulatory provisions; and (5) financial information presented in prescribed forms (AU 623). Appraised liquidation values are not usually considered a comprehensive basis of accounting other than GAAP.

Answers (A), (B), and (C) are incorrect because a special report may be issued on specified elements, accounts, or items of a financial statement, compliance with contractual agreements, or price-level basis financial statements.

5. An auditor should provide a list of procedures performed and related findings but should not provide an opinion or negative assurance about fair presentation when (s)he is requested to report on the

A. Compilation of prospective financial statements.

B. Compliance with the provisions of the Foreign Corrupt Practices Act.

C. Results of applying agreed-upon procedures to an account within unaudited financial statements.

D. Audit of historical financial statements.

The correct answer is (C). *(CPA, adapted)*

REQUIRED: The report in which a list of procedures and related findings is provided but an opinion or negative assurance is not.

DISCUSSION: An engagement to perform specific agreed-upon procedures on the specific subject matter of specified elements, accounts, or items of a financial statement does not entail performance of an audit. The auditor does not express an opinion or provide negative assurance about fair presentation of the specified elements, accounts, or items. For example, the auditor should not state "nothing came to my attention that caused me to believe that the specified element, account, or item is not fairly stated in accordance with GAAP." Moreover, the absence of an exception should also not be expressed in the form of negative assurance. Instead, the report should be in the form of procedures and findings.

Answer (A) is incorrect because a compilation provides no findings. Answer (B) is incorrect because an auditor should not provide findings about compliance with the FCPA. Such compliance requires a legal determination (AT 400, *Reporting on an Entity's Internal Control over Financial Reporting*). Answer (D) is incorrect because an audit is a form of examination. It is undertaken to afford a reasonable basis for a positive opinion (AT 100, *Attestation Standards*).

6. An auditor's report on financial statements prepared in accordance with a comprehensive basis of accounting other than GAAP should include all of the following except

A. Reference to the note to the financial statements that describes the basis of presentation.

B. A statement that the basis of presentation is a comprehensive basis of accounting other than GAAP.

C. An opinion as to whether the basis of accounting used is appropriate under the circumstances.

D. An opinion as to whether the financial statements are presented fairly, in all material respects, in conformity with the other comprehensive basis of accounting.

The correct answer is (C). *(CPA, adapted)*

REQUIRED: The item not in a report on statements prepared on a comprehensive basis other than GAAP.

DISCUSSION: In a report on such statements, the independent auditor should include a title with the word independent; a paragraph stating that the statements were audited, that the financial statements are the responsibility of management, and that the auditor is responsible for expressing an opinion thereon; a scope paragraph; a paragraph stating the basis of the presentation, referring to the footnote describing that basis, and stating that the basis is a comprehensive one other than GAAP; a paragraph expressing or disclaiming an opinion (an explanatory paragraph(s) may be needed); and, in some cases, a paragraph restricting distribution. The auditor should not express an opinion on the propriety of the basis of accounting used.

Answers (A), (B), and (D) are incorrect because the report should refer to the note describing the basis of accounting, state that this basis is not GAAP, and express an opinion.

7. Which of the generally accepted auditing standards of reporting normally applies to an auditor's special report on cash-basis statements?

	Conformity with GAAP	Consistency	Adequacy of Disclosure
A.	No	Yes	Yes
B.	Yes	Yes	Yes
C.	No	No	Yes
D.	No	No	No

The correct answer is (A). *(Publisher)*

REQUIRED: The GAAS applicable to special reports on cash-basis statements.

DISCUSSION: According to AU 623, an auditor should indicate in the report that the financial statements on which (s)he is reporting are prepared on a comprehensive basis of accounting other than GAAP. The cash basis is such a comprehensive basis. The first reporting standard, which is concerned with whether the financial statements are presented in accordance with GAAP, therefore does not apply (AU 150, *Generally Accepted Auditing Standards*). However, the second reporting standard (consistency), the third standard (disclosure), and the fourth (regarding the degree of responsibility taken) are applicable.

Answers (B), (C), and (D) are incorrect because the consistency and disclosure standards apply, but the standard related to conformity with GAAP does not.

8. When an auditor reports on financial statements prepared on an entity's income tax basis, the auditor's report should

A. Disclaim an opinion on whether the statements were examined in accordance with generally accepted auditing standards.

B. Not express an opinion on whether the statements are presented in conformity with the other comprehensive basis of accounting (OCBOA) used.

C. Include an explanation of how the results of operations differ from the cash receipts and disbursements basis of accounting.

D. State that the basis of presentation is a comprehensive basis of accounting other than GAAP.

The correct answer is (D). *(CPA, adapted)*

REQUIRED: The content of a report on financial statements prepared on the income tax basis.

DISCUSSION: A separate paragraph of the auditor's special report on financial statements prepared on a comprehensive basis of accounting other than GAAP, e.g., the income tax basis, should state the basis of the presentation, refer to a note to the statements explaining the basis chosen, and state that the basis of the presentation is a comprehensive basis other than GAAP. An OCBOA may be the tax basis, the cash basis, the requirements of a regulatory agency, or a definite set of criteria having substantial support and applied to all material financial statement items (AU 623).

Answer (A) is incorrect because the auditor applies GAAS in the engagement. Answer (B) is incorrect because the auditor expresses an opinion on whether the statements are presented in conformity with the OCBOA. Answer (C) is incorrect because a note in the financial statements should explain how the basis of accounting differs from GAAP, but the report need only refer to that note.

9. Delta Life Insurance Co. prepares its financial statements on an accounting basis insurance companies use pursuant to the rules of a state insurance commission. If Wall, CPA, Delta's auditor, discovers that the statements are not suitably titled, Wall should

A. Disclose any reservations in an explanatory paragraph and qualify the opinion.

B. Apply to the state insurance commission for an advisory opinion.

C. Issue a special statutory basis report that clearly disclaims any opinion.

D. Explain in the notes to the financial statements the terminology used.

The correct answer is (A). *(CPA, adapted)*

REQUIRED: The proper action when statements prepared on an OCBOA are not suitably titled.

DISCUSSION: Terms such as balance sheet, statement of income, or similar unmodified titles are ordinarily understood to apply to statements presented in conformity with GAAP. Consequently, the auditor of statements prepared under an OCBOA should consider whether the statements are suitably titled. If (s)he believes they are not, the auditor should disclose any reservations in an explanatory paragraph and qualify the opinion (AU 623).

Answer (B) is incorrect because AU 623 does not require the auditor to apply to the state insurance commission for an advisory opinion. Answer (C) is incorrect because the opinion should be qualified. Answer (D) is incorrect because the notes are the responsibility of management, not the auditor.

10. An auditor is reporting on cash-basis financial statements. These statements are best referred to in the opinion by which of the following descriptions?

A. "Financial position" and "results of operations arising from cash transactions."

B. "Assets and liabilities arising from cash transactions" and "revenue collected and expenses paid."

C. "Balance sheet" and "income statement resulting from cash transactions."

D. "Cash balance sheet" and "statement of cash flows."

The correct answer is (B). *(CPA, adapted)*

REQUIRED: The best description of cash-basis financial statements in an auditor's report.

DISCUSSION: Terms such as balance sheet, statement of financial position, statement of operations, income statement, statement of cash flows, and similar unmodified titles suggest that the statements were prepared in conformity with GAAP. According to AU 623, appropriate titles for comparable cash-basis statements are statement of assets and liabilities arising from cash transactions and statement of revenue collected and expenses paid.

Answers (A), (C), and (D) are incorrect because terms such as financial position, results of operations, balance sheet, income statement, and statement of cash flows imply that the statements were prepared in conformity with GAAP.

11. Which of the following statements is correct with respect to an auditor's report expressing an opinion on a specific item on a financial statement?

A. Materiality must be related to the specified item rather than to the financial statements taken as a whole.

B. Such a report can only be issued if the auditor is also engaged to audit the entire set of financial statements.

C. The attention devoted to the specified item is usually less than it would be if the financial statements as a whole were being audited.

D. The auditor who has expressed an adverse opinion on the financial statements as a whole can never express an opinion on a specified item in these financial statements.

The correct answer is (A). *(CPA, adapted)*

REQUIRED: The true statement about expressing an opinion on specified elements of financial statements.

DISCUSSION: In an engagement to express an opinion on one or more specified elements, accounts, or items of a financial statement, materiality must be measured in relation to each element, account, or item reported on rather than in relation to their aggregate or to the financial statements as a whole (AU 623).

Answer (B) is incorrect because this form of special report is not contingent upon a complete audit. Answer (C) is incorrect because the attention devoted to the specified item is usually greater (not less). Answer (D) is incorrect because, although piecemeal opinions are prohibited, the auditor is allowed to express an opinion on specific items after expressing an adverse opinion if the specified items do not constitute a major portion of the financial statements.

12. Entities may be required by contractual agreements, such as loan agreements, or by regulatory agencies to furnish compliance reports by independent auditors. For example, loan agreements usually impose on borrowers a variety of covenants involving matters such as payments into sinking funds, maintenance of current ratios, restrictions of dividend payments, and the use of proceeds of sales of property. In such a report,

A. The independent auditor normally expresses an opinion on the applicable covenants.

B. The assurance must be given in one or more paragraphs of the auditor's report accompanying the financial statements.

C. The assurance may be given only if the auditor has audited the financial statements.

D. If a separate report provides negative assurance, it should contain a paragraph stating that the financial statements were not audited in accordance with GAAS.

The correct answer is (C). *(Publisher)*

REQUIRED: The true statement about reports on compliance with aspects of contractual agreements.

DISCUSSION: Reports based upon compliance with aspects of contractual agreements or regulatory provisions should be provided in conjunction with an ordinary audit of financial statements. The report envisioned provides negative assurance that may be given in the report on the financial statements or in a separate report. But this assurance should not be given unless an audit of the statements has been made and should not extend to any covenants relating to matters that have not been audited.

Answer (A) is incorrect because negative assurance, not an opinion, is appropriate relative to covenants in such agreements. Answer (B) is incorrect because the auditor may issue a separate report or include a separate paragraph providing the assurance on compliance. Answer (D) is incorrect because, if a separate report is issued, it should indicate that the financial statements have been audited in accordance with GAAS, give the date of the report on the financial statements, and disclose any departure from the standard report on those statements.

13. Whenever a special report, filed on a printed form designed by authorities, calls upon the independent auditor to make an assertion that the auditor believes is not justified, the auditor should

A. Reword the form or attach a separate report.

B. Submit a standard report with explanations.

C. Submit the form with questionable items clearly omitted.

D. Withdraw from the engagement.

The correct answer is (A). *(CPA, adapted)*

REQUIRED: The auditor action when asked to make an unjustified assertion in a prescribed form.

DISCUSSION: Printed forms designed by the bodies with which they will be filed often prescribe the wording of the auditor's report. Many are unacceptable to auditors because they conflict with reporting standards. When a report form calls for an unjustified assertion, an auditor should reword the form or attach a separate report (AU 623).

Answer (B) is incorrect because a standard report is not appropriate for a special reporting situation. Answer (C) is incorrect because omission of questionable items does not meet the auditor's reporting responsibility; these items should be resolved. Answer (D) is incorrect because withdrawal from the engagement is an extreme measure unnecessary in most circumstances.

14. An auditor may express an opinion on an entity's accounts receivable balance even if the auditor has disclaimed an opinion on the financial statements taken as a whole provided the

A. Report on the accounts receivable discloses the reason for the disclaimer of opinion on the financial statements.

B. Distribution of the report on the accounts receivable is restricted to internal use only.

C. Auditor also reports on the current asset portion of the entity's balance sheet.

D. Report on the accounts receivable is presented separately from the disclaimer of opinion on the financial statements.

The correct answer is (D). *(CPA, adapted)*

REQUIRED: The condition for expressing an opinion on an account balance despite disclaiming an opinion on the financial statements as a whole.

DISCUSSION: An auditor may be requested to express an opinion on one or more specified elements, accounts, or items of a financial statement. The report should be a special report (AU 623). However, the auditor may not express such an opinion after disclaiming an opinion on the financial statements if such reporting is tantamount to a piecemeal opinion on the financial statements. Nevertheless, an auditor may be able to express an opinion in these circumstances if a major portion of the financial statements is not involved. For example, an auditor who has disclaimed an opinion on the financial statements may be able to express an opinion on the accounts receivable balance. Moreover, the report should be presented separately.

Answer (A) is incorrect because the report on accounts receivable should disclose the departure from the standard report on the financial statements if it is considered relevant, but any reasons for the departure need not be described. Answer (B) is incorrect because the report need not be restricted to internal use unless the presentation does not conform with GAAP or another comprehensive basis of accounting. Answer (C) is incorrect because a report may be presented on one or more specified elements, accounts, or items of a financial statement.

15. When an engagement involves applying agreed-upon procedures to specified elements, accounts, or items of a financial statement,

A. All GAAS apply.

B. No GAAS apply.

C. Only the general standards and the first standard of field work (adequate planning and supervision) apply.

D. The field work and reporting standards apply but not the general standards.

The correct answer is (C). *(Publisher)*

REQUIRED: The GAAS that apply to engagements to apply agreed-upon procedures to specified elements, accounts, or items of a financial statement.

DISCUSSION: The second and third standards of field work and the standards of reporting do not apply. The auditor is not responsible for understanding internal control and assessing control risk or for the collection of sufficient competent evidence to afford a reasonable basis for an opinion because only findings related to specified procedures will be provided. Also, conformity with GAAP, consistency, adequacy of disclosure, and expression of an opinion on the statements taken as a whole are not at issue because only specified elements, accounts, or items are involved. However, interpretive guidance related to application of the third standard of field work should be followed. Moreover, reporting standards addressed in the SAS on such engagements should be followed (AU 622, *Engagements to Apply Agreed-Upon Procedures to Specified Elements, Accounts, or Items of a Financial Statement*).

Answer (A) is incorrect because all GAAS do not apply. Answers (B) and (D) are incorrect because only the general standards and the first standard of field work apply.

16. An auditor may accept an engagement to perform specified procedures on the specific subject matter of specified elements, accounts, or items of a financial statement if

A. The report does not list the procedures performed.

B. The financial statements are prepared in accordance with a comprehensive basis of accounting other than GAAP (OCBOA).

C. Distribution of the report is restricted.

D. The auditor is also the entity's continuing auditor.

The correct answer is (C). *(CPA, adapted)*

REQUIRED: The condition of an engagement to apply agreed-upon procedures, specified elements, accounts, or items.

DISCUSSION: In such an engagement, users of the report assume responsibility for the sufficiency of the procedures because they best understand their own needs. As a consequence of the role of users in establishing the procedures to be performed, the report should clearly indicate that its use is restricted to those users.

Answer (A) is incorrect because the procedures performed must be enumerated. Answer (B) is incorrect because the financial statements need not be prepared in accordance with an OCBOA. Answer (D) is incorrect because the auditor need not be a continuing auditor.

17. A report may be based upon applying agreed-upon procedures to specified elements, accounts, or items of a financial statement. The users of the report should be specified and should participate in establishing the procedures to be performed. If the auditor cannot discuss the procedures directly with all specified users who will receive the report, (s)he may

A. Discuss the procedures to be applied with appropriate representatives of the users involved.

B. Review relevant correspondence from the specified users.

C. Compare the procedures to be applied with written requirements of the specified users.

D. All of the answers are correct.

The correct answer is (D). *(Publisher)*

REQUIRED: The procedure(s) for determining that users participate in establishing the procedures to be performed.

DISCUSSION: The usual method is to have a direct discussion with the specified users. Sometimes, however, the auditor must satisfy this requirement by alternative means. Each of the identified actions represents a possible procedure that the auditor may perform. The auditor should also consider distributing a draft of the report or a copy of the engagement letter to the specified users with a request for their comments.

Answers (A), (B), and (C) are incorrect because discussing the procedures with representatives of the users, reviewing relevant contracts with or correspondence from the parties, and comparing the procedures with written requirements of the users are appropriate.

8.2 Condensed Statements and Other, Supplementary, and Accompanying Information

18. Which of the following best describes "other information" in documents containing audited financial statements?

A. Supplemental information required by the FASB or GASB.

B. Information contained in a registration statement filed under the Securities Act of 1933.

C. Information presented in addition to the audited financial statements, such as the president's letter, history of the firm, and explanatory material.

D. Footnotes to the financial statements.

The correct answer is (C). *(Publisher)*

REQUIRED: The best description of other information.

DISCUSSION: An entity may publish various documents that contain information in addition to audited financial statements. This material is defined as other information by AU 550, *Other Information in Documents Containing Audited Financial Statements*.

Answer (A) is incorrect because the auditor's responsibilities regarding supplementary information required by the FASB or GASB differ from those regarding other information. Answer (B) is incorrect because AU 550 does not apply to registration statements. Rather, the procedures described in AU 711, *Filings under Federal Securities Statutes*, should be followed. Answer (D) is incorrect because the footnotes are integral to the statements.

19. The other information in a published report containing audited financial statements may be relevant to an independent auditor. With respect to other information,

A. The auditor's responsibility does not extend beyond the financial information identified in the report.

B. The auditor is obligated to perform auditing procedures to corroborate other information contained in a document.

C. The auditor need not be concerned with the other information.

D. The auditor must include the other information in the report.

The correct answer is (A). *(Publisher)*

REQUIRED: The auditor's responsibility for other information.

DISCUSSION: AU 550 states that the auditor's responsibility does not extend beyond the financial information identified in his/her report. AU 550 is not applicable, however, to SEC registration statements.

Answer (B) is incorrect because the auditor need not perform auditing procedures to corroborate other information. Answer (C) is incorrect because the auditor should read the other information and consider whether it or its presentation is materially inconsistent with the audited financial statements. Answer (D) is incorrect because such information ordinarily is not included. However, one of the auditor's options when the other information is materially inconsistent with the audited statements and the client does not revise it is to include an explanatory paragraph.

20. When audited financial statements are presented in a document containing other information, the auditor

A. Has an obligation to perform auditing procedures to corroborate the other information.

B. Is required to express a qualified opinion if the other information has a material misstatement of fact.

C. Should read the other information to consider whether it is inconsistent with the audited financial statements.

D. Has no responsibility for the other information because it is not part of the basic financial statements.

The correct answer is (C). *(CPA, adapted)*

REQUIRED: The auditor's responsibility for other information.

DISCUSSION: AU 550 states that the auditor should read the other information and consider whether it and its manner of presentation are consistent with the financial statements on which (s)he is expressing an opinion or whether it contains a material misstatement. AU 550 is not applicable, however, to registration statements.

Answer (A) is incorrect because the auditor must read but need not corroborate the other information. Answer (B) is incorrect because, if the audited information is presented fairly, the opinion should be unqualified. However, the auditor should request the client to revise other information that is materially misstated. If revision is not made, (s)he should consider modifying the report to include an explanatory paragraph, withholding use of the report, or withdrawing from the engagement. Answer (D) is incorrect because the auditor should read the other information to consider whether it is inconsistent with the audited financial statements.

21. An auditor concludes that there is a material inconsistency in the other information in an annual report to shareholders containing audited financial statements. If the auditor concludes that the financial statements do not require revision, but the client refuses to revise or eliminate the material inconsistency, the auditor may

A. Revise the auditor's report to include a separate explanatory paragraph describing the material inconsistency.

B. Express a qualified opinion after discussing the matter with the client's directors.

C. Consider the matter closed because the other information is not in the audited statements.

D. Disclaim an opinion on the financial statements after explaining the material inconsistency in a separate paragraph.

The correct answer is (A). *(CPA, adapted)*

REQUIRED: The auditor action when the client presents other information with a material inconsistency.

DISCUSSION: If the other information contains a material inconsistency, the auditor should determine whether the statements or the report need revision. If they do not, (s)he should request the client to revise the other information. If revision is not made, (s)he should consider revising the report to include an explanatory paragraph, withholding use of the report, or withdrawing from the engagement. The action taken will depend on the circumstances and the significance of the inconsistency.

Answer (B) is incorrect because the opinion is expressed on the financial statements only. The inconsistency in the other information does not affect that opinion. Answer (C) is incorrect because the auditor may not ignore a material inconsistency in other information. Answer (D) is incorrect because the auditor's decision to disclaim an opinion is not affected by the other information.

22. The auditor's inquiries of management regarding required supplementary information should be directed to the judgments made concerning

A. Relevance and validity.

B. Measurement and presentation.

C. Accuracy and objectivity.

D. Rights and obligations.

The correct answer is (B). *(CPA, adapted)*

REQUIRED: The direction of auditor inquiries about supplementary data.

DISCUSSION: Certain entities may be required by the FASB or GASB to present supplementary information. Thus, authoritative guidelines for its measurement and presentation have been established. The auditor should inquire about (1) whether the information is within the guidelines, (2) whether methods of measurement or presentation have changed and the reasons therefor, and (3) any significant assumptions or interpretations (AU 558, *Required Supplementary Information*).

Answer (A) is incorrect because the relevance of data is for management to decide. The validity of assertions is a concern in an audit. Answer (C) is incorrect because AU 558 specifically refers to measurement and presentation rather than accuracy and objectivity. Answer (D) is incorrect because an auditor's concern with rights and obligations is appropriate to an audit of basic financial statements.

23. What is an auditor's responsibility for supplementary information required by the GASB that is placed outside the basic financial statements?

A. Label the information as unaudited and expand the auditor's report to include a disclaimer on the information.

B. Add an explanatory paragraph to the auditor's report and refer to the information as required supplementary information.

C. Apply limited procedures to the information and report deficiencies in, or the omission of, the information.

D. Audit the required supplementary information in accordance with generally accepted governmental auditing standards.

The correct answer is (C). *(CPA, adapted)*

REQUIRED: The auditor's responsibility for required supplementary information.

DISCUSSION: Required supplementary information differs from other information outside the basic statements because the FASB or GASB considers it to be an essential part of the financial reporting of certain entities. The auditor should apply limited procedures and should report deficiencies in, or the omission of, such information (AU 558).

Answer (A) is incorrect because only if the required supplementary information is not presented outside the basic financial statements should it be labeled as unaudited. If the information is presented within the financial statements and is not clearly labeled, the auditor should expand the report to include a disclaimer. Answer (B) is incorrect because an explanatory paragraph should not be added unless (1) the information is omitted, (2) the information departs materially from prescribed guidelines, (3) the prescribed procedures were not completed by the auditor, or (4) there are unresolved substantial doubts about adherence to prescribed guidelines. Answer (D) is incorrect because an audit is inappropriate.

24. If management declines to present supplementary information required by the Governmental Accounting Standards Board (GASB), the auditor should express

A. An adverse opinion.

B. A qualified opinion with an explanatory paragraph.

C. An unqualified opinion.

D. An unqualified opinion with an additional explanatory paragraph.

The correct answer is (D). *(CPA, adapted)*

REQUIRED: The effect on the opinion of the client's failure to disclose required supplementary information.

DISCUSSION: Failure to present supplementary information required by the FASB or GASB does not affect the auditor's opinion because such information does not change the standards of financial accounting and reporting that were followed in preparing the financial statements (AU 558). Instead, the auditor should express an unqualified opinion with an additional explanatory paragraph stating that required supplementary information was omitted. The information itself need not be presented by the auditor.

Answers (A) and (B) are incorrect because the auditor should expand the report but not change the opinion. Answer (C) is incorrect because the opinion should include an additional explanatory paragraph.

25. If management chooses to place supplementary information required by the FASB or GASB in footnotes attached to the financial statements, this information should be clearly marked as

A. Unaudited.

B. Supplementary information required by the FASB or GASB.

C. Disclosures required by the FASB or GASB.

D. Audited financial data required by generally accepted accounting principles.

The correct answer is (A). *(CPA, adapted)*

REQUIRED: The proper marking of required supplementary information.

DISCUSSION: Required supplementary information should be distinct from the audited statements, but management may choose not to place it outside of the basic financial statements. In that event, the information should be clearly marked as unaudited. If it is not, the report must be expanded to include a disclaimer on the information (AU 558).

Answer (B) is incorrect because, although the information should be clearly identifiable, much flexibility is allowed regarding presentation. However, the information must be clearly marked as unaudited if it appears in footnotes. Answer (C) is incorrect because the auditing standards do not prescribe how the information should be identified, only that it be labeled as unaudited. Answer (D) is incorrect because the information is not audited, although the auditor should apply certain limited procedures.

26. Which of the following best describes the auditor's reporting responsibility concerning information accompanying the basic financial statements in an auditor-submitted document?

A. The auditor has no reporting responsibility concerning information accompanying the basic financial statements.

B. The auditor should report on the information accompanying the basic financial statements only if the auditor participated in its preparation.

C. The auditor should report on the information accompanying the basic financial statements only if the auditor did not participate in its preparation.

D. The auditor should report on all the information included in the document.

The correct answer is (D). *(CPA, adapted)*

REQUIRED: The auditor's reporting responsibility for information accompanying the basic financial statements.

DISCUSSION: AU 551, *Reporting on Information Accompanying the Basic Financial Statements in Auditor-Submitted Documents*, concerns information presented outside the basic statements and not deemed necessary for their fair presentation in conformity with GAAP, e.g., additional details or explanations of items in or related to the statements, consolidating information, statistical data, historical summaries, etc. However, when an auditor submits a document containing audited financial statements to the client or to others, (s)he must report on all the information included in the document.

Answers (A), (B), and (C) are incorrect because the auditor has an unconditional obligation to report on all information in an auditor-submitted document.

27. Investment and property schedules are presented for purposes of additional analysis in an auditor-submitted document. The schedules are not required parts of the basic financial statements, but accompany the basic financial statements. When reporting on such additional information, the measurement of materiality is the

A. Same as that used in forming an opinion on the basic financial statements as a whole.

B. Lesser of the individual schedule of investments or schedule of property by itself.

C. Greater of the individual schedule of investments or schedule of property by itself.

D. Combined total of both the individual schedules of investments and property as a whole.

The correct answer is (A). *(CPA, adapted)*

REQUIRED: The measure of materiality required for the purpose of reporting on information presented for additional analysis in an auditor submitted-document.

DISCUSSION: "When reporting in this manner, the measurement of materiality is the same as that used in forming an opinion on the basic financial statements taken as a whole. Accordingly, the auditor need not apply procedures as extensive as would be necessary to express an opinion on the information taken by itself" (AU 551).

Answers (B), (C), and (D) are incorrect because the measurement of materiality is the same as that in forming an opinion on the basic financial statements as a whole.

28. When financial statements audited by the independent auditor contain footnotes that are captioned "unaudited" or "not covered by the auditor's report," the auditor

A. May refer to these notes in the auditor's report.

B. Has no responsibility with respect to information contained in these notes.

C. Must refer to these notes in the auditor's report.

D. Is precluded from referring to these notes in the auditor's report.

The correct answer is (A). *(CPA, adapted)*

REQUIRED: The auditor's responsibility when financial statements include notes labeled "unaudited."

DISCUSSION: Financial statements sometimes contain unaudited information, such as pro forma calculations or other similar disclosures. If these disclosures are unnecessary to fair presentation of the statements, they may be identified as "unaudited" or "not covered by the auditor's report." If they are properly identified, the auditor is not required by any pronouncement to refer to them in the report. However, a reference to these footnotes is not expressly prohibited. If the content is inconsistent with the financial statements or otherwise misleading, (s)he should provide an explanation in a separate explanatory paragraph.

Answer (B) is incorrect because the auditor must ascertain that unaudited notes are clearly labeled as unaudited. Answers (C) and (D) are incorrect because the auditor may, but is not required to, refer to unaudited footnotes in the report.

29. According to AU 552, *Reporting on Condensed Financial Statements and Selected Financial Data*, an auditor should

A. Issue the same report on both the condensed statements and the complete statements from which they are derived.

B. Express no opinion on the condensed statements.

C. Not report on selected financial data derived from audited financial statements.

D. Express an opinion as to whether the selected financial data were fairly stated.

The correct answer is (D). *(Publisher)*

REQUIRED: The auditor's obligation regarding condensed statements and selected financial data.

DISCUSSION: AU 552 concerns reporting in a client-prepared document on (1) condensed statements derived from audited statements of a public entity required to file complete audited statements with a regulatory agency and (2) selected financial data of a public or nonpublic entity. The auditor's report should indicate that the auditor has expressed an opinion on the complete statements, the type of opinion expressed, and an opinion as to whether the information set forth is fairly stated in all material respects in relation to the complete statements. In the case of condensed statements, the report should also indicate the date of the report on the complete statements.

Answer (A) is incorrect because the report on condensed statements is typically a two-paragraph report. Answer (B) is incorrect because an opinion is expressed stating that the information is fairly stated in all material respects in relation to the complete statements. Answer (C) is incorrect because a report on selected financial data must be presented.

30. In the standard report on condensed financial statements that are derived from a public entity's audited financial statements, a CPA should indicate that the

A. Condensed financial statements are prepared in conformity with another comprehensive basis of accounting.

B. CPA has audited and expressed an opinion on the complete financial statements.

C. Condensed financial statements are not fairly presented in all material respects.

D. CPA expresses limited assurance that the financial statements conform with GAAP.

The correct answer is (B). *(CPA, adapted)*

REQUIRED: The indication in a standard report on condensed financial statements.

DISCUSSION: The report should state that the auditor has audited and expressed an opinion on the complete statements, the date of that report, the type of opinion expressed, and an opinion as to whether the condensed statements are fairly stated in all material respects in relation to the complete statements (AU 552).

Answer (A) is incorrect because condensed financial statements are prepared from GAAP-based financial statements. Answer (C) is incorrect because condensed financial statements may be fairly presented. Answer (D) is incorrect because the CPA expresses an opinion.

8.3 Interim Financial Information

31. The objective of a review of interim financial information of a public entity is to provide an accountant with a basis for reporting whether

A. A reasonable basis exists for expressing an updated opinion regarding the financial statements that were previously audited.

B. Material modifications should be made to conform with generally accepted accounting principles.

C. The financial statements are presented fairly in accordance with standards of interim reporting.

D. The financial statements are presented fairly in accordance with generally accepted accounting principles.

The correct answer is (B). *(CPA, adapted)*

REQUIRED: The objective of a review of interim financial information.

DISCUSSION: The review provides the accountant, based on application of his/her knowledge of reporting practices to significant accounting matters of which (s)he becomes aware through inquiries and analytical procedures, with a basis for reporting whether material modifications should be made for such information to conform with GAAP. According to AU 722, this objective differs significantly from that of an audit, which is to provide a basis for an opinion.

Answer (A) is incorrect because the review of interim financial information does not provide a reasonable basis for expressing an opinion. Answers (C) and (D) are incorrect because reporting on whether the statements are fairly presented is the expression of an opinion.

32. Auditors of public companies are often requested to report on interim financial statements. A review of interim financial information consists primarily of

A. Vouching and tracing.

B. Reconciling and reperforming.

C. Inquiries and analytical procedures.

D. Confirmation and observation.

The correct answer is (C). *(Publisher)*

REQUIRED: The procedures performed in a review of interim financial information.

DISCUSSION: Timeliness is an important element of interim reporting. The development of documentation and information underlying the report is necessarily less extensive at interim dates than at year-end. Consequently, "procedures for making a review of interim financial information generally are limited to inquiries and analytical procedures, rather than search and verification procedures, concerning significant accounting matters relating to the financial information to be reported" (AU 722).

Answers (A), (B), and (D) are incorrect because vouching and tracing, reconciling and reperforming, and confirmation and observation are more extensive procedures than those listed in AU 722.

33. Which of the following statements is not included in an auditor's report on the interim financial statements of a public entity?

A. "We conducted our review in accordance with generally accepted auditing standards."

B. "A review of interim financial information consists principally of applying analytical procedures to financial data and making inquiries of management."

C. "Based on our review, we are not aware of any material modifications that should be made to the accompanying financial statements for them to be in conformity with GAAP."

D. "These financial statements are the responsibility of the company's management."

The correct answer is (A). *(Publisher)*

REQUIRED: The statement not in a report on a review of interim financial information.

DISCUSSION: The scope of a review of interim financial information is less than the scope of an audit. The accountant's report should therefore include a statement that a review of financial information is substantially less in scope than an audit in accordance with GAAS, the objective of which is an expression of an opinion on the statements as a whole, and that no such opinion is expressed. The report should also contain a statement that the review was made in accordance with AICPA standards (AU 722).

Answers (B), (C), and (D) are incorrect because a description of the procedures, a statement about whether the accountant is aware of any material modifications that should be made, and a statement that the financial statements are the responsibility of management are proper elements of the report.

34. Procedures for a review of interim financial information are ordinarily limited to inquiries and analytical procedures, rather than search and verification procedures, concerning significant accounting matters relating to the financial information to be reported. The extent to which the procedures are to be applied depends on each of the following considerations except

A. The accountant's time budget allotted for the tests.

B. The issuance of new accounting pronouncements.

C. Litigation, claims, and assessments.

D. Questions raised in performing other procedures.

The correct answer is (A). *(Publisher)*

REQUIRED: The matter not considered in determining the extent of procedures applied.

DISCUSSION: The procedures in a review of interim financial information include (1) inquiry about internal control and changes therein, (2) analytical procedures, (3) reading the minutes of meetings, (4) reading the interim information, (5) obtaining reports of other accountants who have reviewed interim information of components of the entity, (6) inquiry of officers and others with responsibility for financial and accounting matters, and (7) obtaining written representations from management. The extent of procedures depends on the accountant's knowledge of changes in accounting practices or in the nature or volume of the client's business activities, e.g., business combinations or disposal of a segment. However, the accountant's time budget should not be a determining factor.

Answer (B) is incorrect because accounting changes may affect the extent of procedures. Answer (C) is incorrect because an inquiry of the client's lawyer may be appropriate if the accountant learns that the interim financial information may contain a departure from GAAP related to litigation, claims, or assessments. Answer (D) is incorrect because, if the accountant has reason to question whether the interim information conforms with GAAP, (s)he should make additional inquiries or employ other appropriate procedures.

35. A clear understanding should be established with the client regarding the nature of the service to be performed in a review of interim financial information and the responsibilities to be assumed. Accordingly, the accountant may wish to confirm the nature and scope of the engagement in a letter to the client. The letter would normally include all of the following except

A. A general description of the procedures.

B. An explanation that such procedures are substantially less in scope than an audit made in accordance with GAAS.

C. A description of the form of the report.

D. The nature and content of the working papers that will be maintained by the accountant.

The correct answer is (D). *(Publisher)*

REQUIRED: The topic not included in an engagement letter for a review of interim financial information.

DISCUSSION: The form and content of the working papers are the responsibility of the accountant and are inappropriate for discussion in an engagement letter. The form or content of the working papers that the accountant should prepare cannot be specified because circumstances differ from one engagement to another. The working papers should document the performance and results of procedures performed (AU 722).

Answer (A) is incorrect because a general description of the procedures to be performed in conjunction with the review should be given in the engagement letter. Answer (B) is incorrect because the accountant must communicate that the scope of the review is less than that of an audit. Answer (C) is incorrect because the accountant should describe the responsibility assumed and the form of the report to be issued.

36. A modification of the accountant's report on a review of interim financial information of a publicly held company is necessitated by which of the following?

A. An uncertainty.

B. Lack of consistency.

C. Use of another accountant's report.

D. Inadequate disclosure.

The correct answer is (D). *(CPA, adapted)*

REQUIRED: The reason for modifying a review report on interim financial information.

DISCUSSION: Modification of the report on a review of interim financial information is necessary for departures from GAAP, including inadequate disclosure. But many circumstances that preclude the issuance of an unmodified report on audited statements do not cause a modification of a review report (AU 722).

Answers (A) and (B) are incorrect because AU 722 specifically states that neither an uncertainty nor lack of consistency is a cause for modification if appropriately disclosed. Answer (C) is incorrect because the use of the report of another accountant may result in, but does not require, modification of the report. The accountant may be able to conclude, after considering the guidance in AU 543, *Part of Audit Performed by Other Independent Auditors*, that referring to the other accountant's report is not necessary.

37. Lara Green, CPA, is aware that her name is to be included in the interim report of National Company, a publicly held entity. National's quarterly financial statements are contained in the interim report. Green has not audited or reviewed these interim financial statements. Green should request that

I. Her name not be included in the communication

II. The financial statements be marked as unaudited, with a notation that no opinion is expressed on them

A. I only.

B. II only.

C. Both I and II.

D. Either I or II.

The correct answer is (D). *(CPA, adapted)*

REQUIRED: The request(s) of an accountant who is associated with financial statements of a public entity that (s)he has not audited or reviewed.

DISCUSSION: If Green is aware that her name is to be included in a client-prepared written communication of a public company containing financial statements that she has not audited or reviewed, she should request either (1) that her name not be included in the communication or (2) that the financial statements be marked as unaudited and that a notation be included to the effect that she does not express an opinion on them (AU 504, *Association with Financial Statements*).

Answers (A), (B), and (C) are incorrect because the accountant may request that his/her name not be included in the communication or that the statements be marked as unaudited, with a notation that no opinion is expressed.

38. A company includes selected interim financial information in a footnote to its annual financial statements. The independent auditor has made a review of the information and is satisfied with its presentation. Under these circumstances, the auditor's report on the annual financial statements

A. Should be modified to refer to the review and the selected interim financial information.

B. Need not be modified to refer to the review but should be modified to refer to the selected financial information.

C. Should be modified to refer to the review but not the selected interim financial information.

D. Need not be modified to refer to the review or the selected interim financial information.

The correct answer is (D). *(CPA, adapted)*

REQUIRED: The effect on the audit report of including interim financial information in a footnote.

DISCUSSION: According to AU 722, "The auditor ordinarily need not modify the report on the audited financial statements to refer to his/her review or to the interim financial information." The interim information has not been audited and is not necessary for the fair presentation of the statements in conformity with GAAP. Modification is necessary, however, when quarterly data required by SEC Regulation S-K are omitted or have not been reviewed. Regulation S-K specifies nonfinancial statement information to be reported.

Answers (A), (B), and (C) are incorrect because the audit report need not refer either to the review or to the interim information.

8.4 Unaudited Statements, Compilations, and Reviews

39. An accountant may compile a nonpublic entity's financial statements that omit all of the disclosures required by GAAP only if the omission is

I. Clearly indicated in the accountant's report

II. Not undertaken with the intention of misleading the financial statement users

A. I only.

B. II only.

C. Both I and II.

D. Either I or II.

The correct answer is (C). *(CPA, adapted)*

REQUIRED: The situation in which an accountant may compile a nonpublic entity's financial statements that omit all of the disclosures required by GAAP.

DISCUSSION: An accountant may accept an engagement to compile financial statements that omit substantially all disclosures required by GAAP "provided the omission is clearly indicated in the report and is not, to his/her knowledge, undertaken with the intention of misleading those who might reasonably be expected to use such financial statements" (AR 100, *Compilation and Review of Financial Statements*).

Answers (A), (B), and (D) are incorrect because the omission must be clearly indicated and not made with deceptive intent.

40. When an independent CPA assists in preparing the financial statements of a publicly held entity, but has not audited or reviewed them, the CPA should issue a disclaimer of opinion. The CPA has no responsibility to apply any procedures beyond

A. Ascertaining whether the financial statements are in conformity with generally accepted accounting principles.

B. Determining whether management has elected to omit substantially all required disclosures.

C. Documenting that internal control is not being relied on.

D. Reading the financial statements for obvious material misstatements.

The correct answer is (D). *(CPA, adapted)*

REQUIRED: The procedure applied to public-company financial statements that the CPA has assisted in preparing.

DISCUSSION: AU 504 states that the accountant has no responsibility to apply any procedures beyond reading the financial statements for obvious material misstatements. Any procedures applied should not be described.

Answer (A) is incorrect because an audit is conducted to ascertain whether the financial statements are in conformity with GAAP. Answer (B) is incorrect because the disclaimer is modified if the accountant concludes on the basis of facts known to him/her that the unaudited financial statements do not conform with GAAP. Lack of adequate disclosure is a departure from GAAP. Answer (C) is incorrect because the CPA in these circumstances need not consider internal control and therefore has no responsibility for documentation.

41. Statements on Standards for Accounting and Review Services (SSARSs) establish standards and procedures for which of the following engagements?

A. Assisting in adjusting the books of account for a partnership.

B. Reviewing interim financial data required to be filed with the SEC.

C. Processing financial data for clients of other accounting firms.

D. Compiling an individual's personal financial statement to be used to obtain a mortgage.

The correct answer is (D). *(CPA, adapted)*

REQUIRED: The accounting service for which SSARSs establish standards or procedures.

DISCUSSION: The preparation of financial statements from an entity's (here an individual's) records is a compilation service. AR 100 describes the accountant's procedures and reporting responsibilities relative to this service. (AR 600, *Reporting on Personal Financial Statements Included in Written Personal Financial Plans*, provides an exemption from the SSARSs for personal financial statements under certain conditions.) Before issuing a report on the compilation of financial statements, the accountant should read the statements to consider whether they are free from obvious material errors.

Answers (A) and (C) are incorrect because AR 100 specifically does not apply to preparing a working trial balance, assisting in adjusting the books of account, or processing financial data for clients of other accounting firms. Answer (B) is incorrect because AU 722 describes the accountant's responsibilities for interim financial information of public companies.

42. A CPA is required to comply with the provisions of Statements on Standards for Accounting and Review Services (SSARSs) when

	Processing Financial Data for Clients of Other CPA Firms	Consulting on Accounting Matters
A.	Yes	Yes
B.	Yes	No
C.	No	Yes
D.	No	No

The correct answer is (D). *(CPA, adapted)*

REQUIRED: The circumstances in which a CPA is required to comply with SSARSs.

DISCUSSION: AR 100 states that the following services are not subject to SSARSs: (1) preparing a working trial balance; (2) assisting in adjusting the books of account; (3) consulting on accounting, tax, and similar matters; (4) preparing tax returns; (5) providing various manual or automated bookkeeping or data processing services unless the output consists of financial statements; and (6) processing financial data for clients of other accounting firms.

Answers (A), (B), and (C) are incorrect because processing financial data for clients of other accounting firms and consulting on accounting matters are not subject to SSARSs.

43. Statements on Standards for Accounting and Review Services (SSARSs) require an accountant to report when the accountant has

A. Typed client-prepared financial statements, without modification, as an accommodation to the client.

B. Provided a client with a financial statement format that does not include dollar amounts, to be used by the client in preparing financial statements.

C. Proposed correcting journal entries to be recorded by the client that change client-prepared financial statements.

D. Generated, through the use of computer software, financial statements prepared in accordance with a comprehensive basis of accounting other than GAAP.

The correct answer is (D). *(CPA, adapted)*

REQUIRED: The situation in which an accountant must issue a report.

DISCUSSION: AR 100 requires the accountant to issue a report when presenting to a client or others financial statements that the accountant has generated either manually or through the use of computer software or modified by materially changing account classifications, amounts, or disclosures directly on client-prepared financial statements. This principle applies whether the financial statements are based on GAAP or on a comprehensive basis of accounting other than GAAP.

Answer (A) is incorrect because AR 100 states, "Typing or reproducing client-prepared financial statements, without modification, as an accommodation to a client" does not constitute a submission of financial statements. Answer (B) is incorrect because, without dollar amounts, the presentation is not a financial statement. Answer (C) is incorrect because journal entries are not a financial statement.

44. Statements on Standards for Accounting and Review Services (SSARSs) define the compilation and review of financial statements of a nonpublic entity and provide guidance concerning the standards and procedures applicable to such engagements. For the purposes of SSARSs, which of the following is a nonpublic entity?

A. One whose securities trade on a stock exchange or over the counter, including securities quoted only regionally or locally.

B. One that makes a filing with a regulatory agency in preparation for a sale of any class of securities to the public.

C. A subsidiary, corporate joint venture, or other entity controlled by a public entity.

D. A closely held corporation.

The correct answer is (D). *(Publisher)*

REQUIRED: The entity not considered a public entity for purposes of SSARSs.

DISCUSSION: A private entity is one whose shares are not traded in a public market, that has not made a filing with a regulatory body preparatory to public sale of its securities, and that is not controlled by a public entity. For example, a proprietorship, partnership, or closely held corporation might be considered a nonpublic entity.

Answers (A), (B), and (C) are incorrect because an entity whose shares are traded; an entity that makes a filing with a regulatory agency in preparation for a sale of any class of securities to the public; and a subsidiary, corporate joint venture, or other entity controlled by a public entity are considered to be public entities for the purposes of SSARSs.

45. A CPA who is not independent may issue a

A. Review report.

B. Comfort letter.

C. Report expressing a qualified opinion.

D. Compilation report.

The correct answer is (D). *(CPA, adapted)*

REQUIRED: The report that a CPA who is not independent may issue.

DISCUSSION: A compilation is the presentation in statement form of information that is the representation of management without expressing any assurance thereon. A CPA who is not independent may issue a compilation report if (s)he discloses the lack of independence (AR 100).

Answer (A) is incorrect because an accountant may not issue a review report if (s)he is not independent. A review entails the expression of limited assurances based on inquiries and analytical procedures. Answer (B) is incorrect because a letter for underwriters (a comfort letter) cannot be issued by a CPA who lacks independence (AU 634, *Letters for Underwriters and Certain Other Requesting Parties*). Answer (C) is incorrect because GAAS prohibit a CPA from expressing any opinion when not independent.

46. Which of the following representations does an accountant make implicitly when issuing the standard report for the compilation of a nonpublic entity's financial statements?

A. The accountant is independent with respect to the entity.

B. The financial statements have not been audited.

C. A compilation consists principally of inquiries and analytical procedures.

D. The accountant does not express any assurance on the financial statements.

The correct answer is (A). *(CPA, adapted)*

REQUIRED: The implicit representation in a standard compilation report.

DISCUSSION: Although an accountant who lacks independence is not precluded from issuing a compilation report, (s)he should specifically disclose the lack of independence in the report. Thus, the standard report is silent with respect to independence.

Answers (B) and (D) are incorrect because a compilation explicitly states that the financial statements have not been audited and that no assurance is expressed. Answer (C) is incorrect because a compilation does not include application of inquiry and analytical procedures.

47. When compiling the financial statements of a nonpublic entity, an accountant should

A. Review agreements with financial institutions for restrictions on cash balances.

B. Understand the accounting principles and practices of the entity's industry.

C. Inquire of key personnel concerning related parties and subsequent events.

D. Perform ratio analyses of the financial data of comparable prior periods.

The correct answer is (B). *(CPA, adapted)*

REQUIRED: The accountant's responsibility before undertaking a compilation.

DISCUSSION: The accountant should acquire "a level of knowledge of the accounting principles and practices of the industry in which the entity operates that will enable him/her to compile financial statements that are appropriate in form for an entity operating in that industry." Also, (s)he should possess an understanding of the nature of the entity's business, its accounting records, the qualifications of its accounting personnel, and the content and accounting basis of the financial statements.

Answers (A) and (C) are incorrect because procedures to obtain evidence about restrictions on cash balances and inquiries about related parties and subsequent events are appropriate in an audit. Answer (D) is incorrect because analytical procedures are necessary in review and audit engagements.

48. The accountant's knowledge of the accounting principles and practices of the client's industry should enable him/her to compile appropriate financial statements. Also, the accountant should understand the nature of the entity's business, its accounting records, the qualifications of its personnel, the accounting basis of the financial statements, and their content. To acquire such knowledge, the accountant does not normally

A. Consult Audit and Accounting Guides.

B. Read industry publications and consult textbooks and periodicals.

C. Obtain an understanding of internal control and assess control risk.

D. Make inquiries of the entity's personnel.

The correct answer is (C). *(Publisher)*

REQUIRED: The procedure not normally performed to acquire the knowledge of the industry and the client.

DISCUSSION: The consideration of internal control is not necessary to perform compilation services. No auditing procedures need be applied in a compilation. The financial statements, however, should be read to determine whether they are in an appropriate form and free of obvious material errors, such as clerical mistakes or departures from GAAP, including inadequate disclosure.

Answers (A) and (B) are incorrect because AICPA Audit and Accounting Guides, industry publications, textbooks, and periodicals are appropriate sources of the knowledge of the accounting principles and practices of the industry required to perform a compilation. Answer (D) is incorrect because inquiries of the entity's personnel are the primary procedures employed to gain an understanding of the client's business accounting records, and the basis on which it intends to report.

49. An accountant's compilation report should be dated as of the date of

A. Completion of field work.

B. Completion of the compilation.

C. Transmittal of the compilation report.

D. The latest subsequent event referred to in the notes to the financial statements.

The correct answer is (B). *(CPA, adapted)*

REQUIRED: The date of a compilation report.

DISCUSSION: When an accountant has performed a compilation for a private company, the date of the report should be the completion date of the compilation (AR 100).

Answer (A) is incorrect because field work is performed in attestation engagements, such as a financial statement audit or a review, not a compilation. Answer (C) is incorrect because the date of the transmittal of the compilation report, which refers to the time of its communication to the user, is not appropriate. Answer (D) is incorrect because the dates of subsequent events may be significant for an audit but not a compilation.

50. Which of the following should not be included in an accountant's standard report based upon the compilation of an entity's financial statements?

A. A statement that a compilation is limited to presenting in the form of financial statements information that is the representation of management.

B. A statement that the compilation was performed in accordance with Statements on Standards for Accounting and Review Services.

C. A statement that the accountant has not audited or reviewed the statements.

D. A statement that the accountant does not express an opinion but provides only limited assurance on the statements.

The correct answer is (D). *(CPA, adapted)*

REQUIRED: The statement not made in the standard compilation report.

DISCUSSION: A compilation report does not express an opinion or any other form of assurance. Any procedures that the accountant may have performed should not be described because readers may be misled into believing that the statements have been subjected to review or audit.

Answer (A) is incorrect because the report should include a statement that a compilation is limited to presenting in the form of financial statements information that is the representation of management. Answer (B) is incorrect because the report should include a statement that the compilation was performed in accordance with SSARSs issued by the AICPA. Answer (C) is incorrect because the report should include a statement that the accountant has not audited or reviewed the statements.

51. Each page of the financial statements compiled by an accountant should include a reference such as

A. See Accompanying Accountant's Footnotes.

B. Unaudited, See Accountant's Disclaimer.

C. See Accountant's Compilation Report.

D. Subject to Compilation Restrictions.

The correct answer is (C). *(CPA, adapted)*

REQUIRED: The reference on each page of compiled financial statements.

DISCUSSION: According to AR 100, "Each page of the financial statements compiled by the accountant should include a reference such as 'See Accountant's Compilation Report.'"

Answers (A), (B), and (D) are incorrect because See Accompanying Accountant's Footnotes; Unaudited, See Accountant's Disclaimer; and Subject to Compilation Restrictions are not appropriate references to be included on each page of compiled financial statements.

52. In performing a compilation of financial statements of a nonpublic entity, the accountant decides that modification of the standard report is not adequate to indicate deficiencies in the financial statements taken as a whole, and the client is not willing to correct the deficiencies. The accountant should therefore

A. Perform a review of the financial statements.

B. Issue a special report.

C. Withdraw from the engagement.

D. Express an adverse audit opinion.

The correct answer is (C). *(CPA, adapted)*

REQUIRED: The appropriate action when modification of the compilation report is inadequate.

DISCUSSION: If the accountant becomes aware that information supplied by the entity is incorrect, incomplete, or otherwise unsatisfactory, (s)he should request the client to provide additional or revised information. If the client is not willing to correct the deficiencies, the accountant is advised to withdraw from the engagement.

Answer (A) is incorrect because the accountant is under no obligation to upgrade the service to a review. Answer (B) is incorrect because a special report (as contemplated by AU 623) can be issued only in conjunction with auditing services. Answer (D) is incorrect because an opinion may be expressed only after an audit.

53. An accountant has been asked to compile the financial statements of a nonpublic company on a prescribed form that omits substantially all the disclosures required by generally accepted accounting principles. If the prescribed form is a standard preprinted form adopted by the company's industry trade association, and is to be transmitted only to such association, the accountant

A. Need not advise the industry trade association of the omission of all disclosures.

B. Should disclose the details of the omissions in separate paragraphs of the compilation report.

C. Is precluded from issuing a compilation report when all disclosures are omitted.

D. Should express limited assurance that the financial statements are free of material misstatements.

The correct answer is (A). *(CPA, adapted)*

REQUIRED: The accountant's responsibility when (s)he compiles statements on a prescribed form.

DISCUSSION: AR 300, *Compilation Reports on Financial Statements Included in Certain Prescribed Forms*, provides for an alternative form of the standard compilation report when a prescribed form or related instructions call for departure from GAAP by specifying a measurement principle not in conformity with GAAP or failing to require disclosures in accordance with GAAP. The presumption is that the information required in a prescribed form is sufficient to meet the needs of the body that designed or adopted the form. In the standard report on statements included in such a form, the accountant should indicate that the statements are in a prescribed form and that they may differ from those presented in accordance with GAAP, but (s)he need not describe the differences.

Answer (B) is incorrect because this disclosure is unnecessary. Answer (C) is incorrect because the report may be issued in these circumstances. Answer (D) is incorrect because a compilation report expresses no assurance.

54. When an accountant compiles a nonpublic entity's financial statements that omit substantially all disclosures required by generally accepted accounting principles, the accountant should indicate in the compilation report that the financial statements are

A. Restricted for internal use only by the entity's management.

B. Not to be given to financial institutions for the purpose of obtaining credit.

C. Compiled in conformity with a comprehensive basis of accounting other than generally accepted accounting principles.

D. Not designed for those who are uninformed about the omitted disclosures.

The correct answer is (D). *(CPA, adapted)*

REQUIRED: The language in the report when compiled statements omit disclosures required by GAAP.

DISCUSSION: The accountant may not accept the engagement unless two conditions are satisfied: (s)he must modify the standard compilation report to clearly indicate that substantially all disclosures required by GAAP have been omitted, and the omission must not be made to mislead users of the statements. The language given is a quotation from the compilation report when substantially all disclosures are omitted (AR 100).

Answer (A) is incorrect because the CPA need not indicate in the compilation report that the financial statements are restricted for internal use only. Answer (B) is incorrect because the statements may be given to financial institutions for the purpose of obtaining credit. Answer (C) is incorrect because the omission of disclosures required by GAAP does not result in conformity with a comprehensive basis of accounting other than GAAP.

55. Miller, CPA, is engaged to compile the financial statements of Web Co., a nonpublic entity, in conformity with the income tax basis of accounting. If Web's financial statements do not disclose the basis of accounting used, Miller should

A. Disclose the basis of accounting in the accountant's compilation report.

B. Clearly label each page "Distribution Restricted--Material Modifications Required."

C. Issue a special report describing the effect of the incomplete presentation.

D. Withdraw from the engagement and provide no further services to Web.

The correct answer is (A). *(CPA, adapted)*

REQUIRED: The effect on a compilation report of failure to disclose the basis of accounting used.

DISCUSSION: Although the auditor is expected to perform no procedures, if (s)he is aware of misapplications of GAAP or the absence of required disclosures, (s)he should disclose that information in the compilation report.

Answer (B) is incorrect because each page of the financial statements should contain the statement, "See accountant's compilation report." Answer (C) is incorrect because a special report is issued in conjunction with an audit. Answer (D) is incorrect because the auditor need not withdraw from the engagement.

56. When unaudited financial statements of a nonpublic entity are presented in comparative form with audited financial statements in the subsequent year, the unaudited financial statements should be clearly marked to indicate their status, and

I. The report on the unaudited financial statements should be reissued.

II. The report on the audited financial statements should include a separate paragraph describing the responsibility assumed for the unaudited financial statements.

A. I only.

B. II only.

C. Both I and II.

D. Either I or II.

The correct answer is (D). *(CPA, adapted)*

REQUIRED: The appropriate reporting when unaudited financial statements of a nonpublic entity are presented in comparative form with audited financial statements.

DISCUSSION: The financial statements that have not been audited should be clearly marked to indicate their status and either (1) the report on the prior period should be reissued or (2) the report on the current period should include as a separate paragraph an appropriate description of the responsibility assumed for the financial statements of the prior period (AU 504).

Answers (A), (B), and (C) are incorrect because either form of reporting is appropriate.

57. An accountant's standard report on a review of the financial statements of a nonpublic entity should state that the accountant

A. Does not express an opinion or any form of limited assurance on the financial statements.

B. Is not aware of any material modifications that should be made to the financial statements for them to conform with GAAP.

C. Obtained reasonable assurance about whether the financial statements are free of material misstatement.

D. Examined evidence, on a test basis, supporting the amounts and disclosures in the financial statements.

The correct answer is (B). *(CPA, adapted)*

REQUIRED: The statement in a standard review report.

DISCUSSION: The standard review report states, "Based on my review, I am not aware of any material modifications that should be made to the accompanying financial statements in order for them to be in conformity with generally accepted accounting principles" (AR 100).

Answer (A) is incorrect because a review provides negative assurance. Answer (C) is incorrect because an audit provides reasonable assurance about whether the financial statements are free of material misstatement. Answer (D) is incorrect because an audit entails gathering sufficient competent evidence to support the amounts and disclosures in the financial statements.

58. Which of the following procedures is an accountant least likely to perform during an engagement to review the financial statements of a nonpublic entity?

A. Observing the safeguards over access to and use of assets and records.

B. Comparing the financial statements with anticipated results in budgets and forecasts.

C. Inquiring of management about actions taken at the board of directors' meetings.

D. Studying the relationships of financial statement elements expected to conform to predictable patterns.

The correct answer is (A). *(CPA, adapted)*

REQUIRED: The procedure least likely to be performed during a review engagement.

DISCUSSION: A review does not contemplate (1) obtaining an understanding of internal control or assessing control risk, (2) testing accounting records or responses to inquiries by obtaining corroborating evidence, or (3) other tests ordinarily performed in an audit (AR 100).

Answers (B) and (D) are incorrect because a review contemplates the application of analytical procedures. Comparing financial statements with anticipated results and studying relationships among the significant financial statement items are analytical procedures. Answer (C) is incorrect because a review encompasses inquiries to management about numerous operating activities.

59. In a review engagement, the accountant should establish an understanding with the client, preferably in writing, regarding the services to be performed. The understanding should include all of the following except a

A. Description of the nature and limitations of the services to be performed.

B. Description of the report the accountant expects to render.

C. Provision that the engagement cannot be relied upon to disclose errors, fraud, or illegal acts.

D. Provision that any errors, fraud, or illegal acts that come to the accountant's attention need not be reported.

The correct answer is (D). *(Publisher)*

REQUIRED: The false statement about the accountant's understanding with the client in a review engagement.

DISCUSSION: Although the engagement cannot be relied upon to disclose errors, fraud, or illegal acts, the accountant should indicate to the client that any such acts discovered will be reported to management or the directors unless the acts are clearly inconsequential (AR 100).

Answers (A), (B), and (C) are incorrect because a description of the nature and limitations of the services to be performed, a description of the report the accountant expects to issue, and a provision that the engagement cannot be relied upon to disclose errors, fraud, or illegal acts should be included in the understanding with the client.

60. Which of the following inquiry or analytical procedures ordinarily is performed in an engagement to review a nonpublic entity's financial statements?

A. Analytical procedures designed to test the accounting records by obtaining corroborating evidential matter.

B. Inquiries concerning the entity's procedures for recording and summarizing transactions.

C. Analytical procedures designed to test management's assertions regarding continued existence.

D. Inquiries of the entity's attorney concerning contingent liabilities.

The correct answer is (B). *(CPA, adapted)*

REQUIRED: The procedure ordinarily performed during a review of a nonpublic entity's financial statements.

DISCUSSION: These procedures consist of (1) inquiries about accounting principles and practices and the methods of applying them; (2) inquiries about procedures for recording, classifying, and summarizing transactions, and accumulating information for disclosure; (3) analytical procedures; (4) inquiries about actions at directors' meetings, etc.; (5) reading the statements; (6) obtaining reports from other accountants, if any; and (7) inquiries of responsible persons about preparation of the statements in conformity with GAAP, accounting changes, changes in business activities, subsequent events, and questions arising while applying the foregoing procedures (AR 100).

Answers (A), (C), and (D) are incorrect because a review does not require gathering corroborating evidence, testing assertions about continued existence, or making inquiries of the entity's attorney.

61. Which of the following procedures should an accountant perform during an engagement to review the financial statements of a nonpublic entity?

A. Communicating reportable conditions discovered during the assessment of control risk.

B. Obtaining a client representation letter from members of management.

C. Sending bank confirmation letters to the entity's financial institutions.

D. Examining cash disbursements in the subsequent period for unrecorded liabilities.

The correct answer is (B). *(CPA, adapted)*

REQUIRED: The procedure performed in a review.

DISCUSSION: A review consists of inquiries and analytical procedures. In support of the inquiries, the accountant "is required to obtain a representation letter from members of management who the accountant believes are responsible for and knowledgeable about the matters covered" (AR 100).

Answer (A) is incorrect because reportable conditions must be communicated in an audit, not a review. Answer (C) is incorrect because confirmations to financial institutions are normally sent in an audit, not a review. Answer (D) is incorrect because tests of details, e.g., tests of subsequent payments, are performed in an audit, not a review.

62. A review does not provide assurance that the accountant will become aware of all significant matters that would be disclosed in an audit. However, if the accountant becomes aware that information coming to his/her attention is incorrect, incomplete, or otherwise unsatisfactory, (s)he should

A. Withdraw immediately from the engagement.

B. Perform the additional procedures (s)he deems necessary to achieve limited assurance.

C. Perform a complete audit and issue a standard audit report with appropriate qualifications.

D. Downgrade the engagement to a compilation and issue the appropriate report.

The correct answer is (B). *(Publisher)*

REQUIRED: The accountant's response to unsatisfactory information in a review.

DISCUSSION: In a review, the accountant makes inquiries and applies analytical procedures. If information appears unsatisfactory, (s)he should perform the additional procedures deemed necessary to achieve limited assurance that no material modifications need be made to the statements for them to conform with GAAP. These procedures are left to the judgment of the accountant (AR 100).

Answer (A) is incorrect because the accountant should withdraw only after (s)he has concluded that the financial statements are not in conformity with GAAP and that modification of the standard report is inadequate. Answer (C) is incorrect because the accountant cannot decide to perform a complete audit; (s)he must be engaged to do so by the client. Answer (D) is incorrect because unsatisfactory information is not a basis for changing the engagement if the accountant can perform necessary procedures.

63. Appendix A of AR 100 lists more than 75 questions that may be appropriate to address to management in a review engagement. Which of the following is true concerning this list?

A. The list is intended to be a checklist or program so that all appropriate questions will be addressed.

B. The questions are all-inclusive and should be applied in every engagement.

C. It may be necessary to make several inquiries to answer one question.

D. The questions cover only general management procedures rather than specific account balances.

The correct answer is (C). *(Publisher)*

REQUIRED: The true statement concerning the inquiries listed in AR 100.

DISCUSSION: The inquiries to be made in a review of financial statements are a matter of the accountant's judgment. The accountant may believe it is necessary to make several inquiries to answer one of the questions listed.

Answers (A) and (B) are incorrect because AR 100 indicates specifically that the list is not intended to be a program or a checklist or to be all-inclusive. Answer (D) is incorrect because the questions range from general questions concerning procedures for recording, classifying, and summarizing transactions to specific questions concerning the accounts on the income statement and balance sheet.

64. Which of the following would not be included in an accountant's report based upon a review of the financial statements of a nonpublic entity?

A. A statement that the review was in accordance with GAAS.

B. A statement that all information included in the financial statements is the representation of management.

C. A statement describing the principal procedures performed.

D. A statement describing the accountant's conclusions based upon the results of the review.

The correct answer is (A). *(CPA, adapted)*

REQUIRED: The statement not included in an accountant's report based upon a review.

DISCUSSION: The report should include a statement that the review is substantially less in scope than an audit in accordance with GAAS. GAAS apply to audits, not reviews. A review consists principally of inquiries and analytical procedures applied to financial data (AR 100).

Answers (B), (C), and (D) are incorrect because a statement that all information included in the financial statements is the representation of management, a description of the principal procedures performed, and the accountant's conclusions based upon the results of the review are included in the standard report.

65. Baker, CPA, was engaged to review the financial statements of Hall Company, a nonpublic entity. Evidence came to Baker's attention that indicated substantial doubt as to Hall's ability to continue as a going concern. The principal conditions and events that caused the substantial doubt have been fully disclosed in the notes to Hall's financial statements. Baker

A. Is not required to modify the accountant's review report.

B. Is not permitted to modify the accountant's review report.

C. Should issue an accountant's compilation report instead of a review report.

D. Should express a qualified opinion in the accountant's review report.

The correct answer is (A). *(CPA, adapted)*

REQUIRED: The reporting responsibility in a review given a substantial doubt about the going concern assumption.

DISCUSSION: AR 100 states, "Normally, neither an uncertainty nor an inconsistency in the application of accounting principles would cause the accountant to modify the standard report provided the financial statements appropriately disclose such matters. Nothing in this statement, however, is intended to preclude an accountant from emphasizing in a separate paragraph of the report a matter regarding the financial statements."

Answer (B) is incorrect because an accountant may emphasize a matter in a separate paragraph. Answer (C) is incorrect because, if appropriate procedures have been applied and the accountant has formed a conclusion, a review report may be issued. Answer (D) is incorrect because, unless an audit has been conducted, an opinion may not be expressed.

66. During an engagement to review the financial statements of a nonpublic entity, an accountant becomes aware of a material departure from GAAP. If the accountant decides to modify the standard review report because management will not revise the financial statements, the accountant should

A. Express negative assurance on accounting principles not conforming with GAAP.

B. Disclose the departure from GAAP in a separate paragraph of the report.

C. Express an adverse or a qualified opinion, depending on materiality.

D. Express positive assurance on accounting principles conforming with GAAP.

The correct answer is (B). *(CPA, adapted)*

REQUIRED: The accountant's reporting responsibility in a review engagement given a material departure from GAAP and management's refusal to revise the statements.

DISCUSSION: AR 100 states that, if the accountant concludes that a departure from GAAP will result in a modified review report, the report should contain a separate paragraph disclosing the departure, including its effects on the financial statements if they have been determined by management or are known as the result of the accountant's procedures.

Answer (A) is incorrect because the accountant provides negative assurance when no departures from GAAP exist. Answers (C) and (D) are incorrect because a review does not result in the expression of any form of positive assurance, including an opinion.

67. Each page of a nonpublic entity's financial statements reviewed by an accountant should include the following reference:

A. See Accountant's Review Report.

B. Reviewed, No Accountant's Assurance Expressed.

C. See Accompanying Accountant's Footnotes.

D. Reviewed, No Material Modifications Required.

The correct answer is (A). *(CPA, adapted)*

REQUIRED: The reference on each page of financial statements reviewed by an accountant.

DISCUSSION: Each page should include a reference such as "See Accountant's Review Report" (AR 100).

Answer (B) is incorrect because a review report ordinarily expresses limited assurance. Answer (C) is incorrect because footnotes are part of the financial statements, not the accountant's report. Answer (D) is incorrect because the review report states that the accountant is not aware of any modifications that should be made other than those indicated in the report.

68. An accountant has been engaged to review a nonpublic entity's financial statements that contain several departures from GAAP. If the financial statements are not revised and modification of the standard review report is not adequate to indicate the deficiencies, the accountant should

A. Withdraw from the engagement and provide no further services concerning these financial statements.

B. Inform management that the engagement can proceed only if distribution of the report is restricted to internal use.

C. Determine the effects of the departures from GAAP and issue a special report on the financial statements.

D. Issue a modified review report provided the entity agrees that the financial statements will not be used to obtain credit.

The correct answer is (A). *(CPA, adapted)*

REQUIRED: The effect of uncorrected departures from GAAP when modifying the review report is not adequate.

DISCUSSION: If the accountant believes that modification of the standard report is not adequate to indicate the deficiencies in the financial statements taken as a whole, and if the client is unwilling to correct the deficiencies, (s)he should withdraw from the engagement and provide no further services with respect to those financial statements. The accountant may wish to consult with legal counsel in such circumstances. The standards do not provide for an adverse review report (AR 100).

Answers (B) and (D) are incorrect because no report should be issued in this situation. Answer (C) is incorrect because a special report is an audit report on financial statements prepared in conformity with an other comprehensive basis of accounting; specified elements, accounts, or items of a financial statement; etc.

69. An accountant has been asked to issue a review report on the balance sheet of a nonpublic company but not to report on the other basic financial statements. The accountant may not do so

A. Because compliance with this request would result in a violation of the ethical standards of the profession.

B. Because compliance with this request would result in an incomplete review.

C. If the review of the balance sheet discloses material departures from GAAP.

D. If the scope of the inquiry and analytical procedures has been restricted.

The correct answer is (D). *(CPA, adapted)*

REQUIRED: The situation in which an accountant may not issue a review report on a single financial statement.

DISCUSSION: "An accountant may be asked to issue a review report on one financial statement, such as the balance sheet, and not on other related financial statements, such as the statements of income, retained earnings, and cash flows. (S)he may do so if the scope of the inquiry and analytical procedures has not been restricted" (AR 100).

Answers (A) and (B) are incorrect because the accountant may report on one financial statement. Answer (C) is incorrect because, if the review discloses material departures from GAAP, the accountant may issue a modified report.

70. Davis, CPA, accepted an engagement to audit the financial statements of Tech Resources, a nonpublic entity. Before the completion of the audit, Tech requested Davis to change the engagement to a review of financial statements. Before Davis agrees to change the engagement, Davis is required to consider the

	Additional Audit Effort Necessary to Complete the Audit	Reason Given for Tech's Request
A.	No	No
B.	Yes	Yes
C.	Yes	No
D.	No	Yes

The correct answer is (B). *(CPA, adapted)*

REQUIRED: The matter(s) to be considered before changing an engagement from an audit to a review.

DISCUSSION: Before an accountant who was engaged to perform an audit in accordance with GAAS agrees to change the engagement to a compilation or a review, at least the following should be considered: (1) the reason given for the client's request, particularly the implications of a restriction on the scope of the audit, whether imposed by the client or by circumstances; (2) the additional audit effort required to complete the audit; and (3) the estimated additional cost to complete the audit (AR 100).

Answers (A), (C), and (D) are incorrect because the additional audit effort and the reason for the request should be considered prior to the change in engagement.

71. An accountant who had begun an audit of the financial statements of a nonpublic entity was asked to change the engagement to a review because of a restriction on the scope of the audit. Given reasonable justification for the change, the accountant's review report should refer to the

	Scope Limitation That Caused the Changed Engagement	Original Engagement That Was Agreed To
A.	Yes	No
B.	No	Yes
C.	No	No
D.	Yes	Yes

The correct answer is (C). *(CPA, adapted)*

REQUIRED: The reference(s) in a review report issued after a change of the engagement.

DISCUSSION: An accountant may be asked to change the engagement from a higher to a lower level of service. If the accountant concludes that the change is reasonably justified and if (s)he complies with the standards applicable to the changed engagement, the accountant may issue the appropriate review report. The report on the changed engagement should not mention the original engagement, any auditing procedures performed, or scope limitations that led to the changed engagement.

Answers (A), (B), and (D) are incorrect because neither the scope limitation that caused the changed engagement nor the original engagement that was agreed to should be disclosed in the report.

72. During a compilation, the client requests that the accountant test certain cash disbursement transactions. The accountant agrees and performs such procedures. The procedures

A. Are part of an auditing service and change the scope of the engagement to that of an audit in accordance with GAAS.

B. Are part of an accounting service and are not performed for the purpose of conducting an audit in accordance with GAAS.

C. Are not permitted when the purpose of the engagement is to compile financial statements and the work to be performed is not in accordance with GAAS.

D. Would require the accountant to issue a report indicating that the audit was conducted in accordance with GAAS but was limited in scope.

The correct answer is (B). *(Publisher)*

REQUIRED: The true statement about audit procedures performed during an engagement to compile statements.

DISCUSSION: Accountants may perform other accounting services in connection with a compilation or review of unaudited financial statements of a nonpublic entity (AR 100). Similarly, an accountant who is associated with statements of a public entity (s)he has not audited or reviewed may have performed some procedures (AU 504).

Answer (A) is incorrect because testing transactions does not convert the engagement to an audit. An audit entails comprehensive procedures to understand internal control and assess control risk, test accounting records, etc. Answer (C) is incorrect because the accountant is allowed to perform additional procedures when compiling statements, but such procedures may not be disclosed in the report. Answer (D) is incorrect because the accountant must prepare a report stating that the statements have not been audited or reviewed.

73. When an accountant performs more than one level of service (for example, a compilation and a review, or a compilation and an audit) concerning the financial statements of a nonpublic entity, the accountant ordinarily should issue the report that is appropriate for

A. The lowest level of service rendered.

B. The highest level of service rendered.

C. A compilation engagement.

D. A review engagement.

The correct answer is (B). *(CPA, adapted)*

REQUIRED: The report issued when an accountant performs more than one level of service.

DISCUSSION: The report should indicate the degree of responsibility, if any, that the accountant accepts regarding the financial statements. If an accountant performs a compilation or review of the statements of a nonpublic entity, (s)he should report in accordance with the SSARSs. But if more than one service is performed, (s)he "should issue the report that is appropriate for the highest level of service rendered" (AR 100). An exception is permitted, however, if an accountant has both compiled and reviewed the financial statements of a nonpublic entity and if the compilation report for the same period concerns financial statements included in a prescribed form that requires a departure from GAAP (AR 300).

Answers (A), (C), and (D) are incorrect because the report issued should usually be appropriate for the highest level of service rendered.

74. During the course of an audit of financial statements, the client informs the accountant that (s)he may not correspond with the client's legal counsel. Under these circumstances, the accountant

A. May issue the standard review report with no mention of a scope limitation.

B. Should refuse to issue a review report but would not ordinarily refuse to issue a compilation report.

C. Should ordinarily refuse to issue either a review or a compilation report.

D. Should mention the scope limitation in the review report.

The correct answer is (C). *(Publisher)*

REQUIRED: The effect of a client-imposed scope restriction.

DISCUSSION: The accountant must consider that the information affected by the restriction may be incorrect, incomplete, or otherwise unsatisfactory. An accountant who has been engaged to audit the financial statements ordinarily should refuse to issue either a review or a compilation report when not allowed to consult with the client's legal counsel (AR 100).

Answers (A), (B), and (D) are incorrect because the accountant is not allowed to issue a review or compilation report, however modified, when not allowed to consult with the client's legal counsel.

75. A continuing accountant is one who has been engaged to audit, review, or compile and report on the financial statements of the current period and one or more consecutive periods immediately prior to the current period. A continuing accountant who performs the same or a higher level of service with respect to the financial statements of the current period should

A. Update his/her report on the financial statements of a prior period.

B. Disclaim any assurance on the prior periods' statements.

C. Reissue the report on the financial statements of a prior period.

D. Express an adverse opinion with respect to the prior period's financial statements.

The correct answer is (A). *(Publisher)*

REQUIRED: The report by a continuing accountant.

DISCUSSION: When a continuing accountant performs the same or a higher level of service, an updated report should be issued that considers information of which (s)he becomes aware during the current engagement and that reexpresses the previous conclusions or, depending on the circumstances, expresses different conclusions on the financial statements of a prior period as of the date of the current report (AR 200, *Reporting on Comparative Financial Statements*).

Answer (B) is incorrect because the previous conclusions should be reexpressed unless circumstances require otherwise. Answer (C) is incorrect because a reissued report results when the continuing accountant performs a lower-level service in the current period. A reissued report bears the same date as the original report but may be revised for the effects of certain events. In that case, the report may be dual dated. Answer (D) is incorrect because opinions do not result from compilations and reviews.

76. When the financial statements of a prior period have been compiled or reviewed by a predecessor whose report is not presented, the successor should refer in an additional paragraph of the report on the current-period financial statements to the predecessor's report on the prior-period financial statements. This reference should include the date of the report and all of the following except

A. A statement that the financial statements of the prior period were compiled or reviewed by another accountant.

B. A description of the standard form of disclaimer or limited assurance, as applicable, included in the report.

C. A description of the procedures applied by the other auditor.

D. A description of any modifications of the standard report and of any paragraphs emphasizing a matter.

The correct answer is (C). *(Publisher)*

REQUIRED: The matter in a predecessor's review or compilation report that should not be included in a successor's report.

DISCUSSION: The procedures applied by the other auditor should not be described or discussed in the successor's report. Such a description might be misleading to the users of the report.

Answer (A) is incorrect because a statement that the financial statements of the prior period were compiled or reviewed by another accountant should be included in the successor's reference to the predecessor's report when that report is not presented. Answer (B) is incorrect because a description of the standard form of disclaimer or limited assurance, as applicable, should be included in the report. Answer (D) is incorrect because a description of any modifications of the standard report and of any paragraphs emphasizing a matter regarding the financial statements should be included in the report.

77. AR 400, *Communications between Predecessor and Successor Accountants*, provides guidance regarding compilations and reviews. A successor accountant

A. Must communicate with the predecessor before accepting the engagement.

B. Must not communicate with the predecessor. Communication would be a breach of confidentiality.

C. Need not communicate with a predecessor but may decide to do so.

D. Must communicate but not until after accepting the engagement.

The correct answer is (C). *(Publisher)*

REQUIRED: The true statement concerning predecessor-successor communication.

DISCUSSION: The successor accountant is not required to communicate with the predecessor. If the successor decides that communication is useful, (s)he should obtain the consent of the client and ask appropriate questions of the predecessor either orally or in writing. This inquiry allows the successor accountant to make a decision as to whether to accept the engagement.

Answers (A), (B), and (D) are incorrect because the standards permit but do not require the successor to communicate with the predecessor.

78. An accountant who has reviewed statements that did not omit the disclosures required by GAAP may subsequently be requested to compile statements for the same period that do omit substantially all of those disclosures when they are presented in comparative financial statements. In these circumstances, the accountant may report on the comparative compiled financial statements that omit such disclosures if (s)he

A. Does not mention the omissions.

B. Does not mention the prior report.

C. Includes in the report an additional paragraph indicating the nature of the previous service rendered.

D. States in the report that (s)he is not aware of any material modifications that should be made for the financial statements to be in conformity with GAAP.

The correct answer is (C). *(Publisher)*

REQUIRED: The basis for reporting on comparative compiled statements that omit disclosures required by GAAP that appeared in previously reviewed statements.

DISCUSSION: The accountant may report on the comparative compiled statements that omit these disclosures if the compilation report includes the date of the previous report and a paragraph that explains the prior service provided (AR 200).

Answer (A) is incorrect because the compilation report must mention the omission of the disclosures. Answer (B) is incorrect because the prior report based upon another accounting service should be referred to and its date given. Answer (D) is incorrect because limited assurance is provided in a report on a review of financial statements, not a compilation.

79. Clark, CPA, compiled and properly reported on the financial statements of Green Co., a nonpublic entity, for the year ended March 31, 1997. These statements omitted substantially all disclosures required by GAAP. Green asked Clark to compile the statements for the year ended March 31, 1998, and to include all GAAP disclosures for the 1998 statements only, but otherwise present both years' statements in comparative form. Clark may

A. Not report on the comparative financial statements because the 1997 statements are not comparable with the 1998 statements that include the GAAP disclosures.

B. Report on the comparative financial statements provided the 1997 statements have no obvious material misstatements.

C. Report on the comparative financial statements provided an explanatory paragraph is added to Clark's report on the comparative financial statements.

D. Report on the comparative financial statements provided Clark updates the report on the 1997 statements.

The correct answer is (A). *(CPA, adapted)*

REQUIRED: The accountant's responsibility when compiled financial statements are presented comparatively but the earlier year's statements omit most disclosures required by GAAP.

DISCUSSION: Compiled financial statements that omit substantially all of the disclosures required by GAAP are not comparable to financial statements that include such disclosures. Accordingly, the accountant should not issue a report on comparative financial statements when statements for one or more, but not all, of the periods presented omit substantially all of the disclosures required by GAAP (AR 200).

Answers (B), (C), and (D) are incorrect because the comparative statements are not comparable and should not be reported on.

80. One of the conditions required for an accountant to submit a written personal financial plan containing unaudited financial statements to a client without complying with the requirements of AR 100 is that the

A. Client agrees that the financial statements will not be used to obtain credit.

B. Accountant compiled or reviewed the client's financial statements for the immediate prior year.

C. Engagement letter acknowledges that the financial statements will contain departures from GAAP.

D. Accountant expresses limited assurance that the financial statements are free of any material misstatements.

The correct answer is (A). *(CPA, adapted)*

REQUIRED: The condition for an accountant to submit a written personal financial plan.

DISCUSSION: The accountant must have an understanding with the client, preferably written, that the statements "will be used solely to assist the client and the client's advisers to develop the client's personal financial goals and objectives" and that they "will not be used to obtain credit or for any purposes other than developing these goals and objectives." Nothing must come to the accountant's attention during the engagement that indicates a use of the statements that violates the understanding (AR 600).

Answer (B) is incorrect because the accountant need not be a continuing accountant or have audited, reviewed, or compiled the statements. Answer (C) is incorrect because the accountant's report should indicate that the statements may be incomplete or contain a departure from GAAP, but AR 600 establishes no such requirement for the engagement letter. Answer (D) is incorrect because the accountant expresses no assurance on these statements.

8.5 Reports on Internal Control

81. Which of the following best describes a CPA's engagement to report on an entity's internal control over financial reporting?

A. An attestation engagement to examine and report on management's written assertion about the effectiveness of its internal control.

B. An audit engagement to express an opinion on the entity's internal control.

C. A prospective engagement to project, for a period of time not to exceed one year, and report on the expected benefits of the entity's internal control.

D. A consulting engagement to provide constructive advice to the entity on its internal control.

The correct answer is (A). *(CPA, adapted)*

REQUIRED: The best description of an engagement to report on an entity's internal control over financial reporting.

DISCUSSION: In an attestation engagement to examine and report on management's written assertion about the effectiveness of its internal control over financial reporting, the practitioner's objective is to express an opinion about whether the assertion regarding internal control as a whole is fairly stated, in all material respects, based upon the control criteria.

Answer (B) is incorrect because the CPA's responsibility is to express an opinion on management's assertion about internal control, not on internal control itself. Answer (C) is incorrect because the opinion expressed by the CPA should not extend into the future. Answer (D) is incorrect because consulting engagements do not result in the expression of an opinion.

82. A practitioner may accept an engagement to examine and report on management's assertion about the effectiveness of an entity's internal control over financial reporting only if certain conditions are met. Which of the following is not such a condition?

A. Management accepts responsibility for the effectiveness of internal control.

B. Management evaluates the effectiveness of the entity's internal control using reasonable criteria.

C. Management provides assurance that inherent limitations in the existing internal control have been eliminated.

D. Management presents its written assertion about the effectiveness of internal control.

The correct answer is (C). *(Publisher)*

REQUIRED: The item not a condition of examining and reporting on management's assertion about internal control.

DISCUSSION: A practitioner may express an opinion on the fairness of management's written assertion about the effectiveness of its internal control in effect as of a specified date or in effect during a specified period of time. The conditions for engagement performance do not include management assurances about elimination of inherent limitations in internal control. These limitations cannot be eliminated. Hence, the standard report states that errors and irregularities may not be detected because of inherent limitations (AT 400).

Answers (A), (B), and (D) are incorrect because the conditions for examining and reporting in a general-use document about management's assertion are that (1) management accept responsibility for the effectiveness of internal control, (2) management evaluate effectiveness based on reasonable criteria established by a recognized body, (3) sufficient competent evidence exists or can be developed to support management's evaluation, and (4) management present its assertion in a separate written report, accompanying the practitioner's report.

83. The practitioner's standard report expressing an opinion on management's assertion about the effectiveness of an entity's internal control over financial reporting need not include

A. An identification of management's assertion about the effectiveness of the entity's internal control.

B. A paragraph stating that, because of inherent limitations of any internal control, errors or irregularities may occur and not be detected.

C. A statement that the examination was made in accordance with standards established by the AICPA.

D. A statement that the entity's internal control is consistent with that of the prior year given subsequent changes.

The correct answer is (D). *(Publisher)*

REQUIRED: The information not in a report on management's assertion about the effectiveness of an entity's internal control.

DISCUSSION: The standard report on management's assertion about the effectiveness of internal control over financial reporting does not contain a statement about consistency. Moreover, lack of consistency is not listed as a basis for modification of the standard report (AT 400).

Answer (A) is incorrect because the introductory paragraph of the standard report identifies management's assertion by referring to the title used by management. Answer (B) is incorrect because the inherent limitations paragraph states that, in any internal control, errors or irregularities may occur and not be detected. It also states that conditions may change and that the degree of compliance with policies and procedures may deteriorate. Answer (C) is incorrect because the scope paragraph states that the examination was made in accordance with standards established by the AICPA.

84. How do the scope, procedures, and purpose of an engagement to express an opinion on management's assertion about an entity's internal control compare with those for the consideration of internal control in a financial statement audit?

	Scope	Procedures	Purpose
A.	Similar	Different	Similar
B.	Different	Similar	Similar
C.	Different	Different	Different
D.	Different	Similar	Different

The correct answer is (D). *(CPA, adapted)*

REQUIRED: The comparison of an engagement to express an opinion on management's assertion about an entity's internal control and the understanding of internal control in an audit.

DISCUSSION: The purpose of an examination of management's assertion about internal control is to express an opinion. The purpose of the consideration of internal control in a financial statement audit is to enable the auditor to plan the audit. The two engagements also differ in scope. In the latter, the auditor is only required to obtain an understanding of internal control and assess control risk. Accordingly, the consideration in an audit is usually more limited than that undertaken to express an opinion. However, the procedures typically performed are similar.

Answers (A), (B), and (C) are incorrect because the scope and purposes of the two engagements are different, but the procedures are similar.

85. When an independent auditor reports on management's assertion about internal control based on criteria established by a regulatory agency, the report should

A. State that the practitioner assumes responsibility for the comprehensiveness of the criteria if they have not been subjected to due process procedures.

B. Modify the inherent limitations paragraph.

C. Limit the distribution of the report if the criteria have not been subjected to due process procedures.

D. Identify the control criteria in the introductory paragraph if they have been subjected to due process procedures.

The correct answer is (C). *(Publisher)*

REQUIRED: The true statement about a report on internal control based on established criteria.

DISCUSSION: If management's assertion is based on criteria established by a regulatory agency after following due process procedures, including broad distribution of proposed criteria for public comment, one of the standard forms of reporting may be used. If the control criteria have not been subjected to due process procedures, the appropriate form of the standard report must be modified. The principal modification is a limitation on distribution stated in a paragraph following the opinion paragraph.

Answer (A) is incorrect because the practitioner assumes no responsibility for the control criteria, but (s)he must report material weaknesses that come to his/her attention even if they are not covered by the criteria. Answer (B) is incorrect because AT 400 lists seven conditions for modification of the standard reports, but none requires omission or amendment of the inherent limitations paragraph. Answer (D) is incorrect because the control criteria are mentioned only in the opinion paragraph of the standard reports unless they have not been subjected to due process procedures.

86. A practitioner has been engaged to report on management's assertion about an entity's internal control without performing an audit of the financial statements. The assertion is contained in a separate report that will accompany the practitioner's report and is based on control criteria that have been subjected to due process procedures. What restrictions, if any, should the practitioner place on the use of this report?

A. This report should be restricted for use by management.

B. This report should be restricted for use by the audit committee.

C. This report should be restricted for use by a specified regulatory agency.

D. The practitioner does not need to place any restrictions on the use of this report.

The correct answer is (D). *(CPA, adapted)*

REQUIRED: The restrictions, if any, on the use of a report on management's assertion about internal control.

DISCUSSION: Practitioners are allowed to provide assurances that management's assertion about internal control is fairly stated in all material respects in accordance with the control criteria. Such a report will have no restrictions on its use if the assertion is based upon criteria that have been subjected to due process procedures and is included in a separate report that accompanies the practitioner's report. However, if the assertion is presented only in a representation letter to the practitioner, the asserter's responsibility may not be sufficiently clear to permit distribution to third parties. In this case, the report should limit distribution. A similar limitation is necessary when the control criteria have been established by a regulatory agency that did not follow due process.

Answers (A), (B), and (C) are incorrect because this report need not be restricted.

87. A practitioner's report on internal control is least likely to be issued as a result of

A. An engagement to examine management's assertion based on criteria established by a regulatory body.

B. A review of the annual financial statements of a large corporation.

C. A request to apply agreed-upon procedures relating to management's assertion about the effectiveness of internal control.

D. A request by management to report on the fairness of its assertion about the effectiveness of internal control.

The correct answer is (B). *(CPA, adapted)*

REQUIRED: The engagement that would least likely result in a report related to internal control.

DISCUSSION: A review is appropriate for nonpublic entities that seek a report expressing only limited assurance. Thus, a report related to internal control is not likely to be issued because a "review of the annual financial statements of a large corporation" is itself unlikely. Moreover, a review does not contemplate consideration of internal control (AR 100). According to AT 400, a practitioner may examine or apply agreed-upon procedures relating to, but not review, management's assertion about the effectiveness of internal control.

Answer (A) is incorrect because a regulatory body may establish its own criteria, which may or may not have been subjected to due process procedures. Answer (C) is incorrect because a practitioner may apply agreed-upon procedures relating to the assertion. However, the report should be in the form of procedures and findings and not provide positive or negative assurance. Answer (D) is incorrect because a practitioner may examine and express a positive opinion on the assertion.

88. A practitioner's client is subject to the jurisdiction of a regulatory agency. The client has requested the practitioner to examine and report on its separate written assertion about internal control based on criteria established by the agency. These control criteria have not been subjected to due process procedures. The auditor completes the examination but discovers a material weakness in control not covered by the criteria. Which of the following statements about the engagement is true?

A. The practitioner should include the weakness in the report.

B. The practitioner assumes responsibility for the comprehensiveness of the criteria.

C. The practitioner need not limit the distribution of the report.

D. Because the criteria were not subject to due process procedures, the practitioner should not accept the engagement.

The correct answer is (A). *(Publisher)*

REQUIRED: The true statement concerning a practitioner's report based on control criteria established by a regulatory body.

DISCUSSION: The practitioner should "report any condition that comes to his/her attention during the course of the examination that (s)he believes is a material weakness, even though it may not be covered by the criteria" (AT 400).

Answer (B) is incorrect because the agency, not the practitioner, assumes responsibility for the comprehensiveness of the criteria. Answer (C) is incorrect because the control criteria were not subjected to due process. Thus, the report should include a paragraph limiting distribution to the client and agency. Answer (D) is incorrect because the practitioner may accept the engagement.

89. AU 324, *Reports on the Processing of Transactions by Service Organizations*, relates to audits of service organizations and of clients of service organizations. It provides guidance when a service organization executes client transactions and maintains the recorded accountability, records transactions and processes related data, or performs various combinations of these services for the client. Which of the following is a true statement about a service auditor's report?

A. It provides the user auditor with assurance regarding whether controls have been placed in operation at the client organization.

B. It should include an opinion.

C. If it proves to be inappropriate for the user auditor's purposes, (s)he must personally apply procedures at the service organization.

D. A user auditor need not inquire about the service auditor's professional reputation.

The correct answer is (B). *(Publisher)*

REQUIRED: The true statement about a service auditor's report regarding internal control.

DISCUSSION: A service auditor's report on controls at the service organization should be helpful in providing a sufficient understanding to plan the audit of the user organization. The service auditor's report may express an opinion on the fairness of the description of the controls placed in operation at the service organization and whether they were suitably designed. If the service auditor has also tested controls, the report may also express an opinion on their operating effectiveness.

Answer (A) is incorrect because a service auditor's report is helpful to the user auditor in obtaining an understanding of internal control at the service organization, including whether relevant controls have been placed in operation, but it does not provide assurance regarding conditions at the client organization. Answer (C) is incorrect because audit procedures at the service organization may be applied by the service auditor on the request of (and under the direction of) the user auditor. Answer (D) is incorrect because the user auditor should inquire about the service auditor's professional reputation. AU 543 gives appropriate sources of information.

90. Lake, CPA, is auditing the financial statements of Gill Co. Gill uses the Technology Service Center, Inc. to process its payroll transactions. Technology's financial statements are audited by Cope, CPA, who recently issued a report on Technology's internal control. Lake is considering Cope's report in assessing control risk on the Gill engagement. What is Lake's responsibility concerning making reference to Cope as a basis, in part, for Lake's own opinion?

A. Lake may refer to Cope only if Lake is satisfied as to Cope's professional reputation and independence.

B. Lake may refer to Cope only if Lake relies on Cope's report in restricting the extent of substantive tests.

C. Lake may refer to Cope only if Lake's report indicates the division of responsibility.

D. Lake may not refer to Cope under the circumstances above.

The correct answer is (D). *(CPA, adapted)*

REQUIRED: The reference, if any, in an auditor's report to a service auditor's report on internal control.

DISCUSSION: The service auditor was not responsible for examining any portion of the user organization's financial statements. Hence, the user auditor should not refer to the service auditor's report as a basis in part for his/her own opinion on those financial statements (AU 324).

Answer (A) is incorrect because, although the user auditor should make inquiries concerning the service auditor's professional reputation and consider the service auditor's independence, no reference to the service auditor should be made in the user auditor's report. Answer (B) is incorrect because the user auditor should not refer to the service auditor's report even if (s)he uses that report in assessing control risk and determining the nature, timing, and extent of the substantive tests. Answer (C) is incorrect because the user auditor should not divide responsibility with the service auditor.

91. A service organization's internal control may interact with that of the client. The user auditor

A. Is not required to evaluate the service organization's controls.

B. Should obtain absolute assurance that the service organization's internal control will prevent or detect errors or fraud.

C. Should not consider weaknesses in the service organization's internal control to be weaknesses in the client's system.

D. Need not be concerned with the service organization's internal control if the client has effective controls related to service organization processing.

The correct answer is (D). *(Publisher)*

REQUIRED: The true statement about the interaction of controls at the service and client organizations.

DISCUSSION: When the client has effective controls related to service organization processing, the user auditor may be able to assess control risk at an acceptably low level and forgo the service auditor's report.

Answer (A) is incorrect because, when controls of the client and service organizations interact, the service organization's controls must be evaluated in conjunction with the client's. Answer (B) is incorrect because reasonable, not absolute, assurance should be obtained that the service organization's controls will prevent or detect errors and fraud. Answer (C) is incorrect because the user auditor should consider the combination of controls at the client and service organizations.

92. A service auditor's report on internal control may be issued on controls placed in operation or on controls placed in operation and tests of operating effectiveness. Which of the following is true of a report on controls placed in operation?

A. It should disclaim an opinion on whether internal control, taken as a whole, meets the control objectives.

B. It should include an opinion concerning the design of internal control as well as conclusions from tests of controls.

C. It will include a list of all errors and fraud found.

D. It need not be restricted in its use and may be made available to any third party.

The correct answer is (A). *(Publisher)*

REQUIRED: The true statement about a service auditor's report on internal control.

DISCUSSION: A service auditor's report on controls placed in operation should contain a disclaimer of opinion on operating effectiveness and an opinion on whether the service organization's description of control objectives and controls fairly presents, in all material respects, the relevant aspects of the controls placed in operation at a specific date. It also includes an opinion on whether they were suitably designed to provide reasonable assurance that the control objectives would be achieved if complied with satisfactorily (AU 324).

Answer (B) is incorrect because no tests of controls have been performed. Thus, no conclusions as to effectiveness can be expressed. Answer (C) is incorrect because clearly inconsequential errors and fraud that have been detected and corrected need not be identified. Answer (D) is incorrect because a service auditor's report is intended solely for the use of service organization management, client organizations, and their independent auditors.

8.6 Prospective and Pro Forma Financial Information

93. A financial forecast consists of prospective financial statements that present an entity's expected financial position, results of operations, and cash flows. A forecast

A. Is based on the most conservative estimates.

B. Presents estimates given one or more hypothetical assumptions.

C. Unlike a projection, may contain a range.

D. Is based on assumptions reflecting conditions expected to exist and courses of action expected to be taken.

The correct answer is (D). *(Publisher)*

REQUIRED: The true statement about a financial forecast.

DISCUSSION: According to AT 200, a financial forecast consists of prospective financial statements "that present, to the best of the responsible party's knowledge and belief, an entity's expected financial position, results of operations, and cash flows." A forecast is based on "the responsible party's assumptions reflecting conditions it expects to exist and the course of action it expects to take."

Answer (A) is incorrect because the information presented is based on expected (most likely) conditions and courses of action. Answer (B) is incorrect because a financial projection (not a forecast) is based on assumptions by the responsible party reflecting expected conditions and courses of action, given one or more hypothetical assumptions (a condition or action not necessarily expected to occur). Answer (C) is incorrect because both forecasts and projections may be stated as point estimates or ranges.

94. The AICPA recommends that the format of prospective financial statements be similar to

A. Traditional financial statements, such as income statements, balance sheets, and statements of cash flows.

B. Worksheet formats so that adjustments can be readily made.

C. Specialized schedules that do not resemble financial statements.

D. Computer printouts so that the sophisticated nature of forecasting can be demonstrated.

The correct answer is (A). *(Publisher)*

REQUIRED: The recommended format appropriate for prospective financial statements.

DISCUSSION: The AICPA states that information in prospective financial statements should be communicated by using the format of traditional financial statements, unless the responsible party and potential users agree on another format. This information should be put in the form of income statements, balance sheets, and statements of cash flows to facilitate comparisons with prior periods as well as with the actual financial statements for the prospective period (AT 200)

Answers (B), (C), and (D) are incorrect because worksheet formats, specialized schedules, and computer printouts are inappropriate for prospective financial statements.

95. AT 200 provides for minimum presentation guidelines for prospective financial information that

A. Permit prospective financial statements to be limited to certain minimum items.

B. Apply to pro forma statements.

C. Apply to partial presentations distributed for general use.

D. Require the usual footnotes associated with historical statements, including summaries of significant accounting policies and assumptions.

The correct answer is (A). *(Publisher)*

REQUIRED: The correct provision of the minimum presentation guidelines.

DISCUSSION: Under the guidelines, prospective financial statements may take the form of complete basic statements or be limited to the following minimum items: (1) sales or gross revenues; (2) gross profit or cost of sales; (3) unusual or infrequently occurring items; (4) provision for income taxes; (5) discontinued operations or extraordinary items; (6) income from continuing operations; (7) net income; (8) primary and fully diluted earnings per share; (9) significant cash flows; (10) a description of what management intends the statements to present, a statement that the assumptions are based on information about circumstances and conditions existing at the time of preparation, and a caveat about achievability; (11) summary of significant assumptions; and (12) summary of significant accounting policies.

Answer (B) is incorrect because pro forma statements demonstrate the effect of a consummated or hypothetical transaction or event by showing how it might have affected the historical statements if it had occurred during the period covered by those statements. Answer (C) is incorrect because a presentation is partial if it omits one or more of items (1) through (9) above. A partial presentation is ordinarily not appropriate for general use. The presentation is not deemed to be partial and the provisions of AT 200 still apply if items (10) through (12) are omitted. Answer (D) is incorrect because the details of each statement may be summarized or condensed, and the usual footnotes need not be included as such.

96. Which of the following statements concerning prospective financial statements is correct?

A. Only a financial forecast would normally be appropriate for limited use.

B. Only a financial projection would normally be appropriate for general use.

C. Any type of prospective financial statements would normally be appropriate for limited use.

D. Any type of prospective financial statements would normally be appropriate for general use.

The correct answer is (C). *(CPA, adapted)*

REQUIRED: The true statement about prospective financial statements.

DISCUSSION: Limited use of prospective financial statements means use by the responsible party and those with whom that party is negotiating directly, for example, in a submission to a regulatory body or in negotiations for a bank loan. These third parties are in a position to communicate directly with the responsible party. Consequently, AT 200 states, "Any type of prospective financial statements that would be useful in the circumstances would be appropriate for limited use."

Answer (A) is incorrect because projections as well as forecasts are appropriate for limited use. Answers (B) and (D) are incorrect because only a forecast is appropriate for general use.

97. An accountant's compilation report on a financial forecast should include a statement that

A. The forecast should be read only in conjunction with the audited historical financial statements.

B. The accountant expresses only limited assurance on the forecasted statements and their assumptions.

C. There will usually be differences between the forecasted and actual results.

D. The hypothetical assumptions used in the forecast are reasonable in the circumstances.

The correct answer is (C). *(CPA, adapted)*

REQUIRED: The statement included in an accountant's compilation report on a financial forecast.

DISCUSSION: The standard report states that a compilation is limited in scope and does not enable the accountant to express an opinion or any other form of assurance. It adds that there will usually be differences between the forecasted and actual results (AT 200).

Answer (A) is incorrect because a forecast may stand alone. Answer (B) is incorrect because a compilation provides no assurance. Answer (D) is incorrect because a financial projection, not a financial forecast, contains hypothetical assumptions.

98. The accountant's standard report on the examination of prospective financial statements should include all of the following except

A. An identification of the prospective financial statements presented and a statement that the examination was made in accordance with AICPA standards.

B. A statement that the accountant assumes no responsibility to update the report for events and circumstances after the report date.

C. The accountant's opinion that the statements are in conformity with AICPA presentation guidelines and that the underlying assumptions provide a reasonable basis for the projection given the hypothetical assumptions or a reasonable basis for the forecast.

D. The accountant's opinion that the prospective results will be attained.

The correct answer is (D). *(Publisher)*

REQUIRED: The inappropriate element in a report on prospective financial statements.

DISCUSSION: Whenever an accountant submits prospective financial statements that (s)he has assembled that reasonably might be expected to be used by a third party or reports on such statements, (s)he should examine, compile, or apply agreed-upon procedures to the statements. An examination is a professional service involving evaluation of the preparation of the statements, of the support underlying the assumptions, and of the presentation of the statements in conformity with AICPA guidelines. It also entails issuance of a report. However, the accountant should provide a caveat that the prospective results may not be attained (AT 200).

Answers (A), (B), and (C) are incorrect because each item should appear in the standard report.

99. An accountant's standard report on a compilation of a projection should not include a

A. Statement that a compilation of a projection is limited in scope.

B. Disclaimer of responsibility to update the report for events occurring after the report's date.

C. Statement that the accountant expresses only limited assurance that the results may be achieved.

D. Separate paragraph that describes the limitations on the presentation's usefulness.

The correct answer is (C). *(CPA, adapted)*

REQUIRED: The item not in an accountant's standard report on a compilation of a projection.

DISCUSSION: Limited assurance (e.g., based on a review) should not be provided by the accountant based on any prospective financial statement service.

Answer (A) is incorrect because the report should state that a compilation is limited in scope and does not provide any form of assurance. Answer (B) is incorrect because the report should contain a statement that the accountant assumes no responsibility to update the report for events and circumstances occurring after the report date. Answer (D) is incorrect because, if the accountant has reservations about the usefulness of the statements (e.g., the statements fail to provide footnotes), (s)he should so indicate in a separate paragraph.

100. When an accountant examines a financial forecast that fails to disclose several significant assumptions used to prepare the forecast, the accountant should describe the assumptions in the accountant's report and express

A. An "except for" qualified opinion.

B. A "subject to" qualified opinion.

C. An unqualified opinion with a separate explanatory paragraph.

D. An adverse opinion.

The correct answer is (D). *(CPA, adapted)*

REQUIRED: The appropriate opinion if a forecast fails to disclose several significant assumptions.

DISCUSSION: An examination entails evaluating the preparation of the statements, the support underlying the assumptions, and the presentation of the statements for conformity with AICPA guidelines. It also involves issuance of a report stating the accountant's opinion on whether (1) the presentation conforms with AICPA guidelines and (2) the assumptions provide a reasonable basis for the forecast. If assumptions that appear to be significant at the time are not disclosed in the presentation, including the summary of assumptions, the accountant must express an adverse opinion. Moreover, an accountant should not examine a presentation that omits all such disclosures.

Answer (A) is incorrect because omission of assumptions that appear significant requires an adverse opinion. Other departures from the presentation guidelines, however, may justify either a qualified or an adverse opinion. Answer (B) is incorrect because the language "subject to" is never permissible. Answer (C) is incorrect because an explanatory paragraph is insufficient when significant assumptions are omitted (AT 200).

101. The party responsible for assumptions identified in the preparation of prospective financial statements is usually

A. A third-party lending institution.

B. The client's management.

C. The reporting accountant.

D. The client's independent auditor.

The correct answer is (B). *(CPA, adapted)*

REQUIRED: The party responsible for assumptions identified in the preparation of prospective statements.

DISCUSSION: Management is usually the responsible party, that is, the person(s) responsible for the assumptions underlying prospective financial statements. However, the responsible party may be a party outside the entity, such as a possible acquirer.

Answers (A), (C), and (D) are incorrect because management is usually the responsible party.

102. Which of the following is a prospective financial statement for general use upon which an accountant may appropriately report?

A. Financial projection.

B. Partial presentation.

C. Pro forma financial statement.

D. Financial forecast.

The correct answer is (D). *(CPA, adapted)*

REQUIRED: The prospective financial statement for general use upon which an accountant may report.

DISCUSSION: Prospective financial statements are for general use if they are for use by persons with whom the responsible party is not negotiating directly, e.g., in an offering statement of the party's securities. Only a report based on an examination of a financial forecast is appropriate for general use.

Answer (A) is incorrect because a projection is appropriate only for limited use, i.e., by the responsible party or by those with whom that party is negotiating directly. The reason is that it is based on one or more hypothetical assumptions. Answer (B) is incorrect because a presentation not in compliance with minimum guidelines is not appropriate for general use. Answer (C) is incorrect because pro forma statements are essentially historical, not prospective, statements.

103. Given one or more hypothetical assumptions, a responsible party may prepare, to the best of its knowledge and belief, an entity's expected financial position, results of operations, and cash flows. Such prospective financial statements are known as

A. Pro forma financial statements.

B. Financial projections.

C. Partial presentations.

D. Financial forecasts.

The correct answer is (B). *(CPA, adapted)*

REQUIRED: The prospective statements based on one or more hypothetical assumptions.

DISCUSSION: Prospective statements include forecasts and projections. The difference between a forecast and a projection is that only the latter is based on one or more hypothetical assumptions, which are conditions or actions not necessarily expected to occur.

Answer (A) is incorrect because pro forma statements are essentially historical, not prospective, statements. Answer (C) is incorrect because partial presentations are not prospective statements. They do not meet the minimum presentation guidelines. Answer (D) is incorrect because forecasts are based on assumptions about conditions the responsible party expects to exist and the course of action it expects to take.

104. Accepting an engagement to examine an entity's financial projection most likely would be appropriate if the projection were to be distributed to

A. All employees who work for the entity.

B. Potential shareholders who request a prospectus or a registration statement.

C. A bank with which the entity is negotiating for a loan.

D. All shareholders of record as of the report date.

The correct answer is (C). *(CPA, adapted)*

REQUIRED: The situation in which acceptance of an engagement to examine a projection is appropriate.

DISCUSSION: A projection is based on one or more hypothetical assumptions and therefore should be considered for limited use only. Limited use of prospective financial statements means use by the responsible party and those with whom that party is negotiating directly. Examples of appropriate use include negotiations for a bank loan and submission to a regulatory body.

Answers (A), (B), and (D) are incorrect because a projection is inappropriate for distribution to those who will not be negotiating directly with the responsible party.

105. An accountant's compilation report on a financial forecast should include a statement that the

A. Compilation does not include evaluation of the support for the assumptions underlying the forecast.

B. Hypothetical assumptions used in the forecast are reasonable.

C. Range of assumptions selected is one in which one end of the range is less likely to occur than the other.

D. Prospective statements are limited to presenting, in the form of a forecast, information that is the accountant's representation.

The correct answer is (A). *(CPA, adapted)*

REQUIRED: The true statement about a compilation report on a financial forecast.

DISCUSSION: A compilation of a financial forecast involves assembling, to the extent necessary, the statements based on the responsible party's assumptions, performing required compilation procedures, and issuing a compilation report. The procedures include reading the statements and considering whether they meet AICPA presentation guidelines and are not obviously inappropriate. The standard report states that a compilation "does not include evaluation of the support for the assumptions."

Answer (B) is incorrect because a compilation does not enable the accountant to express an opinion or any other form of assurance. Answer (C) is incorrect because AT 200 states, "When a forecast contains a range, the range is not selected in a biased or misleading manner, for example, a range in which one end is significantly less expected than the other." Answer (D) is incorrect because the representations in the forecast are those of management.

106. An accountant may perform an agreed-upon procedures attestation engagement regarding prospective financial statements provided that

A. Use of the report is to be restricted to the specified users.

B. The prospective financial statements are also examined.

C. Responsibility for the sufficiency of the procedures performed is taken by the accountant.

D. Negative assurance is expressed on the prospective financial statements taken as a whole.

The correct answer is (A). *(CPA, adapted)*

REQUIRED: The condition for performing an agreed-upon procedures attestation engagement regarding prospective financial statements.

DISCUSSION: AT 200 establishes conditions for performing such an engagement: (1) the accountant is independent, (2) the specified users have participated in establishing the procedures and take responsibility for their sufficiency, (3) the statements include a summary of significant assumptions, (4) the accountant and the users have agreed upon the criteria to be used in determining findings, (5) the procedures are expected to result in findings capable of reasonably consistent estimation or measurement using the criteria, (6) use of the report is restricted to those users, and (7) evidence is expected to exist providing a reasonable basis for expressing the findings.

Answer (B) is incorrect because the accountant should state that the work performed does not constitute an examination. Answer (C) is incorrect because the specified users must assume responsibility for the sufficiency of the procedures. Answer (D) is incorrect because the accountant should not provide negative assurance.

107. When third party use of prospective financial statements is expected, an accountant may not accept an engagement to

A. Perform a review.

B. Perform a compilation.

C. Perform an examination.

D. Apply agreed-upon procedures.

The correct answer is (A). *(CPA, adapted)*

REQUIRED: The engagement regarding prospective statements that may not be accepted.

DISCUSSION: AT 200 does not provide for the review form of engagement with regard to prospective statements.

Answer (B) is incorrect because a compilation may be performed provided the report does not express any form of assurance. Answer (C) is incorrect because an examination report may express an opinion on presentation in conformity with AICPA guidelines and the reasonableness of assumptions. Answer (D) is incorrect because an agreed-upon procedures engagement is permissible, but the report must state that the work performed does not constitute an examination.

108. Which of the following presents what the effects on historical financial data might have been if a consummated transaction had occurred earlier?

A. Prospective financial statements.

B. Pro forma financial information.

C. Interim financial information.

D. A financial projection.

The correct answer is (B). *(Publisher)*

REQUIRED: The presentation that reflects the results of a consummated transaction had it occurred earlier.

DISCUSSION: According to AT 300, *Reporting on Pro Forma Financial Information*, pro forma information shows "what the significant effects on historical financial information would have been had a consummated or proposed transaction (or event) occurred at an earlier date." Examples of these transactions include a business combination, disposal of a segment, change in the form or status of an entity, and change in capitalization.

Answers (A) and (D) are incorrect because forecasts and projections are not presentations of historical information. Answer (C) is incorrect because interim financial information states actual results.

109. An accountant may report on an examination of pro forma financial information if the related historical financial statements have been

A. Audited.

B. Audited or reviewed.

C. Audited, reviewed, or compiled.

D. Reviewed or compiled.

The correct answer is (A). *(Publisher)*

REQUIRED: The service(s) on historical statements permitting an examination of pro forma financial information.

DISCUSSION: An accountant may examine or review pro forma financial information if (1) the document includes or incorporates by reference the complete historical statements, (2) the assurance provided is limited to that given on the historical statements, and (3) the reporting accountant is knowledgeable about the reporting practices of each significant part of the combined entity. Thus, an examination of pro forma information is appropriate only if the historical statements have been audited (AT 300).

Answer (B) is incorrect because, if the historical statements have been reviewed, only a review of the pro forma information is appropriate. Answers (C) and (D) are incorrect because a compilation of the historical statements provides no assurance; it does not provide a basis for examining or reviewing the pro forma statements.

110. The accountant's report on an examination of pro forma financial information

A. Should have the same date as the related historical financial statements.

B. Should be added to the report on the historical financial statements.

C. Need not mention the report on the historical financial statements.

D. May state an unqualified, qualified, or adverse opinion.

The correct answer is (D). *(Publisher)*

REQUIRED: The true statement about the accountant's report on an examination of pro forma financial information.

DISCUSSION: The report should include an opinion on whether (1) management's assumptions provide a reasonable basis for the significant effects attributable to the transaction or event, (2) the pro forma adjustments give appropriate effect to the assumptions, and (3) the pro forma column reflects the proper application of those adjustments to the historical data. Scope limitations, uncertainties, reservations about the assumptions or the presentation (including inadequate disclosure), and other matters may lead to modification of the opinion or a disclaimer (AT 300).

Answer (A) is incorrect because the report should be dated as of the completion of procedures. Answer (B) is incorrect because the report may appear separately. If it is combined with the report on the historical statements, the combined report may need to be dual-dated. Answer (C) is incorrect because the report should refer to the financial statements and state whether they were audited or reviewed.

111. An accountant's report on a review of pro forma financial information should include a

A. Statement that the entity's internal control was not relied on in the review.

B. Disclaimer of opinion on the financial statements from which the pro forma financial information is derived.

C. Caveat that it is uncertain whether the transaction or event reflected in the pro forma financial information will ever occur.

D. Reference to the financial statements from which the historical financial information is derived.

The correct answer is (D). *(CPA, adapted)*

REQUIRED: The statement that should be included in a review of pro forma financial information.

DISCUSSION: An accountant's report on pro forma information should include (1) an identification of the pro forma information, (2) a reference to the financial statements from which the historical financial information is derived and a statement as to whether such financial statements were audited or reviewed, (3) a statement that the review was made in accordance with standards established by the AICPA, (4) a caveat that a review is substantially less in scope than an examination and that no opinion is expressed, (5) a separate paragraph explaining the objective of pro forma financial information and its limitations, and (6) the accountant's conclusion providing negative assurance (AT 300).

Answer (A) is incorrect because the report should not mention internal control. Answer (B) is incorrect because the accountant should disclaim an opinion on the pro forma financial information. Answer (C) is incorrect because the transaction may already have occurred.

8.7 SEC Reporting and Letters for Underwriters and Certain Other Requesting Parties

112. The Securities and Exchange Commission has authority to

A. Prescribe specific auditing procedures to detect fraud concerning inventories and accounts receivable of companies engaged in interstate commerce.

B. Deny lack of privity as a defense in third-party actions for gross negligence against the auditors of public companies.

C. Determine accounting principles for the purpose of financial reporting by companies offering securities to the public.

D. Require a change of auditors of governmental entities after a given period of years as a means of ensuring independence.

The correct answer is (C). *(CPA, adapted)*

REQUIRED: The authority of the SEC.

DISCUSSION: The SEC has the authority to regulate the form and content of all financial statements, notes, and schedules filed with the SEC, and also the financial reports to shareholders if the company is subject to the Securities Exchange Act of 1934. The SEC has stated that financial statements conforming to FASB standards will be presumed to be in accordance with GAAP. However, the SEC reserves the right to substitute its principles for those of the accounting profession and to require such additional disclosures as it deems necessary.

Answer (A) is incorrect because the SEC may not prescribe specific auditing procedures. Answer (B) is incorrect because the SEC may not deny lack of privity as a defense. Answer (D) is incorrect because the SEC may not require a change of auditors of governmental entities.

113. Accountants are often called upon to confer with clients, underwriters, and their respective counsel concerning the accounting and auditing requirements of the Securities Act of 1933 and of the SEC. A service often requested is the issuance of letters for underwriters and certain other requesting parties, commonly called comfort letters. Which of the following statements is true?

A. Comfort letters by the accountant are required under the Securities Act of 1933.

B. Comfort letters should not state that the accountant carried out procedures that (s)he considered necessary in the circumstances.

C. Copies of comfort letters should be filed with the SEC.

D. All of the answers are correct.

The correct answer is (B). *(Publisher)*

REQUIRED: The true statement about comfort letters.

DISCUSSION: Much of the uncertainty and consequent risk of misunderstanding with regard to the nature and scope of comfort letters has arisen from the necessary limitations on the comments that accountants are permitted to make with respect to financial information in a registration statement that has not been audited. What constitutes a reasonable investigation of unaudited financial information sufficient for the purposes of an underwriter or other requesting party has never been authoritatively established. Consequently, the underwriter or other party should establish those procedures necessary for his/her purposes. However, the accountants cannot provide any assurance about the sufficiency of those procedures, and they should avoid any implication that they are carrying out such procedures as they consider necessary (AU 634).

Answer (A) is incorrect because comfort letters are not required by the SEC. They are requested by underwriters and certain others. Answer (C) is incorrect because comfort letters need not be filed with the SEC. Answer (D) is incorrect because two statements are false.

114. Comfort letters ordinarily are addressed to

A. The Securities and Exchange Commission.

B. The intermediary who negotiated the agreement with the client.

C. Creditor financial institutions.

D. The client's audit committee.

The correct answer is (B). *(CPA, adapted)*

REQUIRED: The addressee of a comfort letter.

DISCUSSION: The letter should not be addressed or given to anyone other than the client and the named underwriters, broker-dealer, intermediary, or buyer or seller. "The appropriate addressee is the intermediary who has negotiated the agreement with the client, and with whom the accountants will deal in discussions regarding the letter" (AU 634).

Answers (A), (C), and (D) are incorrect because the comfort letter should be addressed to the client and the named underwriters, broker-dealer, intermediary, or buyer or seller.

115. Underwriters or other requesting parties occasionally request the accountants to repeat in the comfort letter their report on the audited financial statements included in the registration statement. They may also request negative assurance regarding the accountants' report. When these requests are made, the accountants should

A. Honor both requests.

B. Not honor either request.

C. Honor the request to repeat the report, but not provide negative assurance.

D. Provide negative assurance, but not repeat the report.

The correct answer is (B). *(Publisher)*

REQUIRED: The appropriate response to a request to repeat the audit report or to provide negative assurance concerning the report.

DISCUSSION: "Because of the special significance of the date of the accountants' report, the accountants should not repeat their opinion." Also, accountants should not provide negative assurance regarding their report. "Because accountants have a statutory responsibility with respect to their opinion as of the effective date of the registration statement, and because the additional significance, if any, of negative assurance is unclear and such assurance may therefore give rise to misunderstanding, accountants should not give such negative assurance" (AU 634).

Answers (A), (C), and (D) are incorrect because the auditor should not honor either request.

116. Comfort letters ordinarily are signed by the client's

A. Independent accountants.

B. Underwriters of securities.

C. Audit committee.

D. Senior management.

The correct answer is (A). *(CPA, adapted)*

REQUIRED: The persons who sign a comfort letter.

DISCUSSION: A common condition of an underwriting agreement in connection with the offering for sale of securities registered with the SEC under the Securities Act of 1933 is that the accountants furnish a comfort letter to the underwriters. Hence, the independent accountants sign the comfort letter.

Answers (B), (C), and (D) are incorrect because comfort letters are provided by accountants.

117. When an accountant issues to an underwriter a comfort letter containing comments on data that have not been audited, the underwriter most likely will receive

A. Positive assurance on supplementary disclosures.

B. Negative assurance on capsule information.

C. A disclaimer on prospective financial statements.

D. A limited opinion on pro forma financial statements.

The correct answer is (B). *(CPA, adapted)*

REQUIRED: The most likely assurance or lack thereof provided in a comfort letter commenting on unaudited data.

DISCUSSION: According to AU 634, capsule information is unaudited summarized interim information for subsequent periods used to supplement the audited financial statements or unaudited condensed interim financial information in a registration statement. The accountant may give negative assurance regarding conformity with GAAP if the capsule information is in accordance with the disclosure requirements of APB 28, *Interim Financial Reporting*, and if the accountants have performed an AU 722 review of the underlying financial statements.

Answer (A) is incorrect because a comfort letter expresses, at most, negative assurance. Answer (C) is incorrect because prospective statements do not appear in a registration statement. Answer (D) is incorrect because a limited opinion is not a permissible form of reporting.

118. Which of the following matters is covered in a typical comfort letter?

A. Negative assurance concerning whether the entity's control activities operated as designed during the period audited.

B. An opinion regarding whether the entity complied with laws and regulations under *Government Auditing Standards* and the Single Audit Act.

C. Positive assurance concerning whether unaudited condensed financial information complied with GAAP.

D. An opinion as to whether the audited financial statements comply in form with the accounting requirements of the SEC.

The correct answer is (D). *(CPA, adapted)*

REQUIRED: The item in a typical comfort letter.

DISCUSSION: A typical comfort letter expresses an opinion on whether audited financial statements and schedules "included in the registration statement comply as to form in all material respects with the applicable accounting requirements of the Act and the related published rules and regulations" (AU 634). However, the comfort letter does not state or repeat an opinion about the fairness of presentation of the statements.

Answers (A), (B), and (C) are incorrect because comfort letters concern financial information contained in registration statements filed with the SEC under the Securities Act of 1933.

119. A comfort letter to underwriters or other requesting parties provided by a CPA may use which of the following terms to describe the work performed?

	Audited	Read	Made General Review
A.	Yes	Yes	Yes
B.	No	No	No
C.	Yes	No	Yes
D.	Yes	Yes	No

The correct answer is (D). *(Publisher)*

REQUIRED: The terms an accountant may use in a letter for underwriters or other requesting parties.

DISCUSSION: The accountant performs a reasonable investigation to provide negative assurance in a comfort letter. "Terms of uncertain meaning (such as general review, limited review, reconcile, check, or test) should not be used in describing the work unless the procedures comprehended by these terms are described in the comfort letter" (AU 634).

Answers (A), (B), and (C) are incorrect because terms such as audited and read have specific meaning.

120. A CPA should not express negative or limited assurance in a standard

A. Compilation report on financial statements of a nonpublic entity.

B. Review report on financial statements of a nonpublic entity.

C. Review report on interim financial statements of a public entity.

D. Comfort letter on financial information included in a registration statement of a public entity.

The correct answer is (A). *(CPA, adapted)*

REQUIRED: The report in which a CPA should not express negative or limited assurance.

DISCUSSION: The standard compilation report states that the financial statements have not been audited or reviewed and, accordingly, the accountant does not express an opinion or any other form of assurance (AR 100).

Answers (B) and (C) are incorrect because a review report provides limited assurance. Answer (D) is incorrect because the standard comfort letter regarding such information may contain negative assurance, which "consists of a statement by accountants that, as a result of specified procedures, nothing came to their attention that caused them to believe that specified matters do not meet a specified standard" (AU 634).

121. Which of the following is a true statement about the accountant's responsibility for letters to underwriters and certain other requesting parties?

A. An accountant who states in the letter that (s)he is independent may have an interest of the type requiring disclosure in the prospectus or registration statement.

B. An accountant may comment in the letter on compliance as to form in regard to any information contained in a registration statement.

C. An accountant may issue a draft comfort letter regarding a single shelf registration statement filed to cover delayed offerings of securities over an extended period.

D. Certain reports previously issued by an accountant may be repeated in the letter if they are not included in the registration statement.

The correct answer is (C). *(Publisher)*

REQUIRED: The accountant's responsibility for letters to underwriters and certain other parties.

DISCUSSION: A shelf registration statement permits a company to register "a designated amount of securities for continuous or delayed offerings during an extended period." At the date of the registration, an underwriter may not have been chosen but the client or legal counsel for the underwriting group may request a comfort letter. Because only the underwriter can determine the procedures necessary for its purposes, the accountants should not issue a letter addressed to the client, legal counsel, or a nonspecific addressee, but they may issue a draft describing procedures performed and comments based thereon with a statement that the final letter will depend on procedures requested by the underwriter.

Answer (A) is incorrect because Regulation S-X lists the interests that must be disclosed. An accountant with one or more of these interests cannot be independent. Answer (B) is incorrect because an accountant should comment on compliance with SEC rules and regulations as to form only with respect to those requirements that apply to the form and content of financial statements and schedules. Answer (D) is incorrect because certain reports previously issued by an accountant may be attached to, but not repeated in, a letter for underwriters if they are not included in the registration statement.

122. An item typically included in a comfort letter is

A. The independence of the CPA.

B. Permission to distribute the letter to interested parties.

C. Positive assurance about whether the financial statements are fairly presented in conformity with GAAP.

D. Negative assurance about information included in management's discussion and analysis (MD&A).

The correct answer is (A). *(Publisher)*

REQUIRED: The item a CPA would typically refer to when writing a comfort letter.

DISCUSSION: The independence of the CPA is a matter customarily addressed in comfort letters. The following example of a statement about independence is given in AU 634: "We are independent CPAs with respect to The Blank Co., Inc., within the meaning of the Act and the applicable published rules and regulations thereunder." The allusion is to the Securities Act of 1933.

Answer (B) is incorrect because the letter should include a statement that the "letter is solely for the information of the addressees and to assist the underwriters." Answer (C) is incorrect because the CPA should not repeat the audit opinion in the comfort letter. Answer (D) is incorrect because, although the accountant may refer to an examination or review of MD&A information, no assurance should be included in the comfort letter. Furthermore, the accountant should not refer to any restricted use report, such as a report on agreed-upon procedures.

123. Whenever negative assurance is provided by a CPA, it is based upon

A. An absence of nullifying evidence.

B. A presence of substantiating evidence.

C. An objective audit in accordance with generally accepted auditing standards.

D. A judgmental determination in accordance with guidelines promulgated by the AICPA.

The correct answer is (A). *(CPA, adapted)*

REQUIRED: The basis upon which a CPA would provide negative assurance.

DISCUSSION: "Negative assurance consists of a statement by accountants that, as a result of specified procedures, nothing came to their attention that caused them to believe that specified matters do not meet a specified standard" (AU 634). For example, this phrasing might suggest the absence of evidence that financial statements are not fairly presented.

Answer (B) is incorrect because substantiating evidence would be the basis for positive assurance. Answer (C) is incorrect because negative assurance is provided by the application of procedures substantially more limited than those in an audit in accordance with GAAS. Answer (D) is incorrect because, although the authority to permit negative assurance rests with the AICPA, the basis for rendering it is the lack of nullifying evidence.

124. An independent accountant's report is based on a review of interim financial information. If this report is presented in a registration statement, a prospectus should include a statement clarifying that the

A. Accountant's review report is not a part of the registration statement within the meaning of the Securities Act of 1933.

B. Accountant assumes no responsibility for subsequent events.

C. Accountant's review was performed in accordance with rules and regulations adopted by the Securities and Exchange Commission.

D. Accountant obtained corroborating evidence to determine whether material modifications are needed for such information to conform with GAAP.

The correct answer is (A). *(CPA, adapted)*

REQUIRED: The statement in a review report on interim financial information included in a registration statement.

DISCUSSION: According to AU 711, when an independent accountant has reviewed interim information and his/her report is presented or incorporated by reference in a registration statement, the SEC requires that a prospectus containing a statement about the accountant's involvement clarify that the report "is not a 'report' or 'part' of the registration statement within the meaning of sections 7 and 11 of the Securities Act of 1933." The prospectus should state that reliance on the report should be restricted given the limited procedures applied and that the accountant is not subject to the liability provisions of section 11.

Answer (B) is incorrect because the registration statement contains audited financial statements. Thus, procedures should be extended from the date of the audit report to the effective date of the filing. Answer (C) is incorrect because the wording suggested by AU 711 is that "the independent public accountants have reported that they have applied limited procedures in accordance with professional standards for a review of such information." Answer (D) is incorrect because accountants make inquiries and apply analytical procedures to determine whether modifications are needed for financial information to conform with GAAP. They do not collect corroborating evidence in a review.

125. When an independent audit report is incorporated by reference in an SEC registration statement, a prospectus that includes a statement about the independent accountant's involvement should refer to the independent accountant as

A. Auditor of the financial reports.

B. Management's designate before the SEC.

C. Certified preparer of the report.

D. Expert in auditing and accounting.

The correct answer is (D). *(CPA, adapted)*

REQUIRED: The reference to an independent accountant in a prospectus.

DISCUSSION: In filings under the Securities Act of 1933, the prospectus often states that certain information included in the registration statement is in reliance on the report of a named expert. Accordingly, the prospectus may state that reliance has been placed on the report of the independent public accountant, given on his/her authority as an expert in auditing and accounting (AU 711).

Answers (A), (B), and (C) are incorrect because an independent accountant should be referred to as an expert in auditing and accounting.

126. An audit of the financial statements included in Form 10-Q is not required. However, an external auditor's involvement with a Form 10-Q that is being prepared for filing with the SEC would most likely consist of

A. A compilation report on the financial statements included in Form 10-Q.

B. A comfort letter that covers stub-period financial data.

C. An opinion on internal controls under which the Form 10-Q data were developed.

D. A review of the interim financial statements included in Form 10-Q.

The correct answer is (D). *(CMA, adapted)*

REQUIRED: The external auditor's most likely involvement with Form 10-Q.

DISCUSSION: Form 10-Q is the quarterly report to the SEC. It must be filed for each of the first three quarters of the year within 45 days after the end of the quarter. It need not contain audited or reviewed financial statements, but it should be prepared in accordance with APB 28. However, some entities must present certain quarterly supplementary data. The independent accountant who has audited the annual financial statements for the periods for which such data are presented should review the selected quarterly data. A review by an accountant based on inquiries and analytical procedures would permit an expression of negative assurance that no material modifications need to be made to the statements for them to be in conformity with GAAP. A review would help satisfy the SEC requirement of "adequate and accurate disclosure of material facts."

Answer (A) is incorrect because a compilation provides no assurance and would thus not satisfy the SEC requirement stated above. Answer (B) is incorrect because comfort letters are addressed to underwriters, not the SEC. Answer (C) is incorrect because the SEC does not require an external auditor's opinion on internal control.

127. Form 10-K is filed with the SEC to update the information a company supplied when filing a registration statement under the Securities Exchange Act of 1934. Form 10-K is a report filed

A. Within 90 days of the end of a company's fiscal year.

B. Within 45 days of the end of each quarter.

C. Within 2 weeks of the end of each month.

D. Within 15 days of significant events.

The correct answer is (A). *(CMA, adapted)*

REQUIRED: The true statement about filing Form 10-K.

DISCUSSION: Form 10-K is the annual report to the SEC. It must be filed within 90 days after the corporation's year-end. It must contain audited financial statements and be signed by the principal executive, financial, and accounting officers and by a majority of the board. The content is essentially that in the Basic Information Package.

Answers (B), (C), and (D) are incorrect because Form 10-K must be filed within 90 days after the corporation's year-end.

128. SEC Form S-3 is an optional, short-form registration statement that relies on the incorporation by reference of periodic reports required by the Securities Exchange Act of 1934. Form S-3 offers substantial savings in filing costs over other forms because minimal disclosures are required in the prospectus. The SEC permits the use of Form S-3 only by those large public firms that have filed periodic reports with the SEC for at least 3 years if the registrant

A. Does not have stock held by nonaffiliates.

B. Does not qualify for Form S-1.

C. Is widely followed and actively traded.

D. Has not had to file Form 8-K during the most recent 2-year period.

The correct answer is (C). *(CMA, adapted)*

REQUIRED: The requirement for use of Form S-3.

DISCUSSION: Form S-1 is used for a first registration and for any securities for which no other form is authorized. Form S-2 is used by companies that have filed timely reports for 3 years. Incorporation by reference from the annual shareholders' report of Basic Information Package disclosures is allowed in Form S-2. If a company meets the requirements for use of Form S-2 and a specified amount in value of its stock is held by nonaffiliates (or it meets the requirements for total stock outstanding and for annual trading volume), Form S-3 may be used. It allows most information to be incorporated by reference to other SEC filings.

Answer (A) is incorrect because Form S-3 may not be used unless nonaffiliates hold the company's stock. Answer (B) is incorrect because Form S-1 is used for original filings. Answer (D) is incorrect because not having to file Form 8-K during the most recent 2-year period is not a requirement for use of Form S-3.

129. Form 8-K must be filed within

A. 90 days after the end of the fiscal year covered by the report.

B. 45 days after the end of each of the first three quarters of each fiscal year.

C. 90 days after the end of an employee stock purchase plan fiscal year.

D. 15 days of significant events.

The correct answer is (D). *(CMA, adapted)*

REQUIRED: The filing deadline for Form 8-K.

DISCUSSION: Form 8-K is a current report used to disclose material events affecting a company. It must be filed within 15 days after the occurrence of a material event that is required to be reported (5 business days after a change of external auditors or resignation of a director). An extension may be obtained for filing financial statements and pro forma information required for an acquisition. Material events include changes in control, bankruptcy, acquisition or disposition of significant assets not in the ordinary course of business, a change in the independent auditors, etc.

Answers (A), (B), and (C) are incorrect because Form 8-K must be filed within 15 days of significant events.

130. In an effort to consolidate the registration process, the SEC has adopted new security forms. However, these forms do not cover all circumstances. A registrant would use Form S-4 to register securities

A. In connection with mergers and related business-combination transactions.

B. When the registrant does not qualify for Form S-1.

C. When the registrant has not had to file Form 8-K during the most recent 2-year period.

D. Of real estate investment trusts.

The correct answer is (A). *(CMA, adapted)*

REQUIRED: The circumstance under which a registrant would use Form S-4.

DISCUSSION: Form S-4 is a simplified form for business combinations, such as mergers. It is part of the integrated disclosure system established to simplify reporting requirements under the Securities Act of 1933 and the Securities Exchange Act of 1934. Thus, Form S-4 may incorporate much information by reference to other reports already filed with the SEC. The integrated disclosure system permits many companies to use the required annual report to shareholders (if prepared in conformity with Regulations S-X and S-K) as the basis for the annual report to the SEC on Form 10-K. Some may even use this report as the basis for registration statements.

Answers (B), (C), and (D) are incorrect because Form S-4 is a simplified form for business combinations, such as mergers.

8.8 Governmental Auditing

131. Financial audits of certain governmental entities are required to be performed in accordance with generally accepted government auditing standards (GAS). These standards do not require, as part of an auditor's report, the inclusion of

A. A statement as to whether the tests performed provide sufficient evidence to support an opinion on internal controls.

B. The reportable conditions, with identification of material weaknesses.

C. Sampling methods used to test the controls designed to detect errors and fraud.

D. A description of the scope of testing of internal controls.

The correct answer is (C). *(CPA, adapted)*

REQUIRED: The item not required by GAS to be identified in an audit report.

DISCUSSION: The General Accounting Office (GAO) promulgates *Government Auditing Standards* (the Yellow Book). They apply not only to financial audits (financial statement and financial-related audits) but also to performance audits (economy and efficiency audits and program audits). GAS incorporate GAAS for reporting and field work for financial audits and also state additional standards. They do not require that the report identify specific sampling techniques used to test the controls.

Answer (A) is incorrect because auditors should state whether tests provided sufficient evidence to support an opinion on internal control, although such an opinion is not required. Answer (B) is incorrect because auditors should report deficiencies considered to be reportable conditions, with identification of those individually or cumulatively deemed to be material weaknesses. Answer (D) is incorrect because the report on the financial statements should describe the scope of testing of compliance with laws and regulations and internal controls and present the results of those tests or refer to separate reports containing that information.

132. In governmental accounting, emphasis is placed on

A. Total assets owned by the governmental entity.

B. Generating income from funds employed.

C. Expenditures of funds.

D. The flow of funds through the income statement.

The correct answer is (C). *(CIA, adapted)*

REQUIRED: The emphasis of governmental accounting.

DISCUSSION: Compliance with applicable laws in providing services to the public is the primary focus of governmental accounting. Accounting for expenditures demonstrates that monies were spent in accordance with the law.

Answer (A) is incorrect because emphasis is on individual funds, not total assets. Answer (B) is incorrect because earning a return on investment is emphasized by private sector entities. Answer (D) is incorrect because governmental accounting does not focus on earnings.

133. An auditor who is engaged to audit the financial statements of a governmental entity should

A. Design the audit to provide reasonable assurance that the statements are free of material misstatements resulting from illegal acts having direct or indirect effects.

B. Obtain an understanding of the possible financial statement effects of laws and regulations having direct and material effects on amounts reported.

C. Assume responsibility for assuring that the entity complies with applicable laws and regulations.

D. Assess control risk with respect to each component of internal control.

The correct answer is (B). *(Publisher)*

REQUIRED: The responsibility of an auditor of the statements of a governmental entity.

DISCUSSION: According to AU 801, *Compliance Auditing Considerations in Audits of Governmental Entities and Recipients of Governmental Financial Assistance*, the auditor must obtain this understanding. The auditor must also assess whether management has identified laws and regulations that might have such effects. Procedures to obtain the understanding and make the assessment include, but are not limited to, considering knowledge from prior audits; obtaining written management representations; discussions with the entity's legal counsel, chief financial officer, or grant administrators; and reviewing minutes of the appropriate legislative body.

Answer (A) is incorrect because auditors are primarily concerned with direct and material effects on financial statement amounts. Answer (C) is incorrect because management should assume responsibility for assuring that the entity complies with applicable laws and regulations. Answer (D) is incorrect because control risk should be assessed with respect to financial statement assertions.

134. Governmental auditing may extend beyond expressions of opinion on the fairness of financial presentation to include

	Program Audits	Compliance Considerations	Economy and Efficiency Audits
A.	Yes	Yes	No
B.	Yes	Yes	Yes
C.	No	Yes	Yes
D.	Yes	No	Yes

The correct answer is (B). *(CPA, adapted)*

REQUIRED: The scope of a governmental audit.

DISCUSSION: Under *Government Auditing Standards*, an audit may be a financial audit or a performance audit. Financial audits result not only in opinions on financial statements but also in reporting the results of tests of compliance with laws and regulations and of internal controls. Performance audits include economy and efficiency audits and program audits.

Answers (A), (C), and (D) are incorrect because, under *Government Auditing Standards*, an audit may be a financial audit or a performance audit.

135. An auditor was engaged to conduct a performance audit of a governmental entity in accordance with *Government Auditing Standards*. These standards do not require which of the following to be included in this auditor's report?

A. A statement of the audit objectives and a description of the audit scope.

B. Instances of noncompliance and abuse discovered during the audit.

C. The pertinent views of the entity's responsible officials concerning the auditor's findings.

D. A concurrent opinion on the financial statements taken as a whole.

The correct answer is (D). *(CPA, adapted)*

REQUIRED: The action not required of an auditor in a performance audit.

DISCUSSION: Performance audits include economy and efficiency and program audits. There is no requirement that a financial audit be conducted simultaneously or concurrently with a performance audit.

Answers (A), (B), and (C) are incorrect because the reporting standards for performance audits require auditors to report the audit objectives and the audit scope and methodology, all significant instances of noncompliance and abuse, and the views of responsible officials about auditors' findings, conclusions, and recommendations, as well as corrections planned.

136. The purpose of governmental effectiveness or program auditing is to determine if the desired results of a program are being achieved. The first step in conducting such an audit is to

A. Evaluate the system used to measure results.

B. Determine the time frame to be audited.

C. Collect quantifiable data on the program's success or failure.

D. Identify the legislative intent of the program being audited.

The correct answer is (D). *(CIA, adapted)*

REQUIRED: The first step in conducting a governmental effectiveness or program audit.

DISCUSSION: A program audit of a government program obtains information about the costs, outputs, benefits, and effects of the program. It attempts to measure the accomplishments and relative success of the undertaking. However, this measurement depends on the actual intent of the legislation that established the program.

Answers (A), (B), and (C) are incorrect because evaluating the system used to measure results, determining the time frame to be audited, and collecting quantifiable data on the program's success or failure are subsequent steps in a program audit.

137. Because of the pervasive effects of laws and regulations on the financial statements of governmental units, an auditor should consider obtaining written representations from management regarding

A. Completeness of management's identification of laws and regulations that have a direct and material effect on its financial statements.

B. Implementation of controls designed to detect all illegal acts.

C. Expression of both positive and negative assurance to the auditor that the entity complied with all laws and regulations.

D. Employment of internal auditors who can report their findings, opinions, and conclusions objectively.

The correct answer is (A). *(CPA, adapted)*

REQUIRED: The audit procedure that should be considered in a governmental audit.

DISCUSSION: The auditor should obtain an understanding of the possible financial statement effects of laws and regulations widely recognized by auditors as having direct and material effects. The auditor should also assess whether management has identified such laws and regulations. Thus, the auditor may consider obtaining written representations from management about the completeness of management's identification (AU 801).

Answer (B) is incorrect because internal control typically safeguards assets and promotes the reliability of financial statements but, given its inherent limitations, cannot be expected to prevent or detect all illegal acts. Answer (C) is incorrect because management does not express assurance, either positive or negative, that it has complied with all laws and regulations in an audit. Answer (D) is incorrect because the entity will decide whether to employ internal auditors.

138. The Single Audit Act is intended to be the definitive legislation concerning the audit of federal financial assistance programs for state and local governments and nonprofit organizations. Which of the following statements is a false statement about the act?

A. The single audit concept changes the focus from individual grants to grant recipients.

B. The act requires federal auditors to rely on single audit findings, to base any supplemental auditing on them, and to pay any additional auditing costs.

C. The recipient must designate one of the grant providers as a cognizant agency to act as a liaison between the auditee and the federal agencies providing funds.

D. Audit reporting should cover an opinion on the fairness of the financial statements, a report on internal control, and a report on compliance with grant requirements.

The correct answer is (C). *(Publisher)*

REQUIRED: The false statement concerning the Single Audit Act.

DISCUSSION: A recipient expending more than $25 million per year in federal awards must have a cognizant agency for audit. The designated agency is the federal awarding agency that provides the predominant amount of direct funding, unless the OMB specifies another cognizant agency or the cognizant agency reassigns cognizance to another federal awarding agency. The cognizant agency overseeing the audit process acts as a liaison among the auditor, the auditee, and the granting agencies. Guidance for the application of the Single Audit Act is provided in OMB Circular A-133, *Audits of States, Local Governments, and Non-Profit Organizations*. Generally accepted governmental auditing standards (GAS) and generally accepted auditing standards (GAAS) apply when appropriate.

Answer (A) is incorrect because the single audit concept changes the focus of audits from individual grants to the grant recipients. Answer (B) is incorrect because the act requires federal auditors to rely on single audit findings. Answer (D) is incorrect because the audit report should cover the financial statements, internal control, and compliance with grant requirements.

139. When performing an audit of a city that is subject to the requirements of the federal Single Audit Act, an auditor should adhere to

A. Governmental Accounting Standards Board General Standards.

B. Governmental Finance Officers Association Governmental Accounting, Auditing, and Financial Reporting Principles.

C. *Government Auditing Standards*.

D. Securities and Exchange Commission Regulation S-X.

The correct answer is (C). *(CPA, adapted)*

REQUIRED: The standards for an audit of a city.

DISCUSSION: The Single Audit Act establishes audit requirements for recipients of federal financial assistance. The act requires that audits of such entities be in accordance with *Government Auditing Standards* promulgated by the GAO. OMB Circular A-133 and the related AICPA statement of position are also applicable. The act and the circular also state certain requirements that exceed those of the GAO's Standards.

Answers (A), (B), and (D) are incorrect because an audit of a city should adhere to *Government Auditing Standards*.

140. In auditing compliance with requirements governing major federal financial assistance programs under the Single Audit Act, the auditor's consideration of materiality differs from materiality under generally accepted auditing standards. Under the Single Audit Act, materiality is

A. Calculated in relation to the financial statements taken as a whole.

B. Determined separately for each major federal financial assistance program.

C. Decided in conjunction with the auditor's risk assessment.

D. Ignored, because all account balances, regardless of size, are fully tested.

The correct answer is (B). *(CPA, adapted)*

REQUIRED: The materiality determination under the Single Audit Act.

DISCUSSION: Under the Single Audit Act, the emphasis of the audit effort is on major programs related to financial assistance. Materiality is determined in relation to each major program for the purposes of testing and reporting. When reaching a conclusion as to whether noncompliance is material, the auditor considers its nature and the amount affected in relation to the nature and amount of the major program.

Answer (A) is incorrect because, in a for-profit financial statement audit, materiality is related to the financial statements taken as a whole. Answer (C) is incorrect because, although risk and materiality are closely related, the materiality judgment is based upon the expenditures of the major program. Answer (D) is incorrect because materiality must be considered in determining the appropriate tests to be applied.

141. Tell, CPA, is auditing the financial statements of Youth Services Co. (YSC), a not-for-profit organization, in accordance with *Government Auditing Standards*. Tell's report on YSC's compliance with laws and regulations is required to contain statements of

	Positive Assurance	Negative Assurance
A.	Yes	Yes
B.	Yes	No
C.	No	Yes
D.	No	No

The correct answer is (D). *(CPA, adapted)*

REQUIRED: The assurance, if any, provided regarding compliance in a report on a financial statement audit in accordance with GAS.

DISCUSSION: The third additional GAS reporting standard for financial statement audits states that the report should either (1) describe the scope of the auditors' testing of compliance with laws and regulations and present the results of those tests or (2) refer to a separate report containing that information. No statement of assurance is required.

Answers (A), (B), and (C) are incorrect because no statement of assurance is required.

142. In an audit under *Government Auditing Standards*, procedures have disclosed material instances of noncompliance with regulations. The report should

A. Also disclose immaterial instances of noncompliance.

B. Indicate that the audit was designed to provide reasonable assurance that illegal acts that could result in criminal prosecution would be detected.

C. Be qualified.

D. Place the findings in proper perspective.

The correct answer is (D). *(Publisher)*

REQUIRED: The necessary element of a report given material noncompliance.

DISCUSSION: To give the reader a basis for judging consequences of material instances of noncompliance, the instances identified should be related to the universe of the number of cases examined and be quantified in terms of dollar amounts, if appropriate.

Answer (A) is incorrect because instances of immaterial noncompliance need not be disclosed in the report but must be included in a separate communication to the audited entity, preferably in writing. However, under the Single Audit Act relating to federal financial assistance programs, the auditor should report all known questionable costs and instances of noncompliance. Answer (B) is incorrect because the auditor's duty regarding illegal acts by clients as defined by AU 317, *Illegal Acts by Clients*, is to design the audit to consider the possibility of, and to detect, such acts. Answer (C) is incorrect because the report does not express an opinion.

143. Reporting on internal control under *Government Auditing Standards* differs from reporting under generally accepted auditing standards in that *Government Auditing Standards* requires a

A. Written report describing the entity's controls specifically designed to prevent fraud, abuse, and illegal acts.

B. Written report describing each reportable condition observed including identification of those considered material weaknesses.

C. Statement of negative assurance that the controls not tested have an immaterial effect on the entity's financial statements.

D. Statement of positive assurance that controls designed to detect material errors and fraud were tested.

The correct answer is (B). *(CPA, adapted)*

REQUIRED: The difference between GAS and GAAS regarding reports on internal control.

DISCUSSION: GAS states that auditors should identify reportable conditions that are individually or cumulatively material weaknesses. However, AU 325, *Communication of Internal Control Related Matters Noted in an Audit*, does not require the separate identification and communication of material weaknesses.

Answer (A) is incorrect because identification of specific controls is not required under GAS or GAAS. Answers (C) and (D) are incorrect because GAS does not require expression of any form of assurance on internal control.

144. An auditor most likely would be responsible for assuring that management communicates significant deficiencies in the design of internal control

A. To a court-appointed creditors' committee when the client is operating under Chapter 11 of the Federal Bankruptcy Code.

B. To shareholders with significant influence (more than 20% equity ownership) when the reportable conditions are deemed to be material weaknesses.

C. To the Securities and Exchange Commission when the client is a publicly held entity.

D. To specific legislative and regulatory bodies when reporting under *Government Auditing Standards*.

The correct answer is (D). *(CPA, adapted)*

REQUIRED: The auditor's responsibility for assuring communication of significant deficiencies in internal control outside the audited entity.

DISCUSSION: An auditor is required to include reportable conditions in a report prepared under *Government Auditing Standards*. Under the fifth additional GAS reporting standard for financial audits, the report is required to be distributed to the appropriate officials of the organization audited, officials of the organizations requiring or arranging for the audits, other officials who have legal oversight authority or who may be responsible for taking action, and others who may be authorized to receive the report.

Answer (A) is incorrect because management would be responsible for providing audited financial statements to a creditors' committee. Answer (B) is incorrect because the auditor's communication of internal-control-related matters noted in an audit is to the audit committee, management, or others in the organization, not to external parties. Answer (C) is incorrect because management is responsible for providing audited financial information to the SEC.

145. Under the Single Audit Act, the auditor must report on compliance with laws and regulations that may have a material effect on each audited major federal financial assistance program from which the auditee receives funding. In accordance with the act and OMB Circular A-133, which contains policies, procedures, and guidelines to implement the act, the auditor

A. Is responsible for identifying major and nonmajor federal programs.

B. Must apply a concept of materiality in the audit of major federal programs that is similar to that in an audit under GAAS.

C. Must determine whether the recipient has engaged in activities to which particular types of compliance requirements apply.

D. Is required to restrict control risk and assess inherent and detection risk.

The correct answer is (C). *(Publisher)*

REQUIRED: The true statement about compliance auditing of major federal financial assistance programs.

DISCUSSION: OMB Circular A-133 and the related Compliance Supplement list 14 types of compliance requirements, e.g., activities allowed or unallowed; allowable costs/cost principles; cash management; eligibility; matching, level of effort, earmarking; and reporting. The data collection form submitted by the auditee should include, for each federal program, a yes or no statement as to whether there are audit findings for each of the types of compliance requirements and the total of any questioned costs.

Answer (A) is incorrect because management has the responsibility for identifying major and nonmajor federal programs. Answer (B) is incorrect because, under the act, materiality is determined with respect to each program, not the financial statements. Answer (D) is incorrect because the auditor assesses inherent and control risk and restricts detection risk.

146. An auditor is auditing an entity's compliance with requirements governing a federal financial assistance program. The auditor may be required to

	Report Findings Related to Compliance	Express an Opinion on Compliance
A.	Yes	Yes
B.	Yes	No
C.	No	Yes
D.	No	No

The correct answer is (A). *(Publisher)*

REQUIRED: The reporting in a compliance audit of a federal financial assistance program.

DISCUSSION: The auditor ordinarily must test compliance with requirements governing federal financial assistance programs. The form of the report and the assurance to be given vary with the requirements of the agency or program. Thus, when reporting on compliance, an auditor may be required to report findings related to compliance or to express an opinion on whether the recipient has complied with the requirements applicable to its major federal financial assistance programs (AU 801).

Answers (B), (C), and (D) are incorrect because, depending on the requirements of the agency or program, the auditor may need to report findings or to express an opinion.

147. Which of the following is a documentation requirement that an auditor should follow when auditing in accordance with *Government Auditing Standards*?

A. The auditor should obtain written representations from management acknowledging responsibility for correcting instances of fraud, abuse, and waste.

B. The auditor's working papers should contain sufficient information so that an experienced auditor can ascertain the evidence supporting significant conclusions.

C. The auditor should document the procedures that assure discovery of all illegal acts and contingent liabilities resulting from noncompliance.

D. The auditor's working papers should contain a caveat that all instances of material errors and irregularities may not be identified.

The correct answer is (B). *(CPA, adapted)*

REQUIRED: The documentation requirement under GAS.

DISCUSSION: The additional working paper GAS standard for financial audits states, "Working papers should contain sufficient information to enable an experienced auditor having no previous connection with the audit to ascertain from them the evidence that supports the auditors' significant conclusions and judgments."

Answer (A) is incorrect because the auditor must report on certain instances of fraud, abuse, and waste but need not gain acknowledgment from management of its responsibility for correction. Answer (C) is incorrect because assurance of discovery of all illegal acts is impossible given the nature of the audit process. Answer (D) is incorrect because a caveat that all instances of material errors and irregularities may not be identified is appropriate for the required description of the scope of testing of internal control but need not be stated in the auditor's working papers.

8.9 Compliance Attestation

148. According to Statement on Standards for Attestation Engagements 3, *Compliance Attestation* (AT 500),

A. The field work and reporting but not the general attestation standards apply to this type of engagement.

B. The practitioner may accept an examination engagement only if management's written assertion is in a representation letter to the practitioner.

C. A compliance attestation engagement is intended to result in a legal determination of an entity's compliance with specified requirements.

D. Compliance attestation engagements are restricted to providing assurance concerning management's written or nonwritten assertion about compliance requirements.

The correct answer is (B). *(Publisher)*

REQUIRED: The true statement about compliance attestation engagements.

DISCUSSION: If an examination is performed and the report is intended for general use, the assertion must be in a representation letter and in a separate report that will accompany the practitioner's report. If the report on an examination is not intended for general use, the assertion need only be in the representation letter.

Answer (A) is incorrect because the general attestation standards also apply. Answer (C) is incorrect because a report issued in accordance with AT 500 does not provide a legal determination on compliance with specified requirements, but it may be useful to legal counsel or others in making such determinations. Answer (D) is incorrect because compliance attestation engagements provide assurance concerning management's written assertion.

149. A practitioner may accept a compliance attestation engagement to perform

	Agreed-Upon Procedures	An Examination	A Review
A.	Yes	Yes	Yes
B.	No	Yes	Yes
C.	Yes	Yes	No
D.	No	No	Yes

The correct answer is (C). *(Publisher)*

REQUIRED: The type(s) of compliance attestation engagements.

DISCUSSION: The practitioner may accept an agreed-upon procedures attestation engagement as long as the specified users participate in establishing the procedures to be applied and take responsibility for the sufficiency of such procedures for their purposes. The practitioner may also conduct an examination in which (s)he gathers evidence to support an opinion. Both types of engagements may be performed with respect to a written assertion about compliance with specified requirements or about the effectiveness of internal control over compliance. However, AT 500 does not provide for a review engagement.

Answers (A), (B), and (D) are incorrect because AT 500 permits agreed-upon procedures and examination engagements but not a review.

150. A practitioner's report on agreed-upon procedures related to management's assertion about an entity's compliance with specified requirements should contain

A. A statement of restrictions on the use of the report.

B. An opinion about whether management's assertion is fairly stated.

C. Negative assurance that control risk has not been assessed.

D. An acknowledgment of responsibility for the sufficiency of the procedures.

The correct answer is (A). *(CPA, adapted)*

REQUIRED: The statement in a report on a compliance attestation engagement to apply agreed-upon procedures.

DISCUSSION: The fourth attestation standard of reporting states, "The report on an engagement to apply agreed-upon procedures should contain a statement limiting its use to the parties who have agreed upon such procedures." Nevertheless, if the report is a matter of public record, the practitioner should so indicate.

Answer (B) is incorrect because agreed-upon procedures typically result in a summary of findings, not an opinion. Answer (C) is incorrect because negative assurance is not permitted in reports on applying agreed-upon procedures. Answer (D) is incorrect because the parties who agreed to the procedures are responsible for their sufficiency.

151. The objective of a practitioner's examination of management's assertion about compliance with specified requirements is the expression of an opinion. For this purpose, (s)he accumulates sufficient evidence to limit attestation risk to an appropriately low level. An attestation risk is the risk that

A. Material noncompliance with specified requirements could occur, assuming no related controls over compliance exist.

B. Material noncompliance that could occur will not be prevented or detected on a timely basis by the entity's controls.

C. The practitioner may unknowingly fail to modify appropriately the opinion on management's assertion.

D. The practitioner's procedures will lead to the conclusion that material noncompliance does not exist when, in fact, such noncompliance does exist.

The correct answer is (C). *(Publisher)*

REQUIRED: The nature of attestation risk.

DISCUSSION: Attestation risk is the risk that the practitioner may unknowingly fail to modify appropriately the opinion on management's assertion. Its components are inherent risk, control risk, and detection risk.

Answer (A) is incorrect because inherent risk is the risk that material noncompliance with specified requirements could occur, assuming no related controls over compliance exist. Answer (B) is incorrect because control risk is the risk that material noncompliance that could occur will not be prevented or detected on a timely basis by the entity's controls. Answer (D) is incorrect because detection risk is the risk that the practitioner's procedures will lead to the conclusion that material noncompliance does not exist when, in fact, such noncompliance does exist.

8.10 Management's Discussion and Analysis

152. AT 700, *Management's Discussion and Analysis*, provides guidance for an engagement regarding management's discussion and analysis (MD&A) prepared under the rules and regulations adopted by the SEC. A practitioner who undertakes such an engagement

A. May review but not apply agreed-upon procedures to MD&A.

B. Must comply with the general and reporting but not the field work attestation standards.

C. May perform services regarding MD&A of a public but not a private entity.

D. Must have audited the entity's financial statements for the latest period to which MD&A relates if the service provided is an examination.

The correct answer is (D). *(Publisher)*

REQUIRED: The true statement about an engagement to provide services regarding MD&A.

DISCUSSION: A practitioner may examine MD&A if (s)he has performed an audit in accordance with GAAS of the financial statements for at least the most recent period to which the presentation relates. Furthermore, the financial statements for the other periods covered by the presentation must have been audited by the practitioner or a predecessor auditor. A base knowledge of the entity obtained in this way is necessary to provide knowledge sufficient to evaluate the results of the examination. A practitioner may also review MD&A of a public entity for an annual period if (s)he has audited the statements for the latest annual period and if the other statements covered by the presentation were audited by the practitioner or a predecessor auditor. In addition, a practitioner may review MD&A of a public entity for an interim period if (1) (s)he has reviewed the historical statements for the related comparative interim periods or audited the interim statements and (2) MD&A for the most recent fiscal year has or will be examined or reviewed.

Answer (A) is incorrect because agreed-upon procedures may be performed if the practitioner applies AT 600 or AU 622. Answer (B) is incorrect because the attestation standards for field work must be followed. Answer (C) is incorrect because attest services may be provided regarding an MD&A presentation of a nonpublic entity whose management furnishes a written assertion that it was prepared using the rules and regulations adopted by the SEC.

153. The practitioner's objective in an examination of a management's discussion and analysis (MD&A) presentation is to

A. Express an opinion as to whether the historical financial amounts are fairly presented, in all material respects, in accordance with GAAP.

B. Express an opinion as to whether the underlying assumptions provide a reasonable basis for the disclosures.

C. Report whether any information came to his/her attention indicating that the elements required by the SEC are not included.

D. Report whether any information came to his/her attention indicating that the underlying information and estimates of the entity do not provide a reasonable basis for the disclosures.

The correct answer is (B). *(Publisher)*

REQUIRED: The practitioner's objective in an examination of MD&A.

DISCUSSION: In an examination, the objective is to express an opinion on the presentation taken as a whole by reporting whether (1) it includes, in all material respects, the required elements of the rules and regulations adopted by the SEC; (2) the historical financial amounts have been accurately derived, in all material respects, from the entity's financial statements; and (3) the underlying information, determinations, estimates, and assumptions of the entity provide a reasonable basis for the disclosures.

Answer (A) is incorrect because one objective is to express an opinion as to whether the historical financial amounts have been accurately derived, in all material respects, from the entity's financial statements. Answers (C) and (D) are incorrect because an examination involves expressing an opinion, not providing negative assurance.

CHAPTER NINE
INTERNAL AUDITING

This chapter concerns the following pronouncements of The Institute of Internal Auditors:

1. *Code of Ethics*
2. Statement of Responsibilities of Internal Auditing (SRIA)
3. Standards for the Professional Practice of Internal Auditing (SPPIA)
4. Statements on Internal Auditing Standards (SIASs)

Other questions unique to internal auditing are also included. The concepts and terminology used are from The IIA's pronouncements and may differ from those found in other authoritative literature. Most citations are to the SPPIA, which consist of five general standards and 25 specific standards.

Still other questions from the CIA exam and internal auditing questions from the CMA and CPA exams appear in the chapters that cover subject matter common to both external and internal auditing:

Chapter 3 -- Internal Control
Chapter 4 -- Audit Evidence and Procedures
Chapter 5 -- Information Systems
Chapter 6 -- Statistical Sampling

9.1 Introduction to Internal Auditing

1. The proper organizational role of internal auditing is to

A. Assist the external auditor in order to reduce external audit fees.

B. Perform studies to assist in the attainment of more efficient operations.

C. Serve as the investigative arm of the audit committee of the board of directors.

D. Serve as an appraisal function to examine and evaluate activities as a service to the organization.

The correct answer is (D). *(CIA, adapted)*

REQUIRED: The role of internal auditing.

DISCUSSION: According to the SRIA, "Internal auditing is an independent appraisal function established within an organization to examine and evaluate its activities as a service to the organization. The objective of internal auditing is to assist members of the organization in the effective discharge of their responsibilities."

Answer (A) is incorrect because reducing external audit fees may be a direct result of internal audit work, but it is not a reason for staffing an internal audit department. Answer (B) is incorrect because the primary role of internal auditing includes but is not limited to assessing the efficiency of operations. Answer (C) is incorrect because internal auditors serve management as well as the audit committee.

2. Internal auditing is a dynamic profession. Which of the following best describes the scope of internal auditing as it has developed to date?

A. Internal auditing involves appraising the economy and efficiency with which resources are employed.

B. Internal auditing involves evaluating compliance with policies, plans, procedures, laws, and regulations.

C. Internal auditing has evolved to verifying the existence of assets and reviewing the means of safeguarding assets.

D. Internal auditing has evolved to more of an operational orientation from a strictly financial orientation.

The correct answer is (D). *(CIA, adapted)*

REQUIRED: The scope of internal auditing.

DISCUSSION: Internal auditing encompasses the examination and evaluation of internal control and the quality of performance in carrying out assigned responsibilities. It includes the audit of (1) financial and operating information; (2) compliance with policies, plans, procedures, laws, regulations, and contracts; (3) the means of safeguarding assets and verifying their existence; (4) the economy and efficiency with which resources are employed; and (5) operations or programs to ascertain whether results are consistent with established objectives and goals and whether they are being carried out as planned.

Answers (A) and (B) are incorrect because appraising economy and efficiency and evaluating compliance are incomplete descriptions of the scope of internal auditing. Answer (C) is incorrect because verifying the existence of assets and reviewing the means of safeguarding assets are not the only functions of internal auditors.

3. Of the following, which is the major objective of The Institute of Internal Auditors (IIA)?

A. Cultivate, promote, and disseminate information concerning internal auditing and related subjects.

B. Oversee the activities of internal auditors.

C. Promulgate standards that must be followed by all corporations.

D. Investigate accusations that Certified Internal Auditors have violated The Institute of Internal Auditors *Code of Ethics*.

The correct answer is (A). *(CIA, adapted)*

REQUIRED: The major objective of The IIA.

DISCUSSION: The articles of incorporation of The IIA state its purposes: "To cultivate, promote, and disseminate knowledge and information concerning internal auditing and subjects related thereto; to establish and maintain high standards of integrity, honor, and character among internal auditors; to furnish information regarding internal auditing and the practice and methods thereof to its members, and to other persons interested therein, and to the general public; to cause the publication of articles relating to internal auditing and practices and methods thereof; to establish and maintain a library and reading rooms, meeting rooms and social rooms for the use of its members; to promote social inter-course among its members; and to do any and all things which shall be lawful and appropriate in furtherance of any of the purposes hereinbefore expressed."

Answer (B) is incorrect because The IIA is not a regulatory agency. Answer (C) is incorrect because the Standards are not compulsory. Answer (D) is incorrect because investigating ethics violations is not a major objective.

4. Individuals holding the CIA designation can expect all of the following benefits except

A. Participation in a recognized professional group.

B. Recognition as an expert management accountant.

C. Recognition among peers for the attainment of the designation.

D. A credential for professional advancement.

The correct answer is (B). *(Publisher)*

REQUIRED: The benefit not received from the CIA designation.

DISCUSSION: The CIA designation signifies compe-tence in internal auditing, principles of management, and disciplines related to internal auditing. However, it does not imply expertise in management accounting. The Certified Management Accountant (CMA) designation, conferred by the Institute of Certified Management Accountants (ICMA), signifies proficiency in management accounting.

Answer (A) is incorrect because the CIA designation is a recognized professional designation. Answer (C) is incorrect because the CIA designation provides recognition among peers for expertise in internal auditing. Answer (D) is incor-rect because the CIA designation is a credential that can be used in the employment market as evidence of attainment of certain educational and professional objectives.

5. One of the purposes of the Standards for the Professional Practice of Internal Auditing as stated in the introduction to the Standards is to

A. Encourage the professionalization of internal auditing.

B. Establish the independence of the internal audit department and emphasize the objectivity of internal auditing.

C. Encourage external auditors to make more extensive use of the work of internal auditors.

D. Establish the basis for guidance and measurement of internal auditing performance.

The correct answer is (D). *(CIA, adapted)*

REQUIRED: The purpose of the SPPIA.

DISCUSSION: The introduction states the following purposes of the Standards:

1. Impart an understanding of the role and responsibilities of internal auditing to all levels of management, boards of directors, public bodies, external auditors, and related professional organizations.
2. Establish the basis for guidance and measurement of internal auditing performance.
3. Improve the practice of internal auditing.

Answer (A) is incorrect because the professionalization of internal auditing is important but is not a purpose of the Standards. Answer (B) is incorrect because independence and objectivity are but two aspects of the basis for guidance and measurement of internal auditing performance. Answer (C) is incorrect because the Standards do not formally encourage external auditors to make more extensive use of the work of internal auditors.

6. Which of the following is considered a major reason for establishing an internal audit function?

A. To relieve overburdened management of the responsibility for establishing an effective control structure.

B. To safeguard resources entrusted to the organization.

C. To ensure the accuracy, reliability, and timeliness of financial and operating data used in management's decision making.

D. To assist members of the organization in the measurement and evaluation of the effectiveness of the established internal control.

The correct answer is (D). *(CIA, adapted)*

REQUIRED: The major reason for establishing an internal auditing function.

DISCUSSION: According to the SRIA, "The scope of internal auditing should encompass the examination and evaluation of the adequacy and effectiveness of the organization's system of internal control."

Answer (A) is incorrect because management is responsible for the establishment of internal control. Answer (B) is incorrect because controls, not the internal auditors, safeguard the organization's resources. The internal auditors are not charged with custody of assets, but they should review the means of safeguarding assets and verify the existence of such assets. Answer (C) is incorrect because internal auditors cannot ensure that certain conditions exist. Their responsibility is to report on the status of operations.

7. The internal auditing profession is believed to have advanced primarily as a consequence of

A. Increased interest by graduating students and experienced auditors.

B. The limitation of external audit scope.

C. Job qualification specifications that include added emphasis on background knowledge and skills.

D. Increased complexity and sophistication of business operations.

The correct answer is (D). *(CIA, adapted)*

REQUIRED: The reason for the internal auditing profession's increasing importance.

DISCUSSION: The increased complexity and sophistication of business operations have required management to rely on an internal audit system that functions as an appraisal control by measuring and evaluating other controls; internal auditing provides assurance that what management wants to happen is happening.

Answer (A) is incorrect because increased interest by graduating students and experienced auditors is not the primary reason for the advancement of the internal audit profession, but it contributes to, or results from, such advancement. Answer (B) is incorrect because a limitation on audit scope does not contribute to the profession's advancement. Answer (C) is incorrect because improved qualifications of internal auditors are a result of increased complexity and sophistication of business operations.

8. The audit committee can serve several important purposes, some of which directly benefit internal auditing. The most significant benefit provided by the audit committee to the internal auditor is

A. Protecting the independence of the internal auditor from undue management influence.

B. Reviewing annual audit plans and monitoring audit results.

C. Approving audit plans, scheduling, staffing, and meeting with the internal auditor as needed.

D. Reviewing copies of the procedures manuals for selected company operations and meeting with company officials to discuss them.

The correct answer is (A). *(CIA, adapted)*

REQUIRED: The most significant benefit provided by the audit committee to the internal auditor.

DISCUSSION: The audit committee is a subcommittee of outside directors who are independent of corporate management. Its purpose is to help keep external and internal auditors independent of management and to assure that the directors are exercising due care. This committee often selects the external auditors, reviews their overall audit plan, and examines the results of external and internal audits.

Answers (B), (C), and (D) are incorrect because, although the audit committee may participate in some of the identified activities, none is as beneficial as protecting auditor independence.

9.2 Independence, Status, Objectivity

9. According to the Statement of Responsibilities, the authority of the internal auditing department is limited to that granted by

A. The board of directors and the controller.

B. Senior management and the Standards.

C. Management and the board of directors.

D. The audit committee and the chief financial officer.

The correct answer is (C). *(CIA, adapted)*

REQUIRED: The source of authority of the internal auditing department.

DISCUSSION: According to the SRIA, internal auditing "functions under the policies established by senior management and the board. The director of internal auditing should seek approval of the charter by senior management as well as acceptance by the board. The charter should make clear the purposes of the internal audit department, specify the unrestricted scope of its work, and declare that auditors are to have no authority or responsibility for the activities they audit."

Answer (A) is incorrect because the controller is not the only member of management. Answer (B) is incorrect because the Standards provide no actual authority to internal auditors. Answer (D) is incorrect because management and the board, not a committee of the board and a particular manager, endow internal auditing with its authority.

10. A medium-sized publicly owned corporation operating in Country X has grown to a size that the directors of the corporation believe warrants the establishment of an internal auditing department. Country X has legislated internal auditing requirements for government-owned companies. The company changed the corporate bylaws to reflect the establishment of the internal auditing department. The directors decided that the director of internal auditing must be a certified internal auditor and will report directly to the newly established audit committee of the board of directors. Which of the items discussed above will contribute the most to the new audit director's independence?

A. The establishment of the internal auditing department is documented in corporate bylaws.

B. Country X has legislated internal auditing requirements.

C. The director will report to the audit committee of the board of directors.

D. The director is to be a certified internal auditor.

The correct answer is (C). *(CIA, adapted)*

REQUIRED: The item that contributes most to an audit director's independence.

DISCUSSION: According to Standard 100, independence is achieved through organizational status and objectivity. The director should be responsible to an individual with sufficient authority to promote independence. The board of directors is the highest authority in the organization.

Answer (A) is incorrect because documentation in the bylaws does little to promote independence. Answer (B) is incorrect because legislated internal auditing requirements in Country X do not promote independence. Answer (D) is incorrect because independence is achieved through organizational status and objectivity.

11. During an audit of the organization's accounts payable function, an internal auditor plans to confirm balances with suppliers. What is the source of authority for such contacts with units outside the organization?

A. Internal auditing department policies and procedures.

B. The Standards.

C. The Statement of Responsibilities of Internal Auditing.

D. The internal auditing department's charter.

The correct answer is (D). *(CIA, adapted)*

REQUIRED: The source of authority for an internal auditor to contact units outside the organization.

DISCUSSION: According to Standard 110, "The purpose, authority, and responsibility of the internal audit department should be defined in a formal written document (charter). The charter should establish the department's position within the organization; authorize access to records, personnel, and physical properties relevant to the performance of audits; and define the scope of internal audit activities." The charter should prescribe internal auditing's relationships to other units within and outside the organization.

Answer (A) is incorrect because departmental policies and procedures guide the audit staff in the consistent compliance with the department's standards of performance. Answer (B) is incorrect because the Standards do not grant authority to auditors. Answer (C) is incorrect because the SRIA recommends that a formal charter define the authority of the department.

12. The auditor has planned an audit of the effectiveness of the quality assurance function as it affects the receiving of goods, the transfer of the goods into production, and the scrap costs related to defective items. The auditee argues that such an audit is not within the scope of the internal auditing function and should come under the purview of the quality assurance department only. What would be the most appropriate audit response?

A. Refer to the auditing department charter and the approved audit plan that includes the area designated for audit in the current time period.

B. Because quality assurance is a new function, seek the approval of management as a mediator to set the scope of the audit.

C. Indicate that the audit will examine the function only in accordance with the standards set by, and approved by, the quality assurance function.

D. Terminate the audit because an operational audit will not be productive without the auditee's cooperation.

The correct answer is (A). *(CIA, adapted)*

REQUIRED: The most appropriate response to an assertion that an audit is beyond the scope of internal auditing.

DISCUSSION: The charter should define the purpose, authority, and responsibility of the internal auditing department. Among other matters, it should define the scope of internal audit activities. Furthermore, the director should submit annually to management for approval and to the board for its information a summary of the department's audit work schedule, staffing plan, and financial budget (Standard 110).

Answer (B) is incorrect because the auditee does not determine the scope of the audit. Answer (C) is incorrect because other objectives may be established by management and the auditor. The audit should not be limited to the specific standards set by the quality assurance department, but it should consider such standards in the development of the audit program. Answer (D) is incorrect because the auditor should conduct the audit and communicate any scope limitations to management and the board.

13. The director of internal auditing routinely presents an activity report to the board of directors as part of the board meeting agenda each quarter. Senior management has asked to review the director's board presentation before each board meeting so that any issues or questions can be discussed beforehand. The director should

A. Provide the activity report to senior management as requested and discuss any issues that may require action to be taken.

B. Withhold disclosure of the activity report to senior management because such matters are the sole province of the board.

C. Disclose to the board only those matters in the activity report that pertain to expenditures and financial budgets of the internal auditing department.

D. Provide information to senior management that pertains only to completed audits and findings available in published audit reports.

The correct answer is (A). *(CIA, adapted)*

REQUIRED: The action that should be taken regarding the review of internal auditing reports by management.

DISCUSSION: Standard 110 states, "The director of internal auditing should submit activity reports to management and to the board annually or more frequently as necessary. Activity reports should highlight significant findings and recommendations and should inform management and the board of any significant deviations from approved audit work schedules, staffing plans, and financial budgets, and the reasons for them."

Answer (B) is incorrect because the Standards require that activity reports be presented to management. Answer (C) is incorrect because the report should not be restricted to expenditures and financial budgets. Information about significant deviations from audit work schedules and staffing plans should be included. Answer (D) is incorrect because the Standards do not require the information to be limited in this manner.

14. According to the Standards, internal auditors must be objective in performing audits. Assume that the internal audit director received an annual bonus as part of that individual's compensation package. The bonus may impair the audit director's objectivity if

A. The bonus is administered by the board of directors or its salary administration committee.

B. The bonus is based on dollar recoveries or recommended future savings as a result of audits.

C. The scope of internal auditing work is reviewing control rather than account balances.

D. All of the answers are correct.

The correct answer is (B). *(CIA, adapted)*

REQUIRED: The conditions under which a bonus may impair the audit director's objectivity.

DISCUSSION: Objectivity may be impaired if the bonus is based on dollar recoveries or recommended future savings as a result of audits. A bonus based on either of these criteria could unduly influence the type of audits performed or the recommendations made. Furthermore, The IIA *Code of Ethics* requires objectivity and prohibits activities that may constitute a conflict of interest.

Answer (A) is incorrect because the board of directors should determine the director's compensation. Answer (C) is incorrect because the scope of internal auditing should include reviewing control. Answer (D) is incorrect because objectivity is not impaired if the board determines the director's compensation or if the scope of internal auditing is reviewing control rather than account balances.

15. Management has requested the internal auditing department to perform an operational audit of the telephone marketing operations of a major division and to recommend procedures and policies for improving management control over the operation. The auditor should

A. Not accept the engagement because recommending controls would impair future objectivity of the department regarding this auditee.

B. Not accept the engagement because audit departments are presumed to have expertise on accounting controls, not marketing controls.

C. Accept the engagement but indicate to management that, because recommending controls impairs audit independence, future audits of the area will be impaired.

D. Accept the audit engagement because independence will not be impaired.

The correct answer is (D). *(CIA, adapted)*

REQUIRED: The acceptability of an operational audit engagement to recommend standards of control.

DISCUSSION: The director of internal auditing should accept the engagement; assign staff with the knowledge, skills, and disciplines essential to the performance of this audit; and make appropriate recommendations. Recommending standards of control does not impair objectivity (Standard 120).

Answer (A) is incorrect because the auditor should accept the engagement. Recommending controls is not considered a violation of the auditor's independence or objectivity. Answer (B) is incorrect because the auditor should accept the engagement. Auditors should have control knowledge that is not limited to accounting controls. Answer (C) is incorrect because audit independence is not impaired by making control recommendations.

9.3 Professional Proficiency

16. It would be appropriate for internal auditing departments to use outside service providers with expertise in health care benefits when the internal auditing department is

A. Conducting an audit of the organization's estimate of its liability for postretirement benefits, which include health care benefits.

B. Comparing the cost of the organization's health care program with other programs offered in the industry.

C. Training its staff to conduct an audit of health care costs in a major division of the organization.

D. All of the answers are correct.

The correct answer is (D). *(CIA, adapted)*

REQUIRED: The reason(s) for using outside service providers with expertise in health care benefits.

DISCUSSION: The internal auditing staff should collectively possess the knowledge and skills essential to the practice of the profession. Thus, it should have employees or use outside service providers who are qualified in the disciplines relevant to audit activities. Accordingly, if the audit staff lacks expertise with regard to health care costs, outside service providers should be employed who can provide the requisite knowledge and skills. They can provide assistance in estimating the company's liability for postretirement benefits, in developing a comparative analysis of health care costs, and in training the staff to audit health care costs.

Answers (A), (B), and (C) are incorrect because audit activities pertaining to health care costs may require the use of outside service providers.

17. An internal auditing director for a large manufacturing company is considering revising the department's charter with respect to the minimum educational and experience qualifications required. The director wants to require all staff auditors to possess specialized training in accounting and a professional auditing certification such as the Certified Internal Auditor (CIA, adapted) or the Chartered Accountant (CA). One of the disadvantages of imposing this requirement would be

A. The policy might negatively affect the department's ability to perform quality examinations of the company's financial and accounting systems.

B. The policy would not promote the professionalism of the department.

C. The policy would prevent the department from using outside consultants when the department did not have the skills and knowledge required in certain audit situations.

D. The policy could limit the range of activities that could be audited by the department due to the department's narrow expertise and backgrounds.

The correct answer is (D). *(CIA, adapted)*

REQUIRED: The disadvantage of requiring all staff auditors to possess specialized training in accounting and a professional auditing certification.

DISCUSSION: According to Standard 220, "The internal auditing department should have employees or use outside service providers who are qualified in such disciplines as accounting, auditing, economics, finance, statistics, information technology, engineering, taxation, law, environmental affairs, and such areas as needed to meet the department's audit responsibilities. Each member of the department, however, need not be qualified in all disciplines." Thus, internal auditing departments should have an appropriate balance of experience, training, and skills to permit the audit of a wide range of activities.

Answer (A) is incorrect because the policy might result in better audits of financial and accounting systems. Answer (B) is incorrect because setting minimum professional standards promotes professionalism. Answer (C) is incorrect because this requirement would not affect whether consultants were used.

18. The best control over the work on which audit opinions are based is

A. Supervisory review of all audit work.

B. Preparation of time budgets for auditing activities.

C. Preparation of working papers.

D. Staffing of audit activities.

The correct answer is (A). *(CIA, adapted)*

REQUIRED: The best control over the work on which audit opinions are based.

DISCUSSION: "Supervision includes ensuring that the auditors assigned possess the requisite knowledge and skills; providing appropriate instructions during the planning of the audit and approving the audit program; seeing that the approved audit program is carried out unless changes are both justified and authorized; determining that audit working papers adequately support the audit findings, conclusions, and reports; ensuring that audit reports are accurate, objective, clear, concise, constructive, and timely; ensuring that audit objectives are met; and providing opportunities for developing internal auditors' knowledge and skills" (Standard 230). Hence, supervision is a control that encompasses all aspects of audit work.

Answer (B) is incorrect because, although useful in controlling audit time, time budgets do not assure the adequacy of work supporting opinions. Answer (C) is incorrect because working papers provide the basis for audit opinions, but review is necessary to ensure the adequacy of work. Answer (D) is incorrect because staffing is required, but audit work reviews are essential to ensure an adequate basis for audit opinions.

19. The ability to apply knowledge to situations likely to be encountered and to deal with them without extensive recourse to technical research and assistance is required of all internal auditors in applying

A. Internal auditing procedures and techniques.

B. Accounting principles and techniques.

C. Management principles.

D. Quantitative methods.

The correct answer is (A). *(CIA, adapted)*

REQUIRED: The organizational discipline that matches the skill level described.

DISCUSSION: Standard 250 states, "Proficiency in applying internal auditing standards, procedures, and techniques is required in performing internal audits. Proficiency means the ability to apply knowledge to situations likely to be encountered and to deal with them without extensive recourse to technical research and assistance."

Answer (B) is incorrect because proficiency in accounting principles and techniques is required only of auditors who work extensively with financial records and reports. Answer (C) is incorrect because an internal auditor is required to have an understanding of, not a proficiency in, management principles. Answer (D) is incorrect because an internal auditor is required to have only an appreciation of quantitative methods.

20. The ability to apply broad knowledge to situations likely to be encountered, to recognize significant deviations, and to be able to carry out the research necessary to arrive at reasonable solutions is required of all internal auditors in applying

A. Internal auditing procedures and techniques.

B. Accounting principles and techniques.

C. Management principles.

D. Quantitative methods.

The correct answer is (C). *(CIA, adapted)*

REQUIRED: The organizational discipline that matches the skill level described.

DISCUSSION: Standard 250 states, "An understanding of management principles is required to recognize and evaluate the materiality and significance of deviations from good business practice. An understanding means the ability to apply broad knowledge to situations likely to be encountered, to recognize significant deviations, and to be able to carry out the research necessary to arrive at reasonable solutions."

Answer (A) is incorrect because proficiency, not an understanding, is required in applying internal auditing procedures and techniques. Answer (B) is incorrect because proficiency in accounting principles and techniques is required only of auditors who work extensively with financial records and reports. Answer (D) is incorrect because an internal auditor is required to have only an appreciation of quantitative methods.

21. Communication skills are important to internal auditors. According to the Standards, the auditor should be able to effectively convey all of the following to the auditee except

A. The audit objectives designed for a specific auditable entity.

B. The audit evaluations based on a preliminary survey of an auditable entity.

C. The risk assessment used in selecting the area for audit investigation.

D. Recommendations that are generated in relationship to a specific auditable entity.

The correct answer is (C). *(CIA, adapted)*

REQUIRED: The matter that an auditor need not communicate to the auditee.

DISCUSSION: According to Standard 260, "Internal auditors should be skilled in oral and written communications so that they can clearly and effectively convey such matters as audit objectives, evaluations, conclusions, and recommendations." However, the auditor's risk assessment is not specifically mentioned in Standard 260.

Answers (A), (B), and (D) are incorrect because the auditor should be able to convey effectively audit objectives, conclusions, evaluations, and recommendations.

22. The Standards state that internal auditors are "responsible for continuing their education in order to maintain their proficiency." Which of the following is correct regarding the continuing education requirements of the practicing internal auditor?

A. Internal auditors are required to obtain 40 hours of continuing professional development each year and a minimum of 120 hours over a 3-year period.

B. CIAs have formal requirements that must be met in order to continue as CIAs.

C. Attendance, as an officer or committee member, at formal Institute of Internal Auditors meetings does not meet the criteria of continuing professional development.

D. In-house programs meet continuing professional development requirements only if they have been preapproved by The Institute of Internal Auditors.

The correct answer is (B). *(CIA, adapted)*

REQUIRED: The true statement about continuing professional education (CPE) requirements.

DISCUSSION: To maintain the CIA designation, the CIA must commit to a formal program of CPE and report to the Certification Department of The IIA.

Answer (A) is incorrect because the Standards do not state formal hour requirements for internal auditors. The intent of the Standards is to provide flexibility in meeting the requirements. Answer (C) is incorrect because continuing education may be obtained by participation in professional societies (Standard 270). Answer (D) is incorrect because prior approval of The IIA is not necessary for CPE courses.

23. An auditor has some suspicion, but no evidence, of potential misstatement. The standard of due professional care would be violated if the auditor

A. Identified potential ways in which an error could occur and ranked the items for audit investigation.

B. Informed the audit manager of the suspicions and asked for advice on how to proceed.

C. Did not test for possible misstatement because the audit program had already been approved by audit management.

D. Expanded the audit program, without the auditee's approval, to address the highest ranked ways in which a misstatement may have occurred.

The correct answer is (C). *(CIA, adapted)*

REQUIRED: The act in violation of the due professional care standard.

DISCUSSION: Due professional care requires the exercise of the care and skill expected of a reasonably prudent and competent auditor in similar circumstances (Standard 280). Because audit programs are expected to be modified to reflect changing circumstances, the auditor would fail to exercise due care if (s)he did not investigate a suspected misstatement solely because the audit program had already been approved.

Answers (A) and (B) are incorrect because ranking the ways in which the error could occur and seeking advice are consistent with the due professional care standard. Answer (D) is incorrect because the auditor does not need the auditee's approval to expand the audit test.

9.4 Fraud

24. According to the Standards, which of the following best describes the two general categories or types of fraud that concern most internal auditors?

A. Improper payments (such as bribes and kickbacks) and tax fraud.

B. Fraud designed to benefit the organization and fraud perpetrated to the detriment of the organization.

C. Acceptance of bribes or kickbacks and improper related-party transactions.

D. Acceptance of kickbacks or embezzlement and misappropriation of assets.

The correct answer is (B). *(CIA, adapted)*

REQUIRED: The best description of the two general types of fraud that concern most internal auditors.

DISCUSSION: "Fraud encompasses an array of irregularities and illegal acts characterized by intentional deception. It can be perpetrated for the benefit of or to the detriment of the organization and by persons outside as well as inside the organization" (SIAS 3).

Answers (A), (C), and (D) are incorrect because improper payments, tax fraud, improper related-party transactions, embezzlement, and misappropriation of assets are specific kinds of fraud, not general categories.

25. A significant employee fraud took place shortly after an internal audit. The internal auditor may not have properly fulfilled the responsibility for the deterrence of fraud by failing to note and report that

A. Policies, practices, and procedures to monitor activities and safeguard assets were less extensive in low-risk areas than in high-risk areas.

B. A system of control that depended upon separation of duties could be circumvented by collusion among three employees.

C. There were no written policies describing prohibited activities and the action required whenever violations are discovered.

D. Divisional employees had not been properly trained to distinguish between bona fide signatures and cleverly forged ones on authorization forms.

The correct answer is (C). *(CIA, adapted)*

REQUIRED: The failure to deter fraud.

DISCUSSION: According to SIAS 3, "Internal auditing is responsible for assisting in the deterrence of fraud by examining and evaluating the adequacy and the effectiveness of control, commensurate with the extent of the potential exposure/risk in the various segments of the entity's operations. In carrying out this responsibility, internal auditing should, for example, determine whether written corporate policies (e.g., a code of conduct) exist that describe prohibited activities and the action required whenever violations are discovered."

Answer (A) is incorrect because, for cost-benefit reasons, control activities are more extensive in high-risk areas. Answers (B) and (D) are incorrect because even the best internal control can often be circumvented by collusion or forgery.

26. The primary responsibility for preventing fraud in an organization lies with

A. Management.

B. The internal auditor.

C. Security personnel.

D. The audit committee of the board of directors.

The correct answer is (A). *(CIA, adapted)*

REQUIRED: The person(s) primarily responsible for preventing fraud.

DISCUSSION: Fraud prevention consists of those actions taken to discourage the perpetration of fraud and to limit the exposure if fraud does occur. The principal mechanism for preventing fraud is control. Primary responsibility for establishing and maintaining control rests with management (SIAS 1). Ultimately, prevention is a matter of the policies and procedures established by management.

Answers (B) and (C) are incorrect because the internal auditor and security personnel work within the environment established by management. Answer (D) is incorrect because the responsibility of preventing fraud must lie within the organization, not with outside directors.

27. After noting some red flags, an auditor has an increased awareness that fraud may be present. Which of the following best describes the auditor's responsibility?

A. Expand activities to determine whether an investigation is warranted.

B. Report the possibility of fraud to top management and ask them how they would like to proceed.

C. Consult with external legal counsel to determine the course of action to be taken, including the approval of the proposed audit program to make sure it is acceptable on legal grounds.

D. Report the matter to the audit committee and request funding for outside specialists to help investigate the possible fraud.

The correct answer is (A). *(CIA, adapted)*

REQUIRED: The auditor's responsibility after noting some fraud indicators.

DISCUSSION: According to SIAS 3, an internal auditor's responsibilities for detecting fraud include evaluating fraud indicators and deciding whether any additional action is necessary or whether an investigation should be recommended.

Answers (B) and (D) are incorrect because the auditor should notify the appropriate authorities within the organization only if (s)he has determined that the indicators of fraud are sufficient to recommend an investigation. Answer (C) is incorrect because the internal auditor does not have the authority to consult with external legal counsel.

28. Red flags are conditions that indicate a higher likelihood of fraud. Which of the following would not be considered a red flag?

A. Management has delegated the authority to make purchases under a certain dollar limit to subordinates.

B. An individual has held the same cash-handling job for an extended period without any rotation of duties.

C. An individual handling marketable securities is responsible for making the purchases, recording the purchases, and reporting any discrepancies and gains/losses to senior management.

D. The assignment of responsibility and accountability in the accounts receivable department is not clear.

The correct answer is (A). *(CIA, adapted)*

REQUIRED: The item not a red flag.

DISCUSSION: Delegating the authority to make purchases under a certain dollar limit to subordinates is an acceptable and common practice intended to limit risk while promoting efficiency. It is not, by itself, considered a red flag.

Answer (B) is incorrect because lack of rotation of duties or cross-training for sensitive jobs is a red flag. Such a person may have a greater opportunity to commit and conceal fraud. Answer (C) is incorrect because an inappropriate combination of duties is a red flag. Answer (D) is incorrect because establishing clear lines of authority and accountability not only helps to assign culpability but also has preventive effects.

29. The Standards require that, when an internal auditor identifies multiple factors linked with possible fraudulent conditions and suspects that fraud has taken place, the auditor should

A. Immediately notify senior management and the board.

B. Immediately inform the audit committee.

C. Notify the appropriate authorities within the company and recommend an investigation.

D. Extend audit tests to determine the extent of the fraud.

The correct answer is (C). *(CIA, adapted)*

REQUIRED: The auditor's responsibility when (s)he suspects fraud.

DISCUSSION: According to SIAS 3, the internal auditor's responsibilities for detecting fraud when conducting an audit assignment are to have sufficient knowledge of the indicators of fraud; to be alert to opportunities, such as control weaknesses, that could allow fraud; to conduct additional tests directed toward detection of fraud if significant weaknesses are found; to evaluate the indicators and decide whether further action is necessary or an investigation should be recommended; and to "notify the appropriate authorities within the organization if a determination is made that there are sufficient indicators of the commission of a fraud to recommend an investigation."

Answers (A) and (B) are incorrect because immediate notification of the board is required once additional testing has established that a fraud has taken place. Answer (D) is incorrect because tests to determine the extent of fraud are performed after the fraud has in fact been determined, not suspected.

30. According to the Standards, an internal auditor should be involved in fraud investigations as a(n)

A. Sole investigator.

B. Part of an investigation team.

C. Independent observer.

D. Nonparticipant.

The correct answer is (B). *(CIA, adapted)*

REQUIRED: The status of internal auditors in fraud investigations.

DISCUSSION: According to SIAS 3, "Investigation consists of performing extended procedures necessary to determine whether fraud, as suggested by the indicators, has occurred. It includes gathering sufficient evidential matter about the specific details of a discovered fraud. Internal auditors, lawyers, investigators, security personnel, and other specialists from inside or outside the organization are the parties that usually conduct or participate in fraud investigations."

Answers (A), (C), and (D) are incorrect because internal auditors usually participate in fraud investigations as part of a team.

31. Which of the following is the most appropriate activity for an internal auditor involved in a fraud investigation?

A. Supervising the activities of security personnel and other investigators.

B. Serving as liaison with law enforcement and the press.

C. Designing procedures to identify the perpetrators and causes of the fraud.

D. Conducting public interrogations of suspected perpetrators.

The correct answer is (C). *(CIA, adapted)*

REQUIRED: The most appropriate activity for an internal auditor involved in a fraud investigation.

DISCUSSION: In fraud investigations, internal auditing should (1) assess the probable level and the extent of complicity in the fraud within the organization; (2) determine the knowledge, skills, and disciplines needed for an effective investigation; (3) assess the qualifications and the skills of the internal auditors and specialists available to participate in the investigation; (4) design procedures to identify the perpetrators, the extent of the fraud, the techniques used, and the cause of the fraud; (5) coordinate activities with management, legal counsel, and other specialists; and (6) be aware of the rights of alleged perpetrators and personnel (SIAS 3).

Answer (A) is incorrect because internal auditors, as such, do not act in a supervisory role. Answer (B) is incorrect because serving as liaison with law enforcement and the press is not an internal audit function. Answer (D) is incorrect because interrogations should be private and conducted by specialists.

32. If there is fraud in the marketing department, which of the following would be beyond the scope of the auditor's responsibility?

A. Informing the wrongdoer of his/her legal rights.

B. Determining the effects of the wrongdoing.

C. Discussing the wrongdoing with an appropriate level of management.

D. Including the wrongdoing in a report that will go to the audit committee.

The correct answer is (A). *(CIA, adapted)*

REQUIRED: The action beyond the scope of the auditor's responsibility regarding fraud.

DISCUSSION: The auditor is responsible for having sufficient knowledge of fraud to be able to identify indicators that fraud might have been committed. In the investigation of fraud, the internal auditor should assess the probable level and the extent of complicity in the fraud and should design procedures to identify the perpetrators, the extent of the fraud, the techniques used, and the cause. However, the criminal investigation is the responsibility of external authorities. The auditor does not have the responsibility or the right to inform the wrongdoer of his/her legal rights.

Answer (B) is incorrect because determining the effects of the wrongdoing is a responsibility of the auditor. Answer (C) is incorrect because discussing the wrongdoing with the appropriate level of management is a responsibility of the auditor. Answer (D) is incorrect because including the wrongdoing in a report to the audit committee is a responsibility of the auditor.

33. The internal auditing department has concluded a fraud investigation that revealed a previously undiscovered materially adverse impact on the financial position and results of operations for 2 years on which financial statements have already been issued. The director of internal auditing should immediately inform

A. The external audit firm responsible for the financial statements affected.

B. The appropriate governmental agency.

C. Appropriate management and the audit committee of the board of directors.

D. The accounting function ultimately responsible for corrective journal entries.

The correct answer is (C). *(CIA, adapted)*

REQUIRED: The parties informed of the results of a fraud investigation.

DISCUSSION: SIAS 3 states, "The results of a fraud investigation may indicate that fraud has had a previously undiscovered materially adverse effect on the financial position and results of operations of an organization for one or more years on which financial statements have already been issued. Internal auditing should inform appropriate management and the audit committee of the board of directors of such a discovery."

Answers (A), (B), and (D) are incorrect because management should communicate with the external auditors, governmental agencies, and the accounting function.

34. Internal auditing is responsible for reporting fraud to senior management or the board when

A. The incidence of fraud of a material amount has been established to a reasonable certainty.

B. Suspicious activities have been reported to internal auditing.

C. Irregular transactions have been identified and are under investigation.

D. The review of all suspected fraud-related transactions is complete.

The correct answer is (A). *(CIA, adapted)*

REQUIRED: The responsibility of internal auditing for reporting fraud to senior management or the board.

DISCUSSION: According to SIAS 3, the internal auditor's responsibilities for detecting fraud when conducting an audit assignment are to have sufficient knowledge of the indicators of fraud; to be alert to opportunities, such as control weaknesses, that could allow fraud; to conduct additional tests directed toward detection of fraud if significant weaknesses are found; to evaluate the indicators and decide whether further action is necessary or an investigation should be recommended; and to notify the appropriate authorities within the organization if a determination is made that there are sufficient indicators of the commission of a fraud to recommend an investigation.

Answer (B) is incorrect because reporting is not required when suspicious acts are reported to the auditor. Answer (C) is incorrect because irregular transactions under investigation do not require reporting until the investigation is completed. Answer (D) is incorrect because reporting should occur when a material fraud has been established with reasonable certainty.

35. After completing an investigation, internal auditing has concluded that an employee has stolen a material amount of cash. A draft of the proposed report on this finding should be reviewed by

A. Legal counsel.

B. The audit committee of the board of directors.

C. The president of the organization.

D. The external auditor.

The correct answer is (A). *(CIA, adapted)*

REQUIRED: The person(s) who should receive a draft of the proposed report on a fraud investigation.

DISCUSSION: Review by legal counsel reduces the possibility of inclusion (and dissemination) of a statement for which the accused employee could sue the organization. If internal auditing wants to invoke client privilege, the report should be addressed to legal counsel.

Answer (B) is incorrect because the audit committee should receive a final draft of the report after it has been reviewed and approved by legal counsel. Answer (C) is incorrect because, if appropriate, the president may receive a final draft of the report after it has been reviewed and approved by legal counsel. Answer (D) is incorrect because, if sending the outside auditors copies of all internal audit reports is customary, they should receive final drafts approved by legal counsel.

36. According to the Standards, a fraud report is required

A. At the conclusion of the detection phase.

B. At the conclusion of the investigation phase.

C. At the conclusion of both the detection and the investigation phases.

D. Neither at the conclusion of the detection phase nor at the conclusion of the investigation phase.

The correct answer is (B). *(CIA, adapted)*

REQUIRED: The situation in which a fraud report is required.

DISCUSSION: According to SIAS 3, "A written report should be issued at the conclusion of the investigation phase. It should include all findings, conclusions, recommendations, and corrective action taken."

Answers (A) and (C) are incorrect because a fraud report is authorized, but not required, at the conclusion of the detection phase. Answer (D) is incorrect because a fraud report is required at the end of the investigation.

37. According to the Standards, which of the following is the correct listing of information that must be included in a fraud report?

A. Purpose, scope, results, and, when appropriate, an expression of the auditor's opinion.

B. Criteria, condition, cause, and effect.

C. Background, findings, and recommendations.

D. Findings, conclusions, recommendations, and corrective action.

The correct answer is (D). *(CIA, adapted)*

REQUIRED: The correct listing of information that must be included in a fraud report.

DISCUSSION: According to SIAS 3, "A written report should be issued at the conclusion of the investigation phase. It should include all findings, conclusions, recommendations, and corrective action taken."

Answer (A) is incorrect because purpose, scope, results, and, when appropriate, an opinion are included in every final written report. This definition does not include corrective action. Answer (B) is incorrect because criteria, condition, cause, and effect are the elements of a finding. A fraud report includes more than findings. Answer (C) is incorrect because the inclusion of background is recommended but not required for inclusion in a final audit report, and there is no mention of it in a fraud report. Conclusions and corrective action are omitted, so the listing is incomplete.

9.5 Internal Control

38. Auditors regularly evaluate controls. Which of the following best describes the concept of control as recognized by internal auditors?

A. Management regularly discharges personnel who do not perform up to expectations.

B. Management takes action to enhance the likelihood that established goals and objectives will be achieved.

C. Control represents specific procedures that accountants and auditors design to ensure the correctness of processing.

D. Control procedures should be designed from the "bottom up" to ensure attention to detail.

The correct answer is (B). *(CIA, adapted)*

REQUIRED: The best description of the concept of control as recognized by internal auditors.

DISCUSSION: "A control is any action taken by management to enhance the likelihood that established goals and objectives will be achieved. Management plans, organizes, and directs the performance of sufficient actions to provide reasonable assurance that objectives and goals will be achieved. Thus, control is the result of proper planning, organizing, and directing by management" (SIAS 1).

Answer (A) is incorrect because termination of employees who perform unsatisfactorily is not a comprehensive definition of control. Answer (C) is incorrect because control is not limited to processing. Moreover, it is instituted by management, not auditors. Answer (D) is incorrect because some control procedures may be designed from the bottom up, but the concept of control flows from management down through the organization.

39. SIAS 1, *Control: Concepts and Responsibilities*, adds a guideline to the Standards. Which of the following is a summary of that guideline?

A. Control is the result of proper planning, organizing, and directing by management.

B. Controls are the broadest statements of what the organization chooses to accomplish.

C. Control is provided when cost-effective actions are taken to restrict deviations to a tolerable level.

D. Control accomplishes objectives and goals in an accurate and timely fashion with minimal use of resources.

The correct answer is (A). *(CIA, adapted)*

REQUIRED: The guideline added by SIAS 1.

DISCUSSION: "A control is any action taken by management to enhance the likelihood that established objectives and goals will be achieved. Management plans, organizes, and directs the performance of sufficient actions to provide reasonable assurance that objectives and goals will be achieved. Thus, control is the result of proper planning, organizing, and directing by management" (SIAS 1).

Answer (B) is incorrect because objectives are the broadest statements of what the organization chooses to accomplish. Answer (C) is incorrect because reasonable assurance is provided when cost-effective actions are taken to restrict deviations to a tolerable level. Answer (D) is incorrect because efficient performance accomplishes objectives and goals in an accurate and timely fashion with minimal use of resources.

40. Corporate directors, management, external auditors, and internal auditors all play important roles in creating a proper control environment. Top management is primarily responsible for

A. Establishing a proper environment and specifying an overall system of internal control.

B. Reviewing the reliability and integrity of financial information and the means used to collect and report such information.

C. Ensuring that external and internal auditors adequately monitor the control environment.

D. Implementing and monitoring controls designed by the board of directors.

The correct answer is (A). *(CIA, adapted)*

REQUIRED: The best description of top management's responsibility.

DISCUSSION: According to SIAS 1, "Management plans, organizes, and directs in such a fashion as to provide reasonable assurance that established goals and objectives will be achieved." Also, "Management establishes and maintains an environment that fosters control."

Answer (B) is incorrect because internal auditing is responsible for reviewing the reliability and integrity of financial information and the means used to collect and report such information. Answer (C) is incorrect because management cannot delegate its responsibilities for control to auditors. Answer (D) is incorrect because the board has oversight responsibilities but ordinarily does not become involved in the details of operations.

41. Which group has the primary responsibility for the establishment, implementation, and monitoring of adequate controls in the posting of accounts receivable?

A. External auditors.

B. Accounts receivable staff.

C. Internal auditors.

D. Accounting management.

The correct answer is (D). *(CIA, adapted)*

REQUIRED: The group responsible for controls over accounts receivable.

DISCUSSION: Management is responsible for establishing goals and objectives, developing and implementing control procedures, and accomplishing desired results.

Answer (A) is incorrect because external auditors are responsible for the independent outside audit of financial statements. Answer (B) is incorrect because accounts receivable staff is responsible for daily transaction handling. Answer (C) is incorrect because internal auditors are responsible for examining and evaluating the adequacy and effectiveness of internal control.

42. Which of the following features of a large manufacturing company's organization structure is a control weakness?

A. The information systems department is headed by a vice president who reports directly to the president.

B. The chief financial officer is a vice president who reports to the chief executive officer.

C. The audit committee of the board consists of the chief executive officer, the chief financial officer, and a major shareholder.

D. The controller and treasurer report to the chief financial officer.

The correct answer is (C). *(CIA, adapted)*

REQUIRED: The control weakness in a large manufacturing company's organization structure.

DISCUSSION: The audit committee has a control function because of its oversight of internal as well as external auditing. It should consist of directors who are independent of management. The authority and independence of the audit committee strengthen the position of internal auditing. The board should concur in the appointment or removal of the director of internal auditing, who should have direct, regular communication with the board (Standard 110).

Answer (A) is incorrect because this reporting relationship is a strength. It prevents the information systems operation from being dominated by a user. Answers (B) and (D) are incorrect because each is a normal and appropriate reporting relationship.

43. Controls can be classified according to the functions they are intended to perform; for example, to discover the occurrence of an unwanted event (detective), to avoid the occurrence of an unwanted event (preventive), or to ensure the occurrence of a desirable event (directive). Which of the following is a directive control?

A. Preparing monthly bank statement reconciliations.

B. Requiring dual signatures on all disbursements over a specific dollar amount.

C. Recording every transaction on the day it occurs.

D. Requiring all members of the internal auditing department to be CIAs.

The correct answer is (D). *(CIA, adapted)*

REQUIRED: The directive control.

DISCUSSION: Requiring all members of the internal auditing department to be CIAs is a directive control. The control is designed to encourage a desirable event to occur, i.e., to enhance the professionalism and level of expertise of the internal auditing department.

Answer (A) is incorrect because monthly bank statement reconciliation is a detective control. The events under scrutiny have already occurred. Answer (B) is incorrect because requiring dual signatures on all disbursements over a specific dollar amount is a preventive control. The control is designed to deter an undesirable event. Answer (C) is incorrect because recording every transaction on the day it occurs is a preventive control. The control is designed to deter an undesirable event.

9.6 Scope of Work

44. When the executive management of an organization decided to form a team to investigate the adoption of an activity-based costing (ABC) system, an internal auditor was assigned to the team. The best reason for including an internal auditor would be the auditor's knowledge of

A. Activities and cost drivers.

B. Information processing procedures.

C. Current product cost structures.

D. Internal controls alternatives.

The correct answer is (D). *(CIA, adapted)*

REQUIRED: The auditor's knowledge that is the best reason for including him/her in a team investigating ABC.

DISCUSSION: An internal auditor is concerned about the reliability of the information contained in the company's operating reports. Accordingly, the internal auditors' overall scope of work extends to the examination and evaluation of the organization's system of internal control and the quality of performance in carrying out assigned responsibilities (Standard 300), and the audit objective includes promoting effective control at reasonable cost (SRIA).

Answer (A) is incorrect because an engineer has more knowledge about activities and cost drivers. Answer (B) is incorrect because an information systems expert has more knowledge about information needs and information processing procedures. Answer (C) is incorrect because a management accountant has more knowledge about a company's current product cost.

45. The primary difference between operational auditing and financial auditing is that in operational auditing

A. The auditor is not concerned with whether the audited activity is generating information in compliance with financial accounting standards.

B. The auditor is seeking to help management use resources in the most effective manner possible.

C. The auditor starts with the financial statements of an activity being audited and works backward to the basic processes involved in producing them.

D. The auditor can use analytical skills and tools that are not necessary in financial auditing.

The correct answer is (B). *(CIA, adapted)*

REQUIRED: The main distinction between operational and financial auditing.

DISCUSSION: Financial auditing is primarily concerned with forming an opinion on the fairness of the financial statements. Operational auditing evaluates compliance with policies, plans, procedures, laws, regulations, and contracts; accomplishment of established objectives and goals for operations or programs; and economical and efficient use of resources.

Answer (A) is incorrect because the reliability and integrity of financial information are important in operational auditing. Information systems provide data for decision making, control, and compliance with external requirements. Answer (C) is incorrect because using financial statements as a starting point describes financial auditing. Answer (D) is incorrect because analytical skills are necessary in all types of auditing.

46. According to the Standards, internal auditors should review the means of physically safeguarding assets from losses arising from

A. Misapplication of accounting principles.

B. Procedures that are not cost justified.

C. Exposure to the elements.

D. Underusage of physical facilities.

The correct answer is (C). *(CIA, adapted)*

REQUIRED: The cause of losses giving rise to physical safeguards that should be reviewed by the auditor.

DISCUSSION: According to Standard 330, "Internal auditors should review the means used to safeguard assets from various types of losses such as those resulting from theft, fire, improper or illegal activities, and exposure to the elements."

Answer (A) is incorrect because misapplication of accounting principles relates to the reliability of information and not physical safeguards. Answer (B) is incorrect because procedures that are not cost justified relate to efficiency, not effectiveness, of operations. Answer (D) is incorrect because underusage of facilities relates to efficiency of operation.

47. In conducting an appraisal of the economy and efficiency with which resources are employed, an internal auditor is responsible for

A. Determining whether operating standards have been established.

B. Verifying the existence of assets.

C. Reviewing the reliability of operating information.

D. Verifying the accuracy of asset valuation.

The correct answer is (A). *(CIA, adapted)*

REQUIRED: The internal auditor's responsibility for assessing economic and efficient use of resources.

DISCUSSION: Standard 340 concerns the economic and efficient use of resources. It states that management is responsible for setting operating standards. Internal auditors are responsible for determining that (1) such standards have been established, (2) the standards are being met, (3) deviations are being identified and communicated, and (4) corrective action has been taken.

Answer (B) is incorrect because verifying existence relates to the safeguarding of assets (Standard 330). Answers (C) and (D) are incorrect because the reliability of operating information and the accuracy of asset valuation concern the reliability and integrity of information (Standard 310).

48. According to the Standards, an internal auditor's role with respect to operating objectives and goals includes

A. Approving the operating objectives or goals to be met.

B. Determining whether underlying assumptions are appropriate.

C. Developing and implementing control procedures.

D. Accomplishing desired operating program results.

The correct answer is (B). *(CIA, adapted)*

REQUIRED: The auditor's role regarding operating objectives and goals.

DISCUSSION: According to Standard 350, "Internal auditors can provide assistance to managers who are developing objectives, goals, and systems by determining whether the underlying assumptions are appropriate; whether accurate, current, and relevant information is being used; and whether suitable controls have been incorporated into the operations or programs."

Answers (A), (C), and (D) are incorrect because operational matters are the responsibility of management.

49. Management has requested the audit department to conduct an audit of the implementation of its recently developed company code of conduct. In preparing for the audit, the auditor reviews the newly developed code and compares it with several others for comparable companies and concludes that the newly developed code has severe deficiencies. Based on this conclusion, the auditor should

A. Plan an audit for the implementation of management's code of conduct and also for compliance with the "best practices" from the other codes since this represents the best available criteria.

B. Report the nature of the deficiencies in a formal report to management.

C. Inform management of the problems with the existing code and report that it would be inappropriate to conduct an audit until the code is revised to incorporate the "best practices" from industry.

D. Conduct the audit as requested by management, reporting only noncompliance with the code.

The correct answer is (B). *(CIA, adapted)*

REQUIRED: The responsibility of the auditors when requested to audit a new company code of conduct.

DISCUSSION: Management is responsible for establishing criteria to determine if objectives and goals have been accomplished. If the internal auditors believe that the established criteria are inadequate, they should report such conditions to the appropriate levels of management and may recommend appropriate courses of action (SIAS 10).

Answer (A) is incorrect because the auditors should not conduct an audit of compliance with criteria that have never been communicated to the auditees. Answer (C) is incorrect because conducting the audit is appropriate if management wants feedback about the implementation of its code. Answer (D) is incorrect because the auditor must communicate the deficiencies to management.

50. The president wants to know whether the purchasing function is properly meeting its charge to "purchase the right material at the right time in the right quantities." Which of the following types of audits addresses the president's request?

A. A financial audit of the purchasing department.

B. An operational audit of the purchasing function.

C. A compliance audit of the purchasing function.

D. A full-scope audit of the manufacturing operation.

The correct answer is (B). *(CIA, adapted)*

REQUIRED: The type of audit that determines whether the purchasing function is effective and efficient.

DISCUSSION: According to *Sawyer's Internal Auditing* (The IIA 1996, p. 4), an operational audit involves a "comprehensive review of the varied functions within an enterprise to appraise the efficiency and economy of operations and the effectiveness with which those functions achieve their objectives."

Answer (A) is incorrect because a financial audit involves the analysis of the economic activity of an entity as measured and reported by accounting methods. Answer (C) is incorrect because a compliance audit is a review of both financial and operating controls and transactions to determine conformity with established standards. It tests adherence to management's policies, procedures, and plans designed to ensure certain actions. Answer (D) is incorrect because an audit of the manufacturing operation has financial, compliance, and operational aspects. It exceeds the president's request.

51. An operational audit of the production function includes an audit procedure to compare actual costs with standard costs. The purpose of this operational audit procedure is to

A. Determine the accuracy of the system used to record actual costs.

B. Measure the effectiveness of the standard cost system.

C. Assess the reasonableness of standard costs.

D. Assist management in its evaluation of effectiveness and efficiency.

The correct answer is (D). *(CIA, adapted)*

REQUIRED: The purpose in an operational audit of the production function of comparing actual and standard costs.

DISCUSSION: A standard cost system costs the product at standard (predetermined) costs and compares expected with actual cost. This comparison allows deviations (variances) from expected results to be identified and investigated. Responsibility can then be pinpointed and corrective action taken. A standard cost system can be used in both job-order and process-costing systems.

Answers (A), (B), and (C) are incorrect because the comparison will not determine the accuracy of actual costs, the effectiveness of the system, or the reasonableness of standard costs.

52. A determination of cost savings is most likely to be an objective of

A. Program auditing.

B. Financial auditing.

C. Compliance auditing.

D. Operational auditing.

The correct answer is (D). *(CIA, adapted)*

REQUIRED: The form of auditing in which a determination of cost savings is an objective.

DISCUSSION: The scope of internal auditing extends to (1) safeguarding assets; (2) compliance with policies, plans, procedures, laws, and regulations; (3) accomplishment of goals; (4) reliability and integrity of data; and (5) economical and efficient use of resources. Operational auditing emphasizes operational efficiency and effectiveness (items 2, 3, and 5). Accordingly, operational auditing is most likely to address a determination of cost savings by focusing on economy and efficiency.

Answer (A) is incorrect because program auditing addresses accomplishment of program objectives. Answer (B) is incorrect because financial auditing concerns the safeguarding of assets and the reliability and integrity of information. Answer (C) is incorrect because compliance auditing relates to compliance with legal, regulatory, procedural, and other requirements.

53. Internal auditors are often called upon to either perform, or assist the external auditor in performing, a due diligence review. A due diligence review is

A. A review of interim financial statements as directed by an underwriting firm.

B. An operational audit of a division of a company to determine if divisional management is complying with laws and regulations.

C. A review of operations as requested by the audit committee to determine whether the operations comply with audit committee and organizational policies.

D. A review of financial statements and related disclosures in conjunction with a potential acquisition.

The correct answer is (D). *(CIA, adapted)*

REQUIRED: The nature of a due diligence review.

DISCUSSION: Due diligence is a defense by accountants to liability under the Securities Act of 1933 when a material fact has been misstated in, or omitted from, a registration statement. Accountants who prepare or certify financial statements used in registration statements or other disclosures need only prove due diligence regarding the work they perform. The accountants must show that, after conducting a reasonable investigation, they had reasonable grounds to believe, and did believe, that the registration statement was true and contained no material omissions of fact when it became effective. Standards such as GAAP provide evidence, which is not conclusive, about the nature of a reasonable investigation.

Answer (A) is incorrect because, although the reviews may be used by the underwriter, they are not directed by the underwriter. Answers (B) and (C) are incorrect because the due diligence review is not an operational audit or a review for compliance with company policies.

54. Assume your company is considering purchasing a small toxic waste disposal company. As an internal auditor, you are part of the team doing a due diligence review for the acquisition. Your scope (as auditors) would most likely not include

A. An evaluation of the merit of lawsuits currently filed against the waste company.

B. A review of the purchased company's procedures for acceptance of waste material and comparison with legal requirements.

C. Analysis of the company's compliance with, and disclosure of, loan covenants.

D. Assessment of the efficiency of the waste company's operations and profitability.

The correct answer is (A). *(CIA, adapted)*

REQUIRED: The procedure not included in a due diligence review for an acquisition.

DISCUSSION: An evaluation of the merit of lawsuits requires legal expertise. At most, an internal auditor is required to have an appreciation of the fundamentals of commercial law, that is, an ability to recognize the existence of problems and to determine the assistance to be obtained. Hence, the auditors' responsibility is limited to using consultants to evaluate the merits of the lawsuits.

Answers (B) and (C) are incorrect because compliance with both legal requirements and loan covenants is within the scope of internal auditing. Answer (D) is incorrect because appraising the economy and efficiency with which resources are employed and reviewing the accomplishment of objectives and goals are within the scope of work of internal auditors.

9.7 Planning an Internal Audit

55. According to Standard 410, internal auditors should plan each audit. Audit planning should be documented and the planning process should include all the following except

A. Establishing audit objectives and scope of work.

B. Obtaining background information about the activities to be audited.

C. Collecting audit evidence on all matters related to the audit objectives.

D. Determining how, when, and to whom the audit results will be communicated.

The correct answer is (C). *(CIA, adapted)*

REQUIRED: The item not part of the planning process.

DISCUSSION: Planning should include "establishing audit objectives and scope of work; obtaining background information about the activities to be audited; determining the resources necessary to perform the audit; communicating with all who need to know about the audit; performing, as appropriate, an on-site survey to become familiar with the activities and controls to be audited, to identify areas for audit emphasis, and to invite auditee comments and suggestions; writing the audit program; determining how, when, and to whom audit results will be communicated; and obtaining approval of the audit work plan." Evidence is collected during field work, not planning.

Answers (A), (B), and (D) are incorrect because the planning process includes establishing audit objectives and scope of work, obtaining background information, and determining how, when, and to whom the audit results will be communicated.

56. According to the Standards, documentation required to plan an internal auditing assignment should include evidence that

A. Resources needed to complete the audit were considered.

B. Planned audit work will be completed on a timely basis.

C. Intended findings have been clearly identified.

D. Internal auditing department resources are efficiently and effectively employed.

The correct answer is (A). *(CIA, adapted)*

REQUIRED: The evidence included in the documentation required to plan an internal auditing assignment.

DISCUSSION: Planning should be documented with regard to establishing audit objectives and scope of work, obtaining background information about auditee activities, determining the resources required for the audit, communicating with auditees, identifying areas of audit emphasis through an on-site survey, writing the audit program, communicating audit results, and obtaining approval of the audit work plan (Standard 410).

Answer (B) is incorrect because whether the planned work will actually be completed on time cannot be known in the planning phase. Answer (C) is incorrect because intended findings should be identified when determining the scope of work to be performed. Answer (D) is incorrect because documenting the economic and efficient use of resources can be done only on completion of the assignment.

57. Which of the following auditable activities represents the greatest risk to a post-merger manufacturing corporation and would therefore most likely be subjected to an audit?

A. Combining imprest funds.

B. Combining purchasing functions.

C. Combining legal functions.

D. Combining marketing functions.

The correct answer is (B). *(CIA, adapted)*

REQUIRED: The activity representing the greatest risk.

DISCUSSION: During the planning phase of an audit, the auditor must assess risks to identify significant areas of audit emphasis. Purchasing functions represent the greatest exposure to loss and are therefore most likely to be subjected to an audit. The financial exposure in the purchasing function is ordinarily greater than in, for example, the legal and marketing functions. After a merger, risk is heightened because of the difficulty of combining the disparate systems of the two companies. Thus, the likelihood of an audit is increased.

Answer (A) is incorrect because imprest funds are typically immaterial in amount. Answer (C) is incorrect because legal functions do not typically represent a risk of loss as great as the purchasing functions. Answer (D) is incorrect because marketing functions do not typically represent a risk of loss as great as the purchasing functions.

58. In planning an audit, an on-site survey could assist with all of the following, except

A. Obtaining auditee comments and suggestions on control problems.

B. Obtaining preliminary information on internal controls.

C. Identifying areas for audit emphasis.

D. Evaluating the effectiveness of the system of internal controls.

The correct answer is (D). *(CIA, adapted)*

REQUIRED: The audit planning item with which an on-site survey would not assist.

DISCUSSION: According to SIAS 12, "A survey is a process for gathering information, without detailed verification, on the activity being examined." A survey may involve discussions with the auditee, documenting key control activities, and identifying significant audit issues. A survey does not help in evaluating the effectiveness of internal control except to the extent the auditor gains familiarity with the controls. Evaluation requires testing.

Answers (A), (B), and (C) are incorrect because a survey could assist with obtaining auditee comments and suggestions on control problems, obtaining preliminary information on internal controls, and identifying areas for audit emphasis.

59. The preliminary survey indicates that severe staff reductions have resulted in extensive amounts of overtime among accounting staff. Accounting payrolls are nearly equal to prior years, and many key controls, such as segregation of duties, are no longer in place. The accounting supervisor now performs all operations within the cash receipts and posting process and has no time to review and approve transactions generated by the remaining members of the department. Journal entries since the staff reductions show increasing numbers of prior-month adjustments and corrections. The auditor should

A. Discuss these findings with audit management to determine whether further audit work would be an efficient use of audit resources at this time.

B. Proceed with the scheduled audit but add audit personnel based on the expected number of findings and anticipated lack of assistance from local accounting management.

C. Evaluate the costs and benefits of outsourcing needed services.

D. Suspend further audit work because the findings are obvious and issue the report.

The correct answer is (A). *(CIA, adapted)*

REQUIRED: The auditor action given the absence of many key controls.

DISCUSSION: A preliminary survey allows the auditor to become familiar with activities, risks, and controls; to identify areas for audit emphasis; and to invite auditee comments and suggestions. Among many other matters, the summary of results prepared at the conclusion of the survey should identify, when applicable, reasons for not continuing the audit (SIAS 12). In this case, additional planning is necessary to modify the audit for the difficult circumstances discovered during the preliminary survey and to address the responsibilities of the audit department.

Answer (B) is incorrect because what additional audit work will be necessary is not clear in these circumstances. Answer (C) is incorrect because management has not accepted this plan of action. Answer (D) is incorrect because issuing a report would violate the Standards, including those relating to objectivity, due professional care, and performance of audit work.

60. As a means of controlling projects and avoiding time-budget overruns, decisions to revise time budgets for an audit should normally be made

A. Immediately after the preliminary survey.

B. When a significant deficiency has been substantiated.

C. When inexperienced audit staff are assigned to an audit.

D. Immediately after expanding tests to establish reliability of findings.

The correct answer is (A). *(CIA, adapted)*

REQUIRED: The timing of decisions to revise time budgets for an audit.

DISCUSSION: Planning entails, among other things, conducting "an on-site survey to become familiar with the activities and controls to be audited, to identify areas for audit emphasis, and to invite auditee comments and suggestions" (Standard 410). The preliminary survey provides the auditor with the information needed to identify any time-budget constraints or overruns and to revise the time budget.

Answer (B) is incorrect because, when a deficiency has been substantiated, no further audit work is required. Answer (C) is incorrect because the assignment of inexperienced staff should have no effect on the decision to revise the time budget. Answer (D) is incorrect because expanded tests should have no effect on the time budget; the budget would have already been expanded as necessary.

61. In the preparation of an audit program, which of the following items is not essential?

A. The performance of a preliminary survey.

B. A review of material from prior audit reports.

C. The preparation of a budget identifying the costs of resources needed.

D. A review of performance standards set by management.

The correct answer is (C). *(CIA, adapted)*

REQUIRED: The item not essential to preparing the audit program.

DISCUSSION: The audit program should state the resources necessary to carry out the detailed tasks specified. However, quantification of costs is not essential to writing the audit program.

Answer (A) is incorrect because the preliminary survey provides necessary background information about activities and controls. Answer (B) is incorrect because audit reports contain, among other things, information about findings of prior audits and corrective actions taken. Answer (D) is incorrect because auditors who appraise the economy and efficiency of operations are responsible for considering operating standards (Standard 340).

9.8 Audit Evidence

62. Of the following, audit evidence is best described as

A. The records of preliminary planning and surveys, the audit program, and the results of field work.

B. The information documented by the auditors and obtained through observing conditions, interviewing people, and examining records.

C. An intermediate fact, or group of facts, from which the auditor can infer the fairness of an assertion being audited.

D. Detailed documentation for systems that do not achieve desired objectives, actions that were taken improperly, and actions that should have been taken but were not.

The correct answer is (B). *(CIA, adapted)*

REQUIRED: The best description of audit evidence.

DISCUSSION: Standard 420 states that internal auditors should collect, analyze, interpret, and document information to support audit results. The definition given properly implies the inclusion of physical, testimonial, documentary, and analytical evidence.

Answer (A) is incorrect because the records of preliminary planning and the audit program do not constitute audit evidence. Answer (C) is incorrect because an intermediate fact, or group of facts, from which the auditor can infer the fairness of an assertion is circumstantial evidence. This definition excludes direct evidence. Answer (D) is incorrect because deficiency findings concern detailed documentation for ineffective systems, improper actions, and actions that were not taken. Evidence underlies positive, as well as negative, findings.

63. Which of the following is an essential factor in evaluating the sufficiency of evidence? The evidence must

A. Be well documented and cross-referenced in the working papers.

B. Be based on references that are considered reliable.

C. Bear a direct relationship to the finding and include all of the elements of a finding.

D. Be convincing enough for a prudent person to reach the same decision.

The correct answer is (D). *(CIA, adapted)*

REQUIRED: The essential factor in evaluating the sufficiency of evidence.

DISCUSSION: According to Standard 420, "Sufficient information is factual, adequate, and convincing so that a prudent, informed person would reach the same conclusions as the auditor."

Answer (A) is incorrect because documentation and cross-referencing are desirable but have no specific relationship to any of the characteristics of evidence (sufficiency, competence, relevance, and usefulness). Answer (B) is incorrect because reliability is a characteristic of competent evidence. Answer (C) is incorrect because relevant evidence supports audit findings.

64. The Standards define competent information as

A. Supporting the audit findings and being consistent with the audit objectives.

B. Assisting the organization in meeting prescribed goals.

C. Factual, adequate, and convincing so that a prudent person would reach the same conclusion as the auditor.

D. Reliable and the best available through the use of appropriate audit techniques.

The correct answer is (D). *(CIA, adapted)*

REQUIRED: The definition of competent information.

DISCUSSION: Under Standard 420, competent evidence is reliable and the best available though the application of appropriate audit procedures. An original document is the prime example of such evidence.

Answer (A) is incorrect because relevant information supports audit findings and is consistent with audit objectives. Answer (B) is incorrect because useful information assists the organization in meeting goals. Answer (C) is incorrect because sufficient information is factual, adequate, and convincing to a prudent person.

65. An internal auditor is auditing the corporate advertising function. The company has engaged a medium-sized local advertising agency to place advertising in magazine publications. As part of the review of the audit working papers, the internal auditing supervisor is evaluating the evidence collected. The auditor reviewed the language in the advertising for its legality and compliance with fair trade regulations by interviewing the firm's advertising manager, the product marketing director (who may not have been objective), and five of the firm's largest customers (who may not have been knowledgeable). The supervisor can justifiably conclude that the evidence is

A. Competent.

B. Irrelevant.

C. Conclusive.

D. Insufficient.

The correct answer is (D). *(CIA, adapted)*

REQUIRED: The conclusion about the audit evidence.

DISCUSSION: Standard 420 states, "Information should be sufficient, competent, relevant, and useful to provide a sound basis for audit findings and recommendations. Sufficient information is factual, adequate, and convincing so that a prudent, informed person would reach the same conclusions as the auditor. Competent information is reliable and the best attainable through the use of appropriate audit techniques. Relevant information supports audit findings and recommendations and is consistent with the objectives for the audit. Useful information helps the organization meet its goals." Testimonial evidence from individuals who may be neither objective nor knowledgeable is unlikely to be sufficient.

Answer (A) is incorrect because the firm's advertising director and the firm's product marketing director are not objective. Answer (B) is incorrect because the information is relevant but not sufficient. Answer (C) is incorrect because the evidence is not sufficient. Hence, it cannot be conclusive. The inherent limitations of audits require that auditors rely on evidence that is merely persuasive rather than convincing beyond all doubt.

66. Audit information is usually considered relevant when it is

A. Derived through valid statistical sampling.

B. Objective and unbiased.

C. Factual, adequate, and convincing.

D. Consistent with the audit objectives.

The correct answer is (D). *(CIA, adapted)*

REQUIRED: The circumstance in which audit information is usually considered relevant.

DISCUSSION: "Information should be sufficient, competent, relevant, and useful to provide a sound basis for audit findings and recommendations. Relevant information supports audit findings and recommendations and is consistent with the objectives for the audit" (Standard 420).

Answer (A) is incorrect because whether sampling is appropriate and the results are valid are issues related to the determination of sufficiency and competence rather than relevance. Answer (B) is incorrect because objectivity and lack of bias do not assure that information will support audit findings. Answer (C) is incorrect because sufficient evidence is factual, adequate, and convincing.

67. What standard of evidence is satisfied by an original signed document?

A. Sufficiency.

B. Competence.

C. Relevance.

D. Usefulness.

The correct answer is (B). *(CIA, adapted)*

REQUIRED: The standard of evidence satisfied by an original signed document.

DISCUSSION: Competent evidence is reliable and the best available through the application of appropriate audit procedures. An original document is the prime example.

Answer (A) is incorrect because sufficient evidence is factual, adequate, and convincing. The information contained on the document may be none of those things. Answer (C) is incorrect because relevance concerns the relationship of the evidence to some objective of the audit. No audit objective is disclosed in the question. Answer (D) is incorrect because usefulness means that the evidence helps the organization (the auditor) to accomplish predetermined goals. No such goals are specified.

68. An auditor has set an audit objective of determining whether all cash receipts are deposited intact daily. To satisfy this objective, the auditor interviewed the controller who assured the auditor that all cash receipts are deposited as soon as is reasonably possible. As evidence that can be used to satisfy the audit objective stated above, the controller's assurances are

A. Sufficient but not competent or relevant.

B. Sufficient, competent, and relevant.

C. Not sufficient, competent, or relevant.

D. Relevant but not sufficient or competent.

The correct answer is (D). *(CIA, adapted)*

REQUIRED: The characteristics of audit evidence.

DISCUSSION: Competent evidence is both valid and relevant, and the sufficiency of evidence is determined by professional judgment. The controller's assurance is relevant because it pertains to the cash receipts. However, it lacks competence because it was not obtained from an independent source. Furthermore, the evidence is not sufficient because, by itself, it does not provide a reasonable basis for a conclusion.

Answers (A), (B), and (C) are incorrect because the evidence is relevant but not sufficient or competent.

69. While auditing an organization's cash controls, the auditor found that cash deposits are not deposited intact daily. A comparison of a sample of cash receipts lists revealed that each cash receipts list equaled cash journal entry amounts but not daily bank deposits amounts, and cash receipts list totals equaled bank deposit totals in the long run. This evidence as support for the auditor's findings is

A. Sufficient but not competent or relevant.

B. Sufficient, competent, and relevant.

C. Not sufficient, competent, or relevant.

D. Relevant but not sufficient or competent.

The correct answer is (B). *(CIA, adapted)*

REQUIRED: The characteristics of audit evidence.

DISCUSSION: The bank deposits can be verified by examining bank statements obtained directly from the bank. Evidence obtained from an independent source is usually more reliable (competent) than evidence secured solely within the entity. Moreover, it is obviously relevant to the issue of whether cash receipts are deposited intact. A reasonable auditor would find that the comparison of company records with independently obtained bank statements is persuasive of the proposition that cash receipts are not deposited intact. Thus, the evidence is also sufficient.

Answers (A), (C), and (D) are incorrect because the evidence is sufficient, competent, and relevant.

70. An auditor has set an audit objective of identifying the existence of personality conflicts that are detrimental to productivity. Which of the following audit techniques will best meet this objective?

A. Inspection of documents.

B. Observation.

C. Inquiry.

D. Analytical review.

The correct answer is (C). *(CIA, adapted)*

REQUIRED: The audit technique for identifying personality conflicts detrimental to productivity.

DISCUSSION: By interviewing selected individuals about the causes of inefficiencies, the internal auditor can obtain evidence as to the existence and seriousness of personality conflicts that inhibit efficient and effective work.

Answers (A), (B), and (D) are incorrect because inquiry is the best technique to identify personality conflicts.

71. An auditor has set an audit objective of determining whether mail room staff is fully used. Which of the following audit techniques will best meet this objective?

A. Inspection of documents.

B. Observation.

C. Inquiry.

D. Analytical review.

The correct answer is (B). *(CIA, adapted)*

REQUIRED: The audit technique for determining whether mail room staff is fully used.

DISCUSSION: By observing mail room operations at various times on various days of the week, the internal auditor can note whether incoming or outgoing mail backlogs exist, and whether mail room staff are busy on mail room activities, idle, or working on other projects.

Answers (A), (C), and (D) are incorrect because observation is the best technique to determine if the staff is fully used.

72. A letter to the auditor in response to an inquiry is an example of

A. Physical evidence.

B. Testimonial evidence.

C. Documentary evidence.

D. Analytical evidence.

The correct answer is (B). *(CIA, adapted)*

REQUIRED: The kind of evidence represented by a letter to the auditor in response to an inquiry.

DISCUSSION: Audit evidence may consist of authoritative documentation, calculations by the auditor, internal control, interrelationships among the data, physical existence, subsequent events, subsidiary records, and testimony by the auditee and third parties. Oral or written statements (e.g., letters to the auditor) derived from inquiries or interviews are testimonial evidence.

Answer (A) is incorrect because verification of the actual existence of something by observation, inspection, or count is physical evidence. Answer (C) is incorrect because documentary evidence exists in permanent form, such as checks or invoices. It includes both external evidence, e.g., bills of lading from common carriers, and documents originating with the auditee. Answer (D) is incorrect because analytical evidence derives from the study and comparison of relationships among data.

73. The director of internal auditing is reviewing the working papers produced by an auditor during a fraud investigation. Among the items contained in the working papers is a description of an item of physical evidence. Which of the following is the most probable source of this item of evidence?

A. Observing conditions.

B. Interviewing people.

C. Examining records.

D. Computing variances.

The correct answer is (A). *(CIA, adapted)*

REQUIRED: The most probable source of physical evidence.

DISCUSSION: Verification of the actual existence of things, activities, or individuals by observation, inspection, or count is physical evidence. It may take the form of photographs, maps, charts, or other depictions.

Answer (B) is incorrect because interviewing produces testimonial evidence. Answer (C) is incorrect because the examination of records produces documentary evidence. Answer (D) is incorrect because computations and verifications lead to analytical evidence.

74. Which of the following is an example of documentary evidence?

A. A photograph of an auditee's workplace.

B. A letter from a former employee alleging a fraud.

C. A page of the general ledger containing irregularities placed there by the perpetrator of a fraud.

D. A page of the auditor's working papers containing the computations that demonstrate the existence of an error or irregularity.

The correct answer is (C). *(CIA, adapted)*

REQUIRED: The example of documentary evidence.

DISCUSSION: Documentary evidence exists in permanent form, such as checks, invoices, shipping records, receiving reports, and purchase orders. It includes both external evidence, e.g., shipping documents provided by carriers, and documents originating with the auditee.

Answer (A) is incorrect because photographic evidence is physical. Answer (B) is incorrect because responses to inquiries or interviews are testimonial. Answer (D) is incorrect because the study and comparison of relationships among data is analytical evidence.

75. In an audit of travel expenses for salesmen, the auditor calculates average travel expenses per day traveled for all salesmen and then examines detailed receipts for salesmen with high averages. These procedures represent the use of which types of audit evidence?

A. Documentary and physical evidence.

B. Analytical and physical evidence.

C. Documentary and analytical evidence.

D. Physical and testimonial evidence.

The correct answer is (C). *(CIA, adapted)*

REQUIRED: The types of audit evidence.

DISCUSSION: Audit evidence consists of four categories: physical, testimonial, documentary, and analytical. Physical evidence is obtained by observing people, property, and events. Testimonial evidence consists of letters or statements in response to inquiries or interviews. Documentary evidence includes accounting records, outgoing correspondence, receiving reports, etc. Analytical evidence results from analysis and verification and includes computations and comparisons. The travel expense receipts are documentary evidence. The calculations of average travel expenses are analytical evidence.

Answers (A) and (B) are incorrect because physical evidence is not involved. Answer (D) is incorrect because neither physical evidence nor testimonial evidence is involved.

76. During an audit, the internal auditor should consider the following factor(s) in determining the extent to which analytical procedures should be used:

A. Adequacy of the system of internal control.

B. Significance of the area being examined.

C. Precision with which the results of analytical audit procedures can be predicted.

D. All of the answers are correct.

The correct answer is (D). *(CIA, adapted)*

REQUIRED: The factors the auditor should consider in determining the extent of analytical procedures.

DISCUSSION: According to SIAS 8, in determining the extent to which analytical procedures should be used, the auditor should consider the significance of the area being examined, the adequacy of the system of internal control, the availability and reliability of financial and nonfinancial information, the precision with which the results of analytical auditing procedures can be predicted, the availability and comparability of information regarding the industry in which the organization operates, and the extent to which other auditing procedures provide support for audit results.

Answers (A), (B), and (C) are incorrect because the adequacy of the system of internal control, the significance of the area being examined, and the precision with which the results of analytical audit procedures can be predicted should all be considered.

77. An inexperienced internal auditor notified the senior auditor of a significant variance from the auditee's budget. The senior told the new auditor not to worry because the senior had heard that there had been an unauthorized work stoppage that probably accounted for the difference. Which of the following statements is most appropriate?

A. The new auditor should have investigated the matter fully and not bothered the senior.

B. The senior used proper judgment in curtailing what could have been a wasteful investigation.

C. The senior should have halted the audit until the variance was fully explained.

D. The senior should have aided the new auditor in formulating a plan for accumulating appropriate evidence.

The correct answer is (D). *(CIA, adapted)*

REQUIRED: The senior auditor's proper response to a significant budget variance.

DISCUSSION: The variance was not adequately investigated or explained. According to SIAS 8, "When analytical auditing procedures identify unexpected results or relationships, the internal auditor should examine and evaluate such results or relationships. The examination and evaluation should include inquiries of management and the application of other auditing procedures until the internal auditor is satisfied that the results or relationships are sufficiently explained. Unexplained results or relationships may be indicative of a significant condition such as a potential error, irregularity, or illegal act."

Answer (A) is incorrect because Standard 230 states that the extent of supervision varies with the proficiency of the auditor and the difficulty of the assignment. An inexperienced auditor should refer this matter to the senior. Answer (B) is incorrect because the facts given do not support the conclusion that accumulating additional evidence would be wasteful. Answer (C) is incorrect because the variance needs explanation, but the audit should continue.

9.9 Working Papers

78. According to the Standards, the director of internal auditing should establish policies for

A. Indexing and the type of working-paper files maintained.

B. Defining the audit hours available for individual audits.

C. Defining standardized tick marks and ensuring compliance with them.

D. Ensuring the written documentation of all conversations held throughout the audit.

The correct answer is (A). *(CIA, adapted)*

REQUIRED: The policies required by the Standards.

DISCUSSION: According to SIAS 6, "The director of internal auditing should establish policies for the types of audit working-paper files maintained, stationery used, indexing, and other related matters. Standardized audit working papers, such as questionnaires and audit programs, may improve the efficiency of an audit and facilitate the delegation of audit work."

Answer (B) is incorrect because the time devoted to an audit depends on its complexity and other unique circumstances. Answer (C) is incorrect because defining standardized tick marks and ensuring compliance with them is not required. Answer (D) is incorrect because only conversations relevant to the audit must be documented.

79. Internal auditors often include summaries within their working papers. Which of the following best describes the purpose of such summaries?

A. Summaries are prepared to conform with the Standards.

B. Summaries are usually required to complete each section of an audit program.

C. Summaries distill the most useful information from several working papers into a more usable form.

D. Summaries document that the auditor has considered all relevant evidence.

The correct answer is (C). *(CIA, adapted)*

REQUIRED: The purpose of working-paper summaries.

DISCUSSION: Working papers document an audit. They contain the records of planning, the preliminary survey, the audit program, the results of field work, and other related matters. When preparing working papers, auditors periodically summarize findings. Summaries are beneficial in tying together working papers that relate to a particular point. Thus, they provide for an orderly and logical flow of information and facilitate supervisory review.

Answer (A) is incorrect because summaries are not required by the Standards. Answer (B) is incorrect because summaries are not usually required by audit programs. Answer (D) is incorrect because summaries are not necessary to document that the auditor has considered all relevant evidence.

80. An adequately documented working paper should

A. Be concise but complete.

B. Follow a unique form and arrangement.

C. Contain examples of all forms and procedures used by the auditee.

D. Not contain copies of auditee records.

The correct answer is (A). *(CIA, adapted)*

REQUIRED: The characteristic of an adequately documented working paper.

DISCUSSION: Audit working papers provide the principal evidential basis for the audit report (SIAS 6). They are the auditor's documentation of audit activities. They record the information obtained and the analyses made and should support the bases for the findings and recommendations reported (Standard 420). Clarity, conciseness, and accuracy are desirable qualities of working papers, but SIAS 6 emphasizes completeness and support for conclusions.

Answer (B) is incorrect because working papers should be uniform and consistent. Answer (C) is incorrect because working papers should contain only information related to an audit objective. Answer (D) is incorrect because copies of auditee records should be included whenever necessary.

81. A feasibility study is being completed to determine whether an internal auditing department should convert to electronic working papers. Decision criteria will be based primarily on the requirements of internal auditing standards and the experience of other audit departments. Internal auditing standards specify that, for working papers on media other than paper,

A. Conversion to paper should occur no later than the time of final review.

B. Consideration should be given to generating backup copies of working papers.

C. The media selected should determine working paper design and content.

D. Working paper retention should be solely a function of the media used.

The correct answer is (B). *(CIA, adapted)*

REQUIRED: The true statement about working papers on media other than paper.

DISCUSSION: Audit working papers may be in the form of paper, tapes, disks, diskettes, films, or other media. For media other than paper, consideration should be given to generating backup copies (SIAS 6).

Answer (A) is incorrect because conversion to a paper medium is not specified by the standards. Answer (C) is incorrect because the nature of the audit determines working-paper design and content. Answer (D) is incorrect because retention policies are a function of several concerns, e.g., legal guidelines.

82. When audit conclusions are challenged, the auditor's factual rebuttal is best facilitated by

A. Summaries in the audit program.

B. Pro forma working papers.

C. Cross-referencing of the working papers.

D. Explicit procedures in the audit program.

The correct answer is (C). *(CIA, adapted)*

REQUIRED: The best means of facilitating factual rebuttal when audit conclusions are challenged.

DISCUSSION: SIAS 6 states that each working paper should have an index or reference number. Indexing permits cross-referencing, which simplifies supervisory review either during the audit or subsequently by creating an audit trail of related items through the working papers. It thus facilitates preparation of the final report, later audits of the same auditee, peer review, and factual rebuttal of challenges by clearly identifying sources and locations of facts.

Answers (A) and (D) are incorrect because the audit program guides the collection of evidence, but appropriately cross-referencing evidence in the working papers assists in the factual rebuttal of challenges. Answer (B) is incorrect because pro forma working papers save time in the evidence collection process by guiding the auditor to ensure that all significant points are covered.

83. To control working papers properly, the auditor should not

A. Share the results of an audit with the auditee.

B. Permit access to external auditors.

C. Permit access to government auditors.

D. Make them available to people who have no authority to use them.

The correct answer is (D). *(CIA, adapted)*

REQUIRED: The practice that does not result in proper control of working papers.

DISCUSSION: According to SIAS 6, "Audit working-paper files should ordinarily remain under the control of the internal auditing department and should be accessible only to authorized personnel." Audit working papers may be shown to other members of the organization and to external auditors subject to the approval of the director of internal auditing. Approval for access should be given by senior management or legal counsel, as appropriate.

Answer (A) is incorrect because audit working papers may be shown to the auditee to assist the auditors in evaluating significance, perspective, accuracy, and relevance. Answers (B) and (C) are incorrect because external auditors may be given access to avoid duplicate work.

84. Which of the following statements relating to the retention of audit working papers is an inappropriate policy?

A. Working papers should be disposed of when they have no further use.

B. Working papers on fraud audits should be retained indefinitely.

C. Working papers retention schedules should be approved by legal counsel.

D. Working papers retention schedules should consider legal and contractual requirements.

The correct answer is (B). *(CIA, adapted)*

REQUIRED: The inappropriate policy relating to the retention of audit working papers.

DISCUSSION: SIAS 6 states, "The director of internal auditing should develop retention requirements for audit working papers. The retention requirements should be consistent with the organization's guidelines and any pertinent legal or other requirements." Thus, approval by the organization's legal counsel is appropriate. Although working papers pertaining to a fraud audit might be kept apart from others, no working paper will have to be kept indefinitely. Those discarded should be disposed of according to organizational policies.

Answer (A) is incorrect because the duration of retention should be determined by usefulness. Answer (C) is incorrect because approval by legal counsel is appropriate. Answer (D) is incorrect because legal and contractual requirements may determine the retention period.

85. A fire destroyed a large portion of a company's inventory. Management is filing an insurance claim and needs to use the internal auditors' working papers in preparing the claim. According to the Standards, management

A. May not use the working papers in preparing the claim.

B. May use the working papers in preparing the claim, but such use should be approved by the director of internal auditing.

C. Should be precluded from preparing the claim, and such function should be given to the internal auditing department.

D. May use the working papers in preparing the claim, but such use should be approved by the company's external independent auditors.

The correct answer is (B). *(CIA, adapted)*

REQUIRED: The true statement about working-paper requests.

DISCUSSION: SIAS 6 states, "Management and other members of the organization may request access to audit working papers. Such access may be necessary to substantiate or explain audit findings or to use audit documentation for other business purposes. The director of internal auditing should approve these requests." Accordingly, the insurance claim is an "other business purpose," and management may use the internal auditors' working papers in preparing the claim.

Answer (A) is incorrect because the Standards allow working papers to be used for "other business purposes." Answer (C) is incorrect because management, not the internal auditing department, should prepare the insurance claim. Answer (D) is incorrect because the approval of external independent auditors is not needed.

86. Working papers should include

A. Documentation of the examination and evaluation of the adequacy and effectiveness of the system of internal control.

B. Copies of all source documents examined in the course of the audit.

C. Copies of all procedures that were reviewed during the audit.

D. All working papers prepared during a previous audit of the same area.

The correct answer is (A). *(CIA, adapted)*

REQUIRED: The items included in working papers.

DISCUSSION: Working papers document planning; the examination and evaluation of the adequacy and effectiveness of the system of internal control; the procedures performed, the information obtained, and the conclusions reached; review; reporting; and follow-up (SIAS 6).

Answer (B) is incorrect because many documents may be examined that prove to be irrelevant to the audit objectives. These documents need not be included. Answer (C) is incorrect because in many circumstances the exact wording of a procedure is not needed to support a finding. A reference to the procedure in the working papers may be adequate. Answer (D) is incorrect because some previous working papers may be outdated. However, parts of previous audit working papers may be included in current working papers subject to updating.

87. Employees using personal computers have been reporting occupational injuries and claiming substantial workers' compensation benefits. The working papers of an operational audit to determine the extent of company exposure to such personal injury liability should include

A. Analysis of claims by type of equipment and extent of use by individual employees.

B. Confirmations from insurance carriers as to claims paid under workers' compensation policies in force.

C. Reviews of documentation supporting purchases of personal computers.

D. Listings of all personal computers in use and the employees who use them.

The correct answer is (A). *(CIA, adapted)*

REQUIRED: The item included in the working papers of an operational audit to determine the extent of company exposure to personal injury liability.

DISCUSSION: Claims analysis is appropriately included because it permits determination of the importance of the two key factors (equipment in use and time spent by employees at such equipment) leading to claims.

Answer (B) is incorrect because confirmations of workers' compensation claims fail to identify exposure to risks; they only support claims paid by the carrier under the workers' compensation policies. Answer (C) is incorrect because documentation supporting purchases of personal computers cannot be expected to address risk assessments. Answer (D) is incorrect because listings of all personal computers in use and the employees using them fail to indicate the risks associated with the extent of usage and the type of equipment.

88. Which of the following should be identified as a deficiency by an audit supervisor when reviewing a set of working papers?

A. A memorandum explaining why the time budget for a part of the audit was exceeded.

B. An audit finding recorded in the working papers and report draft that omits the criteria used for evaluation.

C. A memorandum explaining why an audit program step was omitted.

D. A letter to the auditee outlining the scope of the audit.

The correct answer is (B). *(CIA, adapted)*

REQUIRED: The deficiency in a set of working papers.

DISCUSSION: Standard 230 states that audit supervision includes determining that working papers adequately support findings, conclusions, and reports. Findings include four attributes: criteria, condition, cause, and effect. Thus, omitting evaluation criteria fails to support findings adequately.

Answers (A), (C), and (D) are incorrect because reasons for exceeding a time budget, an explanation of the omission of an audit program step, and a letter outlining the scope of the audit are appropriate for inclusion in working papers.

89. An internal audit manager is reviewing the audit working papers prepared by the staff. Which of the following review comments is true?

A. Each working paper should include the actual and the budgeted time related to such audit work.

B. Including copies of all the forms and directives of the auditee department constitutes over-documentation.

C. Conclusions need not be documented in the working papers when the audit objectives are achieved.

D. Each working paper should include a statement regarding the auditees' cooperation during the conduct of the audit.

The correct answer is (B). *(CIA, adapted)*

REQUIRED: The review comment that is true.

DISCUSSION: Reviewing working papers includes determining whether the findings, conclusions, and reports are adequately supported. However, adequate support includes only those forms and directives that are relevant to the audit or to the audit findings. Thus, including copies of all the forms and directives of the auditee department constitutes over-documentation.

Answer (A) is incorrect because actual and budgeted audit time is documented in the budget section of the working papers and not on each working paper. Answer (C) is incorrect because audit conclusions should be documented in the working papers whether or not the audit objectives are achieved. Answer (D) is incorrect because only noncooperation is likely to be documented.

90. A significant part of the auditor's working papers will be the conclusions reached by the auditor regarding the audit area. In some situations, the supervisor might not agree with the conclusions and will ask the staff auditor to perform more work. Assume that after subsequent work is performed, the staff auditor and the supervisor continue to disagree on the conclusions documented in the working paper developed by the staff auditor. Which of the following audit department responses would not be appropriate?

A. Both the staff auditor and the supervisor document their reasons for reaching different conclusions. Retain the rationale of both parties in the working papers.

B. Note the disagreement and retain the notice of disagreement and follow-up work in the audit working papers.

C. Present both conclusions to the director of internal auditing for resolution. The director may resolve the matter.

D. Present both conclusions in the audit report and let management and the auditee react to both.

The correct answer is (D). *(CIA, adapted)*

REQUIRED: The inappropriate audit department response to a dispute between the auditor and his/her supervisor.

DISCUSSION: The director of internal auditing should determine the most reasonable conclusion and present it to the auditee and management. Disagreements documented in the working papers should not necessarily affect reports unless the director believes that both conclusions are equally appropriate and that reporting both would enhance management's understanding of the issues.

Answers (A) and (B) are incorrect because an assistant may document his/her disagreement with the conclusions reached. Answer (C) is incorrect because the director of internal auditing is ultimately responsible for the supervision of the audit staff as well as the quality of the working papers.

9.10 Communicating Results and Following Up

91. In which section of the final report should the internal auditor describe the audit objectives?

A. Purpose.

B. Scope.

C. Criteria.

D. Condition.

The correct answer is (A). *(CIA, adapted)*

REQUIRED: The final report section describing audit objectives.

DISCUSSION: According to SIAS 2, *Communicating Results*, "audit reports should present the purpose, scope, and results of the audit; and, if appropriate, reports should contain an expression of the auditor's opinion. Purpose statements should describe the audit objectives and may, if necessary, inform the reader why the audit was conducted and what it was expected to achieve."

Answer (B) is incorrect because scope statements identify the audited activities and describe the nature and extent of auditing performed. Answer (C) is incorrect because criteria are the "standards, measures or expectations used in making an evaluation and/or verification (what should exist)." Answer (D) is incorrect because a condition is the "factual evidence that the internal auditor found in the course of the examination (what does exist)."

92. Which of the following is a proper element in an audit results section of a report?

A. Status of findings from prior reports.

B. Personnel used.

C. Significance of deficiencies.

D. Engagement plan.

The correct answer is (C). *(CIA, adapted)*

REQUIRED: The proper element in an audit results section of a report.

DISCUSSION: A deficiency is a difference between criteria (what should exist) and condition (what does exist). The significance of deficiencies is an audit finding that belongs in the audit results section of the report.

Answer (A) is incorrect because the status of prior findings, such as corrective action taken since the last audit, appears in another section of the report. Answer (B) is incorrect because personnel used is not a finding. Answer (D) is incorrect because the engagement plan precedes the audit results section of the report.

93. According to the Standards, a report issued by an internal auditor should contain an expression of opinion when

A. The area of the audit is the financial statements.

B. The internal auditors' work is to be used by external auditors.

C. A full-scope audit has been conducted in an area.

D. An opinion will improve communications with the reader of the report.

The correct answer is (D). *(CIA, adapted)*

REQUIRED: The circumstances in which a report should contain an expression of opinion.

DISCUSSION: The evaluation of the impact of audit findings on audited activities is the statement of conclusions (opinion). A statement of conclusions (opinion) is required only when appropriate (Standard 430). The criterion of appropriateness is improvement in communications.

Answer (A) is incorrect because the area of the audit is irrelevant to decisions about whether an overall opinion is appropriate. Answer (B) is incorrect because whether the internal auditors' work is to be used by external auditors is irrelevant. The external auditors cannot depend on an overall opinion but must examine evidence to form their own opinion. Answer (C) is incorrect because an overall opinion is not mandatory.

94. The internal auditing department for a chain of retail stores recently concluded an audit of sales adjustments in all stores in the southeast region. The audit revealed that several stores are costing the company an estimated $85,000 per quarter in duplicate credits to customers' charge accounts. The audit report, published 8 weeks after the audit was concluded, included the internal auditors' recommendations to store management that should prevent duplicate credits to customers' accounts. Which of the following standards for reporting has been disregarded in the above case?

A. The follow-up actions were not adequate.

B. The auditors should have implemented appropriate corrective action as soon as the duplicate credits were discovered.

C. Auditor recommendations should not be included in the report.

D. The report was not timely.

The correct answer is (D). *(CIA, adapted)*

REQUIRED: The standard that was disregarded.

DISCUSSION: According to Standard 430, "Reports should be objective, clear, concise, constructive, and timely." SIAS 2 adds, "Timely reports are those that are issued without delay and enable prompt effective action." The report, which was not published until 8 weeks after the audit was concluded, was not timely, given the significance of the findings and the need for prompt, effective action.

Answer (A) is incorrect because there is not enough information to evaluate the effectiveness of follow-up. Answer (B) is incorrect because auditors may properly make recommendations for improvements but should not implement corrective action. Answer (C) is incorrect because auditor recommendations are an element of an audit finding.

95. The auditor completed work on a segment of the audit program. It was clear that a problem existed that would require a modification of the organization's distribution procedures. The auditee agreed and has implemented revised procedures. The internal auditor should

A. Research the problem and recommend in the audit report measures that should be taken.

B. Jointly develop and report an appropriate recommendation.

C. Report the problem and assume that management will take appropriate action.

D. Indicate in the audit report that the auditee determined and implemented corrective action.

The correct answer is (D). *(CIA, adapted)*

REQUIRED: The action an internal auditor should take when an auditee has implemented changes.

DISCUSSION: Audit reports may include recommendations for improvements and acknowledge satisfactory performance and corrective action. This information may be necessary to represent the existing conditions fairly and to provide a proper perspective and appropriate balance to the audit report (SIAS 2).

Answers (A), (B), and (C) are incorrect because the audit report should indicate that the auditee has already determined and implemented corrective action.

96. SIAS 2 addresses the internal auditor's obligation to report findings and conclusions. According to SIAS 2, which of the following is not a correct statement with respect to the use of interim audit reports? Interim audit reports

A. Are used to communicate information that requires immediate attention.

B. Are used to communicate a change in audit scope for the activity under review.

C. Keep management informed of audit progress when audits extend over a long period of time.

D. Eliminate the need for issuing a final report.

The correct answer is (D). *(CIA, adapted)*

REQUIRED: The false statement about interim reports.

DISCUSSION: According to SIAS 2, "Interim reports may be used to communicate information which requires immediate attention, to communicate a change in audit scope for the activity under review, or to keep management informed of audit progress when audits extend over a long period. The use of interim reports does not diminish or eliminate the need for a final report."

Answers (A), (B), and (C) are incorrect because interim reports are used to communicate information that requires immediate attention, to communicate a change in audit scope for the activity under review, and to keep management informed of audit progress when audits extend over a long period of time.

97. Assume that an auditor's findings are so serious that, in the auditor's view, they require immediate action by management. Which of the following statements regarding the auditor's responsibility with respect to reporting and follow-up are correct?

I. The conditions should be actively monitored by the internal auditor until corrected.

II. The initial findings should be communicated to senior management and the audit committee even if the audit of the activities is not complete.

III. The auditor should test the actions implemented by management to determine if they remedy the problem.

A. I only.

B. II only.

C. II and III only.

D. I, II, and III.

The correct answer is (D). *(CIA, adapted)*

REQUIRED: The true statement(s) regarding the auditor's responsibility for reporting and following up findings requiring immediate action.

DISCUSSION: SIAS 13 states, "Certain reported findings may be so significant as to require immediate action by management. These conditions should be monitored by internal auditors, until corrected, because of the effect they may have on the organization." SIAS 2 states, "Interim reports may be used to communicate information that requires immediate attention." SIAS 13 also states that the director of internal auditing should establish procedures to determine a time frame within which management's response to the audit findings is required, to evaluate the response, to verify the response, to conduct a follow-up audit, and to transmit unsatisfactory responses or actions to the appropriate management levels.

Answers (A), (B), and (C) are incorrect because the auditor should communicate the findings to the audit committee and management even if the audit is not complete. The conditions should be monitored by the auditor, and any corrective action implemented by management should also be tested by the auditor to determine if the action remedies the problem.

98. An internal auditing director has noticed that staff auditors are presenting more oral reports to supplement written reports. The best reason for the increased use of oral reports by the auditors is that they

A. Reduce the amount of testing required to support audit findings.

B. Can be delivered in an informal manner without preparation.

C. Can be prepared using a flexible format thereby increasing overall audit efficiency.

D. Permit auditors to counter arguments and provide additional information that the audience may require.

The correct answer is (D). *(CIA, adapted)*

REQUIRED: The best reason for the increased use of oral reports by the auditors.

DISCUSSION: Interim reports may be given orally. These reports provide a format in which the auditors can receive and respond to feedback. Because the reports permit face-to-face responses, the auditors are able to respond immediately to auditee objections or needs for further information.

Answer (A) is incorrect because the amount of testing required to support audit findings is not related to the format of reports. Answer (B) is incorrect because the oral report should be delivered in a formal manner and be carefully prepared. Answer (C) is incorrect because oral reports should be adapted to the audience. Oral reports do not improve overall audit efficiency.

99. The Standards specify that final audit reports should be reviewed and approved by the

A. Auditee or the person to whom the auditee reports.

B. Auditor-in-charge.

C. Internal auditing director or designee.

D. Chief financial officer.

The correct answer is (C). *(CIA, adapted)*

REQUIRED: The person who should review and approve final audit reports.

DISCUSSION: According to Standard 430, the director of internal auditing or a designee should review and approve and may sign the final audit report before issuance and should decide to whom the report will be distributed. According to SIAS 2, if specific circumstances warrant, consideration should be given to having the auditor-in-charge, supervisor, or lead auditor sign the report as a representative of the director.

Answers (A) and (D) are incorrect because final reports should be reviewed by the director or a designee. Answer (B) is incorrect because the auditor-in-charge should not approve final reports unless designated by the director.

100. The internal auditing unit has recently completed an operational audit of its company's accounts payable function. The audit director decided to issue a summary report in conjunction with the final report. Who would be the most likely recipient(s) of just the summary audit report?

A. Accounts payable manager.

B. External auditor.

C. Controller.

D. Audit committee of the board of directors.

The correct answer is (D). *(CIA, adapted)*

REQUIRED: The most likely recipient(s) of the summary audit report.

DISCUSSION: According to SIAS 2, "Audit reports should be distributed to those members of the organization who are able to ensure that audit results are given due consideration. This means that the report should go to those who are in a position to take corrective action or to ensure that corrective action is taken. The final audit report should be distributed to the head of each audited unit. Higher-level members in the organization may receive only a summary report." Thus, summary written reports are usually intended for audit committees or higher-level management.

Answer (A) is incorrect because the accounts payable manager is best served by receiving a copy of the full final audit report. Answer (B) is incorrect because the external auditor needs the details in the full report. Answer (C) is incorrect because the controller is responsible for the accounting function and is more likely to receive the full report than is the audit committee.

101. The Standards require that the director of internal auditing or designee decide to whom the final audit report will be distributed. Findings concerning significant internal control weakness are included in an audit report on the accounts payable system of a company whose securities are publicly traded. Which of the following is the most likely reason that the director of internal auditing has chosen to send copies of this audit report to the audit committee and the external auditor?

A. The audit committee and external auditor are normally sent copies of all internal audit reports as a courtesy.

B. The audit committee and external auditor will need to take corrective action on the deficiency findings.

C. The activities of the audit committee and external auditor may be affected because financial statements may be misstated.

D. A regulatory agency requires distribution.

The correct answer is (C). *(CIA, adapted)*

REQUIRED: The most likely reason for distributing copies of an audit report containing findings of significant control weaknesses in the accounts payable system.

DISCUSSION: According to SIAS 2, "Audit reports should be distributed to those members of the organization who are able to ensure that audit results are given due consideration." SIAS 2 states, "Reports may also be distributed to other interested or affected parties such as external auditors or the audit committee." The potential for misstated financial statements created by the internal control deficiencies should be of interest to the audit committee and the external auditors.

Answer (A) is incorrect because normal distribution is to department heads of units audited and others in a position to take corrective action or ensure that corrective action is taken. Answer (B) is incorrect because operating management is responsible for taking corrective action. Answer (D) is incorrect because no regulatory agency requires distribution to the audit committee and the board.

102. Which of the following combinations of participants would be most appropriate to attend an exit conference?

A. The responsible internal auditor and representatives from management who are knowledgeable of detailed operations and those who can authorize implementation of corrective action.

B. The director of internal auditing and the executive in charge of the activity or function audited.

C. Staff auditors who conducted the field work and operating personnel in charge of the daily performance of the activity or function audited.

D. Staff auditors who conducted the field work and the executive in charge of the activity or function audited.

The correct answer is (A). *(CIA, adapted)*

REQUIRED: The combination of participants most appropriate to attend an exit conference.

DISCUSSION: The internal auditor should discuss conclusions and recommendations at appropriate levels of management before issuing final reports (Standard 430). Although the level of participants in the discussions and reviews may vary, they will usually include those individuals who are knowledgeable about detailed operations and who have the authority to implement corrective action (SIAS 2).

Answer (B) is incorrect because the director of internal auditing and the executive in charge of the activity audited may not be knowledgeable about the details. Answer (C) is incorrect because staff auditors and operating personnel might not have the necessary perspectives and/or authority. Answer (D) is incorrect because the staff auditors might lack the proper perspective and authority.

103. Follow-up activity may be required to ensure that corrective action has taken place for certain findings. The internal auditing department's responsibility to perform follow-up activities as required should be defined in the

A. Internal auditing department's written charter.

B. Mission statement of the audit committee.

C. Engagement memo issued prior to each audit assignment.

D. Purpose statement within applicable audit reports.

The correct answer is (A). *(CIA, adapted)*

REQUIRED: The authoritative source defining the internal auditing department's responsibility to perform follow-up activities.

DISCUSSION: According to SIAS 13, "Follow-up is defined as a process by which internal auditors determine the adequacy, effectiveness, and timeliness of actions taken by management on reported audit findings. Such findings also include relevant findings made by external auditors and others. Responsibility for follow-up should be defined in the internal auditing department's written charter."

Answer (B) is incorrect because follow-up is not specified in the content of the audit committee's mission statement. Answer (C) is incorrect because the engagement memo may contain a statement about responsibility for follow-up, but it should be based on the wording and authority of the departmental charter. Answer (D) is incorrect because follow-up authority and responsibility may be cited in applicable audit reports, but the definition should be stated first in the departmental charter.

Questions 104 and 105 are based on the following information. An internal audit team recently completed an audit of the company's compliance with its lease-versus-purchase policy concerning company automobiles. The audit report noted that the basis for several decisions to lease rather than purchase automobiles had not been documented and was not auditable. The report contained a recommendation that operating management ensure that such lease agreements not be executed without proper documentation of the basis for the decision to lease rather than buy. The internal auditors are about to perform follow-up work on this audit report.

104. The primary purpose of performing a follow-up review is to

A. Ensure timely consideration of the internal auditors' recommendations.

B. Ascertain that appropriate action is taken on reported findings.

C. Allow the internal auditors to evaluate the effectiveness of their recommendations.

D. Document what management is doing in response to the audit report and close the audit file in a timely manner.

The correct answer is (B). *(CIA, adapted)*

REQUIRED: The primary purpose of performing a follow-up review.

DISCUSSION: Standard 440 states, "Internal auditors should follow up to ascertain that appropriate action is taken on reported findings. Internal auditors should determine that corrective action was taken and is achieving the desired results, or that management or the board has assumed the risk of not taking corrective action on reported findings."

Answers (A) and (C) are incorrect because the primary emphasis is on the audit findings, not the auditor's recommendations. Answer (D) is incorrect because internal auditing's clerical functions are secondary to the action taken on audit findings.

105. Assume that senior management has decided to accept the risk involved in failure to document the basis for lease-versus-purchase decisions involving company automobiles. In such a case, what would be the auditors' reporting obligation?

A. The auditors have no further reporting responsibility.

B. Management's decision and the auditors' concern should be reported to the company's board of directors.

C. The auditors should issue a follow-up report to management clearly stating the rationale for the recommendation that the basis for lease-versus-purchase decisions be properly documented.

D. The auditors should inform the external auditor and any responsible regulatory agency that no action has been taken on the finding in question.

The correct answer is (A). *(CIA, adapted)*

REQUIRED: The auditor's reporting obligation given management's decision not to document the basis for lease-versus-purchase decisions.

DISCUSSION: Senior management has assumed the risk of not correcting the reported condition because of cost or other considerations. Moreover, the board should be informed of senior management's decision on all significant findings (SIAS 13). However, the facts do not indicate that the finding regarding documentation of lease-versus-purchase decisions is significant.

Answer (B) is incorrect because reporting management's decision is necessary only if the finding is significant. Answer (C) is incorrect because senior management has already indicated that it understands and has accepted the related risk. Answer (D) is incorrect because reporting to anyone outside the organization is neither required nor appropriate.

106. An internal auditor has completed an audit of an organization's activities and is ready to issue a report. However, the auditee disagrees with the internal auditor's conclusions. The auditor should

A. Withhold the issuance of the audit report until agreement on the issues is obtained.

B. Perform more work, with the auditee's concurrence, to resolve areas of disagreement. Delay the issuance of the report until agreement is reached.

C. Issue the audit report and indicate that the auditee has provided a scope limitation that has led to a difference as to the conclusions.

D. Issue the audit report and state both the auditor and auditee positions and the reasons for the disagreement.

The correct answer is (D). *(CIA, adapted)*

REQUIRED: The action to be taken when an auditee disagrees with an auditor's conclusions before the report is issued.

DISCUSSION: According to SIAS 2, which interprets Standard 430, if the auditor and the auditee disagree on the auditor's conclusions, the auditor should issue the report and include both positions and the reasons for the disagreement. The auditee's written comments may be included in an appendix, or the auditee's views may be stated in the report or in a cover letter.

Answer (A) is incorrect because, if the audit is completed, the report should be communicated in a timely manner. Moreover, agreement with the auditee is not mandatory. Answer (B) is incorrect because, if the auditor is satisfied with the conclusions drawn from the audit, there is no reason to perform more work. Answer (C) is incorrect because the disagreement on conclusions is not a scope limitation.

9.11 Managing the Internal Auditing Department

107. According to the Standards, the director of internal auditing should establish goals that have two basic qualities. What are the traits of internal auditing goals?

A. Measurable and attainable.

B. Budgeted and approved.

C. Planned and attainable.

D. Requested and approved.

The correct answer is (A). *(CIA, adapted)*

REQUIRED: The traits of internal auditing goals.

DISCUSSION: Standard 520 requires that goals be capable of accomplishment within given operating plans and budgets, and that they be measurable to the extent possible. They should be accompanied by measurement criteria and targeted dates of accomplishment.

Answer (B) is incorrect because goals should be attainable within budget constraints. However, approval of goals is not mentioned in this Standard. Answer (C) is incorrect because the establishment of goals is part of the overall planning process for the internal auditing department. Answer (D) is incorrect because goals are not usually requested. Instead, they are established by the director of internal auditing.

108. What is the audit director's most logical definition of risk of loss to be used in selecting auditees?

A. Amount of risk exposure times the probability of loss.

B. Amount of annual costs in a department.

C. Probability of loss.

D. Amount of assets in a department.

The correct answer is (A). *(CIA, adapted)*

REQUIRED: The audit director's most logical definition of risk of loss to be used in selecting auditees.

DISCUSSION: To facilitate development of an audit work schedule, the director of internal auditing should perform a risk assessment. Risk is the probability that an event or action may adversely affect the organization (SIAS 9). For this purpose, risk of loss is most logically defined as an expected value. It equals the amount at risk times the probability of loss.

Answers (B) and (D) are incorrect because the amount of assets or costs in a department is not necessarily the amount exposed to a risk of loss. Answer (C) is incorrect because the probability of a loss must be multiplied by the amount exposed to possible loss.

109. The first phase of the risk assessment process is to identify and catalog the auditable activities of the organization. Which of the following would not be considered an auditable activity?

A. The agenda established by the audit committee for one of its quarterly meetings.

B. General ledger account balances.

C. Computerized information systems.

D. Statutory laws and regulations as they affect the organization.

The correct answer is (A). *(CIA, adapted)*

REQUIRED: The item not an auditable activity.

DISCUSSION: The director of internal auditing should assess the risks facing the organization. Thus, (s)he must identify auditable activities and relevant risk factors. A prioritized work schedule can then be developed. Auditable activities consist of the subjects, units, or systems capable of being defined and evaluated. They include the items listed in (B), (C), and (D); policies, procedures, and practices; responsibility centers; major contracts and programs; organizational units; business functions; transaction systems; and financial statements (SIAS 9). The audit committee's agenda for an audit committee meeting is not an auditable activity, but it may contain auditable activities.

Answers (B), (C), and (D) are incorrect because general ledger account balances, computerized information systems, and laws and regulations are auditable activities.

110. The director of internal auditing for an organization has just completed a risk assessment process, identified the areas with the highest risks, and assigned an audit priority to each. Which of the following conclusions logically follow(s) from such a risk assessment and is(are) consistent with the Standards?

I. Items should be quantified as to risk in the rank order of quantifiable dollar exposure to the organization.

II. The risk priorities should be in order of major control deficiencies.

III. The risk process, though quantified, is the result of professional judgments about both exposures and probability of occurrences.

A. I only.

B. III only.

C. II and III only.

D. I, II, and III.

The correct answer is (B). *(CIA, adapted)*

REQUIRED: The conclusion(s) logically following from a risk assessment process.

DISCUSSION: SIAS 9 states that risk assessment entails identifying auditable activities and relevant risk factors. Higher audit priorities are usually assigned to activities with higher risks. However, SIAS 9 also states that it does not prescribe a rigid process specifying how the assessment is to be conducted. Risk assessment is defined as "a systematic process for assessing and integrating professional judgments about probable adverse conditions and/or events." Thus, although risk factors may be weighted to determine their relative significance, SIAS 9 does not stipulate a ranking based on such specific criteria as dollar exposure or control deficiencies.

Answers (A), (C), and (D) are incorrect because conclusions I and II are not consistent with SIAS 9.

111. Which of the following represent(s) appropriate internal auditing action in response to the risk assessment process?

I. The low-risk areas may be delegated to the external auditor, but the high-risk areas should be performed by the internal auditing function.

II. The high-risk areas should be integrated into an audit plan along with the high-priority requests of management and the audit committee.

III. The risk analysis should be used in determining an annual audit work plan; therefore the risk analysis should be performed only on an annual basis.

A. I only.

B. II only.

C. III only.

D. I and III only.

The correct answer is (B). *(CIA, adapted)*

REQUIRED: The appropriate internal auditing action in response to a risk assessment.

DISCUSSION: The risk assessment is preliminary to the development of the audit work schedule. Higher audit priorities are usually assigned to activities with higher risks (SIAS 9). Other matters to be considered in establishing the audit work schedule are the date and result of the last audit, financial exposure, requests by management, major changes, opportunities to achieve operating benefits, and capabilities of the auditors (Standard 520).

Answers (A), (C), and (D) are incorrect because work should be coordinated with the external auditor to avoid duplication of effort and to ensure adequate audit coverage, but allocation of tasks is not necessarily risk based. Moreover, changing conditions may require updating the risk assessment during the year.

112. The internal auditor is considering performing risk analysis as a basis for determining which areas of the organization ought to be examined. Which one of the following statements is correct regarding risk analysis?

A. The extent to which management judgments are required in an area could serve as a risk factor in assisting the auditor in making a comparative risk analysis.

B. The highest risk assessment should always be assigned to the area with the largest potential loss.

C. The highest risk assessment should always be assigned to the area with highest probability of occurrence.

D. Risk analysis must be reduced to quantitative terms in order to provide meaningful comparisons across an organization.

The correct answer is (A). *(CIA, adapted)*

REQUIRED: The true statement about risk analysis.

DISCUSSION: Risk factors are the criteria used to determine the relative significance and probability of occurrence of conditions or events that may adversely affect an organization. According to SIAS 9, the auditor could appropriately consider the extent of management judgments and accounting estimates as a risk factor.

Answer (B) is incorrect because risk analysis should consider both the potential loss (or damages) and the probability of occurrence. An area with the largest potential loss may have a very low expected loss. Answer (C) is incorrect because a high probability of occurrence may be associated with a small potential loss. Answer (D) is incorrect because the concept of risk analysis is not limited to quantitative measures.

113. The internal auditing department's planning process involves establishing staffing plans and financial budgets. When determining the number and experience level of an internal audit staff to be assigned to an audit, the director should consider all of the following except the

A. Complexity of the audit assignment.

B. Available audit resources.

C. Training needs of internal auditors.

D. Lapsed time since the last audit.

The correct answer is (D). *(CIA, adapted)*

REQUIRED: The least appropriate criterion for assigning a staff auditor to a specific audit.

DISCUSSION: Staffing plans and budgets, "including the number of auditors and the knowledge, skills, and disciplines required to perform their work, should be determined from audit work schedules, administrative activities, education and training requirements, and audit research and development efforts" (Standard 520). However, lapsed time since the last audit is a factor affecting audit scheduling, not staffing.

Answers (A), (B), and (C) are incorrect because the complexity of the audit, available audit resources, and the training needs of individual auditors are factors in a staffing decision.

114. According to the Standards, an internal auditing department's activity reports should

A. List the material findings of major audits.

B. List unresolved findings.

C. Report the weekly activities of the individual auditors.

D. Compare audits completed with audits planned.

The correct answer is (D). *(CIA, adapted)*

REQUIRED: The true statement about an internal auditing department's activity reports.

DISCUSSION: According to Standard 520, "Activity reports should be submitted periodically to management and to the board. These reports should compare (1) performance with the department's goals and audit work schedules and (2) expenditures with financial budgets. They should explain the reasons for major variances and indicate any action taken or needed."

Answers (A), (B), and (C) are incorrect because material findings, unresolved findings, and weekly activities are not included in an activity report.

115. The Standards require that, in most cases, an internal auditing department have documented policies and procedures to ensure the consistency and quality of audit work. The exception to this requirement is directly related to

A. Departmentalization.

B. Division of labor.

C. Span of control.

D. Authority.

The correct answer is (C). *(CIA, adapted)*

REQUIRED: The exception to the requirement that, in most cases, an internal auditing department have documented policies and procedures.

DISCUSSION: Span of control concerns the number of employees directed. According to Standard 530, "Formal administrative and technical audit manuals may not be needed by all internal audit departments. A small internal audit department may be managed informally. Its audit staff may be directed and controlled through daily, close supervision and written memoranda. In a large internal audit department, more formal and comprehensive policies and procedures are essential to guide the audit staff in the consistent compliance with the department's standards of performance."

Answer (A) is incorrect because departmentalization can improve communications among team members, but sufficient direct supervision may be lacking if spans of control are large. Answer (B) is incorrect because division of labor produces highly specialized individuals, but formalized guidance is necessary for newer employees if the department is large. Answer (D) is incorrect because, regardless of the degree of authority wielded by the audit director, formal policies are needed in a large department.

116. Standard 540 states, "The director of internal auditing should establish a program for selecting and developing the human resources of the internal audit department." This program should include

A. Continuing education opportunities and performance appraisals.

B. Counseling and an established career path.

C. An established training plan and a charter.

D. Job descriptions and competitive salary increases.

The correct answer is (A). *(CIA, adapted)*

REQUIRED: The director of internal auditing's responsibilities for the human resource development program.

DISCUSSION: The program "should provide for developing written job descriptions for each level of the audit staff, selecting qualified and competent individuals, training and providing continuing educational opportunities for each internal auditor, appraising each internal auditor's performance at least annually, and providing counsel to internal auditors on their performance and professional development" (Standard 540).

Answer (B) is incorrect because counseling is an attribute of the program, but an established career path is not. Answer (C) is incorrect because planning is an overall part of the development program, but a charter is not specified. Answer (D) is incorrect because written job descriptions, but not salary increases, are required.

117. Which of the following is not a true statement about the relationship between internal auditors and external auditors?

A. Oversight of the work of external auditors is the responsibility of the director of internal auditing.

B. There may be periodic meetings between internal and external auditors to discuss matters of mutual interest.

C. There may be an exchange of audit reports and management letters between internal and external auditors.

D. Internal auditors may provide audit programs and working papers to external auditors.

The correct answer is (A). *(CIA, adapted)*

REQUIRED: The false statement about the relationship between internal and external auditors.

DISCUSSION: SIAS 5, *Internal Auditors' Relationship with Independent Outside Auditors*, states, "Oversight of the work of the independent outside auditor, including coordination with internal auditing, is generally the responsibility of the audit committee or its equivalent. Actual coordination should be the responsibility of the director of internal auditing." However, according to SIAS 17, *Assessment of Performance of External Auditors*, the board in the exercise of its oversight role may request that the director assess the performance of the external auditors. Ordinarily, this assessment is made in the context of the director's function or coordinating internal and external auditing efforts.

Answers (B), (C), and (D) are incorrect because Standard 550 states that coordination between internal and external auditors involves (1) periodic meetings to discuss matters of mutual interest; (2) access to each other's audit programs and working papers; (3) exchange of audit reports and management letters; and (4) common understanding of audit techniques, methods, and terminology.

118. Which statement is true regarding coordination of internal and external audit efforts?

A. The director of internal audit should not give information about illegal acts to an external auditor because external auditors may be required to report the matter to the board and/or regulatory agencies.

B. Ownership and the confidentiality of the external auditor's working papers prohibit their review by internal auditors.

C. The director of internal audit should determine that appropriate follow-up and corrective action was taken by management when required on matters discussed in the external auditor's management letter.

D. If internal auditors provide assistance to the external auditors in connection with the annual audit, the audit work is not subject to the SPPIA.

The correct answer is (C). *(CIA, adapted)*

REQUIRED: The true statement about coordination of internal and external audit efforts.

DISCUSSION: According to SIAS 5, which interprets Standard 550, *External Auditors*, "Internal auditors need access to independent outside auditors' management letters. Matters discussed in management letters assist internal auditing in planning the areas to emphasize in future internal audit work. After review of the management letter and initiation of any needed corrective action by management and the board of directors, the director of internal auditing should ensure that appropriate follow-up and corrective action have been taken."

Answer (A) is incorrect because internal auditors should give external auditors access to their audit programs, working papers, and reports. Information about illegal acts should be communicated to the external auditor. Answer (B) is incorrect because the Standards allow review of internal audit working papers by external auditors. Answer (D) is incorrect because all work done by internal auditors should be done in accordance with the Standards.

119. The Standards would not require the director of internal auditing to

A. Contribute resources for the annual audit of financial statements.

B. Coordinate audit work with that of the external auditors.

C. Communicate to senior management and the board the results of evaluations of the coordination between internal and external auditors.

D. Communicate to senior management and the board the results of evaluations of the performance of external auditors.

The correct answer is (A). *(CIA, adapted)*

REQUIRED: The action by the director of internal auditing not required by the Standards.

DISCUSSION: According to SIAS 5, "Internal auditing may agree to perform work for the independent outside auditors in connection with their annual audit of the financial statements. Work performed by internal auditing to assist the independent outside auditors in fulfilling their responsibility is subject to all relevant provisions of the SPPIA."

Answer (B) is incorrect because actual coordination of audit efforts should be the responsibility of the director of internal auditing. Answers (C) and (D) are incorrect because, according to SIAS 7, "The director of internal auditing should communicate the results of evaluations of the coordination between the internal and external auditor to senior management and the board along with any relevant comments about the performance of the external auditor."

120. Which of the following activities are designed to provide feedback on the effectiveness of an internal audit department?

I. Proper supervision
II. Proper training
III. Internal reviews
IV. External reviews

A. I, II, III.

B. II, III, IV.

C. I, III, IV.

D. I, II, III, IV.

The correct answer is (C). *(CIA, adapted)*

REQUIRED: The activities designed to provide feedback on the effectiveness of internal auditing.

DISCUSSION: A quality assurance program of an internal auditing department provides reasonable assurance that audit work conforms with applicable standards. Standard 560 states that the purpose of a quality assurance program "is to provide reasonable assurance that audit work conforms with these standards, the internal auditing department's charter, and other applicable standards." A quality assurance program should include supervision, internal reviews, and external reviews.

Answers (A), (B), and (D) are incorrect because proper training is an aspect of personnel management and development (Standard 540). It is not a feedback mechanism.

121. The Standards specify that supervision of the work of internal auditors be "carried out continually." Which of the following statements regarding supervision is(are) correct?

I. "Continually" indicates that supervision should be performed throughout the planning, examination, evaluation, report, and follow-up stages of the audit.

II. Supervision should also be extended to training, time reporting, and expense control, as well as similar administrative matters.

III. The extent and nature of supervision needs to be documented, preferably in the appropriate working papers.

A. I only.

B. I and III only.

C. II only.

D. I, II, and III.

The correct answer is (D). *(CIA, adapted)*

REQUIRED: The true statements about supervision.

DISCUSSION: Standard 560 requires continual supervision of the work of internal auditors to ensure conformity with internal auditing standards, departmental policies, and audit programs. Supervision includes documenting and retaining appropriate evidence of supervision. The language in statements I and II is found in SIAS 4, *Quality Assurance*, which interprets Standard 560.

Answers (A), (B), and (C) are incorrect because statements I, II, and III are in accordance with Standard 560.

122. The Standards require the performance of periodic internal reviews by members of the internal auditing staff. This function is designed primarily to serve the needs of

A. The audit committee.

B. The director of internal auditing.

C. Management.

D. The internal auditing staff.

The correct answer is (B). *(CIA, adapted)*

REQUIRED: The person(s) primarily served by formal internal reviews.

DISCUSSION: According to SIAS 4, "Internal quality assurance reviews primarily serve the needs of the director of internal auditing, but can also provide senior management and the audit committee with an assessment of the internal auditing function. These reviews should be structured to evaluate the degree of compliance with the Standards, level of audit effectiveness, and extent of compliance with the organization and departmental policies and standards. The review should also provide recommendations for improvement."

Answers (A) and (C) are incorrect because the audit committee and management are indirect beneficiaries of the reviews. Answer (D) is incorrect because the audit staff benefits indirectly by having deficiencies addressed more promptly.

9.12 Ethics

123. A primary purpose for establishing a code of conduct within a professional organization is to

A. Reduce the likelihood that members of the profession will be sued for substandard work.

B. Ensure that all members of the profession perform at approximately the same level of competence.

C. Demonstrate acceptance of responsibility to the interests of those served by the profession.

D. Require members of the profession to exhibit loyalty in all matters pertaining to the affairs of their organization.

The correct answer is (C). *(CIA, adapted)*

REQUIRED: The purpose of a code of conduct.

DISCUSSION: The preamble to The IIA *Code of Ethics* includes the following: "PURPOSE: A distinguishing mark of a profession is acceptance by its members of responsibility to the interests of those it serves. Members of The Institute of Internal Auditors (Members) and Certified Internal Auditors (CIA, adapted) order to effectively discharge this responsibility. The Institute of Internal Auditors (Institute) adopts this *Code of Ethics* for Members and CIAs."

Answer (A) is incorrect because reducing the probability of being sued may result from establishing a code of conduct, but it is not the primary purpose. Answer (B) is incorrect because a code of conduct may influence standards of competence, but legislating equality of competence is impossible. Answer (D) is incorrect because, in some situations, responsibility to the public at large may conflict with, and be more important than, loyalty to one's organization.

124. The Standards of Conduct set forth in the *Code of Ethics*

A. Provide basic principles in the practice of internal auditing.

B. Are guidelines to assist internal auditors in dealing with auditees.

C. Are rules that must be obeyed in all circumstances.

D. Provide a general understanding of the responsibilities of internal auditing.

The correct answer is (A). *(CIA, adapted)*

REQUIRED: The true statement about The IIA *Code of Ethics*.

DISCUSSION: The applicability section of the preamble to The IIA *Code of Ethics* states, "The standards of conduct set forth in this *Code of Ethics* provide basic principles in the practice of internal auditing. Members and CIAs should realize that their individual judgment is required in the application of these principles."

Answer (B) is incorrect because internal auditors should observe the Standards of Conduct to discharge their responsibility to all those whom they serve. Auditees are not the only parties served by internal auditing. Answer (C) is incorrect because judgment is required in applying the Standards of Conduct. Answer (D) is incorrect because the Statement of Responsibilities of Internal Auditing (SRIA) is intended to provide a general understanding of the responsibilities of internal auditing.

125. The *Code of Ethics* requires IIA members to exercise three particular qualities in the performance of their duties. These qualities are

A. Honesty, objectivity, and diligence.

B. Timeliness, sobriety, and clarity.

C. Knowledge, skills, and disciplines.

D. Punctuality, loyalty, and dignity.

The correct answer is (A). *(CIA, adapted)*

REQUIRED: The qualities required of IIA members.

DISCUSSION: According to Standard of Conduct I of The IIA *Code of Ethics*, "Members and CIAs shall exercise honesty, objectivity, and diligence in the performance of their duties and responsibilities."

Answer (B) is incorrect because timeliness, sobriety, and clarity are not mentioned in the Code. Answer (C) is incorrect because knowledge, skills, and disciplines are mentioned in Standards 220 and 250 but not in the Code. Answer (D) is incorrect because punctuality is not mentioned in the Code.

126. Which of the following would be permissible under The IIA *Code of Ethics*?

A. Disclosing confidential, audit-related, information that is potentially damaging to the organization in a court of law in response to a subpoena.

B. Using audit-related information in a decision to buy stock issued by the employer corporation.

C. Accepting an unexpected gift from an employee whom you have praised in a recent audit report.

D. Not reporting significant findings about illegal activity to the audit committee because management has indicated it will handle the issue.

The correct answer is (A). *(CIA, adapted)*

REQUIRED: The action permissible under The IIA *Code of Ethics*.

DISCUSSION: Under Standard of Conduct II, "Members and CIAs shall exhibit loyalty in all matters pertaining to the affairs of their organization or to whomever they may be rendering a service. However, Members and CIAs shall not knowingly be a party to any illegal or improper activity." Thus, the requirement of loyalty does not override the legal obligation to respond to a validly issued and enforceable subpoena.

Answer (B) is incorrect because Standard of Conduct VIII prohibits internal auditors from using confidential information for personal gain. Answer (C) is incorrect because Standard of Conduct V prohibits internal auditors from accepting anything of value from other employees that would impair or be presumed to impair their professional judgment. Answer (D) is incorrect because Standard of Conduct II prohibits knowingly being a party to any illegal or improper activity.

127. An internal auditor for a large regional bank holding company was asked to serve on the board of directors of a local bank. The bank competes in many of the same markets as the bank holding company but focuses more on consumer financing than on business financing. In accepting this position, the auditor

I. Violates The IIA *Code of Ethics* because serving on the board may be in conflict with the best interests of the auditor's employer.

II. Violates The IIA *Code of Ethics* because the information gained while serving on the board of directors of the local bank may influence recommendations regarding potential acquisitions.

A. I only.

B. II only.

C. I and II.

D. Neither I nor II.

The correct answer is (C). *(CIA, adapted)*

REQUIRED: The possible violation(s), if any, of The IIA *Code of Ethics*.

DISCUSSION: Under Standard of Conduct IV, "Members and CIAs shall refrain from entering into any activity that may be in conflict with the interest of their organization or that would prejudice their ability to carry out objectively their duties and responsibilities." Accordingly, service on the board of the local bank constitutes a conflict of interest and may prejudice the internal auditor's ability to carry out objectively his/her duties regarding potential acquisitions.

Answers (A), (B), and (D) are incorrect because serving on the board of the local bank creates a conflict of interest and may prejudice the internal auditor's ability to perform his/her duties.

128. During the course of an audit, an auditor discovers that a clerk is embezzling company funds. Although this is the first embezzlement ever encountered and the organization has a security department, the auditor decides to personally interrogate the suspect. If the auditor is violating the *Code of Ethics*, the rule violated is most likely

A. Failing to show due diligence.

B. Lack of loyalty to the organization.

C. Lack of competence in this area.

D. Failing to comply with the law.

The correct answer is (C). *(CIA, adapted)*

REQUIRED: The ethics rule most likely violated.

DISCUSSION: The Code requires members and CIAs to refrain from undertaking services that cannot be reasonably completed with professional competence (Standard of Conduct VI). Internal auditors may not have and are not expected "to have knowledge equivalent to that of a person whose primary responsibility is to detect and investigate fraud" (SIAS 7).

Answer (A) is incorrect because the due diligence requirement does not override the professional competence standard of conduct or the need to use good judgment. Answers (B) and (D) are incorrect because interrogation of a suspect, by itself, does not constitute disloyalty or a violation of the law.

129. In some countries, governmental units have established audit standards. For example, in the United States, the General Accounting Office has developed standards for the conduct of governmental audits, particularly those that relate to compliance with government grants. In performing governmental grant compliance audits, the auditor should

A. Be guided only by the governmental standards.

B. Be guided only by The IIA Standards because they are more encompassing.

C. Be guided by the more general standards that have been issued by the public accounting profession.

D. Follow both The IIA Standards and any additional governmental standards.

The correct answer is (D). *(CIA, adapted)*

REQUIRED: The standards an auditor follows when performing governmental grant compliance audits.

DISCUSSION: Standard of Conduct VII of The IIA *Code of Ethics* states, "Members and CIAs shall adopt suitable means to comply with the Standards for the Professional Practice of Internal Auditing." Furthermore, an auditor is legally obligated to adhere to governmental auditing standards when performing governmental grant compliance audits.

Answers (A), (B), and (C) are incorrect because the auditor should follow both The IIA Standards and governmental auditing standards.

130. A new staff auditor was told to perform an audit in an area with which the auditor was not familiar. Because of time constraints, there was no supervision of the audit. The auditor was given the assignment because it represented a good learning experience, but the area was clearly beyond the auditor's competence. Nonetheless, the auditor prepared comprehensive working papers and reported the results to management. In this situation

A. The auditing department violated the Standards by hiring an auditor without proficiency in the area.

B. The auditing department violated the Standards by not providing adequate supervision.

C. The director of internal auditing has not violated the *Code of Ethics* because the Code does not address supervision.

D. The Standards and the *Code of Ethics* were followed by the auditing department.

The correct answer is (B). *(CIA, adapted)*

REQUIRED: The effect of failing to supervise an auditor who lacks proficiency in the area being audited.

DISCUSSION: Although The IIA *Code of Ethics* does not address supervision directly, it does require that the Standards be followed (Standard of Conduct VII). Moreover, Standard 500 requires the director of internal auditing to ensure that audit work conforms to the Standards, and Standard 230 requires the department to provide appropriate supervision.

Answer (A) is incorrect because all auditors need not be proficient in all areas. The department should have an appropriate mix of skills. Answer (C) is incorrect because the Code requires compliance with the Standards, and the Standards require appropriate supervision. Answer (D) is incorrect because the Standards and the Code were not followed.

131. Which situation most likely violates the *Code of Ethics* and the Standards?

A. The director of internal auditing disagrees with auditee management about the finding and recommendation in a sensitive area. The director discusses the detail of the finding and the proposed recommendation with a fellow audit director from another firm.

B. A company's audit charter requires the director of internal auditing to present the yearly audit plan to the audit committee for its approval and suggestions.

C. The audit manager has removed the most significant finding and recommendation from the audit report. The in-charge auditor opposed the removal, explaining that (s)he knows the reported condition exists. The in-charge auditor agrees that, technically, the audit lacks sufficient evidence to support the finding, but management cannot explain the condition and the finding is the only reasonable conclusion.

D. Because the internal auditing department lacks skill and knowledge in a specialty area, the audit director has hired an expert. The audit manager has been asked to review the expert's approach to the assignment. Although knowledgeable about the area under review, the manager is hesitant to accept the assignment because of lack of expertise.

The correct answer is (A). *(CIA, adapted)*

REQUIRED: The situation most likely to be considered a violation of the *Code of Ethics*.

DISCUSSION: According to Standard of Conduct VIII of The IIA *Code of Ethics*, "Members and CIAs shall be prudent in the use of information acquired in the course of their duties. They shall not use confidential information for any personal gain or in any manner that would be contrary to law or detrimental to the welfare of their organization." Consequently, discussion of sensitive matters with an unauthorized party is the situation most likely to be considered a Code violation. The information conveyed might be used to the detriment of the organization.

Answer (B) is incorrect because approval of the audit plan by the audit committee or management is required by the Standards. Answer (C) is incorrect because the Standards require sufficient evidence to support findings. Answer (D) is incorrect because the Standards allow use of experts when needed.

132. In a review of travel and entertainment expenses, a certified internal auditor questioned the business purposes of an officer's reimbursed travel expenses. The officer promised to compensate for the questioned amounts by not claiming legitimate expenses in the future. If the officer makes good on the promise, the internal auditor

A. Can ignore the original charging of the non-business expenses.

B. Should inform the tax authorities in any event.

C. Should still include the finding in the audit report.

D. Should recommend that the officer forfeit any frequent flyer miles received as part of the questionable travel.

The correct answer is (C). *(CIA, adapted)*

REQUIRED: The internal auditor's action when an officer agrees to compensate for questionable expenses by not claiming legitimate expenses in the future.

DISCUSSION: According to Standard of Conduct IX of The IIA *Code of Ethics*, "Members and CIAs, when reporting on the results of their work, shall reveal such material facts known to them which, if not revealed, could either distort reports of operations under review or conceal unlawful practices."

Answer (A) is incorrect because the possibly fraudulent behavior of the officer is a material fact that should be reported regardless of whether the questioned expenses are reimbursed. Answer (B) is incorrect because the Standards require the director of internal auditing to distribute audit reports to those members of the organization who can take appropriate action. Answer (D) is incorrect because management should determine what constitutes just compensation.

Questions 133 through 135 are based on the following information. A company with a whistle-blowing hotline has received an anonymous tip that three senior internal auditors are in violation of The IIA's *Code of Ethics*. The company has adopted The IIA's Code as a part of the corporate ethical code. Among the allegations against the auditors were the following:

1. Auditor 1 has a part-time job outside of office hours as a visiting professor at a local community college.
2. Auditor 1 owns stock in the employer company.
3. Auditor 1 told his next-door neighbor to start looking for a new job because an audit of the executive office indicated that the neighbor's division was going to be closed down in about 6 months.
4. Auditor 2 received an item of value from a local nonprofit organization of purchasing agents for whom he gave a speech.
5. Auditor 2 received an item of value from a customer of the employer.
6. Auditor 2 has a part-time job as president of a local charitable organization.
7. Auditor 2 shared audit techniques with auditors from another company while attending a professional meeting.
8. A buyer accepted a kickback of $500 to give bid amounts to a supplier to enable that supplier to bid the contract. Auditor 2 omitted this information from the audit report since the contract amount was not material to the financial statements.
9. Auditor 3 received royalties from a publisher for authoring a professional book on internal auditing.
10. Auditor 3 has a part-time job as a real estate broker, and his real estate firm recently received a commission from the employer company.
11. Auditor 3 received an item of value from a fellow employee in the same company whose department has never been audited and whose department is not scheduled to be audited in the foreseeable future.
12. Auditor 3 did not include in an audit report that the bottlenecks in a shipping department were caused by the absence of the supervisor. The supervisor was the auditor's friend and neighbor who had a hospitalized child requiring him to miss work off and on for several weeks.

133. How many of the allegations about Auditor 1 represent violations of The IIA's *Code of Ethics*?

A. None.

B. One.

C. Two.

D. Three.

The correct answer is (B). *(CIA, adapted)*

REQUIRED: The number of ethics violations by Auditor 1.

DISCUSSION: According to Standard of Conduct VIII, "Members and CIAs shall be prudent in the use of information acquired in the course of their duties. They shall not use confidential information for any personal gain nor in any manner which would be contrary to law or detrimental to the welfare of their organization." Thus, discussing the plant closing with a neighbor violates the *Code of Ethics*. Teaching at a local community college presents no conflict of interest. Such activity is consistent with the duty to strive for improvement in proficiency. Furthermore, owning stock in the employer company may enhance loyalty to the organization.

Answers (A), (C), and (D) are incorrect because telling the neighbor about the plant closing is the only violation of the *Code of Ethics*.

134. How many of the allegations about Auditor 2 represent violations of The IIA's *Code of Ethics*?

A. One.

B. Two.

C. Three.

D. Four.

The correct answer is (B). *(CIA, adapted)*

REQUIRED: The number of ethics violations by Auditor 2.

DISCUSSION: According to Standard of Conduct V, "Members and CIAs shall not accept anything of value from an employee, client, customer, supplier, or business associate of their organization which would impair or be presumed to impair their professional judgment." Accepting an item of value from a customer violates this standard. Standard of Conduct IX states, "Members and CIAs, when reporting on the results of their work, shall reveal such material facts known to them which, if not revealed, could either distort reports of operations under review or conceal unlawful practices." Failing to disclose the kickback violates this standard. Receiving an item of value in exchange for speaking to a nonprofit group of purchasing agents is not presumed to impair professional judgment. The group is not an employee, client, customer, supplier, etc. Serving as an officer of a charity likewise provides no basis for a conflict of interest.

Answers (A), (C), and (D) are incorrect because accepting an item of value from a customer of the employer and failing to disclose a kickback are the only violations of the *Code of Ethics*.

135. How many of the allegations about Auditor 3 represent violations of The IIA's *Code of Ethics*?

A. One.

B. Two.

C. Three.

D. Four.

The correct answer is (C). *(CIA, adapted)*

REQUIRED: The number of ethics violations by Auditor 3.

DISCUSSION: According to Standard of Conduct IV, "Members and CIAs shall refrain from entering into any activity which may be in conflict with the interest of their organization or which would prejudice their ability to carry out objectively their duties and responsibilities." The part-time job as a real estate broker for a company that does business with the employer is a violation of this standard. Standard of Conduct V states, "Members and CIAs shall not accept anything of value from an employee, client, customer, supplier, or business associate of their organization which would impair or be presumed to impair their professional judgment." The receipt of an item of value from a fellow employee violates this standard. Standard of Conduct IX states, "Members and CIAs, when reporting on the results of their work, shall reveal such material facts known to them which, if not revealed, could either distort reports of operations under review or conceal unlawful practices." Failing to report the reason for the bottlenecks in shipping violates this standard.

Answer (A), (B), and (D) are incorrect because receiving royalties from a book publisher is the only action that is not a violation of the *Code of Ethics*. The receipt of royalties is not a violation because the publisher is not an employee, client, etc.

136. During an audit, an employee with whom you have developed a good working relationship informs you that she has some information about top management that would be damaging to the organization and may concern illegal activities. The employee does not want her name associated with the release of the information. Which of the following actions would be considered inconsistent with The IIA *Code of Ethics* and Standards?

A. Assure the employee that you can maintain her anonymity and listen to the information.

B. Suggest the employee consider talking to legal counsel.

C. Inform the employee that you will attempt to keep the source of the information confidential and will look into the matter further.

D. Inform the employee of other methods of communicating this type of information.

The correct answer is (A). *(CIA, adapted)*

REQUIRED: The action considered inconsistent with The IIA's *Code of Ethics* and Standards.

DISCUSSION: An internal auditor cannot guarantee anonymity. Information communicated to an internal auditor is not subject to a testimonial privilege. Moreover, Standard of Conduct IX states, "Members and CIAs, when reporting on the results of their work, shall reveal such material facts known to them that, if not revealed, could either distort reports of operations under review or conceal unlawful practices." The identity of the informant may be such a material fact.

Answer (B) is incorrect because suggesting that the person seek expert legal advice from a qualified individual is appropriate. Answer (C) is incorrect because promising merely to attempt to keep the source of the information confidential is allowable. This promise is not a guarantee of confidentiality. Answer (D) is incorrect because the employee could be directed to other methods of communicating the information in order to maintain her anonymity.

137. Today's internal auditor will often encounter a wide range of potential ethical dilemmas, not all of which are explicitly addressed by The Institute of Internal Auditors' *Code of Ethics*. If the auditor encounters such a dilemma, the auditor should always

A. Seek counsel from an independent attorney to determine the personal consequences of potential actions.

B. Consider all parties affected and the potential consequences of actions, and take an action consistent with the objectives of internal auditing and the concepts embodied in The IIA's *Code of Ethics*.

C. Seek the counsel of the audit committee before deciding on an action.

D. Act consistently with the code of ethics adopted by the organization even if such action would not be consistent with The IIA's *Code of Ethics*.

The correct answer is (B). *(CIA, adapted)*

REQUIRED: The action taken when an auditor encounters an ethical dilemma.

DISCUSSION: Internal auditors' actions should be consistent with the concepts embodied in The IIA Code. Standard of Conduct XI states, "Members shall abide by the Bylaws and uphold the objectives of the Institute."

Answer (A) is incorrect because seeking the advice of legal counsel on all ethical decisions is impracticable. Answer (C) is incorrect because seeking the advice of the audit committee on all ethical decisions is impracticable. Furthermore, the advice might not be consistent with the profession's standards. Answer (D) is incorrect because, if the company's standards are not consistent with, or as high as, the profession's standards, the internal auditor is held to the standards of the profession.

APPENDIX A
CHAPTER CROSS-REFERENCES
TO AUDITING TEXTBOOKS

The next nine pages contain the tables of contents of current auditing textbooks with cross-references to the related modules or chapters in this study manual. The books are listed in alphabetical order by the first author. As you study a particular chapter in your auditing textbook, you can easily determine which module(s) to study in this manual. You should review all questions in the module.

Professors, students, and accounting practitioners should all note that, even though new editions of the texts listed below may be published as you use this book, the new tables of contents usually will be very similar, if not the same. Thus, this edition of *Auditing & Systems Exam Questions and Explanations* will remain current and useful.

AUDITING TEXTBOOKS

1. Arens and Loebbecke, *Auditing, Revised*, Seventh Edition, Prentice Hall, Inc., 1997.
2. Boynton and Kell, *Modern Auditing*, Sixth Edition, John Wiley & Sons, Inc., 1996.
3. Carmichael, Willingham, and Schaller, *Auditing Concepts and Methods*, Sixth Edition, McGraw-Hill Book Company, 1996.
4. Guy, Alderman, and Winters, *Auditing*, Fourth Edition, the Dryden Press, 1996.
5. Guy, Carmichael, and Whittington, *Audit Sampling: An Introduction*, Fourth Edition, John Wiley & Sons, Inc., 1998.
6. Hermanson, Strawser, and Strawser, *Auditing Theory and Practice*, Sixth Edition, Richard D. Irwin, 1993.
7. Kiger and Scheiner, *Auditing*, Second Edition, Houghton Mifflin Co., 1997.
8. Knechel, *Auditing*, First Edition, South-Western College Publishing, 1998.
9. Konrath, *Auditing Concepts and Applications: A Risk Analysis Approach*, Fourth Edition, South-Western Publishing Co., 1999.
10. Messier, *Auditing: A Systematic Approach*, First Edition, McGraw-Hill Book Company, 1996.
11. Pany and Whittington, *Auditing*, Second Edition, Richard D. Irwin, 1997.
12. Ricchiute, *Auditing Assurances & Services*, Fifth Edition, South-Western Publishing Co., 1999.
13. Rittenberg and Schwieger, *Auditing: Concepts for a Changing Environment*, Second Edition, The Dryden Press, 1997.
14. Robertson, *Auditing*, Eighth Edition, Richard D. Irwin, 1996.
15. Sawyer and Dittenhofer, *Sawyer's Internal Auditing*, Fourth Edition, The Institute of Internal Auditors, Inc., 1996.
16. Taylor and Glezen, *Auditing: An Assertions Approach*, Seventh Edition, John Wiley & Sons, Inc., 1997.
17. Thomas, Ward, and Henke, *Auditing: Theory and Practice*, Third Edition, PWS-Kent Publishers, 1991.
18. Wallace, *Auditing*, Third Edition, South-Western Publishing Company, 1995.
19. Whittington and Pany, *Principles of Auditing*, Twelfth Edition, Richard D. Irwin, 1997.

SYSTEMS TEXTBOOKS

Chapter 5, Information Systems, covers the material in systems textbooks.

CHAPTER CROSS-REFERENCES TO AUDITING TEXTBOOKS

Professors, students, and accounting practitioners should all note that even though new editions of the texts listed below may be published as you use this book, the new tables of contents usually will be very similar, if not the same. Thus, this edition of *Auditing & Systems Exam Questions and Explanations* will remain current and useful.

Arens and Loebbecke, *Auditing, Revised*, Seventh Edition, Prentice Hall, Inc., 1997.

Part I: The Auditing Profession
- Chapter 1 The Auditing Profession - 1.1-1.9
- Chapter 2 Audit Reports - 1.4, Ch. 7, Ch. 8, 9.10
- Chapter 3 Professional Ethics - 1.5-1.8, 9.3
- Chapter 4 Legal Liability - 1.9, 2.3, 2.4

Part II: The Auditing Process
- Chapter 5 Audit Responsibilities and Objectives - Ch. 1, Ch. 2, 3.1, 3.2
- Chapter 6 Audit Evidence - 2.2, 2.5, 3.4, 3.5, 3.14, Ch. 4, Ch. 6, 9.8
- Chapter 7 Audit Planning and Documentation - Ch. 2, 3.14
- Chapter 8 Materiality and Risk - 1.4, 2.3, 3.2, 4.1
- Chapter 9 The Study of the Client's Internal Control and Assessment of Control Risk - 2.3, 3.1-3.4
- Chapter 10 Overall Audit Plan and Audit Program - 2.2, 4.1

Part III: Application of the Auditing Process to the Sales and Collection Cycle
- Chapter 11 Audit of the Sales and Collection Cycle: Tests of Controls and Substantive Tests of Transactions - 3.6, 4.3
- Chapter 12 Audit Sampling for Tests of Controls and Substantive Tests of Transactions - Ch. 6
- Chapter 13 Completing the Tests in the Sales and Collection Cycle: Accounts Receivable - 3.6, 4.3
- Chapter 14 Audit Sampling for Tests of Details of Balances - Ch. 6

Part IV: Auditing Complex EDP Systems
- Chapter 15 Auditing Complex EDP Systems - Ch. 5

Part V: Application of the Auditing Process to Other Cycles
- Chapter 16 Audit of the Payroll and Personnel Cycle - 3.8, 4.11
- Chapter 17 Audit of the Acquisition and Payment Cycle: Tests of Controls, Substantive Tests of Transactions, and Accounts Payable - 3.7, 4.4
- Chapter 18 Completing the Tests in the Acquisition and Payment Cycle: Verification of Selected Accounts - 3.7, 4.4
- Chapter 19 Audit of the Inventory and Warehousing Cycle - 3.10, 4.6
- Chapter 20 Audit of the Capital Acquisition and Repayment Cycle - 3.7, 3.11, 4.4, 4.7
- Chapter 21 Audit of Cash Balances - 3.6, 3.7, 4.3-4.5

Part VI: Completing the Audit and Offering Other Services
- Chapter 22 Completing the Audit - 3.12, 4.12-4.16
- Chapter 23 Other Audit, Attestation Services, and Compilation Engagements - 1.11-1.13, 8.1-8.7, 8.9
- Chapter 24 Internal Government Financial Auditing and Operational Auditing - 8.8, 8.9, Ch. 9

Boynton and Kell, *Modern Auditing*, Sixth Edition, John Wiley & Sons, Inc., 1996.

Part One: The Auditing Environment
- Chapter 1 Auditing and the Public Accounting Profession - 1.1
- Chapter 2 Financial Statement Audits and Auditors' Responsibilities - 1.2-1.4
- Chapter 3 Professional Ethics - 1.5-1.8, 9.12
- Chapter 4 Auditor's Legal Liability - 1.9, 2.3, 2.4

Part Two: Audit Planning
- Chapter 5 Audit Objectives, Evidence, and Working Papers - 1.1-1.4, 2.5, Ch. 4
- Chapter 6 Accepting the Engagement and Planning the Audit - 2.1, 2.2
- Chapter 7 Materiality, Risk, and Preliminary Audit Strategies - 1.4, 2.3, 3.2, 4.1
- Chapter 8 Understanding the Internal Control Structure - 3.1-3.4

Part Three: Audit Testing Methodology
- Chapter 9 Assessing Control Risk/Tests of Controls - 2.3, 3.5
- Chapter 10 Detection Risk and the Design of Substantive Tests - 2.3, 4.1-4.11, 6.1-6.3, 6.8
- Chapter 11 Audit Sampling in Tests of Controls - 6.1-6.5
- Chapter 12 Audit Sampling in Substantive Tests - 6.1-6.4, 6.6
- Chapter 13 Auditing Electronic Data Processing Systems - Ch. 5

Part Four: Auditing the Transaction Cycles
- Chapter 14 Auditing the Revenue Cycle - 3.6, 4.3
- Chapter 15 Auditing the Expenditure Cycle - 3.7, 4.4
- Chapter 16 Auditing the Production and Personnel Services Cycles - 3.8, 3.10, 3.11, 4.6, 4.7, 4.11
- Chapter 17 Auditing the Investing and Financing Cycles - 3.9, 4.9, 4.10
- Chapter 18 Auditing Cash Balances - 3.6, 3.7, 4.3-4.5

Part Five: Completing the Audit, Reporting, and Other Services
- Chapter 19 Completing the Audit/Postaudit Responsibilities - 3.12, 4.12-4.16
- Chapter 20 Reporting on Audited Financial Statements - 1.4, Ch. 7
- Chapter 21 Other Services and Reports - 1.8, 1.11-1.13, Ch. 8
- Chapter 22 Internal, Operational, and Governmental Auditing - 8.5, 8.8, 8.9, Ch. 9
- Chapter 23 The Independent Accountant and the Securities and Exchange Commission - 8.7

Carmichael, Willingham, and Schaller, *Auditing Concepts and Methods*, Sixth Edition, McGraw-Hill Book Company, 1996.

- Chapter 1 The Audit Function -- An Overview - 1.1-1.9
- Chapter 2 Professional Ethics and the Auditing Environment - 1.1-1.9
- Chapter 3 Legal Liability - 1.9, 2.3, 2.4
- Chapter 4 The Elements of Auditing - 1.3-1.8
- Chapter 5 Understanding the Client and General Planning - 1.1-1.3, 2.1-2.3
- Chapter 6 Understanding the Internal Control Structure and Assessing Control Risk - 2.3, 3.1-3.4
- Chapter 7 Planning Tests of Details of Transactions and Balances - 2.2, 4.1, 6.1-6.6
- Chapter 8 Audit Sampling - Ch. 6
- Chapter 9 The Effects of Computers on the Audit - Ch. 5
- Chapter 10 Tests of Transaction Classes and Related Balances - 3.6-3.11, 4.3-4.11, 6.6-6.8
- Chapter 11 Direct Tests of Balances - 6.2-6.7
- Chapter 12 Completion of the Audit - 3.12, 4.12-4.16
- Chapter 13 The Auditor's Report - 1.4, Ch. 7, Ch. 8, 9.10
- Chapter 14 Attestation Services, Unaudited Financial Statements and Specialized Reporting - 1.12, 1.13, Ch. 8
- Chapter 15 Operational Auditing - 8.5, 9.1, 9.2

Guy, Alderman, and Winters, *Auditing*, Fourth Edition, The Dryden Press, 1996.

Part One: The Auditing Environment
- Chapter 1 The Audit Function in Society - 1.1-1.9
- Chapter 2 Professional Ethics - 1.5-1.8, 9.12
- Chapter 3 The Auditor's Legal Liability - 1.9, 2.3, 2.4

Part Two: Auditing Concepts
- Chapter 4 The Audit Evidence Process - 2.2-2.5, 3.4, 3.5, 3.14, Ch. 4, Ch. 6, 9.8
- Chapter 5 Obtaining and Documenting Audit Evidence - 3.14, Ch. 4
- Chapter 6 Consideration of the Internal Control Structure - 2.3, 3.1-3.4
- Chapter 7 The Computer Environment and the Internal Control Structure - 5.1-5.12

Part Three: Auditing Tools and Techniques
- Chapter 8 Auditing in a Computer Environment - Ch. 5
- Chapter 9 Audit Sampling Concepts - 6.2
- Chapter 10 Audit Sampling Applications - 6.3-6.7
- Chapter 11 Analytical Procedures - 4.2

Part Four: The Audit Engagement
- Chapter 12 Planning the Engagement - 2.1-2.3
- Chapter 13 Understanding the Internal Control Structure and Assessing Control Risk: The Revenue Cycle - 2.3, 3.6, 4.3
- Chapter 14 Substantive Tests of Cash Balances and the Revenue Cycle - 4.3-4.5
- Chapter 15 Understanding the Internal Control Structure, Assessing Control Risk, and Performing Substantive Tests: The Expenditure Cycle - 2.3, 3.7, 4.4
- Chapter 16 Understanding the Internal Control Structure and Assessing Control Risk: The Conversion Cycle - 2.3, 3.10, 3.11, 4.6, 4.7
- Chapter 17 Substantive Tests of the Conversion Cycle Balances and Transactions - 4.6, 4.7, 6.5, 6.6
- Chapter 18 Understanding the Internal Control Structure, Assessing Control Risk, and Performing Substantive Tests: The Financing and Investing Cycle - 2.3, Ch. 3, 6.5
- Chapter 19 Completing the Engagement - 3.12, 4.12-4.16

Part Five: Reporting Responsibilities
- Chapter 20 Reporting on Auditing Financial Statements - 1.4, Ch. 7
- Chapter 21 Other Reports - Ch. 8, 9.10
- Chapter 22 Compilation and Review Engagements - 8.4, 8.9

Part Six: Internal, Operational, and Governmental Audits
- Chapter 23 Compliance Auditing - 8.8, 8.9
- Chapter 24 Internal and Operational Auditing - 8.5, Ch. 9

Guy, Carmichael, and Whittington, *Audit Sampling: An Introduction*, Fourth Edition, John Wiley & Sons, Inc., 1998.

- Chapter 1 Overview of Audit Sampling - 6.1-6.3
- Chapter 2 Selecting a Representative Sample - 6.4
- Chapter 3 Attribute Sampling - 6.5
- Chapter 4 Using Variable Sampling for Accounting Estimation - 6.6
- Chapter 5 Using Variable Sampling for Audit Hypothesis Testing - 6.6
- Chapter 6 Probability Proportional to Size Sampling - 6.7
- Chapter 7 Nonstatistical Audit Sampling - Ch. 6

Hermanson, Strawser, and Strawser, *Auditing Theory and Practice*, Sixth Edition, Richard D. Irwin, 1993.

Part I: The Auditing Environment
- Chapter 1 The CPA and the Auditing Environment - 1.1-1.9
- Chapter 2 The Code of Professional Conduct - 1.5-1.8, 9.12
- Chapter 3 Auditors' Legal Liability - 1.9, 2.3, 2.4

Part II: The Audit Process
- Chapter 4 Audit Planning - Ch. 2
- Chapter 5 Internal Control Structure - 3.1-3.4
- Chapter 6 Evidence and Working Papers - 2.4, 2.5, 4.1, 4.2
- Chapter 7 Introduction to Sampling and Attribute Sampling - 6.1-6.5
- Chapter 8 Variables Estimation Sampling - 6.6
- Chapter 9 Computer Controls and Audit Techniques - Ch. 5

Part III: Audit Procedures
- Chapter 10 Cash - 3.6, 3.7, 4.3-4.5
- Chapter 11 Receivables - 3.6, 4.3
- Chapter 12 Inventories - 3.10, 4.6
- Chapter 13 Other Types of Assets - 3.9, 3.11, 4.7, 4.8
- Chapter 14 Liabilities - 3.7, 3.8, 4.9, 4.11
- Chapter 15 Stockholders' Equity, Operations, and Completing the Audit - 3.12, 4.10, 4.12-4.16

Part IV: Auditors' Communications
- Chapter 16 The Auditor's Report - 1.4, Ch. 7
- Chapter 17 Other Reporting Issues - Ch. 8, 9.10
- Chapter 18 Management Letters and Recent Developments in Auditing - 4.12

Part V: Other Types of Auditing
- Chapter 19 Compliance, Internal, and Operational Auditing - 8.5, 8.8, 8.9, Ch. 9

Kiger and Scheiner, *Auditing*, Second Edition, Houghton Mifflin Company, 1997.

- Chapter 1 Introduction to Auditing - 1.1-1.9
- Chapter 2 Professional Standards - 1.2-1.4
- Chapter 3 Reporting on Financial Statements - 1.4, Ch. 7, Ch. 8, 9.10
- Chapter 4 Auditors' Legal Responsibilities - 1.9, 2.3, 2.4
- Chapter 5 Professional Conduct - 1.5-1.8, 9.12
- Chapter 6 A Risk-Based Audit Approach - 2.3
- Chapter 7 Gathering and Evaluating Audit Evidence - 2.2-2.5, 3.4, 3.5, 3.14, Ch. 4, Ch. 6, 9.8
- Chapter 8 Assessing Control Risk - 2.3, 3.2
- Chapter 9 Managing an Engagement - 2.2, 2.3, 2.6, 9.11
- Chapter 10 Auditing in a Computer Environment - Ch. 5
- Chapter 11 Sales and Collections Cycle: Tests of Controls - 3.6
- Chapter 12 Audit Sampling for Tests of Controls - 3.5, 6.1-6.5
- Chapter 13 Substantive Tests of Sales, Accounts Receivable, and Cash Balances - 4.3, 4.5
- Chapter 14 Audit Sampling for Substantive Tests - 6.1-6.4, 6.6
- Chapter 15 Acquisitions and Payments Cycle - 3.7, 4.4, 4.5
- Chapter 16 The Payroll and Personnel and the Production and Warehousing Cycles - 3.8, 3.10, 3.11, 4.6-4.8, 4.11
- Chapter 17 The Investing and Financing Cycle - 3.9, 4.9, 4.10
- Chapter 18 Completing the Audit - 3.12, 4.12-4.16
- Chapter 19 Specialized Reporting - Ch. 8, 9.10
- Chapter 20 Operational, Compliance, Internal, and Governmental Auditing - 8.5, 8.8, 8.9, Ch. 9

Knechel, *Auditing*, First Edition, South-Western College Publishing, 1998.

Chapter 1 Accounting, Attestation and Auditing - 1.1, 1.6-1.13
Chapter 2 Overview of the Audit Process - 1.3-1.4, 2.3, Ch. 3, 4.1, 4.12, Ch. 7
Chapter 3 Client Acceptance and Preliminary Engagement Planning - 2.1-2.4, 3.2
Chapter 4 Understanding the Client's Business - 3.4
Chapter 5 Internal Control and Control Risk - Ch. 3
Chapter 6 Preliminary Analytical Procedures - 4.2
Chapter 7 Planning Audit Testing - 2.3, 4.1
Chapter 8 The Revenue Process: Audit of Sales, Receivables and Cash - 3.6, 4.3, 4.5
Chapter 9 The Resource Acquisition Process: Audit of Expenses, Disbursements, Assets and Liabilities - 3.7, 3.8, 3.11, 4.4, 4.7, 4.9, 4.11
Chapter 10 The Conversion, Financing, and Investing Processes: Audit of Inventory, Investments, Debt and Equity - 3.9-3.10, 4.6, 4.9-4.10
Chapter 11 Completing the Audit and Communicating Results - 1.4, 3.12, 4.12, Ch. 7
Chapter 12 Statistical Methods of Evidence Gathering Used in Auditing - Ch. 6
Chapter 13 Auditor Judgment and Professional Decision Making - 1.6-1.11
Chapter 14 Other Attestation Engagements - 1.13, Ch. 8

Konrath, *Auditing Concepts and Applications: A Risk-Analysis Approach*, Fourth Edition, South-Western Publishing Company, 1999.

Chapter 1 An Overview of Auditing - 1.1-1.3
Chapter 2 Professional Responsibility: Defining the Quality of Assurance Services - 1.5-1.8, 9.12
Chapter 3 Professional Responsibility: Maintaining the Quality of Assurance Services - 1.9, 2.3, 2.4
Chapter 4 Audit Evidence and Audit Programs - 2.2-2.5, 3.4, 3.5, 3.14, Ch. 4, Ch. 6, 9.8
Chapter 5 Materiality and Audit Risk - 2.3, 3.2
Chapter 6 Internal Control: Concepts - 3.1-3.4
Chapter 7 Internal Control: Assessment of Control Risk - 2.3, 3.2
Chapter 8 Internal Control and EDP - 5.1-5.13
Chapter 9 Statistical Sampling for Testing Control Procedures - 3.5, 6.1-6.5
Chapter 10 Statistical Sampling for Substantive Testing - 6.1-6.4, 6.6
Chapter 11 Substantive Audit Testing: Revenue Cycle - 3.6, 4.3, 4.5
Chapter 12 Substantive Audit Testing: Expenditure Cycle - 3.7, 4.4, 4.5
Chapter 13 Substantive Audit Testing: Financing and Investing Cycle and Completing the Audit Field Work - 3.9, 4.9, 4.10
Chapter 14 Audit Reports - 1.4, Ch. 7
Chapter 15 Other Assurance Services - 1.8, 1.11-1.13, Ch. 8, 9.10
Chapter 16 Operational and Governmental Compliance Auditing - 8.5, 8.8, 8.9, Ch. 9

Messier, *Auditing: A Systematic Approach*, First Edition, McGraw-Hill Book Company, 1996.

Part I: Introduction to Auditing and Financial Statement Audits
- Chapter 1 An Introduction to Auditing - 1.1
- Chapter 2 An Overview of Financial Statements - N/A

Part II: Basic Auditing Concepts: Materiality, Audit Risk, and Evidence
- Chapter 3 Materiality and Audit Risk - 2.3
- Chapter 4 Evidential Matter, Types of Audit Evidence, and Workpaper Documentation - 2.5, Ch. 4

Part III: Planning the Audit and Understanding Internal Control
- Chapter 5 Audit Planning and Types of Audit Tests - 2.2, 3.5, 4.2-4.16
- Chapter 6 Internal Control in a Financial Statement Audit - Ch. 3
- Chapter 7 The Effect of Computer Processing on the Audit Function - Ch. 5

Part IV: Statistical Tools for Auditing
- Chapter 8 Audit Sampling: An Overview and Application to Tests of Control - 3.5, 6.1-6.6
- Chapter 9 Audit Sampling: An Application to Substantive Tests of Account Balances - Ch. 6

Part V: Auditing Accounting Applications and Related Accounts
- Chapter 10 Auditing the Revenue Cycle - 3.6, 4.3
- Chapter 11 Auditing Accounts Receivable and Related Accounts - 3.6, 4.3
- Chapter 12 Auditing the Purchasing Cycle and Related Accounts - 3.7, 4.4
- Chapter 13 Auditing the Payroll Cycle and Related Accounts - 3.8, 4.11
- Chapter 14 Auditing the Inventory Cycle and Related Accounts - 3.10, 4.6
- Chapter 15 Auditing Selected Asset Accounts: Prepaid Expenses and Property, Plant and Equipment - 3.11, 4.7-4.8
- Chapter 16 Auditing Long-Term Liabilities, Stockholders' Equity, and Income Statement Accounts - 3.9, 4.9-4.10
- Chapter 17 Auditing Cash and Investments - 3.6-3.7, 4.5, 4.8

Part VI: Completing the Audit and Reporting Responsibilities
- Chapter 18 Completing the Engagement - 3.12, 4.12-4.16
- Chapter 19 Reports on Audited Financial Statements and Special Reporting Issues - Ch. 7, Ch. 8

Part VII: Professional Responsibilities and Other Forms of Services
- Chapter 20 The Code of Professional Conduct and Quality Control Standards - 1.5-1.8
- Chapter 21 Legal Liability - 1.9
- Chapter 22 Attestation Engagements and Other Accounting Services - 1.13

Pany and Whittington, *Auditing*, Second Edition, Richard D. Irwin, 1997.

Part 1: Professional Responsibilities
- Chapter 1 The Role of the Auditor in the American Economy - 1.1
- Chapter 2 Professional Standards - 1.2-1.4, 1.10, 2.4, 7.1, 7.2
- Chapter 3 Auditors' Reports - Ch. 7
- Chapter 4 Professional Ethics - 1.5-1.8, 1.11, 9.12
- Chapter 5 Legal Liability of Auditors - 1.9

Part 2: The Design of Audits
- Chapter 6 Audit Evidence and Documentation - 2.1-2.5, Ch. 4
- Chapter 7 Planning the Audit; Designing Audit Programs - 2.2-2.4, 4.17
- Chapter 8 Internal Control - 3.1-3.5, 3.12-3.14

Part 3: Technology and Sampling Approaches
- Chapter 9 Consideration of Internal Control In a Computer Environment - Ch. 5
- Chapter 10 Audit Sampling – Concepts and Techniques - 6.1-6.5, 6.8
- Chapter 11 Audit Sampling – Applications for Substantive Testing - 6.6-6.8

Part 4: Testing Cycle Controls and Performing Substantive Tests
- Chapter 12 Revenue Cycle – Obtaining an Understanding and Testing Controls - 3.6
- Chapter 13 Revenue Cycle – Substantive Tests - 4.3, 4.4
- Chapter 14 Auditing the Acquisition Cycle - 3.7, 4.4, 4.5
- Chapter 15 Auditing the Conversion and Payroll Cycles - 3.8, 3.10, 4.6, 4.11
- Chapter 16 Auditing the Financing Cycle - 4.9-4.10
- Chapter 17 Auditing the Investment Cycle - 3.9, 3.11, 4.7, 4.8
- Chapter 18 Auditing Operations and Completing the Audit - 3.12, 4.13, 4.15, 7.4

Part 5: Other Responsibilities
- Chapter 19 Other Attestation and Accounting Services - 1.13, 8.1-8.7
- Chapter 20 Internal, Operational, and Compliance Auditing - 8.5, 8.8, 8.9, Ch. 9

Ricchiute, *Auditing Assurances and Services*, Fifth Edition, South-Western Publishing Co., 1999.

Part 1: Responsibility
- Chapter 1 Introduction to Assurance Services - 1.1
- Chapter 2 Professional Standards - 1.2-1.4
- Chapter 3 Reports - 1.4, Ch. 7, Ch. 8, 9.10
- Chapter 4 Professional Ethics - 1.5-1.8, 9.12
- Chapter 5 Legal Liability - 1.9, 2.3, 2.4

Part 2: Technology
- Chapter 6 Evidence - Ch. 4, 9.8
- Chapter 7 Internal Control and Computer Information Services - 3.1-3.4, 5.1-5.13
- Chapter 8 Sampling in Tests of Controls - 3.5, 6.1-6.4
- Chapter 9 Sampling in Substantive Tests - 6.1-6.4

Part 3: Method
- Chapter 10 Tests of Controls in the Revenue/Receipt Cycle: Sales and Cash Receipts Transactions - 3.6, 6.5
- Chapter 11 Substantive Tests in the Revenue/Receipt Cycle: Sales, Receivables, Cash, and Management Discretion in Revenue Recognition - 4.3, 4.5
- Chapter 12 Tests of Controls of the Expenditure/Disbursement Cycle: Purchases and Cash Disbursements Transactions - 3.7, 6.5
- Chapter 13 Substantive Tests of the Expenditure/Disbursement Cycle: Payables, Prepaids, Accrued Liabilities, and Management Discretion in Accounting - 4.4, 4.5
- Chapter 14 Tests of Controls and Substantive Tests of Personnel and Payroll, and Management Discretion in Accounting for Postretirement Health Care - 3.8, 4.11, 6.5, 6.6
- Chapter 15 Tests of Controls and Substantive Tests of the Conversion Cycle: Inventory, Fixed Assets, and Management Discretion in Accounting for Impaired Assets - 3.10, 3.11, 4.6, 4.7, 6.5, 6.6
- Chapter 16 Tests of Controls and Substantive Tests of the Financing Cycle: Investments, Debt, Equity, and Management Discretion in Accounting for Financial Instruments - 3.9, 4.9, 4.10, 6.5, 6.6
- Chapter 17 Completing an Engagement - 3.12, 4.12-4.16, Ch. 7

Part 4: Assurance and Attestation Services, Compliance and Internal Auditing
- Chapter 18 Assurance and Attestation Services - 1.13, 8.9
- Chapter 19 Compliance Auditing and Internal Auditing - 8.5, 8.8, Ch. 9

Rittenberg and Schwieger, *Auditing: Concepts for a Changing Environment*, Second Edition, Dryden Press, 1997.

- Chapter 1 Introduction to the Auditing Profession - 1.1
- Chapter 2 Audit Services and Standards - 1.2-1.4
- Chapter 3 Professional Ethics: Maintaining Quality and Public Trust - 1.5-1.8, 9.12
- Chapter 4 Auditor Liability and Exposures - 1.9, 2.3, 2.4
- Chapter 5 Marketing Public Accounting Services - 1.5-1.8, 2.1
- Chapter 6 Understanding Audit Responsibilities and Planning - 1.4, 2.3, 3.2, 4.1
- Chapter 7 Obtaining Evidence to Minimize Audit Risk - 2.2-2.5, 3.4, 3.5, 3.14, Ch. 4, Ch. 6, 9.8
- Chapter 8 Assessing Control Risk: An Overview - 2.3, 3.2
- Chapter 9 Assessing Risk in Computerized Applications - 5.1-5.13
- Chapter 10 Computer-Assisted Auditing: Today's Environment for Efficient Auditing - 5.12
- Chapter 11 Assessing Control Risk: Revenue Cycle - 3.6
- Chapter 12 Introduction to Audit Sampling - 6.1-6.4
- Chapter 13 Substantive Testing in the Revenue Cycle - 4.3, 4.5
- Chapter 14 Sampling for Substantive Tests of Account Balances - 6.6, 6.7
- Chapter 15 Audits of Cash, Marketable Securities, and Other Instruments - 3.9, 4.8
- Chapter 16 Audit of Acquisition Cycle and Inventory - 3.7, 3.10, 4.4-4.6
- Chapter 17 Audit of Employee Compensation and Related Benefits - 3.8, 4.11
- Chapter 18 Audit of Other Assets and Long-Term Financing - 3.11, 4.7, 4.8
- Chapter 19 Audit of Financial Institutions - 3.9
- Chapter 20 Completing the Audit and Assessing Overall Risk and Materiality - 2.3, 3.12, 4.12-4.16
- Chapter 21 Audit Reports, Compilations, and Reviews - 1.4, Ch. 7, 8.1-8.4, 8.6, 8.7
- Chapter 22 Special-Purpose Reporting Situations: Expansion of the Attest Function - 8.9
- Chapter 23 Internal, Operational, Governmental, and Compliance Auditing - 8.5, 8.8, Ch. 9

Robertson, *Auditing*, Eighth Edition, Richard D. Irwin, 1996.

Part I: Introduction to Auditing and Public Practice
- Chapter 1 Professional Practice - 1.1
- Chapter 2 Attestation, Audit, and Quality Control Standards - 1.2-1.4, 1.10-1.13
- Chapter 3 Reports on Audited Financial Statements - 1.4, Ch. 7

Part II: Basic Concepts and Techniques of Auditing
- Chapter 4 Audit Objectives, Procedures, and Working Papers - Ch. 2, 3.4, 3.5, 3.14, Ch. 4, Ch. 6, 9.7
- Chapter 5 Audit Planning with Analytical Procedures, Risk, and Materiality - 1.4, 2.3, 3.2, 4.1
- Chapter 6 Internal Control Evaluation: Assessing Control Risk - 2.3, 3.1-3.4
- Chapter 7 Audit Sampling - 6.1-6.4
- Chapter 8 Fraud Awareness Auditing - 2.4, 9.4
- Chapter 9 Revenue and Collection Cycle - 3.6, 4.3

Part III: Audit Applications
- Chapter 10 Acquisition and Expenditure Cycle - 3.7, 4.4
- Chapter 11 Production and Payroll Cycle - 3.8, 3.10, 3.11, 4.6, 4.7, 4.11
- Chapter 12 Finance and Investment Cycle - 3.9, 4.9, 4.10
- Chapter 13 Completing the Audit - 3.12, 4.12-4.16

Part IV: Statistical Sampling and Computer Auditing
- Chapter 14 Test of Controls with Attribute Sampling - 3.5, 6.5
- Chapter 15 Test of Balances with Dollar-Value Sampling - 6.6, 6.7
- Chapter 16 Audit Planning in a Computer Environment - 5.1-5.13
- Chapter 17 Auditing in a Computer Environment - 5.1-5.13

Part V: Professional Services and Responsibilities
- Chapter 18 Other Public Accounting Services and Reports - 1.11, 1.12, Ch. 8, 9.10
- Chapter 19 Operational Auditing: Governmental and Internal Audits - 8.5, 8.8, Ch. 9
- Chapter 20 Professional Ethics - 1.5-1.8, 9.12
- Chapter 21 Legal Liability - 1.9, 2.3, 2.4

Sawyer and Dittenhofer, *Sawyer's Internal Auditing*, Fourth Edition, The Institute of Internal Auditors, Inc., 1996.

Part One: Introduction to Internal Auditing
- Chapter 1 The Nature of Internal Auditing - 9.1
- Chapter 2 Control - 9.5

Part Two: Techniques of Internal Auditing
- Chapter 3 Preliminary Surveys - 9.7
- Chapter 4 Audit Programs - 9.7
- Chapter 5 Field Work - 9.8
- Chapter 6 Audit Findings - 2.4
- Chapter 7 Working Papers - 2.5

Part Three: Scientific Methods
- Chapter 8 Risk Assessment - 2.3, 3.2
- Chapter 9 Sampling - Ch. 6
- Chapter 10 Analytical and Quantitative Methods - 9.8
- Chapter 11 Computer Auditing - 5.1
- Chapter 12 Using Computers in Auditing - 5.12

Part Four: Reporting
- Chapter 13 Reports - 8.5, 9.10
- Chapter 14 Audit Report Reviews and Replies - 3.12
- Chapter 15 Reports to Executive Management and the Board - 3.12

Part Five: Administration
- Chapter 16 Establishing the Auditing Organization - 9.7
- Chapter 17 Selecting and Developing the Staff - 9.7
- Chapter 18 Preparing Long-Range Schedules - 9.7
- Chapter 19 Controlling Audit Projects - 9.4, 9.7
- Chapter 20 Quality Assurance - 9.6, 9.7

Part Six: Other Matters Relating to Internal Auditing
- Chapter 21 Principles of Management - 9.7, 9.11
- Chapter 22 Employee and Management Fraud - 2.4
- Chapter 23 Dealing with People - 9.10
- Chapter 24 Relationships with External Auditors - 3.13
- Chapter 25 Relationships with Boards of Directors and Audit Committees - 9.10
- Chapter 26 Standards, Responsibilities, Code of Ethics - 9.2, 9.3

Taylor and Glezen, *Auditing: An Assertions Approach*, Seventh Edition, John Wiley & Sons, Inc., 1997.

Chapter 1 The Audit Function - 1.1-1.4
Chapter 2 The Public Accounting Profession and Auditing Standards - 1.1-1.4, 1.13
Chapter 3 The Auditor's Ethical Environment - 1.5-1.8, 9.12
Chapter 4 The Auditor's Legal Environment - 1.9, 2.3, 2.4
Chapter 5 The Auditor's Responsibility - Fraudulent Financial Reporting - 2.3, 2.4
Chapter 6 Audit Objectives and Audit Documentation - 1.1-1.4, Ch. 2
Chapter 7 Basic Auditing Concepts - 4.1
Chapter 8 Planning the Audit - 2.1, 2.2
Chapter 9 Internal Control - Obtaining an Understanding - 3.1-3.4
Chapter 10 Internal Control - Testing, Assessing Control Risk, and Designing Substantive Tests - 3.5, 6.1-6.5
Chapter 11 Obtaining an Understanding of Internal Control in a Computer Environment - 5.1-5.12
Chapter 12 Testing Controls and Gathering Evidence in a Computer Environment - 5.9, 5.10, 6.5
Chapter 13 Evidence of Financial Statement Assertions - 4.1, 4.12
Chapter 14 Sampling for Substantive Tests of Account Balances -- Nonstatistical and Statistical - 6.3, 6.6, 6.7
Chapter 15 Auditing the Working Capital Assertions -- Part I - 3.5-3.11, 4.2-4.11
Chapter 16 Auditing the Working Capital Assertions -- Part II - 3.5-3.11, 4.2-4.11
Chapter 17 Auditing the Capital Asset and Financing Base Assertions - 3.7, 3.11, 4.4, 4.7
Chapter 18 Auditing the Operations, Contingencies, and Subsequent Events Assertions - 4.13, 4.15
Chapter 19 The Standard Audit Report - 7.5, 7.8
Chapter 20 Modifications of the Standard Audit Report - 7.6, 7.7, 7.9-7.12
Chapter 21 Other Types of Reports - Ch. 8, 9.10
Chapter 22 Operational and Compliance Auditing - 8.5, Ch. 9

Thomas, Ward, and Henke, *Auditing: Theory and Practice*, Third Edition, South-Western Publishing Co., 1991.

Part One: The Audit: Its Nature and Environment
- Chapter 1 Conceptual Framework Underlying the Audit - 1.1
- Chapter 2 AICPA Auditing and Quality Control Standards - 1.2-1.4, 1.10
- Chapter 3 Professional Ethics - 1.5-1.8, 9.12
- Chapter 4 Accountants' Legal Liability - 1.9, 2.3, 2.4

Part Two: The Financial Statement Audit: Process and Principles
- Chapter 5 Evidence, Audit Risk, and Materiality - 1.4, 2.2-2.5, 3.2, 3.4, 3.5, 3.14, Ch. 4, Ch. 5, 9.7
- Chapter 6 Audit Objectives and Procedures - 2.4
- Chapter 7 Planning the Audit - 2.2
- Chapter 8 The Effects of the Control Structure on the Audit - 3.1-3.4
- Chapter 9 The Computer Environment and the Control Structure - 5.1-5.13

Part Three: Auditing Tools and Techniques
- Chapter 10 The Computer as an Auditing Tool - 5.11
- Chapter 11 Sampling Techniques and Internal Control Evaluation - 3.5, 6.1-6.5
- Chapter 12 Sampling Techniques and Substantive Tests of Details - 6.1-6.4, 6.6

Part Four: The Application of Audit Theory in Practice
- Chapter 13 The Revenue and Collections System - 3.6, 4.3
- Chapter 14 The Acquisitions and Expenditures System - 3.7, 4.4
- Chapter 15 The Audit of Selected Accounts in the Acquisitions and Expenditures System - 3.7, 4.4
- Chapter 16 The Payroll System and Related Accounts - 3.8, 4.11
- Chapter 17 The Production and Conversion System - 3.10, 3.11, 4.6, 4.7
- Chapter 18 The Financing and Investing System - 3.9, 4.9, 4.10
- Chapter 19 The Audit of Cash - 3.6, 3.7, 4.3-4.5
- Chapter 20 Completing the Audit - 3.12, 4.12-4.16

Part Five: Reports and Other Services
- Chapter 21 The Audit Report - 1.4, Ch. 7
- Chapter 22 Other Types of Reports - Ch. 8, 9.10
- Chapter 23 Nonaudit Services and Reports - 1.11-1.13, 8.4, 8.6, 8.7
- Chapter 24 Internal, Operational, and Governmental Auditing - 8.5, 8.8, 8.9, Ch. 9

Wallace, *Auditing*, Third Edition, South-Western Publishing Company, 1995.

Part One: The Meaning of Auditing within Its Environment
- Chapter 1 What is Auditing? - 1.1-1.4, 9.1
- Chapter 2 The Auditor's Report -- The "Product" - 1.4, Ch. 7, Ch. 8, 9.10
- Chapter 3 Structure and Standards of the Auditing Profession - 1.2-1.4
- Chapter 4 The Code of Professional Conduct - 1.5-1.8, 9.12
- Chapter 5 The Auditor and Litigation - 1.9, 2.3, 2.4

Part Two: Components of the Audit Process
- Chapter 6 Engagement Planning - 2.1-2.4
- Chapter 7 Audit Evidence, Procedures, and Working Papers - Ch. 2, 3.4, 3.5, 3.14, Ch. 4, Ch. 6, 9.9
- Chapter 8 Materiality, Audit Risk, and Development of the Audit Program - 1.4, 2.2, 2.3

Part Three: Tools for Assessing Inherent Control and Detection Risk
- Chapter 9 Internal Control Structure - 3.1-3.4
- Chapter 10 Auditing in a Computer Environment - 5.1-5.13
- Chapter 11 Sampling Concepts and Attributes Testing - 6.1-6.5
- Chapter 12 Variables Sampling and Regression Analysis - 6.6

Part Four: Audit Applications to Operating, Financing, and Investment Activities
- Chapter 13 Cycle Chapters: The Revenue Cycle - 3.6, 4.3
- Chapter 14 The Cost of Sales or Production Cycle - 3.7, 3.10, 3.11, 4.4, 4.6, 4.7
- Chapter 15 The Finance and Administrative Cycle - 3.8, 3.9, 4.9, 4.10

Part Five: Special Audit Risk Considerations and Other Attestation Services
- Chapter 16 Special Concerns Posing Audit Risk - 2.3
- Chapter 17 Other Types of Engagements - 1.11-1.13, Ch. 8

Appendix A: A Brief Topical Outline of Official Statements on Standards

Whittington and Pany, *Principles of Auditing*, Twelfth Edition, Richard D. Irwin, 1997.

- Chapter 1 The Role of the Auditor in the American Economy - 1.1
- Chapter 2 Professional Standards - 1.2-1.4
- Chapter 3 Professional Ethics - 1.5-1.8, 9.12
- Chapter 4 Legal Liability of Auditors - 1.9, 2.3, 2.4
- Chapter 5 Audit Evidence - 4.1
- Chapter 6 Planning the Audit; Designing Audit Programs - 2.1-2.4
- Chapter 7 Internal Control - 3.1-3.4
- Chapter 8 Consideration of Internal Control in a Computer Environment - 5.1-5.13
- Chapter 9 Audit Sampling - Ch. 6
- Chapter 10 Audit Working Papers: Examination of the General Records - 2.5
- Chapter 11 Cash and Marketable Securities - 3.6, 3.7, 3.9, 4.3-4.5, 4.8
- Chapter 12 Accounts Receivable, Notes Receivable, and Sales Transactions - 3.6, 4.3
- Chapter 13 Inventories and Cost of Goods Sold - 3.10, 4.6
- Chapter 14 Property, Plant, and Equipment: Depreciation and Depletion - 3.11, 4.7
- Chapter 15 Accounts Payable and Other Liabilities - 3.7, 4.4
- Chapter 16 Debt and Equity Capital; Loss Contingencies - 4.9, 4.10, 4.13
- Chapter 17 Auditing Operations and Completing the Audit - 3.12, 4.12-4.16
- Chapter 18 Auditors' Reports - 1.4, Ch. 7, Ch. 8, 9.10
- Chapter 19 Other Attestation and Accounting Services - 1.11-1.13, 8.1-8.4, 8.6, 8.7
- Chapter 20 Internal, Operational, and Compliance Auditing - 8.5, 8.8, 8.9, Ch. 9

APPENDIX B
AUDITING & SYSTEMS CPE

Courses Available	Average Comp. Time	CPE Credit
1. Audit Standards, Ethics, Planning, and Risk	700 min.	14 hours
2. Internal Control	600 min.	12 hours
3. Audit Evidence and Procedures	800 min.	16 hours
4. Information Systems	900 min.	18 hours
5. Statistical Sampling	400 min.	8 hours
6. Audit Reports	600 min.	12 hours
7. Special Reports and Other Reporting Issues	400 min.	8 hours
8. Internal Auditing	500 min.	10 hours
	Total CPE Credit	98 hours

---

1. Registration: The cost of this Auditing & Systems CPE program is $125.

   A. If you have made your payment, then you are pre-registered and in addition to this book you have one machine-readable answer sheet that you can use to submit up to eight Auditing & Systems CPE courses at one time. Should you decide to take fewer than eight courses, you will need to purchase an additional answer sheet for $25 in order to submit additional courses.

   B. If you are not pre-registered as described in A. above, you can register to participate by photocopying and completing the form below and mailing it, along with a $110 remittance, to:

      Gleim Publications, Inc.
      CPE Division
      P.O. Box 12848, University Station
      Gainesville, FL 32604

      1) If you are using a credit card, you can fax us at (352) 375-6940.

      2) Gleim Publications will process your registration and send you one machine-readable answer sheet that you can use to submit up to eight Auditing & Systems CPE courses at one time. Should you decide to take fewer than eight courses, you will need to purchase an additional answer sheet for $25 in order to submit additional courses.

Gleim's Auditing & Systems CPE Registration Form

Name of Participant ______________________________

Social Security No. (for recordkeeping purposes) ______________

Mailing Address ______________________________

____

City ______________ State ________ ZIP __________

Daytime Telephone ____________ E-mail Address ______________

Remit $25 registration fee by check, money order, or VISA/MC/AMEX/DISC.

Credit Card No. ______-______-______-______ Exp. Date ___/___

Signature ______________________________

2. Follow the specific instructions on the next four pages that describe exactly what must be done to earn CPE credit for each of the eight courses.

PROCEDURES TO OBTAIN CPE CREDIT

Follow the instructions presented at the opening of **each** course you have chosen. Also, read these introductory pages carefully. In general, the procedure listed below is recommended.

1. Comply with the registration requirement described on page 623.
2. Work through each multiple-choice question in the pertinent modules of *Auditing & Systems Exam Questions and Explanations*, 8th edition. Do not skip questions.
   a. Study the adjacent answer explanations for the questions you answered incorrectly or had difficulty answering.
   b. Make study notes in the margins as you work through the questions and explanations.
3. When you complete the assigned material, turn to the appropriate course in this CPE section and take the open-book final exam.
   a. The best procedure is to answer the questions in the order they appear.
   b. If you are unsure of some answers, consult the questions and answer explanations in *Auditing & Systems Exam Questions and Explanations*, 8th Edition.
   c. Circle your answer for each CPE question. Wait until you have answered all of the questions for a course before **carefully transferring** your answers to our machine-readable answer sheet.
      1) Do not make a mistake in this transfer (i.e., skip a line, start on the wrong line, etc.). Read the instructions in the next section and at the beginning of each course, and follow them carefully.
4. When you are ready to submit completed courses in this program, mail the machine-readable answer sheet in the special pre-addressed protective envelope accompanying your answer sheet to Gleim Publications, Inc., CPE Division, P.O. Box 12848, University Station, Gainesville, FL 32604. You may take one or more courses at a time using the answer sheet provided when you purchased this program. **Additional answer sheets are available for $25 and may be used for additional courses not submitted on the single answer sheet provided with the purchase of this program.**
   a. Please complete the course evaluation sheet and send it with your answer sheet.
   b. **Same day grading service** available Monday through Friday: Send your materials and $50 prepayment ($100 if out of the U.S.) (check, VISA/MC/AMEX/DISC) via Federal Express (priority, so we receive it by noon) or UPS Next Day Letter Service to 4201 N.W. 95th Blvd., Gainesville, FL 32606. We will hand-grade your answer sheet and arrange to have the results in your hands by the following afternoon. Add $10 if you request Saturday delivery.

MACHINE-READABLE ANSWER SHEET

We have contracted with the Office of Instructional Resources at the University of Florida to read your answer sheet with optical scanning equipment that will record your responses. Computerization of the grading and grade analysis means that you must fill out the answer sheet carefully and correctly.

1. Fill out all of the required information on page 2 of the answer sheet completely. You must write in the required information **AND** darken appropriate circles. Note that the answer sheet is four pages long. On page 2, fill in the following data:

   a. Last name, first initial, middle initial. If your last name is over 15 characters long, use only the first 15 characters.

   b. Sex, so we can computer-generate a Mr. or Ms. in our correspondence

   c. Social Security number

   d. Course number(s)--**THIS IS VERY IMPORTANT**. Note the four-digit code in the following table for each Auditing & Systems CPE course you will be asking us to grade on this answer sheet. "B" means leave that circle blank.

	Course	Code
1.	Audit Standards, Ethics, Planning, and Risk	B 0 B 1
2.	Internal Control	B 0 B 2
3.	Audit Evidence and Procedures	B 0 B 3
4.	Information Systems	B 0 B 4
5.	Statistical Sampling	B 0 B 5
6.	Audit Reports	B 0 B 6
7.	Special Reports and Other Reporting Issues	B 0 B 7
8.	Internal Auditing	B 0 B 8
	All Eight Courses	B 0 B 1, 2, 3, 4, 5, 6, 7, 8

   NOTE: If you wish to take all eight courses, fill in 1, 2, 3, 4, 5, 6, 7, and 8 in the fourth column.

   e. Total CPE credit hours for which you are applying on this answer sheet.

      1) You may ignore this. Your Certificate of Completion will automatically reflect the proper amount of credit (see page 627).

2. **Sign and date** the self-certification statement on page 1 of the machine-readable answer sheet.

• Self-certification: I confirm that I have studied all of the required material and answered all the required questions for the course(s) for which I am seeking CPE credit. I also have studied the answer explanations to questions I answered wrong or had difficulty understanding.

_______________________ Signature _______________ Date

3. If your answer sheet is not completed properly, it will be returned to you for correction.
4. Again, a single answer sheet may be used to take as many courses in a program as you wish, but it may be submitted only once. CPE participants may **NOT** mix courses from different programs on the same answer sheet. If you decide to submit this answer sheet for grading of only one or a few courses, but you would like to take more Auditing & Systems CPE courses in the future, simply enclose $25 with the answer sheet you submit for grading, and we will send you another blank answer sheet separately from the results of your CPE tests.

GRADING YOUR CPE EXAM FOR CPE CREDIT

After we receive the results from the machine grading,

1. We will send you a Certificate of Completion if you achieve at least a 70% score.
   a. For every question you answered incorrectly, we will send a synopsis of the concept tested.
   b. When you receive your results, take the time to read through these synopses to be sure you have no miscomprehension of basic concepts or principles.
2. If you do not get a score of at least 70%, we will return your answer sheet and a list of the question numbers incorrectly answered. A $25 regrading fee is payable upon resubmission of the corrected answer sheet. You cannot obtain credit until you obtain at least a 70% success rate.

RECORD RETENTION AND DUPLICATE CERTIFICATES

Gleim Publications, Inc. will retain your answer sheet(s) and a record of your course completions for 5 years. You must notify us **within 60 days** if you have not received your Certificate of Completion. After 60 days, we will charge $25 to send you a duplicate certificate.

You should retain your Certificate of Completion to document completion of your CPE course(s). You should also retain your *Auditing & Systems Exam Questions and Explanations* book containing this CPE section, which has your completed answers and notes.

ADDITIONAL INFORMATION ABOUT THIS CPE PROGRAM

Prerequisites and Advance Preparation -- A participant must have an undergraduate major in business or an equivalent.

Program Objectives -- Upon completion of this program, the participant will have at least an entry-level knowledge of the basic principles in each area studied as well as familiarity with current pronouncements and auditing philosophies.

Change of Address -- Please notify us of any changes in your shipping and/or mailing addresses by writing to

Gleim Publications, Inc.
CPE Division
P.O. Box 12848, University Station
Gainesville, FL 32604

Time Limit on Completion of This CPE Program -- You have at least 1 year from the date of purchase to complete the courses in this CPE program. We will notify you at your permanent address (see the discussion on the previous page) when the program goes out of date and/or is superseded by a replacement program. You will have 30 days after our mailing to submit your final answer sheet. Thus, while we will allow you to use this CPE program until, in our opinion, it is no longer current, you should plan on completing the courses you desire within 1 year. Our intent is to serve you better than the competition; i.e., if a CPE program is not out of date in 1 year, why cancel it? We are committed, however, to provide up-to-date CPE programs, a commitment which requires us to retire out-of-date courses as we develop new (current) editions.

Limit on Amount of Correspondence Course CPE Credit -- We are concerned that some individuals may misuse our program (as is probably the case for all CPE programs). While we have not instituted limits on the maximum number of hours available through this CPE program, we ask that you do not misuse our programs. In addition, some state boards of accountancy have placed limits on the number of hours of CPE credit that may be fulfilled through individual study or correspondence courses.

Additionally, our Certificate of Completion lists maximum credit for both formal self-study measurement principles: average completion time and one-half average completion time. Thus, if your time spent on any course is less than the "recommended maximum hours of CPE credit," we suggest that you **report your actual hours consistent with the rules and procedures of the agency or organization to which you are reporting.**

Our approach permits you to take simple courses or courses already familiar to you for review purposes "just to make sure." When you use less than the average time, you can so indicate. We have explained our approach to the various agencies/organizations requiring CPE.

FORMAL SELF-STUDY CPE PROGRAM CREDIT MEASUREMENT

The AICPA standard for measuring CPE credit for formal, noninteractive self-study CPE programs states that CPE credit should equal one-half of the average completion time, as determined by the program developer through pretesting. For example, a course that takes an average of 800 minutes to complete is recommended for 8 contact hours of CPE credit. The recommended credit we indicate is based on this AICPA standard.

Note, however, that about a third of CPE jurisdictions that require reporting of CPE credit will allow "full credit" for our programs; i.e., a course that takes an average of 800 minutes to complete is recommended for 16 contact hours of CPE credit. Thus, our Certificate of Completion lists both measures of credit, i.e., **average completion time** and **one-half average completion time**. We encourage you to verify the measurement standard (as it relates to Gleim's self-study courses) with your reporting jurisdiction(s) so you can properly report your credit.

Call us for assistance: **(800) 87-GLEIM.**

COURSE 1
AUDIT STANDARDS, ETHICS, PLANNING, AND RISK

This introductory course is most appropriate for an accountant/auditor who has either been away from the auditing profession for some time or has no prior experience in auditing. It contains 331 questions, of which 70 constitute the final examination. As continuing professional education, 7 hours of CPE credit are recommended based on one-half the average completion time. If any of the CPE agencies you report to measures self-study CPE in terms of average completion time (rather than one-half average completion time), your certificate of completion will indicate 14 hours of maximum recommended CPE credit. Additional discussion regarding self-study credit measurement is provided in the introduction.

Date Completed	Time (Minutes)
______	______

1. Work through each question in Chapters 1 and 2 (pages 25 through 115) in *Auditing & Systems Exam Questions and Explanations*, 8th Edition.
   a. Cover the answer explanations, which appear to the right of each question, with a piece of paper. Do not skip questions.
   b. Answer each question: circle your answer or write "T" or "F" next to the alternative answer choices.
   c. Lift the cover sheet and compare your choice with the correct answer in the first line of the answer explanation.
   d. Study the answer explanation.

______ ______

2. Take the final exam by answering questions 1 through 70 on the following pages.
3. Carefully transfer your answers for these 70 questions to the CPE final exam answer sheet. Be sure you use the circles numbered 1 through 70.
4. Mark **B 0 B 1** (B means Blank) as the course number on page 2 of the answer sheet. See example at right.
5. Refer to the INTRODUCTION chapter in this book for instructions on how to complete the remainder of the machine-readable answer sheet.
6. Please complete the accompanying course evaluation and submit it with your answer sheet.

COURSE NUMBER(S)			
	0		1
0	●	0	0
1	1	1	●
2	2	2	2
3	3	3	3
4	4	4	4
5	5	5	5
6	6	6	6
7	7	7	7
8	8	8	8
9	9	9	9

Total Time ______ (Carry this amount to your CPE course evaluation form.)

1. The primary objective of an independent, external audit of financial statements is to

A. Detect and report fraud.

B. Provide an independent assessment of management's performance.

C. Express an opinion on the financial statements taken as a whole.

D. Express an opinion on management's assertion about internal control.

2. The Boards of Accountancy primarily

A. Issue auditing standards.

B. Issue accounting pronouncements.

C. Issue licenses of CPAs.

D. Prepare and grade professional examinations.

3. The Auditing Standards Board is the senior technical committee of the AICPA authorized to issue pronouncements in connection with

A. Unaudited financial statements of a nonpublic entity.

B. Government auditing standards.

C. Attest services.

D. Consulting services.

4. State CPA societies

A. Provide continuing education programs.

B. Issue interpretations of auditing pronouncements.

C. May suspend or revoke licenses to practice.

D. Conduct professional examinations.

5. Which of the following statements best describes an attribute of Statements on Auditing Standards (SASs)?

A. They reflect the consensus among independent auditors.

B. They are considered standards of the profession by state boards of accountancy and the courts.

C. They interpret the 10 generally accepted auditing standards (GAAS) but do not have the status of GAAS.

D. They are specific audit objectives generally accepted for audit engagements.

6. Requirements in GAAS for the use of due professional care are stated in the

A. General standards.

B. Field work standards.

C. Reporting standards.

D. Compliance standards.

7. Normal functions in the performance of audit services would include all the following except

A. Guaranteeing the outcome.

B. Conducting additional research.

C. Consulting with others.

D. Supervising assistants.

8. An external auditor of financial statements should be

	Objective	Independent in Appearance
A.	Yes	Yes
B.	Yes	No
C.	No	Yes
D.	No	No

9. A CPA who lacks independence with respect to an audit of financial statements should

A. Express a qualified opinion.

B. Downgrade the engagement to another form of attest service.

C. Express the appropriate opinion if (s)he is objective.

D. State specifically that (s)he is not independent.

10. GAAS for reporting require the report to state whether the financial statements are presented in accordance with GAAP. Which of the following conclusions can be drawn based on this requirement?

A. The principles selected and applied have general acceptance and are the most conservative in the circumstances.

B. The principles used are appropriate in the specific circumstances.

C. The auditor's report will present a statement of fact that the statements comply with GAAP.

D. The audit was performed in accordance with GAAS.

11. According to AU 230, the performance of audit work with due care requires that each person in the auditor's organization observe the

A. Reporting and general standards only.

B. Field work and reporting standards only.

C. Field work standards only.

D. General standards only.

12. The AICPA Code of Professional Conduct contains two sections, rules that govern the performance of professional services and

A. A list of acts discreditable to the profession.

B. AICPA bylaws that describe administration of the profession.

C. Ethics rulings that interpret the rules.

D. Principles that are goal-oriented and nonbinding.

13. Which Rule is included in the Code of Professional Conduct?

A. *Encroachment.*

B. *Offers of Employment.*

C. *Form of Organization and Name.*

D. *Responsibilities to Colleagues.*

14. A source of information concerning a specific CPA firm may be found in

A. Information available from the Division for CPA Firms on the firm's enrollment in a practice-monitoring program.

B. Proceedings of the Professional Ethics Division regarding complaints currently being investigated.

C. The reports by the National Commission on Fraudulent Financial Reporting.

D. The Anderson Committee report.

15. A CPA's financial interest in a client does not impair his/her independence if the interest

A. Consists of a dependent's ownership of stock in the client at the time of the engagement.

B. Is a material indirect interest at the time of the engagement.

C. Is direct and is disposed of during the engagement.

D. Existed during the period covered by the financial statements but was disposed of before commencement of the engagement.

16. The independence of a member of the AICPA is least likely to be impaired if (s)he

A. Is designated a trustee of a trust that had a material indirect financial interest in a client.

B. Purchases stock of a client and places it in trust for his/her dependent child.

C. Holds a direct investment in a nonclient that has a material investment in a client.

D. Holds a material indirect investment in a non-client that has a material investment in a client.

17. The independence of a CPA is most likely impaired if

A. A client's note receivable arising from fees charged for the prior year's audit is unpaid when the current year's report is issued.

B. The client is a financial institution with which the CPA has a fully insured depository relationship.

C. The CPA is designated as the executor of an estate having a material indirect financial interest in the client.

D. The CPA provides actuarial services for the client.

18. Which statement is most likely true concerning the independence of CPAs?

A. Independence is not impaired if the CPA accepts more than a token gift from a client.

B. Independence is impaired if a CPA joins a client trade association even if the CPA does not participate in management.

C. A CPA's independence is not impaired if (s)he merely reviews business processes for operational efficiency and effectiveness.

D. Service as a client's general counsel does not constitute acting in a management capacity.

19. According to the AICPA, the independence of a member is most likely to be impaired if

A. The member is the auditor of a credit union to which (s)he belongs.

B. A client's management has expressed an intent to begin litigation against the member for deficient audit work although such litigation is not probable.

C. The member maintains client accounting records in computer format.

D. The member holds a small amount of the debt issued by a client municipality.

20. A CPA is the auditor of a financial institution's financial statements. Which new loan made under normal leading procedures, terms, and requirements and kept current at all times as to all terms may the CPA obtain from the client without impairment of independence?

A. An automobile lease not collateralized by the automobile.

B. A credit card balance of $4,000.

C. A home mortgage.

D. Any secured loan.

21. A CPA may be a director of a not-for-profit organization, which is also an audit client, if certain conditions are met. Which of the following is a condition that must be met for the CPA to be independent?

A. The CPA's name is not included on the organization's letterhead.

B. The directorship is not disclosed.

C. The CPA does not vote or participate in management functions.

D. The CPA does not take part in the audit.

22. When a CPA enters into a lease with a client, independence is least likely to be impaired with respect to that client if

A. The lease meets all the criteria of a capital lease, and the client is the lessor.

B. The lease meets all the criteria of an operating lease, and the client is the lessee.

C. The lease meets all the criteria of a capital lease, and the terms are not comparable to those of similar leases.

D. The lease meets all the criteria of an operating lease, and the terms are not comparable to those of similar leases.

23. A CPA violates the AICPA Code of Professional Conduct Rule 102, *Integrity and Objectivity*, if (s)he

A. Maintains an insured account at a client bank.

B. Has an immaterial interest in a mutual fund that owns some stock in a client.

C. Knowingly misrepresents facts.

D. Recommends in good faith a tax return position that is unlikely to be sustained.

24. Which of the following is most likely to be considered confidential client information and should not be disclosed under the AICPA Code of Professional Conduct?

A. Information not required to be disclosed in financial statements.

B. Information requested by a federal court by subpoena.

C. Information about an audit client requested in an AICPA-authorized peer review.

D. Comment in an audit report that the client failed to provide adequate disclosure.

25. A CPA has completed an engagement for which fees have not been paid. If the client demands specified information, which of the following actions by the CPA is most likely to be a violation of the Code of Professional Conduct?

A. Retaining working papers consisting of schedules prepared by the client at the CPA's request.

B. Retaining working papers prepared in lieu of a general ledger.

C. Retaining information consisting of adjusting and closing entries prepared by the CPA.

D. Retaining working papers containing client financial information not reflected in the client's books.

26. Under certain circumstances a CPA can accept a contingent fee for a(n)

	Review	Compilation	Audit
A.	Yes	No	Yes
B.	No	No	No
C.	No	Yes	No
D.	Yes	Yes	No

27. The advertising activity by an AICPA member considered improper is

A. Comparative advertising.

B. Publishing self-laudatory statements.

C. Offering free advice for certain issues or problems.

D. A claim to be endorsed by the AICPA.

28. Under Conduct Rule 503, *Commissions and Referral Fees*, a CPA may

A. Receive but not pay a referral fee.

B. Pay but not receive a referral fee.

C. Receive a referral fee if it is disclosed to the client.

D. Pay a referral fee whether or not it is disclosed to the client.

29. Under Conduct Rule 503, *Commissions and Referral Fees*, a CPA may receive a disclosed commission if the CPA performs for the client

A. A review of a financial statement.

B. An examination of a financial statement.

C. A compilation of a financial statement if the report mentions lack of independence.

D. An examination of prospective financial information.

30. A member of the AICPA may practice public accounting only in a form of organization

A. Permitted under federal law.

B. Wholly owned by CPAs.

C. In which any non-CPA owners are passive investors.

D. In which any non-CPA owners are responsible for completing work-related CPE requirements.

31. If a member of the AICPA permits the publisher of a tax booklet to attribute it to him/her, the CPA

A. Has committed an act discreditable.

B. Has violated Conduct Rule 502, Advertising and Other Forms of Solicitation.

C. Has not violated the Code of Professional Conduct if (s)he has no reason to believe that the attributed information is incorrect.

D. Has not violated the Code of Professional Conduct if (s)he has a reasonable basis for believing that the attributed information is not false, misleading, or deceptive.

32. Which action by a member is considered a violation of the AICPA Code of Professional Conduct?

A. A member who is a defendant in a sexual harassment suit has lost a final appeal of an adverse verdict.

B. A member forms a partnership for the practice of public accounting with non-CPAs.

C. A member who is also a licensed attorney simultaneously practices both professions. The member does not use separate letterheads.

D. A member solicits clients by direct telephone contact.

33. A registration statement omitted a material fact for which the auditors were responsible. They are now defendants in a suit brought under the Securities Act of 1933 by a purchaser of the securities covered by the registration statement. The plaintiff is able to prove a loss occurred in a transaction involving the securities. To prevail, the

A. Auditors must prove due diligence.

B. Plaintiff must prove negligence.

C. Plaintiff must prove privity.

D. Plaintiff must prove reliance.

34. Which of the following would not be contained in an audit engagement letter?

A. A management representation letter.

B. The nature and the scope of the services to be rendered by the auditor.

C. Responsibilities of management.

D. Amount of fees to be charged by the auditor.

35. Elements of quality control for a CPA firm include

	Acceptance and Continuance of Clients and Engagements	Internal Control	Independence, Integrity, and Objectivity
A.	Yes	No	Yes
B.	Yes	Yes	No
C.	No	No	Yes
D.	Yes	No	No

36. Statements on Quality Control Standards require firms to adopt policies and procedures to provide reasonable assurance that the firm will comply with applicable professional standards for which services?

	Audits	Reviews	Tax Services
A.	Yes	No	No
B.	Yes	Yes	No
C.	Yes	Yes	Yes
D.	No	Yes	Yes

37. A CPA firm adopted quality control policies and procedures related to monitoring. The primary objective of these policies and procedures is to provide assurance that

A. All staff members are properly trained for the duties assigned.

B. New audit clients are evaluated as to integrity prior to acceptance.

C. Working papers are sufficient to support audit reports rendered.

D. Other elements of quality control are being effectively applied.

38. A condition of AICPA membership is

A. Membership in the PCPS.

B. Membership in the Division for CPA Firms.

C. Membership in the SEC Practice Section.

D. Participation in an approved peer review program.

39. A CPA firm has one SEC client. According to the AICPA, membership in which of the following is required?

	SEC Practice Section	PCPS
A.	Yes	Yes
B.	Yes	No
C.	No	Yes
D.	No	No

40. If a member of the AICPA prepares a tax return for another person but does not receive compensation,

A. Treasury Regulations require that (s)he sign the return.

B. The Internal Revenue Code requires that (s)he sign the return.

C. The Code of Professional Conduct requires that (s)he sign the return.

D. (S)he is not required to sign the return.

41. A CPA has prepared a client's federal income tax returns for several years. When the CPA discovers a material error in a previously filed return, (s)he should

	Inform IRS	Inform Client
A.	Yes	No
B.	No	Yes
C.	No	No
D.	Yes	Yes

42. When preparing a federal income tax return, a CPA

A. May rely on oral information provided by the client.

B. Is obligated to examine or verify supporting data.

C. Should perform certain limited procedures on the supporting data.

D. Must document supporting data obtained from the client.

43. According to a Statement on Responsibilities in Tax Practice, which of the following is a basis for a good faith belief that a tax return position is likely to be sustained?

A. An IRS General Counsel Memorandum.

B. Usefulness as a bargaining point in negotiations with the IRS.

C. A low probability of an IRS audit.

D. Full disclosure even if the position is frivolous.

44. Consulting services include all of the following except

A. Tax preparation and planning services.

B. Transaction services.

C. Staff and support services.

D. Implementation services.

45. Which of the following general standards identified in Conduct Rule 201 apply to consulting services?

	Professional Competence	Sufficient Relevant Data	Independence
A.	Yes	Yes	Yes
B.	Yes	Yes	No
C.	No	No	Yes
D.	No	No	No

46. A major difference between GAAS and the attestation standards is that GAAS require

A. Independence; the attestation standards do not.

B. Adequate planning of the work and proper supervision of assistants; the attestation standards do not.

C. Collection of sufficient competent evidence; the attestation standards do not.

D. Consideration of GAAP; the attestation standards do not.

47. Management's Discussion and Analysis (MD&A) is presented in the client's annual report. In accordance with the attestation standards, a practitioner may

A. Review the MD&A provided the review report is to be filed with the SEC.

B. Treat the MD&A as a written assertion to which (s)he may attest.

C. Examine or review an MD&A only if it has been prepared pursuant to FASB pronouncements.

D. Not perform attest services regarding the MD&A of a nonpublic entity.

48. Assurance services do not

A. Evolve naturally from attestation services.

B. Improve the quality of information.

C. Encompass consulting services.

D. Apply to engagements in which one party wants to monitor another.

49. The AICPA has developed business plans for certain assurance services, including

A. Health care delivery and risk assessment.

B. Information systems design and financial forecasting.

C. Reporting on SEC engagements and performing operational audits.

D. Performance measurement and reporting on management's discussion and analysis.

50. According to the AICPA, the CPA WebTrust seal indicates that the CPA has audited the client organization and its Web site in the area(s) of

	Disclosure of of Business Practices	Protection of Customer Information	Fair Presentation of Financial Statements
A.	Yes	Yes	Yes
B.	Yes	Yes	No
C.	No	Yes	Yes
D.	No	No	Yes

51. A successor auditor is most likely to inquire of the predecessor auditor about

A. Issues bearing on management's integrity.

B. The profitability of the client.

C. The sufficiency of evidence to collect.

D. Appropriate timing of substantive tests.

52. The first standard of field work requires adequate planning and proper supervision. This standard is most closely related to the requirement for

A. Proper education and experience in auditing.

B. A written audit program.

C. An attitude of judicial impartiality.

D. Maintaining independence in mental attitude.

53. An audit program is the basic tool used by the auditor in controlling the audit work. It

A. Records the hours of staff time and expenses incurred for particular engagements.

B. Constitutes the agreement between the auditor and client concerning the nature and scope of the audit.

C. Primarily serves to set forth specific audit objectives.

D. Sets forth audit procedures in reasonable detail.

54. In planning the audit engagement, the auditor should

A. Obtain a written representation letter from client management.

B. Explicitly quantify audit risk.

C. Consider the conditions likely to require extension or modification of audit tests.

D. Consider the kind of opinion (unqualified, qualified, or adverse) that will likely be expressed.

55. Most of the independent auditor's work consists of

A. Obtaining and examining underlying accounting data and corroborating information.

B. Planning the engagement and writing the audit program.

C. Searching for fraud.

D. Gathering information for management control purposes.

56. Audit risk is the risk that the auditor may unknowingly fail to appropriately modify the opinion on financial statements that are materially misstated. The audit risk formula explicitly includes

	Inherent Risk	Sampling Risk	Control Risk
A.	Yes	No	Yes
B.	Yes	No	No
C.	No	Yes	Yes
D.	Yes	Yes	Yes

57. Inherent risk is

A. Affected by the choice of audit procedures.

B. The risk that the auditor will not detect a material misstatement.

C. The susceptibility of an assertion to material misstatement in the absence of an internal control structure.

D. The risk that the auditor may modify the opinion when the financial statements are not materially misstated.

58. The detection risk for a substantive test of details encompasses which, if any, of the following risks?

I. The risk that analytical procedures and other relevant substantive tests will fail to detect misstatements equal to tolerable misstatement
II. The allowable risk of incorrect rejection for the substantive test of details

A. Neither I nor II.

B. I but not II.

C. II but not I.

D. I and II.

59. Changing the extent of substantive tests, such as by using a larger sample, is most appropriate when

A. Control risk decreases.

B. Inherent risk decreases.

C. The acceptable level of detection risk decreases.

D. The risk that other substantive tests will not detect material misstatements decreases.

60. Which of the following statements is true concerning the concept of materiality?

A. Materiality is measured according to AICPA standards.

B. Materiality has greater application to the standards of reporting than to the other generally accepted auditing standards.

C. Materiality judgments involve both quantitative and qualitative considerations.

D. Materiality requires that relatively more time be directed to those areas that are more susceptible to fraud.

61. Assume the overall allowable audit risk (AR) is 5%, inherent risk (IR) is 100%, control risk (CR) is 50%, and the detection risk associated with analytical procedures and other relevant substantive tests (AP) is 30%. The allowable risk of incorrect acceptance associated with a particular substantive test of details (TD) is

A. 5%.

B. 15%.

C. 33⅓%.

D. Indeterminable.

62. In an audit conducted with professional skepticism, the auditor

A. Assumes that management is dishonest.

B. Assumes that the financial statements are fairly presented.

C. Assumes that fraud has occurred.

D. Neither assumes that management is dishonest nor assumes unquestioned honesty.

63. An auditor should plan and perform the audit to provide what level(s) of assurance, if any, that misstatements material to the financial statements, whether caused by errors or fraud, are detected?

A. Positive assurance about errors and negative assurance about fraud.

B. Positive assurance about errors and no assurance about fraud.

C. Reasonable assurance about errors and absolute assurance about fraud.

D. Reasonable assurance about errors and fraud.

64. Which factor most likely indicates increased audit risk?

A. Operating decisions are made by numerous people.

B. Financing decisions are made by numerous people.

C. Management is slow to correct known material control weaknesses.

D. Senior management turnover is low.

65. An audit in accordance with GAAS

A. Requires that the auditor use statistical sampling techniques.

B. Ordinarily should be conducted with the intention of reporting fraud to outside authorities.

C. May involve a reconsideration of the initial risk assessment if the auditor discovers a condition differing adversely from expectations.

D. Does not require assessment of the risk of material fraud.

66. According to AU 316, an auditor should consider fraud risk factors relating to misstatements arising from fraudulent reporting and misappropriation of assets. Which specific categories of risk factors related to fraudulent reporting should the auditor consider?

I. Controls
II. Operating characteristics
III. Management's characteristics

A. I only.

B. I and II only.

C. II and III only.

D. I, II, and III.

67. An audit in accordance with GAAS is least likely to include audit procedures designed to detect material illegal acts by the client relating to its

A. Tax returns.

B. Operating aspects.

C. Accounting policies.

D. Financial affairs.

68. Audit working papers

A. Should contain a working trial balance that eliminates the details found in the lead schedules.

B. Should be adequate substitutes for the client's records.

C. Are the primary support for the financial statements being audited.

D. Should demonstrate how the engagement was planned.

69. Which of the following is most likely to be included in the permanent section of the auditor's working papers?

A. Analysis designed to be a part of the client's accounting records.

B. Summary of the prior year's receivable confirmations.

C. Schedules supporting the current year's adjusting entries.

D. Flowcharts describing internal control.

70. What audit working paper is prepared for several days before and after the audit period to determine that both parts of a transaction are recorded appropriately?

A. Carryforward schedule.

B. Working trial balance.

C. Expense and revenue summary.

D. Interbank transfer schedule.

COURSE 2
INTERNAL CONTROL

This course primarily covers AU 319, *Consideration of the Internal Control in a Financial Statement Audit*, and related auditing standards. It contains 280 questions, of which 60 constitute the final examination. As continuing professional education, 6 hours of CPE credit are recommended based on one-half the average completion time. If any of the CPE agencies you report to measures self-study CPE in terms of average completion time (rather than one-half average completion time), your certificate of completion will indicate 12 hours of maximum recommended CPE credit. Additional discussion regarding self-study credit measurement is provided in the introduction.

Date Completed	Time (Minutes)	
________	________	1. Work through each question in Chapter 3 (pages 117 through 188) in *Auditing & Systems Exam Questions and Explanations*, 8th Edition. a. Cover the answer explanations, which appear to the right of each question, with a piece of paper. Do not skip questions. b. Answer each question: circle your answer or write "T" or "F" next to the alternative answer choices. c. Lift the cover sheet and compare your choice with the correct answer in the first line of the answer explanation. d. Study the answer explanation.
________	________	2. Take the final exam by answering questions 71 through 130 on the following pages.

3. Carefully transfer your answers for these 60 questions to the CPE final exam answer sheet. Be sure you use the circles numbered 71 through 130.
4. Mark **B 0 B 2** (B means Blank) as the course number on page 2 of the answer sheet. See example at right.
5. Refer to the INTRODUCTION chapter in this book for instructions on how to complete the remainder of the machine-readable answer sheet.
6. Please complete the accompanying course evaluation and submit it with your answer sheet.

COURSE NUMBER(S)

	0		2
0	●	0	0
1	1	1	1
2	2	2	●
3	3	3	3
4	4	4	4
5	5	5	5
6	6	6	6
7	7	7	7
8	8	8	8
9	9	9	9

Total Time ________ (Carry this amount to your CPE course evaluation form.)

71. As defined by Generally Accepted Auditing Standards, which of the following is one of the five components of internal control?

A. The organizational structure.

B. Assignment of authority and responsibility.

C. Risk assessment.

D. External influences.

72. The control environment component of internal control is important because it

A. Enhances management's decision-making processes.

B. Affects the auditor's assessment of inherent risk.

C. Is the foundation for the other components of internal control.

D. Provides for the elimination of fraudulent activities.

73. The categories of the control activities component of internal control include

A. Human resources policies.

B. Performance reviews.

C. An internal auditing function.

D. Monitoring.

74. Which control component assesses the performance of internal control over time?

A. Risk assessment.

B. Monitoring.

C. Control environment.

D. Legal environment.

75. An entity's internal control can be expected to provide reasonable assurance regarding achievement of objectives in the categories of

	Compliance with Laws and Regulations	Efficiency of Operations	Reliability of Financial Reporting
A.	Yes	Yes	Yes
B.	Yes	No	Yes
C.	No	Yes	No
D.	No	No	No

76. The CPA must test the effectiveness of controls in an engagement to

	Audit Financial Statements	Report on Internal Control
A.	No	No
B.	No	Yes
C.	Yes	No
D.	Yes	Yes

77. When considering internal control in a financial statement audit, one of the auditor's responsibilities is to

A. Search for reportable conditions.

B. Assess control risk.

C. Plan the audit to provide reasonable assurance of detecting reportable conditions.

D. Report violations of the Foreign Corrupt Practices Act to the SEC.

78. Inherent limitations are evident in any internal control system. Which of the following would not be considered an inherent limitation?

A. Segregation of duties may not be operationally efficient.

B. Faulty judgment may be applied in decision making.

C. Simple errors or mistakes may be made by staff personnel.

D. There is a potential for management override.

79. A higher acceptable level of detection risk is most likely to result in

A. Elimination of tests of controls.

B. Elimination of all substantive tests.

C. Changing the nature of substantive tests.

D. A higher assessed level of control risk.

80. A firm employed a division of duties and responsibilities so that no one person had responsibility to authorize, record, and maintain assets related to a transaction process. In order to gain confidence that the risk of fraud for this process was minimized, the auditor would be most interested to know that

A. One of the employees in the process was bonded.

B. Employees knew their responsibilities and were trained to perform their duties.

C. Employees were separated geographically and had little contact with one another.

D. Employees participated in performance evaluations each year.

81. Competent personnel are imperative to an organization's control environment. Which of the following is not a factor in providing for competent personnel?

A. Actions to correct employee deficiencies.
B. Appropriate compensation of employees.
C. Periodic evaluation of employees.
D. Use of surveillance equipment to monitor employees.

82. Transaction authorization within an organization may be either specific or general. An example of general transaction authorization is the

A. Authorization of promotion of middle management personnel.
B. Granting of customer credit to those who meet established requirements.
C. Authorization of a sales transaction by the sales manager.
D. Approval of a detailed construction budget for a warehouse.

83. Which of the following expresses a general concept of internal control?

A. The costs of safeguarding assets should not exceed the expected benefits.
B. As risk increases, the importance of controls decreases.
C. Controls are more important for preventing errors than fraud.
D. The auditor and management share in the responsibility for maintenance of controls.

84. An auditor's consideration of internal control in a financial statement audit includes obtaining an understanding. Which of the following is most likely to be done while obtaining the understanding?

A. Gathering client documents.
B. Determining the quality of performance.
C. Determining whether internal control is operating as planned.
D. Evaluating the economy and efficiency of management decision processes.

85. An internal auditing department

A. Permits the independent auditor to substitute the work of the internal auditors for his/her own.
B. Should be independent in the same sense as the external auditors.
C. Is part of the monitoring component of internal control.
D. Does not affect the work of the external auditors.

86. The auditor must obtain an understanding of the client's internal control. Accordingly, the auditor

A. Should assess management's ability to manage efficiently.
B. Should assess control risk at less than the maximum whenever controls are properly designed.
C. May conclude that the risk of material misrepresentation is so great that an audit cannot be conducted.
D. Must disclose reportable conditions to the major shareholders.

87. The auditor assessed control risk at the maximum for the processing of purchase transactions. The auditor most likely

A. Will eliminate substantive tests.
B. Will perform additional procedures to gain an understanding of internal control.
C. Did not perform tests of controls.
D. Did not gain a sufficient understanding of internal control.

88. According to AU 319, *Consideration of Internal Control in a Financial Statement Audit*, an auditor who seeks a further reduction in the assessed level of control risk should consider

A. Changing the assessment of inherent risk.
B. Reducing the audit effort devoted to tests of controls.
C. Whether sufficient additional evidence is likely to be available.
D. Performing additional procedures related to understanding internal control.

89. Which audit procedure is a test of controls?

A. Tracing vouchers to entries in the voucher register.

B. Confirming inventory held in warehouse.

C. Performing a cutoff test.

D. Sending an inquiry letter to the client's attorney.

90. If the sample obtained in a test of controls contains proportionately fewer control deviations than the population,

A. The rate of misstatements in the accounting records exceeds the rate of deviations in the sample.

B. The efficiency but not the effectiveness of the audit is most likely to be diminished.

C. Control risk may be assessed too low.

D. Control risk may be assessed too high.

91. An auditor tests to determine that all sales invoices are present based on the sequence of the sales invoice number. The financial statement assertion being tested by this test of control would most likely be

A. Completeness.

B. Rights and obligations.

C. Valuation or allocation.

D. Presentation and disclosure.

92. If internal control over the revenue cycle is ineffective, fictitious transactions may be recorded. The result is most likely to be

	Receivables	Revenues
A.	Overstated	Overstated
B.	Overstated	Understated
C.	Understated	Understated
D.	Understated	Overstated

93. An auditor took a sample of sales invoices and compared them with the related bills of lading indicating shipment of goods to customers. This test provides evidence that

A. All goods that were shipped were also invoiced.

B. All invoices were recorded as a sale.

C. Accounts receivable balances exist for all invoiced amounts.

D. Invoices represent valid sales.

94. Which of the following fraudulent activities most likely could be perpetrated due to the lack of effective internal control over the revenue cycle?

A. Fictitious transactions may be recorded that cause an overstatement of revenues and an understatement of receivables.

B. Duplicate payments are made to vendors because supporting documentation is not canceled.

C. Approval of credit memos by personnel who receive cash may permit the misappropriation of cash.

D. The failure to transmit billing documents may cause an overstatement of receivables balances.

95. For internal control purposes, the billing department should most likely report to the

A. Sales manager.

B. Cashier.

C. Controller.

D. Credit manager.

96. The least effective procedure to prevent lapping is to

A. Have all payments sent directly to the company's bank.

B. Place all monies in the custody of the treasurer.

C. Have the accounts receivable bookkeeper open the mail so that fewer people have access to the checks.

D. Require that checks be made payable to the company.

97. Which of the following describes an appropriate activity?

A. Postdated checks are safeguarded by the controller.

B. Accounts receivable employees use remittance advices to make entries in the subsidiary ledger.

C. The treasurer reconciles the monthly bank statement.

D. Customers return defective merchandise to the sales department.

98. For proper control, all checks received by an organization should be

A. Sent immediately to the treasurer.

B. Sent immediately to the controller.

C. Endorsed "For Deposit Only."

D. Stapled to a remittance advice.

99. If the cash receipts function is effectively controlled, the amount of the daily bank deposit should equal

A. Daily cash receipts minus daily cash disbursements.

B. Daily cash receipts plus daily cash disbursements.

C. Daily cash receipts.

D. Total daily sales.

100. Controls to help assure that a firm does not order obsolete materials include

A. Requiring purchasing to obtain a bid for all materials purchased.

B. Review of all purchase orders for completeness prior to issuance.

C. Systematic reporting of product changes to appropriate personnel.

D. Requiring requisitions prior to preparation of purchase orders.

101. An auditor examines a purchase requisition to determine that

A. The related goods were received.

B. The related vendor invoice was received.

C. A purchase order was sent to a supplier.

D. A user department authorized a purchase.

102. Effective purchasing departments should

A. Use prescribed forms to document transfer of goods from the purchasing department to other departments.

B. Employ economic order quantity techniques.

C. Have purchase orders approved by internal auditing.

D. Primarily emphasize reduction of ordering costs.

103. A firm wishes to determine whether it has received the proper terms (discounts, prices, etc.) from vendors. Which documents display the terms for purchases of goods and services?

A. Remittance advices.

B. Invoices.

C. Receiving reports.

D. Purchase requisitions.

104. Which of the following is an appropriate control procedure for the purchase of merchandise?

A. The receiving department accepts all merchandise received from the usual company vendors.

B. The receiving department accepts all merchandise approved by the warehouse supervisor.

C. The receiving department accepts merchandise to the extent of the quantity listed on its copy of the purchase order.

D. The receiving department should have a blind copy of the purchase order.

105. By requiring competitive bidding, an entity can minimize the risk that purchasing agents will

A. Show favoritism to a vendor.

B. Obtain the best price.

C. Use the same vendor for subsequent purchases of the same item.

D. Consider all sources for the items needed.

106. Which of the following is an appropriate procedure related to cash disbursements?

A. Record keepers have no access to signed checks.

B. Accounting personnel mail payments directly to payees.

C. The check preparer signs the checks.

D. Payments should be made in cash whenever possible.

107. A company that makes partial payments to vendors is having difficulty keeping track of the amounts still due. The best remedy for this problem is to

A. Cancel vouchers upon payment.

B. Establish a voucher register.

C. Use an accounts payable subsidiary ledger.

D. Match invoices, receiving reports, and purchase orders before disbursing funds.

108. For the most effective control, the person who signs a check should also

A. Mail the check.

B. Prepare the voucher.

C. Record the check.

D. Perform the bank reconciliation.

109. Which of the following is an appropriate control related to purchase and payment transactions?

A. The accounting department mails the checks.

B. The petty cash fund is reimbursed daily.

C. Legal counsel has control of the check-signing machine.

D. All checks are signed by the treasurer on a timely basis.

110. Effective internal control over the cash payroll function would require which of the following?

A. Separation of the preparation of the payroll register from the maintenance of payroll records.

B. Approval of employee time records by the payroll accounting department.

C. Separation of time keeping and payroll preparation.

D. Temporary retention of unclaimed payroll cash by the personnel department.

111. A responsibility compatible with the normal duties of the personnel department is the

A. Preparation of the payroll from job time tickets.

B. Review of payroll calculations.

C. Authorization of pay rate changes.

D. Distribution of payroll checks.

112. Internal control is most likely to be ineffective when

A. The payroll department approves all hiring decisions.

B. Job time tickets identify labor hours as direct or indirect.

C. The personnel and payroll functions are segregated.

D. Payroll department employees are rotated periodically.

113. To maintain effective internal control, a supervisor of a manufacturing department performs all the following duties except

A. Approve the hours worked by subordinates.

B. Evaluating the performance of subordinates.

C. Distributing paychecks to subordinates.

D. Assigning tasks to subordinates.

114. Which of the following is a weakness in internal control for securities?

A. Custody is assigned to a trust company.

B. The board approves temporary stock purchases.

C. Securities are held in the name of an individual.

D. The internal auditors reconcile the detail of securities.

115. Which of the following procedures is appropriate for the protection of securities?

A. Securities are held in bearer form.

B. The corporate controller approves all purchases and sales of securities.

C. The corporate controller and corporate treasurer should have sole access to the securities.

D. Custody of securities should not be assigned to persons who have the responsibility of accounting for them.

116. Which of the following is a control weakness in the purchasing of inventory?

A. Purchase requisitions are not used.

B. Perpetual inventory records are maintained for large dollar value items.

C. The company maintains an open purchase order file.

D. Prenumbered production orders are signed by supervisors.

117. For several years, a client's physical inventory count has exceeded recorded quantities. The inventory problem may result from failing to record

A. Consignment sales.

B. Sales discounts allowed.

C. Purchases.

D. Purchases returned to vendors.

118. A client maintained a just-in-time inventory system. As a result of this system, the auditor would expect

A. Inventory receipt and usage records to be more accurate.

B. Inventory levels to be minimal at the time of physical count.

C. Management use of a two-bin system to determine need.

D. A difficult time in determining whether inventory was as lower of cost or market.

119. Which control procedure is relevant to the initiation and execution of transactions?

A. Major acquisitions are subject to competitive bidding.

B. Access to equipment is restricted.

C. The internal auditors take a full physical inventory periodically.

D. The formal budgeting system isolates variances.

120. Which of the following is an appropriate policy or procedure relevant to fixed assets?

A. User departments are authorized to initiate removal work orders and to dispose of equipment.

B. Equipment replacements are usually made when estimated useful lives have expired.

C. All purchases are made by user departments.

D. Checks issued in payment of purchases are signed by the controller.

121. The investigation of variances within a budgeting system will likely disclose all of the following except

A. Equipment purchases that were misclassified as repairs expense.

B. Repairs expense misclassified as equipment purchases.

C. Repairs budgeted and recorded but never actually performed.

D. Equipment budgeted and purchased but never recorded.

122. A report issued on reportable conditions

A. May state that no reportable conditions or material weaknesses were found.

B. Must identify material weaknesses separately.

C. Must provide assurance regarding the degree to which internal control is free of material weaknesses.

D. May state that the reportable conditions are not material weaknesses.

123. A report on reportable conditions should state all the following except the

A. Auditor's opinion on internal control.

B. Definition of reportable conditions.

C. Restrictions on the distribution of the report.

D. Purpose of the report.

124. What matter(s) must be communicated by an auditor to a client's audit committee?

I. Significant accounting policies
II. Disagreements with management
III. Basis for assessing control risk

A. I, II, III.

B. I, II.

C. I, III.

D. III.

125. The work of the internal auditor may affect the nature, timing, and extent of the independent auditor's work. Accordingly, the independent auditor should

A. Assist in the hiring of the internal auditor.

B. Assist in managing the work of the internal auditor.

C. Provide training to the internal auditor.

D. Gain an understanding of the work of the internal auditor.

126. The external auditor may evaluate the competence and objectivity of the internal auditors. To evaluate competence, the external auditor should consider the internal auditors'

A. Access to the board of directors.

B. Working papers, reports, and recommendations.

C. Organizational status (reporting level).

D. Independence.

127. The independent auditor may use internal auditors to

A. Evaluate significant accounting estimates.

B. Assist in performing substantive tests and tests of controls.

C. Determine sufficiency of evidence.

D. Assess audit risk.

128. The auditor's documentation of the client's internal control

A. Must document the basis for a conclusion that the assessed level of control risk for a specific assertion is at the maximum.

B. Must document the basis for a conclusion that the assessed level of control risk for a specific assertion is below the maximum.

C. Need not document the conclusion that the assessed level of control risk for a specific assertion is at the maximum.

D. Need not document the conclusion that the assessed level of control risk is below the maximum.

129. When documenting the client's internal control, the independent auditor sometimes prepares a symbolic representation of the system. This representation is best described as a(n)

A. Decision table.

B. Systems flowchart.

C. Organization chart.

D. Program flowchart.

130. Auditors often use a questionnaire in the assessment of control risk. Which of the following is an advantage of a questionnaire?

A. A questionnaire helps assure that the auditor does not overlook important control considerations.

B. A questionnaire is flexible in application.

C. A questionnaire presents a series of sequential processes.

D. A questionnaire provides a pictorial representation of the transaction flows.

COURSE 3
AUDIT EVIDENCE AND PROCEDURES

This course includes the basic auditing procedures and the Statements on Auditing Standards (mostly codified under AU 300) relevant to the audit evidence gathering and evaluation process. It primarily applies to the sales-receivables cycle; purchases-payables cycle; cash; inventories; property, plant, and equipment; other assets; long-term debt and other liabilities; owners' equity; and personnel and payroll. This course contains 366 questions, of which 80 constitute the final examination. As continuing professional education, 8 hours of CPE credit are recommended based on one-half the average completion time. If any of the CPE agencies you report to measures self-study CPE in terms of average completion time (rather than one-half average completion time), your certificate of completion will indicate 16 hours of maximum recommended CPE credit. Additional discussion regarding self-study credit measurement is provided in the introduction.

Date Completed	Time (Minutes)	
________	______	1. Work through each question in Chapter 4 (pages 189 through 284) in *Auditing & Systems Exam Questions and Explanations*, 8th Edition.

a. Cover the answer explanations, which appear to the right of each question, with a piece of paper. Do not skip questions.

b. Answer each question: circle your answer or write "T" or "F" next to the alternative answer choices.

c. Lift the cover sheet and compare your choice with the correct answer in the first line of the answer explanation.

d. Study the answer explanation.

Date Completed	Time (Minutes)	
________	______	2. Take the final exam by answering questions 131 through 210 on the following pages.

3. Carefully transfer your answers for these 80 questions to the CPE final exam answer sheet. Be sure you use the circles numbered 131 through 210.

4. Mark **B 0 B 3** (B means Blank) as the course number on page 2 of the answer sheet. See example at right.

COURSE NUMBER(S)

0 3

5. Refer to the INTRODUCTION chapter in this book for instructions on how to complete the remainder of the machine-readable answer sheet.

6. Please complete the accompanying course evaluation and submit it with your answer sheet.

Total Time ______ (Carry this amount to your CPE course evaluation form.)

131. To which assertion category does management refer when it states that assets, liabilities, equity, revenues, and expenses have been included in the financial statements at their appropriate amounts?

A. Valuation or allocation.

B. Existence or occurrence.

C. Completeness.

D. Presentation and disclosure.

132. The third standard of field work requires the auditor to collect sufficient competent evidential matter in support of the opinion. Which of the following are mentioned in this standard?

A. Inquiries.

B. Reconciliations.

C. Vouching.

D. Tracing.

133. According to AU 326, *Evidential Matter*, underlying accounting data include

A. Confirmations.

B. Spreadsheets supporting cost allocations.

C. Checks stored in electronic form.

D. Minutes of meetings.

134. Audit objectives define specific desired accomplishments, whereas audit procedures provide a(n)

A. Means of achieving audit objectives.

B. Set of broad general guidelines.

C. Framework for documenting the objectives.

D. Alternative way to define the objectives.

135. Competent evidence is

A. That provided by high-level management.

B. Both valid and relevant.

C. Of a nature that proves an intermediate fact.

D. Desirable but typically not attainable by the auditor.

136. Which procedures are performed to restrict detection risk to an acceptable level?

A. Tests of controls.

B. Substantive tests.

C. Objective tests.

D. Documentation tests.

137. Cost-benefit considerations relate most closely to which characteristic of audit evidence?

A. Validity.

B. Competence.

C. Sufficiency.

D. Relevance.

138. The audit procedure of observation is most effective for testing the assertion of

A. Completeness.

B. Obligations and rights.

C. Statement presentation and disclosure.

D. Existence.

139. When an auditor evaluates the reasonableness of an accounting estimate, (s)he normally concentrates on key factors and assumptions that are

A. Objectively determined.

B. Based on criteria established by an external authority.

C. Consistent with historical patterns.

D. Subjective and susceptible to misstatement.

140. Which of the following is a true statement about the auditor's concerns prior to applying substantive tests to balance sheet items at an interim date?

A. The auditor must consider the propriety of the auditee's procedures for adjusting accounts and establishing cutoffs.

B. The assessment of inherent risk must be below the maximum.

C. Significant events may occur subsequent to the balance sheet date that will affect the choice of interim tests.

D. The assessment of control risk must be at the maximum.

141. Analytical procedures are most likely to involve

A. Tests of the details of transactions and balances.

B. A study of plausible relationships.

C. Identifying weaknesses in internal control.

D. Vouching transactions to supporting documentation.

142. According to professional standards, analytical procedures are required to be applied

A. During the final review stage of the audit.

B. Only in the initial planning phase of the audit.

C. To test the details of transactions.

D. In the substantive testing phase of the audit.

143. Analytical procedures used in the

A. Planning stage of the audit should assist in assessing the validity of the conclusions reached.

B. Planning stage of the audit should enhance the understanding of transactions and events since the last audit.

C. Final review stage of the audit should achieve audit objectives related to specific assertions in the financial statements.

D. Final review stage of the audit should focus on identifying areas of specific audit risk.

144. Analytical procedures are required in a

I. Compilation of financial statements
II. Review of interim financial information
III. Review of financial statements of a private entity

A. I and II only.

B. I and III only.

C. II and III only.

D. I, II, and III.

145. The auditor should evaluate significant unexpected differences revealed by analytical procedures. The first step is

A. Consider changing the audit report.

B. To reconsider methods used and to make inquires of management.

C. Gain a further understanding of internal control.

D. Perform additional tests of controls.

146. The client's accounts receivable turnover increased significantly from the prior year. This result could have been caused by a

A. Decrease in cash sales.

B. Change in terms from net 60 days to net 30 days.

C. Liberalization of credit policy.

D. Decrease in the cash discount allowed.

147. What is the effect on the accounts receivable turnover ratio of an increase in cash sales offset by a reduction in credit sales?

A. The accounts receivable turnover ratio will increase.

B. The accounts receivable turnover ratio will decrease.

C. The accounts receivable turnover ratio will remain constant.

D. The effect cannot be determined.

148. An auditor who wishes to detect the overstatement of sales should

A. Vouch sales journal entries to bills of lading.

B. Compare bills of lading with sales invoices.

C. Compare accounts receivable entries with sales journal entries.

D. Compare sales journal entries with entries in the general ledger.

149. An auditor examines recorded sales for several days prior to and subsequent to the balance sheet date. The purpose of this procedure is to

A. Determine the net realizable value of accounts receivable.

B. Verify the existence of recorded receivables.

C. Test the completeness assertion about sales.

D. Detect concealment of a cash shortage.

150. An auditor wishes to determine whether all invoiced sales were actually shipped. The auditor should

A. Compare a sample of invoices with bills of lading.

B. Trace a sample of bills of lading to invoices.

C. Vouch a sample of entries in the sales journal to invoices.

D. Trace a sample of invoices to the sales journal.

151. A client shipped merchandise costing $60,000 to a customer on December 30, 19x1. The shipment was made FOB destination. The client recognized the sale and billed the customer for $100,000 on January 2, 19x2. On December 31, 19X1, the client's physical inventory was taken, and cost of sales was recorded using the periodic method. The goods shipped on December 30, 19X1 were not counted. What, if any, correcting entry will likely be required?

A. Credit to sales and debit to accounts receivable.

B. Credit to sales and debit to inventory.

C. Debit to inventory and credit to cost of sales.

D. None.

152. An auditor may appropriately develop audit objectives with respect to which assertion(s) about accounts receivable?

	Existence	Completeness	Rights
A.	Yes	Yes	Yes
B.	Yes	Yes	No
C.	Yes	No	No
D.	No	No	Yes

153. The use of confirmations of accounts receivable balances is likely to be effective with respect to the existence assertion and the

A. Completeness assertion.

B. Obligations assertion.

C. Rights assertion.

D. Presentation assertion.

154. An independent auditor who confirms receivables

A. May decide to use the blank form of negative confirmation.

B. Is applying a generally accepted auditing procedure.

C. Should use positive confirmations only when the combined assessed level of inherent risk and control risk is low.

D. Should use negative confirmations only when balances are large.

155. Which of the following most accurately compares positive and negative accounts receivable confirmations?

A. A nonreply is assumed to indicate agreement when positive but not negative confirmations are used.

B. Negative confirmation is preferable when recipients are unlikely to give confirmations appropriate consideration.

C. Negative confirmation requires a reply but positive confirmation does not.

D. Positive confirmation is the more effective procedure.

156. An auditor need not confirm receivables when

A. Other evidence is sufficient to reduce audit risk to an acceptably low level.

B. The combined assessed level of inherent risk and control risk is high.

C. They are material in total but not individually.

D. Response rates are likely to be high.

157. An auditor has received replies to all but one of the positive confirmation requests sent to a client's customers. Although the auditor is satisfied with the confirmation process, she decides to gather additional evidence as to the existence of the unconfirmed receivable. If no response has been made to a second request, the auditor will most likely choose from all of the following procedures except

A. Inspecting a copy of the bill of lading for the shipment.

B. Examining subsequent collections from the customer.

C. Inspecting the copy of the customer order filed in the sales department.

D. Examining the physical inventory to determine that goods are no longer in inventory for the quantities claimed to be shipped.

158. The completeness assertion is the primary emphasis in an audit of

A. Purchases of inventory for cash.

B. Accounts payable.

C. Cash receipts.

D. Trading securities.

159. An auditor is most likely to confirm accounts payable when

A. The accounts are unsecured.

B. The client has made large purchases from the creditors.

C. The combined assessed level of inherent risk and control risk is low.

D. Balances are immaterial.

160. Which of the following is the most important information in determining whether goods in transit should be included in a client's inventory?

A. The date the client obtains physical possession of the goods.

B. The date the purchase is paid for.

C. The date the purchase is invoiced.

D. The freight terms.

161. The search for unrecorded liabilities, especially accounts payable, will typically be conducted

A. At an interim date if controls are strong.

B. A few days prior to year-end, as part of cutoff tests.

C. While obtaining the understanding of internal control.

D. After the balance sheet date.

162. Which procedure is most likely to detect unrecorded liabilities?

A. Review of shipping records.

B. Reconciling vendors' statements to the file of receiving reports.

C. Recomputation of interest expense.

D. Recomputation of depreciation expense.

163. The auditor chooses accounts payable accounts with small or zero balances for confirmation because

A. Materiality is not an issue in an audit of accounts payable. Every understatement is automatically considered to be material.

B. The auditor is concerned with understatement of accounts payable, and accounts with small balances are more likely to be understated.

C. The sampling methods used by accountants work best when accounts have small balances.

D. Creditors respond more readily when balances are small rather than large.

164. Which procedure is least likely to reveal the existence of unrecorded liabilities?

A. Examination of cash disbursements made after year-end.

B. Sending confirmations to vendors with zero balances.

C. Review of unvouchered vendor invoices.

D. Review of unmatched sales invoices.

165. Which of the following would most likely increase the auditor's concern about verifying the existence of assets?

A. The client uses demand deposit accounts.

B. Both cash and negotiable securities are on hand.

C. Compensating balances are required.

D. The client has foreign currency accounts.

166. An audit client has significant balances denominated in foreign currencies. The auditor is evaluating the exchange rates and conversions at the balance sheet date. This concern is directly linked to tests of which management assertion?

A. Valuation.

B. Existence.

C. Completeness.

D. Rights and obligations.

167. An auditor sent the AICPA Standard Form to Confirm Account Balance Information with Financial Institutions to a client's bank. What information is least likely to be obtained from the bank's response?

A. Year-end balance of a demand deposit account.

B. Description of collateral for a loan noted on the form.

C. Contingent liabilities.

D. Direct liabilities on loans.

168. A proof of cash is most appropriate

A. If the auditor is unable to control negotiable securities during the count of cash.

B. When controls related to cash are ineffective.

C. When the cash balance is material.

D. In every audit because it is a required procedure.

169. To verify deposits in transit and outstanding checks listed on the client's bank reconciliation, the auditor should most likely

A. Send a standard confirmation request to all banks.

B. Analyze a cutoff bank statement.

C. Inspect the contents of the client's safe deposit box.

D. Prepare a schedule of interbank transfers.

170. Recording a deposit from an interbank transfer in the current period but intentionally failing to record the disbursement in the same accounting period is

A. Lapping.

B. Disproving cash.

C. Window dressing.

D. Kiting.

171. An auditor discovered the following interbank cash transfer while examining a schedule of bank transfers for a company with a December 31 year end:

Disbursing Bank (Month/Day)		Receiving Bank (Month/Day)	
Per Bank	Per Books	Per Bank	Per Books
1/5	12/30	1/4	1/3

This transfer indicates that

A. A deposit in transit should appear on the December 31 bank reconciliation of the disbursing bank.

B. The company's cash balance at year-end was understated.

C. The receiving bank has made a recording error.

D. Lapping has probably occurred.

172. An auditor examines vendors' invoices, consignment agreements, and contracts primarily to test which assertion about inventory?

A. Valuation and allocation.

B. Completeness.

C. Presentation and disclosure.

D. Rights and obligations.

173. When well-kept perpetual inventory records are periodically checked by comparisons with physical counts taken by the client, and control risk is low, the auditor's observation procedures

A. May be performed at interim dates.

B. May be performed by the client's personnel if errors are well documented.

C. May be performed by outside specialists.

D. Must be performed at year-end.

174. If the number of items reflected in the perpetual inventory balance is larger than the physical count, the cause of the difference may be unrecorded

A. Purchases.

B. Sales returns.

C. Sales.

D. Sales discounts.

175. During the observation of the client's physical count of inventories, the auditor should be alert for damaged or obsolete inventory. The auditor's major concern in this regard is to test management's assertion about

A. Rights and obligations.

B. Valuation.

C. Statement presentation and disclosure.

D. Completeness.

176. If the client uses a sampling method in the taking of the physical inventory, the auditor

A. Must disclaim an opinion because of the scope limitation.

B. Must qualify the opinion because of the departure from GAAP.

C. Must express an adverse opinion because of the departure from GAAP.

D. May be able to express an unqualified opinion if (s)he concludes that the results are reasonable.

177. The auditor should evaluate the assignment and allocation of costs to ensure that the balances for manufactured inventory contain

A. Direct materials, direct labor, and manufacturing overhead.

B. Assets, liabilities and owners' equity.

C. Revenues and costs.

D. Direct materials, work-in-process, and finished goods.

178. Fewer but larger shipments with many returns most likely indicate

A. Unrecorded returns.

B. Lapping.

C. Fictitious cash sales.

D. Consignments.

179. When testing the rights assertion about real estate, the auditor should consider performing all of the following procedures except

A. Inspecting public records.

B. Examining deeds.

C. Evaluating closing statements representing purchases.

D. Obtaining appraisals from independent specialists.

180. The auditor usually substantiates the balance of the property, plant, and equipment account instead of performing tests of controls. The principal reason is that

A. The beginning balance has been audited and subsequent transactions are few.

B. The dollar balance is usually small.

C. Inspection of the assets is often difficult.

D. The account usually has numerous transactions.

181. In an audit of property, plant, and equipment, which of the following is most likely to detect unrecorded additions?

A. Inspection of lease agreements.

B. Recomputations.

C. Investigation of reductions in insurance coverage.

D. Obtaining management representations.

182. In an audit of property, plant, and equipment, the repairs and maintenance expense account should be reviewed. A large debit in the account could suggest that

A. Gains on disposal of assets have been misstated.

B. Repairs have been deferred to future periods.

C. Maintenance expenses have been understated.

D. An asset has been improperly expensed.

183. Excessive recurring gains on the retirement of plant equipment suggest that

A. Assets were originally recorded at an amount exceeding the cost of the equipment.

B. Asset lives used to determine depreciation were greater than the economic lives of the equipment.

C. Income in prior periods was understated.

D. Assets are being retired but not replaced.

184. The auditor is testing assertions relating to the client's available-for-sale securities. The auditor should determine that

A. All securities are in the physical custody of the client.

B. Physical documents exist to support all securities.

C. The securities are reported at fair value.

D. Management has the authority to convert the securities into cash.

185. The client reports a significant amount of publicly traded stocks classified as trading securities. The auditor will most likely seek evidence to support the recorded valuation by

A. Confirming the amount of securities with the custodian.

B. Obtaining year-end market quotations.

C. Reviewing the controls implemented to assure proper valuation.

D. Obtaining representations from members of the client's board of directors.

186. Which audit procedure provides assurance of the existence and validity of the securities balance?

A. Examining paid checks issued in payment of securities purchased.

B. Confirming securities held by the client as collateral.

C. Counting securities when officials of the client are not present.

D. Vouching changes in the account to supporting documents.

187. If an acquisition of another company is accounted for under the pooling-of-interests method, an auditor should ascertain that assets and liabilities are recorded at

A. Fair values.

B. Carrying values.

C. Appraisal values.

D. Cost.

188. The objectives of the audit of prepaid insurance include determining that amounts shown

A. Do not include amortization of premium refunds.

B. Are expected to provide future benefits.

C. Represent the best rates available for the coverage received.

D. Reflect premium rates that have been confirmed with an independent broker.

189. The client has a material asset recorded in an account classified as "deferred charges." The auditor's primary objective in the examination of this asset will most likely be to determine whether the amount

A. Is properly chargeable to future periods.

B. Was originally incurred.

C. Corresponds to actual physical assets.

D. Represents rights held by the client.

190. Which of the following would the auditor usually not find in a bond trust indenture?

A. Sinking-fund requirements.

B. Provisions for retirement.

C. Current financial ratios.

D. Interest rates.

191. Which audit procedure is most closely related to management's assertions about the presentation and disclosure of liabilities?

A. Tracing cash received from a bond issue to the accounting records.

B. Confirmation with the bond trustee of amounts owed on a private placement of bonds.

C. Reviewing the renewal of a note payable immediately after the balance sheet date.

D. Inspection of public records of lien balances.

192. Which of the following is a permissible basis for accruing a contingent liability?

A. A threat of expropriation.

B. The existence of unspecified business risks.

C. An uncertainty inherent in the accounting process.

D. The possibility of a loss is remote but can be reasonably estimated.

193. An audit of shareholders' equity ordinarily should include

A. Tracing individual dividend payments to the capital stock records.

B. Reviewing minutes of board meetings to determine the number of shares outstanding.

C. Confirming shares outstanding with state officials.

D. Determining that dividend declarations comply with debt agreements.

194. The audit procedure to determine that stock dividends have been properly authorized is to inspect the

A. Equity section of the balance sheet.

B. Stock certificate book.

C. Registrar's records.

D. Minutes of board of directors' meetings.

195. Which audit procedure is most closely related to management's assertions about the presentation and disclosure of shareholders' equity?

A. Determining whether restrictions have been imposed on retained earnings.

B. Counting treasury stock certificates.

C. Inspecting minutes of meetings of the board of directors to verify that cash dividends were declared.

D. Establishing that treasury stock is valued at cost.

196. The objectives of an audit of payroll include which of the following?

I. Conclude whether payments are made to bona fide employees
II. Determine whether rates of pay are justified
III. Determine whether paychecks are distributed to all employees

A. I.

B. I and II.

C. II and III.

D. I, II, and III.

197. To provide direct evidence as to the accuracy of the payroll journal, the auditor should

A. Read the labor variance report.

B. Reconcile the payroll bank account.

C. Vouch a sample of journal entries to records of wage rates and authorized deductions.

D. Perform appropriate analytical procedures.

198. Production employees may be paid for hours that they did not work if

A. Distribution of paychecks is not made by the paymaster.

B. The payroll bank account is not reconciled promptly.

C. Department supervisors do not approve time cards.

D. The personnel department does not maintain authorized pay rates.

199. The management representation letter should ordinarily be dated as of the date of the

A. Issuance of the financial statements.

B. Auditor's report.

C. Balance sheet.

D. Transmission of the letter to the auditor.

200. If management refuses to provide essential written representations, but the auditor has no reason to believe that the financial statements are not fairly presented, the auditor

A. Should treat the refusal as a scope limitation and not express an unqualified opinion.

B. Should treat the refusal as a scope limitation and express an adverse opinion.

C. May express an unqualified opinion but should include an explanatory paragraph.

D. May not express an opinion.

201. The scope of an audit is limited when the client's lawyers limit their response to the letter of audit inquiry to matters

I. To which they have given substantive attention in the form of legal consultation or representation
II. That are material
III. Concerning asserted claims and pending litigation

A. I only.

B. II only.

C. III only.

D. I, II, and III.

202. When the client's lawyers refuse to provide information requested in a letter of audit inquiry, what is the effect on the audit report?

A. An unqualified opinion is precluded.

B. An unqualified opinion may be expressed, but only if an explanatory paragraph is included.

C. The auditor most likely should withdraw from the engagement.

D. Modification of the report is unnecessary.

203. Which of the following is considered a specialist according to AU 336, *Using the Work of a Specialist*?

A. An internal auditor.

B. A staff accountant of the client.

C. An engineer.

D. An attorney representing the client in litigation.

204. The auditor may be able to rely on the work of a specialist who is related to the client

A. If the auditor assesses the objectivity and competence of the specialist as acceptable.

B. If the auditor refers to the relationship in the audit report and indicates that responsibility for the report is being shared with the specialist.

C. If the specialist is an internal auditor with a CIA designation.

D. In no circumstances.

205. An audit report may refer to a specialist if it

	Includes an Explanatory Paragraph	Departs from an Unqualified Opinion
A.	Yes	Yes
B.	Yes	No
C.	No	Yes
D.	No	No

206. If the balance sheet date is December 31, 1998, the financial statements were completed on February 1, 1999, the audit field work began on February 5, 1999 and was completed on March 11, 1999, and the audit report was issued on March 18, 1999, the subsequent events period ended on

A. February 1, 1999.

B. February 5, 1999.

C. March 11, 1999.

D. March 18, 1999.

207. Which of the following audit procedures is/are ordinarily appropriate for a subsequent events review?

	Sending Follow-up Receivable Confirmation Requests	Obtaining a Client Representation Letter	Testing the Effectiveness of Controls
A.	No	Yes	No
B.	Yes	Yes	No
C.	No	No	Yes
D.	No	No	No

208. Which of the following is a transaction that may indicate the existence of related parties?

A. Selling realty at a price materially different from its appraised value.

B. Writing inventory down to lower of cost or market.

C. The sale of equipment to another corporation with a similar name.

D. A large loan with scheduled repayment terms.

209. Which of the following conditions is most likely to motivate a transaction outside the ordinary course of business between related parties?

A. Mutual benefit to both parties.

B. No excess capacity.

C. Lack of sufficient working capital.

D. A strong credit rating.

210. Cash receipts from which of the following are not classified as cash inflows from operating activities?

A. Sale of services.

B. Collection of interest on a loan.

C. Dividends on equity securities.

D. Collection of the principal of a loan.

COURSE 4
INFORMATION SYSTEMS

This course covers the basic principles at the entry level concerning the information systems environment, as well as the auditing of information systems. It contains 404 questions, of which 90 constitute the final examination. As continuing professional education, 9 hours of CPE credit are recommended based on one-half the average completion time. If any of the CPE agencies you report to measures self-study CPE in terms of average completion time (rather than one-half average completion time), your certificate of completion will indicate 18 hours of maximum recommended CPE credit. Additional discussion regarding self-study credit measurement is provided in the introduction.

Date Completed	Time (Minutes)	
________	________	1. Work through each question in Chapter 5 (pages 285 through 386) in *Auditing & Systems Exam Questions and Explanations*, 8th edition.

   a. Cover the answer explanations, which appear to the right of each question, with a piece of paper. Do not skip questions.

   b. Answer each question: circle your answer or write "T" or "F" next to the alternative answer choices.

   c. Lift the cover sheet and compare your choice with the correct answer in the first line of the answer explanation.

   d. Study the answer explanation.

Date Completed	Time (Minutes)	
________	________	2. Take the final exam by answering questions 211 through 300 on the following pages.

3. Carefully transfer your answers for these 90 questions to the CPE final exam answer sheet. Be sure you use the circles numbered 211 through 300.

4. Mark **B 0 B 4** (B means Blank) as the course number on page 2 of the answer sheet. See example at right.

5. Refer to the INTRODUCTION chapter in this book for instructions on how to complete the remainder of the machine-readable answer sheet.

6. Please complete the accompanying course evaluation and submit it with your answer sheet.

COURSE NUMBER(S)			
	0		4
0	●	0	0
1	1	1	1
2	2	2	2
3	3	3	3
4	4	4	●
5	5	5	5
6	6	6	6
7	7	7	7
8	8	8	8
9	9	9	9

Total Time ________ (Carry this amount to your CPE course evaluation form.)

211. A decision support system assists managers in making decisions

A. In a human way.

B. Involving structured tasks.

C. By automating the decision process.

D. That are long-term, nonroutine, and often unstructured.

212. Which parties, if any, are ultimately responsible for the implementation of cost-effective information systems within an organization?

	Client Operating Management	Independent Auditor
A.	No	No
B.	Yes	No
C.	Yes	Yes
D.	No	Yes

213. An advantage of a microcomputer-based system is that

A. Unauthorized individuals have difficulty in accessing and altering files.

B. Once programmed, similar transactions are processed in a similar manner.

C. The division of responsibilities allows for more effective control than in a manual system.

D. Errors can be completely eliminated from processing.

214. Information system control activities may be classified as general controls and application controls. Which of the following are general controls?

A. Report distribution controls.

B. Access security controls.

C. Output controls.

D. Input controls.

215. Which of the following is true of a computerized information system?

A. Files may be altered without documentation.

B. The greatest risk to business is equipment malfunction.

C. The potential for systematic error is ordinarily less than in a manual system.

D. The risks of data concentration are reduced from that in a manual system.

216. Which controls primarily address the most common computer-related problem confronting organizations?

A. Controls related to high-level management fraud.

B. Input controls.

C. Output controls.

D. Hardware controls.

217. Which data entry technique is often used by retailers?

A. Bar coding.

B. MICR.

C. Keydisk.

D. Printer.

218. A modem is

A. A switching device that channels data flow.

B. A device that converts digital information into sound waves.

C. A programmable communications control unit consisting of a small computer that relieves the main computer of routine data transfer tasks.

D. Used to control the physical flow of data between the input/output devices and the processor.

219. The time interval between the moment at which a computer instruction initiates a call for data and the moment at which delivery of the data is completed is

A. Read/write time.

B. Access time.

C. Recall interval.

D. Execution time.

220. Magnetic tape storage is a popular storage medium because it

	Is Inexpensive	Is Reusable	Provides for Direct Access
A.	Yes	Yes	No
B.	Yes	Yes	Yes
C.	Yes	No	No
D.	No	Yes	No

221. Memory with read-only stored instructions that can be erased is

A. EPROM.

B. RAM.

C. ROM.

D. COM.

222. A compiler can be used to translate

A. Object programs into source programs.

B. Assembly language programs into English-like statements.

C. Source code into machine language.

D. Machine language into utility programs.

223. Which of the following is a data manipulation language?

A. SQL.

B. Unix.

C. C.

D. DOS.

224. A utility program

A. Oversees the interaction of the hardware components of a computer system.

B. Is a standardized subroutine.

C. Converts source programs into object programs.

D. Produces customized reports.

225. Macro programs are typically used to perform

A. Multiprocessing.

B. Repetitive tasks.

C. Logic tests.

D. Diagnostic procedures.

226. Which of the following is the lowest in the data hierarchy?

A. Byte.

B. Field.

C. Record.

D. File.

227. In a single flat file structure,

A. Relations are defined in a tree organization.

B. Attributes are related in a network format.

C. One attribute is related to many others in a hierarchical format.

D. Field lengths are the same in all records.

228. If each prior record must be bypassed to read the record of interest, the file is most likely a(n)

A. Parallel file.

B. Online file.

C. Random file.

D. Sequential file.

229. Source documents typically printed by a computer system as output and then later returned for use as machine-readable input are

A. Echo documents.

B. Redundant documents.

C. Closed-loop documents.

D. Turnaround documents.

230. A database system

A. Permits application programs to be independent of the logical arrangement of the data.

B. Increases data redundancy.

C. Provides separate files for different application programs.

D. Uses a traditional flat file structure.

231. Linked list file organization provides for file processing by

A. Random access only because records are not in physical order.

B. Sequential access only although records need not be in physical order.

C. Both sequential and random access.

D. Neither sequential nor random access.

232. Which of the following are most likely to be found in a relational database?

A. Magnetic tape storage media.

B. Sequential files.

C. Trees and indexes.

D. Two-dimensional tables.

233. Which of the following is a true statement about an inverted file?

A. A randomizing formula must be used to create addresses for the records in the file.

B. It is based on a primary key.

C. It is based on a secondary key.

D. It can be processed sequentially starting at the end of the file.

234. A protocol

A. Prescribes the manner by which data are transmitted between a sending and a receiving device.

B. Allows multiple parties to use a single line for communication.

C. Makes terminals compatible with the mainframe.

D. Is the set of procedures designed to protect against computer viruses.

235. When confidential data are transmitted over public or shared communication networks, the best form of security is

A. Encryption.

B. Electronic mail services.

C. Asynchronous transmissions.

D. EDI.

236. Which of the following is false concerning electronic funds transfer (EFT)?

A. EFT is based on electronic data interchange (EDI) concepts.

B. EFT services are offered by financial institutions worldwide.

C. The cost per transaction is lower than in manual processing.

D. Human intervention is important at points during the processing to prevent errors and to speed the process.

237. A firm is moving to a just-in-time (JIT) inventory management system and wants to improve relationships and communications with its suppliers. It would be most interested in

A. Fiber optics.

B. A local area network (LAN).

C. A PBX system.

D. Electronic data interchange (EDI).

238. Gateways are hardware or software products that

A. Determine the best path for data.

B. Translate between two protocol families.

C. Connect local area networks.

D. Strengthen signals.

239. Which term best describes the systems design approach that begins with obtaining an understanding of the organization's environment and significant activities?

A. Prototyping.

B. Feasibility analysis.

C. Bottom-up method.

D. Top-down method.

240. Which approach to writing computer programs is specifically based on self-contained reusable parts?

A. Structured English.

B. Prototyping.

C. Pseudocode.

D. Object technology.

241. Allowing end-users to develop their own applications

A. Ensures data consistency.

B. Facilitates locating data.

C. Improves integration with other information systems.

D. Decentralizes control.

242. Which systems development approach salvages reusable components of existing systems and restructures them?

A. Prototyping.

B. Structured English.

C. Reengineering.

D. Parallel operation.

243. Computer-aided software engineering

A. Can generate program documentation.

B. Cannot generate program code.

C. Cannot generate program logic design.

D. Can generate information requirements.

244. Proper segregation of duties in a computer environment suggests which of the following duties for a computer operator?

	Programming Computer Applications	Systems Design
A.	Yes	Yes
B.	No	Yes
C.	Yes	No
D.	No	No

245. Formal lines of authority are depicted in a(n)

A. Systems flowchart.

B. Organization chart.

C. Program flowchart.

D. Gantt chart.

246. Information about jobs processed, job start and stop times, and problems encountered is contained in the

A. Console log.

B. Computer run book.

C. Program run manual.

D. Systems documentation.

247. Which of the following is a weakness in internal control for computer operations?

A. A data control group distributes computer reports.

B. Systems analysts have access to flowcharts.

C. Console operators have access to the file library containing programs.

D. Programmers do not have access to the file library containing programs.

248. Computer operations centers have been targets of sabotage. Thus, all of the following actions are appropriate except

A. Maintaining a low profile concerning computer processing.

B. Downplaying the importance of the computer center.

C. Monitoring the activities of known saboteurs.

D. Disguising the computer center facility.

249. One of the database administrator's responsibilities is to

A. Review output for errors.

B. Protect the database.

C. Develop database applications.

D. Distribute output.

250. Backup of files used in online systems

A. Is provided by a rollback and recovery technique.

B. Requires that the files be dumped onto a computer printout.

C. Requires that the files be dumped onto magnetic disks.

D. Is typically provided by the grandfather-father-son technique.

251. A checkpoint and restart procedure is used to

A. Implement the grandfather-father-son technique.

B. Eliminate the need to rerun a complete program that was in use when a power failure occurred.

C. Require the use of an auxiliary computer facility.

D. Protect a company if its computer facilities are destroyed.

252. Proper external labels on file media are important to prevent

A. Unauthorized access to a file.

B. Abuse of a file.

C. Erasing a file.

D. Theft of a file.

253. Boundary protection

A. Prevents electrical power loss interruptions.

B. Permits the sending of more than one message on a communication line.

C. Increases the use of a computer's memory by bringing data from disk storage into main memory only when it is needed.

D. Prevents interference with programs or data caused by activity related to other programs or data.

254. Program documentation should include

I. Systems flowcharts
II. Gantt charts
III. Approval and change sheets

A. I and II only.

B. I and III only.

C. II and III only.

D. I, II, and III.

255. Which step in the development of an information system requires approval by the management of a user department?

A. Design of hardware controls.

B. System conversion.

C. Hiring of computer personnel.

D. Drafting of operating instructions for computer personnel.

256. A company's data or programs are most likely to contract a virus as a result of

A. Message switching within the firm's system.

B. Reading electronic mail in a local area network.

C. Downloading software from an electronic bulletin board.

D. Using add-in boards.

257. Unexplained losses of data and involuntary changes in files in a computer system are most likely due to

A. The lack of adequate documentation.

B. Encryption.

C. Improper labeling of files.

D. The presence of a virus.

258. A system flowchart emphasizes

A. Reporting relationships.

B. Decision matrices.

C. Data flow.

D. Computer program logic.

259. As part of the documentation of an information system, a decision table may be used to represent the

A. Possible combinations of alternative logic conditions and corresponding courses of action for each condition in a computer program.

B. Flow of sequential processes in a system.

C. Conversion of source programs written in a higher-level language into a machine-readable object program.

D. Sequence of logical operations performed during the execution of a computer program.

260. Structured analysis

A. Uses data flow diagrams.

B. Is a bottom down approach.

C. Relies on decision tables and program flowcharts.

D. Uses graphical aids to depict an entire system, not just the flow of data.

261. The offline storage symbol is

A.

B. 

C. 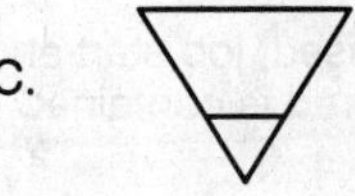

D. 

262. A parallelogram is the flowcharting symbol that represents

A. A manual operation.

B. A computer disk file.

C. General input and output.

D. Processing.

263. An appropriate password security measure is to

A. Prohibit certain character strings.

B. Print passwords on hard copy output.

C. Changing passwords infrequently.

D. Complete and immediate deletion of old password values.

264. Which of the following most directly guards against theft of software licensed to an organization by vendors?

A. An integrated test facility.

B. Antivirus software.

C. Monitoring of access attempts.

D. Diskless workstations.

265. A firm that allows users to communicate via telephone into the LAN file server should maintain

A. Online backup copies of all application software.

B. An access log of all successful and unsuccessful attempts to use the system.

C. Utility software.

D. Fingerprint biometric authorization before allowing access.

266. Biometric technologies are improving computer system security. Which of the following is a biometric technology?

A. Randomly assigned passwords.

B. Hand geometry.

C. Key cards.

D. Device authorization.

267. Device authorization tables are

A. Application controls.

B. Access controls.

C. Limit controls.

D. Production controls.

268. Resetting the values of memory locations to zero

A. Cannot be done if a callback feature is part of the control structure.

B. Is a characteristic of asynchronous transmission.

C. Prevents scavenging for residual information.

D. Permits equalization of modems.

269. A company maintains files on a server. Certain employees are not allowed access to these files. The company currently uses passwords to limit access. An additional control that could be implemented to minimize the risk that employees will be able to view the files is to use

A. Secondary keys.

B. Primary keys.

C. Scavenging.

D. Encryption.

270. A computer with dial-up capabilities is exposed to the additional risk that unauthorized persons may gain access to the computer if they have the telephone number. Which of the following help to control this additional risk?

I. High baud rate lines
II. Automatic call forwarding
III. Access codes
IV. Dial-back capability
V. Data encryption

A. I, II, III.

B. I, III, V.

C. II, IV, V.

D. III, IV, V.

271. Which set of controls relate to specific tasks performed by the computer processing department?

A. Application controls.

B. Access controls.

C. Software controls.

D. Life-cycle controls.

272. The acronym GIGO relates to which of the following?

A. No matter how good the computer hardware, if programming is not sufficient, the system will produce poor results.

B. No matter how good the computer system is, if input is inappropriate, the output will be inappropriate.

C. No matter how good the computer operators are at their jobs, if programmers are not qualified, the system will not produce satisfactory results.

D. No matter how good the programmers are at their jobs, if computer operators are not qualified, the system will not produce satisfactory results.

273. In a batch processing application, a printout showing exceptions and control totals is generated during

A. Input validation.

B. Batching of source documents for processing.

C. Performance of backup procedures.

D. Echo checking.

274. Online data conversion is difficult to audit because

A. Magnetic tape may be substituted for magnetic disk.

B. The audit trail is often invisible.

C. The audit trail is in the form of computer printouts.

D. Optical scanners may be used.

275. A hash total

A. Is a data output validation routine.

B. Results from adding numbers not normally added.

C. Reconciles financial totals.

D. Provides access control.

276. One type of control is the establishment of batch or control totals. Control totals include

A. Terminal logs.

B. Match counts.

C. Record counts.

D. Transaction logs.

277. A check digit is most likely used to

A. Check the character length of a field.

B. Detect errors made in the conversion of source documents to machine-readable form.

C. Check for the consistency of fields.

D. Test whether a value is outside a range.

278. Field checks would be most useful in the detection of

A. Entering the hours worked as 94 rather than 49.

B. Entering the quantity sold as 3R rather than 38.

C. Entering item number 1736 as 1376.

D. The assignment of a valid identification code to the wrong customer.

279. A test to ensure that all data elements are entered before processing is a(n)

A. Sequence check.

B. Validity check.

C. Completeness test.

D. Echo check.

280. Which of the following errors would most likely be detected by a limit check?

A. Keying an invalid number for the customer number.

B. Keying employee number 582 as C82.

C. Miskeying a customer's name from the source document.

D. Entering 734 as an account number when the accounts are numbered from 001 to 500.

281. This portion of a program flowchart depicts

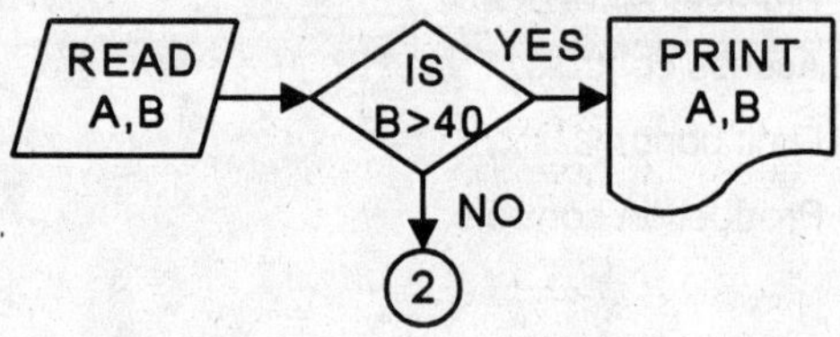

A. A tape to disk transfer.

B. A limit test.

C. An unconditional "go to" instruction.

D. A program loop.

282. Displaying a document on screen with blanks for data items to be provided by the user is

A. Preformatting.

B. Echo checking.

C. Validity checking.

D. Desk checking.

283. A computer system echoes back to the user certain input information. The purpose of this procedure is for the user to confirm that the transaction has been entered properly. This control is best described as

A. Visual display.

B. A desk check.

C. A sequence check.

D. Closed-loop verification.

284. To assess the control risk of a computer processing system at less than the maximum, the auditor must

A. Test the effectiveness of the controls.

B. Test the efficiency of the controls.

C. Perform substantive tests of the output of the system.

D. Rely on the work of the internal auditors.

285. Which procedures are performed in an audit of the manual aspects of an information system?

A. Inquiries of personnel, completion of a questionnaire, observation, and review of documents.

B. Identification and evaluation of critical records and processes and use of test decks.

C. Inquiries of personnel and parallel simulation.

D. Completion of a questionnaire and use of generalized audit software.

286. In the test data approach to testing a computerized accounting system, which, if any, transaction types are developed?

	Valid Transactions	Invalid Transactions
A.	Yes	Yes
B.	No	Yes
C.	No	No
D.	Yes	No

287. Parallel simulation involves

A. Tracing and mapping.

B. Auditing around and through the computer.

C. Simultaneous operation of an entity's old and new information systems.

D. Duplicate processing of the client's data using a program controlled by the auditor.

288. Which of the following audit techniques will require auditing through the computer?

A. Considering the segregation of duties in the computer processing department.

B. Using an integrated test facility.

C. Reviewing system documentation.

D. Desk checking programs.

289. The snapshot technique

A. Identifies program statements not executed, the CPU time for each statement executed, and the number of times each statement was executed.

B. Is most useful in parallel simulation.

C. Tags and traces live transactions through the processing system and evaluates the impact of the transactions on the output.

D. Captures data used in processing at a specific point in the stream of processing.

290. An embedded audit module

A. Reports code usage within a program.

B. Calls audit routines to perform processing for audit activity.

C. Is useful for debugging applications.

D. Selects transactions meeting specified criteria.

291. If an audit client's financial data are processed by an external computer service organization,

A. Control risk for the assertions contained in the data processed by the service organization must be assessed at the maximum level.

B. The independent auditor is required by GAAS to obtain the report of another external auditor regarding control risk at the service organization.

C. The independent auditor is required by GAAS to audit through the service organization.

D. Control risk may be reduced because of the greater segregation of duties.

292. The file containing records relating to specified data items and the list of the programs used to process them is the

A. Data dictionary.

B. Database management system.

C. Decision table.

D. Data entry monitor.

293. Currently, the least likely use of generalized audit software packages is to

A. Select and summarize records.

B. Extract, compare, and analyze file data.

C. Audit systems with diverse computers and programming languages.

D. Test extensions and footings.

294. An auditor is most likely to use generalized audit software to

A. Assess control risk.

B. Evaluate segregation of duties.

C. Prepare spreadsheets.

D. Develop custom software for each engagement.

295. Auditors may find utility programs useful for

A. Sorting and copying records.

B. Converting source code to object code.

C. Performing applications such as recording and posting transactions.

D. Enhancing the understanding of internal control.

296. The job content of information systems (IS) auditors has which of the following domains?

I. Information Systems Organization and Management
II. Information Systems Process
III. Information Entry, Processing, and Output

A. I only.

B. I and II.

C. I and III.

D. I, II, and III.

297. When an information systems audit manager is engaged in audit planning, (s)he

A. Will most likely draw upon the work of an external auditor regarding the safeguarding of company assets.

B. Will most likely draw upon the work of an external auditor regarding the promotion of operational efficiency.

C. Does not know what areas are to appear on the IS audit plan until a risk analysis is completed.

D. Should meet with the audit committee before a risk analysis of areas of exposure has been undertaken.

298. A characteristic of distributed data processing (DDP) systems is that

A. Communications functions are increasingly performed by software.

B. They minimize the need for audit risk analysis.

C. They reduce the complexity of the audit.

D. End-user software may be susceptible to errors by unskilled users.

299. A hotsite is a service bureau where data centers obtain processing services in case of a disaster. The organization's least concern regarding a hotsite is that

A. Availability of facilities is limited.

B. It does not have the most recently updated version of the operating system.

C. Files are adequately protected.

D. It has many subscribers.

300. A firm is in the process of selecting a service bureau to meet its data processing needs. To assess the financial stability of the service bureau, the firm might request that the service bureau

A. Submit to an audit.

B. Maintain a compensating balance with a bank.

C. Provide a set of its latest financial statements.

D. File with the SEC.

COURSE 5
STATISTICAL SAMPLING

This course covers statistical sampling applications to auditing including basic concepts, sampling methodology, sample selection, and dollar-unit sampling. It also covers AU 350. This course contains 166 questions, of which 40 constitute the final examination. As continuing professional education, 4 hours of CPE credit are recommended based on one-half the average completion time. If any of the CPE agencies you report to measures self-study CPE in terms of average completion time (rather than one-half average completion time), your certificate of completion will indicate 8 hours of maximum recommended CPE credit. Additional discussion regarding self-study credit measurement is provided in the introduction.

Date Completed	Time (Minutes)	
________	________	1. Work through each question in Chapter 6 (pages 387 through 432) in *Auditing & Systems Exam Questions and Explanations*, 8th edition.
		a. Cover the answer explanations, which appear to the right of each question, with a piece of paper. Do not skip questions.
		b. Answer each question: circle your answer or write "T" or "F" next to the alternative answer choices.
		c. Lift the cover sheet and compare your choice with the correct answer in the first line of the answer explanation.
		d. Study the answer explanation.
________	________	2. Take the final exam by answering questions 301 through 340 on the following pages.
		3. Carefully transfer your answers for these 40 questions to the CPE final exam answer sheet. Be sure you use the circles numbered 301 through 340.
		4. Mark **B 0 B 5** (B means Blank) as the course number on page 2 of the answer sheet. See example at right.
		5. Refer to the INTRODUCTION chapter in this book for instructions on how to complete the remainder of the machine-readable answer sheet.
		6. Please complete the accompanying course evaluation and submit it with your answer sheet.

COURSE NUMBER(S)			
	0		5
0	●	0	0
1	1	1	1
2	2	2	2
3	3	3	3
4	4	4	4
5	5	5	●
6	6	6	6
7	7	7	7
8	8	8	8
9	9	9	9

Total Time ________ (Carry this amount to your CPE course evaluation form.)

301. The auditor may select either statistical or nonstatistical sampling. Which of the following is a true statement concerning the two approaches?

A. Nonstatistical sampling involves risk that statistical sampling does not.

B. Either approach can provide sufficient competent evidence.

C. The choice of methods directly affects the auditor's decisions about auditing procedures.

D. Statistical sampling provides more competent evidence than nonstatistical sampling.

302. The primary advantage of statistical sampling is that it allows the auditor to

A. Eliminate auditor judgment.

B. Eliminate the causes of nonsampling risk.

C. Design more efficient samples.

D. Evaluate the competence of evidential matter.

303. The application of statistical sampling techniques is most closely related to the

A. Field work standards.

B. General standards.

C. Independence standards.

D. Reporting standards.

304. An example of nonsampling risk is

A. Drawing an erroneous conclusion from the sample data.

B. Improperly applying a proper auditing procedure.

C. The existence of a smaller ratio of monetary misstatements in the sample than in the account balance tested.

D. The existence of a greater ratio of control deviations in the sample than in the class of transactions tested.

305. In substantive testing, the incorrect acceptance of a false hypothesis is

A. An alpha error.

B. A Type II error.

C. A Type I error.

D. An aspect of nonsampling risk.

306. The complement of the confidence level for

A. Attribute sampling is the risk of assessing control risk too high.

B. Attribute sampling is the risk of incorrect acceptance.

C. Variables sampling is the risk of assessing control risk too low.

D. Variables sampling is the risk of incorrect rejection.

307. In statistical sampling the concept of materiality is most closely related to the

A. Tolerable misstatement.

B. Control risk assessment.

C. Probability of misstatement.

D. Inherent risk assessment.

308. In substantive testing, a higher acceptable level of audit risk

A. Permits the auditor to plan to find larger misstatements.

B. Results from assessing control risk too high.

C. Increases the tolerable rate of deviations.

D. Decreases tolerable misstatement.

309. The standard error of the mean for a statistical sample is

A. Increased by stratifying the population.

B. Decreased by reducing the sample size.

C. Decreased by increasing the estimate of the population standard deviation.

D. Decreased by decreasing the estimated variability of the population.

310. The sampling method that calculates the average value of items in the sample and multiplies the average value times the number of items in the population to estimate the population value is

A. Discovery sampling.

B. Attribute sampling.

C. Stratified sampling.

D. Mean-per-unit sampling.

311. Ratio estimation should be used when

A. The auditor is concerned with the frequency of deviations.

B. Book values are not available for each sample item.

C. Misstatements tend to be in one direction.

D. Misstatements are frequent and in both directions.

312. Stop-or-go sampling may be used to

A. Test the effectiveness of controls.

B. Search for critical errors that have an expected occurrence rate of 0%.

C. Estimate quantities or dollar amounts.

D. Stratify the population.

313. Systematic sample selection

A. Samples blocks of items rather than individual items.

B. Requires that every item in the sample correspond to a random number.

C. Requires increased time to locate an individual item compared with random number selection.

D. Selects every nth item. The value of n equals the number of items in the population divided by the sample size.

314. Stratified sample selection is used to

A. Eliminate the need for auditor judgment in the statistical sampling process.

B. Make random selections of groups of items as the sampling units.

C. Sample normally distributed populations only.

D. Reduce the effect of high variability in the population.

315. Stratification of a population is done by

A. Dividing it into subpopulations.

B. Combining it with other populations.

C. Choosing every nth item.

D. Blocking the sample.

316. Block sampling selects groups of items rather than individual items. A drawback of block sampling is that

A. The sample may be biased if homogeneous blocks are selected.

B. Locating items in the sample is more time-consuming than when using other methods.

C. Sample sizes are larger than those drawn using other methods.

D. The sample may be biased if heterogenous blocks are selected.

317. That random numbers and items in the population need not correspond is an advantage of

A. Block sampling over systematic sampling.

B. Cluster sampling over random number sampling.

C. Random number sampling over attribute sampling.

D. Attribute sampling over variables sampling.

318. The auditor uses attribute sampling to

A. Determine whether a balance is fairly stated.

B. Test a management assertion about valuation.

C. Test the effectiveness of a control.

D. Determine whether a book value appears to be reasonable.

319. After taking an attribute sample, the auditor counts the deviations in the sample. These deviations can best be described as

A. Overstatements or understatements of a balance.

B. Failures of control.

C. Miscounts.

D. Valuations of assets or liabilities.

320. Which of the following is a possible application of attribute sampling?

A. Estimate the number of times a required approval for purchase orders was not obtained.

B. Estimate the amount of inventory on hand at year end.

C. Estimate the dollar value of the fixed assets account.

D. Determine the accounts receivable selected for confirmation.

Questions 321 through 323 are based on the following information. The diagram below depicts the auditor's estimated maximum deviation rate compared with the tolerable rate, and also depicts the true population deviation rate compared with the tolerable rate.

Auditor Estimate Based on Sample Results	True Sate of Population	
	Deviation Rate is Less than Tolerable Rate	Deviation Rate Exceeds Tolerable Rate
Maximum Deviation Rate Exceeds Tolerable Rate	I.	III.
Maximum Deviation Rate is Less than Tolerable Rate	II.	IV.

321. As a result of an attribute test, the auditor assesses control risk too high and thereby increases substantive testing. This situation is illustrated by

A. I.

B. II.

C. III.

D. IV.

322. As a result of an attribute test, the auditor correctly assesses control risk as high and thereby increased substantive testing. This situation is illustrated by

A. I.

B. II.

C. III.

D. IV.

323. As a result of an attribute test, the auditor correctly assesses control risk at less than the maximum and thereby decreases substantive testing. This situation is illustrated by

A. I.

B. II.

C. III.

D. IV.

324. While executing an attribute sampling plan, the auditor discovers several documents with supervisors' signatures that appear to be forged. The auditor most likely will

A. Count the deviations twice in the assessment of the upper deviation limit.

B. Convert the sampling plan to a discovery sampling plan.

C. Give special consideration to the qualitative aspects of the sampled items.

D. Discard the sample and select a new sample.

325. An auditor has determined the tolerable rate of deviations from a prescribed control procedure to be 5% and the expected rate to be 3%. If the sample rate is 6% but the true population rate is 2%, the auditor will be most likely to

A. Increase the acceptable level of detection risk.

B. Incorrectly accept the account balance.

C. Assess control risk too high.

D. Commit a beta error.

326. A test of 400 documents, selected randomly by the auditor, revealed 20 that contained erroneously coded customer identification numbers. At the 95.5% confidence level, what precision (rounded to the nearest hundredth) can be assigned if the confidence coefficient is 2.00?

A. ± .00

B. ± .02

C. ± .03

D. ± .05

327. In an audit of a company's numerous receivables, the auditor drew a random sample of 20 items based on a variables sampling plan. What is the effect of the use of this size sample?

A. The risk of assessing control risk too low is decreased.

B. The risk of incorrect acceptance is decreased.

C. The risk of incorrect rejection is decreased.

D. The risk that the sample is unrepresentative is increased.

328. The auditor most likely uses variables sampling, such as difference estimation, to

A. Estimate the value of a population.

B. Test the effectiveness of a control.

C. Determine whether fraudulent transactions have occurred.

D. Reduce the need for judgment in the audit process.

329.

Sample size	100 items
Average sample item	\$80
Estimated standard deviation	\$15

Assuming a two-tailed 90% confidence level (C = 1.64), the upper confidence limit for the average sample item, given the information above, is

A. \$77.54

B. \$80.25

C. \$81.64

D. \$82.46

330. In dollar-unit (probability-proportional-to-size) sampling, all the following are true except

A. Every nth dollar in the population is selected.

B. Each dollar has a known probability of being selected.

C. The probability of selection of a sampled item is inversely related to the value of the item.

D. More than one dollar may be selected from a sample item.

331. An account receivable with a zero balance will not be included in a dollar-unit sample in the absence of special design considerations. The reason is that

A. It cannot be understated.

B. It contains no sampling units.

C. No account in the general ledger with a zero balance needs to be audited.

D. The auditor will omit the account even if its inclusion is indicated by the sample selection method.

332. Which of the following are advantages of dollar-unit sampling?

I. It easily considers population items with zero or negative values.
II. It allows the auditor to estimate deviation rates.
III. It is particularly appropriate for the audit of account balances that are more likely to be overstated than understated.

A. III only.

B. I and III.

C. II and III.

D. I and II.

333. If BV is the book value, RF the reliability factor, and TM the tolerable misstatement, the basic sample size formula for a probability-proportional-to-size sampling application is

A. TM ÷ RF.

B. BV ÷ (TM x RF).

C. (BV x RF) ÷ TM.

D. BV ÷ TM.

334. In dollar-unit sampling, the upper misstatement limit (UML) is the sum of the allowance for precision gap widening, the basic precision, and the

A. Total projected misstatement.

B. Tolerable misstatement.

C. Sampling interval.

D. Reliability factor.

335. Dual-purpose testing is customarily used when the

A. Actual rate of deviations from a control is expected to exceed the tolerable rate.

B. Assessed level of control risk is at the maximum.

C. Sample provides evidence for tests of controls and substantive testing.

D. Sample required for attribute testing is the same as that for variables testing.

336. The sample size for a test of controls will most clearly increase if the

A. Expected population deviation rate decreases and the tolerable rate decreases.

B. Expected population deviation rate increases and the tolerable rate increases.

C. Allowable risk of assessing control risk too low decreases and the expected population deviation rate decreases.

D. Allowable risk of assessing control risk too low decreases and the tolerable rate decreases.

337. The sample size varies _____ with changes in confidence level and _____ with changes in precision.

A. Inversely; inversely.

B. Inversely; directly.

C. Directly; inversely.

D. Directly; directly.

338. An auditor is statistically sampling a population for an attribute. If the auditor uses a confidence level of 95.5%, a confidence coefficient of 2.00, an expected error rate of 8%, and a desired precision interval of ±4%, the required sample size is approximately

A. 736

B. 368

C. 184

D. 92

339. An increase in population size

A. Decreases the effect of the finite population correction factor on the sample size.

B. Decreases the sample size.

C. Has no effect on sample size.

D. Has no effect on the finite population correction factor.

340. If n equals the sample size, BV equals the book value of a client's accounts receivable, RF is the appropriate risk factor, TM is tolerable misstatement (a nonzero amount), EF is the expansion factor, and AM is anticipated misstatement (a nonzero amount), the sample-size formula for an application of probability-proportional-to-size (PPS) sampling (also called dollar-unit sampling) is best stated as

A. $n = \dfrac{BV \times RF}{AM - (TM \times EF)}$

B. $n = \dfrac{BV \times RF}{EF\ (TM - AM)}$

C. $n = \dfrac{BV \times RF}{TM - (AM \times EF)}$

D. $n = \dfrac{BV \times EF}{RF\ (TM - AM)}$

COURSE 6
AUDIT REPORTS

This course covers the principal issues with respect to audit reports, including adherence to GAAP, disclosure, consistency, the types of opinions, scope limitations, and other matters. Certain other kinds of reports (e.g., special reports) are addressed in Course 7. Course 6 contains 280 questions, of which 60 constitute the final examination. As continuing professional education, 6 hours of CPE credit are recommended based on one-half the average completion time. If any of the CPE agencies you report to measures self-study CPE in terms of average completion time (rather than one-half average completion time), your certificate of completion will indicate 12 hours of maximum recommended CPE credit. Additional discussion regarding self-study credit measurement is provided in the introduction.

Date Completed	Time (Minutes)
______	______

1. Work through each question in Chapter 7 (pages 433 through 510) in *Auditing & Systems Exam Questions and Explanations*, 8th Edition.
   a. Cover the answer explanations, which appear to the right of each question, with a piece of paper. Do not skip questions.
   b. Answer each question: circle your answer or write "T" or "F" next to the alternative answer choices.
   c. Lift the cover sheet and compare your choice with the correct answer in the first line of the answer explanation.
   d. Study the answer explanation.

______ ______

2. Take the final exam by answering questions 341 through 400 on the following pages.
3. Carefully transfer your answers for these 60 questions to the CPE final exam answer sheet. Be sure you use the circles numbered 341 through 400.
4. Mark **B 0 B 6** (B means Blank) as the course number on page 2 of the answer sheet. See example at right.
5. Refer to the INTRODUCTION chapter in this book for instructions on how to complete the remainder of the machine-readable answer sheet.
6. Please complete the accompanying course evaluation and submit it with your answer sheet.

COURSE NUMBER(S)			
	0		6
0	●	0	0
1	1	1	1
2	2	2	2
3	3	3	3
4	4	4	4
5	5	5	5
6	6	6	●
7	7	7	7
8	8	8	8
9	9	9	9

Total Time ______ (Carry this amount to your CPE course evaluation form.)

341. Which of the following is one of the four standards of reporting included in GAAS?

A. Due professional care is to be exercised in the performance of the audit and the preparation of the report.

B. The report shall state whether the financial statements are presented in accordance with GAAP.

C. Sufficient competent evidential matter is to be obtained to afford a reasonable basis for an opinion regarding the financial statements under audit.

D. The report shall state that GAAS have been followed in the conduct of the audit.

342. According to the fourth reporting standard of GAAS, the report should

A. Express an opinion on the financial statements taken as a whole or disclaim an opinion.

B. Express a single opinion or disclaim an opinion on the full set of financial statements but not on individual statements.

C. Express an opinion or disclaim an opinion on individual financial statements but not on the full set of statements.

D. Express an opinion on specific items in the financial statements taken as a whole.

343. The standard audit report explicitly states, "These financial statements are the responsibility of the

A. Independent auditor."

B. SEC."

C. Company's management."

D. Internal auditor."

344. Which of the following statements concerning GAAP is false?

A. GAAP represents conventions and procedures that define accounting practice.

B. GAAP may evolve and change over time.

C. GAAP is primarily established by governmental agencies.

D. GAAP attempts to provide uniform standards to measure financial presentations.

345. Officially established accounting principles (GAAP) for state and local governments include

A. All FASB and GASB Statements and Interpretations.

B. GASB Statements and GASB Interpretations.

C. AICPA Industry Audit and Accounting Guides.

D. Prevalent industry practices.

346. Material unjustified departures from GAAP may result in a(n)

	Adverse Opinion	Qualified Opinion	Disclaimer of Opinion
A.	No	No	No
B.	Yes	Yes	No
C.	Yes	No	Yes
D.	Yes	Yes	Yes

347. An auditor may express an unqualified opinion while describing a departure from GAAP in a separate paragraph of the report when the financial statements contain a

A. Material, unjustified departure from GAAP.

B. Immaterial departure from GAAP.

C. Material, justified departure from GAAP.

D. Never.

348. The financial statements of regulated companies are often based on a comprehensive basis other than GAAP. When reporting on the non-GAAP statements of a regulated company that are intended for general distribution, the auditor

A. May express an unqualified opinion if the statements are audited in accordance with GAAS.

B. May issue a special report with an unqualified opinion.

C. Should use the standard form of report modified as appropriate for departures from GAAP.

D. Must disclaim an opinion.

349. AU 625, *Reports on the Application of Accounting Principles*, provides guidance to a reporting accountant

A. Who reports in writing to intermediaries on the application of accounting principles to hypothetical transactions.

B. In an engagement to provide expert testimony.

C. In an engagement to advise other public accountants.

D. Who is reporting in financial statements prepared in accordance with a comprehensive basis of accounting other than GAAP.

350. The client has changed from one generally accepted accounting principle to another but has failed to justify the change. Which type of report may be appropriate?

	Unqualified	Qualified	Adverse
A.	Yes	Yes	No
B.	Yes	Yes	Yes
C.	No	Yes	No
D.	No	Yes	Yes

351. Which of the following accounting changes does not require modification of the audit report?

A. Failure to restate prior year statements after a pooling of interests.

B. Change in accounting estimate.

C. Error correction involving a principle.

D. A change in the presentation of cash flows that involves determination of the items treated as cash equivalents.

352. Which of the following accounting changes requires a consistency modification of the audit report?

A. Accounting for a substantially different transaction or event.

B. Changes in classifications and reclassifications.

C. Changes in the reporting entity.

D. Error correction not involving a principle.

353. Which of the following accounting changes would require restatement of prior financial statements presented comparatively?

A. A change from LIFO to any other inventory valuation method.

B. A change to LIFO from any other inventory valuation method.

C. A change in the useful lives of depreciable assets.

D. A change in principle inseparable from a change in estimate.

354. If a company changes from deferring and amortizing a cost to recording it as an expense when incurred because future benefits of the cost have become doubtful, the auditor should

A. Modify the report as to consistency. This is a change in principle inseparable from a change in estimate.

B. Modify the report as to consistency. This is a correction of an error in principle.

C. Not modify the report as to consistency. This is a change in accounting principle.

D. Not modify the report as to consistency. This is a change in estimate.

355. If management fails to disclose information required by GAAP in the financial statements, the auditor should

A. Express an unqualified opinion if the information is reported elsewhere by management.

B. Disclaim an opinion.

C. Modify the introductory, scope, and opinion paragraphs of the report.

D. Disclose the information in the audit report.

356. If the client issues statements of financial position and income but omits the cash flow statement, the auditor will most likely

A. Add a footnote to correct the improper financial statement presentation.

B. Qualify the opinion, explain the reason in a separate paragraph, but not prepare the omitted statement.

C. Express an adverse opinion and prepare the omitted statement.

D. Conclude that the statements taken as a whole are unfairly presented.

357. If single-year statements only are presented for the year of a pooling, a footnote should disclose certain information about the pooled entities for the preceding year on a combined basis. If these disclosures are omitted, the audit report should contain

A. A qualified opinion and two explanatory paragraphs.

B. An unqualified opinion and one explanatory paragraph.

C. A qualified opinion and one explanatory paragraph.

D. An unqualified opinion and two explanatory paragraphs.

358. Subsequent events that provide additional evidence with respect to conditions that existed at the balance sheet date and that affect the estimates inherent in the process of preparing the financial statements should be

A. Reflected in the current financial statements.

B. Included in the auditor's report.

C. Disclosed in the footnotes only.

D. Reported separately to the SEC.

359. If an auditor concludes that a substantial doubt exists about the auditee's ability to continue as a going concern, (s)he must consider the adequacy of disclosure and modify the report. If disclosure is adequate, the auditor should

A. Specifically use the phrases "substantial doubt" and "going concern" in an explanatory paragraph.

B. Use conditional language in expressing the conclusion about the substantial doubt.

C. Express a qualified or adverse opinion as a result of the substantial doubt.

D. Express a qualified opinion or disclaim an opinion as a result of the substantial doubt.

360. If material segment disclosures are omitted from the audited financial statements, and the auditor believes the information should be included, the auditor must

	Modify the Opinion	Describe the Information	If Practicable, Provide the Information in the Report
A.	Yes	Yes	No
B.	Yes	Yes	Yes
C.	No	Yes	Yes
D.	No	No	No

361. The standard audit report mentions GAAP in the

	Introductory Paragraph	Scope Paragraph	Opinion Paragraph
A.	Yes	Yes	No
B.	No	Yes	Yes
C.	Yes	No	No
D.	No	No	Yes

362. An auditor emphasizes a matter in an explanatory paragraph but expresses an unqualified opinion. Matters suitable for this treatment include

A. Significant related party transactions but not subsequent events.

B. That the entity is a component of a larger enterprise but not significant related party transactions.

C. Accounting matters affecting comparability but not that the entity is a component of a larger enterprise.

D. Accounting matters affecting comparability but not failure to follow GAAP.

363. Which of the following phrases may appropriately be included in the opinion paragraph?

	With the Exception of	Except for	With the Foregoing Explanation
A.	Yes	Yes	No
B.	Yes	No	Yes
C.	No	Yes	Yes
D.	No	Yes	No

364. An audit report expresses a qualified opinion. The separate paragraph should

A. State that the auditor is independent.

B. State the reason the client used accounting principles that were not generally accepted.

C. Indicate that the financial statements are not intended for external use.

D. State the principal effects on the financial statements of the subject matter of the qualification.

365. A CPA who is not independent but has disclosed the lack of independence

A. May express an unqualified opinion on financial statements.

B. May express a qualified or an adverse opinion on financial statements.

C. Should disclaim an opinion on financial statements.

D. Should not issue a report of any kind.

366. Financial statements that are fairly presented should be

I. Neither too detailed nor too condensed
II. Based on the most conservative principles available
III. Subject to no material uncertainties
IV. Presented to reflect the underlying transactions within a range of acceptable limits

A. I and II only.

B. I and IV only.

C. II and III only.

D. III and IV only.

367. When an auditor expresses an adverse opinion, the

A. Opinion paragraph should give all the substantive reasons for the opinion.

B. Opinion paragraph should state the principal effects of the subject matter of the opinion, if practicable.

C. Explanatory paragraph should precede the opinion paragraph and state the principal effects of the subject matter of the opinion, if practicable.

D. Explanatory paragraph should follow the opinion paragraph and state all the substantive reasons for the opinion.

368. Which of the following most likely does not preclude the expression of an unqualified opinion on the complete set of financial statements?

A. The auditor did not observe the beginning inventory but has become satisfied by using alternative procedures.

B. Certain material transactions cannot be tested because of management's records retention policy.

C. The client's legal counsel has declined to state whether an act by the client having material financial statement effects is illegal.

D. The client would not sign the management representation letter.

369. A qualified opinion is not expressed because of

A. A departure from GAAP.

B. A lack of sufficient competent evidence.

C. An uncertainty unrelated to a departure from GAAP or a scope limitation.

D. A restriction on the scope of the audit.

370. The reason that an auditor may refer to a specialist in a modified audit report is to

A. Share the risk with the specialist.

B. Divide the responsibility for the report findings.

C. Provide additional assurance in the report.

D. Facilitate the understanding of the reason for the modification.

371. A report disclaiming an opinion on financial statements is similar to a report on a compilation of unaudited financial statements because

A. Both offer limited assurance.

B. Both require the auditor to be independent.

C. Neither refers to all financial statements presented.

D. Neither describes the procedures performed.

372. An auditor must not disclaim an opinion when

A. The financial statements contain a material departure from GAAP.

B. Significant uncertainties affect the financial statements.

C. (S)he is associated with unaudited and unreviewed financial statements.

D. A scope restriction was imposed by circumstances, such as the timing of the work.

373. A CPA would not necessarily be deemed associated with the client's financial statements

A. If (s)he consents to the use of his/her name with them.

B. If (s)he helps prepare them.

C. When (s)he has provided consulting services regarding computer processing procedures.

D. When (s)he only reviews them.

374. An auditor has expressed an adverse opinion on the financial statements taken as a whole but has included a statement that working capital appears to be fairly stated. This type of reporting is deemed inappropriate because the report constitutes a(n)

A. Piecemeal opinion.

B. Qualified adverse opinion.

C. Adverse opinion with two explanatory paragraphs.

D. Limited scope engagement report.

375. An unqualified opinion is most likely to be expressed when the

A. Timing of the audit precludes performance of all necessary procedures.

B. Accounting records are inadequate.

C. Auditor has been engaged to report on one basic financial statement only.

D. Client has imposed a restriction on the audit.

376. Which of the following is true concerning a report that includes an opinion qualified because of a scope limitation?

A. The opinion paragraph should indicate that the qualification pertains to the possible effects on the financial statements.

B. The opinion paragraph should indicate that the qualification is based on the scope limitation itself.

C. The explanatory paragraph should indicate that the qualification pertains to the possible effects on the financial statements.

D. The scope paragraph should indicate that the qualification is based on the scope limitation itself.

377. An auditor is most likely to express an unqualified opinion when

A. The client refuses to allow its lawyer to reply to the letter of audit inquiry.

B. The auditor owns only an immaterial amount of client stock.

C. Management precludes the auditor from obtaining sufficient evidence about whether an illegal act has occurred.

D. The auditor cannot confirm accounts receivable and must become satisfied by applying other procedures.

378. The audit report is not normally addressed to the

A. Chair of the board of directors of a corporation.

B. Partners of a partnership.

C. Proprietor of a proprietorship.

D. Shareholders of a closely held corporation.

379. The date of the auditor's report should normally coincide with the date

A. Stated in the engagement letter.

B. Of the completion of subsequent events procedures.

C. Of the financial statements.

D. The client is billed for the audit.

380. Dual dating an auditor's report implies that

A. The specific event referred to is unaudited.

B. The auditor is extending his/her responsibility for all events occurring subsequent to the completion of field work up to and including the specific event referred to.

C. The auditor is assuming no responsibility for events occurring subsequent to the completion of field work.

D. The auditor performed all subsequent events procedures up through the earliest of the two dates.

381. A predecessor auditor has agreed to reissue the report on the prior-period financial statements of a privately held company. They are to be presented comparatively with the audited statements for the current period. The date of the prior-period report will be used for the reissued report. With regard to the period between the original issuance and reissuance of the report, the predecessor auditor

A. Must obtain an updating representation letter from management.

B. Must perform standard subsequent events procedures.

C. Has no responsibility to carry out any procedures relating to events occurring after the report date.

D. Must perform standard review procedures.

382. A departure from GAAP caused an adverse opinion to be expressed on the prior year's financial statements. However, those statements have been restated during the current year in accordance with GAAP. The continuing auditor should

A. Change the opinion on the prior year's financial statements in the updated report.

B. Not change the prior opinion but refer to the restatement of the prior-period information in the updated report.

C. Not change the prior opinion or refer to the restatement of the prior-period information in the updated report.

D. Report only on the current financial statements and avoid reference to the prior report.

383. When financial statements for the current period are presented comparatively with those for the immediately preceding period, the continuing auditor should

I. Reissue the report for the prior period
II. Update the report for the prior period
III. If appropriate, include an opinion different from that previously expressed
IV. Not include an opinion different from that previously expressed

A. I and III.

B. I and IV.

C. II and III.

D. II and IV.

384. The phrase "applied on a basis consistent with that of the preceding year" should

A. Be included in the audit report on comparative financial statements.

B. Be included in the audit report on single-year financial statements.

C. Be included in the report only if a change in accounting principle was made during the year.

D. Not be included in the standard auditor's report.

385. An auditor reports on current-year financial statements. The prior year's statements were audited by another CPA and are not presented. Assuming no other basis for modifying the report on the single-year statements exists, the auditor should

A. Express an unqualified opinion and not refer to the prior year's statements or the report thereon.

B. Express an unqualified opinion and refer to the prior year's statements and the report thereon.

C. Modify the opinion for failure to present comparative statements.

D. Modify the opinion and refer to the prior year's statements and the report thereon only if the predecessor auditor did not express an unqualified opinion.

386. An auditor has reported on current-year financial statements that are presented comparatively with unaudited statements for the prior year. These comparative statements are presented in documents filed with the SEC. Thus,

I. The report on the comparative statements should refer to the unaudited statements
II. The unaudited statements should be clearly marked as unaudited
III. The report on the prior period should be reissued

A. I only.

B. II only.

C. III only.

D. II and III only.

387. A predecessor auditor who reissues a report on a prior period's financial statements should

A. Refer to the work and the report of the successor auditor.

B. Obtain a representation letter from the successor auditor.

C. Obtain a representation letter from the client's lawyer.

D. Modify the report to include a paragraph describing the scope of procedures performed before reissuing the report.

388. What condition is indicative of related party transactions?

A. A reduction in the amount of short-term debt with a corresponding increase in long-term debt.

B. Replacement of fully-depreciated assets.

C. Nonmonetary exchange of property.

D. Transactions with the U.S. government.

389. A material sales transaction has been concluded by an audit client with a related party. The client has reported this transaction as a normal sale but has disclosed information about it in the footnotes to the financial statements. The auditor will most likely

A. Ask the client to remove the footnote.

B. Ask the client to change the accounting treatment of the sale.

C. Ask the client not to make any future sales to the related party.

D. Do nothing because the treatment of the transaction was appropriate.

390. The auditee represents in a footnote that material related party transactions were consummated on terms similar to those obtainable in transactions with unrelated parties. If the auditor cannot draw a conclusion about the propriety of the footnote, (s)he should consider expressing

A. A qualified opinion or disclaiming an opinion.

B. A qualified or an adverse opinion.

C. An unqualified opinion but referring to an explanatory paragraph using the phrase "with the foregoing explanation."

D. An adverse opinion or disclaiming an opinion.

391. How may a material subsequent event relevant to a condition arising after the balance sheet date but before issuance of the audit report be treated?

I. Adjustment of the financial statements
II. Footnote disclosure
III. Presentation of pro forma data
IV. Reference by the auditor in an explanatory paragraph in the report

A. I, II, III.

B. I, II, IV.

C. II, III, IV.

D. III, IV.

392. After completion of the audit field work but prior to the issuance of the report, an auditor received information about the culmination of a condition existing at the balance sheet date. If the condition materially affects the financial statements, the auditor should request management to

A. Disclose the event in the financial statements and label it as unaudited.

B. Adjust the financial statements to reflect the event.

C. Disclose the event by presenting pro forma financial statements.

D. Include the information in a footnote.

393. After the balance sheet date but prior to the issuance of the audit report, the auditor learned of a material subsequent event. This event did not provide evidence about conditions existing at the balance sheet date. Management refuses to disclose this information. The auditor should

A. Insist that management present supplemental, pro forma financial statements.

B. Take no action if insurance will prevent a loss.

C. Provide the information in the report and express an unqualified opinion.

D. Modify the opinion.

394. The audit report had just been issued when a significant lawsuit that had been properly disclosed was settled. The auditor should

A. Request that the client notify the shareholders of the change in the audit report.

B. Issue a new audit report.

C. Notify the shareholders directly that the audit report will be updated.

D. Do nothing because resolution of a contingency is not deemed to be new information.

395. After issuing the report, the auditor became aware of newly discovered facts having a material effect on the financial statements. The auditor has verified the reliability of this information and determined its effects promptly. Accordingly, (s)he

A. Should recall the original financial statements and related audit report.

B. Must reissue corrected financial statements.

C. Has no further obligation because the nature of the transaction was discovered after issuance of the report.

D. Should urge the client to issue revised statements as soon as practicable.

396. An auditor is asked to reissue the report. The auditor is aware that an event subsequent to the issuance of the report has occurred that requires disclosure in but not adjustment of the financial statements. The proper action of the auditor is to

A. Reissue the report with the original date and have the client disclose in a footnote that the subsequent event was audited.

B. Reissue the report as of the date of the subsequent event if no additional audit work was performed.

C. Reissue the report with the original date and disregard the subsequent event.

D. Dual date the report if further audit work is performed.

397. If the principal auditor decides to refer to the work of another auditor, the modification to the report results in

A. An adverse opinion.

B. A qualified opinion.

C. A scope limitation.

D. No change in the nature of the opinion expressed.

398. The principal auditor should inquire about the professional reputation and independence of the other auditor when the principal auditor decides

	To Refer to the Audit of the Other Auditor	Not to Refer to the Audit of the Other Auditor
A.	No	No
B.	No	Yes
C.	Yes	No
D.	Yes	Yes

399. The division of responsibility between the portion of the financial statements covered by the principal auditor's own audit and that covered by the other auditor will be specifically stated as percentages or dollar amounts in which paragraph(s)?

	Introductory	Scope	Opinion
A.	Yes	Yes	Yes
B.	Yes	No	Yes
C.	No	No	Yes
D.	Yes	No	No

400. Pring, CPA, is the principal auditor of Awed Co. Otho, CPA, has audited a wholly owned subsidiary of Awed and expressed a qualified opinion. Pring

A. Must refer to Otho's qualified opinion.

B. May still express an unqualified opinion without referring to Otho's opinion if the qualification is not material to the consolidated statements.

C. May not refer to Otho's opinion if Pring expresses an unqualified opinion.

D. May only express a qualified or adverse opinion.

COURSE 7
SPECIAL REPORTS AND OTHER REPORTING ISSUES

This course covers independent auditor reports on matters other than audited financial statements. It includes special reports, compilations, reviews, reports on internal control, SEC reporting, letters to underwriters and other requesting parties, prospective financial information, and governmental auditing. This course contains 193 questions, of which 40 constitute the final examination. As continuing professional education, 4 hours of CPE credit are recommended based on one-half the average completion time. If any of the CPE agencies you report to measures self-study CPE in terms of average completion time (rather than one-half average completion time), your certificate of completion will indicate 8 hours of maximum recommended CPE credit. Additional discussion regarding self-study credit measurement is provided in the introduction.

Date Completed	Time (Minutes)	
________	________	1. Work through each question in Chapter 8 (pages 511 through 562) in *Auditing & Systems Exam Questions and Explanations*, 8th Edition. a. Cover the answer explanations, which appear to the right of each question, with a piece of paper. Do not skip questions. b. Answer each question: circle your answer or write "T" or "F" next to the alternative answer choices. c. Lift the cover sheet and compare your choice with the correct answer in the first line of the answer explanation. d. Study the answer explanation.
________	________	2. Take the final exam by answering questions 401 through 440 on the following pages. 3. Carefully transfer your answers for these 40 questions to the CPE final exam answer sheet. Be sure you use the circles numbered 401 through 440. 4. Mark **B 0 B 7** (B means Blank) as the course number on page 2 of the answer sheet. See example at right. 5. Refer to the INTRODUCTION chapter in this book for instructions on how to complete the remainder of the machine-readable answer sheet. 6. Please complete the accompanying course evaluation and submit it with your answer sheet.
Total Time	________	(Carry this amount to your CPE course evaluation form.)

COURSE NUMBER(S)

	0		7
0	●	0	0
1	1	1	1
2	2	2	2
3	3	3	3
4	4	4	4
5	5	5	5
6	6	6	6
7	7	7	●
8	8	8	8
9	9	9	9

401. Which of the following items is included when reporting on audited statements prepared in accordance with a comprehensive basis of accounting other than GAAP?

A. An opinion on whether the statements were fairly presented in accordance with GAAP.

B. Reference to the note to the financial statements that describes the basis of presentation.

C. An opinion on the propriety of the basis of accounting used.

D. A scope paragraph indicating that the audit was not in accordance with GAAS.

402. An auditor's report issued in connection with which of the following is considered to be a special report?

A. Specified elements from a balance sheet.

B. Compiled financial statements prepared in accordance with an appraised liquidation value.

C. Limited use prospective financial statements such as financial projections.

D. Application of accounting principles to specified transactions.

403. Comprehensive bases of accounting other than GAAP include the

	Cash Basis	Income Tax Basis
A.	Yes	No
B.	No	No
C.	Yes	Yes
D.	No	No

404. An auditor has been engaged to report on a specified element that is not a major portion of the financial statements. The auditor may appropriately express an opinion on the specified element

A. Only if (s)he has performed an audit of the financial statements.

B. Only if materiality is measured in relation to the financial statements as a whole.

C. Only if (s)he has not expressed an adverse opinion on the financial statements.

D. Although (s)he has expressed an adverse opinion on the financial statements.

405. The distribution of a special report must be restricted if it is based on

A. Agreed-upon procedures applied to specified accounts in the financial statements.

B. An audit of financial statements prepared using a basis of accounting specified by a regulatory agency.

C. An audit of specified accounts in the financial statements.

D. An audit by an auditor who is not a continuing auditor.

406. An auditor determines that other information in an annual report to shareholders is materially inconsistent with the audited financial statements on which (s)he is expressing an opinion. If the other information is not revised, the auditor's options include

A. Withholding use of the report or withdrawing from the engagement.

B. Expressing an adverse opinion on the financial statements or withdrawing from the engagement.

C. Modifying the opinion on the financial statements or withholding use of the report.

D. Disclaiming an opinion on the financial statements, expressing a qualified or adverse opinion, or withholding use of the report.

407. Certain entities may be required by the FASB or GASB to present supplementary information in addition to the financial statements. The audit report should include an explanatory paragraph if the information

A. Is placed outside the financial statements and is clearly labeled.

B. Is placed within the financial statements and is clearly labeled.

C. Departs materially from prescribed guidelines.

D. Has not been audited.

408. A report on condensed financial statements should state that

A. No opinion can be expressed because they are not in conformity with GAAP.

B. The auditor has expressed an opinion on the complete financial statements.

C. The condensed statements are derived from interim financial information.

D. They are prepared in conformity with another comprehensive basis of accounting.

409. The standard review report states that nothing caused the accountant to believe that material modifications should be made to the financial statements for them to conform with GAAP. This report contains

A. An opinion.

B. Positive assurance.

C. Negative assurance.

D. No assurance.

410. The standard report on a review of interim financial information should include a statement that

A. A review of interim financial information is substantially less in scope than an audit in accordance with GAAS.

B. The financial statements are presented fairly in accordance with generally accepted accounting principles.

C. No assurance is provided.

D. Search and verification procedures were performed.

411. The purpose of an engagement letter for a review of interim financial information of a public company is to

A. Describe the specific procedures to be applied.

B. Provide an understanding of the nature of the service to be performed.

C. Describe the content of the working papers that will be maintained.

D. Describe the type of opinion that will be expressed in the report.

412. The standard report on a review of interim financial information is most likely to be modified because of

A. An undisclosed uncertainty.

B. Lack of consistency.

C. Failure of the accountant to confirm receivables.

D. Use of the report of another accountant.

413. When a CPA has assisted in preparing, but has not audited or reviewed, the financial statements of a public company, (s)he should

A. Describe in the report any procedures that may have been applied and express limited assurance.

B. Read the financial statements for obvious misstatements and consider internal control.

C. Disclaim an opinion and not describe in the report any procedures that may have been applied.

D. Express a modified opinion or disclaim an opinion as circumstances warrant.

414. Providing automated bookkeeping services does not constitute a compilation service under SSARSs unless

A. The accountant also provides tax consulting.

B. The output of the processing consists of financial statements.

C. A working trial balance is prepared.

D. The accountant enters the data into the system.

415. For the purposes of the SSARSs, which of the following might be considered a private entity?

A. An entity whose shares are traded in a public market.

B. A partnership.

C. A joint venture controlled by a public entity.

D. An entity whose shares are traded over the counter but are quoted only locally.

416. Before compiling the financial statements of a nonpublic entity, an accountant should

A. Perform analytical procedures.

B. Obtain an understanding of internal control.

C. Possess an understanding of the nature of the entity's business.

D. Assess control risk.

417. The accountant should withdraw from a review engagement if

A. A written engagement letter is not obtained.

B. (S)he cannot gain an understanding of internal control.

C. The client refuses to correct substantial deficiencies in the financial statements.

D. The client has made changes in accounting principles that materially affect comparability.

418. An accountant has compiled a nonpublic entity's financial statements from which most disclosures required by GAAP have been omitted. The accountant may not accept the engagement unless the

	Standard Compilation Report is Modified	Omissions are Not Made to Mislead Users
A.	Yes	Yes
B.	Yes	No
C.	No	Yes
D.	No	No

419. The procedures ordinarily performed during a review of a nonpublic entity's financial statements include

A. Analytical procedures.

B. Cut-off tests.

C. Examining cash.

D. Confirmations.

420. An accountant applies additional procedures in a standard review of the financial statements of a nonpublic entity when

A. (S)he becomes aware that information forthcoming is incorrect, incomplete, or unsatisfactory.

B. The client does not provide adequate documentation for internal control.

C. The review engagement is changed to a compilation engagement.

D. (S)he wishes to state that GAAS were followed in the review process.

421. An accountant has reviewed the financial statements of a nonpublic entity. A material uncertainty and an inconsistency in the application of accounting principles have both been fully disclosed. The accountant must modify the review report because of the

	Uncertainty	Inconsistency
A.	Yes	Yes
B.	Yes	No
C.	No	Yes
D.	No	No

422. Before an accountant who was engaged to perform an audit in accordance with GAAS agrees to change the engagement to a review, (s)he must consider the

I. Implications of a restriction on the audit scope.
II. Additional audit effort to complete the audit

A. I only.

B. II only.

C. I and II.

D. Neither I nor II.

423. A continuing accountant performed a lower level of service for financial statements of the current period than for those of the preceding period. The accountant should

A. Update the report on the prior period's financial statements.

B. Reissue the report on the prior period's financial statements.

C. Provide no assurance about the prior period's financial statements.

D. Issue no report on the prior period's financial statements.

424. Which of the following are included in a standard report on management's assertion about the effectiveness of internal control?

I. A statement that the examination was made in accordance with AICPA standards
II. A statement that conditions may change
III. A statement that the degree of compliance may deteriorate
IV. A statement that errors may occur and not be detected

A. I and II.

B. II and III.

C. II, III, and IV.

D. I, II, III, and IV.

425. An independent auditor has been engaged to report on management's assertion about the effectiveness of internal control based on criteria established by a regulatory agency. Which of the following statements is true?

A. The assertion must be presented only in a letter of representation to the practitioner.

B. The assertion must be presented only in a separate management report.

C. If the control criteria have not been subjected to due process procedures, the appropriate form of the standard report must be modified.

D. If the control criteria have not been subjected to due process procedures, an inherent limitations paragraph is deleted from the standard report.

426. With respect to management's assertion about the effectiveness of internal control, a practitioner may

A. Examine or apply agreed-upon procedures to, but not review, the assertion.

B. Apply agreed-upon procedures to the assertion and provide negative assurance.

C. Examine or review, but not apply agreed-upon procedures to, the assertion.

D. Review the assertion and disclaim a positive opinion.

427. A service auditor issues a report on the internal control of an organization processing transactions for the user auditor's client. The report may be important to the user auditor in

A. Gaining an understanding of the controls related to client transactions.

B. Sharing responsibility for the audit opinion with the service auditor.

C. Providing reports on controls to the SEC.

D. Providing assurances in comfort letters.

428. A prospective financial statement based on assumptions by the responsible party reflecting the conditions it expects to exist and the course of action it expects to take is a

A. Financial projection.

B. Financial forecast.

C. Pro forma financial statement.

D. Partial presentation.

429. AT 200, *Financial Forecasts and Projections*, provides for minimum presentation guidelines for prospective financial information. A presentation is considered to be partial if it omits

A. A summary of significant accounting policies.

B. A summary of significant assumptions.

C. A description of what management intends the statements to present.

D. Primary and fully diluted earnings per share.

430. Prospective financial statements may be examined,

A. Reviewed, or subjected to agreed-upon procedures.

B. Compiled, or subjected to agreed-upon procedures.

C. Reviewed, or compiled.

D. Reviewed, compiled, or subjected to agreed-upon procedures.

431. Who is most likely to be responsible for the assumptions underlying prospective financial statements?

A. The potential acquirer of the client organization.

B. The client's management and the external auditor.

C. The internal auditor.

D. The SEC.

432. If the related historical financial statements have been audited, pro forma financial information may be

	Examined	Reviewed
A.	Yes	Yes
B.	Yes	No
C.	No	Yes
D.	No	No

433. In a typical comfort letter prepared for underwriters, the accountant

A. States an opinion on the fairness of presentation of financial statements.

B. States that the procedures performed were those (s)he deemed necessary in the circumstances.

C. Provides positive assurance as to whether interim financial statements are presented in conformity with GAAP.

D. Provides negative assurance based on a reasonable investigation.

434. When an independent accountant has reviewed interim information and his/her report is presented in a registration statement, the accountant's

A. Report is not considered to be a "report" but is "part" of the registration statement.

B. Services must be performed in accordance with GAO standards.

C. Responsibility extends to the effective date of the filing.

D. Status is that of management's designate before the SEC.

435. A company would report the change in independent auditors in a

A. Form S-1.

B. Form 8-K.

C. Form 10-Q.

D. Form 10-K.

436. The Single Audit Act and OMB Circular A-133 apply to audits of recipients of federal financial assistance. The auditor's responsibilities under the act include

A. Designating the cognizant agency.

B. Submitting a data collection form.

C. Identifying major and nonmajor federal programs.

D. Reporting on internal control.

437. The report on a financial statement audit performed in accordance with *Government Auditing Standards* should

I. Describe the scope of tests of compliance with laws and regulations and present the results
II. Refer to a separate report describing the scope and results of compliance tests
III. Provide positive assurance about compliance with laws and regulations

A. I or II.

B. I and III.

C. II and III.

D. II only.

438. Which set of documentation from a governmental audit "should contain sufficient information to enable an experienced auditor having no previous connection with the audit" to conclude that sufficient evidence was collected?

A. Client's procedures manual.

B. Auditor's working papers.

C. Client's financial statements.

D. Auditor's engagement letter.

439. A practitioner has accepted an engagement to examine management's written assertion about compliance with the requirements of specified laws and regulations. If the practitioner's report is intended for general use, the assertion must be in a

I. Representation letter to the practitioner
II. Separate report accompanying the practitioner's report

A. I only.

B. II only.

C. I or II.

D. I and II.

440. An engagement to report on management's discussion and analysis (MD&A) prepared under SEC rules and regulations may take which form(s)?

	Examination	Review	Application of Agreed-Upon Procedures
A.	Yes	Yes	Yes
B.	Yes	Yes	No
C.	Yes	No	No
D.	No	No	Yes

COURSE 8
INTERNAL AUDITING

This course emphasizes authoritative pronouncements by The Institute of Internal Auditors, including The IIA Code of Ethics, the Statement of Responsibilities of Internal Auditing (SRIA), and the Standards for the Professional Practice of Internal Auditing (SPPIA). These documents can be obtained from The Institute of Internal Auditors, 249 Maitland Avenue, Altamonte Springs, Florida 32701 (407) 830-7600. Also included are issues unique to internal auditing. This course contains 187 questions, of which 50 constitute the final examination. As continuing professional education, 5 hours of CPE credit are recommended based on one-half the average completion time. If any of the CPE agencies you report to measures self-study CPE in terms of average completion time (rather than one-half average completion time), your certificate of completion will indicate 10 hours of maximum recommended CPE credit. Additional discussion regarding self-study credit measurement is provided in the introduction.

Date Completed	Time (Minutes)	
________	________	1. Work through each question in Chapter 9 (pages 563 through 610) in *Auditing & Systems Exam Questions and Explanations*, 8th Edition. a. Cover the answer explanations, which appear to the right of each question, with a piece of paper. Do not skip questions. b. Answer each question: circle your answer or write "T" or "F" next to the alternative answer choices. c. Lift the cover sheet and compare your choice with the correct answer in the first line of the answer explanation. d. Study the answer explanation.
________	________	2. Take the final exam by answering questions 441 through 490 on the following pages.
		3. Carefully transfer your answers for these 50 questions to the CPE final exam answer sheet. Be sure you use the circles numbered 441 through 490.
		4. Mark **B 2 B 8** (B means Blank) as the course number on page 2 of the answer sheet. See example at right.
		5. Refer to the INTRODUCTION chapter in this book for instructions on how to complete the remainder of the machine-readable answer sheet.
		6. Please complete the accompanying course evaluation and submit it with your answer sheet.

COURSE NUMBER(S)

	0		8
⓪	●	⓪	⓪
①	①	①	①
②	②	②	②
③	③	③	③
④	④	④	④
⑤	⑤	⑤	⑤
⑥	⑥	⑥	⑥
⑦	⑦	⑦	⑦
⑧	⑧	⑧	●
⑨	⑨	⑨	⑨

Total Time ________ (Carry this amount to your CPE course evaluation form.)

441. Which of the following best describes the objective of internal auditing?

A. To assist members of the organization in the effective discharge of their responsibilities.

B. To assist management with the design and implementation of accounting and control systems.

C. To examine and evaluate an organization's accounting system as a service to management.

D. To monitor the organization's internal control system on behalf of the external auditors.

442. According to the Statement of Responsibilities of Internal Auditing, which of the following is not included in the scope of the internal audit function?

A. Appraising the economy and efficiency with which resources are employed.

B. Reviewing the strategic management process, assessing the quality of management decision making both quantitatively and qualitatively, and reporting the results to the audit committee.

C. Reviewing the means of safeguarding assets and, as appropriate, verifying the existence of such assets.

D. Reviewing operations or programs to ascertain whether results are consistent with established objectives and goals and whether the operations or programs are being carried out as planned.

443. Which of the following is within the scope of an internal auditing function?

A. Reviewing the means of safeguarding assets and verifying their existence.

B. Instituting internal control.

C. Setting operating standards.

D. Establishing criteria to determine if objectives have been met.

444. One of the purposes of the Standards for the Professional Practice of Internal Auditing as stated in the Introduction to the Standards is to

A. Establish the independence of internal auditing.

B. Impart an understanding of the responsibilities of internal auditing to all levels of management.

C. Establish the objectivity of internal auditing.

D. Encourage external auditors to make more extensive use of the work of internal auditors.

445. Independence permits internal auditors to render impartial and unbiased judgments. The best way to achieve independence is through

A. Individual knowledge and skills.

B. Organizational status and objectivity.

C. Supervision within the organization.

D. Organizational knowledge and skills.

446. The charter of the internal auditing department is a formal written document that

A. Establishes staff policies and procedures.

B. Helps establish the department's position in the organization.

C. Is approved by the director of internal auditing and accepted by the controller.

D. Grants operational authority over the activities audited.

447. It has been established that an internal auditing charter is one of the more important factors positively affecting the internal auditing department's independence. The Standards help clarify the nature of the charter by providing guidelines as to the contents of the charter. Which of the following is not suggested in the Standards as part of the charter?

A. The department's access to records within the organization.

B. The scope of internal auditing activities.

C. The length of tenure for the internal auditing director.

D. The department's access to personnel within the organization.

448. The authority and independence of the internal auditing department are most likely strengthened

A. Through the exercise of due professional care.

B. By requiring internal auditors to achieve and maintain professional proficiency.

C. Through proper staffing and effective supervision.

D. When the board of directors concurs in the appointment or removal of the internal auditing department director.

449. An internal auditor's objectivity is not compromised by

A. A conflict of interest.

B. Auditor implementation of controls.

C. Auditor assumption of operational duties on a temporary basis.

D. Employment of outside service providers who have skills the internal auditor lacks.

450. A director of internal auditing has reviewed credentials, checked references, and interviewed a candidate for a staff position. The director concludes that the candidate has a thorough understanding of internal auditing techniques, accounting, and management. However, the candidate has limited knowledge of economics and computer science. Which action is most appropriate?

A. Reject the candidate because of the lack of knowledge required by the Standards.

B. Offer the candidate a position despite lack of knowledge in certain essential areas.

C. Encourage the candidate to obtain additional training in economics and computer science and then reapply.

D. Offer the candidate a position if other staff members possess sufficient knowledge in economics and computer science.

451. Under Standard 230, audit supervision includes

A. Preparing activity reports.

B. Determining that working papers support findings.

C. Performing an on-site survey.

D. Periodically rotating audit managers.

452. Which of the following activities does not constitute audit supervision?

A. Preparing a preliminary audit program.

B. Providing appropriate instructions to the auditors.

C. Reviewing audit working papers.

D. Seeing that audit objectives are achieved.

453. According to Standard 250, *Knowledge, Skills, and Disciplines*, each internal auditor is required to

A. Be proficient in accounting.

B. Have an understanding of the application of auditing standards.

C. Have an understanding of the application of auditing techniques.

D. Have an appreciation of quantitative methods.

454. Fraud is best defined as an irregularity or illegal act

A. Involving intentional deception.

B. Perpetrated for the benefit of the organization.

C. By parties inside the organization.

D. By parties outside the organization.

455. According to the Standards, internal auditing has a responsibility for helping to deter fraud. Which of the following best describes how this responsibility is usually met?

A. By coordinating with security personnel and law enforcement agencies in the investigation of possible fraud.

B. By testing for fraud in every audit and following up as appropriate.

C. By assisting in the design of control systems to prevent fraud.

D. By evaluating the adequacy and effectiveness of controls in light of the potential exposure or risk.

456. Internal auditors are more likely to detect fraud if they improve their

A. Knowledge of fraud indicators.

B. Ability to interrogate fraud perpetrators to discover why the fraud was committed.

C. Design of control systems implemented to prevent fraud.

D. Supervision of security personnel.

457. When conducting fraud investigations, internal auditing should

A. Clearly indicate the extent of internal auditing's knowledge of the fraud when questioning suspects.

B. Assign personnel to the investigation in accordance with the audit schedule established at the beginning of the fiscal year.

C. Perform its investigation independent of lawyers, security personnel, and specialists from outside the organization who are involved in the investigation.

D. Assess the probable level and extent of complicity in the fraud within the organization.

458. In accordance with internal auditing pronouncements, control is the result of

A. Effective administration of the internal auditing department.

B. Peer reviews in accordance with AICPA standards.

C. Planning, organizing, and directing by management.

D. Coordination of internal and external auditing efforts.

459. According to The IIA, a basic concept of internal control is

A. Oversight of management's performance by internal auditing.

B. Top management's review of the reliability and integrity of financial information.

C. Reasonable assurance of achieving objectives.

D. Prevention of employee collusion.

460. Senior management has requested a compliance audit of the company's employee benefits package. Which of the following audit objectives would be considered the primary objective by both internal audit and senior management?

A. The level of company contributions is adequate to meet the program's demands.

B. Individual programs are operating in accordance with corporate policy and government regulations.

C. Participation levels support continuation of individual programs.

D. Benefit payments, when appropriate, are accurate and timely.

461. A company's new president meets the director of internal auditing for the first time and asks the director to briefly describe the department's overall scope. The director states that internal auditing's overall scope is to

A. Examine and evaluate internal control and the quality of performance in carrying out assigned responsibilities.

B. Review the means of safeguarding assets and, as appropriate, verify the existence of such assets.

C. Ensure compliance with policies, plans, procedures, laws, and regulations that could have a significant impact on operations and reports.

D. Review the reliability and integrity of financial and operating information and the means used to identify, measure, classify, and report such information.

462. Which type of internal audit involves a comprehensive review of unit activities, systems, and controls within an enterprise to reach economic, efficiency, effectiveness, or other objectives?

A. Operational.

B. Program results.

C. Financial.

D. Compliance.

463. Which type of internal audit emphasizes the reliability and integrity of information?

A. Operational.

B. Functional.

C. Financial.

D. Compliance.

464. The scope of an internal audit is initially defined by the

A. Audit objectives.

B. Scheduling and time estimates.

C. Preliminary survey.

D. Audit program.

465. When planning an audit, an on-site survey is appropriate for

A. Evaluating the effectiveness of internal control.

B. Identifying areas for audit emphasis.

C. Detailed verification of information.

D. Determining to whom results will be communicated.

466. Writing an audit program occurs at which stage of the audit process?

A. During the planning stage.

B. Subsequent to testing internal control to determine whether to rely on the controls or audit around them.

C. As the audit is performed.

D. At the end of each audit when the standard audit program should be revised for the next audit to ensure coverage of noted problem areas.

467. Which of the following is most essential to the development of audit programs?

A. Considering operating standards set by management.

B. Testing internal control before writing the audit program.

C. Preparing a budget identifying the costs of resources needed.

D. Taking a preliminary survey immediately after writing the audit program.

468. Planning an internal auditing assignment involves

A. Determining to whom audit results will be communicated.

B. Collecting audit evidence on all matters related to the audit objectives.

C. Following up on previous audit findings.

D. Preparation of working papers.

469. The most accurate term for evidence that is reliable and the best attainable through the use of appropriate audit techniques is

A. Direct.

B. Competent.

C. Useful.

D. Material.

470. The most accurate term for evidence that supports audit findings and is consistent with audit objectives is

A. Corroborative.

B. Competent.

C. Material.

D. Relevant.

471. The most accurate term for evidence that is factual, adequate, and convincing is

A. Useful.

B. Direct.

C. Sufficient.

D. Material.

472. A written statement derived from an interview is what form of audit evidence?

A. Testimonial.

B. Physical.

C. Documentary.

D. Analytical.

473. What audit evidence derives from a comparison of the relationships among data?

A. Testimonial.

B. Physical.

C. Documentary.

D. Analytical.

474. An internal auditor takes a photograph of the auditee's workplace. The photograph is a form of what kind of evidence?

A. Physical.

B. Testimonial.

C. Documentary.

D. Analytical.

475. According to SIAS 6, *Audit Working Papers*,

A. Working papers should be converted to paper.

B. Summaries of audit programs must be prepared.

C. Standardized working papers may improve efficiency.

D. Standardized tick marks should be defined.

476. Which of the following is an appropriate action by an internal auditor concerning working papers?

A. Maintain them indefinitely.

B. Adhere to retention policies established by the external auditors.

C. Allow the external auditors access to them.

D. Not disclose their contents to the auditee.

477. In general, internal auditing working papers should be

A. Retained according to the guidelines published by the federal government.

B. Retained for 3 years as specified in the Standards.

C. Disposed of in accordance with departmental policy.

D. Disposed of after the performance of two subsequent audits.

478. An internal auditing supervisor, when reviewing a staff member's working papers, found unsupported statement that "the auditee unit was operating inefficiently." What action should the supervisor direct the auditor to take?

A. Remove the comment from the working paper file.

B. Obtain the auditee's concurrence with the statement.

C. Research and identify evaluation criteria for measuring operating efficiency.

D. Explain that it is the opinion of the staff member.

479. Which of the following would not be included in the statement of scope in an audit report?

A. Period covered by the audit.

B. Audit objectives.

C. Activities not audited.

D. Nature and extent of the auditing performed.

480. The audit committee is most likely to receive

A. No audit report.

B. A full audit report.

C. An oral audit report.

D. A summary audit report.

481. The internal auditor should ordinarily discuss conclusions and recommendations at appropriate levels of management

A. Only during the closing conference or after issuing the final audit report.

B. After the closing conference and the conclusion of the audit.

C. During the course of the audit or at the closing conference.

D. After issuing the final audit report.

482. The internal auditing department should submit periodic activity reports to management and the board. These reports are most likely to

A. Explain major variances.

B. Describe audit findings and conclusions.

C. Include a risk and skill analysis of proposed audit activities.

D. Define the scope of the department's activities.

483. According to the Standards for the Professional Practice of Internal Auditing (SPPIA), a program for developing the human resources of the internal auditing department should include

A. An established career path for each employee.

B. Maintenance of formal technical manuals regardless of the size of the staff.

C. An annual appraisal of each internal auditor's performance.

D. Assurance that all auditors are proficient in each relevant discipline.

484. The capabilities of individual staff members are key features in the effectiveness of an internal auditing department. What is the primary consideration used when staffing an internal auditing department?

A. Background checks.

B. Job descriptions.

C. Continuing education.

D. Organizational orientation.

485. A quality assurance program for an internal auditing department should provide

A. Reasonable assurance that audit work conforms with all generally accepted auditing standards.

B. For coordination of the efforts of the internal and external auditors.

C. For internal but not external reviews.

D. Reasonable assurance that audit [illegible] conforms with the department's charter.

486. In applying the standards of conduct set forth in the *Code of Ethics*, internal auditors are expected to

A. Exercise their individual judgment.

B. Compare them to standards of other professions.

C. Be guided by the desires of the auditee.

D. Use discretion in deciding whether to use them or not.

487. The IIA Code of Ethics specifically requires

A. Avoidance of conflicts of interest.

B. Fulfillment of a duty to serve the general public.

C. Skill, knowledge, and discipline.

D. Loyalty to the organization even though the auditors thereby knowingly become parties to an improper act.

488. An internal auditor of a foreign subsidiary is aware that the social climate of the country is such that "facilitating payments" (bribes) are an accepted part of doing business. The auditor has found significant weaknesses relating to important controls. The division manager offers the auditor a substantial "facilitating payment" to omit these findings from the audit report with a provision that the auditor could revisit the division in 6 months to verify that the problem areas have been addressed. The auditor should

A. Not accept the payment because of a conflict with the *Code of Ethics*.

B. Not accept the payment but omit the findings if a verification visit is made in 6 months.

C. Accept the offer because it is consistent with the ethical concepts of the country in which the division is doing business.

D. Accept the payment because it has the effect of doing the greatest good for the greatest number; the auditor is better off, the division is better off, and the organization is better off because there is strong motivation to correct the deficiencies found by the auditor.

489. The IIA Code of Ethics lists 11 obligations of CIAs and members. Which of the following is permissible under the Code?

A. Revealing all material facts that, if not disclosed, might distort reports of operations.

B. Reporting apparent violations of governmental regulations to parties outside the organization rather than to the audit committee.

C. Using confidential information in a manner detrimental to the welfare of the organization.

D. Accepting consulting fees from a supplier.

490. The IIA Code of Ethics requires members to

A. Be independent of their employer.

B. Abide by the Institute's bylaws.

C. Adhere to generally accepted accounting principles.

D. Observe the accountant-client testimonial privilege.

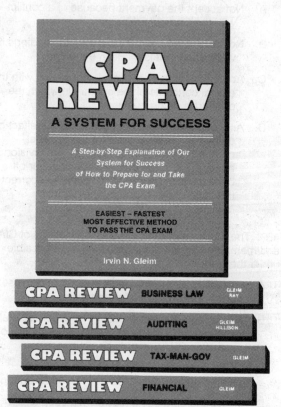

INDEX

Contact Gleim Today!
Post Office Box 12848, Univ. Station
Gainesville, Florida 32604
Call: (800) 87-GLEIM
FAX: (352) 375-6940
E-mail: sales@gleim.com

Five GLEIM CPE Programs Using Objective Question Format

This is a straightforward approach to CPE. Each program contains individual courses based on objective study questions. They are designed to meet the needs of practitioners by providing low-cost, easy-to-use, effective CPE. They offer five advantages:

FIRST, a self-diagnosis of your knowledge

SECOND, a formal program of learning that constitutes a review and study of what professional accountants need to know to provide competent professional service to their clients

THIRD, challenging multiple-choice questions with thorough, easy-to-understand explanations if you have difficulty

FOURTH, a programmed learning format organized from general to specific, easy to difficult, etc.

FIFTH, periodic revisions to keep the programs up-to-date and in compliance with the currency standards of NASBA, AICPA, etc.

EASY TO USE

You are formally registered when we receive your order, which is shipped to you the next business day. With each program, you receive an objective questions and explanations study book, the CPE final exam and instructions, and a machine-readable final exam answer sheet and return envelope. From there, you simply follow these three steps:

FIRST, study the assigned questions and explanations when and where you want.

SECOND, take a final exam (open book) and record your answers on Gleim's machine-readable answer sheet.

THIRD, return the answer sheet and an evaluation form to Gleim. If you score 70% or above, we will send you a certificate of completion. In the event of a failure, your answer sheet will be returned to you for correction after your additional study. Our charge for **regrading** is $25.

NOTE: In each program, you have the option of taking all of the courses, just one course, or any combination of individual courses. All of the courses in a single program can be completed at no additional charge by using the one answer sheet provided with each program. If you prefer to obtain CPE credit for a few courses at a time, there is a grading fee of just $25 (additional answer sheet) for each subsequent submission.

SAME-DAY GRADING SERVICE!

Available Mon.-Fri.: Send your materials and $50 prepayment for each answer sheet ($100 if out of the U.S.) via UPS Next Day Letter Service (if you use another carrier, we must receive it by noon) to 4201 N.W. 95th Blvd., Gainesville, FL 32606. We will hand-grade your answer sheet and send the results back to you the same day via the next day letter service of our choice. Call (800) 87-GLEIM.

	Credit Hours
AUDITING & SYSTEMS CPE -- 8th Edition	
8 separate courses with up to 49 (or 98*) CPE hours -- **all for $125**	
1. Audit Standards, Ethics, Planning, and Risk	7/14
2. Internal Control	6/12
3. Audit Evidence and Procedures	8/16
4. Information Systems	9/18
5. Statistical Sampling	4/8
6. Audit Reports	6/12
7. Special Reports and Other Reporting Issues	4/8
8. Internal Auditing	5/10
BUSINESS LAW CPE -- 4th Edition	
10 separate courses with up to 48 (or 96*) CPE hours -- **all for $95**	
1. The American Legal System	4/8
2. Criminal Law, Torts, and Insurance	4/8
3. Contracts	5/10
4. Sales, Antitrust, Consumer Protection, and International Business Law	5/10
5. Negotiable Instruments, Credit Law, and Liens and Mortgages	5/10
6. Secured Transactions, Suretyship, and Bankruptcy	5/10
7. Property Law and Environmental Regulation	5/10
8. Agency and Partnership	4/8
9. Corporations and Securities Regulation	5/10
10. Accountants' Legal Responsibilities, Estates and Trusts, and Employment Regulation	6/12
FEDERAL TAX CPE -- 8th Edition	
12 separate courses with up to 64 (or 128*) CPE hours -- **all for $125**	
1. Gross Income and Exclusions	5/10
2. Business Expenses and Losses	4/8
3. Investment and Personal Deductions	6/12
4. Individual Loss Limits, Tax Calculations, and Credits	5/10
5. General Business Credit and Basic Property Transactions	6/12
6. Other Property Transactions	6/12
7. Partnerships	6/12
8. Corporate Formations and Operations	5/10
9. Advanced Corporate Topics	5/10
10. Accounting Methods and Employment Taxes	5/10
11. Estates, Trusts, Tax-Exempt Organizations, and Wealth Transfer Taxes	6/12
12. Tax Preparer Rules, Process, and Procedures	5/10
FINANCIAL ACCOUNTING CPE -- 8th Edition	
13 separate courses with up to 46 (or 92*) CPE hours -- **all for $125**	
1. Basic Concepts and the Accounting Process	5/10
2. Current Assets	4/8
3. Noncurrent Assets	4/8
4. Current and Noncurrent Liabilities	3/6
5. Present Value, Pensions, and Leases	4/8
6. Shareholders' Equity and EPS	4/8
7. Income Tax Allocation, Accounting Changes, Error Corrections	2/4
8. Financial Statements and Disclosures	3/6
9. Statement Analysis, Interim Statements, and Segment Reporting	4/8
10. Investments and Business Combinations	4/8
11. Price-Level Changes and Foreign Exchange	2/4
12. Government and Nonprofit Accounting	4/8
13. Specialized Industry and Partnership Accounting	3/6
MANAGERIAL ACCOUNTING CPE -- 5th Edition	
10 separate courses with up to 41 (or 82*) CPE hours -- **all for $95**	
1. Cost Accounting Overview, Job-Order Costing, and ABC Costing	6/12
2. Process Costing; Spoilage, Scrap, Waste, and Rework	4/8
3. Joint Products and By-Products; Service Cost Allocations; and Absorption and Variable Costing	4/8
4. Cost-Volume-Profit Analysis	3/6
5. Budgeting and Responsibility Accounting	4/8
6. Standard Costs and Variances	4/8
7. Nonroutine Decisions; Inventory Planning and Control	4/8
8. Capital Budgeting	3/6
9. Probability and Statistics; Regression Analysis	5/10
10. Linear Programming and Other Quantitative Approaches	4/8

* See the discussion of determining self-study CPE credit on page 705.

Earn Continuing Education Credit While Preparing for the CIA, CMA, CFM Exams!

Each course consists of two study units containing study outlines and practice questions. Just pass a final exam to receive credit! See the discussion on self-study credit on page 345 and below to determine credit hours. Price includes the appropriate, current CIA, CMA, or CFM text. Customers who already own the current text pay only $25 per five-course program. CIA CPE credit amounts are estimates, call for more information.

CIA Part I: Internal Audit Process
5 separate courses with up to 25 (or 50) hours -- all for $47.95

1: Intro./Independence, Status, and Objectivity 5/10
2: Standards, Proficiency, and Internal Control 5/10
3: Planning, Administering, and Audit Evidence 5/10
4: Managing and Information Tech. Auditing 5/10
5: Ethics and Fraud 5/10

CIA Part II: Internal Audit Skills
5 separate courses with up to 25 (or 50) hours -- all for $47.95

1: Problem Solving and Decision Making 5/10
2: Audit Evidence 5/10
3: Flowcharting/Data Gathering/Using Elec. Media 5/10
4: Working Papers and Communicating Results 5/10
5: Mathematics, Statistics, and Sampling 5/10

CIA Part III: Management Control and Information Technology
5 separate courses with up to 25 (or 50) hours -- all for $47.95

1: Internal Control Concepts and the Controlling Process 5/10
2: Budgeting & Responsibility Accounting 5/10
3: Product Cost Control Sys. & Decision Analysis 5/10
4: Decision Analysis and Information Technology 5/10
5: Information Technology and Control 5/10

CIA Part IV: The Audit Environment
5 separate courses with up to 25 (or 50) hours -- all for $47.95

1: Financial Accounting I 5/10
2: Financial Accounting II 5/10
3: Finance 5/10
4: Managerial Accounting 5/10
5: The Regulatory Environment 5/10

CMA/CFM PART 1: ECONOMICS, FINANCE, AND MANAGEMENT
5 separate courses with up to 25 (or 50) hours -- all for $47.95

1. Economics 5/10
2. Business Environment 5/10
3. Finance 5/10
4. Risk and Organizational Theory 5/10
5. Motivation and Communication 5/10

PART 2CFM: CORPORATE FINANCIAL MANAGEMENT
5 separate courses with up to 25 (or 50) hours -- all for $47.95

1. Financial Statements 5/10
2. Long-Term Financing, Capital Market, and Int. Rates 5/10
3. Investment/Commercial Banking and Fin. Analysis 5/10
4. Business Restructuring and Risk Management 5/10
5. Accounting Standards and Financial Environment 5/10

PART 2CMA: FINANCIAL ACCOUNTING AND REPORTING
5 separate courses with up to 25 (or 50) hours -- all for $47.95

1. Accounting Standards and Financial Statements 5/10
2. Conceptual Framework and Assets 5/10
3. Liabilities and Shareholder's Equity 5/10
4. Other Income Items and Reporting Issues 5/10
5. Financial Statement Analysis and External Auditing 5/10

CMA/CFM PART 3: MGMT. REPORTING/ANALYSIS/BEHAV. ISSUES
5 separate courses with up to 25 (or 50) hours -- all for $47.95

1. Cost 5/10
2. Cost Behavior/SMAs 5/10
3. Planning and Budgeting 5/10
4. Control/Standard Costs and Variance Analysis 5/10
5. Responsibility Accounting and Behavioral Issues 5/10

CMA/CFM PART 4: DECISION ANALYSIS AND INFO SYSTEMS
5 separate courses with up to 25 (or 50) hours -- all for $47.95

1. Decision Analysis and CVP 5/10
2. Capital Budgeting and Decision Making 5/10
3. Quantitative Methods 5/10
4. Information Systems 5/10
5. Internal Control and Internal Auditing 5/10

40 JURISDICTIONS GRANT DOUBLE THE LISTED CREDIT FOR GLEIM CPE PROGRAMS!

The following grant one contact hour for each 50 minutes of completion time for Gleim CPE. Verify the self-study measurement standard with your CPE reporting agencies.

Governmental/Other Organizations

Accreditation Council for Accountancy and Taxation
American Society of Appraisers
Association of Certified Fraud Examiners
Association of Government Accountants
Association of Insolvency Accountants
BAI Foundation (Certified Bank Auditors)
California Dept. of Consumer Affairs, Tax Preparer Program
Certified Government Financial Managers Program
Certified Information Systems Auditor
General Accounting Office
Information Systems Audit and Control Association
Institute of Certified Management Accountants
Institute of Internal Auditors
Internal Revenue Service
National Association of Certified Valuation Analysts
National Association of Enrolled Agents
Oregon Board of Tax Service Examiners
The American College (ChFC and CLU)
U.S. Treasury Department

State Boards of Accountancy

Alabama
Alaska
Arkansas
Colorado
Delaware
Hawaii
Iowa
Maine
Massachusetts
Michigan
Minnesota
Mississippi
Nevada
New Hampshire
Ohio
South Dakota
Tennessee
Utah
West Virginia
Wyoming

CPE Report Generator software saves enormous amounts of time and record-keeping costs so you can concentrate on your clients. Call today for more information at (800) 87-GLEIM or download our fully functional demo program:

http://www.gleim.com/Accounting/CPE/cperg-demo.html

Gleim Publications, Inc.
P.O. Box 12848
Gainesville, FL 32604

TOLL FREE: (800) 87-GLEIM
LOCAL: (352) 375-0772
FAX: (888) 375-6940 (toll free)
INTERNET: http://www.gleim.com
E-MAIL: sales@gleim.com

Customer service is available:
8:00 a.m. - 7:00 p.m., Mon. - Fri.
9:00 a.m. - 2:00 p.m., Saturday
Please have your credit card ready or save time by ordering online!

CPA REVIEW *(98-99 Ed.)*	Books	Audiotapes	**CPA Test Prep** Software	
Auditing	☐ @ $24.50	☐ @ $75.00	☐ @ $35.00	$______
Business Law	☐ @ $24.50	☐ @ $75.00	☐ @ $35.00	______
TAX-MAN-GOV	☐ @ $24.50	☐ @ $75.00	☐ @ $35.00	______
Financial	☐ @ $24.50	☐ @ $75.00	☐ @ $35.00	______

☐ A System for Success (112 pp.) (FREE with any Gleim CPA Review book)

Save 15% on the Complete Gleim CPA System (add $16 S&H below) ...... $457.00 ______
[5 books, 4 audio cassette albums (41 tapes), 4 CPA Test Prep diskettes, and bonus canvas book bag]

CMA/CFM REVIEW	Books	Audiotapes	CMA/CFMTP Software	CPE	
Part 1	☐ @ $22.95	☐ @ $60.00	☐ @ $35.00	☐ @ $25.00	$______
Part 2CMA	☐ @ $22.95	☐ @ $60.00	☐ @ $35.00	☐ @ $25.00	______
Part 2CFM	☐ @ $22.95	☐ @ $60.00	☐ @ $35.00	☐ @ $25.00	______
Part 3	☐ @ $22.95	☐ @ $60.00	☐ @ $35.00	☐ @ $25.00	______
Part 4	☐ @ $22.95	☐ @ $60.00	☐ @ $35.00	☐ @ $25.00	______

CIA REVIEW	Books	CIATP Software	CPE	
Part I, Internal Audit Process	☐ @ $22.95	☐ @ $35.00	☐ @ $25.00	$______
Part II, Internal Audit Skills	☐ @ $22.95	☐ @ $35.00	☐ @ $25.00	______
Part III, Management Control and Information Technology	☐ @ $22.95	☐ @ $35.00	☐ @ $25.00	______
Part IV, The Audit Environment	☐ @ $22.95	☐ @ $35.00	☐ @ $25.00	______

"THE GLEIM SERIES" EXAM QUESTIONS AND EXPLANATIONS BOOKS & CPE

	Book Only	Book & CPE		
Auditing & Systems	☐ $19.95	☐ $125.00	(49-98 hours)	$______
Business Law/Legal Studies	☐ $16.95	☐ $ 95.00	(48-96 hours)	______
Federal Tax	☐ $19.95	☐ $125.00	(51-102 hours)	______
Financial Accounting	☐ $19.95	☐ $125.00	(46-92 hours)	______
Managerial Accounting	☐ $16.95	☐ $ 95.00	(41-82 hours)	______

Shipping (nonrefundable): **First item = $5; each additional item = $1** .... ______
Add applicable sales tax for shipments within Florida. .... ______
Fax or write for prices/instructions for shipments outside the 48 contiguous states. **TOTAL** $______

1. We process and ship orders daily, within one business day over 98.8% of the time. Call by noon for same-day service!
2. Please PHOTOCOPY this order form for use by others.
3. No CODs. Orders from individuals must be prepaid. Library and company orders may be purchased on account.
4. Gleim Publications, Inc. guarantees the immediate refund of all resalable texts and unopened software and audiotapes if returned within 30 days. Applies only to items purchased direct from Gleim Publications, Inc. Our shipping charge is nonrefundable.

NAME (please print) ______________________

ADDRESS ______________________ Apt. ______
(street address required for UPS)

____

CITY ______________ STATE ____ ZIP ______

___ MC/VISA/DISC/AMEX ___ Check/M.O. Daytime Telephone (____)__________

Credit Card No. ______-______-______-______

Exp. ___/___ Signature ______________________
Mo. / Yr.

Printed 8/98. Prices subject to change without notice.

Please forward your suggestions, corrections, and comments concerning typographical errors, etc., to **Irvin N. Gleim • c/o Gleim Publications, Inc. • P.O. Box 12848 • University Station • Gainesville, Florida • 32604**. Please include your name and address so we can properly thank you for your interest.

1.____

2.____

3.____

4.____

5.____

6.____

7.____

8.____

9.____

10.____

11. ____________________

12. ____________________

13. ____________________

14. ____________________

15. ____________________

16. ____________________

17. ____________________

18. ____________________

Remember for superior service: Mail, e-mail, or fax questions about our books or software. Telephone Gleim with questions about orders, prices, shipments, or payments.

Name: ____________________

Address: ____________________

City/State/Zip: ____________________

Telephone: Home: __________ Work: __________ Fax: __________

E-Mail: ____________________

GLEIM BOOKMARK

Dr. Gleim's Orders: Cover the answers and explanations in our book with this bookmark to make sure you do NOT cheat yourself. Answers will not be alongside questions when you take your exam. In class, at home, and everywhere else, cover the right side of the page before answering questions.

SUCCESSFUL
CAREERS IN
ACCOUNTING
BEGIN WITH
THE GLEIM SERIES OF
OBJECTIVE QUESTIONS AND EXPLANATIONS . . .

WITH GLEIM *CPA REVIEW*

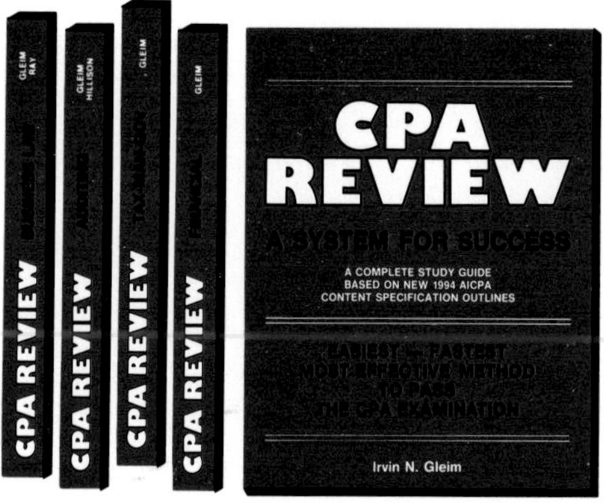

BOOKS ◆ SOFTWARE ◆ AUDIOTAPES

(800) 87-GLEIM
www.gleim.com

GLEIM BOOKMARK

Dr. Gleim's Orders: Cover the answers and explanations in our book with this bookmark to make sure you do NOT cheat yourself. Answers will not be alongside questions when you take your exam. In class, at home, and everywhere else, cover the right side of the page before answering questions.

SUCCESSFUL
CAREERS IN
ACCOUNTING
BEGIN WITH
THE GLEIM SERIES OF
OBJECTIVE QUESTIONS AND EXPLANATIONS . . .

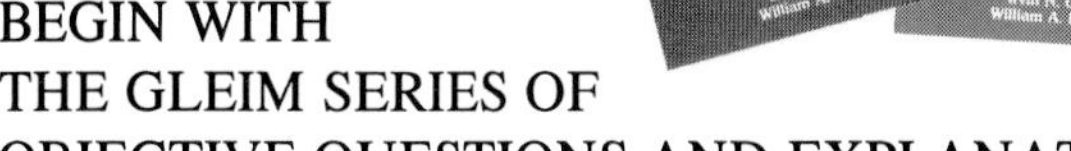

. . . AND ARE ACCELERATED
WITH GLEIM *CPA REVIEW*

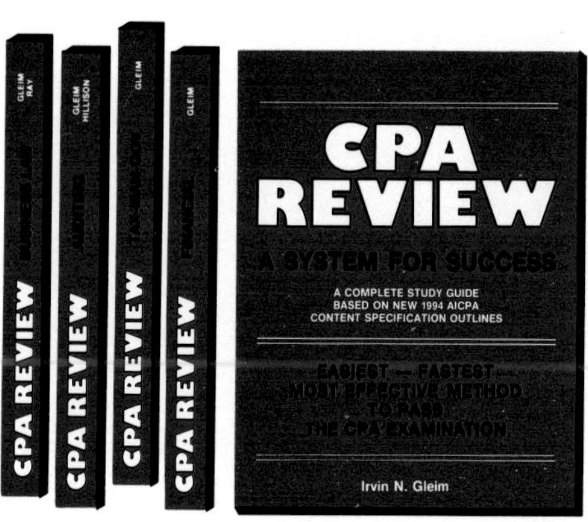

BOOKS ◆ SOFTWARE ◆ AUDIOTAPES

(800) 87-GLEIM
www.gleim.com